May be redeemed in accordance with the conditions overleaf at any of the establishments whose gazetteer entry shows the symbol £

May be redeemed in accordance with the conditions overleaf at any of the establishments whose gazetteer entry shows the symbol £

May be redeemed in accordance with the conditions overleaf at any of the establishments whose gazetteer entry shows the symbol £

May be redeemed in accordance with the conditions overleaf at any of the establishments whose gazetteer entry shows the symbol £

May be redeemed in accordance with the conditions overleaf at any of the establishments whose gazetteer entry shows the symbol £

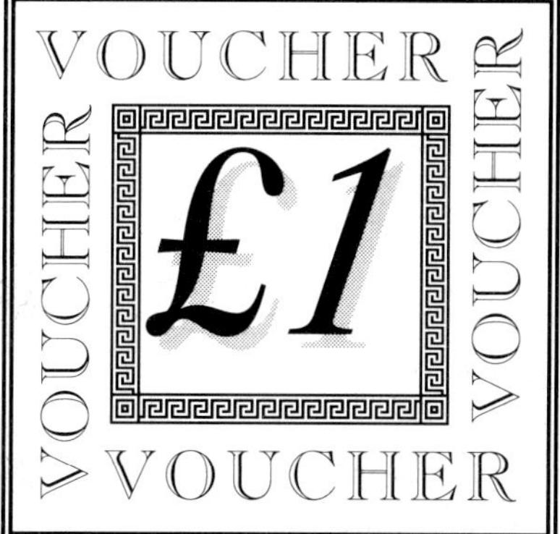

May be redeemed in accordance with the conditions overleaf at any of the establishments whose gazetteer entry shows the symbol £

CONDITIONS

A COPY OF AA INSPECTED BED AND BREAKFAST IN BRITAIN AND IRELAND 1993 MUST BE PRODUCED WITH THIS VOUCHER.. ONLY ONE VOUCHER PER PERSON OR PARTY ACCEPTED. NOT REDEEMABLE FOR CASH. NO CHANGE GIVEN. THE VOUCHER WILL NOT BE VALID AFTER 31ST DECEMBER 1993. USE OF THE VOUCHER WILL ONLY BE ACCEPTED AGAINST ACCOMMODATION AT FULL TARIFF RATES.

CONDITIONS

A COPY OF AA INSPECTED BED AND BREAKFAST IN BRITAIN AND IRELAND 1993 MUST BE PRODUCED WITH THIS VOUCHER.. ONLY ONE VOUCHER PER PERSON OR PARTY ACCEPTED. NOT REDEEMABLE FOR CASH. NO CHANGE GIVEN. THE VOUCHER WILL NOT BE VALID AFTER 31ST DECEMBER 1993. USE OF THE VOUCHER WILL ONLY BE ACCEPTED AGAINST ACCOMMODATION AT FULL TARIFF RATES.

CONDITIONS

A COPY OF AA INSPECTED BED AND BREAKFAST IN BRITAIN AND IRELAND 1993 MUST BE PRODUCED WITH THIS VOUCHER.. ONLY ONE VOUCHER PER PERSON OR PARTY ACCEPTED. NOT REDEEMABLE FOR CASH. NO CHANGE GIVEN. THE VOUCHER WILL NOT BE VALID AFTER 31ST DECEMBER 1993. USE OF THE VOUCHER WILL ONLY BE ACCEPTED AGAINST ACCOMMODATION AT FULL TARIFF RATES.

CONDITIONS

A COPY OF AA INSPECTED BED AND BREAKFAST IN BRITAIN AND IRELAND 1993 MUST BE PRODUCED WITH THIS VOUCHER.. ONLY ONE VOUCHER PER PERSON OR PARTY ACCEPTED. NOT REDEEMABLE FOR CASH. NO CHANGE GIVEN. THE VOUCHER WILL NOT BE VALID AFTER 31ST DECEMBER 1993. USE OF THE VOUCHER WILL ONLY BE ACCEPTED AGAINST ACCOMMODATION AT FULL TARIFF RATES.

CONDITIONS

A COPY OF AA INSPECTED BED AND BREAKFAST IN BRITAIN AND IRELAND 1993 MUST BE PRODUCED WITH THIS VOUCHER.. ONLY ONE VOUCHER PER PERSON OR PARTY ACCEPTED. NOT REDEEMABLE FOR CASH. NO CHANGE GIVEN. THE VOUCHER WILL NOT BE VALID AFTER 31ST DECEMBER 1993. USE OF THE VOUCHER WILL ONLY BE ACCEPTED AGAINST ACCOMMODATION AT FULL TARIFF RATES.

CONDITIONS

A COPY OF AA INSPECTED BED AND BREAKFAST IN BRITAIN AND IRELAND 1993 MUST BE PRODUCED WITH THIS VOUCHER.. ONLY ONE VOUCHER PER PERSON OR PARTY ACCEPTED. NOT REDEEMABLE FOR CASH. NO CHANGE GIVEN. THE VOUCHER WILL NOT BE VALID AFTER 31ST DECEMBER 1993. USE OF THE VOUCHER WILL ONLY BE ACCEPTED AGAINST ACCOMMODATION AT FULL TARIFF RATES.

AA

INSPECTED

BED & BREAKFAST in BRITAIN & IRELAND

1993

PRODUCED BY THE PUBLISHING DIVISION OF THE AUTOMOBILE ASSOCIATION

Directory: compiled by the AA's Hotels and Touring Information Services Department and generated by the AA's Establishment Database.

Maps: prepared by the Cartographic Department of the Automobile Association

Cover design: The Paul Hampson Partnership, Southampton
Colour supplement design: Liz Baldin
Photography: Gordon Hammond ABIPP, Southampton
Chairs kindly loaned by B&Q.
Feature: Putting out the welcome mat by Penny Hicks

Head of Advertisement Sales: Christopher Heard Tel:(0256) 20123
Advertisement Production: Karen Weeks Tel:(0256) 20123

Typeset, printed and bound in Great Britain by William Clowes Ltd, Beccles and London

Colour supplement produced by Sussex Litho Ltd, Chichester

A CIP catalogue record for this book is available from the British Library.

PUBLISHED BY THE AUTOMOBILE ASSOCIATION, FANUM HOUSE, BASINGSTOKE, HAMPSHIRE RG21 2EA

ISBN 0 7495 0542 7

CONTENTS

INTRODUCTION

We are always pleased to welcome new establishments to the guide and regularly feature the regional winners of our Best Newcomer Awards. From the places appearing for the first time in the guide this year, we have chosen eight that we consider to be special. Turn to our colour feature and read all about them.

This year we have also conducted a survey of current trends in bed and breakfast accommodation. We asked proprietors to tell us how they run their business, what their pet hates are and what they like best about their guests, especially children. To find out, turn to our article 'Putting out the welcome Mat' on page 17.

All the establishments listed in the directory are given awards of between one and four 'Q's for quality. More details about the 'Q' awards can be found in the explanation of the Quality Assessment on page 8. Establishments awarded the highest quality rating (four Qs) are highlighted in the directory under the heading 'Selected' and their entries are enclosed in a tinted panel. A full list of the 291 establishments that have achieved the 'Selected' status is given on page 9.

Establishments that offer bed and breakfast for a budget price of £15 or under are indicated by the symbol against their entry. This year we also include a quick-reference list of these establishments on page 474. For more details about the accommodation, consult the directory.

Many one-star hotels offer good-value accommodation on a par with some of our guesthouses and small private hotels. For the first time this year we have included a quick-reference list, taken from the 1993 edition of the AA Hotels and Restaurants in Britain and Ireland guide, on page 477. Please note however that these hotels are not included in the Directory and you will have to write or telephone for details

WHAT IS A GUESTHOUSE?

The term 'guesthouse' can lead to some confusion, particularly when many include the word 'hotel' in their name. For our purposes, we include small and private hotels in this category when they cannot offer all the services required for our star classification system.

This is not to say that guesthouses are inferior to hotels, just that they are different - and many offer a very high standard of accommodation. It is not unusual to be offered en suite bathrooms, for instance, or to find a colour television in your room. It is true that some guesthouses will only offer a set meal in the evening, but many provide a varied and interesting menu, and a standard of service that one would expect of a good restaurant. At the other end of the scale, some guesthouses offer bed and breakfast only, and it would also be wise to check if there are any restrictions to your access to the house, particularly late in the morning and during the afternoon.

Guesthouses in the London section of the book are all small hotels. Of course, London prices tend to be higher than those in the provinces, but those that we list offer cost-conscious accommodation, although normally only bed and breakfast is provided. To allow for all eventualities, we have also included a few which provide a full meal service and the charges for these will naturally be higher.

STAYING AT A FARMHOUSE

Farmhouse accommodation has a special quality, and is particularly noted for being inexpensive and cosy, with a high standard of good home-cooking. Those listed in our book are generally working farms, and some farmers are happy to allow visitors to look around, or even to help feed the animals. However, we must stress that the modern farm is a potentially dangerous place, especially where machinery and chemicals are concerned, and visitors must be prepared to exercise care, particularly if they bring children. Never leave children unsupervised around the farm. Sometimes guest accommodation is run as a separate concern from the farm on which it stands, and visitors are discouraged from venturing on to the working land. In other cases, the land has been sold off. Although the directory entry states the acreage and the type of farming carried out, it is advisable to check when booking to make sure that your requirements are met. As with guest-houses, standards will vary considerably, and are often far above what one would expect.

Some of our farmhouses are grand ex-manor houses furnished with antiques and offering a stylish way of life, others will offer more basic accommodation. All of the farmhouses are listed under town or village names, but obviously many will be some distance from other habitation. Proprietors will, of course, give directions when you book, and we publish a six-figure map reference against the directory entry which can be used in conjunction with Ordnance Survey maps.

INNS

We all know what we can expect to find in a traditional inn - a cosy bar, a convivial atmosphere, good beer and pub food. Nevertheless, we have a few criteria which must be met. Breakfast is a must of course, in a suitable breakfast room, and the inn should also serve at least light meals during licensing hours. Our inn category may also include a number of small, fully licensed hotels, and the character of the properties will vary according to whether they are pretty country inns or larger establishments in towns. Again it is important to check details before you book.

COMMON TO ALL

Whatever the type of establishment, there are certain requirements common to all, including a well-maintained exterior, clean and hygienic kitchens; good standards of furnishing; friendly and courteous service; access to the premises at reasonable times; the use of a telephone; and a full English or Irish breakfast. Bedrooms should be equipped with comfortable beds, a wardrobe, a bedside cabinet, a washbasin with soap, towel, mirror and shaver socket and at least a carpet beside the bed. There should not be an extra charge for the use of baths or lavatories, and heating should be unmetered.

NB Where an establishment shows the central heating symbol, it does not necessarily mean that central heating will be available all year round. Some places only use it in winter, and then at their own discretion.

QUALITY ASSESSMENT

Quality assessment is now made for all the establishments listed in the directory. It is made on a subjective basis, following each inspection, to indicate the overall quality of the facilities and services provided by each establishment.

The quality assessment is shown as follows:

FALMOUTH Cornwall Map **2** SX25

GH QQ **Ram Hotel** High Road XY21 1AB
☎(05036) 4321 Plan 9 C2

FH QQQ Mr & Mrs J Smith **Homestead** DX8 1WY (SX261567)
☎(05036) 3421

Each establishment receives from one to four symbols in ascending order of merit, denoting:

A simple establishment with clean, modest accommodation and adequate bathroom facilities.

QQ

A sound establishment offering a higher standard of accommodation in terms of furnishing, decor and comfort; likely to have some en suite facilities.

QQQ

A well-appointed establishment offering superior accommodation with comfortable public areas. En suite facilities may be provided.

SELECTED

The very best of AA-listed establishments, offering excellent standards of accommodation, a high degree of comfort, good food and hospitable, caring hosts. Many provide a high proportion of en suite facilities.

This year 291 places have been awarded the 'Selected' distinction, and their directory entries are highlighted by means of a tinted panel. A full list of these establishments will be found overleaf.

SELECTED GUESTHOUSES, FARMHOUSES AND INNS

The county index which follows is a list of all the guesthouses, farmhouses and inns - 291 in all - which have been awarded the AA's highest quality rating of 4 Q symbols and the designation 'SELECTED'. You will find full details of each in the directory and the entries are highlighted by means of a tinted panel.

ENGLAND

AVON

Bath	GH	Arden House
Bath	GH	Haydon House
Bath	GH	Holly Lodge
Bath	GH	Laura Place Hotel
Bath	GH	Leighton House
Bath	GH	Old School House
Bath	GH	Paradise House
Bath	GH	Somerset House Hotel & Restaurant
Bath	GH	Underhill Lodge

CHESHIRE

Chester	GH	Redland Private Hotel
Malpas	FH	Tilston Lodge

CO DURHAM

Darlington	FH	Clow Beck House
Fir Tree	GH	Greenhead Country House Hotel

CORNWALL & ISLES OF SCILLY

Crackington Haven	FH	Manor Farm
Crackington Haven	FH	Trevigue
Fowey	GH	Carnethic House
Lizard	GH	Landewednack House
Looe	GH	Harescombe Lodge
Newquay	GH	Towan Beach
Newquay	GH	Windward Hotel
Penryn	GH	Prospect House
Polzeath	FH	Trenderway Farm
St Blazey	GH	Nanscawan House
St Hilary	FH	Ennys Farm
St Just in Roseland	GH	Rose-da-Mar Hotel
St Marys	GH	Brantwood Hotel
St Marys	GH	Carnwethers Country House
Tintagel	GH	Trebrea Lodge

CUMBRIA

Ambleside	GH	Grey Friar Lodge Country House Hotel
Ambleside	GH	Rothay Garth Hotel
Ambleside	GH	Rydal Lodge
Boltongate	GH	The Old Rectory
Borrowdale	GH	Greenbank
Buttermere	GH	Pickett Howe
Caldbeck	GH	High Greenrigg House
Catlowdy	FH	Bessiestown Farm
Cockermouth	GH	Low Hall Country Guest House
Coniston	GH	Coniston Lodge Hotel
Grange over Sands	GH	Greenacres
Kendal	GH	Burrow Hall Country Guest House
Kendal	GH	Lane Head Country House Hotel
Keswick	GH	Applethwaite Country House Hotel
Kirkby Lonsdale	GH	Cobwebs Country House
Kirkby Lonsdale	GH	Hipping Hall
Kirkby Stephen	GH	The Town Head House
Kirkcambeck	FH	Cracop Farm
Kirkoswald	GH	Prospect Hill Hotel
Near Sawrey	GH	Ees Wyke Country House
Near Sawrey	GH	The Garth
Penruddock	FH	Highgate Farm
Watermillock	GH	The Old Church Hotel
Windermere	GH	The Hawksmoor Guest House

DERBYSHIRE

Bakewell	GH	Merlin House Country House Hotel
Buxton	GH	Brookfield on Longhill
Shottle	FH	Dannah Farm

DEVON

Axminster	FH	Millbrook Farmhouse
Bickington	FH	East Burne Farm

Bovey Tracey	FH	Willmead Farm
Colyford	GH	Swallows Eaves Hotel
Croyde	GH	Whiteleaf at Croyde
Dartington	INN	Cott Inn
Dartmouth	GH	Captains House
Dartmouth	GH	Ford House
Holne	FH	Wellpritton Farm
Ilfracombe	GH	Varley House
Kingston	GH	Trebles Cottage Hotel
Lynmouth	GH	Countisbury Lodge Hotel
Lynton	GH	Waterloo House Hotel
Morchard Bishop	FH	Wigham
Mortehoe	GH	Sunnycliffe Hotel
Parkham	GH	The Old Rectory
Payhembury	GH	Colestocks House
Shillingford	GH	The Old Mill
Teignmouth	GH	Thomas Luny House
Tiverton	FH	Lower Collipriest Farm
Torquay	GH	Glenorleigh Hotel
Torquay	GH	Kingston House
Totnes	GH	Lyssers
Totnes	GH	Old Forge at Totnes
Totnes	INN	The Watermans Arms
West Down	GH	The Long House

DORSET

Beaminster	GH	Hams Plot
Bournemouth	GH	Cliff House Hotel
Chideock	GH	Betchworth House Hotel
Dorchester	GH	Yalbury Cottage
Horton	GH	Northill House
Wareham	FH	Redcliffe Farm
Weymouth	GH	Bay Lodge

ESSEX

Thaxted	FH	Piggots Mill

GLOUCESTERSHIRE

Cheltenham	GH	Cleeve Hill Hotel
Cheltenham	GH	Lypiatt House
Clearwell	FH	Tudor Farmhouse
Laverton	GH	Leasow House
Tetbury	GH	Tavern House
Willersey	GH	Old Rectory

GREATER MANCHESTER

Altrincham	GH	Ash Farm

HAMPSHIRE

Hayling Island	GH	Cockle Warren Cottage Hotel
Lyndhurst	GH	Knightwood Lodge
Ringwood	GH	Little Forest Lodge Hotel
Sway	GH	The Tower
Winchester	INN	The Wykeham Arms

HEREFORD & WORCESTER

Bishampton	FH	Nightingale Hotel
Bredwardine	GH	Bredwardine Hall
Hanley Castle	GH	Old Parsonage Farm
Hereford	GH	Hermitage Manor
Leominster	GH	Withenfield
Ruckhall	INN	The Ancient Camp Inn
Ullingswick	GH	The Steppes
Vowchurch	GH	The Croft Country House
Weobley	INN	Ye Olde Salutation Inn
Whitney-on-Wye	INN	The Rhydspence Inn

KENT

Canterbury	GH	Thanington Hotel
Canterbury	GH	The Old Rectory
Canterbury	GH	Thruxted Oast
Cranbrook	GH	Hancocks Farmhouse
Maidstone	GH	Tanyard Hotel
Penshurst	GH	Swale Cottage
Petham	GH	The Old Poor House
Royal Tunbridge Wells	GH	Danehurst House
Sittingbourne	GH	Hampstead House
Tonbridge	GH	Goldhill Mill
West Malling	GH	Scott House

LANCASHIRE

Blackpool	GH	Sunray Private Hotel
Carnforth	GH	New Capernwray Farm
Colne	FH	Higher Wanless Farm
Harrop Fold	FH	Harrop Fold Country Farmhouse Hotel
Slaidburn	GH	Parrock Head Farm House Hotel
Thornton	GH	The Victorian House

LINCOLNSHIRE

Lincoln	GH	D'Isney Place Hotel

LONDON (GREATER)

(Postal Districts)

NW3	GH	The Langorf Hotel
SE3	GH	Vanbrugh
W2	GH	Byron Hotel
W2	GH	Pembridge Court

NORFOLK

Barney	GH	The Old Brick Kilns
Kings Lynn	GH	Russet House Hotel

NORTHUMBERLAND

Alnmouth	GH	Marine House Private Hotel
Haltwhistle	FH	Broomshaw Hill Farm
Kirkwhelpington	FH	Shieldhall
Rothbury	GH	Orchard

NOTTINGHAMSHIRE

North Wheatley	GH	The Old Plough

OXFORDSHIRE

Burford	GH	Andrews Hotel
Chislehampton	INN	The Coach & Horses
Faringdon	GH	Barcote Manor
Kidlington	GH	Bowood House
Kingston Bagpuize	FH	Fallowfields
Lew	FH	The Farmhouse Hotel & Restaurant
Milton-under-Wychwood	GH	Hillborough Hotel
Oxford	GH	Cotswold House
Oxford	GH	Tilbury Lodge Private Hotel
Thame	FH	Upper Green Farm
Woolstone	INN	The White Horse

SHROPSHIRE

Church Stretton	FH	Rectory Farm
Diddlebury	GH	The Glebe
Middleton Priors	GH	Middleton Lodge

SOMERSET

Beercrocombe	FH	Frog Street Farm
Beercrocombe	FH	Whittles Farm
Crewkerne	GH	Broadview
Kilve	INN	The Hood Arms
Langport	GH	Hillards Farm
Minehead	GH	Marston Lodge
Porlock	GH	Gable Thatch
Somerton	GH	The Lynch Country House
Taunton	GH	Meryan House Hotel
Wells	GH	Coach House
Wells	FH	Littlewell Farm
Williton	GH	Curdon Mill

STAFFORDSHIRE

Cheddleton	GH	Choir Cottage & Choir House
Oakamoor	GH	Bank House

SUFFOLK

Gislingham	GH	The Old Guildhall
Higham	GH	The Old Vicarage
Needham Market	GH	Pipp's Ford Farm

SUSSEX (EAST)

Arlington	FH	Bates Green
Brighton	GH	Adelaide Hotel
Hastings & St Leonards	GH	Parkside House
Hove	GH	Claremont House
Rye	GH	Green Hedges
Rye	GH	Holloway House
Rye	GH	Jeakes House
Rye	GH	The Old Vicarage Hotel & Restaurant
Uckfield	GH	Hooke Hall
Uckfield	GH	South Paddock
Winchelsea	GH	The Country House at Winchelsea

SUSSEX (WEST)

Bepton	GH	The Park House Hotel
Billingshurst	FH	Old Wharf
Rogate	FH	Mizzards Farm
Sutton	INN	White Horse

WARWICKSHIRE

Hatton	GH	Northleigh House
Lower Brailles	GH	Feldon House
Shrewley	GH	Shrewley House

WIGHT, ISLE OF

Sandown	GH	St Catherine's Hotel
Shanklin	GH	Chine Lodge
Shanklin	GH	Osborne House

WILTSHIRE

Alderton	FH	Manor Farm
Bradford on Avon	GH	Bradford Old Windmill
Bradford on Avon	GH	Widbrook Grange
Burbage	GH	The Old Vicarage
Lacock	GH	At the Sign of the Angel

Nettleton	GH	Fosse Farmhouse Country Hotel
West Grafton	FH	Mayfield

YORKSHIRE (NORTH)

Grassington	GH	Ashfield House Hotel
Harrogate	GH	Alexa House & Stable Cottages
Kettlewell	GH	Langcliffe House
Kirbymoorside	GH	Appletree Court
Patrick Brompton	GH	Elmfield House
Raskelf	GH	Old Farmhouse Country Hotel
Reeth	GH	Arkleside Hotel
Richmond	FH	Whashton Springs Farm
Scotch Corner	INN	Vintage Hotel
Starbotton	GH	Hilltop Country Guest House
Whitby	GH	Dunsley Hall
York	GH	Arndale Hotel
York	GH	Grasmead House Hotel

WALES

CLWYD

Ruthin	GH	Eyarth Station
St Asaph	FH	Bach-y-Craig

DYFED

Carew	GH	Old Stable Cottage
Gwuan Valley	FH	Tregynon Country Farmhouse Hotel
New Quay	GH	Park Hall
Solva	FH	Lochmeyler Farm

GLAMORGAN (WEST)

Swansea	GH	Tredillon House

GWENT

Abergavenny	GH	Llanwenarth House

GWYNEDD

Aberdovey	GH	Morlan Guesthouse
Betws-y-Coed	GH	Tan-Y-Foel
Bontddu	GH	Borthwnog Hall
Harlech	GH	Castle Cottage Hotel
Llanddeiniolen	FH	Ty'n Rhos Farm
Llandudno	GH	Craiglands Private Hotel
Llanfachreth	GH	Ty Isaf

POWYS

Penybont	GH	Ffaldau Country House & Restaurant
Sennybridge	FH	Brynfedwen Farm

CHANNEL ISLANDS

GUERNSEY

St Peter Port	GH	Midhurst House

JERSEY

St Aubin	GH	The Panorama

SCOTLAND

BORDERS

Jedburgh	GH	The Spinney
Melrose	GH	Dunfermline House
West Linton	GH	Medwyn House

CENTRAL

Brig O'Turk	GH	Dundarroch
Callander	GH	Arran Lodge

DUMFRIES & GALLOWAY

Kirkbean	GH	Cavens House
Kirkcudbright	GH	Gladstone House
Moffat	GH	Gilbert House
Twynholm	GH	Fresh Fields

GRAMPIAN

Aberdeen	GH	Cedars Private Hotel
Keith	FH	The Haughs
Forres	GH	Parkmount House Hotel

HIGHLAND

Boat of Garten	GH	Heathbank House
Carrbridge	GH	Fairwinds Hotel
Contin	GH	Contin House
Drumnadrochit	GH	Polmaily House Hotel
Gairloch	GH	Horisdale House
Grantown-on-Spey	GH	Culdearn House
Grantown-on-Spey	GH	Garden Park
Inverness	GH	Culduthel Lodge
Kirkhill	GH	Moniack View
Muir of Ord	GH	The Dower House
Rogart	FH	Rovie Farm

LOTHIAN

Edinburgh	GH	Dorstan Private Hotel

Edinburgh	GH	The Lodge Hotel

STRATHCLYDE

Ayr	GH	Brenalde Lodge
Cardross	GH	Kirkton House
Connel	GH	Loch Etive Hotel
Machrihanish	GH	Ardell House
Prestwick	GH	Golf View Hotel
Tobermory	GH	Fairways Lodge
Tobermory	GH	Strongarbh House

TAYSIDE

Arbroath	FH	Farmhouse Kitchen
Brechin	FH	Blibberhill Farm
Dundee	GH	Beach House Hotel
Pitlochry	GH	Dundarave House

NORTHERN IRELAND

ANTRIM

Bushmills	GH	White Gables
Lisburn	FH	Brook Lodge
Farmhouse		

TYRONE

Dungannon	GH	Grange Lodge

REPUBLIC OF IRELAND

CARLOW

Milford	T&C	Goleen Country
House		

CLARE

Ballyvaughan	T&C	Rusheen Lodge

CORK

Ballinadee	T&C	Glebe House
Kanturk	GH	Assolas Country House
Kinsale	GH	Old Bank House
Youghal	GH	Ahernes

DUBLIN

Dublin	GH	Aberdeen Lodge
Dublin	GH	Ariel House
Dublin	GH	The Grey Door

KERRY

Killarney	GH	Kathleen's Country House

LOUTH

Ardee	GH	The Gables House Guest House & Restaurant

MAYO

Achill Island	GH	Gray's

OFFALY

Tullamore	GH	Moorhill Country
House		

TIPPERARY

Bansha	FH	Bansha House

WATERFORD

Cappoquin	GH	Richmond House

WEXFORD

Ballymurn	FH	Ballinkeele House
Ferns	FH	Clone House
Gorey	FH	Woodlands Farmhouse
Wexford	T&C	Ardruagh
Wexford	GH	Whitford House

WICKLOW

Wicklow	GH	The Old Rectory Country House & Restaurant

YOUR STAY- WHAT YOU NEED TO KNOW

BOOKING

Book as early as possible, particularly if accommodation is required during the peak holiday period from the beginning of June to the end of September, plus public holidays and, in some parts of Scotland, during the skiing season.

Although it is possible for chance callers to find a night's accommodation, it is by no means a certainty, especially at peak holiday times and in the popular areas, so to be certain of obtaining the accommodation you require, it is always advisable to book as far in advance as possible. Some establishments will also require a deposit on booking.

We have tried to provide as much information as possible about the establishments in our directory, but if you should require further information before deciding to book, you should write to the establishment concerned. Do remember to enclose a stamped addressed envelope, or an international reply-paid coupon if writing from overseas, and please quote this publication in any enquiry.

It is regretted that the AA cannot at the present time undertake to make any reservations.

CANCELLATION

If you later find that you must cancel your visit, let the proprietor know at once, because if the room you booked cannot be re-let, you may be held legally responsible for partial payment.

Whether it is a matter of losing your deposit, or of being liable for compensation, you should seriously consider taking out cancellation insurance, such as AA Travelsure.

COMPLAINTS

AA members who have any cause to complain are urged to do so on the spot. This should provide an opportunity for the proprietor to correct matters. If a personal approach fails, AA members should inform the AA Head Office at Basingstoke.

FIRE PRECAUTIONS

Many of the establishments listed in the Guide are subject to the requirements of the Fire Precautions Act of 1971. As far as we can discover, every establishment in this book has applied for, and not been refused, a fire certificate.

The Fire Precautions Act does not apply to Ireland (see page 454), the Channel Islands, or the Isle of Man, which exercise their own rules regarding fire precautions for hotels.

FOOD AND DRINK

If you intend to take dinner at an establishment, note that sometimes the meal must be ordered in advance of the actual meal time. In some cases, this may be at breakfast time, or even on the previous evening. If you have booked on bed, breakfast and evening meal terms, you may find that the tariff includes a set menu, but you can usually order from the à la carte menu, if there is one, and pay a supplement.

Some establishments in London only provide a Continental breakfast. If a full English breakfast is available, this is indicated in their description.

On Sundays, many establishments serve the main meal at midday, and provide only a cold supper in the evening.

In some parts of Britain, particularly in Scotland, high tea (ie a savoury dish followed by bread and butter, scones, cakes, etc) is sometimes served instead of dinner, which may, however, be available on request. The last time at which high tea or dinner may be ordered on weekdays is shown, but this may be varied at weekends.

LICENCES

The directory entry will show whether or not the establishment is licensed to serve alcoholic drinks. Many places in the guesthouse category hold a residential or restaurant license only, but all inns hold a full licence. Licensed premises are not obliged to remain open throughout the permitted hours, and they may do so only when they expect reasonable trade.

Note that in establishments which have registered clubs, club membership does not come into effect, nor can a drink be bought, until 48 hours after joining.

MONEY-OFF VOUCHER SCHEME
In the front of this book you will find six £1 vouchers which can be redeemed against your bill for accommodation at any of the establishments which show the £ symbol in the directory.

Only one voucher may be presented for one room bill irrespective of the number of nights stayed. You must show your copy of the 1993 Guide in order to claim the discount and it is essential to do this when you check in at reception. The vouchers are not valid if you are already benefitting from a discount under some other scheme, or from special off-peak rates.

The voucher scheme is not applicable in the Republic of Ireland.

PAYMENT
Most proprietors will only accept cheques in payment of accounts if notice is given and some form of identification (preferably a cheque card) is produced. If a hotel accepts credit or charge cards, this is shown in its directory entry (see page 34 for details).

PRICES
It should be noted that daily terms quoted throughout this publication show minimum and maximum prices for both one (sb&b) and two persons (db&b) and include a full breakfast. If dinner is also included this will be indicated in parenthesis (incl dinner). Weekly terms, where available, show minimum and maximum prices per person, which take into account minimum double occupancy and maximum single occupancy, where appropriate, and may include the price of an evening meal (WBDi).

The Hotel Industry Voluntary Code of Booking Practice was revised in 1986, and the AA encourages its use in appropriate establishments. Its prime object is to ensure that the customer is clear about the precise services and facilities s/he is buying and what price will have to be paid, before entering into a contractually binding agreement. If the price has not been previously confirmed in writing, the guest should be handed a card at the time of registration, stipulating the total obligatory charge. The Tourism (Sleeping Accommodation Price Display) Order 1977 compels hotels, motels, guesthouses, farmhouses, inns and self-catering accommodation with four or more letting bedrooms to display in entrance halls the minimum and maximum prices charged for each category of room. This order complements the Voluntary Code of Booking Practice. The tariffs quoted in the directory of this book may be affected in the coming year by inflation, variations in the rate of VAT and many other factors.

You should always confirm the current prices before making a booking. Those given in this book have been provided by proprietors in good faith, and must be accepted as indications rather than firm quotations.

In some cases, proprietors have been unable to provide us with their 1993 charges, but to give you a rough guide we publish the 1992 price, prefixed with an asterisk (*). It is also a good idea to ascertain all that is included in the price. Weekly terms can vary according to the meals that are included. We cannot indicate whether or not you are able to arrive mid-week, so if this is your intention, do check when making your reservation. Where information about 1993 prices is not given, you are requested to make enquiries direct.

VAT is payable, in the United Kingdom and in the Isle of Man, on both basic prices and any service. VAT does not apply in the Channel Islands. With this exception, prices quoted in the Guide are inclusive of VAT (and service where applicable).

Prices for the Republic of Ireland are shown in Irish punts. At the time of going to press, the exchange rate is 1.09 Punts = £1.00 Sterling.

PUTTING OUT THE WELCOME MAT

An entire generation has achieved maturity without ever experiencing the dubious hospitality of the old-fashioned boarding house landlady - the kind who would throw you out after breakfast, whatever the weather, and not allow you back in until tea-time, fill you up with good plain stodge at mealtimes and lock you out if you weren't back by 10 o'clock in the evening. And yet the image seems to persist - she lingers on as a spectre to haunt the modern bed and breakfast establishment in spite of their efforts to shake her off.

To discover whether there are any restrictions in the hospitality business today, we conducted a survey among the establishments in this guide, asking whether children are welcome, what the policy was with regard to meals, smoking, drinking, etc., whether guests were still expected to be out all day, and finally, we asked proprietors what they thought of their guests.

Children Welcome

The friendliness and informality of a bed and breakfast holiday would seem to be ideal for families, and 95 per cent of our establishments say that they welcome children. However, we received more adverse comments from proprietors for this than for any other question in our survey. Are children really just an unruly rabble who create noise, mayhem and a trail of destruction wherever they go?

95% of establishments welcome children.

Well, ask any parent! Perhaps, though, it is telling that the places which merely tolerate children because they can't afford to turn families away, but do not provide any special facilities, are the ones that relate most of the bad experiences; those who say that they actually like children, and provide things to play with, early meals so that parents can eat in peace and the all-important baby-sitting service seem to experience fewer difficulties.

"Having a child in the house is like having a time bomb under your roof."

Of the places which welcome children, about 8 per cent impose an age restriction - some will not accept babies, others will only accept babies; the four to ten age group is the least popular and many will only accept teenagers. Family rooms are not always available, and if children must occupy their own room, a price reduction is unlikely. Neither can you rely on being provided with a cot and/or high chair; some that do provide a cot will charge for it. Sometimes children are not allowed into the dining room in the evening.

"We abhor the British trait of treating children as unwanted appendages"

"We don't allow our friends to smoke here either. Anyone who wants to smoke will have to go outside, even if it's raining."

To Smoke or not to Smoke

Smoking is a contentious issue these days, and smokers would need to know that only 20 per cent of respondents to our survey allowed complete freedom of choice to smokers. Just under 10 per cent imposed a total ban, labelling smokers as "disgusting", "obnoxious" and even "unhygienic". The remaining 70 per cent compromise, with some no-smoking areas - usually the dining room.

In 90% of establishments smoking is allowed somewhere on the premises.

One can sympathise with the asthma sufferer and the one who was afraid for the thatched roof, but it must be safer to have a designated area for smoking than for guests to have a sneaky smoke in the bedroom.

The Demon Drink

Alcohol is another subject which brought some strong sentiments from our B & B hosts, but those who regard it as the demon drink are in a very small minority. What was surprising was the number of proprietors who equate having a drink with drunkenness and bad behaviour, when most people simply want a glass of wine with dinner and a civilised couple of drinks during the evening.

Alcohol is served in 66 % of establishments

For one reason or another, mainly because of licensing restrictions, 34% of our establishments do not supply alcohol.

"We do not want to encourage that kind of guest."

However, most will have no objection to guests bringing their own, and only six places would not have the stuff under their roof at any price.

Around 37 per cent have a full bar service and the rest have a compromise of some sort, such as a table licence or "honesty" bar.

"We have an honesty bar - guests drink more by helping themselves."

Dinner is Served

Two-thirds of the establishments who returned our questionnaire provide evening meals, but you may not always be able to decide what you want to eat and at what time. More than half of those who provide an evening meal serve it at a set time, often as early as 5.30pm, and usually before 7pm.

Most require some advance notice that you will be eating with them: 15 per cent need to know at least 24 hours in advance (one asked for two days' notice and many said the meal must be ordered when booking); 27 per cent take orders for the evening meal at breakfast time; 30 per cent ask for notice of between three and six hours, which could be the most awkward of all because most guests will be out at that time of day. The remainder asked for less than two hours' notice.

As to whether or not you can choose what you eat, in 23 per cent of cases, the answer would be no, and a further 10 per cent only offer a choice at breakfast

Evening meals are provided in 68% of establishments.

time. Where there is no choice, the chances are that they will stick to the safe options, such as roasts and grills, but the proprietor will usually tell guests what is going to be served and will provide an alternative for anyone who doesn't like it. Most will also cater for vegetarians and special dietary needs. Another 11 per cent offer only a limited choice - usually a choice of starters and puddings, but a set main course. This leaves 56 per cent who offer a choice of dishes, which varies from a couple of alternatives at each course to a full *carte*

Printed on a breakfast menu - *"We do not make fried bread and there is no tomato ketchup or brown sauce."*

One of the reasons why people stay in guesthouses and private hotels is in expectation of personal service, but the majority of places are now providing DIY refreshment facilities in bedrooms. Only 8 per cent of our respondents said that they did not do this, with reasons ranging from: "we prefer to offer a personal service and a more friendly approach" to: "guests make a mess in the bedrooms". More than half will also provide personal service.

In 56% of establishments menus offer a choice of dishes.

The Seating Plan

Communal tables are liked by 11 per cent of our respondents - mainly those who like to promote "a house-party atmosphere". In this situation success depends entirely on the ability of a band of complete strangers to get on - a lively and sociable crowd can be real fun, but one opinionated bore can ruin a mealtime for the rest.

Separate tables are provided in 89% of dining rooms.

Some will provide separate tables for guests who wish it - such as the one which offers honeymooners the sole use of the conservatory at breakfast time - but for most people, sitting in conspicuous isolation can be almost as bad as reluctantly joining in. And yet, proprietors tell us that it usually works well, with lots of lively discussions and new friendships forged. Foreigners, it seems, are particularly keen on the arrangement. The majority of places provide separate tables for all as a matter of course, but around 20 per cent will ask you to share when they are very busy. Many told us that, if sharing is unavoidable, they always try to match up people who they think will be compatible. Single people are the most likely to be asked to share - no-one seems to like to see a single woman eating alone, though the privacy of the lone businessman is always respected. It is interesting that all the places that provide separate tables say their guests prefer it and all with a communal table say exactly the same. Are there two distinct breeds of holidaymaker, or do we simply adapt and accept?

"Much more of a private home atmosphere, otherwise guests tend to adopt a funereal whisper in conversation."

Whatever the Weather

The British climate, it has to be said, is not the reason why people holiday here and there could be the odd day when you really don't want to be out of doors all the time. Without exception, our respondents all told us that

"If a guest requires any refreshment I try to supply it, but I don't encourage it. I am a professional chef!"

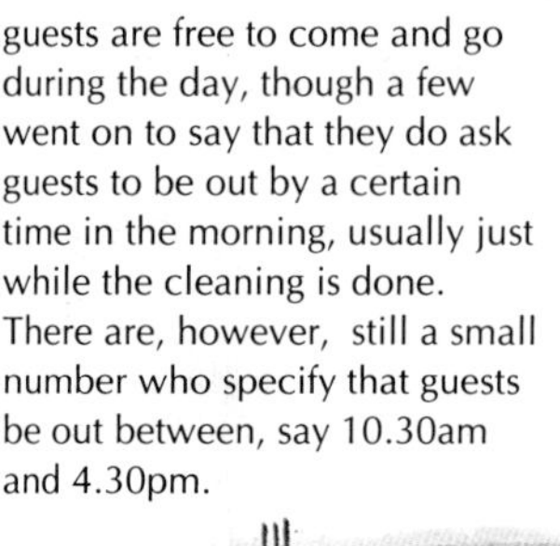

guests are free to come and go during the day, though a few went on to say that they do ask guests to be out by a certain time in the morning, usually just while the cleaning is done. There are, however, still a small number who specify that guests be out between, say 10.30am and 4.30pm.

"Surely no-one gets locked out of hotels these days!"

Every establishment allows (more or less) free access to guests during the day.

The majority also provide guests with a key to the front door. Of those who do not supply keys, many just stay up until the last guest has returned to the fold. We were amazed, however, to discover that there are still one or two who supply no keys and have a set time to lock up at night - sometimes as early as 10.30pm

Rules of the House

One hallmark of the old-fashioned boarding house was the list of do's and don'ts on each bedroom wall. We asked our guesthouses whether or not they had any notices around the place and 20 per cent said they had no notices at all; 25% displayed only tourist information and local entertainment; 8 per cent favoured the information folder in each room.

"Too many rules and regulations frighten guests away."

However, 42 per cent had more varied notices, such as:

Let us know if you want to go into the garden so we can make sure the guard dog is not out.

Let us know when you are taking a bath so that we can ensure there is hot water.

Please allow one hour between baths.

Due to the increase in bed-linen being badly soiled with take-away food, a charge will be made for extra cleaning.

Do not iron on the carpets.

No washing to be done in rooms.

Turn TV down after 10.30pm.

A few replies were less specific about the content of their notices, but one has to wonder about the one which gives guests: "information about our aims in running a hotel and how to get the best out of their stay." Another simply displayed: "a little poetry."

Making friends

It is encouraging, however, to note that 88 per cent of proprietors like to promote a friendly relationship with their guests. Some are more friendly than others - like the guesthouse (not AA) we heard about where guests enjoying a dip in the swimming pool on warm evenings would be joined by their host - completely naked! The vast majority of those hosts who favour the friendly approach, however, confine their enthusiasm to the occasional congenial chat, offering help and advice when it is asked for and sometimes joining them in the evening for a drink. Finally, we gave proprietors the opportunity to tell us what they don't like about the business they are in. Many of them couldn't think of a single thing to complain about.

The majority of proprietors remain enthusiastic and happy in their work.

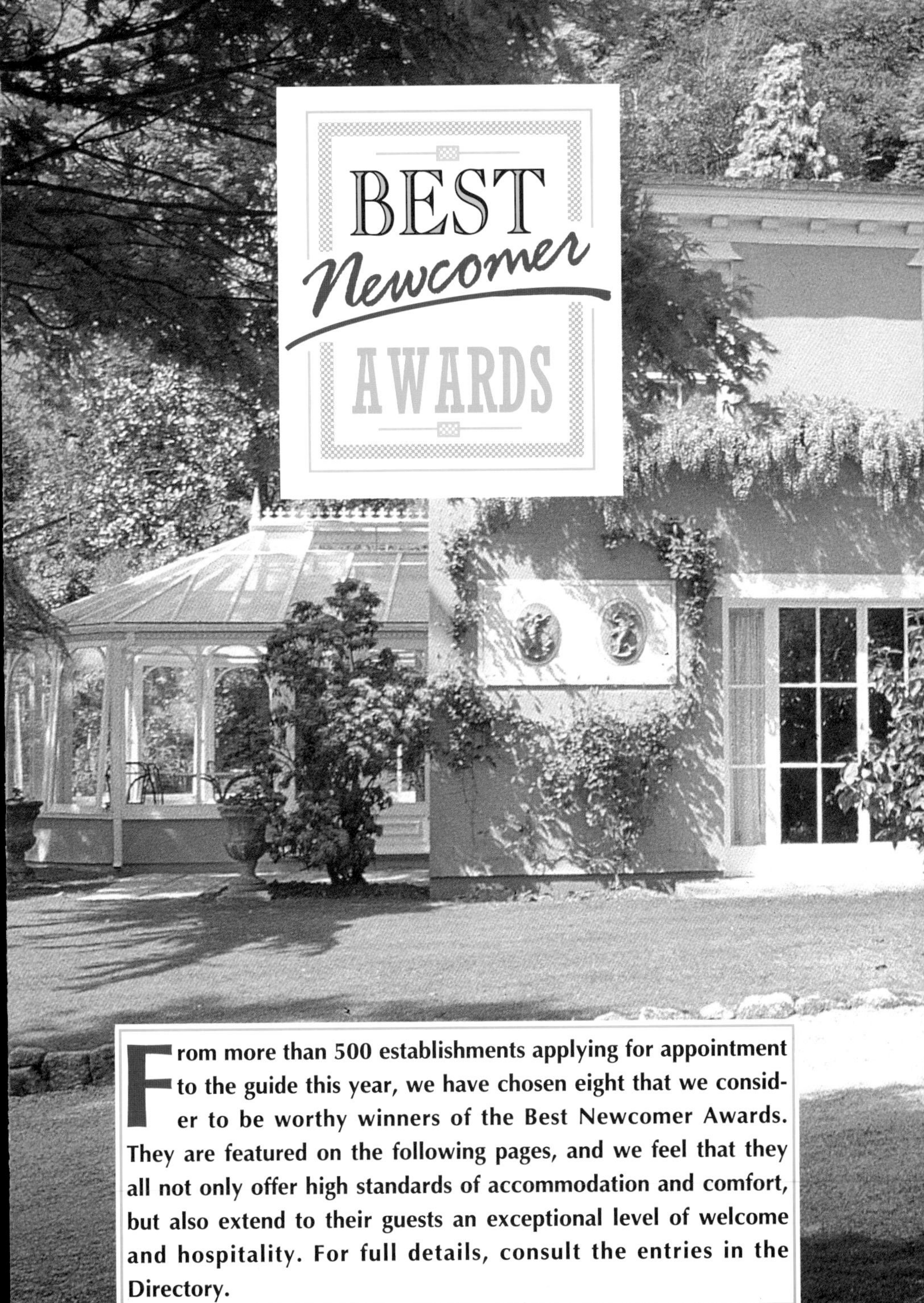

BEST *Newcomer* AWARDS

From more than 500 establishments applying for appointment to the guide this year, we have chosen eight that we consider to be worthy winners of the Best Newcomer Awards. They are featured on the following pages, and we feel that they all not only offer high standards of accommodation and comfort, but also extend to their guests an exceptional level of welcome and hospitality. For full details, consult the entries in the Directory.

THE TOWER
Sway, Hampshire

Dating back to 1885 and built, unusually for that period, entirely of concrete, the Tower stands over 200ft high, its rooms offering a superb outlook over the surrounding countryside. As a guesthouse, this is something quite unique and owners Paul and Julie Atlas have given it an atmosphere of real charm and romance. A winding staircase gives access to the four guest rooms, one to a floor, each decorated with antique furnishings and tapestries, in keeping with the style of the building. These rooms are, you may be glad to know, not on the highest storeys of the tower, but a trip to the 13th floor to admire the splendid views is a must. The evening meal, served in the small dining room, is also an experience to be enjoyed. For relaxation, there is a pleasant lounge or, weather permitting, a delightful walled garden. After a stay in this most unusual guesthouse, no-one could fail to feel revitalised.

NANSCAWEN HOUSE
St Blazey, Cornwall

For the last four years, Keith and Janet Martin have opened the doors to their Cornish home and invited guests in to enjoy warm hospitality and a genuine welcome. Janet is very interested in cooking and combines local produce with vegetables and fruit from their garden. Light, crisp pastry horns filled with wild mushrooms, onions and herbs and a subtle hint of garlic, made a mouthwatering starter for our inspector . Fillets of Cornish sole with a cream sauce, delicately flavoured with saffron, and, for dessert, a compote of summer fruits, completed a memorable meal. Guests will find fruit and mineral water in their bedrooms and can relax in a spa bath, ideal after a long journey or a hectic day's sightseeing. It is obvious that Mr and Mrs Martin thoroughly enjoy looking after guests and it is impossible not to have fond and lasting memories of a stay at Nanscawen.

THE OLD PLOUGH

North Wheatley

Mrs Pasley is an excellent cook and guests will thoroughly enjoy their stay at the Old Plough. Formerly a pub, the tradition of hospitality is still the hallmark of this attractive, grade II listed building. Dinner, served house-party style at a large table in the elegant dining room, is a set, four-course meal, but the dishes change frequently so that there is always something different to try. Smoked haddock, plaice and salmon in a Stilton sauce, or vegetable and fish terrine are typical starters from the imaginative menu. Breakfasts are pretty special too, featuring home-made breads, preserves and honey. Attractive bedrooms are equipped with little extra comforts such as fresh flowers, bowls of fruit and even bathrobes. A comfortable drawing room decorated with prints, pictures and ornaments adds to the relaxing atmosphere of this truly delightful guesthouse.

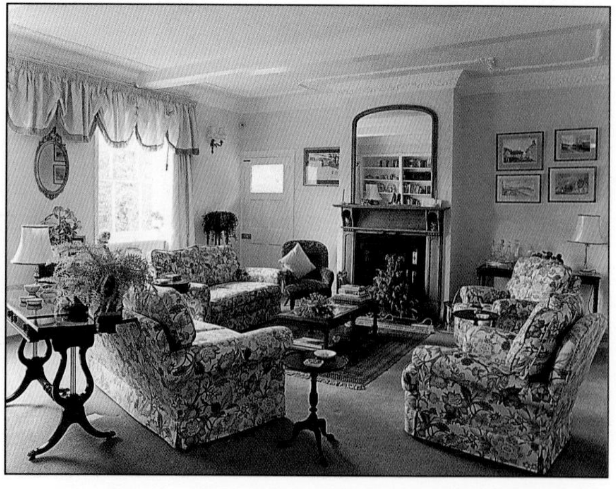

The gardens are a delight at Fayrer Holme, colourful all through the seasons with mature plants, trees and flowering shrubs. The setting is superb too, overlooking Lake Windermere. Iain and Jackie Garside previously owned and ran the Rothay Garden Hotel at Grasmere, but decided to retire from the business and then changed their minds and bought Fayrer Holme. This is very good news for their guests because they have years of experience in making people welcome at this elegant Lakeland stone house in its five acres of grounds. The bedrooms are charming and very comfortable, with en suite facilities, and for a romantic weekend, why not choose the one with a four poster bed and whirlpool bath. Fayrer Holme provides bed and breakfast (served in the attractive conservatory) only but nearby Bowness offers a good choice of restaurants for dinner. All in all a lovely place to stay.

FAYRER HOLME
Windermere, Cumbria

PENGWERN FARM
Llanwnda, Gwynedd

Gwyndaf and Jane Rowlands own and run this lovely old Victorian house, beautifully preserved and impeccably maintained. Set in peaceful surroundings with superb views of Snowdonia and situated on 130 acres of land between the mountains and the sea, Pengwern Farm is very special. Three bedrooms, two with en suite bathrooms, are available. A few yards away from the main house is a single storey cottage, completely self contained with its own lounge, bathroom and kitchen and let as a family unit. Gwyndaf and Jane Rowlands are delighted to welcome guests to Pengwern Farm and Jane prepares excellent meals combining fresh ingredients with home produced beef and lamb. The atmosphere here is one of peace and relaxation. The comment made by our inspector was: "the kind of place I would choose for a private visit".

John and Sandra Caldwell are the owners of this delightful Victorian farmhouse, full of character and charm, where guests are greeted personally and offered refreshments in the comfortable lounge as soon as they arrive. The Farmhouse Kitchen offers bed and breakfast only, but what good, substantial breakfasts they are, with the famous local Arbroath smokies often on the menu. The meal is served in the farmhouse kitchen at a communal table, which makes for a really friendly feel. Two unusual facilities are offered here, one we suspected more popular than the other: for keep-fit addicts there is a rowing machine; for sun seekers a sun bed to give them that Mediterranean tan with which to impress their friends.

FARMHOUSE KITCHEN
Arbroath, Tayside

GRANGE LODGE
Dungannon, Co. Tyrone

An air of peace prevails at this delightful Georgian house, home of Ralph and Norah Brown, and from the moment you arrive you are made to feel at ease, and part of the family. The accommodation is truly special, and it is obvious that great care and attention has been paid to the decorating and furnishing of this elegant house. This same care is carried through to the cooking. Norah Brown takes great pride in producing excellent meals to tempt the appetite of her guests. Smoked salmon or Stuffed pork fillet with fresh vegetables could be a choice for main course. Brandy-snap baskets filled with fresh fruit and ice cream are a regular pudding and one much enjoyed by our inspector, who summed up his visit to Grange Lodge in the one word "Superb".

GREY DOOR
Dublin, Co. Dublin

The Irish are renowned for their hospitality and the owners of this charming guesthouse are no exception to the rule. Patrick Daly and his partner Pierce Wyse are friendly and attentive hosts. The accommodation in this elegant building in the heart of Dublin is of a high standard and very comfortable. It has seven bedrooms, each with their own luxurious bathrooms. Guests have a choice of two restaurants in which to enjoy an excellent meal, the Grey Door itself, or Blushers,a more informal bistro in style. There is a delightful private dining room which can accommodate up to 60 people. The antique furnishings, original plaster ceilings and decoration give a stylish atmosphere to this most relaxing and comfortable place to stay. Comfort is a priority here and nothing is too much trouble to give guests an enjoyable holiday. A stay at the Grey Door is a truly memorable experience.

PREVIOUS AWARD WINNERS 1992

South of England	**Wales**
SWALE COTTAGE	BORTHWNOG HALL
Penshurst, Kent	Bontddu, Dolgellau, Gwynedd
South West of England	**Scotland**
BRADFORD OLD WINDMILL	DOWER HOUSE
Bradford-upon-Avon, Wiltshire	Muir of Ord, Highland
Central England	**Northern Ireland**
BROOKFIELD ON LONGHILL	WHITE GABLES
Buston, Derbyshire	Bushmills, Portballintrae

North of England

THE OLD RECTORY

Bolton Gate, Cumbria

HOW TO USE THE GUIDE

The directory lists place-names alphabetically throughout England, Scotland and Wales, the Isle of Man and the Channel Islands.

Establishments on islands are listed under the appropriate island heading. The example of an entry is to help you find your way through the directory. All the abbreviations and symbols are explained on pages 35 and 36.

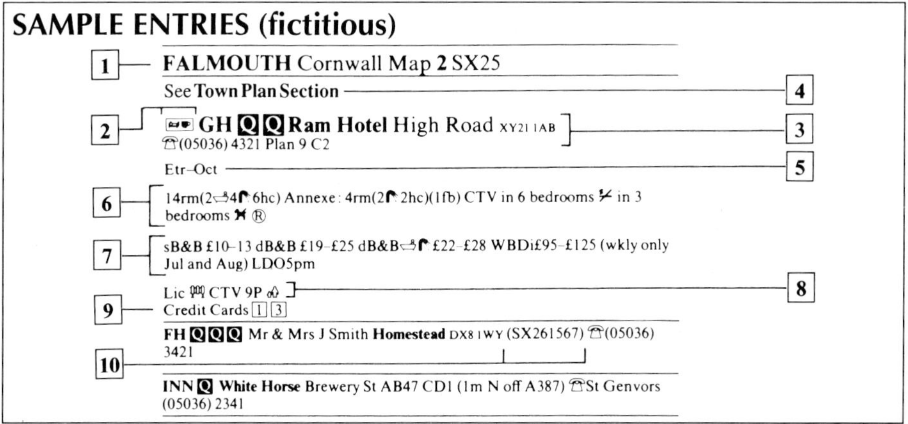

SAMPLE ENTRIES (fictitious)

1 — **FALMOUTH** Cornwall Map **2** SX25

See **Town Plan Section** — 4

2 — **GH Q Q Ram Hotel** High Road XY21 1AB — 3
☎(05036) 4321 Plan 9 C2

Etr–Oct — 5

6 — 14rm(2⇌4🚿6hc) Annexe: 4rm(2🚿2hc)(1fb) CTV in 6 bedrooms ⚟ in 3 bedrooms ✗ ®

7 — sB&B £10–13 dB&B £19–£25 dB&B⇌🚿 £22–£28 WBDi£95–£125 (wkly only Jul and Aug) LDO5pm

Lic 🛉 CTV 9P — 8

9 — Credit Cards 1 3

FH Q Q Q Mr & Mrs J Smith **Homestead** DX8 1WY (SX261567) ☎(05036) 3421

10

INN Q White Horse Brewery St AB47 CD1 (1m N off A387) ☎St Genvors (05036) 2341

1 **Towns** (including London) are listed in strict alphabetical order followed by the county or region. This is the administrative county, or region, and not necessarily part of the correct postal address. Towns on islands (not connected to the mainland by a bridge) are listed under the island name. With Scottish regions or islands, the old county name follows in italics. The map reference denotes first the map number, then the grid reference. To find the location on the atlas, first find the appropriate square (indicated by two letters), then read the 1st figure across and the 2nd figure vertically.

2 This symbol indicates that the establishment expects to provide bed and breakfast for under £15 per person, per night during 1993, but remember that circumstances can change during the currency of the Guide.

3 **Establishment name**, address, postal code and telephone number. When an establishment's name is shown in italics the particulars have not been confirmed by the proprietor. Guesthouses are identified by the letters GH, Farmhouses by FH, Inns by INN and Town and Country by T&C- this is also the order in which they are listed beneath the town headings.

All establishments are now rated for quality on a scale of one to four. This is denoted by the letter Q. See page 8 for a full explanation.

The telephone exchange (STD code) is usually that of the town heading. Where it differs from the town heading the exchange is given after the symbol, and before the dialling code and number. In some areas, numbers are likely to be changed during the currency of this book. In case of difficulty, check with the operator.

4 **Town Plans** There are street plans of some major towns and resorts at the end of the directory. If there is a town plan, each establishment is given a key number and located on the plan. The London street plans, however, appear next to the London entries in the directory.

5 **Opening details** Unless otherwise stated, the establishments are open all year, but where dates are shown they are inclusive: eg 'Apr-Oct' indicates that the establishment is open from the beginning of April to the end of October. Although some places are open all year, they may offer a restricted service during the less busy months, and we indicate this in the gazetteer by using the rs abbreviation. This may mean that there is a reduction in meals served and/or accommodation available, and where not indicated in the text, you should telephone in advance to find out the nature of the restriction.

6 Accommodation details The first figure shows the number of letting bedrooms. Where rooms have en suite bath or shower and wc or hot and cold water (hc), the number precedes the appropriate symbol.

Annexe - bedrooms available in an annexe are shown. Their standard is acceptable, but facilities may not be the same as in the main building, and it is advisable to check the nature of the accommodation and tariff before making a reservation.

⅟ number of bedrooms for non-smokers.

fb - family bedrooms.

CTV/TV - colour or black and white television available in lounge. This may also mean televisions permanently in bedrooms or available on request from the management. Check when making reservations.

no dogs allowed in bedrooms. Some establishments may restrict the size of dogs permitted and the rooms into which they may be taken. Establishments which do not normally accept dogs may accept guide dogs. Generally, dogs are not allowed in the dining room. Check when booking the conditions under which pets are accepted.

7 Prices Bed and breakfast per person/two persons, per night and per person, per week (inclusive of dinner at times). For full explanation see page 15. Prices given have been provided by the proprietor in good faith, and are indications rather than firm quotations. Some establishments offer free accommodation to children provided they share the parents' room. Check current prices before booking. See also page 15.

8 Facilities For key to symbols see pages 35 and 36.

no coaches. This information is published in good faith from details supplied by the establishments concerned. Inns, however, have well-defined legal obligations towards travellers, and any member with cause for complaint should take this up with the proprietor or the local licensing authority.

nc - establishments listed accommodate children of all ages unless a minimum age is given (eg nc 4 yrs), but they may not necessarily be able to provide special facilites. nc by itself indicates 'no children'. For very young children, check before booking about such provisions as cots and high chairs, and any reductions made.

establishments with special facilities for children, which will include babysitting service or baby intercom system, playroom or playground, laundry facilities, drying and ironing facilities, cots, high chairs and special meals.

Note - disabled people may be accommodated, and where this is the case reference to this may be made in the description. Further details for disabled people will be found in the AA's Guide for the Disabled Traveller available from AA shops, free to members, £3.50 to non-members. Intending guests with any form of disability should notify proprietors, so that arrangements can be made to minimise difficulties, particularly in the event of an emergency.

9 Payment details (the following cards or discount vouchers may be accepted, but check current details when booking)

1 - Access/Eurocard/Mastercard
2 - American Express
3 - Barclaycard/Visa
5 - Diners
£ - Establishment accepts AA Money-Off Vouchers as detailed on page 15.

10 Ordnance Survey Map Reference This is shown for farmhouse entries only. As they are often in remote areas, we provide a six-figure map reference which can be used with Ordnance Survey maps.

SYMBOLS AND ABBREVIATIONS

ENGLISH

	Bed and breakfast for £15 or under
Q	Quality assessment (see p. 8)
☎	Telephone number
	Private bath and WC
	Private shower and WC
	Bedrooms set aside for non-smokers
	No dogs
®	Tea/coffee-making facilities in bedrooms
*	1992 prices
	Full central heating
P	Parking for cars
P̸	No parking on premises
	Garage accommodation for . . . cars
	Coach parties not accepted
	Special facilities for children (see p. 34)
	Indoor swimming pool
	Outdoor swimming pool
9 18	9-hole or 18-hole golf course
	Tennis court(s)
	Fishing
U	Riding stables on premises
sB&B	Single room including breakfast per person per night
dB&B	Double room (2 persons sharing a room) including breakfast per night
WB&B	Weekly terms, bed and breakfast, per person
WBDi	Weekly terms bed, breakfast and evening meal, per person
alc	A la carte
CTV	Colour television
Etr	Easter
fb	Family bedroom
fr	From
hc	Number of bedrooms with hot and cold water
LDO	Time last dinner can be ordered
Lic	Licensed
mdnt	Midnight
nc	No children, nc . . . yrs, no children under . . . years of age
rm	Letting bedrooms in main building
rs	Restricted service
T	Direct dial telephones in rooms
TV	Black and white television
1	Credit cards (see p. 34)
£	Voucher scheme (see p. 15)
→	Entry continued overleaf

FRANÇAIS

	Chambre et petit déjeuner pour moins de £15
Q	Symbole AA d'évaluation qualitative (voir p. 8)
☎	Numéro de téléphone
	Salle de bain privée avec WC
	Douche privée et WC
	Chambres réservées aux non-fumeurs
	Chiens interdits
®	Possibilité de faire le thé/le café dans les chambres
*	Prix 1992
	Chauffage central intégral
P	Stationnement pour voitures
P̸	Pas de stationnement sur place
	Garage pour . . . voitures
	Groups en autocar pas reçus
	Facilités spéciales pour enfants – (voir p. 34)
	Piscine à l'intérieur
	Piscine à l'extérieur
9 18	Terrain de golf à 9 ou 18 trous
	Court(s) de tennis
	Pêche
U	Ecuries d'équitation sur les lieux
sB&B	Chambre à un lit et petit déjeuner par personne et par nuit
dB&B	Chambre à deux lits (2 personnes à une chambre) avec petit déjeuner par nuit
WB&B	Prix par semaine et par personne, chambre et petit déjeuner inclus
WBDi	Prix par semaine et par personne, chambre, petit déjeuner et diner inclus
alc	A la carte
CTV	TV en couleurs
Etr	Pâques
fb	Chambre de famille
fr	A partir de
hc	Nombre de chambres avec eau chaude et froide
LDO	Le dîner est à commander avant cette heure
Lic	Licence de boissons
mdnt	Minuit
nc	Enfants pas admis, nc . . . ans, enfants au-dessous de . . . ans pas admis
rm	Nombre de chambres dans le bâtiment principal
rs	Service réduit
T	Téléphone dans la chambre, direct avec l'exterieur
TV	TV en noir et blanc
1	Cartes de crédit (voir p. 34)
£	Bons (voir p. 15)
→	Suite au verso

DEUTSCH

	Bett mit Frühstück für unter £15
Q	AA Katagorisierung der Qualität (siehe S. 8)
☎	Telefonnummer
	Privatbadezimmer mit WC
	Privatdusche mit WC
	Zimmer für Nichtraucher
	Hundeverbot
®	Tee/Kaffeemöglichkeiten im Zimmer
*	1992 Preise
	Vollfernheizung
P	Parkplatz
P̸	Kein Parkplatz
	Garagen für . . . Autos
	Reisebusgesellschaften nicht aufgenommen
	Sonderdientleistungen für Kinder – (siehe S. 34)
	Hallenbad
	Freibad
9 18	Golfplatz mit 9 oder 18 löcher
	Tennisplatz (Platze)
	Angeln
U	Reitstall an Ort und Stelle
sB&B	Übernachtung in einem Einzelzimmer mit Frühstück pro Person
dB&B	Doppelzimmer (2 Personer in einem Zimmer) mit Frühstück pro Nacht
WB&B	Wochenpreis pro Person, Übernachtung mit Frühstück
WBDi	Wochenpreis pro Person, Übernachtung mit Frühstück und Abendessen
alc	A la carte
CTV	Farbfernsehen
Etr	Ostern
fb	Familienzimmer
fr	Von
hc	Zimmer mit Warm- und Kaltwasser
LDO	Letzte Bestellzeit für Abendessen
Lic	Ausschank alkoolischer Getränke
mdnt	Mitternacht
nc	Kinder nicht willkommen, nc . . Jahren, Kinder unter . . Jahren nicht willkommen
rm	Zimmeranzahl im Hauptgebäude
rs	Beschränkte Dienstleistungen
T	Zimmertelefon mit Aussenverbindung über Telefonzentrale
TV	Schwarzweissfernsehen
1	Kreditkarten (seihe p. 34)
£	Gutschein (seihe p. 15)
→	Fortsetzung umseitig

SYMBOLS AND ABBREVIATIONS

ITALIANO

	Camera e prima colazione a meno di 15 sterline
Q	Simbolo di valutrazione qualitativa della AA (vedi p. 8)
☎	Numero telefonica
	Bagno e servizi privati
	Doccia e servizi privati
	Camere per non fumatori
	Proibito ai cani
®	Attrezzatura per fare il té o il caffé nelle camere
✱	Prezzi del 1992
	Riscaldemento centrale in tutte le camere
P	Parcheggio macchine
	Senza parcheggio sul posto
	Garage per . . . macchine
	Non si accettano comitive in gita turistica
	Attrezzature speciali per í bambini – (vedi p. 34)
	Piscina coperta
	Piscina scoperta
▶9▶18	Campo da golf a 9 o 18 buche
	Campo(i) da tennis
	Pesca
U	Scuola d'equitazione sul posto
sB&B	Prezzo di una camera singola con la colazione compresa (per notte)
dB&B	Prezzo di una camera doppia (2 persone per camera) con la colazione compresa (per notte)
WB&B	Tariffe settimanali per persona, camera e prima colazione
WBDi	Tariffe settimanali per persona, sono compresi la camera, la prima colazione e il pranzo
alc	Alla carta
CTV	Televisione a colori
Etr	Pasqua
fb	Camera familiare
fr	Da
hc	Numero di camera con acqua calda e fredda
LDO	Ora in cui si accettano le ultime ordinazioni
Lic	Autorizzato alla vendita alcolici
mdnt	Mezzanotte
nc	Proibito ai bambini, nc . . . anni, proibito ai bambini sottoi . . . anni
rm	Numero di camere nell' edificio principale
rs	Servizio limitato
T	Telefono in camera communicante direttamente con l'esterno
TV	Televisione in bianco e nero
[1]	Carte di credito (vedi p. 34)
(£)	Documento di riduzione (vedi p. 15)
→	La lista delle voci continua a tergo

ESPAÑOL

	Cama y desaguno a menos de 15 libras esterlinas
Q	Simbolo de evaluación calitativa de la AA (Véase p. 8)
☎	Numero de teléfono
	Baño y servicios en cada habitación
	Ducha y servicios en cada habitación
	Habitaciones reservados para los no fumadores
	Se prohibe a los porros
®	Facilidades para hacer el té o el café en los habitaciones
✱	Precios de 1992
	Calafacción central
P	Aparcamiento para automóviles
	No poder estacionarse junto al establecimiento
	Garaje o espacio cubierto para . . . automóviles
	No se aceptan los grupos de viajeros en coches de linea
	Facilidades especialies para los niños (p. 34)
	Piscina cubierta
	Piscina descubierta
▶9▶18	Campo de golf de 9 o 18 hoyos
	Cancha(s) de tenis
	Pesca
U	Escuela hípica
sB&B	Precio por noche de una habitación individual con desayuno incluido
dB&B	Precio por noche de una habitación para dos personas (2 personas compartiendo una habitación) con desayuno incluido
WB&B	Tarifas semanales cama y desayuno
WBDi	Tarifas semanales, el precio incluye a la cama, al desayuna y a la comida
alc	A la carta
CTV	Televisión en colores
Etr	Pascua de Resurrección
fb	Habitación familiar
fr	De
hc	Número de habitaciones con agua fría y caliente
LDO	Últimas ordenes
Lic	Con licencia para vender bebidas alcóholicas
mdnt	Medianoche
nc	Se prohibe le entrada a los niños, nc . . . años, se prohibe la entrada a los niños de menos de . . . años
rm	Número de habitaciones del edifico principal
rs	Servicio limitado
T	Teléfono en la habitación, comunicando con el exterior
TV	Televisión en blanco y negro
[1]	Tarjetas de crédito (véase p. 34)
(£)	Documento de rehaja (véase p. 15)
→	La lista continúa a la vuelta

Directory

ABBOTS BICKINGTON Devon Map 02 SS31

FH QQ Mrs E Bellew **Court Barton** *(SS384133)* EX22 7LQ ☎Milton Damerel(0409261) 214
May-Oct
An impressive stone-built farmhouse standing in its own gardens within a 650- acre mixed farm. The accommodation provides spacious bedrooms and comfortable public rooms. Home produce features in the set menus available in the dining room.
4hc (1fb) ® sB&B£13-£14 dB&B£26-£28 WB&Bfr£84 WBDi£100-£105 LDO 5pm
CTV 10P nc3yrs rough shooting 640 acres arable beef sheep £

ABBOTS BROMLEY Staffordshire Map 07 SK02

FH QQ Mrs M K Hollins **Marsh** *(SK069261)* WS15 3EJ ☎Burton-on-Trent(0283) 840323
Closed Xmas
On the B5013 a mile north of this pleasant village famed for its horn dancing, the farmhouse has been fully modernised but retains its exposed old beams. There are 2 large, well furnished bedrooms, a cosy first-floor lounge and a spacious dining room where afternoon teas are a speciality.
2hc (1fb) ® * dB&B£27-£30 WB&B£90-£100 LDO 5pm
CTV 6P 87 acres mixed £

ABERAERON Dyfed Map 02 SN46

GH QQQ Arosfa 8 Cadwgan Place SA46 0BU ☎(0545) 570120
Arosfa is a guesthouse and teashop (siop te) combined, opposite the car park and the inner yachting harbour. The teashop is popular with tourists and locals, and it is here that breakfast and dinner are served. There are 3 bedrooms in the main house, all en suite or with a private shower room, and a small residents' lounge which features an original fireplace complete with brass fender and black kettle. Some 70yds away is Morawel where there is a further lounge and 3 more bedrooms, and this overlooks the main harbour. The establishment is completely no smoking.
6rm(1 2 3hc) (1fb) in all bedrooms CTV in 3 bedrooms ® (ex guide dogs) * sB&B£12-£17 sB&B £15-£22 dB&B£24-£30 dB&B £30-£36 WB&B£70-£110 WBDi£110-£160 LDO 6pm
CTV

GH QQ Moldavia 7 & 8 Bellevue Ter SA46 0BB ☎(0545) 570107
This very friendly, family-run establishment is superbly situated above the picturesque harbour with a view to the mountains beyond. The 3 bedrooms are well furnished and brightly decorated, and one has a corner bath and separate shower. There is a small conservatory lounge overlooking the garden to the rear, and guests breakfast together at a communal table.
3rm(1 2hc) (1fb) in 1 bedroom CTV in 1 bedroom sB&B£16.50-£20 sB&B £20-£25 dB&B£33 dB&B £38 WB&B£115.50-£133
CTV 3P

ABERDEEN Grampian *Aberdeenshire* Map 15 NJ90

GH QQ Bimini 69 Constitution St AB2 1ET ☎(0224) 646912
Situated in the East End, convenient for the city centre, this small, family- run guesthouse has a friendly atmosphere and offers good value bed and breakfast accommodation. It is a no-smoking house.
7hc (1fb) in all bedrooms CTV in all bedrooms ® (ex guide dogs) * sB&B£16-£20 dB&B£28-£32
CTV 7P
Credit Cards 1 3

SELECTED

GH QQQQ Cedars Private Hotel 339 Great Western Rd AB1 6NW ☎(0224) 583225
In a West End residential area not far from central amenities, this efficiently run bed and breakfast establishment is especially popular with business guests. Bedrooms vary in size but are well furnished in the modern style. There is a comfortable sitting room and an attractive breakfast room with a splendidly ornate ceiling. The housekeeping here is exemplary.
13rm(6 7hc) (2fb) CTV in all bedrooms ® (ex guide dogs) * sB&B £36-£40 dB&B £47-£52 WB&B£238-£266
13P pool table
Credit Cards 1 2 3

GH QQQ Corner House Hotel 385 Great Western Rd AB1 6NY ☎(0224) 313063
A family-run business and holiday hotel, situated in a West End residential area. Bedrooms vary in size but are all comfortably furnished and well equipped, and a relaxed atmosphere prevails.
17 (3fb) CTV in all bedrooms ® T sB&B £35-£48 dB&B £45-£55 WB&B£160-£250 WBDi£220-£310 LDO 8pm
Lic CTV 12P
Credit Cards 1 3

GH QQQ Craiglynn Hotel 36 Fonthill Rd AB1 2UJ ☎(0224) 584050

→

In a south-side residential area, this impressive granite house offers a blend of Victorian elegance with modern comforts and is a popular base for business people. There is a choice of traditional lounges, and well prepared meals are served in the basement dining room. Smoking is not permitted in the comfortable bedrooms.

9rm(7⇨ↄ 2hc) (1fb)⁄ in all bedrooms CTV in all bedrooms ® T ✗ sB&B£32 sB&B⇨ↄ£43 dB&B⇨ↄ£59 LDO 7pm
Lic ♏ CTV 7P
Credit Cards 1 2 3 5

GH QQ Denver 154 Bon-Accord St AB1 2TX ☎(0224) 580617
Situated in a residential area just south of the town centre, this well maintained family-run guesthouse offers good value bed and breakfast accommodation.
8hc (3fb) CTV in all bedrooms ® sB&B£17 dB&B£26
♏ CTV

GH QQQ Fourways 435 Great Western Rd AB1 6NJ ☎(0224) 310218
This attractive grey-stone guesthouse with large bay windows is conveniently situated beside the ring road at the west end of town. Bedrooms are nicely decorated, plain but light and airy, and all offer the expected facilities. Hearty breakfasts are served in the combined lounge/dining room. This is a friendly, family-run establishment which offers good value accommodation.
7rm(6⇨ↄ 1hc) (2fb) CTV in all bedrooms ®
✗ (ex guide dogs) * sB&B⇨ↄ£22-£25 dB&B⇨ↄ£34
♏ CTV 7P

GH QQ Klibreck 410 Great Western Rd AB1 6NR ☎(0224) 316115
Closed Xmas & New Year
A small family-run guesthouse on the main Deeside road, close to the ring road. Good value bed and breakfast accommodation is provided, and there is a friendly atmosphere. Smoking is not permitted.
6hc (1fb)⁄ in all bedrooms ® ✗ * sB&Bfr£18 dB&Bfr£28
♏ CTV 3P

GH QQQ Open Hearth 349 Holburn St AB1 6DQ ☎(0224) 596888
Situated in the west end, this well established commercial guesthouse offers comfortable modern appointments and provides good value bed and breakfast accommodation.
11hc (2fb) CTV in all bedrooms ® sB&B£18.50 dB&B£30
♏ CTV 5P

GH QQ Strathboyne 26 Abergeldie Ter AB1 6EE ☎(0224) 593400
This traditional granite-built semidetached house is situated in a quiet West End residential area, and caters for both commercial visitors and holidaymakers. Recent improvements include the addition of 2 rooms with en suite facilities. Other rooms are modest with practical appointments, but are well equipped. There is also a new comfortable lounge.
7rm(2ↄ 5hc) (1fb) CTV in all bedrooms ® * sB&B£16.50-£17 sB&Bↄ£21.50-£22.50 dB&B£27-£30 LDO 12.30pm
♏ CTV ₽

ABERDOUR Fife Map **11** NT18

GH Q Fairways 17 Manse St KY3 0TT ☎(0383) 860478
Quietly situated at the end of a cul-de-sac between the village centre and the coast, this family-run bed and breakfast establishment offers simply furnished bedrooms and an attractively decorated breakfast room.
5hc (2fb) CTV in all bedrooms ® * sB&Bfr£15 dB&Bfr£30
♏ 3P

Street plans of certain towns and cities will be found in a separate section at the back of the book.

ABERDOVEY Gwynedd Map **06** SN69

GH QQQ Brodawel Tywyn Rd, Brodawel LL35 0SA ☎(0654) 767347
Closed Jan-Feb
Privately owned and personally run, this small, friendly hotel is situated on the A493. The bedrooms vary in size and family accommodation is available. They are well equipped with TV, radio and hairdryers, and all but one have views of the sea across the golf links. Other public areas include a cottage- style dining room, a quiet, cosy lounge and a pleasant garden. Guests are asked not to smoke in all rooms except for an area set aside for that purpose.
6⇨ↄ (1fb)⁄ in all bedrooms CTV in all bedrooms ® *
dB&B⇨ↄ£36-£38 WB&B£119 WBDi£196 LDO noon
Lic ♏ CTV 8P nc6yrs

GH QQ Cartref LL35 0NR ☎(0654) 767273
Located close to the beach and golf course – where guests can benefit from reduced green fees – this detached house offers traditionally furnished accommodation, which includes family rooms, and the majority enjoy sea views. This modest guesthouse is situated on the A493 to the western edge of Aberdovey.
7rm(1⇨ 3ↄ 3hc) (2fb) CTV in 6 bedrooms ® sB&B£16 dB&B£32 dB&B⇨ↄ£36 LDO 5pm
♏ CTV 8P

SELECTED

GH QQQQ Morlan LL35 0SE ☎(0654) 767706
This small, single-storey guesthouse is situated just west of the town on the A493 in an elevated position, with excellent views across the golf course to Cardigan Bay. The rooms are modern, with good quality furniture including some antiques. Each room has a private bathroom and French windows giving direct access to the pleasant garden; one room has a sea view and they are all thoughtfully equipped with several extra touches. There is a log fire in the comfortable lounge, and golf concessions can be arranged at the nearby championship course.
4rm(1⇨ 3ↄ) ⁄ in all bedrooms CTV in all bedrooms ®
✗ (ex guide dogs) * dB&B⇨ↄ£38-£40 WB&B£129-£135 WBDi£199-£206 LDO 2pm
Lic ♏ CTV 10P 🚗 nc16yrs

GH QQ Rossa LL35 0NR ☎(0654) 767545
Closed Dec & Jan
This small, privately owned and personally run guesthouse is situated on the A493, on the western edge of the town; the beach is a short walk away. It provides modern accommodation and is soundly maintained.
4rm(2ↄ 2hc) (2fb) CTV in 2 bedrooms ® * dB&Bfr£26 dB&Bↄfr£30 WB&B£88.50-£102.50 WBDi£137.50-£151.50
♏ CTV 3P

ABERGAVENNY Gwent Map **03** SO21

GH QQ Belchamps 1 Holywell Rd NP7 5LP ☎(0873) 853204
Overlooking the river Gavenny, this small, modest, well run hotel is situated on the edge of town, just off the A40. Parking is limited at the hotel but there is a free car park a short distance away.
5hc (3fb) CTV in all bedrooms ® ✗ (ex guide dogs) sB&B£16-£18 dB&B£32-£36 WB&B£100-£112 WBDi£160-£180 LDO 7pm
♏ CTV 5P

SELECTED

GH QQQQ Llanwenarth House Govilon NP7 9SF
☎Gilwern(0873) 830289
rs Jan-Feb
This imposing 16th-century house is set in a fine situation in the Vale of Usk, with commanding views of the Brecon Beacons, yet only 3 miles from the town. Owners Bruce and Amanda Weatherill have conscientiously renovated their charming home, and offer a welcoming house-guest atmosphere. Bedrooms are spacious, individual and distinctly different, and offer modern facilities in addition to several extra personal touches; the rooms are well equipped and have glorious views. Good home cooking is served by candlelight at an elegant communal mahogany table, accompanied by sparkling silverware and ornate surroundings, nicely set off with wine from an excellent cellar. There is a spacious, well furnished drawing room with a log fire, and the house is surrounded by very pretty mature gardens.
5rm(3⇌2♪) (1fb) CTV in all bedrooms ® ✱
dB&B⇌♪£62-£70 LDO 6.30pm
Lic 🍽 6P nc10yrs

FH QQ Mrs D Miles ***Great Lwynfranc*** *(SO327193)* Llanvihangel Crucorney NP7 8EN (off A465 3m N)
☎Crucorney(0873) 890418
Mar-Nov
Standing on a hillside overlooking the A465 Abergavenny to Hereford road, this attractive house is reached via an uphill, bumpy track. The freshly decorated bedrooms are very clean and all front-facing rooms offer spectacular views of the Llanhtony Valley. Warm hospitality is generated throughout the establishment.
3hc (1fb) ®
🍽 CTV 10P 154 acres mixed

FH QQQ Mrs J Nicholls **Newcourt** *(SO317165)* Mardy NP7 8AU ☎(0873) 852300
Closed Xmas wk
A charming 17th-century stone-built courthouse, part of a working farm situated 2 miles north of Abergavenny, on the edge of the village of Mardy. Rooms in the main house have recently been refurbished and now offer a high standard in quality, facilities and cleanliness. There are 2 comfortable lounges, and the house affords fine views of Sugar Loaf Mountain. Smoking is not permitted.
3⇌♪ ⊁in all bedrooms CTV in all bedrooms ®
✗ (ex guide dogs) ✱ sB&B⇌♪fr£25 dB&B⇌♪£37
WB&Bfr£117.50
🍽 CTV 10P nc10yrs snooker 160 acres arable beef £

INN Q The Great George Cross St NP7 5ER
☎(0873) 854230 or (0831) 107862 FAX (0873) 859261
In the centre of a busy market town, this 16th-century inn provides good, simple bar and restaurant facilities. Bedrooms are modestly furnished, but equipped with modern comforts.
7⇌♪ (2fb) CTV in all bedrooms ® ✗ sB&B⇌♪fr£33
dB&B⇌♪fr£48 Lunch £1.25-£7.95alc Dinner £1.25-£7.95alc
LDO 7.30pm
🍽 50P
Credit Cards 1 3 £

ABERPORTH Dyfed Map **02** SN25

GH QQ Ffynonwen Country SA43 2HT ☎(0239) 810312
Run by the friendly Duckworth family, this busy, converted farmhouse is situated just east of the town. Bedrooms are all neat and comfortable, and en suite rooms are furnished to a good standard. Extensive public rooms include a function suite, with a comfortable lounge bar and a choice of a conservatory lounge or an inner lounge with an inglenook fireplace.
7rm(3⇌1♪3hc) (3fb) CTV in 4 bedrooms ✱ sB&B£16
sB&B⇌♪£18 dB&B£32 dB&B⇌♪£36
Lic 🍽 30P games room

ABERSOCH Gwynedd Map **06** SH32

GH QQ Ty Draw Lon Sarn Bach LL53 7EL
☎(075881) 2647 due to change to (0758) 712647
Etr-end Sep
Mouth-watering home-made bread is the speciality of this house, made by Jean Collins who has been running the guesthouse with her husband, Peter, for several years. Bedrooms are bright and airy, with comfortable duvet-covered beds and modern white furniture. There is a cosy residents' lounge, and guests can relax on the shrub-sheltered lawns in fine weather. A secluded rear car park and the short walk to the sea and shops add to the attraction of this well maintained establishment.
7hc ⊁in 2 bedrooms ✗ (ex guide dogs) sB&B£13-£18
dB&B£26-£36
CTV 10P £

ABERYSTWYTH Dyfed Map **06** SN58

GH QQQ Glyn-Garth South Rd SY23 1JS ☎(0970) 615050
Closed 1 wk Xmas rs Oct-Etr
This double-fronted Victorian terraced house is situated a short distance from the South Promenade and close to both the castle and harbour, a short walk from the town centre. The attractively decorated bedrooms have modern furniture and equipment, and family rooms are also available. One bedroom is located on the ground floor, and the dining room is in the basement. This small personally run hotel is exceptionally well maintained, and offers a cosy bar together with a comfortable, pleasant lounge.
10rm(6⇌♪4hc) (3fb)⊁in 5 bedrooms CTV in all bedrooms ®
✗ ✱ sB&B£16-£17 dB&B£32-£34 dB&B⇌♪£38-£42
Lic 🍽 CTV 4 (£2 per night) £

GH QQ Llety Gwyn Hotel Llanbadarn Fawr SY23 3SX (1m E A44) (0970) 623965
rs 25-26 Dec
This family-run hotel is situated at Llanbadarn just off the A44, east of the town. Six of the bedrooms are located in the grounds, and they are all well decorated and equipped. There is a busy function suite including a bar, and a gymnasium, sauna and solarium which attract a local membership. The hotel also benefits from pleasant lawns and ample car parking.
8rm(4 4hc) Annexe 6rm(1 3 2hc) (3fb) CTV in all bedrooms ® * sB&B£16.50 sB&B fr£20 dB&B£32-£36 dB&B £38-£44 LDO 5pm
Lic CTV 50P snooker sauna solarium gymnasium
Credit Cards 1 3

GH Q Shangri-La 36 Portland St SY23 2DX (0970) 617659
Closed 25 & 26 Dec
This small, mid-terrace Victorian house provides simple accommodation, with family rooms also available. It is situated in a side street of terraced properties close to both the seafront and shopping area. There is no car park and finding street parking space in the vicinity can be a problem during busy periods.
6hc (3fb) TV in all bedrooms ® * sB&Bfr£12 dB&Bfr£22 WB&Bfr£77
CTV

GH QQ Southgate Hotel Penparcau SY23 1SF (0970) 611550
This large detached family-run guesthouse is situated on the A487 Aberaeron road, south of the town. It provides spacious, modern accommodation which includes family rooms and ground floor bedrooms. Other facilities include an attractive dining room, small bar and cosy lounge; there is also a self- contained function room which is popular for wedding receptions, together with a large private car park.
8 (1fb) dB&B £36 WB&B£126 WBDi£168 LDO noon
Lic CTV 40P pool table
Credit Cards 1 3

INN QQ *Talbot Hotel* Market St SY23 1DL (0970) 612575
Situated in the town centre, this is one of the oldest hotels in Aberystwyth and is a popular meeting place for locals. Discos are held regularly, but bedrooms are well insulated against noise. The rooms are spacious and brightly decorated, with TV and tea making facilities. There is a small, well-furnished restaurant and bar meals are also available.
15rm(13) (4fb) CTV in all bedrooms ® (ex guide dogs) LDO 9.30pm
CTV
Credit Cards 1 3

ABINGDON Oxfordshire Map 04 SU49

INN QQ Barley Mow Hotel Clifton Hampden OX14 3EH (through village on road to Didcot) (Chef & Brewer) Clifton Hampden(086730) 7847
An appealing thatched pub dating from 1352 in the village of Clifton Hampden (on the Didcot Road) just outside Abingdon. Bedrooms are well decorated, attractively furnished and have modern facilities. There are small, cosy bars and a panelled dining room where a wide range of food is served.
4rm(1 3hc) CTV in all bedrooms ® T (ex guide dogs) * sB&B £30-£45 dB&B £50-£65 LDO 9.30pm
250P
Credit Cards 1 2 3 5

Every effort is made to provide accurate information, but details can change after we go to print. It is advisable to check prices etc. before you make a firm booking.

ABINGTON Strathclyde *Lanarkshire* Map 11 NS92

FH QQ Mrs M L Hodge **Craighead** *(NS914236)* ML12 6SQ Crawford(08642) 356
May-Oct
This attractive farmhouse lies amid rolling hills by the River Duneaton, to the north of the village, one mile off the B7078 (old A74). There are 2 large and comfortable bedrooms and a smaller one without a wash basin, usually preferred for children.
3rm(2hc) ® (ex guide dogs) sB&B£12.50-£14 dB&B£25-£28 LDO 5pm
CTV 6P 4 600 acres mixed

ACASTER MALBIS North Yorkshire Map 08 SE54

INN QQQ Ship YO2 1JH York(0904) 705609 & 703888
Once frequented by Cromwell's soldiers, this 17th-century coaching house is situated on the banks of the Ouse. This is an attractive brick building, adorned with colourful flowers, and has a garden with children's play equipment. The inn is renowned for its restaurant meals and bar food, as well as its traditional Yorkshire hand-pulled beers. The original oak beams are retained in the tastefully extended bar where a blazing open fire burns in winter. Beams are also apparent in the rustic-style restaurant, which features a ship's figurehead. There are 8 bedrooms – one with a 4-poster bed – decorated with modern fabrics and characteristic scrubbed pine furniture. The rooms are not particularly big but well designed and most have a view of the river. There are private boat moorings and fishing rights available for guests.
8rm(2 6) in all bedrooms CTV in all bedrooms ® (ex guide dogs) * sB&B fr£37.50 dB&B fr£40 WB&Bfr£225 LDO 9.30pm
60P river cruises private moorings
Credit Cards 1 3 £
See advertisement under YORK

AIRDRIE Strathclyde *Lanarkshire* Map 11 NS76

GH QQ Rosslee 107 Forrest St ML6 7AR (0236) 765865
A detached house sitting back from the main road on the eastern side of Airdrie, this guesthouse caters for both the commercial and tourist trade, and is run by enthusiastic owners.
6rm(2 4hc) (2fb) CTV in 5 bedrooms TV in 1 bedroom ® sB&B£17.50-£21 dB&B£35-£42 dB&B £40-£43 LDO 7pm
Lic CTV 8P

AISLABY North Yorkshire Map 08 SE78

GH QQ Blacksmiths Arms Pickering YO18 8PE Pickering(0751) 72182
Closed 4-31 Jan
A former smithy with many original beams and stone walls, parts of which date back to the 17th century. Really a restaurant with rooms, the accommodation is however comfortable and attractive. Three bedrooms have en suite facilities and 2 rooms share a communal bathroom, which is ideal for families. A feature of the bar is the log fire which burns in the forge on winter evenings. The restaurant is situated on the A170, 2 miles west of Pickering.
5rm(1 2 2hc) (1fb) CTV in all bedrooms ® sB&B£19-£22 sB&B £19-£22 dB&B£38-£40 dB&B £42-£44 WB&B£133-£154 WBDi£224-£286 LDO 9pm
Lic 35P
Credit Cards 1 3 £

ALBURY Surrey Map 04 TQ04

INN QQQ *Drummond Arms* The Street GU5 9AG Shere(048641) 2039
This popular inn in the picturesque village offers a high level of comfort and attractive, recently refurbished bedrooms, all with en suite facilities. Interesting bar meals are available in the cosy bar or brighter conservatory extension, providing an alternative to the more formal à la carte restaurant, which has speciality evenings and fondues on Monday nights. During the summer months guests

can sit in the small garden, complete with pond, where ducks roam freely.
7⇌↱ CTV in all bedrooms ✖ (ex guide dogs) LDO 10pm
▥ 30P nc10yrs
Credit Cards [1] [3]

ALCESTER Warwickshire Map **04** SP05

GH QQ ***Coughton Cross*** The Old Post House, Alcester Rd, Coughton B49 5HR ☎(0789) 400166
Situated on the Alcester road, this guesthouse was previously the post office and general store for the area. Accommodation is generally spacious, and those rooms which are not en suite do have private facilities. Public areas are limited, with a small breakfast room.
8↱ (2fb) CTV in all bedrooms ®
Lic

ALDERTON Wiltshire Map **03** ST88

SELECTED

FH QQQQ Mrs V Lippiatt ***Manor*** *(ST840831)* SN14 6NL ☎Malmesbury(0666) 840271
Apr-Oct
This 17th-century mellow stone farmhouse sits in the quiet village of Alderton, convenient for the M4 and the towns of Malmesbury and Castle Combe. Bedrooms are spacious and comfortable, with TV and tea making facilities, and while one has a private bathroom across the landing, the other two are en suites. Personal belongings of the friendly Lippiatt family are evident in the lounge, giving it a homely feel, and breakfast is served in the dining room where guests may eat together or at separate tables.
3rm(2⇌↱1hc) CTV in all bedrooms ® ✖
▥ CTV 10P nc12yrs 600 acres arable beef
See advertisement under MALMESBURY

ALKMONTON Derbyshire Map **07** SK13

FH QQQ Mr A Harris **Dairy House** *(SK198367)* DE6 3DG ☎Great Cubley(0335) 330359
Closed Xmas
Mr and Mrs Harris provide a friendly welcome and stay at their comfortably modernised 16th-century farmhouse, which is found 3 miles up Woodyard Lane after turning off the A50 at Foston.
7rm(1⇌3↱3hc) (1fb)⊘in all bedrooms ® ✖ (ex guide dogs) ✱ sB&B£16 sB&B⇌↱£22 dB&B£32 dB&B⇌↱£38 WB&B£105-£126 WBDi£175-£196 LDO 8pm
Lic ▥ CTV 8P nc5yrs ⛳ bowls croquet 82 acres stock Ⓔ

ALMONDSBURY Avon Map **03** ST68

GH QQQ **Abbotts Way** Gloucester Rd BS12 4JB ☎(0454) 613134
Situated on the A38, 2 miles north of junction 16 on the M5, this large modern house is set in 12 acres and has fine views of the surrounding countryside. Bedrooms are comfortable and well furnished, and the spacious conservatory/dining room is a delightful setting in which to enjoy the delicious breakfasts.
6rm(1⇌↱5hc) (1fb) sB&Bfr£18 sB&B⇌↱£25 dB&B⇌↱£40 LDO breakfast
▥ CTV 10P
Credit Cards [1] [3] [5] Ⓔ

ALNMOUTH Northumberland Map **12** NU21

GH QQQ **Blue Dolphins** 11 Riverside Rd NE66 2SD ☎Alnwick(0665) 830893
Overlooking the mouth of the River Aln, this is a spacious, warm and friendly guesthouse with a lovely home-from-home feel to it. Bedrooms are especially well furnished and a delightful lounge is provided.
5rm(2⇌3↱) ⊘in all bedrooms CTV in all bedrooms ® ✱ sB&B⇌↱fr£20 dB&B⇌↱fr£40 WB&Bfr£130
5P Ⓔ

GH QQ **High Buston Hall** High Buston NE66 3QH ☎Alnwick(0665) 830341
Mar-Dec
All those who have an affection for days gone by and things authentically old fashioned, will love Alison Edward's fine Georgian country mansion with its cosy lived in feel, which is being enthusiastically restored to its former glory with antiques and period objets d'art. The bedrooms are well proportioned, each retaining its original cast-iron fireplace, and give delightful views of the Northumberland coast. The bathroom is just across the corridor. There is an attractive drawing room, whilst meals are taken in the dining room around a large table. High Buston Hall sits in 5 acres of gardens and paddock, in the hamlet from which it takes its name, off the A1068 between Alnmouth and Warkworth.
3rm(1⇌1hc) ⊘in all bedrooms ® ✖ (ex guide dogs) ✱ dB&Bfr£45 dB&B⇌fr£55 WB&B£135-£165 WBDi£240-£270 LDO 9am
Lic ▥ CTV 9P nc13yrs

SELECTED

GH QQQQ **Marine House Private Hotel** 1 Marine Dr NE66 2RW ☎Alnwick(0665) 830349
This substantial, listed, ivy-clad building has an interesting history: originally a granary 200 years ago, it was then converted to a vicarage. Many original features remain, particularly on the upper floors, where woodwork and various nooks and crannies show evidence of its working days. It is now run as a holiday hotel by the Inkster family, and son Iain, a chef, offers a fine 4- course set-price dinner, also presenting the occasional gourmet evenings; table sharing may be necessary. Bedrooms vary in size and style, but are all bright and modern. There is a small residents' bar in a novel location on the stair landing between the ground and first floor. There is a comfortable lounge with a selection of board games, and a games room in the cellar provides pool, table tennis and darts. The hotel overlooks the golf links and provides limited parking.
10⇌↱ (4fb) ✱ dB&B⇌↱£72-£78 (incl dinner) WBDi£234-£254 LDO 4pm
Lic ▥ CTV 12P nc3yrs Ⓔ

See advertisement on page 43

ALNWICK Northumberland Map **12** NU11

GH QQQ **Aln House** South Rd NE66 2NZ ☎(0665) 602265
Set in its own well tended gardens, this Victorian house is situated on the main road leading into town from the south. The bedrooms are equipped with bright, modern facilities, and there is an attractive lounge.
8rm(3⇌↱5hc) (3fb) CTV in 6 bedrooms TV in 2 bedrooms ® ✱ sB&Bfr£15 dB&Bfr£30 dB&B⇌↱fr£35
Lic ▥ CTV 8P nc4yrs

GH QQ ***Aydon House*** South Rd NE66 2NT ☎(0665) 602218
This semidetached Victorian house is situated on the main road leading into town from the south. Some bedrooms are spacious and comfortable, others are more compact and plainly furnished. There is a comfortable lounge and a neat dining room.
10rm(4⇌↱6hc) (4fb) CTV in all bedrooms LDO 5pm
Lic ▥ 12P

GH QQ **Bondgate House Hotel** Bondgate Without NE66 1PN ☎(0665) 602025 FAX (0665) 602554
This 3-storey Georgian town house is situated on the main road to the southeast and a couple of minutes' walk from the centre. The dining room has a tasteful blue colour scheme which mirrors the character of the house, but the bedrooms are modern.
→

8rm(3↑5hc) (3fb) CTV in all bedrooms ® ✗ (ex guide dogs) sB&B↑£22-£36 dB&B£33-£34 dB&B↑£34-£36 WB&B£115.50-£126 WBDi£171.50-£182 LDO 4.30pm
Lic ⊞ CTV 8P £

ALTON Hampshire Map **04** SU73

INN QQ White Hart London Rd, Holybourne GU34 6EX ☎(0420) 87654

A busy, traditional inn set in the village of Holybourne. The refurbished bars offer a wide range of snacks, and there are 4 attractive, comfortable bedrooms.

4hc CTV in all bedrooms ® ✗ (ex guide dogs) sB&B£25 dB&B£40 WB&Bfr£120 WBDifr£170 Lunch £1.50-£7.95alc Dinner £2.95-£10alc LDO 10pm
⊞ 40P
Credit Cards 1 3

ALTRINCHAM Greater Manchester Map **07** SJ78

SELECTED

GH QQQQ Ash Farm Park Ln, Little Bollington WA14 4TJ ☎061-929 9290
Closed Xmas

Although peacefully situated in the village of Little Bollington (turn off the A56 beside the Stamford Arms) and surrounded by the Cheshire countryside, this small, former 19th-century farmhouse is very convenient for the motorway network, Manchester airport and the city centre. Carefully restored, it has been modernised to provide good quality, extremely well equipped accommodation by the owners David and Janice Taylor. The charming bedrooms have hand-made pine furniture and offer all modern amenities in addition to several thoughtful extras including fruit, toiletries and bathrobes. An inviting lounge/dining room with deep sofas, an open fire and a large library is the setting for Jan's generous home-made meals which are served around the communal table: breakfast is a veritable feast. One of the outbuildings has been converted into a snooker room with a championship table, which guests are welcome to use.

2⇌↑ (2fb) CTV in all bedrooms ® ✗ (ex guide dogs) ✱ sB&B⇌↑£35-£40 dB&B⇌↑£40-£50 WB&Bfr£230 WBDifr£300 LDO 9.30pm
Lic ⊞ 4P nc9yrs snooker
Credit Cards 1 2 3 5

GH Q *Bollin Hotel* 58 Manchester Rd WA14 4PJ ☎061-928 2390

Situated beside the A56 and close to the town centre, this friendly commercial guesthouse offers modestly appointed but well maintained bed and breakfast accommodation. Some bedrooms are fairly compact, but there is a comfortable lounge in which to relax.

10hc (2fb) CTV in all bedrooms ®
⊞ CTV 10P

INN QQQ *The Old Packet House* Navigation Rd, Broadheath WA14 1LW ☎061-929 1331

Pleasantly situated adjacent to the Bridgewater canal, this whitewashed 18th- century inn is thought to derive its name from the 'Packet Boats' en route from Chester to Manchester, for which the hostelry provided a staging post. The commendable bedrooms are all identical in style with rich red and green soft fabrics enhancing the dark wood fittings. Good facilities are thoughtfully provided and the bathrooms are modern, imitating the Victorian style. Off-street parking is available.

5rm(1↑4hc) CTV in all bedrooms ® ✗ (ex guide dogs) LDO 9pm
⊞ CTV 10P

ALYTH Tayside *Perthshire* Map **15** NO25

INN QQ Losset Losset Rd PH11 8BT ☎(08283) 2393

A friendly, family-run inn standing close to the centre of this small country town and only 6 miles from the better known tourist centre of Blairgowrie, the Losset has compact bedrooms which are neat and fresh, with practical modern furnishings and fittings and there is a cosy lounge bar.

3↑ CTV in all bedrooms ® sB&B↑£20 dB&B↑£40 WB&B£100 Lunch £3.50-£8 Dinner £3.50-£10 LDO 9pm
⊞ 10P

AMBLESIDE Cumbria Map **07** NY30

GH QQQ Compston House Hotel Compston Rd LA22 9DJ ☎(05394) 32305

A well run guesthouse offering good home comforts by the caring owners Mr and Mrs Smith. It is situated on a corner site in the town centre, overlooking a small golf course and tennis courts. Bedrooms are modern in style, and there is a cosy lounge.

8↑ (1fb)⊘in 2 bedrooms CTV in all bedrooms ® ✗ (ex guide dogs) ✱ dB&B↑£31-£49 WB&B£108-£171.50 WBDi£168-£231 LDO 5pm
Lic ⊞ P̸ nc5yrs £

GH QQQ Gables Private Hotel Compston Rd LA22 9DJ ☎(05394) 33272
Closed Dec rs Jan & Feb

Family owned for 40 years, the Gables provides friendly and courteous service. There are 2 comfortable lounges, traditional English meals in the dining room, and the individually fitted bedrooms offer good facilities including central heating, tea-making facilities and colour TV. Not far from the village and situated close to the church, overlooking parkland.

13⇌↑ (4fb) CTV in all bedrooms ® ✱ sB&B⇌↑£18.25-£22 dB&B⇌↑£36.50-£44 WB&Bfr£127.75 WBDifr£203 LDO 5pm
Lic ⊞ CTV 10P

SELECTED

GH QQQQ Grey Friar Lodge Country House Hotel Brathay LA22 9NE (1m W off A593) ☎(05394) 33158
Mar-Oct

Formerly known as Brathay vicarage this lovely, lakeland stone house dating back to 1819 is now a small, well furnished country hotel. It stands in its own grounds surrounded by woodlands overlooking the River Brathay. The bedrooms are a good size, individually decorated with coordinating fabrics. All are equipped with TV, radio alarm, hairdryer and tea/coffee-making facilities. There are 2 very comfortable lounges provided, with lots of antiques around the hotel. A set dinner is served in the attractive dining room each evening, and Mr and Mrs Sutton offer a warm welcome to their home.

8⇌↑ ⊘in all bedrooms CTV in all bedrooms ® ✗ sB&B⇌↑fr£42 dB&B⇌↑£70-£86 (incl dinner) WBDi£225-£285 LDO 7.30pm
Lic ⊞ 12P nc12yrs £

GH QQ Hillsdale Hotel Church St LA22 0BT ☎(05394) 33174

A helpful and friendly service is provided at this comfortable, family-owned and run guesthouse, close to the town centre. There is a cosy, attractive lounge and all the bedrooms are equipped with colour TV and tea-making facilities.

8rm(1⇌7hc) CTV in all bedrooms ® ✗ ✱ sB&B£20-£24 dB&B£30-£32 dB&B⇌£38-£40
⊞ P̸

GH QQQ The Horseshoe Hotel Rothay Rd LA22 0EE ☎(05394) 32000

Town-centre guesthouse overlooking park. Recently extended to offer en suite bedrooms. Traditional or wholefood breakfast is available.

→

19rm(17⇌↱2hc) (4fb) CTV in all bedrooms Ⓡ ✱
sB&B⇌↱£27.50-£31.50 dB&B£54-£57 dB&B⇌↱£57-£61
LDO 8.30pm
Lic CTV 19P
Credit Cards [1] [2] [3]

GH QQQ Lyndhurst Hotel Wansfell Rd LA22 0EG ☎(05394) 32421

This pleasant lakeland stone house is situated reasonably close to the town centre. The 8 attractive, en suite bedrooms, 2 of which are located in a separate house next door, are equipped with colour TV and radio, and one has a 4-poster bed. Well produced home cooking is served. There is a cosy lounge and a well stocked bar. There is ample car parking space.

6↱ Annexe 2↱ (2fb)ⅎin 1 bedroom CTV in all bedrooms Ⓡ
✗ dB&B↱£37-£48 WB&B£128-£160 WBDi£185-£210
LDO 8pm
Lic 🍴 8P Ⓔ

GH QQQ Riverside Lodge Country House Rothay Bridge LA22 0EH ☎(05394) 34208

A charming early-Georgian house, delightfully situated on the banks of the River Rothay, a short walk from the village yet surrounded by 3 acres of grounds. The bedrooms have good facilities including TV and telephones, and there is a cosy lounge.

5rm(3⇌2↱) (1fb) CTV in all bedrooms Ⓡ T ✗
dB&B⇌↱£40-£57 WB&B£140-£176
Lic 🍴 20P ♪
Credit Cards [1] [3] Ⓔ

SELECTED

GH QQQQ Rothay Garth Hotel Rothay Rd LA22 0EE ☎(05394) 32217 FAX (05394) 34400

An attractive and well maintained family-run hotel, situated in well tended gardens on the edge of the village. A feature of the hotel is the elegant restaurant, where a 5-course fixed-price menu is available for both residents and non-residents. The bedrooms are individually furnished and decorated to a high standard; they are also particularly well equipped and have private bathrooms. There is a very comfortable lounge and a cocktail bar, and staff are most helpful and courteous.

16rm(14⇌↱2hc) (3fb)ⅎin 12 bedrooms CTV in all bedrooms Ⓡ T sB&B£38.50-£46.50 sB&B⇌↱£44.50-£52.50 dB&B£65-£81 dB&B⇌↱£77-£93 (incl dinner)
WBDi£232-£309 LDO 8pm
Lic 🍴 CTV 17P
Credit Cards [1] [2] [3] [5] Ⓔ

GH QQQ Rowanfield Country House Kirkstone Rd LA22 9ET ☎(05394) 33686
Closed Jan & Feb

This lakeland period house is situated overlooking the village in its own well cared for gardens, complete with views including Windermere, the Hundreds and Coniston Old Man. The house is delightfully furnished throughout with lots of care given to the décor. All bedrooms are en suite except for one with its own facilities across the landing, and each has a TV and tea-making equipment. A well produced dinner is served each evening by the resident owners Mr and Mrs Butcher, who are warm, attentive hosts. Rowanfield is a no-smoking house.

7rm(1⇌5↱1hc) (1fb)ⅎin all bedrooms CTV in all bedrooms
Ⓡ dB&B⇌↱£44-£54 WB&B£154-£168 WBDi£210-£225
LDO 5pm
🍴 8P nc5yrs
Credit Cards [1] [3] Ⓔ

SELECTED

GH QQQQ *Rydal Lodge Hotel* LA22 9LR (2m NW A590) ☎(05394) 33208
Closed 7 Jan-4 Feb

This attractive lodge set in delightful grounds beside the River Rothay is located on the A591, north of Ambleside. It has 2 lounges, one of them is on the first floor and has lovely views over the garden and surrounding hills. A well produced home-cooked dinner is served in the attractive dining room. The bedrooms are individually furnished and decorated, complete with TV and tea-making facilities. The attentive manner of the owners is one of the reasons why guests return year after year to this charming guesthouse.

8rm(2↱6hc) (1fb) LDO 7pm
Lic CTV 12P ♪
Credit Cards [1] [3]

GH QQ Rysdale Hotel Rothay Rd LA22 0EE ☎(05394) 32140 FAX (05394) 31111

Family owned and run, this small comfortable hotel is situated close to the town centre and overlooking a park. The prettily decorated bedrooms are all equipped with TV, tea-making facilities and the majority are en suite. A very inviting lounge is available and there is a separate bar furnished with comfy settees. Home-cooked dinners are served in the elegant dining room.

9rm(1⇌5↱3hc) (2fb)ⅎin all bedrooms CTV in all bedrooms
Ⓡ ✗ (ex guide dogs) ✱ sB&B£16-£20 sB&B⇌↱£25
dB&B£32-£34 dB&B⇌↱£38-£48 WB&B£107-£160
WBDi£180-£230 LDO 10am
Lic 🍴 CTV 2P nc8yrs
Credit Cards [1] [3]

GH QQ Smallwood Hotel Compston Rd LA22 9DJ ☎(05394) 32330

A spacious, detached house offering comfortable accommodation, with a pleasant lounge. The guesthouse is well maintained and located close to the town centre, with parking facilities at the rear.

12rm(5⇌↱7hc) Annexe 1⇌ (3fb) CTV in 8 bedrooms Ⓡ ✱
sB&Bfr£16 dB&Bfr£32 dB&B⇌↱fr£36 WBDifr£155
LDO 7pm
Lic 🍴 CTV 13P Ⓔ

See advertisement on page 43

GH Q *Thrang House* Compston Rd LA22 9DJ ☎(05394) 32112
Mar-Dec

This friendly guesthouse is close to the town centre, overlooking the miniature golf course. It has a small car park to the rear.

6rm(2↱4hc) CTV in all bedrooms Ⓡ ✗ LDO 6pm
🍴 5P nc9yrs

INN QQQ Drunken Duck Barngates LA22 0NG ☎Hawkshead(09666) 347

This 300-year-old inn is set in its own 60 acres, surrounded by beautiful open countryside, about 3 miles from Ambleside. The décor throughout is delightful and the bedrooms are tastefully furnished and have en suite facilities. An extensive range of meals is available in the old-world bars, and a small, cosy restaurant is provided (booking essential).

8⇌ Annexe 2↱ CTV in all bedrooms Ⓡ T ✱ sB&B⇌↱£40-£45 dB&B⇌↱£65-£74 LDO 8.45pm
🍴 40P ♪
Credit Cards [1] [3]

ANCASTER Lincolnshire Map 08 SK94

FH Q Mrs F Mival **Woodlands** *(SK966437)* West Willoughby NG32 3SH (off the A153 between Sleaford and Grantham, 1m W of Ancaster) ☎Loveden(0400) 30340
Etr-Oct

→

Woodlands Farm is set well back from the A153 a mile west of Ancaster and the junction with the B6403. It offers peace, comfort, a warm greeting and limited facilities.
2rm(1hc) (1fb) TV in all bedrooms Ⓡ ✱ sB&B£14-£16 dB&B£26-£28 WB&B£98-£112 WBDi£147-£168
LDO previous day
♨ CTV 3P 12 acres mixed (£)

ANDOVER Hampshire Map **04** SU34

GH QQ ***Istana*** 4 Eversfield Close, off The Avenue SP10 3EN ☎(0264) 351454
Check for directions to this modern bed and breakfast establishment, in a leafy residential cul-de-sac. Within, bedrooms are neat and tidy and the hallway walls have Mrs Collins' own eye-catching paintings on display.
3hc (1fb) 🚭 in all bedrooms CTV in all bedrooms Ⓡ
✖ (ex guide dogs) LDO 5.30pm
♨ CTV 10P 1🚗 🏊

ANGLESEY, ISLE OF Gwynedd Map **06**

BEAUMARIS Map **06** SH67

GH QQ Sea View 10 West End LL58 8BG ☎(0248) 810384
Closed Xmas
A small, spotlessly clean and well maintained guesthouse at the western end of town, with impressive views of Snowdonia, across the Menai Straits – a view which 3 of the bedrooms share. The accommodation is old fashioned and simple but is nevertheless very well maintained, with proprietors Jenny and Philip Gower being justifiably house proud. Smoking is not permitted.
6hc 🚭 in all bedrooms ✖ ✱ sB&B£16-£17 dB&B£30-£32
LDO 2pm
CTV 5P nc10yrs

HOLYHEAD Map **06** SH28

GH QQ ***Monravon*** Porth-Y-Felin Rd LL65 1PL
☎(0407) 762944
This much extended and modernised semidetached house is situated in a residential area convenient for access to both the port area and the town centre. Its proximity to the ferry terminal makes it popular with travellers to and from Ireland. Personally run by resident owners Len and Margaret Williams, the accommodation is modern, and facilities include a pool table in the lounge. Smoking is not permitted in the bedrooms.
5🚿 (2fb) 🚭 in all bedrooms CTV in all bedrooms Ⓡ ✖
♨ CTV 5P pool table

GH QQ Offaly 20 Walthew Av LL65 1AF ☎(0407) 762426
This small, privately owned and personally run detached guesthouse is close to the harbour and conveniently placed for the ferry terminal. It provides well maintained accommodation.
5rm(1🚿 4hc) (2fb) Ⓡ ✖ ✱ sB&B£12-£14 sB&B🚿£13-£14
LDO 3pm
♨ CTV 3P (charged)

GH Q Wavecrest 93 Newry St LL65 1HU ☎(0407) 763637
This small guesthouse is personally run by young proprietors and is conveniently located for the harbour, ferry terminal and town centre. Street parking presents no problem.
4hc (1fb) CTV in all bedrooms Ⓡ ✱ sB&B£12-£20 dB&B£24-£28 WB&B£80-£90 WBDi£120-£130 LDO 3pm
♨ CTV 1P

RHOSCOLYN Map **06** SH27

GH QQQ The Old Rectory LL65 2DQ (left off A5 at Valley)
☎Trearddur Bay(0407) 860214
Closed 21 Dec-19 Jan
This lovely old Georgian house stands in its own pleasant gardens, with both sea and rural views and the surrounding area is abounding with footpaths, being popular with bird-watchers. The guesthouse has fine bedrooms, all with en suite facilities and equipped with TV, radio and tea-making equipment. Family rooms are also available. In addition to the cosy dining room, where guests sit around a large communal table, there is a choice of comfortable lounges, both having open fires burning in the cold weather, and one designated no smoking.
5🛁🚿 (3fb) CTV in all bedrooms Ⓡ sB&B🛁🚿£28-£29 dB&B🛁🚿£46-£48 WB&B£150-£175 LDO 5pm
Lic ♨ CTV 8P
Credit Cards [1] [3]

TREARDDUR BAY Map **06** SH27

GH QQ Moranedd Trearddur Rd LL65 2UE ☎(0407) 860324
This large detached house surrounded by attractive gardens is quietly situated in a residential cul-de-sac, within a short walk of the beach. The accommodation is not luxurious, but the bedrooms are modern and most are quite spacious; family rooms are also available. Separate tables are provided in the breakfast room and there is a choice of 2 lounges, one being a sun lounge.
6hc (1fb) Ⓡ ✱ sB&B£13-£15 dB&B£26-£30
Lic ♨ CTV 10P

ANGMERING West Sussex Map **04** TQ00

GH QQQ Cherrymead Station Rd BN16 4HY
☎Worthing(0903) 782119
In the peaceful village of Angmering, about 1.5 miles from the sea and the South Downs, this pleasant guesthouse is set in pretty, well tended gardens. It is personally run by Mrs Dawson and offers comfortable bedrooms and an attractive lounge and breakfast room filled with reproduction furniture and family mementoes. There is also a sunny terrace where guests may enjoy the good weather during summer months.
5rm(4🛁🚿 1hc) Ⓡ ✖ sB&B£30-£34 sB&B🛁🚿£32-£34 dB&B£54-£58 dB&B🛁🚿£56-£58
♨ CTV 6P
Credit Cards [1] [3] (£)

ANNAN Dumfries & Galloway *Dumfriesshire* Map **11** NY16

GH QQ Ravenswood Private Hotel St Johns Rd DG12 6AW
☎(0461) 202158
Situated in a residential street between the station and the town centre, this red-sandstone, private hotel boasts comfortable accommodation. The bedrooms are generally spacious and traditionally furnished, while public areas include a small bar in addition to a well proportioned lounge. Bar suppers and evening meals both offer a choice of reasonably priced dishes.
8hc (2fb) CTV in all bedrooms Ⓡ ✖ (ex guide dogs) ✱ sB&B£16.50-£17 dB&B£30-£31 LDO 8pm
Lic ♨ CTV P̸

ANSTRUTHER Fife Map **12** NO50

GH QQQ The Spindrift Pittenweem Rd KY10 3DT
☎(0333) 310573
Closed Xmas
Formerly the home of a sea-faring owner, one of the features of this Victorian stone-built house is the Captain's Room, a second-floor room completely wood lined to create a replica of a ship master's cabin, and with superb views of the coastline. Several of the other bedrooms enjoy fine views, and all rooms are tastefully furnished and individually decorated. Well proportioned public rooms include a comfortable and inviting lounge and a bright, fresh dining room with bamboo tables and chairs. The guesthouse is no smoking throughout and is situated on the western approach to the small fishing town.
8rm(7🛁 1🚿) (3fb) 🚭 in all bedrooms CTV in all bedrooms Ⓡ
✖ dB&B🛁🚿£47-£50 WB&B£164.50-£175 WBDi£210-£283.50 LDO 7pm
Lic ♨ CTV 12P
Credit Cards [1] [3]

INN Q ***The Royal Hotel*** 20 Rodger St KY10 3DU
☎(0333) 310581 FAX (0333) 310270
A friendly family-owned inn situated close to the harbour of this pretty coastal town. New owners are beginning to improve the modest acccommodation.
11rm(2⇌7↱2hc) (1fb) CTV in 6 bedrooms ®
✖ (ex guide dogs) LDO 9pm
🏛 CTV 6P
Credit Cards 1 2 3 5

ANSTY Wiltshire Map **03** ST92

INN QQQ ***Maypole*** SP3 5PY ☎Tisbury(0747) 870607 & 871227
This attractive inn overlooks the village duck pond in the quaint village of Ansty, close to the A30. Three bedrooms have been tastefully decorated with modern colours and bright fabrics, and all have private bathrooms, colour TV and tea-making facilities. Home-cooked dishes are served in the character open-plan bar or in the adjoining restaurant.
3⇌ CTV in all bedrooms ® ✖ (ex guide dogs) LDO 9.30pm
CTV 50P nc12yrs
Credit Cards 1 3

APPLEBY-IN-WESTMORLAND Cumbria Map **12** NY62

GH QQ ***Bongate House*** Bongate CA16 6UE
☎Appleby(07683) 51245
Closed Xmas & New Year
This fine Georgian house stands in an acre of garden, part of which provides a home for 2 goats and 2 pot-bellied pigs. Bright bedrooms with good quality beds and a lounge with lots of books complete the picture.
8rm(1⇌4↱3hc) (4fb) ® ✖ (ex guide dogs) LDO 6pm
Lic 🏛 CTV 8P 2🚗 nc7yrs croquet & putting lawn

ARBROATH Tayside *Angus* Map **12** NO64

GH Q Kingsley 29 Market Gate DD11 1AU ☎(0241) 73933
This compact commercial guesthouse is just off the town centre. As well as a guests' lounge with a large screen TV, there is a games room with a pool table and dart board.
14hc (8fb) ✱ sB&B£13-£14 dB&B£25 WB&B£85-£90 WBDi£120-£125 LDO 7.30pm
Lic 𝍖 CTV 4P snooker solarium childrens play ground

SELECTED

FH QQQQ Mrs S A Caldwell **Farmhouse Kitchen** *(NO582447)* Grange of Conon DD11 3SD
☎Carmyllie(02416) 202
A delightful Victorian farmhouse set amidst peaceful rolling countryside. Bedrooms are elegantly furnished, with attractive modern fabrics used to good effect, and have been thoughtfully equipped with useful extras. There is a cosy sun lounge overlooking the landscaped garden, and hearty Scottish breakfasts are served at the communal table in the farmhouse kitchen. Upstairs, the games room offers billiards, table tennis, a rowing exercise machine and a sun bed. The farmhouse is situated some 6 miles north of Arbroath and is signposted from the A933 just beyond Colliston. Best Newcomer for Scotland 1992–3, see colour section.
3hc (1fb) ⊬in all bedrooms CTV in all bedrooms ®
✖ (ex guide dogs) ✱ sB&B£25-£30 dB&B£40-£50
𝍖 CTV 4P nc3yrs ↲ snooker solarium games room 560 acres arable £

ARDBRECKNISH Strathclyde *Argyllshire* Map **10** NN02

FH QQQ ***Rockhill*** *(NN072219)* PA33 1BH
☎Kilchrenan(08663) 218
May-Sep
This 17th-century stone-built cottage-style country house sits in its own attractive gardens on the south side of Loch Awe. Reached by a single track from the village, this secluded farm enjoys splendid views and is full of character. The lounge is well stocked with books and games, and the small, neat dining room offers an honesty drinks counter. The bedrooms are simply decorated and furnished, but thoughtfully equipped; two ground-floor rooms are reached from the kitchen area.
5rm(1⇨↱4hc) (3fb) CTV in all bedrooms ®
✖ (ex guide dogs) LDO 7pm
Lic 8P nc8yrs ↲ 200 acres horses sheep

ARDERSIER Highland *Inverness-shire* Map **14** NH85

FH QQQ Mrs L E MacBean ***Milton-of-Gollanfield*** *(NH809534)* Gollanfield IV1 2QT ☎(0667) 62207 due to change to 462207
May-Nov
A substantial Victorian farmhouse standing in its own garden just off the A96 between Inverness and Nairn. It is an ideal base for the tourist, offering enjoyable home cooking and sound traditional comforts.
3hc ⊬in all bedrooms ® ✖ (ex guide dogs)
CTV P 360 acres mixed arable beef sheep

ARDGAY Highland *Sutherland* Map **14** NH58

GH QQQ Ardgay House IV24 3DH ☎(08632) 345
Apr-15 Dec rs 16 Dec-Mar
Set in its own garden beside the main road overlooking the Dornoch Firth, this substantial Victorian house has been sympathetically converted to provide comfortable accommodation for the tourist. Public rooms have been tastefully furnished with fine antiques, and the well equipped bedrooms offer a combination of modern and traditional furnishings.
6rm(4⇨↱2hc) (2fb) CTV in all bedrooms ®
✖ (ex guide dogs) sB&B£16-£24 sB&B⇨↱£20-£24 dB&B£26-£28 dB&B⇨↱£36 WBDi£168-£196 LDO 7pm
Lic 𝍖 9P £

ARLINGTON East Sussex Map **05** TQ50

SELECTED

FH QQQQ Mrs C McCutchan **Bates Green** *(TQ553077)* BN26 6SH ☎Polegate(0323) 482039
This charming brick-built, tile-hung farmhouse has been restored and enlarged since its beginnings as an 18th-century gamekeeper's cottage. Owner Carolyn McCutchan is a gardening enthusiast and the garden is regularly open for all to enjoy under the National Gardens Scheme. The 3 bedrooms, named after her daughters, are decorated and furnished in a cottagey style without being fussy, and all have smart en suite bathrooms. There is a choice of lounges, one on the first floor and another downstairs with a real log fire. Mrs McCutchan knows how to look after guests, with tea and home-made cake on arrival and a wonderful breakfast with freshly squeezed juice, locally cured bacon, old-fashioned sausages, free range eggs and a choice of excellent home-made preserves.
3⇨↱ ⊬in all bedrooms ® ✖ ✱ dB&B⇨↱£38-£40
𝍖 CTV 3P nc10yrs ℛ(hard)150 acres sheep turkey

ARRAN, ISLE OF Strathclyde *Buteshire* Map **10**

BRODICK Map **10** NS03

GH QQQ Allandale KD27 8BJ ☎(0770) 2278
Closed Nov-Dec
This detached house sits in its own gardens in an elevated position on the southern outskirts of town. The bedrooms are practical and modern with 2 annexe rooms larger than those in the house. There is a comfortable lounge and a neat dining room with a small dispenser bar.
4rm(2⇨2↱) Annexe 2⇨ (1fb) CTV in all bedrooms ®
LDO 6pm
Lic 𝍖 12P

GH QQQ Dunvegan Dunvegan Shore Rd KA27 8AJ
☎(0770) 2811
This detached Victorian house sits on the seafront looking out across Brodick Bay. It has been carefully renovated to feature its period characteristics, and yet provide modern amenities.
6hc (1fb) ⊬in all bedrooms CTV in all bedrooms ®
✖ (ex guide dogs) ✱ sB&B£15-£18 dB&B£30-£34 LDO 4pm
Lic CTV 8P

LOCHRANZA Map **10** NR95

GH Q ***Kincardine Lodge*** KA27 8HL ☎(077083) 267
Apr-Oct
Conveniently placed for the Claonaig ferry, this guesthouse has pleasant views of the bay and castle. The bedrooms are fairly spacious and modestly furnished and there are 2 traditional lounges, one with TV. The house features an attractive wooden staircase.
7hc (4fb) ®
CTV 6P

ARROCHAR Strathclyde *Dunbartonshire* Map **10** NN20

GH QQQ Mansefield Country House G83 7AG ☎(03012) 282
With lovely views out over Loch Long, this detached, period house sits in its own grounds well back from the Helensburgh road. It has a very comfortable lounge and a neat, little dining room with an attractive fireplace. The proprietors Robin and Charintorn Campbell who took over the guesthouse in mid- 1991, are in the process of upgrading the bedrooms and adding en suite facilities, which they expect to be available in 1993.

5rm(1🚿4hc) (2fb)🚭in all bedrooms CTV in all bedrooms ® ✱ sB&B£22-£27 sB&B🚿fr£27 dB&B£30-£32 dB&B🚿£36-£38 WB&B£100-£125 WBDi£170-£190 LDO 6pm
🔥 CTV 8P

ARUNDEL West Sussex Map **04** TQ00

GH QQ Arden 4 Queens Ln BN18 9JN ☎(0903) 882544
This friendly hotel is quietly situated off the main road but is within easy walking distance of the castle and town centre. The bedrooms are freshly decorated, neat and well equipped, and the attractive breakfast room has pine furniture.
8rm(2🚿6hc) (1fb) CTV in all bedrooms ® 🐕 (ex guide dogs) sB&B£16-£18 sB&B🚿£20-£24 dB&B£30-£32 dB&B🚿£32-£37
🔥 4P nc2yrs

GH QQ Bridge House 18 Queen St BN18 9JG
☎(0903) 882142 & 882779
Closed Xmas wk
This family-run guesthouse with a 16th-century cottage annexe is centrally situated, with views of the castle, the River Arun and the South Downs. Bedrooms vary considerably in size and are simply furnished, some being old fashioned in style. Many of the rooms now have private bathrooms, and 3 new bedrooms with additional en suite facilities are being provided. There is a small bar lounge, and evening meals are available in the dining room.
16rm(12🛁🚿3hc) Annexe 3🛁🚿 (6fb)🚭in 4 bedrooms CTV in all bedrooms ® sB&B£20 sB&B🛁🚿£25 dB&B£28-£30 dB&B🛁🚿£36-£40 LDO 8pm
Lic 🔥 CTV 9P 4🚗
Credit Cards 1 3

INN QQ Swan Hotel High St BN18 9AG ☎(0903) 882314 FAX (0798) 831716
This popular free house is situated towards the end of the high street of the historic town. The beamed bar is furnished in traditional pub style with red dralon banquette seating, bar stools and polished tables, and there is an adjoining restaurant area with cosy booths. Bedrooms are similar and modern in style, but those in the new extension are more compact.
13rm(11🛁2🚿) (1fb) CTV in all bedrooms ® T
🐕 (ex guide dogs) sB&B🛁🚿£42.50 dB&B🛁🚿£55 Lunch £9&alc Dinner £10&alc LDO 9.30pm
🔥
Credit Cards 1 2 3 5 £

ASHBOURNE Derbyshire

See **Waterhouses**

ASHBURTON Devon Map **03** SX76

See also Bickington
GH QQQ Gages Mill Buckfastleigh Rd TQ13 7JW
☎(0364) 52391
Feb-Nov
This is an attractive whitewashed former wool mill from the 14th century, situated on the edge of the Dartmoor National Park in its own well kept gardens. It is near the A38 with easy access to both Exeter and Plymouth. The bedrooms are spotlessly clean, brightly decorated and furnished. All offer tea-making facilities and central heating; all are now en suite. At the entrance there is a cosy reception lounge with bare stone walls next to a more spacious sitting room with a small dispenser bar. Home-cooked dishes are served in the relaxed atmosphere of the dining room and the proprietors, Chris and Anne Moore extend a warm welcome to guests in their comfortable home.
8🛁🚿 (1fb) ® 🐕 (ex guide dogs) ✱ sB&B🛁🚿£19.50-£20.50 dB&B🛁🚿£39-£41 WB&B£112-£126 WBDi£185-£192.50 LDO 3pm
Lic 🔥 CTV 10P nc5yrs

FH Q Mrs H Young **Bremridge** *(SX785701)* Woodland TQ13 7JX (2m E unclass towards Denbury) ☎(0364) 52426 FAX (0364) 53589
Feb-Nov
A simply appointed farmhouse, peacefully situated about a mile from the A38 and 2 miles from Ashburton. The Young family are enthusiastic and welcoming.
5rm(1⇌4hc) (3fb) sB&B£16.50-£18.50 sB&B⇌£16.50-£18.50 dB&B£33-£37 dB&B⇌£33-£37 WB&B£95-£105 WBDi£105-£115 LDO 6pm
CTV 6P 8 acres mixed £

ASHBY-DE-LA-ZOUCH Leicestershire Map **08** SK31

INN Q ***Ashby Court Hotel*** 35 Wood St LE6 5LE ☎Ashby(0530) 415176
Located near the south-east edge of town on the busy A50, this small inn has recently been updated with the aim of attracting business guests, and has proved a success with local companies. Similarly the restaurant is becoming increasingly more popular, as a result a more ambitious international style menu is planned. The owners and management actively encourage an informal, friendly environment, with particular efforts to meet individual requests. The compact bedrooms are equipped to a good standard but tend to be modestly furnished.
10⇌ (1fb) in all bedrooms CTV in all bedrooms ® (ex guide dogs) LDO 10pm
16P nc15yrs
Credit Cards 1 3

ASHFORD Kent Map **05** TR04

GH QQQ **Croft Hotel** Canterbury Rd, Kennington TN25 4DU ☎(0233) 622140
Spacious, family-style, modern accommodation set in 2 acres of well kept grounds combines with a choice of well equipped bedrooms in the main house. A bar and a tastefully furnished lounge augment the cosy Croft Restaurant, which serves moderately priced à la carte dishes and grills. All the garden rooms have generous and very comfortable sitting areas, which provide real home comforts for the tourist and business guest. Service is supervised by the very helpful and agreeable resident proprietors, Mr and Mrs John Ellerington.
15⇌ Annexe 13⇌ (3fb) CTV in all bedrooms ® * sB&B⇌£32.50-£40 dB&B⇌£42.50-£50 LDO 8pm
Lic CTV 30P croquet
Credit Cards 1 3

ASHOVER Derbyshire Map **08** SK36

FH QQ Mr J A Wootton **Old School** *(SK323654)* Uppertown S45 0JF ☎Chesterfield(0246) 590813
Mar-Oct
With all rooms on the ground floor, this modern stone-built farmhouse is ideal for young children and elderly guests. Surrounded by farmland it stands on the opposite side of the A632 from the village of Ashover.
4hc (2fb) in all bedrooms CTV in all bedrooms * sB&Bfr£14 dB&Bfr£28 WB&Bfr£98 WBDifr£140 LDO 9.30am
CTV 10P 45 acres poultry sheep

ASHTON-UNDER-LYNE Greater Manchester Map **07** SJ99

GH QQQ **Welbeck House Hotel** 324 Katherine St OL6 7BD ☎061-344 0751 FAX 061-343 4278
A small private hotel in a residential area close to the town centre, with a comfortable lounge bar and a small dining room. Some of the modern bedrooms, though well equipped, are fairly compact.
8⇌ (2fb) CTV in all bedrooms ® T * sB&B⇌£29.50-£35 dB&B⇌£42-£45 LDO 8pm
Lic CTV 12P games room
Credit Cards 1 2 3 5 £

ASTBURY Cheshire Map **07** SJ86

INN Q ***Egerton Arms Hotel*** CW12 4RQ ☎Congleton(02602) 73946
This much extended old inn stands next to the village church and has its own driveway from the A34. Facilities include a large and pleasant lounge bar, a small cottage-style dining room, and a children's play area in the grounds and gardens. The simple modern bedrooms are comfortable and soundly maintained, and at the time of our inspection work was about to commence on providing all bedrooms with en suite facilities.
7hc CTV in all bedrooms ® LDO 9.30pm
CTV 100P
Credit Cards 1 3 5

ASTHALL Oxfordshire Map **04** SP21

INN QQQ **Maytime** OX8 4HW (0.25m N off A40) ☎(0993) 822068
Situated in the Windrush Valley, this was once a local hostelry, dating back to the 16th century. A spacious bar with its flagstone floor has a friendly, comfortable atmosphere and offers an extensive range of meals and snacks. The attractive ground-floor bedrooms are conveniently situated for the car park and are furnished with hand-built elm furniture. All rooms are equipped with TV, telephone, tea-making facilities and radio alarm. The inn is popular with locals and tourists alike.
Annexe 6⇌ CTV in all bedrooms ® T * sB&B⇌£43.60 dB&B⇌£48-£56.50 Lunch £5-£15 Dinner £5-£15 LDO 10pm
100P
Credit Cards 1 2 3

ASTON Staffordshire Map **07** SJ74

GH QQ ***Larksfield Country Accommodation*** Stoniford Ln TF9 4JB ☎Pipe Gate(063081) 7069
A modern farmhouse in a peaceful rural setting conveniently positioned for the main Shropshire, Staffordshire and Cheshire tourist areas. Expert shotgun tuition is available.
7rm(5 2hc) (4fb) CTV in all bedrooms ®
CTV 10P nc12yrs clay pigeon shooting pitch & putt
Credit Cards 3

ASTON MUNSLOW Shropshire Map **07** SO58

GH QQQ **Chadstone** SY7 9ER ☎Munslow(058476) 675
Mar-Oct
A modern dormer-style bungalow in a small hamlet on the B4368 near the Craven Arms pub. It offers neat rooms and the elegant dining room has panoramic views of the countryside. The resident proprietors are genuinely hospitable and provide attentive service.
5rm(2⇌ 3hc) in all bedrooms CTV in 1 bedroom ® sB&B£22 dB&B£40 dB&B⇌£44 LDO 7pm
Lic CTV 6P nc12yrs £

ASWARBY Lincolnshire Map **08** TF03

INN QQQ **Tally Ho** NG34 8SA ☎Culverthorpe(05295) 205
Located in pleasant open countryside, this stone 17th-century listed inn stands in neatly tended gardens, which include a barbecue and children's play area. Under new owners it has become a popular venue for food, particularly bar meals, chosen from a menu or blackboard selections of interesting country dishes. Exposed beams and stone walls are prominent features in the attractive bar, which also boasts a log fire. The newly restored dining room has been decorated to reflect the original character of the inn, with polished wooden floors, attractive rich bold drapes, complementary cushion seating and copper pans displayed in the fireplace. All the neat, bright bedrooms are housed in an annexe building and are equipped with modern en suites, TV and tea-making facilities.
Annexe 6rm(2⇌4) (2fb) CTV in all bedrooms ® sB&B⇌£28-£32 dB&B⇌£42-£46 WB&B£175-£203 Lunch £9.25-£17.50alc Dinner £9.25-£17.15alc LDO 10pm

♨ 40P
Credit Cards [1] [3] £

AUCHTERMUCHTY Fife Map **11** NO21

FH QQQ Mrs I Steven **Ardchoille** *(NO248096)* Dunshalt KY14 7EY ☎(0337) 28414
Closed Xmas & New Year
Situated just outside the village of Dunshalt on the B936, this modern farmhouse is the home of Mrs Steven, an enthusiastic cook who offers guests a warm welcome and imaginative meals. Guests dine around a communal table, elegantly set with china and crystal, and then relax in the comfortable lounge. Bedrooms, while not spacious, are cleanly maintained and provided with numerous thoughtful extras.
3rm(2↱ 1hc) (1fb) CTV in all bedrooms ® ✗ (ex guide dogs) ✱ sB&B£30-£38 dB&B↱£44-£60 LDO 6pm
♨ CTV 8P U 2 acres horses

AUDLEY Staffordshire Map **07** SJ75

FH QQQ Mrs E E Oulton **Domvilles** *(SJ776516)* Barthomley Rd ST7 8HT ☎Stoke-on-Trent(0782) 720378
Closed 25 Dec
This large farmhouse is beautifully furnished and immaculately maintained. The gardens and farmyard are also well tended, and guests are offered friendly service and comfortable accommodation. To find the house, leave the M6 at junction 16, follow signs to Barthomley, turn left at the White Lion Inn to Audley.
5rm(4⇌↱ 1hc) (2fb)⊬in 3 bedrooms CTV in all bedrooms ® ✗ (ex guide dogs) ✱ sB&B£20-£22 sB&B⇌↱£20-£22 dB&Bfr£32 dB&B⇌↱fr£32 WB&B£112-£140 WBDi£168-£196 LDO 6pm
CTV 8P table tennis 225 acres dairy mixed
See advertisement under STOKE-ON-TRENT

AULDGIRTH Dumfries & Galloway Map **11** NX98

FH QQ Mr P A Burford ***Allanton House*** *(NX915840)* DG2 0RY ☎(038774) 509
This large 16th-century mansion house situated off the A76 south of the town offers spacious and characterful accommodation with lofty bedrooms and public rooms filled with antiques. Guests are encouraged to explore the farm with its collection of animals, and are also able to purchase from a selection of bric- a-brac, a reflection of the proprietor's other interests.
3hc (1fb)⊬in 1 bedroom ® LDO 6pm
♨ CTV P 20 acres beef sheep

AUSTWICK North Yorkshire Map **07** SD76

FH QQ Mrs M Hird ***Rawlinshaw*** *(SD781673)* LA2 8DD ☎Settle(0729) 823214
Etr-Sep
Comfortable accommodation is provided in the family house of this true working farm and pony trekking centre, situated just off the A65 at the northern end of the Settle bypass. It is almost opposite the Dales Falconry, so look out for the distinctive green sign.
2hc (1fb) ® ✗ (ex guide dogs)
♨ CTV 10P U 206 acres beef dairy horses sheep

AVIEMORE Highland *Inverness-shire* Map **14** NH81

GH QQQ **Corrour House** Inverdruie PH22 1QH ☎(0479) 810220
Closed Nov-26 Dec
Stone-built house standing in tree-studded grounds half a mile east of Aviemore on B970.
8rm(3⇌5↱) (2fb) CTV in all bedrooms ® **T** sB&B⇌↱£24-£30 dB&B⇌↱£44-£56 WBDi£215-£275 LDO 8.30pm
Lic ♨ 15P nc1yr
Credit Cards [1] [3]

GH QQ ***Craiglea*** Grampian Rd PH22 1RH ☎(0479) 810210
Centrally situated beside the main road close to the railway station, this detached, small villa stands in its own grounds and offers unpretentious bed and breakfast accommodation at reasonable rates. The bedrooms vary in size and shape and although plainly decorated they have colourful fabrics with modern furniture. The lounge and dining room are furnished in a more traditional style.
11rm(1↱ 10hc) (4fb) ®
CTV 12P sauna

GH QQ **Ravenscraig** Grampian Rd PH22 1RP ☎(0479) 810278
Situated at the northern end of the main street, this friendly, family-run and neatly maintained bed and breakfast establishment offers a good standard of accommodation at reasonable rates. There is a comfortable lounge and newly extended breakfast room, while the bedrooms, furnished in a modern style, are either contained in the original house or a single-storey annexe to the rear.
6↱ Annexe 6↱ (2fb) CTV in all bedrooms ®
♨ CTV 12P

AXBRIDGE Somerset Map **03** ST45

FH Q Mr L F Dimmock ***Manor*** *(ST420549)* Cross BS26 2ED ☎(0934) 732577
Closed Xmas
This period farmhouse is very much part of a working sheep farm and is situated at the junction of the A38 and A371. The accommodation is very basic but reasonable, and the proprietors offer genuine, uncomplicated hospitality. Bedrooms are currently being brightened and modernised: they remain simple, but the soft furnishings are pretty and fresh. The farmhouse is very much a hard-working, no-nonsense place, where guests are cared for in a down-to-earth manner.
7rm(2hc) (2fb) ® LDO 5pm
CTV 10P 250 acres beef horses sheep
See advertisement on page 53

AXMINSTER Devon Map **03** SY29

SELECTED

FH QQQQ Mrs S Gay **Millbrook Farmhouse** *(SY304987)* Chard Rd EX13 5EG ☎(0297) 35351
Closed Xmas, 2wks autumn & 3wks spring
This pretty thatched farmhouse dates from around 900AD and combines the character and charm of an old building with the comforts of modern facilities. Rurally situated, it is a peaceful retreat, yet convenient for the market town and the coast. Hosts Sybil and John Gay are a charming couple who offer guests a warm welcome to their home. Bedrooms have high ceilings, oak beams and whitewashed walls, and are filled with handsome antique furniture and pretty, soft fabrics. All are well equipped with modern amenities. Breakfasts are hearty, and evening meals can be arranged, with fruit and vegetables freshly picked from the garden. Guests dine around a communal table in a relaxed and jovial atmosphere. Public areas are in the style of a traditional farmhouse, cosy and comfortable, and for the energetic, there are croquet, badminton and mini-golf facilities outside in the flower-filled gardens. This is a no- smoking establishment.
3rm(1hc) (2fb)⊬in all bedrooms CTV in all bedrooms ® ✗ (ex guide dogs) ✱ sB&B£18 dB&B£29 LDO 5pm
♨ CTV P 1🚗 putting croquet

Q is for quality. For a full explanation of this AA quality award, consult the Contents page.

AYR Strathclyde *Ayrshire* Map **10** NS32

GH QQ ***Arrandale Hotel*** 2-4 Cassillis St KA7 1DW
☎(0292) 289959
rs Winter
Within walking distance of the seafront, this small enthusiastically run hotel attracts both tourist and commercial clientèle. There are several nice bedrooms, a comfortable lounge and a dining room with a small residents' bar and a pool table.
13rm(1⇨2↱10hc) (6fb) CTV in all bedrooms
✗ (ex guide dogs) LDO 3pm
Lic ꟸ CTV ₱

SELECTED

GH QQQQ Brenalder Lodge 39 Dunure, Doonfoot KA7 4HR ☎(0292) 43939
rs during props holiday
Brenda and Albert Taylor's modern bungalow on the A719 just south of Ayr is popular with business people, golfers and tourists alike. The 5 attractive bedrooms are enhanced by pretty, soft fabrics and thoughtfully equipped with hairdryers, radio alarm clocks and TV. The dining room and lounge are shared with the proprietors, and hearty dinners are available with 24 hours' notice and are excellent value. Smoking is only permitted in the lounge.
5⇨↱ (1fb)⊁in all bedrooms CTV in all bedrooms ® ✱ sB&B⇨↱£35-£50 dB&B⇨↱£50-£60 WB&B£161-£210 WBDi£273-£322 LDO 24hrs prior
ꟸ CTV 9P nc7yrs

GH QQ Craggallan 8 Queens Ter KA7 1DU
☎(0292) 264998
Conveniently placed between the town centre and the seafront, this pleasant guesthouse features attractively decorated and nicely furnished bedrooms.
7hc (1fb)⊁in 4 bedrooms CTV in all bedrooms ® sB&B£14-£16 dB&B£28-£30 WBDi£125-£135 LDO 5pm
ꟸ CTV 4P

GH QQ Dargill 7 Queens Ter KA7 1DU ☎(0292) 261955
Cheery modern bedrooms, a cosy dining room and an attractive, comfortable lounge are provided by a compact terraced hotel located between sea and town centre.
4hc (2fb) CTV in all bedrooms ® ✱ sB&B£16-£18 dB&B£28-£30 WB&B£98-£105 WBDi£120-£140 LDO 2pm
ꟸ CTV nc3yrs

GH QQQ Glenmore 35 Bellvue Crescent KA7 2DP
☎(0292) 269830
This mid-terrace, 2-storey house, with a small rose garden at the front, is in a quiet residential crescent close to the town centre. It has been extensively refurbished to provide a high standard of décor, furnishings and fittings, with bold use of colours and patterns. There is a separate spacious lounge and a smaller dining room, both with fine fireplaces, and owner, Mrs Reid, ensures that guests have the best of facilities. Street parking is available, and while restrictions can apply, permits are available. Bedrooms are very well equipped, all en suite, with a good range of equipment.
4⇨↱ (2fb)⊁in all bedrooms CTV in all bedrooms ® **T** ✗ ✱ sB&B⇨↱fr£22 dB&B⇨↱fr£36 LDO 7.30pm
ꟸ

GH QQ Langley Bank 39 Carrick Rd KA7 2RD
☎(0292) 264246
This substantial period house appeals to the business person as well as the tourist. Bedrooms have telephones and radio alarm clocks, and the bathrooms are elegant and modern, some having bidets.
6rm(4↱2hc) (1fb) CTV in all bedrooms ® ✗ (ex guide dogs) ✱ sB&B£20-£40 dB&B£30-£45 dB&B↱£40-£45
ꟸ 4P
Credit Cards 1 3

GH QQ ***Windsor Hotel*** 6 Alloway Place KA7 2AA
☎(0292) 264689
Within walking distance of both the town centre and the seafront, this terraced house with bright, attractive bedrooms is full of character.
10rm(7⇨↱3hc) (4fb) CTV in all bedrooms ® LDO 6pm
ꟸ CTV ₱
Credit Cards 1 3

AYTON, GREAT North Yorkshire Map **08** NZ51

INN QQ ***Royal Oak Hotel*** High Green TS9 6BW
☎(0642) 722361 FAX (0642) 724047
An 18th-century coaching inn situated in the centre of the village, which has historical associations with Captain Cook. An à la carte and table d'hôte restaurant and wide-ranging bar meals are features of the inn. Bedrooms are well furnished, all with en suite facilities, colour TV, telephones and tea- making equipment.
5⇨↱ CTV in all bedrooms ® LDO 9.15pm
ꟸ ₱
Credit Cards 1 3

BABELL Clwyd Map **07** SJ17

FH QQ Mrs M L Williams **Bryn Glas** *(SJ155737)* CH8 7PZ
☎Caerwys(0352) 720493
Feb-Nov
This dormer-style bungalow is located opposite the Black Lion Inn, next to the original farmhouse and buildings, and is surrounded by farmland. It offers 2 nicely maintained rooms which are equipped with black and white TV and tea- making facilities.
2hc (1fb)⊁in all bedrooms TV in all bedrooms ® ✱ sB&Bfr£15 dB&Bfr£25 WB&Bfr£86
ꟸ CTV 2P pony trekking 40 acres beef mixed sheep horses

BAKEWELL Derbyshire Map **08** SK26

GH QQ Castle Cliffe Private Hotel Monsal Head DE4 1NL
☎Great Longstone(0629) 640258
A friendly guesthouse situated at Monsal Head, a few miles northwest of Bakewell. It offers personal service, home-cooked interesting regional British dishes and sound accommodation. Some of the bedrooms have superb views over Monsal Dale.
9rm(2↱7hc) (2fb) CTV in 2 bedrooms ® ✗ (ex guide dogs) sB&B£19-£30 dB&B£38-£42 dB&B↱£41-£45 WB&B£118-£128 WBDi£180-£200 LDO 5pm
Lic CTV 12P 3🚗
Credit Cards 1 3 £

GH QQ Cliffe House Hotel Monsal Head DE45 1NL
☎Great Longstone(0629) 640376
Situated at the top of Monsal Dale, this house has some lovely panoramic views out across the dale and surrounding Peak District. The proprietors are actively involved, which helps to create a friendly, relaxed environment. Guests can enjoy the traditional, freshly prepared home cooking, then adjourn to relax in the TV lounge.
10rm(5⇨5↱) (3fb) CTV in all bedrooms ® ✗ (ex guide dogs) sB&B⇨↱£30-£32 dB&B⇨↱£40-£44 WB&B£130-£136 WBDi£190-£200 LDO 10am
Lic ꟸ CTV 14P
Credit Cards 1 3 £

SELECTED

GH QQQQ Merlin House Ashford Ln, Monsal Head DE45 1NL ☎Great Longstone(0629) 640475
Mar-Oct
A small, immaculately kept guesthouse in an lovely rural location at Monsal Head, 3 miles northwest of Bakewell. Bedrooms are light and fresh, with high standards of housekeeping and maintenance; the sizes and styles of rooms vary. There is a small comfortable lounge with a good range of

books and some board games, and an adjoining conservatory with cane furniture and matching soft fabrics overlooking the well tended lawns.
2⌐ TV in all bedrooms ✱ dB&B⌐£40-£46 WB&B£140 ▥ 4P nc

BALA Gwynedd Map **06** SH93

GH Q Frondderw Stryd-y-Fron LL23 7YD ☎(0678) 520301
Mar-Nov
This charming period mansion dates back to 1680, and from its elevated position on the western outskirts of town, it commands lovely views of the Berwyn Mountains and the lake. The accommodation is fairly simple, but some rooms have en suite facilities.
8rm(1⇌3⌐4hc) (3fb) ® ✱ (ex guide dogs) sB&B£16-£17 sB&B⇌⌐£16-£17 dB&B£24-£26 dB&B⇌⌐£32-£34 WB&B£80.50-£115.50 WBDi£133-£168 LDO 5pm
Lic ▥ CTV 10P ⓔ

See advertisement on page 55

FH QQ Mrs E Jones **Eirianfa** *(SH967394)* Sarnau LL23 7LH (4m N on A494) ☎Llandderfel(06783) 389
Mar-Dec (ex Xmas)
This modern, single-storey property stands next to Penbryn farmhouse, which is owned by the same family and is also used to accommodate guests. The farm is on the A494, northeast of Bala on the outskirts of Sarnau village, and from its elevated position there are good views of the Berwyn Mountains. The bedrooms are simple but soundly maintained, with a mixture of modern and traditional furniture. One room is equipped for family occupancy. Comfortable seating is provided in a combined lounge/dining room, where breakfast is also served.
3hc (1fb) ® ✱ ✱ sB&B£14-£15 dB&B£26-£27 LDO 5pm
▥ CTV 4P ✓ 150 acres mixed

FH **QQ** Mrs M E Jones **Penbryn** *(SH498723)* Sarnau LL23 7LH ☎LLandderfel(06783) 297

This pleasant, well maintained farmhouse is situated on the A494, to the northeast of Bala, on the outskirts of Sarnau village. There are good views of the Berwyn Mountains from its elevated position, and the accommodation is modern and attractively decorated.

6hc (1fb) ✖ ✻ sB&Bfr£15 dB&Bfr£26 WB&Bfr£87.50 WBDifr£136.50 LDO 6pm

♨ CTV 10P ✓ 200 acres beef mixed sheep

BALLACHULISH Highland *Argyllshire* Map **14** NN05

GH **QQQ** **Fern Villa** East Laroch PA39 4JE ☎(08552) 393

Closed Xmas & New Year

An attractive granite-built Victorian house, situated in the centre of the village, which owners John and Beryl Clement have recently upgraded. Bedrooms, though compact, are comfortably furnished and all have private bathrooms. Local produce features on the daily changing set-price dinner menu, served at separate tables in the pleasant dining room. This is a no-smoking establishment.

5⇌⌐ 🚭in all bedrooms ® ✖ (ex guide dogs) dB&B⇌⌐£50-£54 (incl dinner) WB&B£115-£123 WBDi£165-£179 LDO 6.30pm

Lic ♨ CTV 5P nc16yrs

GH **QQQ** ***Lyn-Leven*** White St PA39 4JP ☎(08552) 392

Closed Xmas

Set in its own well tended gardens just off the A82, this friendly, comfortable family-run guesthouse is a modern bungalow enjoying wonderful views over Loch Leven and the Glencoe Mountains. Bedrooms, though compact, are comfortably appointed, and well cooked traditional food is served in the spacious dining room which overlooks the loch.

8rm(7⌐1hc) Annexe 5⇌⌐ (1fb) CTV in 8 bedrooms ® LDO 8pm

Lic ♨ 12P

BALLANTRAE Strathclyde *Ayrshire* Map **10** NX08

GH **QQQ** **Balkissock Lodge** KA26 0LP ☎(0465) 83537

Formerly a shooting lodge serving the local estate, this extended country house has been converted to a guesthouse by Janet and Adrian Beale and sits amidst farmland in a lovely, peaceful setting. The bedrooms are named after renowned painters and are thoughtfully equipped. The upstairs room has a single room leading off and makes an ideal family unit, whilst the ground floor rooms are more compact but sensibly furnished. Janet Beale's cooking will be a highlight of a visit to Balkissock, and the delightful little restaurant, created out of the original sitting room with a low ceiling and open fireplace, will come as a pleasant surprise. There is an à la carte and set-price dinner menu, served between 7pm and 9pm, and the latter might be smoked salmon paté followed by Ewenique pie (lamb) and perhaps banana pancakes with maple syrup for dessert. Breakfast also offers an impressive choice and vegetarians are catered for. Teas, coffees and snacks are served at reasonable times either in the bedrooms or in the small lounge.

3⇌⌐ (1fb)🚭in all bedrooms CTV in all bedrooms ® ✖ (ex guide dogs) ✻ sB&B£19.50-£24.50 dB&B⇌⌐fr£39 WBDi£175-£195 LDO 9pm

♨ P

Credit Cards [1] [3]

BALLATER Grampian *Aberdeenshire* Map **15** NO39

GH **QQQ** **Moorside** Braemar Rd AB35 5RL ☎(03397) 55492

Mar-Nov

This granite-stone former church manse has been sympathetically restored and stands on the main road west of the town. The bright, airy bedrooms, some of which are quite spacious, are complemented by a vast dining room and lounge. It has a welcoming atmosphere and offers enjoyable home cooking.

9rm(3⇌6⌐) (3fb) CTV in all bedrooms ® ✻ sB&B⇌⌐fr£24 dB&B⇌⌐fr£36 WB&Bfr£117

Lic ♨ 10P

Credit Cards [1] [3]

GH **QQ** **Netherley** 2 Netherley Place AB35 5QE ☎(03397) 55792

Closed Nov-Jan rs Feb

Situated in a residential street beside the village green, this family-run guesthouse forms part of a terrace, and is a popular base for tourists and golfers. Bedrooms vary in size and are simply appointed; some have private bathrooms and are equipped with TV and tea-making facilities. There is a friendly atmosphere with a choice of comfortable lounges, where smoking is not permitted.

9rm(4⇌⌐5hc) (3fb) CTV in 4 bedrooms ® ✻ sB&B£16-£18 dB&B£28-£32 dB&B⇌⌐£34-£38 LDO 5pm

CTV P̸ nc4yrs

BALLOCH Strathclyde *Dumbartonshire* Map **10** NX39

GH **QQQ** **Arbor Lodge** Old Luss Rd G83 8QW ☎Alexandria(0389) 56233

A modern house with thoughtfully equipped bedrooms, just 400yds from the main Glasgow to Loch Lomond road. It has no lounge.

4⌐ CTV in all bedrooms ® ✖ (ex guide dogs) ✻ dB&B⌐£36-£40 WBDi£252-£280

♨ 8P

Credit Cards [1] [3]

BALQUHIDDER Central *Perthshire* Map **11** NN52

INN **QQ** **Monachyle Mhor** FK19 8PQ (4m SW) ☎Strathyre(08774) 622

Apart from the occasional house, this 17th-century, fully licensed farmhouse lies in splendid isolation at the head of Loch Voil. It is reached by a 4-mile single-track road which meanders along the lochside. The house retains much of its original character, particularly the bedrooms, which while simply decorated and furnished do have modern facilities such as en suite bathrooms, central heating and hairdryers. Good Scottish country cooking can be sampled in the original dining room around a refectory table or at individual tables in the small conservatory. The cosy bar is the focal point of the house and its popularity combined with the service of meals to non-residents gives the atmosphere of a country inn. Private fishing, stalking and grouse shooting can be arranged.

4⇌⌐ ® ✖ (ex guide dogs) ✻ dB&B⇌⌐fr£38 WBDi£217-£238 Lunch £5-£20 Dinner £14-£17.50 LDO 10pm

♨ CTV 12P nc10yrs ✓

Credit Cards [1] [3]

BAMFORD Derbyshire Map **08** SK28

INN **QQ** **Ye Derwent Hotel** Main Rd S30 2AY ☎Hope Valley(0433) 51395

10rm(1⇌1⌐8hc) (1fb) CTV in all bedrooms ® ✻ sB&B£25-£30 sB&B⇌⌐£32.50 dB&B£40 dB&B⇌⌐£45 WB&B£126-£189 WBDi£175-£208 Lunch £5.85-£12.30 Dinner £5.85-£12.95 LDO 9.15pm

♨ 40P boat for hire

Credit Cards [1] [3] £

BAMPTON Devon Map **03** SS92

See also Shillingford

GH **QQ** ***Courtyard Hotel & Restaurant*** 19 Fore St EX16 9ND ☎(0398) 331536

Closed Xmas & New Year

An attractive stone building enjoying a central location in the town. Rooms are simple but well equipped with modern facilities, whilst public rooms are in keeping with the original style of the property. The busy restaurant is open to non-residents, and offers an à la carte menu.

6rm(2⇌1⌐3hc) (1fb) CTV in all bedrooms ® ✖ LDO 9pm

Lic ♨ CTV 35P

Credit Cards [1] [2] [3] [5]

INN QQQ Exeter Tiverton Rd EX16 9DY ☏(0398) 331345
This old family-run inn is full of character, and is well situated in the Exe valley, on the A396 between Bampton and Tiverton. The bedrooms have been attractively decorated and furnished, and are all well equipped with telephones, TVs, hairdryers and tea-making facilities. There is an extensive choice of bar snacks available, whilst an à la carte menu is offered in the more formal restaurant. Salmon and trout fishing is available, and clay-pigeon shooting can be arranged.
8rm(4⇌3↱1hc) CTV in all bedrooms ® T ✗ (ex guide dogs)
✱ sB&B⇌↱fr£27.50 dB&B⇌↱fr£49.50 WB&Bfr£172.50
WBDifr£250 Lunch fr£7.95alc Dinner fr£9.95alc LDO 9pm
50P ⚲ U clay pigeon & game shooting
Credit Cards 1 3 £

BAMPTON Oxfordshire Map **04** SP30

INN QQ *Talbot Hotel* Market Square OX8 2HA
☏Bampton Castle(0993) 850326
In the heart of the pretty Cotswold village, this inn offers modern, well equipped bedrooms, along with cosy traditional public areas. Extensive meal times and a varied choice of table d'hôte, à la carte and bar-snack menus ensure that guests won't go hungry.
6rm(5↱1hc) CTV in all bedrooms ® ✗ (ex guide dogs)
LDO 10pm
Credit Cards 1 3

BANBURY Oxfordshire Map **04** SP44

GH QQ Belmont 34 Crouch St OX16 9PR ☏(0295) 262308
This Victorian town house is conveniently situated close to the town centre and the famous Banbury Cross. Bed and breakfast only are offered, and bedrooms are comfortable, clean and simply appointed. Some are en suite, and all have TV.
8rm(5↱3hc) (1fb) CTV in all bedrooms ® ✗ (ex guide dogs)
✱ sB&B£18-£25 sB&B↱£22-£30 dB&B£28-£35 dB&B↱£35
Lic 6P 1 nc7yrs
Credit Cards 1 3

GH QQ Calthorpe Lodge 4 Calthorpe Rd OX16 8HS
☏(0295) 252325
This small Victorian terraced house is on the south side of town, behind the Moat House. It has recently been renovated and refurnished to provide good, modern standards in the bedrooms, some of which have private bathrooms. The breakfast room is also freshly decorated, and the accommodation is spotlessly clean.
6rm(4⇌↱2hc) (1fb) CTV in all bedrooms ® sB&Bfr£22.50
sB&B⇌↱£25-£30 dB&B⇌↱£35-£40
CTV 6P
Credit Cards 1 3 5 £

GH QQ *Fairlawns* 60 Oxford Rd OX16 9AN ☏(0295) 262461
This turn-of-the-century detached house has neat gardens and private parking. The bedrooms have been professionally colour coordinated, and provide modern facilities, and there is a spacious breakfast room.
10rm(1⇌4↱5hc) (3fb) CTV in all bedrooms ®
CTV 9P
Credit Cards 1 2 3

GH QQQ La Madonette Country OX15 6AA (3m W off B4035) ☏(0295) 730212
This pretty miller's house, dating from 1640, is delightfully set in rural surroundings just 2.5 miles west of Banbury, and boasts an outdoor swimming pool in addition to a mill stream. The spacious bedrooms offer a good range of modern facilities as well as comfortable beds and chairs, and there is an attractive breakfast room and reception lounge.
5⇌↱ (1fb) CTV in all bedrooms ® T ✗ (ex guide dogs) ✱
sB&B⇌↱£28-£37.50 dB&B⇌↱£42-£55
Lic CTV 20P ⛱(heated)
Credit Cards 1 3

INN QQQ ***The Blinking Owl*** Main St, North Newington OX15 6AE ☎(0295) 730650

This 16th-century stone-built inn sits in the village of North Newington, about 2 miles from the centre of Banbury, surrounded by open countryside. Bedrooms, though perhaps a little compact, are comfortable and have en suite facilities, and are located in the converted barn adjacent to the inn. There is a restaurant below the rooms, offering a choice of dishes, while bar snacks are available in the atmospheric inn.

3rm(1⇌2♪) CTV in all bedrooms ✗ LDO 9pm
▥ 12P nc8yrs

BANTHAM Devon Map **03** SX64

INN QQQ Sloop TQ7 3AJ ☎Kingsbridge(0548) 560489 & 560215

Dating back to the 16th century, this inn was originally a farmhouse and was owned by a famous smuggler. Situated in the village centre close to the beach, the property retains its character, with many original features. Bedrooms are spotlessly clean, comfortably furnished and equipped with a good range of modern facilities and en suite bathrooms. The popular bar is full of character and there is a panelled family restaurant where a comprehensive range of imaginative home-cooked food is available, including a good choice of fresh fish, shellfish and rich puddings.

5⇌♪ (2fb) CTV in all bedrooms ® ✱ sB&B⇌♪£22.50-£30 dB&B⇌♪£45-£53 WBDi£255-£270 Lunch £6-£10alc Dinner £6-£15alc LDO 10pm
▥ 35P

BARDON MILL Northumberland Map **12** NY76

FH QQ Judy Davidson **Crindledykes** *(NY787672)* Nr Housesteads NE47 7AF (on unclass rd, between A69 and B6318) ☎Haltwhistle(0434) 344316

In a magnificent rural location between the A69 and B6318 Roman road, this traditional stone-built farmhouse offers very neat, cosy bedrooms, an inviting lounge and dining room and friendly service.

2rm ✗ ✱ sB&B£18-£20 dB&B£28-£32 LDO noon
▥ CTV 10P 475 acres stock ⓔ

BARMOUTH Gwynedd Map **06** SH61

GH QQ Cranbourne Hotel 9 Marine Pde LL42 1NA ☎(0341) 280202

A small, professionally run hotel on the seafront, within a short walk of the town centre, catering mainly for holidaymakers.

10rm(8⇌♪2hc) (6fb) CTV in all bedrooms ® ✗ ✱ sB&B£15-£17.50 dB&B⇌♪£35-£40 WB&B£122-£147 WBDi£185-£200 LDO 5pm
Lic ▥ CTV 4P (85p per day)
Credit Cards 1 3

GH Q Endeavour Marine Pde LL42 1NA ☎(0341) 280271
Closed mid Dec-mid Jan

This personally run guesthouse is situated on the seafront, overlooking the beach, and is within a short walk of the town centre. It provides simple but nicely maintained accommodation and caters mainly for holidaymakers.

9rm(5♪4hc) CTV in 8 bedrooms TV in 1 bedroom ® ✗ (ex guide dogs) ✱ sB&B£13.50-£16 dB&B£27-£32 dB&B♪£29-£33 WB&B£95-£110 WBDi£125-£145 LDO 4pm
Lic ▥ CTV
Credit Cards 1 3

GH QQ Morwendon Llanaber LL42 1RR ☎(0341) 280566
Closed Jan-Mar rs Oct-Dec

A small, personally run hotel providing comfortable accommodation about 1.5 miles north of the town on the A496 coast road. Several bedrooms enjoy good sea views.

6♪ (3fb) CTV in all bedrooms ® ✗ (ex guide dogs) ✱ sB&B♪£17 dB&B£30-£34 dB&B♪£34 WB&B£105-£112 WBDi£140-£160 LDO 5pm
Lic ▥ CTV 7P

INN Q ***Tal-y-Don*** St Anne's Square LL42 1DL ☎(0341) 280508

Situated in the town centre, this is a small public house providing simple accommodation. It also offers a choice of 3 bars and a beer garden to the rear.

7hc (3fb) CTV in all bedrooms ® ✗
▥ CTV P̸

BARNARD CASTLE Co Durham Map **12** NZ01

GH QQQ The Homelands 85 Galgate DL12 8ES ☎Teesdale(0833) 38757

A licensed restaurant and guesthouse situated on the main road into the town centre. The charming bedrooms are individually designed, and there is a comfortable lounge and an impressive restaurant. The dinner menu offers a selection of imaginative dishes, prepared by the delightful proprietors.

4rm(2♪2hc) CTV in all bedrooms ® ✗ (ex guide dogs) ✱ sB&Bfr£16 sB&B⇌♪fr£20 dB&B⇌♪fr£35 WB&B£122.50 WBDi£192.50 LDO 8.15pm
Lic ▥ 5P

FH Q R & Mrs D M Lowson **West Roods** *(NZ022141)* Boldron DL12 9SW ☎Teesdale(0833) 690116
Mar-Dec

A modest farmhouse situated in a delightful rural location with direct access from the A66.

3rm(2♪1hc) (1fb)⊬in all bedrooms CTV in all bedrooms ® ✗ (ex guide dogs) ✱ sB&B£17-£20 dB&B♪fr£34 WB&Bfr£100 LDO 6pm
▥ 6P 58 acres dairy
Credit Cards 1 2 3 ⓔ

INN QQQ The Fox and Hounds Country Inn & Restaurant Cotherstone DL12 9PF ☎Teesdale(0833) 50241 & 50811

A charming village inn that has earned a good reputation for its imaginative menus. Bedrooms are most attractive and well equipped. The bar lounges and restaurants, while modernised, retain their original character and atmosphere.

3⇌♪ ⊬in all bedrooms CTV in all bedrooms ® T ✗ (ex guide dogs) sB&B⇌♪£35-£40 dB&B⇌♪£45-£55 Lunch £10.45-£10.95&alc Dinner £12.50-£15&alc LDO 9pm
▥ CTV 30P nc9yrs
Credit Cards 1 3 ⓔ

BARNEY Norfolk Map **09** TF93

SELECTED

GH QQQQ The Old Brick Kilns Little Barney NR21 0NL ☎Thursford(0328) 878305

This guesthouse is northeast of Fakenham, off the A148 towards Barney, first left down a narrow lane which ends at the Brick Kilns. Tessa Gent greets her guests at the car door and leads them into her home with an offer of refreshments in the lounge – a large room with pale gold dralon armchairs and sofas, colour TV in a cabinet, a log fire and Copenhagen china figurines. The dining room is a modern extension with patio doors overlooking the well tended lawns and shrubbery. The 3 bedrooms have period furniture and high, thick mattresses on bedsteads of polished dark wood. There are modern tiled en suite facilities, and the house is immaculate throughout with gleaming surfaces and fresh flowers.

3rm(1⇌2♪) CTV in all bedrooms ® ✗ (ex guide dogs) sB&B⇌♪£18-£21 dB&B⇌♪£36-£42 WB&B£126 WBDi£217 LDO 10am
Lic ▥ CTV 10P ⓔ

BARNSTAPLE Devon Map **02** SS53

[⇔●] **GH QQ Cresta** 26 Sticklepath Hill EX31 2BU
☏(0271) 74022
At the top of Sticklepath Hill and about a mile from the centre of town, you will find this simple but comfortable accommodation. A cosy residents' lounge is provided. The proprietor Mrs Curtis is a member of the 'British Sugarcraft Guild' and sometimes examples of her hobby are on display. Good car parking is available on site.
5rm(1↑4hc) Annexe 1⇔ (1fb) CTV in all bedrooms Ⓡ ✗ sB&B£15-£17 sB&B⇔↑£18-£20 dB&B£25-£30 dB&B⇔↑£28-£34 WB&B£77-£105
▥ CTV 6P nc £

[⇔●] **GH Q West View** Pilton Causeway EX32 7AA
☏(0271) 42079
Excellent value for money is provided by this end-of-terrace, red-brick Edwardian house, which is situated just a short walk from the town centre, on the road to Lynton. The bedrooms are simply furnished and each is equipped with TV, radio alarm and tea-making facilities.
7hc (2fb) CTV in all bedrooms Ⓡ sB&B£13-£15 dB&B£26-£30 WB&B£91-£105 WBDi£122.50-£130 LDO 7pm
▥ 6P 1⌂
Credit Cards [1] [3] £

GH QQQ Yeodale Hotel Pilton Bridge EX31 1PG
☏(0271) 42954
This 3-storey listed building, with its elegant iron balcony, dates back partly to the 16th century. Geoffrey and Irene Smith have carried out major alterations to create attractive bedrooms, equipped with hairdryers and radio alarms, in addition to other facilities. The table d'hôte dinner menu offers a choice of home-cooked dishes. Conveniently situated, an easy level walk takes you into the centre of the town. There is adjacent on-street parking available.
10rm(1⇔5↑4hc) (3fb) CTV in all bedrooms Ⓡ sB&B£16-£20 sB&B⇔↑£24.50-£28.50 dB&B£36 dB&B⇔↑£42-£52 WB&B£112-£140 WBDi£171.50-£199.50 LDO 5pm
Lic ▥ CTV P̸
Credit Cards [1] [2] [3] £

[⇔●] **FH QQ** Mr & Mrs J Dallyn **Rowden Barton** *(SS538306)* Roundswell EX31 3NP (2m SW B3232)
☏(0271) 44365
This relatively modern farmhouse has lovely views across open countryside, and is popular with gardening enthusiasts visiting nearby Rosemore and Marwood Hill. The 2 bedrooms, which share a bathroom, are freshly painted and provide comfortable, good quality beds, and the 2 lounges are pleasantly informal. Mr and Mrs Dallyn provide true farmhouse hospitality and wholesome home cooking.
2rm ⊘in all bedrooms Ⓡ ✗ (ex guide dogs) sB&Bfr£14 dB&Bfr£28 WB&Bfr£98 WBDifr£154 LDO 5pm
▥ CTV 4P 90 acres beef sheep £

BATH Avon Map **03** ST76

See Town Plan Section
See also Frome, Keynsham and Timsbury

SELECTED

GH QQQQ *Arden Hotel* 73 Great Pulteney St BA2 4DL
☏(0225) 466601 & 330039 FAX (0225) 465548
Closed mid Dec-2 Jan
This very elegant Grade I listed building is set in a delightful row of Georgian town houses, and only a short walk from the city centre. The hotel is classically furnished throughout and richly decorated, in keeping with the grandness and architecture of the building. The bedrooms are well proportioned with many original features retained. The majority boast stylish French furniture, all with pretty Austrian ruche curtains and have a good range of modern facilities including TV, direct-line telephones and bright en suites. During the season Florizel's restaurant is open in the basement, where imaginative food is served.
10⇔↑ (2fb) CTV in all bedrooms Ⓡ **T** ✗ (ex guide dogs)
Lic ▥ CTV P̸
Credit Cards [1] [3]

GH Q Arney 99 Wells Rd BA2 3AN ☏(0225) 310020
Situated a mile from the city centre on the A36 Wells road, this small Victorian terraced house offers modest, value-for-money bed and breakfast accommodation.
7rm(1↑6hc) (3fb) ✱ sB&B£19-£22 dB&B£29-£32.01
▥ CTV P̸ £

GH QQ Ashley Villa Hotel 26 Newbridge Rd BA1 3JZ
☏(0225) 421683 & 428887
Closed 2 wks Xmas
There has been continued good work and upgrading at this friendly small hotel, and at the time of our last visit the bedroom décor was being softened with coordinated fabrics, to go with the good range of modern facilities provided. Personally run by the enthusiastic proprietors Mr and Mrs Kitcher, Ashley Villa has the added benefit of a patio garden, secluded outdoor swimming pool and a car park. It is conveniently positioned on the A4 west of the city and caters well for both business and tourist guests.
14rm(4⇔10↑) (3fb) CTV in all bedrooms Ⓡ **T** ✗ (ex guide dogs) sB&B⇔↑£35-£39 dB&B⇔↑£45-£59 WB&B£207-£247 LDO 9pm
Lic ▥ CTV 10P ≈(heated)
Credit Cards [1] [3] £

See advertisement on page 59

GH Q Astor House 14 Oldfield Rd BA2 3ND ☏(0225) 429134
Apr-Oct
Particularly popular with overseas visitors, this establishment is set in a pleasant residential area of the city, yet is convenient for the centre and all amenities. The accommodation is simple and functional, representing good value for money. A friendly atmosphere is created by the owners, Mr and Mrs Johnson, and car parking is available.
7hc Ⓡ ✗ (ex guide dogs) dB&B£30-£36
▥ CTV 4P nc7yrs £

GH QQQ The Bath Tasburgh Warminster Rd, Bathampton BA2 6SH ☏(0225) 425096
Built in 1890, this large Victorian house with canal frontage is situated on the A36, a mile from the city centre, and surrounded by 2 acres of well tended gardens and 5 acres of pasture. Rooms have some superb views and are individually styled and decorated, with good facilities including bright, modern en suites. There is a comfortable, tastefully furnished lounge with an attractive conservatory extension. Proprietors Brian and Audrey Archer are friendly hosts with a professional staff.
13rm(12⇔↑1hc) (4fb)⊘in 2 bedrooms CTV in all bedrooms Ⓡ **T** ✗ ✱ sB&Bfr£32 sB&B⇔↑£40-£48 dB&B£44-£45 dB&B⇔↑£50-£68
Lic ▥ CTV 15P ✿ croquet
Credit Cards [1] [2] [3] [5] £

See advertisement on page 59

GH QQQ Bloomfield House 146 Bloomfield Rd BA2 2AS
☏(0225) 420105 FAX (0225) 481958
This Georgian house was built in 1820 with mellow Bath stone, and stands in its own grounds on the southern outskirts of the city, enjoying excellent views. It has been extensively and tastefully restored to its former elegance by owners John Pascoe and Titos Argiris; bedrooms feature ornate canopied and half-tester beds and some fine pieces of period furniture, and modern brass-fitted mahogany panelled private bathrooms have bathrobes and several
→

extra touches. The entrance hall has been imaginatively decorated with stylish hand painted murals and there is a comfortable, sunny breakfast room; the adjacent sitting room overlooks the garden.
5⇔↱ (1fb)⊬in 3 bedrooms CTV in all bedrooms ®
✗ (ex guide dogs) sB&B⇔↱£26-£35 dB&B⇔↱£35-£65
▥ 9P
Credit Cards [1] [3] £

GH QQQ Brocks 32 Brock St BA1 2LN ☎(0225) 338374
Closed Xmas & 2 wks Jan
This very attractive Georgian Grade II listed building is a little gem. It is personally run by Marion Dodd and offers spotlessly clean, bright and comfortable bedrooms, all individually decorated and equipped with a good range of modern facilities. There is a cosy little lounge and a breakfast room where handsome English breakfasts are taken. The location, just off Bath's famous Circus, is ideal for both tourists and business people.
8rm(4⇔↱2hc) (2fb) CTV in all bedrooms ®
✗ (ex guide dogs) sB&B£19-£20 sB&B⇔↱£30-£40 dB&B£40-£42 dB&B⇔↱£44-£50
▥ CTV 2🚗 £

GH QQQ Brompton House Hotel St John's Rd BA2 6PT
☎(0225) 420972 & 448423
Closed Xmas & New Year
New owners David and Sue Selby have undertaken an enthusiastic renovation and upgrading programme to restore this attractive Victorian house to its former glory, while providing modern standards of comfort. Suitable for tourists and business guests, it is in a convenient city-centre location and has its own secluded gardens and car park.
19⇔↱ (1fb) CTV in all bedrooms ® T ✗ (ex guide dogs) ✱
sB&B⇔↱£32-£39 dB&B⇔↱£56-£69
Lic ▥ 20P nc7yrs
Credit Cards [1] [3] £

GH QQQ Carfax Hotel Great Pulteney St BA2 4BS
☎(0225) 462089 FAX (0225) 443257
There has been continued good work at this elegant terrace of 3 Regency houses, on the famous Great Pulteney Street close to the centre. Bedrooms have been upgraded to promote comfortable modern standards and a good range of modern facilities. Public rooms are bright and comfortable and there is an attractive ground-floor restaurant.
39rm(34⇔↱5hc) (3fb)⊬in 5 bedrooms CTV in all bedrooms ® T ✗ (ex guide dogs) sB&B£22-£25 sB&B⇔↱£35-£47.50 dB&B£40-£44.50 dB&B⇔↱£48-£68 WB&B£126-£214 WBDi£164.50-£245.50 LDO 7.50pm
lift ▥ CTV 13P 4🚗 (£2 per day) ⌂ games room
Credit Cards [1] [2] [3] £

GH QQQ *Cedar Lodge* 13 Lambridge, London Rd BA1 6BJ
☎(0225) 423468
Closed 24-27 Dec
Conveniently situated 50yds west of the A46 (London Road) junction, this double-fronted Georgian house has been restored by Derek and Maria Beckett to provide commendable comfort while retaining much of its original character, including fine interior architecture, stained glass windows and Adam fireplaces. There are only 3 bedrooms, and although they are not fully en suite, they are spacious and well furnished with assorted antiques and quality furniture. Cedar Lodge is a no-smoking, personally run and very friendly establishment offering a good bed and breakfast service.
3rm(1↱2hc) (1fb)⊬in all bedrooms CTV in all bedrooms
✗ (ex guide dogs)
▥ CTV 6P ⌂ U

GH QQQ Cheriton House 9 Upper Oldfield Park BA2 3JX
☎(0225) 429862
Closed Xmas & New Year
A large semidetached Victorian villa situated south of the city centre in a residential area off the A367 Wells road, with some fine views over the city. Carefully restored and modernised, it now
→

The Bath Tasburgh Hotel

WARMINSTER ROAD, BATHAMPTON, BATH BA2 6SH
TEL & FAX: 0225 425096 (3 LINES)

A beautiful Victorian Mansion built for a Photographer to the Royal Family and set in 7 acres of lovely gardens and grounds with canal frontage and breathtaking views. All rooms have en-suite bathrooms, tea/coffee facilities, colour TV, telephone, radio/alarm and there are King-size beds and a Four-Poster. Fine sitting room and conservatory. Private CAR PARK. A relaxed setting so convenient to main attractions.

This Fine House is recommended in many Good Guides.

ETB HIGHLY COMMENDED — AA LISTED QQQ

Personally managed by the Resident Owners – Brian & Audrey Archer

Ashley Villa Hotel, Bath

26 Newbridge Road, Bath BA1 3JZ
Telephone: (0225) 421683 & 428887

Comfortably furnished licensed hotel with relaxing informal atmosphere, situated close to the city centre. All bedrooms have en suite facilities, colour television, direct dial telephone, tea and coffee making.

This small friendly hotel has recently been refurbished throughout. It has a **heated swimming pool** (summer only), with garden patio and car park.

You can be sure of a warm welcome from the resident owners,
Rod and Alex Kitcher, M.H.C.I.M.A

provides intimate and comfortable public areas and well equipped bedrooms with private bathrooms.
9rm(2⇌7♠) CTV in all bedrooms ® ✗ (ex guide dogs) sB&B⇌♠£32-£38 dB&B⇌♠£47-£58
♨ 9P nc
Credit Cards [1] [3] £

GH QQ Cranleigh 159 Newbridge Hill BA1 3PX
☎(0225) 310197
This attractive Victorian building of Bath stone is set in its own gardens in a very convenient city location. Bedrooms are spotlessly clean, well proportioned and airy, retaining the original fireplaces and decorative plasterwork. The owners have enhanced these features with pastel walls and good use of bold, colour-coordinating fabrics. All rooms are individually styled, with lots of personal touches and objets d'art. A friendly, family-run establishment, this is an ideal base for touring the city and surrounding area.
4⇌♠ (3fb)⚡in all bedrooms CTV in all bedrooms ®
✗ (ex guide dogs) sB&B⇌♠£30-£40 dB&B⇌♠£48-£58
Lic ♨ 4P nc6yrs
Credit Cards [1] [3]

GH QQ Devonshire House 143 Wellsway BA2 4RZ
☎(0225) 312495
This cosy little bed and breakfast establishment has 3 comfortable, personally styled bedrooms furnished in stripped pine, set off by an abundance of Victoriana, objets d'art and some antiques. The owners also run the adjacent antique shop. The rooms have bright coordinating décor and a good range of modern facilities, 2 have en suite facilities while the remaining single has a private bathroom. The little breakfast room is also furnished in Victorian style. There is useful on-site parking and an enclosed rear courtyard, and the location on the Wells road is convenient, though on the outskirts of the city.
3⇌♠ (1fb)⚡in all bedrooms CTV in all bedrooms ® ✗
sB&B⇌♠£20-£25 dB&B⇌♠£38-£40 WB&B£115-£120
♨ 6P
Credit Cards [1] [3] £

GH QQQ Dorian House 1 Upper Oldfield Park BA2 3JX
☎(0225) 426336
Built in 1890, this guesthouse enjoys an elevated position off the A367, with fine views over the city and surrounding hills. Bedrooms are individually decorated with quality in mind. En suite facilities are modern and well kept, and extras include telephones and hairdryers. The cosy sitting room is open all hours, and a small bar is licenced to open in the evenings. Breakfasts are taken in the attractive dining room, and are well worth getting up for. Doreen and Ian Bennetts are charming hosts who maintain excellent standards throughout.
7rm(4⇌3♠) (2fb) CTV in all bedrooms ® T
✗ (ex guide dogs) sB&B⇌♠£35-£45 dB&B⇌♠£49-£72
Lic ♨ 8P 2🚘
Credit Cards [1] [2] [3] [5] £

GH QQQ Dorset Villa 14 Newbridge Rd BA1 3JZ
☎(0225) 425975
Conveniently positioned on the main A4 to the west of the city, this small, personally run hotel has recently been refurbished and now offers bright, comfortable bedrooms. It is well furnished throughout, the atmosphere is friendly and there is on-site parking.
7rm(5♠2hc) (1fb) CTV in all bedrooms ✱ sB&B£28-£30 sB&B♠£33-£35 dB&B£38-£40 dB&B♠£43-£45 WB&B£114-£210 WBDi£170-£288.40 LDO 9pm
Lic ♨ CTV 6P
Credit Cards [1] [3] £

GH QQQ Eagle House Church St, Bathford BA1 7RS (3m NE A363) ☎(0225) 859946
Closed 23-30 Dec
John and Rosamund Napier have painstakingly restored this fine Georgian listed house by John Wood the Elder, which lies in the very attractive village of Bathford, 3 miles from Bath. Once a boys' school, this large family home is set back in 1.5 acres of mature attractive gardens, with commanding views across the city. There is a comfortable, spacious drawing room, second sitting room and pleasant breakfast room. Bedrooms are of varying shapes and sizes but well equipped with modern facilities. The recent addition of a walled-garden cottage is an ideal retreat, with full use of the main house available. Well sited for touring, this is very much a family home where guests are treated as house rather than hotel guests.
6⇌♠ Annexe 2⇌♠ (2fb) CTV in all bedrooms ® T
sB&B⇌♠£27.50-£39.50 dB&B⇌♠£40-£62.50
Lic ♨ 10P croquet lawn £

GH QQQ Edgar Hotel 64 Gt Pulteney St BA2 4DN
☎(0225) 420619
Conveniently situated in the centre of Great Pulteney Street, this Regency town house provides comfortable bed and breakfast accommodation close to the city centre. Bedrooms are simply styled with compact modern en suites and a good range of facilities, and there is a modest breakfast room on the ground floor.
14♠ (1fb) CTV in all bedrooms ® ✗ ✱ sB&B♠£25-£30 dB&B♠£35-£55
Lic ♨ CTV 𝒫
Credit Cards [1] [3] £

GH QQQ Gainsborough Hotel Weston Ln BA1 4AB
☎(0225) 311380
Closed 1 wk Xmas
16rm(12⇌4♠) (2fb) CTV in all bedrooms ® T ✗
sB&B⇌♠£28-£40 dB&B⇌♠£48-£60 WBDi£150-£190
Lic ♨ 18P
Credit Cards [1] [2] [3]

GH QQ Grove Lodge 11 Lambridge, London Rd BA1 6BJ
☎(0225) 310860
Conveniently situated on the A4 London Road, and only a mile from the city centre, this bed and breakfast guesthouse is strictly no smoking. The building is a fine example of Regency

→

architecture, set back from the road in its own secluded gardens. On-street parking is available close by.
8hc (2fb)⅟in all bedrooms CTV in all bedrooms
✱ (ex guide dogs) ✻ sB&B£20-£25 dB&B£38-£45 WB&B£125-£145
Lic P̸ Ⓔ

SELECTED

GH QQQQ Haydon House 9 Bloomfield Park BA2 2BY
☎(0225) 444919 & 427351 FAX (0225) 469020
This unassuming Edwardian house belies a wealth of hospitality, elegance and commendable standards of comfort; tucked away in a quiet residential area. Each bedroom is individually styled and furnished to retain the character and charm of the building and is equipped with a high range of modern creature comforts including TV, direct-line telephone and bright modern en suites. Delightful personal touches are added to greet the guests, such as a complimentary decanter of sherry and home-made shortbread biscuits. The cosy public rooms are elegantly furnished with Chesterfields and include a delightful sitting room overlooking the lovely garden, and a small writing room. Breakfast, which is the only meal available and served on a communal table, is a treat in itself. It includes such delicacies as porridge with whisky and scrambled egg with salmon. Smoking is prohibited throughout the house.
4rm(3⨍ 1hc) ⅟in all bedrooms CTV in all bedrooms Ⓡ **T**
✱ sB&B⨍£40-£45 dB&B⨍£52-£65
卌 1🚗 nc6yrs
Credit Cards 1 3 Ⓔ

GH QQQ Highways House 143 Wells Rd BA2 3AL
☎(0225) 421238 FAX (0225) 481169
Closed 24-27 Dec
Spotlessly clean and enthusiastically run by the resident owners Mr and Mrs James, this small hotel offers a comfortable and hospitable environment. The Victorian house is set back in its own small gardens, it offers bright bedrooms, a particularly pleasant lounge and good on-site parking.
7rm(6⇌⨍ 1hc) CTV in all bedrooms Ⓡ ✱ (ex guide dogs)
sB&B£33-£36 dB&B⇌⨍£48-£58
卌 8P nc5yrs
Credit Cards 1 3 Ⓔ

SELECTED

GH QQQQ Holly Lodge 8 Upper Oldfield Park
BA2 3JZ ☎(0225) 424042 FAX (0225) 481138
Carrolle Sellick's immaculately styled Victorian town house is a little gem. Squeaky clean throughout, the 6 bedrooms are exceptionally comfortable, beautifully decorated and furnished with pleasing colours and fabrics, and adorned with pictures and objets d'art. Two of the rooms have sumptuous marble-finished bathrooms, and all the en suites are equipped with fluffy towels and perfumed toiletries. The richly furnished lounge and bright conservatory dining room are equally attractive and offer views over the terrace to the city beyond. Carrolle and her partner George provide a warm hospitable welcome and personal but unobtrusive service. Neatly tucked away with useful car parking and a pretty garden, the house is well positioned for the city and for touring the region.
6⇌⨍ ⅟in all bedrooms CTV in all bedrooms Ⓡ **T** ✱
sB&B⇌⨍£46-£48 dB&B⇌⨍£65-£85
卌 8P
Credit Cards 1 2 3 5

Book as early as possible for busy holiday periods.

GH QQQ Kennard Hotel 11 Henrietta St BA2 6LL
☎(0225) 310472 FAX (0225) 442456
Situated close to Great Pulteney Bridge and the city centre, this period house is part of an attractive terrace, and has benefited from recent upgrading by the conscientious owners. Bedrooms have bright, modern en suite showers, rich décor and bold coordinating fabrics. The bright and attractive breakfast room has a garden theme, and although there is no parking, the guesthouse is in a convenient position for both the tourist and business guest.
12rm(9⨍ 3hc) (2fb) CTV in all bedrooms Ⓡ sB&B£25-£35
dB&B⨍£40-£55
卌 P̸
Credit Cards 1 2 3 Ⓔ

SELECTED

GH QQQQ Laura Place Hotel 3 Laura Place, Great Pulteney St BA2 4BH ☎(0225) 463815
Mar-21 Dec
This elegant and beautifully preserved Georgian town house is in an exceptionally convenient location. It is tastefully decorated and furnished with many antique pieces, with good use of coordinating colour schemes and rich fabrics. Spotlessly clean, the bedrooms tend to range from enormous to reasonably well proportioned and boast modern en suites. All bedrooms are equipped with a good range of facilities including a remote-control TV, direct-line telephone and early morning tea. A bright breakfast room and small reception lounge are equally stylish. The house is personally run by the conscientious Bull family, who provide good quality bed and breakfast. An additional bonus for this part of the city is a small number of reserved parking spaces.
8rm(7⇌⨍ 1hc) (1fb) CTV in all bedrooms Ⓡ **T**
✱ (ex guide dogs) sB&B⇌⨍£50 dB&B£50
dB&B⇌⨍£65-£80
卌 10P (£5 per week) nc11yrs
Credit Cards 1 2 3 Ⓔ

SELECTED

GH QQQQ Leighton House 139 Wells Rd BA2 3AL
☎(0225) 314769
rs May-Oct
A fine Victorian residence in an elevated position 10 minutes' walk from the city centre. The surrounding garden is beautifully kept and full of colour in the summer. Dave and Kathy Slape, along with their daughter Debbie and son-in-law Patrick, have carefully upgraded their home to provide 8 en suite bedrooms of considerable quality, with many thoughtful extras provided for guests' comfort. There is an elegant lounge and a dining room where breakfast, and dinner by arrangement, is served.
8⇌⨍ (2fb) CTV in all bedrooms Ⓡ **T** ✱ (ex guide dogs)
✻ sB&B⇌⨍£42-£46 dB&B⇌⨍£54-£62 WB&B£175-£196 LDO 2pm
Lic 卌 8P
Credit Cards 1 3 Ⓔ

GH QQQ Meadowland 36 Bloomfield Park BA2 2BX
☎(0225) 311079
Spotlessly bright and clean, this elegant no-smoking residence is a large family home set in about half an acre of secluded grounds and lovely gardens just on the outskirts of the city in a very convenient location. Personally restored, it is enthusiastically owned and run by Catherine Andrew, who offers individually styled bedrooms of distinct charm with coordinated décor in bold colours and quality furnishings. There is an elegant lounge with a selection of books and magazines. Breakfasts are hearty with an

imaginative menu, and special diets can be catered for with advance notice. Useful car parking is available on site.
3[bath/shower] (1fb)[no smoking] in all bedrooms CTV in all bedrooms ® [no dogs]
dB&B[bath/shower]£45-£55
[central heating] CTV 4P
Credit Cards [1] [3]

GH QQ Millers Hotel 69 Great Pulteney St BA2 4DL
☎(0225) 465798
Closed Xmas wk
Situated on the renowned Great Pulteney Street, Millers Hotel offers simply appointed bed and breakfast accommodation close to all amenities.
14rm(6[bath/shower]8hc) (3fb) CTV in 8 bedrooms [no dogs] (ex guide dogs)
* sB&B£23-£25 sB&B[bath/shower]£36-£38 dB&B£34-£38
dB&B[bath/shower]£45-£52
Lic [central heating] CTV [no parking]
Credit Cards [1] [3] £

GH QQQ Monkshill Shaft Rd, Monkton Combe BA2 7HL
☎Combe Down(0225) 833028
Though built in 1902, there is a strong Victorian influence in the style of this guesthouse, both architecturally and in décor. The building is perched in an elevated position on the outskirts of the city, with superb, uninterrupted views of beautiful landscape designated as being of outstanding natural beauty. Within the elegant walls, there is a cosy atmosphere in every stylish room. The 3 bedrooms are prettily decorated, with colourful flowing drapes, antique and stripped pine furniture and brass bedsteads. Roll-topped Victorian baths complement the modern facilities. The elegant, congenial drawing room features a Victorian fireplace, comfortable Chesterfields and a piano. In all, this is a most restful retreat.
3rm(2[bath/shower]1hc) (1fb) [no dogs] (ex guide dogs) * sB&B£25
sB&B[bath/shower]£30 dB&B£40 dB&B[bath/shower]£50
6P nc2yrs croquet lawn

See advertisement on page 65

GH QQQ Oldfields 102 Wells Rd BA2 3AL ☎(0225) 317984
FAX (0225) 444471
Personally run by owners Mr and Mrs O'Flaherty, this hotel provides a hospitable and friendly retreat. The detached Victorian house has been sympathetically restored; public rooms are cosy and full of character, and bedrooms are individually styled, richly furnished and equipped with modern comforts. Good parking is provided in the drive and the hotel is only 10 minutes' walk from the Roman Baths and Abbey.
14rm(1[bath]7[shower]6hc) CTV in all bedrooms ® [no dogs] (ex guide dogs) *
sB&B£35 sB&B[bath/shower]£45 dB&B£50 dB&B[bath/shower]£58
[central heating] 10P
Credit Cards [1] [3]

See advertisement on page 65

SELECTED

GH QQQQ Old School House Church St, Bathford
BA1 7RR (3m NE on A363) ☎(0225) 859593
This delightful former Victorian school, which has been tastefully converted into a no-smoking hotel, is positioned in a peaceful village setting, boasting glorious views over the Avon valley. Upgraded by Sonia and Rodney Stone, this cosy little retreat offers 4 spotlessly clean and bright bedrooms, individually styled and furnished with rich pine/mahogany furniture, pretty drapes and coordinating soft fabrics. All bedrooms are equipped with bright modern en suites, plus a range of facilities including remote-control TV and direct-line telephones. An elegant country-style lounge with log fires and rich leather Chesterfields, leads on to the mahogany-furnished dining room and pretty conservatory – which is quite a sun trap – overlooking the well tended gardens. The proprietors take great pride in their house, creating a very welcoming and hospitable atmosphere.
→

4⇌↑ ⊁in all bedrooms CTV in all bedrooms ® T ✕
sB&B⇌↑£40-£45 dB&B⇌↑£59-£64 WB&B£187.50-£202.50 WBDi£317-£332 LDO noon
Lic 🍽 6P nc10yrs
Credit Cards 1 3 £

GH QQQ *Orchard House Hotel* Warminster Rd (A36), Bathampton BA2 6XG ☎(0225) 466115

Conveniently situated 2 miles from the city centre on the Warminster road at Bathampton, this small purpose-built hotel and restaurant has attractive open- plan public areas, which are comfortably furnished and afford good views over the city. Bedrooms are bright, spacious and equipped for the discerning traveller. Additional facilities include good on-site parking and a small health area with a sauna and solarium. New owners Mr and Mrs Hannay run the house on the same friendly lines as before.

14⇌↑ (3fb) CTV in all bedrooms ® LDO 7.45pm
Lic 🍽 16P sauna solarium
Credit Cards 1 2 3 5

GH Q *Oxford Private Hotel* 5 Oxford Row Lansdown Rd BA1 2QN ☎(0225) 314039

Situated close to the centre of the town, in a Regency terrace on Lansdowne Road, this establishment offers convenient bed and breakfast accommodation.

11rm(4↑7hc) (3fb) CTV in 7 bedrooms ® ✕ LDO 10pm
Lic 🍽 P̸ nc5yrs

SELECTED

GH QQQQ Paradise House Hotel Holloway BA2 4PX ☎(0225) 317723 FAX (0225) 482005

Closed 20-28 Dec

This beautifully restored, elegant Georgian house boasts one of the finest views over the city and offers commendable bed and breakfast accommodation. The cosy public rooms are styled with rich colours, deep furnishings and complementary fabrics, and the building features a fine staircase, moulded ceilings and decorative cornices. The lounge overlooks the city and highlights the splendid walled garden, and a hearty breakfast is served in the bright attractive breakfast room every morning. The bedrooms are particularly comfortable, individually styled – again with good use of bold colours and fabrics. All are equipped to a high standard and the majority have bright en suite facilities.

10rm(7⇌1↑2hc) (1fb) CTV in all bedrooms ® T ✕
sB&B£40-£46 sB&B⇌↑£52-£60 dB&B£48-£54 dB&B⇌↑£65-£68 WB&B£152-£215
🍽 2P 3🚗 (£2 per night) nc10yrs croquet lawn boules
Credit Cards 1 2 3 £

GH QQ Parkside 11 Marlborough Ln BA1 2NQ ☎(0225) 429444

Closed Xmas wk

In a convenient city-centre location, this attractive Edwardian property is on the edge of Victoria Park and has useful on-street parking close by. Rooms are spacious, bright and comfortable, and the resident proprietors provide a welcoming atmosphere.

5rm(3↑2hc) (2fb)⊁in all bedrooms CTV in 4 bedrooms ®
dB&B£37 dB&B↑£49 WB&B£116.55-£154.35 LDO 5pm
🍽 CTV 3P nc5yrs £

GH QQQ Hotel St Clair 1 Crescent Gdns, Upper Bristol Rd BA1 2NA ☎(0225) 425543

This spacious, semidetached Victorian villa is conveniently located close to Victoria Park and only a few minutes from the city centre, on the Bristol Road, near Royal Crescent. Bedrooms are well equipped and furnished, complemented by bright and pleasant public rooms, providing good value accommodation suitable for the business guest and tourist alike. Car parking is available at the rear of the premises.

10rm(2↑8hc) (1fb) CTV in all bedrooms ® ✕ (ex guide dogs)
✱ sB&B£23-£26 sB&B↑£30-£36 dB&B£35-£40 dB&B↑£40-£46 WB&B£145-£165
Lic 🍽 nc3yrs
Credit Cards 1 3 £

SELECTED

GH QQQQ *Somerset House Hotel & Restaurant* 35 Bathwick Hill BA2 6LD ☎(0225) 466451

A house with a difference – this tall classical Regency guesthouse is in an elevated position with good views over the city and countryside beyond. Being a listed property, the rooms retain their original dimensions. The bedrooms are all named after the children of George III and are brightly decorated in individual styles, complete with nice little touches including rag dolls. There is a choice of sitting rooms, either on the first floor or the ground- floor library/music room. A congenial attractive country dining room in the basement features the original hearth ovens and promotes imaginative and well cooked dishes. The dining room is also open to non-residents. Another feature is the mature large garden, complete with reputedly the oldest Judas tree in the country and the house's own miniature railway. The proprietors operate a no-smoking policy throughout.

10⇌↑ (5fb)⊁in all bedrooms ® LDO 6.30pm
Lic 🍽 CTV 12P nc10yrs
Credit Cards 1 2 3

SELECTED

GH QQQQ *Underhill Lodge* Warminster Rd, Bathampton BA2 6XQ ☎(0225) 464992

rs Xmas wk

This imposing late-Victorian villa is conveniently positioned 2 miles from the city centre on the Warminster road at Bathampton, and enjoys commanding views of the valley. Personally and tastefully restored by the present owners, June and Don Mather, luxury-hotel standards are provided, with an abundance of personal touches throughout. Bedrooms are a treat: spotlessly clean and furnished with antiques, comfortable armchairs, pretty drapes and canopies and sumptuous Victorian bathrooms with brass fittings. Each room is equipped with TV, direct-dial telephones, books and good quality cotton bed linen. The house is enhanced by a profusion of Eastern artefacts which the owners have collected on their travels; these are nicely set off by Chesterfields, bright décor and coordinating soft furnishings. Carefully prepared, home-cooked meals are served in the conservatory dining room at the communal table. There is an attractive terraced rear garden and orchard, with a paddock, and ample car parking on site. Smoking is discouraged, but a separate room is provided for those who wish to smoke.

4⇌↑ ⊁in all bedrooms CTV in all bedrooms ® ✕
LDO noon
Lic 🍽 10P nc10yrs
Credit Cards 1 3

See advertisement on page 67

GH QQQ Villa Magdala Private Hotel Henrietta Rd BA2 6LX ☎(0225) 466329

Closed Xmas

A beautifully maintained house of distinct charm, converted from 2 early- Victorian houses and very conveniently situated 100 yards from Great Pulteney Street and the city centre. Many of the original features are retained, in particular the attractive sweeping Italian-style staircase and the moulded cornices. The well proportioned, brightly decorated bedrooms are spotlessly clean and

→

THE OXFORD HOTEL

5 Oxford Row, Lansdown Road, Bath BA1 2QN Avon.
Telephone: Bath (STD 0225) 314039

An 18th Century House-Hotel in the City Centre (near the Assembly rooms). Most rooms with TV & coffee/tea making facilities.

Proprietress: Diana Thomas

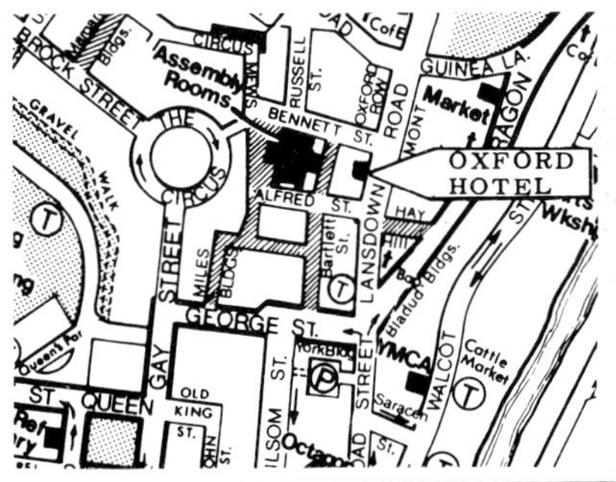

OLDFIELDS

ELEGANT & TRADITIONAL BED & BREAKFAST

Oldfields, a restored Victorian family house, overlooks Bath and surrounding hills. We offer a clean, comfortable and relaxed atmosphere (there's Mozart at breakfast), attentive service with free coffee and tea and biscuits.
Each bedroom has colour TV and central heating, with en suite shower room and W.C. in eight rooms – all with Laura Ashley prevailing!

Parking in drive. Ten minutes walk to Roman Baths and Abbey.

102 Wells Road, Bath
(at the corner of Upper Oldfield Park)
Telephone: 0225 317984
Fax: 0225 444471

Situated in a conservation area overlooking the beautiful Avon valley, the Old School House offers high quality accommodation with en suite bathrooms and all facilities. Candle-lit dinners and log fires in an informal and friendly atmosphere.
Residential licence. Special breaks November-March. Brochure available.

A Non-Smoking House
The Old School House Church Street
Bathford BATH Avon BA1 7RR
Telephone: Bath (0225) 859593

ETB
Highly Commended

AA
QQQQ selected

MONKSHILL GUEST HOUSE

SHAFT ROAD MONKTON COMBE
BATH BA2 7HL
TELEPHONE: 0225 833028

Monkshill is a grand Edwardian country house hotel located two miles from the city centre of Bath. It is surrounded by woodlands and gardens, close by are golf courses and a variety of old country inns and has the most magnificent views across one of Bath's finest landmarks; the Limpley Stoke valley. All of its bedrooms, two of which are en suite, are luxuriously furnished and the house's idyllic location belies the fact that it is so close to the heart of the city.

comfortable, with private bathrooms and a good range of modern facilities. The house stands in its own well tended grounds overlooking the park, and has the additional advantage of private parking.
17rm(13⇌4⚐) (3fb) CTV in all bedrooms ® T ✗ ✱ sB&B⇌⚐fr£42 dB&B⇌⚐£56-£72
🏘 13P 2🚗 (£3 per night)
Credit Cards 1 3

GH QQ Waltons 17 Crescent Gardens, Upper Bristol Rd BA1 2NA ☎(0225) 426528
A simple guesthouse conveniently positioned only a few minutes from the city centre and close to Victoria Park. The bedrooms are modestly appointed and furnished, providing good value accommodation popular with commercial guests and tourists.
15hc (3fb) sB&B£18-£22 dB&B£28-£32
🏘 CTV ✗

GH QQQ Wentworth House 106 Bloomfield Rd BA2 2AP ☎(0225) 339193
Closed mid Dec-mid Jan
This attractive, character Victorian house is set back in its own grounds of three quarters of an acre, complete with an outdoor swimming pool. The house is personally owned and run by Mr and Mrs Kitching, who create a friendly, welcoming atmosphere and provide a high standard of cleanliness and comfort. The bedrooms are well furnished and adequately equipped, with the majority having en suite facilities. A hearty English breakfast and dinner (by prior arrangement only) is served in the stylish conservatory dining room, and a cosy congenial bar, richly decorated and furnished, is provided for guests.
20rm(7⇌9⚐4hc) (2fb) CTV in all bedrooms ® T ✱ sB&B£20-£24 sB&B⇌⚐£35-£38 dB&B£36-£40 dB&B⇌⚐£46-£54
LDO 10.30am
Lic 🏘 20P nc 5yrs ⛱
Credit Cards 1 3

INN Q *County Hotel* 18-19 Pulteney Rd BA2 4DN ☎(0225) 425003 & 466493
Closed 25 & 26 Dec
A conveniently positioned hotel close to the city centre, with popular bars. Bedrooms are well equipped and currently being upgraded and redecorated. Bar snacks are available at lunch time, and more substantial meals are offered during the evenings in the restaurant.
22rm(1⇌11⚐10hc) (5fb) CTV in all bedrooms ®
🏘 CTV 60P
Credit Cards 1 3

BATTLE East Sussex Map 05 TQ71

GH QQQ Netherfield Hall Netherfield TN33 9PQ (3 m NW of B2096) ☎(04246) 4450 due to change to (0424) 774450
Closed Feb
In a pretty village setting, opposite the parish church this appealing coach house has been adapted to provide comfortable accommodation. There is a small coffee lounge where proprietor Mrs Blake serves home-made scones and cake, and an attractive dining room for breakfast – both rooms have doors leading into the garden. Guests can also share the lounge; Mr Blake has a large selection of pictures and china that guests can buy as souvenirs.
3rm(2⚐1hc) Annexe 1⚐ CTV in 1 bedroom TV in 2 bedrooms ® ✱ dB&Bfr£35 dB&B⚐£45 WB&B£105-£135
🏘 CTV 6P £

GH QQ *Priory House* 17 High St TN33 0EA ☎(04246) 3366 due to change to (0424) 773366
This small hotel dates back, in parts, to pre-Tudor days and provides traditionally furnished and comfortable rooms, most of which are en suite. Ideally situated in the High Street of this historic town, the simple restaurant offers a good selection of home-cooked dishes, and there is a cosy bar/lounge.
6rm(2⇌3⚐1hc) (3fb) TV in all bedrooms ® ✗ (ex guide dogs) LDO 9pm
Lic 🏘
Credit Cards 1 3

FH QQQ Paul & Alison Slater **Little Hemingfold Farmhouse Hotel** *(TQ774149)* Telham TN33 0TT (2.5m SE on N side of A2100) ☎(04246) 4338 due to change to (0424) 774338
This delightful farmhouse hotel is set in 40 acres of woodland and walks and benefits from its own trout lake and grass tennis court. The coach-house bedrooms are individually decorated in a cosy, cottage style, surrounding the leafy courtyard; the rooms are particularly well equipped, and some have original wood-burning stoves. A 4-course meal is served in the style of a dinner party, but a separate table can be requested. Coffee is served in the comfortable lounge with its welcoming log fire. The owners also specialise in house parties for 24 people.
3⇌ Annexe 9rm(7⇌) CTV in all bedrooms ® T dB&B£65-£70 dB&B⇌£65-£70 WB&B£200-£230 WBDi£260-£296 LDO 7pm
Lic 🏘 30P ⚑18 🎾(grass) ✓ boules swimming in lake croquet 40 acres mixed
Credit Cards 1 3 £

INN QQQ *Abbey Hotel* 84 High St TN33 0AQ (Shepherd) ☎(04246) 2755 due to change to (0424) 772755
8rm(3⇌5⚐) (5fb) CTV in all bedrooms ® LDO 9.30pm
🏘
Credit Cards 1 3

BEAMINSTER Dorset Map 03 ST40

SELECTED

GH QQQQ Hams Plot Bridport Rd DT8 3LU ☎(0308) 862979
Apr-Oct
An interesting Regency house with some earlier parts in an attractive walled garden containing a hard tennis court, croquet lawn and swimming pool. Bedrooms are spacious, furnished with antiques and comfortable chairs and (mostly) large bathrooms. In addition to the dining room there are 2 splendid lounges, the cool, formal sitting room and the cosy, cluttered library.
3rm(2⇌1⚐) ® ✗ sB&B⇌⚐£36 dB&B⇌⚐£50
Lic 🏘 CTV 7P nc10yrs ⛱ 🎾(hard)croquet £

BEAMISH Co Durham Map 12 NZ25

GH QQ *Coppy Lodge* Coppy Farm, Beamish Lodge DH6 0RQ ☎Stanley(0207) 231479
An attractive stone-built house in a riding stable complex, situated in Beamish Park, close to the golf club and the open-air museum. Bedrooms are modern and functional, and there is an open-plan ground-floor area with a dining area, bar lounge and a full-size snooker table.
6rm(2⇌4⚐) TV available ® LDO 9pm
Lic 🏘 40P U snooker

BEATTOCK Dumfries & Galloway *Dumfriesshire* Map 11 NT00

FH QQ Mr & Mrs Bell ***Cogrie's*** *(NY106974)* DG10 9PP (3m S off A74) ☎Johnstone Bridge(05764) 320
Mar-Nov
Peacefully situated, although just off the A47 south of the town, this family- run dairy and mixed farm offers pleasantly appointed, comfortable accommodation in the traditionally furnished 18th-century farmhouse.
4hc (3fb)⊬in all bedrooms ® ✗ LDO 6pm
🏘 CTV 6P 275 acres dairy mixed

BEAULY Highland *Inverness-shire* Map **14** NH54

GH QQ Arkton Hotel Westend IV4 7BT ☎(0463) 782388

This personally run, licensed guesthouse is conveniently situated at the south end of the village square and attracts both tourists and commercial visitors. The Arkton offers good value, practical accommodation in 8 bedrooms that are equipped with tea-making facilities. There is a dining room and TV lounge provided for guests, accompanied by a friendly atmosphere throughout.

8hc (1fb) CTV in 3 bedrooms ® ✱ sB&B£14-£18 dB&B£28-£36 WB&B£98-£126 WBDi£161-£189 LDO 8pm

Lic 🍴 CTV 8P nc6yrs

GH QQQ Chrialdon Hotel Station Rd IV4 7EH ☎Inverness(0463) 782336

Enthusiastic owners Anthony and Jennifer Bond extend a warm welcome to all who visit their fine, turreted Victorian house, which stands in its own garden beside the main road. Drinks are provided in the comfort of the quiet lounge, and imaginative Scottish dishes, prepared from best local produce, are served at the shared tables in the elegant dining room. The bedrooms are constantly being improved and are furnished in a blend of traditional and modern styles. Most of them have en suite facilities and all have TV and tea/coffee-making facilities.

9rm(1⇌5⇡3hc) (2fb) CTV in all bedrooms ® ✱ sB&B£19.50 dB&B£39 dB&B⇌⇡£47-£51 WB&B£137 WBDi£206.50-£220.50 LDO 7.30pm

Lic 🍴 CTV 18P

Credit Cards 1 3

GH QQQ Heathmount Station Rd IV4 7EQ ☎(0463) 782411

Closed Xmas & New Year

This detached, sandstone Victorian house stands in its own garden beside the main road, close to central amenities. It offers good value bed and breakfast accommodation in spacious, modern bedrooms with bright, cheery soft furnishings. The attractive

→

lounge invites peaceful relaxation and a hearty breakfast is served at individual tables in the tastefully appointed dining room.
5hc (2fb) CTV in all bedrooms ® sB&B£13-£15 dB&B£26-£30 WB&B£82-£95
🍽 CTV 5P

BEAUMARIS

See **ANGLESEY, ISLE OF**

BEDALE North Yorkshire Map **08** SE28

See also Hunton and Patrick Brompton

FH QQQ Mrs D I Knox **Blairgowrie Country House** *(SE241921)* Crakehall DL8 1JZ ☎Richmond(0748) 811377
Closed Xmas & New Year
This charming farmhouse is set in its own well tended gardens, surrounded by farmland where cattle graze, just one mile north of the village of Crakehall. While not a working farm, the owners and their family have farmed in the area for many years, so the friendly and welcoming atmosphere of a traditional farmhouse prevails. Comfortable bedrooms are prettily and tastefully decorated, and there is a comfortable guests' lounge and a smaller lounge leading out to the garden. A beautiful dresser stands along one wall of the dining room where guests eat around a large antique table.
2rm(1🚿1hc) ⊬in all bedrooms ® 🐕 ✱ sB&Bfr£20 sB&B🚿fr£20 dB&Bfr£30 dB&B🚿£32 WB&Bfr£105
🍽 CTV 6P nc10yrs 🎣 3 acres small holding

BEDFORD Bedfordshire Map **04** TL04

GH QQ Bedford Oak House 33 Shakespeare Rd MK40 2DX ☎(0234) 266972
A sympathetically extended 1930s house set back from a residential link road near the centre of town offering bed and breakfast accommodation. The entrance hall and breakfast room feature period wood panelling, complemented by plates, ornaments and books. The bedrooms are bright, simply furnished and well equipped, and located on the ground and first floors (a couple are reached through the car park).
15rm(9🚿6hc) (1fb) CTV in all bedrooms 🐕 (ex guide dogs) ✱ sB&B£19-£22 sB&B🚿£27.50-£32.50 dB&B£31-£34 dB&B🚿£36-£42
🍽 CTV 17P
Credit Cards 1 2 3 £

GH QQ Clarendon House Hotel 25/27 Ampthill Rd MK42 9JP ☎(0234) 266054
Closed 24 Dec-2 Jan
A small private hotel on the A6 south of the town centre. The accommodation is on 3 floors: room sizes vary, but all are neat and nicely equipped. Downstairs there is a cheerful open-plan lounge and breakfast room.
17rm(13🚿4hc) CTV in all bedrooms ® 🐕 (ex guide dogs) ✱ sB&B£21.50 sB&B🚿£26-£33.50 dB&B🚿£35.50-£43 LDO 7.45pm
Lic 🍽 CTV 15P
Credit Cards 1 2 3 5 £

GH QQ *Hertford House Hotel* 57 De Parys Av MK40 2TR ☎(0234) 50007 & 54470
Closed 24 Dec-2 Jan
An Edwardian villa in a tree-lined avenue near the town centre. Bedrooms are on three floors and vary in size; they are in good decorative order, in mixed furnishing styles. There is a comfortable lounge on the ground floor with a gas coal fire. Outside there is a new gravel car park, together with the garden and patio.
16rm(5⇌2🚿9hc) (2fb) CTV in all bedrooms ®
🍽 CTV 4P
Credit Cards 1 2 3 5

GH QQQ Kimbolton Hotel 78 Clapham Rd MK41 7PN ☎(0234) 54854
Closed 25-31 Dec
A large, detached Victorian house set in its own grounds, situated on the A6 just north of the town centre. It has recently been refurbished, and now provides full en suite facilities with the bedrooms. A limited menu is offered in the dining room, and there is a lounge and a well stocked bar.
14rm(3⇌11🚿) CTV in all bedrooms ® 🐕 ✱ sB&B⇌🚿£15-£42.30 dB&B⇌🚿£30-£54 WB&Bfr£241.50 LDO 7.30pm
Lic 🍽 CTV 15P nc3yrs beauty salon steam cabinet sun bed
Credit Cards 1 2 3 £

BEER Devon Map **03** SY28

GH Q *Bay View* Fore St EX12 3EE ☎Seaton(0297) 20489
Etr-mid Nov
Property at the end of the village overlooking the beach and sea.
6hc (1fb) ®
🍽 CTV P̸ nc5yrs

BEERCROCOMBE Somerset Map **03** ST32

SELECTED

FH QQQQ Mrs V A Cole **Frog Street Farm** *(ST317197)* Frog St TA3 6AF ☎Hatch Beauchamp(0823) 480430
Mar-Nov
Still a working farm set in 160 acres, this property dates back to 1436 and is an attractive Somerset longhouse, clad in wisteria. The bedrooms are good sizes and have pretty individual décor. One room – a converted cider house – has a separate lounge with TV. There is a comfortable residents' lounge with log-burning stoves, but the heart of the farmhouse is undoubtedly in the kitchen and dining room, where Veronica Cole serves delicious home-cooked food. Outside, the swimming pool is in a sheltered spot and the garden is very pretty, filled with spring flowers and well kept. Run by the attentive Cole family, the whole house is extremely well presented and has a very friendly, cosy atmosphere.
3rm(2⇌1🚿) ® 🐕 ✱ sB&B⇌🚿fr£27 dB&B⇌🚿fr£50 LDO 2pm
🍽 CTV P nc11yrs ⛱(heated) 160 acres dairy mixed stud £

SELECTED

FH QQQQ Mr & Mrs Mitchem **Whittles** *(ST324194)* TA3 6AH ☎Hatch Beauchamp(0823) 480301
mid Feb-Nov
John and Clare Mitchem welcome guests to their ivy-clad, period house, amidst 200 acres of dairy and beef farmland. The attractive en suite bedrooms are individually furnished and decorated, offering flexibility with zip and linked beds – smoking is not permitted in the bedrooms. Dinner is served by arrangement, cooked by Mrs Mitchem using fresh local produce, in the cosy rear dining room, while breakfast is taken around a large table in the front-facing breakfast room. Guests have their own comfortable drawing room, with a feature fireplace and are asked to help themselves to drinks from the honesty bar.
3⇌ CTV in all bedrooms ® 🐕 sB&B⇌£26-£28 dB&B⇌£40-£42 WB&B£136-£147 WBDi£241-£255.50 LDO 6.30pm(previous day)
Lic 🍽 4P nc12yrs 200 acres beef dairy

BEESTON Nottinghamshire Map **08** SK53

GH Q *Brackley House Hotel* 31 Elm Av NG9 1BU
☎Nottingham(0602) 251787
Closed Xmas & New Year
A continental atmosphere prevails at this well furnished guesthouse set in a quiet side road. Good, all-round facilities are provided.
15rm(12⇌ 3hc) (1fb) CTV in all bedrooms ® ✗
LDO 8.15pm
Lic CTV 15P nc9yrs (heated) sauna
Credit Cards 1 2 3

GH Q Fairhaven Private Hotel 19 Meadow Rd NG9 1JP
☎Nottingham(0602) 227509
Closed 25-26 Dec
A clean, modest hotel on the edge of the town situated close to Beeston station. There is a really comfortable lounge in which to relax and watch TV.
10rm(1 9hc) (1fb) CTV in 1 bedroom ® ✗ * sB&B£18-£21.50 dB&B£28-£30 dB&B £35-£37.50 WBDi£178.50-£196
LDO 2pm
Lic CTV 12P

BEITH Strathclyde *Renfrewshire* Map **10** NS35

GH QQ *Garnock Lodge* Boydstone Rd, Loamhead, Lochwinnoch PA12 4JT ☎(05055) 3680 & 2161
A well maintained detached private house sitting amidst open farming land just off the A737, one mile north of Beith. Bedrooms are compact but thoughtfully equipped, and there is a guests' lounge. Meals are taken round a communal table in the dining area and vegetarians are readily catered for.
3hc (2fb) CTV in all bedrooms ® ✗ (ex guide dogs) LDO 6pm
CTV 4P

BELL BUSK North Yorkshire Map **07** SD95

GH QQ Tudor House BD23 4DT ☎Airton(0729) 830301
mid Feb-mid Nov
Surrounded by the beautiful countryside of the Dales, this Tudor-style, family house is situated in the tiny hamlet of Bell Busk, alongside the Settle- Carlisle railway. The dining room, which looks out over the track, was once part of the platform and the very comfortable lounge, with colour TV, was the booking office. The bedrooms are modern in style with attractive, coordinated fabrics and have full central heating. There is a friendly residents' lounge and a small bar in the foyer, providing a relaxing atmosphere.
4rm(1 3hc) (1fb) ® ✗ (ex guide dogs) sB&B£14-£16 dB&B£28-£30 dB&B £32-£34 WB&B£90-£105 WBDi£145-£160
Lic CTV 6P games room £

BELLINGHAM Northumberland Map **12** NY88

GH QQQ *Westfield House* NE48 2DP
☎Hexham(0434) 220340
Mar-Nov
A well furnished country house, now a comfortable small hotel personally owned and run. Bedrooms are very well furnished, and good home cooking is provided. It is situated within the village, close to the Pennine Way and surrounded by beautiful countryside. Smoking is not permitted.
5rm(2 3hc) (1fb) in all bedrooms ® ✗ (ex guide dogs)
LDO noon
CTV 10P

BELPER Derbyshire Map **08** SK34

See also Shottle

GH QQ *The Hollins* 45 Belper Ln DE5 2UQ ☎(0773) 823955
This is a small family home situated on the outskirts of the town in a quiet residential area, within easy access of several stately homes and beautiful Peak District countryside. The 2 guest bedrooms are comfortable, light and fresh: non-smokers are preferred. Owner Mrs Emery creates a hospitable environment and takes pride in serving a substantial breakfast which includes home-made bread, free range eggs and locally cured bacon.
2hc in all bedrooms CTV in all bedrooms ®
✗ (ex guide dogs)
1P nc4yrs

BEPTON (NEAR MIDHURST) West Sussex Map **04** SU81

SELECTED

GH QQQQ The Park House Hotel GU29 0JB
☎Midhurst(0730) 813543 FAX (0730) 815643
Parts of this delightful country-house hotel date back to the 1600s, and the charm and tranquility of the hotel is enhanced by extensive rural views and a very convenient location for racing and polo. The well kept grounds include an outdoor swimming pool, 2 grass tennis courts, a 9-hole golf course, pitch and putt and croquet. The spacious and comfortable bedrooms are tastefully decorated, some furnished with antiques, and offer many modern facilities. The elegant drawing room has thick Chinese rugs and soft lighting and the dining room offers polished tables, gilt-framed mirrors and Mrs O'Brien's cooking, which is not to be missed.
10rm(8⇌2) Annexe 2⇌ CTV in 11 bedrooms ® T
sB&B⇌ £52-£57 dB&B⇌ £90-£99 LDO noon
Lic CTV 25P (heated) (grass)croquet pitch & putt
Credit Cards 1 3
See advertisement under MIDHURST

BERE REGIS Dorset Map **03** SY89

GH QQQ Culeaze BH20 7NR ☎(0929) 471209
Apr-Oct
This charming family manor house, dating back over 100 years, is situated 1.5 miles from the town and is surrounded by the estate and farmland. The bedrooms are tastefully and individually decorated in a comfortable, attractive style. Guests may use the drawing room or the flower-filled conservatory, and a choice of English or continental breakfast is served around a communal dining table. The well tended gardens and countryside are peaceful and the River Piddle runs through the estate: fishing is available by prior arrangement. Telephone reservations are strongly advised.
4rm(1⇌2hc) ® ✗ * sB&Bfr£22 sB&B⇌fr£22.50 dB&Bfr£45 dB&B⇌fr£48
P nc10yrs

BERKELEY Gloucestershire Map **03** ST69

FH QQQ Mrs B A Evans **Greenacres** *(ST713008)*
Breadstone GL13 9HF (2m W off A38) ☎Dursley(0453) 810348
Closed 4 Dec-2 Jan
Well situated for touring the Cotswolds and visiting Bristol and Gloucester, this modern farmhouse sits in an elevated position just off the A38, close to junctions 13 and 14 of the M5. Rooms are attractively decorated with coordinated soft fabrics and pine furniture, and have modern en suite facilities. Generous breakfasts are served in the dining room overlooking the garden, and there is also a comfortable lounge with TV.
4rm(1⇌3) in all bedrooms ✗ sB&B⇌ £17-£18.25 dB&B⇌ £33-£35 WB&B£112-£120
CTV 10P nc10yrs snooker sauna 47 acres horse breeding £

See advertisement on page 71

BERRYNARBOR Devon Map **02** SS54

GH QQQ The Lodge Country House Hotel EX34 9SG
(Berrynarbor 1.5m W of A399) ☎Combe Martin(0271) 883246
Closed Xmas
Guests return year after year to this well established Victorian house with attractive gardens set in an award-winning Best Kept Village. Spacious bedrooms are comfortable and well equipped, many with modern bath or shower facilities. There is a quiet lounge and a neat dining room, but Mrs Prater's good home cooking is the →

main attraction. Fresh produce, some from the garden, is skilfully prepared to a high standard.
7rm(2⇌3♠2hc) (2fb) CTV in all bedrooms ® ✱ sB&B£16.50-£20 dB&B£33-£40 dB&B⇌♠£39-£46 WB&B£99-£120 WBDi£145.20-£175 LDO 6pm
Lic 🍽 8P nc2yrs 9 hole putting £
See advertisement under COMBE MARTIN

BETTISCOMBE Dorset Map **03** SY39

GH QQQ ***Marshwood Manor*** DT6 5NS
☎Bridport(0308) 68442
Mar-Nov
A 19th-century country manor house set in 10 acres of well-kept grounds which include a heated pool, croquet and a putting green. Spacious, well furnished bedrooms are very clean and comfortable, and many rooms have views of the Marshwood Vale. The lounge is an elegant and well proportioned room, with Chinese rugs and log fires, and home-cooked food using local produce is served in the dining room.
8rm(5⇌♠3hc) (5fb) CTV in all bedrooms ®
Lic 🍽 15P ⛱croquet putting
See advertisement under BRIDPORT

BETWS-Y-COED Gwynedd Map **06** SH75

GH Q **Bryn Llewelyn** Holyhead Rd LL24 0BN
☎(0690) 710601
A small family-run guesthouse in the centre of the village, with ample parking ; it is a good base for touring the Snowdonia National Park, with the beaches at Llandudno within a half-hour drive. Bedrooms are neat and tidy, and there is a comfortable lounge.
7rm(1♠6hc) (3fb) CTV in 1 bedroom ® sB&Bfr£13 dB&B£26-£32 dB&B♠£30-£36 WB&B£77-£94.50
🍽 CTV 11P nc2yrs £

GH QQQ **The Ferns** LL24 0AN ☎(0690) 710587
Young and enthusiastic owners, Keith and Teresa Roobottom, have considerably modernised and improved this stone-built house, which stands on the A5 close to the famous Waterloo Bridge. The bedrooms are modern and equipped to a standard more usually found in a 2-star hotel. Home-cooked meals are served in the spacious dining room, where individual tables are provided. A cosy lounge is available, as well as a small private car park – a great asset in this popular village. This is a no-smoking establishment.
9rm(7♠2hc) (2fb) CTV in all bedrooms ® sB&B£15-£18 dB&B£28-£32 dB&B♠£30-£36
Lic 🍽 CTV 10P nc4yrs £

GH Q ***Summer Hill Non Smokers Guesthouse*** Coedcynhelier Rd LL24 0BL ☎(0690) 710306
This large, detached, stone-built house dates back to 1874 and is situated in an elevated position close to River Llugwy. The shops and other amenities of this popular village are within a few minutes' walk. Family owned and run, it provides modest accommodation suitable for climbers, walkers and other tourists visiting this part of Snowdonia. The hotel has the advantage of having its own private car park.
7hc (1fb)⁄in all bedrooms ®
Lic 🍽 CTV 6P

SELECTED

GH QQQQ **Tan-y-Foel** Capel Garmon LL26 0RE 3m SE
☎(0690) 710507 FAX (0690) 710681
The new owners, Janet and Peter Pitman, took over this establishment in 1991 and, we are delighted to say, have shown that they could even improve on the already very high standards. The views are spectacular from the front of this lovely part 16th-century house, looking north up the Conway valley. The warm lounges are fully carpeted with richly coloured scatter rugs added, and log fires burn on chilly days. The menu is small but gives a perfectly balanced choice of usually 2 items for each course. Our inspector sampled wild duck breast with a salad of peppers and onion macerated in olive oil, followed by a large portion of poached monkfish garnished with carrot and orange butter sauce. A hearty grilled breakfast is served with a wide choice of cereals and fruit available. The bedrooms are all en suite and the majority are furnished with stripped pine and decorated in pastel shades. One bedroom has been created from the previous billiard room and is quite spectacular, with an enormous bed, rich, high quality soft furnishings, and shows a real touch of dramatic design. This is a no-smoking establishment.
9⇌♠ ⁄in 7 bedrooms ® T ✗ ✱ sB&B⇌♠£48 dB&B⇌♠£76 WBDi£280-£345 LDO 6.30pm
Lic 🍽 18P 1🚗 nc9yrs ⛾(heated)
Credit Cards 1 2 3
See advertisement in colour supplement

GH QQQ **Tyn-Y-Celyn** Llanwrst Rd LL24 0HD
☎(0690) 710202 FAX (0690) 710800
rs Jan-Mar
This impeccably maintained, family-run guesthouse provides good quality, well equipped accommodation. It is situated just north of Betwys-y-Coed on the A470, and enjoys spectacular views across the Conwy valley. The bedrooms are well equipped and all have private bathrooms.
8rm(2⇌6♠) (2fb) CTV in all bedrooms ® ✱ dB&B⇌♠£36-£40
Lic 🍽 CTV 10P £

BEXHILL East Sussex Map **05** TQ70

GH QQ **The Arosa** 6 Albert Rd TN40 1DG
☎(0424) 212574 & 732004
Situated close to the seafront, shops and all local amenities, this small hotel is run by friendly proprietors Mr and Mrs Bayliss. Bedrooms are all freshly decorated and comfortable, and a few now have en suite facilities. There is a cosy lounge, and dinner, cooked by Mr Bayliss, offers a good variety of dishes.
9rm(3⇌♠6hc) (1fb) CTV in all bedrooms ®
✗ (ex guide dogs) sB&B£13-£17 sB&B⇌♠£16.50-£23 dB&B£22-£27 dB&B⇌♠£32-£37 WB&B£78-£140 WBDi£113-£175 LDO noon
🍽 CTV P̸
Credit Cards 1 3 £

GH QQQ ***Park Lodge*** 16 Egerton Rd TN39 3HH
☎(0424) 216547 & 215041
Located adjacent to Egerton Park and just off the seafront, this very well kept guesthouse comprises bright and comfortable bedrooms, generally equipped with en suite facilities and extensive modern amenities. A cosy and very comfortable lounge augments the separate dining room, attractively appointed with lace cloths and fresh flowers, where the evening meal is taken. Mrs Rogers provides a daily menu composed from fresh ingredients. Car parking can be a little difficult at certain times of the day.
10rm(6⇌♠4hc) (2fb)⁄in all bedrooms CTV in all bedrooms ® ✗ (ex guide dogs) LDO 3pm
Lic 🍽
Credit Cards 1 3

BEYTON Suffolk Map **05** TL96

FH QQ Mrs E Nicholson **The Grange** *(TL940632)* Tostock Rd IP30 9AG ☎(0359) 70184
Centrally located towards the village green, this farmhouse stands in its own well maintained grounds. It offers a peaceful retreat with spacious, comfortable rooms, one, with en suite facilities, enjoying ground-floor access. This is a no-smoking establishment.
2rm(1⇌1♠) Annexe 1⇌ ⁄in all bedrooms CTV in 2 bedrooms ® ✗ sB&B⇌♠£18-£20 dB&B⇌♠£36 LDO By arrangement
🍽 CTV 5P 4 acres non-working £

BICKINGTON (NEAR ASHBURTON) Devon Map **03** SX77

SELECTED

FH QQQQ Mrs E A Ross **East Burne** *(SX799711)* TQ12 6PA ☎Bickington(0626) 821496

Closed Xmas & New Year

A Grade II listed medieval house situated in a peaceful, unspoilt valley only a mile from the A38. The bedrooms are well decorated and comfortable, with a host of reading material provided. The house is full of character, with exposed beams, stone walls and open fireplaces; several of the barns outside have been sympathetically converted to provide self-catering accommodation. A cobbled courtyard leads to a secluded garden with a heated, well fenced outdoor swimming pool. The owners provide bed and breakfast only, but are happy to advise of local places to eat.

3rm(2↱1hc) ⊁in all bedrooms ® ✱ (ex guide dogs) ✱ sB&B£15-£20 sB&B↱£15-£20 dB&B£30-£40 dB&B↱£30-£40 WB&Bfr£100

CTV 8P ⇋(heated) 40 acres sheep horses

BIDEFORD Devon Map **02** SS42

See also Westward Ho!

GH Q Kumba Chudleigh Rd, East-the-Water EX39 4AR ☎(0237) 471526

An Edwardian property in an elevated position with views across the river. There is a relaxed atmosphere created by Mr and Mrs Doughty, and the accommodation is cosy with many of the proprietors' pieces decorating the public areas.

9rm(1⊷3↱5hc) (5fb)⊁in 2 bedrooms CTV in 7 bedrooms ® ✱ sB&B£15-£20 dB&B£28-£30 dB&B⊷↱£32-£35 WB&B£95-£110

Lic CTV 14P 2➚ ⌂ putting green Ⓕ

See advertisement on page 73

GH QQ Mount Private Hotel Northdown Rd EX39 3LP ☎(0237) 473748

This small, interesting Georgian building is set in its own walled gardens, only a 5 minute walk to the town centre. An elegant hall with a sweeping staircase leads to the comfortable TV lounge, furnished with quality dralon- covered chairs and sofas. In the pleasant dining room Janet and Mike Taylor pride themselves on good home cooking. All the bedrooms are comfortable, restfully decorated and some have en suite facilities.

8rm(1⊷4↱3hc) (2fb)⊁in all bedrooms ® ✱ (ex guide dogs) ✱ sB&Bfr£19 sB&B⊷↱£21.25-£23 dB&B£33-£37 dB&B⊷↱£38-£41 WB&B£115-£140 WBDi£168-£230 LDO 5pm

Lic ꟼ CTV 4P

Credit Cards 1 3 Ⓕ

GH QQQ Pines at Eastleigh Old Barnstaple Rd, Eastleigh EX39 4PA (3m E off A39 at East-the-Water) ☎Instow(0271) 860561 FAX (0271) 861166

Originally an 18th-century farmhouse, this small family-run hotel is set in a secluded location with 7 acres of grounds, on the edge of the village, approximately 4 miles from Bideford. Bedrooms, some of which have recently been converted from the outbuildings, are well equipped, each with small but modern private bathrooms. There is a comfortable lounge with an additional sun lounge bar, and a bright, traditional dining room, where a choice of home-cooked meals is available.

6rm(1⊷2↱3hc) Annexe 5⊷↱ (2fb) CTV in all bedrooms ® **T** ✱ sB&B£23 sB&B⊷↱£27 dB&B£42 dB&B⊷↱£50 WB&B£100-£132 WBDi£178-£200 LDO 9pm

Lic ꟼ CTV 12P art courses

Credit Cards 1 3 Ⓕ

BILLINGSHURST West Sussex Map 04 TQ02

GH QQ Newstead Hall Hotel Adversane RH14 9JH
☏(0403) 783196 & 784734 FAX (0403) 784228

This house, in a very convenient location on the A24, can be traced back to the 12th century. It has been slightly extended and upgraded, and now offers a refurbished restaurant, bar, lounge and reception facilities as well as 10 new bedrooms. Chef Michel Alliot has come straight from a Paris restaurant and offers a classical style of à la carte cooking and daily fixed-price menus. Service is well managed and personally supervised by the resident proprietors. More refurbishment is underway to complete all the accommodation to the same standard.

15🛁🚿 CTV in all bedrooms Ⓡ **T** sB&B🛁🚿£32-£36 dB&B🛁🚿£42-£46 LDO 9pm
Lic ™ 60P 1🚗
Credit Cards [1] [2] [3] [5]

SELECTED

FH QQQQ Mrs M Mitchell **Old Wharf** *(TQ070256)* Wharf Farm, Wisborough Green RH14 0JG
☏Horsham(0403) 784096
Closed 2 wks Xmas & New Year

Originally a warehouse at the busy terminus of the Arun Navigation Company, this historic canalside building was built in 1839, and has been lovingly converted by Mara and David Mitchell into a charming home, with the primary features retained. Each of the 4 bedrooms has its own colour scheme and is attractively furnished with antique pine: the Primrose suite has its own sitting room and enjoys lovely canal views; all the rooms have smart en suite facilities. Guests have their own sitting room with a cosy log-burning stove and French doors out to the canalside. The unusual home-made continental breakfast can include a more hearty meal for a small extra charge. There is a no-smoking policy throughout.

4🛁🚿 🚭in all bedrooms CTV in all bedrooms Ⓡ **T** 🐕✗ ✱ sB&B🛁🚿£40 dB&B🛁🚿£45-£60
™ CTV 6P nc12yrs 🐴 200 acres sheep
Credit Cards [1] [2] [3]

BINGLEY West Yorkshire Map 07 SE13

GH QQQ Hall Bank Private Hotel Beck Ln BD16 4DD
☏Bradford(0274) 565296
Closed Xmas

This huge Victorian manse is set within its own grounds in a quiet residential area, just yards away from the Liverpool-Leeds canal and the 5 rises (staircase) locks, and with superb views toward Haworth and the Druid's Altar. Bedrooms are comfortable and offer facilities more often associated with a 2- star hotel, including trouser presses. Public areas include a book-lined lounge, a games room with a pool table, and a dining room with well polished dark wood tables and offering a 2-choice table d'hôte menu.

10rm(9🛁🚿1hc) (2fb) CTV in all bedrooms Ⓡ **T** 🐕✗ sB&B🛁🚿£25-£40 dB&B🛁🚿£40-£50 WB&B£140-£195 LDO 7.30pm
Lic ™ CTV 20P nc4yrs games room Ⓔ

BIRKENHEAD Merseyside Map 07 SJ38

GH Q Gronwen 11 Willowbank Rd, Devonshire Park L42 7JU
☏051-652 8306

Situated in a residential area close to Tranmere Rovers football ground and the Glenda Jackson Theatre, this small unpretentious guesthouse offers modest accommodation in pleasant surroundings.

5hc (1fb) CTV in all bedrooms Ⓡ ✱ sB&B£15-£16 dB&B£28-£30 WB&B£105 WBDi£140 LDO 7.30pm
™ CTV 𝓟

BIRMINGHAM West Midlands Map 07 SP08

See **Town Plan Section**
See also Blackheath

GH QQ Ashdale House Hotel 39 Broad Rd, Acock's Green B27 7UX ☏021-706 3598

A Victorian property in a residential area overlooking the park, yet convenient for access to the NEC and M42. Rooms can be compact but are well furnished, mainly with stripped pine. A comfortable guest lounge is provided, as well as a breakfast room where organic English breakfasts are served. The friendly hosts make guests feel welcome.

9rm(4🚿5hc) (2fb) CTV in all bedrooms Ⓡ sB&B£20 sB&B🚿£25 dB&B£30 dB&B🚿£35 WB&B£120-£155
™ CTV 3P
Credit Cards [1] [3] Ⓔ

GH Q Awentsbury Hotel 21 Serpentine Rd, Selly Park B29 7HU
☏021-472 1258

Standing in a quiet residential area close to the university, Awentsbury has bedrooms which are simply furnished with good facilities.

16rm(6🚿10hc) (2fb) CTV in all bedrooms Ⓡ **T** sB&B£24-£34 sB&B🚿£34 dB&B£38-£46 dB&B🚿£46 LDO 6pm
™ 13P 1🚗 (charged) 🏠
Credit Cards [1] [2] [3] Ⓔ

GH QQ ***Bearwood Court Hotel*** 360-366 Bearwood Rd, Warley B66 4ET ☏021-429 9731 & 021-429 6880
FAX 021-429 6175

Situated on a busy road within easy reach of the city centre and the A456, the hotel is run by the Doyle family who are friendly, helpful hosts. The accommodation varies, but rooms are well equipped and maintained.

24rm(20🛁🚿4hc) (2fb) CTV in all bedrooms Ⓡ
🐕✗ (ex guide dogs) LDO 6pm
Lic ™ CTV 24P
Credit Cards [1] [3]

GH QQ Beech House Hotel 21 Gravelly Hill North, Erdington B23 6BT ☏021-373 0620
Closed 2wks Xmas & New Year

A small, privately owned hotel in a convenient location close to Spaghetti Juntion on the M6. Rooms vary in size and styles: en suite bedrooms have TV, which are available for hire in other rooms. There are 2 lounges, one for non- smokers and the other with a TV. The emphasis here is on personal service provided by the proprietor.

9rm(4🛁🚿5hc) (2fb) CTV in 4 bedrooms Ⓡ sB&B£25.85-£27.50 sB&B🛁🚿£32.90-£34.50 dB&B£39.95-£41.50 dB&B🛁🚿£47-£49.50 WB&B£180.95-£192.50 WBDi£228.95-£240.50 LDO noon
™ CTV 10P nc5yrs
Credit Cards [1] [3]

GH QQQ Bridge House Hotel 49 Sherbourne Rd, Acocks Green B27 6DX ☏021-706 5900
Closed Xmas & New Year

The Hopwood family continue to make improvements at their comfortable private hotel, conveniently placed for access to the city centre, the M42 and NEC. Bedrooms are very well equipped. Public areas are attractive and include the small 'movie bar', restaurant, conservatory and guest lounge.

30rm(2🛁28🚿) (1fb) CTV in all bedrooms Ⓡ **T** 🐕✗ ✱ sB&B🛁🚿£29.37 dB&B🛁🚿£44.65 LDO 8.30pm
Lic ™ CTV 48P
Credit Cards [1] [2] [3] [5] Ⓔ

GH QQ Cape Race Hotel 929 Chester Rd, Erdington B24 OHJ
☏021-373 3085

Conveniently placed for access to the M5, M6, NEC and the city centre, this hotel has its own outdoor swimming pool and tennis court. The rooms, although limited for space, are well equipped and the proprietors' personal service is assured.

9rm(8↱1hc) CTV in all bedrooms ® T ✗ (ex guide dogs) sB&B£24-£29 sB&B↱£24-£29 dB&B£30-£40 dB&B↱£30-£40 LDO 8.30pm
Lic 🍴 CTV 15P ⛵(heated) 🎾(hard)
Credit Cards [1] [3] £

GH QQ Elston 751 Washwood Heath Rd, Ward End B8 2JY ☎021-327 3338
rs Sat & Sun
This popular commercial guesthouse is in a convenient location on the A47, 4 miles from the city centre and close to Spaghetti Junction. It is run by Elsie and Tony Bennett who provide a relaxed and friendly atmosphere. Rooms are centrally heated and double glazed, and have a mixture of décor and furnishings. There is a comfortable guests' lounge and a very small dining room, overlooking the rear garden, where both breakfast and evening meals are served. Car parking is provided.
11rm(1↱9hc) CTV in all bedrooms LDO 8pm
🍴 CTV 11P

GH QQQ Fountain Court Hotel 339-343 Hagley Rd, Edgbaston B17 8NH ☎021-429 1754 FAX 021-429 1209
This family-owned and run hotel, on the busy Hagley road, is converted from 3 houses. Rooms vary in size and have modest décor and furnishings, and all are well equipped with en suite facilities. Public areas are extensive with a dining room, bar and residents' lounge, and Mr and Mrs Smith are friendly hosts.
25⇌↱ CTV in all bedrooms ® ✱ sB&B⇌↱£30-£39 dB&B⇌↱£40-£55 WB&B£210 WBDi£300 LDO 8.30pm
Lic 🍴 CTV 20P
Credit Cards [1] [2] [3]

GH QQ Heath Lodge Hotel Coleshill Road, Marston Green B37 7HT ☎021-779 2218
A conveniently located hotel 1.5 miles from the NEC and airport, with easy access to the motorway network. Room standards vary: several bedrooms and shower rooms are compact, but new rooms →

are all of a good standard, and there is a comfortable TV lounge and a small bar.
15rm(9↱6hc) (1fb) CTV in 16 bedrooms ® **T** ✱ sB&B£25-£29 sB&B↱£35-£39 dB&B£35-£42 dB&B↱£4-£50 LDO 8.30pm
Lic ▥ CTV 15P
Credit Cards [1] [2] [3] (£)

GH QQ Lyndhurst Hotel 135 Kingsbury Road, Erdington B24 8QT ☎021-373 5695
A private hotel in a convenient location, within easy reach of Spaghetti Junction and the city centre. Accommodation is modest but well maintained; several of the rooms have en suite showers. The restaurant overlooks the garden and offers an extensive menu.
14rm(1⇔11↱2hc) (3fb)⊘in 5 bedrooms CTV in all bedrooms ® ✗ (ex guide dogs) sB&B£29.95-£32.50 sB&B⇔↱£36.50-£39.50 dB&B⇔↱£42.50-£49.50 WB&Bfr£199 WBDifr£270 LDO 8.15pm
Lic ▥ CTV 15P
Credit Cards [1] [2] [3] [5] (£)

GH QQ Robin Hood Lodge Hotel 142 Robin Hood Ln, Hall Green B28 0JX ☎021-778 5307
Situated on the A4040, 5 miles from the city centre, this commercial guesthouse offers well equipped bedrooms, most of which have shower units. Additional accommodation is provided in 2 adjoining houses nearby.
7rm(1⇔2↱4hc) (1fb) CTV in all bedrooms ® ✱ sB&Bfr£22 sB&B⇔↱£27-£29 dB&B£33-£47 dB&B⇔↱£42-£47 LDO 7.30pm
Lic ▥ CTV 11P
Credit Cards [1] [3] [5] (£)

GH Q Rollason Wood Hotel 130 Wood End Road, Erdington B24 8BJ ☎021-373 1230 FAX 021-382 2578
35rm(1⇔10↱24hc) (4fb) CTV in all bedrooms ® sB&B£17-£29.40 sB&B⇔↱£30-£34.50 dB&B£28.50-£45 dB&B⇔↱£40-£50 WB&B£117-£200 LDO 8.30pm
Lic ▥ CTV 35P games room
Credit Cards [1] [2] [3] [5] (£)

GH Q Tri-Star Hotel Coventry Road, Elmdon B26 3QR ☎021-782 1010 & 021-782 6131
Conveniently situated on the A45, midway between the NEC and airport, this privately owned guesthouse has simple and well maintained accommodation.
15rm(11↱4hc) (3fb) CTV in all bedrooms ® ✗ ✱ sB&B£28.20-£37.60 sB&B↱£37.60 dB&B£42.30 dB&B↱£47 LDO 8pm
Lic ▥ CTV 25P pool table
Credit Cards [1] [2] [3]

GH QQ Willow Tree Hotel 759 Chester Rd, Erdington B24 0BY ☎021-373 6388 & 021-384 7721
rs Xmas
A pleasant, well established guesthouse in a convenient location close to the motorway network and city centre. Accommodation is well kept, with an impressive array of modern facilities.
7rm(5↱2hc) (2fb) CTV in all bedrooms ® **T** ✗ (ex guide dogs) ✱ sB&B£26 sB&B↱£32 dB&B£46 dB&B↱£46 LDO 8pm
Lic ▥ CTV 7P
Credit Cards [1] [3] (£)

BIRNAM Tayside Map 12 NO04

GH QQQ Oronsay House Oak Rd PH8 0BL ☎Dunkeld(0350) 727294
Apr-Oct
This fine detached Victorian house stands secluded in its own gardens down a quiet private lane from the village centre, close to the Birnam Hotel. The bedrooms are spacious, comfortable and well equipped with thoughtful items such as hairdryers, radios, fruit and tissues, and one has retained its original fireplace. The River Tay – separating Birnam from Dunkeld – is just 50yds from the house, which is a no-smoking establishment.
3rm(2↱1hc) ⊘in all bedrooms TV in 1 bedroom ® ✗ (ex guide dogs)
▥ CTV 4P

BIRTLEY Tyne & Wear Map 12 NZ25

INN QQ Portobello Lodge Durham Rd DH3 2PF ☎091-410 2739
This large roadside public house offers a good standard of newly refurbished bedrooms. An extensive range of bar meals is available all day and evening.
11⇔↱ (1fb) CTV in all bedrooms ® ✗ (ex guide dogs) ✱sB&B⇔↱ fr £20 dB&B⇔↱fr £30 LDO 10pm
▥
Credit Cards [1] [2] [3]

BISHAMPTON Hereford & Worcester Map 03 SO95

SELECTED

FH QQQQ Mrs H K Robertson **Nightingale Hotel** *(SO988512)* WR10 2NH ☎Evesham(0386) 82521 & 82384
This mock-Tudor farmhouse lies in 200 acres of land now turned over to the breeding of Aberdeen Angus. The restaurant, also popular locally, serves prime Angus beef and also specialises in genuine Shetland smoked salmon. There is a choice of several very comfortable lounges which are due to be extended shortly. Bedrooms are very well equipped and furnished, and extra rooms are also planned. The farm is set in pleasant lawns and gardens and is situated in a quiet village between Evesham and Worcester. Mr and Mrs Robertson continue to provide warm and genuine hospitality to their guests, many of whom return regularly.
4⇔↱ (1fb) CTV in all bedrooms ® ✗ sB&B⇔↱£32 dB&B⇔↱£45 LDO 9pm
Lic ▥ 30P ▶ 18 U snooker 200 acres beef arable
Credit Cards [1] [3]

BISHOP'S CLEEVE Gloucestershire Map 03 SO92

GH Q The Old Manor House 43 Station Rd GL52 4HH ☎(024267) 4127
Set in the heart of the village, this house is full of character and offers modest accommodation in spacious bedrooms and comfortable public areas.
6hc (3fb) ® ✗
CTV 8P U

BISHOP'S STORTFORD Hertfordshire Map 05 TL42

GH QQQ Cottage 71 Birchanger Ln, Birchanger CM23 5QA ☎(0279) 812349
A charming 17th-century Grade II listed cottage which has been carefully modernised to retain its character. Set in a quiet rural location yet close to Bishop's Stortford, the accommodation is attractively decorated and furnished and well equipped. The panelled lounge is comfortable, and the delightful conservatory/dining room overlooks the garden.
10rm(8↱1hc) ⊘in all bedrooms CTV in all bedrooms ® ✗ (ex guide dogs) sB&B↱£34 dB&B↱£44 WB&Bfr£140 LDO 9.30am
Lic ▥ 10P croquet
Credit Cards [1] [3] (£)

Street plans of certain towns and cities will be found in a separate section at the back of the book.

BISHOPSTON West Glamorgan Map **02** SS58

See also Langland Bay and Mumbles

GH QQQ ***Winston Hotel*** 11 Church Ln, Bishopston Valley SA3 3JC ☎(044128) 2074

Closed 24-29 Dec

This modern hotel is situated in a peaceful and secluded wooded valley, and it is run by the very friendly Clarke family. Bedrooms are comfortable and the public rooms are spacious and include the use of an indoor swimming pool and a snooker table.

14rm(3⌐3hc) Annexe 5rm(4⇌1⌐) (2fb) CTV in 5 bedrooms ® LDO 10.30am

Lic ⊞ CTV 20P ⊡(heated) snooker sauna solarium

Credit Cards 1 3

BLACKHEATH West Midlands Map **07** SO98

GH QQ **Highfield House Hotel** Holly Rd, Rowley Regis B65 0BH ☎021-559 1066

A commercial guesthouse with easy access to junction 2 of the M5 motorway. The proprietors are friendly and welcoming, the accommodation is functional, and though evening meals are not served, snacks are available.

14rm(2⇌⌐12hc) CTV in all bedrooms ® ✗ (ex guide dogs) ✱ sB&B£23-£26 sB&B⇌⌐£35 dB&B£40-£46 dB&B⇌⌐£44-£55 LDO 7.45pm

Lic ⊞ CTV 12P nc5yrs

Credit Cards 1 3

BLACKPOOL Lancashire Map **07** SD33

See **Town Plan Section**

GH QQ ***Arosa Hotel*** 18-20 Empress Dr FY2 9SD ☎(0253) 52555

Situated in a quiet side street in a residential area close to the seafront, this large guesthouse offers friendly and pleasant service. The bedrooms are modern, and there is a cosy front lounge, an attractive dining room and a friendly bar.

20rm(3⇌16⌐1hc) (7fb) CTV in all bedrooms ® LDO 5pm

Lic ⊞ CTV 5P

GH QQ **Ashcroft Private Hotel** 42 King Edward Av FY2 9TA ☎(0253) 51538

A small, modern hotel situated in a quiet side road just off the North Promenade.

10hc (3fb) ® ✱ sB&B£15-£18 dB&B£30-£36 WB&B£98-£119 WBDi£123-£151 LDO 2pm

Lic ⊞ CTV 3P

Credit Cards 1 3 £

GH QQ **Berwick Private Hotel** 23 King Edward Av FY2 9TA ☎(0253) 51496

Closed 20 Mar-7 Nov

A small, modern hotel situated in a quiet side road just off the North Promenade. Bedrooms are bright and fresh, and there is a cosy lounge. Guests are well cared for by the resident owners.

8rm(6⌐2hc) ® ✗ sB&B£16-£18 dB&B£30-£34 dB&B⌐£32-£36 (incl dinner) WB&B£98-£107 WBDi£112-£119 LDO 3pm

Lic ⊞ CTV 4P nc3yrs

GH QQ **Brooklands Hotel** 28-30 King Edward Av FY2 9TA ☎(0253) 51479

A well furnished and comfortable double-fronted small hotel situated in a side road just off the North Promenade. Bedrooms are well furnished and there is a comfortable lounge with a small bar. Family owned and run, it offers friendly service.

18rm(12⌐6hc) (3fb) CTV in all bedrooms ® ✗ (ex guide dogs) sB&B£15-£18 sB&B⌐£18-£21.50 dB&B£30-£36 dB&B⌐£36-£42 WB&B£105-£126 WBDi£126-£147 LDO 3.30pm

Lic ⊞ 5P £

GH QQQ **Burlees Hotel** 40 Knowle Av FY2 9TQ ☎(0253) 54535

Feb-Nov

Just a short stroll from the North Promenade is this well preserved house, situated in a peaceful residential area. The bedrooms are equipped with good facilities which include TV, hairdryer, radio and most are en suite. A comfortable lounge is provided, also there is a separate bar and the attractive dining room features pine tables. The proprietors, Mr and Mrs Lawrence, are very friendly and look after their guests well.

10rm(7⌐3hc) (2fb) CTV in all bedrooms ® ✗ sB&B£16.40-£19 sB&B⌐£19.55-£21 dB&B£32.80-£38 dB&B⌐£39.10-£42 WB&B£106.80-£145 WBDi£154-£193 LDO 4pm

Lic ⊞ CTV 5P 1⌂

Credit Cards 1 3 £

GH Q **Claytons** 28 Northumberland Av, off Queens Promenade FY2 9SA ☎(0253) 55397

This is a small, family-owned and run guesthouse, offering value for money. The bedrooms are simply furnished but are equipped with colour TV and radio. A comfortable lounge is provided, and good home cooking is served in the cosy dining room.

6⌐ (1fb)⊬in 1 bedroom CTV in all bedrooms ® ✗ (ex guide dogs) sB&B⌐£15.50-£17.50 dB&B⌐£31-£35 WB&B£96.50-£102.50 LDO 4pm

⊞ nc7yrs

Credit Cards 1 3 £

GH QQ **Cliff Head Hotel** 174 Queens Promenade, Bispham FY2 9JN ☎(0253) 591086

Overlooking the seafront, this is a small, well preserved hotel. The bedrooms are prettily decorated and all have en suite facilites, together with a TV and tea-making equipment. There is a cosy, comfortable TV lounge, with big picture windows facing the sea. Service is very friendly and helpful.

7⇌⌐ (1fb) CTV in all bedrooms ® ✱ sB&B⇌⌐£17-£21 dB&B⇌⌐£34-£42 LDO 5.30pm

Lic ⊞ CTV 3P £

GH QQ **The Colby Hotel** 297 The Promenade FY1 6AL ☎(0253) 45845

Etr & May-Nov

This modern-fronted family-owned hotel stands on the seafront of Blackpool's South Shore. Bedrooms are modestly furnished but offer good facilities including colour TV, radio, tea-making facilities and central heating. A spacious bar and sun lounge are provided.

14⌐ (5fb) CTV in all bedrooms ® ✗ sB&B⌐£14-£23.50 dB&B⌐£25-£44 LDO 5pm

Lic ⊞ CTV 3P pool table

Credit Cards 1 3

GH QQ **Denely Private Hotel** 15 King Edward Av FY2 9TA ☎(0253) 52757

A small, friendly, privately run hotel situated in a quiet side road just off the North Promenade. Bedrooms are cosy, and there is a pleasant lounge for guests' use.

9rm(2⌐7hc) (2fb) ® ✗ ✱ sB&B£15-£16.50 sB&B⌐£21-£32.50 dB&B£30-£33 dB&B⌐£36-£39 WB&B£105 WBDi£135 LDO 3.30pm

⊞ CTV 6P

GH QQ **Derwent Private Hotel** 8 Gynn Av FY1 2LD ☎(0253) 55194

A small, comfortable hotel situated in a quiet side street on the north side of town, close to the seafront. Bedrooms are modern and freshly decorated, and there is a cosy lounge. Well maintained accommodation and good service is provided by the resident owners.

12rm(4⌐8hc) (2fb) ® sB&B£17.50-£20 sB&B⌐£20.50-£23.50 dB&B£29-£34 dB&B⌐£35-£40 (incl dinner) WB&B£75-£95 WBDi£95-£115 LDO 2pm

Lic ⊞ CTV 4P

Credit Cards 1 3

GH QQ **The Garville Hotel** 3 Beaufort Av, Bispham FY2 9HQ (2m N) ☎(0253) 51004

A comfortable, friendly guesthouse offering good value for money, located in a quiet side road on the north side of town, close to the seafront.

7rm(2⇨5hc) (3fb)⅟in 3 bedrooms CTV in 6 bedrooms ® sB&B£12-£14 dB&B£24-£26 dB&B⇨£26-£28 WB&B£84-£98 Lic CTV 5P £

GH QQQ Hartshead Hotel 17 King Edward Av FY2 9TA ☎(0253) 53133 & 57111

Closed end Nov-2 wk Dec

A small, friendly guesthouse situated in a quiet side road 200yds from the North Shore and within easy reach of the town centre. The bedrooms are bright and fresh, with private bathrooms, TV, radio and direct-dial telephones. There is a pleasant lounge furnished with antiques and fine paintings. A home-cooked dinner is provided in the early evening, offering a limited choice.

10rm(1⇨9↱) (3fb)⅟in all bedrooms CTV in all bedrooms ® **T** (ex guide dogs) LDO 3pm

Lic CTV 6P nc3yrs

Credit Cards 1 3 £

GH QQ Inglewood Hotel 18 Holmfield Rd FY2 9TB ☎(0253) 51668

A pleasant small hotel offering very good value for money, situated on a quiet side road on the North Shore, close to the sea. The house is comfortable and well furnished throughout, and service is friendly.

10↱ (2fb) CTV in all bedrooms ® (ex guide dogs) ✻ sB&B↱£14.50-£21 dB&B↱£29-£42 WB&B£90-£109 WBDi£110-£130 LDO 10am

Lic CTV nc2yrs £

GH QQQ ***Lynstead Private Hotel*** 40 King Edward Av FY2 9TA ☎(0253) 51050
Closed 1st 2 wks Jan
The resident owners, Mr and Mrs Shearer, offer a very caring and friendly service at this small, well maintained hotel, which is situated in a side road off the North Shore. The bedrooms are pleasantly decorated and all have en suite facilities. A main feature of this house is the unique Tramcar bar, presenting a superb collection of toy trams and buses. The very comfortable sitting room has a delightful sun lounge, enhanced with a selection of plates, and a further collection of teapots are on show in the cosy dining room.
10♠ (4fb) ® ✗ (ex guide dogs) LDO 3pm
Lic lift 𝍖 CTV ₱ nc3yrs

GH QQQ Lynwood 38 Osborne Rd FY4 1HQ ☎(0253) 44628
Closed Xmas & New Year
A small, neat guesthouse situated close to the Sandcastle Centre and Pleasure Park and providing very good value for money. Run by Mr and Mrs Cowley, good home cooking is served in the pleasant dining room, which leads into a comfortable lounge. The well equipped bedrooms are bright, modern and comfortable, and most have private bathrooms.
8rm(1⇌5♠2hc) (1fb) CTV in all bedrooms ® ✗ ✱ sB&B£13-£15 sB&B⇌♠£16-£20 dB&B£26-£30 dB&B⇌♠£30-£32 WB&B£90-£105 WBDi£112-£130 LDO breakfast
𝍖 ₱
Credit Cards 1 2 3 £

GH Q Motel Mimosa 24A Lonsdale Rd FY1 6EE ☎(0253) 41906
Closed 21-31 Dec
A small, modern motel set in a side street not far from the promenade and central pier. Bedrooms all have private bathrooms and TV. Breakfast is delivered to the room each morning as there is no breakfast room. Parking is available at the rear.
15⇌♠ (3fb) CTV in all bedrooms ® ✱ sB&B⇌♠£20-£30 dB&B⇌♠£27-£40 WB&B£110-£210 WBDi£130-£240 LDO 8.30pm
Lic 𝍖 CTV 14P 2🚘
Credit Cards 1 3 £

GH QQ The New Esplanade Hotel 551 New South Promenade FY4 1NF ☎(0253) 41646
Etr-Nov & Xmas/New Year
Standing in a good corner position, on the South Shore promenade, overlooking the sea, this is a purpose-built hotel. The modern bedrooms vary in size and all are centrally heated with tea/coffee-making facilities. There are 2 lounges provided – one has a TV and games room – and both conform to the modern style of this hotel.
15rm(5♠10hc) (3fb) CTV in 5 bedrooms ® ✗ ✱ sB&B£13-£20 dB&B£26-£40 dB&B♠£33-£50 WB&B£91-£130 WBDi£119-£140 LDO 2pm
Lic 𝍖 CTV 20P games room
Credit Cards 1 3

GH QQ ***North Mount Private Hotel*** 22 King Edward Av FY2 9TD ☎(0253) 55937
A semidetached house situated in a quiet side road, with unrestricted parking. Bedrooms vary in style and colour and are brightly decorated and modern. There is a comfortable lounge and good home cooking is provided in the cosy dining room. Family owned and run, the guesthouse is conveniently located on the North Shore.
8hc (1fb) ® LDO 3pm
Lic 𝍖 CTV 1P

GH QQQ The Old Coach House 50 Dean St FY4 1BP ☎(0253) 44330
rs Nov-Mar
A detached Tudor-style house standing in a quiet side road, convenient for the beach and Sandcastle Centre. The house was built in 1851 and is surrounded by well kept gardens which are a riot of colour in summer. The spacious bedrooms are very well equipped and provide several extra facilities including telephones; they all have private bathrooms. There is an attractive conservatory lounge which is a useful addition to the house.
5♠ (2fb) CTV in all bedrooms ® T ✗ (ex guide dogs) ✱ sB&B♠£19.50-£22.50 dB&B♠£37-£43 WB&B£129.50 WBDi£164.50 LDO 2pm
𝍖 10P
Credit Cards 1 3

GH Q Park Lodge 98 Park Rd FY1 4ES ☎(0253) 751218
An end-of-terrace house situated on one of the main approach roads to the town, some way from the sea. Bedrooms are pleasantly furnished, and there is a pretty breakfast room. Friendly service is provided by the resident owners.
4rm(2♠2hc) (1fb) CTV in all bedrooms ® ✗ (ex guide dogs) ✱ sB&B£15-£18 dB&B£13-£28 dB&B♠£30-£32 WB&B£105-£112
𝍖 3P 1🚘 £

GH Q ***Sunny Cliff*** 98 Queens Promenade, North Shore FY2 9NS ☎(0253) 51155
Etr-9 Nov & 4 days Xmas
This guesthouse is situated on the North Shore seafront, and has easy access to all amenities. There is a sun lounge bar and TV lounge available for guests, and the resident owners are well established and offer friendly service.
12hc (4fb) ® LDO 5pm
Lic CTV 8P

SELECTED

GH QQQQ Sunray Private Hotel 42 Knowle Av, Queens Promenade FY2 9TQ ☎(0253) 51937
Closed 15 Dec-5 Jan
Jean and John Dodgson are justifiably proud of their inviting little guesthouse, situated in a quiet side road just off the promenade on Blackpool's North Shore. The bright, freshly decorated bedrooms have just about everything that guests could need; TV, tea-making facilities, direct- dial telephones, radio and hairdryers, and all of the bedrooms are en suite. There are comfortable armchairs and settees in the cosy lounge, which is brightly decorated, and a well produced evening meal is provided in time for guests to get to one of Blackpool's many shows. Warm and friendly attention is assured at this little gem of a guesthouse.
9rm(1⇌8♠) (2fb) CTV in all bedrooms ® T sB&B⇌♠£24-£27 dB&B⇌♠£48-£54 WB&B£144-£162 WBDi£204-£222 LDO 3pm
𝍖 CTV 6P
Credit Cards 1 3 £

GH QQ Surrey House Hotel 9 Northumberland Av FY2 9SB ☎(0253) 51743
Apr-Oct rs Mar & early Nov
Located in a quiet side road, just off the North Promenade, you will find this large semidetached house. The bright, fresh bedrooms vary in size and comfort but all are provided with hairdryers and tea-making facilities, plus the majority are equipped with en suite. There is a comfortable TV lounge and a separate sun lounge to the front. A friendly and caring service is offered at all times.
12rm(2⇌9♠1hc) (2fb)⅟in 1 bedroom ® ✱ sB&B£12.50-£15 sB&B⇌♠£13.50-£16 dB&B⇌♠£27-£35 WB&B£91-£105 WBDi£112-£133 LDO 4.30pm
𝍖 CTV 6P 1🚘 (charged) nc3mths table tennis pool table £

GH QQ The Windsor & Westmorland Hotel 256 Queens Promenade FY2 9HB ☎(0253) 54974
Located in a select area of the promenade, this canopied, licensed hotel is situated on the North Shore with many of its rooms overlooking the sea. The majority also have en suite facilities, and all have colour TV, radio and tea- making facilities. There is a lift to all floors.
→

SUNRAY HOTEL

42 Knowle Avenue, Blackpool. Telephone: (0253) 51937
Proprietors: Jean and John Dodgson – personal attention

- ★ All Bedrooms En-suite with Colour TV and radio
- ★ Tea/Coffee/Hot Chocolate making facilities
- ★ Direct dialling Telephone in each Bedroom
- ★ Hair Drier each bedroom — Use of Trouser Press
- ★ Full Central Heating — Electric Blankets
- ★ Ample Free Car Parking at the premises
- ★ Delightful small South facing well-used Garden
- ★ Unlicensed — Quiet Peaceful and very Friendly
- ★ Just off Queens Promenade and near Golf Course
- ★ Winter Bargain Rates and OAP's April to August

"Motel Mimosa"

24A LONSDALE ROAD,
BLACKPOOL FY1 6EE
Tel: (0253) 41906

An immaculate luxuriously appointed establishment with 15 bedrooms all with private facilities (bath/shower, toilet), colour TV, radio/intercom, tea/coffee facilities, coffee table and lounge chair. Five rooms on the ground floor suitable for senior citizens. Breakfast served in your own suite. Free car park at the rear. Central heating. Situated midway between the Tower and Sandcastle complex/pleasure beach and 250 yards from the Promenade. Ideal for business and conferences.
Open all year.
Bed & Breakfast only.
Access from M55 link road through Bloomfield No. 4 car park.

Personally supervised by the owner W. Patterson

Overlooking the sea

Ample Parking

98 Queens Promenade
Blackpool FY2 9NS
Tel: 0253 51155

Very pleasant lounge bar, TV lounge and sun lounge. Mainly traditional menus, freshly prepared for evening meal at 6pm. Many come for Roy's bread and butter pudding alone! Early breakfasts available for conferences etc. Singles no extra, dogs allowed in bedrooms by arrangement.

Proprietors: Pauline and Roy Star

LYNSTEAD HOTEL

The better place to stay

A small hotel where good food, service, cleanliness & comfort in a pleasant atmosphere are assured. Convenient for town centre & all amenities. All rooms, toilet & shower en suite, tea & coffee making facilities. Single rooms available. Chairlift first to second floor. Lounge with colour TV. Separate bar lounge, spacious dining room. Open all year. Ideal for conference and business representatives.

Resident Proprietors: Jim & Doreen Shearer
40 King Edward Avenue, Blackpool FY2 9TA
Telephone: (0253) 51050

32rm(26⇌↱4hc)(13fb) CTV in 31 bedrooms ® ✱
dB&B⇌↱£54 (incl dinner) WBDi£140 LDO 7pm
Lic lift ⌘ CTV 14P
Credit Cards [1] [3]

⊞ GH QQ **Woodleigh Private Hotel** 32 King Edward Av, North Shore FY2 9TA ☎(0253) 593624
Mar-Oct
A friendly guesthouse situated in a quiet road just off the North Promenade. Some bedrooms are fairly compact but they are modern in style, and there is a delightful lounge. The dining room is quite small and guests may have to share tables.
10rm(7↱3hc) (3fb) CTV in all bedrooms ® ✗ sB&B£13-£16 dB&B£26-£32 dB&B↱£30-£35.70 WB&B£90-£122.50 WBDi£115-£136.50 LDO 2pm
⌘ CTV P̸ Ⓔ

BLACKWOOD Gwent Map **03** ST19

INN QQ ***Plas*** Gordon Rd NP2 1D ☎(0495) 224674
Originally a farmhouse, this family-run inn stands above the town and has good views of the valley. Bedrooms are attractive and well equipped, and the bars are full of character, with stone walls and an inglenook fireplace.
6rm(4↱2hc) (1fb) CTV in 6 bedrooms ® LDO 9.45pm
⌘ 50P
Credit Cards [1] [3] [5]

BLAGDON Avon Map **03** ST55

INN QQQ ***Seymour Arms*** Bath Rd BS18 6TH ☎(0761) 62279
Situated in the heart of the village, on the main Bath road, this Victorian inn has been completely refurbished to provide attractive open-plan public areas and pretty bedrooms, many with good en suite facilities.
4rm(3↱1hc) (1fb) CTV in all bedrooms ® ✗ (ex guide dogs) LDO 9.30pm
⌘ 30P nc5yrs

BLAIR ATHOLL Tayside *Perthshire* Map **14** NN86

GH QQ The Firs Saint Andrews Crescent PH18 5TA ☎(0796) 481256
Etr-mid Oct
Set in half an acre of grounds in a quiet residential area, this substantial, detached house was built around the turn of the century and is efficiently run by the friendly owners Kirstie and Geoff Crerar. Considerable improvements have been carried out in recent years to provide comfortably furnished bedrooms and a cosy TV lounge where guests can relax in front of the log fire. There is a dining room available where smoking is prohibited, which also applies to the bedrooms.
4⇌↱ (2fb)⊬in all bedrooms ® ✗ (ex guide dogs) ✱
sB&B⇌↱fr£17.50 WB&Bfr£105 WBDifr£168
⌘ CTV 6P

BLAIRGOWRIE Tayside *Perthshire* Map **11** NO14

GH QQQ Ivybank House Boat Brae, Rattray PH10 7BH ☎(0250) 873056
Ivybank lies in its own grounds, off the main road, and most of the bedrooms here have been tastefully upgraded, offering superior accommodation reflecting the Victorian character of this detached house – some retaining beautiful Victorian fireplaces. There is a small lounge for guests to use.
5rm(3⇌↱2hc) (2fb) CTV in 6 bedrooms ® ✱ sB&B£15-£18 sB&B⇌↱£16.50 dB&B£30-£36 dB&B⇌↱£33 LDO 6pm
⌘ CTV 6P ♪(hard)
Credit Cards [2]

GH QQQ The Laurels Golf Course Rd, Rosemount PH10 6LH ☎(0250) 874920
Closed Dec
Situated on the A93 on the southern outskirts of the town, this modern stone house is well maintained throughout. The bright, airy bedrooms have white furniture, complete with trouser press, hairdryer, and thoughtful extras such as cotton wool balls and tissues are provided. Four of the bedrooms have top- quality en suites with power showers. There is a comfortable lounge and small dining room, where dinner is served offering a good range of dishes as does the breakfast menu, and a selection of wines, beers and spirits is available.
6rm(4↱2hc) ® ✗ ✱ sB&B£14-£15 dB&B£28-£30 dB&B↱£32-£34 LDO 5.45pm
Lic ⌘ CTV 6P nceyrs
Credit Cards [1] [2] [3] [5]

GH QQQ Rosebank House Balmoral Rd PH10 7AF ☎(0250) 872912
last wk Jan-Oct
Charles and Sue Collings put a commendable emphasis on cleanliness, hospitality and food at their detached Georgian house, where guests are really cosseted and Sue's home cooking has won much praise. The bright, airy bedrooms vary in size and a large public area accommodates the lounge at one end and a dining room at the other. Rosebank House sits in its own gardens, well back from the A93.
7rm(5↱1hc) (2fb)⊬in all bedrooms CTV in 6 bedrooms ® ✗ (ex guide dogs) sB&B£21-£23.50 sB&B↱£22.50-£25 dB&B£36-£41 dB&B↱£39-£44 WB&B£101-£129 WBDi£171-£202.50 LDO 7pm
Lic ⌘ CTV 10P nc10yrs

GH QQQ Tay Farm House PH2 6EE ☎Meikleour(0250) 883345
A house-party atmosphere prevails at this recently renovated country house which stands beside the A984 west of the village. The bedrooms have been tastefully furnished and thoughtfully equipped, including en suite facilities. The lounge, with its welcoming open fire, invites peaceful relaxation, and competent country-house cooking, prepared from wholesome ingredients, is served at the communal table in the attractive dining room.
3rm(2⇌1↱) CTV in all bedrooms ® sB&B⇌↱£16-£30 dB&B⇌↱£32-£40 WB&B£112-£210 WBDi£217-£322 LDO 7pm
⌘ 6P nc12yrs

BLAKENEY Gloucestershire

See **Lydney**

BLAKENEY Norfolk Map **09** TG04

GH QQ Flintstones Wiveton NR25 7TL ☎Cley(0263) 740337
Closed 25 & 26 Dec
This is a 1960s bungalow with a flintstone façade in a quiet village setting. To find it, take the A149 to Blakeney and at the crossroads by St Peters church turn right on to the B1156 for a mile. The bedrooms are modern with fresh, bright décor, and though they tend to be compact they have good lighting, mirrors and plenty of power points. Local kippers appear on the breakfast menu, and an evening meal is available. Smoking is not permitted here.
5↱ (3fb)⊬in all bedrooms CTV in all bedrooms ® ✱ dB&B↱£34 WB&B£105 WBDi£168 LDO 5pm
Lic ⌘ 5P

BLANDFORD FORUM Dorset Map **03** ST80

GH QQQ ***Fairfield House*** Church Rd DT11 8UB ☎(0258) 456756 FAX (0258) 480053
This attractive Georgian house is quietly located along a country lane, surrounded by its own well tended gardens, in the village of Pimperne, near the A354. Bedrooms are bright and fresh with a good selection of modern facilities, yet retain much character and charm. There is a cosy lounge complete with piano, games and books. The restaurant, open to non-residents, is beginning to gain a good reputation with locals and guests alike; there is a select à la

carte menu. One bedroom is well suited to disabled guests and is located in the stable block, complete with ramps and easy access. The hotel is steadily being improved and upgraded to a consistent, comfortable standard and the amiable proprietors endeavour to make their guests welcome.
5⇌ (1fb) in 4 bedrooms CTV in all bedrooms ® (ex guide dogs) LDO 6pm
Lic 10P nc7yrs
Credit Cards 1 2 3

BLEDINGTON Gloucestershire Map **04** SP22

INN QQQ Kings Head Inn & Restaurant The Green OX7 6HD ☎Kingham(0608) 658365
'Beware of the ducks' is the unusual sign in the centre of the village, aimed to protect them as they parade from one side of the green to the brook in front of the inn. The village is one of the Cotswolds 'best kept' award winners and the Kings Head, with its tidy garden, is a centre of attraction for visitors. The bar is full of character; besides the real ale there is lovingly polished wood, stone-flagged floors, a huge inglenook fireplace complete with blazing log fire for most of the year, and lots of antique cooking implements. There are plenty of those heavy dark oak beams, put in when folk were rather shorter, and which now catch the unwary over 5'8". The spacious bedrooms have pretty coordinated fabrics, pine furniture and lots of unexpected extras such as fresh flowers, direct-dial phones, remote-control TV and modern bathrooms – but, once again, look out for those low beams!
6⇌ (2fb) in 3 bedrooms CTV in all bedrooms ® **T** (ex guide dogs) * sB&B⇌£28-£30 dB&B⇌£49-£55 Bar Lunch £3.95-£8.50 Dinner £5.95-£8.95&alc LDO 9.45pm
CTV 70P ⓕ

BLICKLING Norfolk Map **09** TG12

INN QQQ *Buckinghamshire Arms Hotel* Blickling, Aylsham NR11 6NF ☎Aylsham(0263) 732133
Overlooking Blickling Hall, this 17th-century inn offers spacious accommodation in 3 bedrooms furnished with 4-poster or tester beds, well used and comfortable leather armchairs or sofas, and pine furniture. The shared bathroom features an attractive claw-foot bath. Public areas are comfortable and convivial; the inn is popular locally for its bar food and restaurant menu, and everywhere is furnished with pine furniture and Liberty print fabrics. Some 83 original Vanity Fair prints adorn the walls.
3hc (1fb) CTV in all bedrooms ® (ex guide dogs) LDO 9.30pm
80P
Credit Cards 1 3

BLOCKLEY Gloucestershire Map **04** SP13

GH QQQ Lower Brook House GL56 9DS ☎Evesham(0386) 700286
4⇌ CTV in all bedrooms ® sB&B⇌£30 dB&B⇌£40
10P ⓕ

BOAT OF GARTEN Highland *Inverness-shire* Map **14** NH91

SELECTED

GH QQQQ Heathbank House PH24 3BD
☎(047983) 234
Closed Nov & 1-26 Dec
Set in its own garden on the fringe of the village, Heathbank is a Victorian house of considerable character and charm. A genuine welcoming atmosphere prevails and everywhere you will find parts of a fascinating collection of bric-a-brac and objets d'art. Each bedroom has its own colour scheme, like the gold and blue room, with its lovely Edwardian open-work bedspread and collection of framed lace. Other rooms have a Victorian look and two rooms on the top floor are different again, decorated in pastel tones with views over the Abernethy →

Forest RSPB Reserve and the Cairngorms. The cosy lounge has books, magazines and board games. The set 4-course menu is prepared from good local produce which makes dining in the lovely Victorian dining room a pleasure.
8rm(4⌐4hc) (2fb)⊬in all bedrooms Ⓡ ✗ (ex guide dogs) sB&B£17-£19 dB&B£34-£38 dB&B⌐£40-£48 WB&B£119-£168 WBDi£203-£259 LDO 5pm
Lic ꟾ CTV 8P

GH QQQ Moorfield House Hotel Deshar Rd PH24 3BN ☎(047983) 646
Situated in its own garden in the centre of the village, this sturdy Victorian house is an ideal base for the tourist. Enthusiastic owners Ron and Liz Gould are welcoming hosts and work hard to improve and maintain standards. The house is comfortably furnished throughout and enjoyable home cooking is served in the small dining room, which also has a dispense bar.
4rm(1⇌3⌐) (1fb)⊬in 3 bedrooms Ⓡ ✱ sB&B⇌⌐£16-£19 dB&B⇌⌐£32 WB&B£101 WBDi£152 LDO 3pm
Lic ꟾ CTV 8P

BODENHAM Hereford & Worcester Map **03** SO55

FH QQQ Mr & Mrs P J Edwards **Maund Court** *(SO561505)* HR1 3JA ☎(056884) 282
Closed mid Dec-mid Jan
Originally built around 1400 and extended in 1775, this very well maintained farmhouse is situated east of Leominster, just off the A417. Bedrooms are all en suite, comfortable and modern, and there is a pleasant lounge. Outside, guests can enjoy the swimming pool or croquet in season.
4rm(3⇌1⌐) CTV in all bedrooms Ⓡ ✱ sB&B⇌⌐£15-£16 dB&B⇌⌐£30-£32 WB&B£100-£102
ꟾ CTV 6P ⛱(heated) croquet 130 acres mixed

BODLE STREET GREEN East Sussex Map **05** TQ61

FH Q Mr & Mrs P Gentry **Stud** *(TQ652144)* BN27 4RJ ☎Herstmonceux(0323) 833201
Closed Xmas
Set in 70 acres of farmland, accommodation in this simply furnished farmhouse consists of three bedrooms, one with an en suite shower room, the others sharing an old-fashioned bathroom. There is a comfortable lounge with a TV, and breakfast is served in the sun lounge.
3rm(1⌐2hc) ⊬in all bedrooms CTV in 1 bedroom Ⓡ ✗ sB&B£22-£25 dB&B£34-£38 WB&B£119-£175
ꟾ CTV 3P 70 acres cattle sheep

BODMIN Cornwall & Isles of Scilly Map **02** SX06

GH QQ Mount Pleasant Moorland Hotel Mount PL30 4EX ☎Cardinham(020882) 342
Apr-Sep
A 17th-century Cornish stone farmhouse in a peaceful setting on the edge of Bodmin Moor surrounded by farmland. There are well presented bedrooms with good facilities, and public areas include a cosy, stone-walled bar area, a sunny conservatory lounge complete with indoor garden and vines, and a well furnished TV lounge. A home-cooked evening meal is available.
7rm(1⇌5⌐1hc) (1fb)⊬in all bedrooms Ⓡ ✗ sB&B£15-£17 dB&B⇌⌐£35-£37 WB&B£100-£129 WBDi£125-£169 LDO 7pm
Lic ꟾ CTV 10P Ⓔ

FH QQQ Mrs P A Smith **Treffry** *(SW073637)* Lanhydrock PL30 5AF ☎(0208) 74405
Closed Xmas rs 20 Oct-Mar
A 16th-century stone and slate farmhouse set in mature gardens adjoining National Trust property, and part of a working dairy farm. Bedrooms are comfortable, well equipped and attractively decorated. Fresh, home-cooked meals are provided using home-grown produce; award-winning self-catering accommodation is also available.
3rm(2⌐1hc) ⊬in all bedrooms CTV in all bedrooms Ⓡ ✗ (ex guide dogs) dB&B£38 WB&B£125 WBDi£185 LDO noon
ꟾ CTV 4P nc6yrs 200 acres dairy Ⓔ

BOLLINGTON Cheshire Map **07** SJ97

INN QQ Turners Arms Hotel 1 Ingersley Rd SK10 5RE ☎(0625) 573864
This stone-built public house stands in a residential area at the edge of the town, on the road leading to Pott Shrigley and Whaley Bridge. The accommodation has recently benefited from extensive refurbishment, including more en suite facilities. The bedrooms, while not luxurious, are modern and comfortable. There are 2 bars and a separate dining room which offers good value, wholesome dishes. The hotel caters for, and is popular with mainly commercial visitors.
8rm(2⇌3⌐3hc) (2fb) CTV in all bedrooms Ⓡ ✱ sB&B£25-£28 sB&B⇌⌐£35-£40 dB&B£40-£48 dB&B⇌⌐£45-£55 Lunch £4.50-£12alc High tea £1.60-£7.50alc Dinner £7.50-£14.50alc LDO 9.30pm
ꟾ 2P 1🚗 pool darts
Credit Cards 1 2 3 Ⓔ

BOLTONGATE Cumbria Map **11** NY24

SELECTED

GH QQQQ The Old Rectory CA5 1DA ☎Low Ireby(09657) 647
Closed early Dec-late Jan
This lovely old house is set amidst magnificent Lakeland scenery in the hamlet of Boltongate. Part of the house dates back to the 15th century and this is now the study. The 3 guest bedrooms are lovingly furnished and tastefully decorated. There is very much the feeling of being a guest in a private house. Kathleen and Anthony Peacock are fine hosts. Cooking is quite superb using all fresh ingredients, including herbs, from the garden. Food is served in the 17th-century dining room with stone walls, oak beams and a roaring log fire. Quite simply a unique guesthouse and fully deserving our selected award.
3rm(2⌐1hc) Ⓡ ✗ (ex guide dogs) ✱ sB&B⌐£32-£33.50 dB&B£64 dB&B⌐£67 LDO 4pm
Lic ꟾ CTV 10P nc14yrs
Credit Cards 1 3

BO'NESS Central *West Lothian* Map **11** NS98

FH QQQ Mrs A Kirk **Kinglass** *(NT006803)* Borrowstoun Rd EH51 9RW ☎(0506) 822861 & 824185 FAX (0506) 824433
Situated off the B903 to the south of the town and convenient for junction 3 of the M9, this friendly stone-built farmhouse enjoys splendid views across the Firth of Forth. Two of the comfortable bedrooms are located in a neighbouring bungalow, but all are individually furnished and equipped with modern amenities. Public areas include a neat dining room with a licenced bar, and a cosy lounge.
6rm(2⌐4hc) (1fb) CTV in all bedrooms Ⓡ **T** dB&Bfr£33 dB&B⌐fr£50 LDO 5.30pm
Lic ꟾ CTV 20P 120 acres arable

BONSALL Derbyshire Map **08** SK25

GH QQ Sycamore 76 High St, Town Head DE4 2AA ☎Wirksworth(0629) 823903
Guests can relax on the front lawn of this 18th-century house which enjoys an elevated position overlooking the village. There is a choice of meals in the evening and prepared lunches are available.

6rm(2⇔1↑3hc) (1fb) CTV in all bedrooms ® ✗ (ex guide dogs) sB&B£17 sB&B⇔↑£27 dB&B£32 dB&B⇔↑£42-£44 WB&B£114-£183.50 WBDi£179-£214 LDO noon
Lic ⅲ 7P nc10yrs (£)

BONTDDU Gwynedd Map **06** SH61

SELECTED

GH QQQQ Borthwnog Hall Hotel LL40 2TT
☎(034149) 271
Closed Xmas

This 17th-century Regency house on the A496 is set in beautiful grounds overlooking the Mawddach Estuary and the massive Cader Idris mountain range beyond. Some bedrooms have estuary views and they all have fine furniture chosen by proprietors Vicki and Derek Hawes, with large bathrooms, TV and tea making facilities. The drawing room has some lovely antiques, together with fine paintings and an open fire. There is a wide selection of pictures in the library which is now a Gallery displaying the work of many local artists, available for sale. The excellent meals provided by Vicki Hawes are popular with locals, offering a small imaginative menu depending on local produce, especially seafood. Winner of the AA 1992 Best Newcomer Award, Borthwnog Hall continues to provide accommodation of the highest quality.

3⇔↑ CTV in all bedrooms ® ✱ dB&B⇔↑£40-£45 WB&B£295-£330 LDO 8.15pm
Lic ⅲ 6P
Credit Cards [1] [3]

BOROUGHBRIDGE North Yorkshire Map **08** SE36

INN QQQ The Crown Roecliffe YO5 9LY ☎(0423) 322578 FAX (0423) 324060

This delightful country inn is situated in the village of Roecliffe and features attractive, modern bedrooms that are furnished and decorated to a high standard. Bar meals are served in the beamed bars, or evening meals can be taken in the formal restaurant, renowned for its duck and steak menu. Owned and run by the Barker family, the Crown Inn aims to ensure guests feel welcome and relaxed at all times.

12⇔↑ CTV in all bedrooms ® T ✱ sB&B⇔↑£25-£45 dB&B⇔↑£30-£55 WB&B£150-£200 WBDi£200-£250 Lunch £5.50-£8.60&alc Dinner £9-£11&alc LDO 9.30pm
ⅲ 70P ⌂ ⅃
Credit Cards [1] [3] (£)

BORROWDALE Cumbria Map **11** NY21

GH QQ *The Grange* CA12 5UQ ☎(07687) 77251
19 Mar-Oct

A very attractive house, with its own well kept garden, in the centre of Grange in the Borrowdale valley. Family-run, it offers good all round facilities and friendly service from Mr and Mrs Jenkinson.

7rm(1⇔6hc) (1fb) ® ✗ (ex guide dogs)
ⅲ 8P

SELECTED

GH QQQQ Greenbank CA12 5UY ☎(07687) 77215
Closed 6-28 Jan & 29 Nov-26 Dec

This beautifully situated Lakeland house has excellent views over the Borrowdale Valley. The house is in its own well kept grounds and gardens and is delightfully furnished offering 2 comfortable lounges, one with colour TV, both with inviting log fires. Bedrooms have pine furniture and are prettily decorated and furnished with matching fabrics. All are en suite. A well produced 5-course dinner prepared by Mrs Lorton is served each evening.

10rm(9⇔1↑) (1fb)⁄in all bedrooms ® ✗ sB&B⇔↑£20.50 dB&B⇔↑£41-£47 WB&B£115.50-£136.50 WBDi£192.50-£213.50 LDO 5pm
Lic ⅲ CTV 15P (£)

GH QQ *Mary Mount Hotel* CA12 5UU (Stakis)
☎Keswick(07687) 77223 Telex no 64305 FAX (07687) 77343
Mar-Oct

A pleasant hotel under the same management as the nearby Lodore Swiss Hotel, where guests may want to book dinner. It offers good bed and breakfast accommodation in a peaceful setting in the Borrowdale Valley.

7⇔↑ Annexe 6⇔ CTV in all bedrooms ®
Lic ⅲ 40P
Credit Cards [1] [2] [3] [5]
See advertisement under KESWICK

BORTH Dyfed Map **06** SN68

GH QQ Glanmor Hotel Princess St SY24 5JP ☎(0970) 871689

This small personally run hotel is situated on the seafront, with a safe sandy beach, and close to the golf course. Run by the friendly Elliott family, it provides well maintained accommodation, with modern furnishings and equipment in the bedrooms, 4 of which have sea views; family rooms are also available. The dining room has separate tables, and there is a residents' bar in the cosy lounge.

7rm(2↑5hc) (3fb) CTV in 4 bedrooms ® sB&B£17.50 dB&B£35 dB&B↑£35 WB&B£122.50 WBDi£182 LDO 5pm
Lic CTV 10P 2⌂ (£)

BOSCASTLE Cornwall & Isles of Scilly Map **02** SX09

GH QQ *Lower Meadows House* Penally Hill PL35 0HF
☎(0840) 250570

A modern detached house conveniently situated next to the main car park and a short walk from the harbour. Most of the bedrooms are on the ground floor and are simply furnished in a modern style. The first floor bar offers a varied selection of snacks and light meals throughout the day and there is a TV lounge. Service is supervised by Mr and Mrs Justin Smith, the proprietors, and family.

5hc (2fb)⁄in 1 bedroom LDO 9.30pm
Lic ⅲ CTV P̸
Credit Cards [1] [3]

GH QQQ Melbourne House New Rd PL35 0DH
☎(0840) 250650

Within half a mile of the historic harbour, this fine Georgian house has excellent views of the Jordan Valley. The house is attractively furnished, retaining much of its original character, including a fine tiled entrance hall. Bedrooms are individually furnished and have colour TV, tea and coffee making equipment and en suite shower facilities or sole use of a bathroom with WC. There is a comfortable lounge and a well furnished dining room. The atmosphere is peaceful and relaxing, and there is plenty of car parking space.

6rm(1⇔2↑3hc) CTV in all bedrooms ® sB&B£15-£19 sB&B⇔↑£15-£19 dB&B£30-£38 dB&B⇔↑£30-£42 WB&B£95-£132 WBDi£151-£189 LDO 6pm
Lic ⅲ 8P nc7yrs
Credit Cards [1] [3] (£)

See advertisement on page 85

GH QQQ Old Coach House Tintagel Rd PL35 0AS
☎(0840) 250398
Closed 23 Dec-2 Jan rs Nov-Mar

Built 300 years ago, this historic coaching inn has been skilfully converted to provide modern facilities, whilst retaining its original character. A new extension has added convenient ground floor bedrooms and a bright, double-glazed dining room. Bedrooms all have TV, clock radios and tea-making facilities and are well

→

equipped and furnished. The resident proprietors Allan and Sue Miller are friendly and helpful, and ample car parking is provided.
6rm(1⇨5♠) (1fb) CTV in all bedrooms ® ✗ (ex guide dogs) sB&B⇨♠£14-£22 dB&B⇨♠£28-£44 WB&B£87-£143
Lic 🍽 7P nc6yrs
Credit Cards 1 2 3 £

GH QQQ St Christophers Country House Hotel High St PL35 0BD ☎(0840) 250412
Closed Jan & Feb
A former manor house built over 200 years ago, situated at the top of the village overlooking the valley below. Tastefully converted, much of its original character has been retained, and the standard of housekeeping is very high. Bedrooms are modern and individually furnished, most with en suite shower rooms. Cooking is based on local fresh produce, and light refreshments are available throughout the day; vegetarians are also well catered for. Dogs are welcome here, there is a small car park nearby, and proprietors Brian and Brenda Thompson provide a very friendly, informal style of service.
9rm(7♠2hc) CTV in all bedrooms ® ✱ sB&B£15.50-£18.50 sB&B♠£17.50-£18.50 dB&B♠£35-£37 WBDi£158-£192.50 LDO 8pm
Lic 🍽 CTV 8P nc12yrs
Credit Cards 1 3 £

GH QQQ *Tolcarne Hotel* Tintagel Rd PL35 0AS ☎(0840) 250654
Etr-Oct
A Victorian house retaining much of the original character, and traditionally furnished. The bedrooms vary in style; most have orthopaedic beds and very good en suite facilities. Both the lounge and dining room give fine headland views, and outside there are mature terraced gardens, a croquet lawn and ample car parking. Smoking is not permitted in the dining room, and home-cooked meals are provided by the proprietor, Mrs Stephens.
9rm(8⇨♠1hc) (1fb) CTV in all bedrooms ® LDO 5.30pm
Lic 🍽 CTV 15P croquet
Credit Cards 1 2 3

BOSTON SPA West Yorkshire Map 08 SE44

INN QQQ The Royal Hotel 182 High St LS23 7AY (Chef & Brewer) ☎(0937) 842142 FAX (0937) 541036
This busy village inn dates from 1771, today it offers comfortable bedrooms with modern facilities. An extensive range of bar snacks is available and more substantial meals are served in the Coach House Grill restaurant.
13⇨♠ CTV in all bedrooms ® T ✗ (ex guide dogs) ✱ sB&B⇨♠£30-£45 dB&B⇨♠£50-£70 Lunch fr£8.50alc Dinner £12.50-£18.50alc LDO 10pm
🍽 65P
Credit Cards 1 2 3 5

BOURNEMOUTH Dorset Map 04 SZ09

See **Town Plan Section**
See also Christchurch and Poole

GH QQ *Albemarle Private Hotel* BH2 5PH ☎(0202) 551351
Conveniently close to the Bournemouth International Centre, shops and sea, this terraced Victorian house has steadily been improved by the resident proprietors. The comfortably equipped bedrooms are prettily decorated in coordinated colour schemes. There is a ground floor lounge in addition to the basement bar and dining room, where evening meals are offered.
12rm(5♠7hc) (3fb) CTV in all bedrooms ® ✗ (ex guide dogs) LDO 11am
Lic 🍽 CTV P̸
Credit Cards 1 3

GH QQQ Alum Grange Hotel 1 Burnaby Rd, Alum Chine BH4 8JF ☎(0202) 761195
Closed Nov
A well run hotel with enthusiastic and welcoming proprietors. The bedrooms are freshly decorated and have modern facilities. There is a bar and sun lounge as well as a smart dining room where a short à la carte menu supplements the daily table d'hote.
14rm(5⇨7♠2hc) (7fb)⊬in 4 bedrooms CTV in all bedrooms ® sB&B£21.37-£35 dB&B⇨♠£42.74-£70 (incl dinner) WB&B£105-£140 WBDi£149.62-£199.50 LDO noon
Lic 🍽 CTV 10P
Credit Cards 3 £

GH QQQ Amitie 1247 Christchurch Rd BH7 6BP ☎(0202) 427255
This very smart, spotlessly clean and well run establishment is located midway between Christchurch and Bournemouth. The pretty bedrooms are fresh and bright, each is equipped with modern conveniences such as TV, tea making facilities and double glazing – also 2 rooms have been fitted with new en suite bathrooms. There is a cosy breakfast room, with interesting treasures adorning the walls. The resident proprietors are very helpful and ensure guests are well received.
8rm(2⇨2♠4hc) (2fb) CTV in all bedrooms ® ✗ (ex guide dogs) ✱ sB&B£13-£15 dB&B£26-£30 dB&B⇨♠£28-£32 WB&B£90-£98
🍽 8P nc3yrs
Credit Cards 1 3 £

GH QQ *Braemar Private Hotel* 30 Glen Rd BH5 1HS ☎(0202) 396054
Mar-Oct
This family run guesthouse is situated in a quiet residential street, close to the seafront and shopping centre. Bedrooms are freshly decorated and nicely presented, and public areas include a cosy bar area and dining room where a home cooked evening meal is offered. There is some forecourt parking, which is useful in this area.
10rm(1⇨5♠4hc) (4fb) CTV in all bedrooms ® ✗ LDO 6pm
Lic 🍽 CTV 6P

GH QQQ Cairnsmore Hotel 37 Beaulieu Rd, Alum Chine BH4 8HY ☎(0202) 763705
Owned by 2 amiable gentlemen who have successfully restored the house to its former Edwardian style, this guesthouse is quietly situated near Alum Chine. Bedrooms are nicely decorated and some have good views out across the woods and the suspension bridge. Most have well presented en suite facilities. The lounge area is particularly pretty, filled with comfortable sofas and antiques, and is a popular meeting place with guests. There is a small bar area and dining room where the home-cooked evening meals are much appreciated.
10rm(9⇨♠1hc) (1fb) CTV in all bedrooms ® dB&B⇨♠£32-£42 WB&B£89-£128 WBDi£124-£163 LDO 4pm
Lic 🍽 CTV 4P nc5yrs £

GH QQ *Carisbrooke Hotel* BH2 5NT ☎(0202) 290432
Telex no 310499
Feb-Dec
Conveniently close to the BIC, Winter Gardens and the centre of town, this guesthouse is neatly presented and offers bright, comfortable bedrooms with modern equipment. Public areas include a traditional lounge and a pretty dining room where a home-cooked meal may be served. Some forecourt parking is a bonus.
22rm(19⇨♠3hc) (6fb) CTV in all bedrooms ® ✗ (ex guide dogs) LDO 7pm
Lic 🍽 CTV 18P
Credit Cards 1 2 3

SELECTED

GH QQQQ *Cliff House Hotel* 113 Alumhurst Rd BH4 8HS ☎(0202) 763003

Mar-Nov & Xmas

This spacious guesthouse sits high above the sea at Alum Chine, and some rooms have private balconies from which guests can enjoy spectacular sea views. The large light rooms are spotlessly clean and well furnished, and bedrooms are also spacious, with private bathrooms and tea and coffee-making facilities. The licensed restaurant serves a good choice of main courses and desserts if ordered in advance, and private parking is provided at the rear.

12rm(2⇌9♠ 1hc) (4fb) CTV in all bedrooms ® ✗
LDO 6.30pm
Lic lift 12P nc7yrs snooker

GH QQ **Cransley Private Hotel** 11 Knyveton Rd BH1 3QG ☎(0202) 290067

Apr-Oct

This private hotel is located in a quiet tree-lined avenue in a residential area of town, close to the railway station and Eastcliff. Bedrooms are simple in style and décor and most have private bathrooms; public areas are comfortable. A home cooked evening meal is also offered.

12rm(10⇌♠ 2hc) (2fb)⊁in all bedrooms CTV in all bedrooms ® sB&B£15-£21 sB&B⇌♠£15-£24 dB&B£30-£42 dB&B⇌♠£30-£48 WB&B£85-£140 WBDi£110-£165
Lic 10P
Credit Cards 1 3

GH QQQ *Croham Hurst Hotel* 9 Durley Rd South BH2 5JH
☎(0202) 552353
Closed Jan
Conveniently situated on the West Cliff side of town, this hotel offers nicely presented rooms, many of which have modern furniture and coordinating décor and fabrics. Public rooms are equally attractive and include a comfortable bar and lounge area. A table d'hôte style menu with a varied choice of dishes is served in the smart dining room. There is a lift to all floors and a large parking area. The cheerful proprietors are involved in the daily running of the hotel, and offer a warm welcome to new and returning guests.
40⇨↱ (7fb) CTV in all bedrooms ® ✕ LDO 7.15pm
Lic lift 🍽 20P
Credit Cards [1] [3]

GH QQQ *Dene Court* 19 Boscombe Spa Rd BH5 1AR
☎(0202) 394874
Conveniently situated close to the town centre of Boscombe, this establishment has much to offer. Bedrooms and public areas are fresh, bright and well presented. In addition to a small games room and cosy bar, there is a neat dining room where wholesome home-cooked fare is served. The resident proprietors Mr and Mrs Mills are a friendly couple who take a pride in their hotel and run it professionally but with an informal approach to their guests, many of whom return time and time again so booking is advisable.
16rm(14⇨↱) (7fb) CTV in all bedrooms ® ✕
🍽 CTV 15P snooker
Credit Cards [1]

[Ⓖ] GH QQ Derwent House 36 Hamilton Rd BH1 4EH
☎(0202) 309102
This detached Victorian house is conveniently placed for shopping in Boscombe. The bedrooms are freshly decorated and some have private bathrooms. There is a small TV lounge and a separate, larger, bar/lounge.
9rm(5↱4hc) (3fb) CTV in all bedrooms ® sB&B£13-£17 sB&B↱£15-£19 dB&B£26-£34 dB&B↱£30-£38 WB&B£70-£110 WBDi£100-£140 LDO 5pm
Lic 🍽 CTV 10P
Credit Cards [1] [3] (£)

[Ⓖ] GH QQ Dorset House 225 Holdenhurst Rd BH8 8DD
☎(0202) 397908
Closed 25 Dec
On the main road into town, conveniently close to the railway station, the enthusiastic proprietors have steadily improved this small guesthouse. Bedrooms are fresh, bright and pretty, and more en suite facilities are planned. Breakfast is the only meal offered, but this is a hearty, freshly cooked meal providing a good choice.
6rm(2⇨↱4hc) ⊁in 2 bedrooms CTV in all bedrooms ® ✕ sB&B£14-£17 sB&B⇨↱£17 dB&B£26-£28 dB&B⇨↱£27-£30 WB&B£91-£98
🍽 6P nc

GH QQQ Golden Sands Hotel BH4 8HR ☎(0202) 763832
Mar-Oct & Xmas
Close to Alum Chine, this well maintained and nicely presented guesthouse offers bright and clean bedrooms, reasonably equipped in addition to a comfortable, traditional lounge area and dining room. A home-cooked evening meal is offered and the resident proprietors take great pride in running this small hotel.
11⇨↱ (2fb) CTV in all bedrooms ® ✕ (ex guide dogs) sB&B⇨↱£18.50-£23.50 dB&B⇨↱£37-£47 WB&B£115-£140 WBDi£150-£183 LDO 4.30pm
Lic 🍽 10P nc2yrs

GH QQ Hawaiian Hotel 4 Glen Rd BH5 1HR ☎(0202) 393234
mid Apr-Oct
A well established hotel where an older clientèle return year after year to enjoy the quiet atmosphere and genial company of the resident proprietors.
12rm(8⇨↱4hc) (3fb) CTV in all bedrooms ®
✕ (ex guide dogs) sB&Bfr£19 sB&B⇨↱fr£19 dB&Bfr£36 dB&B⇨↱fr£38 WB&Bfr£100 WBDifr£130 LDO 6pm
Lic 🍽 CTV 7P (£)

GH QQQ Highclere Hotel 15 Burnaby Rd BH4 8JF
☎(0202) 761350
Apr-Sep
A popular choice for families with children, this establishment is quietly located in Alum Chine and run by the cheerful Mr and Mrs Baldwin. Bedrooms, some of which enjoy sea views, are neat and fresh, and the public areas are decorated in keeping with the late Victorian period of the house. There is a small bar in one corner of the dining room, where guests can enjoy drinks before dinner – at which a choice of dishes is available – and liqueurs with their coffee. Car parking is available in the forecourt.
9rm(4⇨5↱) (5fb) CTV in all bedrooms ® T
sB&B⇨↱£20.95-£23.50 dB&B⇨↱£41.90-£47 WB&B£140-£161 WBDi£145-£165 LDO 4pm
Lic 🍽 CTV 7P nc3yrs
Credit Cards [1] [2] [3] (£)

GH QQQ Holmcroft Hotel 5 Earle Rd BH4 8JQ
☎(0202) 761289
Close to Alum Chine, this well presented, neat hotel is owned by young, friendly proprietors. Bedrooms are bright, clean and well equipped, whilst public areas are comfortably laid out, with plenty of green plants and personal ornaments giving the hotel a warm, welcoming feel. A home-cooked evening meal is offered in the attractive dining room.
19⇨↱ (3fb) CTV in all bedrooms ® T ✱ sB&B⇨↱£29-£34.50 dB&B⇨↱£58-£69 (incl dinner) WB&B£126-£151.20 WBDi£167-£189 LDO 5pm
Lic 🍽 CTV 13P
Credit Cards [1] [3] (£)

GH QQ Kelmor Lodge 30 Stourcliffe Av, Southbourne BH6 3PT ☎(0202) 424061
This small family hotel is situated in a quiet residential area close to the sea and Boscombe shopping centre. It offers simple, neat and comfortable accommodation with cosy bedrooms and a nicely appointed dining room.
8rm(2⇨↱6hc) (1fb) CTV in all bedrooms ® ✕ ✱
sB&B£13.50-£16.50 dB&B£25-£31 dB&B⇨↱£28-£34 WB&B£82-£103 WBDi£114-£131 LDO 9am
Lic 🍽 CTV 6P nc8yrs (£)

GH QQQ Linwood House Hotel BH5 1ND ☎(0202) 397818
Mar-Oct
A detached house with a neat garden, in a quiet residential area near the beach and Boscombe. Bedrooms are simply furnished but are cosy, clean and well kept. There is a spacious comfortable lounge and the smart dining room has a small bar.
10rm(7↱3hc) (2fb) CTV in 6 bedrooms ® dB&B£36-£44 dB&B↱£40-£48 WB&B£84-£112 WBDi£126-£152 LDO 9.30am
Lic 🍽 CTV 7P nc6yrs

GH QQQ *Lynthwaite Hotel* 10 Owls Rd BH5 1AF
☎(0202) 398015
A Victorian villa dating back to 1876, conveniently situated between the seafront and Boscombe town centre. Bedrooms are very nicely presented, well equipped, bright and fresh. Public areas include a first floor lounge and balcony, a traditional bar area and dining room.
14rm(10⇨1↱3hc) (3fb) CTV in all bedrooms ® ✕ LDO 5pm
Lic 🍽 CTV 17P nc3yrs
Credit Cards [1] [2] [3]

GH Q Mae-Mar Hotel 91/95 West Hill Rd BH2 5PQ
☎(0202) 553167 FAX (0202) 311919
Convenient for the town, on the West Cliff side, this large guesthouse is gradually being upgraded. The proprietor Mr Cleaver does the work himself and has so far added en suite

facilities to the majority of the rooms and built a smart basement bar. Further improvements are planned, and while bedrooms are simply furnished, the accommodation is moderately priced.
40rm(4⇨24ſ12hc) (11fb) CTV in all bedrooms Ⓡ sB&B£16-£20 sB&B⇨ſ£18.50-£22.50 dB&B£32-£40 dB&B⇨ſ£37-£45 WBDi£160-£175 LDO 5.30pm
Lic lift 🍴 CTV
Credit Cards [1] [2] [3] (£)

🛏♥ **GH QQ Mayfield Private Hotel** 46 Frances Rd BH1 3SA ☎(0202) 551839
Closed Dec
Situated in a residential area, this small guesthouse offers cosy, comfortable accommodation. Public areas have recently gained from the addition of a small no smoking lounge. The proprietors are very involved in the day-to-day running of the hotel and do their best to ensure that guests enjoy their stay.
8rm(4ſ4hc) (1fb) CTV in all bedrooms Ⓡ sB&B£13-£15 dB&B£26-£30 dB&Bſ£31-£35 WB&B£70-£85 WBDi£102-£120 LDO 9am
Lic 🍴 CTV 5P nc7yrs (£)

GH QQ New Dorchester Hotel 64 Lansdowne Rd North BH1 1RS ☎(0202) 551271
Closed 24 Dec-4 Jan
A large, detached Victorian villa with a huge stained glass window; located along the Lansdowne Road. Bedrooms are practical, plainly decorated and light, with modern equipment; some single rooms are rather compact. Public areas are smart, with an elegant, comfortable and well furnished lounge. The dining room overlooks a pretty garden, and there is plenty of forecourt parking.
8rm(3⇨2ſ3hc) CTV in all bedrooms Ⓡ Ħ ✱ sB&B£16-£20 sB&B⇨ſ£20-£25 dB&B⇨ſ£30-£40 WB&B£96-£120 WBDi£145-£169 LDO 6pm
Lic 🍴 10P nc12yrs
Credit Cards [1] [2] [3] [5] (£)

GH QQQ Newfield Private Hotel 29 Burnaby Rd BH4 8JF ☎(0202) 762724
Situated in the residential area of Alum Chine, this friendly guesthouse has a cheerful atmosphere. The bedrooms are neat with coordinated décor and the majority are en suite, equipped with modern facilities. A comfortable lounge and nicely appointed dining room, with a cosy bar at one end, are also offered. The helpful proprietors provide a friendly, relaxed atmosphere.
11rm(1⇨7ſ3hc) (4fb) CTV in all bedrooms Ⓡ ✱ sB&B£17-£22 sB&B⇨ſ£19-£24 dB&B£30-£40 dB&B⇨ſ£34-£44 WB&B£119-£154 WBDi£148-£180
Lic 🍴 CTV 4P
Credit Cards [1] [2] [3] (£)

🛏♥ **GH Q Norland Private Hotel** 6 Westby Rd BH5 1HD ☎(0202) 396729
A deceptively large semidetached Victorian house conveniently located close to the town centre. The modest but adequate bedrooms vary in size, and are relatively comfortable although compact, and generally freshly decorated. A front-facing lounge with bright décor and a simply appointed dining room are provided, together with a small bar, and some forecourt parking is also available.
9rm(3⇨ſ6hc) (2fb) CTV in all bedrooms Ⓡ sB&B£13-£17 dB&B£26-£34 dB&B⇨ſ£30-£38 WB&B£80-£105 WBDi£105-£135 LDO 4.30pm
Lic 🍴 CTV 8P (£)

GH QQ Northover Private Hotel 10 Earle Rd BH4 8JQ ☎(0202) 767349
This small Victorian building is quietly located in Alum Chine. Bedrooms are spotlessly clean, fresh and neat, and some have en suite facilities. Public areas are cosy and comfortable, and filled with plants and flowers. Car parking is available.
10rm(6ſ4hc) (6fb) TV available Ⓡ ✱ sB&B£17-£21 sB&Bſ£19-£24 dB&B£34-£42 dB&Bſ£38-£48 WB&B£102-£126 WBDi£140-£190 LDO 5pm
Lic 🍴 CTV 11P nc3yrs (£)

GH QQ Oak Hall Private Hotel 9 Wilfred Rd BH5 1ND ☎(0202) 395062
Closed 3wks Oct rs Nov, Jan & Feb
A detached house situated in a quiet residential area, yet conveniently close to the beach and shops at Boscombe. The bedrooms are comfortable and bright, with conventional décor and furnishings and modern facilities. A home-cooked evening meal with a small choice is offered, and in addition to a cosy lounge, there is also a small bar.
13rm(9⇨ſ4hc) (4fb) CTV in all bedrooms Ⓡ ✱ WB&Bfr£129.50 WBDi£156.50-£173.75 LDO 3pm
Lic 🍴 CTV 9P
Credit Cards [1] [3] (£)

GH QQ St John's Lodge Hotel 10 St Swithun's Rd South BH1 3RQ ☎(0202) 290677
This family-run hotel is conveniently located close to the railway and bus stations, and within walking distance of the Chine and pier. Bedrooms are simply furnished and vary in size, but are freshly decorated and some have private bathrooms. There is a cocktail bar and a spacious dining room, where a simple table d'hôte menu is offered.
15rm(5ſ10hc) (2fb) CTV in all bedrooms Ⓡ Ħ sB&B£16.50-£17.50 sB&Bſ£20-£21 dB&B£33-£35 dB&Bſ£40-£42 WB&B£105-£135 WBDi£130-£160 LDO 4pm
Lic 🍴 CTV 13P sauna
Credit Cards [1] [3] (£)

Book as early as possible for busy holiday periods.

GH QQ Sea-Dene Hotel 10 Burnaby Rd BH4 8JF
☎(0202) 761372
Mar-Oct & Xmas
This small, friendly guesthouse is situated close to the beach at Alum Chine, in a quiet residential area. The house dates back to 1906 and bedrooms vary: those on the top floor are especially attractive and unusual, others are light and airy and enjoy sea views. All the rooms are freshly decorated and nicely presented: some have new showers recently installed, and further improvements are steadily being made by Mr and Mrs Harfoot. Comfortable public areas include a lounge providing books and games and a rear terrace with flowers in season. There is limited forecourt car parking.
7rm(5♠2hc) (3fb) CTV in all bedrooms ® ✗ (ex guide dogs) ✱ sB&B£14-£17 sB&B♠£17-£19 dB&B£28-£34 dB&B♠£34-£38 WB&B£89-£125 WBDi£134-£162 LDO 6.30pm
Lic 𝍢 CTV 4P nc3yrs
Credit Cards 1 3 £

GH QQQ Silver Trees Hotel BH3 7AL ☎(0202) 556040
This Victorian house has an elegant façade and pretty gardens to the front, while the rear gardens are beautifully kept with an abundance of colourful flowers and an ornamental pond. Bedrooms, most of which are en suite, have a bright, fresh décor and very comfortable beds and armchairs. Public areas include a cosy lounge and a pretty dining room. Evening meals are not available, but guests may be served snacks and light refreshments during the day and evening.
8rm(5♠3hc) (2fb)⊬in 4 bedrooms CTV in all bedrooms ® ✗ sB&B£25-£27 sB&B♠£28-£30 dB&B£36-£38 dB&B♠£40-£42 WB&B£170-£200
𝍢 10P
Credit Cards 1 3

GH QQ Hotel Sorrento 16 Owls Rd BH5 1AG
☎(0202) 394019
rs Xmas
This holiday hotel, in a residential area midway between Boscombe shopping centre and the seafront, offers a relaxed and friendly atmosphere. Bedrooms vary in size and are neat, bright and well equipped. There is an attractive lounge area, cosy bar and sunny dining room, along with a pretty garden and car parking facilities.
17rm(12⇌♠5hc) (5fb) CTV in all bedrooms ® sB&B£14-£19 sB&B⇌♠£16.50-£21.50 dB&B£28-£38 dB&B⇌♠£33-£43 WB&B£83-£135.50 WBDi£125-£177.50 LDO 6pm
Lic 𝍢 CTV 19P nc2yrs solarium gymnasium
Credit Cards 1 3 £

GH Q Telstar 1257 Christchurch Rd BH7 6BP
☎(0202) 428626
Situated along the busy, main Christchurch road, midway between Christchurch and Boscombe, this simple guesthouse offers 2 bedrooms, both neatly presented, modestly furnished and offering a few modern facilities. Breakfast is the only meal served and this is taken in the small, front-facing dining room which is well stocked with local tourist information. Limited car parking is available on the front forecourt.
2hc (1fb) CTV in all bedrooms ® ✗ (ex guide dogs) sB&B£14.50-£15.50 dB&B£27-£29 WB&B£84-£91
2P nc13yrs

GH QQQ Tudor Grange Hotel BH1 3EE ☎(0202) 291472 & 291463
A mock-Tudor house set in neat, well kept gardens on the East Cliff. The public areas are very handsome, with fine panelled walls, ornate ceilings and a comfortable lounge area. Bedrooms are prettily decorated and have well maintained modern facilities. An evening meal is offered, cooked by Mrs Heeley, who enjoys welcoming guests into her home, many of whom return year after year.
12rm(11⇌♠1hc) (4fb) CTV in all bedrooms ® T ✱ sB&B£27.25 sB&B⇌♠£25.25-£29.75 dB&B⇌♠£50.50-£59.50 WB&B£144-£187 WBDi£194-£237 LDO 7pm
Lic 𝍢 CTV 11P
Credit Cards 1 3 £

GH QQQ Valberg Hotel 1a Wollstonecraft Rd BH5 1JQ
☎(0202) 394644
An unusual looking house with a Spanish style exterior, quietly situated in a pleasant area close to the sea and shops. Clean and freshly decorated bedrooms provide en suite facilities together with comfortable beds; the top 2 bedrooms have access to a large balcony. The lounge and dining room, with a small bar, overlook the attractive garden.
10♠ (2fb) CTV in all bedrooms ® ✗ ✱ dB&B♠£30-£40 WB&B£84-£111 WBDi£133-£160 LDO 12pm
Lic 𝍢 CTV 9P nc4yrs

GH QQQ Weavers Hotel 14 Wilfred Rd BH5 1ND
☎(0202) 397871
Apr-Oct
This is a well presented 1920s detached house, freshly decorated throughout and with high standards of housekeeping. There is a small quiet lounge in addition to the smart bar lounge and light spacious dining room. Bedrooms vary a little in size but most have modern fully tiled showers. Situated in a tree- lined street in a pleasant residential area, it is close to Boscombe's shops and beach.
7rm(6♠1hc) (1fb) CTV in all bedrooms ® ✗ sB&B£21.50-£23 dB&B♠£43-£46 (incl dinner) WB&B£125-£135 WBDi£135-£145 LDO 5pm
Lic 𝍢 7P nc7yrs

GH QQQ *West Dene Private Hotel* 117 Alumhurst Rd BH4 8HS ☎(0202) 764843
Mar-Oct
On a cliff close to Alum Chine and enjoying superb views out to sea, this hotel offers comfortable bedrooms, a small, sunny bar area and a home-cooked evening meal. The resident proprietors are keen to oblige and are justly proud of their well kept and nicely presented hotel.
17rm(5⇌7♠5hc) (4fb) CTV in 15 bedrooms ® ✗
LDO 3.30pm
Lic 𝍢 CTV 17P nc4yrs
Credit Cards 1 2 3 5

GH QQQ West Hill Court Hotel 121 West Hill Rd, West Cliff BH2 5PH ☎(0202) 551125
Etr-Oct
Dating back over 150 years, this property stands on the West Cliff, conveniently close to the BIC, seafront and town centre. Personally run by the Battey family, this well presented, comfortable guesthouse offers spick and span bedrooms that are freshly decorated with pretty coordinating themes and some have smart, modern en suite shower rooms. An evening meal and English breakfast is served in the pleasant dining room, at separate tables, on the lower ground level, and an intimate bar is also found on the same floor. On the ground floor above is a well furnished lounge, where guests may relax and enjoy a chat. Some on street parking is available nearby, but it is advised to discuss this with the proprietors when reserving your room. West Hill Court has a warm, friendly atmosphere that prevails throughout.
12rm(6♠6hc) (2fb) CTV in all bedrooms ® ✗ (ex guide dogs) ✱ sB&B£18-£25.50 dB&B£39-£48 dB&B♠£45-£54 (incl dinner) WB&B£96-£125 WBDi£117-£146 LDO 4.30pm
Lic CTV nc8yrs
Credit Cards 1 3

GH QQ Woodford Court Hotel 19-21 Studland Rd BH4 8HZ
☎(0202) 764907 FAX (0202) 761214
Situated in a quiet, residential area close to Alum Chine, this hotel offers neat, bright bedrooms with modern en suite facilities. The proprietor Mrs Peters cooks the evening meal and runs the hotel with her husband and family. A smart new bar area provides guests with a cosy corner, and this holiday hotel offers good value for money.

35rm(8⇌18↱9hc) (11fb) CTV in all bedrooms ® **T**
sB&Bfr£17 sB&B⇌↱£22 dB&Bfr£34 dB&B⇌↱£44
WB&B£120-£152 WBDi£141-£195 LDO 6.15pm
Lic ♨ CTV 18P nc2yrs
Credit Cards 1 2 3

GH QQ ***Woodlands Hotel*** 28 Percy Rd, Boscombe BH5 1JG
☎(0202) 396499

A pretty house in a quiet residential area quite close to the sea with individually decorated bedrooms. The dining room and bar have recently been refurbished and there is a cosy lounge.

11rm(5↱6hc) (3fb) CTV in all bedrooms ® LDO 6.15pm
Lic ♨ CTV 7P
Credit Cards 1 3

GH QQQ Wood Lodge Hotel 10 Manor Rd BH1 3EY
☎(0202) 290891
Etr-Oct

This hotel is situated in a quiet avenue on the East Cliff side of town and is well run by the resident proprietors. Set in its own well kept gardens, complete with a mini-golf/putting area, ample car parking is an added bonus here. The public areas and bedrooms are bright, fresh and neatly presented; bedrooms are well equipped with modern facilities. A home cooked evening meal is served, and there is a cosy bar area.

15rm(14⇌↱1hc) (5fb) CTV in all bedrooms ® sB&B£21.50-£26.75 sB&B⇌↱£23-£28.75 dB&B⇌↱£46-£57.50
WB&B£135-£169 WBDi£175-£208 LDO 6pm
Lic ♨ CTV 12P 9 hole putting green
Credit Cards 1 3 £

BOURTON-ON-THE-WATER Gloucestershire Map **04** SP12

GH QQQ Coombe House Rissington Rd GL54 2DT
☎Cotswold(0451) 821966

Personally run by enthusiastic hoteliers Graham and Diana Ellis – who are ex farmers and horticulturists, this cosy, no-smoking house stands in its own pretty lawned gardens, combined with some unusual plants depicting the Ellis' expertise in this field. There are 7 spotlessly clean, bright and comfortable bedrooms, individually dedorated and furnished with pretty duvets and coordinating fabrics that complement the high standard of modern facilities, including the bright en suites with thick towels and perfumed toiletries. The cosy lounge has a sunny patio and the breakfast room where delicious croissants and preserves, in addition to a hearty breakfast are served, has views of the garden.

7⇌↱ (2fb)⊁in all bedrooms CTV in all bedrooms ® ✗
sB&B⇌↱£33-£40 dB&B⇌↱£49-£56 WB&B£160-£185
Lic ♨ 10P

BOVEY TRACEY Devon Map **03** SX87

GH Q Blenheim Hotel Brimley Rd TQ13 9DH ☎(0626) 832422
rs 25 & 26 Dec

A fine detached Victorian property on the edge of the moorland town of Bovey Tracey, standing within its own secluded 2 acres of gardens and grounds. The bedrooms are clean, if simply furnished and decorated, and there is a choice of comfortable lounges, one with TV.

5hc (1fb) CTV in 4 bedrooms sB&B£21 dB&B£42 WB&B£135 WBDi£210 LDO 7.30pm
Lic ♨ CTV 8P £

SELECTED

FH QQQQ Mrs H Roberts **Willmead** *(SX795812)*
TQ13 9NP ☎Lustleigh(06477) 214
Closed Xmas & New Year

This charming 15th-century thatched cottage is next to 31 acres of woodland, and boasts a duck pond and plenty of hens and guinea fowl roaming freely. Bedrooms have uneven, whitewashed walls, oak beams and comfortable, good quality furniture. One has a fully tiled en suite shower. Public areas have exposed stone and whitewashed walls, inglenook fireplaces and plenty of oak beams. There is a comfortable lounge, a delightful dining room, a library and a hall complete with Minstrel's Gallery. Furniture and ornaments all enhance the rustic style of the building, and include some very interesting pieces. The breakfasts include free range eggs and a wide range of home-made preserves.

3rm(1↱2hc) ⊁in all bedrooms ✗ sB&Bfr£30 dB&Bfr£40 dB&B↱fr£46
♨ CTV 10P nc10yrs 32 acres beef

BOWNESS-ON-WINDERMERE Cumbria

See **Windermere**

BRADFORD West Yorkshire Map **07** SE13

GH QQ Maple Hill Hotel 3 Park Dr, Heaton BD9 4DP
☎(0274) 544061 FAX (0274) 481154

Maple Hill is situated just off Keighley Road adjacent to Lister Park in a leafy residential area. It is an imposing Victorian house in weathered local stone surrounded by a wonderful garden. Inside the period features are intact: moulded panels, coving, roses and some original tiled fireplaces. Just off the well stocked bar is a domed Victorian conservatory with stained leaded windows perfect for the summer. The bedrooms are quite simply furnished in a mixture of styles and coordinated colour schemes with a light, fresh look.

12rm(2↱9hc) (1fb)⊁in 1 bedroom CTV in all bedrooms ®
sB&B£30.55 sB&B↱£36.43 dB&B£42.30 dB&B↱£48.18
WB&B£213.85-£255.01 WBDi£291.97-£333.13
Lic ♨ 20P 2🚗 half size snooker table £

BRADFORD ON AVON Wiltshire Map **03** ST86

SELECTED

GH QQQQ Bradford Old Windmill 4 Masons Ln BA15 1QN ☎(0225) 866842

Part of a group of distinctly different places to stay, this unique home of Peter and Priscilla Roberts sits high above the picturesque town of Bradford-on-Avon in its own pretty gardens. A converted windmill built in 1806 and more recently lovingly restored, the character of the building has been retained with the décor and furnishings chosen in keeping with the style, creating a wealth of interest. All the bedrooms are memorable in some way, including one with a circular bed and another with a water bed. The majority are en suite and all are comfortably equipped with tea making facilities. There is an attractively furnished circular lounge with a log fire burning on cold winter nights and literature provided for guests to enjoy. Home cooked meals are served around a communal refectory table in the tastefully furnished dining room. The mill is strictly no smoking throughout.

4rm(1⇌2♨1hc) (1fb)⅟in all bedrooms ® ✗ sB&B£30-£39 sB&B⇌♨£45-£50 dB&B£45-£49 dB&B⇌♨£59-£65 WB&B£127.50-£197.50 LDO previous day

卌 4P nc6yrs £

SELECTED

GH QQQQ Widbrook Grange Trowbridge Rd BA15 1UH ☎(02216) 3173 & 2899 FAX (02216) 2890

An attractive 18th-century farmhouse, one mile from the town on the Trowbridge road, yet set in rolling countryside. The house is impressive and very comfortable, with attractively furnished bedrooms, complemented by thoughtful extras and period furnishings; some of the bedrooms are outside in a recently converted stable block. The owners only provide bed and breakfasts, but are happy to help guests find a suitable restaurant for dinner.

4rm(3⇌♨1hc) Annexe 11⇌♨ (2fb)⅟in 4 bedrooms CTV in all bedrooms ® T ✗ sB&Bfr£30 sB&B⇌♨£49-£55 dB&B⇌♨£60-£79 LDO noon

Lic 卌 50P 10🚗

Credit Cards 1 2 3 £

BRADING

See **WIGHT, ISLE OF**

BRAEMAR Grampian *Aberdeenshire* Map **15** NO19

GH QQ Callater Lodge Hotel 9 Glenshee Rd AB35 5YQ ☎(03397) 41275

Jan-Oct

Under the ownership of Peter and Mary Nelson gradual improvements are taking place at this converted Victorian lodge, which is set in its own grounds beside the A93 at the southern edge of the village. The spacious lounge has a welcoming open fire, and enjoyable 4-course dinners are served in the recently refurbished dining room. Bedrooms vary in size and offer a mixture of modern and conventional appointments. The hotel is well situated for climbing, fishing, touring, golfing and ski-ing, with the Glenshee Ski Centre and Balmoral both nearby.

8rm(2♨6hc) ® sB&B£16-£18 sB&B♨£21 dB&B£32-£36 dB&B♨£42 WB&B£103.60-£116.55 WBDi£208.60-£221.55 LDO 7pm

Lic 卌 14P

Credit Cards 1 3 £

BRAITHWAITE Cumbria Map **11** NY22

GH QQQ Cottage in the Wood Whinlatter Pass CA12 5TW ☎Keswick(07687) 78409

mid Mar-mid Nov

7⇌♨ (2fb)⅟in all bedrooms ® dB&B⇌♨£54-£59 WB&B£175-£192.50 WBDi£235-£250 LDO 6.30pm

Lic 卌 15P

GH QQQ Maple Bank CA12 5RY ☎(07687) 78229

Closed mid Nov-mid Dec

An attractive Lakeland stone detached house standing just off the A66 to the north of Keswick, it has been tastefully decorated and furnished with quality coordinated fabrics and wallpapers. There is a comfortable lounge, and well prepared meals are served in the pretty dining room.

7♨ (1fb) CTV in all bedrooms ® ✗ sB&B♨£22-£25 dB&B♨£39-£45 WB&B£122.85-£141.75 WBDi£192.50-£210 LDO 4pm

Lic 卌 CTV 10P nc8yrs

Credit Cards 1 3 £

See advertisement under KESWICK

BRAMPTON Cumbria Map **12** NY56

See also Castle Carrock and Kirkcambeck

GH QQQ Oakwood Park Hotel Longtown Rd CA8 2AP ☎(06977) 2436

A comfortable and well furnished Victorian house standing in its own grounds, a short way from Brampton on the Longtown road. Bedrooms all have private bathrooms and good facilities. Good home cooking is provided, and there is a pleasant lounge.

5rm(2⇌3♨) (1fb)⅟in all bedrooms CTV in all bedrooms ® ✗ (ex guide dogs) ✱ sB&B⇌♨fr£24 dB&B⇌♨£33-£39 WB&Bfr£97 WBDifr£159 LDO 8pm

Lic 卌 CTV 7P ♂(hard)

Credit Cards 1 3 £

INN QQQ The Blacksmiths Arms Talkin Village CA8 1LE ☎(06977) 3452

A typical Cumbrian inn situated in the centre of the village of Talkin, 2 miles south east of Brampton. Bedrooms are well furnished and attractively decorated, and a good range of food is available in either the bar or restaurant.

5rm(3⇌2♨) CTV in all bedrooms ® ✗ (ex guide dogs) sB&B⇌♨£28 dB&B⇌♨£42 WB&B£126-£168 Lunch £6-£15alc Dinner £6-£15alc LDO 9pm

12P games room

Credit Cards 1 3 £

BRAMSHAW Hampshire Map **04** SU21

INN QQ Bramble Hill Hotel SO43 7JG ☎Southampton(0703) 813165

Etr or 1 Apr-15 Jan

12rm(7⇌♨5hc) (3fb) CTV in 9 bedrooms TV in 1 bedroom ® ✱ sB&B£35-£45 sB&B⇌♨£45-£55 dB&Bfr£37.50 dB&B⇌♨£57.50-£77.50 Lunch £7-£10&alc Dinner £10-£15&alc LDO 9pm

卌 CTV 70P U

Credit Cards 1 3 £

BRANSGORE Hampshire Map **04** SZ19

GH QQQ Tothill House off Forest Rd BH23 8DZ ☎(0425) 74414

You will need to phone for directions to find this fine Edwardian house, hidden down a long drive, amid a pine plantation. The bedrooms enjoy relaxing views and are generally spacious, decorated with a mixture of period furnishings, ornaments and pictures. Breakfast only is available and is taken informally around a communal table. The guesthouse has new owners who are at present restoring the house and grounds.

3rm(2 1hc) in all bedrooms CTV in all bedrooms ® (ex guide dogs) sB&B £25-£30 dB&B£50 dB&B fr£50 WB&B£148.75
10P nc15yrs (£)

BRAUNTON Devon Map **02** SS43

GH QQQ ***Alexander Brookdale Hotel*** 62 South St EX33 2AN
(0271) 812075
Tucked away close to the town centre, this friendly guesthouse provides unpretentious, neat bedrooms, a spacious lounge/bar and an attractive first floor lounge.
8hc (2fb) in all bedrooms CTV in all bedrooms ®
(ex guide dogs) LDO 11am
Lic CTV 9P 2 nc8yrs
Credit Cards 2

FH QQQ Mr & Mrs Barnes **Denham Farm & Country House** *(SS480404)* North Buckland EX33 1HY
Croyde(0271) 890297
Closed 18-28 Dec
This characterful farmhouse has been recently refurbished to provide bright, well equipped bedrooms with TV and tea-making facilities and modern en suite shower rooms. Good home-cooked meals are offered in the informal restaurant. Set in a quiet village location, this provides a good touring base for north Devon, with a Championship golf course nearby.
10 (2fb) CTV in all bedrooms ® * sB&B fr£30 dB&B £40-£42 WB&Bfr£133 WBDifr£190 LDO 6pm
Lic CTV 8P 3 games room table tennis skittle alley 160 acres beef sheep

(£) Remember to use the money-off vouchers.

BRECHIN Tayside *Angus* Map **15** NO56

SELECTED

FH QQQQ Mrs M Stewart **Blibberhill** *(NO553568)* DD9 6TH (5m WSW off B9134) ☎Aberlemno(030783) 225

This well maintained 18th-century farmhouse is reached off the B9134 Brechin- Aberlemno road, and there are fine views of the Vale of Strathmore. Two of the comfortably furnished bedrooms have private bathrooms, and the third room is particularly spacious. There is a pleasant lounge and an attractive small conservatory overlooking the garden. Good home cooking is served at a communal table, and the farm offers tremendous value for money.

3rm(2⇌🚿1hc) ⚟in all bedrooms Ⓡ ✗ (ex guide dogs) sB&Bfr£16 dB&Bfr£27 dB&B⇌🚿fr£32
CTV 4P 300 acres arable beef mixed

BRECON Powys Map **03** SO02

GH QQ Beacons 16 Bridge St LD3 8AH ☎(0874) 623339

Near the River Usk and a short walk from the town centre, the Beacons is run by the very friendly Cox family. Many bedrooms are attractively pine furnished, some of them still have their original fireplaces and one bedroom has a four-poster bed. The rear of the house was originally 17th-century weavers' cottages and much of the character remains. There is a modern lounge, a bar in what was once a meat cellar and a coffee lounge which is open to passing trade during the summer.

10rm(7⇌🚿3hc) Annexe 1⇌🚿 (2fb) CTV in all bedrooms Ⓡ ✱ sB&B£16-£19 sB&B⇌🚿fr£19 dB&Bfr£32 dB&B⇌🚿fr£38 WB&B£96-£114 WBDi£147-£165 LDO 6.30pm
Lic CTV 12P
Credit Cards 1 2 3

GH QQ Borderers Inn 47 The Watton LD3 7EG ☎(0874) 623559
Closed Dec

Once a Drovers inn dating from the 17th century, the original courtyard and entrance of this inn still remains and is now used as a car park. It has been converted to a bed and breakfast guesthouse and many original beams and timbers are evident throughout. The neat bedrooms are well decorated, and there is a small but very cosy sitting room. Although it is called 'Borderers Inn', this guesthouse is not open as a public house.

5rm(3🚿2hc) Annexe 2rm(1⇌1🚿) (2fb)⚟in 3 bedrooms CTV in all bedrooms Ⓡ ✱ sB&B£18 sB&B⇌🚿£20 dB&B£30 dB&B⇌🚿£34 WB&B£100-£135
Lic CTV 6P nc5yrs

GH QQQ The Coach Orchard St, Llanfaes LD3 8AN ☎(0874) 623803
Closed 22 Dec-7 Jan

Once an 18th-century inn, this mid-terrace guesthouse is run by the very friendly Ashton family and is situated opposite the town's Christ College. Everything is spotless and newly decorated. The bedrooms have recently been re-furbished with dark fitted furniture and pretty floral fabrics. There is a very comfortable residents' lounge, furnished with modern 3 piece suites, which features a genuine Victorian fireplace.

6⇌🚿 (2fb)⚟in all bedrooms CTV in all bedrooms Ⓡ T ✗ (ex guide dogs) ✱ dB&B⇌🚿£35-£36 LDO 7pm
Lic 5P nc

GH QQ Flag & Castle 11 Orchard St, Llanfaes LD3 8AN ☎(0874) 625860

Not far from the Usk and once a tavern, this establishment offers clean, plain accommodation and a genuine welcome from Pat and Arthur Jones. A very comfortable atmosphere prevails, and guests dine together at the communal table.

6rm(1🚿5hc) (1fb) CTV in 1 bedroom Ⓡ sB&B£15-£16 dB&B£28-£30 dB&B🚿£30-£34 WB&B£90-£110
Lic CTV 2P

BREDWARDINE Hereford & Worcester Map **03** SO34

SELECTED

GH QQQQ Bredwardine Hall HR3 6DB ☎Moccas(09817) 596 due to change to (0981) 500596
Mar-mid Nov

A warm welcome is assured from Wendy and Maurice Jancey at this 18th-century manor house with its magnificent reception hall and staircase. Set in its own wooded grounds with well kept lawns, most rooms have rural views. There is an elegant drawing room with several floor to ceiling windows, furnished with brown dralon seating, and the cosy dining room has an honesty bar. The majority of bedrooms are spacious, fitted with good quality furniture and all have en suite or private bathrooms, along with TV and tea making facilities.

5rm(3⇌1🚿1hc) CTV in all bedrooms Ⓡ ✗ (ex guide dogs) sB&B£27-£29 sB&B⇌🚿£27-£29 dB&B£42-£46 dB&B⇌🚿£42-£46 WB&B£142-£156 WBDi£215.50-£229.50 LDO 4.30pm
Lic 7P nc10yrs Ⓔ

See advertisement under HEREFORD

BRENDON Devon Map **03** SS74

GH Q Brendon House Hotel EX35 6PS ☎(05987) 206
2 Mar-mid Nov

Positioned at the entrance to this sleepy village, Brendon House is an unpretentious, friendly guesthouse. Home-cooked dinners are provided and a tea shop service is offered throughout the day.

5rm(1⇌3🚿1hc) (1fb) Ⓡ ✱ sB&Bfr£17 sB&B⇌🚿fr£18 dB&Bfr£34 dB&B⇌🚿fr£36 WB&Bfr£109 WBDifr£172 LDO 5pm
Lic CTV 5P Ⓔ

GH QQQ *Millslade Country House Hotel* EX35 6PS ☎(05987) 322

Quietly situated on the edge of the village, this attractive house is run by friendly, courteous proprietors and provides nicely furnished, cosy bedrooms, combined with a comfortable, inviting lounge and a very popular restaurant that offers an impressive menu.

6hc (1fb) CTV in all bedrooms Ⓡ LDO 9pm
Lic CTV 50P
Credit Cards 1 2 3 5

BRENT ELEIGH Suffolk Map **05** TL94

FH QQQ Mrs J P Gage **Street** *(TL945476)* CO10 9NU ☎Lavenham(0787) 247271
Closed Dec-mid Feb

A 16th-century farmhouse with a well tended walled garden situated in the centre of the village, but with immediate access from the A1141 Lavenham/Hadleigh road. The accommodation is of excellent quality and the lounge has a beautiful inglenook fireplace and log fire.

3rm(2⇌🚿1hc) ⚟in all bedrooms Ⓡ ✗ ✱ dB&B£34 dB&B⇌🚿£36
CTV 4P nc12yrs 143 acres arable Ⓔ

BRIDESTOWE Devon Map **02** SX58

FH QQ Mrs J E Down **Little Bidlake** *(SX494887)* EX20 4NS ☎(083786) 233
Etr-Oct

Two comfortable bedrooms are offered at this friendly, stone-built farmhouse, set back off the A30 at Bridestowe but with direct access to it. There is also a cosy lounge and an informal dining room where dinner is available in the evening on request.

2hc ⚟in all bedrooms Ⓡ ✗ (ex guide dogs) sB&Bfr£15 dB&Bfr£26 WB&Bfr£77 WBDifr£120 LDO 7.30pm
CTV P putting 150 acres beef dairy mixed Ⓔ

FH QQ Mrs M Hockridge **Week** *(SX519913)* EX20 4HZ
☏(083786) 221

A large 17th century farmhouse set in peaceful and attractive Devon countryside, yet convenient for the A30. Some private bathrooms have recently been installed, and there is a cosy lounge and dining room. The farm's welcoming atmosphere makes this a good touring base for Dartmoor National Park and an en route stopover to the south west.

6rm(3↱3hc) (3fb) CTV in 3 bedrooms Ⓡ ✱ sB&B£15-£16 dB&B£30-£32 dB&B↱£36-£38 LDO 5pm
䦨 CTV 10P 180 acres dairy sheep
Credit Cards [2] Ⓔ

BRIDGNORTH Shropshire Map **07** SO79

GH QQQ **Haven Pasture** Underton WV16 6TY
☏(074635) 632

Once a farm worker's cottage, Haven Pasture has been modernised and extended and is set against a backdrop of mature trees in a very rural location in the hamlet of Underton off the B4364 southwest of the town. There are attractive lawns and gardens and a swimming pool for the good weather. Three pine furnished bedrooms are available, each with access to a patio area. Guests eat together in the open-plan sitting room and dining room with its beams and brick inglenook fireplace where logs burn in cold weather. Pat and David Perks offer genuine hospitality to guests in their lovely home.

3rm(1↱2hc) (2fb) CTV in all bedrooms Ⓡ sB&B£18.50 dB&B£30 dB&B↱£35 LDO 8pm
䦨 CTV 7P ⛆(heated)

GH QQQ ***Severn Arms Hotel*** Underhill St, Low Town WV16 4BB ☏(0746) 764616
Closed 23 Dec-2 Jan

This tall, terraced house is situated close to the cliff railway which links Low Town to High Town. The front rooms have lovely views of the old bridge across the river Severn at Low Town. Home-cooked meals are served in the dining room.

9rm(2⇔3↱4hc) (5fb) CTV in 7 bedrooms TV in 1 bedroom Ⓡ LDO 7pm
Lic 䦨 CTV ♪
Credit Cards [1] [2] [3]

INN Q ***Kings Head Hotel*** Whitburn St WV16 4QN
☏(0746) 762141

A 17th-century inn situated just off the main street of High Town, down a narrow road. Retaining many of its original features, the inn is full of character and offers good value accommodation.

5hc (3fb) CTV in all bedrooms Ⓡ ✗ (ex guide dogs) LDO 8pm
䦨 8P

BRIDGWATER Somerset Map **03** ST33

GH QQ **Brookland Hotel** 56 North St TA6 3PN
☏(0278) 423263
Closed 24 Dec-1 Jan

Just away from the centre of town along the Minehead road in a prominent corner position stands this popular and busy licensed commercial guesthouse, which offers simply appointed, neatly presented bedrooms, some of which are en suite. The dining room is compact but well furnished and evening meals are available; the small bar is well stocked. Quality leather seating in the lounge, which has a TV, makes for comfort. Ample car parking is available and manager Mr O'Toole is a cheerful host.

8rm(3↱5hc) (1fb) CTV in all bedrooms Ⓡ ✱ sB&B£25-£30 sB&B↱£35-£40 dB&B£40-£45 dB&B↱£45-£50 WB&B£210-£280 LDO 6pm
Lic 䦨 CTV 10P
Credit Cards [1] [2] [3]

BRIDLINGTON Humberside Map **08** TA16

GH QQQ Bay Ridge Hotel Summerfield Rd YO15 3LF
☎(0262) 673425

With a cream stucco façade, this 1920s house appears to be a very jolly establishment, with friendly proprietors Mr and Mrs Myford going out of their way to meet the needs of all guests. The bedrooms are simply furnished in melamine and are gradually being upgraded with coordinating fabrics, offset by plain emulsioned walls, and towels chosen to match. All rooms have TV with Sky channels available. There is a lovely, large lounge with a Chesterfield suite and brass inlaid teak coffee tables. A separate small lounge, designated no smoking, is also available. The large central bar is furnished with deep 3- piece suites, bar billiards and music, and there is entertainment provided in season. An honest, interesting menu with a strong appeal is served in the restaurant.

14rm(6⇌6↱2hc) (5fb) CTV in all bedrooms Ⓡ ✱ sB&B£21.50-£22.50 dB&B⇌↱£43-£45 (incl dinner) WB&B£115-£120 WBDi£140-£150 LDO 5.45pm
Lic ᵯ CTV 6P 1🚗 (£2 per day) bar billiards darts board games library
Credit Cards 1 3 (£)

GH QQQ ***Langdon Hotel*** Pembroke Ter YO15 3BX
☎(0262) 673065

With a distinctive façade of yellow brick, this mid-terrace house is set between the harbour and the Spa Theatre, separated from the beach by a small park. This large establishment boasts a high percentage of modern, well fitted, tiled en suites in bedrooms of simple white melamine furnishings, coordinated colour schemes and pretty floral bedding – the front rooms have double glazing. The restaurant opens into the bar, and there is a huge lounge with strong blue and brown colour coordination. All the public areas have the added advantage of overlooking the sea. The proprietor Mrs Smith, continues to upgrade the hotel each year and the same care is reflected in the cleanliness.

20rm(11↱9hc) (8fb) CTV in all bedrooms Ⓡ
✗ (ex guide dogs) LDO 5pm
Lic lift ᵯ

GH QQQ ***Southdowne Hotel*** South Marine Dr YO15 3NS
☎(0262) 673270

Situated on the seafront in a quiet, mainly residential area, this 1920s red brick house tends to attract the older holidaymaker, who appreciates quiet and rest with modern facilities. The bedrooms have a multitude of designs and colour schemes and the furniture is mainly melamine. All the rooms have en suite facilities tiled and coordinated in pastel shades. There is a large sitting room with a mixed range of comfortable armchairs and imitation onyx tables, leading to a TV lounge. A small bar doubles up with the reception desk in the hallway and the dining room is truly sunny, both in position and colour scheme. The proprietor, Mrs Kemp, keeps a very good house with genuine old- fashioned care and hospitality.

12rm(8↱4hc) (2fb) TV in 1 bedroom Ⓡ ✗ LDO 5.30pm
Lic ᵯ CTV 10P

GH QQQ The Tennyson 19 Tennyson Av YO15 2EU
☎(0262) 604382

A pleasant mellow brick Victorian terraced house set at right angles to the promenade, north of the town. Each of the spacious, high-ceilinged rooms has been carefully furnished to provide comfortable accommodation with matching soft furnishings: Mrs Stalker has a keen eye for detail and presentation. Bedroom 2 is very distinctive, with a carved American 4-poster bed heavily swathed in gold fabric, setting off the ebony-inlaid period furniture. There is a pretty blue and white dining room and comfortable lounge.

6rm(3⇌2↱1hc) ⊬in all bedrooms CTV in all bedrooms Ⓡ sB&B⇌↱£16-£23 dB&B£26-£28 dB&B⇌↱£32-£34 WB&B£80-£100 WBDi£125-£150 LDO 8.30pm
Lic ᵯ 2P 1🚗 nc9yrs
Credit Cards 1 3 5 (£)

BRIDPORT Dorset Map **03** SY49

See also Bettiscombe, Chideock & Nettlecombe

GH QQQ Britmead House 154 West Bay Rd DT6 4EG
☎(0308) 22941

Britmead is in a pleasant location between the centre of Bridport and the harbour of West Bay, and the rear bedrooms and public areas particularly enjoy pretty rural views. Bedrooms are comfortable and offer plenty of extras, there is a comfortable lounge and a neat dining room. The menu is appreciated by many returning guests, who enjoy the fresh, quality ingredients and well cooked dishes. A popular ground floor bedroom is available, and car parking is provided.

7rm(6⇌↱1hc) (1fb) CTV in all bedrooms Ⓡ sB&B£22-£28 sB&B⇌↱£27-£32 dB&B£34-£39 dB&B⇌↱£44-£46 WB&B£110.25-£147 WBDi£187.25-£227.50 LDO 6pm
Lic ᵯ 8P
Credit Cards 1 2 3 5 (£)

BRIGHTON & HOVE East Sussex Map **04** TQ30

See **Town Plan Section**
See also Rottingdean

SELECTED

GH QQQQ Adelaide Hotel 51 Regency Square BN1 2FF
☎Brighton(0273) 205286 FAX (0273) 220904
Closed 23-30 Dec

This attractive end-of-terrace Regency building has a distinctive smart exterior and a pretty display of hanging baskets. Many of the freshly decorated and tastefully furnished bedrooms have canopied beds, and all are equipped with every modern facility. Public areas include a comfortable lounge with a marble fireplace and an elegant basement dining room where welcoming proprietors Ruth and Clive Buxton will happily serve snacks at any time.

12⇌↱ (1fb) CTV in all bedrooms Ⓡ **T** ✗ sB&B⇌↱£38-£60 dB&B⇌↱£59-£75 LDO 5pm
Lic ᵯ P̸
Credit Cards 1 2 3 5 (£)

GH QQQ Allendale Hotel 3 New Steine BN2 1PB
☎Brighton(0273) 675436 FAX (0273) 602603

Situated on a pleasant garden square close to the seafront and local amenities, this small Regency house is run by charming proprietors Mr and Mrs Keeble. The smart, modern bedrooms are attractively appointed with coordinating floral fabrics, and they are all exceptionally well equipped, making the hotel a popular choice for business people. There is a small cosy lounge adjoining the dining room, where Mrs Keeble will happily provide dinner by prior request.

13rm(6↱5hc) (5fb)⊬in 2 bedrooms CTV in all bedrooms Ⓡ **T** sB&B£27-£30 sB&B↱£35-£50 dB&B£44 dB&B↱£54-£66 WB&B£120-£168 WBDi£176-£224 LDO 4pm
Lic ᵯ P̸ nc8yrs
Credit Cards 1 2 3 5 (£)

GH QQ Alvia Hotel 36 Upper Rock Gardens BN2 1QF
☎Brighton(0273) 682939

Undergoing considerable upgrading, this family-run bed and breakfast establishment has a friendly and informal atmosphere, with the personal touch added by David Scourfield and his family. The room sizes vary but all are furnished in a modern style. Guests have a choice of cooked English breakfast dishes, and an enclosed car park at the rear of the building is provided.

9rm(7⇌↱2hc) (1fb)⊬in 3 bedrooms CTV in all bedrooms Ⓡ ✗ (ex guide dogs) ✱ sB&B£16-£18 sB&B⇌↱£25-£30 dB&B£26-£30 dB&B⇌↱£36-£40 WB&B£112-£140
ᵯ 5P
Credit Cards 1 2 3 5 (£)

GH QQQ Ambassador Hotel 22 New Steine BN2 1PD
☎Brighton(0273) 676869 FAX (0273) 689988
Situated close to the Palace Pier and seafront, and within walking distance of the town, this family-run hotel offers a range of neat, well equipped bedrooms with private bathrooms. On the ground floor there is a TV lounge with a bar.
9rm(2🛁7🚿) (4fb) CTV in all bedrooms ® T ✈ ✱
sB&B🛁🚿£23-£30 dB&B🛁🚿£42-£57
Lic 🍴 CTV 🅿̸
Credit Cards 1 2 3 5 £

GH QQ Amblecliff Hotel 35 Upper Rock Gardens BN2 1QF
☎Brighton(0273) 681161 & 676945
This attractive Victorian terraced house is centrally situated for all amenities. The bedrooms are pleasantly decorated in pastel shades with coordinating fabrics, and many have en suite facilities. On the ground floor, guests have their own small lounge and a bright dining room for full English breakfast, or for a more leisurely start friendly proprietor Mrs Kelman will bring a continental breakfast to your room. Amblecliff has a residential licence, though there is no bar as such.
11rm(8🛁🚿3hc) ⊁in 4 bedrooms CTV in all bedrooms ® T ✈ (ex guide dogs) ✱ sB&B£16-£18 dB&B🛁🚿£36-£50
WB&B£96-£150
Lic 🍴 CTV 3P (£1.50-£2) nc4yrs
Credit Cards 1 2 3 £

GH QQQ Arlanda Hotel 20 New Steine BN2 1PD
☎Brighton(0273) 699300 FAX (0273) 600930
Situated in an attractive garden square overlooking the sea, this family-run terraced Regency-style house offers a mixed style of accommodation. Single rooms are generally compact, with more spacious family rooms. Each room has assorted furnishings but benefits from full en suite facilities, TV and direct dial telephones. Breakfast, snacks and an evening meal are served in the dining room/lounge, which also has a residental licence.
12rm(2🛁10🚿) (4fb) CTV in all bedrooms ® T
✈ (ex guide dogs) sB&B🛁🚿£28-£38 dB&B🛁🚿£38-£66
WB&B£120-£250 WBDi£175-£336 LDO 4pm
Lic 🍴 🅿̸
Credit Cards 1 2 3 5 £

GH QQQ Ascott House Hotel 21 New Steine, Marine Pde BN2 1PD ☎Brighton(0273) 688085 FAX (0273) 623733
Ideally situated in a garden square close to the seafront and town, this small hotel is personally run by proprietors Michael and April Strong. Bright, freshly decorated bedrooms offer a good standard of comfort and they are all equipped with every modern facility. There is also a comfortable lounge adjoining the breakfast room, and a small bar.
12rm(11🛁🚿1hc) (8fb) CTV in all bedrooms ® T ✈ sB&B£22-£25 sB&B🛁🚿£30-£35 dB&B£42-£48 dB&B🛁🚿£50-£70
LDO 4pm
Lic 🍴 🅿̸ nc3yrs
Credit Cards 1 2 3 5 £

GH QQQ Bannings 14 Upper Rock Gardens, Kemptown BN2 1QE ☎Brighton(0273) 681403
Just away from the seafront, in a smart area of town, this elegant town house has been attractively restored to provide comfortable, though rather compact, bedrooms. Geoff Norris and his son enjoy running the guesthouse and they have many returning guests. Breakfast is the only meal served, and it is a hearty one, taken in the prettily furnished, basement breakfast room. Two rooms are designated no-smoking, and there is plenty of on-street parking which requires easily purchased vouchers.
6rm(3🛁🚿3hc) (3fb)⊁in 2 bedrooms CTV in all bedrooms ®
✱ sB&B£18-£23 sB&B🛁🚿£25-£32 dB&B£36-£42
dB&B🛁🚿£38-£44
🍴 nc12yrs
Credit Cards 1 2 3 5 £

See advertisement on page 97

GH QQ Cavalaire House 34 Upper Rock Gardens, Kemptown BN2 1QF ☎Brighton(0273) 696899 FAX (0273) 600504
Closed Xmas-mid Jan
Immediately noticeable by its bright blue exterior, this small terraced house is conveniently situated for all amenities. Freshly decorated bedrooms offer satisfactory comforts and a few have smart en suite shower rooms. There is a bright breakfast room adjoining a homely lounge with an attractive marble fireplace.
9rm(3↱6hc) (2fb) CTV in all bedrooms ® sB&B£17-£19 dB&B£27-£34 dB&B↱£34-£44
nc9yrs
Credit Cards 1 2 3 5 £

SELECTED

GH QQQQ *Claremont House* Second Av BN3 2LL ☎Brighton(0273) 735161
This attractive Victorian house is situated in a select residential area close to the seafront. Bedrooms vary in size but are all furnished to the same high standard, with coordinated soft furnishings and every modern facility. En suite bathrooms are smart and modern, and guests have the choice of a corner or spa bath. The attractive and spacious bar lounge features the original marble fireplace and ornate cornices. There is also a pretty dining room where Mrs Humber's varied menu is served, a secluded garden to the rear, and ample street parking. Service is at hand throughout the day, and the atmosphere is friendly and informal.
12⇌↱ (2fb) CTV in all bedrooms ® LDO 10pm
Lic CTV
Credit Cards 1 2 3 5

GH QQ Cornerways Private Hotel 18-20 Caburn Rd BN3 6EF ☎Brighton(0273) 731882
A large Victorian corner house, Cornerways, offers a variety of accommodation, mostly furnished in traditional style. There is a small bar, cosy TV lounge and a traditional dining room.
10rm(1↱9hc) (2fb) CTV in 3 bedrooms ® ✱ sB&Bfr£16 dB&Bfr£32 dB&B↱fr£37 WB&Bfr£102 WBDi£137 LDO 2pm
Lic CTV £

GH QQ Croft Hotel 24 Palmeira Av BN3 3GB ☎Brighton(0273) 732860 FAX (0273) 820775
Quietly situated in a residential area but only a few minutes' walk to the seafront, this small guesthouse offers bedrooms that are simply furnished with shared facilities, but all are equipped with a TV, hairdryer and tea-making amenities. An attractive dining room leads to the patio garden and there is a small TV lounge in the basement.
11hc (2fb) CTV in all bedrooms ® sB&B£23-£25 dB&B£40-£42
Lic CTV £

GH QQ Dudley House 10 Madeira Place BN2 1TN ☎Brighton(0273) 676794
Situated close to the seafront and local amenities, this small Victorian terraced guesthouse is run by friendly proprietors Mr and Mrs Lacey. Bedrooms vary in size from spacious, complete with an en suite shower room, to a more compact standard room; they are all comfortable and well maintained. There is a small sitting area adjoining the attractive dining room, where smoking is not permitted.
6rm(3↱3hc) (3fb)⊬in 4 bedrooms CTV in all bedrooms ® (ex guide dogs) ✱ sB&B£20-£25 sB&B↱£27-£30 dB&B£30-£36 dB&B↱£40-£50 WB&B£95-£180
CTV nc5yrs £

GH QQQ George IV Hotel 34 Regency Square BN1 2FJ ☎Brighton(0273) 21196
Elegantly situated at the top of this prominent Regency square, overlooking the gardens and sea, this small hotel has been totally restored to provide smartly furnished bedrooms with modern bathrooms and every conceivable facility. A further benefit is the lift to all floors, which is unusal in a hotel of this size. A full English breakfast is served in the small but pretty dining room and the reception combines with the lounge area.
8⇌↱ (3fb) CTV in all bedrooms ® T sB&B⇌↱£30-£45 dB&B⇌↱£45-£65 WB&B£250-£350 LDO by arrangement
Lic lift CTV
Credit Cards 1 2 3 5 £

GH QQ Georjan 27 Upper Rock Gardens BN2 1QE ☎Brighton(0273) 694951
Just a short walk away from the seafront and local amenities, this small guesthouse offers freshly decorated bedrooms, some of which have their own en suite shower rooms. The friendly proprietor Mr Flegg is happy to provide snacks and beverages throughout the day.
5rm(3↱2hc) (1fb)⊬in 2 bedrooms CTV in all bedrooms ® sB&B↱£17-£24 dB&B↱£34-£48 WB&B£105-£150
Credit Cards 1 2 3 £

GH QQQ Gullivers 10 New Steine BN2 1PB ☎Brighton(0273) 695415 FAX (0252) 372774
This mid-terrace Regency residence is close to the seafront and all amenities. The attractively decorated bedrooms feature floral duvets that coordinate with the curtains and all have direct-dial telephones, with the majority benefiting from en suite facilities. Breakfast is served in the bright dining room by the friendly owner, Sally Gannaway.
9rm(5↱4hc) (3fb) CTV in all bedrooms ® T ✱ sB&B£22-£24 sB&B↱£35-£37 dB&B£42-£44 dB&B↱£48-£54
Credit Cards 1 2 3 5 £

GH QQ *Harvey's* 1 Broad St BN2 1TJ ☎Brighton(0273) 699227
Closed Xmas
A well maintained guesthouse situated close to the seafront and run by friendly owners Mr and Mrs Harvey. Bedrooms are all attractively decorated in pastel shades, and provide a good level of comfort.
7hc (3fb)⊬in 4 bedrooms CTV in all bedrooms
nc5yrs

GH QQ Kempton House Hotel 33/34 Marine Pde BN2 1TR ☎Brighton(0273) 570248
Directly opposite the sea, these 2 Regency houses have been combined and now operate as a small hotel run by welcoming proprietors Mr and Mrs Swaine. Bedrooms are bright, modern and well equipped: all but one have a private bathroom, and those at the front benefit from fine sea views. There is a small restaurant bar adjoining the breakfast room, and guests are offered the option of a leisurely continental breakfast in their room.
13rm(12↱1hc) (4fb) CTV in all bedrooms ® T ✱ sB&B↱£30-£40 dB&B↱£44-£52 LDO 9am
Lic
Credit Cards 1 2 3 5 £

GH QQ Malvern Hotel 33 Regency Square BN1 2GG ☎Brighton(0273) 24302
A well maintained guesthouse which offers comfortable rooms equipped with most modern conveniences including en suite facilities. There is a small residents' bar and a pleasant lounge.
12↱ CTV in all bedrooms ® T sB&B↱£30-£38 dB&B↱£45-£55 WB&B£150-£240
Lic
Credit Cards 1 2 3 5 £

GH QQ *Marina House Hotel* 8 Charlotte St, Marine Pde BN2 1AG ☎Brighton(0273) 605349 & 679484 FAX (0273) 605349
A single-fronted Victorian mid-terrace building just off the Marine Parade and a short walk to all the town's tourist and conference

venues. The well equipped bedrooms are situated on four floors and are simply furnished. In the lower ground floor dining room, English, Indian, Chinese and vegetarian meals are available by prior arrangement.
10rm(7♠ 3hc) (2fb) CTV in all bedrooms ® ✗ LDO 4pm
Lic 🍽 CTV
Credit Cards 1 2 3 5

GH Q Marine View 24 New Steine BN2 1PD
☎Brighton(0273) 603870
Situated in one of Brighton's smartest Regency squares, this small guesthouse has recently been taken over by Mr and Mrs Miyake. The bedrooms are all freshly decorated in pastel shades and are furnished in a simple, modern style. The four singles share a general bathroom, whilst the others have their own shower unit. There is a combined dining room and sitting area on the ground floor.
10rm(3♠ 7hc) ⊁in 2 bedrooms CTV in all bedrooms ® ✗ ✱ sB&B£17-£20 dB&B£36-£38 dB&B♠£38-£40 WB&B£119-£140
🍽 CTV nc15yrs
Credit Cards 1 3

GH QQ Melford Hall Hotel 41 Marine Pde BN2 1PE
☎Brighton(0273) 681435
In a prime position overlooking the sea, this small hotel has benefited from recent upgrading. Bedrooms are freshly decorated in a modern style with white furniture, floral duvets and coordinating curtains, and the majority are en suite. English breakfast is served in the basement dining room and there is a guests' lounge to the front. Car parking facilities, though limited, are an added bonus.
25rm(23⇌♠ 2hc) (4fb) CTV in all bedrooms ®
✗ (ex guide dogs) sB&B£23-£25 sB&B⇌♠£25-£35 dB&B⇌♠£44-£50 WB&B£140-£170
🍽 CTV 12P
Credit Cards 1 2 3 5 £

GH QQQ New Steine Hotel 12a New Steine, Marine Pde BN2 1PB ☎Brighton(0273) 681546
Mar-mid Dec rs Xmas & New Year
Run by friendly proprietors Ron and Andy, this attractive Regency house offers smart, comfortable accommodation and is ideally situated for both the seafront and the shops. Guests can relax in the cosy lounge, and breakfast is served in the basement dining room.
11rm(4♠ 7hc) (2fb) CTV in all bedrooms ® ✱ sB&Bfr£17 sB&B♠fr£25 dB&B♠£39-£42
🍽 CTV ₱ nc8yrs £

GH QQ Paskins Hotel 19 Charlotte St BN2 1AG
☎Brighton(0273) 601203 FAX (0273) 621973
This is an elegant Georgian mid-terrace house situated in a peaceful street which is just a short distance from the seafront and the town centre. Many of the bedrooms are attractively decorated in co-ordinated colour schemes and the others are due for refurbishment in the immediate future. All but three are en suite and particularly well equipped. Public areas include a ground floor reception and lounge and there is a basement dining room and adjoining bar furnished in a bright modern style.
19rm(16⇌♠ 3hc) (2fb) CTV in all bedrooms ® T ✱ sB&B£20-£22 sB&B⇌♠£27.50-£32 dB&B£30-£32 dB&B⇌♠£42-£55 WB&B£90-£165 WBDi£160-£235 LDO 5.30pm
Lic 🍽
Credit Cards 1 3 £

See advertisement on page 99

GH QQQ Pier View Hotel 28 New Steine BN2 1PD
☎Brighton(0273) 605310 FAX (0273) 688604
A prime position, with views overlooking the sea and Palace Pier, makes this smart, Regency terraced house a convenient choice for all attractions. Bedrooms are freshly decorated in pastel shades with coordinating duvets and most are en suite. The pleasant breakfast room combines with a small lounge, which is comfortably

furnished and the King family always create a welcoming atmosphere.
10rm(7⇋3hc) (3fb) CTV in all bedrooms ® ✗ (ex guide dogs) sB&B£22-£24 sB&B⇋fr£30 dB&Bfr£39 dB&B⇋£43-£58
LDO 5pm
CTV
Credit Cards 1 2 3 £

GH QQ Prince Regent Hotel 29 Regency Square BN1 2FH
☎Brighton(0273) 29962 FAX (0273) 748162
Closed 24-25 & 31 Dec & 1 Jan
This elegant hotel, overlooking the sea, offers a range of bedrooms to suit every taste. Some are spacious and ornately decorated in the Regency style, while others are bright and compact. All have en suite facilities and are well equipped. Breakfast is served in the basement dining room and there is a small residents' bar.
20⇌⇋ in 1 bedroom CTV in all bedrooms ® T
✗ (ex guide dogs) sB&B⇌⇋£30-£50 dB&B⇌⇋£50-£80
Lic CTV nc12yrs
Credit Cards 1 2 3 5 £

GH QQ Queensbury Hotel 58 Regency Square BN1 2GB
☎Brighton(0273) 25558 FAX (0273) 24800
Closed 1wk Xmas
A single fronted period property in a classical square opening onto the seafront. Simply furnished bedrooms are on the 4 floors above ground floor, they have comfortable modern beds, TV and tea-making facilities. Breakfast is served in the lower ground floor dining room.
16rm(6⇌⇋1hc) (8fb) CTV in all bedrooms ® * sB&B£18-£25 sB&B⇌⇋£30-£35 dB&B⇌⇋£35-£50
CTV
Credit Cards 1 3 £

GH QQ *Regency Hotel* 28 Regency Square BN1 2FH
☎Brighton(0273) 202690 FAX (0273) 220438
Situated in Regency Square directly facing the sea, this small family-run hotel offers a range of simply furnished bedrooms, some of which have recently been upgraded. There is an elegant dining room with an adjoining, traditionally styled lounge and small bar.
14rm(1⇌10⇋3hc) (1fb) CTV in all bedrooms ®
✗ (ex guide dogs) LDO noon
Lic CTV
Credit Cards 1 2 3 5

GH QQQ Trouville Hotel 11 New Steine, Marine Pde BN2 1PB ☎Brighton(0273) 697384
Closed Jan
Situated close to the town centre and seafront, this family-run guesthouse offers freshly decorated bedrooms which vary in size. A cosy lounge adjoins the pleasant breakfast room.
9rm(2⇋7hc) (2fb) CTV in all bedrooms ® ✗ sB&B£18 dB&B£32-£35 dB&B⇋£42-£46 WB&B£108-£150
Lic CTV
Credit Cards 1 2 3 £

GH QQQ Twenty One 21 Charlotte St, Marine Pde BN2 1AG
☎Brighton(0273) 686450
Situated close to the seafront in the Kemp Town area, this early Victorian town house offers a choice of exceptionally well equipped bedrooms, all but one being en suite. There is an impressive 4-poster bedroom with period furniture and in the basement a charming double room with its own ivy-clad courtyard. Breakfast and evening meals (by prior arrangement only) are enjoyed in the bright ground floor dining room and there is a comfortable furnished lounge downstairs.
6rm(5⇋1hc) CTV in all bedrooms ® ✗ (ex guide dogs) sB&B⇋£35-£50 dB&B⇋£46-£68 LDO 9am
Lic nc9yrs
Credit Cards 1 2 3 £

GH QQ Westbourne Hotel 46 Upper Rock Gardens BN2 1QF
☎Brighton(0273) 686920
Within walking distance of all local amenities, this listed Victorian terrace house offers a range of bright comfortable bedrooms, which are simply furnished and many have en suite facilities. The neat dining room has a small corner bar for residents only and there is a guests' lounge provided.
10rm(6⇋4hc) (4fb) CTV in all bedrooms ® ✗ * sB&B£16-£25 dB&Bfr£30 dB&B⇋£40 WB&Bfr£105 WBDifr£150
LDO 6pm
Lic
Credit Cards 1 2 3 £

BRIG O'TURK Central *Perthshire* Map 11 NN50

SELECTED

GH QQQQ Dundarroch Trossachs FK17 8HT
☎Trossachs(08776) 200
rs Dec-Feb
Charmingly situated midway between Callander and Aberfoyle in the heart of the Trossachs, this delightful, small country house which dates back to 1843, has been tastefully furnished to provide comfortable and nicely appointed accommodation. There is a most attractive dining room, furnished with polished tables and antiques, with views of Ben Venue. Equally attractive is the lounge with its feature stone wall, large Victorian fireplace and wood burning stove. The bedrooms are comfortably furnished and equipped with a wide range of useful accessories, thoughtful extras such as fruit and biscuits are also provided. The breakfast menu features fresh fish, and apart from Tuesdays, when the owner Mrs Morna Williams prepares a 'hostess supper', evening meals are not served, although these may be taken in the neighbouring Byrs Inn, a characterful Victorian bar and restaurant, with whom a special arrangement exists.
3⇌⇋ CTV in all bedrooms ® T ✗ (ex guide dogs) * sB&B⇌⇋£29.75-£39.75 dB&B⇌⇋£46-£51 WB&B£160-£165 LDO 8.45pm
6P nc3mths
Credit Cards 1 3 £

BRIGSTEER (NEAR KENDAL) Cumbria Map 07 SD48

FH QQ Mrs B Gardner ***Barrowfield*** *(SD484908)* LA8 8BJ
☎Crosthwaite(04488) 336
Apr-Oct
A lovely Elizabethan farmhouse situated on a dairy farm, in a beautiful and peaceful area of lakeland, just north of the village. It is found by taking the Kendal road from Brigsteer up the hill, then turn on the bend along a Forestry Commission road. Very warm and friendly service is provided.
3rm(2hc) (1fb) ✗
CTV 6P 180 acres dairy sheep

BRISTOL Avon Map 03 ST57

See **Town Plan Section**
GH QQQ Aaron Lodge 425 Fishponds Rd, Fishponds BS16 3AP ☎(0272) 653132
Closed Xmas & New Year
9rm(1⇌5⇋3hc) (2fb) CTV in all bedrooms ® ✗ * sB&B£24.70-£34 sB&B⇌⇋fr£34 dB&Bfr£39 dB&B⇌⇋£51-£65 LDO 5.30pm
Lic CTV 6P solarium £

GH QQ Alandale Hotel Tyndall's Park Rd, Clifton BS8 1PG
☎(0272) 735407
Closed 2wks Xmas
An attractive Victorian house centrally situated close to the university and shops, directly opposite the BBC. Personally owned and run, the guesthouse offers functional accommodation and is popular with commercial visitors. Bedrooms tend to vary in size

and spaciousness, but are nicely styled, bright and comfortable, all with private bathrooms and a good range of facilities, including TV and direct dial telephones. There is a comfortable, spacious lounge with an honesty bar for residents, and useful on site car parking.
17rm(5⇔12↱) CTV in all bedrooms ® T sB&B⇔↱£28-£38 dB&B⇔↱£38-£48
Lic 10P
Credit Cards [1] [3] (£)

GH QQ Alcove 508-510 Fishponds Rd, Fishponds BS16 3DT ☎(0272) 653886 & 652436
A friendly, pleasant guesthouse in a residential location, northeast of the city and convenient for both the city and the M32/M4. The accommodation is well kept and comfortable, with some modern facilities. There is a cosy little breakfast room at the rear, and street car parking adjacent.
9rm(2↱7hc) (2fb) CTV in all bedrooms ® (ex guide dogs) sB&B£19-£25 sB&B↱£25-£30 dB&B£30-£36 LDO 4pm
CTV 8P 1 (£)

GH QQ Birkdale Hotel 11 Ashgrove Road, Redland BS6 6LY ☎(0272) 733635 & 736332 FAX (0272) 739964
Closed Xmas wk
Situated off Whiteladies road a mile from the city centre, this hotel is unusual in that the majority of its bedrooms are situated in separate houses nearby and the main building is used for food and drink services. The spacious lounge-bar is comfortable and the bedrooms are well equipped, most of them having modern en suite facilities.
42rm(34⇔8↱) CTV in all bedrooms ® ✱ sB&Bfr£35.25 sB&B⇔↱fr£41.12 dB&Bfr£58.75 dB&B⇔↱fr£68.15
LDO 8pm
Lic 16P
Credit Cards [1] [3] (£)

GH Q Chesterfield Hotel 3 Westbourne Place, Clifton BS8 1LX ☎(0272) 734606 Telex no 449075 FAX (0272) 741082
Situated on the edge of Clifton, this nice terraced house provides low-cost, comfortable accommodation, ideal for the businessman. Evening meals are available at a nearby sister hotel.
13hc (2fb) CTV in all bedrooms ® ✱ sB&B£18-£21 dB&B£33-£35
🅿̸
Credit Cards [1] [2] [3] [5]

GH QQQ Downlands 33 Henleaze Gardens, Henleaze BS9 4HH ☎(0272) 621639
An attractive Victorian house in a quiet residential position very close to the Downs, and a short drive from Clifton and the city centre. It provides spotlessly clean, comfortable bed and breakfast accommodation, with well decorated, nicely furnished bedrooms and a cosy breakfast room. The owners Mr and Mrs Newman create a friendly atmosphere, and there is on street parking adjacent.
10rm(2↱8hc) (1fb) CTV in all bedrooms ® sB&B£321-£25 dB&Bfr£38 dB&B↱fr£44
🅿̸
Credit Cards [1] [3] (£)

GH Q *Oakfield Hotel* 52-54 Oakfield Rd, Clifton BS8 2BG ☎(0272) 735556
Closed 23 Dec-1-Jan
Personally owned and run by Mrs Hurley, this established hotel deserves top marks for spotless cleanliness and refreshingly traditional methods. The bedrooms are simply styled and furnished, and have central heating and remote control colour TV, but no en suite facilities. Good old-fashioned service includes early morning tea and hot drinks served in the evening. The guesthouse is very conveniently positioned close to Whiteladies Road, the BBC, Clifton and the university.
27hc (4fb) CTV in all bedrooms ® LDO 7pm
CTV 4P 2

See advertisement on page 101

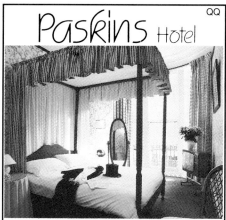

GH QQ *Rowan Lodge* 41 Gloucester Rd North, Filton Park BS7 0SN ☎(0272) 312170
Closed Xmas & New Year
A large detached house situated north of the city on the junction of the A38 with Bronksea road, close to the suburb of Filton and Bristol's new business complex. This friendly guesthouse is spotlessly clean, with bright, cosy, comfortable bedrooms. There is a car park at the rear.
6rm(3↱3hc) (2fb) CTV in all bedrooms
8P
Credit Cards 1 3

GH QQ Washington Hotel 11-15 St Pauls Rd, Clifton BS8 1LX ☎(0272) 733980 Telex no 449075 FAX (0272) 741082
Closed 23 Dec-3 Jan
A large, rambling, unlicensed private hotel in a very convenient position for Clifton, the shops and university. There is a range of well equipped bedrooms: some have received recent upgrading to a good modern standard, whilst others are more modest in comfort and furnishings. The breakfast room is bright and cosy, and guests can also dine at the Racks restaurant located in the sister hotel The Clifton. There is limited but unrestricted car parking in the opposite street.
46rm(34⇔↱12hc) (5fb) CTV in all bedrooms ® sB&Bfr£27.50 sB&B⇔↱£45 dB&Bfr£46.50 dB&B⇔↱£61
Lic 20P
Credit Cards 1 2 3 5 £

GH QQQ Westbury Park Hotel 37 Westbury Rd, Westbury-on-Trym BS9 3AU ☎(0272) 620465
9rm(2⇔3↱4hc) (1fb) CTV in all bedrooms ® **T** (ex guide dogs) ✱ sB&B£25-£28 sB&B⇔↱£33-£38.50 dB&B£36-£40 dB&B⇔↱£43-£48.50 WB&B£165-£250 WBDi£240-£330 LDO 8.30pm
Lic CTV 4P
Credit Cards 1 3 £

BRIXHAM Devon Map **03** SX95

See **Town Plan Section**

GH QQQ Harbour Side 65 Berry Head Rd TQ5 9AA ☎(0803) 858899
This friendly guesthouse is situated up a flight of steps from the road, with beautiful views over the marina and Torbay beyond. Bedrooms are bright and comfortable, with tea-making facilities and TV; one room has a brass 4-poster bed, and one family room has a private bathroom. Dinner is available on request, and a good choice is offered at breakfast; smoking is not permitted in the dining room.
5rm(1↱4hc) (2fb) CTV in all bedrooms ® (ex guide dogs) sB&B£15-£17 dB&B£27-£31 dB&B↱£31-£35 LDO 10am
CTV £

GH Q Harbour View Hotel 65 King St TQ5 9TH ☎(0803) 853052
Providing a good vantage point for Brixham's harbour, this 250-year-old house was once the former home of a harbour master. The public areas are limited to an open-plan lounge/dining room, where breakfast is served and evening meals are only available in August. Simply furnished bedrooms are equipped with colour TV and tea making facilities. Limited parking is available.
9hc (1fb) CTV in all bedrooms ® ✱ sB&Bfr£16 dB&B£30-£35
2P (£1 per night)
Credit Cards 1 3

GH QQ Raddicombe Lodge 105 Kingswear Rd TQ5 0EX ☎(0803) 882125
14 Apr-14 Oct
A friendly guesthouse quietly situated midway between Brixham and Dartmouth, with views of the countryside and the sea in the distance from some rooms. Varied and imaginative choices are served at breakfast in the pretty dining room, and bedrooms are individually decorated and furnished.
8rm(3↱5hc) (2fb) CTV in all bedrooms ® sB&B£15.50-£22 sB&B↱£18.70-£22 dB&B£31-£37.60 dB&B↱£37.40-£44 WBDi£108.50-£142.10
CTV 9P
Credit Cards 1 3 £

GH QQ Ranscombe House Hotel Ranscombe Rd TQ5 9UP ☎(0803) 882337
A detached property dating back to 1743, located in a residential area with views over the harbour, and the benefit of its own car park. Bedrooms are very comfortable and well equipped, each with a private bathroom. A choice of menus is offered in the elegant restaurant, and there is a cosy bar in the cellar.
9⇔↱ (2fb) CTV in all bedrooms ® **T** (ex guide dogs) ✱ sB&B⇔↱£21-£27 dB&B⇔↱£42-£54 WBDi£147-£189 LDO 4pm
Lic 16P
Credit Cards 1 2 3

GH QQ Sampford House 59 King St TQ5 9TH ☎(0803) 857761
Mar-Oct rs Nov-Feb
A cosy, family-run, terraced period house overlooking the inner harbour. While there is no private parking, limited parking is available on the quay. Bedrooms are simply furnished and fairly compact. The rear dining room overlooks a colourful courtyard, and there is a small lounge. Bed and breakfast accommodation is provided.
6hc (1fb) CTV in 5 bedrooms TV in 1 bedroom ® ✱ sB&B£14-£16 dB&B£28-£32 LDO 10am
CTV 2P (£2 per night) £

GH QQQ Woodlands Parkham Rd TQ5 9BU ☎(0803) 852040
Apr-Oct
You are now entering a clean, smoke-free environment. Perched overlooking Brixham, this Victorian house is only a short walk from the harbour and town centre. Each of the 5 bedrooms is en suite, and there is a fridge on the first floor landing for cold drinks available on an honesty basis. Breakfast is served in the dining room which has a lovely view. Dutch is spoken.
5↱ (1fb) in all bedrooms CTV in all bedrooms ® sB&B↱£17.50-£19.80 dB&B↱£35-£39 WB&B£108-£125
4P
Credit Cards 1 3 £

BROAD HAVEN (NEAR HAVERFORDWEST) Dyfed Map **02** SM81

GH QQ Broad Haven Hotel SA62 3JN ☎Haverfordwest(0437) 781366 FAX (0437) 781070
This large family holiday hotel stands opposite the sandy beach of the small resort. Bedrooms are modestly furnished but provide modern facilities, and most are en suite. The bars are popular with tourists and locals, and there are extensive leisure facilities including an outdoor pool.
39rm(34⇔↱5hc) (7fb) CTV in all bedrooms ® **T** ✱ sB&Bfr£25 sB&B⇔↱£30 dB&Bfr£40 dB&B⇔↱£50 WB&B£129.50-£164.50 WBDi£196-£234.50 LDO 8pm
Lic CTV 100P (heated) solarium table tennis pool table
Credit Cards 1 2 3
See advertisement under HAVERFORDWEST p 197

BROADSTAIRS Kent Map **05** TR36

GH QQQ Bay Tree Hotel 12 Eastern Esplanade CT10 1DR ☎Thanet(0843) 862502 FAX (0843) 860589
An attractive Victorian house with tastefully modernised accommodation. The bedrooms are comfortable and well maintained, some have en suite facilities and most have magnificent sea views; one room has its own balcony. There is a comfortable combined bar lounge and an attractive separate dining room. Car parking is provided at the rear, and service is friendly and helpful.

11⇌↱ CTV in all bedrooms ® ✗ (ex guide dogs)
sB&B⇌↱£20-£25 dB&B⇌↱£40-£50 WB&B£120-£130
WBDi£165-£170 LDO 4pm
Lic 𝍸 12P nc10yrs
Credit Cards [1] [3] £

GH QQ Devonhurst Hotel Eastern Esplanade CT10 1DR
☎Thanet(0843) 863010

A friendly, family-run hotel overlooking the sea. Bedrooms have been skilfully upgraded, and are furnished and equipped to the same high standard, with double glazing and pretty, individual décor. The comfortable lounge/sitting area has a balcony with stunning views of the sea and coastline: a feature which 2 of the bedrooms share.

9↱ (1fb) CTV in all bedrooms ® ✗ (ex guide dogs)
dB&B↱£39-£46 WB&B£119-£140 WBDi£149-£169 LDO 6pm
Lic 𝍸 P̸ nc6yrs
Credit Cards [1] [2] [3] £

GH Q East Horndon Private Hotel 4 Eastern Esplanade CT10 1DP ☎Thanet(0843) 868306
Mar-Nov

A small, old-fashioned licensed hotel facing the sea, in a quiet position 5 minutes walk from the town centre. There is a cosy bar/lounge, dining room and adequately furnished and well equipped bedrooms, with some new en suite facilities. Service is helpful and friendly.

11rm(4⇌↱4hc) (6fb) CTV in 9 bedrooms TV in 1 bedroom ®
✱ sB&Bfr£18 dB&Bfr£36 dB&B⇌↱fr£40 WB&Bfr£120
WBDifr£140 LDO noon
Lic 𝍸 P̸
Credit Cards [1] [3]

GH QQQ *Gull Cottage* 5 Eastern Esplanade CT10 1DP
☎Thanet(0843) 861936
Closed Nov-Mar

Quietly situated facing the sea, this popular commercial guesthouse has a no smoking policy in all areas. The accommodation has been extensively upgraded and consists of a choice of attractive bedrooms and a delightful first-floor lounge overlooking the sea. Service is provided by the proprietors Mr and Mrs Watling, and the comfortable dining room benefits from Mr Watling's professional cooking standards and home-made breads.

9rm(5↱4hc) ⊁in all bedrooms CTV in 6 bedrooms ®
✗ (ex guide dogs)
Lic 𝍸 CTV 6P nc8yrs
Credit Cards [1] [3]

See advertisement on page 103

BROADWAY Hereford & Worcester Map **04** SP03

SELECTED

GH QQQQ Leasow House WR12 7NA BROADWAY
☎Stanton(038673) 526
(For full entry see Laverton)

See advertisement on p 103

GH QQQ Milestone House Hotel 122 High St WR12 7AJ
☎(0386) 853432
Closed 27 Dec-Jan

A small guesthouse with a popular restaurant. Bedrooms, some with wall timbers and beams, are well furnished and equipped with modern facilities. There is a small cocktail bar and the attractive restaurant is in 2 parts. To the rear are pleasant lawns and a small car park.

4rm(2⇌2↱) (1fb) CTV in all bedrooms ® ✗ (ex guide dogs)
✱ dB&B⇌↱£49.50-£55 WBDifr£252 LDO 9.30pm
Lic 𝍸 8P
Credit Cards [1] [3] £

See advertisement on page 103

SELECTED

GH QQQQ Old Rectory Church St WR12 7PN BROADWAY ☎(0386) 853729
(For full entry see Willersey)

GH QQ Olive Branch Guest House 78 High St WR12 7AJ ☎(0386) 853440
Closed 24-31 Dec
Dating back to the 16th century, this pleasant hotel has its own large car park and a secluded walled garden to the rear. The rooms, situated above some shops, are bright and well furnished, and there is a comfortable old-fashioned lounge for residents.
9rm(7⚑2hc) (2fb) CTV in all bedrooms ® ✗ (ex guide dogs) sB&B£17.50-£19.50 dB&Bfr£35 dB&B⚑£37-£40 WB&B£119-£129 LDO 7.30pm
CTV 9P
Credit Cards [2] £

GH QQQ Small Talk Lodge 32 High St WR12 7DP ☎Evesham(0386) 858953
Situated in the centre of the village, set back off the high street, with a small private car park, this guesthouse offers modern bedrooms in excellent decorative order. The very friendly owner/chef Lin Scrannage, as well as creating some mouthwatering dishes for her guests, makes ice cream, marmalade and yoghurt. A typical menu could consist of twice baked cheese soufflé and corn fed chicken breast stuffed with ginger and chestnuts. There is a very comfortable lounge for guests to relax in after dinner.
8rm(6⇌⚑2hc) (1fb) CTV in all bedrooms ®
✗ (ex guide dogs) ✱ sB&B⇌⚑fr£20 dB&B£36-£42 dB&B⇌⚑£40-£48
Lic CTV 8P
Credit Cards [1] [3] £

GH QQ Whiteacres Station Rd WR12 7DE ☎(0386) 852320
Mar-Oct
Whiteacres is situated a short walk from the popular Cotswold village, and has its own car park. The dining room has an interesting plate collection and opens out onto the rear patio and lawns. It has a modern lounge and a good range of bedrooms, all en suite; 2 rooms with 4-poster beds and one with its own sitting room.
6⇌⚑ ⚟in all bedrooms CTV in all bedrooms ®
✗ (ex guide dogs) dB&B£38-£42 WB&B£120-£132
🍽 6P nc12yrs £

BRODICK

See **ARRAN, ISLE OF**

BROMLEY Greater London London plan **4** F2 (pages 248-249)

GH QQ Glendevon House 80 Southborough Rd, Bickley BR1 2EN (2m E off A22) ☎081-467 2183
This detached period house is in a residential street near Bickley station and Bromley shopping centre. Bedrooms vary in size and are simply decorated and soundly equipped. Downstairs is a comfortable lounge, and evening snacks are available.
11rm(3⇌⚑8hc) (2fb) CTV in 8 bedrooms ® ✱ sB&B£20-£27 sB&B⇌⚑£29.50 dB&B£37-£42 dB&B⇌⚑£42 LDO 9pm
🍽 CTV 7P
Credit Cards [1] [3] £

BROMPTON REGIS Somerset Map **03** SS93

FH Q Mrs G Payne **Lower Holworthy** *(SS978308)* TA22 9NY ☎(03987) 244
Closed Xmas
This 200-acre livestock farm is situated on the outskirts of the village about 5 miles from Dulverton and overlooks Wimbleball lake, in Exmoor National Park. The 3 bedrooms are simple and modestly furnished but enjoy lovely panoramic views. The cosy lounge has a log fire and TV, and proprietors Mr and Mrs Payne are friendly hosts. Traditional farmhouse food is served, with ample portions using local produce; the 4-course dinner and hearty breakfast are popular with the regular returning fishermen enjoying its location near the lake.
3rm(2hc) ® ✗ (ex guide dogs) ✱ sB&B£15 dB&B£30
🍽 CTV 6P 200 acres beef sheep

BROMSGROVE Hereford & Worcester Map **07** SO97

INN Q ***The Forest*** 290 Birmingham Rd B61 0XO ☎(0527) 72063
Closed Xmas
A large, popular inn situated at the junction of the A38 and M42. The modestly appointed bedrooms are clean and equipped with modern facilities. The restaurant and bar offer a good choice of reasonably priced meals, and a function room is also available.
9hc CTV in all bedrooms ® LDO 9.15pm
🍽 70P
Credit Cards [1] [2] [3]

BROMYARD Hereford & Worcester Map **03** SO65

FH QQ Mrs Patsy Morgan **Nether Court** *(SO619494)* Stoke Lacy HR7 4HJ ☎Hereford(0432) 820247
This solid red brick Victorian farmhouse is on the A465 some 10 miles from Hereford. It has its own outdoor tennis court and lake, and is peacefully located overlooking rolling countryside. Rooms are individually decorated with sturdy antique pieces. There is a guests' reading room with TV, and the breakfast room is quite fascinating with its range, antiques and curios – like a mini museum – and guests breakfast around a communal table.
3rm(1⇌2hc) (1fb) CTV in 2 bedrooms TV in 1 bedroom ® ✗ ✱ sB&B£15-£18 sB&B⇌£18-£20 dB&B£28-£30 dB&B⇌£28-£30 LDO 24hr notice
TV P 🎾(grass) ✓ 360 acres mixed

BRONLLYS Powys Map **03** SO13

GH QQ Beacons Edge Country Hotel Pontithel LD3 0RY ☎Brecon(0874) 711182
A family run hotel situated alongside the A438 Brecon to Hereford road. The restaurant offers a good choice of food and is popular locally, and the bedrooms, although on the small side, are comfortably appointed.
7rm(1⇌6⚑) (1fb) CTV in all bedrooms ® ✱ sB&B⇌⚑£27-£30 dB&B⇌⚑£50-£60 WB&B£150-£180 WBDi£195-£230 LDO 9.30pm
Lic 🍽 24P
Credit Cards [1] [3] [5]

BRORA Highland *Sutherlandshire* Map **14** NC90

GH QQ ***Lynwood*** Golf Rd KW9 6QS ☎(0408) 621226
Closed Jan & Feb
Set in its own walled garden overlooking the harbour and close to the golf course, this friendly family-run guesthouse is an ideal base for the touring holidaymaker. Bedrooms, three of which have en suite facilities, are tastefully decorated and comfortably furnished in a modern style. One room, with external access, is suitable for disabled guests. There is a cosy lounge where guests relax and enjoyable home cooking is served at the communal table in a smart dining room.
3hc Annexe 1⚑ (1fb)⚟in all bedrooms CTV in all bedrooms ®
🍽 CTV 4P

BROUGH Cumbria Map **12** NY71

FH QQQ Mrs J M Atkinson **Augill House** *(NY814148)* CA17 4DX ☎(07683) 41305
A well furnished and comfortable farmhouse situated in attractive gardens just off Brough bypass at its eastern end.
→

3rm(1 2hc) in all bedrooms CTV in all bedrooms ® (ex guide dogs) * dB&B £34 WB&B£105 WBDi£165 LDO 4pm
CTV 6P nc12yrs 40 acres mixed £

BUCKFAST Devon Map **03** SX76

GH QQ *Furzeleigh Mill Country Hotel* Dart Bridge TQ11 0JP
Buckfastleigh(0364) 43476

A 16th-century converted mill house located in a pleasant rural spot beside the A38 between the villages of Buckfast and Dartmoor. Now a small, pleasant family-run hotel, it offers compact but bright and comfortable bedrooms, equipped with TV and tea making facilities, many with private bathrooms. Pleasant public rooms include a cosy lounge, and informal residents' bar and an attractive beamed restaurant where both table d'hôte and à la carte menus are served.

15rm(13 2hc) (2fb) CTV in all bedrooms ® LDO 8pm
Lic CTV 32P
Credit Cards 1 2 3

BUCKFASTLEIGH Devon Map **03** SX76

GH QQ *Dartbridge Manor* 20 Dartbridge Rd TQ11 0DZ
(0364) 43575

A friendly guesthouse, situated beside the A38 about halfway between Exeter and Plymouth, and close to Buckfast Abbey. The bedrooms are clean and comfortable, and the public areas of this 400-year-old former manor house ooze character and charm.

10 (2fb)
CTV 30P

BUDE Cornwall & Isles of Scilly Map **02** SS20

GH Q *Beach House Hotel* Widemouth Bay EX23 0AW
Widemouth Bay(0288) 361256
Etr-Sep

Having a unique foreshore position, with its own private access to the beach, this long established hotel has been personally supervised by Roy and Pat Wilkins for over 27 years. There is a very popular residents' bar where lunches are available. The attractive, comfortable dining room with sea views, serves snacks and cream teas together with full Sunday lunches (only in the winter months). Other public areas include a sun and TV lounge plus a games room. The well presented bedrooms have facilities for making tea, and several are furnished particularly with families in mind – 2 rooms have balconies. The friendly and helpful Wilkins family provide a relaxed and informal atmosphere.

13rm(8 5hc) (5fb) ® LDO 7pm
Lic CTV 20P games room childrens play area

GH QQQ *Cliff Hotel* Maer Down, Crooklets Beach EX23 8NG (0288) 353110
Apr-Oct

Occupying a good position 200 yards from Crooklets beach, this hotel provides extensive outdoor and indoor leisure facilities, including an all weather tennis court and indoor swimming pool. Spacious, modern bedrooms offer good family accommodation and all are equipped with TV, radio, telephone and tea/coffee making facilities. The first floor rooms have balconies, while ground floor bedrooms with easy access add a further benefit for less mobile guests. There are extensive public rooms including a spacious bar lounge and an attractive well furnished dining room. Snacks are available throughout the day and an early morning tea service to the bedrooms can be arranged.

15 (12fb) CTV in all bedrooms LDO 6pm
Lic CTV 15P 1 (heated) (hard)solarium indoor spa pool putting

GH QQQ Dorset House Hotel 47 Killerton Rd EX23 8EN
(0288) 352665

Full of character and retaining much of the original Victorian cherry and oak wood panelling, this pleasant guesthouse is quietly situated in its own garden and small car park. The bedrooms are furnished in the older style with ranging degrees of comfort and only one room has full en suite facilities. A cosy lounge blends well with the lively bar and snooker/games room. The dining room provides an elegant setting for evening meals and good quality home-cooked food is served. The proprietors Eric and Lorna Hatch offer a very warm welcome to children.

6rm(1 5hc) (2fb) in all bedrooms ® * sB&B£17-£18 dB&B£34-£36 WB&B£108-£118 WBDi£130-£162 LDO 6.30pm
Lic CTV 6P games room
Credit Cards 1 3 £

GH Q Links View 13 Morwenna Ter EX23 8BU
(0288) 352561
Closed Dec

Partly overlooking the golf links, this popular, terraced guesthouse offers a very cordial atmosphere and is ideal for family holidays. The bedrooms are comfortable and some have en suite shower rooms and colour TV. There is a cosy TV lounge, separate dining room and licensed bar.

7hc (2fb) CTV in all bedrooms ® (ex guide dogs) * sB&B£13-£14 dB&B£26-£28 WB&B£84-£91 WBDi£120-£126 LDO 5pm
Lic CTV 2P 1 £

GH QQ Pencarrol 21 Downs View EX23 8RF
(0288) 352478
Closed Dec rs Jan-Mar & Nov

Long established and very comfortable this house enjoys a corner location overlooking the downs and golf course. The accommodation includes 2 convenient ground floor bedrooms, equipped with TV to avoid climbing the stairs to the cosy first floor lounge, and all the rooms have tea making facilities. Good home-cooked meals, including light suppers, are served in the dining room and special diets can be arranged. Children of all ages are welcome. A relaxed and informal service is provided at this friendly establishment, which is open all year round.

8rm(2 6hc) (1fb) CTV in 2 bedrooms ® (ex guide dogs) sB&B£13.50-£20 dB&B£27-£40 dB&B £31-£44 WB&B£81-£120 WBDi£126-£162 LDO 5pm
CTV 1 £

GH QQ Trelawny Hotel Marine Dr, Widemouth Bay EX23 0AH Widemouth Bay(0288) 361328
Etr-Oct

Occupying an excellent roadside location directly facing the bay, this popular hotel provides comfortable bedrooms with colour TV, hot drink-making equipment, double glazing and pretty fabrics. The bar lounge augments the dining room with an extensive range of bar food, and a separate popular café is open all day for light refreshments. Ample car parking and surfing gear hire are available.

10 (3fb) CTV in all bedrooms ® sB&B £20-£22 dB&B £40-£44 WB&B£140-£154 WBDi£180-£199 LDO 7pm
Lic 12P
Credit Cards 1 3

FH QQ Mrs S Trewin **Lower Northcott** *(SS215087)* Poughill EX23 7EL (0288) 352350
Closed Dec

This is a remote and secluded farmhouse, set in a valley with views of the coastline. It is ideal for children, who are particularly welcome to explore the farm and see the cows being milked. The bright, no-smoking bedrooms are simply furnished and bunk beds can be provided for the children. There is a cosy TV lounge, plus a games room and the dining room has a communal table. The proprietors, Sally and William Trewin, create a very relaxed and informal atmosphere.

5rm(1 3 1hc) (3fb) ® (ex guide dogs) * sB&Bfr£14 dB&B fr£28 WB&Bfr£98 WBDifr£148 LDO 6.30pm
CTV 4P 470 acres arable beef dairy sheep £

BUDLEIGH SALTERTON Devon Map **03** SY08

GH QQQ Copperfields 7 Upper Stoneborough Ln EX9 6SZ
☎(0395) 443430
Etr-Sep
This delightful Victorian house is set in a quiet location just five minutes' walk from the sea and town centre. Whilst retaining its original charm, Copperfields offers modern-day comfort, including bright bedrooms with en suite showers, wc and television.
6rm(4⌐ 2hc) (1fb) CTV in all bedrooms ® ✱ sB&B£17-£17.50 dB&B£32-£33 dB&B⌐£37-£39 WB&B£102-£122 WBDi£154-£178 LDO 5pm
Lic 𝍖 8P nc9yrs

GH QQQ Long Range Hotel Vale's Rd EX9 6HS
☎(0395) 443321
Apr-Oct rs Nov-Mar
Situated in a quiet residential area only 15 minutes' walk from the town centre, this attractive, modern detached building is the home of Sue and Paul Griffin who offer friendly and attentive service. Bedrooms are all soundly maintained and well equipped, and guests may choose to relax in the comfortable sitting room or the separate sun lounge. Menus offer a choice for each of the 3 courses at dinner, which is served at 7pm.
7rm(2⇌4⌐ 1hc) (1fb) CTV in all bedrooms ® ✗ ✱ sB&B£21 sB&B⇌⌐fr£21 dB&B£42 dB&B⇌⌐fr£42 WB&B£140 WBDi£195 LDO 7pm
Lic 𝍖 CTV 8P 2🚗 nc Ⓔ

GH QQ Willowmead 12 Little Knowle EX9 6QS
☎(0395) 443115
Mrs Barker welcomes guests, many of whom return regularly, to her comfortable home tucked away in a quiet residential area. Home-cooked meals, with a choice, are served in the cosy dining room, and there is a comfortable first-floor sitting room. Bedrooms vary in size and the en suite facilities are compact and well installed.
6rm(4⌐ 2hc) ® sB&B⌐£16-£17.50 dB&B⌐£32-£35 WB&B£98-£110 WBDi£138-£145
𝍖 CTV 6P nc5yrs

BUNESSAN

See **MULL, ISLE OF**

BURBAGE Wiltshire Map **04** SU26

SELECTED

GH QQQQ The Old Vicarage SN8 3AG
☎Marlborough(0672) 810495 FAX (0672) 810663
Closed Xmas & New Year
This fine brick and flint-built former Victorian vicarage dates from 1853 and is set in its own pretty gardens beside the church. Each of the 3 bedrooms has been tastefully decorated and furnished in the period of the house, with many thoughtful extra touches. The resident proprietors are charming and extend a warm welcome into their home, where the high standard of tasteful décor and furnishings is evident throughout. The drawing room is elegant and comfortable, stocked with a wealth of reading material and beautiful fresh flower arrangements, together with a log fire; drinks are served here before dinner. Guests dine together around a large antique table in the candlelit dining room; home cooked dinners showing imagination and flair are served, using top quality fresh produce. Breakfast is informal, with a good choice of cooked and continental dishes. Smoking is not permitted.
3⇌ ⊬in all bedrooms CTV in all bedrooms ®
✗ (ex guide dogs) sB&B⇌fr£35 dB&B⇌fr£60 LDO noon
𝍖 CTV 10P nc18yrs
Credit Cards 1 2 3 Ⓔ

BURFORD Oxfordshire Map **04** SP21

SELECTED

GH QQQQ **Andrews Hotel** High St OX18 4QA
☎(099382) 3151
Closed 25 & 26 Dec
Conveniently situated in the high street of this famous Cotswold town, within walking distance of many pubs and restaurants, this attractive stone, Tudor timbered building dates back to the 15th century. Comfortable en suite bedrooms retain their characterful features and are prettily decorated with quality fabrics and furniture. The elegant lounges and breakfast room, together with a flower filled courtyard, set the scene for the splendid afternoon tea, that is very popular with non residents – comprising excellent home-made cakes, tarts and scones with thick Devonshire clotted cream and a choice of teas.
10⇌↱ (1fb)⊁in all bedrooms CTV in all bedrooms ✖ (ex guide dogs) ✱ sB&B⇌↱£40-£70 dB&B⇌↱£60-£80
Lic 𝍖 CTV P̸
Credit Cards 1 3 5

GH QQQ **Elm Farm House** Meadow Ln, Fulbrook OX18 4BW
☎(0993) 823611
Closed 14 Dec-Jan
A fine example of a Cotswold manor-style farmhouse, built in 1897 from mellow stone, with a stonesfield slate roof, gables and mullion windows. The house sits in a well kept garden, situated at the end of a quiet lane in the pretty village of Fulbrook, 1 mile from Burford. The bedrooms have been refurbished by the resident owners and are clean and comfortable, with TV and telephones; several have private bathrooms. One of the lounges has TV and is reserved for non-smokers, and the other has French windows opening on to the terrace and gardens, which include a croquet lawn. There is a small bar, and good home cooking using local produce is served in the dining room.
7rm(4⇌↱3hc) (2fb)⊁in all bedrooms CTV in all bedrooms ® T ✖ sB&B£30.50-£36 sB&B⇌↱£33-£36 dB&B£43-£59 dB&B⇌↱£45-£59 WB&B£206.50-£245 WBDi£252-£308 LDO 10am
Lic 𝍖 CTV 10P nc1-10yrs
Credit Cards 1 2 3

BURNLEY Lancashire Map **07** SD83

GH QQQ **Ormerod Hotel** 121/123 Ormerod Rd BB11 3QW
☎(0282) 23255
This attractive Victorian residence, with colourful flower baskets and shrubs on its forecourt patio, occupies a corner site opposite Queens Park, about 5 minutes' walk from the town centre. The bedrooms feature modern furnishings, fabrics and colour schemes, with comfortable chairs and other practical facilities. There is an elegant guests' lounge with deep armchairs and settees and a very attractive wood panelled dining room where breakfast is served. Unrestricted kerbside parking is available nearby.
9rm(3⇌6↱) (2fb) CTV in all bedrooms ® ✱ sB&B⇌↱£18-£22 dB&B⇌↱£33
𝍖 CTV 8P

BURNOPFIELD Co Durham Map **12** NZ15

GH QQQ ***Burnbrae*** Leazes Villas NE16 6HN ☎((0207) 70432
Surrounded by its own attractive gardens, this handsome stone-built Edwardian house offers most appealing bedrooms all individually decorated and furnished. Both the lounge and dining room are most inviting, and a good sized rear car park is provided.
6rm(2⇌2↱2hc) (1fb)⊁in 12 bedrooms CTV in all bedrooms ® ✖ (ex guide dogs)
𝍖 CTV 5P 1🚗
Credit Cards 1 3

BURNSALL North Yorkshire Map **07** SE06

GH Q ***Manor House*** BD23 6BW ☎(075672) 231
Closed Jan
A family-run private hotel on the B6160 as it approaches the village from the Grassington direction. Bedrooms are on 2 floors and although none have en suite facilities, bathrooms and toilets are adjacent. There is a licensed bar and a comfortable residents' lounge.
7hc (2fb) ✖ LDO 5pm
Lic 𝍖 CTV 7P ⌡ U solarium

BURRELTON Tayside *Perthshire* Map **11** NO23

INN QQQ **Burrelton Park** High St PH13 9NX ☎(08287) 206
This popular roadside hotel is in the centre of the village and has a reputation for hearty catering. Most of the dishes are home-made and food is available from 11am to 10pm in either the bar or restaurant. Bedrooms are modern and comfortable.
6⇌↱ (1fb) CTV in all bedrooms ® sB&B⇌↱fr£30 dB&B⇌↱fr£45 WB&Bfr£252 WBDifr£301 Lunch £6-£12alc High tea £4-£9alc Dinner £9-£15alc LDO 10.30pm
𝍖 CTV 28P
Credit Cards 1 3 £

BURROWBRIDGE Somerset Map **03** ST32

GH Q ***The Old Bakery*** TA7 0RB ☎(082369) 234
Mar-24 Dec
The Old Bakery is situated between Burrow Mump and the River Parrett on the A361, in the centre of the village which is surrounded by typical Somerset Levels scenery. Bedrooms are simple, clean and comfortable; the menu offers an extensive choice, and the welcome is warm and friendly.
6rm(1⇌5hc) (2fb)⊁in all bedrooms ✖ (ex guide dogs) LDO 9.30pm
Lic 𝍖 CTV 8P
Credit Cards 1 3

BURRY PORT Dyfed Map **02** SN40

INN QQQ **The George** Stepney Rd SA16 0BH
☎(0554) 832211
This very popular family-run inn and restaurant lies in the centre of the town and has been carefully modernised in recent years. The 'Friendship' lounge is named after the seaplane flown by Amelia Earhart when she arrived in the estuary after becoming the first woman to fly the Atlantic in 1928. A wide choice of food is available, staff are friendly, and the bedrooms, mostly spacious, are modern and comfortable.
5rm(4⇌↱) (2fb) CTV in all bedrooms ® ✖ (ex guide dogs) ✱ sB&B⇌↱£19.50-£29.50 dB&B⇌↱£34-£40 Lunch £4.94-£16.38alc Dinner £8.90-£19.35alc LDO 10.15pm
𝍖

BURTON BRADSTOCK Dorset Map **03** SY48

GH QQQ ***Common Knapp House*** Coast Rd DT6 4RJ
☎(0308) 897428
Closed Dec-Jan
Just on the fringe of the village along the coast road, this modern well presented property enjoys sea views from many rooms. The fresh, bright bedrooms are spacious and generally well furnished, mostly in a modern, smart style and the majority are en suite with well kept shower facilities. The public rooms are comfortable and there is a cosy bar area, in addition to a spacious dining room where a set dinner is served. It should be noted this is a no-smoking establishment and particularly well suited to guests who require peace and quiet in a relaxed, friendly atmosphere.
12rm(9↱3hc) (1fb)⊁in all bedrooms CTV in 9 bedrooms ® ✖ (ex guide dogs) LDO 4pm
Lic 𝍖 12P nc4yrs

BURTON UPON TRENT Staffordshire Map **08** SK22

GH QQQ Delter Hotel 5 Derby Rd DE14 1RU
☎(0283) 35115
A fully modernised house situated on the edge of town, on the busy Derby road. The bedrooms are bright and clean, and in the small basement bar snacks are served in the evening.
5rm(1⇌4♠) CTV in all bedrooms ® ✗ (ex guide dogs) ✱ sB&B⇌♠£26 dB&B⇌♠£38 LDO 6pm
Lic 🍽 CTV 8P
Credit Cards 1 3 £

GH QQ Edgecote Hotel 179 Ashby Rd DE15 0LB
☎Burton on Trent(0283) 68966
Very much a family-run hotel, the Edgecote is situated on the A50 road, the Leicester side of the town. Bedrooms are bright and modern, and the panelled dining room is an interesting feature.
12rm(3♠9hc) (2fb)⁄in all bedrooms CTV in all bedrooms ® sB&B£18.50-£24.50 sB&B♠£25.50-£28.50 dB&B£34-£36 dB&B♠£37-£45 LDO 8pm
Lic 🍽 CTV 6P 2🚗
Credit Cards 1 2 3 £

BURWASH East Sussex Map **05** TQ62

FH Q Mrs E Sirrell **Woodlands** *(TQ656242)* TN19 7LA
☎(0435) 882794
Etr-Oct
This 16th-century farmhouse is remotely situated but easy to find along its private track with access from the main road. Accommodation is modern but simple, although one room has an attractive 4-poster bed. Breakfast is taken at the communal dining table and guests can share Mr and Mrs Sirrell's lounge.
4rm(1♠1hc) ✗ ✱ sB&Bfr£16.50 dB&Bfr£24 dB&B♠fr£35 LDO am
🍽 CTV 4P 55 acres mixed

BURY ST EDMUNDS Suffolk Map **05** TL86

See also Beyton

GH QQQ The Chantry Hotel 8 Sparhawk St IP33 1RY
☎(0284) 767427 FAX (0284) 760946
rs wknds
The Chantry is a listed Georgian house with a linked Tudor annexe. To find it from the abbey, follow signs for the A45 and Newmarket around the one way system and it is located on the left, with the car park through the wrought iron gateway. The bar and dining room are attractive with good quality blue carpeting and coordinated tub-style chairs. The bedrooms have modern en suite bathrooms, but vary from the plainly decorated and furnished to the super suite, prettily done out in Coloroll with a small split-level lounge area and antique furniture.
14rm(5⇌9♠) Annexe 3⇌♠ (1fb) CTV in all bedrooms ® T sB&B⇌♠£32.50-£39.50 dB&B⇌♠£45-£49.50 WB&Bfr£157.50 LDO 6.45pm
Lic 🍽 16P
Credit Cards 1 3 £

GH QQQ Dunston House Hotel 8 Springfield Rd IP33 3AN
☎(0284) 767981
Situated in a quiet residential area of the town, this well maintained Victorian guesthouse has been sympathetically extended, and is run by the Dakin family. There is a comfortable lounge with an adjacent conservatory and an attractive restaurant. Bedrooms are bright, well equipped and modern.
11rm(6♠5hc) Annexe 6rm(2♠4hc) (5fb) CTV in all bedrooms ® ✗ ✱ sB&B£18-£20 sB&B♠£25-£27.50 dB&B£32-£34 dB&B♠£36-£40 WB&B£126-£192.50 WBDi£196-£262.50 LDO 10pm previous day
Lic 🍽 CTV 12P £

GH QQQ The Olde White Hart Hotel 35 Southgate St IP33 2AZ ☎(0284) 755547
Easily found by following directions from the Abbey Square to Newmarket, or leaving the A45 at the most easterly exit, then about 0.3 mile from the roundabout taking the last turning – the white painted exterior of the Tudor inn stands immediately to the roadside. Just basic services are offered, and the accommodation has character with its timbered walls but also offers good modern en suite facilities. Three spacious rooms have recently been added, these have pretty papered décor with a frieze, and while dressing tables are limited, the dining-style tables are useful for the commercial user. Renovation of the public areas and car park will further enhance the establishment.
10⇌♠ (2fb) CTV in all bedrooms ® T ✗ (ex guide dogs) sB&B⇌♠£39.50-£42.50 dB&B⇌♠£49.50-£55
Lic 🍽 10P 4🚗
Credit Cards 1 2 3 £

BUTLEIGH Somerset Map **03** ST53

FH QQ Mrs Atkinson **Court Lodge** *(ST517339)* BA6 8SA
☎Baltonsborough(0458) 50575
This pretty house nestles in secluded gardens in the village of Butleigh and has commanding views of the surrounding countryside. The rooms have traditional style and charm, and substantial breakfasts are served in the bright dining room.
2rm TV available ✱ dB&Bfr£25
🍽 CTV 4P 110 acres beef £

FH QQQ Mrs J M Gillam **Dower House** *(ST517333)* BA6 8TG ☎Baltonsborough(0458) 50354
Feb-Nov
Attractive 18th-century farmhouse with friendly atmosphere.
3rm(1⇌2hc) (1fb) ® ✗ (ex guide dogs) ✱ sB&B£16 dB&B£30 dB&B⇌£34 LDO 4.30pm
🍽 CTV 6P 80 acres non-working £

BUTTERMERE Cumbria Map 11 NY11

SELECTED

GH QQQQ Pickett Howe Brackenthwaite, Buttermere Valley CA13 9UY ☎Cockermouth(0900) 85444
end Mar-Nov
Nestling peacefully at the end of a long track amongst 15 acres of hillside, wood and pasture, this Cumbrian longhouse, dating back to 1650, is full of character and charm with its slate floors, oak beams and mullioned windows, and has been carefully restored. There are 2 lovely lounges with log fires, and dinner is a special occasion served in the intimate dining room complete with candles and chamber music. The menu is very interesting with everything being home-made. Beautifully combining the old with the new, the bedrooms have old brass bedsteads, direct dial telephones and are very pretty in appearance. David and Dani Edwards offer a warm welcome and care greatly for their guests' comfort and well being, thus a worthy holder of our 'Selected' award.
4⇌↱ ⊬in all bedrooms CTV in all bedrooms ® T ✖ dB&B⇌↱£96-£100 (incl dinner) WB&B£217 WBDi£329 LDO 7.15pm
Lic 🍽 10P nc10yrs ⤶ badminton short tennis court
Credit Cards [1] [3]

BUXTON Derbyshire Map 07 SK07

SELECTED

GH QQQQ *Brookfield On Longhill* Brookfield Hall, Long Hill SK17 6SU ☎(0298) 24151
A Victorian retreat, just over a mile from Buxton, in 10 acres of gardens and woodlands amid beautiful Peak District countryside. Brookfield Hall is a quality small country hotel with period furnishings and antique pieces, but modern facilities and hospitable service. The restaurant is fast becoming popular for its interesting menus and good food and wines.
4⇌↱ CTV in all bedrooms ® LDO 10.30pm
Lic 🍽 CTV 35P U
Credit Cards [1] [2] [3]

GH QQ *Buxton Lodge Private Hotel* 28 London Rd SK17 9NX ☎(0298) 23522
This modern hotel is close to the town centre, on the main road out of Buxton towards Ashbourne. Families are encouraged and a children's room is provided. On summer evenings barbecues are held in the garden.
7rm(3↱4hc) (1fb) CTV in all bedrooms ® LDO 4pm
Lic 🍽 CTV 5P ♧
Credit Cards [3]

GH QQ Buxton View 74 Corbar Rd SK17 6RJ ☎(0298) 79222 FAX (0298) 79222
Mar-Nov
A stone-built house in a quiet residential area on the north side of the town. Aptly named, it has well equipped accommodation, a neat colourful garden and private car parking.
5⇌↱ (1fb)⊬in all bedrooms CTV in all bedrooms ® sB&B⇌↱£21-£26 dB&B⇌↱£30-£36 WB&Bfr£95 WBDifr£165 LDO 9am
🍽 CTV 5P 2🚘

GH Q *Griff* 2 Compton Rd SK17 9DN ☎(0298) 23628
Situated in a residential area convenient for the town centre, this guesthouse provides modest accommodation and car parking facilities.
5hc (1fb) CTV in all bedrooms ® LDO noon
🍽 CTV 5P

GH QQQ The Grosvenor House Hotel 1 Broad Walk SK17 6JE ☎(0298) 72439
This guesthouse is well situated in a quiet yet central location, overlooking the Pavilion Gardens and within 2 minutes' walk of the Opera House and town centre. The friendly proprietors provide cheerful service, with particular attention paid to both housekeeping and maintenance. Bedrooms are tastefully furnished and decorated, with pleasant light pastel colours, matching soft furnishings and Edwardian antique furniture; each room has a good modern en suite bathroom, TV and radio alarm. Smoking is not permitted in bedrooms. There is a nicely appointed lounge and a small dispense bar in the dining room. Dinner is available by arrangement, and there is a small coffee shop attached to the hotel which is a popular meeting place for locals and tourists.
8⇌↱ (2fb)⊬in all bedrooms CTV in all bedrooms ® ✖ (ex guide dogs) sB&B⇌↱fr£35 dB&B⇌↱fr£40 WBDifr£205 LDO am
Lic 🍽 6P
Credit Cards [1] [3]

GH Q Hawthorn Farm Fairfield Rd SK17 7ED ☎(0298) 23230
Apr-Oct
This charming, fully converted farmhouse and its outbuildings are fronted by well kept gardens and lawns, and stands on the outskirts of Buxton.
5hc Annexe 6rm(4↱2hc) (1fb) ® sB&B£17-£18 dB&B£34-£36 dB&B↱£40-£42
🍽 CTV 12P 2🚘 (£)

GH QQQ Lakenham 11 Burlington Rd SK17 9AL ☎(0298) 79209
This guesthouse is located in a quiet residential avenue overlooking the Pavilion Gardens. Public rooms and bedrooms are Victorian in style, tastefully furnished with some lovely antiques, but providing modern facilities in comfortable and very clean surroundings.
6rm(1⇌5↱) (3fb) CTV in all bedrooms ® ✱ sB&B⇌↱£25-£32 dB&B⇌↱£40 WB&B£126
9P
Credit Cards [1] [3] (£)

GH Q The Old Manse Private Hotel 6 Clifton Rd, Silverlands SK17 6QL ☎(0298) 25638
Closed Xmas & New Year
Close to the town centre this stone-built semidetached house provides simple accommodation with a comfortable atmosphere and the advantage of having its own small car park.
8rm(4↱4hc) (2fb) ® sB&B£16-£17 dB&B£32-£34 dB&B↱£37-£39 LDO 5pm
Lic 🍽 CTV 4P nc2yrs (£)

GH Q Roseleigh Private Hotel 19 Broad Walk SK17 6JR ☎(0298) 24904
Closed Xmas-Jan rs Feb & Dec
Roseleigh has an enviable position overlooking the Pavilion Gardens and lake. Small and comfortable, the hotel has vehicular access via Hartington Road as Broad Walk is for pedestrians only.
13rm(9⇌↱4hc) (1fb) CTV in all bedrooms ® ✱ sB&B£20 dB&B⇌↱£40-£42 WB&B£140-£152 WBDi£185-£190 LDO 5pm
Lic CTV 12P

GH QQ Swanleigh 7 Grange Rd SK17 6NH ☎(0298) 24588
Closed Xmas
Centrally situated in a quiet residential area, this semidetached house offers attractive, well-equipped rooms and bright, comfortable public rooms. The friendly proprietors give personal and professional service.
7hc (1fb) TV in all bedrooms ® ✖ (ex guide dogs) ✱ sB&B£16-£18 dB&B£32-£36 WB&B£100-£110
🍽 CTV 6P

GH QQ Templeton 13 Compton Rd SK17 9DN
☎(0298) 25275
rs Nov-Etr
A semi-detached house in a quiet residential area, Templeton provides bright, warm and well-equipped accommodation close to the town centre. Good home-cooked meals are provided and there is ample parking space.
6rm(2⌐4hc) (2fb) CTV in all bedrooms ® ✗ ✱ dB&Bfr£33 dB&B⌐fr£38 WB&B£98-£115 WBDi£148-£165 LDO noon
Lic 🍽 CTV 6P nc14yrs £

GH QQQ Thorn Heyes Private Hotel 137 London Rd SK17 9NW ☎(0298) 23539
Closed last 2 wks Nov & Jan
Set in large attractive gardens, this Victorian house provides guests with almost every convenience they require on holiday. Mrs Green prepares the meals, and her husband has a store of local knowledge, having lived in Buxton all his life.
8⌐ (2fb) CTV in all bedrooms ® ✱ sB&B⌐£20-£28 dB&B⌐fr£40 WB&Bfr£136
Lic 🍽 12P nc14yrs
Credit Cards 1 3

GH QQQ Westminster Hotel 21 Broadwalk SK17 6JT
☎(0298) 23929
Feb-Nov & Xmas
Set in a quiet residential area with views of the lake in the Pavilion Gardens, this friendly hotel provides well-equipped accommodation. Because Broad Walk is closed to traffic the hotel is approached via Hartington Road.
12rm(5⇌7⌐) CTV in all bedrooms ® ✗ (ex guide dogs) sB&B⇌⌐£24-£26 dB&B⇌⌐£40-£42 WB&B£140-£168 WBDi£180-£204 LDO 3pm
Lic 🍽 14P
Credit Cards 1 2 3 £

FH QQQ Mrs M A Mackenzie ***Staden Grange*** *(SK075717)* Staden Ln SK17 9RZ (1.5m SE off A515) ☎(0298) 24965
FAX (0298) 72067
Don't be put off by the approach to this spacious farm, as once through the industrial estate, you will be in a very rural district. Superior accommodation is offered here, as well as a caravan site and self-catering accommodation.
14⇌⌐ (4fb) CTV in all bedrooms ® LDO 4pm
Lic 🍽 CTV 30P ✓ U sauna spa pool 250 acres beef/sheep

BYRNESS Northumberland Map **12** NT70

FH QQ Mrs A Anderson ***Blakehope Burnhaugh*** *(NT783002)* Otterburn NE19 1SW (1.5m along A68 towards Rochester)
☎Otterburn(0830) 20267
A pleasant farmhouse located in a beautiful forest setting. The house is very comfortable and a good standard of hospitality is provided by the resident owners.
3hc (1fb) ® LDO 4pm
🍽 CTV 5P 3🚗 150 acres beef

CADNAM Hampshire Map **04** SU21

FH QQQ Mrs A M Dawe ***Budds*** *(SU310139)* Winsor Rd, Winsor SO4 2HN ☎Southampton(0703) 812381
Apr-Oct
With its very pretty front garden, this thatched farmhouse stands discreetly back from the road. The first floor bedrooms are a good size and very comfortable. Downstairs there is a TV lounge and the attractive dining room enjoys a display of plates and bric-a-brac on the sideboards. The hostess, Mrs Dawe, is a cheerful, bustling lady who extends a warm welcome.
2hc (1fb)⊬in all bedrooms ✗ (ex guide dogs)
🍽 CTV 3P 200 acres beef dairy

Book as early as possible for busy holiday periods.

FH QQQ Mrs A Dawe **Kents** *(SU315139)* Winsor Rd, Winsor SO4 2HN ☎Southampton(0703) 813497
Apr-Oct
A 16th-century thatched farmhouse renovated to provide 2 attractive and comfortable bedrooms for bed and breakfast accommodation. Set in well tended cottage gardens and surrounded by its own pastureland, the farmhouse offers comfortable cottage-style décor, with oak beams and an inglenook fireplace. There is a pleasant lounge where guests are joined by the friendly owners, who can recommend one of the many New Forest pubs or restaurants.
2rm(1⇌1⌐) (1fb)⊬in all bedrooms ✗ ✱ dB&B⇌⌐£30
🍽 CTV 4P nc2yrs 200 acres beef dairy

CAERNARFON Gwynedd Map **06** SH46

See also Llanddeiniolen

GH QQQ Caer Menai 15 Church St LL55 1SW ☎(0286) 2612
Mar-Dec
This small, personally run guesthouse is quietly situated, within a short walk of both the harbour and castle. The modern style accommodation is impeccably maintained, and family rooms are available. In addition to the attractive dining room, there is also a comfortable, cosy lounge.
7rm(3⌐4hc) (2fb)⊬in 3 bedrooms CTV in all bedrooms ®
✗ (ex guide dogs) sB&B£16.50-£17 dB&B£28-£29 dB&B⌐£35-£36
CTV ℙ solarium £

GH QQ Menai View Hotel North Rd LL55 1BD ☎(0286) 4602 due to change to 674602
This small personally run guesthouse is situated on the A487, just north of the town, and overlooks the Menai Straits. Recent improvements include the provision of 2 en suite bathrooms and a ground floor bedroom. Four of the bedrooms enjoy views across to Anglesey, and family rooms are also available; all the rooms have TV. Other facilities include a residential bar.
8rm(2⌐6hc) (5fb) CTV in all bedrooms ® ✱ sB&Bfr£14 dB&Bfr£23 dB&B⌐fr£31 WB&Bfr£75 LDO 7.30pm
Lic 🍽 CTV ℙ

CALDBECK Cumbria Map **11** NY33

SELECTED

GH QQQQ High Greenrigg House CA7 8HD
☎(06998) 430
Mar-Oct
Set in an ideal location for the hiking enthusiast, this delightful 17th- century farmhouse, situated at the foot of Caldbeck Fells, is only half a mile from the Cumbria Way. Full of interest, the house provides 2 lounges – one with stone flag flooring, a superb old fireplace and a piano, the other equipped with a TV. There are lots of books and games available, plus a separate games room with a bar. A set dinner menu is served by Mrs Jacobs in the bright dining room, with its pine tables. Old beams and open stone walls feature in the attractive, en suite bedrooms. This is an ideal place to stay for peace and tranquility.
7⇌⌐ ⊬in all bedrooms sB&B⇌⌐£17-£20 dB&B⇌⌐£34-£40 WB&B£102-£120 LDO 5pm
Lic 🍽 CTV 8P
Credit Cards 1 3

CALLANDER Central *Perthshire* Map **11** NN60

GH QQ Abbotsford Lodge Stirling Rd FK17 8DA
☎(0877) 30066
Set back from the A84 on the eastern approach to the town, this guesthouse is popular with touring holidaymakers. It offers a range of accommodation, from traditionally furnished spacious rooms to more functional, compact, but modern bedrooms.
→

19rm(4⇌3↱12hc) (7fb) ® ✱ sB&Bfr£19.75 sB&B⇌↱fr£23.50 dB&Bfr£30.50 dB&B⇌↱fr£38 WBDi£169-£193 LDO 7pm
Lic Ⅲ CTV 20P

GH QQ Annfield 18 North Church St FK17 8EG
☎(0877) 30204

A detached Victorian house in a quiet side street just 2 minutes' walk from the town centre. It offers comfortable public areas and traditionally styled bedrooms.

8rm(2↱6hc) (2fb) ® ✱ sB&B£14 dB&B£28 dB&B↱£32
Ⅲ CTV 9P nc10yrs

GH QQQ Arden House Bracklinn Rd FK17 8EQ
☎(0877) 30235
Feb-Nov

Situated in its own grounds close to the golf course and overlooking the town, this detached stone-built house was used in the making of Dr Finlay's Casebook; it offers comfortable, traditional accommodation which proves popular with a returning clientèle.

8⇌↱ (3fb)⌿in all bedrooms ® ✱ sB&B⇌↱£18-£22 dB&B⇌↱£32-£36 WBDi£155-£170 LDO 7pm
Ⅲ CTV 12P ⌂ putting green £

SELECTED

GH QQQQ Arran Lodge Leny Rd FK17 8AJ
☎(0877) 30976
Closed 5-13 Dec & 9-17 Jan

Enjoying lovely views over the River Leny, which flows past the bottom of the well tended gardens and where visitors can fish, this 150 year-old bungalow has been refurbished to provide a high standard of accommodation. Particularly well kept and spotlessly clean throughout, this establishment is run with enthusiasm by the resident proprietors and offers comfortably furnished public rooms in addition to well appointed bedrooms, which are furnished in a modern style and have smart private bathrooms. Although not licensed, guests may bring their own wine to enjoy with their meal, which is served in the spacious dining room. Residents can only smoke on the covered verandah situated off the lounge.

3rm(2⇌1↱) ⌿in all bedrooms CTV in all bedrooms ® ✘ sB&B⇌↱£34.20-£54.90 dB&B⇌↱£38-£61 WB&B£157.50-£192.50 WBDi£217-£259 LDO 7.30pm
Ⅲ CTV 5P nc12yrs ♪

GH QQQ Brook Linn Country House Leny Feus FK17 8AU
☎(0877) 30103
Etr-Oct

Standing in an elevated position on the western edge of town, with wonderful views of the surrounding countryside, this detached Victorian house is set in 2 acres of grounds. It offers comfortable bedrooms and attractively decorated and appointed public areas. Smoking is not permitted.

7rm(5↱2hc) (2fb)⌿in all bedrooms CTV in all bedrooms ® ✱ sB&B↱£15-£17 dB&B↱£36-£42 LDO 4pm
Lic Ⅲ 10P

GH Q Greenbank 143 Main St FK17 8BH ☎(0877) 30296

This small roadside bed and breakfast guesthouse is situated in the town centre and offers modest standards of accommodation.

3hc (1fb) CTV in 1 bedroom TV in 1 bedroom ® sB&B£15-£20 dB&B£24-£32 WB&B£75-£100 WBDi£150-£200 LDO 6pm
Lic Ⅲ CTV 5P ⌂

GH QQ Rock Villa 1 Bracklinn Rd FK17 8EH ☎(0877) 30331
mid Mar-mid Nov

Improvements continue to be made to this friendly bed and breakfast guesthouse which stands in its own grounds to the east of the town centre. Bedrooms are not spacious but they are simple and comfortable, and there is a lounge and a bright, airy dining room where home cooked meals are provided.

6rm(3↱3hc) (1fb) CTV in 3 bedrooms ® ✱ sB&B£15-£17 dB&B£28-£30 dB&B↱£34-£36
Ⅲ CTV 7P

CALLINGTON Cornwall & Isles of Scilly Map 02 SX36

INN QQQ Manor House Rilla Mill PL17 7NT
☎Liskeard(0579) 62354

Peacefully situated in the village of Rilla Mill, the accommodation at this 300-year-old inn is contained in 6 chalet style cottages, built during 1991. All are named after Cornish rivers – 2 enjoying a river frontage – and each chalet contains 2 bedrooms, an open-plan lounge/diner and facilities to enable self catering if required. Home-cooked bar meals and an extensive à la carte are available at the inn.

Annexe 6⇌↱ (6fb) CTV in 6 bedrooms ® ✱ sB&B⇌↱fr£20 dB&B⇌↱fr£40 Lunch £7.15-£15alc Dinner £7.15-£15alc LDO 9.30pm
Ⅲ CTV 50P ⌂
Credit Cards 1 3

CAMBRIDGE Cambridgeshire Map 05 TL45

See also Little Gransden

GH QQ Assisi 193 Cherry Hinton Rd CB1 4BX
☎(0223) 211466 & 246648
Closed 15 Dec-5 Jan

Within easy distance of the city centre towards the east, the Assisi has well equipped accommodation, a good standard of cleanliness and a friendly atmosphere. Mainly commercial though usefully sited for leisure visitors to the city.

17⇌↱ (2fb) CTV in all bedrooms ✘ (ex guide dogs) sB&B⇌↱£23-£28 dB&B⇌↱£35-£38 WB&Bfr£175 WBDifr£238 LDO 7.30pm
Ⅲ CTV 15P
Credit Cards 1 2 3 £

GH QQ Avimore 310 Cherry Hinton Rd CB1 4AU
☎(0223) 410956

This small, family-run guesthouse is near the junction of the Cherry Hinton road and the ring road, it is also conveniently situated within half a mile of Addenbrookes Hospital, and three quarters of a mile from the town centre. Bedrooms are brightly decorated and very well equipped. There is a modern dining room with limited lounge facilities adjacent, and evening meals are available with prior notice.

4rm(2↱2hc) (2fb) CTV in all bedrooms ® ✘ (ex guide dogs) ✱ sB&B£17-£25 sB&B↱£25 dB&B£30 dB&B↱£36 LDO 6.30pm
Ⅲ CTV 5P
Credit Cards 1 3

GH QQ Benson House 24 Huntingdon Rd CB3 0HH
☎(0223) 311594

A converted terraced house conveniently situated near New Hall and Fitzwilliam House, on the A604 Huntingdon road, not far from the city centre. Public rooms and bedrooms tend to be compact, but it provides sound, clean accommodation and the bonus of its own rear car park.

5rm(2↱3hc) (3fb) CTV in all bedrooms ® ✱ sB&B£17-£20 dB&B£28-£32 dB&B↱£35-£40
Ⅲ 5P £

GH QQ Bon Accord House 20 St Margarets Square CB1 4AP
☎(0223) 411188 & 246568
Closed Xmas & New Year

This guesthouse is situated in a quiet residential cul-de-sac just off the Cherry Hinton road, and provides comfortable accommodation with good housekeeping throughout. There is a large dining room and a small but comfortable lounge. Smoking is not permitted.

9rm(1↱8hc) (1fb)⌿in all bedrooms CTV in all bedrooms ® ✘ sB&B£19.50-£23 dB&B£33-£36 dB&B↱£38-£42

🅿 12P 2🚗
Credit Cards 1 3 £

GH QQ Brooklands 95 Cherry Hinton Rd CB1 4BS
☎(0223) 242035
A cosy family run guesthouse on the Cherry Hinton road out of the city. Bedrooms are pretty and very well equipped with modern facilities, and there is a comfortable lounge for residents.
6rm(1⇌2⌐3hc) (1fb)⊁in 2 bedrooms CTV in all bedrooms ® ✗ (ex guide dogs) ✱ sB&Bfr£19 sB&B⇌⌐fr£26 dB&Bfr£32 dB&B⇌⌐£38-£42 LDO noon
🅿 CTV
Credit Cards 1 2 3 5 £
See advertisement on page 113

GH QQ Cristina's 47 St. Andrews Rd CB4 1DL
☎(0223) 65855 & 327700
Closed 25-27 Dec
Located to the north of the city centre in a residential street close to the large Philips factory. Helpful proprietors provide bright, clean accommodation with en suite shower facilities. A cosy lounge is available and there is private car parking to the rear of the building.
6rm(5⌐1hc) (2fb) CTV in all bedrooms ® ✗ ✱ sB&B£22-£24 dB&Bfr£34 dB&B⌐£38-£40
🅿 CTV 8P
See advertisement on page 113

GH QQ Fairways 141-143 Cherry Hinton Rd CB1 4BX
☎(0223) 246063 FAX (0223) 212093
Closed 24-26 Dec
A family-owned guesthouse where the proprietors work hard not only to maintain the good standard of existing facilities, but also to improve their range. Latest additions are more en suites, and the attractive refurbishment of the lounge which includes a well stocked bar. Bar meals and a small à la carte selection offering →

popular dishes are served from 6-9pm. This is a sought after place, particularly with those working in the area.
16rm(8🚿8hc) (2fb)🚭in 2 bedrooms CTV in all bedrooms ®
✗ (ex guide dogs) sB&B£20.50-£27 sB&B🚿£25-£27 dB&B£32-£35 dB&B🚿£37-£40 WB&B£136.50-£150 LDO 8pm
Lic 🍴 CTV 20P pool table
Credit Cards [1] [3]

GH QQ De Freville House 166 Chesterton Rd CB4 1DA
☎(0223) 354993 FAX (0223) 321890
This friendly family-run Victorian house is maintained in its original character, the comfortable lounge being a good example. The basement dining room is light and fresh, providing a pleasant environment for breakfast. Some of the bedrooms have modern en suite shower rooms. Smoking is not permitted.
9rm(5🛁🚿4hc) (1fb)🚭in all bedrooms CTV in all bedrooms ®
✗ sB&B£16-£19 sB&B🛁🚿£20-£24 dB&B£32-£34 dB&B🛁🚿£36-£42
🍴 CTV 2🚗 nc6yrs Ⓛ

GH QQ Hamden 89 High St, Cherry Hinton CB1 4LU
☎(0223) 413263
Located in the village of Cherry Hinton about 2 miles east of the city, this 1960s detached and extended house offers very good accommodation and simple bed and breakfast service. The professional Italian proprietors have an especially high standard of cleanliness.
4🚿 🚭in all bedrooms CTV in all bedrooms ®
✗ (ex guide dogs) sB&B🚿£25 dB&B🚿£35-£40
🍴 6P nc12yrs

GH QQ *Hamilton Hotel* 156 Chesterton Rd CB4 1DA
☎(0223) 65664
A popular establishment that succeeds in providing value for money for most customers. Smart public areas offer a range of services, a licensed bar, snacks and bar meals; most bedrooms have en suite facilities though some rooms are rather compact. Professional standards are reflected throughout, and car parking is available at the rear of the building.
10rm(5🚿5hc) (3fb) CTV in all bedrooms ® ✗ LDO noon
Lic 🍴 10P nc4yrs
Credit Cards [3]

GH QQQ Helen Hotel 167-169 Hills Rd CB2 2RJ
☎(0223) 246465 FAX (0223) 214406
Closed 15 Dec-5 Jan
About a mile east from the city centre (Parkers Piece, follow signs to A604 Colchester), on a busy, tree-lined main road. Helen and Gino Agodino are a friendly Italian couple who strive to maintain a good reliable standard. The accommodation is very well equipped and represents good value for the city.
22🛁🚿 Annexe 6rm(5🚿1hc) (4fb) CTV in all bedrooms ® **T**
✱ sB&B£35 sB&B🛁🚿£43-£44 dB&B£50-£52 dB&B🛁🚿£55 WB&Bfr£240 WBDifr£310 LDO 7.30pm
Lic 🍴 CTV 20P
Credit Cards [1] [3] Ⓛ

See advertisement on page 115

GH QQQ Lensfield Hotel 53 Lensfield Rd CB2 1EN
☎(0223) 355017 Telex no 818183 FAX (0223) 312022
Closed 2wks Xmas
A friendly, family-run hotel situated on the ring road, a few minutes' walk from the city centre. Improved accommodation now provides more bedrooms and a newly styled restaurant. The bedrooms vary in size, some rooms being compact, but they are all very well equipped. The new restaurant on the lower ground floor is popular with both guests and local residents, and offers a good range of English, French and Greek dishes. There is a large car park to the rear.
36rm(2🛁18🚿16hc) (4fb) CTV in all bedrooms ® **T** ✗ ✱
sB&Bfr£35 sB&B🛁🚿fr£45 dB&B🛁🚿£58-£68 WB&B£245-£315 WBDi£297.50-£367.50 LDO 8.45pm
Lic 🍴 CTV 5P 2🚗
Credit Cards [1] [2] [3] [5]

DE FREVILLE HOUSE

AA

QQ

Family run Victorian house, maintained to retain its original character. Convenient for visiting the colleges, City Centre and river. All rooms have central heating, colour T.V., tea/coffee making facilities. Some en suite. English breakfast. Guests' Lounge. Attractive garden. Parking.

NO SMOKING

Mrs. A. Hunter
166 Chesterton Road
Cambridge CB4 1DA
Tel. (0223) 354993

Cristinas Guest House

47 St Andrews Road, Cambridge CB4 1DL
Telephone: (0223) 65855 & 327700

Guests are assured of a warm welcome at Cristinas Guest House, quietly located in the beautiful city of Cambridge, only 15 minutes walk from the City Centre and colleges. There are many places of cultural and historic interest to visit, as well as shops and leisure facilities. All rooms have colour TV and tea/coffee making facilities; some rooms are available with private shower and toilet. The house is centrally heated and there is a comfortable TV lounge. Private car park. Further details on application.

FAIRWAYS GUEST HOUSE

This charming Victorian House, offers you a warm welcome. Full central heating, colour TV in all bedrooms, tea/coffee making facilities.
Most rooms en suite.
Licensed bar & restaurant, also open to non residents.
Large car park. Near to Golf Course and Addenbrooke Hospital.

Proprietors:
Mr & Mrs M R Slatter

QQ

141-143 Cherryhinton Road
Cambridge CB1 4BX
Tel: (0223) 246063 Fax: (0223) 212093

Brooklands Guest House

95 Cherry Hinton Road
Cambridge CB1 4BS
Telephone: (0223) 242035

Bed & breakfast with evening meal by arrangement. Most rooms are en suite. All rooms have satellite TV and telephones for incoming calls. Four poster bed with jacuzzi bath available.

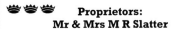

GH QQQ ***Sorrento Hotel*** 196 Cherry Hinton Rd CB1 4AN ☎(0223) 243533 FAX (0223) 213463

A friendly family-run guesthouse with well equipped accommodation, mostly with en suite facilities, and a good standard of cleanliness is maintained. Public areas are spacious and include a well stocked bar and a no-smoking lounge. A good car park is provided for guests.

24rm(5⇌19↱) (5fb) CTV in all bedrooms ® LDO 8.30pm
Lic ꟽ CTV 25P petanque terraine
Credit Cards 1 2 3 5

GH QQQ **Suffolk House Private Hotel** 69 Milton Rd CB4 1XA ☎(0223) 352016

This private hotel is located on the A1309 north of the city centre, within a 15 minute walk. The bedrooms are fresh, attractive and tastefully furnished, all having modern en suite bathrooms, the majority with showers; all the rooms are equipped with TV, radios and tea trays. Proprietors Mr and Mrs Cuthbert work hard to provide high standards of housekeeping and maintenance.

10rm(1⇌9↱) (4fb) CTV in all bedrooms ® ✖ ✱ sB&B⇌↱£35-£50 dB&B⇌↱£45-£65
Lic ꟽ CTV 11P nc4yrs
Credit Cards 1 3 £

CAMPBELTOWN Strathclyde *Argyllshire* Map **10** NR72

GH QQQ **Ballegreggan House** Ballegreggan Rd PA28 6NN ☎(0586) 52062

Considerable renovations and improvements have been carried out at this impressive mansion house, which is set on a hill just outside the town and offers a fine outlook over Campbeltown Loch. The house has been tastefully decorated throughout and is comfortably furnished. At peak periods it may be necessary to share a dining table; it should be noted that smoking is not encouraged in the bedrooms.

6rm(4↱2hc) (1fb)⊁in all bedrooms ® sB&B£18-£22 sB&B↱£22-£26 dB&B£36 dB&B↱£44 WB&B£120-£150 WBDi£190-£220 LDO 6pm
ꟽ CTV 8P ✔

GH Q **Westbank** Dell Rd PA28 6JG ☎(0586) 553660

This neat guesthouse lies in a quiet residential side street off the town centre. Run by an enthusiastic couple who are in the process of refurbishing the house, it is suitable for both tourists and commercial visitors.

7hc ® ✖ (ex guide dogs) sB&B£18 dB&B£32
Lic ꟽ CTV nc3yrs

CANNINGTON Somerset Map **03** ST23

FH QQQ Mrs H Roe ***Swang*** *(ST232388)* TA5 2NJ (2m SW on A39) ☎Spaxton(0278) 67765 FAX (0278) 67747

A garden containing peacocks, pigs and an outdoor swimming pool provides an interesting setting for this attractive old farmhouse, which stands back from the A39. All the bedrooms are on the first floor – 3 are quite spacious, fitted with antique furniture and have modern en suite facilities, while the fourth is more compact. There is a delightful, comfortable lounge with deep sofas and an open fire. An extensive and most appetizing breakfast menu is served around a large communal table.

4⇌↱ (1fb)⊁in 2 bedrooms CTV in all bedrooms ®
ꟽ P ⩯(heated) ✔ solarium 700 acres mixed
See advertisement under BRIDGWATER

CANTERBURY Kent Map **05** TR15

GH Q **Castle Court** 8 Castle St CT1 2QF ☎(0227) 463441

Conveniently located close to the main shopping precinct, a park and all local tourist attractions, this well maintained family guesthouse retains much of its original character and charm, despite rather small bedrooms and a basement breakfast room. Service is friendly and well managed, supervised by the proprietors Mr and Mrs Noble. There is a public car park nearby.

12hc (1fb) sB&B£16-£20 dB&B£30-£34
ꟽ CTV 2P
Credit Cards 1 3 £

GH QQ **Cathedral Gate Hotel** 36 Burgate CT1 2HA ☎(0227) 464381 FAX (0227) 462800

Built in 1438 and overlooking the cathedral's south porch, this historic hostelry has sloping floors, oak beams and winding corridors. Some bedrooms which are reached via a roof top walkway overlook chimney pots and hung-tile roofs. The accommodation offers a choice of standard, basic or better equipped bedrooms overlooking the pedestrian or cathedral precincts. Breakfast is served in the bedrooms or, if preferred, the small dining room. Car access is allowed in order to drop off luggage: the reception is located on the first floor above the shops and restaurant, where a map is provided with directions for the hotel's car park.

12rm(2⇌8hc) (4fb) CTV in all bedrooms ® **T** sB&B£27.50-£28.50 sB&B⇌↱£38.50-£48.50 dB&B£51.50-£53 dB&B⇌↱£59-£75 LDO 9pm
Lic ꟽ 12P (£2 per night)
Credit Cards 1 2 3 5 £

GH QQQ **Ebury Hotel** New Dover Rd CT1 3DX ☎(0227) 768433 FAX (0227) 459187
Closed 25 Dec-14 Jan

The house, which stands in 2 acres of beautifully kept grounds, dates from about 1850 and many of its original features have been restored. Bedrooms are bright, spacious and well equipped; there are well furnished public rooms including an à la carte restaurant, and some very good leisure facilities. Excellent car parking and 2 self-catering units are available.

15⇌↱ (2fb) CTV in all bedrooms ® **T** sB&B⇌↱£41-£46 dB&B⇌↱£59.50-£62 WBDi£225-£250 LDO 8.30pm

→

The Lensfield Hotel

53 Lensfield Road
Cambridge CR2 1EN
Telephone (0223) 355017
Fax (0223) 312022

The Lensfield is a residentially run FAMILY HOTEL centrally situated, within walking distance of the nearby Colleges, river and shops.

All of our bedrooms have bathroom en-suite and are all centrally heated and have Television, Radio and private telephone.

You can sample the superb cuisine of our TABLE d'HOTE and A LA CARTE Restaurant or, should one prefer a mere drink, enjoy the surroundings of our cosy bar.

The main interest at the LENSFIELD is to provide to all guests personal service in a very friendly and relaxing atmosphere.

WE LOOK FORWARD TO WELCOMING YOU!

Helen Hotel

167/169 Hills Road, Cambridge CB2 2RJ
Tel. (0223) 246465 Fax: (0223) 214406

Gino and Helen Agodino welcome you to their family run hotel, situated one mile from city centre. Enjoy a high standard of Italian food, friendly and personal service. All rooms with en suite facilities, telephone, colour TV, tea/coffee facilities and hair dryer. Ample car park. Charming Italian garden.

THE SUFFOLK HOUSE

private hotel

15 minutes' walk from the city centre and Colleges. All rooms are en suite and have colour TV and tea and coffee making facilities. Pleasant secluded garden. Hotel car park. Family run.

69 Milton Road, Cambridge CB4 1XA
Tel: (0223) 352016

VISA

Lic 🍽 CTV 20P 1🚗 (£2) ⛆(heated)
Credit Cards 1 2 3 £

GH QQQ Ersham Lodge 12 New Dover Rd CT1 3AP
☎(0227) 463174 FAX (0227) 455482
Apr-Dec
An attractive ivy-clad, Tudor beamed hotel conveniently located, with good forecourt parking. Very well equipped bedrooms are individually furnished with antiques, and offer good facilities, complemented by particularly good standards of housekeeping. The breakfast room is a no-smoking area, and there is a sitting area with a bar. Service from the French proprietors is personal and helpful.
14rm(2⇨11🚿1hc) (1fb) CTV in all bedrooms ® T
✗ (ex guide dogs) sB&B⇨🚿£43-£52 dB&B⇨🚿£54-£61
Lic 🍽 11P 1🚗 (£3)
Credit Cards 1 2 3 £

GH QQ Highfield Hotel Summer Hill, Harbledown CT2 8NH
☎(0227) 462772
Feb-Nov
Set back off the main London Road in an acre of grounds, this late Victorian house has been home to the Smallwood family for many years. A choice of bedrooms – the old and the new – are furnished in an adequate modern style while retaining some original features and fireplaces. There is a lovely traditional lounge with a writing desk and fresh flowers, and a full breakfast service is provided by the family. Highfield attracts many regular guests from all over the world.
8rm(3🚿5hc) ® ✗ sB&B£27-£30 dB&B£38-£43 dB&B🚿£50-£54
Lic 🍽 12P nc5yrs
Credit Cards 1 3

GH QQQ Magnolia House 36 St Dunstan's Ter CT2 8AX
☎(0227) 765121
This attractive late Georgian detached house is set in a quiet conservation area close to the city centre and cathedral. Each of the 6 bedrooms is individually decorated with pretty colour schemes and coordinating fabrics, and they all have en suite facilities. The dining room looks onto the secluded walled garden and there is also a sitting room where smoking is permitted. Owners Ann and John Davies have refurbished and upgraded their home over the last few years, and the accommodation is comfortable and well maintained.
6⇨🚿 ⊬in all bedrooms CTV in all bedrooms ® ✗
sB&B⇨🚿£30-£35 dB&B⇨🚿£45-£50
🍽 4P
Credit Cards 1 2 3

SELECTED

GH QQQQ The Old Rectory Ashford Rd, Chartham CT4 7HS ☎(0227) 730075
Feb-Oct
Originally a farmhouse and later used by the Church as a rectory, this delightful copy of a Georgian house was built at the turn of the century. Set in almost 2 acres of beautiful lawned gardens, the house has excellent rural views. Bedrooms vary in size, each individually furnished and decorated, with fresh flowers and several extra touches. The daily set menu regularly features fresh fish, with home-made recipes plainly cooked by the proprietor Mrs Creasy. The guesthouse is unlicensed, but guests may bring their own wine, and there is a 1st floor sitting area with TV. Smoking is not permitted.
3rm(2⇨🚿) ⊬in all bedrooms CTV in 1 bedroom
✗ (ex guide dogs) ✱ sB&B£20-£25 sB&B⇨🚿£20-£25 dB&B£34-£40 dB&B⇨🚿£34-£40 WB&B£119-£140 WBDi£180-£200 LDO 4pm
🍽 CTV 5P nc12yrs
Credit Cards 1 3

GH QQ Pointers Hotel 1 London Rd CT2 8LR
☎(0227) 456846 FAX (0227) 831131
Closed Xmas & New Year
Conveniently located close to the city centre, this elegant Georgian house has been tastefully modernised, and offers a choice of well equipped bedrooms all with TV, radio and tea trays. There is a well stocked bar and an attractively furnished comfortable lobby lounge. Dinner is usually available every night in the rear dining room, and light refreshments are provided throughout the day. 24-hour reception includes a night porter, and car parking is also available.
14rm(10⇨🚿4hc) (2fb) CTV in all bedrooms ® T sB&B£30-£33 sB&B⇨🚿£35-£38 dB&B£42-£45 dB&B⇨🚿£46-£54 WB&Bfr£147 WBDifr£180 LDO 8.15pm
Lic 🍽 10P
Credit Cards 1 2 3 5 £

SELECTED

GH QQQQ Thanington Hotel 140 Wincheap CT1 3RY
☎(0227) 453227
Originally a farmhouse, this Georgian house was built around 1800, and is now linked by a conservatory to the bedroom accommodation. It is set in a very convenient location with its own courtyard car park, and facilities now include a games room with a three-quarter size billiard table and darts, and a new indoor swimming pool in the walled garden. The bedrooms are mainly furnished with pine and have been redecorated. Service is personally supervised by the very friendly and helpful David and Jill Jenkins, who also provide a generous choice of breakfasts.
10⇨ (2fb) CTV in all bedrooms ® T ✱ sB&B⇨£38-£45 dB&B⇨£55-£62
Lic 🍽 CTV 8P 2🚗 ⛆(heated) games room
Credit Cards 1 2 3 £

SELECTED

GH QQQQ Thruxted Oast Mystole, Chartham CT4 7BX
☎(0227) 730080
Closed Xmas
Peacefully set in an area surrounded by hop gardens and orchards, only 4 miles from the city, this original 5-bay square kilned oast and barn were built in 1791 and have recently been converted to provide luxurious accommodation, within the family home of the Derouets. The 3 spacious bedrooms feature rafters and stripped pine furniture, together with private bathrooms and a host of extra personal touches. The stunning, very comfortable lounge forms a major part of the house, together with an open plan farmhouse style kitchen/breakfast room, where home-grown produce is served at the communal table. The accommodation also houses a picture-framing workshop, art gallery and gift shop. There is an attractive garden with a terrace and croquet, and ample car parking is provided, along with a very useful location map.
3🚿 ⊬in all bedrooms CTV in all bedrooms ® T
✗ (ex guide dogs) dB&B🚿£60-£70
🍽 8P nc8yrs croquet lawn
Credit Cards 1 2 3 5

INN QQQ *The Pilgrims Hotel* 18 The Friars CT1 2AS
☎(0227) 464531
15⇨🚿 (1fb) CTV in 15 bedrooms ® LDO 11pm
🍽
Credit Cards 1 2 3 5

See advertisement on page 119

THANINGTON HOTEL ♛♛
140 Wincheap, HIGHLY COMMENDED
Canterbury CT1 3RY AA Selected
Tel: 0227 453227

Lovely Georgian (1810) house with walled garden and courtyard car parking. 5 minutes stroll to City Centre and restaurants, 12 minutes to Cathedral.

All bedrooms are en-suite with modern day conveniences. Elegant dining room and lounges. New Snooker room and Indoor Swimming Pool.

Off-season discounted prices and colour brochure on request.

THE OLD RECTORY

Ashford Road, Chartham
Canterbury, Kent CT4 7HS
Telephone: 0227 730075

This elegant family home, formerly a rectory and set in 2 acres, is furnished with antiques. The beautifully decorated rooms have private facilities. Freshly made tea/coffee provided. Within easy reach of Channel ports for Continental travel or day trips to France. Canterbury is only 2½ miles or 4 minutes by train. Safe parking within grounds.
From £18 pp including full English breakfast.

NO SMOKING

POINTERS HOTEL

1 London Road, Canterbury
Tel. 0227-456846 Fax: 0227 831131

Situated only a few minutes' walk from the City Centre and Cathedral and close to the University.

Pointers is a family-run Georgian hotel offering home-produced English meals.

All bedrooms have either bath or shower and each is equipped with colour television, radio, direct-dial telephone and tea and coffee making facilities.

Private car park. AA QQ

36 St Dunstan's Terrace, Canterbury,
Kent CT2 8AX
Telephone: (0227) 765121 ♛♛
HIGHLY COMMENDED

This friendly, family run Georgian house, set in a quiet street, just a few minutes walk from the Westgate Towers and the City centre, with its magnificent Cathedral is ideally situated for the University and touring the Kentish coast and countryside. Enjoy our en suite facilities, varied and delicious breakfasts and relax in the beautiful walled garden. Car parking.

CARDIFF South Glamorgan Map **03** ST17

GH Q Albany 191-193 Albany Rd, Roath CF2 3NU
☎(0222) 494121
Closed Xmas wk
A bright, friendly little guesthouse in a convenient city location, with cosy well equipped bedrooms and a small residents' lounge. The house is personally run by Mrs McMahon and offers good value-for-money accommodation.
12rm(3↱9hc) (3fb) CTV in 3 bedrooms Ⓡ ✗ (ex guide dogs) sB&B£17 dB&B£27 dB&B↱£37
🎹 CTV P

GH Q *Balkan Hotel* 144 Newport Rd CF2 1DJ
☎(0222) 463673
This modestly furnished guesthouse with established owners is in a convenient city location, close to the local Broadway Centre.
14rm(5↱9hc) (3fb) CTV in 13 bedrooms Ⓡ ✗ LDO 7pm
🎹 CTV 18P
Credit Cards [1] [2]

GH QQQ Clare Court Hotel 46/48 Clare Rd CF1 7QP
☎(0222) 344839 FAX (0222) 665856
Closed Xmas Day & Boxing Day
This family-run hotel is situated within walking distance of the city centre. The bedrooms are spacious and well equipped, and there is a comfortable lounge and small bar.
9⇨↱ (2fb) CTV in all bedrooms Ⓡ T ✗ (ex guide dogs) ✱ sB&B⇨↱£26-£28 dB&B⇨↱£36-£40 LDO 7.30pm
Lic 🎹 CTV P̸
Credit Cards [1] [2] [3]

GH QQ Courtfield Hotel 101 Cathedral Rd CF1 9PH
☎(0222) 227701 & 345098
Closed 25-26 Dec & 31 Dec
Near Sophia Gardens and a short walk from the castle and city centre, this hotel offers well equipped bedrooms with modern facilities. There is a comfortable lounge and a cosy bar. A good choice of food is available.
16rm(4↱12hc) (3fb) CTV in all bedrooms Ⓡ ✱ sB&Bfr£22 sB&B↱fr£30 dB&Bfr£32 dB&B↱fr£45 LDO 8.30pm
Lic 🎹 CTV
Credit Cards [1] [2] [3] [5]

GH QQ Domus 201 Newport Rd CF2 1AJ ☎(0222) 495785
20 Jan-20 Dec
This friendly little guesthouse is run by enthusiastic owners who are in the process of upgrading the accommodation. Public rooms are comfortable and the bedrooms are soundly furnished. The Domus is in a convenient city centre location and car parking facilities are provided at the rear.
10rm(2↱8hc) (2fb) CTV in all bedrooms Ⓡ T ✗ (ex guide dogs) sB&B£18-£23 dB&B£35 dB&B↱£40 LDO noon
Lic 🎹 CTV 10P nc2yrs

GH QQQ Ferrier's (Alva) Hotel 130/132 Cathedral Rd CF1 9LQ ☎(0222) 383413
Closed 2wks Xmas & New Year
Only a few minutes' walk from the city centre and close to Sophia Gardens, this friendly, family-owned and run hotel offers bright, clean bedrooms that are equipped to satisfy both tourists and business visitors. A spacious, comfortable lounge and congenial bar are provided for guests, together with useful car parking at the rear. The Ferrier's is a well established, private residence and is nicely maintained throughout.
26rm(6⇨↱20hc) (4fb) CTV in all bedrooms Ⓡ T sB&B£24 sB&B⇨↱£35 dB&B£38-£42 dB&B⇨↱£48 LDO 7.45pm
Lic 🎹 CTV 10P
Credit Cards [1] [2] [3] [5]

GH QQ Tane's Hotel 148 Newport Rd CF2 1DJ
☎(0222) 491755 & 493898
Situated on the busy Newport Road but within walking distance of the city centre, this family-run guesthouse provides simple yet sound, clean accommodation. All the modest bedrooms are equipped with a colour TV, although no en suite is provided. There is a cosy little residents' lounge and a pleasant breakfast room. Unrestricted street parking is close at hand.
9hc (1fb) CTV in all bedrooms Ⓡ ✗ ✱ sB&Bfr£17 dB&Bfr£28 WB&Bfr£119 WBDifr£161 LDO 7pm
Lic 🎹 CTV 10P nc6yrs
Credit Cards [2] [3]

CARDIGAN Dyfed Map **02** SN14

GH QQQ Brynhyfryd Gwbert Rd SA43 1AE
☎(0239) 612861
Just a short walk from the town centre and opposite the tennis courts and bowling green, this semidetached guesthouse has been run by Nesta and Ieuan Davies for many years, and is always well maintained and spotlessly clean. The 7 bedrooms have a floral décor and include a TV and a tea tray, and 2 have modern en suite shower rooms. There is a comfortable cottage-style lounge, and meals are served in the pretty dining room.
7rm(2↱5hc) (1fb) CTV in all bedrooms Ⓡ ✗ (ex guide dogs) sB&B£14-£14.50 sB&B↱£16-£16.50 dB&B£28-£29 dB&B↱£32-£33 WBDi£140-£154 LDO 7.30pm
🎹 CTV Ⓔ

GH QQQ Skippers Tresaith Beach SA43 2JL
☎Aberporth(0239) 810113
Etr-Sep
Situated on the beautiful sandy beach of a secluded cove, this family-run guesthouse has an attractive timbered restaurant and small bar. There are 3 apartments, each with its own lounge and bathroom, available on a self- catering or bed and breakfast basis.
3⇨↱ (3fb) CTV in all bedrooms Ⓡ ✱ sB&B⇨↱£31.95 dB&B⇨↱£63.90 LDO 9pm
Lic CTV 16P
Credit Cards [1] [2] [3] Ⓔ

CARDROSS Strathclyde *Dunbartonshire* Map **10** NS37

SELECTED

GH QQQQ Kirkton House Darleith Rd G82 5EZ (0.5m N of village) ☎(0389) 841951 FAX (0389) 841868
Closed 18 Dec-10 Jan
Overlooking the River Clyde from its quiet rural setting above the village, this sympathetically converted 18th-century farmhouse is a popular base for both business visitors and tourists. Owners Stewart and Gillian MacDonald are unstinting in their efforts to ensure their guests are well cared for, and they have created a warm, welcoming atmosphere. Bedrooms are thoughtfully equipped and very individual in style, and public areas are refreshingly unpretentious and sensibly furnished.
6⇨↱ (4fb) CTV in all bedrooms Ⓡ T ✱ sB&B⇨↱£29.50-£34.50 dB&B⇨↱£49-£52 WB&B£154.35-£163.80 WBDi£259.35-£268.80 LDO 7.30pm
Lic 🎹 CTV 12P U
Credit Cards [1] [3]
See advertisement under HELENSBURGH

GH QQ Westlade Darleith Rd G82 5PG ☎(0389) 841007
Situated in a quiet residential area just off the A814, this small, friendly, family-run guesthouse offers good value bed and breakfast accommodation. The 2 bedrooms have modern appointments, with private shower units. There is also a comfortable lounge/breakfast room, where guests dine at the communal table.
2hc (1fb) Ⓡ ✗ ✱ dB&B£28 WBDi£88
🎹 CTV 3P

ST-Y-NYLL HOUSE

Situated with lovely views of the Vale of Glamorgan, 7 miles Cardiff, 4 miles M4 - close to Welsh Folk Museum. Relax in lovely country house own extensive grounds, plenty of parking. Licensed. Central heating, colour TV, tea/coffee all rooms. Personal supervision resident owners Paul and Monica Renwick. Welsh Tourist Board approved.

St Brides-Super-Ely, South Glamorgan CF5 6EZ
Tel: (0446) 760209

The Albany Hotel

M4 junction 33

14 Victoria Road, Penarth, S Glamorgan CF6 2EF.
Tel: Cardiff (0222) 701242 Telefax: (0222) 701598

Ideally situated in quiet Victorian tree lined surroundings in this attractive coastal resort 3 miles from Cardiff. Only minutes walk away from station, shopping centre, excellent restaurants, breathtaking cliff walks, elegant promenade and pier.

Home of the 'Waverley'. Reasonable rates from £20.00pp. Comfortable rooms, many en suite. All with colour TV, satellite, video channel, room phone, clock radio and tea/coffee facilities. Licensed, extensive menu, full fire certificate and parking. You will find us friendly, convenient, comfortable as well as inexpensive.

FERRIER'S HOTEL

132 Cathedral Road, Cardiff, CF1 9LQ
Tel: (0222) 383413

Ferrier's Hotel is a family-managed hotel set in a Victorian Conservation area and yet within walking distance of the city centre. 26 bedrooms, including 7 on the ground floor. All rooms tastefully furnished and have hot and cold water, central heating, radio, colour TV, tea & coffee making facilities and direct dial telephone. Many rooms with private shower and many en suite. Reasonably priced à la carte menu available Monday to Thursday. Light refreshments are available in the Cane Lounge and well stocked Bar. Residents' Lounge with colour TV. Full fire certificate. Car Park, locked at night.

The Pilgrims Hotel

Canterbury's new quaint hotel. Completely refurbished whilst retaining historical Roman wall. Very tastefully decorated throughout. 4 poster bed. Situated opposite the Marlowe Theatre and five minutes' walk from the Cathedral. The Restaurant/Bar gives a warm welcome to all Pilgrims.

An atmosphere of care awaits you.

Quoted "luxury elegance charm, history and location blend to make the Pilgrims Hotel, Canterbury one of Kent's finest" seeing is believing – give us a call for more information. Parking available.

THE PILGRIMS HOTEL

18 THE FRIARS : CANTERBURY : CT1 2AS

Telephone: 0227 464531
Fax: 0227 762514

AA QQQ

CAREW Dyfed Map **02** SN00

SELECTED

GH QQQQ ***Old Stable Cottage*** 3 Picton Ter SA70 8SL
☎(0646) 651889
Feb-20 Dec
Run by the friendly Lionel Fielder and his wife Joyce, this delightful cottage was originally a stable and cart house for the nearby castle. The trap shed is now the entrance porch which leads to the spacious sitting room. Comfortably furnished with deep sofas and armchairs, this room features an inglenook fireplace and bread oven, and a wrought-iron spiral staircase which leads to the bedrooms. These are furnished in a country style with stripped pine, and feature the original timbers. All have good en suite facilities, 2 of which have attractive brass fittings. Breakfasts and evening meals by arrangement are served in the conservatory, and guests can relax in the games room where there is a mini snooker table.
3rm(2⇌1♠) (1fb)⚟in all bedrooms CTV in all bedrooms ® ✗ (ex guide dogs) LDO 7pm
🝘 2P nc5yrs

CARLISLE Cumbria Map **11** NY45

See also Catlowdy

GH QQ Angus Hotel 14 Scotland Rd CA3 9DG
☎(0228) 23546
rs 24-31Dec
A pleasant and well run guesthouse offering simple, well maintained accommodation, situated on the A7, north of the city centre. Bedrooms have good facilities and home cooking is provided to residents, making this a suitable choice for both tourists and commercial visitors. There is ample free parking nearby.
12rm(7♠5hc) (4fb)⚟in 6 bedrooms CTV in 1 bedroom ® ✱ sB&B£20 sB&B♠£28 dB&B£31 dB&B♠£42 LDO 8.45pm
Lic 🝘 CTV 8🚗
Credit Cards [1] [3]

GH QQ Crossroads House Brisco CA4 0QZ ☎(0228) 28994
Closed Xmas & New Year
A modern, detached house set in open countryside on a crossroads three quarters of a mile from Junction 42 of the M6 – follow signs for Dalston from the roundabout. Formerly used as an office in the 19th century for estate workers, it is now fully modernised, and is nicely decorated throughout. There is a comfortable lounge and sun lounge, and a 100 foot deep Roman well is a feature of the hallway, under the staircase. Smoking is not permitted in the bedrooms and breakfast room.
5hc (1fb)⚟in all bedrooms ✱ sB&Bfr£17 dB&Bfr£32
LDO 10am
Lic 🝘 CTV 6P Ⓕ

GH QQ East View 110 Warwick Rd CA1 1JU
☎(0228) 22112
A family owned and run friendly guesthouse situated on the main road leading into the city centre from Junction 43 of the M6, and only a short walk from the town centre. All bedrooms have private bathrooms, and the house is well maintained and offers good value.
9♠ (3fb) CTV in all bedrooms ® sB&B♠£15-£20 dB&B♠£25-£32 WB&B£100-£140
🝘 4P Ⓕ

GH QQ Kenilworth Hotel 34 Lazonby Ter CA1 2PZ
☎(0228) 26179
A terraced Victorian house offering good comforts and good value for money. Family owned and run, it is spotlessly clean and very well maintained. It is situated on the A6, three quarters of a mile south of the city centre, 2 miles from Junction 42 of the M6.
6hc (2fb) CTV in all bedrooms ® sB&B£13-£15 dB&B£24-£26 WB&B£72-£84
🝘 CTV 5P Ⓕ

GH QQ Kingstown Hotel 246 Kingstown Rd CA3 0DE
☎(0228) 515292
Closed Xmas & New Year
7rm(3⇌♠4hc) (1fb) CTV in all bedrooms ® sB&B£16 sB&B⇌♠£29.50 dB&B£32 dB&B⇌♠£37 LDO 9pm
Lic 🝘 9P
Credit Cards [1] [3] Ⓕ

FH QQ Mr A J Westmorland **Blackwell** *(NY387512)* Blackwell CA2 4SH ☎(0228) 24073
A neat, clean, family-run dairy farm situated 2 miles south of the city, close to the race course. The accommodation is nicely decorated and well maintained, with 2 pleasant bedrooms served by a shared bathroom, together with a comfortable residents' lounge/dining room. To find the farmhouse, leave the M6 at Junction 42 and follow signs to Dalston. After 3 miles, at Durdar, turn right at the Black Lion and continue past the race course to the White Ox Inn. Turn left into Lowry Street and the farm is on the right.
2rm ✗ (ex guide dogs) sB&B£14-£15 dB&B£28-£30 WB&B£90-£100
🝘 CTV 4P 120 acres dairy mixed

CARMARTHEN Dyfed Map **02** SN42

See also Cwmduad & Llanfynydd

FH QQQ Mrs J Willmott **Cwmtwrch Farm Hotel & Four Seasons Restaurant** *(SN497220)* Nantgaredig SA32 7NY (5mE)
☎Nantgaredig(0267) 290238
This small guesthouse, situated east of the town, off the A40 at Nantgaredig, has its own very popular restaurant and bar complex, where a wide choice of food is available. The bedrooms are fully modernised, and there are 3 pine furnished rooms in converted outbuildings, and 3 in the original farmhouse, together with the breakfast room, lounge and new conservatory – where breakfast is served in the summer.
6rm(3⇌3♠) (2fb) CTV in 3 bedrooms ® ✱ sB&B⇌♠£28-£34 dB&B⇌♠£38-£44 WB&B£140-£180 WBDi£240-£280 LDO 9pm
Lic 🝘 CTV 20P ⚘ ▭(heated) 30 acres sheep Ⓕ

CARNFORTH Lancashire Map **07** SD47

SELECTED

GH QQQQ New Capernwray Farm Capernwray LA6 1AD ☎(0524) 734284
A charming 300-year-old stone-built farmhouse set in beautifully kept gardens surrounded by open countryside. This is the home of genial hosts Peter and Sally Townend and guests will enjoy the relaxed, informal atmosphere as well as the excellent 4-course dinners prepared daily by Mrs Townend, served at a communal table in the tiny candlelit dining room – once the farm's dairy. No choice is offered, but the cooking is outstanding, and while there is no drinks licence, guests are encouraged to serve themselves to as much as they like. Each of the 3 bedrooms is well equipped and beautifully furnished. There are lots of thoughtful touches including books, sewing kits, toiletries and writing materials.
3rm(1⇌1♠) ⚟in all bedrooms CTV in all bedrooms ® sB&B⇌♠£36-£39 dB&B⇌♠£52-£58 LDO 5pm
🝘 4P nc10yrs clay pigeon shooting arranged
Credit Cards [1] [3] Ⓕ

See the regional maps of popular holiday areas at the back of the book.

CARRADALE Strathclyde *Argyllshire* Map **10** NR83

GH QQ *Ashbank Hotel* PA28 6RY ☏(05833) 650
Situated close to the village golf course, this cosy little hotel has a wood-panelled bar lounge for residents and diners and a neat dining room where meals are also served to non-residents. Bedrooms are compact, modestly furnished and cheerful.
6rm(3⌐3hc) (1fb) TV in 1 bedroom ®
Lic ▥ 8P

GH QQ Dunvalanree Portrigh Bay PA28 6SE ☏(05833) 226
FAX (05833) 339
Etr-Nov
In the hamlet of Portrigh, this fine Edwardian house overlooks the bay with its gardens almost stretching down to the shore. Spotlessly maintained, with attractive public rooms and neat bedrooms, the original character of the house has been retained by the enthusiastic owners.
14hc (3fb) ® sB&Bfr£16.50 dB&Bfr£33
Lic CTV 19P ▶9

CARRBRIDGE Highland *Inverness-shire* Map **14** NH92

GH QQQ Carrmoor Carr Rd PH23 3AD
☏(047984) 244
This cosy little guesthouse is being progressively upgraded by the enthusiastic owners, and the emphasis is on hospitality and good food.
5rm(2⌐3hc) (3fb)⅟in all bedrooms ® sB&B£13-£19.50
dB&B£26-£29 dB&B⌐£28-£31 WB&B£91-£118.50
WBDi£154-£171.50
Lic ▥ CTV 5P

SELECTED

GH QQQQ Fairwinds Hotel PH23 3AA ☏(047984) 240
Closed 2 Nov-14 Dec
Conveniently situated in the centre of the village some 200 yards back from the main road, this stone-built former manse has been sympathetically renovated and extended to provide every modern comfort and facility. Surrounded by 6 acres of grounds, with a small loch and mature pine woods, superior accommodation is provided by Mr and Mrs Reed, who are constantly making improvements to ensure that standards are maintained. Bedrooms are generally spacious, with individual colour schemes, pine furniture and private bathrooms. Drinks are served in the attractive lounge which is comfortably furnished in the modern style, and hearty dinners with a Scottish flavour are provided in the small neat dining room overlooking the garden.
5⇌⌐ CTV in all bedrooms ® ✗ sB&B⇌⌐£22-£24
dB&B⇌⌐£40-£50 WB&B£126-£168 WBDi£202-£234
LDO 4pm
Lic ▥ 8P nc12yrs
Credit Cards 1 3 £

GH QQQ Feith Mhor Country House Station Rd PH23 3AP
☏(047984) 621
Closed 16 Nov-19 Dec
Set in its own well tended garden 1.25 miles west of the village, this elegant 19th-century house is efficiently run by enthusiastic owners. It has a friendly atmosphere and many guests return regularly. Good home cooking is served in the attractive dining room, and before dinner guests can relax in the comfortable lounge where drinks are served between 6pm and 7pm. Bedrooms are very individual with a mixture of modern and traditional furniture, and all have lovely views of the countryside.
6rm(3⇌3⌐) (1fb) CTV in all bedrooms ® sB&B⇌⌐£20-£21
dB&B⇌⌐£40-£42 WBDi£210-£217 LDO 6.45pm
Lic ▥ 8P nc10yrs

CASTLE CARROCK Cumbria Map **12** NY55

FH Q B W Robinson **Gelt Hall** *(NY542554)* CA4 9LT ☎Hayton(0228) 70260

Neat, clean and tidy accommodation is provided at this friendly little farmhouse which dates back to 1818. Situated in the centre of the village, it has a genuine farmhouse atmosphere.

3rm(1⇨)(1fb) ✗ ✱ sB&B£13-£14 dB&B£26 LDO 5pm
CTV 6P 1🚗 250 acres beef dairy sheep £

CASTLE CARY Somerset Map **03** ST63

INN QQQ **The George Hotel** Market Place BA7 7AH ☎(0963) 50761

One of the 100 oldest inns in Britain, this 15th-century, former coaching inn continues to be upgraded to a pleasing standard, while retaining the comfort and charm of an old-world establishment. The pretty oak-panelled dining room serves delicious dinners and Sunday lunches, while extensive, tasty bar meals are offered at lunchtimes Monday to Saturday. Chef Trevor Parsons has created a varied, interesting à la carte menu, with tempting dishes such as smooth duck liver and orange paté and a good selection of fish dishes, balanced with a range of meat and poultry, and his home-made puddings should not be missed. A well planned, sensibly priced wine list is provided, which gives good value for money, as does the à la carte menu. Modern comforts are supplied in the en suite bedrooms that are individually decorated and furnished. Service is charming and friendly, with a relaxed, easy atmosphere throughout.

12⇨↱ Annexe 3⇨↱ (1fb) CTV in all bedrooms ® **T** ✱ sB&B⇨↱£35-£45 dB&B⇨↱£50-£60 Lunch £7-£8.50 Dinner £7-£8.50&alc LDO 9pm
10P
Credit Cards 1 3 £

CASTLE DONINGTON Leicestershire Map **08** SK42

GH QQ **The Four Poster** 73 Clapgun St DE7 2LF ☎Derby(0332) 810335 & 812418

Tastefully restored and modernised old ivy-clad house in a quiet street.

7rm(3⇨↱4hc) Annexe 4hc ⊬in 7 bedrooms CTV in all bedrooms ® ✱ sB&B£15 dB&B£30-£40 dB&B⇨↱£50
CTV 18P 4🚗 £

GH QQ **Park Farmhouse Hotel** Melbourne Rd, Isley Walton DE74 2RN ☎Derby(0332) 862409 FAX (0332) 862364

Closed Xmas & New Year

8rm(3⇨3↱2hc) (2fb) CTV in all bedrooms ® LDO 8pm
Lic 20P
Credit Cards 1 2 3 5

INN QQ **Le Chevalier Bistro Restaurant** 2 Borough St DE7 2LA ☎Derby(0332) 812005 & 812106 FAX (0322) 811372

A popular little bistro situated in a narrow side street in the centre of the town. Accommodation consists of 4 rooms with access via a courtyard, where guests can enjoy a pre-dinner drink or after-dinner coffee. Rooms are modestly decorated, each with a private bathroom. A friendly, informal atmosphere and a good choice from menus makes this a favourite of both locals and business people. A supplement is charged for a full English breakfast.

4⇨↱ (1fb) CTV in all bedrooms ® ✗ (ex guide dogs) ✱ sB&B⇨↱£23.95-£30.95 dB&B⇨↱£36.90-£46.90 WBDifr£216.65 LDO 10.30pm
CTV 100P 2🚗 pool table
Credit Cards 1 3 £

'Selected' establishments, which have the highest quality award, are highlighted by a tinted panel. For a full list of these establishments, consult the Contents page.

CASTLE DOUGLAS Dumfries & Galloway *Kirkcudbrightshire* Map **11** NX76

GH QQQ **Rose Cottage** Gelston DG7 1SH ☎(0556) 2513

Feb-Oct

This delightful whitewashed cottage is situated at Gelston beside the B727 just over 2 miles from the centre of Castle Douglas. It offers attractive and cosy accommodation all of which is on ground floor level.

3rm(1⇨↱2hc) Annexe 2hc (1fb) TV in 3 bedrooms ® dB&B£30 dB&B⇨↱£35 WB&Bfr£102.50 WBDifr£145 LDO 5pm
CTV 15P

CATLOWDY Cumbria Map **12** NY47

SELECTED

FH QQQQ Mr & Mrs J Sisson **Bessiestown** *(NY457768)* CA6 5QP ☎Nicholforest(0228) 577219

Situated in open countryside, just off the B6318 close to the tiny village and the Scottish border, this is an exceptional farmhouse offering superb hospitality and service. Bedrooms are spacious, with en suite facilities, radios and pretty coordinated fabrics. Spacious public areas include an elegant bar lounge, a cosy TV lounge and a traditional dining room where excellent home cooking is provided. There is even the added luxury of an indoor pool.

4⇨↱ (1fb)⊬in all bedrooms ® ✗ (ex guide dogs) ✱ sB&B⇨↱£24-£25 dB&B⇨↱£38-£40 WB&B£120-£125 LDO 4pm
Lic CTV 10P (heated) games room 80 acres beef sheep £

FH QQ Mr & Mrs Lawson **Craigburn** *(NY474761)* CA6 5QP ☎Nicholforest(0228) 577214

Set in 250 acres of working farmland, this farmhouse dating back to 1760, has been upgraded to provide tasteful, modern accommodation. Bedrooms are bright and fresh, with coordinated furnishings and en suite facilities. There are 2 comfortable lounges complete with books, games and TV, and a spacious farmhouse restaurant. Jack and Jane Lawson are enthusiastic hosts and are always on hand to care for their guests.

6rm(4⇨2↱) (2fb)⊬in all bedrooms ® sB&B⇨↱£22-£23 dB&B⇨↱£34-£36 WB&B£107-£113 WBDi£170-£176 LDO 5.30pm
Lic CTV 20P snooker 250 acres beef mixed sheep £

CHAGFORD Devon Map **03** SX78

GH QQQ **Bly House** Nattadon Hill TQ13 8BW ☎(0647) 432404

Formerly Chagford Rectory, Bly House is set in beautifully kept gardens within walking distance of the village. The house is lovingly furnished with antique pieces and objets d'art and provides quality accommodation of great charm.

6rm(5⇨1↱) CTV in all bedrooms ® sB&B⇨↱£29-£30 dB&B⇨↱£48-£50 WB&Bfr£168
CTV 10P nc12yrs (grass)croquet

GH QQ **Glendarah** TQ13 8BZ ☎(0647) 433270

Mar-Dec

The family home of Edward and Marian Willett, who extend a warm welcome to guests. Glendarah is within walking distance of the village centre. Bedrooms are comfortable and made bright with coordinating soft furnishings. There is a lively atmosphere in the small bar area, and home-cooked dinners are served in the dining room.

6hc Annexe 1⇨ (2fb) CTV in 1 bedroom ® ✗ (ex guide dogs) sB&B£16 dB&B£32 dB&B⇨£40 WB&B£108.50-£136.50
Lic CTV 9P £

CHANNEL ISLANDS Map 16

GUERNSEY Map 16

FOREST

GH QQQ Mon Plaisir Rue Des Landes
☎Guernsey(0481) 64498 FAX (0481) 65999

Conveniently situated close to Petit Bot Valley and beautiful cliff walks, this Guernsey farmhouse dates back to 1830. Spacious modern bedrooms are freshly decorated and comfortably furnished, each equipped with a smart en suite and small fridge, in addition to other amenities. Mr Torode offers a hearty English breakfast in the small dining room which adjoins the guests' sitting room. A secluded garden and greenhouse can be enjoyed on bright days.

4⇌♪ CTV in all bedrooms ® ✗ (ex guide dogs)
dB&B⇌♪£32-£38 WB&B£112-£133
🏛 4P £

ST MARTIN

GH QQQ Hotel La Michelle Les Hubits
☎Guernsey(0481) 38065 FAX (0481) 39492
Apr-Dec

A smartly presented private hotel quietly located in a residential area, not far from the town centre and airport. Bedrooms are all very well equipped and stylishly furnished with quality and comfort in mind. Public areas are also attractive and comfortable, and an evening meal is offered.

14⇌♪ (5fb) CTV in all bedrooms ® ✗ (ex guide dogs)
sB&B⇌♪£19-£28 dB&B⇌♪£38-£56 (incl dinner)
WB&B£133-£196 WBDi£168-£231 LDO 6.45pm
Lic 🏛 CTV 14P nc8yrs
Credit Cards 1 2 3 £

ST PETER PORT

GH QQQ Marine Hotel Well Rd ☎Guernsey(0481) 724978

Situated just a short distance from the North Esplanade in a one-way street, this family-run private hotel offers clean, comfortable accommodation which is constantly being improved. Bedrooms are modestly equipped, spotlessly clean and all are en suite. Breakfast only is served, but the resident proprietors can suggest reasonable local restaurants for the benefit of guests.

11⇌♪ (3fb) ® ✗ (ex guide dogs) ✱ sB&B⇌♪£13.50-£22.50
dB&B⇌♪£27-£42 WB&B£94.50-£147
Lic 🏛 CTV ₱ £

SELECTED

GH QQQQ Midhurst House Candie Rd
☎Guernsey(0481) 724391
mid Apr-mid Oct

Run as a small, private hotel for the last 12 years by enthusiastic proprietors Brian and Jan Goodenough, this Regency town house is situated in a quiet residential area. The 5 bedrooms in the main house are all individually styled with attractive soft furnishings, antique furniture and original fireplaces. The the 3 purpose built rooms are obviously more modern, and they have the advantage of direct access to the small, sheltered, south facing garden; all 8 rooms have en suite facilities. In the cosy dining room chef/ proprietor Brian prepares a short but interesting menu, using the finest, fresh produce. Afterwards guests can relax in the comfortable lounge, designed to create an indoor garden atmosphere with its domed skylight, plants and tiled floor.

5rm(2⇌3♪) Annexe 3♪ (1fb) CTV in all bedrooms ® ✗
sB&B⇌♪£27-£37 dB&B⇌♪£40-£58 WBDi£180-£250
LDO 6.45pm
Lic 🏛 1🚗 nc8yrs

GH QQQ *Les Ozouets Lodge* Ozouets Rd
☎Guernsey(0481) 721288
Mar-Oct

A private hotel dating back to 1903, situated in a quiet residential area, away from the town centre. Run by the chef/patron, it offers excellent cooking complemented by a well chosen wine list. A simple table d'hôte menu and a more imaginative à la carte menu are available to guests and a limited number of non-residents also. The house is grandly furnished downstairs, with handsome antiques and attractive soft furnishings. Bedrooms are comfortable and well presented, with modern facilities. The gardens are outstanding and include bowling and putting greens, and a tennis court.

13rm(5⇌8♪) Annexe 1⇌♪ (3fb) CTV in all bedrooms ® ✗
LDO 7.45pm
Lic 🏛 20P nc5yrs 🎾(grass)bowling green putting green petanques
Credit Cards 1 3

ST SAMPSON

GH QQ Ann-Dawn Private Hotel Route des Capelles
☎Guernsey(0481) 725606
Etr-Oct

Located in a quiet, residential street, some distance from the town and harbour, this guesthouse is surrounded by landscaped gardens. Bedrooms are freshly decorated, simply appointed and reasonably equipped, and housekeeping standards are good. In addition to breakfast, an evening meal is offered, and guests may also enjoy drinks from the residents' bar.

14rm(3⇌9♪2hc) CTV in all bedrooms ® ✗ sB&B£20-£25.50
sB&B⇌♪£22-£27.50 dB&B⇌♪£40-£55 (incl dinner)
WB&B£112-£147 WBDi£140-£192.50 LDO 5pm
Lic 🏛 12P nc12yrs
Credit Cards 1 3 £

JERSEY Map 16

GREVE DE LECQ BAY

GH QQQ Des Pierres JE3 2DT (on B65 near beach)
☎Jersey(0534) 481858 FAX (0534) 485273
Closed Xmas & New Year

Situated on top of a hill overlooking the bay and coastal countryside, this guesthouse offers modern, smartly decorated bedrooms, some of which have superb views; all rooms have good en suite facilities, double glazing, TV, radios, hairdryers and tea trays; several bedrooms are ideal for families. There is a basement bar and dining room, and the daily choice of fresh home- cooked dishes is displayed on a blackboard. Service is personally supervised by the resident proprietors Mr and Mrs Flath, who have owned the guesthouse for many years.

16rm(9⇌7♪) (4fb) CTV in all bedrooms ® ✗ WB&B£119-£161 WBDi£189-£231 LDO 8pm
Lic 🏛 CTV 13P gymnasium
Credit Cards 1 3

GROUVILLE

GH QQQ *Lavender Villa Hotel* Rue A Don
☎Jersey(0534) 54937
Mar-Nov

A well run and maintained, family hotel adjoining the Royal Jersey golf course, and only a short stroll from the beach. The accommodation has been tastefully furnished in the modern style, and bedrooms are particularly well equipped. Spacious public areas include a 'no smoking' traditional TV lounge and separate bar, together with a beamed dining room. Outside there are good leisure facilities and ample car parking.

21rm(10⇌11♪) (3fb) CTV in all bedrooms ® ✗ LDO 7.15pm
Lic 🏛 CTV 20P nc3yrs ⛱
Credit Cards 1 3

ST AUBIN

GH QQ Bryn-y-Mor Route de la Haule
☎Jersey(0534) 20295 FAX (0534) 24262
A small hotel in a prime position overlooking St Aubins Bay, offering a choice of well equipped bedrooms, many with lovely sea views. There is a small TV lounge and a combined bar/dining room. Predominantly English food is served with set menus; lunch is served daily and light refreshments on request. Manager Mr Sousa provides friendly and helpful standards of service, and the hotel is licensed. There are pleasant gardens, a sun terrace and ample parking nearby on the seafront.
14rm(11⇌♠3hc) (4fb) CTV in all bedrooms ® LDO 6.30pm
Lic 6P
Credit Cards [1] [2] [3] [5] £

SELECTED

GH QQQQ The Panorama La Rue du Crocquet
JE3 8BR ☎Jersey(0534) 42429 FAX (0534) 45940
Etr-Nov
Set high above the village and enjoying excellent sea views from most of the bedrooms, this delightful and very popular, family-run guesthouse has a choice of individually decorated and well furnished bedrooms that are thoughtfully equipped with telephones, fridges and microwave ovens. In addition to the comfortable lounge, there is a new tea room, both rooms having exquisite oak carved fireplaces, and a terraced tea garden, where over 90 different varieties of tea are offered. As well as the full choice of afternoon teas, morning coffee and light refreshments are usually served throughout the day and are particularly recommended; this service is also offered to non residents. An excellent breakfast menu includes such dishes as a grand slam 'full house' or crumpets with bacon and maple syrup. A friendly service is personally provided by the enthusiastic proprietors John and Jill Squires. Car parking is limited and is located below the guesthouse at roadside level.
17⇌♠ (2fb) CTV in all bedrooms ® ✗ sB&B⇌♠£18-£35 dB&B⇌♠£36-£60
nc10yrs Tea garden
Credit Cards [1] [2] [3] [5] £

ST HELIER

GH QQQ *Cliff Court Hotel* St Andrews Rd, First Tower
☎(0534) 34919
14 Apr-29 Oct
This hotel is in a quiet location overlooking St Aubins Bay, and provides extensive accommodation; some bedrooms have sea views, and all have private bathrooms. The combined bar/lounge augments the large, bright dining room, and there is a professional Portuguese chef. Outside, the small but secluded terrace and swimming pool provide an enjoyable sun trap. Service is under the personal supervision of the resident proprietors.
16rm(15⇌1hc) (4fb) ® ✗ (ex guide dogs) LDO 7.30pm
Lic CTV 14P (heated)
Credit Cards [3]

GH QQQ *Cornucopia Hotel & Restaurant* Mont Pinel
☎Jersey(0534) 32646
Enjoying a quiet location overlooking adjoining farmland, the accommodation here comprises a choice of bedrooms, some on the ground floor and some family rooms. The restaurant is augmented by 2 bars, and pleasant lounge facilities are available in the quiet 'no smoking' area. Extensive indoor and outdoor leisure facilities are provided, together with private parking.
15rm(4⇌11♠) (2fb) CTV in all bedrooms ® LDO 2.30pm
Lic 21P (heated) solarium gymnasium games room jacuzzi turkish bath
Credit Cards [1] [2] [3]

GH QQ Millbrook House Rue de Trachy JE2 3JN
☎Jersey(0534) 33036 FAX (0534) 24317
Apr-Oct
This Georgian and Colonial-style house is set in 10 acres of mature, and in many parts, wild gardens, 500 yards from the beach. A quiet, family-run hotel, it offers bright, well equipped bedrooms and cosy, traditional lounges. A country-house atmosphere prevails, and the peaceful atmosphere is complemented by wholesome home cooking.
24rm(18⇌6♠) (2fb) CTV in all bedrooms ® T ✗
sB&B⇌♠£20-£29.50 dB&B⇌♠£40-£59 WB&B£140-£206.50 WBDi£175-£241.50 LDO 7pm
Lic lift CTV 20P
Credit Cards [2]

GH QQQ Runnymede Court Hotel 46/52 Roseville St
JE2 4PN ☎Jersey(0534) 20044 FAX (0534) 27880
mid Feb-mid Dec
Conveniently positioned, this established and popular hotel has been extensively refurbished to offer a choice of comfortable, bright, well equipped bedrooms with a good range of facilities; some of the rooms are situated around a rear central garden. The public rooms are well furnished, spacious and comfortable and include a bar, lounge and large dining room. The beach and shopping centre are within easy reach.
57⇌♠ (6fb) CTV in all bedrooms ® T ✗ (ex guide dogs)
sB&B⇌♠£20-£32 dB&B⇌♠£40-£64 (incl dinner)
LDO 7.15pm
Lic lift CTV
Credit Cards [1] [2] [3]

TRINITY

GH QQQ Highfield Country Hotel Route du Ebenezer
JE3 5DS ☎Jersey(0534) 862194 FAX (0534) 865342
30 Mar-30 Oct rs Nov-29 Mar
This bright, spacious hotel, pleasantly situated in a country location, stands in an acre of grounds which include a swimming pool. Bedrooms are pretty and well equipped with modern facilities and private bathrooms. There is a comfortable bar and lounge to complement the well appointed dining room. Ground floor self-catering apartments are also available.
41⇌♠ (20fb) CTV in all bedrooms ® T ✗ sB&B⇌♠£20-£31 dB&B⇌♠£40-£62 (incl dinner) LDO 8pm
Lic lift CTV 41P (heated) (heated) sauna solarium gymnasium games room
Credit Cards [1] [3] [5] £

CHARD Somerset Map 03 ST30

GH QQQ Watermead 83 High St TA20 1QT ☎(0460) 62834
This small establishment at the top of the high street is neat and well kept. The bedrooms are simply furnished and some of them have en suite facilities. There is a comfortable lounge, and a neat breakfast room where evening meals are available by prior arrangement.Guests can be sure of a warm welcome from the proprietor Mrs Plant.
9rm(6♠3hc) in 3 bedrooms CTV in all bedrooms ® *
sB&B£12.50-£13.50 sB&B♠£15-£20 dB&B♠£30-£32
WB&B£80-£100 LDO noon
Lic 9P 2 £

CHARFIELD Gloucestershire Map 03 ST79

INN QQ Huntingford Mill Hotel GL12 8EX
☎Dursley(0453) 843431
Situated one mile from the village in a quiet river setting, this was the last working flour mill in Gloucestershire. Carefully converted to retain the original character, bedrooms are simply appointed and well equipped. There is also a spacious restaurant specialising in North American dishes, and over two miles of private fishing is available to resident guests.

5hc (1fb) CTV in all bedrooms ® ✈ (ex guide dogs) ✱ sB&B£22.50-£25 dB&B£31.50-£35 WB&B£157.50-£175 WBDi£220-£245 Lunch fr£12.95&alc High tea fr£5&alc Dinner fr£12.95&alc LDO 10pm
CTV 25P
Credit Cards [1] [3]

CHARING Kent Map **05** TQ94

FH QQQ Mrs P Pym **Barnfield** *(TQ924477)* TN27 0BN ☎(023371) 2421
Barnfield is a medieval farmhouse with low oak beams and inglenook fireplaces, and is furnished with antique and period furniture. It is the home of the Pym family, and the bedrooms are named after members of the family. Supper is available most evenings, and is taken in the combined lounge and dining room, or with the family. It is a no smoking house throughout. There is a separate converted barn which is available for private hire, and can be used for small meetings and parties.
5rm(4hc) (1fb) in all bedrooms ® ✈ ✱ sB&B£18-£20 dB&B£36-£40 WB&B£108-£120 WBDi£177-£189 LDO 5pm
CTV 100P 1 (hard)500 acres arable sheep

CHARLWOOD Surrey For accommodation details see under **Gatwick Airport**

CHARMOUTH Dorset Map **03** SY39

GH QQQ Newlands House Stonebarrow Ln DT6 6RA ☎(0297) 60212
Mar-Oct
Formerly a 16th-century farmhouse, this property is set in 2 acres of pretty gardens on the edge of this quiet, rural village. The accommodation consists of tastefully furnished and nicely equipped bedrooms, and public areas that have much character and charm. There are 2 comfortably furnished lounges, plus a cosy bar and meals are served in the attractive dining room, cooked by Mrs Vear – guests particularly enjoy her home-made pies and pastries. Her husband is an amiable host and a quiet relaxed atmosphere prevails throughout. Set at the foot of Stonebarrow Hill, this house offers lovely walks nearby.
12rm(11 1hc) (2fb) in all bedrooms CTV in all bedrooms ® sB&B£19.50-£22.50 sB&B £21-£24 dB&B £42-£48 WB&B£133-£151 WBDi£199.50-£220 LDO noon
Lic CTV 12P nc6yrs £

CHEDDLETON Staffordshire Map **07** SJ95

SELECTED

GH QQQQ Choir Cottage and Choir House Ostlers Ln ST13 7HS ☎Churnet Side(0538) 360561
Situated in a rather pretty village, this small delightful house offers an unusual choice of sleeping accommodation. Two bedrooms are housed in the separate cottage, which is over 300 years old and includes the 'Pine Room' which has a 4-poster bed plus 2 small children's rooms, and the 'Roe Room' which has an attractively draped 4-poster bed and a small patio area for summer use. The 'Green Room' is situated in the main house and has its own small conservatory lounge. All bedrooms are equipped with every modern comfort and good quality en suite facilities. Breakfast is served in the pine furnished dining room and dinner is available by prior arrangement. There is a pretty lounge with floral covered seating and for smokers a conservatory is provided, furnished with cane chairs.
2 Annexe 2 (1fb) in all bedrooms CTV in all bedrooms ® T ✈ ✱ sB&B £35-£40 dB&B £40-£46 WB&B£120-£140 LDO 24hrs notice
5P nc4yrs

CHELMSFORD Essex Map **05** TL70

GH QQ Beechcroft Private Hotel 211 New London Rd CM2 0AJ ☎(0245) 352462
Closed Xmas & New Year
This privately owned and run guesthouse provides neatly decorated but simply furnished bedrooms, some of which now have en suite shower rooms. Guests have the choice of 2 lounges, and there is a large car park to the rear.
20rm(8 12hc) (2fb) CTV in 17 bedrooms ® sB&B£26-£27 sB&B £31.40-£34.95 dB&B£39.65-£41.70 dB&B £49.80-£49.50
CTV 15P
Credit Cards [1] [3]

GH QQQ Boswell House Hotel 118-120 Springfield Rd CM2 6LF ☎(0245) 287587
Closed 10 days Xmas
This 19th century Victorian town house has been nicely converted and now offers particularly well equipped bedrooms which have been tastefully furnished with stripped pine; they are all en suite and some have been designated non-smoking. Guests can enjoy traditional home cooking in the attractive, informal restaurant, or alternatively a light snack in the cosy bar. The friendly and enthusiastic proprietors continue to offer efficient service.
13rm(9 4) (2fb) in 9 bedrooms CTV in all bedrooms ® T ✈ (ex guide dogs) ✱ sB&B £41-£45 dB&B £61-£67 LDO 8.30pm
Lic CTV 15P
Credit Cards [1] [2] [3] [5] £

GH QQQ Snows Oaklands Hotel 240 Springfield Rd CM2 6BP ☎(0245) 352004
Situated north of the city off the A12, this attractive detached house has a well kept garden, with a pond and small aviary. Bedrooms come in various shapes and sizes, are well maintained and offer most facilities. Public areas are traditionally furnished in →

an informal style, with a magnificent clock collection owned by the proprietor. Bar snacks (soups and sandwiches) are available during lunch time and for a limited period in the evening.
14rm(13⇨🚿1hc) (3fb) CTV in all bedrooms ® 🚫 (ex guide dogs) ✱ sB&B£28 sB&B⇨🚿£38-£45 dB&B⇨🚿£44-£54 LDO 8pm
Lic 🍴 CTV 14P £

GH QQ *Tanunda Hotel* 219 New London Rd CM2 0AJ ☎(0245) 354295
Closed 2wks Xmas
This commercial guesthouse offers a choice of simply furnished and decorated bedrooms, well equipped with TV and telephones; many also benefit from en suite facilities. There is a traditionally furnished TV lounge, and car parking is available.
20rm(2⇨9🚿9hc) CTV in 12 bedrooms ® LDO 7.25pm
Lic 🍴 CTV 20P

CHELTENHAM Gloucestershire Map 03 SO92

See also Bishop's Cleeve

GH QQ Abbey Hotel 16 Bath Pde GL53 7HN ☎(0242) 516053 FAX (0242) 513034
An early Victorian terraced house, situated behind Sandford Park and close to the town centre, Abbey Hotel has been carefully modernised to provide compact but well equipped bedrooms and cosy public rooms.
11rm(7🚿1hc) (1fb) CTV in all bedrooms ® T sB&B£23-£30 sB&B🚿£33-£35 dB&B£48-£50 dB&B🚿£54-£56 WB&B£150-£160 WBDi£237-£247 LDO 6pm
Lic 🍴 P̸
Credit Cards 1 3 £

GH QQQ Battledown Hotel 125 Hales Rd GL52 6ST ☎(0242) 233881
Standing back in its own well tended gardens, this Victorian colonial-style residence has seen recent significant upgrading. It is spotlessly clean throughout with bright, comfortable bedrooms and modern en suite showers/wcs. There are cosy public rooms with friendly services provided by enthusiastic owners Mr and Mrs Austin. Useful car parking is available and this is an ideal location for the town or for touring the Cotswolds.
4🚿 CTV in all bedrooms ® 🚫 ✱ sB&B🚿£24-£26 dB&B🚿£36-£44 WB&B£126-£142 WBDi£196-£212 LDO 6.30pm
🍴 10P
Credit Cards 1 3 £

GH QQQ Beaumont House Hotel 56 Shurdington Rd GL53 0JE ☎(0242) 245986 FAX (0242) 245986
This attractive Victorian house is set back off the main road in its own small grounds. Its public rooms retain much of their original charm and architectural features. The bedrooms are well proportioned and equipped with modern facilities. The establishment is family owned and hospitable, with prompt, friendly service.
18rm(6⇨11🚿1hc) (3fb) CTV in all bedrooms ® T sB&B£19-£22.50 sB&B⇨🚿£30-£40 dB&B⇨🚿£43-£55 WB&B£129.50-£262.50 WBDi£210-£335 LDO 8pm
Lic 🍴 CTV 20P 1🚗
Credit Cards 1 2 3 £

GH QQQ Beechworth Lawn Hotel 133 Hales Rd GL52 6ST ☎(0242) 522583
An attractive, spacious Victorian house set back from the Broadway road, in its own small grounds, half a mile from the town centre. Public rooms are comfortable, and the bedrooms are well equipped, bright and individually decorated, combining character with modern good quality furnishings and private bathrooms. Spotlessly clean throughout, this congenial guesthouse represents excellent value for money. Private car parking is another asset.
7rm(5🚿2hc) (2fb) CTV in all bedrooms ® sB&B£19.50-£22 sB&B🚿£24-£28 dB&B£36-£38 dB&B🚿£40-£46 WB&Bfr£126 WBDifr£190 LDO 7pm
🍴 CTV 10P £

SELECTED

GH QQQQ Cleeve Hill Hotel Cleeve Hill GL52 3PR ☎(0242) 672052
Closed 23-27 Dec
Perched high towards the summit of Cleeve Hill, this attractive hotel offers views across the valley to the Malvern Hills. Run by Marian and John Enstone, who are enthusiastic, welcoming hosts, they have transformed this characterful home into a delightful retreat. Most of the comfortable bedrooms are richly decorated with pleasing colours and coordinating fabrics, fitted with modern, quality furniture and bright, modern en suite facilities. On the ground floor is an elegant sitting room in restful shades of light green and peach, with an adjacent dispense bar. Delicious breakfasts are served in the sunny conservatory dining room, which overlooks the colourful terraced garden. Hospitality and tasteful, quality surroundings are the hallmarks of this excellent bed and breakfast hotel.
10⇨🚿 (1fb)⚟in 8 bedrooms CTV in all bedrooms ® 🚫 (ex guide dogs) ✱ sB&B⇨🚿£35-£40 dB&B⇨🚿£50-£65
Lic 🍴 12P nc8yrs
Credit Cards 1 2 3

GH Q Crossways Oriel Place, 57 Bath Rd GL53 7LH ☎(0242) 527683
In a convenient central position, this end of terrace bed and breakfast guesthouse offers a friendly, personal atmosphere. Bedrooms are simply furnished with modern equipment.
6rm(3🚿3hc) (3fb) CTV in all bedrooms ® sB&B£17 sB&B🚿£30 dB&B£32 dB&B🚿£40
🍴
Credit Cards 1 3 £

GH QQ Hallery House 48 Shurdington Rd GL53 0JE ☎(0242) 578450 FAX (0242) 529730
This detached, Georgian Grade II listed building, set back from the road, is situated directly adjacent to the A46, within walking distance of the town centre. It provides comfortable spacious public rooms and bright, well furnished bedrooms, equipped with good facilities including modern en suite showers, TV with satellite and direct dial telephone. The nicely furnished restaurant provides imaginative menus. The guesthouse is personally run by the family owners.
16rm(10⇨🚿6hc) (1fb)⚟in 2 bedrooms CTV in all bedrooms ® T sB&B£25-£30 sB&B⇨🚿£35-£50 dB&B£42-£50 dB&B⇨🚿£50-£70 WB&B£165-£325 WBDi£250-£450 LDO 8.30pm
Lic 🍴 20P 🚲 cycle hire
Credit Cards 1 2 3 £

GH QQQ Hannaford's 20 Evesham Rd GL52 2AB ☎(0242) 515181
A well maintained terraced town house on the A435 Evesham road just north of the town. Public rooms include the recent addition of a bright conservatory lounge bar and a comfortable sitting room. Bedrooms are modestly furnished but spacious and well equipped. Personally run by the Crowley family, who continue to make improvements to this welcoming guesthouse.
10rm(9⇨🚿1hc) (1fb) CTV in all bedrooms ® T 🚫 ✱ sB&B£18.50-£25 sB&B⇨🚿£31-£40 dB&B⇨🚿£48-£60 LDO 9.30am
Lic 🍴 CTV P̸
Credit Cards 1 3 £

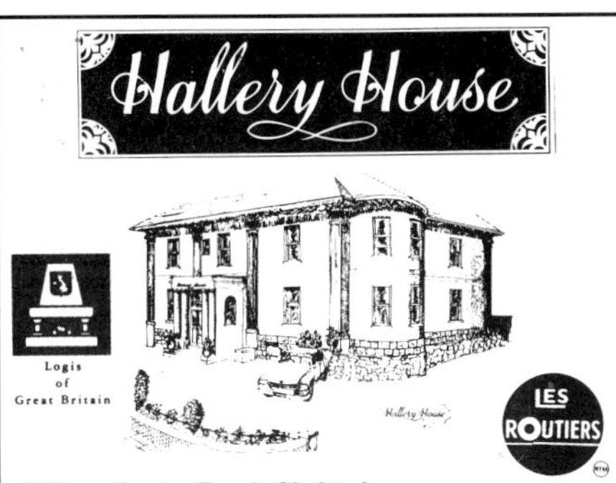

48 Shurdington Road, Cheltenham Spa, Gloucestershire GL53 0JE
Tel: 0242-578450 Fax: 0242 549730

Steve and Angie welcome you to their lovely Victoria home offering

- ★ Comfortable rooms with hot drinks tray – majority en-suite
- ★ Colour TV with satellite in all rooms
- ★ Excellent traditional English or Continental breakfast
- ★ Excellent evening meals and we cater for all diets
- ★ Direct dial telephones ★ Pets and children very welcome
- ★ Large car park

Four times winner of Spa award for customer comfort, excellent food and exceptional hygiene standards. Hallery House is of architectural interest and is situated on the main A46. It is a short walk from Cheltenham centre with all the attractions this beautiful town has to offer. Brochures available. Amex, Visa and Mastercard accepted.

Cycling holiday and short breaks.

A warm friendly team welcomes you to this charming detached, listed Victorian building set in peaceful, picturesque gardens. On the A46, minutes from town centre. All rooms have colour TV with satellite movie channel, hot drinks tray and telephone with radio alarm. En suite available. Our Chef provides our Restaurant with freshly prepared food and a choice from an imaginative daily menu. Licensed bar and private car park.

Conferences and parties catered for.

56 Shurdlington Road, Cheltenham, Glos.
Tel: (0242) 245986

Beechworth Lawn Hotel

133 Hales Road, Cheltenham, Glos.
Telephone: 0242 - 522583

Near the centre and conveniently situated for all amenities, Betty & Brian Toombs offer you a relaxed atmosphere and friendly service at their carefully modernised and quality appointed hotel set in conifer and shrub gardens. Bedrooms have colour TV, beverages, hairdryer, toiletries, clock radio etc. Easy off-street parking, 24 hr. access and traditional English food freshly cooked, ensure your satisfaction.

ABBEY HOTEL

Elegance and taste are the hallmarks which characterise the ambiance of the Abbey Hotel, a regency-style hotel situated in the centre of Cheltenham near the bus terminus, shopping centre, theatres and the museum.

- Excellent table d'hôte dinners from £12.50
- TV in all rooms including Sky News and Sky Sport
- Mastercard, Visa and Eurocard accepted
- French spoken

14/16 Bath Parade, Cheltenham GL53 7HN
Tel: (0242) 516053 Fax: (0242) 513034

GH QQQ *Hollington House Hotel* 115 Hales Rd GL52 6ST
☎(0242) 519718 FAX (0242) 570280
Conveniently positioned just half a mile from the town centre on the Prestbury road, this attractive detached Victorian property is set back within its own small grounds. Built from Cotswold stone, the house offers 9 spacious, well appointed and comfortable bedrooms, the majority with modern en suite bathrooms. Well furnished, pleasant public rooms complement the friendly service in a pleasant and relaxed atmosphere, combined with good quality home- cooked food.
9rm(8↱1hc) (2fb) CTV in all bedrooms ® ✗ LDO 5pm
Lic 🍽 12P nc3yrs
Credit Cards 1 2 3

GH QQ *Ivy Dene* 145 Hewlett Rd GL52 6TS
☎(0242) 521726 & 521776
An attractive detached house set in its own pretty, small garden and providing a nice combination of character and charm with modern comforts. Bedrooms are bright, comfortable and well equipped although none have private bathrooms. Public rooms are cosy, and the guesthouse is spotlessly clean throughout. It is conveniently located close to the town centre and provides good car parking.
9hc (2fb) CTV in all bedrooms ®
🍽 CTV 8P

GH Q Knowle House 89 Leckhampton Rd GL53 0BS
☎(0242) 516091
Closed Xmas
This attractive Edwardian property, set back in its own small garden, offers a friendly atmosphere, bright surroundings and clean modern rooms. It is in a residential area convenient for the city and as a touring base for the Cotswolds.
5rm(2↱3hc) (1fb) ® sB&B£15-£17 dB&B£30-£34 dB&B↱£35-£39
🍽 CTV 6P Ⓔ

GH QQ Lonsdale House Montpellier Dr GL50 1TX
☎(0242) 232379
rs Xmas
In a convenient central location with useful car parking provided, this friendly establishment offers bright accommodation with cosy public rooms, but no en suite bedrooms at present. Lonsdale House is popular with both business guests and tourists.
11rm(3↱8hc) (3fb) CTV in all bedrooms ® ✗ (ex guide dogs) sB&B£17-£19 sB&B↱£22-£25 dB&B£34-£38 dB&B↱£40-£48
🍽 CTV 6P
Credit Cards 1 2 3 Ⓔ

SELECTED

GH QQQQ Lypiatt House Lypiatt Rd GL50 2QW
☎(0242) 224994 FAX (0242) 224996
Closed 22 Dec-2 Jan
An elegant and charming Victorian house set in a pleasant tree-lined location in the Montpellier area. Enthusiastic restoration over the years by the conscientious owners Michael and Susan Malloy has restored it to its former glory, with many of the original features retained. The spacious and impressive drawing room and small, cosy breakfast room are comfortable and well furnished with pleasant coordinating décor, colours and fabrics. The spotlessly clean bedrooms are tastefully furnished with an excellent range of modern facilities and several extra touches. The conservatory lounge bar is a popular recent addition. Hearty breakfasts and light suppers are served to residents in the attractive basement dining room.
10rm(9⇌1↱) CTV in all bedrooms ® T ✗
sB&B⇌↱£44-£50 dB&B⇌↱£62
Lic 🍽 14P nc12yrs
Credit Cards 1 3

GH QQQ Milton House 12 Royal Pde, Bayshill Rd GL50 3AY ☎(0242) 582601 FAX (0242) 222326
An imposing Regency house within the terrace of Royal Parade which is benefiting from careful restoration by the owners Mr and Mrs Milton. Bedrooms are bright and comfortable, individually styled and decorated and furnished in pine, with a good selection of modern creature comforts and facilities. Public rooms are equally attractive, with many of the original features retained. This elegant house is also very conveniently located, with direct rear access to Montpelier, the heart of Cheltenham's excellent shopping area. There is also limited car parking available.
9⇌↱ (4fb)⚟in 6 bedrooms CTV in all bedrooms ® T ✗ ✱
sB&B⇌↱£30-£55 dB&B⇌↱£45-£60 LDO 9am
Lic 🍽 CTV 5P
Credit Cards 1 2 3 Ⓔ

GH QQQ North Hall Hotel Pittville Circus Rd GL52 2PZ
☎(0242) 520589 FAX (0242) 261953
Closed Xmas
An elegant, early Victorian large detached house situated in the Pittville district, close to the town centre. Bedrooms are comfortable and well equipped and many of the attractive public rooms retain the original features. The guesthouse is conveniently located in a prominent central position with good car parking.
20rm(6⇌7↱7hc) (1fb) CTV in all bedrooms ® T sB&Bfr£18 sB&B⇌↱fr£27.50 dB&Bfr£31 dB&B⇌↱fr£43.50 WB&B£126-£192.50 WBDi£192.50-£259 LDO 7.15pm
Lic 🍽 CTV 20P
Credit Cards 1 3 Ⓔ

GH QQQ Regency House Hotel 50 Clarence Square GL50 4JR ☎(0242) 582718 FAX (0242) 262697
Closed Xmas & New Year
An elegant period house situated north of the town, just off the A453 Evesham Road, in a quiet location overlooking a leafy square and gardens. The spacious public rooms have high ceilings, with a grand spiral stone staircase leading to the bedrooms which are well equipped, most of them have private bathrooms and all overlook the square and gardens. Personally owned and run, the guesthouse is in the process of substantial upgrading and renovation.
8⇌↱ (3fb)⚟in 3 bedrooms CTV in all bedrooms ® T
sB&B⇌↱£29-£36 dB&B⇌↱£42-£48 WB&B£142-£206 WBDi£218-£283 LDO noon
Lic 🍽 3P
Credit Cards 1 3 Ⓔ

GH QQQ Stretton Lodge Western Rd GL50 3RN
☎(0242) 528724 & 570771
Initial impressions may be misleading for behind this fairly standard exterior lies a character residence with elegant public rooms and comfortable bedrooms. This large, Victorian semi has been carefully modernised by the owners Mr and Mrs Price to provide good hotel accommodation, retaining much of its charm. The en suite bedrooms are well proportioned, nicely decorated and softened with pleasing flowered drapes and fabrics, blending with a high range of facilities that include TV, direct dial telephone, mini bar and trouser press with iron. There are various comfortable public areas, which are rich in attractive interior architecture with their cornices and marbled fireplaces.
9⇌↱ (3fb)⚟in 6 bedrooms CTV in all bedrooms ® T
✗ (ex guide dogs) sB&B⇌↱£35-£45 dB&B⇌↱£50-£65
WB&B£150-£300 WBDi£235-£375 LDO noon
Lic 🍽 6P
Credit Cards 1 2 3 Ⓔ

GH QQ Willoughby 1 Suffolk Square GL50 2DR
☎(0242) 522798
Closed 2 wks Xmas & New Year
A fine, imposing late-Georgian Cotswold stone property in a prominent position on the square. Bedrooms are spacious and well equipped, and the public areas retain many original features

including a magnificent brass-railed staircase. Useful car parking is available on site.
9rm(7fl 2hc) (1fb) CTV in all bedrooms ® ✱ sB&Bfr£23.50 sB&Bfl£26.50-£35 dB&Bfr£40 dB&Bfl£45-£50 LDO 4pm
CTV 10P £

GH QQ Wishmoor 147 Hales Rd GL52 6TD ☎(0242) 238504
Dating back to the turn of the century, this bright, comfortable guesthouse reflects this charm throughout. Personally run by Mr and Mrs Risborough, it has been continually upgraded to provide bright décor throughout and comfortable, nicely equipped bedrooms. This spotlessly clean house is just off the B4075, set back in its own small gardens, and provides useful off street parking.
10rm(4fl 6hc) (1fb) ⊬in 2 bedrooms CTV in all bedrooms ® ✗ (ex guide dogs) ✱ sB&B£17.50-£18.50 sB&Bfl£26-£30 dB&B£34-£36 dB&Bfl£42-£46 WB&B£122.50-£182 WBDi£196-£255 LDO noon
10P
Credit Cards [1] [3] £

CHEPSTOW Gwent See **Tintern**

CHERITON FITZPAINE Devon Map **03** SS80

FH QQ Mrs D M Lock **Brindiwell** *(SS896079)* EX17 4HR ☎(0363) 866357
A period, pink Devonshire longhouse surrounded by farmland, with its own small garden. Situated on the side of a valley, there are views of the Exe valley and Dartmoor. The bedrooms are comfortable, some with coordinating colour schemes. Guests share one large table for breakfast.
4rm(1hc) (1fb) ⊬in 1 bedroom CTV in 1 bedroom ® ✗ (ex guide dogs) ✱ dB&B£24-£30 WB&Bfr£85 WBDifr£110 LDO 5pm
CTV 4P 1🚗 120 acres sheep £

CHESTER Cheshire Map **07** SJ46

GH QQ Bawnpark Hotel 10 Hoole Rd, Hoole CH2 3NH
☏(0244) 324971 FAX (0244) 310951
This large, semidetached Victorian residence has a rear car park, and stands on the outskirts of Chester. The cheerfully decorated bedrooms have many amenities expected at a hotel.
7rm(5⇌2↱) (2fb) CTV in 5 bedrooms ® ✱ sB&B⇌↱£25-£36 dB&B⇌↱£32-£36
ꟿ CTV 12P
Credit Cards [1] [3] (£)

GH QQQ *Chester Court Hotel* 48 Hoole Rd (A56) CH2 3NL
☏(0244) 320779 & 311098 FAX (0244) 344795
Closed 24 Dec-5 Jan
A fully modernised and extended hotel on the A56 route into the city centre. The bedrooms are smartly furnished and most have en suite facilities; some are in an annexe a few steps from the main house.
8rm(1⇌4↱3hc) Annexe 12rm(6⇌6↱) (2fb) CTV in all bedrooms ® LDO 8pm
Lic ꟿ 25P
Credit Cards [1] [2] [3] [5]

GH QQQ Chester Town House 23 King St CH1 2AH
☏(0244) 350021
A quaint old town house in a conservation area within the city walls. Each room is individually decorated to a high standard and has been thoughtfully furnished to reflect the age of the building. The resident hosts offer a warm welcome, and parking is arranged in a private car park.
3⇌↱ Annexe 1⇌ CTV in all bedrooms ® sB&B⇌↱£32 dB&B⇌↱£45
ꟿ
Credit Cards [1] [3]

GH QQ Dee House 67 Hoole Rd, Hoole CH2 3NJ
☏(0244) 351532
A small, well run guesthouse which is home to the Carter family. It is close to the railway station on the junction of the one-way Westminster Road and Hoole Road. The bedrooms are clean and well decorated and there is a car park at the rear.
5rm(3⇌↱2hc) (1fb) CTV in all bedrooms ® ✖ ✱ sB&B£17-£20 sB&B⇌↱£20 dB&B£30 dB&B⇌↱£32
ꟿ 8P (£)

GH Q Devonia 33-35 Hoole Rd CH2 3NH ☏(0244) 322236
This family-run hotel is on the busy A56 route into the city and has its own private car park. The rooms are simply furnished, clean and warm.
10hc (6fb) CTV in all bedrooms ® ✱ sB&B£17.50-£22.50 dB&B£27.50-£32 LDO 4pm
Lic ꟿ CTV 15P (£)

GH QQ Eaton Hotel 29 City Rd CH1 3AE ☏(0244) 320840
FAX (0244) 320850
A deceptively large hotel situated alongside the Shropshire Union canal, close to the main railway station. Most of the bedrooms are well equipped and have private bathrooms, and the public areas have been attractively refurbished. There is a car park at the rear.
22rm(6⇌7↱9hc) (3fb) CTV in all bedrooms ® T ✱ sB&B£28 sB&B⇌↱£35 dB&B£35 dB&B⇌↱£45 LDO 8pm
Lic ꟿ 8P 1🚗
Credit Cards [1] [2] [3] [5] (£)

GH QQ Egerton Lodge Hotel 57 Hoole Rd, Hoole CH2 3NJ
☏(0244) 320712
Closed 19 Dec-3 Jan
Neat and attractive, this Victorian terraced house is on the A56 route into the city. Bedrooms are compact but well equipped, and central heating and double glazing have recently been installed for guests' comfort. Car parking is provided.
4rm(3↱1hc) (3fb) CTV in all bedrooms ® ✖ ✱ sB&B↱£17.50-£19.50 dB&B↱£28-£32
ꟿ 5P nc3yrs
Credit Cards [1] [2] [3] (£)

GH QQ Eversley Hotel 9 Eversley Park CH2 2AJ
☏(0244) 373744
Closed 24 Dec-2 Jan
A bustling hotel in a quiet residential area off the A5116 signed to Ellesmere Port. There is a bar/dining room serving à la carte meals, and many of the bedrooms have en suite facilities.
11rm(4⇌5↱2hc) (3fb) CTV in all bedrooms ® ✖ ✱ sB&Bfr£23 sB&B⇌↱fr£30 dB&Bfr£40 dB&B⇌↱fr£43 WB&Bfr£150.50 WBDifr£200 LDO 8pm
Lic ꟿ CTV 17P
Credit Cards [1] [3]

GH Q Gables 5 Vicarage Rd, Hoole CH2 3HZ ☏(0244) 323969
Closed 23-27 Dec
This small Victorian house is just off the A56 road into the city, close to the park. The hotel has a small car park and street parking is also available.
6hc (4fb) CTV in all bedrooms ® ✖ ✱ sB&B£16-£20 dB&B£26-£30
CTV 6P (£)

GH QQ Gloster Lodge Hotel 44 Hoole Rd, Hoole CH2 3NL
☏(0244) 348410 & 320231
Closed 24-31 Dec
A friendly, small family-run hotel on the A56 route into town, commonly known as the 'Hotel Road'. The rooms have good amenities and are clean and freshly decorated.
5⇌↱ Annexe 3⇌↱ (2fb) CTV in all bedrooms ® T ✱ sB&B⇌↱£25-£30 dB&B⇌↱£32-£36.50 LDO 8pm
Lic ꟿ 9P
Credit Cards [1] [3]

GH QQQ Green Gables 11 Eversley Park CH2 2AJ
☏(0244) 372243 FAX (0244) 376352
A fully modernised small hotel on the outskirts of Chester, in a quiet area just off the A5116 signed to Ellesmere Port. The bedrooms are smart and the dining room has a Continental feel to it.
4↱ (1fb) 🚭 in all bedrooms CTV in all bedrooms ® T ✖ (ex guide dogs) ✱ sB&B↱£20-£22 dB&B↱£33-£35 LDO 9.30pm
ꟿ CTV 8P 3🚗 (£)

GH QQ Hamilton Court 5-7 Hamilton St CH2 3JG
☏(0244) 345387
Closed 22 Dec-5 Jan
A well appointed, hospitable hotel converted from 2 gabled houses, just off the A56, a mile from the city centre. Evening meals are available by prior booking, and parking can also be arranged.
12rm(6↱6hc) (5fb) CTV in all bedrooms ® ✱ sB&B£19-£20 dB&B£31-£33 dB&B↱£37 LDO 6.30pm
Lic ꟿ CTV 8P 10🚗
Credit Cards [1] [3] (£)

SELECTED

GH QQQQ *Redland Private Hotel* 64 Hough Green CH4 8JY ☏(0244) 671024
Formerly a gentleman's residence, this red brick Victorian house has retained much of its original character and charm. The spacious ground floor public areas, with their fine panelling, moulded cornices and ceilings, are enhanced by tasteful décor and quality antiques. An original staircase is the excellent background for some fine paintings and on the bottom half landing an honesty bar is guarded by a suit of armour! Very individual spacious bedrooms, with tasteful colour schemes, are offered by Theresa White, who is a talented interior designer and her choice of schemes, coupled with the quality of furnishings, makes Redland a unique base for touring the charms of the city.

13⇌↱ (3fb) CTV in all bedrooms ® Lic ꟾꟾꟾ 10P 2⛍ sauna solarium

GH Q ***The Riverside Hotel*** 22 City Walls, Duke St, Off Lower Bridge St CH1 1SB ☎(0244) 326580 & 325278 FAX (0244) 311567

A popular modern hotel on the city walls, next to the river Dee, virtually in the town centre. The hotel is comprised of 2 separate buildings: 1 has the reception and Georgian style restaurant, and the other houses 'Edgar's' coffee shop which serves light snacks throughout the day. All the bedrooms are well furnished, with en suite facilities.

13⇌↱ (2fb)⚟in 1 bedroom CTV in all bedrooms ®
LDO 9pm
Lic ꟾꟾꟾ CTV 25P
Credit Cards [1] [2] [3]

GH QQQ **Vicarage Lodge** 11 Vicarage Rd, Hoole CH2 3HZ ☎(0244) 319533

An attractive house situated in a quiet residential road just off the A56 route into the city centre. The warm and cosy bedrooms are freshly decorated, and the resident proprietors make you welcome. There is a private rear car park.

4rm(1↱3hc) CTV in all bedrooms ® ✗ ✱ dB&Bfr£27 dB&B↱fr£30
ꟾꟾꟾ 7P Ⓕ

CHEWTON MENDIP Somerset Map **03** ST55

FH QQ Mrs B Clothier ***Franklyns*** *(ST601522)* BA3 4NB ☎(0761) 241372
Mar-Oct

Located in a rural position, this stone farmhouse offers mostly very spacious and extremely comfortable bedrooms, that share a bathroom on the same floor. There is a large lounge and a

→

breakfast room that features picture windows overlooking the gardens. Outside, a tennis court is available along with parking facilities.
3hc CTV in all bedrooms ® ✗ (ex guide dogs)
♨ CTV 3P ♈(hard)400 acres arable dairy

CHIDEOCK Dorset Map **03** SY49

SELECTED

GH QQQQ Betchworth House Hotel DT6 6JW
☎(0297) 89478
Mar-Oct
Conveniently situated for the main resorts, this pretty, stone cottage, dating back to 1640, boasts beautiful gardens filled with flowers, and it is here that many people come to enjoy a Dorset cream tea. All the bedrooms are freshly decorated in a light, airy style and the soft furnishings are prettily coordinated. Some rooms are equipped with very good, modern en suite showers, whilst the others share a well kept general bath/shower room. The cosy lounge is comfortably furnished with soft, easy chairs and has a TV along with books/magazines. There is a front facing breakfast room which is double glazed (as are most rooms), furnished with some handsome pieces and freshly decorated. Breakfast and cream teas are the only meals served. Mrs Scott is a friendly host, who works hard to keep the hotel spick and span as well as providing a warm and relaxed atmosphere.
6rm(3↱3hc) (1fb) ® ✗ (ex guide dogs) sB&B£20-£24 dB&B£36-£40 dB&B↱£40-£44 WB&B£122.50-£150.50
Lic ♨ CTV 15P nc7yrs ⓔ

CHILHAM Kent Map **05** TR05

INN QQQ Woolpack High St CT4 8DL (Shepherd)
☎Canterbury(0227) 730208 FAX (0227) 731053
Combining the old with the new, the accommodation here has recently been completely renovated. There is a beamed and wood panelled bar with a lovely inglenook fireplace, a smart modern restaurant with flambé cooking and an à la carte menu. Bar meals are also available from a blackboard selection. The bedrooms are all well furnished; 5 low beamed rooms in the main building, the remainder in the Coach House and Stable annexes.
5⇌ Annexe 10↱ (3fb) CTV in all bedrooms ® T
sB&B⇌↱£40-£45 dB&B⇌↱£50-£60 Lunch £10-£15alc Dinner £12-£17alc LDO 10pm
♨ CTV 30P
Credit Cards [1] [3]

CHIPPENHAM Wiltshire Map **03** ST97

GH QQ *Oxford Hotel* 32/36 Langley Rd SN15 1BX
☎(0249) 652542
A small privately run hotel with easy access to the station and town centre. The bedrooms are simply decorated and some are made attractive with floral soft furnishings. A comfortable bar and conservatory lounge are available for guests' use.
13rm(7↱6hc) (1fb) CTV in all bedrooms ® LDO 5.30pm
Lic ♨ 9P
Credit Cards [1] [2] [3]

CHIPPING CAMPDEN Gloucestershire Map **04** SP13

GH QQQ The Malt House Broad Campden GL55 6UU
☎Evesham(0386) 840295 FAX (0386) 841334
Closed 23 Dec-1 Jan rs Tue
Just a mile from Chipping Campden in the picturesque village of Broad Campden, this quality, comfortable guesthouse was once a row of cottages. The Malt House is lovingly cared for and very clean. Each bedroom is unique, but with the same period character as the gorgeous lounge which overlooks a walled garden. Dinner is also available.
3⇌ CTV in all bedrooms ® ✗ (ex guide dogs) ✱ sB&B£25-£40 dB&B⇌£55-£75 LDO noon
Lic ♨ 8P nc12yrs
Credit Cards [1] [3] ⓔ

CHISELBOROUGH Somerset Map **03** ST41

FH QQ Mrs E Holloway **Manor** *(ST468151)* TA14 6TQ
☎(0935) 881203
Apr-Oct
Built in 1861 as a model farm, this delightful Ham-stone house provides spacious bedrooms with antique furniture and some modern facilities such as TV and tea making facilities. Mrs Holloway has been receiving guests into her home for 22 years now and provides a full English breakfast served at one large table. The lounge is especially comfortable and has an open log fire. There is coarse fishing in the carp pond, and endless country walking for the energetic.
4hc (1fb) CTV in all bedrooms ® ✗ ✱ sB&B£17-£19 dB&B£34-£38 WB&B£106-£109
♨ CTV 4P ✔ 450 acres mixed ⓔ

CHISELDON Wiltshire Map **04** SU17

FH QQ M Hughes **Parsonage** *(SU185799)* SN4 0NJ
☎Swindon(0793) 740204
This attractive stone-built farmhouse is in a quiet position beside the church in the village of Chiseldon, which is only a mile from junction 15 of the M4 and 4 miles from the centre of Swindon. The bedrooms are comfortable and very traditional in style. The public areas are full of character with some tasteful personal touches, and guests share one large antique table in the dining room.
4rm(2⇌↱) ® ✱ sB&B£22.50-£25 sB&B⇌↱£25 dB&B⇌↱£40
♨ CTV 8P 2♠ U 400 acres arable ⓔ

CHISLEHAMPTON Oxfordshire Map **04** SU59

SELECTED

INN QQQQ Coach & Horses Stadhampton Rd OX9 7UX ☎Stadhampton(0865) 890255
FAX (0865) 891995
An attractive 16th-century stone-built inn standing beside the B480, just 7 miles from the city of Oxford. There are 9 bedrooms offering comfortable accommodation in an annexe block around a rear courtyard; all are en suite, with TV and direct dial telephones, and are tastefully decorated and furnished. The public areas, in the original main building, are cosy and inviting, with attractive stone work, oak beams and roaring log fires. There is a choice of interesting dishes available in the popular restaurant, with home-cooked, nicely presented à la carte and table d'hôte menus. Drinks and snacks are also served on the patio in summer. Ample car parking is provided adjacent to the rooms.
9⇌↱ CTV in all bedrooms ® T ✗ (ex guide dogs) ✱ sB&B£37-£52 sB&B⇌↱£41-£55.50 dB&B£52-£69 dB&B⇌↱£54-£72.50 WB&B£196-£314 WBDi£285.50-£404 Lunch fr£12.50&alc Dinner fr£12.50&alc LDO 10pm
42P
Credit Cards [1] [2] [3] [5] ⓔ

CHOLMONDELEY Cheshire Map **07** SJ55

GH QQQ The Cholmondeley Arms SY14 8BT
☎(0829) 720300
This former school building, converted into a simple but pleasant bar/bistro, has retained much of its original character including the lofty ceilings and painted brick walls, now decorated with pictures and a variety of bric a brac. The furniture is a mixture of old, simple pieces including several original school desks. Meals can be selected from a comprehensive menu of hot and cold dishes, supplemented by a blackboard selection. Located in the old school

house across the playground, the attractively decorated bedrooms are something of a contrast with their modern style and en suite facilities.
4↱ (1fb) CTV in all bedrooms ® ✱ sB&B↱fr£30 dB&B↱fr£40 LDO 10pm
Lic 🍴
Credit Cards [1] [3] (£)

CHORLEY Lancashire Map **07** SD51

GH QQQ Astley House Hotel 3 Southport Rd PR7 1LB ☎(0257) 272315
This former family home, situated on the A581 close to the town centre, has recently been renovated in a very elegant Victorian style. The spacious double bedrooms are beautifully decorated, and the breakfast room has many items of antique furniture and other items of bygone days. The bedrooms have TV and tea and coffee making facilities, and 3 of the rooms have private bathrooms. There is a small private car park.
6rm(3⇌↱3hc) CTV in all bedrooms ® ✕ sB&B£17-£22 sB&B⇌↱£20-£22 dB&B⇌↱£34-£40
🍴 1🚘
Credit Cards [1] [2] [3] (£)

CHRISTCHURCH Dorset Map **04** SZ19

See also Bournemouth
GH Q Belvedere Hotel 59 Barrack Rd BH23 1PD ☎(0202) 485978
This large Victorian hotel on the main Christchurch – Bournemouth road has been under the ownership of Mrs Jefferis for the past 38 years. Bedrooms are simply furnished, but with some modern facilites. There is a comfortable lounge area and a neat breakfast room. Conveniently close to the county's rivers, the guesthouse is popular with fishermen, most of whom return each year.
8hc (3fb) CTV in all bedrooms ® ✱ sB&B£16-£18 dB&B£30-£36 WB&B£110-£120 LDO 4pm
Lic 🍴 CTV 12P (£)

CHURCH STOKE Powys Map **07** SO29

FH QQQ Mrs C Richards **The Drewin** *(SO261905)* SY15 6TW ☎(0588) 620325
Apr-Nov rs Etr (if in Mar)
This 300-year-old farmhouse is part of a working farm, with splendid views of the surrounding countryside; Offa's Dyke footpath runs through the farm. Bedrooms are modern and well equipped, and there is a comfortable lounge complemented by the original beams and inglenook fireplace.
2rm(1↱1hc) (2fb) CTV in all bedrooms ® ✕ sB&B£14-£17 sB&B↱£15-£18 dB&B£28-£34 dB&B↱£30-£35 WB&B£98-£120 LDO 7pm
🍴 CTV 6P games room 102 acres mixed (£)

CHURCH STRETTON Shropshire Map **07** SO49

See also Strefford
GH QQQ Belvedere Burway Rd SY6 6DP ☎(0694) 722232
A well-run family hotel on the northwest edge of the town. The house is surrounded by charming gardens, the bedrooms are modern and there is a choice of lounges.
12rm(6↱6hc) (2fb) ® sB&B£20-£23 dB&B£40 dB&B↱£45 WB&B£126-£144.90 WBDi£185.50-£204.40 LDO 6pm
Lic 🍴 CTV 9P 1🚘 ♧
Credit Cards [1] [3] (£)

GH QQQ Brookfields Watling St North SY6 7AR ☎(0694) 722314
This recently established, small, privately owned hotel is situated close to the A49, on the northeast edge of the village. It provides well equipped bedrooms furnished to a high standard, with particularly luxurious en suite facilities. The resident proprietor is a trained chef, and it is hoped to extend the restaurant and bar facilities.
4⇌↱ (1fb)⊬in all bedrooms CTV in all bedrooms ® T ✱ sB&B⇌↱£25-£35 dB&B⇌↱£48-£60 LDO 9pm
Lic 🍴 16P (£)

GH QQ Hope Bowdler Hall Hope Bowdler SY6 7DD ☎(0694) 722041
Mar-Oct rs Nov
Set in 11 acres of grounds with wooded slopes and pleasant lawns, which include a tennis court, this impressive stone manor is situated in the peaceful village of Hope Bowdler, near the church. There are just 2 spacious bedrooms, both comfortably furnished with older stripped pine. The attractive drawing room features an open fire with 3 piece suites displaying loose floral covers, and polished floor boards and oil paintings are prominent in many areas throughout the house.
3hc ⊬in all bedrooms ✕ ✱ sB&B£16-£17.50 dB&B£30-£32
🍴 4P nc10yrs 🎾(hard)

GH QQQ Jinlye Castle Hill, All Stretton SY6 6JP ☎(0694) 723243
Once a crofter's cottage dating back at least 200 years and now extended to provide excellent accommodation, this stone-built property lies in attractive lawns and gardens with the front overlooking the Strettons and the rear set against the sheep-filled mountains. Cream teas are served in the conservatory and on the lawns in good weather, and there are 3 superb sitting rooms, one with a log-burning stone inglenook fireplace, a beamed ceiling and comfortable deep sofas and easy chairs. Bedrooms sparkle with pretty décor and matching fabrics. Family run, the house has a friendly atmosphere and guests are assured of a warm welcome.
3↱ ⊬in all bedrooms ® ✕ ✱ dB&B£32 dB&B↱£48 WB&B£105-£150 WBDi£185-£235 LDO 2pm
🍴 CTV 3P nc12yrs mountain bikes for hire

FH QQQ Mrs C J Hotchkiss **Olde Hall** *(SO509926)* Wall-under-Heywood SY6 7DU ☎Longville(0694) 771253
Feb-Nov
This old farmhouse, dating back to the Elizabethan period, is just off the B4371 Much Wenlock to Church Stretton road. It is home to the Hotchkiss family and their guests, and the rooms have been carefully restored to retain their character.
3hc (1fb) CTV in all bedrooms ® ✕ sB&B£16.50 dB&B£33 WB&B£95
CTV 6P 275 acres dairy

SELECTED

FH QQQQ Mrs J A Davies Rectory *(SO452985)* Woolstaston SY6 6NN (3.5m off B4370 at All Stretton) ☎Leebotwood(0694) 751306
Mar-Nov
Very much a working farm, this beautiful, half timbered farmhouse, built around 1620, is situated on the lower slopes of the Lens Mynd. All areas have an abundance of ceiling beams and exposed timbers, and the dining room with its oak tables features impressive carved wooden wall panels. Two sitting rooms are available, with a fine central fireplace splitting the main one, furnished with modern lounge seating. The en suite bedrooms are well furnished and are equipped with comfortable settees or armchairs. The Davies family continue to provide warm hospitality to all their guests.
3⇌ TV available ® ✕ ✻ sB&B⇌£24 dB&B⇌£36
CTV 10P nc12yrs 170 acres beef

CIRENCESTER Gloucestershire Map 04 SP00

GH QQ ***La Ronde Hotel*** 52-54 Ashcroft Rd GL7 1QX ☎(0285) 654611 & 652216
Personally run by Mr and Mrs Smales, this small, friendly hotel is situated in the heart of the historic town, with car parking on site. Bedrooms are soundly equipped, with cosy public areas including a small restaurant offering a good range of nicely cooked, imaginative dishes.
10⇌♠ (2fb) CTV in all bedrooms ® LDO 9pm
Lic 9P
Credit Cards 1 3

GH QQQ Wimborne House 91 Victoria Rd GL7 1ES ☎(0285) 653890
A friendly, personally owned and run guesthouse catering for non-smokers only. It is conveniently situated 5 minutes' walk from the town centre, and has a private car park and gardens to the front and rear. The comfortable bedrooms are all en suite, with modern facilities.
5⇌♠ ⊁in all bedrooms CTV in all bedrooms ® ✕ ✻ sB&B⇌♠£20-£25 dB&B⇌♠£25-£35 LDO 4pm
8P nc5yrs £

INN QQQ Eliot Arms Clark's Hay, South Cerney GL7 5UA ☎(0285) 860215
Set in the charming hamlet of South Cerney, this stone-built inn has attractive open plan public rooms, a cosy dining area and very attractive and well-equipped en suite bedrooms.
9⇌♠ (1fb) CTV in all bedrooms ® **T** sB&B⇌♠fr£30 dB&B⇌♠fr£45 Lunch £1.50-£10.95alc Dinner £3.95-£10.95alc LDO 10pm
28P
Credit Cards 1 3 £

INN QQQ Masons Arms Meysey Hampton GL7 5JT ☎(0285) 850164
This small, personally run country inn, attractively positioned in a pretty village just outside Cirencester, has recently been acquired and renovated by enthusiastic owners. Bedrooms are spotless and cosy, although some are compact, with a nice blend of antique stripped pine furniture and a good range of modern facilities, including en suite showers. Public rooms comprise a congenial bar and an attractive breakfast room. A good range of home-cooked food is served.
9♠ (2fb)⊁in 2 bedrooms CTV in all bedrooms ® ✻ sB&B⇌♠£17.50-£20 dB&B⇌♠£35 WB&B£105 WBDi£160 Bar Lunch £1.50-£8.25&alc Dinner £6.60-£15alc LDO 10pm
8P
Credit Cards 1 3

CLACTON-ON-SEA Essex Map 05 TM11

GH QQQ Chudleigh Hotel Agate Rd CO15 1RA ☎(0255) 425407
Closed 15 Dec-6 Jan
This small, family run guesthouse is ideally situated between the seafront, pier and town centre. Bedrooms are all freshly decorated and well equipped, the majority having private bathrooms. There is a comfortable lounge and dinner is available. The charming owners offer a warm welcome.
12rm(11⇌♠1hc) (3fb) CTV in all bedrooms ® ✻ sB&B⇌♠£27.50 dB&B⇌♠£45-£50 WB&B£165-£170 WBDi£200 LDO 7pm
Lic 7P nc2yrs
Credit Cards 1 2 3 5 £

GH QQQ Sandrock Hotel 1 Penfold Rd CO15 1JN ☎(0255) 428215
This detached Victorian house is situated just 50 yards from the seafront, and benefits from a small car park to the rear. Bedrooms all have private bathrooms, and are freshly decorated. There is a comfortable lounge, and a daily menu is offered for dinner.
7♠ (3fb) CTV in all bedrooms ® sB&B♠£27 dB&B♠£48 WB&B£135 WBDi£180 LDO 6pm
Lic 6P
Credit Cards 1 3

CLAPHAM North Yorkshire Map 07 SD76

INN QQ The Flying Horseshoe LA2 8ES ☎(05242) 51229
A mile west of the A65 opposite Clapham Railway Station, the Flying Horseshoe offers well equipped bedrooms and an attractive dining room, as well as the lounge bar where a log fire blazes in cold weather.
4rm(1⇌3♠) CTV in all bedrooms ® ✻ sB&B⇌♠£25 LDO 9pm
50P ♪

CLAVERDON Warwickshire Map 04 SP16

GH QQ Woodside Country House Langley Rd CV35 8PJ (0.75m S of B4095) ☎(0926) 842446
Closed Xmas wk
3hc (1fb) CTV in 1 bedroom TV in 1 bedroom ® sB&B£14-£20 dB&B£28-£34 WBDi£181-£222 LDO 2pm
CTV 12P 1🚗 (hard) croquet £

CLAYTON-LE-WOODS Lancashire Map 07 SD52

GH QQQ Brook House Hotel 662 Preston Rd PR6 7EH ☎Preston(0772) 36403
This 19th-century private hotel has recently been extended, and provides immaculate accommodation with every modern facility and friendly, helpful service. There is a residents' lounge bar, a comfortable general lounge and an attractive dining room. Private parking facilities are also provided, and the hotel is situated on the A6 at Clayton-le-Woods, a mile from Junction 29 of the M6.
20rm(16⇌♠4hc) (3fb) CTV in all bedrooms ® **T** ✕ (ex guide dogs) sB&B£25 sB&B⇌♠£33 dB&B£38 dB&B⇌♠£46 LDO 8.30pm
Lic CTV 25P
Credit Cards 1 3 £

CLEARWELL Gloucestershire Map **03** SO50

SELECTED

GH QQQQ Tudor Farmhouse Hotel GL16 8JS
☎Dean(0594) 833046 FAX (0594) 837093
rs Sun
Overlooking its own 15 acres of grounds, Deborah and Richard Fletcher's listed Tudor farmhouse is set right in the heart of this fascinating village and epitomizes character throughout. Due to the age of the property obvious architectural restraints are imposed here but in fact this adds to the cosiness and charm of the house. The original oak spiral staircase leads to the bedrooms in the main house, which boast heavy oak doors, beamed ceilings and uneven floors. Quaint features are blended with modern comforts such as remote control TV, tea making facilities and small en suites. The converted stables which adjoin the cottage garden offer bedrooms with extra space, yet are equally full of charm. The candle-lit cosy restaurant offers a good range of imaginative home-cooked dishes and pre-dinner drinks can be taken in the bright little conservatory lounge. With such a popular retreat, reservations are advisable.
6⇔↱ Annexe 3⇔↱ CTV in all bedrooms ® T
sB&B⇔↱£42.50-£47 dB&B⇔↱£49-£65 LDO 9pm
Lic 🍽 15P 2🚗
Credit Cards [1] [2] [3] £

CLEETHORPES Humberside Map **08** TA30

GH QQ ***Mallow View*** 9-11 Albert Rd DN35 8LX
☎(0472) 691297
Situated between the town centre and steps from the seafront, this long established guesthouse is in a Victorian terrace tucked away behind the library. Well carpeted ground floor areas comprise a poolroom, bar with piano and small dining room. The ground floor bedroom, which has its own bathroom, is the largest. Mrs Meyers is the friendly proprietor.
16rm(1↱15hc) (1fb) CTV in 15 bedrooms ® LDO 7pm
Lic 🍽 CTV ⁄P

CLEVEDON Avon Map **03** ST47

INN QQ The Salthouse Salthouse Rd BS21 7TY
☎(0275) 871482
This is a very lively seafront pub, with a garden play area to the front and commanding views across the bay. Public areas were in the final stages of redecoration at the time of our visit, but it is evidently a popular establishment with a sound range of bar meals available. The 2 bedrooms are quite compact, but well equipped with modern facilities.
2↱ CTV in all bedrooms ® ✗ * dB&B⇔↱£50-£57
WB&Bfr£175 Lunch fr£3.30 Dinner fr£4.75 LDO 8.45pm
🍽 50P nc12yrs ℘(hard)golf driving range
Credit Cards [1] [3]

CLIFTON UPON TEME Hereford & Worcester Map **03** SO76

INN QQ The Lion WR6 6DH
☎Shelsley Beauchamp(08865) 617 & 235
The Lion dates back to 1207 when it started life as a court house and hostelry. Cheerful log fires greet you in the restaurant and both bars, where bar meals augment the regularly changing restaurant menu. There are 2 commendable bedrooms available with modern en suite facilities.
2⇔↱ (2fb) CTV in all bedrooms ® sB&B⇔↱£28-£38
dB&B⇔↱£55 Lunch £8 Dinner £12 LDO 9pm
22P
Credit Cards [1] [3] £

CLIFTONVILLE Kent

See **Margate**

CLITHEROE Lancashire Map **07** SD74

GH QQQ **Brooklyn** 32 Pimlico Rd BB7 2AH ☎(0200) 28268
This detached Victorian town house is situated in a quiet area just a short walk from the centre of the historic market town, and is an ideal base from which to tour the Trough of Bowland, the Yorkshire Dales or even the Lake District. It is an immaculate guesthouse with comfortable modern bedrooms, all tastefully decorated with attractive coordinated Dorma fabrics together with framed prints and dried flower arrangements. Four of the rooms are in an end terrace house opposite, where standards are equally high, and there is also an elegant lounge. The dining room, with 6 polished wooden tables and a pine dresser, is in the main house along with the comfortable lounge bar. There is a neat patio garden at the back, ideal for summer days, and a narrow paved area at the front with garden furniture. Service to guests includes the provision of umbrellas on wet days.
4♠ CTV in all bedrooms ® ✗ (ex guide dogs) sB&B♠£20-£21 dB&B♠£38-£40 WB&Bfr£126 WBDifr£189 LDO 10am
Lic ♨ CTV 1🚗
Credit Cards 1 3 £

CLOUGHTON North Yorkshire Map **08** TA09

GH QQ **Cober Hill** Newlands Rd YO13 0AR ☎Scarborough(0723) 870310
This conference and holiday centre has been used for many years by voluntary, religious and educational groups; it is also popular with tourists during the summer months, and now offers modern bedrooms with full en suite facilities in a recently constructed annexe. The complex stands in 6 acres of grounds, just off the A171, 6 miles north of Scarborough and close to delightful coastal walks on the north Yorkshire moors. Other facilities include tennis, croquet, bowls and clock golf.
44hc Annexe 31rm(17⇌14♠) (13fb) ® sB&B£16.50-£18.50 sB&B⇌♠£23.50 dB&B£33-£37 dB&B⇌♠£47 WB&B£99-£141 WBDi£144-£184 LDO 7pm
Lic ♨ 60P ℛ(hard)bowling green croquet table-tennis

CLOVELLY Devon Map **02** SS32

FH QQQ Mrs E Symons **Burnstone** *(SS325233)* Higher Clovelly EX39 5RX ☎(0237) 431219
An attractive 17th-century Devon longhouse retaining many original features in the spacious, well furnished lounge and dining room. The 2 bedrooms are a good size and share a bathroom and separate toilet.
2hc (2fb) ® LDO 4pm
♨ CTV 3P ✓ 500 acres arable dairy mixed £

CLUN Shropshire Map **07** SO38

FH QQ Mr & Mrs Davies **Lower Duffryn** *(SO229822)* SY7 8PQ ☎(0588) 640239
Mar-Nov
Dating back 300 years, this beautifully preserved and maintained farmhouse is set in the picturesque surrounding of Clun Valley. The comfortable bedrooms are attractively decorated and one has an en suite toilet, while another is furnished for family occupancy. The third and final room is a double but quite compact. In addition to the pleasantly furnished dining room, with exposed ceiling beams, there is a cosy, comfortably furnished lounge with a TV – although reception is unpredictable due to the surrounding hills, not a problem for those wanting to escape to peace and tranquility.
3hc ® ✗ ✱ dB&B£24-£28 WB&B£80 WBDi£120 LDO 3pm
♨ CTV 3P 2🚗 140 acres mixed sheep cattle rearing

CLUNTON Shropshire Map **07** SO38

FH QQ Mrs J Williams **Hurst Mill** *(SO318811)* SY7 0JA ☎Clun(0588) 640224
A more hospitable family than the Williams would be difficult to find. The house has an attractive setting just off the B4368, beside the banks of the river. The rooms are simply furnished, but all the worries of the world evaporate when you unwind at this friendly working farm.
3rm(2hc) (1fb)⚟in 1 bedroom CTV in 1 bedroom TV in 1 bedroom ® ✱ sB&B£13-£15 dB&B£26-£30 WB&B£90-£100 WBDi£145-£150 LDO 6.30pm
CTV 4P 2🚗 ✓ 2 ponies 100 acres mixed £

COCKERMOUTH Cumbria Map **11** NY13

SELECTED

GH QQQQ ***Low Hall Country*** Brandlingill CA13 0RE (3m S on unclass off A5086) ☎(0900) 826654
Mar-Nov
A charming 17th-century farmhouse situated in peaceful surroundings with views of the western fells. The 6 bedrooms are all very attractive, each with a private bathroom and individual style and character. The lounges and dining room are quite delightful, with oak beams, stone walls, open fires and plenty of books and magazines. The home cooked meals include a choice of international dishes as well as traditional Cumbrian recipes. Low Hall is ideally located for touring the Lake district: to find it take the A66, then the A5086 Egremont road, turn left after about 2 miles at the school. The drive is on the right after 1 mile.
6rm(1⇌5♠) ⚟in all bedrooms ® ✗ (ex guide dogs) LDO 7.30pm
Lic ♨ CTV 10P nc10yrs
Credit Cards 1 3

GH QQQ ***Sundawn*** Carlisle Rd, Bridekirk CA13 0PA ☎(0900) 822384
This spacious Victorian family house is set in an elevated position amid green fields, just 2 miles from Cockermouth on the Carlisle road. The bedrooms are comfortably furnished and decorated in a variety of styles, and there is a cosy sun lounge. Guests can be sure of warm, friendly service from the resident proprietors.
4rm(2⇌♠2hc) (1fb)⚟in all bedrooms ® ✗ (ex guide dogs) LDO 9am
♨ CTV 6P

CODSALL Staffordshire Map **07** SJ80

FH QQQ Mrs D E Moreton **Moors Farm & Country Restaurant** *(SJ859048)* Chillington Ln WV8 1QH ☎(0902) 842330
A busy working farm in an isolated position 5 miles northwest of Wolverhampton, between the village of Codsall and Codsall Wood. Many school parties have their first introduction to a variety of farm animals here, with over 100 acres of mixed farming. Bedrooms are attractively decorated, with TV and tea trays. There is a small cosy residents' lounge, an oak beamed bar, and a choice of menus cooked by the very friendly Mrs Moreton is served in the restaurant. The farm is well known in the area for both its accommodation and restaurant.
6rm(2♠4hc) (3fb) CTV in all bedrooms ® ✗ ✱ sB&B£23-£24 sB&B♠£27-£28 dB&B£36-£38 dB&B♠£44-£46 LDO 5pm
Lic ♨ CTV 20P nc4yrs 100 acres mixed

COLCHESTER Essex Map **05** TL92

GH QQ **Four Sevens** 28 Inglis Rd CO3 3HU ☎(0206) 46093
This guesthouse provides simple, cheerful accommodation with well equipped, spacious bedrooms, some with private bathrooms. It is located in a quiet residential area, near the town centre: down the Maldon road, 2nd on the right then 1st left.

6rm(2↱4hc) (1fb) CTV in all bedrooms ® ✗ ✱ sB&Bfr£25 sB&B↱fr£30 dB&Bfr£32 dB&B↱fr£38 LDO 8.30pm
ⓜ 2P (£)

GH QQ 14 Roman Road 14 Roman Rd CO1 1UR
☎(0206) 577905
Closed 23-31 Dec
A semidetached house near the town centre with a cheerful red front door. The three bedrooms are spick and span, well appointed and comfortable. Breakfast is served in the kitchen at a large pine table, and there is a small neat garden outside by the original Roman wall.
3rm(1⇌) ⊁in all bedrooms CTV in all bedrooms ® ✗ ✱ sB&Bfr£20 sB&B⇌fr£24 dB&B£30-£32 dB&B⇌£34-£36
ⓜ 1P

GH QQ Tarquins 26 Inglis Rd CO3 3HU ☎(0206) 579508 FAX (0206) 579508
A Victorian house in a quiet residential side street, run for many years by Mrs Hudson. Bedrooms, on 2 floors, are bright and well kept, and the downstairs rooms include a breakfast room with some shared seating, a TV lounge and a conservatory lounge for smokers, all made cosy with plants and ornaments.
6rm(2↱4hc) (4fb) CTV in all bedrooms ® ✱ sB&B£15-£20 sB&B↱£30 dB&B£30 dB&B↱£38 WB&Bfr£90 LDO 10am
ⓜ CTV 1P nc5yrs (£)

COLEFORD Gloucestershire Map **03** SO51

FH Q Mrs Sylvia Davis **Lower Tump** *(SO588160)* Eastbach, English Bicknor GL16 7EU ☎Dean(0594) 860253
Set in a lovely position close to the beautiful Forest of Dean, this farmhouse provides simply appointed accommodation.
2rm(1⇌1↱) (1fb) CTV in all bedrooms ® ✱ sB&B⇌↱£16-£20 dB&B⇌↱£25-£30 WB&B£175-£185
ⓜ CTV 10P 150 acres mixed (£)

COLESBOURNE Gloucestershire Map **03** SO91

INN QQQ Colesbourne GL53 9NP
☎Cheltenham(0242) 870376 FAX (0242) 870397
This former coaching inn is steeped in history and has rare 'Lunnet' windows to complete the picture of an old Cotswold inn. Situated on the A435 Cirencester to Cheltenham road, it has been converted to offer comfortable, well equipped accommodation.
Annexe 10rm(6⇌4↱) CTV in all bedrooms ® ✱ sB&B⇌↱£29 dB&B⇌↱£49 Lunch £9.95&alc High tea £9.95&alc LDO 10pm
70P
Credit Cards [1] [2] [3] [5] (£)

COLNE Lancashire Map **07** SD84

SELECTED

FH QQQQ Mrs C Mitson **Higher Wanless** *(SD873413)* Red Ln BB8 7JP ☎(0282) 865301
Closed Dec
Set in attractive rural countryside overlooking the canal, with its barges leisurely passing up and down, this quaint 250-year-old whitewashed farmhouse is an ideal base for touring. The house features a wealth of original oak beams and enormous fireplaces where a fire is lit in cooler weather. There is a cosy lounge, and a set dinner menu, offering honest, substantial home-cooked food, is served in the comfortable dining room. Guests approval of the planned dishes is very important to the friendly hosts and alternatives are available if necessary. The spacious bedrooms are attractively decorated and furnished, and very comfortably equipped with TV, radio alarm and beverage-making facilities, plus many little extras. There are several interesting walks nearby and fishing can be enjoyed from the canal bank.
2rm(1↱1hc) (2fb) CTV in 1 bedroom ® ✗ ✱ sB&B£16-£18 sB&B↱£20-£23 dB&B£32-£36 dB&B↱£36-£40 WB&B£100-£126 WBDi£163-£185 LDO 9am
ⓜ CTV 4P nc3yrs 25 acres shire horses sheep (£)

COLWYN BAY Clwyd Map **06** SH87

GH Q *Briar Lea* 44 Greenfield Rd LL29 8EW ☎(0492) 530052
This large semidetached Victorian house has been extensively renovated and converted into 2 private flats on the ground floor and guest accommodation on the first and 2nd floors. The premises also include a workshop at the rear, from which the proprietors run a car valeting business, which some visitors may find useful. The guesthouse is conveniently situated for access to the town centre and is also close to the A55 coastal expressway. The bedrooms are fairly compact and furnished in a variety of styles, and there is a combined dining room and lounge.
4hc (1fb) CTV in all bedrooms
CTV 6P

GH QQQ Cabin Hill Private Hotel College Avenue, Rhos-on-Sea LL28 4NT ☎(0492) 544568 & 874642
Mar-Nov
This modernised Edwardian house, now a personally run private hotel, is situated in a quiet road, close to Rhos-on-Sea promenade. The accommodation is very well maintained and quite well equipped, the majority of rooms having en suite facilities.
10rm(7↱3hc) CTV in all bedrooms ® ✗ sB&Bfr£23.50 sB&B↱£27 dB&Bfr£44 dB&B↱£51 (incl dinner) WB&B£107-£131 WBDi£119-£145 LDO 5pm
Lic ⓜ CTV 6P nc14yrs

GH Q Crossroads 15 Coed Pella Rd LL29 7AT ☎(0492) 530736
Closed 24 Dec-2 Jan
A large Victorian house situated close to the town centre, with a public car park within 100yds. This personally run guesthouse provides simple but sound accommodation, suitable for tourists and commercial visitors alike.
6hc (2fb) CTV in all bedrooms ® ✱ sB&B£12-£13 dB&B£24-£26 WB&B£80-£85
ⓜ CTV solarium
Credit Cards [1] [3]

GH QQ Fairways Hotel 12 Ellesmere Rd LL29 8RP
☎(0492) 530528 FAX (0492) 534558
This small, privately owned and personally run hotel is conveniently situated for access to the town centre, the seafront and other amenities. It provides simple but quite well equipped accommodation, suitable for both tourists and commercial visitors.
9rm(6⇌↱3hc) (4fb) CTV in all bedrooms ® ✱ sB&B£18-£20 sB&B⇌↱£20-£22 dB&B£36-£40 dB&B⇌↱£40-£44 WB&B£118-£132 WBDi£154-£168 LDO 6pm
Lic ⓜ CTV P
Credit Cards [1] [3]

See advertisement on page 139

GH Q Grosvenor Hotel 106-108 Abergele Rd LL29 7PS
☎(0492) 530798 & 531586
This privately owned and personally run hotel provides simple and rather dated accommodation. It is on the main road, close to the town centre, and caters for both tourists and commercial visitors.
18rm(2⇌16hc) (8fb) CTV in 7 bedrooms TV in 3 bedrooms ® sB&B£15.90-£16.90 dB&B£31.80-£33.80 dB&B⇌£36.30-£38.30 WB&B£91-£95 WBDi£132-£139 LDO 7pm
Lic CTV 16P pool table darts
Credit Cards [3]

GH QQ Northwood Hotel 47 Rhos Rd, Rhos-on-Sea LL28 4RS
☎(0492) 549931
Friendly proprietors Gordon and Agnes Palliser look after the guests at this small hotel while their son does the cooking. They have steadily improved the accommodation since acquiring it in 1986. The bedrooms are modern and equipped to a standard more
→

usually found in hotels of a higher classification, and there is a small bar in addition to the comfortable lounge. The hotel is conveniently situated approximately 0.25 mile from the Rhos-on-Sea shops and promenade.

12rm(1⇌10↱1hc) (3fb) CTV in all bedrooms ® sB&B£15.50 sB&B⇌↱£17.50 dB&B⇌↱£35 WB&B£107-£115 WBDi£123-£149 LDO 6.15pm

Lic 🍽 CTV 11P

Credit Cards [1] [3]

COLYFORD Devon Map **03** SY29

SELECTED

GH QQQQ Swallows Eaves Hotel Swan Hill Rd EX13 6QJ ☎Colyton(0297) 553184

John and Jane Beck continue to provide a warm friendly welcome at their charming small hotel, a former gentleman's residence set back from the road in its own small garden and grounds in the attractive East Devon village of Colyford. The bedrooms are well presented, light, airy and very comfortable. Quality toiletries and bowls of fresh fruit are just two of the thoughtful touches. The dining room with its parquet floor and quality tables and chairs is the setting for Jane's honest home cooking which continues to be popular. The lounge is cosy and comfortable and Swallows Eaves is the ideal retreat from which to tour Dorset and South Devon. The Beck's natural friendliness and hospitality will not fail to please.

8⇌↱ ⊁in 4 bedrooms CTV in all bedrooms ®

✗ (ex guide dogs) ✱ sB&B⇌↱£25-£32.50 dB&B⇌↱£50-£60 WB&B£165-£205 WBDi£245-£300 LDO 8pm

Lic 🍽 10P nc14yrs

Credit Cards [2] ⓔ

COMBE MARTIN Devon Map **02** SS54

See also Berrynarbor

GH QQQ Channel Vista EX34 0AT ☎(0271) 883514

Etr-Oct & Xmas

An attractive, well furnished house with a comfortable lounge and small bar in the dining room. Bedrooms are freshly decorated and clean, and all have en suite facilities.

7rm(2⇌5↱) (3fb) CTV in 3 bedrooms ® ✗ (ex guide dogs) sB&B⇌↱£17-£19 dB&B⇌↱£34-£38 WB&B£109.50-£129.50 WBDi£129.50-£149.50 LDO 3pm

Lic 🍽 CTV 9P nc3yrs

Credit Cards [1] [2] [3] ⓔ

GH QQ *The Woodlands* 2 The Woodlands EX34 0AT ☎(0271) 882769

Mar-Oct

This modest but comfortable guesthouse provides neat bedrooms and a spacious lounge bar, in addition to the open-plan lounge and dining room.

8hc (2fb) ✗ LDO 5pm

Lic CTV 8P nc2yrs

Credit Cards [3]

CONISHOLME Lincolnshire Map **09** TF39

GH QQQ Wickham House Church Ln LN11 7LX (9m NE unclass/16m NE class road of Louth) ☎North Somercotes(0507) 358465

Closed Xmas & New Year

This tasteful conversion of 3 19th-century cottages set amidst beautiful gardens is situated in a small, peaceful village beside the B1031. Bedrooms are comfortable and well equipped, complemented by an abundance of fresh flowers, and there is a spacious lounge and a small library. Fresh, competently prepared set evening meals are available. This is a no smoking establishment.

4rm(2⇌2↱) ⊁in all bedrooms CTV in all bedrooms ® ✗ (ex guide dogs) sB&B⇌↱fr£22 dB&B⇌↱fr£35 LDO noon

🍽 4P nc8yrs

CONISTON Cumbria Map **07** SD39

SELECTED

GH QQQQ Coniston Lodge Hotel Sunny Brow LA21 8HH ☎(05394) 41201

rs Sun & Mon pm

Family owned and run this attractive, almost Swiss style, building offers a perfect place to relax and unwind, standing in a quiet side road close to the village. There are 6 modern en suite bedrooms with coordinated colour schemes and fabrics, equipped with thoughtful extras. There is a comfortable lounge, prettily decorated with matching seat covers and curtains. A set 4-course dinner is served each evening in the pleasing dining room, except on Sunday and Monday. The menu is English in style and may include Coniston char (a fish native to the nearby lake).

6⇌↱ ⊁in all bedrooms CTV in all bedrooms ® T ✗ (ex guide dogs) sB&B⇌↱£26-£40 dB&B⇌↱£52-£80 LDO 7.30pm

Lic 🍽 3P 6🚗 nc10yrs

Credit Cards [1] [3] ⓔ

CONNEL Strathclyde *Argyllshire* Map **10** NM93

GH QQQ Ards House PA37 1PT ☎(063171) 255

Mar-Nov rs 1-23 Dec

This detached whitewashed house is situated at the west end of the village on the Oban road, and enjoys a wonderful view overlooking the Firth of Lorne to the Morvern Hills. Spotlessly maintained throughout, it has attractive individually decorated bedrooms with modern private bathrooms; front-facing rooms have splendid loch views. The sitting room is spacious and comfortably furnished, and the pretty dining room with its neat round tables and Victorian fireplace is the setting for John Bowman's home-cooked 4-course dinners.

7rm(6⇌↱1hc) CTV in 1 bedroom ® ✗ ✱ sB&Bfr£30 sB&B⇌↱fr£35 dB&Bfr£40 dB&B⇌↱£48-£55 WB&B£126-£173.25 WBDi£213.50-£260.75 LDO 6pm

Lic 🍽 CTV 12P nc12yrs

Credit Cards [1] [3]

See advertisement under OBAN

SELECTED

GH QQQQ Loch Etive Hotel Main St PA37 1PH ☎(063171) 400

Etr-10 Oct

Françoise Weber and Bill Mossman's small private hotel nestles beside a stream in the centre of the village, some 200 yards from the A85 road, and is well located for touring the beautiful west coast of Scotland. Bedrooms are deceptively spacious, with 2 top floor rooms full of character; they are all comfortable and well maintained. The small lounge is separated from the neat dining room by a trellis, and Bill's 3-course dinners, available only during May, June and July are very good value; a choice of dishes is served at both dinner and breakfast.

6rm(4⇌↱2hc) (2fb) CTV in all bedrooms ® sB&Bfr£23 sB&B⇌↱fr£27 dB&Bfr£39 dB&B⇌↱£45-£48 WB&B£136.50-£168 WBDi£192-£221 LDO 6.30pm

Lic 🍽 7P

See advertisement under OBAN

GH QQQ **Ronebhal** PA37 1PJ ☎(063171) 310
Apr-Oct
This Victorian house lies close to the Connel bridge, with fine views out across Loch Etive. It has been nicely decorated and is well maintained by the enthusiastic young owners.
6rm(3 2hc) (1fb) ® sB&B£14-£19 dB&B£31-£40 dB&B £33-£53
CTV 6P nc5yrs
Credit Cards [1] [3]

CONSETT Co Durham Map **12** NZ15

GH QQQ Greenhead Carterway Heads, (A68), Shotley Bridge DH8 9TP ☎(0207) 55676
Flowing with charm and character this listed guesthouse was built in the 1700s as an inn, now comfortably modernised retaining many of the original beams, wood panelling and internal stone walls. It is conveniently situated just off the A68, 2 miles from Shotley Bridge, in a delightful rural setting.
3 (1fb) CTV in all bedrooms ® ✱ sB&Bfr£16 dB&Bfr£28
Lic CTV P

CONSTANTINE Cornwall & Isles of Scilly Map **02** SW72

INN QQQ Trengilly Wartha Nancenoy TR11 5RP
☎Falmouth(0326) 40332
This traditional country inn is situated in a small hamlet just outside the village, and has recently been significantly upgraded and refurbished. The cosy, individually styled and decorated bedrooms are bright and well equipped, complemented by nice little personal touches. The public bar is very much a rustic Cornish local, with a good range of real ales and bar food, and one of the inn's strengths is the intimate restaurant designed to portray the atmosphere of a French family hotel, with imaginative menus.
6rm(5 1hc) CTV in all bedrooms ® **T** sB&B£32-£38 sB&B £38-£42 dB&B£41-£45 dB&B £49-£55 WB&Bfr£130 WBDifr£225 Bar Lunch £8-£13 Dinner £18-£18alc LDO 9.30pm
55P
Credit Cards [1] [2] [3] (£)

CONTIN Highland *Ross-shire* Map **14** NH45

SELECTED

GH QQQQ *Contin House* IV14 9EB
☎Strathpeffer(0997) 421920 FAX (0997) 421841
Mar-Oct rs Dec-Feb
Surrounded by peaceful pastures and close to the River Blackwater, this former Church of Scotland manse was built in 1794. The house has been sympathetically refurbished to provide high standards of comfort and appointment by Daphne and David Du Boulay who are the most welcoming of hosts. The individually decorated bedrooms have a light and airy feeling; all are thoughtfully equipped with useful extras. The drawing room, with its welcoming log fire and comfortable easy chairs, invites peaceful relaxation, and there is an honesty bar in the adjoining cosy sitting room. Daphne's 5-course set dinners are taken in the candle-lit dining room, an enjoyable experience. In the season fishing parties choose the Contin.
5 CTV in all bedrooms ®
Lic CTV 20P nc8yrs croquet
Credit Cards [1] [3]

Street plans of certain towns and cities will be found in a separate section at the back of the book.

CONWY Gwynedd Map **06** SH77

See also Roewen

GH QQ **Bryn Derwen** Woodlands LL32 8LT
☎Aberconwy(0492) 596134
Closed 15 Dec-3 Jan
This large semidetached Victorian house is situated on the B5106 on the outskirts of town, but within a few minutes' walk of the castle and other amenities. The comfortable bedrooms vary in style and the furniture ranges from simple old to antique pieces. Some of the front rooms enjoy good views. In addition to the small dining room, with its solid pine furniture, there is a cosy lounge on the 2nd floor. The guesthouse is personally run by resident proprietors Neville and Mary Matthews.
6rm(1⇌ 5hc) (2fb) ® ✻ sB&B£12-£18 dB&B£24-£30 dB&B⇌£30-£36 WB&B£72-£102 LDO noon
CTV 8P

GH QQ ***Pen-y-bryn Tearooms*** Lancaster Square LL32 8DE
☎Aberconwy(0492) 596445
This cosy 400-year-old property was previously known as The Old Ship Guesthouse; however, it was changed in early 1992 into a traditional 'olde worlde' tearoom, serving morning coffee, light lunches and afternoon teas. Accommodation is still available in the form of 3 compact but modern bedrooms, 2 of which have en suite shower rooms. All meals except dinner are served in the teashop. Situated in the town centre, it is conveniently close to the station, with parking facilities nearby.
6rm(2 4hc) (3fb)⁄in 2 bedrooms CTV in all bedrooms ®
Lic CTV P

GH QQ **Sunnybanks** Woodlands, Llanwrst Rd LL32 8LT
☎Aberconwy(0492) 593845
This large semidetached house is situated on the B5106, on the outskirts of this famous walled town, and the castle and other attractions are easily accessible. The young proprietors continue to improve the guesthouse which, although not luxurious, is soundly maintained and provides good value for money, with the advantage of its own car park. The simple bedrooms have a mixture of modern and traditional furniture, and there is a small but comfortable lounge with TV.
6rm(3⇌ 3hc) (2fb) CTV in all bedrooms ® ✻ sB&B£12.50-£15.50 sB&B⇌£15.50-£17.50 dB&B£23-£27 dB&B⇌£27-£31 WB&B£85-£110 LDO 8.30pm
Lic CTV 8P 1

COOMBE BISSETT Wiltshire Map **04** SU12

FH QQ A Shering **Swaynes Firs** *(SU068221)* Grimsdyke SP5 5RF ☎Martin Cross(072589) 240
This friendly farmhouse is approximately 7 miles from Salisbury on the A354 Blandford road. The 3 bedrooms offer bright décor and modern facilities. The guests' lounge is comfortable, and the proprietors' personal pieces create a home-from-home feel. Breakfast is served in the relaxed atmosphere of the dining room.
3 (1fb) CTV in all bedrooms ® ✻ sB&B£17-£18 dB&B£34-£36
CTV 6P 11 acres beef horses poultry £

COPMANTHORPE North Yorkshire Map **08** SE54

GH QQ **Duke of Connaught Hotel** Copmanthorpe Grange YO2 3TN ☎Appleton Roebuck(090484) 318
Closed Xmas wk
This hotel was converted from a group of farm buildings and is situated in open countryside off the Appleton/Roebuck/Bishopthorpe road, about 5 miles from the centre of York. All the accommodation has en suite facilities and there is a cosy, beamed lounge bar. Meals are served in the nicely appointed dining room.
14rm(2⇌12) Annexe 4rm (2fb)⁄in 4 bedrooms CTV in 14 bedrooms ® (ex guide dogs) ✻ sB&B⇌£32 dB&B⇌£45 WB&B£150 WBDi£200 LDO 6pm
Lic 40P
Credit Cards 1 3 £

CORBRIDGE Northumberland Map **12** NY96

GH QQQ **Morningside** Riding Mill NE44 6HL
☎Hexham(0434) 682350
This delightful old stone-built house is situated in the heart of the village of Riding Mill, with easy access to Hexham, Corbridge and the A69. Accommodation throughout is attractive and comfortable, and bedrooms are well furnished, with many thoughtful extras.
5rm(1 4hc) (2fb)⁄in all bedrooms CTV in all bedrooms ® ✻ sB&Bfr£16 sB&Bfr£25 dB&Bfr£28 dB&Bfr£34 WB&B£84-£98 WBDi£126-£154 LDO breakfast
CTV 5P £

CORTACHY Tayside *Angus* Map **15** NO35

FH QQ Mrs Joan Grant **Cullew** *(NO387609)* DD8 4QP
☎(05754) 242
Apr-Oct
A substantial stone-built farmhouse set in a secluded position at the south end of the picturesque, isolated Glen Clova. There are 2 good-sized bedrooms, a comfortable sitting room and pleasant dining room. To find the house, follow the Clova road past Dykehead and the farm road is on the right a quarter of a mile along.
2rm (1fb)⁄in all bedrooms CTV in 1 bedroom
(ex guide dogs) sB&B£11.50-£12.50 dB&B£23-£24
CTV 3P fishing permits 850 acres arable mixed

CORWEN Clwyd Map **06** SJ04

GH Q **Coleg-y-Groes** LL21 0AU ☎(0490) 2169 due to change to 412169
Closed 24-27 Dec
This row of former 18th-century alms houses is quietly located behind the church, close to both the town centre and the A5. Now a Christian guesthouse, it provides modest but clean accommodation.
6hc (2fb)⁄in all bedrooms ® ✻ sB&B£13-£15 dB&B£26-£30 WB&B£89 WBDi£138 LDO previous evening
CTV 6P

GH QQ **Corwen Court Private Hotel** London Rd LL21 0DP ☎(0490) 2854 due to change to (0490) 412854
Mar-Nov Closed Xmas-New Year rs Dec-Feb
This former Victorian police station and courthouse was converted into a small private hotel in 1983. Some of the original cells are now bedrooms. It stands on the main A5 in the centre of town.
10rm(4⇌ 6hc) sB&B£13-£14 dB&B⇌£26-£28 WB&B£86.50-£93 WBDi£126.35-£139.65 LDO 5.30pm
CTV P £

GH QQQ **Powys House Estate** Bonwm LL21 9EG
☎(0490) 2367 due to change to 412367
Parts of this impeccably maintained and attractive house date back some 200 years, but most of it was built in the 1920s. It stands in 3 acres of pleasant grounds and gardens, which contain a swimming pool and grass tennis court. Family-owned and run, this small private hotel provides comfortable, good quality accommodation suitable for tourists and commercial visitors alike. It is situated on the A5, just east of Corwen.
3rm(2 1hc) (1fb)⁄in all bedrooms ® (ex guide dogs) sB&B£20-£21 dB&B£30-£32 dB&B£30-£32 WB&B£98-£105 LDO 6pm
CTV 4P (grass) £

COUNTISBURY (NEAR LYNTON) Devon Map **03** SS74

FH QQQ Mrs R Pile **Coombe** *(SS766489)* EX35 6NF
☎Brendon(05987) 236
Apr-Oct rs Nov & Dec
A stone-built farmhouse dating from the 17th century on a sheep farm within the Exmoor National Park, and surrounded by dramatic scenery. An evening meal is available which makes use of fresh local produce, and the comfortable accommodation and

genuine farmhouse hospitality make it an ideal centre for touring the north Devon coastline.
5rm(2↱3hc) (2fb) Ⓡ ✗ (ex guide dogs) ✱ dB&B£33-£35 dB&B↱£39-£42 WB&B£101-£120 WBDi£185-£205 LDO 5pm
Lic ⅢⅡ CTV 6P 365 acres sheep

COVENTRY West Midlands Map **04** SP37

GH Q Ashleigh House 17 Park Rd CV1 2LH ☎(0203) 223804
Closed Xmas
A privately owned and run guesthouse situated in a quiet cul-de-sac, close to the town centre and the railway station. The addition of en suite facilities has improved the accommodation, however furnishings are modest and the rooms compact. There is an attractive dining room with its own small bar, and car parking is available at the rear.
10rm(8↱2hc) (5fb) CTV in all bedrooms Ⓡ ✗ ✱ sB&Bfr£15 sB&B↱£18-£23 dB&Bfr£28 dB&B↱£28-£32 WB&B£90-£105 LDO 8.45pm
Lic ⅢⅡ CTV 12P (£)

GH Q Croft Hotel 23 Stoke Green, Off Binley Rd CV3 1FP ☎(0203) 457846
This pleasant guesthouse is situated just off the Rugby road, a little over a mile away from the town centre. Rooms are gradually being improved with the addition of en suite facilities and redecoration, although some rooms remain modest. Public areas include a bar with a pool table, lounge and dining room. Friendly owners play an active role in providing a personal service to guests.
12rm(4↱8hc) (1fb) CTV in 6 bedrooms Ⓡ ✱ sB&Bfr£25 sB&B↱fr£34 dB&Bfr£42 dB&B↱fr£54 LDO 8.30pm
Lic ⅢⅡ CTV 20P pool table
Credit Cards [1] [3]

GH Q Fairlight 14 Regent St CV1 3EP ☎(0203) 224215
Closed 24 Dec-2 Jan
This terraced property is situated in a residential area close to the railway station and city centre, and provides simple, value-for-money accommodation. Rooms vary in size and although modest are well maintained. There is a pleasant lounge with TV, and the resident proprietors provide a friendly, relaxed atmosphere.
12rm(2↱10hc) (1fb) CTV in 11 bedrooms Ⓡ ✱ sB&Bfr£15 sB&B↱fr£17 dB&Bfr£28 dB&B↱fr£32
ⅢⅡ CTV 6P (£)

GH QQ *Hearsall Lodge Hotel* 1 Broad Ln CV5 7AA ☎(0203) 674543
A professionally run guesthouse situated close to the A45, with easy access to the city centre. The accommodation has been extended and well equipped rooms are provided, making this a suitable choice for the business traveller.
13hc (2fb) CTV in all bedrooms Ⓡ LDO 7.30pm
Lic ⅢⅡ CTV 13P
Credit Cards [1] [3]

GH QQ Three Spires 62 Grosvenor Rd CV1 3FZ ☎(0203) 632596
A new addition to Coventry's guesthouses, the Three Spires is situated just off the Kenilworth road, close to the railway station. Only 2 rooms are being let at present, with bright, fresh décor and a mixture of furnishings, but the proprietors have plans for 2 further bedrooms. Car parking is available on the street and in the NCP opposite.
2hc CTV in all bedrooms Ⓡ ✗ (ex guide dogs) ✱ sB&Bfr£15 dB&Bfr£26
ⅢⅡ
Credit Cards [1] [3] (£)

This guide is updated annually – make sure you use an up-to-date edition.

COWDENBEATH Fife Map **11** NT19

GH Q *Struan Bank Hotel* 74 Perth Rd KY4 9BG ☎(0383) 511057
Situated in a residential area to the north end of town, this licensed family- run commercial hotel also welcomes visiting holiday-makers. Bedrooms are somewhat compact and modest, although the older style furniture is gradually being replaced with smart new pine units. There is a comfortable lounge with a cosy bar area adjoining.
8hc Ⓡ ✗ LDO 6pm
Lic ⅢⅡ CTV 8P

CRACKINGTON HAVEN Cornwall & Isles of Scilly Map **02** SX19

SELECTED

FH QQQQ Mrs M Knight **Manor** *(SX159962)* EX23 0JW ☎St Gennys(08403) 304 due to change to (0840) 230304
Remotely situated in 6 acres of farmland, this fine, period stone-built farmhouse, partly dates from the 11th century. A choice of individual and very comfortable bedrooms is available either in the main house or in a separate wing. They are all furnished throughout with antiques and offer good facilities, with 2 rooms having sole use of an adjacent bath or shower room. There are several lounge areas available including a fine drawing room with dispense bar and a delightful dining room with a separate breakfast room, plus a games room with a full size snooker table. A daily menu is carefully prepared with only the best ingredients. A typical menu might be lightly curried parsnip soup with croutons; casserole of local Hartland pheasant with silverskin onions and chestnuts, followed by home-baked almond slice with an apricot coulis and Cornish clotted cream. Afternoon tea is →

available and guests are asked to refrain from smoking in the house.
4rm(2⇌2hc) Annexe 2♪ ⅄in all bedrooms ✖
sB&B⇌♪£27-£30 dB&B£54-£60 dB&B⇌♪£54-£60
WB&B£189-£210 WBDi£252-£280 LDO 5pm
Lic 🍽 CTV 6P nc18yrs snooker table tennis 30 acres beef

SELECTED

FH QQQQ Mrs J Crocker ***Trevigue** (SX136951)*
EX23 0LQ ☎St Gennys(08403) 418 due to change to (0840) 230418
Mar-Sep
From the ancient burial mounds at the top of the farm, it would appear that there has been a farm at Trevigue for very many centuries, certainly since the Norman Conquest anyway. Built around a cobbled courtyard in the early 16th century, the present farmhouse and restaurant is run by Mrs Janet Crocker. There is a choice of bedrooms, some in the west wing. The beamed and flagstoned interior offers a delightful lounge and breakfast room furnished with antiques, paintings and prints and a log burning stove. The restaurant and tea rooms open for dinner on Fridays and Saturdays. Sample dishes might include home reared pork or beef, free range eggs and home-made clotted cream. Cream of lemon soup, breast of duck a l'orange or venison with red wine, bacon and juniper berries can figure on the menu. Non-residents are welcomed at the fully licensed restaurant. There are also three self-contained cottages on the farm.
4rm(2⇌2♪) CTV in 2 bedrooms ® ✖ LDO 5pm
Lic CTV 20P nc12yrs 500 acres dairy mixed

INN QQQ Coombe Barton EX23 0JG
☎St Gennys(08403) 345 due to change to (0840) 230345
FAX (08403) 510
Mar-Oct rs Nov-Feb
7rm(3⇌4hc) (1fb) CTV in 3 bedrooms ® sB&B£17.50-£19.50 dB&B£35-£39 dB&B⇌£48-£54 WB&B£112-£123 Lunch £6.75-£15alc Dinner £6.75-£15alc LDO 9.30pm
🍽 40P
Credit Cards 1 2 3 £

CRAIL Fife Map **12** NO60

GH QQQ *Caiplie* 51-53 High St KY10 3RA ☎(0333) 50564
Mar-Sep Closed Dec-Jan rs Oct-Nov & Feb-1 Mar
A warm welcome is assured at this popular licensed guesthouse situated in the centre of this picturesque coastal village, within easy walking distance of the attractive harbour. Bedrooms vary in shape and size and all are clean and comfortably furnished, with colourful fabrics and thoughtful extras. There is a cosy lounge on the first floor, and the bright, cheerful dining room overlooks the main road and offers daily changing menus which include a choice of Scottish and continental dishes.
7hc (1fb) ® LDO 4pm
Lic 🍽 CTV ℙ̸

GH QQ *Selcraig House* 47 Nethergate KY10 3TX
☎(0333) 50697
A stone-built house, with roses framing ground floor windows, located in a quiet street in the town centre, close to the picturesque old harbour. Carefully renovated in Edwardian style, there are many nice pieces of period furniture and interesting photographs, with an attractive gas coal-effect fire in the dining room, where Margaret Carstairs serves good home cooking. Bedrooms on the top floor are reached by a steep staircase, whilst those on the 1st floor are more spacious and elegantly furnished.
5hc (2fb) ® LDO noon
CTV

INN QQ Golf Hotel 4 High St KY10 3TA ☎(0333) 50206 & 50500
Closed Dec & Jan
Reputedly one of the oldest inns in Scotland, this hotel at the east end of the High Street retains many original architectural features. Bedrooms have been attractively refurbished by owners Graham and Heather Guthrie and the bars and dining room are popular locally for food and ales.
5♪ CTV in all bedrooms ® ✱ sB&B⇌♪£25-£27 dB&B⇌♪£44-£48 WB&B£140-£175 WBDi£210-£224 Lunch £7.50-£8.50 High tea £6-£6.50 Dinner £12.50-£14 LDO 9pm
CTV 15P ▶18

CRANBROOK Kent Map **05** TQ73

SELECTED

GH QQQQ Hancocks Tilsden Ln TN17 3PH
☎(0580) 714645
Situated just outside the attractive Wealden town of Cranbrook, this well preserved timber-framed listed building dates back to the 16th century and is surrounded by farmland. The 3 bedrooms are tastefully furnished with antiques and pretty fabrics; the 2 on the first floor share a bathroom while the room on the ground floor is en suite. Guests will be welcomed by natural hosts Bridget and Robin Oaten with a pot of tea and home-made cake, served in the drawing room by the inglenook fireplace with its wood-burning stove, or in the garden during the summer. Breakfast is a real treat with home-made bread and rolls, fresh fruit, home-made marmalade and a full cooked meal. Dinner is also available by prior arrangement.
3rm(1♪2hc) ⅄in all bedrooms CTV in 1 bedroom ®
dB&B£34-£40 dB&B♪£40-£44 WB&B£110-£125
WBDi£197.50-£212.50 LDO 2pm
🍽 CTV 3P nc9yrs £

FH QQQ Mrs S Wickham **The Oast** *(TQ755345)* Hallwood Farm TN17 2SP ☎(0580) 712416
Mar-Nov
Forming part of a farm on the outskirts of town amid typical Kent countryside, part of this converted oast house dates from the 16th century. Hops are no longer grown, but soft fruits, corn and sheep are the mainstays of the Wickham family's livelihood. The 2 bedrooms are prettily decorated and very spacious with good modern bathroms. Some original features have been retained on the ground floor, where there is an open-plan dining area with a communal table, and a comfortable sitting room with a wood-burning stove. A garden is available for guests' use.
2⇌♪ ⅄in all bedrooms ® ✖ ✱ sB&B⇌♪£20 dB&B⇌♪£30
WB&B£105-£140 WBDi£175-£210 LDO 24hr notice
🍽 CTV P 🚜 160 acres arable fruit sheep

CRASTER Northumberland Map **12** NU22

INN QQQ Cottage Dunstan Village NE66 3SZ
☎Embleton(0665) 576658
Sitting in its own wooded gardens, this extended single storey inn offers modern, comfortable accommodation equipped to hotel standards. The cosy bar retains the character of an inn, with beams and pews, and a good range of bar meals is served both here and in the bright modern conservatory. There is also an attractive Jacobean-style restaurant which is open to non-residents, and meals can also be taken on the patio. The inn is situated in the tiny hamlet of Dunstan, just northwest of Craster, off the Howick to Embleton road.
10⇌♪ (2fb) CTV in all bedrooms ® **T** ✖ (ex guide dogs)
sB&B⇌♪£35 dB&B⇌♪£57 WB&B£171 Lunch £7.50 Dinner £13.95&alc LDO 9.30pm
🍽 32P
Credit Cards 1 3 £

CRAWFORD Strathclyde *Lanarkshire* Map **11** NS92

GH Q Field End ML12 6TN ☎(08642) 276
Closed Xmas & New Year
An established guesthouse, it overlooks open pasture and is reached from the main village street by way of a rough steep track.
5rm(2⌐3hc) (2fb)⅟in all bedrooms CTV in all bedrooms ® ✖(ex guide dogs) ✱ sB&Bfr£13 sB&B⌐£15-£20 dB&B£26-£30 dB&B⌐£32-£36 WB&B£75-£100 WBDi£110-£135
LDO 7pm
CTV 6P
Credit Cards 1 3

CRAWLEY West Sussex For accommodation details see **Gatwick Airport**

CREDITON Devon Map **03** SS80

FH QQ Mr & Mrs M Pennington ***Woolsgrove*** *(SS793028)*
Sandford EX17 4PJ ☎Copplestone(0363) 84246
Feb-Nov
A large, detached 17th-century farmhouse in a quiet position surrounded by farmland, with views along a valley. The bedrooms are comfortable and there is a cosy lounge. Dinner and breakfast are served at separate tables in the dining room. It is located 3 miles northwest on an unclassified road, one mile north of the A377.
3hc (2fb) ® ✖ (ex guide dogs) LDO 6pm
CTV 4P 150 acres mixed

CREWE Cheshire Map **07** SJ75

FH QQ Mrs Diana Edwards **Balterley Hall** *(SJ765499)*
Balterley CW2 5QG ☎(0270) 820206
Closed Xmas
This large, imposing brick and sandstone house dates back to the mid-17th century and is peacefully situated down the lane opposite
→

the church. It is near the village of Balterley, some 4 miles southeast of Crewe and within easy reach of the M6. The farmhouse is surrounded by a large arable stock farm. Two of the 3 bedrooms are very spacious, and furnishings range from modern fitted furniture to some antique pieces. The combined lounge/ dining room seats up to 6 people at one table, and also has some antique furniture.

3rm(1⌐2hc) (1fb) CTV in all bedrooms ® ✗ (ex guide dogs) ✱ sB&B£15-£20 sB&B⌐fr£20 dB&B£26-£28 dB&B⌐£30-£32 LDO noon

CTV 6P 240 acres arable mixed

Credit Cards [3] £

CREWKERNE Somerset Map **03** ST40

SELECTED

GH QQQQ **Broadview** 43 East St TA18 7AG ☎(0460) 73424

This small colonial-style bungalow is set high above the town in well tended landscaped gardens which include a water garden. Bedrooms are well presented, carefully decorated and furnished and particularly well equipped, with several extra touches; 2 have private bathrooms. The lounge area is very comfortable, with a pretty skylight roof and an array of indoor plants. A substantial home- cooked set dinner is served around a large antique table, making this excellent value for money and a friendly, caring place to stay. No smoking is requested in public areas.

3⇌⌐ CTV in all bedrooms ® sB&B⇌⌐£25 dB&B⇌⌐£37 WB&B£129.50 WBDi£196 LDO 9am

3P 2

CRIANLARICH Central *Perthshire* Map **10** NN32

GH QQQ **Glenardran Guest House** FK20 8QS ☎(08383) 236

Situated beside the A85 on the eastern approach to the village, this friendly family-run guesthouse offers bright, fresh bedrooms and comfortable public areas.

6hc (1fb) in all bedrooms CTV in all bedrooms ® sB&Bfr£18 dB&Bfr£32 WB&Bfr£112 WBDifr£175 LDO 6pm

Lic 6P

Credit Cards [1] [3] £

CRICCIETH Gwynedd Map **06** SH43

GH QQ **Glyn-Y-Coed Private Hotel** Portmadoc Rd LL52 0HL ☎(0766) 522870 FAX (0766) 523341

Closed Xmas & New Year

A family-run guesthouse situated on the A497 just east of the town centre, within a short walk of the beach and castle. It has recently benefited from comprehensive renovation, which includes the provision of double glazing throughout, extensive redecoration and tastefully coordinated soft furnishings. All the bedrooms have private bathrooms, and 4 enjoy sea views. It is popular with both tourists and commercial guests, many of whom are 'regulars' who appreciate the good humour and friendly hospitality of the proprietor Ann Reynolds.

10rm(3⇌7⌐) (5fb) CTV in all bedrooms ® sB&B⇌⌐fr£18 dB&B⇌⌐fr£36 WB&Bfr£120 WBDifr£190 LDO 4pm

Lic CTV 14P

GH QQ **Min-y-Gaer Private Hotel** Porthmadog Rd LL52 0HP ☎(0766) 522151

Mar-Oct

Close to the beach and castle this semidetached house is situated on the A497 east of the town centre. All but one of the bedrooms is equipped with en suite shower and toilet.

10rm(9⌐1hc) (3fb) CTV in all bedrooms ® sB&B£16.25-£17.75 sB&B⌐£18.50-£20 dB&B⌐£37-£40 WB&B£123-£129

Lic CTV 12P

Credit Cards [1] [2] [3] £

GH Q ***Mor Heli Hotel*** Marine Ter LL52 0EF ☎(0766) 522878

Apr-Sep rs Mar & Oct

One of a pair of similar large terraced houses (the other being The Neptune) under the same ownership. Both are situated on the seafront, close to the castle with good views across Cardigan Bay. The bedrooms are simple but soundly maintained: 2 of the rooms have en suite bathrooms and some have TV. Customers are mainly holiday-makers.

10rm(2⇌8hc) (2fb) CTV in 4 bedrooms LDO 5pm

Lic CTV

GH Q ***Neptune Hotel*** Marine Ter LL52 0EF ☎(0766) 522794

Apr-Sep

The sister establishment to Mor Heli, described above, and under the same ownership. Simple but soundly maintained accommodation is provided, and some of the bedrooms overlook Cardigan Bay. The guesthouse provides good value for money and is popular with holidaymakers.

10rm(1⇌3⌐6hc) (2fb) CTV in 4 bedrooms LDO 5pm

Lic CTV

CRICKHOWELL Powys Map **03** SO21

GH QQQ **Dragon House Hotel** High St NP8 1BE ☎(0873) 810362 FAX (0873) 811868

This town centre hotel has been carefully converted and extended to provide very attractive and well-equipped bedrooms. The bar and lounge are both cosy and comfortable and good food, including vegetarian meals, are available.

13rm(8⇌⌐5hc) Annexe 3⇌⌐ (2fb) in 5 bedrooms CTV in 11 bedrooms ® T ✗ (ex guide dogs) ✱ sB&B£21-£30 sB&B⇌⌐£33-£45 dB&B£38-£45 dB&B⇌⌐£49-£53 WB&B£132-£155 WBDi£175-£215 LDO 8.30pm

Lic CTV 15P

Credit Cards [1] [3]

CRICKLADE Wiltshire Map **04** SU09

GH QQQ ***Chelworth Hotel*** Upper Chelworth SN6 6HD ☎Swindon(0793) 750440

Closed mid Dec-mid Jan

This thoughtfully extended 16th-century farmhouse has been refurbished to provide private bathrooms for 6 of the bedrooms, together with TV. The public areas offer a relaxed atmosphere, and a simple choice of menu is available in the beamed dining area of the lounge. Family run by Mr and Mrs Hopkins, this small hotel is conveniently situated a mile from Cricklade and near Swindon.

7rm(6⌐1hc) (1fb) in 2 bedrooms CTV in 6 bedrooms ® ✗ (ex guide dogs) LDO 7pm

Lic CTV 10P

CRIEFF Tayside *Perthshire* Map **11** NN82

GH QQ **Comeley Bank** 32 Burrell St PH7 4DT ☎(0764) 3409

Delightful public rooms are a feature of this little guesthouse, which lies on the main road leading into town from the south. Both the lounge and dining room have been tastefully styled to reflect the Victorian period, particularly the latter with its lace topped tables and old photographic prints on the walls. Bedrooms are simpler in design but bright and cheery.

5hc (2fb) ✱ sB&B£12 dB&B£24

Lic CTV

GH QQQ **Heatherville** 29-31 Burrell St PH7 4DT ☎(0764) 2825

Closed Dec-Jan

This guesthouse is situated on the main road from the south and within walking distance of the town centre. The décor throughout is bright and cheerful and the bedrooms are further enhanced by attractive furnishings. The spacious first-floor lounge has some fine plasterwork and bay windows with views across the garden to the countryside beyond.

5rm(1⇨4hc) (2fb) CTV in 1 bedroom ® ✱ sB&B£13.50-£14 dB&B£27-£28 dB&B⇨£32-£33 WB&B£89.50-£93 WBDi£134.50-£138 LDO noon
Lic 🍽 CTV 5P

CROESGOCH Dyfed Map **02** SM83

FH QQ Mrs A Charles **Torbant** *(SM845307)* SA62 5JN ☎(0348) 831276
rs Nov-Etr
This 17th-century farmhouse is part of a busy working farm, situated just off the ***A487*** *between Fishguard and St David's. Bedrooms are neat and bright, and public rooms are spacious and comfortable and include a function suite.*
6rm(2⇨1⇨3hc) (2fb) ® ✗ (ex guide dogs) ✱ sB&Bfr£16 dB&Bfr£32 dB&B⇨⇨fr£35 WB&Bfr£110 WBDifr£150 LDO 6pm
Lic 🍽 CTV 40P 110 acres dairy
See advertisement under ST DAVID'S

CROMER Norfolk Map **09** TG24

GH Q Chellow Dene 23 MacDonald Rd NR27 9AP ☎(0263) 513251
Mar-Oct
A cheerfully run, simple guesthouse, just steps away from the seafront, where a consistent standard is maintained and a warm welcome assured.
7hc (2fb) CTV in all bedrooms ® ✱ sB&Bfr£17 dB&Bfr£34 LDO 5pm
Lic 🍽 CTV 6P

GH QQQ Morden House 20 Cliff Av NR27 0AN ☎(0263) 513396
Closed 3-4wks Spring/Autumn
A good quality guesthouse with spacious accommodation where the highest level of hospitality is assured from Mr and Mrs Votier and their family. Leisure and commercial guests appreciate the peace achieved by the absence of modern appliances. There is a good menu and fresh food prepared by Mrs Votier.
6rm(4⇨⇨2hc) (1fb) ® ✗ (ex guide dogs) sB&B£18.50 dB&B£37 dB&B⇨⇨£41 WB&Bfr£126 WBDifr£165 LDO 5pm
Lic 🍽 CTV 3P

GH QQ Sandcliff Private Hotel Runton Rd NR27 9AS ☎(0263) 512888
Feb-10 Dec
An imposing Victorian House on the seafront where efforts are constantly made to improve facilities. Some rooms with en suites are available.
24rm(9⇨10⇨5hc) (10fb) CTV in 15 bedrooms ® sB&Bfr£22 sB&B⇨⇨fr£22 dB&Bfr£44 dB&B⇨⇨fr£44 WB&Bfr£150 WBDifr£173 LDO 6pm
Lic CTV 10P

GH QQQ Westgate Lodge Private Hotel 10 MacDonald Rd NR27 9AP ☎(0263) 512840
Mar-29 Nov
Steps away from the seafront, this is a nicely furnished guesthouse with an attractive à la carte restaurant, small bar and full en suite facilities. Proprietors Mr and Mrs Robson take particular pride in their establishment.
11⇨ (4fb) CTV in all bedrooms ® ✗ ✱ dB&B⇨fr£47 WB&Bfr£164.50 WBDifr£185.65 LDO 6.30pm
Lic 🍽 14P nc3yrs

CROMHALL Avon Map **03** ST69

FH QQ Mrs S Scolding **Kimber's Lea** *(ST699905)* Talbots End GL12 8AJ ☎Chipping Sodbury(0454) 294065
Etr-Sep
Tucked away just outside the small village of Cromhall, this stone clad farmhouse provides a good standard of accommodation in attractively decorated rooms.
3rm ⅟in all bedrooms ® ✗ sB&B£15-£16 dB&B£30 WB&B£98
🍽 CTV 3P 75 acres dairy

CROSTHWAITE Cumbria Map **07** SD49

GH QQQ Crosthwaite House LA8 8BP ☎(05395) 68264
mid Mar-mid Nov
A charming Georgian house set in beautiful countryside overlooking the Lythe Valley which is famous for its damson orchards. The house is well furnished and cared for, and offers comfortable bedrooms with private bathrooms.
6⇨ CTV in 3 bedrooms ® ✱ sB&B⇨£20-£22 dB&B⇨£40-£44 WBDi£200-£210 LDO 5pm
Lic 🍽 CTV 10P 2🚗
See advertisement under KENDAL

CROYDE Devon Map **02** SS43

GH QQQ Moorsands House Hotel Moor Ln EX33 1NP ☎(0271) 890781
Apr-Oct
A semidetached Victorian house within walking distance of the beach and village centre, offering neatly decorated and well kept bedrooms with en suite showers and modern facilities. Two attractive lounges, 1 with a bar and the other with TV, retain some original features. A daily menu offering 4 choices is provided in the dining room.
8⇨ (3fb) CTV in all bedrooms ® ✱ sB&B⇨£21-£24 dB&B⇨£36-£42 WB&B£110-£151 WBDi£173-£214 LDO 6pm
Lic 🍽 CTV 8P nc2yrs
Credit Cards 1 3 £

SELECTED

GH QQQQ Whiteleaf At Croyde EX33 1PN ☎(0271) 890266
Closed Jan & 2weeks Apr, Jul & Oct
Amidst its own well kept and colourful gardens, this detached house built in the 1930s, stands adjacent to the golden sands of Croyde Bay. David and Flo Wallington are experienced hosts, Flo providing the excellent service and David cooking to satisfy most tastes. A high standard of cleanliness is maintained throughout. A varied choice of dinner is offered – starters may include smoked salmon or a daily pasta dish and the main courses range through steak and kidney pie, beef Wellington or seafood feuille. A good selection of desserts are also available and the wine list is a treasure trove for the enthusiast. Unusual specialities are also served at breakfast time. Individually furnished and decorated bedrooms are extremely comfortable with attractive colour schemes and are equipped with many facilities including hairdryers, TV, telephones and radio/clocks.
5⇨⇨ (1fb) CTV in all bedrooms ® T sB&B⇨⇨£34.50 dB&B⇨⇨£54 WBDi£280 LDO 6.30pm
Lic 🍽 10P
Credit Cards 1 3 £

CROYDON Greater London London plan **4** D1 (pages 248-249)

GH QQQ Kirkdale Hotel 22 St Peter's Rd CR0 1HD
☎081-688 5898 FAX 081-680 6001
Closed 2wks Xmas
The Wallingfords are the welcoming hosts at this Victorian house, situated in a residential area not far from the town centre. They continue to make improvements and nearly all the rooms have en suite facilities now. Bedrooms vary in size, but are bright, pretty and very well kept, and direct dial telephones have recently been installed. The house has some period features including stained glass on the staircase, ceiling mouldings and a mahogany fire surround in the reception/lounge, where plants and ornaments create a friendly atmosphere. On sunny days guests can sit outside on the patio.
18⮣ CTV in all bedrooms ® **T** ⋈ (ex guide dogs) ✻
sB&B⮣£32-£35 dB&B⮣£45-£50
Lic ⅏ CTV 12P
Credit Cards 1 3

GH QQQ Markington Hotel 9 Haling Park Rd CR2 6NG
☎081-681 6494 FAX 081-688 6530
4 Jan-16 Dec rs Xmas
This guesthouse consists of several houses located in a residential street, now converted into a comfortable and well run hotel with a friendly atmosphere. Bedrooms vary in size and are well furnished and equipped with modern amenities, with the business guest in mind. Standards of housekeeping are high, and the guesthouse is well maintained.
21rm(20⇌⮣1hc) (2fb)⅟in 4 bedrooms CTV in all bedrooms ® **T** ⋈ sB&B⇌⮣£35-£49.50 dB&B⇌⮣£40-£60 LDO 8.30pm
Lic ⅏ CTV 18P
Credit Cards 1 2 3 £

GH QQ *Oakwood Hotel* 69 Outram Rd CRO 6XJ
☎081-654 2835
rs 25 & 26 Dec
This Victorian house, in a quiet residential side street, has been run for many years by Mrs Delve. Bedrooms vary in size but all are clean and bright and have en suite facilities. There is a lounge with a pool table and a combined bar and breakfast room.
17rm(10⇌7⮣) (3fb) CTV in all bedrooms ® LDO 8pm
Lic ⅏ CTV 7P sauna solarium
Credit Cards 1 2 3 5

CUCKNEY Nottinghamshire Map **08** SK57

FH QQ Mrs J M Ibbotson ***Blue Barn*** *(SK539713)* NG20 9JD
☎Mansfield(0623) 742248
Closed 24-25 Dec
Although within easy reach of all the county's attractions, this farm is quite isolated and is reached by a private lane off the A616 out of Cuckney. As well as the comfortable rooms in the house, there is a self-catering cottage in the grounds.
3hc (1fb) ® ⋈ (ex guide dogs)
⅏ CTV 6P 2🚗 250 acres arable beef mixed

CULLODEN MOOR Highland *Inverness-shire* Map **14** NH74

FH QQ Mrs E M C Alexander **Culdoich** *(NH755435)* IV1 2EP
☎Inverness(0463) 790268
May-Oct
This 18th century small traditional farmhouse is situated near the historic battlefield of Culloden, and offers good value accommodation together with enjoyable home cooking.
2hc (1fb) ® ⋈ ✻ dB&Bfr£28 LDO 5pm
CTV P 200 acres mixed

Q is for quality. For a full explanation of this AA quality award, consult the Contents page.

CULLOMPTON Devon Map **03** ST00

GH QQQ Rullands Rull Ln EX15 1NQ ☎(0884) 33356
FAX (0884) 35890
A comfortable 15th-century longhouse set amid rolling countryside, its circular stairway is a fascinating feature and the old cruck beams can be seen on the landing. Bedrooms are individually furnished and decorated, all en suite except for a small room with shower only, and there are ample lounge areas and a cosy bar. The restaurant serves dinner Tuesday to Saturday – home cooking using local produce – and is open to non-residents. Children under 18 months old are accepted at this establishment.
5⇌⮣ (1fb)⅟in all bedrooms CTV in all bedrooms ® ✻
sB&B⇌⮣£25-£32 dB&B⇌⮣£45-£47.50 LDO 9.45pm
Lic ⅏ 20P nc12yrs 🎾(hard)
Credit Cards 1 3 £

CULMINGTON Shropshire Map **07** SO48

GH QQQ *Seifton Court* Culmington SY8 2DG
☎Seifton(058473) 214
Set in pleasant lawns and gardens, situated in the tiny hamlet of Culmington, this delightful 18th-century, stone farmhouse provides a warm welcome to all guests. The bedrooms are attractively furnished in pine, especially the 'Loft' which has an abundance of exposed timbers. A comfortable lounge is available and guests often join Peter and Valerie Humphreys in their own private lounge, such is the at home feeling generated by this friendly couple. Good home cooking is served, using home-grown produce when available.
3rm(2⮣1hc) (1fb)⅟in all bedrooms CTV in 2 bedrooms TV in 1 bedroom ® ⋈ (ex guide dogs) LDO 9am
Lic ⅏ CTV 6P fishing can be arranged

CWMBRAN Gwent Map **03** ST29

FH QQ Mrs B Watkins **Glebe** *(ST325965)* Croes Y Ceiliog NP44 2DE (1.5m E unclass towards Llandegveth village)
☎Tredunnock(063349) 251 & 242
Closed 21 Dec-7 Jan
Popular with guests using the Irish ferries, due to its proximity to the M4, this modern bungalow stands in picturesque surroundings and provides comfortable accommodation together with warm hospitality.
3hc (1fb)⅟in all bedrooms ⋈ ✻ sB&Bfr£17 dB&Bfr£32
⅏ CTV 6P 100 acres beef dairy

CWMDUAD Dyfed Map **02** SN33

GH QQQ Neuadd-Wen SA33 6XJ
☎Cynwyl Elfed(026787) 438
Situated alongside the A484 road, this family-run guesthouse and restaurant lies in a peaceful wooded valley. All bedrooms now have en suite facilities and there are two lounges available for residents.
7rm(6⇌⮣1hc) (2fb) CTV in all bedrooms ✻
sB&B⇌⮣£13.50-£15 dB&B⇌⮣£27-£30 WB&B£80-£88 WBDi£115-£125 LDO 9.30pm
Lic ⅏ CTV 12P
Credit Cards 1 3 £

DALBEATTIE Dumfries & Galloway Map **11** NX86

INN Q Pheasant Hotel 1 Maxwell St DG5 4AH
☎(0556) 610345
New owners are improving this popular town centre inn which provides a good range of reasonably priced meals both in the public bar and 1st floor restaurant. Bedrooms are simply furnished and modestly appointed.
9rm(2⇌⮣7hc) (1fb) CTV in all bedrooms ®
⋈ (ex guide dogs) sB&B£15-£20 sB&B⇌⮣£15-£20 dB&B£25 dB&B⇌⮣£30 Lunch £3.50-£4.50&alc Dinner £3.50-£4.50&alc LDO 9pm
⅏ P̸

DALKEITH Lothian Map **11** NT36

INN Q Barley Bree Motel 3 Easthouses Rd EH22 4DH
☎Edinburgh031-663 3105
This unusual operation combines a comfortable Indian restaurant, that also offers European menus, a public bar, function room and bright, cheerful bedrooms that are nicely equipped. The Barley Bree lies half a mile along the B6482, off the A68, on the southern outskirts of Dalkeith.
4⇌↱ (1fb) CTV in all bedrooms ® ✗ (ex guide dogs) ✱ sB&B⇌↱£20 dB&B⇌↱£35 Lunch £2.50-£15alc High tea £2.50-£15alc Dinner £2.50-£15alc LDO 11.30pm
▥ 40P snooker skittles
Credit Cards 1 3 5

DALMALLY Strathclyde *Argyllshire*

See **Ardbrecknish**

DARLINGTON Co Durham Map **08** NZ21

GH QQ Woodland 63 Woodland Rd DL3 7BQ
☎(0325) 461908
This Victorian terraced house is situated on the A68, giving easy access to the town centre and A1(M). The well maintained bedrooms are comfortable and all have TV; windows on the front-facing rooms are double glazed. There is an inviting spacious lounge, and service is friendly and personal.
8rm(1⇌7hc) (2fb) CTV in all bedrooms ✱ sB&B£18-£28 dB&Bfr£32 dB&B⇌fr£38
▥ CTV Ⓔ

SELECTED

FH QQQQ Mr & Mrs D & A Armstrong **Clow Beck House** *(NZ281100)* Monk End Farm, Croft on Tees DL2 2SW ☎(0325) 721075
This modern stone-faced farmhouse is the home of Heather and David Armstrong and is situated at Croft on Tees just south of Darlington, within easy reach of the A1 and A1(M). All facilities are of the highest standard, with luxuriously furnished bedrooms and a spacious lounge decorated in Wedgewood blue. Dinner is not served but there are plenty of places to eat in the area, and an excellent farmhouse breakfast is served at a large communal table adjoining the kitchen. To find the house, follow the road between the hotel and church which will take you to the farmhouse, standing in its own mature gardens, with an open aspect over fields; the farm is about 200 yards from the house.
3rm(1↱2hc) CTV in all bedrooms ® ✗ ✱ sB&B£24 sB&B↱£34 dB&B£37 dB&B↱£47
▥ CTV 8P ✓ 90 acres mixed

DARTINGTON Devon Map **03** SX76

SELECTED

INN QQQQ Cott TQ9 6HE ☎Totnes(0803) 863777 FAX (0803) 866629
A delightful thatched country inn dating back to 1324, quietly situated in a residential area and ideally positioned for tourists visiting the South Hams of Devon, Dartington Hall and the Cider Press Centre. The 6 cosy, spotlessly clean bedrooms are pretty and well furnished, the majority with private bathrooms. The accommodation is not really suitable for families with small children. The spacious bar is beamed, with flagstone floors, country furniture and a variety of memorabilia; there is a good choice of real ales, wines and farmhouse cider. The cosy restaurant provides a range of home-made traditional dishes: at lunch time there is a buffet service with a choice advertised on a blackboard, and waitress service in the evening complements the extensive supper menu. Staff are very friendly, making this a popular choice for locals and tourists alike. Smoking in bedrooms is not permitted.
6rm(5⇌↱1hc) ⊬in all bedrooms CTV in all bedrooms ® T ✗ (ex guide dogs) ✱ sB&Bfr£50 sB&B⇌↱fr£60 dB&Bfr£55 dB&B⇌↱fr£65 WB&Bfr£315 Lunch £9.70-£10.95alc Dinner £15.95-£20.95alc LDO 9pm
50P nc10yrs
Credit Cards 1 2 3

DARTMOUTH Devon Map **03** SX84

SELECTED

GH QQQQ Captains House 18 Clarence St TQ6 9NW
☎(0803) 832133
A charming small Georgian Grade II listed house built about 1730 and conveniently situated in a quiet street close to the shops, harbour and River Dart. Personally run by the enthusiastic owners Ann and Nigel Jestico, bed and breakfast is provided with good standards of housekeeping throughout. Bedrooms are individually furnished and decorated with character and charm, with modern facilities and several extra touches. Superb English breakfasts using fresh local produce are served in the dining room or bedrooms. There are local car parks nearby, and the guesthouse is within walking distance of the ferry and quayside.
5rm(3⇌2↱) CTV in all bedrooms ® sB&B⇌↱£24-£27 dB&B⇌↱£34-£44 WB&B£102-£140
▥ nc5yrs
Credit Cards 2 Ⓔ

SELECTED

GH QQQQ Ford House 44 Victoria Rd TQ6 9DX
☎(0803) 834047
Mar-Dec
A detached Regency town house situated 500 yards from the harbour and quayside. Two of the 3 bedrooms are on the lower ground floor level and all of them are individually furnished and decorated with flair, featuring a selection of antiques and objets d'art. The rooms are well equipped and have spacious private bathrooms. Dinner is taken around a large mahogany table, with a daily changing set Cordon Bleu menu using fresh local produce, especially fish; a range of vegetarian dishes is also available. An à la carte breakfast is served until midday, and there is an open log fire in the drawing room. Tea is served in the sheltered garden on sunny days, and car parking is available at the rear. The hotel is unlicensed, but will arrange local delivery or guests can bring their own drinks.
3⇌↱ CTV in all bedrooms ® T ✱ sB&B⇌↱£35-£55 dB&B⇌↱£50-£60 WB&Bfr£175 WBDifr£280 LDO noon
▥ 3P 1🚘
Credit Cards 1 3 Ⓔ

GH QQ Sunny Banks 1 Vicarage Hill TQ6 9EN
☎(0803) 832766
A detached property in a residential area, within a short walking distance of the town centre and quay. Bedrooms are well equipped with TV, tea-making facilities and radio alarms. The 10 comfortable bedrooms have pretty soft furnishings, and there is a small lounge and dining room, where a set dinner is available if ordered in advance. A private patio is available for guests' use, and Rosemary and Shaun Pound are friendly owners.
10rm(2⇌3↱5hc) (2fb)⊬in 2 bedrooms CTV in all bedrooms ® sB&B£16-£25 dB&B£32-£40 dB&B⇌↱£36-£44 WB&B£100-£150 WBDi£165-£215 LDO 7.30pm
Lic ▥ CTV 3P 2🚘 (£3 per night)

DATCHET Berkshire Map **04** SU97

GH QQQ The Beeches 19 The Avenue SL3 9DQ ☎Slough(0753) 580722

This semidetached, red brick Victorian house, situated in a residential area, has been recently upgraded to provide comfortable bed and breakfast accommodation. Most of the bedrooms are en suite and all have TV and central heating. Breakfast is served at separate tables in the attractive dining room.

7rm(6⇌↱1hc) (2fb)⊁in all bedrooms CTV in all bedrooms ® ✗ ✱ sB&B⇌↱£28.50 dB&B⇌↱£45

᪤ 10P

Credit Cards 1 3

DAWLISH Devon Map **03** SX97

GH Q *Mimosa* 11 Barton Ter EX7 9QH ☎(0626) 863283

Close to the town centre and beaches, this holiday guesthouse is family run.

9rm(1↱) (4fb) ✗ LDO 3pm

Lic ᪤ CTV 4P nc3yrs

GH QQQ The Old Vicarage Cofton Hill, Cockwood EX6 8RB ☎Starcross(0626) 891354

May-Oct rs Nov-Apr

Set in an elevated position, this stone-built Victorian house has views over the Exe Estuary and Dawlish Warren. Over the last 5 years the owners have fully restored the property to provide comfortable bedrooms that are attractively decorated and each containing a few objets d'art which are for sale. The shared bathroom is Victorian in style and quite a feature. Breakfast is taken in the nicely appointed kitchen, around a large pine table, and an elegantly furnished lounge with TV is provided. Two self-catering cottages are also available.

3hc (1fb) ® ✗ sB&B£20-£25 dB&B£35-£45

᪤ CTV 6P nc13yrs £

DEAL Kent Map **05** TR35

GH QQ *Kingsdown Hotel* Cliffe Rd, Kingsdown CT14 8HS ☎(0304) 373755

Peacefully situated in the village of Kingsdown, this small family-run hotel offers compact, en suite bedrooms which are attractively furnished. Traditionally styled public rooms include an open plan lounge/bar and restaurant with an à la carte menu which specialises in fish.

4↱ (1fb)⊁in all bedrooms CTV in all bedrooms ®

LDO 9.30pm

Lic ᪤ 20P

Credit Cards 1 3

DEBDEN GREEN Essex Map **05** TL53

FH Q Mrs K M Low **Wychbars** *(TL579320)* CB11 3NA ☎Bishops Stortford(0279) 850362

Remotely situated at the end of a long, unclassified lane off the B1051, this 200-year-old moated, whitewashed farmhouse stands in 3.5 acres and offers 2 simply furnished bedrooms with a shared shower room.

2rm CTV in all bedrooms ® ✱ dB&B£32-£34

lift ᪤ CTV 10P 600 acres arable non-working £

DENBIGH Clwyd Map **06** SJ06

GH Q Cayo 74 Vale St LL16 2BW ☎(0745) 812686

Closed Xmas

This mid-Victorian house is situated just south of the town centre. The accommodation is simple but well maintained, and represents good value for money. There is street parking nearby.

5rm(1⇌1↱3hc) (2fb) sB&B£13-£14 sB&B⇌↱£14-£15 dB&B£26-£28 dB&B⇌↱£28-£30 LDO 2pm

Lic ᪤ CTV ℙ̸

Credit Cards 1 3 £

DENNY Central *Stirlingshire* Map **11** NS88

FH QQQ Mr & Mrs Steel **The Topps** *(NS757843)* Fintry Rd FK6 5JF ☎(0324) 822471

Situated just off the B818, 4 miles west of the village, this modern chalet bungalow farmhouse is set amidst beautiful rolling countryside, with spectacular views over the Carron valley. Bedrooms have either traditional or modern furnishings and all of them offer smart en suite facilities. Dinner features local and home-grown produce and is served in a small dining area adjoining the comfortable and spacious lounge.

8rm(1⇌7↱) (1fb)⊁in all bedrooms CTV in all bedrooms ® ✱ sB&B⇌↱fr£25 dB&B⇌↱fr£35 WB&Bfr£110 WBDifr£200 LDO 5pm

Lic ᪤ CTV 12P ♩ 300 acres cashmere goats sheep

Credit Cards 3

See advertisement under STIRLING

DERBY Derbyshire Map **08** SK33

GH Q Dalby House Hotel 100 Radbourne St, off Windmill Hill Ln DE22 3BU ☎(0332) 42353

A large detached house providing modest accommodation in a quiet residential area. Ample enclosed car parking is available.

9hc (2fb) CTV in all bedrooms ® sB&B£17-£19 dB&B£33-£36 LDO 4pm

᪤ CTV 9P 1🚗 ♧ £

GH QQQ Georgian House Hotel 32/34 Ashbourne Rd DE22 3AD ☎(0332) 49806

This small hotel has been tastefully furnished, providing good standards of comfortable and well appointed accommodation. An appetising selection of meals is available in the restaurant, and there is a small cosy bar; the foyer/lounge area has an open fire.

21rm(14⇌↱7hc) (5fb) CTV in all bedrooms ® T ✱ sB&Bfr£23 sB&B⇌↱£40 dB&Bfr£37 dB&B⇌↱£52

LDO 9.30pm

Lic ᪤ CTV 24P ♧ £

GH Q Rangemoor Hotel 67 Macklin St DE1 1LF ☎(0332) 47252

Simple accommodation in a terraced house near town centre.

12hc Annexe 8hc (3fb) CTV in all bedrooms ® ✗ ✱ sB&B£22-£24 dB&B£35-£37

᪤ CTV 18P 2🚗

Credit Cards 1 3

GH QQ *Rollz Hotel* 684-8 Osmaston Rd DE2 8GT (on A514 2m S) ☎(0332) 41026

Situated on the A514 about 2 miles south of the city centre, this large, well maintained house provides light, cheerful bedrooms which are modestly furnished, some being rather compact. There is a comfortable lounge/bar with TV.

14hc (1fb) ® ✗ (ex guide dogs) LDO 9pm

Lic ᪤ CTV 4🚗

DERVAIG

See **MULL, ISLE OF**

DEVIL'S BRIDGE Dyfed Map **06** SN77

FH QQ Mrs E E Lewis **Erwbarfe** *(SN749784)* SY23 3JR ☎Ponterwyd(097085) 251

Etr-Oct

This traditional stone-built farmhouse is very much a working farm, situated just off the A4120, on the Ponterwyd side of the village. There are two cosy bedrooms and a modern, comfortable lounge.

2hc ® ✗ ✱ sB&Bfr£15 dB&Bfr£30 LDO 4pm

᪤ CTV 4P 400 acres beef sheep working farm

DEVIZES Wiltshire Map **04** SU06

GH QQ ***Long Street House*** 27 Long St SN10 1NW
☎(0380) 724245

This family home with a relaxed atmosphere is in a terrace of elegant early Georgian properties close to the town centre. The bedrooms are comfortably furnished and have modern en suite facilities. Guests have the use of a spacious lounge and there is a breakfast room with separate tables. No smoking is permitted in the house.

7rm(5⇔↱2hc) ⚐in all bedrooms CTV in all bedrooms ® ✗ (ex guide dogs)
♨ CTV 7P

GH QQ Pinecroft Potterne Rd (A360) SN10 5DA
☎(0380) 721433 FAX (0380) 728368

Part Georgian and part Edwardian, the house is set in its own garden and offers comfortable accommodation in a family atmosphere. Breakfast is served at one large table in the informal dining room. A short walk from the town and leisure centre.

4rm(1⇔3↱) (1fb)⚐in 3 bedrooms CTV in all bedrooms ® ✗ ✱ sB&B⇔↱£20-£22 dB&B⇔↱£35-£38 WB&B£126-£140 WBDi£182-£196
♨ 6P 1🚗 mountain bikes for hire
Credit Cards [1] [2] [3] £

GH QQQ Rathlin Wick Ln SN10 5DP ☎(0380) 721999

Quietly situated in a residential area, close to the town centre, this 1920s house has been tastefully renovated with flair and style by the resident proprietors. Each of the 4 bedrooms has an individual style and is furnished with antiques, pretty prints, lace and knick-knacks. The public rooms have an Edwardian air about them and the lounge, although small, is cosy and comfortable.

4↱ ⚐in 2 bedrooms CTV in all bedrooms ® ✗ sB&B↱£23 dB&B↱£37 LDO 6pm
♨ 4P £

DIBDEN Hampshire Map **04** SU40

GH QQ Dale Farm Manor Rd, Applemore Hill SO4 5TJ ☎Southampton(0703) 849632
Closed Xmas

This attractive 18th-century former farmhouse lies half hidden behind a riding stables down an unmade road off the Marchwood bypass. Modern bedrooms are bright and cosy, some overlooking the forest, and breakfast is served in a pine-furnished lounge/dining room.

6hc (2fb) TV in 1 bedroom ® ✗ (ex guide dogs) ✱ sB&B£16.50-£18.50 dB&B£29-£33 WB&B£82-£110 WBDi£152-£155 LDO 11am
CTV 20P ⚲ U ⓔ

DIDDLEBURY Shropshire Map **07** SO58

SELECTED

GH QQQQ The Glebe SY7 9DH
☎Munslow(058476) 221
Mar-Oct (closed 10 days early Jun)

Situated near Diddlebury village stream, the pleasant lawns and garden of this impressive 400-year-old Elizabethan farmhouse are overlooked by the church's Norman tower. Three bedrooms are housed in a converted outbuilding and 2 share the character of the house with exposed wall timbers. The panelled sitting room has a welcoming wood burning stove, and an adjacent bar offers similar comfort. Evening meals are available by arrangement only in the flag- stoned dining room, which is furnished with fine period pieces. For many years the Wilkes family have offered their guests warm hospitality and are now assisted by son Adrian.

3⚐ Annexe 3rm(1⚐2hc) ⚟in 2 bedrooms CTV in 5 bedrooms ® ✗ (ex guide dogs) sB&B£19-£26 dB&B£36-£44 dB&B⚐£48-£54
Lic CTV 10P 2⛟ nc8yrs

DINTON Buckinghamshire Map **04** SP71

FH QQQ Mrs J M W Cook **Wallace** *(SP770110)* HP17 8UF ☎Aylesbury(0296) 748660 FAX (0296) 748851

It is advisable to phone for directions to find this delightful 16th-century farmhouse, situated in the heart of the countryside. The comfortable bedrooms are spacious and equipped with en suite or private bathroom. There is a beamed sitting room with an open fire and TV, leading on to the patio. Breakfast is served on a communal table in the kitchen, beside an inglenook fireplace and bread ovens. A further highlight of a stay here is the range of animals at the farm: rare breeds of sheep, an aviary and heavy horses. The lovely grounds include a pond and invite pleasant walks.

3rm(2⚐) (1fb) ® ✗ (ex guide dogs) sB&Bfr£28 dB&B⚐£36-£38
CTV 6P ⚲ 150 acres beef cattle sheep
Credit Cards 1 3 ⓔ

DIRLETON Lothian *East Lothian* Map **12** NT58

INN Q ***Castle*** EH39 5EP ☎(062085) 221
Closed 21 Dec-5 Jan rs Nov-Apr

This small, family-run inn stands beside the village green overlooking the 13th-century castle. Modest accommodation is available in the main building or in an annexe, and there is a choice of bars and lounges. The inn is popular with golfing parties.

4rm(3⚐1⚐) Annexe 4hc ® LDO 8.30pm
CTV 20P
Credit Cards 1 2 3

ⓔ Remember to use the money-off vouchers.

DOCKLOW Hereford & Worcester Map **03** SO55

FH Q Mrs M R M Brooke **Nicholson** *(SO584581)* HR6 0SL ☎Steens Bridge(056882) 269
Mar-early Nov

This rambling 17th-century farmhouse is set back from the A44 east of the village. Very much a working dairy farm, it is run by the jovial Mrs Brooke. Polished oak floorboards, original beams and timbers abound, and there is a comfortable lounge for residents.

2rm(1hc) (1fb) ® ✱ sB&B£15 dB&B£30 WB&Bfr£105 LDO before 2pm
CTV 4P ⚲ snooker 200 acres dairy mixed
Credit Cards 1 3

DODDINGHURST Essex Map **05** TQ59

FH QQQ Mrs S Porter **Red House** *(TQ326247)* Warren Ln CM15 0JD ☎Brentwood(0277) 372336

Set in 9 acres on the outskirts of the village, this charming farmhouse has been traced back to 1590. The attractive bedrooms have been furnished with Victorian pieces and share a modern shower room. There is an elegant dining area, a cosy lounge with chintz sofas and an inglenook fireplace with a wood- burning stove, but breakfast is generally taken at the pine kitchen table. Owner Mrs Porter is the friendly hostess, and her daughter runs the riding school next door.

2rm (2fb)⚟in all bedrooms CTV in all bedrooms ® ✗ ✱ sB&B£20-£25 dB&B£30-£40 WB&B£100-£170 WBDi£150-£220 LDO am
CTV P U 9 acres riding school ⓔ

DOLGELLAU Gwynedd Map **06** SH71

FH QQ Mr & Mrs D I Jones **Fronolau Farm Restaurant** *(SH747176)* Tabor LL40 2PS (2m SE) ☎(0341) 422361

A stone-built farmhouse situated on a sheep-rearing smallholding, 2 miles east southeast of the town. The house, which is some 300 years old, sits on the northern edge of Cader Idris and overlooks the magnificent scenery of the Mawddach Estuary. In addition to the traditionally furnished bedrooms there is a large cottage-style restaurant offering a wide range of dishes, which is popular with locals. There is also a small bar and spacious comfortable lounge.

4hc (2fb) CTV in all bedrooms ® ✱ sB&B£17.50-£18.50 dB&B£29-£31 WB&B£91.35-£146.55 LDO 10pm
Lic 30P ⌂ 40 acres sheep

FH QQ Mrs E W Price **Glyn** *(SH704178)* LL40 1YA ☎(0341) 422286
Mar-Nov

This small, solid stone-built farmhouse is some 300 years old and retains much of its original character. It provides simple accommodation and is reached via the A493, about a mile west of Dolgellau, in a picturesque and peaceful situation.

4hc (2fb) TV in 3 bedrooms ® sB&B£12-£15 dB&Bfr£26 WB&Bfr£77 LDO previous day
6P 150 acres mixed ⓔ

DONCASTER South Yorkshire Map **08** SE50

GH QQ Almel Hotel 20 Christchurch Rd DN1 2QL ☎(0302) 365230 FAX (0302) 341434

This commercial, town centre guesthouse is off Thorne Road in a residential street opposite Christ Church and the Odeon cinema. It is a double-fronted Victorian property with bay windows and decorative herring-bone brickwork. The well stocked bar and coffee lounge are furnished in deep red dralon with dark polished tables, while the large restaurant is simply decorated and fresh looking. The light painted bedrooms are furnished with dark modern units and candlewick bedspreads, and they each have ivory wash handbasins, remote control TV and hairdryers. Rooms are quite compact, especially those with shower cubicles, but immaculate throughout.

30rm(24⚐6hc) (1fb) CTV in all bedrooms ® ✱ sB&B£20-£28 sB&B⚐£26-£28 dB&B£34-£38 dB&B⚐£38 WB&Bfr£119 WBDifr£150.50 LDO 8pm

Lic CTV 8P
Credit Cards [1] [2] [3]

INN QQ Nelsons Hotel Cleveland St DN1 1TR
☎(0302) 344550 FAX (0302) 341596

This small privately owned hotel is situated in the town centre, close to the main shopping areas and within easy walking distance of the railway station. The bright and pleasant bar is busy and popular, and a good range of hot and cold bar meals are served. The bedrooms are soundly decorated and have modern furnishings. There is no car park, but plenty of public facilities are located in the area.

9hc (2fb) CTV in all bedrooms ® sB&B£15-£23 dB&B£22-£32 WB&Bfr£80 WBDifr£100 Lunch £1.50-£3.50 High tea £1.50-£3.50 Dinner £3.50-£8.50 LDO 8pm

Credit Cards [3] £

DORCHESTER Dorset Map **03** SY69

See also Evershot & Winterbourne Abbas

GH QQQ The Creek Ringstead DT2 8NG
☎Warmwell(0305) 852251

This family home offers 2 very pretty bedrooms, nicely decorated and reasonably equipped. The house is located down a private toll road, leading down to Ringstead beach; much of the surrounding land is owned by the National Trust, although the Fisher family own the beach. Guests are offered tea on arrival in the sunny, sea-facing lounge, and a gourmet meal may be ordered, which is recommended, as Mrs Fisher's cooking is renowned. Meals are taken around a communal dining table; smoking is not permitted in bedrooms. Although very much a family home, bookings are advisable. Directions for Ringstead: from Dorchester (coming south) or Wareham (coming west), take the A352 to Warmwell roundabout. Take the A353 towards Weymouth. After 1 mile (through Poxwell), turn sharp left to Ringstead. Just before the top of the hill turn right, signposted to Ringstead beach, on to the toll road. Follow the road, almost to the sea, turn left after the shop/café, past a terrace of 3 cottages and the Creek is the next house.

2rm(1 1hc) in all bedrooms ® (ex guide dogs) * dB&B fr£34 LDO 10am
CTV 4P nc10yrs (heated) £

GH QQQ Westwood House Hotel 29 High West St DT1 1UP
☎(0305) 268018 FAX (0305) 250282

Supposedly built for Lord Ilchester, this handsome, Georgian listed town house has been elegantly and stylishly renovated by the resident, attentive hosts. The individually styled bedrooms have lovely French antique beds and furniture, and are equipped with mini bars, telephones and many extras. The majority have very smart, modern en suite facilities (2 with spa baths). There is a very comfortable, stylish lounge area and a hearty breakfast, including fresh fruit and a wide choice of preserves, is served in the airy conservatory. On-street parking is available or a large public car park is located 100 yards away. A calm, relaxed and friendly atmosphere abounds throughout this guesthouse.

7rm(5 2hc) (1fb) CTV in all bedrooms ® T * sB&B£25-£31 sB&B £30-£36 dB&B£39.50 dB&B £47.50-£58 WB&B£165-£225
Lic CTV
Credit Cards [1] [3] £

SELECTED

GH QQQQ Yalbury Cottage Lower Bockhampton DT2 8PZ ☎(0305) 262382
rs end Dec-end Jan

This thatched country cottage has been extended and restored to create an elegant and comfortable extablishment. Bedrooms are individually furnished in modern styles and are provided with every convenience imaginable, including iron and board, bathrobes and clock radios. Public areas are →

elegantly furnished, and feature original oak beams and inglenook fireplaces. There is a stylish drawing room, and guests dine in the candlelit dining room. A constantly changing menu reflects the individual style of Pauline Voss, an enthusiastic, self-taught cook. Her husband, Rolf Voss has produced a varied and informative wine list and is pleased to assist in guests' choice, and also provides very useful tasting notes.
8⇌ CTV in all bedrooms ® T ✗ sB&B⇌£60-£65 dB&B⇌£84-£100 LDO 8.30pm
Lic 🍽 19P nc16yrs
Credit Cards [1] [2] [3] ⓔ

DORRINGTON Shropshire Map **07** SJ40

GH QQ Ashton Lees Ashton Lees SY5 7JW
☎(0743) 718378
This large detached house was built by the owners as their family home in 1956. It stands in spacious mature gardens on the A49, on the northern edge of Dorrington village, approximately 6 miles south of Shrewsbury. It provides sound accommodation for bed and breakfast guests, who also have a choice of 2 cosy lounges, both with open fires.
3rm(1⇌🚿2hc) CTV in 2 bedrooms TV in 1 bedroom ® sB&B£14.75-£17.50 dB&Bfr£29.50 dB&B⇌🚿fr£35
Lic CTV 6P ⓔ

DORSINGTON Warwickshire Map **04** SP14

FH QQ Mrs M J Walters **Church** *(SP132495)* CV37 8AX
☎Stratford-on-Avon(0789) 720471 & (0831) 504194
Situated in the heart of this pretty village 6.5 miles from Stratford-upon- Avon, this 18th-century house offers comfortable and well equipped accommodation including four en suite bedrooms in a tasteful conversion of the former stable block.
3hc Annexe 4⇌🚿 (2fb)⚟in all bedrooms CTV in 4 bedrooms ® ✗ (ex guide dogs) ✱ dB&B£27-£28 dB&B⇌🚿£32-£34 WB&B£91-£108.50
🍽 CTV 12P 3🚗 ♪ 127 acres mixed

DOUGLAS

See **MAN, ISLE OF**

DOVER Kent Map **05** TR34

GH Q Beulah House 94 Crabble Hill, London Rd CT17 0SA
☎(0304) 824615
This fine Georgian house stands in an acre of beautifully kept gardens overlooking the river. Long established, the old fashioned accommodation retains many original architectural features including some fine stained glass windows. Bedrooms are traditionally furnished and comfortable, the lounge is available to guests, and the breakfast room is designated no-smoking. Service is personally supervised by the resident proprietor Mr Abate.
8hc (3fb) CTV in 1 bedroom ✗ (ex guide dogs) ✱ sB&B£18-£20 dB&B£34-£36 WB&B£91-£98
🍽 CTV 8P 2🚗 (£2 per night) ⓔ

GH QQ Castle House 10 Castle Hill Rd CT16 1QW
☎(0304) 201656 FAX (0304) 210197
This long-established, brick-built terraced house, is conveniently located on a hillside leading up to the castle. The proprietor, Nona Howarth, creates a friendly and relaxed atmosphere. The bedrooms vary in size – most having a shower facility in the room and bathrooms are provided for those without. A full breakfast is served from 7.30am in the basement dining room and a continental overnight tray can be arranged for early risers. A small lounge is available for guests to use. There is no car park, although roadside parking can usually be found.
6rm(4🚿2hc) (1fb)⚟in all bedrooms CTV in all bedrooms ® ✗ sB&B£18-£30 dB&B£28-£40 dB&B🚿£30-£42
Lic 🍽 3P 1🚗 (£3.50)
Credit Cards [1] [3] ⓔ

GH QQQ Charlton Green 12 Frith Rd CT16 2PY
☎(0304) 210647
Built around 1886, this imposing 4-storey house has been extensively renovated and upgraded, and operates a total no smoking policy. Bedrooms have been individually furnished and equipped to a high standard. There is a pretty basement breakfast room and a separate lounge with low-framed doorways. Service is personally provided by the proprietor, Mrs English, who also does the cooking in her award winning 'clean health' kitchen. Ample car parking is provided on the forecourt.
3rm(1🚿2hc) ⚟in all bedrooms CTV in all bedrooms ® ✗ (ex guide dogs) sB&B£15-£20 dB&B£28-£35 dB&B🚿£30-£37 LDO 4pm
🍽 CTV 3P ⓔ

GH QQ Dell 233 Folkestone Rd CT17 9SL
☎(0304) 202422
This long-established, brick-built terraced house faces onto the busy Folkestone road. The bright bedrooms are beautifully maintained and decorated in different colour schemes. A combined lounge and dining room, provides full English breakfast from 7am – continental breakfast is available earlier by arrangement.
6hc (3fb) ® ✗ (ex guide dogs) sB&B£15-£18 dB&B£26-£32
🍽 CTV 6P ⓔ

GH QQ *Gateway Hovertel* Snargate St CT17 9BZ
☎(0304) 205479
Closed 23 Dec-Feb
Midway between the East and West Ferry terminals, with its own ample car parking, this modern hotel has a relaxed and very informal atmosphere and offers a 24-hour service. A continental breakfast buffet is included, with an extra charge for a full English breakfast. Several compact family rooms are available, with travelling cots and bunk beds. Public areas include a small bar, pine-furnished dining room and a small sitting area with TV.
27rm(4⇌23🚿) (7fb) CTV in all bedrooms ✗ (ex guide dogs) LDO 7pm
Lic 🍽 CTV 24P 2🚗
Credit Cards [1] [3]

GH QQQ Number One 1 Castle St CT16 1QH
☎(0304) 202007
This little Georgian house, overlooked by the castle, is ideally located and can provide long term garaging. The accommodation is individually furnished, mostly with antiques, and generous, good value breakfasts are served in the comfort of your room. Adeline and John Reidy provide a personal and very friendly service, and many thoughtful extras are provided in the cosy bedrooms.
5rm(3🚿2hc) (3fb) CTV in all bedrooms ® ✗ dB&B£28-£34 dB&B🚿£32-£36
🍽 2P 4🚗 (£2.50) ⓔ

GH QQQ *Peverall House Hotel* 28 Park Av CT16 1HD
☎(0304) 202573 & 205088
Quietly situated on a hillside north of the town, this informally run and originally Victorian house has been much improved by the present owners, with attractive and individually furnished bedrooms. The wood panelled breakfast room and comfortable lounges combine with additional amenities such as the guests' laundry, snack service and walled garden.
6rm(2⇌4hc) (2fb) CTV in all bedrooms ® ✗ LDO noon
Lic 🍽 CTV 8P

GH QQ St Brelades 80/82 Buckland Av CT16 2NW
☎(0304) 206126
This very friendly and well run guesthouse is gradually being upgraded. En suite shower facilities have recently been added, and more improvements are being planned. Public areas include a small TV lounge and a dining room which accommodates the reception area and a small bar. Authentic home-made curries are among the choices on the dinner menu, and special curry evenings are held on an occasional basis. Catering for private parties and weddings is often undertaken by the proprietors, who are usually on hand to attend to guests throughout the day. There is a small car park behind the house.

6rm(3⛿3hc) (4fb) CTV in all bedrooms ® ✗ sB&B£18-£38 sB&B⛿£30-£42 dB&B£30-£40 dB&B⛿£32-£42 LDO 7.45pm
Lic 🍽 CTV 6P 1🚗 (£3 per night)
Credit Cards [1] [3] £

GH QQ St Martins 17 Castle Hill Rd CT16 1QW
☎(0304) 205938
Closed Xmas

On a hillside in the leas of Dover Castle, this early Victorian terraced house is run by Mr and Mrs Morriss, in conjunction with Ardmore next door. Bright modern bedrooms are offered, some with en suite showers, along with a very comfortable no smoking lounge, and a pine-furnished basement breakfast room. Parking can be a little difficult at certain times of the day.

8hc (2fb) CTV in all bedrooms ® ✗ sB&B£20-£25 dB&B£25-£40
Lic 🍽 1🚗 (£2 per night)

GH QQQ Walletts Court Manor West Cliffe, St Margarets-at-Cliffe CT15 6EW (1.5m NE of A2/A258 junct, off B2058)
☎(0304) 852424 FAX (0304) 853430
Closed 24-27 Dec rs Sun

This is a medieval manor house, dating back to the Doomsday Book, set in 4 acres and surrounded by rural farmland, yet still within easy reach of the ferry terminals. The bedrooms situated in the original house have been furnished to complement the period and the barn extension houses the rest of the bedrooms, which are mostly modern in style, with pine furniture. There is a restaurant and lounge, which features exposed beams, candlelit tables and a log-burning stove. The serious and dedicated standard of cooking, which chef patron Chris Oakley brings to the restaurant, is something not to be missed.

3⇌⛿ Annexe 4⇌⛿ (1fb) CTV in all bedrooms ® T ✗ ✱ sB&B⇌⛿£40-£55 dB&B⇌⛿£48-£65 LDO 8.30pm
Lic 🍽 16P 10🚗 ⌂ 🎾(hard)games room
Credit Cards [1] [3]

DOWNHAM MARKET Norfolk Map **05** TF60

GH QQQ Crosskeys Riverside Hotel Hilgay PE38 0LN
☎(0366) 387777
Situated just south of Downham Market off the A10 at Hilgay, a pretty riverside location, the Crosskeys offers comfortable accommodation with a good range of facilities and especially good en suite bathrooms.
3⇌ Annexe 2⇌ (1fb) CTV in all bedrooms ® ✱ sB&B⇌fr£38 dB&B⇌fr£53 WB&Bfr£159 WBDifr£214 LDO 8pm
Lic 🍽 10P ✔ row boating
Credit Cards 1 3 £

GH QQQ The Dial House 12 Railway Rd PE38 9EB
☎(0366) 388358 FAX (0366) 382198
rs 24-31 Dec
This pleasing 17th-century house, built of Carr stone, is centrally situated on a relatively quiet main road. The proprietors are a friendly family who make every effort to accommodate personal requests, particularly dietary. A comfortable drawing room serves as both a quiet lounge and breakfast room, kept cosy in the winter months by a log burning stove. A no-smoking policy is operated in the bedrooms.
3rm(2⇌🚿1hc) ⚟in all bedrooms TV in all bedrooms ®
✗ (ex guide dogs) sB&B£17 sB&B⇌🚿£21 dB&B£27.50 dB&B⇌🚿£32.50 WB&B£107-£132 WBDi£166.50-£189.50 LDO noon
CTV 5P £

DOWNTON Wiltshire Map **04** SU12

GH QQQ Warren 15 High St SP5 3PG ☎(0725) 20263
Closed 15 Dec-15 Jan
Warren Guesthouse is a 15th-century property opposite the post office in the attractive village of Downton. The beautiful walled garden at the rear is accessible from the breakfast room and affords views to the village church beyond. The house has been lovingly furnished, bedrooms are clean and comfortable, and fresh flowers add colour.
6rm(2⇌🚿4hc) (1fb) ® ✱ dB&B£38 dB&B⇌🚿£42 WB&B£252.70-£279.30
🍽 CTV 8P nc5yrs £
See advertisement under SALISBURY

DROITWICH Hereford & Worcester Map **03** SO86

GH QQ The Larches 46 Worcester Rd WR9 8AJ
☎(0905) 773441
This house dates back to 1729 and lies just 5 minutes walk from the town's famous Brine Bath. It is a small, well looked after guest house, run by the hospitable Downer family, and all guests receive a pot of tea and home-made cake on arrival. The bedrooms are cosy, and car parking is available.
4hc ⚟in all bedrooms CTV in all bedrooms ®
✗ (ex guide dogs) sB&B£22 dB&B£34 WBDi£210-£213 LDO 10am
7P

DROXFORD Hampshire Map **04** SU61

GH QQ *Coach House Motel* Brockbridge SO3 1QT
☎(0489) 877812
An attractive L-shaped Victorian stable block has been converted into comfortable motel-style accommodation, a few yards from the Hurdles pub. Restaurant and bar meals are served, and there is a pine-furnished breakfast room.
8rm(6⇌2🚿) CTV in all bedrooms ® ✗ (ex guide dogs)
🍽 12P
Credit Cards 1 2 3 5

DRUMBEG Highland *Sutherland* Map **14** NC13

GH QQQ Drumbeg House IV27 4NW ☎(05713) 209
In a peaceful setting of 3 acres of grounds on the fringe of a picturesque village, this attractive Victorian house has been sympathetically restored to provide comfortable accommodation. Warmly welcoming, it offers a choice of cosy lounges, and enjoyable home cooking is served at the communal dining table. The individually decorated bedrooms are well kept and furnished in various styles, all en suite and with tea making facilities. Smoking is not permitted.
3🚿 ⚟in all bedrooms ® ✗ ✱ dB&B🚿£60-£65 (incl dinner) WB&Bfr£140 WBDifr£227.50 LDO 7pm
🍽 CTV 6P nc14yrs

DRUMNADROCHIT Highland *Inverness-shire* Map **14** NH52

GH QQQ Linne Dhuinn Lewiston IV3 6UW ☎(04562) 244 due to change to 450244
Situated in Lewiston just south of Drumnadrochit off the A82, this smart modern bungalow stands in its own garden with parking to the rear. The comfortably furnished bedrooms are all on the ground floor, and hearty breakfasts are served at individual tables in the combined lounge/dining room. Linne Dhuinn is a no smoking establishment.
3⇌🚿 (1fb)⚟in all bedrooms CTV in all bedrooms ®
✗ (ex guide dogs) ✱ dB&B⇌🚿£25-£35
🍽 CTV 6P

SELECTED

GH QQQQ Polmaily House Hotel IV3 6XT
☎(04562) 343 due to change to 450343
Apr-Oct
Situated 3 miles west of the village and set in 18 acres of grounds with a tennis court and open-air swimming pool, this lovely Edwardian country house is an ideal base for the holiday-maker seeking perfect peace, comfort and memorable food. The bright, airy bedrooms have been individually decorated and furnished in keeping with the style of the house. Public areas include a drawing room with a welcoming log fire and comfortable armchairs. Upstairs there is a small reading room with well filled bookshelves and colour TV. Drinks are dispensed from the little bar at the front end of the dining room. At dinner Allison Parsons uses the best available fresh local ingredients to good effect in the preparation of her short, daily changing set price menu which regularly features seafood specialities and game in season. Nicholas Parsons personally looks after front of house and is an affable host.
9rm(7⇌2hc) (1fb) CTV in all bedrooms **T**
✗ (ex guide dogs) ✱ sB&B£45 dB&B⇌£100 LDO 9pm
Lic 🍽 CTV 15P 🏠 ⛱ 🎾(hard)
Credit Cards 1 3

INN QQ Lewiston Arms Hotel Lewiston IV3 6UN
☎(04562) 225 due to change to 450225
Situated just off the A82, the Quinn family's old inn has a relaxed, friendly atmosphere. Bedrooms, all of which are en suite, have recently been upgraded. The lounge bar and dining room overlook the garden, and a welcoming coal fire burns on cooler evenings in the cosy lounge.
5rm(1⇌4🚿) Annexe 4🚿 CTV in all bedrooms ®
sB&B⇌🚿£20-£25 dB&B⇌🚿£40-£50 Bar Lunch £2.50-£5alc Dinner £9-£15alc LDO 8.30pm
🍽 30P
Credit Cards 1 3 £

DUDDINGTON Northants Map **04** SK90

INN QQQ ***Royal Oak Hotel*** High St PE9 3QE ☎Stamford(0780) 83267

This attractive 17th-century stone-built inn is close to both the A47 and A43, with access to the A1 some 4.5 miles away. Accommodation has been attractively modernised with cottage-style décor and a mixture of furnishings. All rooms have good facilities, including direct dial telephones and modern en suites. Open-plan public areas include a cosy bar and an attractive dining area, in shades of pink and green, serving a wide range of meals.

6⇌↱ (2fb) CTV in 6 bedrooms ® LDO 9.30pm
🌾 75P
Credit Cards [1] [3]

DULVERTON Somerset Map **03** SS92

See also Oakford

GH QQQ Dassels Country House TA22 9RZ ☎Anstey Mills(03984) 203 FAX (03984) 561

This detached house stands on the edge of the village of East Anstey, 3 miles from Dulverton. The atmosphere is relaxed and friendly, and the proprietor, Mrs Spencer, is an attentive and caring host.

7⇌↱ Annexe 3↱ (3fb) CTV in all bedrooms ® * sB&B⇌↱£21-£30 dB&B⇌↱fr£36 WB&Bfr£126 WBDifr£169
Lic 🌾 CTV 14P

DUMBARTON Strathclyde

See **Cardross**

DUNBAR Lothian *East Lothian* Map **12** NT67

GH QQ Marine 7 Marine Rd EH42 1AR ☎(0368) 63315
Mar-Oct

This guesthouse forms part of a terrace block and is situated in a quiet residential area near the cliffs. Bedrooms are bright and spotlessly clean, and there is a first floor lounge furnished with books and TV. Good value accommodation is to be had at this family-run establishment.

10hc (3fb) * sB&B£14-£15 dB&B£28-£30 WB&B£95-£105
🌾 CTV 🅿̸

GH QQ Overcliffe 11 Bayswell Park EH42 1AE ☎(0368) 64004

Although situated in a residential area, this red sandstone, semi-detached house is just a few yards from the rugged coastline and not far from the town centre. Family run, it has a friendly atmosphere and offers good value accommodation of various types and sizes, making it popular with visiting golfers and holiday makers alike. Meals are served in a charming dining room, although only a restricted liquor licence is available. There is a pleasant residents' lounge, where guests can relax.

6rm(3↱3hc) (3fb) CTV in all bedrooms ® sB&B£16-£18.50 dB&Bfr£30 dB&B↱fr£35 LDO 5pm
Lic 🌾 CTV 2P

GH QQQ ***St Beys*** 2 Bayswell Rd EH42 1AB ☎(0368) 63571
Feb-Dec

Conveniently situated just off the High Street, this welcoming guesthouse is efficiently run by Mrs Dillon. Bedrooms are in sound decorative order and offer comfortable modern appointments together with a range of thoughtful extras. There is also a comfortable first floor lounge with panoramic views.

6hc (3fb) CTV in all bedrooms ® LDO 6pm
🌾 CTV 🅿̸
Credit Cards [3]

GH QQ St Helens Queens Rd EH42 1LN ☎(0368) 63716
Closed Dec-7 Jan

St Helens is an attractive, semidetached house built in 1880 of traditional red sandstone, now tastefully modernised, yet retaining many of its original features. The owners, Joan and Jim Scott, offer mixed, comfortable accommodation and provide good value bed and breakfast.

7rm(1⇌↱6hc) (1fb)⚟in all bedrooms ® * sB&B£14 dB&B£26-£28 dB&B⇌↱£30 WB&B£84-£91
🌾 CTV 4P

GH QQQ Springfield Edinburgh Rd EH42 1NH ☎(0368) 62502
Mar-Oct

A warm and friendly atmosphere prevails at this sturdy Victorian villa, standing in its own garden in a residential area at the west end of the town. Bedrooms are spacious and comfortable, and there is an attractive first floor lounge well stocked with books and board games. Enjoyable home cooking is served in the pine-furnished dining room.

5hc (2fb) CTV in all bedrooms ® sB&B£17 dB&B£32 WB&B£119 WBDi£170 LDO 5pm
Lic 🌾 CTV 7P
Credit Cards [1] [3]

DUNDEE Tayside *Angus* Map **11** NO43

SELECTED

GH QQQQ Beach House Hotel 22 Esplanade, Broughty Ferry DD5 2EQ ☎(0382) 76614 FAX (0382) 480241

A small hotel pleasantly situated overlooking the River Tay. Attractively decorated and furnished, it is unpretentious but adorned with several thoughtful extras. Some of the bedrooms are compact, but they are all extremely well equipped. There is a delightful lounge and a small dining room, where an ample choice of home-cooked dinners is served from 6 until 9pm. Room service comprising drinks, light refreshments and continental breakfast is also available. The hotel is popular with both commercial and leisure guests.

5⇌↱ (2fb) CTV in all bedrooms ® * sB&B⇌↱£35-£38 dB&B⇌↱£40-£48 LDO 9pm
Lic 🌾 1🚗
Credit Cards [1] [3]

GH QQQ Invermark Hotel 23 Monifeith Rd, Broughty Ferry DD5 2RN (3m E A930) ☎(0382) 739430
This large detached period house, offering spacious accommodation and public areas, is set in its own gardens on the left hand side of the main road coming from Dundee.
4rm(2⮣1hc) (1fb)⊬in all bedrooms CTV in all bedrooms ® ✗ (ex guide dogs) sB&Bfr£25 sB&B⮣£30 dB&Bfr£35 dB&B⮣£40 LDO by arrangement
Lic 🍴 14P pool table

DUNKELD Tayside *Perthshire* Map **11** NO04

GH QQ *Waterbury* Murthly Ter PH8 0BG ☎(03502) 324
This guesthouse in the main street offers very clean standards and all expected comforts, set out on 3 levels. The bedrooms are well proportioned and 4 have retained their original Victorian fireplaces. There is a guests' lounge and a dining room furnished with good sized, well spaced tables.
5hc (2fb) ® ✗ (ex guide dogs) LDO 7pm
Lic 🍴 CTV 6P

DUNLOP Strathclyde *Ayrshire* Map **10** NS44

GH QQ *Struther Farmhouse* Newmill Rd KA3 4BA ☎Stewarton(0560) 84946
Closed 2wks spring & autumn rs Sun & Mon
This substantial period farmhouse is set on the edge of the village, 300 yards from the railway station. It is run in the style of a country house, and is a popular venue for locals, with a 3-course dinner offering a wide choice, except on Sundays and Mondays when a set meal is provided only to residents. Bedrooms are comfortable and generally spacious, with several extra touches.
5hc (2fb) LDO 8.30pm
🍴 CTV 16P
See advertisement under STEWARTON

DUNOON Strathclyde *Argyllshire* Map **10** NS17

GH QQQ Cedars Hotel 51 Alexandra Pde, East Bay PA23 8AF ☎(0369) 2425 FAX (0369) 6964
With just its own front garden dividing this small hotel from the seafront, this family-run, tastefully decorated establishment offers bright, attractive bedrooms in various sizes. The larger rooms have bay windows, tables and comfortable chairs, and all are equipped with remote control TV and radio. Upstairs a bedroom has been converted into a lounge and what was once its en suite bathroom now accommodates a writing desk. There is a selection of magazines, tourist information and a pair of binoculars, enabling guests to enjoy the fine views across the Firth of Clyde.
12⇌⮣ (2fb)⊬in 4 bedrooms CTV in all bedrooms ® T ✗ (ex guide dogs) sB&B⇌⮣£27-£28.50 dB&B⇌⮣£44-£47 WBDi£219-£231 LDO 7.30pm
Lic 🍴 P̸
Credit Cards [1] [2] [3] [5] £

DUNSTER Somerset

See **Minehead & Roadwater**

DUNURE Strathclyde *Ayrshire* Map **10** NS21

FH QQQ Mrs R J Reid **Lagg** *(NS281166)* KA7 4LE ☎(029250) 647
May-Oct
Lying just off the main road a mile north of the village, the elevated position of this farmhouse provides fine views of the rugged coastline and out to sea. The house is attractive and well maintained with a tasteful lounge and a dining room with individual tables.
3hc ® ✱ dB&Bfr£26
🍴 CTV 6P 480 acres dairy sheep

DUNVEGAN

See **SKYE, ISLE OF**

DURHAM Co Durham Map **12** NZ24

GH QQ Lothlorien 48/49 Front St, Witton Gilbert DH7 6SY ☎091-371 0067
A quaint roadside cottage situated on the A691 west of the city. Accommodation is unpretentious but pretty and service from the charming proprietress is most friendly.
3hc ® ✗ ✱ sB&B£15-£17 dB&B£30-£34 WB&B£105-£119 WBDi£157.50
🍴 CTV 3P

INN QQ Bay Horse Brandon DH7 8ST ☎091-378 0498
An attractive stone-built inn situated 3 miles from Durham town centre off the A690. The motel-style bedrooms are modern, comfortable and very well equipped. Good value bar meals are served.
Annexe 4⮣ ⊬in all bedrooms CTV in all bedrooms ® T ✱ sB&B⮣£26 dB&B⮣£35 Bar Lunch £1.50-£6.50 Dinner £1.50-£6.50 LDO 9.30pm
🍴 15P
Credit Cards [1] £

DURSLEY Gloucestershire Map **03** ST79

FH QQQ Mr & Mrs St John Mildmay ***Drakestone House*** *(ST734977)* Stinchcombe GL11 6AS (2.5m W off B4060) ☎(0453) 542140
Apr-Oct
Situated between Dursley and Wooton-under-Edge on the B4060, this fine country house retains many original features, which have been enhanced by the fine antiques and objects collected by hosts Hugh and Crystal St John Mildmay during their many years overseas.
3rm(1hc) ⊬in all bedrooms ✗ LDO previous day
🍴 6P 10 acres sheep

DYFFRYN ARDUDWY Gwynedd Map **06** SH52

GH QQQ *Bryntirion Country House* LL44 2HX ☎Ardudwy(03416) 770
This Victorian country house, now a small personally run hotel, is situated in 3.5 acres of grounds and gardens on the A496 to the north of the village, commanding sea views from its elevated position. The traditional bedrooms are not luxurious but comfortable and equipped with many facilities usually only found in larger hotels. There is a cottage-style dining room, a small bar and a cosy Victorian-style lounge.
4rm(3⇌⮣1hc) (1fb) ® ✗ LDO 9.15pm
Lic 🍴 CTV 10P nc5yrs

DYLIFE Powys Map **06** SN89

INN QQ Star SY19 7BW ☎Llanbrynmair(0650) 521345
This remote inn stands in wild and rugged countryside in the mountains of mid Wales between Llanidloes and Machynlleth. Bedrooms are modestly appointed, but the bars are full of character with slate floors and log fires, and a good range of reasonably priced food is available. It is a good centre for touring and the inn has its own pony trekking centre.
7rm(2⇌5hc) (1fb) ® sB&B£17-£25 sB&B⇌£25 dB&B£35 dB&B⇌£38 WB&B£105 WBDi£140 Lunch £2.95-£8.25 High tea £1.50-£2.75 Dinner £2.95-£8.25 LDO 10.30pm
🍴 CTV 30P U boat hire pony trekking
Credit Cards [1] [3]

DYMCHURCH Kent Map **05** TR12

GH QQ *Chantry Hotel* Sycamore Gardens TN29 0LA ☎(0303) 873137
The hotel is situated off the A259, along a private road heading towards the sea wall, in a peaceful and private location close to the beach which is ideal for family holidays. Bedrooms vary : many

have retained their period character, with the original fireplaces, and there are interconnecting rooms for children, who are well catered for with high teas, a large garden, swings, a safe sandy beach and cream teas in summer. Other facilities include a restaurant, bar, lounge and satellite TV. Proprietors Mr and Mrs Paul Airey provide very friendly and helpful service which is usually available throughout the day.
6rm(5⇌🚿1hc) (5fb) CTV in all bedrooms ® LDO 8.30pm
Lic 🍽 CTV 9P
Credit Cards [1] [3]

GH QQ Waterside 15 Hythe Rd TN29 0LN
☎(0303) 872253
An attractive roadside detached building with extensive rear views over Romney Marsh and double-glazed windows. Bedrooms all have TV and tea making facilities and 2 rooms have private showers. The proprietor provides service throughout the day, with an a la carte menu featuring a daily speciality and a vegetarian choice. There is a bar/lounge with a residential licence, and good car parking facilities are provided.
7rm(5hc) (1fb) CTV in 5 bedrooms TV in 2 bedrooms ® 🐕 sB&B£15-£17 dB&B£28-£32 WB&B£99-£113 WBDi£128.10-£195 LDO 8pm
Lic 🍽 CTV 9P Ⓔ

EARDISLAND Hereford & Worcester Map **03** SO45

FH QQ Miss M Johnson **The Elms** *(SO418584)* HR6 9BN
☎Pembridge(05447) 405
This small, renovated farmhouse is set in the centre of the village. Guests are reminded that no smoking is permitted in the house.
4hc ⊘in all bedrooms 🐕 sB&B£16-£22 dB&B£30-£31 WB&B£203-£210
6P nc12yrs 32 acres stock rearing Ⓔ

EARLS COLNE Essex Map **05** TL82

INN QQ Riverside Inn Motel 40/42 Lower Holt St CO6 2PH
☎(0787) 223487 FAX (0787) 222034

This part-timbered, purpose-built motel is situated on the bank of the river Colne, previously the site of old farm buildings. The modern bedrooms are sparsely furnished but well equipped, each with a smart en suite shower room. Breakfast is cooked and served by the friendly proprietor Mr Collyer in the simple breakfast room where guests may have to share tables. Snacks, meals and refreshments are available in the adjacent freehold pub, which is particularly popular in the summer with its terrace, garden and children's play area.

11↱ (3fb) CTV in all bedrooms ® ✱ sB&B⇌↱fr£30 dB&B⇌↱fr£50 WBDifr£250 Lunch £3-£10 Dinner £8-£15 LDO 9.45pm
🏨 11P
Credit Cards 1 3

EASINGWOLD North Yorkshire Map **08** SE56

GH QQ Roseberry View Easingwold Rd, Stillington YO6 1LR
☎(0347) 810795

Just half a mile from Stillington village and sitting in open countryside, this bungalow has 3 sizeable bedrooms which are all comfortably furnished and have tea-making facilities. There is a guests' lounge which doubles as a breakfast room in the morning, and a pretty garden at the front.

3rm(1↱2hc) ⊬in 2 bedrooms CTV in all bedrooms ® ✗ (ex guide dogs) dB&B£25-£28 dB&B↱£29-£32 WB&B£84-£100
5P Ⓕ

EASTBOURNE East Sussex Map **05** TV69

See **Town Plan Section** During the currency of this publication Eastbourne telephone numbers are liable to change.

GH QQQ Bay Lodge Hotel 61 & 62 Royal Pde BN22 7AQ
☎(0323) 32515 FAX (0323) 35009
Mar-Oct

This attractive double-fronted Victorian house overlooks the sea and has neatly appointed, comfortable accommodation and a cosy bar. There are pleasant sun lounges for smokers and non-smokers, and good home cooking is provided.

12rm(9⇌↱3hc) CTV in all bedrooms ® ✗ (ex guide dogs) sB&B£17-£21 dB&B⇌↱£32-£48 WB&B£99-£144 WBDi£145-£189 LDO 6pm
Lic 🏨 CTV ₽ nc7yrs
Credit Cards 1 3 Ⓕ

GH QQQ Beachy Rise 20 Beachy Head Rd BN20 7QN
☎(0323) 639171

Situated in the peaceful conservation area of Meads Village, en route to Beachy Head, this family-run guesthouse offers particularly comfortable accommodation. Bedrooms have been attractively furnished with antique pieces, most retain original fireplaces and each has its own coordinating colour scheme. Proprietor Sue Cooke prepares wholesome English fare, which is served in the elegant dining room overlooking the south-facing sun terrace and garden. Guests also have their own cosy lounge.

6rm(2⇌4↱) CTV in all bedrooms ® ✗ (ex guide dogs) ✱ dB&B⇌↱£36-£44 WB&B£120-£140 WBDi£175-£195 LDO noon
Lic 🏨 ₽
Credit Cards 1 3 Ⓕ

GH QQ *Bourne House Private Hotel* 16 Bourne St BN21 3ER
☎(0323) 21981

Peacefully located away from the crowds, this small guesthouse offers modestly furnished bedrooms and a cosy lounge. The proprietor, Mrs Barnes, is renowned for her hearty English breakfasts and home cooking, served in the licensed dining room.

10rm(1⇌4↱5hc) (1fb) CTV in all bedrooms ® LDO noon
Lic 🏨 CTV ₽
Credit Cards 1 3

GH QQQ Chalk Farm Hotel & Restaurant Coopers Hill, Willingdon BN20 9JD (2m NNE) ☎(0323) 503800

Quietly situated in 2.5 acres, on the outskirts of Eastbourne, this is an attractive, ivy-clad, 17th-century farmhouse. Beamed bedrooms are decorated in a cottage style – many have original brick fireplaces, and all are equipped with modern facilities. There is a cosy lounge with a real coal fire, a comfortable bar and a nicely furnished restaurant, with a choice of menus. Guests can also enjoy the pretty garden with its hand carved picnic tables.

9rm(2⇌5↱2hc) (1fb) CTV in all bedrooms ® **T** ✱ sB&B£27-£32 dB&B£54-£56 dB&B⇌↱£56-£62 WB&B£185-£195 WBDi£250-£300 LDO 9pm
Lic 🏨 CTV 30P
Credit Cards 1 3

GH QQQ Far End Hotel 139 Royal Pde BN22 7LH
☎(0323) 25666
Apr-Oct

A small, friendly guesthouse on the seafront beside Princes Park. Bedrooms are bright and modern and public areas include a comfortable first-floor lounge, a small bar and an attractive dining room where both breakfast and dinner are served.

10rm(4↱6hc) CTV in all bedrooms ® ✱ sB&B£23 dB&B£46 dB&B↱£52 (incl dinner) WB&B£110-£130 WBDi£130-£170 LDO 1pm
Lic 🏨 CTV 8P nc4yrs Ⓕ

GH QQ Flamingo Private Hotel 20 Enys Rd BN21 2DN
☎(0323) 21654 due to change to 721654

This is an attractive looking, detached property, in a quiet street, with good roadside parking. The proprietors have just started to redecorate the modestly furnished bedrooms, which are adequately equipped and have neat en suite facilities. There is a pleasant bar and separate sun lounge, together with a neat dining room, where both breakfast and dinner are served.

12rm(5⇌7↱) (1fb) CTV in all bedrooms ® ✗ (ex guide dogs) sB&B⇌↱fr£21 dB&B⇌↱fr£42 WB&Bfr£133 WBDifr£174 LDO 4.30pm
Lic 🏨 CTV ₽ nc5yrs
Credit Cards 1 3 Ⓕ

GH QQQ Hotel Mandalay 16 Trinity Trees BN21 3LE
☎(0323) 29222

An attractive town centre hotel with its own car park at the rear. The recently refurbished bedrooms offer a good standard of comfort and are well equipped. The fully licensed restaurant Gatsby's has an adjoining bar, and service is friendly and welcoming.

14rm(4⇌10↱) (2fb) CTV in all bedrooms ® ✗ (ex guide dogs) ✱ sB&B⇌↱£24-£29 dB&B⇌↱£48-£58 WB&B£140-£190 WBDi£200-£230 LDO 9pm
Lic 🏨 CTV 15P
Credit Cards 1 3 Ⓕ

GH QQ Mowbray Hotel Lascelles Tce BN21 4BJ
☎(0323) 20012 due to change to 720012
Apr-Dec

In a prime position close to the theatres, Winter Gardens and seafront, this small hotel offers freshly decorated bedrooms, some on the compact side, with a lift to all floors. Evening meals are served in the basement dining room and there is a cosy lounge for guests' use.

15rm(6↱9hc) CTV in all bedrooms ® sB&B£21-£25 dB&Bfr£42 dB&B↱fr£50 WB&B£125-£148 WBDi£163-£183 LDO 5.30pm
lift CTV nc6yrs
Credit Cards 1 3

GH QQQ ***Saffrons Hotel*** 30-32 Jevington Gardens BN21 4HN
☎(0323) 25539
Etr-Oct
This privately run hotel is situated away from the crowds but within easy reach of the seafront and local amenities. Freshly decorated bedrooms are simply furnished and all benefit from en suite facilities. There is a cosy ground floor lounge and the basement dining room and traditionally styled bar are accessible by lift. Live entertainment is provided twice weekly.
25rm(7⇌6↱12hc) (2fb) CTV in all bedrooms ® LDO 7pm
Lic CTV Ᵽ
Credit Cards 1 3

GH QQ Stirling House Hotel 5-7 Cavendish Place BN21 3EJ
☎(0323) 32263
Closed 1st wk Nov, last wk Jan & 1st wk Feb
This is a terraced house, with a smart pink exterior and is situated close to the seafront. The bedrooms are dated in style with mixed furnishings and fabrics, but many benefit from en suite facilities. There is a comfortable bar with floral sofas and basement dining room, split into sections – one of which has an impressive display of Toby jugs. A separate lounge is also available for non smoking guests. The guesthouse is run by the proprietors, who always offer a friendly welcome.
20rm(11↱9hc) (1fb) CTV in all bedrooms ®
✗ (ex guide dogs) sB&B£17-£18 dB&B£34-£36 dB&B↱£38-£40 WB&B£119-£139 WBDi£124-£151 LDO 9am
Lic CTV Ᵽ nc10yrs Ⓔ

EAST CALDER Lothian *Midlothian* Map **11** NT06

FH QQ Mr & Mrs D R Scott **Whitecroft** *(NT095682)*
EH53 0ET ☎Midcalder(0506) 881810 FAX (0506) 884327
A large, detached bungalow sitting by the roadside just east of the village on the B7015. Attached to a smallholding, the house enjoys fine views northwards across the Forth Valley and offers compact accommodation and a comfortable lounge. There is also a farm shop which is run by the friendly owners.
3hc (1fb)⊬in all bedrooms ® ✗ ✱ sB&B£18 dB&Bfr£28
🏠 CTV 8P 5 acres mixed beef sheep Ⓔ
See advertisement under EDINBURGH

EAST DEREHAM Norfolk Map **09** TF91

GH QQQ Clinton House Well Hill, Clint Green, Yaxham
NR19 1RX ☎(0362) 692079
A pretty, part 18th-century house set in the peaceful rural hamlet of Clint Green, 3 miles southeast of East Dereham. Guests have the use of a cosy lounge with deep comfortable armchairs and sofas, TV, video and a log burning stove in winter months. An attractive new conservatory serves as both a breakfast room and quiet reading room, and bedrooms are similarly attractive and appealing, with good quality soft furnishings. The guesthouse succeeds in providing modern comforts whilst still retaining character and charm. This is a no smoking establishment.
3hc Annexe 1⇌↱ (2fb)⊬in 3 bedrooms CTV in 1 bedroom ®
✗ (ex guide dogs) sB&B£17-£19 dB&B£27-£30 dB&B⇌↱£28
WB&B£105-£140
🏠 CTV 8P 🎾(grass) Ⓔ

EAST GRINSTEAD West Sussex Map **05** TQ33

GH QQ ***Cranfield Lodge Hotel*** Maypole Rd RH19 1HW
☎(0342) 321251 & 410371
Set in a residential area, close to all local amenities, this guesthouse has a well kept garden and a small car park. There is a pleasant residents' bar, a comfortable lounge and a dining room where an evening meal is served on request. Bedrooms vary in size, with rather small annexe rooms, but the accommodation is all well maintained and equipped.
11rm(4↱7hc) Annexe 9rm(1⇌6↱2hc) (1fb) CTV in all bedrooms ® LDO 8pm
Lic 🏠 CTV 11P
Credit Cards 1 2 3

EASTLING Kent Map **05** TQ95

INN QQQ Carpenters Arms The Street ME13 0AZ
☎(0795) 890234
This delightful 14th-century village inn is full of character, with brick flooring, inglenook fireplaces and church pews. Bedrooms are located next door in Carpenters cottage, and are all en suite and equipped with thoughtful extras. A popular à la carte menu is offered in the cosy candlelit restaurant, with soups and hot puddings a speciality, and fresh game when in season. Simple snacks and Kentish ales are also available, and live folk music further enhances the atmosphere on Wednesday nights.
Annexe 3⇌↱ (3fb) CTV in all bedrooms ® ✗ ✱
sB&B⇌↱£35 dB&B⇌↱£45 WB&Bfr£141.75
WBDifr£232.75 Lunch £11-£13&alc Dinner £11-£13&alc
LDO 10pm
🏠 20P nc10yrs
Credit Cards 1 2 3 Ⓔ

EBBERSTON North Yorkshire Map **08** SE88

GH QQ Foxholm Hotel YO13 9NJ (on B1258)
☎Scarborough(0723) 859550
Mar-Nov & Xmas
A stone-built former farmhouse standing in its own grounds at the southern end of the main village street off the A170, Foxholm has bedrooms on both the ground and first floor, all traditional in style. There is a cosy bar and a comfortable guests' lounge with TV. The pleasantly appointed dining room seats 20 and offers a daily changing table d'hôte menu and a full English breakfast, an ideal start for touring the North Yorks moors.
9rm(6⇌↱3hc) (1fb) ® sB&B£34-£37 dB&B⇌↱£66-£72 (incl dinner) WBDi£230-£250 LDO 7pm
Lic 🏠 CTV 12P 2🚗 Ⓔ

EDINBURGH Lothian *Midlothian* Map **11** NT27

See **Town Plan Section**

GH QQ Adam Hotel 19 Lansdowne Crescent EH12 5EH ☎031-337 1148
Neat accommodation is provided at this well established guesthouse, conveniently located close to the city centre.
9hc (2fb) CTV in all bedrooms 🐕 (ex guide dogs) ✱ sB&B£19-£20 dB&B£36-£40
Lic ▥ CTV (£)

GH QQQ *The Adria Hotel* 11-12 Royal Ter EH7 5AB ☎031-556 7875
Closed Nov-Dec
Not far from the east end of Princes Street, the Adria forms part of a stylish Georgian terrace, overlooking the trees and gardens of Calton Hill. Under personal supervision of the Kopystynski family, it has a relaxed and friendly atmosphere, offering spacious accommodation in bedrooms that are comfortably furnished and some with en suite facilities. Enjoyable Scottish breakfasts are served in the pleasant dining room and the guests' lounge invites peaceful relaxation.
28rm(2🛁4🚿22hc) (7fb) Ⓡ 🐕
▥ CTV P̸

GH QQQ Allison House 15/17 Mayfield Gardens EH9 2AY ☎031-667 8049 FAX 031-667 5001
Two terraced houses have been linked to create this popular guesthouse, which attracts both business and tourist clientèle. It is situated in a residential area, beside the A7 south of the city centre. The enthusiastic new owners, Mr and Mrs Hinnrichs, have embarked on a phased programme of bedroom improvements, which will include the provision of additional facilities. Downstairs, the renovated lounge now has an honesty bar and an á la carte menu is available in the attractive dining room.
24rm(22🚿2hc) (10fb) CTV in all bedrooms Ⓡ **T** sB&B🚿£20-£35 dB&B🚿£40-£60 LDO 8.30pm
Lic ▥ CTV 12P
Credit Cards [1] [3]

GH QQ Anvilla 1a Granville Ter EH10 4PG ☎031-228 3381
Anvilla is a small detached house run by friendly owners. There is a large bay windowed lounge on the first floor which has a beautiful ornate ceiling and original brass door and window fittings, and the smaller ground floor dining room features its original Victorian fireplace. Car parking is provided on the tarred forecourt, but can be a bit of a squeeze.
6hc (2fb) CTV in all bedrooms Ⓡ ✱ sB&B£15-£16 dB&B£28-£3 WB&B£84-£96 LDO 5pm
▥ CTV 5P

GH QQQ Ashdene House 23 Fountainhall Rd EH9 2LN ☎031-667 6026
Closed Xmas-New Year & 2 wks winter
This compact guesthouse is situated in a quiet residential area on the south side of the city. Bedrooms vary in size but are equipped with telephones and hairdryers. The lounge and dining area share a room but are neatly screened from each other.
5rm(4🚿1hc) (2fb) CTV in all bedrooms Ⓡ 🐕 (ex guide dogs) dB&B🚿£32-£44
▥ 3P nc2yrs

GH Q Ben Doran 11 Mayfield Gardens EH9 2AX ☎031-667 8488
Closed 20-27 Dec
Conveniently situated for access to both the city and the bypass, this unpretentious house provides well maintained accommodation.
9rm(1🛁3🚿5hc) (5fb) CTV in all bedrooms Ⓡ ✱ sB&B£16-£21 dB&B£32-£37 dB&B🛁🚿£34-£40
▥ 6P 2🚗 (£)

GH QQ Boisdale Hotel 9 Coates Gardens EH12 5LG ☎031-337 1134
A pleasant terraced house situated close to the West End of the city in a residential area just off the A8. Well maintained and with a friendly atmosphere, it offers good value accommodation. Bedrooms vary in size but have recently been refurbished and all have private bathrooms.
11rm(5🛁6🚿) (6fb) CTV in all bedrooms Ⓡ ✱ sB&B🛁🚿£25-£32.50 dB&B🛁🚿£50-£65 LDO 7pm
Lic ▥ CTV P̸

GH QQ Bonnington 202 Ferry Rd EH6 4NW ☎031-554 7610
This family-run semidetached Victorian house is situated in a residential area to the north of the city centre. The bedrooms are comfortable and there is a cosy lounge on the first floor. A hearty breakfast is served in the dining room, where it may sometimes be necessary to share a table.
6rm(1🛁1🚿4hc) (3fb) CTV in all bedrooms Ⓡ ✱ dB&B£34-£40 dB&B🛁🚿£40-£50 WB&B£119-£140 LDO 10am
▥ CTV 9P

GH QQQ Brunswick Hotel 7 Brunswick St EH7 5JB ☎031-556 1238
Good value bed and breakfast accommodation is offered at this comfortable family-run guesthouse situated close to the city centre. It offers a high standard of housekeeping, with pleasant, well decorated bedrooms, each with bright, compact shower rooms. There is a comfortable lounge on the top floor, and breakfasts are served in the small basement dining room.
10🚿 (1fb) CTV in all bedrooms Ⓡ 🐕 sB&B🚿£20-£35 dB&B🚿£40-£60
▥ nc2yrs
Credit Cards [1] [2] [3] (£)

GH QQQ Buchan Hotel 3 Coates Gardens EH12 5LG ☎031-337 1045
A charming Victorian guesthouse set in a residential area close to the city centre. Managed by the friendly resident proprietors, the hotel provides attractive, inviting bedrooms, a comfortable lounge and neat dining room.
11rm(5🚿6hc) (5fb)🚭in 2 bedrooms CTV in all bedrooms Ⓡ ✱ sB&B£20-£26 dB&B£36-£42 dB&B🚿£40-£52
▥ CTV P̸
Credit Cards [1] [2] [3]

GH QQ Clifton Private Hotel 1 Clifton Ter, Haymarket EH12 5DR ☎031-337 1002
Situated close to the town centre, this cosy hotel provides well appointed accommodation and a spacious first floor lounge with views to Arthur's Seat.
11rm(4🚿7hc) CTV in all bedrooms Ⓡ sB&B£21 sB&B🚿£25 dB&B£38 dB&B🚿£40-£47
▥ CTV
Credit Cards [1] [3]

GH QQ Crion 33 Minto St EH9 2BT ☎031-667 2708 FAX 031-662 1946
Bright, compact modern bedrooms, a spacious and inviting lounge/dining room and friendly service are provided at this city guesthouse.
6rm(3🚿3hc) (1fb) CTV in all bedrooms Ⓡ 🐕 (ex guide dogs) sB&B£16-£19 dB&B£24-£36 dB&B🚿£32-£48
▥ CTV 1P

🛏☕ **GH QQ Daisy Park House** 41 Abercorn Ter EH15 2DG ☎031-669 2503
An impressive, stone-built house in an elevated position, set well back from the road with gardens at the front. Accommodation throughout is very neat and well maintained.
6hc (2fb) CTV in 5 bedrooms TV in 1 bedroom Ⓡ 🐕 (ex guide dogs) sB&B£14-£17 dB&B£28-£34
▥ CTV P̸

GH QQ Dalwin Lodge & Restaurant 75 Mayfield Rd EH9 3AA ☎031-667 2294
Closed 24-27 Dec
Well tended, unpretentious bedrooms, friendly service and excellent value menus are offered at this family-owned guesthouse. An interesting table d'hôte menu is available at lunch, with an extensive à la carte menu offered at dinner, catering for all palates and pockets.
5hc (1fb) CTV in all bedrooms ® ✗ (ex guide dogs) ✱ sB&B£14-£17 dB&B£28-£34 LDO 8pm
Lic 🍽 Ⓔ

SELECTED

GH QQQQ Dorstan Private Hotel 7 Priestfield Rd EH16 5HJ ☎031-667 6721
Closed 23 Dec-8 Jan
Iain and Mairae Campbell's extended Victorian house stands in a well tended garden south of the city centre. The main house bedrooms are bright with fresh plain décor and light fitted units. Four extension rooms are more practical. The dining room is full of character with booth style seating, and there is also a tastefully furnished lounge where smoking is discouraged.
14rm(12⇌🚿2hc) (2fb) CTV in all bedrooms ®
✗ (ex guide dogs) sB&B£18-£20 sB&B⇌🚿£26-£28 dB&B£40-£42 dB&B⇌🚿£48-£50 LDO 3pm
🍽 8P
Credit Cards 1 3

GH QQ Dunstane House 4 West Coates EH12 5JQ ☎031-337 6169
Closed Xmas-4 Jan

→

This impressive detached house, elevated from the road, has gardens to the front and parking to the rear. Bedrooms are spacious and comfortable, and an inviting lounge is provided.
15rm(4 11hc) (5fb) CTV in all bedrooms ® ✱ sB&B£25-£31.50 dB&B£45-£50 dB&B £60-£70 WB&B£189-£220
Lic CTV 10P
Credit Cards 1 2 3

GH QQ Ecosse International 15 McDonald Rd EH7 4LX ☎031-556 4967
A neat, cosy guesthouse offering well maintained accommodation and delightful service from the resident proprietress.
5 (2fb) in all bedrooms CTV in all bedrooms ® ✱ sB&B £18-£22 dB&B £36-£44 WBDi£126-£154
£

GH QQ Elder York 38 Elder St EH1 3OX ☎031-556 1926
Conveniently situated beside the bus station in the city centre, this efficiently run guesthouse occupies the 3rd and 4th floors at the end of a Georgian terrace block. The well decorated bedrooms are comfortably furnished in a traditional style, and offer the expected amenities.
13rm(3 7hc) (3fb) CTV in all bedrooms ® (ex guide dogs) ✱ sB&B£18-£20 dB&B£32-£40 dB&B £36-£44 WB&B£105-£154

GH QQQ Ellesmere House 11 Glengyle Ter EH3 9LN ☎031-229 4823
A warm welcome is assured by the delightful, cheery proprietor of this comfortable family-run guesthouse, which forms part of a Georgian terrace overlooking extensive parkland. The spacious bedrooms are individually decorated, furnished in various styles and all are equipped with the expected amenities, including comfortable seating. Hearty breakfasts are served at shared tables in the combined lounge/dining room with its two-tone décor and matching settees/easy chairs, in addition a TV is provided for guests further pleasure.
6rm(2 4hc) (2fb) CTV in all bedrooms ®
(ex guide dogs) sB&B£15-£19 dB&B£30-£38 dB&B £40-£50 WB&B£105-£133
CTV £

GH QQ Galloway 22 Dean Park Crescent EH4 1PH ☎031-332 3672
Little more than a gentle stroll from the west end of Princes Street, this friendly, family-run guesthouse forms part of a Victorian terrace. The bedrooms are mostly spacious; offering comfortable, modern furnishings and some have en suite facilities. A hearty breakfast is served in the airy dining room, although at peak times, tables may have to be shared with other guests.
10rm(6 4hc) (6fb) CTV in all bedrooms ® sB&B£22-£30 sB&B £25-£36 dB&B£32-£38 dB&B £38-£44 WB&B£96-£114
£

GH QQ Glendale Hotel 5 Lady Rd EH16 5PA ☎031-667 6588
Conveniently situated for access to both the city centre and bypass, this attractive stone-built house provides bright, cheerful bedrooms, a comfortable lounge and a neat wood-panelled dining room.
7rm(3 4hc) (3fb) CTV in all bedrooms ® (ex guide dogs) sB&Bfr£17 dB&Bfr£30 dB&B fr£35 WB&B£105-£119
LDO noon
CTV 8P
Credit Cards 1 3

GH QQ *Glenisla Hotel* 12 Lygon Rd EH16 5QB ☎031-667 4877 FAX 031-667 4098
This attractive semidetached sandstone house is situated in a quiet residential area on the south side of the city, and is gradually being improved by the friendly owners. There is a spacious and comfortable first floor TV lounge, and good home cooking is served in the dining room. Bedrooms vary in size, most of them have recently been redecorated.
7rm(4 3hc) (2fb) ® LDO 8.15pm
Lic CTV 6P 1
Credit Cards 1 3

GH QQQ *Glenora Hotel* 14 Rosebery Crescent EH12 5JY ☎031-337 1186
Situated just off Haymarket, close to the town centre, this comfortable house provides attractive, well furnished bedrooms and inviting public rooms.
10 (2fb) CTV in all bedrooms ®
Lic CTV
Credit Cards 1 3

GH QQ Glenorchy Hotel 22 Glenorchy Ter EH9 2DH ☎031-667 5708
Close to the city centre but in a quiet residential area, this unpretentious hotel offers spacious accommodation.
9 (2fb) CTV in all bedrooms ® ✱ sB&B £17-£22
CTV
Credit Cards 1 2 3

GH QQQ Greenside Hotel 9 Royal Ter EH7 5AB ☎031-557 0022
Closed Jan & Feb
This friendly, family-run house forms part of a fine Georgian terrace overlooking Calton Hill, near the east end of Princes Street. It offers good value bed and breakfast accommodation in spotlessly maintained bedrooms, each of which is individually decorated and comfortably furnished; the original master rooms are particularly spacious. There is a quiet terraced garden to the rear.
12rm(7 5hc) (3fb) ✱ sB&B£22.50-£24.50 sB&B £24.50-£30.50 dB&B£41-£45 dB&B £45-£55
CTV

GH QQQ *Grosvenor* 1 Grosvenor Gardens EH12 5JU ☎031-337 4143 FAX 031-346 8732
A major refurbishment programme is nearing completion at this Victorian town house which is situated in a desirable residential area in the West End. Soft pastel shades have been used to good effect in the comfortable well equipped bedrooms. A grand piano is the focal point in the comfortable sitting room, and hearty breakfasts are served at shared tables in the attractive basement dining room.
8 (3fb) CTV in all bedrooms ® (ex guide dogs)

Credit Cards 1 2 3

See advertisement on page 165

GH Q Halcyon Hotel 8 Royal Ter EH7 5AB ☎031-556 1033 & 031-556 1032
Forming part of a Georgian terrace, this family-run guesthouse, attracts both tourists and commercial visitors – being situated just east of the city centre. The bedrooms are generally spacious with high ceilings and offer simple but practical furnishings. The dining room has been partly refurbished and serves a hearty breakfast every morning.
16hc (6fb) ® ✱ sB&B£25-£28 dB&B£42-£56
CTV (hard)

GH QQ A Haven 180 Ferry Rd EH6 4NS ☎031-554 6559
This small guesthouse is situated close to the town centre and offers friendly service, well appointed bedrooms and a comfortable open-plan lounge/dining room.
10rm(5 5hc) (4fb) CTV in all bedrooms ® sB&B£18-£24 dB&B£30-£39 dB&B £40-£59
Lic CTV 6P
Credit Cards 1 3

GH QQ Heriott Park 256 Ferry Rd EH5 3AN ☎031-552 6628
This recently converted, well established guesthouse is situated in the main road at the northern end of the city. It offers warm, friendly service, well maintained, modern bedrooms, an attractive dining room and an inviting lounge.
→

6rm(2↱4hc) (4fb) CTV in all bedrooms ® sB&B£20-£30 sB&B↱£30-£40 dB&B£28-£40 dB&B↱£36-£46
Lic 𝍪 CTV P

GH QQQ International 37 Mayfield Gardens EH9 2BX ☎031-667 2511
This family-run guesthouse forms part of a Victorian terrace and is conveniently situated on the south side of the city beside the A7, with easy access to the city centre. It has a friendly atmosphere and offers good value bed and breakfast accommodation.
7⇌↱ (3fb) CTV in all bedrooms ® (no dogs) (ex guide dogs) ✻ sB&B⇌↱£20-£26 dB&B⇌↱£30-£50 LDO 7.30pm
𝍪 3P

GH QQ *Kariba* 10 Granville Ter EH10 4PQ ☎031-229 3773
Situated to the south of the city, this guesthouse offers modest but neat accommodation.
9rm(2↱7hc) (2fb) CTV in all bedrooms ®
𝍪 CTV 4P

GH QQ Kilmaurs 9 Kilmaurs Rd EH16 5DA ☎031-667 8315
Situated in a southside residential area, this family-run guesthouse offers good value bed and breakfast accommodation. Bedrooms vary in size and have light modern furnishings and all the expected amenities. The lounge and dining room are combined and at peak times it may be necessary to share a table with other guests for breakfast.
5rm(3↱2hc) (2fb) CTV in all bedrooms ® ✻ dB&B£28-£40 dB&B↱£32-£40 WB&B£95-£135
𝍪 P̸ nc3yrs

GH QQ Kingsley 30 Craigmillar Park, Newington EH16 5PS ☎031-667 8439
Conveniently situated between the bypass and the city centre, this establishment provides well tended bedrooms, a spacious lounge and a neat dining room.
6rm(4↱2hc) (3fb) CTV in all bedrooms ® (no dogs) dB&B£28-£36 WB&B£91-£119
𝍪 CTV 6P nc6yrs
Credit Cards 1 3

GH Q The Lairg 11 Coates Gardens EH12 5LG ☎031-346 1050 FAX 031-346 2167
Conveniently situated for access to both the city centre and by-pass, this friendly establishment offers unpretentious, neat accommodation.
10rm(8↱2hc) (3fb) CTV in all bedrooms ® ✻ sB&B£16-£21 sB&B↱£16-£21 dB&B£32-£42 dB&B↱£32-£42
Lic 𝍪 CTV
Credit Cards 1 3

GH QQ Lindsay 108 Polwarth Ter EH11 1NN ☎031-337 1580 FAX 031-337 9174
This guesthouse on the west side of the city has a nice little dining room and comfortable bedrooms.
8rm(3↱5hc) (2fb) CTV in all bedrooms ® ✻ sB&B£18.50-£20 dB&B£37 dB&B↱£44
𝍪 6P
Credit Cards 1 2 3

SELECTED

GH QQQQ The Lodge Hotel 6 Hampton Ter, West Coates EH12 5JD ☎031-337 3682
Enthusiastic owners George and Linda Jarron have lovingly improved their admirable Georgian town house to create this small, elegant hotel, which is conveniently situated in the West End. The bright airy bedrooms are individually decorated, using coordinated fabrics and the majority are comfortably furnished with well polished Stag units. In addition to the restful lounge, with its soothing soft pink colour scheme, there is a cosy cocktail bar where guests can meet and enjoy a quiet drink. A set menu prepared from fresh, local produce is offered in the attractive dining room, along with a friendly and courteous service, which is equally matched by the impeccable standards of housekeeping and maintenance.
10↱ ⚟in 6 bedrooms CTV in all bedrooms ® (no dogs) ✻ sB&B↱£40-£48 dB&B↱£50-£75 LDO 7pm
Lic 𝍪 10P
Credit Cards 1 3

GH QQ *Marchhall Hotel* 14-16 Marchhall Crescent EH16 5HL ☎031-667 2743 FAX 031-662 0777
The Marchhall is in a residential area on the south side of the city just off the A68. The bedrooms are well equipped and those with en suite facilities are particularly comfortable. Lounge space is limited, but there is a lounge bar open to both residents and non-residents in the evenings.
13rm(6⇌↱7hc) (3fb) CTV in all bedrooms ® LDO 3pm
Lic 𝍪 CTV P̸
Credit Cards 1 3

GH QQ Mardale 11 Hartington Place EH10 4LF ☎031-229 2693 & 031-229 8616
This compact terraced guesthouse has an unusual layout of half landings. It has been sympathetically decorated with many nice little touches, and soft furnishings used to great effect. There is no lounge.
6hc (3fb) CTV in all bedrooms ® ✻ sB&B£14-£17 dB&B£28-£34 WBDi£98-£119
𝍪

GH QQ Meadows 17 Glengyle Ter EH3 9LN ☎031-229 9559
Closed 18-28 Dec
Gloria and John Stuart extend a warm welcome to all who stay at their comfortable, terraced guesthouse, which is situated in a residential area, overlooking Bruntsfield Links park. The tastefully decorated bedrooms are spacious with various styles of →

The Lodge is a small elegant family run hotel with friendly personal service. Each bedroom is furnished to a high standard with all facilities en suite. Superbly decorated public rooms assure the complete comfort of all our guests. Residential licence. Good Scottish cooking with emphasis on the use of fresh produce. Private car park. We are situated on A8 only 5 mins from City centre and 10 mins from Airport. Come and enjoy our warm Scottish hospitality at The Lodge.
For details please contact proprietors: Linda & George Jarron, The Lodge Hotel, 6 Hampton Terrace, West Coates, Edinburgh EH12 5JD. Telephone: 031-337 3682.

KARIBA HOUSE

10 Granville Terrace, Edinburgh
Tel: 031-229 3773

Pleasantly situated, within walking distance of Princess Street. Three rooms have ensuite, the other six, have showers, central heating, colour TV and tea & coffee making facilities. Extensive Scottish breakfast.

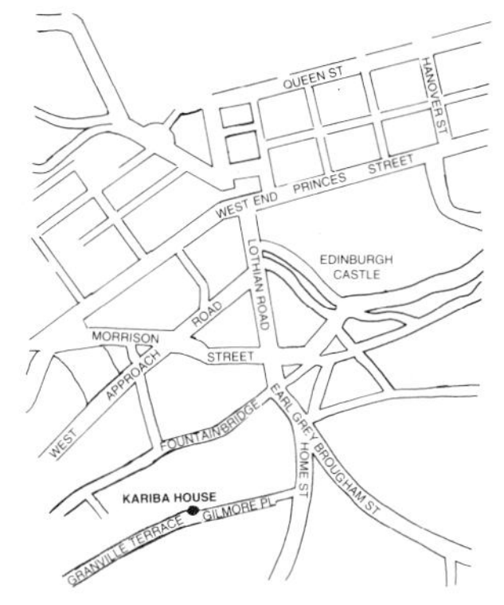

Kingsley Guest House

30 Craigmillar Park, Edinburgh EH16 5PS
Telephone: 031-667 8439

Proprietors: Wilma & Bill Hogg

You are assured of a warm welcome and personal attention at this family run guest house, which is open all year. The pleasant Victorian terraced villa offers 6 comfortable rooms, 4 of which have shower and toilet en-suite. All are well equipped with colour T.V., tea/coffee making facilities etc., and there is a residents lounge. Full central heating. Conveniently situated on the south side of the city centre (A701) in the residential university area. There is an excellent bus service from the door and a private car park. Reduced rates for families and small groups. Off season and weekly terms on application.

THE Grosvenor

Gardens Hotel

1 Grosvenor Gardens
Edinburgh, EH12 5JU
Tel: 031 313 3415
Fax: 031 346 8732

Close to city centre & all amenities, yet located in a quiet cul-de-sac. All spacious rooms have private facilities. Tea/Coffee making Facilities TV, & Hairdryers. Residents sitting room.

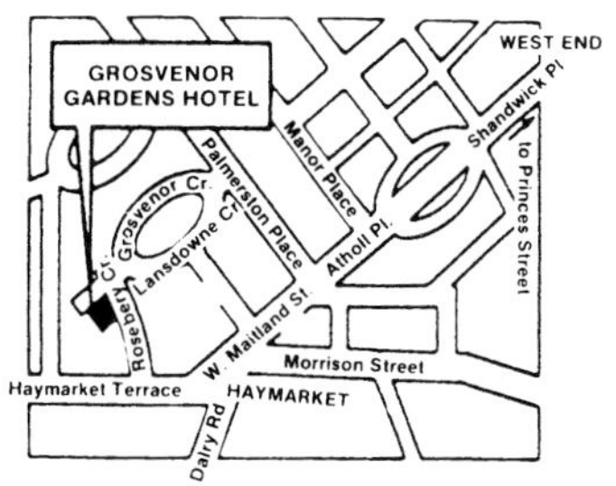

furniture and have been thoughtfully equipped. Hearty breakfasts are served in the attractive dining room, where tables are shared with other guests.

7rm(5 2hc) (3fb) CTV in all bedrooms ® ✱ sB&Bfr£20 sB&B £35 dB&Bfr£40 dB&B £48

Credit Cards 1 3

GH QQ Mrs Rooneys 11 McDonald Rd EH7 4LX ☎031-556 3443

Occupying the ground and lower ground floors of a tenement block in the east end of the city, and not far from the city centre, this small family-run guesthouse offers good value bed and breakfast accommodation.

5rm(2 3hc) (1fb) TV in all bedrooms ® ✱ sB&Bfr£18 sB&B fr£24 dB&Bfr£32 dB&B fr£36 LDO 8pm

GH QQQ *The Newington* 18 Newington Rd EH9 1QS ☎031-667 3356

The Newington is a well established, reliable guesthouse offering delightful accommodation. The bedrooms are individually styled with good quality furnishings and lots of character. The impressive first floor lounge and ground floor restaurant are filled with antiques.

8rm(3 5hc) (1fb) CTV in all bedrooms ®

Lic 3P

GH QQQ Parklands 20 Mayfield Gardens EH9 2BZ ☎031-667 7184

This solid, terraced house has comfortable, mainly spacious bedrooms and a combined dining room and lounge, all very clean.

6rm(5 1hc) (1fb) ® (ex guide dogs) dB&B£36-£40 dB&B £36-£44

CTV

GH QQ Park View Villa 254 Ferry Rd EH5 3AN ☎031-552 3456

Forming part of a stone-built terrace of houses, this family-run guesthouse is situated in a residential area north of the town centre, and offers good value bed and breakfast accommodation. Bedrooms, some with private bathrooms, are generally spacious and provide TV and tea making facilities. Front-facing rooms enjoy views across parkland to the castle beyond. There is ample car parking space, and the owners will arrange sightseeing tours of the city.

7rm(4 3hc) (3fb) CTV in all bedrooms ® (ex guide dogs) ✱ sB&B£20 sB&B £26 dB&B£30-£32 dB&B £36-£40

CTV

Credit Cards 1 3

GH QQ Ravensdown 248 Ferry Rd EH5 3AN ☎031-552 5438

This comfortable, spacious house lies on the main road on the northern side of Edinburgh overlooking the city. Bedrooms are generally of a good size with comfortable seating, and there is an attractive lounge and a well laid out dining room.

7hc (5fb) in 3 bedrooms CTV in all bedrooms ® ✱ dB&B£30-£36

Lic CTV 4P

GH QQQ Ravensnuek 11 Blacket Av EH9 1RR ☎031-667 5347

A tastefully restored semidetached Victorian house in a quiet avenue on the south side of the city. The attractive bedrooms feature the original fireplaces and are thoughtfully furnished with several extra touches. There is a comfortable lounge in which breakfast is served.

6hc (2fb) ® ✱ dB&B£30-£44

CTV 4P

GH QQ *Rosebery Private Hotel* 13 Rosebery Crescent, West End EH12 5JY ☎031-337 1085

Just off the A8 at the western end of the city, this Victorian terraced house features spacious bedrooms and an attractive dining room.

5hc Annexe 1 (1fb) CTV in all bedrooms ®

CTV

GH QQ Rowan 13 Glenorchy Ter EH9 2DQ ☎031-667 2463

This well maintained stone-built semidetached house is situated in a quiet side road to the south of the city, just off the A7. Bedrooms are bright and clean, and a good all round standard of accommodation is provided by the resident owners. Breakfast is served in the lounge which also has TV and tea making facilities.

9rm(2 7hc) (2fb) CTV in all bedrooms ® ✱ sB&B£17-£20 dB&B£30-£36 dB&B £36-£42

CTV P £

GH QQ St Margaret's 18 Craigmillar Park EH16 5PS ☎031-667 2202

Feb-Dec

Some of the bedrooms at St Margaret's are very large and all are enhanced by tasteful soft furnishings and coordinated fabrics; there is also an attractive lounge. The guesthouse is on the A7 on the south side of the city centre.

8rm(2 6hc) (3fb) in 2 bedrooms CTV in all bedrooms ® ✱ sB&B£25 dB&B£28-£40

CTV 7P

Credit Cards 1 3 £

GH QQQ Salisbury Hotel 45 Salisbury Rd EH16 5AA ☎031-667 1264

Closed Xmas-New Year

Situated in a quiet southside residential area, 2 Georgian town houses have been combined to create this friendly, family-run guesthouse. The bedrooms are bright and cheery with comfortable, modern furnishings, and in the evenings guests can relax in the spacious lounge, which also contains a dispense bar.

12rm(9 3hc) (3fb) CTV in all bedrooms ® sB&B £20-£25 dB&B £36-£44 WB&Bfr£120

Lic CTV 12P

GH QQQ Salisbury View Hotel 64 Dalkeith Rd EH16 5AE ☎031-667 1133

rs 23-28 Dec

An attractive detached house with private parking at the rear. Accommodation throughout is tastefully decorated and fitted, with comfort in mind, and the bedrooms are very well appointed with many extra touches.

8rm(7 1hc) (2fb) CTV in all bedrooms ® ✱ sB&B£19-£23 sB&B £26-£36 dB&B £42-£54 LDO 8pm

Lic 8P sauna

Credit Cards 1 3

GH Q Sherwood 42 Minto St EH9 2BR ☎031-667 1200

Closed Xmas & New Year

A friendly terraced house south of the city centre catering essentially for the budget bed and breakfast market. Facilities are modest and functional, but the guesthouse is well maintained and spotlessly clean. Payment is requested on arrival.

6hc (3fb) CTV in all bedrooms ®

3P £

GH QQ Southdown 20 Craigmillar Park EH16 5PS ☎031-667 2410

Feb-Nov

Friendly service is provided at this city guesthouse which offers spacious, individually styled bedrooms, a cosy lounge and an attractive dining room.

6hc (2fb) CTV in all bedrooms ® (ex guide dogs) sB&B£18-£25 dB&B£30-£40

CTV 7P

GH QQ Strathmohr 23 Mayfield Gardens EH9 2BX ☎031-667 8475

mid May-Sep

Strathmohr is a family-run guesthouse with mainly spacious bedrooms equipped with radios and haridryers as well as en suite shower rooms.

7rm(5↱2hc) (4fb) CTV in all bedrooms ® ✕ (ex guide dogs) ✱ sB&B£13-£23 sB&B↱£15-£25 dB&B£30-£44 dB&B↱£32-£48
♨ 5P
Credit Cards [1] [3]

GH QQQ Stra'ven 3 Brunstane Rd North, Joppa EH15 2DL ☎031-669 5580
This fine semidetached Victorian house is only 100yds from the beach and promenade, and 3 miles east of the city centre.
7⇌↱ CTV in all bedrooms ® ✕ (ex guide dogs) ✱ sB&B⇌↱£15-£22 dB&B⇌↱£30-£44
♨ CTV P̸

GH QQQ *Stuart House* 12 East Claremont St EH7 4JP ☎031-557 9030 FAX 031-557 0563
Closed 18-27 Dec
Situated north of the city, in a residential terraced row of town houses, this pretty and comfortable house is run by Gloria Stuart. The well appointed bedrooms all have their own en suite facilities, except a small single room which has exclusive use of the bathroom. Breakfast is served at two communal tables in the large front-facing room on the ground floor, and there is also a small lounge area. A strict no-smoking policy is enforced.
7rm(6⇌↱1hc) (1fb) 🚭 in all bedrooms CTV in all bedrooms ® ✕ LDO 9pm
♨
Credit Cards [1] [3]

GH QQQ Thrums Private Hotel 14 Minto St, Newington EH9 1RQ ☎031-667 5545
Closed Xmas & New Year
This hotel has 2 styles. The main house is cosy and full of character, with a comfortable lounge, a little residents' and diners' bar and a small dining room with conservatory extension. Bedrooms here are cosy while those in the adjacent annexe are large and lofty, reflecting the period styling of the main house. All the rooms offer a good range of equipment and several thoughtful litle extras. The hotel is open to all for lunch and dinner.
8⇌↱ Annexe 7rm(6⇌↱1hc) (5fb) CTV in all bedrooms ® T LDO 7.45pm
Lic ♨ 12P

GH Q Tiree 26 Craigmillar Park EH16 5PS ☎031-667 7477 FAX 031-662 1608
Situated close to the bypass and with easy access to the city, this impressive stone-built house provides unpretentious accommodation.
7rm(4↱3hc) (2fb) CTV in all bedrooms ® ✱ sB&B£12-£16 dB&B£26-£32 dB&B↱£28-£40
♨ 7P

See advertisement on page 169

ELIE Fife Map **12** NO40

GH QQ The Elms 14 Park Place KY9 1DH ☎(0333) 330404
Apr-Sep
An attractive detached house dating from 1880, situated in this picturesque coastal village; it sits back from the main road and there is a well tended walled garden to the rear. Bedrooms vary in size and style, some of them have private bathrooms. There is a comfortable first floor lounge and the pleasant dining room has a fine plaster frieze.
7rm(1⇌3↱3hc) (2fb) CTV in 4 bedrooms ® ✱ sB&B£22.50 dB&B£34 dB&B⇌↱£46 WB&B£119-£159 WBDi£175-£215 LDO 6.30pm
Lic ♨ CTV P̸ nc10yrs Ⓔ

See the regional maps of popular holiday areas at the back of the book.

ELTERWATER Cumbria Map **07** NY30

INN QQQ Britannia LA22 9HP ☎Langdale(09667) 210 due to change to (05394) 37210 FAX (09667) 311 due to change to (05394) 37311

Closed 25 & 26 Dec

In the summer months, this very attractive, black and white painted inn, is distinguished by its colourful window boxes. The bedrooms are very well furnished with modern, dark wood units and have a TV and direct dial telephone. An extensive range of food is available, both at lunch and dinner, served in the small restaurant (booking is essential), and in the summer, meals are served on the lawns and patio outside. Other public areas are provided and each is full of old world charm.

9rm(6⇂3hc) CTV in all bedrooms ® **T** sB&B£22-£49.50 dB&B£44-£55 dB&B⇂£50-£61 WB&B£154-£203 WBDi£269-£318.50 Bar Lunch £3.45-£4.90alc Dinner £16.50-£17.50 LDO 7.30pm

🏠 10P

Credit Cards 1 3 £

ELY Cambridgeshire Map **05** TL58

GH Q Castle Lodge Hotel 50 New Barns Rd CB7 4PW ☎(0353) 662276

This family-owned and run hotel is situated in a residential area, yet is within walking distance of the cathedral and town centre. The public areas are quite comfortable, clean and well maintained, and there is a well stocked bar. Rooms on the 1st floor are simply furnished, some with private bathrooms; the 2nd-floor rooms are quite basic and due for renovation.

10rm(1⇨2⇂7hc) (1fb) CTV in all bedrooms ® ✕ (ex guide dogs) * sB&B£22-£35 sB&B⇨⇂£35 dB&B£42 dB&B⇨⇂£47-£50 WB&B£140 WBDi£190 LDO 7.30pm

Lic 🏠 8P

Credit Cards 1 3 £

FH QQQ Mrs Alison Morbey **Forge Cottage** *(TL554784)* Lower Rd, Stuntney CB7 5TN ☎(0353) 663275

Located in the small village of Stuntney, this 18th-century farmhouse sits in a peaceful part of the village with 2.5 acres of landscaped gardens and grounds. During the summer months, guests are welcome to view the Shire horses put out to graze, and the hard tennis court is available for guests to use. The quality bedrooms are all no smoking, furnished with a nice mixture of antiques and superior, chintz style soft furnishings, blending with matching fabrics and colour coordinated throughout – even extending into the modern, generous sized bathrooms. There is a dining room and lounge that interchange with the seasons, so visitors can enjoy the comfort of the large open log fire in winter months. Both rooms are nicely decorated with rich colours that complement the oak beams and antique furniture. Guests dine communally at a highly polished table and dinners are only available by prior arrangement; alternatively the family have good connections with a local restaurant and can generally make bookings for guests.

2rm(1⇨1⇂) ⊁in all bedrooms CTV in all bedrooms ® ✕ (ex guide dogs) * sB&B⇨⇂£22.50 dB&B⇨⇂£45 WB&B£150

🏠 2P 2🚗 nc10yrs 🎾(hard)U 2500 acres arable vegetables

EMSWORTH Hampshire Map **04** SU70

GH QQ Jingles Hotel 77 Horndean Rd PO10 7PU ☎(0243) 373755

An extended Victorian house in a tree lined road. Bedrooms are bright and well kept: 2 are on the ground floor. There is a comfortable drawing room, and a garden with rural views outside.

13rm(5⇂8hc) CTV in all bedrooms ® sB&Bfr£23 sB&B⇂fr£31 dB&Bfr£40 dB&B⇂fr£48 WB&Bfr£145 WBDifr£199 LDO 7pm

Lic 🏠 CTV 14P

Credit Cards 1 3 £

GH QQ *Merry Hall Hotel* 73 Horndean Rd PO10 7PU ☎(0243) 372424

Closed 25 Dec-3 Jan

This small privately owned hotel is situated in a residential area north of the town. Bedrooms are compact but well equipped, and the open plan bar and dining room lead out to a patio and large garden.

10rm(7⇨3⇂) (2fb) CTV in all bedrooms ® ✕ LDO 7.30pm

Lic 🏠 CTV 12P putting green

Credit Cards 1 3

EPSOM Surrey Map **04** TQ26

GH QQ Epsom Downs Hotel 9 Longdown Rd KT17 3PT ☎(0372) 740643 FAX (0372) 723259

This charming hotel is located in a peaceful residential area, with bedroom accommodation which is modern and well equipped. In addition to the pleasant bar, there is a comfortable lounge and an attractive dining room.

14rm(3⇨9⇂2hc) CTV in all bedrooms ® **T** ✕ sB&B£22-£38.78 sB&B⇨⇂£32.45-£64.63 dB&B⇨⇂£43.45-£71.50 WB&B£340 WBDi£415 LDO 9pm

Lic 🏠 CTV 11P

Credit Cards 1 2 3 5

GH QQ *The White House* Downs Hill Rd KT18 5HW ☎(0372) 722472 FAX (0372) 744447

15rm(4⇨3⇂2hc) (1fb) CTV in all bedrooms ® ✕ (ex guide dogs) LDO 8.30pm

Lic 🏠 CTV 15P

Credit Cards 1 3

ERLESTOKE Wiltshire Map **03** ST95

FH QQQ Mrs P Hampton **Longwater Park** *(ST966541)* Lower Rd SN10 5UE ☎Devizes(0380) 830095

Closed Xmas & New Year

A modern, red-brick farmhouse, detached from the working farm, close to Salisbury Plain. It overlooks an ornamental fishing lake which is available for guests' use. The bedrooms are well equipped and have private bathrooms, and there is a choice of comfortable lounges.

3⇨⇂ (1fb) CTV in all bedrooms ® sB&B⇨⇂£21 dB&B⇨⇂£38 WB&B£116.50-£130 WBDi£190-£210 LDO 5pm

Lic 🏠 CTV 6P ♩ 166 acres beef waterfowl organic £

ETTINGTON Warwickshire Map **04** SP24

FH QQ Mrs B J Wakeham **Whitfield** *(SP265506)* CV37 7PN ☎Stratford on Avon(0789) 740260

Closed Dec

A spacious farmhouse on the A429 just north of the A422 roundabout, 7 miles from Stratford-upon-Avon. Accommodation is comfortable, and the newly created ground floor bedroom is particularly attractive. The Wakeham family are friendly, welcoming hosts.

3rm(2⇂1hc) (1fb) ® ✕ (ex guide dogs) sB&B£15-£17.50 dB&B£26-£27 dB&B⇂£30-£32

🏠 CTV 3P 220 acres mixed £

EVERSHOT Dorset Map **03** ST50

GH QQQ Rectory House Fore St DT2 0JW ☎(093583) 273

Closed Xmas

A charming 18th century stone built house in the centre of this famous Dorset village. There are 6 en suite bedrooms: 4 are in a converted stable annexe, with access through the garden to the main house. All the rooms have been tastefully decorated and comfortably furnished. There is a choice of lounges, one where a log fire blazes on chilly evenings and the other has a TV. The emphasis in the dining room is on good quality, fresh, home-cooked food served as a set meal each evening.

6⇌↱ CTV in all bedrooms ® ✗ (ex guide dogs) dB&B⇌↱£54-£64 WB&B£185-£195 WBDi£240-£260 LDO 6.30pm

Lic ♈ TV 6P nc12yrs

Credit Cards [1] [3] (£)

See advertisement under DORCHESTER p 153

EVESHAM Hereford & Worcester Map **04** SP04

GH QQQ Church House Greenhill Park Rd WR11 4NL ☏(0386) 40498

Antiques and family mementoes add to the friendly, country house atmosphere provided by Veronica and Michael Shaw, in this large semidetached house set back from the A435 in a residential area close to the town centre. Bedrooms are furnished with good quality fabrics and interesting antique pieces, including Victorian dressing tables and wardrobes. Guests are well prepared for the day with a substantial breakfast served at the large ornate table in the dining room. For dinner, the proprietors have a good knowledge of local restaurants and pubs.

3⇌↱ (1fb) CTV in all bedrooms ® sB&B⇌↱£25-£30 dB&B⇌↱£35-£42

♈ 3P (£)

GH QQQ The Croft 54 Greenhill WR11 4NF ☏(0386) 446035

This large Georgian house is set in pleasant gardens on the outskirts of the town. Simon de Montfort is reputed to have died in its grounds. Bedrooms are very well furnished, 2 have en suite facilities and the third, a little smaller, has the private use of a bathroom. There are 2 comfortable lounges and guests breakfast together on a communal basis.

3rm(2⇌↱1hc) (1fb) CTV in all bedrooms ® ✱ sB&B£25-£30 sB&B⇌↱£30-£35 dB&B⇌↱£35-£42

♈ CTV 5P (£)

GH QQQ *Lyncroft* 80 Greenhill WR11 4NH ☏(0386) 442252

Feb-Nov

The Lyncroft is set in pleasant gardens alongside the A435 north of the town centre. Run by the very friendly McLean family it provides a comfortable residents' lounge and bright, well equipped bedrooms.

5rm(1⇌4↱) CTV in all bedrooms ® ✗

♈ 10P nc5yrs

INN QQ Park View Hotel Waterside WR11 6BS ☏(0386) 442639

Closed 25 Dec-1 Jan

28hc (2fb) sB&B£18.50-£20.50 dB&B£34.50-£39 Bar Lunch £1.50-£3.50 Dinner £9-£11 LDO 7pm

CTV 40P

Credit Cards [1] [2] [3] (£)

EXETER Devon Map **03** SX99

See **Town Plan Section**

GH Q *Braeside* 21 New North Rd EX4 4HF ☏(0392) 56875

Closed 25-26 Dec

A terraced property, an easy walk from the city centre, offering simply furnished bedrooms and breakfast served in an informal dining room.

7rm(3↱4hc) (1fb) CTV in all bedrooms ® LDO 4pm

♈ ⊬

GH QQQ The Edwardian 30/32 Heavitree Rd EX1 2LQ ☏(0392) 76102 & 54699

Closed Xmas & New Year

A town house within an easy walk of the cathedral, city centre, theatre and other amenities. The hotel has been redecorated and provides simply furnished bedrooms, comfortable public areas and a large public car park across the road.

13rm(10⇌↱3hc) (2fb) CTV in all bedrooms ® T sB&B£19-£20 sB&B⇌↱£25-£28 dB&B£32-£34 dB&B⇌↱£35-£44

♈ 4P

Credit Cards [1] [3] (£)

GH QQQ Hotel Gledhills 32 Alphington Rd EX2 8HN
☎(0392) 430469 & 71439
Closed 2 wks Xmas
This Victorian red-brick semidetached house, with stained glass and leaded windows, is situated on the edge of the city. Following recent improvements, most of the comfortable bedrooms now offer en suite facilities, all with colour TV and controllable central heating. A cosy lounge/bar has been added, adjacent to the TV lounge, and home-cooked dishes are served in the informal yet attractive dining room. A warm welcome is assured from Mr and Mrs Greening.
12rm(11↱1hc) (4fb) CTV in all bedrooms Ⓡ ✗ ✱ sB&B£20-£22 sB&B↱£25-£27.50 dB&B↱£39-£43 LDO 7pm
Lic ▥ CTV 11P 2🚗
Credit Cards 1 3

GH QQ Park View Hotel 8 Howell Rd EX4 4LG
☎(0392) 71772 & 53047
Closed Xmas
A personally managed small hotel close to the city centre, station, university and cathedral, yet away from the noise. Bedrooms are particularly well equipped, there is an attractive lounge, and breakfast is served in a bright, airy dining room.
10rm(2⇨2↱6hc) Annexe 5↱ (2fb)⊬in 1 bedroom CTV in all bedrooms Ⓡ T ✗ (ex guide dogs) ✱ sB&B£18-£22 sB&B⇨↱£28-£32 dB&B£35 dB&B⇨↱£43-£45
▥ CTV 6P
Credit Cards 1 3 £

GH QQ Sunnymede 24 New North Rd EX4 4HF
☎(0392) 73844
Closed 24 Dec-1 Jan
A Georgian house conveniently located for the city, which has been refurbished and provides bright, well equipped bedrooms, a cosy lounge and a breakfast room, in a welcoming atmosphere.
9rm(5↱4hc) (1fb) CTV in all bedrooms ✗ sB&B£18-£21 sB&B↱£21 dB&B£29-£31 dB&B↱£31 LDO 9pm
▥ CTV ⱣP £

GH Q Telstar Hotel 77 St Davids Hill EX4 4DW
☎(0392) 72466
Closed 2 wks Xmas
A small, family-run guesthouse in a terrace of small hotels, close to the university, station and city centre. Bedrooms are clean and comfortable, and the friendly proprietors serve breakfast in the attractive dining room.
9hc (1fb) Ⓡ ✱ sB&B£13-£16 dB&B£24-£26 dB&B£26-£30
▥ CTV 5P £

GH QQ *Trees Mini Hotel* 2 Queen's Crescent, York Rd EX4 6AY ☎(0392) 59531
A family-run guesthouse, close to all the amenities and just a short walk from the city centre, where the simple bedrooms are spotlessly clean and comfortable. There is a quiet lounge and a set evening meal is now available in the dining room. Devonshire hospitality comes naturally to the resident proprietors.
10rm(1⇨9hc) (1fb) CTV in all bedrooms Ⓡ ✗ LDO 10am
▥ CTV 1🚗
Credit Cards 1 3

GH Q Trenance House Hotel 1 Queen's Crescent, York Rd EX4 6AY ☎(0392) 73277
Closed Xmas
This small family-run hotel offers simply appointed accommodation, within walking distance of the city centre.
15rm(1⇨2↱6hc) (2fb) CTV in all bedrooms Ⓡ ✱ sB&B£17-£23 sB&B⇨↱£18-£23 dB&Bfr£25 dB&B⇨↱£31-£33
LDO noon
▥ CTV 7P
Credit Cards 1 3

EXMOUTH Devon Map 03 SY08

GH Q *Blenheim* 39 Morton Rd EX8 1BA ☎(0395) 264230
Closed 24-26 Dec
A small, modestly appointed and personally run guesthouse conveniently positioned close to the seafront.
6hc (2fb) CTV in all bedrooms Ⓡ ✗ (ex guide dogs)
LDO 4.30pm
Lic ▥ CTV 1P
Credit Cards 1 3

GH QQQ Carlton Lodge Hotel Carlton Hill EX8 2AJ
☎(0395) 263314
A pleasant, small hotel just off the seafront offering friendly service in a relaxed atmosphere, with good car parking on site. Bedrooms, whilst not spacious, are bright and very well equipped, each with a private bathroom. There is a popular bar and a cosy little steak restaurant, with a good range of value-for-money dishes available in both.
6rm(2⇨2↱2hc) (3fb) CTV in all bedrooms Ⓡ ✱ sB&B£24-£26 sB&B⇨↱£30-£32 dB&B£36-£38 dB&B⇨↱£45-£48 WB&B£120-£180 WBDi£162-£222 LDO 9pm
Lic ▥ 14P
Credit Cards 1 3 £

EYE Suffolk Map 05 TM17

INN QQQ The White Horse Stoke Ash IP23 7ET
☎Occold(037971) 222
This 17th-century coaching inn is situated alongside the A140 midway between Ipswich and Norwich. There are 2 bars, both with an abundance of exposed timbers and a central inglenook log fire, and 2 restaurants, all offering an extensive menu. Seven bedrooms are in a completely modern annexe block and 2 are in the main building, one of which is a family suite, and all are very well furnished and equipped. Outside there is a patio and an attractive landscaped garden.
2⇨ Annexe 7⇨ (1fb) CTV in all bedrooms Ⓡ
✗ (ex guide dogs) ✱ sB&B⇨↱£30 dB&B⇨↱£40 Lunch £7.15-£16.25 Dinner £7.15-£16.25 LDO 9.30pm
▥ 60P
Credit Cards 1 3

EYNSHAM Oxfordshire Map 04 SP40

GH QQQ All Views Main A40 OX8 1PU
☎Oxford(0865) 880891
A new bungalow on the A40 offering 4 ground floor bedrooms which are clean and very well equipped; en suite bathrooms provide both bath and shower, with very pretty Italian tiles. Guests share 2 tables in the open plan kitchen and breakfast room, and the comfortable lounge has a log burner for the winter months.
4⇨↱ CTV in all bedrooms Ⓡ T ✗ (ex guide dogs) ✱ sB&B⇨↱£30 dB&B⇨↱£40
▥ CTV 20P nc10yrs
Credit Cards 1 3 £

FAIRBOURNE Gwynedd Map 06 SH61

GH Q Sea View Friog LL38 2NX ☎(0341) 250388
This small guesthouse is situated on the A493 in the tiny hamlet of Friog, 9 miles southwest of Dolgellau. The accommodation is quite simple and functional, but suitable for both commercial and leisure use, and facilities include a small bar. The rear bedrooms have distant views of the sea, and there are sandy beaches and mountain walks close by.
8rm(4↱4hc) (3fb)⊬in 1 bedroom CTV in all bedrooms Ⓡ ✗ ✱ sB&Bfr£15 sB&B↱fr£16 dB&Bfr£30 dB&B↱fr£32 WB&Bfr£95 WBDifr£140 LDO 8pm
Lic ▥ CTV ⱣP

FAKENHAM Norfolk

See **Barney**

FALFIELD Avon Map **03** ST69

GH QQ Green Farm GL12 8DL ☎(0454) 260319
Situated on the A38, just half a mile north of junction 14 on the M5, this large house is set back in its own pleasant grounds which include a tennis court and outdoor swimming pool. Parts of the house date back to the 16th century, and it was formerly the principal house of a large farm; some of the original character has been retained, with flagstone floors, exposed beams and open fires. Bedrooms vary in size and are simple, bright and soundly appointed.
8rm(1⇔7hc) Ⓡ ✱ sB&Bfr£18 sB&B⇔fr£29 dB&Bfr£27 dB&B⇔fr£36 LDO 8.30pm
▥ CTV 10P ≈℘(hard)

FALMOUTH Cornwall & Isles of Scilly Map **02** SW83

See **Town Plan Section**

GH QQQ Cotswold House Hotel 49 Melvill Rd TR11 4DF ☎(0326) 312077
Personally run for many years by its resident owners, this modern hotel is situated between the beaches and town centre. Public rooms include a well stocked cocktail bar and a comfortable lounge. Most of the cheerful bedrooms have private bathrooms, and housekeeping standards are high.
10rm(8⇔↱2hc) (2fb) CTV in all bedrooms Ⓡ ✗ ✱ sB&B£17.50-£18.50 dB&B£34-£37 dB&B⇔↱£36-£40 WB&B£119-£124 WBDi£144-£159 LDO 7pm
Lic 10P nc4yrs

GH QQQ Gyllyngvase House Hotel Gyllyngvase Rd TR11 4DJ ☎(0326) 312956
Mar-Oct
This privately-owned hotel, close to the centre of town and the seafront, is run by the charming French proprietor and his English wife. Quite compact bedrooms are comfortable with a pretty, fresh décor. They are each well equipped, with modern facilities including direct dial telephones. Lounge areas are spacious and comfortable, overlooking the rear garden and enjoying the afternoon sunshine. Housekeeping is of a high standard, and the home-cooked evening meals are enjoyed by many returning guests.
15rm(12⇔↱3hc) (2fb) CTV in all bedrooms Ⓡ ✱ sB&B£18-£19 sB&B⇔↱£22-£30 dB&B⇔↱£40-£42 WBDi£165-£188 LDO 7pm
Lic ▥ CTV 15P (£)

GH QQ Ivanhoe 7 Melvill Rd TR11 4AS ☎(0326) 319083
This family run bed and breakfast stands in an Edwardian terrace between the town centre and beaches. There is a comfortable lounge downstairs, and well kept bedrooms on the 2 floors above, vary in size and headroom but all are brightly decorated with colourful duvets.
7rm(4↱3hc) (2fb) CTV in all bedrooms Ⓡ ✗ ✱ sB&B£12.50-£13 dB&B↱£30-£32 WB&B£85-£105
▥ CTV 4P
Credit Cards [1] [3] (£)

GH QQ Melvill House Hotel 52 Melvill Rd TR11 4DQ ☎(0326) 316645
Closed 23 Dec-1 Jan
This pink, semidetached Victorian villa is in the town between the shops and the sea. The cheerful bedrooms are on 3 floors and all have en suite facilities. The dining room is pretty, and the lounge has comfortable chairs, plants and dried flowers. Two fine palms guard the front entrance, and there is general parking to the rear.
7rm(5⇔2↱) (3fb)⊬in all bedrooms CTV in all bedrooms Ⓡ ✗ ✱ sB&B⇔↱£17.50-£20 dB&B⇔↱£28-£35 WB&B£100-£130 WBDi£129-£154 LDO 5.30pm
Lic ▥ CTV 9P

GH QQQ Penmere "Rosehill", Mylor Bridge TR11 5LZ
☎(0326) 374470

A traditional Cornish house standing in attractive gardens, with delightful views over Mylor Bridge Creek. There is a bright, comfortable lounge and breakfast room. The bedrooms have pretty fabrics, pine furniture and some Victorian fireplaces, and are named after local areas. For the benefit of watersport enthusiasts, the owner teaches at the nearby sailing school.

6rm(4⇌↱2hc) (2fb) CTV in all bedrooms ®
✗ (ex guide dogs) ✱ sB&Bfr£19 sB&B⇌↱fr£23 dB&Bfr£38 dB&B⇌↱fr£46 WB&B£119.70-£144.90
₩ 7P £

GH QQQ ***Penty Bryn Hotel*** 10 Melvill Rd TR11 4AS
☎(0326) 314988
Etr-Oct

This small family-run hotel is conveniently located for both the centre of town and the seafront. Bedrooms are nicely presented, well maintained with modern facilities in each and some enjoy good sea views. A traditional lounge area is complemented by a cosy bar and breakfast room. The guesthouse is personally run by the friendly and warm resident proprietor, Mrs Jane Wearne.

7rm(5↱2hc) (3fb) CTV in all bedrooms ®
Lic ₩ CTV 2P 1🚗
Credit Cards 1 3

GH QQQ Westcott Hotel Gyllyngvase Hill TR11 4DN
☎(0326) 311309
3 Jan-Oct rs Jan-Mar

This agreeable and well maintained family-run house is located close to the beach. Bedrooms are clean and comfortable, and several have sea views. Public areas include a welcoming lounge and a reception hall with an interesting collection of plates.

10rm(6⇌4↱) Annexe 1⇌ (2fb)⊬in all bedrooms CTV in all bedrooms ® ✗ sB&B⇌↱£20-£25 dB&B⇌↱£36-£44 WB&B£106-£140 WBDi£155-£189 LDO 6pm
₩ CTV 9P nc5yrs

FALSTONE Northumberland Map 12 NY78

INN QQQ Pheasant Stannersburn NE48 1DD
☎Bellingham(0434) 240382
rs Jan-Mar

Originally a farm, this delightful country pub, with its beamed ceilings, brasses and natural stone, prides itself on serving real ale. The bedrooms are contained in what used to be the barn and outbuildings, which can be seen in their original appearance in old photographs on the bar wall. They are simply decorated and furnished in a bright, modern style, although 2 rooms feature the original arched windows and exposed stone and 5 rooms have en suite shower facilities. A 3-course meal is available in the cosy, pine furnished dining room, and meals are also served in the bar.

Annexe 10rm(5↱5hc) (1fb)⊬in all bedrooms CTV in 5 bedrooms ® sB&B£19-£22 sB&B↱£30 dB&B£38-£40 dB&B↱£48-£52 Lunch £5-£10&alc Dinner £11-£13.50&alc LDO 8.50pm
₩ 40P pool room darts £

FAREHAM Hampshire Map 04 SU50

GH QQQ Avenue House Hotel 22 The Avenue PO14 1NS
☎(0329) 232175 FAX (0329) 232196

This private hotel is conveniently located close to major road and motorway links and the railway station. The resident proprietors have been converting the house from a private residence into a very smart and comfortable hotel since 1988. Bedrooms are individual in style and thoughtfully designed and equipped, with spotlessly clean modern en suite facilities and several extra touches. Dinner is not served here, but there are plenty of restaurants nearby in the town. Of particular note is the specially equipped ground floor room for disabled guests, suitable for wheelchairs, and there are 3 other rooms on the ground floor.

13⇌↱ (3fb) CTV in all bedrooms ® sB&B⇌↱£26-£43 dB&B⇌↱£33-£54
₩ CTV 13P
Credit Cards 1 2 3 £

FARINGDON Oxfordshire Map 04 SU29

SELECTED

GH QQQQ Barcote Manor Buckland SN7 8PP
☎Buckland(036787) 260 & 330
Apr-Oct

A most impressive red brick Victorian manor house, standing in 35 acres of beautifully kept gardens and grounds. The house is approached by a long tree- lined drive off the A420, with easy access to both Oxford and Swindon. The 3 spacious bedrooms are comfortably furnished and equipped, 2 of the bedrooms have private bathrooms decorated in Victorian style, in keeping with the striking architecture. The Great Hall has a splendid stained glass window, and all the public rooms are oak panelled, with lovely ornate ceilings. Breakfast is served around one large table in the elegant dining room, where the resident proprietors Mr and Mrs Tennant-Eyles extend a warm welcome.

3hc ⊬in all bedrooms ® sB&B£30-£35 dB&B£40-£50
₩ CTV 3P nc6yrs sauna croquet
Credit Cards 1 2 3 £
See advertisement under OXFORD

GH QQQ Faringdon Hotel Market Place SN7 7HL
☎(0367) 240536

A substantial hotel with a smart exterior offering well equipped bedrooms with modern facilities including satellite television. In addition to accommodation in the main building there are five bedrooms in the cottage-style annexe. The public areas are rather limited, but nevertheless pleasantly furnished. The hotel enjoys an international and commercial clientèle.

17rm(11⇌6↱) Annexe 5rm(1⇌4↱) (3fb) CTV in all bedrooms ® T ✱ sB&B⇌↱£46.50 dB&B⇌↱£56.50 LDO 9pm
Lic ₩ 5P
Credit Cards 1 2 3 5

GH QQQ Westbrook House 18 Gravel Walk SN7 7JW
☎(0367) 241820

A warm welcome awaits guests to this interesting and cosy family home. Dating from 1705, the house has a spacious lounge/breakfast room and antique furnished bedrooms, it is centrally located, a short walk from the town centre and provides off street parking.

3⇌↱ (1fb) CTV in 1 bedroom ® ✗ (ex guide dogs) ✱ sB&B⇌↱£18 dB&B⇌↱£30
₩ CTV 5P

FARMBOROUGH Avon Map 03 ST66

GH QQQ Streets Hotel The Street BA3 1AR
☎Mendip(0761) 471452
Closed 23 Dec-1 Jan

An attractive 17th-century house set in a picturesque village, this small private hotel offers some of its accommodation in a converted coaching house. Rooms are well furnished and decorated and have some good modern facilities. An acre of garden is the perfect setting for the swimming pool.

3⇌↱ Annexe 5⇌↱ CTV in all bedrooms ® T ✗ ✱ sB&B⇌↱£42-£50 dB&B⇌↱£52-£62 LDO 8.50pm
Lic ₩ CTV 8P 2🚗 nc6yrs ⛱(heated) solarium
Credit Cards 1 2 3

Book as early as possible for busy holiday periods.

FAR SAWREY Cumbria Map **07** SD39

GH QQQ West Vale Country LA22 0LQ
☎Windermere(05394) 42817
Mar-Oct
This well run family guesthouse, with friendly resident owners, is set in its own grounds with fine views towards Grizedale Forest and the mountains beyond. Bedrooms are comfortably furnished and good lounges are available.
8rm(7 1hc) (3fb) ® (ex guide dogs) sB&B fr£19.50 dB&B fr£39 WB&Bfr£136.50 WBDifr£189 LDO 4pm
Lic CTV 8P nc7yrs £

FAVERSHAM Kent Map **05** TR06

INN QQ White Horse The Street, Boughton ME13 9AX (Shepherd) ☎Canterbury(0227) 751343 FAX (0227) 751090
13rm(7 6) (2fb) CTV in 13 bedrooms ® **T** sB&B £40-£45 dB&B £50-£60 Lunch £10-£15alc Dinner £12-£17alc LDO 9.30pm
35P
Credit Cards 1 3

FAZELEY Staffordshire Map **04** SK20

GH Q Buxton Hotel 65 Coleshill St B78 3RG
☎Tamworth(0827) 285805 & 284842
Closed 25-26 Dec rs 1 Jan
Originally a doctor's residence on the Peel Estate (Sir Robert), the house is situated alongside the A4091 just south of its junction with the A5. Bedrooms are modestly appointed but all have TV and telephones. There is an oak panelled bar, the dining room features an ornately carved wooden fireplace, and the spacious lounge includes a full size snooker table.
15rm(4 9 2hc) (4fb) CTV in all bedrooms ® **T** * sB&B£23-£27 sB&B £25-£35 dB&B£33-£36 dB&B £35-£42 LDO 8.45pm
Lic CTV 16P
Credit Cards 1 3 £

FELINDRE (NEAR SWANSEA) West Glamorgan Map **02** SN60

FH QQQ Mr F Jones ***Coynant*** *(SN648070)* SA5 7PU (4m N of Felindre off unclass rd linking M4 j unc 46 and Ammanford)
☎Ammanford(0269) 595640 & 592064
Rather isolated and reached by a gated concrete road, this comfortably appointed and family-run farmhouse is well worth the journey. It is set in spectacular countryside, with pursuits such as fishing and pony riding available to guests, children particularly may enjoy feeding the farm pets.
5rm(3 2hc) (2fb) in all bedrooms CTV in all bedrooms ® (ex guide dogs) LDO 7pm
Lic 10P games room 150 acres mixed

FELIXSTOWE Suffolk Map **05** TM33

INN QQ Fludyer Arms Hotel Undercliff Rd East IP11 7LU
☎(0394) 283279 FAX (0394) 670754
8rm(4 4hc) (1fb) CTV in all bedrooms ® sB&B£18 sB&B £26 dB&B£32 dB&B £40 Lunch £5-£12 Dinner £5-£12 LDO 9pm
8P
Credit Cards 1 2 3 £

FILEY North Yorkshire Map **08** TA18

GH QQ Abbots Leigh 7 Rutland St YO14 9JA
☎Scarborough(0723) 513334
An attractive small guesthouse set in a quiet side road close to the beach, gardens and town centre. The tastefully furnished and decorated bedrooms all have private bathrooms, TV, clock radios and tea-making facilities: smoking is not permitted in the bedrooms or dining room. A 5-course dinner is served in the pretty dining room, offering a varied choice including a vegetarian menu.
6 (3fb) in all bedrooms CTV in all bedrooms ® (ex guide dogs) dB&B £32 WB&B£102-£171 WBDi£149-£220 LDO 4pm
Lic 4P nc3yrs
Credit Cards 1 3 £

GH QQ *Downcliffe Hotel* The Beach YO14 9LA
☎Scarborough(0723) 513310
Apr-Oct
A detached, 3-storey stone-built Victorian house situated on the seafront. Bedrooms are plainly decorated but comfortable, many overlooking the bay. Public rooms all have fine sea views, and 5-course evening meals are served in the spacious dining room, with local and home-made produce very much in evidence.
17rm(1 6 10hc) (9fb) CTV in all bedrooms ® LDO 6pm
Lic CTV 8P 2
Credit Cards 1 3

GH QQ Seafield Hotel 9/11 Rutland St YO14 9JA
☎Scarborough(0723) 513715
Improvements continue to be made to this family-run private hotel situated in a quiet road of Victorian terraced houses just off the Esplanade. It offers pleasant, if compact, bedrooms, a small lounge bar and an attractive dining room.
13rm(3 6 4hc) (7fb) CTV in all bedrooms ®
sB&B£21.50-£23.50 sB&B £23.50-£25.50 dB&B£43-£47 dB&B £47-£51 (incl dinner) WB&B£124-£128 WBDi£145-£159 LDO 4pm
Lic CTV 8P £

This is one of many guidebooks published by the AA. The full range is available at any AA Shop or good bookshop.

FIR TREE Co Durham Map **12** NZ13

SELECTED

GH QQQQ Greenhead Country House Hotel DL15 8BL
☎Bishop Auckland(0388) 763143
Tucked away just off the A68 between Darlington and Corbridge, this delightful white-washed hotel is run by resident proprietors, Anne and Paul Birbeck, who ensure that both the general atmosphere and the service are friendly and relaxed. The pretty bedrooms are bright, modern and very well equipped. All are similarly furnished but with individual touches. The very comfortable beamed lounge and bar are separated by a large stone chimney breast. Dinner is not served, but hot and cold snacks are always available.
8⇌↱ (1fb) CTV in 7 bedrooms ® ✗ (ex guide dogs) ✱ sB&B⇌↱£30-£35 dB&B⇌↱£40-£45 WB&B£140-£155 LDO 5pm
Lic ꟾꟾꟾ CTV 18P 2🚗 (£2 per night) nc13yrs
Credit Cards [1] [3]

FLAX BOURTON Avon Map **03** ST56

INN QQQ Jubilee Main Rd BS19 3QX ☎(0275) 462741
Closed 25 Dec evening
A popular inn conveniently positioned on the A370 at the edge of the village, on the outskirts of Bristol. The 3 cosy, bright bedrooms are comfortable, with some nice extra touches, and there is a spacious residents' lounge on the first floor. The public areas are full of character, with congenial bars and a good range of home-cooked meals to suit all palates and pockets. Ample car parking is provided on site.
3hc ® sB&B£28-£30 dB&B£56-£60 Lunch £8-£15alc Dinner £8-£15alc LDO 10pm
CTV 51P nc14yrs

FOREST

See **GUERNSEY under CHANNEL ISLANDS**

FORGANDENNY Tayside *Perthshire* Map **11** NO01

FH QQQ Mrs M Fotheringham ***Craighall** (NO081176)* PH2 9DF (0.5m W off B935 Bridge of Earn-Forteviot Rd)
☎Bridge of Earn(0738) 812415
This modern bungalow is situated on the driveway leading to the farm, amidst peaceful countryside yet only 15 minutes by car to Perth. Bedrooms are brightly decorated, and though 2 are quite small, they do have the advantage of modern en suite showers.
3rm(2↱1hc) (1fb)⁄in all bedrooms ® ✗ LDO 9pm
ꟾꟾꟾ CTV 4P ♩ 1000 acres beef mixed sheep

FORRES Grampian *Morayshire* Map **14** NJ05

SELECTED

GH QQQQ *Parkmount House Hotel* St Leonards Rd IV36 0DW ☎(0309) 673312
Closed Xmas & New Year
Set in its own garden in a residential area just south of the town centre, this charming house, built in 1868, has undergone sympathetic refurbishment and offers comfortable, modern accommodation. Bedrooms all have private bathrooms and are comfortably furnished and well equipped. Enjoyable meals prepared from fresh local produce are served in the attractive dining room, and Mr and Mrs Steer are welcoming hosts.
8⇌↱ (1fb)⁄in 1 bedroom CTV in all bedrooms ®
LDO 5pm
Lic ꟾꟾꟾ 25P ⌂ ▶ 18 special rate car hire is available to guests
Credit Cards [1] [3]

FORT WILLIAM Highland *Inverness-shire* Map **14** NN17

GH QQQ Ashburn House Achintore Rd PH33 6RQ
☎(0397) 70600
Jan-Oct
Conveniently situated beside the A82 just south of the town centre, this detached Victorian house stands in its own grounds overlooking Loch Linnhe. Recently modernised and refurbished it offers comfortable accommodation in bedrooms which are tastefully furnished and well equipped. Non-smoking public rooms include an attractive dining room and a comfortable pine-clad conservatory, both of which enjoy loch views.
6rm(5⇌↱) (2fb)⁄in all bedrooms CTV in all bedrooms ® ✱ sB&B£18-£40 sB&B⇌↱£25-£40 dB&B⇌↱£30-£60 WB&B£130-£200 WBDi£230-£30 LDO 8pm
ꟾꟾꟾ 8P ⌂
Credit Cards [1] [3]

GH QQ Benview Belford Rd PH33 6ER ☎(0397) 702966
Mar-Nov
This friendly, family-run guesthouse is situated beside the A82 just north of the town centre. Several of the bedrooms have en suite facilities and TV, and there are 2 comfortable lounges, one with TV. Enjoyable home cooking is served in the spacious dining room which looks out on to Ben Nevis.
13rm(3⇌3↱7hc) CTV in 6 bedrooms ® ✗ (ex guide dogs) ✱ sB&B£16-£19 dB&B£32-£36 dB&B⇌↱£32-£40 WB&B£105-£120
ꟾꟾꟾ CTV 20P

GH QQ Glenlochy Nevis Bridge PH33 6PF ☎(0397) 702909
Situated beside the A82 near the entrance to Glen Nevis, this friendly family- run guesthouse stands in its own grounds opposite the Distillery. It has been fully modernised and offers good value bed and breakfast accommodation, and is an ideal base for touring and hillwalking.
10rm(8↱2hc) (2fb)⁄in 2 bedrooms CTV in all bedrooms ® ✗ (ex guide dogs) ✱ dB&B£26-£36 dB&B↱£30-£42 WB&B£91-£144
ꟾꟾꟾ CTV 12P Ⓔ

GH QQ Guisachan Alma Rd PH33 6HA ☎(0397) 703797
Closed 16 Dec-4 Jan
This guesthouse with a comfortable lounge and an attractive dining room enjoys an elevated position which affords fine views across the town and Loch Linnhe.
13rm(2⇌9↱2hc) (3fb) CTV in 11 bedrooms ® ✗ ✱ sB&B£16-£20 sB&B⇌↱£18-£24 dB&B⇌↱£34-£48 WB&Bfr£45 LDO 5.30pm
Lic ꟾꟾꟾ CTV 15P

GH QQQ Lochview Heathercroft, Argyll Rd PH33 6RE
☎(0397) 703149
Etr-Oct
This former crofthouse has been extended and modernised and is situated on the hillside above the town, with lovely views across Loch Linnhe to the Ardgour hills. The bedrooms all have private bathrooms and are individually decorated and comfortably furnished. The pleasant lounge overlooks the loch, and hearty breakfasts are served in the adjoining dining room. There is a large garden and parking is provided.
8⇌↱ ⁄in all bedrooms CTV in all bedrooms ® ✗ dB&B⇌↱£35-£40 WB&B£119-£140
ꟾꟾꟾ 8P

GH Q Rhu Mhor Alma Rd PH33 6BP ☎(0397) 702213
Etr-Sep
Good value accommodation is offered at this well established family-run guesthouse which is set on a hill overlooking the town. Bedrooms, though simply furnished, are comfortable, and there is a choice of lounges. Good home cooking is served at shared tables in the dining room.
7hc (2fb) ✱ sB&B£13-£15 dB&B£26-£30 LDO 5pm
ꟾꟾꟾ CTV 7P Ⓔ

FOWEY Cornwall & Isles of Scilly Map **02** SX15

GH QQ Ashley House Hotel 14 Esplanade PL23 1HY
☎(0726) 832310
Etr-Oct
This small establishment sits in the heart of the picturesque harbour town, close to the quay and the seafront. Bedrooms are bright and sunny and many have en suite facilities. Recently extended and much improved, public areas include a cosy lounge, an attractive bar area and a small dining room where home-cooked meals are served. There is a small garden, and a sunny terrace on the first floor. There is a public car park nearby, and easy access into town by bus or taxi.
6rm(3⇌1🚿2hc) (6fb) CTV in all bedrooms ®
🐕 (ex guide dogs) LDO 6pm
Lic 🍴 CTV 🅿̸
Credit Cards [1] [3]

SELECTED

GH QQQQ Carnethic House Lambs Barn PL23 1HQ
☎(0726) 833336
Closed Dec-Jan
Located just on the outskirts of this pretty harbour village, an elegant Regency manor house set in beautiful, award-winning gardens. The charming owners Mr and Mrs Hogg have restored and modernised the house, and bedrooms are well equipped and furnished in a practical, modern style, with pretty coordinating décor. The lounge/bar and dining room are comfortable and well furnished, with home-cooked dishes offered. Outside, a variety of leisure pursuits include a sheltered, heated swimming pool, putting, croquet, bowls and tennis. The atmosphere here is that of a house party, and due to the hotel's popularity with appreciative returning guests, early bookings are advised.
8rm(5🚿3hc) (2fb)⊬in 1 bedroom CTV in all bedrooms ®
sB&B£27-£30 sB&B🚿£35-£40 dB&B£40-£44 dB&B🚿£46-£54 WB&B£133-£182 WBDi£208-£257 LDO 8pm
Lic 🍴 20P 🏠 ⛵(heated) 🎾(grass)badminton putting pool table short tennis
Credit Cards [1] [2] [3] [5] £

See advertisement on page 177

GH QQQ Wheelhouse 60 Esplanade PL23 1JA
☎(0726) 832452
Mar-Oct rs Nov-Feb
Standing in an elevated position with breathtaking views over the Estuary, this neat, well presented Victorian terraced house has an attractive front garden filled with flowers and some seats are provided for guests to enjoy the splendid panoramic views. Bedrooms are well equipped and individually furnished, several having front-facing positions enjoying the view. An evening meal can be served on request by Mrs Sixton, a cheerful host who cares well for her guests.
6hc (1fb) CTV in 4 bedrooms ® 🐕 ✱ sB&B£15-£17.50 dB&B£30-£35 WB&B£105-£122.50 WBDi£160-£175 LDO noon
Lic 🍴 CTV 🅿̸ £

INN QQQ King of Prussia Town Quay PL23 1AT (St Austell Brewery) ☎St Austell(0726) 832450
Situated on the town quay, this inn dates back to 1765, and enjoys picturesque harbour views. The bedrooms have all been refurbished to a high standard, and are well presented, with good modern facilities and magnificent sea views over the estuary and quay. Meals are served in a pretty rustic dining room, complete with scrubbed pine tables and dried flowers, and is good value for money.
6⇌🚿 (4fb)⊬in all bedrooms CTV in all bedrooms ®
🐕 (ex guide dogs) LDO 9.30pm
🍴
Credit Cards [1] [2] [3]

FOWNHOPE Hereford & Worcester Map **03** SO53

GH QQQ Bowens Country House HR1 4PS ☎(0432) 860430
Closed New Year
A 17th-century creeper-clad house set in pleasant lawns and gardens opposite the village church. Bedrooms are well furnished and include several ground floor rooms suitable for disabled guests. There is a comfortable lounge and a pine furnished dining room.
8rm(3⇌🚿5hc) Annexe 4⇌🚿 (2fb) CTV in all bedrooms ® sB&Bfr£19.50 sB&B⇌🚿fr£24.50 dB&Bfr£39 dB&B⇌🚿fr£43 WB&Bfr£119 WBDifr£199.50 LDO 8pm
Lic 🍴 15P nc10yrs ♪(grass)9 hole putting
Credit Cards [1] [3] £

FOYERS Highland *Invernesshire* Map **14** NH42

GH QQQ Foyers Bay House Lochness IV1 2YB
☎Gorthleck(04563) 624 FAX (04563) 337
Set in 4 acres of grounds overlooking Loch Ness, this lovely Victorian house has been sympathetically refurbished to provide excellent accommodation. Bedrooms, all with private bathrooms, are comfortably appointed and well equipped, and the attractive conservatory café/restaurant overlooking the loch offers snacks and meals all day.
3⇌🚿 CTV in all bedrooms ® T ✗ (ex guide dogs) ✱ sB&B⇌🚿£20-£26 dB&B⇌🚿£30-£42 WBDi£126-£175 LDO 7.30pm
🍴 CTV 6P
Credit Cards [1] [3]

FRANT East Sussex Map **05** TQ53

SELECTED

GH QQQQ The Old Parsonage Frant TN3 9DX
☎Tunbridge Wells(0892) 750773
This former rectory dates from 1820 and has been beautifully restored and furnished by the hospitable new proprietors, Tony and Mary Dakin. Public rooms capture the atmosphere of earlier times when two Canadian prime ministers were entertained on pilgrimages to the grave of Colonel By who is buried in the churchyard. Bedrooms are spacious and comfortable with a host of extras.
3⇌🚿 ⊬in all bedrooms CTV in all bedrooms ✱ sB&B⇌🚿£25-£35 dB&B⇌🚿£45-£49
🍴 CTV 12P £

FRESHWATER

See **WIGHT, ISLE OF**

FRINTON-ON-SEA Essex Map **05** TM21

GH Q Forde 18 Queens Rd CO13 9BL ☎(0255) 674758
Closed Dec
This small, family run guesthouse offers modest, old-fashioned accommodation which is well maintained and provides adequate comfort. There is a cosy guests' lounge and unrestricted street parking.
6hc (1fb) ✱ sB&B£19.50 dB&B£30 WB&B£105
🍴 CTV 1P nc5yrs £

FROGMORE Devon Map **03** SX74

INN QQ Globe TQ7 2NR ☎Kingsbridge(0548) 531351
In a rural location 3 miles from Kingsbridge on the A379 Dartmouth road, the Globe is in an excellent position from which to tour this picturesque part of south Devon. Bedrooms are gradually being upgraded and are clean and comfortable. The bars are characterful, the restaurant caters for family budgets and there are many facilities for children.
6rm(2🚿4hc) (1fb) CTV in all bedrooms ® ✱ sB&B£20-£25 sB&B🚿£25 dB&B£34 dB&B🚿£40 WB&B£85-£100 Lunch £8-£16alc Dinner £8-£16alc LDO 9.30pm
🍴 CTV 20P
Credit Cards [1] [3] £
See advertisement under KINGSBRIDGE

FROME Somerset Map **03** ST74

GH QQ Wheelbrook Mill Laverton, Nr Bath BA3 6QY
☎(0373) 830263
This charming country home is a 200-year-old stone-built mill just off the A36 within easy reach of Bath. The mill is set well back from a quiet lane overlooking the brook and open fields, with only the ducks to disturb the peace. A spacious double room is offered to guests, providing a good range of facilities, and a more modest single room is also available in conjunction with the double. Owners Andrew and Shelley Weeks and their 2 young sons treat guests as friends of the family; dinner is taken around a long communal table in the cluttered country kitchen and Andrew and Shelley are likely to join their guests. A typical dinner may start with mushrooms in a brandy, cream and bacon sauce, followed by cream of beef in horseradish, and a dessert such as apple and plum crumble or tarte au citron. An informal and relaxed atmosphere prevails.
2rm(1⇌) ⊬in all bedrooms CTV in 1 bedroom ® ✗ ✱ sB&B£15-£20 dB&B⇌£40-£50
🍴 CTV P

GAIRLOCH Highland *Ross & Cromarty* Map **14** NG87

GH QQ Bain's House Strath IV21 2BZ ☎(0445) 2472
Noticable by its pretty, flowering window boxes, this whitewashed house is conveniently situated beside the shops and offers good value bed and breakfast accommodation. The compact bedrooms are fitted with a mixture of modern and old style furnishings and guests are welcome to share the owners comfortable lounge.
5hc (1fb) CTV in 4 bedrooms ® ✱ sB&B£13-£14 dB&B£24-£26
🍴 CTV 6P sea angling

GH QQQ Birchwood IV21 2AH ☎(0445) 2011
Apr-mid Oct
Set in an elevated position in its own grounds, overlooking Old Gairloch Harbour, this comfortable guesthouse offers good value bed and breakfast accommodation. The en suite bedrooms are bright and cheery with comfortable, modern furniture. As well as the attractive lounge, there is a small sun porch which overlooks the harbour, and hearty breakfasts are served in the small dining room. Proprietor Mrs Elsie Ramsay personally runs this friendly establishment and provides a warm welcome.
6🚿 (1fb)⊬in all bedrooms ® dB&B🚿£50-£52
🍴 CTV 6P

SELECTED

GH QQQQ Horisdale House Strath IV21 2DA
☎(0445) 2151
May-Sep
This modern, detached villa lies off the B8021 in its own gardens, and commands breathtaking views across the bay to the distant mountains. Run by Amelia Windsor and Patricia Strack for the past 13 years, the dedication and enthusiasm of these charming American ladies have encouraged guests to return year after year. Bedrooms vary in size, but all are brightly decorated, soundly furnished and spotlessly clean. Public rooms are spacious and have superb views, and dinners are also of note, for the ladies are as enthusiastic about food as they are about the care of their guests.
6hc (1fb)⊬in all bedrooms ® ✗ sB&B£16 dB&B£30 LDO 9am
🍴 10P nc7yrs

GALSTON Strathclyde *Ayrshire* Map **11** NS53

FH QQ Mrs J Bone **Auchencloigh** *(NS535320)* KA4 8NP (5m S off B7037-Scorn Rd) ☎(0563) 820567
Apr-Oct
This well maintained farmhouse sits amidst rolling countryside, with views of the Ayrshire coast and the Isle of Arran on clear days. Mrs Bone is a cheerful and enthusiastic hostess.
2rm (1fb)⊁in all bedrooms Ⓡ ✱ sB&B£14-£16 dB&B£28-£32 WB&Bfr£98 LDO 4pm
CTV 4P 4🚘 sauna 240 acres beef mixed sheep

GARBOLDISHAM Norfolk Map **05** TM08

GH QQQ Ingleneuk Lodge Hopton Rd IP22 2RQ ☎(095381) 541
rs Xmas
Modern bungalow set in 10 acres of quiet wooded countryside.
11rm(10⇆↾1hc) (2fb)⊁in 4 bedrooms CTV in all bedrooms Ⓡ **T** sB&B£21 sB&B⇆↾£30.50-£35 dB&B£34 dB&B⇆↾£47 WB&B£112-£203 WBDi£203-£287 LDO 1pm
Lic 20P
Credit Cards 1 2 3 £

GARGRAVE North Yorkshire Map **07** SD95

GH QQ Kirk Syke 19 High St BD23 3RA ☎Skipton(0756) 749356
Closed 16 Dec-2 Jan
The attractive surroundings of this large Victorian house are complemented by the River Aire flowing close by. The accommodation is split between the main house and a bungalow-style annexe. The bedrooms in the house have a selection of décors but the bungalow rooms are all furnished in a modern style. All the rooms are a good size and very comfortable, with most having a small refrigerator. There are 2 dining rooms, one with light modern furnishings, the other with mahogany tables and upholstered

→

chairs, where a 4-course home- cooked evening meal is served (provided it is ordered by 10am). Sited in the main house, a very comfortable lounge is provided for guests to relax after dinner.
6rm(3⇨3hc) Annexe 6⇨⇘ CTV in all bedrooms ® ✖
sB&B£25 sB&B⇨⇘£27 dB&B£36 dB&B⇨⇘£40
WB&B£132-£180 WBDi£216-£264 LDO 10am
Lic ⌘ CTV 12P nc5yrs
Credit Cards [1] [3]

GARSTANG Lancashire Map **07** SD44

FH QQ Mrs J Higginson **Clay Lane Head** *(SD490474)* Cabus, Preston PR3 1WL (2m N on A6) ☎(0995) 603132
Mar-23 Dec
An ivy-clad farmhouse alongside the A6 just north of Garstang with open countryside and meadows beyond. All bedrooms have washbasins and there is a cosy lounge overlooking the lawn and garden.
3rm(2⇨⇘1hc) (1fb) CTV in 2 bedrooms ® ✖ (ex guide dogs)
sB&B£16 sB&B⇨⇘£22-£24 dB&B£28 dB&B⇨⇘£36
WB&B£91-£119
⌘ CTV 4P 1🚗 30 acres beef £

GATEHOUSE OF FLEET Dumfries & Galloway *Kirkcudbrightshire* Map **11** NX55

GH QQ Bobbin 36 High St DG7 2HP ☎(0557) 814229
Well maintained accommodation is offered at this terraced guesthouse in the main street. Bedrooms are comfortable and traditionally furnished and there is a cosy lounge and a small dining room which is used as a coffee shop during the day.
6rm(2⇘4hc) (3fb) CTV in all bedrooms ® sB&B£19.50-£21.50
sB&B⇘£21.50-£23 dB&B£37-£40 dB&B⇘£44-£48
WB&B£126-£140 WBDi£189-£200 LDO 5pm
⌘ CTV 8P
Credit Cards [1] [3]

INN Q Bank Of Fleet Hotel 47 High St D97 2HR
☎Gatehouse(0557) 814302
Situated in the main street, this family run small private hotel offers modest accommodation but a good range of meals, both in the restaurant and lounge bar.
5hc (1fb) ® ✱ sB&Bfr£17.50 dB&Bfr£35 WBDifr£105
LDO 9pm
CTV
Credit Cards [1] [3]

GATESHEAD Tyne & Wear Map **12** NZ26

GH QQ *Victoria* 681 Durham Rd, Lowfell NE9 6HB
☎091-482 3172
This Victorian house is situated close to the motorway and has easy access to Newcastle. It provides neat, unpretentious and individually styled bedrooms, a cosy lounge and a breakfast room.
6hc (2fb) CTV in all bedrooms ®
⌘ CTV 4P
Credit Cards [1] [2] [3] [5]

GATWICK AIRPORT (LONDON) West Sussex Map **04** TQ24

GH QQ Barnwood Hotel Balcombe Rd, Pound Hill RH10 7RU
☎Crawley(0293) 882709 FAX (0293) 886041
Closed Xmas-1 Jan
This purpose-built hotel is situated on the B2036, south of the airport. Bedrooms are simply furnished with modern facilities, and 10 have been upgraded to a good standard. There is a fully licensed lounge bar and a restaurant, both of which overlook the garden. Reception facilities are available 24 hours a day, and there is good car parking.
35⇨⇘ (3fb) CTV in all bedrooms ® **T** ✖ (ex guide dogs)
sB&B⇨⇘fr£35 dB&B⇨⇘fr£45 LDO 9pm
Lic ⌘ 50P
Credit Cards [1] [2] [3] [5]

GH QQQ Chalet 77 Massetts Rd RH6 7EB
☎Horley(0293) 821666 FAX (0293) 821619
A small, friendly guesthouse in a good location near the airport and Horley town centre. Proprietor Daphne Shortland provides beautifully clean, well maintained bedrooms with fresh décor and good quality, pretty coordinating fabrics. It has a small breakfast room and lounge, and the kitchen has provisions for guests to make tea and coffee as required.
6rm(4⇘2hc) (1fb) CTV in all bedrooms ® ✖ (ex guide dogs)
✱ sB&Bfr£22 sB&B⇘fr£29.50 dB&B⇘fr£40
⌘ CTV 12P
Credit Cards [1] [3] £

GH QQQ Gainsborough Lodge 39 Massetts Rd RH6 7DT (2m NE of airport adjacent A23) ☎Horley(0293) 783982
This attractive house offers comfortable en suite bedrooms furnished in traditional style. Breakfast is served in the spacious dining room and there is a cosy lounge and rear garden for guests' use.
13⇨⇘ (3fb) CTV in all bedrooms ® ✖ (ex guide dogs)
sB&B⇨⇘£27.50-£36.50 dB&B⇨⇘£38.50-£46.50
⌘ 16P
Credit Cards [1] [2] [3] £

GH QQ Gatwick Skylodge London Rd, County Oak RH11 0PF (2m S of airport on A23) ☎Crawley(0293) 544511
Telex no 878307 FAX (0293) 611762
Closed 25-29 Dec
Situated on the A23, just south of Gatwick, this purpose-built hotel offers a courtesy coach service to and from the airport. All but 4 of the bedrooms have been recently refurbished, and accommodation is modern and uniform, with en suite facilities. There is also a small open-plan lounge bar and restaurant. A full English breakfast is available at an extra charge.
51⇨ (7fb) CTV in all bedrooms ® ✖ (ex guide dogs) ✱
sB&B⇨fr£38 dB&B⇨fr£51 LDO 9.15pm
Lic ⌘ 60P (£2.35 nightly)
Credit Cards [1] [2] [3] £

GH QQQ The Lawn 30 Massetts Rd RH6 7DE
☎Horley(0293) 775751
Closed Xmas
A charming Victorian house situated close to the town centre. The bedrooms are all freshly decorated and well maintained: many of the original fireplaces have been retained, lending character to most rooms. Breakfast is served in the tastefully appointed dining room, and the owners Mr and Mrs Stock make guests feel most welcome.
7rm(4⇘3hc) ⊘in all bedrooms CTV in all bedrooms ®
sB&B£24 sB&B⇘£31 dB&B£35 dB&B⇘£42
⌘ 10P
Credit Cards [1] [2] [3] [5] £

GH QQQ Little Foxes Ifield Woods, Ifield Rd RH11 0JY
☎Crawley(0293) 552430
Set in 5 acres, this purpose-built bungalow offers smart, modern bedrooms attractively furnished with pine, the majority having neat, fully tiled shower rooms. There is a small lounge area adjoining the dining room, where English breakfast is available from 7am. Extensive service is provided by the owners, including a courtesy coach to and from Gatwick, and up to 14 days free car parking is included in the room rate.
12rm(10⇨⇘2hc) (2fb) CTV in all bedrooms ® ✖ sB&Bfr£35
sB&B⇨⇘£40 dB&B£45 dB&B⇨⇘£49
⌘ 20P
Credit Cards [1] [2] [3] £

GH QQ *Massetts Lodge* 28 Massetts Rd RH6 7DE
☎Crawley(0293) 782738
A small, friendly guesthouse which offers good overnight accommodation: bedrooms are cosy and well equipped, with TV, coffee-making facilities, and many have smart private bathrooms. Convenient for Gatwick airport, public areas are limited, but there is a pleasant dining room where a range of traditional evening meals are available on request.
8rm(5⇨♪3hc) (2fb) CTV in all bedrooms ® ✖ (ex guide dogs) LDO 7.45pm
🍽 10P ⛆(heated)
Credit Cards 1 2 3

GH QQ Mill Lodge 25 Brighton Rd, Salfords RH1 6PP
☎Crawley(0293) 771170
This guesthouse is situated on the A23 between Redhill and Horley and benefits from car parking facilities. Cheerful bedrooms offer adequate comfort, although a couple are compact in size.
10rm(2⇨♪8hc) (1fb) CTV in all bedrooms ® ✖ (ex guide dogs) ✱ sB&Bfr£25 sB&B⇨♪fr£36 dB&Bfr£36 dB&B⇨♪fr£43
🍽 CTV 30P (£15 per week) 3🚗 (£20 per week)

GH QQ Rosemead 19 Church Rd RH6 7EY
☎Horley(0293) 784965 FAX (0293) 820438
This small guesthouse offers bright, modestly furnished bedrooms which are well maintained. The friendly proprietor Mrs Wood offers a substantial breakfast served in the cheerful dining room, and guests are made to feel at home. A Continental breakfast is served before 7.30am, after this time, a full English breakfast is available.
6hc (2fb) CTV in all bedrooms ® sB&B£23 dB&B£35
🍽 10P
Credit Cards 1 3 £

GH QQQ Vulcan Lodge 27 Massetts Rd RH6 7DQ
☎Horley(0293) 771522
Originally a farmhouse dating from the late 17th century, this guesthouse offers easy access to both Gatwick airport and the town centre from its secluded location off the main road. The individually furnished bedrooms have been stylishly decorated with imagination and great attention to detail; rooms are comfortable and clean, all with TV, radio alarms and tea trays. There is a cosy lounge and breakfast room, where smoking is not permitted. Forecourt car parking is available, and owner Mrs Pike and her friendly staff provide helpful service and a warm welcome.
4rm(3♪1hc) CTV in all bedrooms ® ✖ ✱ sB&B£24 sB&B♪£31 dB&B♪£40-£44
🍽 10P (charged)
Credit Cards 1 3

GH QQ Woodlands 42 Massetts Rd RH6 7DS
☎Horley(0293) 782994 & 776358
This small guesthouse provides bright, comfortable bedrooms with en suite shower rooms. Continental breakfast is available for early risers travelling to Gatwick, and those requiring English breakfast pay a supplement. Owner Mr Moore operates a strict no smoking policy throughout.
5♪ (2fb)⊬in all bedrooms CTV in all bedrooms ® ✖
🍽 20P (£10 per wk) 2🚗 (£15 per wk) nc5yrs £

GAYHURST Buckinghamshire Map 04 SP84

FH QQ Mrs K Adams **Mill** *(SP852454)* MK16 8LT (1m S off B526 unclass rd to Haversham)
☎Newport Pagnell(0908) 611489
This attractive 17th-century farmhouse will certainly suit the tennis enthusiast, as the extensive grounds provide the guests with their own court to play on. The bedrooms are a fair size and have been decorated to give a warm, comfortable feeling. There is a combined lounge and breakfast room, adorned with pictures and ornaments, and a choice of comfortable chairs are provided.
3rm(1⇨♪2hc) (1fb)⊬in 1 bedroom CTV in all bedrooms ® sB&B£15-£20 dB&B£30-£35 dB&B⇨♪£30-£35 LDO 4pm
🍽 CTV 10P 3🚗 ⌂ 🎾(hard) ⚲ U 550 acres mixed £

GIGGLESWICK North Yorkshire Map 07 SD86

INN QQ Black Horse Hotel Church St BD24 0BE
☎Settle(0729) 822506
A small hospitable inn by the village church with cosy bars, a separate dining room, and a residents' TV lounge upstairs. Home-cooked meals are served in the bars at lunch time and in the small restaurant during the evening. Traditional hand pulled ales are also available.
3rm(1⇨2♪) ® ✖ dB&B⇨♪£40 WB&B£126 WBDi£213.50 LDO 8.45pm
🍽 CTV 20P
Credit Cards 1 3 5

INN QQQ The Old Station Brackenbar Ln BD24 0EA
☎Settle(0729) 823623
This well furnished inn stands on the A65 Settle by-pass. It offers comfortable bedrooms with good quality pine furniture and en suite facilities. A range of bar meals is provided in the spacious bar.
8rm(1⇨7♪) (1fb) CTV in all bedrooms ® sB&B⇨♪£30-£35 dB&B⇨♪£51-£65 Lunch £6.50-£15alc High tea £6.50-£15alc Dinner £6.50-£15alc LDO 9.45pm
🍽 CTV 40P
Credit Cards 1 3 £

GILWERN Gwent Map 03 SO21

FH QQQ Mr B L Harris **The Wenallt** *(SO245138)* NP7 0HP (.75m S of A465 Gilwern by pass) ☎(0873) 830694
Situated south of the A465 Gilwern bypass, this 16th-century Welsh longhouse has lovely views of the Usk Valley. Spacious comfortable bedrooms are provided together with good public rooms.
3rm(1⇨2hc) Annexe 4rm(1⇨3♪) ® ✱ sB&B£18 sB&B⇨♪£25 dB&B£32.90 dB&B⇨♪£40 WB&B£105.15-£130 WBDi£183.28-£208.13 LDO 6pm
Lic 🍽 CTV 10P 8🚗 50 acres sheep

GISLINGHAM Suffolk Map 05 TM07

SELECTED

GH QQQQ The Old Guildhall Mill St IP23 8JT
☎Mellis(0379) 783361
Closed Jan
This immaculately maintained, thatched 15th-century guildhall lies in the centre of the village. Original features include beams, timbers and fireplaces. Bedrooms are full of character, 3 having very low ceilings and the 4th room is reached by a spiral staircase; they all have modern en suite bathrooms. The comfortable lounge has a small but well equipped bar, and a snooker room is also available for meetings. Ray and Ethel Tranter ensure that their guests have a warm welcome, with a family atmosphere prevailing.
3⇨ CTV in all bedrooms ® dB&B⇨£50 WB&B£150 WBDi£200 LDO 6pm
Lic 🍽 5P

GLAN-YR-AFON (NEAR CORWEN) Gwynedd Map 06 SJ04

FH Q Mrs G B Jones ***Llawr-Bettws*** *(SJ016424)* Bala Rd
☎Maerdy(049081) 224
This stone-built farmhouse dates back to 1918; the farm is situated close to the A494 (Bala road) approximately 2 miles south of its junction with the A5, and a caravan site also operates from the premises. The accommodation is rather dated, but is in keeping with the age and style of the house. The traditionally furnished bedrooms are quite attractively decorated, and though

they lack modern equipment and facilities they are comfortable. There is a cosy lounge with an open fire and a pleasant dining room with some good pieces of antique furniture.
4hc (2fb) ✗ LDO 7pm
CTV 3P 18 acres mixed beef sheep

GLASBURY Powys Map **03** SO13

FH QQ Mrs B Eckley **Ffforddfawr** *(SO192398)* HR3 5PT ☎(0497) 847332
Mar-Nov
On the B4350 Brecon road just 3 miles west of Hay-on-Wye, this 17th-century stone-built farmhouse is bordered by the river Wye. Very much a working farm, there are spacious lounges and comfortable bedrooms.
2hc CTV in all bedrooms ® ✗ ✱ dB&B£28-£30
CTV 4P 280 acres mixed

GLASGOW Strathclyde *Lanarkshire* Map **11** NS56

GH QQ ***Albion Hotel*** 405-407 North Woodside Rd, Kelvin Bridge G20 6NN ☎041-339 8620
This hotel caters for residents only, and is situated in a cul-de-sac right next to the Great Western road on the northwest side of the city. Bedrooms are very well equipped, with facilities including a trouser press, hair dryer, radio alarm clock, TV, direct dial telephone and tea making equipment, and service is friendly and informal. A limited choice of bar-style evening meals is available in the bar/dining room. Parking is easy, and the underground is only 2 minutes' walk away.
16⟟ (5fb) CTV in all bedrooms ® ✗ (ex guide dogs)
Lic
Credit Cards [1] [2] [3]

See advertisement on page 183

GH QQQ **Ambassador** 7 Kelvin Dr G20 8QJ ☎041-946 1018 FAX 041-945 5377

This tastefully decorated and furnished hotel has attractive, very well equipped bedrooms with facilities including a trouser press, hair dryer, radio alarm clock, TV, direct dial telephone and tea making equipment; some rooms however provide only a stool and no chair. A limited choice of bar-style evening meals is available in the bar/dining room. The hotel caters for residents only, and is situated close to the BBC studios and the botanical gardens on the northwest side of the city.

16🚿 ⚡in 4 bedrooms CTV in all bedrooms ® T ✗ (ex guide dogs) sB&B🚿£30-£35 dB&B🚿£45-£50 WB&B£180-£220 LDO 9.30pm

Lic CTV 8P

Credit Cards 1 3

GH QQ **Botanic Hotel** 1 Alfred Ter, Great Western Rd G12 8RF ☎041-339 6955

Spacious, comfortable bedrooms are a feature of this well run terraced hotel, situated high above the Great Western Road on the right hand side entering the city. Parking is only available in the terraces on the opposite side of the road.

11rm(3🚿7hc) (4fb) CTV in all bedrooms ® ✱ sB&B£25-£32 sB&B🚿£30-£39 dB&B£37-£42 dB&B🚿£45-£49 WB&B£157.50-£201.60

🏛

Credit Cards 1 3

GH QQQ ***Dalmeny Hotel*** 62 St Andrews Dr, Nithsdale Cross G41 5EZ ☎041-427 1106 & 6288

Closed 1 wk New Year

The bedrooms are comfortable and thoughtfully equipped at this small, family-run hotel, situated in a residential area on the city's southern side. The attractive public rooms, including a restaurant open to non-residents, highlight the house's period features.

8rm(2🛁1🚿5hc) CTV in all bedrooms ®

Lic 🏛 CTV 20P

Credit Cards 1 2 3

GH QQQ **Hotel Enterprise** 144 Renfrew St G3 6BF ☎041-332 8095

Situated in a tenement row in the heart of the city close to Glasgow School of Art, this small, private hotel offers a good standard of accommodation. The bedrooms are comfortable and fitted with quality furnishings and fabrics, and are equipped to a good standard, having remote control TVs, telephones and fully tiled en suites, a trouser press and a hairdryer are available. Parking can be difficult but there is a multi-story car park within 150 yards.

6🛁🚿 (2fb)⚡in 1 bedroom CTV in all bedrooms ® T ✗ (ex guide dogs) sB&B🛁🚿£35-£45 dB&B🛁🚿£50-£70

🏛

Credit Cards 1 3

GH QQ **Kelvin Private Hotel** 15 Buckingham Ter, Hillhead G12 8EB ☎041-339 7143

In a terraced row off Great Western Road, on the northwest side of the city, this commercial guesthouse offers rooms which vary in size and standard. The dining room has been moved from the basement to upstairs and a new residents' lounge has been created.

21rm(1🛁8🚿12hc) (5fb) CTV in all bedrooms ® sB&B£24-£26 sB&B🛁🚿£30-£32 dB&B£40-£44 dB&B🛁🚿£46-£52

🏛 5P

Credit Cards 1 3

GLASTONBURY Somerset Map 03 ST53

FH QQQ Mrs J I Nurse **Berewall Farm Country Guest House** *(ST516375)* Cinnamon Ln BA6 8LL ☎(0458) 831451 & 833132

Don't expect antiques or old masters at this farmhouse, south of Glastonbury Tor with glorious views over the surrounding countryside. The bedrooms are simply furnished, all en suite, with colour TV and tea-making facilities. Mrs Nurse does the cooking and a choice is offered and ordered from a blackboard in the lounge. Guests may bring their own horses; Mrs Nurse owns about 6, which can be hired. Rides can be arranged to suit ability, and an outdoor pool and hard tennis court are available to guests.

9🛁🚿 (3fb) CTV in all bedrooms ® ✗ (ex guide dogs) ✱ sB&B🛁🚿fr£22.50 dB&B🛁🚿fr£40 WBDifr£195 LDO 7.30pm

Lic 🏛 12P ⛱ 🎾(hard) U 30 acres grazing

Credit Cards 1 2 3

FH QQQ Mrs H T Tinney **Cradlebridge** *(ST477385)* BA16 9SD ☎(0458) 831827

Closed Xmas

Mrs Tinney continues to provide high standards of comfort and cleanliness at this modern farmhouse overlooking the Levels, a little more than a mile from the town centre, to the west near the River Brue. The 2 bedrooms are on ground floor level, and have comfortable, good quality beds, and there is a sitting area with large armchairs and doors leading onto a patio.

Annexe 2hc (2fb) CTV in all bedrooms ® ✗ ✱ sB&Bfr£20 dB&Bfr£32 WB&Bfr£96

🏛 6P 200 acres dairy £

GLENCOE Highland *Argyllshire* Map 14 NN15

GH QQ **Scorrybreac** PA39 4HT ☎Ballachulish(08552) 354

A friendly, family-run guesthouse set in its own peaceful gardens on a hillside above the village, with a splendid view over Loch Leven. It offers good value accommodation and is a popular base for both tourists and climbers. There is a small TV lounge, and evening meals are available by prior arrangement only. Smoking is not permitted.

5rm(2🚿3hc) (1fb)⚡in all bedrooms CTV in 1 bedroom TV in 1 bedroom ® sB&B£14-£18 sB&B🚿£15-£20 dB&B£26-£28 dB&B🚿£28-£35 LDO 10am

🏛 CTV 8P £

GLENMAVIS Strathclyde *Lanarkshire* Map 11 NS76

FH Q Mrs M Dunbar **Braidenhill** *(NS742673)* ML6 0PJ ☎Glenboig(0236) 872319

Do not be deterred by first impressions of this unassuming working farm. The accommodation is modest, but there is a comfortable lounge and a separate dining room, and Mrs Dunbar's cheery hospitality is second to none. The farm lies on the Coatbridge side of the B803.

3hc (1fb) ® ✗ sB&Bfr£13 dB&Bfr£26

🏛 CTV 4P 50 acres arable mixed

GLOUCESTER Gloucestershire Map 03 SO81

GH Q **Claremont** 135 Stroud Rd GL1 5LJ ☎(0452) 529540 & 529270

After 24 years in the city, Mrs Powell has built up a regular clientèle for her small, spotlessly clean guesthouse. Bed and breakfast is offered, the latter served in the cosy dining room, and the house is conveniently situated on the Stroud road.

6hc (2fb) CTV in all bedrooms ® ✗ ✱ sB&B£12.50-£15 dB&B£24-£27 WB&Bfr£84

🏛 CTV 6P £

GOATHLAND North Yorkshire Map 08 NZ80

GH QQQ **Heatherdene Hotel** YO22 5AN ☎Whitby(0947) 86334

Apr-Dec

Commanding beautiful views over the surrounding countryside, and situated in the moorland village of Goathland, this delightful country house was once the local vicarage. Spacious, comfortable and tastefully decorated bedrooms are very much a feature, modern in many respects yet retaining much of the character of the house. The large lounge, with a small bar in one corner, provides fine views of the moors and valleys, and the attractive dining room, with individual tables, is an ideal setting for the traditional home-

cooked meals provided by proprietors Lisa and John Pearson-Smith.
6rm(2⇌2ℕ2hc) (3fb)⊁in 1 bedroom CTV in all bedrooms ® LDO 4pm
Lic ⅏ CTV 10P solarium

GORRAN HAVEN Cornwall & Isles of Scilly Map **02** SX04

INN QQ Llawnroc PL26 6NU ☎Mevagissey(0726) 843461
Closed 25-26 Dec
The inn stands in its own grounds above the village providing sea and rural views. Personally run by Mr and Mrs Gregory, the atmosphere is friendly and relaxed and there is a choice of 2 comfortable bars and an eating area, exclusively no smoking, designed for families. Overnight guests find well equipped, modern and bright bedrooms and an attractively presented breakfast room.
6rm(2⇌3ℕ1hc) (2fb) CTV in all bedrooms ®
✗ (ex guide dogs) sB&B⇌ℕ£20-£26 dB&B£32-£40 dB&B⇌ℕ£36-£44 WB&B£126-£154 Lunch £5-£15alc Dinner £5-£15alc LDO 9.30pm
⅏ CTV 40P pool darts
Credit Cards 1 2 3 5 £
See advertisement under MEVAGISSEY

GRAMPOUND Cornwall & Isles of Scilly Map **02** SW94

GH QQ Perran House Fore St TR2 4RS
☎St Austell(0726) 882066
Enthusiastic young proprietors provide a cheery welcome at this neat and tidy guesthouse on the A390 between St Austell and Truro. They offer simply furnished but well presented bedrooms along with a comfortable modern breakfast room and lounge area. Cream teas are served on the sunny terrace in summer and there is car parking at the rear.
→

5rm(2⇌1↱2hc) (1fb)⊬in all bedrooms CTV in all bedrooms ® ✗ (ex guide dogs) sB&B£13-£14.50 dB&B£26-£29 dB&B⇌↱£28-£33 WB&B£90-£105
♨ 8P
Credit Cards [1] [3] (£)

GRANGE-OVER-SANDS Cumbria Map **07** SD47

GH Q Birchleigh Kents Bank Rd LA11 7EX ☎(05395) 32592
Closed Jan
A small, friendly guesthouse situated in the town centre, with guests well cared for by the owner Mrs Smith.
5rm(1⇌4↱) (2fb)⊬in all bedrooms TV in all bedrooms ® ✱ dB&B⇌↱fr£33 WB&Bfr£100 WBDi£128-£149
♨ (£)

SELECTED

GH QQQQ *Greenacres* Lindale LA11 6LP (2m N)
☎(05395) 34578
Closed 15 Nov-Dec
This charming white painted 19th-century cottage is situated in the centre of Lindale village about 2 miles from Grange-over-Sands. Mr and Mrs Danson are attentive hosts, and guests can be sure of a well produced home-cooked dinner. The colour coordinated bedrooms are all en suite, each has colour TV, and lots of thoughtful extras are provided. The comfortable lounges have open log fires in the winter months, and the establishment has a residential licence. Greenacres offers excellent value for money and is well situated for exploring southern Lakeland and the beautiful Morecambe Bay area.
5rm(4⇌1↱) Annexe 1⇌ (1fb) CTV in all bedrooms ® ✗
LDO 3pm
Lic ♨ CTV 6P

GRANTOWN-ON-SPEY Highland *Morayshire* Map **14** NJ02

GH QQQ *Ardconnel* Woodlands Ter PH26 3JU ☎(0479) 2104
Closed Nov-Dec
New owners Barbara and Jim Casey have settled in well at this lovely Victorian house, formerly called Umaria. The house stands in its own well tended garden, just south of the town centre and is an ideal base for the touring holiday- maker. The comfortable bedrooms are fitted with modern and traditional furniture, and the quiet lounge invites peaceful relaxation. A no smoking policy has now been introduced.
8hc (3fb)⊬in all bedrooms ® LDO 4.30pm
Lic ♨ CTV 9P croquet

GH QQ Brooklynn Grant Rd PH26 3LA ☎(0479) 3113
Apr-Oct
Good value holiday accommodation is offered at this friendly family-run Victorian villa, which is situated in a residential area, just a short walk from central amenities. The bedrooms are in good decorative order with a mixture of furnishings, and there is a cosy TV lounge where one can relax and enjoy the company of other guests.
6rm(2↱4hc) (1fb) ® ✗ ✱ sB&B£14-£15 dB&B£28-£30 dB&B↱£34-£36 WB&B£98-£119 WBDi£154-£175 LDO by arrangement
♨ CTV 6P

SELECTED

GH QQQQ Culdearn House Woodlands Ter PH26 3JU
☎(0479) 2106
Feb-Oct
Many guests return year after year to Alasdair and Isobel Little's delightful granite-built villa which stands in its own landscaped garden on the southern fringe of the town easily recognised at night by the glow from the small table lamps in every front window. The attractive lounge, has been redecorated and here you can relax with a quiet drink in front of the log fire. Isobel competently prepares the evening meals with local produce like venison, beef, lamb and salmon and offers three choices at each course, served in the elegant dining room. Bedrooms are spotless with mixed appointments and the expected amenities. Special golf, angling and riding packages can be arranged.
9rm(2⇌7↱) (1fb) CTV in all bedrooms ®
✗ (ex guide dogs) sB&B⇌↱£38-£50 dB&B⇌↱£75-£90 (incl dinner) WBDi£265-£315 LDO 6pm
Lic ♨ 9P
Credit Cards [1] [3]

GH QQQ *Dar-Il-Hena* Grant Rd PH26 3LA ☎(0479) 2929
Etr-Oct
This charming Victorian house stands in its own extensive grounds, enjoying an elevated position in a quiet residential road close to the centre of town. Wood panelling is a feature of the spacious, comfortable accommodation, and good home cooking is provided.
7hc (3fb) ®
♨ CTV 10P ⌂

SELECTED

GH QQQQ Garden Park Woodside Av PH26 3JN
☎(0479) 3235
Set in its own attractive gardens in a quiet residential area close to the town centre, this delightful Victorian house has been sympathetically extended and modernised to provide comfortable accommodation. Bedrooms, although compact, are bright and cheerful with en suite facilities and many rooms have lovely views over pine forests to the Cromdale hills. There are 2 comfortable lounges, one with TV and the other well stocked with books. Enjoyable home cooking using fresh ingredients is served in the smart dining room.
5⇌↱ CTV in 2 bedrooms ® ✗ (ex guide dogs) dB&B⇌↱£38.60-£41 WB&B£128.40-£136.40 WBDi£180-£191.90 LDO 5pm
Lic ♨ CTV 8P nc12yrs

GH QQQ Kinross House Woodside Av PH26 3JR
☎(0479) 2042
Mar-Nov
Attentive service combined with genuine hospitality are just part of the appeal of this attractive modernised Victorian house, situated in a quiet residential area. Tastefully decorated throughout, it offers comfortable, well equipped bedrooms together with a cosy sitting room where a welcoming log fire burns on cooler evenings. This is a no-smoking establishment.
7rm(4↱3hc) (2fb)⊬in all bedrooms CTV in all bedrooms ® ✗ (ex guide dogs) sB&B£17-£20 dB&B£32-£38 dB&B↱£38-£44 WB&B£112-£133 WBDi£178-£199 LDO 4pm
Lic ♨ 6P nc7yrs

GH QQ Pines Hotel Woodside Av PH26 3JR ☎(0479) 2092
This friendly family-run holiday guesthouse is set in its own garden in a quiet residential area. It has a relaxed atmosphere and offers good value accommodation, ideal for touring families.
9rm(5↱4hc) (3fb) CTV in all bedrooms ® sB&Bfr£16 dB&Bfr£32 dB&B↱fr£42 WB&B£112-£147 WBDi£160-£190 LDO 3pm
Lic ♨ 9P (£)

Street plans of certain towns and cities will be found in a separate section at the back of the book.

GRASMERE Cumbria Map **11** NY30

GH QQQ Bridge House Hotel Stock Ln LA22 9SN
☎(05394) 35425
mid Mar-mid Nov
Bridge House is in the heart of the village, yet enjoys a peaceful setting in its spacious grounds bordering the River Rothay. It is built of Lakeland stone and has a spacious dining room, overlooking the garden, where a 5-course dinner is served. There is a charming lounge with an attractive fireplace, and a cosy residents' bar. Bedrooms are mainly spacious with modern décor and furniture. Mr and Mrs Leech are sympathetic hosts who ensure that their guests are well looked after.
12rm(10⇌🚿2hc) CTV in all bedrooms ® ✗ ✱ sB&B⇌🚿£39-£43 dB&B⇌🚿£78-£86 (incl dinner) WBDi£245-£260.01 LDO 7pm
Lic 🍴 20P nc5yrs
Credit Cards 1 3

GH QQ Lake View Country House Lake View Dr LA22 9TD
☎(05394) 35384
Mar-Nov rs Dec-Feb
An attractive house and grounds in a quiet side road in the centre of the village, with a view of the lake as the name suggests. It is pleasantly furnished throughout and offers good value for money.
6rm(3🚿3hc) CTV in all bedrooms ® sB&B£26.50 dB&B£45 dB&B🚿£53 WB&B£150-£178 WBDi£214-£242 LDO noon
11P nc12yrs Ⓔ

GH QQQ Raise View Whitebridge LA22 9RQ
☎(05394) 35215
A traditional Lakeland house, on the edge of the village, where the service is warm and friendly. Bedrooms are pleasantly furnished, all have good views, and a comfortable lounge is available.
6rm(4🚿2hc) (1fb) CTV in all bedrooms ® ✗ dB&B£30-£32 dB&B🚿£34-£36 WB&B£94.50-£113.40
🍴 CTV 6P nc5yrs

GRASSINGTON North Yorkshire Map **07** SE06

SELECTED

GH QQQQ Ashfield House Hotel BD23 5AE
☎(0756) 752584
mid Feb-Oct
A lovely stone-built 17th-century house set in a secluded location, just off the village square. Bedrooms are furnished in pine, with comfortable beds and pretty duvets and curtains; most have private bathrooms and all have TV and tea-making facilities; smoking is not permitted in bedrooms or the dining room. A well-produced set 4-course dinner is provided in the cottage-style dining room, which has the original beams and mullioned windows, together with polished wooden tables and fresh flowers. The 2 delightful lounges both have log fires, beams and plenty of books: one lounge is no-smoking. There are spacious lawns and gardens at the rear, with private car parking.
7rm(6🚿1hc) ⊬in all bedrooms CTV in all bedrooms ® ✗ (ex guide dogs) sB&B£36.25 dB&B£61.50-£69 dB&B🚿£69-£76.50 WBDi£215-£243 LDO 5.30pm
Lic 🍴 7P nc5yrs Ⓔ

GH QQQ Greenways Wharfeside Av BD23 5BS
☎Skipton(0756) 752598
Apr-Oct
A family residence situated on the banks of the River Wharfe with the dining room and some bedrooms overlooking one of the most spectacular stretches of the river. Greenways is located in Threshfield; from the Skipton direction, turn left at the school and follow the road to the bottom.
5hc (1fb) ® ✱ sB&B£19-£25 dB&Bfr£38 WB&B£119.70-£149.70 WBDi£189-£219 LDO 5pm
Lic 🍴 CTV 8P nc7yrs

See advertisement on page 187

GH QQ The Lodge 8 Wood Ln BD23 5LU ☎(0756) 752518
Mar-Oct rs Dec
Situated on the edge of this popular, attractive Dales village, this detached, grey stone Victorian house is well known for its excellent 4-course dinners cooked by the proprietors Binnie and Jack Lingard. A small dining room, with individual tables, is provided where guests can savour delicious meals, and a cosy lounge with a coal gas fire is provided for relaxing afterwards. The bedrooms are pleasantly styled and most have views of the surrounding countryside. Parking is available at the side of the house.
8rm(1⇌2🚿5hc) TV in 1 bedroom ® ✱ dB&B£30-£40 dB&B⇌🚿£40 WBDi£165-£200 LDO 2pm
🍴 CTV 7P

GRAVESEND Kent Map **05** TQ67

GH QQ The Cromer 194 Parrock St DA12 1EW
☎(0474) 361935
Closed 24 Dec-2 Jan
A Victorian style house conveniently situated very close to the town centre, with its own private car park. The accommodation is well furnished and maintained, complemented by a spacious lounge and attractive dining room. Bedrooms are bright, well equipped and comfortable. A choice of menus is offered at breakfast and an early morning tea service is available on request. Credit cards are not accepted.
11rm(1⇌10hc) (3fb)⊬in 3 bedrooms CTV in all bedrooms ✗ ✱ sB&B£15-£16 dB&B£27-£28 dB&B⇌£34
🍴 CTV 15P nc9yrs

GH QQQ Overcliffe Hotel 15-16 The Overcliffe DA11 0EF
☎(0474) 322131 Telex no 965117 FAX (0474) 536737
Located on the west side of town on the A226, this Victorian house has been skilfully extended and comprises a variety of bedrooms, a candlelit basement restaurant and bar lounge. The Victoria Lodge annexe is some distance from the main hotel but offers superior accommodation. Car parking facilities are available and the restaurant has its own entrance from the car park.
19🚿 Annexe 10🛁🚿 CTV in all bedrooms ® **T** ✱
sB&B🛁🚿£56-£60 dB&B🛁🚿£60-£65 LDO 9.30pm
Lic 🍽 45P
Credit Cards 1 2 3 5

GREAT Placenames incorporating the word 'Great', such as Gt Yarmouth, will be found under the actual placename, ie Yarmouth.

GREENHEAD Northumberland Map **12** NY66

FH QQ Mrs P Staff **Holmhead** *(NY659661)* Hadrians Wall CA6 7HY ☎Brampton(06977) 47402
Closed 19 Dec-9 Jan
Standing on the foundations of Hadrian's Wall, this attractive farmhouse is made of the same stone as the Wall, and the effect is warm and welcoming. Although no longer a working farm in the full sense, the atmosphere remains, helped by the sight of sheep grazing in the field as you approach the house. Bedrooms are bright and cheerful and have en suite showers. There is a comfortable lounge with an honesty bar, and meals are taken around one large table in the dining room. Here you will find the longest breakfast menu ever seen, running to 127 items!
4🚿 (1fb)✗in all bedrooms ® ✗ dB&B🚿£39-£41
WB&Bfr£128 WBDifr£240 LDO 3pm
Lic 🍽 CTV 6P ♪ table tennis 300 acres breeding sheep cattle
Credit Cards 1 2 3

GRETNA (WITH GRETNA GREEN) Dumfries & Galloway *Dumfriesshire* Map **11** NY36

GH QQQ The Beeches Loanwath Rd CA6 5EP
☎Gretna(0461) 37448
Closed 8 Dec-14 Jan
Panoramic views of the Solway Firth and Lakeland hills make this no-smoking former farmhouse special. Each of the two bedrooms has a double and single bed and a shower room, and there is a small but comfortable lounge where breakfast is served by Mrs Donabie.
2🚿 (1fb)✗in all bedrooms CTV in all bedrooms ® ✗ ✱
dB&B🚿£32-£34 WB&B£112-£119
🍽 CTV 4P nc10yrs

GH QQ Greenlaw CA6 5DU ☎Gretna(0461) 38361
Within easy walking distance of the famous old smithy, this red-brick, detached house is conveniently sited for both the M74 and A75. The bedrooms are generally compact and modestly furnished, although a new honeymoon room offers a 4-poster bed and en suite facilities. There is a comfortable lounge, situated in the foyer, with an open fire and a separate breakfast room is provided.
8rm(1🚿7hc) (1fb) CTV in 6 bedrooms ® ✱ sB&B£15-£16
dB&B£25-£26 dB&B🚿£33-£34 WB&B£80-£86
🍽 CTV 12P 1🚗

GH QQ *Surrone House* Annan Rd CA6 5DL
☎Gretna(0461) 38341
Set back from the main road, in the romantic border town of Gretna, this one- time farmhouse, with connections dating back to Viking times, now offers modern accommodation. The bedrooms are generally spacious, nicely equipped and have good bathrooms, while the public areas include 2 small but comfortable lounges and a steak bar style room open to non residents.
6rm(5🛁🚿1hc) (4fb) CTV in all bedrooms ® LDO 8pm
Lic 🍽 CTV 16P

GREVE DE LECQ BAY

See **JERSEY under CHANNEL ISLANDS**

GROUVILLE

See **JERSEY under CHANNEL ISLANDS**

GUERNSEY

See **CHANNEL ISLANDS**

GUILDFORD Surrey Map **04** SU94

GH QQ Blanes Court Hotel Albury Rd GU1 2BT
☎(0483) 573171 FAX (0483) 32780
Closed 1wk Xmas
Peacefully situated in a residential area, this family-run guesthouse has modest, traditionally furnished bedrooms, many of which are en suite. A buffet-style breakfast is served in the simply furnished conservatory, which becomes a bar in the evening and offers a limited range of snacks and sandwiches.
20rm(4🛁10🚿6hc) (3fb) CTV in all bedrooms ® sB&B£25-£30
sB&B🛁🚿£40-£45 dB&Bfr£45 dB&B🛁🚿£55-£60
WB&B£150-£240
Lic 🍽 CTV 22P
Credit Cards 1 2 3 £

GH QQ Quinns Hotel 78 Epsom Rd GU1 2BX ☎(0483) 60422
Telex no 859754 FAX (0483) 578551
This attractive Victorian house is close to the town centre and benefits from ample car parking. Bedrooms are modestly furnished but are equipped with the commercial traveller in mind. There is a comfortable lounge in addition to the wood-panelled breakfast room.
12rm(7🛁🚿5hc) (3fb) CTV in all bedrooms ® **T** ✗ ✱
sB&B£35-£38 sB&B🛁🚿£45-£48 dB&B£50-£56
dB&B🛁🚿£60-£68 WB&Bfr£250 WBDifr£350 LDO 6pm
🍽 CTV 14P
Credit Cards 1 2 3 5 £

GUNNISLAKE Cornwall & Isles of Scilly Map **02** SX47

GH QQQ Hingston House Country Hotel St Anns Chapel PL18 9HB ☎Tavistock(0822) 832468
Standing in an elevated position in the centre of the village, this late- Georgian property enjoys splendid wide views out across to Plymouth and the Tamar Valley. The freshly decorated bedrooms, most of which are en suite, are reasonably equipped and all are comfortable but simply furnished. There is a very comfortable lounge filled with books, flowers and plants, which has open fires, as does the characterful, cosy bar. A set meal, using fresh ingredients, is cooked and served by Mrs Shelvey, and a relaxed, friendly atmosphere prevails throughout.
10rm(8🚿2hc) (1fb) CTV in all bedrooms ® sB&B£22.25-£25.75 sB&B🚿£29.25-£31.25 dB&B£39-£43 dB&B🚿£45.50-£50.50 WB&B£135.50-£197 WBDi£228.25-£289.75 LDO 7pm
Lic 🍽 CTV 12P croquet putting green
Credit Cards 1 3 £

GWAUN VALLEY Dyfed Map **02** SN03

SELECTED

FH QQQQ Mr P Heard & Mrs M J Heard **Tregynon Country Farmhouse Hotel** *(SN054345)* SA65 9TU (4m E of Pontfaen, off unclass road joining B 4313)
☎Newport(0239) 820531 FAX (0239) 820808
Closed 2wks winter
This 16th-century farmhouse is situated in the scenic Gwaun Valley, in the heart of Pembrokeshire. It has a very attractive lounge with an inglenook fireplace, and features authentic wooden settles in addition to comfortable modern seating. The restaurant is in 2 parts and wholesome food plus vegetarian dishes are highlighted on the menu. There are a few bedrooms in the main house, which are rather on the small side, although →

the 5 bedrooms in the converted outbuilding are larger. All are very well decorated and furnished with mainly pine furniture. Each room has modern en suite facilities and is equipped with a TV and telephone.

3↱ Annexe 5⇔ (4fb) CTV in all bedrooms ® T ✗ ✱ dB&B⇔↱£44-£59 WBDi£230-£290 LDO 6pm

Lic 🍽 20P 10 acres sheep

Credit Cards [1] [3]

HADDINGTON Lothian *East Lothian* Map **12** NT57

FH QQ Mrs K Kerr **Barney Mains Farmhouse** *(NT523764)* Barney Mains EH41 3SA (off A1, 1m S of Haddington)
☎Athelstaneford(062088) 310 FAX (062088) 639

Apr-Nov

Set well back from the A1, about one mile east of Haddington, this 18th- century Georgian house enjoys a fine outlook over the surrounding countryside. The individually decorated bedrooms are spacious and comfortably furnished in a traditional style. There is also a comfortable lounge and hearty farmhouse breakfasts are served at the communal table in the dining room.

3rm ⊬in all bedrooms ® ✗ (ex guide dogs) ✱ sB&B£15-£20 dB&B£28-£36

CTV 8P 580 acres arable beef sheep

HADLEIGH Suffolk Map **05** TM04

GH QQ Odds & Ends 131 High St IP7 5EJ
☎Ipswich(0473) 822032

A delightful 16th-century town house on the main thoroughfare with a walled rear garden. A private dwelling until recent years, Ann Stephenson has successfully converted the public areas into a busy restaurant, the décor and furnishings accentuating the period charm. The garden rooms are popular with disabled people.

6rm(2⇔4hc) Annexe 3↱ CTV in all bedrooms ® sB&Bfr£18 sB&B⇔↱fr£30 dB&Bfr£36 dB&B⇔↱fr£40 LDO 5.30pm

Lic 🍽 3P nc8yrs

Credit Cards [1] [3] £

INN QQ The Marquis of Cornwallis Upper Layham IP7 5JZ
☎(0473) 822051

Dating back to the 16th century, this roadside inn is just over a mile from the town at Upper Layham. Three very spacious bedrooms are available with exposed timbers and ceiling beams, they are fitted with solid furniture and have good beds and comfortable armchairs. There are 2 bars, both timbered with inglenook fireplaces, and an intimate à la carte restaurant serving home- cooked food with vegetarian meals always available. At the rear of the inn there is a large lawn running down to the River Brett.

3↱ (2fb) CTV in all bedrooms ® ✗ (ex guide dogs) ✱ sB&B£20 dB&B£35 dB&B⇔↱£41 Lunch £6.25-£12alc Dinner £6.25-£15alc LDO 9.30pm

22P nc5yrs ♪

Credit Cards [1] [2] [3] [5]

HAINTON Lincolnshire Map **08** TF18

GH QQ The Old Vicarage School Ln LN3 6LW
☎Burgh-on-Bain(0507) 313660

Standing in an acre of its own grounds with neatly tended gardens in a pleasant wolds village, this quiet, relaxing guesthouse is an elegant blend of Georgian and Victorian architecture. The public areas are thoughtfully furnished and comfortable, particularly the light, spacious lounge with its open log fire ; this room is only available to guests from 2.30pm. The friendly proprietors have a wealth of local knowledge, and further information is displayed in the entrance hall. Home cooked evening meals are available by arrangement, using local produce. The brightly decorated bedrooms are nicely equipped including TV, radio alarms and tea making facilities. This is a no smoking establishment.

3hc ⊬in all bedrooms CTV in all bedrooms ® ✗ sB&B£14.50 dB&B£29-£32 WB&B£90 WBDi£139 LDO 3pm

🍽 6P nc12yrs £

HALFORD Warwickshire Map **04** SP24

INN QQ Halford Bridge Fosse Way CV36 5BN
☎Stratford on Avon(0789) 740382

This spacious Cotswold stone road-house, situated on the A429, offers pretty, well-equipped bedrooms and public areas that have character. A wide choice of food is available in either the bars or the dining room.

6hc (1fb) CTV in all bedrooms ® ✗ (ex guide dogs) ✱ sB&B£17.50-£25 dB&B£35-£46 Lunch £1.90-£12.50&alc LDO 9pm

50P

Credit Cards [1] [3] £

HALSTOCK Dorset Map **03** ST50

See also Yeovil

GH QQQ Halstock Mill BA22 9SJ
☎Corscombe(0935) 891278

Closed Dec

An attractive 17th-century cornmill, quietly situated in 10 acres of garden and paddocks. Tastefully converted, it now provides individually furnished bedrooms, some with en suite facilities. The lounge and dining room retain many original features including beams and fireplaces. Fresh local produce and some home-grown fruit and vegetables are served at dinner.

4⇔ CTV in all bedrooms ® ✗ (ex guide dogs) sB&B⇔£27-£30 dB&B⇔£44-£50 WB&B£154-£175 WBDi£238-£259 LDO am

Lic 🍽 20P nc5yrs

Credit Cards [1] [2] [3] £

HALTWHISTLE Northumberland Map **12** NY76

GH QQ ***Ashcroft*** NE49 0DA ☎(0434) 320213

Closed 23 Dec-2 Jan

This impressive stone-built house stands above the A69 within its own award- winning gardens. It offers spacious, no smoking accommodation and friendly service.

6hc (3fb)⊬in all bedrooms ✗

🍽 CTV 15P croquet lawn

GH QQ Burnhead The Burnhead, Cawfields NE49 9PJ
☎Hexham(0434) 321671

Guests are made to feel very much at home at this attractive, small bed and breakfast establishment, situated beside Hadrian's Wall, just off the B6318. Converted from a derelict farm building by the Shentons, it provides 2 cosy bedrooms which share a smart modern bathroom, and thoughtful extras like bathrobes are provided. The area is popular with walkers and their needs can be well catered for, including being met at Haltwhistle station.

2rm ⊬in 3 bedrooms CTV in 1 bedroom ® ✗ dB&B£30

🍽 CTV 3P

FH QQQ Mrs J I Laidlow **Ald White Craig** *(NY713649)* Shield Hill NE49 9NW ☎(0434) 320565 & 321175

This extended farmhouse sits in its own well tended garden high above the town, overlooking the valley. To find it, turn off the A69 at the eastern junction for the town and turn right uphill. Run by the friendly and enthusiastic Mrs Laidlow, the attractive farmhouse is full of character and comfort. Bedrooms, though not large, are nicely decorated and furnished in a pretty cottage style. The 2 at the front enjoy the view whilst one at the side has the advantage of patio doors leading out to the garden. The attractive lounge and dining room are open plan, the latter also having patio doors to the garden, and breakfast is served around one large circular table.

3⇔↱ ⊬in all bedrooms CTV in all bedrooms ® ✗ (ex guide dogs) dB&B⇔↱£37-£40 WB&Bfr£125

🍽 3P nc60 acres stock rearing rare breeds £

SELECTED

FH QQQQ Mrs J Brown **Broomshaw Hill** *(NY706654)* Willia Rd NE49 9NP ☎(0434) 320866
Apr-Oct
Situated on the fringe of the town in a peaceful rural setting, this impressive stone-built farmhouse offers bright, attractive bedrooms, all individually decorated and providing useful extras. Public areas feature polished wood floors with good quality rugs, chunky stone walls, a wood- burning stove, antique and reproduction furniture, delightful pictures and interesting bric-à-brac. A relaxing atmosphere prevails, and a warm welcome with attentive service is assured from the friendly proprietress.
3hc (1fb) CTV in all bedrooms ® * sB&B£16-£18 dB&B£28-£30 WB&Bfr£100 WBDifr£145 LDO 10am
CTV 4P 2 7 acres livestock horses £

HALWELL Devon Map **03** SX75

GH Q ***Stanborough Hundred Hotel*** TQ9 7JG ☎East Allington(054852) 236
20 Mar-15 Oct
A family-run cottage guesthouse set amid interesting gardens next to the site of an old hill fort, midway between Totnes and Kingsbridge. Bedrooms are simply furnished and well equipped, and imaginative home-cooking is served.
5rm(3⇌2hc) (2fb) CTV in all bedrooms ® ✕ (ex guide dogs) LDO 6.30pm
Lic CTV 10P nc5yrs

HAMPTON-IN-ARDEN West Midlands Map **04** SP28

GH QQ **Cottage** Kenilworth Rd B92 0LW ☎(0675) 442323 FAX (0675) 443323
A cosy, friendly guesthouse, conveniently situated for access to the M6 and M42 motorways, and the NEC. Accommodation is generally compact but has been attractively decorated and thoughtfully furnished.
9rm(5 4hc) (2fb) CTV in all bedrooms ® * sB&B£18-£22 sB&B £22-£25 dB&B£34-£36 dB&B £36-£39
CTV 14P £

HAMSTERLEY Co Durham Map **12** NZ13

GH QQQ ***Grove House*** Hamsterley Forest DL13 1NL ☎Witton-le-Wear(038888) 203
Closed Aug, Xmas & New Year
Delightfully situated in the heart of Hamsterley Forest, this handsome stone- built house offers quaint bedrooms, elegant public rooms and interesting home- cooked dinners.
4hc in all bedrooms ® ✕ LDO 7.30pm
CTV 8P nc6yrs

HANLEY CASTLE Hereford & Worcester Map **03** SO84

SELECTED

GH QQQQ **Old Parsonage Farm** WR8 0BU ☎Hanley Swan(0684) 310124
Closed 21 Dec-2 Feb
An 18th-century country residence, finished with mellow brick, on the outskirts of the village. It affords beautiful views of the castle and the Malvern Hills. Genuine hospitality is provided by Ann and Tony Addison; Ann is responsible for the imaginative cooking and Tony is an accredited wine expert. Over 100 wines are available and wine tasting sessions are often held in the old cider mill next to the house. Bedrooms are spacious and well furnished and there are 2 comfortable sitting rooms for residents.
3⇌ (1fb) ✕ sB&B⇌fr£29 dB&B⇌£42-£47 WB&B£140-£156 WBDi£240-£256
Lic CTV 6P nc10yrs
Credit Cards 2 £

HANMER Clwyd Map **07** SJ44

FH Q C Sumner & F Williams-Lee ***Buck*** *(SJ435424)* SY14 7LX ☎(094874) 339
Situated midway between Wrexham and Whitchurch on the A525, this 16th century timber-framed farmhouse has a wealth of charm and character and is surrounded by 8 acres of delightful gardens and woodland. The accommodation is modest, but the imaginative cuisine reflects the proprietors' extensive international travels.
4hc (1fb) in all bedrooms ✕ (ex guide dogs) LDO previous day
CTV 12P 8 acres non-working

HARBERTON Devon Map **03** SX75

GH QQQ **Ford Farm** TQ9 7SJ ☎Totnes(0803) 863539
Situated on the edge of this quiet village on a quiet road, this cottage dates back to 1690 and provides comfortable bed and breakfast accommodation in bedrooms that are attractively coordinated. A full range of beverages is provided on a help yourself basis in the first floor sitting room and breakfast is served in the dining room around a large table. Two self-catering flats are also available.
3rm(1 2hc) * sB&B£18-£20 dB&B£34-£38 dB&B £34-£40
CTV 6P nc12yrs

HARLECH Gwynedd Map **06** SH53

SELECTED

GH QQQQ **Castle Cottage Hotel** Pen Llech LL46 2YL ☎(0766) 780479
This small hotel is reputed to be one of the oldest houses in Harlech; it stands a few hundred yards from the famous castle and is personally run by new, young proprietors Glyn and Jacqueline Roberts. The small but comfortable bedrooms have cottage-style furniture and pretty, coordinating soft furnishings, with modern en suite bathrooms and thoughtful extra touches. There is a small bar with a welcoming log fire and 2 cosy lounges with TV, books and views of Snowdon. Glyn makes good use of fresh local produce in a range of imaginative and very nicely presented dishes, served in the recently enlarged, pleasant restaurant.
6rm(4⇌ 2hc) ® sB&Bfr£20 sB&B⇌ fr£38 dB&B⇌ fr£44 LDO 9pm
Lic CTV
Credit Cards 1 3

GH QQQ ***Gwrach Ynys Country*** Ynys, Talsarnau LL47 6TS ☎(0766) 780742
Feb-Nov
This beautifully restored Edwardian house is situated on the A496, 2 miles north of the town. The name means 'Dwarf Island' and dates back to the time when this lowland area was covered by the sea, with just 5 islands rising above it. It offers comfortable, nicely appointed accommodation with attractively decorated bedrooms in varying sizes and styles of furnishing. Other facilities include a choice of comfortable lounges, one with TV.
7rm(1⇌5 1hc) (2fb) CTV in all bedrooms ® LDO noon
CTV 10P

FH Q Mrs E A Jones **Tyddyn Gwynt** *(SH601302)* LL46 2TH (2.5m off B4573 (A496)) ☎(0766) 780298
Most of this small friendly farmhouse was built about 100 years ago, but some parts are considerably older. It is set in a remote location some 1.5 miles southeast of Harlech, surrounded by spectacular mountain scenery. The modest bedrooms are simply furnished, and the small cosy lounge has TV and a welcoming log →

fire in the winter. A variety of bric-a-brac enhances the historic ambience of the house, which provides an ideal base for walkers.
2hc (1fb) Ⓡ ✱ sB&Bfr£13 dB&Bfr£25 LDO 7pm
CTV 6P 3 acres small holding

INN Q *Rum Hole Hotel* Ffordd Newydd LL46 2UB
☎(0766) 780477
Closed 23 Dec-2 Jan
A family-run inn on the A496 below the famous castle. It is popular with golfers being close to St Davids golf course.
8rm(2⇌3↱3hc) (5fb) CTV in all bedrooms Ⓡ
⋈ (ex guide dogs) LDO 9.30pm
CTV 25P

HARLESTON Norfolk Map **05** TM28

INN QQ Swan Hotel 19 The Thoroughfare IP20 9DQ
☎(0379) 852221
13rm(10⇌3hc) (1fb) CTV in all bedrooms Ⓡ **T** ✱ sB&Bfr£25 sB&B⇌↱fr£30 dB&B⇌↱fr£42 Lunch £1.25-£5 Dinner £5-£7 LDO 9pm
🍽 CTV 75P
Credit Cards 1 3 5

HARROGATE North Yorkshire Map **08** SE35

GH QQQ Acacia Lodge 21 Ripon Rd HG1 2JL
☎(0423) 560752
The mellow, grey stone, semidetached Victorian house is situated in well tended gardens just a few minutes walk from the town centre. It is very attractively furnished and decorated throughout, offering comfortable bedrooms of a very high standard, containing a tasteful blend of antique and modern furniture, as well as coordinated fabrics. The extremely comfortable guests' lounge has a TV and lots of literature, and award winning breakfasts are served in the pretty dining room, with its antique tables and colourful décor. Ample space for parking is available on the premises.
5rm(1⇌4↱) (1fb) CTV in all bedrooms Ⓡ ⋈ (ex guide dogs) ✱ sB&B⇌↱fr£27 dB&B⇌↱fr£44
CTV 6P Ⓕ

SELECTED

GH QQQQ Alexa House & Stable Cottages 26 Ripon Rd HG1 2JJ ☎(0423) 501988 FAX (0423) 504086
Built in 1830 for Baron de Ferrier, this attractive, Victorian detached house is the home of Roberta and John Black, who provide true Yorkshire hospitality in very congenial surroundings. The bedrooms are furnished to a high standard with many modern features, yet retaining the character and comfort of the house. Some rooms are in a converted stable block at the rear and are particularly convenient for those who do not like stairs. There is a comfortable lounge with settees, armchairs and a TV. Delicious, fresh food is served in the attractive dining room, with its individual polished tables and a beautiful dresser boasting a display of china, which makes this an ideal setting to enjoy Roberta Black's cooking.
9rm(2⇌7↱) Annexe 4↱ (1fb) CTV in all bedrooms Ⓡ **T** ⋈ (ex guide dogs) ✱ sB&B⇌↱£25-£28 dB&B⇌↱£46-£50 LDO 6.30pm
Lic 🍽 CTV 14P
Credit Cards 1 3 Ⓕ

GH Q *Argyll House* 80 Kings Rd HG1 5JX ☎(0423) 562408
This semidetached Victorian house is situated almost opposite the Conference Centre and close to the town centre and shops. The simply decorated bedrooms vary in shape and size, and are equipped with telephones, TV, radios, hairdryers and tea and coffee-making facilities. There is a comfortable Victorian-style lounge, and a breakfast room with individual tables. Private parking is provided at the back of the premises.
6hc (1fb) Ⓡ LDO 4pm
🍽 CTV 6P

GH QQQ Ashley House Hotel 36-40 Franklin Rd HG1 5EE
☎(0423) 507474 & 560858
Closed 20 Dec-2 Jan
This attractive, private hotel has been converted from 3 Victorian town houses and is situated within easy walking distance of the conference centre and shops. A friendly hotel, with particularly well equipped bedrooms, most of which have private bathrooms and all with TV, telephone, radio alarm and tea making facilities. Attractively decorated throughout, public areas include a nicely appointed dining room, 2 comfortable lounges and a cosy bar. There is also a small car park at the rear.
16rm(13⇌↱3hc) (2fb) CTV in all bedrooms Ⓡ **T** sB&B£23.50-£32 sB&B⇌↱£27.50-£32 dB&B£42-£45 dB&B⇌↱£50-£56 WB&B£145-£180 WBDi£205-£250 LDO noon
Lic 🍽 CTV 6P
Credit Cards 1 3 Ⓕ

GH QQQ Ashwood House 7 Spring Grove HG1 2HS
☎(0423) 560081
Closed 24 Dec-1 Jan
Converted from 2 Edwardian houses, this hotel has 2 bay windows, twin gables and a terraced rockery at the front, and is situated in a quiet cul-de-sac behind the International Conference Centre. Bedrooms are mostly spacious and comfortably furnished with attractive coordinated fabrics, there is pine furniture in some and louvre-door wardrobes in others, while the large room at the front has a pine 4-poster bed. The dining room is very attractive, painted in Wedgewood blue, with blue linen and white lace tablecloths, fresh flowers and plants. The guests' lounge is small but cosy, with books and magazines to read. A small car park is provided at the back.
10rm(8⇌↱2hc) (2fb)⊬in 1 bedroom CTV in all bedrooms Ⓡ ⋈ ✱ sB&B£20-£22 sB&B⇌↱£25-£27 dB&B£40-£44 dB&B⇌↱£42-£46 WB&B£140-£161
Lic 🍽 CTV 5P Ⓕ

GH QQ The Dales Hotel 101 Valley Dr HG2 0JP
☎(0423) 507248
A welcoming hotel overlooking the renowned Valley Gardens and within easy walking distance of the town centre and conference halls. The hotel is licensed and also provides a nicely furnished dining room and a comfortable residents' lounge overlooking the gardens.
8rm(4↱4hc) (2fb) CTV in all bedrooms Ⓡ ✱ sB&B£22-£24 sB&B↱£38-£40 dB&B↱£42-£44 LDO 9am
Lic 🍽 CTV 1P
Credit Cards 1 3 Ⓕ

GH QQQ Delaine Hotel 17 Ripon Rd HG1 2JL
☎(0423) 567974
Featuring very attractive flower gardens, this family-run, Victorian semidetached house is situated just north of the town centre. The tastefully decorated bedrooms have modern, coordinated colour schemes with attractive fabrics and 2 rooms are in a converted coach house in the grounds. There is a very comfortable lounge, plus a small bar and a dining room with individual tables, where a 3-course, home-cooked evening meal is served. The hotel has its own private car park.
8rm(2⇌6↱) Annexe 2rm(1⇌1↱) (2fb)⊬in 3 bedrooms CTV in all bedrooms Ⓡ ⋈ ✱ sB&B⇌↱£30-£33 dB&B⇌↱£47-£50
Lic 🍽 CTV 12P
Credit Cards 1 3 Ⓕ

GH Q *Gillmore Hotel* 98 Kings Rd HG1 5HH ☎(0423) 503699
This old-established private hotel, has been converted and extended to provide very well maintained accommodation. Situated just 5 minutes' walk from the Conference Centre, it has been under the same ownership since 1967. Some of the bedrooms have private bathrooms and they all have tea and coffee making facilities. There is ample car parking space.

22rm(2⇌4⌐16hc) (8fb) CTV in 9 bedrooms ® LDO 4pm
Lic 🍽 CTV 20P snooker

GH QQQ Glenayr 19 Franklin Mount HG1 5EJ
☎(0423) 504259

This late Victorian terraced house is situated in a quiet tree-lined road a short walk from the Conference Centre and shops. Like other properties in the road, its name is carved into the gatestone. Apart from 2 smallish singles, bedrooms are spacious and comfortable, tastefully decorated and pleasantly furnished. There is a comfortable lounge downstairs at the back, and a large dining room with a bay window at the front with individual tables for about 15 covers. Home-cooked dinners are freshly prepared each day and a substantial English breakfast is also served. There is a residential licence and drinks can be served in the lounge before dinner. A small car park at the rear can take 4 cars, but there is also unrestricted kerbside parking.

6rm(5⌐1hc) CTV in all bedrooms ® ✗ (ex guide dogs) ✱
sB&B£17.50-£18.50 dB&B⌐£41-£45 WB&B£140 WBDi£200
LDO 4.30pm
Lic 🍽 3P
Credit Cards 1 2 3 £

GH QQQ Knox Mill House Knox Mill Ln, Killinghall
HG3 2AE ☎(0423) 560650

Set in a delightful, peaceful location, yet only one mile north of Harrogate town centre. This former miller's residence, built around 1785, is adjacent to Knox Mill, with its original waterwheel and millrack, on the banks of an attractive stream, with meadows and open countryside beyond. The bedrooms, all of which face south, are attractively decorated, comfortable and very well maintained, and a feature downstairs, as well as the spacious lounge, is a tiny alcoved library with shelves of books for guests to read. The hotel is just off the A61, Ripon Road.

3rm(2⌐1hc) ® ✗ ✱ dB&Bfr£32 dB&B⌐fr£36
🍽 CTV 4P nc10yrs £

GH QQ Lamont House 12 St Mary's Walk HG2 0LW
☎(0423) 567143
Closed Xmas

This late Victorian house is located at the end of a terrace, but with all the appearance of being detached, and is situated in a quiet residential area of the town with neat terraced gardens at the front. Friendly and family run, it is within easy reach of the town centre and shops. Bedrooms are tastefully furnished, modern and fresh, with 2 recently added rooms on the lower ground floor. There is a small guests' lounge, with leather armchairs and a chesterfield, and a selection of books and games for guests' use. The breakfast room with a bay window, has a display of decorative plates, and individual tables, overlooks the garden and patio.

9rm(2⌐7hc) (2fb) CTV in all bedrooms ® sB&Bfr£20
dB&Bfr£30 dB&B⌐£45-£50
Lic 🍽
Credit Cards 1 £

GH QQ *Prince's Hotel* 7 Granby Rd HG1 4ST
☎(0423) 883469

This impressive late Victorian terraced house is situated just off the A59 as it enters The Stray from the Knaresborough direction. The spacious double and family rooms feature very comfortable chairs, central heating, double glazing and some antique pieces. One room has a king sized 4-poster bed with fully closing drapes. There is a very comfortable Victorian-style lounge with ample armchairs and sofas, and although there is no bar there is a table licence. The proprietors pride themselves on the standard of their traditional home cooking, prepared without the use of convenience foods. Dinner is served in the elegant dining room at 6.30pm and the price includes 3 courses and coffee. Special diets can also be catered for.

8rm(2⇌2⌐4hc) (1fb)⊁in 1 bedroom CTV in all bedrooms ®
✗ LDO 9am
Lic 🍽 CTV ⊮ nc3yrs

GH QQ The Richmond 56 Dragon View, Skipton Rd HG1 4DG ☎(0423) 530612
A Victorian house set back from the A59 Skipton road towards the end of The Stray. Most of the bedrooms have en suite facilities; there is a comfortable lounge and an attractive dining room.
6rm(5🚿 1hc) (1fb) CTV in all bedrooms ® ✗ (ex guide dogs) sB&B🚿£18-£20 dB&B🚿£36-£40 WB&B£126-£140
🍴 CTV 2P (£)

GH QQ Roan 90 Kings Rd HG1 5JX ☎(0423) 503087
Closed 25-26 Dec
Conveniently situated close to the Conference Centre and the main shopping area, this friendly guesthouse offers traditionally furnished bedrooms, in addition to a comfortable guests' lounge and a spacious dining room where 4- course dinners are served.
7rm(3🚿 4hc) (1fb) CTV in all bedrooms ® ✗ ✱ sB&Bfr£18 dB&Bfr£34.50 dB&B🚿fr£39 LDO 4.30pm
🍴 CTV no parking nc7yrs (£)

GH Q Roxanne 12 Franklin Mount HG1 5EJ ☎(0423) 569930
Closed 24 Dec-2 Jan
This semidetached Victorian house is situated just minutes' walk from the Conference Centre and provides well maintained accommodation.
5hc (1fb) CTV in 1 bedroom TV in 2 bedrooms
✗ (ex guide dogs) ✱ sB&B£15-£17 dB&B£30-£34 WB&B£105-£119 WBDi£140-£154 LDO 4pm
🍴 CTV 1P 1🚗
Credit Cards [1] [3] (£)

GH QQQ Scotia House Hotel 66/68 Kings Rd HG1 5JR ☎(0423) 504361 FAX (0423) 526578
A well furnished private hotel opposite the conference centre, where bedrooms are provided with colour TV, direct dial telephones and tea-making facilities. There is a cosy lounge with a bar and an attractive dining room.
14rm(1🛁 10🚿 3hc) (1fb) no smoking in 6 bedrooms CTV in all bedrooms ® T ✱ sB&B£22.50-£24 sB&B🛁🚿£24.50-£26 dB&B🛁🚿£48-£52 LDO 6pm
Lic 🍴 CTV 8P nc7yrs
Credit Cards [1] [3]

GH Q *Shelbourne* 78 Kings Rd HG1 5JX ☎(0423) 504390
This semidetached Victorian house almost overlooks the conference centre, and is only a few minutes' walk from the town centre and shops. Bedrooms have been nicely decorated and feature a number of interesting prints as well as colourful borders. All are centrally heated and have electric blankets. The lounge is spacious and lofty, with sofas, armchairs, prints, paintings and a colour TV. The dining room, with a small bar in one corner, has substantial polished draw-leaf tables and seating for about 12. There is limited private parking at the rear.
7hc (2fb) ® LDO noon
Lic 🍴 CTV 1P

GH QQQ Stoney Lea 13 Spring Grove HG1 2HS ☎(0423) 501524
Closed Xmas & New Year
A substantial semidetached house, with a mixed facade of stone and Tudor-style timbers, situated in a quiet cul de sac just behind the conference centre. Bedrooms are spacious and particularly comfortable, all with private bathrooms, TV, clock radio, mini bar and facilities for making tea and coffee. There is a cosy lounge downstairs with TV, books and magazines, and a nicely appointed dining room with separate tables, where breakfast is served. There is ample, unrestricted parking, but pets are not allowed.
7🛁🚿 CTV in all bedrooms ® ✗ (ex guide dogs) ✱ sB&B🛁🚿£24-£27 dB&B🛁🚿£40 WB&B£140-£189
🍴 CTV 3P nc4yrs (£)

(£) Remember to use the money-off vouchers.

GH QQQ Wharfedale House 28 Harlow Moor Dr HG2 0JY ☎(0423) 522233
This immaculate hotel is situated in a pleasant location overlooking Valley Gardens, and is also convenient for the town centre and various conference facilities. Bedrooms are exceedingly well appointed, all with en suite facilities, TV, telephones, radio and tea-making facilities. Downstairs there is a very attractive dining room and comfortable lounge, where drinks are served. The owners are both trained chefs, and meals are often prepared to individual requirements.
8rm(1🛁 7🚿) (2fb) CTV in all bedrooms ® T sB&B🛁🚿fr£25 dB&B🛁🚿fr£46 WBDi£200 LDO 4pm
Lic 🍴 3P 🏠 (£)

GH QQQ Wynnstay House 60 Franklin Rd HG1 5EE ☎(0423) 560476
A very comfortable, spotlessly clean late-Victorian terraced house, with particularly well appointed bedrooms including TV, radios, tea making facilities, hairdryers and modern, en suite facilities. Public rooms include a guests' lounge and an attractive dining room in which hearty breakfasts are served.
5🚿 (2fb) CTV in all bedrooms ® sB&B🚿£20 dB&B🚿£40 WB&B£126 WBDi£175 LDO 2pm
🍴
Credit Cards [1] [3] (£)

HARROP FOLD Lancashire Map 07 SD74

SELECTED

FH QQQQ Mr & Mrs P Wood ***Harrop Fold Country Farmhouse Hotel** (SD746492)* BBY 4PJ
☎Bolton-by-Bowland(02007) 600 Telex no 635562
Closed Jan
Guests were first welcomed to this delightful old farmhouse by Peter and Victoria Wood in 1970, and since then many improvements have been made but the genuine, warm atmosphere and hospitality remains. Named after flowers and wild plants, the individually furnished bedrooms have fresh flowers and a welcoming glass of wine, as well as personally designed towels, perfumed bath gel and soaps. The old farmhouse lounge, with its oak beams and brasses, is furnished with comfortable Victorian, button-back chairs, and the stable loft, with views over the farmland, has an interesting collection of maritime photographs and other nautical items. An excellent standard of cooking is provided by Victoria, served in the pretty, candlelit dining room and a memorable breakfast is provided, in addition to afternoon teas.
5🛁 Annexe 2rm(1🛁 1🚿) CTV in all bedrooms ® ✗
LDO 7pm
Lic 🍴 16P nc280 acres sheep
Credit Cards [1] [3]

HARROW Greater London London plan 4 B5 (pages 248-249)

GH Q *Central Hotel* 6 Hindes Rd HA1 1SJ ☎081-427 0893
Near the town centre, this converted Edwardian house offers accommodation on 3 floors; the rooms are simply furnished and vary in size.
10rm(3🚿 7hc) (3fb) CTV in all bedrooms ® ✗
🍴 CTV 12P
Credit Cards [1] [3]

GH QQ *Crescent Lodge Hotel* 58/62 Welldon Crescent HA1 1QR ☎081-863 5491 & 081-863 5163 FAX 081-427 5965
This family-run commercial hotel is set in a quiet residential crescent. Bedrooms come in many different sizes and are cheerfully decorated, well equipped and clean. There is a bar/lounge with comfortable, deep sofas and a bright breakfast room overlooking the garden.
21rm(12🚿 9hc) (2fb) CTV in all bedrooms ®
✗ (ex guide dogs) LDO 8.30pm

Lic 🍽 CTV 8P 1🚗 (£2 per night) ⛳
Credit Cards 1 3

GH Q Hindes Hotel 8 Hindes Rd HA1 1SJ ☎081-427 7468 FAX 081-424 0673

This owner-run guesthouse is located in a residential street near the town centre. The compact bedrooms are on 3 floors and are simply furnished. Plants adorn the pleasant lounge which has a TV and the kitchen/breakfast room is open plan.

13rm(1⚐12hc) (2fb) CTV in all bedrooms ® ✗ ✱ sB&Bfr£29 sB&B⚐fr£38 dB&Bfr£39 dB&B⚐fr£49
🍽 CTV 5P
Credit Cards 1 2 3 £

HARTFIELD East Sussex Map **05** TQ43

FH QQQ Mrs C Cooper **Bolebroke Watermill** *(TQ481373)* Perry Hill, Edenbridge Rd TN7 4JP (off B2026 1m N of Hartfield) ☎(0892) 770425

Mar-Nov rs Dec

This charming and quite unique watermill is set in 6.5 acres of secluded woodlands, with an ancient history dating back to King William in 1086. The tools and machinery are still much in evidence. The bedrooms are reached by very steep staircases and are completely unsuitable for anybody with restricted mobility. The bedrooms are comfortable and well appointed, and all have private facilities. There is a comfortable lounge, and dinner, available by prior arrangement, is served in the adjoining mill house.

2⇌⚐ Annexe 2⇌⚐ ⚟in all bedrooms CTV in all bedrooms ® ✗ sB&B⇌⚐£43-£53 dB&B⇌⚐£48-£58 LDO 10am
🍽 CTV 16P nc7yrs 6 acres smallholding
Credit Cards 1 2 3

HARTLAND Devon Map **02** SS22

GH QQ Fosfelle EX39 6EF ☎(0237) 441273

A 17th-century former manor house in well kept gardens and lovely countryside, a short drive from the sea. Two lakes provide trout and coarse fishing, which are both popular. The bedrooms have comfortable beds and are furnished in country style and some antiques, but with modern facilities including telephones and tea making facilities. The bar supports a local darts team, and sometimes entertainment is provided in the barn, or a barbeque on the patio. The spacious dining room offers both à la carte and table d'hôte menus.

7rm(1⇌1⚐5hc) (2fb) CTV in 3 bedrooms TV in 2 bedrooms ® ✗ sB&B£17-£19 dB&B£34-£38 dB&B⇌⚐£36-£40 WB&B£105-£120 WBDi£145-£165 LDO 9pm
Lic 🍽 CTV 20P ⛳ ♩ snooker
Credit Cards 1 3 £

HASELEY KNOB Warwickshire Map **04** SP27

GH QQQ Croft CV35 7NL ☎(0926) 484447

Situated in the small village of Haseley Knob, 5 miles northwest of Warwick, The Croft is equally suitable for tourists and business guests, being close to Stratford as well as the NAC, NEC, M6, M40, and M42. Two interconnecting ground floor rooms are available, 1 of which opens into the garden at the rear of the building. Public areas include 2 lounges and an attractive conservatory dining room, where dinner is usually served at a communal table. Guests are requested not to smoke in the house.

5rm(4⚐1hc) (2fb)⚟in all bedrooms CTV in 4 bedrooms ® ✱ sB&B⚐£19.50-£28 dB&B£33-£37 dB&B⚐£37-£42 LDO 2pm
🍽 CTV 8P £

See advertisement under WARWICK

This is one of many guidebooks published by the AA. The full range is available at any AA Shop or good bookshop.

HASTINGS & ST LEONARDS East Sussex Map **05** TQ80

GH Q Argyle 32 Cambridge Gardens TN34 1EN
☎(0424) 421294
Closed Xmas
This mid-terrace house is close to the railway station and town centre, and has a ground floor TV lounge and a basement breakfast room. Three of the simply furnished bedrooms have en suite facilities.
8rm(3⬈5hc) (1fb) ® ✱ sB&Bfr£15 sB&B⬈fr£18 dB&Bfr£26 dB&B⬈fr£30 WB&Bfr£77
CTV P nc4yrs

GH QQ *Bryn-y-Mor* 12 Godwin Rd TN35 5JR
☎Hastings(0424) 722744 FAX (0424) 445933
The atmosphere of a past and gracious era is created in this attractive Victorian house, that is located in a quiet residential area and set in beautiful landscaped gardens with a heated swimming pool. There is a small library/lounge in addition to the spacious lounge bar with its adjoining conservatory adorned with plants. Breakfast is served in the grand dining room, which gives a panoramic view of the old town and the sea, and dinner is available by prior arrangement. The 3 bedrooms are ornately furnished in period style, one is en suite while the others share a super bathroom with its generous sized tub. Two self-catering garden apartments are also available to let.
3rm(1⬈2hc) CTV in all bedrooms ® ✱ LDO 4.30pm
Lic CTV (heated) snooker

GH QQQ Eagle House Pevensey Rd TN38 0JZ
☎(0424) 430535 & 441273
Peacefully located in a residential area within walking distance of Warrior Square railway station, this detached Victorian house benefits from a car park and a rear garden where the proprietor's hens wander freely. Bedrooms have been furnished in a traditional style with mostly reproduction furniture, candlewick bedspreads and flock décor – all are very well equipped, and all but three more simply furnished rooms are en suite. Public areas are similar in style and décor, recreating something like the Victorian elegance with crystal chandeliers, original cornices and a marble fireplace in the lounge bar. Dinners are available or the proprietors will bring a supper tray to your room.
23rm(20⇌⬈3hc) (2fb) CTV in all bedrooms ® ✱ sB&B£29 sB&B⇌⬈£31.60 dB&B⇌⬈£47 WB&Bfr£149.50 WBDifr£243 LDO 8.30pm
Lic 13P
Credit Cards 1 2 3 5 £

GH QQQ Norton Villa Hill St, Old Town TN34 3HU
☎Hastings(0424) 428168
This pretty house, built in 1847, is situated high above the town with views across the rooftops and out to sea. It is in the centre of a particularly historic area which is popular with artists. Bedrooms are bright, attractive and equipped with modern facilities. There is a cosy lounge which is filled with flowers and ornaments, as is the sunny dining room where breakfast is served. An evening meal is not provided as there is a wealth of restaurants both in the Old Town and the centre of Hastings. Overnight parking is available but space is limited, so guests may not return their cars until after 4pm. The proprietors prefer guests not to smoke in their rooms.
4rm(3⇌⬈1hc) CTV in all bedrooms ® ✱ ✱ sB&B⇌⬈£18-£32 dB&B⇌⬈£32-£40 WB&B£115-£129
CTV 6P (£1.50 per day) nc8yrs

SELECTED

GH QQQQ Parkside House 59 Lower Park Rd TN34 2LD ☎Hastings(0424) 433096
This elegant Victorian house is situated in a residential area and an elevated position opposite Alexandra Park. Bedrooms are individually decorated with colour coordinated fabrics and a mixture of modern and antique furniture. Many have had smart en suite facilities added, and all accommodate every conceivable extra, so guests may travel light. Breakfast and the set dinner are served in the attractively furnished dining room, and guests can relax in the adjoining TV lounge which features the original marble fireplace, or in the quiet sun lounge.
5rm(4⬈1hc) (1fb) ✗ in all bedrooms CTV in all bedrooms ® T ✱ (ex guide dogs) sB&B£20-£30 sB&B⬈£30-£35 dB&B⬈£40-£48 WB&B£135-£195 WBDi£195-£220 LDO 3pm
Lic CTV P £

GH QQ *The Ridge Guest House & Restaurant* 361 The Ridge TN34 2RD ☎Hastings(0424) 754240 & 753607
A family-run guesthouse set in an elevated position in a residential area, close to the new Conquest Hospital. It offers a range of purpose-built bedrooms which are basically furnished, but all have modern en suite facilities; a further six rooms are presently being built. The dining room doubles as a Fish and Chips restaurant at weekends, and there is a small bar and a simply furnished lounge.
11⬈ (2fb) CTV in all bedrooms ® ✱ LDO 9.15pm
CTV 40P
Credit Cards 1 2

GH QQQ Tower Hotel 28 Tower Rd West TN38 0RG
☎(0424) 427217
Quietly located above St Leonards-on-Sea, this Victorian house has been skillfully extended to provide a choice of bedrooms, some of which are on the ground floor. The rooms are individually decorated, some with private bathrooms, and all have TV and tea trays. A freshly prepared set menu is provided in the attractive, well furnished dining room, and other public rooms include a conservatory breakfast room, small well stocked bar, and a spacious comfortable lounge. Service is particularly helpful, available throughout the day from resident proprietors Roy and Joan Richards. There is no car park, but unrestricted street parking is readily available.
10rm(8⇌⬈2hc) (2fb) CTV in all bedrooms ® sB&B£17.50-£25.50 sB&B⇌⬈£20.50-£28.50 dB&B£35-£41 dB&B⇌⬈£41-£47 WB&B£105-£151 WBDi£164.50-£210.50 LDO 4pm
Lic CTV P
Credit Cards 1 3 £

GH QQ Waldorf Hotel 4 Carlisle Pde TN34 1JG
☎(0424) 422185
This small family-run hotel is in a prime seafront location and offers freshly decorated bedrooms, several with en suite facilities. Breakfast and traditional evening meals are served in the dining room, and there is a comfortable adjoining lounge area with a dispenser bar.
12rm(3⇌2⬈7hc) (3fb) CTV in all bedrooms ®
✱ (ex guide dogs) sB&B£19-£21 sB&B⇌⬈£22-£24 dB&B£32-£36 dB&B⇌⬈£38-£42 WB&B£110-£138 WBDi£159-£187 LDO 11.30am
Lic CTV P

FH QQQ Mrs B Yorke **Filsham Farmhouse** *(TQ784096)* 111 Harley Shute Rd TN38 8BY ☎(0424) 433109
Closed Xmas & New Year
Although in what is now a residential area, Filsham is an archetypal grade II 17th century farmhouse retaining much of its rural and historic charm. Each of the three bedrooms has its own charm – all are furnished with quality antiques and pretty soft furnishings. The 4 poster room is en suite whilst the other two share a large bathroom with separate showers and another has a WC with washbasin. The large hall combines as an dining room and lounge with a charming French Bergere suite, assorted antiques and objets d'art, original beams and an impressive inglenook fireplace with a real log fire. Mrs Yorke is a natural hostess and plays her part in ensuring a memorable stay.
3rm ✗ in all bedrooms CTV in all bedrooms ® ✱ sB&B£20 dB&B£30-£35 WB&Bfr£87.50
CTV 4P 1 acres non-working £

INN QQQ **Highlands** 1 Boscobel Rd TN38 0LU
☎(0424) 420299
Quietly situated on a steep hillside, this impressive listed building offers freshly decorated, modern bedrooms with en suite facilities. There is a popular public bar and a basement restaurant run by friendly proprietors Mr and Mrs Bayes.
9⇔🚿 (1fb) CTV in all bedrooms ® ✗ (ex guide dogs) sB&B⇔🚿fr£28 dB&B⇔🚿fr£46 WB&Bfr£175 WBDifr£231 Lunch £3.25-£7 Dinner £5-£12&alc LDO 9.30pm
🍽 CTV 8P
Credit Cards 1 3 £

HATHERSAGE Derbyshire Map **08** SK28

FH QQ Mr & Mrs P S Wain **Highlow Hall** *(SK219802)* S30 1AX ☎Hope Valley(0433) 50393
Friendly proprietors and generally large bedrooms are features at this 16th- century manor house farm, which is set in lovely countryside. A comfortable lounge with television is available, and breakfast is served in the adjacent small dining room. To find the farm, take the B6001 to Bakewell from Hathersage, then the turn signed for Abney – the farm is on this country lane.
6hc (2fb) ® sB&B£20 dB&B£40-£50 WB&B£120-£150 WBDi£204-£234 LDO 7pm
Lic CTV 12P 900 acres mixed sheep

HATTON Warwickshire Map **04** SP26

SELECTED

GH QQQQ **Northleigh House** Five Ways Rd CV35 7HZ
☎Warwick(0926) 484203
Closed 15 Dec-30 Jan
Enjoying a peaceful location tucked away in the countryside, this guesthouse has a setting that belies its proximity to the Midlands motorway network and the NEC. The 6 bedrooms are individually named – reflecting the décor and theme – for example the 'Victorian room' and the 'Gold room'. All rooms have modern en suite facilities and are equipped with thoughtful extras such as a wide range of teas and coffees plus a fridge. Breakfast is served in a pretty dining room, adjacent to a sitting room furnished with comfortable sofas. High standards are maintained by proprietor Sylvia Fenwich, who is sure to make guests extremely welcome with her hospitable manner.
6⇔🚿 ⊬in all bedrooms CTV in all bedrooms ®
sB&B⇔🚿£29-£37 dB&B⇔🚿£42-£54
🍽 CTV 8P £
See advertisement under WARWICK

HATTON HEATH Cheshire Map **07** SJ46

GH QQQ **Golborne Manor** Platts Ln CH3 9AN
☎Chester(0829) 70310
This beautifully preserved and tastefully modernised mid-Victorian country house is set in 3.5 acres of grounds and gardens in a rural area south of Chester. It provides bed and breakfast accommodation in 2 spacious bedrooms, one of which is furnished in a modern style with twin beds and has private use of a bathroom and WC. The other room is traditionally furnished with family beds and has an en suite shower and WC. Breakfast is served in a pleasant room with period furniture where guests share one large table. There is also a very attractive, comfortable and quiet lounge. The house can be difficult to find, despite its proximity to the main road: turn west off the A41, 6 miles south of Chester, near Demon Tweeks tyre depot, into Platt Lane which is signed for Bruera, Saighton and Aldford, and the manor is on the left after about a quarter of a mile.
2rm(1🚿1hc) (1fb) CTV in all bedrooms ® ✗ ✱ sB&B🚿£25 dB&B🚿£35 WB&B£140
🍽 6P

HAVANT Hampshire Map **04** SU70

See also Emsworth

GH QQ **Holland House** 33 Bedhampton Hill PO9 3JN
☎(0705) 475913 FAX (0705) 470134
This neat and tidy guesthouse is located on the Bedhampton side of Havant. Downstairs there is a comfortable lounge with TV and a no-smoking breakfast room where light snacks are served early in the evening; upstairs are 4 well kept bedrooms.
4rm(1🚿3hc) CTV in 2 bedrooms ® ✗ ✱ sB&B£15-£20 dB&B£27-£30 dB&B🚿£30-£34 WB&Bfr£90 LDO 6.45pm
🍽 CTV 4P £

HAVERFORDWEST Dyfed

See **Broad Haven also advertisement on p 197**

HAVERIGG Cumbria Map **07** SD17

GH QQQ **Dunelm Cottage** Main St LA18 4EX
☎Millom(0229) 770097
Closed Jan
This charming cottage-style guesthouse is situated in the centre of the quaint village. Three tastefully decorated bedrooms are available, along with a cosy lounge and there is a long wooden table for dining. There is adequate free parking just over the road.
3hc ® ✱ (incl dinner) WB&Bfr£115 WBDifr£175
LDO 6.30pm
🍽 CTV ⊬ nc10yrs

HAWES North Yorkshire Map **07** SD88

GH QQQ **Steppe Haugh** Town Head DL8 3RJ
☎Wensleydale(0969) 667645
A 17th-century stone-built house standing on the edge of the village. Managed by the charming resident proprietors, it offers small and cosy bedrooms with lovely views, an inviting spacious →

lounge with a log fire and colour TV, and an attractive dining room.
6rm(2↱4hc) CTV in 2 bedrooms ® ✗ * sB&B£20 dB&B£28 dB&B↱£36 WB&Bfr£98 WBDifr£185.50 LDO 5pm
Lic 🍽 CTV 8P nc10yrs

HAWKSHEAD Cumbria Map **07** SD39

GH QQ *Greenbank Country House Hotel* Main St LA22 0NS ☎(05394) 36497
A former farmhouse dating back to the 17th century on the northern edge of the village, now a small hotel offering a good all round standard of service and comfort.
10rm(2↱8hc) (1fb) ® LDO 4.30pm
Lic 🍽 CTV 12P

GH QQ Ivy House LA22 0NS ☎(05394) 36204
20 Mar-7 Nov
An attractive Georgian house in the village centre, it has a carved staircase leading to well furnished bedrooms. A comfortable lounge is available and good home cooking is provided.
6rm(3⇌3↱) Annexe 5rm(3⇌2↱) (3fb) CTV in 5 bedrooms ® sB&B⇌↱£33-£35 dB&B⇌↱£66-£70 (incl dinner) WB&B£166.25-£180.25 WBDi£210-£224 LDO 6pm
Lic 🍽 CTV 14P 🎣

GH QQQ Rough Close Country House LA22 0QF ☎(05394) 36370
Apr-Oct rs Mar
A lovely house set in well tended gardens about a mile south of the village. It offers good accommodation and very friendly personal service. A good standard of home cooking is provided.
5⇌↱ 🚭in all bedrooms ® ✗ (ex guide dogs) sB&B⇌↱£37-£39 dB&B⇌↱£64-£68 (incl dinner) WB&B£164.50 WBDi£224 LDO 7pm
Lic 🍽 CTV 10P nc5yrs
Credit Cards [1] [3] (£)

INN Q Kings Arms Hotel LA22 0NZ ☎(05394) 36372
A character inn at the centre of the charming village. Bedrooms are well furnished and offer good facilities. A wide range of food is available in either the bar or dining room.
9rm(4↱5hc) (2fb) CTV in all bedrooms ® **T** * sB&B£27 sB&B↱£29 dB&B£44 dB&B↱£54 Dinner £12-£22alc LDO 9pm
🍽
Credit Cards [1] [3]

INN QQ Red Lion The Square LA22 0HB ☎(05394) 36213
Closed 25 Dec
A 15th-century coaching inn situated at the northern end of the village. All the bedrooms have en suite facilities, colour television and tea-making facilities.
8↱ (2fb) CTV in all bedrooms ® ✗ LDO 9pm
🍽 8P
Credit Cards [1] [3] (£)

HAWORTH West Yorkshire Map **07** SE03

GH QQ Ferncliffe Hotel Hebden Rd BD22 8RS ☎(0535) 643405
Overlooking the valley and hills, this semidetached 1950s building on the Hebden Bridge road offers colour coordinated, comfortable accommodation. The large dining room is the focal point, enjoying a sunny, elevated position and decorated in soft colours, with local landscape prints on the walls. Popular with locals for home-cooked meals, it also features a small but well stocked bar.
6↱ (1fb) CTV in all bedrooms ® * sB&B↱£21-£25 dB&B↱£42 WB&B£147-£175 WBDi£213-£241.50 LDO 8.30pm
Lic 🍽 CTV 12P
Credit Cards [1] [3]

HAYFIELD Derbyshire Map **07** SK08

INN Q *Sportsman* Kinder Rd SK12 5EL ☎New Mills(0663) 742118
Traditional country inn, with well-furnished, modern bedrooms, in the valley of the River Set on the approach to Kinder Scout.
7rm(5↱2hc) (1fb) CTV in all bedrooms ® LDO 9.30pm
🍽 20P
Credit Cards [1] [3]

HAYLING ISLAND Hampshire Map **04** SZ79

SELECTED

GH QQQQ Cockle Warren Cottage Hotel 36 Seafront PO11 9HL ☎(0705) 464961
Diane and David Skelton have been running their small, award-winning hotel for some years, and in their own special way offer a high level of attentive service, as well as always seeking new improvements. Built in a farmhouse style, it stands in a large garden at the eastern end of the seafront and provides prettily decorated bedrooms that are generously equipped, including many little extras and 2 have 4-poster beds. There is a comfortable lounge, full of memorabilia and plants, with a log fire burning in winter. Meals are taken in a small, foliaged black and white conservatory that overlooks the patio and swimming pool. Breakfast and the set 4-course dinner are cooked by Diane, who uses fresh ingredients to prepare dishes based on French provincial cuisine.
4rm(1⇌↱3hc) Annexe 1hc 🚭in all bedrooms CTV in all bedrooms **T** ✗ (ex guide dogs) * sB&B⇌↱£35-£55 dB&B⇌↱£60-£74 WB&B£210-£259 LDO 4.30pm
Lic 🍽 7P 2🚗 nc12yrs 🏊(heated) ⛳ 18
Credit Cards [1] [3]

HAY-ON-WYE Powys Map **03** SO24

GH QQQ York House Hardwick Rd, Cusop HR3 5QX (1m SE in England) ☎(0497) 820705
rs Xmas
This fine stone house is set in an acre of peaceful gardens and is only a short walk from the town centre on the Peterchurch road. The bedrooms are all pretty and comfortable, and there is a pleasant lounge; several of the original fireplaces remain, adding to the character of the house.
5rm(3⇌↱2hc) (2fb)🚭in all bedrooms CTV in all bedrooms ® dB&B£33-£35 dB&B⇌↱£38-£42 WB&B£103.95-£132.30 WBDi£173.25-£201.60 LDO 5pm
🍽 8P nc8yrs
Credit Cards [1] [3]

HEASLEY MILL Devon Map **03** SS73

GH QQQ Heasley House EX36 3LE ☎North Molton(05984) 213
Closed Feb
Peacefully situated in the remote village of Heasley Mill, just 4 miles from the North Devon link road and with easy access to Exmoor and the coast, this family-run hotel offers a relaxed atmosphere and comfortable accommodation. The bedrooms, most of which are en suite, vary in size and all provide tea making facilities, although June and Trevor Tate prefer to get to know their guests over tea in one of the attractive lounges. Home-cooked dishes make up the predominantly set menus and are served around a large table in the dining room.
8rm(2⇌3↱3hc) sB&Bfr£32.50 sB&B⇌↱fr£34 dB&Bfr£65 dB&B⇌↱fr£68 (incl dinner) WB&B£140-£150 WBDi£220-£230 LDO 5pm
Lic 🍽 CTV 11P
Credit Cards [1] [3] (£)

HEATHROW AIRPORT Greater London London plan **4** A3 (pages 248-249)

See also Slough

GH QQ ***The Cottage*** 150 High St, Cranford TW5 9PD
☎081-897 1815

Set in a quiet cul-de-sac off Cranford High Street, this guesthouse offers clean, comfortable and well maintained accommodation on the ground and first floors. There is an informal and relaxed atmosphere under the proprietor Mrs Parry's personal supervision.

6hc (1fb) CTV in all bedrooms ✗ (ex guide dogs)
🅿 20P

HEBDEN BRIDGE West Yorkshire Map **07** SD92

GH QQQ Redacre Mill Redacre, Mytholmroyd HX7 5DQ
☎Halifax(0422) 885563

Closed Dec-Jan

A lovingly converted mill standing beside the tranquil Rochdale canal, in Calderdale. Bedrooms are exceptionally well furnished and equipped, and the resident owners offer a warm Yorkshire welcome to all their guests.

5rm(2⇌3♪) (1fb)⚡in all bedrooms CTV in all bedrooms ® ✗ (ex guide dogs) ✱ sB&B⇌♪£35-£40 dB&B⇌♪£45-£50 WB&B£160-£240 WBDi£225-£310 LDO 8pm
Lic 🅿 8P
Credit Cards [1] [3] £

This guide is updated annually – make sure you use an up-to-date edition.

HELENSBURGH Strathclyde *Dunbartonshire*

See **Cardross**

HELMSLEY North Yorkshire Map **08** SE68

FH QQ Mrs M E Skilbeck **Middle Heads** *(SE584869)* Rievaulx YO6 5LU ☎Bilsdale(04396) 251
Mar-Nov

This comfortable and hospitable stone farmhouse in a lovely rural setting can be hard to find. It is three miles from Helmsley, including a mile of farm track and 1m E of the B1257 Stokesley road. Three spacious bedrooms share a modern bathroom and a shower room. All of the bedrooms have tea/coffee making facilities. There is a comfortable lounge and a choice of breakfasts is offered in a beamed sitting room.

3rm ⅟in all bedrooms ® ✗ ✱ dB&B£26-£30 WB&Bfr£91
🍽 CTV 6P nc5yrs 170 acres arable beef mixed sheep

HELSTON Cornwall & Isles of Scilly Map **02** SW62

FH QQ Iris White ***Little Pengwedna*** *(SW638318)* Little Pengwedna Farm TR13 0BA ☎Leedstown(0736) 850649
Etr-Oct

A friendly farmhouse with bright, well decorated bedrooms and modern facilities. There is a traditional lounge and dining room. It is located about four miles outside Helston on the B3303 Camborne road, and provides a good touring base for south west Cornwall.

3hc ⅟in all bedrooms ® ✗ (ex guide dogs) LDO 9am
CTV 6P 74 acres cattle

HENFIELD West Sussex Map **04** TQ21

FH QQ Mrs M Wilkin **Great Wapses** *(TQ242192)* Wineham BN5 9BJ ☎(0273) 492544

This attractive farmhouse is about half a mile off the B2116 to Albourne. It dates back to the 16th century with a Georgian extension. The rooms are furnished with assorted traditional pieces and mixed fabrics giving a modest appearance, all have private facilities. Breakfast is served at a communal dining table.

3rm(2⇌1♠) (1fb) CTV in all bedrooms ® sB&B⇌♠£22-£24 dB&B⇌♠£34-£36
🍽 7P ♨(hard)33 acres mixed
Credit Cards 2

HENLEY-IN-ARDEN Warwickshire Map **07** SP16

GH QQQ ***Ashleigh House*** Whitley Hill B95 5DL ☎(0564) 792315 FAX (0564) 794133

This attractive ivy-clad property is set back in its own gardens from the A4095. Bedrooms have quality coordinated décor and varied furnishings, including some nice antique pieces, and there are finishing touches such as dried flowers and sugared almonds. The lovely light dining room has been refurbished by the present owners and has a huge dresser displaying blue and white china. The cosy lounge provides a good degree of comfort and even has its own gramophone.

6rm(2⇌4♠) Annexe 4♠ CTV in all bedrooms ®
✗ (ex guide dogs)
🍽 CTV 11P nc14yrs
Credit Cards 1 3

HENLEY-ON-THAMES Oxfordshire Map **04** SU78

See also Nettlebed

GH Q ***Flohr's Hotel & Restaurant*** Northfield End RG9 2JG ☎(0491) 573412

A listed Georgian town house dating back to 1750, just 5 minutes' walk from the town centre. Bedrooms are bright and simply furnished with individual décor and TV. A choice of interesting dishes is available from the table d'hôte menu in the formal restaurant which has character and quality.

9rm(1⇌2♠6hc) (4fb) CTV in all bedrooms ® LDO 10pm
Lic 🍽 CTV 6P
Credit Cards 1 2 3 5

GH QQ Slater's Farm Peppard Common RG9 5JL ☎Rotherfield Greys(0491) 628675

Situated 4 miles west of Henley on the B481 at Peppard, it is best to ring for detailed directions to Slaters Farm as it is not easy to find. Though no longer a farmhouse, it is a charming detached property, 270 years old in parts, with a pretty garden offering tennis and croquet in a conservation area. Very much a home which is open to guests, the house has a gracious breakfast room and lounge with a feature fireplace, together with smart new bathrooms and cosy bedrooms. It is a good base for touring, and direct, high- speed trains to London from nearby Reading take only half an hour. The area has many good pubs for dinner.

3hc ⅟in all bedrooms ✱ sB&B£18-£20 dB&B£35-£40
🍽 3P nc8yrs ♨(hard)

HENSTRIDGE Somerset Map **03** ST71

FH QQQ Mrs P J Doggrell **Toomer** *(ST708192)* Templecombe BA8 0PH ☎Templecombe(0963) 250237

Amidst 400 acres of mixed farmland, this 300-year-old farmhouse, surrounded by neat gardens, lies back from the A30 west of the village. The good sized bedrooms are on the first floor and provide pleasant accommodation. Breakfast is taken around a communal table in a lovely dining room, and there is a separate lounge with a TV and deep comfortable sofas.

3rm(1♠2hc) (2fb) CTV in all bedrooms ® ✗ (ex guide dogs)
✱ sB&B£14.50-£17 dB&B♠fr£30
🍽 CTV 6P ✓ 400 acres arable dairy £

HEREFORD Hereford & Worcester Map **03** SO54

See also Bodenham & Little Dewchurch

GH QQ Ferncroft Hotel 144 Ledbury Rd HR1 2TB ☎(0432) 265538
Closed mid Dec-2 Jan

This attractive family hotel is set in pleasant grounds on the A438 Ledbury road. Bedrooms are all well equipped with modern facilities, there is a very comfortable residents lounge and a small foyer bar.

11rm(6⇌♠5hc) (2fb) CTV in all bedrooms ® ✗ ✱ sB&B£20 sB&B⇌♠£27.50 dB&B£30-£35 dB&B⇌♠£45 LDO 9pm
Lic 🍽 CTV 8P
Credit Cards 1 3

SELECTED

GH QQQQ Hermitage Manor Canon Pyon HR4 8NR (3.5m NW off A4110 towards Canon Pyon) ☎(0432) 760317
Mar-mid Dec

With 11 acres of grounds, sheltered by extensive deer woodlands, this impressive manor house is set in an elevated position overlooking rural Herefordshire. It has a magnificent oak panelled lounge and hall with polished floorboards and a cheerful wood burning stove, plus a second no smoking lounge, featuring an interesting carved wooded fireplace, and a small TV lounge, all furnished with modern comfortable seating. Most bedrooms are exceptionally large, well furnished in mixed styles, equipped with en suite bathrooms and TV.

3rm(2⇌1♠) CTV in all bedrooms ® ✗ dB&B⇌♠£38-£46
🍽 CTV 12P nc9yrs bowling croquet

GH QQ Hopbine Hotel Roman Rd HR1 1LE ☎(0432) 268722

Situated alongside the A4103 Roman road, north of the town, a short distance from its junction with the A49, the hotel has smart lawns to the front, and a large lawn and car park at the rear. There is a spacious dining room and small TV lounge, both modestly furnished, and simple but well equipped bedrooms with remote control TV, tea trays, clock radios and hairdryers. The Hopbine is particularly popular with the commercial sector.

10rm(3⇨7hc) (1fb) CTV in all bedrooms ® ✻ sB&B£17-£19 sB&B⇨£21-£24 dB&B£28-£30 dB&B⇨£32-£34 WBDi£160-£170 LDO before noon
Lic CTV 20P £

FH QQQ Mr D E Jones **Sink Green** *(SO542377)* Rotherwas HR2 6LE ☎Holme Lacy(0432) 870223
Closed Xmas
Run by the friendly Jones family, this immaculate 16th-century ivy-clad farmhouse stands alongside the B4399 3 miles southeast of the town. Three excellent bedrooms including a 4-poster room are available for guests, all en suite. There is a large lounge for residents and ceiling beams and timbers abound.
3rm(2⇨1↱) ⅍in all bedrooms CTV in all bedrooms ®
✈ (ex guide dogs) sB&B⇨↱£18-£21 dB&B⇨↱£34-£44
CTV 10P 180 acres beef sheep £

HERSTMONCEUX East Sussex Map **05** TQ61

GH QQ ***Cleavers Lyng Country Hotel*** Church Rd BN27 1QJ ☎(0323) 833131
Closed 24 Dec-1 Jan
A charming 16th-century house set in its own attractive grounds. The bedrooms are traditionally furnished but provide adequate comfort. There is a cosy lounge and the beamed dining room, with a log fire in cold weather, is full of character.
8hc ® LDO 6pm
Lic CTV 15P

HEXHAM Northumberland Map **12** NY96

GH QQ ***Westbrooke Hotel*** Allendale Rd NE46 2DE ☎(0434) 603818
A detached house set in a pleasant residential area on the edge of the town on the Allendale road. The bedrooms are adequately furnished and there is a public bar as part of the hotel.
11rm(5↱6hc) (2fb)⅍in 2 bedrooms CTV in all bedrooms ®
→

Lic CTV 3P snooker
Credit Cards [1] [3]

FH QQQ Elizabeth Anne Courage **Rye Hill** *(NY958580)* Slaley NE47 0AH (5m S, off B6306) ☎Slaley(0434) 673259

Bed and breakfast and self-catering accommodation are provided in the skilfully converted barn and cow shed of this farmhouse. Bedrooms are bright, modern and sensibly furnished, and include a lovely family room. The main building houses a small lounge area, a super games room and a dining room where guests take their meals around 2 pine refectory tables. Patio doors lead out to the garden which enjoys delightful views over the valley. There is also a small campsite on the farm.

6⇔↱ (2fb)⊬in all bedrooms CTV in all bedrooms ® ✱ sB&B⇔↱fr£18 dB&B⇔↱fr£33 WB&Bfr£103.95 WBDifr£157.95 LDO 6pm
Lic 🍽 CTV 6P snooker games room 30 acres sheep Ⓔ

HEYSHAM Lancashire Map 07 SD46

GH QQ ***Carr-Garth*** Bailey Ln LA3 2PS ☎(0524) 51175 due to change to 851175
Etr-mid Oct

An attractive 17th-century residence situated in neat gardens close to Heysham village. Bedrooms are nicely decorated and very well maintained and there are 2 lounges, one with colour TV, and a dining room with separate tables.

8hc (2fb) ® LDO 4pm
CTV 8P

HIGHAM Suffolk Map 05 TM03

GH QQQ The Bauble Higham CO7 6LA ☎Colchester(0206) 37254

Set on the edge of this very pretty village in the heart of Constable country, The Bauble is converted from 2, 16th-century cottages. It is surrounded by a lovely garden, rich in colour in the summer months, with patio doors leading from the lounge – which was being refurbished at the time of our visit, but will have ample deep armchairs and sofas. The dining room has a communal mahogany table with brass inlaid period chairs, and all around the house there are gleaming, polished antiques and other fine items, such as Dalton figures, and the Indian hand-painted figures on rice paper on the staircase to the bedrooms. Each of the bedrooms is colour themed, with soft furnishings in either Laura Ashley or Sanderson prints, and Mrs Watkins has exercised her considerable talent for combining practicality with style – as close to perfection as one can imagine.

3hc CTV in all bedrooms ® ✗ sB&B£20-£25 dB&B£35-£40
🍽 5P nc12yrs ⇒(heated) ℘(hard) Ⓔ

SELECTED

GH QQQQ The Old Vicarage CO7 6JY ☎(020637) 248

Approaching the village from the A12 (1.5 miles), turn left at the green and the Old Vicarage is the distinctive ochre washed and timbered house on the right with leaded windows. The dignified, high-ceilinged rooms look out onto lovely gardens with manicured lawns and colourful shrubberies tended by Mrs Parker. The same talented green fingers are evident in the lounge where, on our last visit, an orange tree was in fruit and the most glorious orchids were in bloom among the fine antiques. Despite the finery, the house has a lived in and welcoming atmosphere. The bedrooms are similar, really comfortable and colour coordinated, but curiously mixed with raffia matting covered in rugs, and cane next to an antique dresser. The Parkers are renowned for their hospitality and it is a pleasure to stay with them.

3rm(2⇔1hc) (1fb) CTV in all bedrooms ® ✱ dB&B£40-£46 dB&B⇔£46-£54
🍽 CTV 10P ⇒℘(hard)✓ boats

HIGH CATTON North Yorkshire Map 08 SE75

FH QQ Mr & Mrs Foster ***High Catton Grange*** *(SE128541)* YO4 1EP ☎Stamford Bridge(0759) 71374
Closed Xmas & New Year

An attractive farmhouse with its own working mixed farm, situated one mile east of High Catton crossroads towards Pocklington. The bedrooms have been tastefully decorated and some have antique furniture. One room has a wash- basin and there is a modern bathroom. Outside, the well kept garden has a large duckpond.

3rm(1hc) (1fb)
🍽 CTV 6P ⌂ 300 acres arable beef dairy sheep

HIGH WYCOMBE Buckinghamshire Map 04 SU89

GH Q ***Amersham Hill*** 52 Amersham Hill HP13 6PQ ☎(0494) 20635
Closed Xmas & New Year

This simply appointed town house has bright and comfortable bedrooms on 3 floors. There is a neat garden at the rear.

8rm(1↱7hc) CTV in all bedrooms ® ✗
🍽 CTV 9P

GH QQQ Clifton Lodge Hotel 210 West Wycombe Rd HP12 3AR ☎(0494) 440095 & 29062 FAX (0494) 536322

This extended gabled house stands on the A40 on the outskirts of town. Bedrooms are on 3 floors and vary in size although all are smartly modernised and comfortable, with good facilities. The Honeymoon suite has a 4-poster bed and a spa bath, and many other rooms have full en suite facilities. Downstairs are a bright, comfortable lounge with a TV, a licenced bar and a smart dining room with a lovely conservatory extension. Other features include a sauna and spa bath, ample parking and pleasant gardens with a barbecue area.

32rm(12⇔8↱12hc) (2fb) CTV in all bedrooms ® **T** ✗ (ex guide dogs) ✱ sB&B£30-£46 sB&B⇔↱£46 dB&B£52 dB&B⇔↱£65 WB&B£210-£322 LDO 8.45pm
Lic 🍽 CTV 28P sauna jacuzzi
Credit Cards [1] [2] [3] [5] Ⓔ

HIMBLETON Hereford & Worcester Map 03 SO95

FH QQ Mrs P Havard **Phepson** *(SO941599)* WR9 7JZ ☎(090569) 205
Closed Xmas & New Year

Popular with business travellers and tourists alike, this traditional 17th- century rambling farmhouse is set in the heart of the country, yet is only 5 miles from the M5. There is a very comfortable lounge with a good selection of games. Bedrooms are cosy and simple, and both rooms in the Granary annexe have good en suite facilities.

3hc Annexe 2⇔ (1fb) CTV in 2 bedrooms ® ✱ sB&Bfr£17.50 sB&B⇔fr£19.50 dB&Bfr£30 dB&B⇔fr£34
🍽 CTV 6P 170 acres beef sheep Ⓔ

HINCKLEY Leicestershire Map 04 SP49

GH QQQ Ambion Court Hotel The Green, Dadlington CV13 6JB (3m NW) ☎(0455) 212292 FAX (0455) 213141

This small hotel is set in a quiet village overlooking the green, about 2 miles north of Hinckley. The red-brick main house is a converted farm building, and some bedrooms are located here, with others on the ground floor, situated across in the courtyard annexe. All rooms have modern en suite facilities, and the annexe rooms have modern furniture, light décor and a good range of facilities such as direct dial telephones, TV, radio and hairdryers; rooms in the main house are similarly equipped, and furnished in pine. The lounge has exposed brickwork, comfortable chairs, TV, a piano, books and board games. There is a small bar, and a varied à la carte menu is available offering English country cooking with an international flair.

2↱ Annexe 5rm(1⇔4↱) CTV in all bedrooms ® **T** ✱ sB&B⇔↱£30-£45 dB&B⇔↱£45-£60 WB&B£180-£270 WBDi£250-£350 LDO 8.30pm

Lic ⊞ CTV 8P
Credit Cards [1] [3] ⓔ

GH ▣▣ Woodside Farm Ashby Rd, Stapleton LE9 8JE
☎Market Bosworth(0455) 291929

A Georgian farmhouse set in a smallholding of 16 acres, 1 mile north of the village and 3 miles from Hinckley. Bedrooms are continually being improved and are well maintained and equipped with radio/alarm and TV. The redecoration includes floral prints and period furniture. Home-cooked meals with an à la carte menu are served in a smart dining room with a conservatory extension, and drinks are available from a small dispense bar in the comfortable lounge.

6rm(3⌐3hc) (1fb)⊘in 1 bedroom CTV in all bedrooms ® ✕ sB&Bfr£18 sB&B⌐fr£22.50 dB&Bfr£32.50 dB&B⌐fr£36
LDO 9.30pm
Lic ⊞ CTV 20P 2⌂
Credit Cards [1] [3]

HINTON CHARTERHOUSE Avon Map **03** ST75

GH ▣▣▣ Green Lane House Green Ln BA3 6BL
☎Limpley Stoke(0225) 723631

John and Lucille Baxter have tastefully converted this property, which was once two early 18th-century cottages, into a cosy and comfortable guesthouse situated close to the village centre.

4rm(2⌐2hc) ® ✕ (ex guide dogs) sB&B£22-£30 sB&B⌐£29-£35 dB&B£34-£40 dB&B⌐£39-£47
⊞ CTV 2P 2⌂
Credit Cards [1] [2] [3] ⓔ

▣ is for quality. For a full explanation of this AA quality award, consult the Contents page.

See gazetteer under Hinckley

HITCHAM Suffolk Map **05** TL95

FH Mrs B Elsden **Wetherden Hall** *(TL971509)* IP7 7PZ Bildeston(0449) 740412
Feb-Nov
Situated on the outskirts of the village towards Kettlebaston, this attractive traditional farmhouse is set on a working farm and offers comfortable, very clean and modest accommodation. A large flock of mixed geese occupy the immediate grounds.
2rm (1fb) sB&B£15-£16 dB&B£27-£29 WB&Bfr£75
CTV 6P nc9yrs 300 acres mixed £

HITCHIN Hertfordshire Map **04** TL12

GH **Firs Hotel** 83 Bedford Rd SG5 2TY (0462) 422322 FAX (0462) 432051
rs 25 Dec-2 Jan
Originally a manor house, this pleasant family run hotel is situated on the A600 close to the town centre. The varied accommodation includes modern bedroom extensions, and although some of the ground floor rooms are compact; they are all well equipped and most have private barthrooms. Public areas include an attractive bar lounge and an Italian restaurant with an à la carte menu offering an interesting choice of dishes. Extensive car parking is available at the rear.
30rm(24 6hc) (2fb) CTV in all bedrooms ® T * sB&B£31-£49 sB&B £37-£49 dB&B£47 dB&B £54-£61
LDO 9.30pm
Lic CTV 30P
Credit Cards 1 2 3 5 £

HOARWITHY Hereford & Worcester Map **03** SO52

FH Mrs C Probert ***The Old Mill*** *(SO546294)* HR2 6QH Carey(043270) 602
This small, attractive, white-painted farmhouse set in the middle of the village is some 250 years old and contains a wealth of original beams and wall timbers. Bedrooms are pretty and well decorated and the comfortable residents' lounge has a log burning stove.
6hc in 1 bedroom LDO 7pm
CTV 6P

HOLBEACH Lincolnshire Map **09** TF32

GH **Pipwell Manor** Washway Rd, Saracens Head PE12 8AL (0406) 23119
This period farmhouse is set amid arable farmland eastwards from the A17 at Saracens Head, on the left and just around the bend. Lesley Honnor greets her guests warmly, and invites each of them on arrival to tea and cake in the lounge – a sunny room furnished with highly polished tables and book-lined walls surrounding the pine mantle and leaded fireplace. The dining room is dominated by a central oak table, and original Georgian panelling is accentuated by candy stripe wallpaper, while greenery and dried flower arrangements in huge baskets add further appeal. The bedrooms, 2 of which are really roomy, all have an armchair or sofa; the soft furnishings and décor are totally coordinated and quite lavish in either Laura Ashley or Sanderson fabrics. The house is immaculate and lovely to look at but, more important, very comfortable and welcoming.
4rm(1hc) in all bedrooms ® * sB&B£17 sB&B£19 dB&B£34 dB&B£36
CTV 4P £

HOLLYBUSH Strathclyde *Ayrshire* Map **10** NS31

FH Mrs A Woodburn **Boreland** *(NS400139)* KA6 7ED Patna(0292) 531228
Jun-Sep
This farmhouse is just off the main road south of the village amid fine open farmland. The bedrooms are spacious and served by a modern bathroom, and there is a comfortable lounge.
3rm (2fb) ® * sB&B£15 dB&B£26-£28
CTV 6P 190 acres dairy

HOLMFIRTH West Yorkshire Map **07** SE10

INN **White Horse** Scholes Road, Jackson Bridge HD7 7HF (0484) 683940
Closed 24-25 Dec & 31 Jan
This typical Yorkshire pub is featured in the television programme 'The Last Of The Summer Wine', and offers a characteristic Yorkshire welcome and atmosphere. It is located two miles from Holmfirth, just off the A616 at Jackson Bridge. Bedrooms are well equipped, and there is a good range of bar meals.
5 (3fb) CTV in all bedrooms ® (ex guide dogs) sB&B £23-£25 dB&B £40 Lunch £2.35-£6alc Dinner £2.35-£6alc LDO 9.30pm
12P 2 £

HOLNE Devon Map **03** SX76

SELECTED

FH Mrs S Townsend **Wellpritton** *(SX716704)* TQ13 7RX Poundsgate(03643) 273
Closed 25-26 Dec
This peacefully situated Devonshire longhouse on the edge of Dartmoor is conveniently located for the south coast of Devon and the National Park. Sue and Jim Townsend provide a warm welcome, and the atmosphere they have created in their well maintained farmhouse is relaxing and friendly. Bedrooms have been tastefully decorated and furnished, with many thoughtful extras provided, such as fruit juices, biscuits and tea and coffee trays; most rooms have private bathrooms. There is a cosy TV lounge, and home-cooked, traditional farmhouse meals are served in the dining room.
4rm(1 2 1hc) (2fb) in all bedrooms ® (ex guide dogs) * sB&B£16-£17 sB&B £16-£17 dB&B£32-£34 dB&B £32-£34 WB&B£105 WBDi£140 LDO 4pm
CTV 6P games room snooker table-tennis skittles 15 acres mixed £

HOLSWORTHY Devon Map **02** SS30

GH **Coles Mill** EX22 6LX (0409) 253313
Mar-mid Oct
An attractive stone-built 18th-century mill with an adjoining accommodation wing, situated on the edge of town, giving easy access to the north coasts of both Devon and Cornwall. The 5 well equipped bedrooms are spotless, and offer en suite showers, TV and tea making facilities. The lounge and dining room still retain some original features, and home cooked meals are served by the resident proprietors.
5 TV in all bedrooms ® (ex guide dogs) sB&B £18-£21 dB&B £31-£34 WB&B£99-£110
Lic CTV 12P nc6yrs

FH Mr & Mrs E Cornish **Leworthy** *(SS323012)* EX22 6SJ (0409) 253488
A friendly family farmhouse set in an attractive large garden facing south, giving good views over the countryside. Bedrooms are simply styled, there is a rustic bar and lounge and a bright dining room.
10rm(3 7hc) (5fb) ® (ex guide dogs) * sB&B£15-£18 dB&B£30-£36 dB&B £34-£40 WBDi£165-£186 LDO 6pm
Lic CTV 20P 2 (hard) badminton skittles archery shooting pitch & putt 235 acres mixed £

HOLT Norfolk Map **09** TG03

GH **Lawns Private Hotel** Station Rd NR25 6BS (0263) 713390
This delightful red brick former farmhouse is just minutes from the town centre. Mr and Mrs Tuck, the proprietors, are a gregarious couple whose desire to excel has resulted in constant improvement and investment. Now operating as a hotel, there is an elegant

dining room with linen clothed tables, and a small well stocked bar leading off. The large, sunny lounge has deep armchairs and sofas and polished mahogany tables. No 2 bedrooms are alike, some are truly huge, and there is a penchant for Laura Ashley papers, fabrics and tiles. All the rooms are cheerful and stylish, with good dressing tables and occasional tables. Facilities include TV, telephones and tea- making facilities.

11⇌↱ (2fb)⚟in all bedrooms CTV in all bedrooms ® **T** sB&B⇌↱fr£35 dB&B⇌↱fr£58 WB&B£185-£245 WBDi£295-£310 LDO 8.30pm

Lic 🍴 12P

Credit Cards [1] [2] [3] [5] £

HOLYHEAD

See **ANGLESEY, ISLE OF**

HOLYWELL Clwyd Map **07** SJ17

See also Babell

[🛏] FH QQQ Mrs M D Jones **Green Hill** *(SJ186776)* CH8 7QF ☎(0352) 713270

Mar-Nov

Situated on a 120-acre mixed and dairy farm on the outskirts of town, this farmhouse has excellent views across the Dee Estuary to the Wirral. Parts of this charming old house date back to the late 15th century and it has a wealth of character, which is enhanced by exposed wall and ceiling timbers.

3rm(1⇌2hc) (1fb) ® ✗ sB&Bfr£14 dB&Bfr£28 dB&B⇌fr£32 LDO 9am

CTV 6P ♧ snooker table childrens play area 120 acres dairy mixed £

HONITON Devon Map **03** ST10

See also Payhembury

FH QQ Mrs I J Underdown ***Roebuck*** *(ST147001)* EX14 0PB (western end of Honiton-by-pass) ☎(0404) 42225

Comfortable accommodation is provided in this farmhouse situated in a dominent position at the western end of the Honiton bypass. Bed and breakfast only is provided in a warm atmosphere. Tea-making facilities and colour TV are available in bedrooms on request.

4rm(3hc) (1fb) CTV in 1 bedroom ®

🍴 CTV P 180 acres dairy mixed

INN QQQ The Heathfield Walnut Rd EX14 8UG ☎(0404) 45321 & 45322

This beautifully restored thatched 16th-century longhouse is approached through a modern housing estate. There are spacious lounge bar areas where an interesting selection of bar meals is offered from a blackboard menu, and a separate à la carte restaurant featuring local specialities. Bedrooms are large and particularly well equipped, including the bridal suite with its locally hand-crafted pine 4-poster bed.

5⇌↱ CTV in all bedrooms ® **T** ✗ (ex guide dogs) ✱ sB&B⇌↱£29.38 dB&B⇌↱£41.13 LDO 10pm

🍴 50P nc14yrs pool table skittle alley

Credit Cards [1] [2] [3]

INN QQQ Monkton Court Monkton EX14 9QH (2m E A30) ☎(0404) 42309

This characterful roadside inn has seen quite a transformation since its change of ownership. The Taylors have furnished and equipped the property well with bright modern-styled bedrooms, complete with en suite facilities. The cosy bar and restaurant offer a good range of wholesome food. The Monkton Court Inn is a friendly, personally run establishment conveniently situated adjacent to the A30.

8rm(2⇌4↱2hc) (1fb) CTV in all bedrooms ® **T** ✗ (ex guide dogs) sB&B£23.40-£26 sB&B⇌↱£32.40-£36 dB&B£33.50-£39.50 dB&B⇌↱£42.15-£49.50 WB&B£163.80-£252 WBDi£245-£336 Lunch £7-£12.65alc Dinner £12.95&alc LDO 9.30pm

🍴 100P

Credit Cards [1] [3] £

HOOK Hampshire Map **04** SU75

GH QQ Cedar Court Country Reading Rd RG27 9DB ☎Basingstoke(0256) 762178

To find this guesthouse follow the Hook bypass and pick up the Reading road. Cedar Court lies well away from the main road, and its 6 ground floor bedrooms are in a wing set in a peaceful garden. Shower room facilities are at the end of the corridor, near a residents' lounge with TV, comfortable sofas and an aquarium.

6hc (1fb) CTV in 1 bedroom ® ✗ (ex guide dogs) sB&B£17-£21 dB&B£28-£35

🍴 CTV 6P £

GH QQ Cherry Lodge Reading Rd RG27 9DB ☎Basingstoke(0256) 762532

Closed Xmas

Cherry Lodge is a small, extended bungalow on the northern edge of the village. Being completely family run and lacking any pretentions, it has become a home from home for travelling business people. The modern bedrooms all have en suite facilities and direct dial telephones. There is a comfortable TV lounge with deep armchairs and a simple conservatory-type dining room where the set 2-course dinner is of the hearty British 'meat and 2 veg' variety.

6⇌↱ (1fb) ® ✱ sB&B⇌↱£22.50-£25 dB&B⇌↱£32.50-£35 LDO 3pm

🍴 CTV 10P

Credit Cards [1] [2] [3] [5]

GH QQ Oaklea London Rd RG27 9LA ☎(0256) 762673 FAX (0256) 762150

A family-run detached Victorian house with a delightful large walled garden. Bedrooms vary in size and are modestly appointed but they are all spick and span. The rooms with private bathrooms →

also provide a TV and tea-making facilities. Downstairs is a licensed bar area, and a cheerful TV lounge. To find the guesthouse, take the Basingstoke road from the centre of Hook, and Oaklea is located shortly on the right.
10rm(4↱6hc) (1fb)⊬in 4 bedrooms CTV in 5 bedrooms ®
sB&B£23.50 sB&B↱£37 dB&B£33 dB&B↱£41-£48
WB&B£152-£240 LDO noon
Lic CTV 11P ⌂ Ⓔ

HOPTON Derbyshire Map **08** SK25

GH QQQ Henmore Grange DE4 4DF
☎Carsington(062985) 420
Standing in a natural butterfly garden of 2.5 acres, this charming house has been fully extended and now incorporates a popular restaurant serving English fruit wines and afternoon cream teas.
14rm(12⇌↱2hc) (2fb) ® sB&B£20-£31 sB&B⇌↱£31
dB&B£36-£55 dB&B⇌↱£36-£55 WB&B£196 WBDi£259-£287 LDO 6pm
Lic 🍽 CTV 14P
Credit Cards [2] Ⓔ

HORLEY Surrey For accommodation details see under **Gatwick Airport, London**

HORNCHURCH Greater London Map **05** TQ58

INN QQ The Railway Hotel Station Ln RM12 6SB
☎(0708) 476415 FAX (0708) 437315
This gabled, Tudor-style pub stands adjacent to the railway station near the town centre of Hornchurch. Life downstairs revolves around the popular bars, one of which offers snacks. Upstairs are the good sized, comfortable bedrooms which are smartly decorated with dark wood furniture and have modern facilities with private bathrooms.
11⇌↱ CTV in all bedrooms ® ✗ (ex guide dogs) ✱
sB&B⇌↱£30-£45 dB&B⇌↱£40-£65 Bar Lunch £2.75-£3.50alc Dinner £2.75-£9alc LDO 9pm
🍽 60P
Credit Cards [1] [2] [3] [5]

HORSFORD Norfolk Map **09** TG11

GH QQQ Church Farm Church St NR10 3DB
☎Norwich(0603) 898020 & 898582
A family-run establishment just off the A140 north of Norwich, in a quiet rural location. Church Farm offers a warm welcome and clean, well equipped accommodation.
6↱ (3fb) CTV in all bedrooms ® ✗ (ex guide dogs) ✱
sB&B↱£17-£20 dB&B↱£32-£36 WB&B£84-£105
🍽 CTV 20P Ⓔ

HORSHAM West Sussex Map **04** TQ13

GH QQQ *Blatchford House* 52 Kings Rd RH13 5PR
☎(0403) 65317
Closed Xmas
An impressive Grade II listed Georgian house situated near the station and within a short drive of Gatwick. The modern bedrooms are all freshly decorated and comfortable; most are en suite, with direct dial telephones and cable TV. An attractive new conservatory now provides the dining room, with set dinners available, and guests have their own spacious lounge. Friendly hosts Mr and Mrs Pedder also run a toning salon in the basement making this a popular choice for business guests and tourists alike.
11↱ CTV in all bedrooms ®
🍽 14P
Credit Cards [1] [3]

See the regional maps of popular holiday areas at the back of the book.

HORSHAM ST FAITH Norfolk Map **09** TG21

GH QQQ Elm Farm Chalet Hotel Norwich Rd NR10 3HH
☎Norwich(0603) 898366 FAX (0603) 897129
rs 25-26 Dec
A former farmhouse in the centre of the village, just off the A140 north of Norwich, with a pleasant restaurant and good accommodation in the 2 adjacent barns.
Annexe 18rm(16⇌↱) (2fb)⊬in 10 bedrooms CTV in all bedrooms ® **T** ✗ (ex guide dogs) sB&B⇌↱£29.50-£35
dB&Bfr£45 dB&B⇌↱£52 WB&B£199.50-£245
WBDi£269.50-£315 LDO 6.30pm
Lic 🍽 CTV 20P
Credit Cards [1] [2] [3] Ⓔ

HORTON Dorset Map **04** SU00

SELECTED

GH QQQQ Northill House BH21 7HL
☎Witchampton(0258) 840407
Closed 20 Dec-mid Feb
This handsome property, built in 1858 and originally part of Lord Shaftesbury's estate, is now owned and personally run by the welcoming Garnsworthy family. Bedrooms are pretty and very well equipped, with thoughtful extras such as shortbread and fresh milk on the tea tray, and hot water bottles. Some are located in the annexe and one of these is well equipped for disabled guests. Public areas are comfortable and have a warm, relaxed atmosphere. A set evening meal is served in the airy dining room, which has a conservatory extension overlooking the pretty gardens.
9rm(7⇌2↱) (1fb) CTV in all bedrooms ® **T**
✗ (ex guide dogs) sB&B⇌↱£35 dB&B⇌↱£60
WB&B£189-£220.50 WBDi£267.75-£299.25 LDO 7pm
Lic 🍽 9P nc8yrs
Credit Cards [1] [2] [3]
See advertisement under WIMBORNE MINSTER

INN QQQ *Horton* Cranborne Rd BH21 5AD
☎Witchampton(0258) 840252
A large, detached 17th-century inn on hilltop crossroads with sweeping views of open farmland. Bedrooms are spacious and well proportioned, comfortable and well equipped. The restaurant serves à la carte food, and informal meals are available in the bar, which has an open fire.
5rm(2⇌3hc) ⊬in 1 bedroom CTV in all bedrooms ®
✗ (ex guide dogs) LDO 10pm
🍽 100P
Credit Cards [1] [3]

HORTON-CUM-STUDLEY Oxfordshire Map **04** SP51

FH QQQ Mrs J R Hicks **Studley** *(SP615126)* Arncott Rd OX33 1BP ☎Stanton St John (086735) 286 due to change to (0865) 351286 FAX (086735) 631 due to change to (0865) 351631
This smart farmhouse is ideally situated for people preferring a rural setting, but needing access to major routes and the town centre. It is signposted Horton-cum-Studley 4.5 miles on the Headington roundabout, on the Oxford ring road, and is seven miles from the M40. Bedrooms are pretty and comfortable, with en suite facilities planned, if not already installed. The proprietors are keen to provide a good service, and offer guests a warm welcome; smoking is not permitted.
3rm(2⇌↱) ⊬in all bedrooms CTV in 2 bedrooms ✗
sB&B£22-£25 sB&B⇌↱£30-£35 dB&B£38-£40
dB&B⇌↱£40-£45
🍽 CTV 6P nc12yrs 50 acres arable
Credit Cards [1] [3]

HORTON IN RIBBLESDALE North Yorkshire Map **07** SD87

INN QQ Crown Hotel BD24 0HF ☎(0729) 860209

Situated in the beautiful Ribble Valley, the Crown is noted for its traditional Dales hospitality. It provides comfortable accommodation in double, single or family size rooms, some with en suite facilities. There is a good selection of bar and restaurant meals, a garden and childrens' play area at the back, and 2 cosy residents' lounges as well as the beamed bars.

10rm(2↱3hc) (4fb) ® LDO 6.30pm

CTV 15P

HOUNSLOW Greater London London plan **4** B3 (pages 248-249)

GH QQ Shalimar Hotel 215-221 Staines Rd TW3 3JJ ☎081-577 7070 & 081-572 2816 FAX 081-569 6789

The Shalimar provides useful accommodation, with simply decorated bedrooms on several floors, some overlooking the main road, others the garden. Residents have a smart bar/lounge downstairs which features interesting pictures of Indian rugs.

31rm(22↱9hc) (7fb) CTV in all bedrooms ® **T** sB&Bfr£34 sB&B↱fr£38 dB&Bfr£44 dB&B↱fr£48 LDO noon

Lic CTV 8P

Credit Cards 1 2 3 5 £

HOUSESTEADS Northumberland Map **12** NY87

GH QQQ Beggar Bog NE47 6NN ☎Haydon Bridge(0434) 344320

The public rooms of this tastefully converted farmhouse, are a real delight. There is a small conservatory looking out onto the gardens, an upstairs lounge with lofted ceiling, parquet floor and open fire, and a beamed dining room, where guests eat around one large table and which features a large vaulted stone fireplace. There are 2 modern bedrooms on the ground floor, and one more traditionally furnished upstairs. Hadrian's Wall and the Roman fort of Housteads are near by, and there are uninterrupted views of the moorlands in every direction.

3hc (1fb) sB&B£16-£22 dB&B£32 LDO 3pm

CTV 6P £

HOVE East Sussex

See **Brighton & Hove**

HUBY North Yorkshire Map **08** SE56

GH QQ The New Inn Motel Main St YO6 1HQ ☎Easingwold(0347) 810219

This modern brick built motel offering chalet style accommodation with functional bedrooms, is situated behind an inn of the same name (but not connected), in the main street of this small Yorkshire village. There is a small breakfast room, and convenient parking is available outside the chalets.

8↱ (2fb) CTV in all bedrooms ® ✱ sB&B↱£20-£25 dB&B↱£30-£36 WB&B£105-£120 WBDi£147-£175 LDO 4pm

Lic CTV 15P £

HUCKNALL Nottinghamshire Map **08** SK54

INN QQ Station Hotel Station Rd NG15 7TQ ☎(0602) 632588

This large, early Victorian public house is situated approximately a quarter of a mile from the high street. It has been considerably modernised and restored to provide pleasant bar facilities and spacious bedrooms, all with central heating and colour TV.

6hc (2fb) CTV in all bedrooms ® (ex guide dogs) ✱ sB&B£25 dB&B£40 Lunch £1.95-£5 High tea £3-£8alc Dinner £6.95&alc LDO 9.30pm

20P

Credit Cards 1 3 £

HUDDERSFIELD West Yorkshire Map **07** SE11

GH QQ Elm Crest 2 Queens Rd, Edgerton HD2 2AG ☎(0484) 530990 FAX (0484) 516227

This stone-built house has a friendly atmosphere and a no smoking rule. It is well signed off the A629 leading to Huddersfield, when using junction 24 off the M62, and there is a floodlit car park to the side and an attractive rose garden at the front.

8rm(5↱3hc) (2fb)in all bedrooms CTV in all bedrooms ® **T** sB&B£22-£24 sB&B↱£32-£34 dB&B£42-£44 dB&B↱£57-£60 WB&Bfr£300 WBDifr£360 LDO 7pm

Lic CTV 12P nc5yrs

Credit Cards 1 2 3 £

HULL Humberside Map **08** TA02

GH QQ Earlesmere Hotel 76/78 Sunny Bank, Spring Bank West HU3 1LQ ☎(0482) 41977 Telex no 592729 FAX (0482) 473714

Closed Xmas rs wknds

This small, privately owned hotel is a mile northwest of the city centre, just off Spring Bank West. It provides sound, well maintained accommodation and is popular with commercial guests.

15rm(7↱8hc) (4fb) CTV in all bedrooms ® ✱ sB&B£18.80-£21.15 sB&B↱£27.02 dB&B↱£41.12-£47 WB&Bfr£131.60 WBDifr£230 LDO 6pm

Lic CTV

Credit Cards 1 3 £

HUNGERFORD Berkshire Map **04** SU36

GH QQQ Marshgate Cottage Hotel Marsh Ln RG17 0QX ☎(0488) 682307 FAX (0488) 685475

Closed 25 Dec-17 Jan

Tucked away down a country lane beside the canal, yet less than a mile from the town centre, a barn conversion attached to this 17th-century thatched house provides cosy bedrooms and public areas full of character. A host of thoughtful extras add to guests' comfort, and the resident proprietors like their guests to relax and enjoy the informal, friendly atmosphere.

9rm(1⇌6↱2hc) (2fb)in 3 bedrooms CTV in all bedrooms ® **T** (ex guide dogs) sB&Bfr£25.50 sB&B⇌↱fr£35.50 dB&Bfr£39.50 dB&B⇌↱fr£48.50 LDO 7.30pm

Lic 7P 2 nc5yrs bike hire

Credit Cards 1 2 3 £

HUNSTANTON Norfolk Map **09** TF64

GH QQQ Claremont 35 Greevegate PE36 6AF ☎(0485) 533171

A detached house a few minutes walk from both shops and seafront. The guesthouse has been totally refurbished with thought and care. Each bedroom is individually decorated in a pretty cottage style, and some rooms are larger and furnished with armchairs or sofas; en suite facilities are good and well maintained. Public rooms include a cheerful dining room, separate lounge and a small bar.

7rm(4⇌3↱) (1fb)in all bedrooms CTV in all bedrooms ® ✱ sB&B⇌↱fr£21 dB&B⇌↱£34-£42 WB&B£112-£140 WBDi£163-£191 LDO 6pm

Lic CTV 3P nc5yrs

Credit Cards 1 3

GH QQQ Pinewood Hotel 26 Northgate PE36 6AP ☎(0485) 533068

Closed Xmas

Popular with commercial and leisure users, the Pinewood offers well furnished accommodation and a relaxed, informal atmosphere. The restaurant uses fresh ingredients with a simple à la carte menu, supplemented by specials of the day.

→

8rm(4⬚4hc) (4fb)⬚in 2 bedrooms CTV in all bedrooms ® sB&B£14.50-£33 sB&B⬚£18.50-£37 dB&B£29-£35 dB&B⬚£33-£40 WB&B£95-£120 WBDi£155-£180 LDO 8.30pm
Lic ⬚ 6P
Credit Cards 1 2 3 £

GH QQQ Sutton House Hotel 24 Northgate PE36 6AP
☎(0485) 532552
Closed 6-31 Jan
A large, stone-built house in an elevated, peaceful location, with fine sea views from most of the bedrooms and the first floor lounge. Most bedrooms have private bathrooms, and there is a variety of dishes on the well chosen menu.
7rm(5⬚⬚2hc) (2fb) CTV in all bedrooms ® sB&B£20-£25 sB&B⬚⬚£20-£30 dB&B£36-£42 dB&B⬚⬚£39-£48 WB&B£125-£170 WBDi£180-£240 LDO 7.30pm
Lic ⬚ CTV 5P
Credit Cards 1 3 £

HUNTLY Grampian *Aberdeenshire* Map **15** NJ53

GH QQQ Dunedin 17 Bogie St AB54 5DX ☎(0466) 794162
This comfortable tourist and commercial guesthouse is in the East End, just a few minutes' walk from the main shopping area and central amenities. Bedrooms, all with en suite facilities, are furnished in a modern style. There is a cosy lounge and an attractive breakfast room where, on occasions, it may be necessary to share a table with other residents.
6⬚ (1fb)⬚in all bedrooms CTV in all bedrooms ® ⬚
sB&B⬚fr£21.25 dB&B⬚fr£33
⬚ CTV 8P

HUNTON North Yorkshire Map **07** SE19

INN QQQ The Countryman's DL8 1PY
☎Bedale(0677) 50554
This delightful mellow stone built inn is situated in the small village of Hunton, just north of the A684 between Bedale and Leyburn. The bars are full of character, with beamed ceilings, open fires and stone walls. There is a separate dining room which displays a collection of unusual china teapots, and paintings for sale. Residents also have the use of a comfortable lounge away from the bar areas. Bedrooms are particularly well appointed with modern furniture and attractive papered walls, and one room has a 4-poster bed.
6⬚⬚ ⬚in all bedrooms CTV in all bedrooms ® ⬚
sB&B⬚⬚fr£25 dB&B⬚⬚£40-£40 Lunch £6-£9.50alc Dinner £7-£15alc LDO 9.30pm
⬚ 20P nc14yrs pool table
Credit Cards 1 3

HURSLEY Hampshire Map **04** SU42

INN Q *Kings Head Hotel* SO21 2JW ☎Winchester(0962) 75208
Closed 25 Dec
This large and popular pub stands in the centre of the busy, attractive village of Hursley and offers simply furnished first floor bedrooms.
5hc (1fb) ® ⬚ (ex guide dogs) LDO 9.30pm
⬚ CTV 30P nc1yr
Credit Cards 1 3

HUTTON-LE-HOLE North Yorkshire Map **08** SE79

GH QQ The Barn Hotel & Tearooms YO6 6UA
☎Lastingham(07515) 311
Feb-Nov
This attractive stone-built guesthouse and tea room was, as its name suggest, once a barn and with its pretty inner courtyard and rough stone walls, is well known to tourists from all over the world. It is at the centre of the village in which sheep roam at will, on the edge of the North Yorkshire Moors. Bedrooms are mostly compact each individually and attractively decorated with modern features. The guests lounge is warm and relaxing with an open fire in winter. Meals are served in an attractive dining area separated from the tea rooms. A private car park at the rear leads to the guests' entrance and reception.
8rm(3⬚⬚5hc) ⬚in all bedrooms ® ⬚ (ex guide dogs) ✱ sB&B£18 dB&B£36 dB&B⬚⬚£44 LDO 10am
Lic ⬚ CTV 15P
Credit Cards 1 3 £

HYDE Greater Manchester Map **07** SJ99

FH QQQ Mr & Mrs I Walsh **Needhams** *(SJ968925)* Uplands Rd, Werneth Low, Gee Cross SK14 3AQ
☎061-368 4610 FAX 061-367 9106
This 16th-century farmhouse is at the end of a long rough farm track (Uplands Road) off the Werneth Low road. It is surrounded by open countryside, yet is within reach of Manchester and the airport, to which a courtesy service is available. Bedrooms are fairly compact but equipped with modern facilities. The cosy, beamed dining room has a small bar and is the setting for home-made meals featuring fresh produce.
6rm(5⬚1hc) (1fb) CTV in all bedrooms ® **T** ✱ sB&B£18-£21 sB&B⬚£20-£22 dB&B£32-£34 dB&B⬚£34-£38 LDO 9.30pm
Lic ⬚ CTV 12P 2⬚ ⬚9 ⬚ 30 acres beef
Credit Cards 1 3 £

HYTHE Kent Map **05** TR13

GH QQ The White House 27 Napier Gardens CT21 6DD
☎(0303) 266252
Only 2 and a half minutes walk from the sea, this comfortable family-run guesthouse is situated overlooking the cricket club. The bedrooms are individually furnished in mixed styles, and a top floor lounge provides a quiet retreat. Proprietor Margaret Kennett cooks the breakfast and personally provides friendly service. With Folkestone close by and access to Hythe sea fishing, there's plenty to do on a holiday break.
3hc (1fb)⬚in 2 bedrooms CTV in all bedrooms ®
⬚ (ex guide dogs) ✱ sB&B£18-£20 dB&B£32-£34 WB&Bfr£95
⬚ CTV 4P

ILFORD Greater London London plan **4** F4 (pages 248-249)

GH QQ *Cranbrook Hotel* 24 Coventry Rd IG1 4QR
☎081-554 6544 & 4765 FAX 081-518 1463
Conveniently situated a few minutes from the town centre, this hotel has bedrooms on 3 floors: simply furnished, they are well maintained and equipped, in varying sizes. The combined dining room and bar has a pool table.
16rm(13⬚3hc) (7fb) CTV in all bedrooms ® LDO 7.30pm
Lic ⬚ CTV 11P 2⬚
Credit Cards 1 2 3
See advertisement under LONDON

GH QQ Park Hotel 327 Cranbrook Rd IG1 4UE
☎081-554 9616 & 7187 FAX 081-518 2700
The Park Hotel is a converted detached house on a main road in a residential area. Bedrooms are on the ground and first floors and come in a variety of sizes and styles. This year has seen the introduction of more en suite facilities and further bedroom redecoration.
20rm(8⬚8⬚4hc) (3fb) CTV in all bedrooms ® ✱ sB&B£30 sB&B⬚⬚£37.50 dB&B£38 dB&B⬚⬚£46.50 LDO 8pm
Lic ⬚ CTV 23P
Credit Cards 1 3

Every effort is made to provide accurate information, but details can change after we go to print. It is advisable to check prices etc. before you make a firm booking.

ILFRACOMBE Devon Map **02** SS54

See **Town Plan Section**
See also West Down

GH QQ **Cavendish Hotel** 9-10 Larkstone Ter EX34 9NU
☎(0271) 863994
Etr-Oct
The Cavendish provides splendid views of the picturesque harbour and St Nicholas chapel from the public rooms and many of the bedrooms. Rooms are spacious, well decorated and very clean. Sensible, plain English food is served in the dining room and there is a well stocked bar, TV lounge and games room. This family hotel enjoys an elevated position with panoramic views. The bedrooms are comfortable and the service friendly.
23rm(15⬆8hc) (5fb) CTV in all bedrooms ® ✱ sB&B£19-£21.50 dB&B£28-£33 dB&B⬆£38-£43 WB&B£90-£135 WBDi£115-£160 LDO 5pm
Lic CTV 20P snooker
Credit Cards 1 3

GH Q ***Chalfont Private Hotel*** 21 Church Rd EX34 8BZ
☎(0271) 862224
Feb-Nov rs Dec-Jan
Sid and Lynda Fisk provide a warm welcome at Chalfont, their Victorian home. The bedrooms are well decorated and most have modern en suite showers and WCs. Public rooms comprise a small bar, a comfortable lounge and a well furnished dining room.
8rm(6⬆2hc) (2fb) ® LDO 4pm
Lic 🍽 CTV ₱
Credit Cards 1 3

GH QQ **Collingdale Hotel** Larkstone Ter EX34 9NU
☎(0271) 863770
Mar-Oct
A Victorian terrace house perched high above the town with fine views of the sea and harbour. Bedrooms are spacious, plainly decorated and very clean. There is a small bar full of cricketing memorabilia and a more comfortable TV lounge.
9rm(3⬆6hc) (6fb) ® ✗ sB&B£15-£18 sB&B⬆£16.50-£19.50 dB&B£30 dB&B⬆£33-£38 WB&B£100-£105 WBDi£125-£140 LDO 5.30pm
Lic CTV ₱
Credit Cards 1 3 £

GH QQ ***Cresta Private Hotel*** Torrs Park EX34 8AY
☎(0271) 863742
mid May-Sep
A large detached Victorian house with its own garden, orchard and ample parking, a fairly level walk from the harbour and sea. Bedrooms are freshly decorated and many have modern en suite showers. The lounge retains some original features and the bar has a dance floor where entertainment is provided 3 times a week.
24rm(15⬆9hc) (10fb) TV available ® LDO 6.30pm
Lic lift 🍽 CTV 30P putting green
Credit Cards 1

GH QQ **Dedes Hotel** 1-3 The Promenade EX34 9BD
☎(0271) 862545
Closed 23-26 Dec
Dedes is in a convenient central location opposite the beach, and many of the rooms have lovely sea views. An extensive range of catering includes an informal café serving fast food, with a carvery at night, plus a more formal restaurant serving steak and lobster. There is also a small first-floor lounge and a busy public bar. Bedrooms tend to be small but are generally well decorated with quality modern beds. The hotel specialises in clay shooting holidays.
17rm(10⇌2⬆5hc) (6fb) CTV in all bedrooms ® LDO 9.45pm
Lic CTV 6P
Credit Cards 1 2 3 5 £

GH Q **Lympstone Private Hotel** Cross Park EX34 8BJ
☎(0271) 863038
Mar-Oct rs Mar-May
The resident proprietors of this well established guesthouse provide a friendly welcome and individually designed bedrooms that are comfortably old-fashioned in style, as is the guests' lounge. A pleasant dining room offers bright and cheerful surroundings.
15rm(9⬆6hc) (4fb) CTV in all bedrooms ® ✱ sB&B£13-£15 sB&B⬆£15-£17 dB&B£26-£30 dB&B⬆£30-£34 WB&B£84-£98
Lic CTV 10P £

GH QQQ **Merlin Court Hotel** Torrs Park EX34 8AY
☎(0271) 862697
Peacefully situated in its own terraced gardens, this handsome property was built as a coastal retreat in the early 1800s. The house has been carefully modernised to retain its original atmosphere and provides well furnished bedrooms, a comfortable lounge and an attractive restaurant. There is also a skittle alley for guests' use.
14rm(2⇌9⬆3hc) (5fb) CTV in all bedrooms ®
✗ (ex guide dogs) sB&B£18-£22 sB&B⇌⬆£20-£24 dB&B£36-£44 dB&B⇌⬆£40-£48 WB&B£126-£168 WBDi£160-£185 LDO 5pm
Lic 🍽 14P skittle alley
Credit Cards 1 3 £

GH QQ **Southcliffe Hotel** Torrs Park EX34 8AZ
☎(0271) 862958
Spring BH-17 Sep rs Mar-Apr
A small family-run hotel within walking distance of the harbour, beaches and town centre. Bedrooms have coordinating soft furnishings, and there is a comfortable TV lounge and bar. A choice of hot dishes is offered in the dining room, and there is a games room for children.

→

13↱ (8fb) ® ✗ sB&B↱£23-£25.85 dB&B↱£46-£51.70 (incl dinner) WBDi£161-£169.20 LDO 6pm
Lic CTV 12P ⌂ games room childrens play area & room £

GH QQ Strathmore Private Hotel 57 St Brannocks Rd EX34 8EQ ☎(0271) 862248

A brick-built Victorian semidetached house on the St Brannocks road, within a short walk of the town centre, harbour and beaches. Bedrooms are well equipped and furnished, most with en suite facilities. There is a comfortable lounge and a cosy bar, and a choice of home-cooked fare is available in the bright dining room; snacks and hot drinks are also available throughout the evening. Limited car parking is provided on site.

9rm(2⇌6↱1hc) (2fb) CTV in all bedrooms ® sB&B£15-£18 sB&B⇌↱£17-£19 dB&B£30-£36 dB&B⇌↱£34-£38 WB&B£98-£106 WBDi£143-£166 LDO 5pm
Lic 🍴 7P
Credit Cards 1 2 3 5 £

SELECTED

GH QQQQ Varley House 13 Chambercombe Ter, Chambercombe Park EX34 9QW ☎(0271) 863927
mid Mar-Oct

Quietly located in a residential area close to the swimming pool, this well managed establishment provides a very warm welcome from resident proprietors Roy and Barbara Gables. The comfortable bedrooms are individually designed, and there is an inviting lounge and small adjoining cocktail bar. Barbara's home-cooked 5-course dinner is especially recommended; guests are given a choice of menu and the decision isn't easy, as all the dishes are imaginative and interesting. Varley House offers outstanding value for money.

9rm(8⇌↱1hc) (3fb) CTV in all bedrooms ® sB&B£17-£18 dB&B⇌↱£37-£42 WBDi£165-£185 LDO 5.30pm
Lic 🍴 CTV 7P nc5yrs
Credit Cards 1 3 £

GH QQQ Westwell Hall Hotel Torrs Park EX34 8AZ ☎(0271) 862792

An early Victorian property prominently set in its own gardens high above the town and harbour, commanding lovely views. The spacious bedrooms, all of which have en suite facilities, are comfortable, brightly decorated and simply furnished, with TV and tea making facilities; one room has a Victorian 4- poster bed. The bar and lounge are on the lower ground floor, and imaginative home-cooked meals are served in the attractive dining room. A games room is provided for children, who are made very welcome, and meals are served on the patio on sunny days. There is ample car parking provided in the grounds.

9⇌↱ (1fb) CTV in all bedrooms ® sB&B⇌↱£20 dB&B⇌↱£40 WB&B£140 WBDi£196 LDO 7pm
Lic 🍴 14P snooker croquet table tennis
Credit Cards 1 3 £

INGLEBY GREENHOW North Yorkshire Map 08 NZ50

FH QQQ Mrs M Bloom **Manor House** *(NZ586056)* TS9 6RB ☎Great Ayton(0642) 722384
Closed 21-29 Dec

Standing at the foot of the Cleveland Hills, this is an 18th-century farmhouse built of Yorkshire stone, offering spacious and comfortable accommodation. Bedrooms are full of character, with interior stonework and wooden beams as well as every modern comfort. There is an attractive dining room, and a cosy lounge with a wood-burning stove and a view of the lawns and the woodland where wildlife includes rabbits, partridges, pheasants, wild ducks and the occasional deer. To find the house, take the B1257 Stokesley – Helmsley road, turning east at the Great Broughton crossroads, and continuing for 2.5 miles before taking the Manor road by the church.

3rm(1⇌2hc) ⊬in all bedrooms ® ✗ ✱ sB&B£31-£34 dB&B£62-£68 dB&B⇌£65-£72 (incl dinner) LDO 5pm
Lic 🍴 CTV 40P 10🚗 nc12yrs ✔ rough shooting & stabling for guests horses 164 acres mixed £

INGLETON North Yorkshire Map 07 SD67

GH QQ Langber Country Tatterhorne Ln LA6 3DT ☎(05242) 41587
Closed 24 Dec-3 Jan

To find the guesthouse turn off at the Masons Arms on the A65, it is situated in open countryside, a mile west of the village with splendid views of the surrounding farmland and hills. Some bedrooms have en suite facilities, there is a large lounge with TV and a small dining room overlooking the lawn.

7rm(2⇌1↱4hc) (3fb)⊬in all bedrooms ® ✱ sB&B£14.50-£16.50 dB&B£28-£32 dB&B⇌↱£32-£38 WB&B£92-£97 WBDi£121-£134 LDO 5pm
🍴 CTV 6P ⌂ £

GH QQQ Oakroyd Old Rectory Hotel Main St LA6 3HJ ☎(05242) 41258

This comfortable, friendly small hotel was formerly a rectory and is situated on the edge of the village just off the A65. Bedrooms are attractively decorated and have private bathrooms, TV and tea making facilities. The hotel is licensed and there is a cosy bar and a comfortable lounge; pride is taken in the standard of the home-cooked meals.

6↱ (2fb) CTV in all bedrooms ® ✗ (ex guide dogs) dB&B↱£50 WB&B£155 WBDi£225 LDO 5.30pm
Lic 🍴 CTV 6P nc11yrs £

GH QQQ ***Pines Country House Hotel*** LA6 3HN ☎(05242) 41252

A small private hotel in an elevated position next to the A65 on the edge of the village. The double glazed bedrooms have lovely views of the surrounding countryside, and there is an elegant lounge with an open fire. The hotel features a productive 80-year-old grapevine in the conservatory dining room and a pitch pine staircase in the entrance hall.

4⇌↱ (1fb) CTV in all bedrooms ® LDO 6pm
Lic 🍴 CTV 14P 2🚗 (£2 per night)

GH QQQ Springfield Private Hotel Main St LA6 3HJ ☎(05242) 41280
Jan-Oct

This detached grey stone, twin gabled, late-Victorian house has its original conservatory still in situ at the front. On the main street about 200yds from the A65 (turn off at the Bridge Hotel), it is a friendly establishment offering traditional bedrooms, some with an extra bed for family occupancy. Rooms at the back have views of the River Greta and the Pennine Hills. The Victorian-style lounge comfortably seats 10 and features a fine wooden fireplace and a dado picked out in gold leaf. There are individual tables in the dining room, which is also decorated in sympathy with the period. The hotel is licensed and offers a good range of wines at competitive prices, and private parking is available at the rear.

5↱ (3fb) CTV in all bedrooms ® ✱ sB&B↱£20 dB&B↱£38-£40 WB&B£110-£120 WBDi£177-£185 LDO 5pm
Lic 🍴 CTV 12P £

INGLEWHITE Lancashire Map 07 SD54

FH QQ Mrs R Rhodes **Park Head** *(SD542395)* Bilsborrow Ln PR3 2LN ☎Brock(0995) 40352

A 200-year-old farmhouse situated in open countryside, a short distance from both the M6 and A6. It features attractively decorated bedrooms, all with wash-basins and TV, and offers true Lancashire hospitality. It is located by leaving the M6 at junction 32, turn north on the A6 and within a short distance turn right at Broughton traffic lights, B5269, and look for the signs to Inglewhite. Alternatively, continue on the A6 to Bilsborrow, turning right at the Roebuck.

3hc (1fb) CTV in all bedrooms ® ✖ ✱ sB&Bfr£12 dB&Bfr£24 WB&Bfr£80
🍽 10P 255 acres dairy £

INSTOW Devon Map **02** SS43

GH QQ Anchorage Hotel The Quay EX39 4HX
☎(0271) 860655 & 860475
Mar-Dec
An attractive Victorian building with 2 spacious and elegant lounges affording fine views over the Taw and Torridge estuary. Bedrooms vary in size but all have the same modern facilities; there is a small bar and an appealing dining room which offers a fixed price menu of fresh home-cooked dishes. Jon and Margaret Cann provide personal service, and concessionary green fees at the nearby Royal North Devon and Saunton golf courses.
17rm(2⇌15⌐) (6fb) CTV in 2 bedrooms ® T ✱ sB&B⇌⌐£35-£37.65 dB&B⇌⌐£70-£75.30 (incl dinner) WB&B£141-£150 WBDi£210-£225.90 LDO 9.30pm
Lic 🍽 CTV 18P
Credit Cards 1 3 £

INVERGARRY Highland *Inverness-shire* Map **14** NH30

GH QQQ Craigard PH35 4HG ☎(08093) 258
Standing in its own neatly maintained grounds, beside the road leading to the Isle of Skye, this sturdy, detached stone house offers a choice of lounges – one for non smokers – together with spacious comfortable bedrooms. The guesthouse is licensed and provides a friendly atmosphere throughout.
7hc ® ✖ (ex guide dogs) ✱ sB&Bfr£15 dB&Bfr£30 WB&Bfr£105 WBDifr£196 LDO 11am
Lic CTV 10P nc8yrs

GH Q *Faichem Lodge* PH35 4HG ☎(08093) 314
Mar-Oct
An attractively modernised 19th-century stone-built farmhouse peacefully situated in pleasant rural countryside about one mile from the village. It offers good value practical accommodation and a friendly atmosphere.
4hc (1fb)⊁in all bedrooms ® LDO 4pm
🍽 CTV 5P

GH QQ *Forest Lodge* South Laggan PH34 4EA (3m SW A82)
☎(08093) 219
This friendly, family-run, purpose-built guesthouse is situated beside the A82, 3 miles south of the village and offers good value holiday accommodation. Recent improvements include the provision of en suite showers in 5 rooms.
7rm(5⌐2hc) (2fb) ® LDO 6.30pm
🍽 CTV 10P

INVERKEITHING Fife Map **11** NT18

GH QQQ Forth Craig Private Hotel 90 Hope St KY11 1LL
☎(0383) 418440
Situated on the southern approach to the town, close to the Forth bridges, this small, purpose-built private hotel offers practical accommodation popular with both business people and tourists. Bedrooms are not large, but they are very neatly maintained and comfortable. There is a small, cosy lounge and a pleasant dining room with views of the Firth of Forth.
5⌐ CTV in all bedrooms ® ✱ sB&B⌐£19-£21 dB&B⌐£32-£36 LDO 6pm
Lic 🍽 8P
Credit Cards 1 3

'Selected' establishments, which have the highest quality award, are highlighted by a tinted panel. For a full list of these establishments, consult the Contents page.

INVERNESS Highland *Inverness-shire* Map **14** NH64

See **Town Plan Section**

GH QQQ *Aberfeldy Lodge* 11 Southside Rd IV2 3BG
☎(0463) 231120
Situated in a residential area not far from the centre, this stone-built detached house has a warm and friendly atmosphere created by Mr and Mrs Hayes. Bedrooms all have en suite facilities, and are decorated in soft pastel shades, with modern furnishings.
9⌐ (4fb) CTV in all bedrooms ® ✖ LDO 4pm
🍽 9P

GH QQQ Ardmuir House 16 Ness Bank IV2 4SF
☎(0463) 231151
This attractive Georgian guesthouse is situated on the east bank of the River Ness, within a short walk of the town centre. Jean and Tony Gatcombe offer a warm welcome and provide tastefully decorated accommodation with all the expected amenities. There is a comfortable, relaxing lounge, and enjoyable home cooking is served in the attractive dining room.
11⌐ (2fb) CTV in all bedrooms ® sB&B⌐£27.50-£31.50 dB&B⌐£43-£49 WBDi£196-£231 LDO 7pm
Lic 🍽 4P
Credit Cards 1 3 £

GH QQ *Ardnacoille House* 1A Annfield Rd IV2 3HP
☎(0463) 233451
Apr-Oct
Good value bed and breakfast accommodation and home comforts are offered at this sturdy semidetached Victorian house, situated in a residential area south of the town centre.
6hc (2fb) ✖
🍽 CTV 8P nc7yrs

GH QQ Brae Ness Hotel 17 Ness Bank IV2 4SF
☎(0463) 712266
Etr-15 Nov
A Georgian house on the riverfront has been converted to create this comfortable family-run private hotel. The bedrooms are gradually being upgraded to offer modern comforts and amenities, and enjoyable home cooking is served in the river-facing dining room.
10rm(9⇨↱1hc) (2fb)⚡in 4 bedrooms CTV in all bedrooms ® ✠ (ex guide dogs) * sB&B⇨↱£20-£30.50 dB&B⇨↱£40-£53 WBDi£192-£238 LDO 7pm
Lic ꙮ 6P 2🚘

GH QQQ Craigside 4 Gordon Ter IV2 3HD ☎(0463) 231576
In a residential area overlooking the castle, this attractive Victorian house has a friendly atmosphere and offers good value bed and breakfast accommodation in comfortable, compact bedrooms.
6rm(4⇨↱2hc) CTV in all bedrooms ® ✠ (ex guide dogs) * sB&B£13-£16 sB&B⇨↱£16-£18 dB&Bfr£26 dB&B⇨↱fr£32 WB&B£85-£100
ꙮ 4P nc9yrs Ⓔ

SELECTED

GH QQQQ Culduthel Lodge 14 Culduthel Rd IV2 4AG
☎(0463) 240089
Set in its own well tended garden in a residential area not far from the town centre, this attractive Georgian house has been carefully converted to provide superior accommodation. Recent improvements include the addition of 6 new bedrooms, each individually decorated and furnished to a high standard. Fresh flowers add to the appeal of the charming sitting room, and delicious home cooking including Scottish fare and local produce is offered at dinner in the elegant dining room.
12⇨↱ (1fb)⚡in 9 bedrooms CTV in all bedrooms ® **T** ✠ (ex guide dogs) LDO 8pm
Lic ꙮ 13P nc5yrs
Credit Cards [1] [3]

GH QQ Four Winds 42 Old Edinburgh Rd IV2 3PG
☎(0463) 230397
Closed Xmas wk & New Year
This fine Victorian house is set in its own well tended garden in a residential area within 10 minutes' walk of the central amenities. It offers good value bed and breakfast accommodation and has a relaxed, friendly atmosphere. Bedrooms, some of which have en suite facilities, are practically furnished and equipped with colour TVs and tea-makers. The first-floor lounge, with its well filled bookshelves, provides traditional comforts.
7rm(4↱3hc) (2fb) CTV in all bedrooms ® * sB&B↱£17 dB&B↱£34 WB&Bfr£107
ꙮ CTV 16P

GH QQ Hebrides 120a Glenurquhart Rd IV3 5TD
☎(0463) 220062
Situated on the A82 beside the Caledonian Canal, this friendly family-run guesthouse offers good value bed and breakfast accommodation. Non smokers are especially welcome.
2rm(1↱1hc) (1fb)⚡in all bedrooms CTV in all bedrooms ® **T** ✠ sB&Bfr£15 sB&B↱£16 dB&Bfr£28 dB&B↱£32 WB&B£91-£98
ꙮ 4P Ⓔ

GH QQ Leinster Lodge 27 Southside Rd IV2 4XA
☎(0463) 233311
Closed Xmas & New Year
Good value bed and breakfast accommodation is offered at this 19th-century guesthouse, situated in a residential area not far from the town centre. Bedrooms, which for the most part are spacious, are practically furnished in a mixture of styles, and there is a TV lounge on the ground floor.
6rm(1↱5hc) (2fb) CTV in 1 bedroom ® * sB&B£14 dB&B£28 dB&B↱£32 WB&B£98
ꙮ CTV 8P

GH QQ Murellan Drumchardine IV5 7PX ☎(0463) 83679
Mar-Oct
This comfortable, detached house is situated seven miles west of Inverness, just off the A862 near the village of Inchmore. It offers good value holiday accommodation; breakfast is served at the communal table in the neatly appointed dining room.
3rm(1↱2hc) (1fb)⚡in 2 bedrooms ✠ (ex guide dogs) dB&B£25 dB&B↱£27 WB&B£70-£78
ꙮ 3P

GH QQQ The Old Rectory 9 Southside Rd IV2 3BG
☎(0463) 220969
Closed 21 Dec-5 Jan
With its own pleasant rear garden, this small, friendly family-run guesthouse is situated in a residential area just a short drive from the town centre. The brightly decorated bedrooms with cheery fabrics, are comfortably fitted with modern furniture. There is a quiet lounge displaying an ample supply of books and board games for guests' relaxation, and for further comfort, smoking is not encouraged throughout the house.
4rm(3↱1hc) (1fb)⚡in all bedrooms ® ✠ (ex guide dogs) dB&B£32-£34 dB&B↱£35
ꙮ CTV 5P nc7yrs

GH QQQ *Riverside House Hotel* 8 Ness Bank IV2 4SF
☎(0463) 231052
A relaxed, friendly atmosphere prevails at this friendly, family-run guesthouse, situated on the east bank of the river convenient for the town centre. It has a small, comfortable lounge and hearty breakfasts are served in the bright dining room overlooking the river. Bedrooms are well maintained and offer modern furnishings, though they do vary in size.

→

Where every Prospect Pleases

Craigside Lodge

4 Gordon Terrace, Inverness IV2 3HD
Tel. (0463) 231576

Comfortable detached and spacious Victorian house in residential area yet only few minutes walk to town centre. Beautiful views of town, river. Castle and countryside from lounge. All six bedrooms (four with private facilities) are fitted to please the discerning visitor. Craigside assures its guest of good food, comfort and experienced, courteous service. Central heating. Parking. Fire Certificate.

Brochure with pleasure from Wilf & Janette Skinner. SAE please.

BRAE NESS HOTEL

INVERNESS

Ideally situated beside the River Ness. 5 minutes walk from the town centre. Excellent home cooking with fresh produce served in our non-smoking dining room with table licence. All rooms have private bathroom, TV, tea making facilities and some rooms are reserved for non smokers.

Margaret & John Hill,
Ness Bank, Inverness IV2 4SF
Telephone (0463) 712266

Culduthel Lodge

14 Culduthdel Road, Inverness IV2 4AG
Telephone: (0463) 240089

Overlooking the River Ness with superb views of the surrounding countryside, Culduthel Lodge places great emphasis on good food, comfort and a quiet friendly atmosphere. The public rooms are tastefully decorated and furnished and our bedrooms are most comfortable each having bathroom, telephone, TV, hospitality tray, and hair drier. Car parking and residents licence.

Please write or telephone for colour brochure.

11rm(5⇔5🚿1hc) (3fb) CTV in all bedrooms ® LDO 7pm
Lic 🍽 CTV 🚭

GH QQQ *St Ann's Hotel* 37 Harrowden Rd IV3 5QN
☎(0463) 236157
This is a traditional detached stone-built house in a quiet residential area which has been extended and modernised to provide comfortable holiday accommodation. Most bedrooms have en suite facilities and all have colour TV and teamakers. The attractive dining room overlooks the pretty garden, and there is also a cosy lounge.
6rm(5⇔🚿1hc) (3fb) CTV in all bedrooms ® LDO 3.30pm
Lic 🍽 CTV 3P

GH QQQ **Sunnyholm** 12 Mayfield Rd IV2 4AE
☎(0463) 231336
Close to the town centre in a residential area, this house has recently been extended to provide 4 bedrooms, all with private shower rooms and predominantly pine furniture. A cosy lounge overlooking the small rear garden is available, and breakfast is served at pine tables in a pleasant room in the original house. From the south (A9) take the junction signed Hilton and Kingmills and follow signs for the town centre. At the traffic lights, take the left turn, then first right, the house is on the left hand side.
4🚿 CTV in all bedrooms ® 🐕 (ex guide dogs) dB&B🚿£30-£36
🍽 CTV 6P

GH QQQ *Villa Fontana* 13 Bishops Rd IV3 5SB
☎(0463) 232999
Situated in a quiet residential area near to the Eden Court Theatre, this comfortably furnished Victorian house has a welcoming atmosphere and offers good value bed and breakfast accommodation.
4hc (2fb) CTV in all bedrooms ®
🍽 4P

GH QQ *Windsor House Hotel* 22 Ness Bank IV2 4SF
☎(0463) 233715 FAX (0463) 713262
This personally run tourist and commercial hotel is situated on the south bank of the river Ness, within easy walking distance of the town centre. It has an attractive new sun lounge, and bedrooms vary in size but are comfortable and well equipped.
18rm(15⇔🚿3hc) CTV in all bedrooms ® 🐕 (ex guide dogs) LDO 6pm
Lic 🍽 20P

INN QQ *Heathmount* Kingsmills Rd IV2 3JU
☎(0463) 235877
Closed 31 Dec-2 Jan
Situated in a residential area not far from the town centre, this friendly, family-run inn is a popular base for visiting business people and tourists. Bedrooms are comfortably furnished in a modern style, and the bars ensure a lively atmosphere.
5⇔🚿 (1fb) CTV in all bedrooms ® LDO 9.15pm
🍽 20P solarium
Credit Cards 1 3

INN QQ *Smithton Hotel* Smithton IV1 2NL ☎(0463) 791999
This friendly, family-run hotel stands on the edge of the village, just over three miles east of Inverness off the A96. Modern and well furnished, it offers a choice of bars and well equipped, pine-furnished bedrooms, all of which have en suite facilities.
10rm(2⇔8🚿) (1fb) CTV in all bedrooms ® 🐕 (ex guide dogs) LDO 8.30pm
CTV 50P pool tables
Credit Cards 1 3

Street plans of certain towns and cities will be found in a separate section at the back of the book.

IPSWICH Suffolk Map **05** TM14

GH QQQ **Bentley Tower Hotel** 172 Norwich Rd IP1 2PY
☎(0473) 212142
Closed 24 Dec-4 Jan
An imposing Victorian detached building set back from the A1156 on an arterial route just outside the city centre, with a car park at the front. Bedrooms are en suite, well equipped and comfortable, and the high-ceilinged public rooms are elegant, light and spacious.
11🚿 (2fb) CTV in all bedrooms ® 🐕 sB&B🚿£35-£40 dB&B🚿£48-£50 WB&B£245-£280 LDO 8.45pm
Lic 🍽 12P
Credit Cards 1 3 £

GH QQ **Cliffden Hotel** 21 London Rd IP1 2EZ
☎(0473) 252689
A detached house in a residential street, located a convenient distance from the town centre. The accommodation is bright and clean, with compact, modestly appointed bedrooms. Well cooked, generous breakfasts are a feature, and the house is colourful in summer with many hanging baskets and pots.
16hc CTV in all bedrooms ® 🐕 (ex guide dogs) * sB&Bfr£17 dB&Bfr£29
🍽 6P
Credit Cards 1 2 3

GH QQQ **Highview House Hotel** 56 Belstead Rd IP2 8BE
☎(0473) 601620 & 688659
A commercial, family-owned guesthouse situated in a quiet area of the city above the railway station. Bedrooms are very well equipped and a high standard of cleanliness is maintained. Dinner is provided with a small simple à la carte menu in a pleasant dining room, which leads into a sitting area with a full-sized metered snooker table.
11rm(7⇔🚿4hc) (1fb) CTV in all bedrooms ® **T** sB&Bfr£33 sB&B⇔🚿fr£38.50 dB&B⇔🚿fr£49.50 LDO 7.30pm
Lic 🍽 CTV 15P
Credit Cards 1 3 £

IRONBRIDGE Shropshire Map **07** SJ60

GH QQQ **Broseley** The Square, Broseley TF12 5EW
☎Telford(0952) 882043
A comfortable guesthouse in the centre of the town with adjacent public car park. The rooms are well equipped and have all the facilities required by the business or tourist visitor.
6⇔🚿 CTV in all bedrooms ® **T** sB&B⇔🚿£25-£30 dB&B⇔🚿£40-£50 LDO by arrangement
Lic 🍽
Credit Cards 1 3 £

GH QQQ **The Library House** 11 Severn Bank TF8 7AN
☎Telford(0952) 432299
Closed Xmas
Situated just 100yds from the famous landmark, this small family-run guesthouse was until 1960 the local library. The lounge now occupies this spot and is furnished with deep modern easy chairs and settees, with a drinks table for diners. The quarry tiled dining room is pine furnished and dates from 1750, and was once a doctor's surgery. Bedrooms are individually decorated with coordinated fabrics and have comfortable armchairs. There are terraced gardens to the rear with fine views of the local church, and free car parking is available nearby. George and Chris Maddocks are a very friendly couple and offer warm hospitality at their totally no smoking establishment.
3⇔🚿 (1fb)🚭in all bedrooms CTV in all bedrooms ® * sB&B⇔🚿fr£30 dB&B⇔🚿fr£42 LDO 4pm
Lic 🍽 CTV 🚭

ISLE OF Places incorporating the words 'Isle of' or 'Isle' will be found under the actual name, eg Isle of Wight is listed under Wight, Isle of.

IVER HEATH Buckinghamshire Map **04** TQ08

GH QQQ Bridgettine Convent Fulmer Common Rd SL0 0NR ☎Fulmer(0753) 662073 FAX (0753) 662645

This very attractive, Tudor-style timbered house sits in its own well kept gardens and is run by an order of Sisters from the House of St Bridget. Bedrooms are simply appointed, bright and spotlessly clean. There is a small TV lounge, and guests are welcome to use the library and chapel. Peace and tranquility are assured here.

13hc (3fb) ✖ LDO 2pm

CTV P Ⓔ

JACOBSTOWE Devon Map **02** SS50

FH QQ Mrs J King **Higher Cadham** *(SS585026)* EX20 3RB ☎Exbourne(083785) 647

Closed Xmas rs Nov-Feb

An attractive 16th-century Devonshire longhouse, peacefully set at the end of an unmade road close to the village. The emphasis here is on family holidays, and a lot of thought has gone into providing amenities for children. The bedrooms are comfortable, and lounges cosy with log fires. A range of snack meals or a full dinner is available at one large table in the dining room.

4hc (1fb) Ⓡ ✖ ✱ sB&B£12-£12.50 dB&B£24-£25 WB&B£78-£80 WBDi£115-£118 LDO 5pm

Lic CTV 6P nc3yrs games room 139 acres beef sheep Ⓔ

JEDBURGH Borders *Roxburghshire* Map **12** NT62

GH QQ Ferniehirst Mill Lodge TD8 6PQ ☎(0835) 63279 due to change to 863279

This modern, purpose-built lodge is situated 3 miles south of the town off the A68, in a secluded valley beside the River Jed, surrounded by 25 acres of land. Drinks are served in the spacious lounge which overlooks the river, and home cooking is offered at shared tables in the pine dining room. Bedrooms are neat, if compact, most having private bathrooms and all equipped with tea trays and telephones.

11rm(5⇌3♠3hc) Ⓡ T ✱ sB&B£21 sB&B⇌♠£21 dB&B£42 dB&B⇌♠£42 WB&B£140 WBDi£220 LDO 8pm

Lic CTV 10P ✓ U

Credit Cards 1 3

GH QQQ 'Froylehurst' Friars TD8 6BN ☎(0835) 62477 due to change to 862477

Mar-Nov

Situated on a hillside in a quiet residential area above the town centre, this handsome Victorian house stands in its own gardens and offers good value bed and breakfast accommodation. Attractive fabrics have been used to good effect in the spacious bedrooms, which are individually decorated and furnished. There is a comfortable, well-furnished lounge and hearty Scottish breakfasts are served at the communal table in the smart dining room.

5hc (3fb) CTV in all bedrooms Ⓡ ✖ ✱ sB&Bfr£16.50 dB&Bfr£27

CTV 5P nc5yrs

GH QQQ Kenmore Bank Hotel Oxnam Rd TD8 6JJ ☎(0835) 62369 due to change to 862369

From its elevated position, just off the A68, this friendly, family run guesthouse enjoys an outlook over the River and Abbey. The compact bedrooms are brightly decorated and furnished in a modern style and all are equipped with TV, tea making facilities and en suite showers. There is an 'at home' feeling in the lounge with a dispense bar offering drinks to residents, and a choice of dishes is available from the menu, served in the attractive dining room.

6⇌♠ (2fb) CTV in all bedrooms Ⓡ sB&B⇌♠£16.50-£27 dB&B⇌♠£33-£38 WB&B£115-£133 WBDi£210-£227 LDO 8pm

Lic 6P ✓

Credit Cards 1 3

See advertisement on page 215

SELECTED

GH QQQQ The Spinney Langlee TD8 6PB (2m S on A68) ☎(0835) 63525 due to change 863525
Mar-2nd wk Nov
This delightful house, formerly 2 cottages, stands on the A68, 2 miles south of the town. Inviting, tastefully fitted and individually decorated bedrooms are a feature, and both the lounge and dining room have been nicely furnished with comfort in mind. There are attractive lawns and gardens, and service from the resident proprietors is friendly and spontaneous.
3rm(2🚿) ⅄in all bedrooms ® ✗ (ex guide dogs) ✻ dB&B🚿fr£34
🍽 CTV P

GH QQQ Willow Court Willow Court, The Friars TD8 6BN ☎(0835) 63702 due to change to 863702
A comfortable, family-run guesthouse standing in 2 acres of gardens on a hillside above the town centre. Bedrooms are compact but comfortably furnished in a modern style, with attractive décor and mixed furnishings; 2 rooms have private bathrooms and TV is available on request. There are 2 comfortable sitting rooms, 1 with TV and the other has a selection of books, magazines and board games. Enjoyable home cooking using fresh garden and local produce is served in the attractive conservatory which overlooks the town. Maintenance and housekeeping standards throughout are impeccable, with a warmly welcoming atmosphere prevailing.
4rm(3⇌🚿1hc) ⅄in all bedrooms CTV in all bedrooms ® ✻ sB&B£20-£25 sB&B⇌🚿£20-£25 dB&B£30-£36 dB&B⇌🚿£32-£36 WB&B£100-£126 WBDi£156-£182 LDO 6.45pm
🍽 CTV 5P

JERSEY

See **CHANNEL ISLANDS**

KEIGHLEY West Yorkshire Map **07** SE04

GH QQ Bankfield 1 Station Rd, Cross Hills BD20 7EH ☎Cross Hills(0535) 632971
A detached house with a small attractive rear garden and parking area. The rooms are spacious and freshly decorated. It is found by turning right at Barclays Bank into Station Road in the village of Cross Hills.
3rm(1🚿2hc) (1fb)⅄in all bedrooms CTV in 1 bedroom ® sB&B£16-£18 sB&B🚿£16-£18 dB&B£32-£36 dB&B🚿£32-£36 WB&B£112
🍽 CTV 4P 1🚗 ⌂ Ⓔ

KEITH Grampian *Banffshire* Map **15** NJ45

SELECTED

FH QQQQ Mrs J Jackson **The Haughs** *(NJ416515)* AB55 3QN (1m from Keith off A96) ☎(05422) 2238
Apr-Oct
Many regulars who return year after year to this establishment are attracted by the genuine warm welcome extended by Mrs Jackson. This mixed working farm engages in rotational cropping, beef, cattle and sheep, with the sturdy, white farmhouse at the centre of the complex. Bright, cheery bedrooms with individual décor and furniture, provide the expected comforts and amenities. The lounge with blue soft furnishings and various comfortable chairs and settees, invites peaceful relaxation, while hearty, home cooked food is served in the sunny dining room, which has a large window offering extensive views of the surrounding countryside.
4rm(3⇌🚿1hc) (1fb)⅄in all bedrooms CTV in all bedrooms ® ✗ (ex guide dogs) dB&B£26-£27 dB&B⇌🚿£30-£32 LDO 3pm
🍽 10P 165 acres beef mixed sheep

KELMSCOT Oxfordshire Map **04** SU29

FH QQ Mrs A Amor ***Manor Farm*** *(SU253995)* GL7 3HJ ☎Faringdon(0367) 52620
A warm and friendly atmosphere is offered at this farmhouse, well run along informal lines by Mrs Amor, set in an arable and dairy farm. Each of the two bedrooms are spacious and reasonably equipped, suitable for families but a comfortable choice for business travellers too. Situated 10-12 miles from the M4 (exit 15), it enjoys a quiet setting but is close to major routes and larger towns such as Oxford, Lechlade and Swindon.
2hc (2fb)⅄in all bedrooms ® ✗ LDO noon
🍽 CTV 4P 315 acres arable dairy

KENDAL Cumbria Map **07** SD59

See also Brigsteer

SELECTED

GH QQQQ Burrow Hall Country Guest House Plantation Bridge LA8 9JR ☎Staveley(0539) 821711
Built in 1648, Burrow Hall has recently been sympathetically extended to include modern comforts yet retains its old-fashioned charm. The principal lounge boasts original oak beams, an enormous feature fireplace and very comfortable seating. The smaller TV lounge is equally comfortable and tastefully furnished. There are 3 compact but cosy bedrooms, all enjoying private facilities. Paul and Honor Brind are congenial hosts who enjoy having guests in their home, and they are justifiably proud of the interesting dinner menu they produce. Whilst the main course gives no choice, there is a mouth- watering range of starters and puddings, and a small wine list is available. The breakfast is also impressive, offering a good selection of dishes.
3🚿 ✗ dB&B🚿£45 WB&B£140 WBDi£220 LDO 7pm
Lic 🍽 CTV 12P nc16yrs
Credit Cards [1] [3]

GH QQQ Higher House Farm Oxenholme Ln, Natland LA9 7QH ☎Sedgewick(05395) 61177
There is a very friendly atmosphere throughout this lovely old 17th-century house, and guests are treated as friends of the family. The 3 bedrooms are prettily furnished and have lots of little extras provided. There is a delightful lounge where afternoon teas are served and dining is around a large polished table. Higher House Farm is situated in the centre of Natland village just off the A65. Within easy reach of the M6, off junction 36.
3rm(1⇌1🚿) (1fb)⅄in all bedrooms CTV in 1 bedroom ® ✗ (ex guide dogs) ✻ sB&Bfr£15 sB&B⇌🚿£21.50 dB&Bfr£30 dB&B⇌🚿£43 LDO 1pm
🍽 CTV 9P

SELECTED

GH QQQQ Lane Head Country House Hotel Helsington LA9 5RJ (0.5m S off A6) ☎(0539) 731283 & 721023
Closed Nov
This charming 17th-century house, full of character and warmth, is peacefully situated overlooking the town surrounded by an acre of grounds which incorporate a knot garden. The elegant lounge is booklined and there is an open fire for cool evenings. One of the bedrooms is on the ground floor, all are individually furnished and decorated. Colour TV, radio and direct dial telephones are provided and all are en suite. This hotel is carefully run by Mr and Mrs Craig to offer a peaceful base for touring southern Lakeland.

7rm(4⇌3♪) (1fb) CTV in all bedrooms ® ✗ (ex guide dogs) sB&B⇌♪£35-£40 dB&B⇌♪£50-£60 LDO 5pm
Lic 🍽 10P
Credit Cards [1] [2] [3] £

GH QQQ *Martindales* 9-11 Sandes Av LA9 4LL ☎(0539) 724028
This very comfortable guesthouse, on the north side of the town near the railway station, is owned and personally run by Mr and Mrs Martindale. The modern bedrooms all have en suite shower facilities and colour TV, and a cosy lounge/bar is provided, with an open fire on colder evenings.
8♪ (1fb) CTV in all bedrooms ® ✗ (ex guide dogs) LDO 1pm
Lic 🍽 6P 1🚗 nc

FH Q Mrs S Beaty ***Garnett House*** *(SD500959)* Burneside LA9 5SF ☎(0539) 724542
Closed Xmas & New Year
A typical Cumbrian farmhouse offering a good standard of accommodation. Mrs Beaty is a charming lady and welcomes her guests with warmth and hospitality. This is very much a working farm, on the edge of the village of Burneside to the north of Kendal.
5hc (2fb) CTV in all bedrooms ® ✗ LDO 5pm
CTV 6P 750 acres dairy sheep

FH QQ Mrs J Ellis **Gateside** *(NY494955)* Windermere Rd LA9 5SE ☎(0539) 722036
Closed Xmas & New Year
An attractive, white-painted well maintained farmhouse with attached farm buildings, situated on the A591, 2 miles north of Kendal. Bedrooms are well equipped with colour TV and tea making facilities, and the lounge and dining room are attractive and comfortable.
5hc (1fb) CTV in all bedrooms ® sB&Bfr£13 dB&Bfr£26 LDO 4.30pm
🍽 6P 280 acres dairy sheep £

FH QQ Mrs E M Gardner **Natland Mill Beck** *(SD520907)* LA9 7LH (1m from Kendal on A65) ☎(0539) 721122
Mar-Oct
A lovely Cumbrian farmhouse with a long history, situated just off the A65 a mile from Kendal. It is very well furnished in all areas, the lounge being particularly pleasant, and Mrs Gardner looks after her guests very well.
3rm(2hc) ® ✗
🍽 CTV 3P 100 acres dairy £

KENILWORTH Warwickshire Map **04** SP27

GH QQQ Abbey 41 Station Rd CV8 1JD ☎(0926) 512707
Situated in a residential area just off the high street, this gabled property is the home of Angela and Trevor Jefferies, who provide a warm welcome for guests. The bedrooms vary in size, the majority have plain but bright, fresh décor and modern furnishings. The public areas consist of a small dining room with cheery poppy wallpaper and a comfortable lounge with TV, games and books.
7rm(2♪5hc) (1fb) CTV in all bedrooms ® ✗ (ex guide dogs) sB&B£18 dB&B£32 dB&B♪£38 LDO 7pm
Lic 🍽 CTV 2P £

GH QQQ Castle Laurels Hotel 22 Castle Rd CV8 1NG ☎(0926) 56179 FAX (0926) 54954
Closed 24 Dec-2 Jan
An attractive, spacious Victorian house opposite the castle and Abbey Fields. The accommodation is well equipped and maintained: room sizes vary. Public areas include a cosy lounge and dining room.
12♪ (1fb) ⚹in all bedrooms CTV in all bedrooms ® T ✗ (ex guide dogs) ✱ sB&B♪£27-£35 dB&B♪£43-£47 LDO 7pm
Lic 🍽 CTV 14P
Credit Cards [1] [3] £

Book as early as possible for busy holiday periods.

GH QQQ Ferndale 45 Priory Rd CV8 1LL ☎(0926) 53214
Improvements continue at this predominantly commercial guesthouse, situated in a residential area not far from the town centre. Accommodation is attractive and comfortable, and all the rooms now have private bathrooms.
8⇌♪ (2fb) CTV in all bedrooms ® ✱ sB&B⇌♪£17 dB&B⇌♪£30-£32
Lic 🍽 CTV 8P £

GH QQQ Hollyhurst 47 Priory Rd CV8 1LL ☎(0926) 53882
Proprietors Bev and Kathy Abley offer a friendly welcome to their comfortable guesthouse, which is situated in a residential area not far from Abbey Fields Park. Bright, fresh bedrooms, with a mixture of furniture, provide a good range of facilities. There is a comfortable lounge with a TV and Hi-fi which leads through to a smaller dining area with a corner bar.
8rm(3♪5hc) (2fb) CTV in all bedrooms ® ✱ sB&B£18 sB&B♪£18 dB&B£32 dB&B♪£36 WB&B£90-£100 LDO noon
Lic 🍽 CTV 9P £

GH QQQ Victoria Lodge Hotel 180 Warwick Rd CV8 1HU ☎0926 512020 FAX (0926) 58703
This delightful, privately run hotel, situated on the main stretch through Kenilworth, is a welcome addition to this year's guide. The house has been carefully renovated to offer attractive, individually styled guest rooms with modern en suite facilities and a good range

→

of equipment. Public areas include a comfortable lounge and cosy dining room where a wide choice of meals is served. Proprietors Malcolm and Joyce Chilvers are charming hosts, and the pride they take in the hotel is evident in the excellent standard of cleanliness and maintenance throughout.
5⇨🚿 ⚡in all bedrooms CTV in all bedrooms ® **T**
✗ (ex guide dogs) ✱ sB&B⇨🚿£29-£30 dB&B⇨🚿£44-£46
LDO 8pm
Lic 🍽 CTV 9P 2🚗 nc14yrs
Credit Cards 1 2 3 £

KENTALLEN Highland *Argyllshire* Map **14** NN05

FH QQ Mrs D A MacArthur ***Ardsheal Home*** *(NN996574)*
PA38 4DZ ☎Duror(063174) 229
Apr-Oct
This farmhouse has a pretty garden with lovely views of Loch Linnhe and the mountains. One of the 3 bedrooms is on the ground floor. Breakfast is served around a stripped wood table in the former living room.
3rm(1hc) (1fb) ®
🍽 CTV 5P 1000 acres beef dairy sheep mixed

KESWICK Cumbria Map **11** NY22

See **Town Plan Section**

GH QQQ Acorn House Hotel Ambleside Rd CA12 4DL
☎(07687) 72553
Feb-Nov
This Georgian house is furnished in traditional style and offers good all- round comfort. The bedrooms are individually styled and have good quality beds – including one 4-poster. All rooms are en suite (one has facilities across the landing), and colour TV, radio alarms and tea-making facilities are provided. There is a comfortable lounge where guests can relax and meet new friends and, while the house is quietly situated, there are many restaurants and pubs just a few minutes' walk away in the town centre.
10rm(9⇨🚿1hc) (4fb)⚡in all bedrooms CTV in all bedrooms
® ✗ (ex guide dogs) ✱ sB&B⇨🚿fr£25 dB&B⇨🚿£40-£55
WB&B£130-£170
Lic 🍽 10P nc5yrs
Credit Cards 1 3

GH QQ Albany House 38 Lake Rd, The Heads CA12 5DQ
☎(07687) 73105
Situated in a row of lakeland houses, this family-owned and run guesthouse offers good all round comfort and service.
8rm(2🚿6hc) (4fb) CTV in 1 bedroom ® ✱ sB&B£18.50
dB&B£32 dB&B🚿£36 WB&B£110-£120 WBDi£160-£180
LDO 4.30pm
Lic CTV 5P £

GH QQQ Allerdale House 1 Eskin St CA12 4DH
☎(07687) 73891
A very well furnished, friendly house, set in a quiet side road a short way from the town centre, personally run by the resident proprietors. The bedrooms have good facilities and a lovely lounge is provided for guests use. Strictly no smoking in the house.
6⇨🚿 (2fb)⚡in all bedrooms CTV in all bedrooms ® **T**
sB&B⇨🚿£28.50 dB&B⇨🚿£57 (incl dinner) WB&B£140
WBDi£199.50 LDO 4.30pm
Lic 🍽 2P 4🚗 nc5yrs
Credit Cards 1 3

SELECTED

GH QQQQ Applethwaite Country House Hotel
Applethwaite CA12 4PL ☎(07687) 72413
Feb-Nov
Formerly known as The Gales Country House Hotel, this private hotel is now under new ownership, but the style has not changed, with the emphasis on friendly hospitality. This splendid Victorian house stands in magnificent gardens with panoramic views over Derwent Water and the Borrowdale Valley. Public areas include a cosy bar, an elegant drawing room and the Garden Room with an attractive tented ceiling. Most of the individually designed bedrooms have private bathrooms, and enjoyable 4-course dinners are provided in the attractive dining room. Bowls, putting and croquet are available on the lawns. The hotel is situated about 1.5 miles from Keswick. Approach from the east via the A66 to a large roundabout, then take the third exit A591 and turn immediately right, signed to Underscar.
14rm(7⇨5🚿2hc) (4fb) CTV in all bedrooms ® ✗
sB&B⇨🚿fr£31 dB&B⇨🚿fr£56 WBDi£255-£270
LDO 6.45pm
Lic 🍽 CTV 10P bowling green putting croquet lawn
Credit Cards 1 3 £

GH QQQ Beckside 5 Wordsworth St CA12 4HU
☎(07687) 73093
This small, friendly guesthouse is situated in a quiet side road and is one of a row of terraced cottages. It has been completely refurbished to a good standard offering 3 bright, fresh bedrooms, complete with en suite. TV and tea-making facilities. A small, cosy lounge is provided on the top floor, and the resident owners have a no smoking policy throughout.
3🚿 ⚡in all bedrooms CTV in all bedrooms ®
✗ (ex guide dogs) ✱ dB&B🚿fr£32 WB&Bfr£110 WBDifr£160
LDO 4pm
🍽 nc5yrs

GH QQ Brierholme 21 Bank St CA12 5JZ ☎(07687) 72938
A well run end of terrace house in the centre of town. Bedrooms are provided with good facilities and offer value-for-money accommodation.
6rm(5⇨🚿1hc) (2fb) CTV in all bedrooms ® ✱ dB&B£32-£34
dB&B⇨🚿£36-£40 LDO 3pm
Lic 🍽 6P

GH QQQ Charnwood 6 Eskin St CA12 4DH (0.5m S off A6)
☎(07687) 74111
rs Nov-Mar wknds only
A well furnished, comfortable guesthouse situated in a quiet side road a short walk from the town centre. Bedrooms are spacious, with good facilities, and there are fine Victorian fireplaces in both the lounge and dining room.
6🚿 (2fb)⚡in all bedrooms CTV in all bedrooms ® ✗
dB&B🚿£32-£36 WB&B£105-£120 WBDi£161-£175 LDO 4pm
Lic 🍽 nc8yrs £

GH QQQ Claremont House Chestnut Hill CA12 4LT
☎(07687) 72089
Pretty, well furnished bedrooms are a feature of this guesthouse, which stands in its own grounds on the main A591 Windermere road about a mile from the town. A well produced 5-course dinner is available.
5⇨🚿 ⚡in all bedrooms ® ✗ sB&B£22.50-£24
dB&B⇨🚿£45-£48 LDO 4pm
Lic 🍽 CTV 8P nc3yrs

GH QQQ Clarence House 14 Eskin St CA12 4DQ
☎(07687) 73186
This detached stone-built Victorian property is tucked away in a side road close to the town centre. Bedrooms are plainly decorated but bright and fresh, with modern furniture and TV; most have private bathrooms. A good standard of home cooking is provided in the attractive dining room, and there is a pleasant residents' lounge. Smoking is not permitted.
8rm(7🚿1hc) (3fb)⚡in all bedrooms CTV in all bedrooms
✗ (ex guide dogs) sB&B£14.50-£15.50 dB&B🚿£36-£40
🍽 CTV P̸

GH QQQ Craglands Penrith Rd CA12 4JL ☎(07687) 74406
Closed Xmas
This traditional Lakeland house with a white painted pebbledash exterior is situated on the main A591 (Windermere road). The house has recently been refurbished to a very good standard and has pretty bedrooms, mostly with coordinated fabrics. All have quality duvets, radio/alarm and hairdryers provided. A comfortable lounge with settees is available and a well produced dinner is served in the fresh, nicely furnished dining room. There are parking facilities to the side of the house.
5rm(1⇌2↱2hc) ⊁in all bedrooms CTV in all bedrooms ® ✕ (ex guide dogs) ✱ sB&Bfr£15 sB&B⇌↱fr£16 dB&Bfr£30 dB&B⇌↱fr£32 LDO 6pm
♨ 6P nc8yrs

GH QQQ Dalegarth House Country Hotel Portinscale CA12 5RQ ☎(07687) 72817
This hotel is situated in the village of Portinscale, in its own grounds amidst beautiful scenery. It offers spacious accommodation and bedrooms are brightly decorated, with good facilities. There are 2 comfortable lounges, and the hotel commands fine views of Derwentwater.
10rm(7⇌3↱) ⊁in all bedrooms CTV in all bedrooms ® ✕ (ex guide dogs) ✱ sB&B⇌↱£24-£26 dB&B⇌↱£48-£52 WB&B£160-£175 WBDi£230-£245 LDO 5.30pm
Lic ♨ CTV 12P nc5yrs
Credit Cards 1 3 £

GH QQ Edwardene 26 Southey St CA12 4EF ☎(07687) 73586
This attractive double-fronted stone house is in a quiet side road, yet close to the town centre. The bedrooms are bright and attractive and there are 2 lounges available to guests. Service is warm and friendly.
11rm(3↱8hc) (3fb) ® ✕ (ex guide dogs) sB&B£14-£15 dB&B£28-£30 dB&B↱£34-£36 WB&B£95-£110 WBDi£150-£180 LDO 6pm

→

Lic 🍽 CTV
Credit Cards 1 3 £

GH QQQ Fell House 28 Stanger St CA12 5JU
☎(07687) 72669
Closed 25 Dec rs Nov-Mar
An attractive Victorian house set in a quiet side road just a short walk from the town centre. The accommodation is of a good standard and the resident owners provide friendly service.
6rm(2↱4hc) (1fb) CTV in all bedrooms ® ✗ (ex guide dogs) sB&B£13.50-£16 dB&B£25-£29 dB&B↱£31-£36 WB&B£81.50-£110
🍽 CTV 4P

GH Q Foye House 23 Eskin St CA12 4DQ ☎(07687) 73288
A mid-terraced Victorian house situated within easy reach of the town centre. The accommodation is clean and well maintained, and bedrooms all have TV and tea-making facilities. Smoking is not permitted here.
7hc (2fb)⊬in all bedrooms CTV in all bedrooms ® ✱ sB&B£12-£15 dB&B£24-£30 WB&B£82-£90 WBDi£130-£140 LDO 4pm
Lic 🍽 CTV ⱣP £

GH QQQ The Great Little Tea Shop 26 Lake Rd CA12 5DQ
☎(07687) 73545
This charming teashop/guesthouse is situated in a cul de sac in the centre of the town. The bedrooms are rather compact but the facilities are good. A wide range of home-cooked goodies is available in the teashop.
7⇌↱ ⊬in all bedrooms CTV in all bedrooms ®
✗ (ex guide dogs) sB&B⇌↱£18-£25 dB&B⇌↱£30-£36 WB&B£115-£135 WBDi£160-£180 LDO 9pm
Lic 🍽 CTV 3P
Credit Cards 1 3 £

GH QQQ Greystones Ambleside Rd CA12 4DP
☎(07687) 73108
Closed 1 Dec-31 Jan
A spacious end-of-terrace house situated in a quiet location yet close to the town centre. The hotel is enthusiastically managed to provide stylish and comfortable accommodation and a friendly atmosphere. Good traditional home cooking is produced in the bright, attractive dining room.
9⇌↱ CTV in all bedrooms ® ✗ (ex guide dogs) dB&B⇌↱£39 LDO 2pm
Lic 🍽 7P 2🚘 nc8yrs £

GH QQ Hazeldene Hotel The Heads CA12 5ER
☎(07687) 72106
Mar-Nov
A large guesthouse in a good position on the edge of town looking up the Borrowdale Valley. The bedrooms have good facilities and a lounge and games room are provided.
22rm(19⇌↱3hc) (5fb) CTV in all bedrooms ® T ✱ sB&B£21-£25 sB&B⇌↱£23-£27 dB&B£42-£50 dB&B⇌↱£46-£54 WB&B£140-£179 WBDi£238-£277 LDO 4pm
Lic 🍽 CTV 18P £

GH QQQ *Holmwood House* The Heads CA12 5ER
☎(07687) 73301
mid Mar-mid Nov
A well furnished and comfortable small hotel facing the Borrowdale Valley. The resident owners provide a friendly service.
7hc (1fb) ✗ (ex guide dogs) LDO 2pm
Lic 🍽 CTV 3P nc5yrs

GH QQ Latrigg House St Herbert St CA12 4DF
☎(07687) 73068
6rm(3↱3hc) (2fb)⊬in all bedrooms CTV in all bedrooms ® sB&B£12.50-£15.50 sB&B↱£20-£25 dB&B£25-£31 dB&B↱£30-£37 WB&B£87.50-£113 WBDi£135-£155
Lic 🍽 CTV 2P £

GH QQ Leonards Field 3 Leonards St CA12 4EJ
☎(07687) 74170
Closed 23 Dec-Jan rs Feb
An attractive little guesthouse, a short distance from the town centre, well kept by the proud and friendly owners. Bedrooms are furnished to a high standard and good facilities are provided. In summer the front of the house is very pretty with flowers and hanging baskets. Smoking is not permitted here.
8rm(3↱5hc) (1fb) CTV in all bedrooms ® ✱ sB&B£13.50-£14.50 dB&B£26-£28 dB&B↱£30-£33 WB&B£94.50-£115.50 WBDi£147.50-£168 LDO 4.30pm
Lic 🍽 nc5yrs

GH QQ Lincoln House 23 Stanger St CA12 5J
☎(07687) 72597
Value for money accommodation is offered at this small guesthouse, situated in an elevated position close to the town centre.
6hc (2fb) CTV in all bedrooms ® ✱ sB&B£14-£15 dB&B£28-£30
Lic 🍽 CTV 5P £

GH QQQ Lynwood 12 Ambleside Rd CA12 4DL
☎(07687) 72081 FAX (07687) 75021
A large, mid-terrace Victorian house in a residential area, close to the town centre. Lovingly cared for by the friendly and helpful owners, it has very well equipped bedrooms and a cosy lounge for guests.
7rm(6↱1hc) (1fb)⊬in all bedrooms CTV in all bedrooms ® ✗ sB&B£17.50 dB&B↱£38-£45 WB&Bfr£133 WBDifr£199.50 LDO 2pm
Lic 🍽 ⱣP
Credit Cards 1 3 £

GH QQ Melbreak House 29 Church St CA12 4DX
☎(07687) 73398
Occupying a corner site in a quiet road, this attractive stone house is only a short distance from the town. The bright, fresh bedrooms are furnished with a mixture of styles and all have a TV and tea making facilities. There is a very comfortable, newly furnished lounge available for guests' convenience.
13rm(5⇌↱8hc) (3fb)⊬in 10 bedrooms CTV in all bedrooms ® ✱ sB&B£13.50 sB&B⇌↱£14.50 dB&B£27 dB&B⇌↱£29 LDO 4pm
Lic 🍽 CTV ⱣP

GH QQQ Ravensworth Hotel 29 Station St CA12 5HH
☎(07687) 72476
Closed 1 Dec-Jan rs Feb
A well furnished and comfortable small hotel situated in the centre of the town. Bedrooms are tastefully furnished and offer good facilities. There is a separate lounge bar and good home-cooked meals are taken in the pretty dining room. Warm and friendly service is provided by the resident owners.
8rm(1⇌7↱) (2fb) CTV in all bedrooms ® ✗ dB&B⇌↱£34-£44 WB&B£119-£140 WBDi£192.50-£206.50 LDO 6pm
Lic 🍽 CTV 5P nc6yrs
Credit Cards 1 3

GH QQ Richmond House 37-39 Eskin St CA12 4DG
☎(07687) 73965
Closed Xmas
Situated in a quiet side road near to the town centre, this is a pleasantly furnished family-run guesthouse offering good home comforts. Smoking is not permitted in the house.
10rm(6↱4hc) (1fb)⊬in all bedrooms CTV in all bedrooms ® ✗ (ex guide dogs) sB&Bfr£14.25 dB&B£28.50-£36 dB&B↱£32-£41 WB&B£90-£120 WBDi£150-£170 LDO 5pm
Lic 🍽 CTV ⱣP nc8yrs
Credit Cards 1 3 £

GH QQQ Rickerby Grange Country House Hotel Portinscale CA12 5RH ☎(07687) 72344
Closed 24-26 Dec
A well furnished and comfortable private hotel situated in the village of Portinscale, close to Keswick and Derwentwater. The bedrooms are brightly decorated and well equipped, most with private bathrooms. There is a cosy lounge, and good home cooking is provided in the spacious restaurant.
13rm(12⇌🚿 1hc) (3fb) CTV in all bedrooms ® T sB&B£21-£22.50 sB&B⇌🚿£24 dB&B£42 dB&B⇌🚿£48 WB&B£137-£163 WBDi£210-£230 LDO 5pm
Lic 🍴 20P ⓕ

GH QQQ Skiddaw Grove Hotel Vicarage Hill CA12 5QB ☎(07687) 73324
Closed 20-28 Dec
This delightful family-run hotel is in a quiet backwater of Keswick. It has superb views of Skiddaw (Lakeland's third highest mountain), and the house is bright, fresh and comfortable. Home cooking is served in the pleasant dining room, and an outdoor pool is available in the summer.
10rm(8⇌2🚿) (1fb)⚡in all bedrooms CTV in all bedrooms ® ✗ (ex guide dogs) ✱ sB&B⇌🚿£20-£22 dB&B⇌🚿£40-£44 WB&B£140-£147 WBDi£210-£230 LDO 7pm
Lic 🍴 12P ⛱(heated)

GH QQ *Squirrel Lodge* 43 Eskin St CA12 4DG ☎(07687) 73091
In a terraced row, this compact family-run guesthouse offers bright, modestly furnished bedrooms. There is no lounge.
7hc ⚡in all bedrooms CTV in all bedrooms ®
✗ (ex guide dogs) LDO 5pm
Lic 🍴 P̸
Credit Cards 1 2 3

GH QQQ Stonegarth 2 Eskin St CA12 4DH ☎(07687) 72436
Stonegarth is a family-run guesthouse with well-equipped bedrooms, an attractive dining room and a comfortable lounge. There is also a private car park. The Victorian building itself is of special architectural interest.
9⇌ (3fb) CTV in all bedrooms ® T sB&B⇌fr£21 dB&B⇌fr£40 WBDi£195-£200 LDO 6pm
Lic 9P nc5yrs
Credit Cards 1 3 £

GH QQ Sunnyside 25 Southey St CA12 4EF ☎(07687) 72446
Closed 15 Dec-15 Feb rs 15 Nov-15 Dec
Within walking distance of the town centre in a residential area, this deceptively spacious house is under the personal supervision of the resident proprietors.
8hc (2fb) CTV in all bedrooms ® ✗ (ex guide dogs) ✱ sB&B£15-£16 dB&B£30-£32 WB&B£90-£96
8P
Credit Cards 1 3

GH QQ *Swiss Court* 25 Bank St CA12 5JZ ☎(07687) 72637
A small guesthouse close to the town centre, it offers well equipped bedrooms and a warm, friendly welcome.
7hc ✗
CTV 3P nc6yrs

GH QQQ Thornleigh 23 Bank St CA12 5JZ ☎(07687) 72863
A pleasant house close to the town centre where friendly service is provided by the proprietors. Bedrooms are well furnished and there is a good guests' lounge available.
6⇌ ⊁in 2 bedrooms CTV in all bedrooms ® ✗ ✱ dB&B⇌£37-£42 LDO 2.30pm
3P nc16yrs
Credit Cards 1 3 £

GH QQ Twa Dogs Penrith Rd CA12 4JU ☎(07687) 72599
This traditional Lakeland stone inn is situated on the main approach road from Windermere. It offers plainly decorated modern bedrooms, each with colour TV, and a good range of food in the spacious public bar. A full Cumbrian breakfast is served in the breakfast room upstairs, and service is friendly and helpful.
5hc (2fb) CTV in all bedrooms ✗ (ex guide dogs) sB&B£15-£20 dB&B£30-£40 LDO 8.45pm
Lic 20P nc5yrs games room £

KETTERING Northamptonshire Map **04** SP87

GH QQ *Headlands Private Hotel* 49-51 Headlands NN15 7ET ☎(0536) 524624 FAX (0536) 83367
This Victorian property is situated in the conservation area of the town, but only 5 minutes' walk from the centre. Accommodation is modest and some single rooms are compact. There is a guests' lounge, and the cosy dining room displays a large collection of footwarmers and Victorian china.
13rm(2⇌4 7hc) (3fb) CTV in all bedrooms ® LDO 5pm
10P
Credit Cards 1 3

KETTLEWELL North Yorkshire Map **07** SD97

SELECTED

GH QQQQ Langcliffe House BD23 5RJ ☎(0756) 760243
Closed Jan
This delightful house stands in its own gardens on the edge of the lovely village of Kettlewell and has excellent views of Wharfedale and surrounding fells. The house has been tastefully furnished throughout and an attractive conservatory has been added to take advantage of the views. Bedrooms have individual colour schemes, and most are fully en suite. There is a self- contained cottage within the grounds designed for the disabled. An elegant lounge with a log fire offers many books and games; and dinner is well produced and served either on a large communal table, or at separate tables in the conservatory. The resident owners are attentive hosts, and many guests return year after year.
6rm(2⇌2 2hc) Annexe 1⇌ (1fb) CTV in all bedrooms ® T ✱ sB&B£27.50 sB&B⇌£29 dB&B£45 dB&B⇌£48 WB&B£156 WBDi£230 LDO 7pm
Lic 7P
Credit Cards 1 3 £

KEXBY North Yorkshire Map **08** SE75

FH QQ Mrs K R Daniel **Ivy House** *(SE691511)* YO4 5LQ ☎York(0904) 489368
Situated on the A1079 York-Hull road, this attractive farmhouse offers comfortable, neat bedrooms and cosy public rooms, with a friendly owner.
3hc (1fb) CTV in all bedrooms ✗
CTV 5P 132 acres mixed

KEYNSHAM Avon Map **03** ST66

GH QQQ Grasmere Court Hotel 22/24 Bath Rd BS18 1SN ☎Bristol(0272) 862662 FAX (0272) 862762
Situated on the edge of the town, this hotel has been totally refurbished to a good standard. It offers public areas of quality, and well-equipped bedrooms, many of which have good, modern en suite facilities.
16⇌ (3fb)⊁in all bedrooms CTV in all bedrooms ® T ✗ ✱ sB&B⇌£36-£45 dB&B⇌£48-£65 LDO 7.30pm
Lic CTV 18P 1
Credit Cards 1 3 £

FH Q Mrs L Sparkes **Uplands** *(ST663664)* Wellsway BS18 2SY ☎Bristol(0272) 865764 & 865159
Closed Dec
Conveniently situated for touring this beautiful part of the country, this 19th-century stone farmhouse has simple accommodation with large, airy rooms. Mrs Sparkes is providing bed and breakfast only this year.
9rm(2 7hc) (4fb) CTV in all bedrooms ® T ✗ ✱ sB&B£17.50-£20 sB&B fr£20 dB&Bfr£35 dB&B fr£40 WB&Bfr£75
CTV 20P 200 acres dairy £

KIDDERMINSTER Hereford & Worcester Map **07** SO87

GH QQQ Cedars Hotel Mason Rd DY11 6AL ☎(0562) 515595 FAX (0562) 751103
Closed 25-31 Dec
Close to the A442, just north of the town centre, this well maintained private hotel provides good quality, well equipped accommodation. Small conferences can be accommodated.
20rm(1⇌19) (6fb)⊁in 7 bedrooms CTV in all bedrooms ® T sB&B⇌£30.70-£41.60 dB&B⇌£35.90-£44.75 LDO 8.30pm
Lic 23P
Credit Cards 1 2 3 5 £

GH Q Gordonhouse Hotel 194 Comberton Rd DY10 1UE ☎(0562) 822900
Closed 24 Dec-1 Jan
This predominantly commercial hotel is situated on the A448, just a short walk from the railway station and the Severn Valley line. Accommodation varies, and public areas include a comfortable lounge and small breakfast room overlooking the rear garden. There is a car park for guests' use.
15rm(1 14hc) Annexe 3hc (2fb) CTV in all bedrooms ® sB&B£18-£20 sB&B £26-£29 dB&B£29-£32 dB&B £38-£40 WB&B£118-£126 LDO 7pm

Lic 🍽 CTV 25P
Credit Cards [1] [2] [3] (£)

KIDLINGTON Oxfordshire Map **04** SP41

SELECTED

GH QQQQ Bowood House 238 Oxford Rd OX5 1EB
☎Oxford(0865) 842288 FAX (0865) 841858
Closed 24 Dec-1 Jan

This modern, detached property is on the A423 in the village of Kidlington, just 4 miles from Oxford city centre. Comfortable, well decorated rooms have good facilities, including telephones and radio alarms, and many have en suite facilities. Some are located in the garden wing annexe connected to the main building by a covered walkway. Public areas include a cosy lounge, a well stocked bar and an informal restaurant which provides an à la carte menu and has access to the garden.

10rm(8⇌🚿2hc) Annexe 12⇌🚿 (4fb) CTV in all bedrooms ® ✗ sB&B£25-£32 sB&B⇌🚿£35-£54 dB&B⇌🚿£55-£60 LDO 8.30pm
Lic 🍽 25P
Credit Cards [1] [3]
See also advertisement under OXFORD

KILBARCHAN Strathclyde *Renfrewshire* Map **10** NS46

GH QQ *Ashburn* Milliken Park Rd PA10 2DB ☎(05057) 5477

This substantial detached period house is set in its own gardens in a quiet road overlooking farmland. Bedrooms are mostly spacious and the lounge has a self-service honesty bar. Ashburn is best approached off the A737; it is convenient for Glasgow airport and the railway station for Glasgow trains is only 3 minutes' walk away.

→

6rm(2⇌4hc) (3fb) CTV in all bedrooms ® LDO 11am
Lic 𝍢 CTV 8P
Credit Cards [1] [3] [5]

KILBURN North Yorkshire Map **08** SE57

INN QQQ ***Forresters Arms Hotel*** YO6 4AH
☎Coxwold(03476) 386
This attractive inn, dating from the 12th century, is in the centre of the village, beneath the famous white horse and next to the church. Bedrooms are particularly well furnished, all have en suite facilities and 2 have 4-poster beds. An extensive range of bar meals is served in the 2 bars and there is a cosy restaurant for residents.
8⇌ (2fb) CTV in all bedrooms ® LDO 9.30pm
𝍢 40P
Credit Cards [1] [3]

KILLIECRANKIE Tayside *Perthshire* Map **14** NN96

GH QQ Dalnasgadh House PH16 5LN
☎Pitlochry(0796) 473237
Etr-Oct
This detached period house is set in its own grounds off the main road (the old A9) half a mile north of the village. It is spotlessly clean and has some fine woodwork which exemplifies the character of the house.
5hc ⊁in all bedrooms ® ✗ (ex guide dogs) ✱ sB&Bfr£18.50 dB&Bfr£33
𝍢 CTV 10P
See advertisement under PITLOCHRY

KILLIN Central *Perthshire* Map **11** NN53

GH QQQ Breadalbane House Main St FK21 8UT
☎(05672) 386 due to change to (0567) 820386
Conveniently situated in the centre of the village, this recently restored guesthouse is an ideal touring base. The bedrooms are comfortably furnished in the modern style (no smoking is encouraged in the rooms), and offer a comprehensive range of facilities. There is a spacious lounge which invites peaceful relaxation.
5rm(1⇌4⇌) (2fb)⊁in all bedrooms CTV in all bedrooms ® ✱ dB&B⇌⇌£34-£36 WB&B£113.40
𝍢 CTV

KILMARNOCK Strathclyde *Ayrshire* Map **10** NS43

GH QQ Burnside Hotel 18 London Rd KA3 7AQ
☎(0563) 22952
This detached period house sitting just east of the town centre is a well run commercial guesthouse with spacious bedrooms, a bright, cheerful dining room and a comfortable lounge.
11rm(2⇌⇌9hc) (4fb) CTV in all bedrooms ® ✱ sB&B£17-£25 sB&B⇌⇌£25-£30 dB&B£30-£40 dB&B⇌⇌£35-£45
LDO noon
𝍢 CTV 10P
Credit Cards [1] [3]

GH QQ The Eriskay 2 Dean Ter KA3 1RJ ☎(0563) 32061
A friendly, unassuming commercial and tourist guesthouse lying north of the town centre off the Glasgow road. The bright, well equipped bedrooms are a feature here, but there is no lounge.
6rm(2⇌4hc) (3fb) CTV in all bedrooms ® ✱ sB&B£14-£16 sB&B⇌£16-£18 dB&B£28 dB&B⇌£34 WB&B£90-£110
𝍢 CTV 12P

KILMUN Strathclyde *Argyllshire* Map **10** NS18

GH QQ ***Fern Grove*** Fern Grove PA23 8SB ☎(036984) 334
A small guesthouse overlooking Holy Loch offering a high standard of cuisine provided by proprietor Estralita Murray. The cuisine is Scottish, with fish and other local produce featured in the short à la carte menu, served in the elegant Victorian dining room. Two of the 3 bedrooms overlook the loch; they are all a mixture of modern and traditional styles, and comfortably furnished. There is a pleasant lounge stocked with plenty of books and magazines of local interest, and drinks are also dispensed here.
3⇌⇌ (1fb)⊁in all bedrooms CTV in all bedrooms ®
✗ (ex guide dogs) LDO 9pm
Lic 𝍢 5P Argyll safaris
Credit Cards [1] [2] [3] [5]

KILVE Somerset Map **03** ST14

SELECTED

INN QQQQ Hood Arms TA5 1EA
☎Holford(027874) 210
Closed 25 Dec
Between Bridgwater and Minehead on the A39, this popular inn has been run by the resident proprietors for many years and has built a reputation locally for friendliness and hospitality. Bedrooms are tastefully decorated, comfortable and supplied with thoughtful extras. All are en suite with good, modern facilities. Public areas are cosy and full of character. Being so popular, the atmosphere is always convivial. Guests may eat in the bar areas or in the attractive restaurant and will find that the comprehensive menus, like the accommodation, offer good value for money.
5⇌ CTV in all bedrooms ® **T** sB&B⇌£35-£38 dB&B⇌£58-£64 Bar Lunch £2.75-£5&alc Dinner £4.50-£6&alc LDO 10pm
𝍢 12P nc7yrs
Credit Cards [1] [3] £

KINCRAIG Highland *Inverness-shire* Map **14** NH80

GH QQ March House Lagganlia, Feshie Bridge PH21 1NG
☎(0540) 651388
Closed 21 Oct-26 Dec
In picturesque Glen Feshie 2 miles east of the village, this family-run guesthouse is an ideal base for the touring holiday-maker, with a range of outdoor pursuits in the vicinity. It has a relaxed atmosphere and offers good value accommodation.
6rm(5⇌⇌1hc) (1fb)⊁in all bedrooms ® sB&B£30 sB&B⇌⇌£30-£31 dB&B£52-£54 dB&B⇌⇌£52-£54 (incl dinner) WB&B£110-£120 WBDi£168-£182 LDO 6pm
𝍢 8P

KINGHAM Oxfordshire Map **04** SP22

GH QQQ Conygree Gate Church St OX7 6YA
☎(0608) 658389
Closed 25 Dec-1 Jan
Set in the centre of this quiet Cotswold village, this former farmhouse with leaded windows and stone fireplaces, dates back to 1648, and is now run as a small hotel by Brian and Kathryn Sykes. Four bedrooms are on the ground floor and all exhibit Kathryn's original style of decoration. Meals are served in the country-style dining room, offering a choice of starters and desserts, and generally a traditional roast for the main course.
10rm(1⇌7⇌2hc) (3fb) CTV in all bedrooms ® ✱ sB&B£25 dB&B£44 dB&B⇌⇌£48 LDO 5pm
Lic 𝍢 12P
Credit Cards [1] [3] £

KINGHORN Fife Map **11** NT28

INN QQQ ***Long Boat*** 107 Pettycur Rd KY3 9RU
☎(0592) 890625
This friendly, family-run inn enjoys magnificent views over the Firth of Forth to Edinburgh and the Lothian hills. Bedrooms are attractive, with cane furniture and corner baths. Two of the rooms also have balconies from which to enjoy the views. There is a spacious restaurant, a comfortable bar with a collection of copper and china bric-a-brac, and an increasingly popular 'Hide away' wine bar, sitting on the water's edge and offering a good range of informal meals throughout the day and evening. Functions are held

in the fine suite which has been built to resemble the inside of an old sailing ship.
6⇌ ꟳ CTV in all bedrooms ® LDO 9.30pm
꧁ CTV 10P
Credit Cards 1 2 3 5

KINGSBRIDGE Devon Map **03** SX74

GH QQQ Ashleigh House Ashleigh Rd, Westville TQ7 1HB ☎(0548) 852893
rs Nov-Mar
This friendly guesthouse is situated on the edge of the town off the Salcombe road, and is an ideal base for touring the South Hams. The first-floor bedrooms feature patchwork quilts, all have tea-making facilities, and colour TV is available by prior arrangement. Home-cooked dishes are served daily in the spacious dining room, and Mike and Jenny Taylor are always on hand to assist guests.
8rm(3ꟳ4hc) (1fb)⊁in all bedrooms ® ✻ sB&B£14.75-£15.75 dB&Bꟳ£33.50-£35.50 LDO 4pm
Lic CTV 5P nc5yrs
Credit Cards 1 3 £

KINGS CAPLE Hereford & Worcester Map **03** SO52

INN Q British Lion Fawley HR1 4UQ ☎Carey(0432) 840280
There are only 3 inns of this name in Great Britain and this one, believed to originate from the coming of the railways, is remotely situated south of Hereford. Accommodation is simple but clean, and there is a cosy country public bar where guests can mix with the locals.
3rm(2hc) ® ✻ sB&B£9.50-£10 dB&B£19-£20 LDO 9pm
꧁ CTV 20P

KINGSDOWN Kent Map **05** TR34

GH QQQ Blencathra Country Kingsdown Hill CT14 8EA ☎Deal(0304) 373725
Quietly situated, with a pleasant garden, this well maintained modern country guesthouse has been steadily upgraded by the new proprietors. Bedrooms are traditionally furnished and brightly decorated, and the lounge is spacious and very comfortable. Service is helpful and friendly.
7rm(4ꟳ3hc) (3fb)⊁in 4 bedrooms CTV in all bedrooms ® ✗ (ex guide dogs) sB&B£17-£20 sB&Bꟳ£20 dB&B£36 dB&Bꟳ£38 WB&B£119-£133
Lic CTV 7P croquet lawn

KINGSEY Buckinghamshire Map **04** SP70

FH QQQ Mr & Mrs N M D Hooper **Foxhill** *(SP748066)* HP17 8LZ ☎Haddenham(0844) 291650
Feb-Nov
The Hoopers offer a friendly welcome at their white-painted, listed farmhouse, which is set back in lovely grounds complete with duck pond. An added bonus is the swimming pool, which is available for use during warmer weather. The first floor bedrooms are spacious with oak-beamed ceilings, and pleasantly furnished. Downstairs there is an entrance hall with polished quarry tiles and a cheerful lounge/breakfast room.
3hc ⊁in all bedrooms CTV in all bedrooms ®
✗ (ex guide dogs) ✻ sB&B£17-£21 dB&B£34-£36
꧁ CTV 40P nc5yrs ⩯(heated) 4 acres non-working £

KINGSGATE Kent Map **05** TR37

GH QQ *Marylands Hotel* Marine Dr CT10 3LG ☎Thanet(0843) 61259
Apr-Oct
In a good location facing the sea, with its own garden leading to a sandy beach with safe bathing, this extended Victorian house retains many of its original features. Bedrooms are slowly being upgraded, many have en suite showers and one has very low attic beams. Public areas include a TV lounge with video, and a lounge bar with a pool table, extending into the dining room. Marylands has a residential licence, and an evening meal can be provided in the summer months.
9rm(1⇌5ꟳ3hc) (3fb) CTV in 6 bedrooms ® LDO noon
Lic CTV 12P snooker

KING'S LYNN Norfolk Map **09** TF62

GH QQ Beeches 2 Guanock Ter PE30 5QT ☎(0553) 766577 FAX (0553) 776664
Family run, this pleasant guesthouse offers nicely equipped accommodation that is plainly decorated and fitted with a mixture of pine and older style furniture. Breakfast and a set home-cooked evening meal are served in the dining room, that opens on to the garden with its summer house. The Beeches is conveniently siutated close to the town centre.
7rm(4⇌ꟳ3hc) (2fb) CTV in all bedrooms ® sB&Bfr£19 sB&B⇌ꟳfr£24 dB&Bfr£29 dB&B⇌ꟳfr£37 LDO 4.30pm
Lic ꧁ CTV 3P

GH QQQ Fairlight Lodge 79 Goodwins Rd PE30 5PE ☎(0553) 762234
Closed 24-26 Dec
From the A17 to the town centre, take the last exit to Gaywood and Fairlight Lodge is a little after Russett House (see separate entry) on the same side. It is an attractive mellow brick-built Victorian house set in neat gardens which are really colourful in summer. Mr Rowe is a professional host who maintains high standards throughout. The décor and furnishings are in immaculate condition and housekeeping is very precise. Each of the bedrooms is light and fresh with Dorma soft furnishings in keeping with the pine furniture and comfortable cane-backed chairs. The dining room is similarly furnished in pine with cottage-style plate shelves, and a good breakfast includes kedgeree and kippers.
6rm(4ꟳ2hc) (1fb) CTV in all bedrooms ® sB&B£15 sB&Bꟳfr£18 dB&Bfr£27 dB&Bꟳfr£35 LDO noon
꧁ 8P £

GH QQ Guanock Hotel South Gate PE30 5JG ☎(0553) 772959
Just within the town gate, south of the town centre, this commercial guesthouse also provides a set evening meal. The bedrooms are quite compact and each is fitted in either white or teak effect melamine, with plain painted walls offset by coordinated curtains, headboard and bed cover, and crisp, creaseless bed linen. While there are no en suite facilities, the general bathrooms are gleaming and regularly cleaned, and the overall impression of the accommodation is good – fresh, neat and spotless. There is a pool room with pink banquette seating, and a small bar to the rear.
17hc (5fb) CTV in all bedrooms ® ✗ (ex guide dogs) sB&B£22-£24 dB&B£32-£34 WB&B£154-£168 WBDi£182-£196 LDO 5pm
Lic ꧁ 12🚗 (£1 per day) pool room
Credit Cards 1 2 3 5 £

GH QQ Havana 117 Gaywood Rd PE30 2PU ☎(0553) 772331
Closed Xmas
To find the Havana, from the A17 to the town centre, take the last exit at the mini roundabout to Gaywood and continue to the very end, turn right at the T-junction and the guesthouse is a few yards along on the left. It is a small terraced property continually improved by proprietors Mr and Mrs Breed. All the bedrooms have now been redecorated using the Country Diary wild flowers scheme with matching fabrics and décor, together with pastel painted chairs and marble effect vanity shelves. The dining room and lounge are combined, the tables set with colourful waxed cloths.
7rm(2ꟳ5hc) (1fb)⊁in 1 bedroom CTV in all bedrooms ® ✗ sB&B£15-£16 dB&B£25-£26 dB&Bꟳ£30-£32 WB&B£86-£105
꧁ CTV 8P £

GH Q **Maranatha** 115 Gaywood Rd PE30 2PU
☎(0553) 774596

Next door to the Havana (see separate entry), this terraced commercial guesthouse is run by proprietor Mrs Bastone. The bedrooms, on 2 floors, are fresh looking but small and each has grey laminated units and papered dusky pink walls with a dado. The lounge, with colour TV, has a recently acquired electric organ, and a feature brick and dark wood shelf which is to be replaced by a gas fire. The dining room has simple décor and red clothed tables.

6rm(1⮡5hc) (2fb) CTV in all bedrooms ® sB&B£15 dB&B£20-£22 dB&B⮡£24 LDO 6pm
CTV 12P £

SELECTED

GH QQQQ **Russet House Hotel** Vancouver Ave, 53 Goodwins Rd PE30 5PE ☎(0553) 773098
Closed Xmas & New Year

This detached red-brick Victorian house has fresh white and green sills, gardens and a pebbled car park, and is run as a small hotel by the very friendly Rae and Barry Muddles. The lounges and restaurant, though extended, have retained the attractive original features. The dining room has a huge sparkling chandelier, and French windows with decorative swags lead to a smaller lounge and a cosy bar decorated in warm terracotta colours. The main lounge has a fine marble fireplace and original coving. Each of the bedrooms is unique, though similarly furnished with good armchairs, light laminated furniture and floral fabrics, and personal touches such as pot pourri, sewing kits, tissues and magazines. To find the hotel from the A17 to the town centre, turn right at the mini roundabout signed to Gaywood, and it is about 0.5 mile further along on the left.

12rm(8⇌4⮡) (1fb) in 1 bedroom CTV in all bedrooms ® T (ex guide dogs) * sB&B⇌⮡£34.50-£41.50 dB&B⇌⮡£46.50-£70 LDO 7.30pm
Lic 14P
Credit Cards 1 2 3 5

KINGSTON Devon Map **02** SX64

SELECTED

GH QQQQ **Trebles Cottage Hotel** TQ7 4PT
☎Bigbury-on-Sea(0548) 810268

Hidden along a myriad of country lanes (good directions given when reservation is confirmed), this pretty cottage stands at the top of a quaint and tranquil village, yet is only 12 miles from Plymouth. The cottage style bedrooms vary in size and furnishings but all are well equipped. A comfortable, nicely presented lounge/dining area adjoins the cosy bar leading out to a tiny, flower filled patio. Resident proprietors Georgiana and David Kinder are jolly hosts, with Mrs Kinder providing enjoyable meals using fresh produce, whilst her husband cares for guests front of house.

5⇌⮡ CTV in all bedrooms ® sB&B⇌⮡£36-£38 dB&B⇌⮡£45-£55 WBDi£220-£250 LDO 4pm
Lic 10P nc12yrs
Credit Cards 1 2 3

KINGSTON BAGPUIZE Oxfordshire Map **04** SU49

SELECTED

GH QQQQ **Fallowfields** Southmoor OX13 5BH
☎Longworth(0865) 820416 Telex no 83388
FAX (0865) 820629
Apr-Sep rs Wed

Dating back over 300 years, this stone-built family home stands in 12 acres of well kept gardens, with direct access to the A420. Once the home of the Begum Aga Khan, it has since been extended and now presents an early Victorian Gothic southern aspect and a late Victorian northern elevation. Spacious bedrooms are stylishly furnished and have en suite facilities. There is a choice of lounges, all with a cosy atmosphere and comfortably furnished with antique pieces. Log fires blaze in winter months and doors open out on to the gardens in warmer weather. The proprietor, Mrs Crowther, offers a choice of dishes for evening meals using vegetables, fruit and herbs from the garden. Outdoor facilities include tennis courts, a croquet lawn and a heated swimming pool.

4⇌⮡ CTV in all bedrooms ® T * sB&B⇌⮡fr£36.50 dB&B⇌⮡£56-£62 LDO 6.30pm
Lic CTV 15P nc10yrs (heated) (hard)
Credit Cards 1 3

KINGSTON UPON THAMES Greater London London plan **4** B2 p 248

GH QQQ **Chase Lodge** 10 Park Rd, Hampton Wick KT1 4AS
☎081-943 1862 FAX 081-943 9393

5⇌⮡ Annexe 4rm(2⮡) (1fb) in 1 bedroom CTV in all bedrooms ® * sB&B⇌⮡£35-£46 dB&B⇌⮡£44-£80 LDO 9pm
Lic CTV 1 (charged)
Credit Cards 1 2 3 £
See advertisement in colour supplement

KINGSWELLS Grampian *Aberdeenshire* Map **15** NJ80

FH QQQ Mrs M Mann ***Bellfield*** *(NJ868055)* AB1 8PX
☎Aberdeen(0224) 740239
Closed Dec

Set in gentle rolling countryside just four miles west of Aberdeen beside the A944, this traditional farmhouse has been tastefully modernised and provides comfortable excellent value accommodation, with an attractive lounge, thoughtfully equipped cheerful bedrooms and a friendly atmosphere.

3hc (2fb) CTV in all bedrooms ®
CTV 200 acres arable beef

KINGUSSIE Highland *Inverness-shire* Map **14** NH70

GH QQ **Craig An Darach** High St PH21 1JE ☎(0540) 661235
Closed Nov-Dec

This family-run guesthouse is set in an elevated position in 3 acres of grounds overlooking the Spey Valley. It has a friendly atmosphere and offers good value bed and breakfast accommodation. Smoking is not permitted throughout the house.

3⮡ (1fb) in all bedrooms ® * dB&B⮡£32-£36
CTV 6P

GH QQ **Homewood Lodge** Newtonmore Rd PH21 1HD
☎(0540) 661507
Closed Xmas

From its elevated position on the southern fringes of the town, this sturdy Victorian house enjoys a fine outlook over the Spey Valley. Bedrooms, all en suite, are spacious, and there is a quiet lounge as well as an attractive pine furnished dining room where imaginative home-cooked fare is served. Homewood Lodge is a no smoking establishment.

3⮡ (2fb) in all bedrooms ® sB&B⮡£22 dB&B⮡£39-£44 LDO 8pm
Lic CTV 6P

GH QQ ***Sonnhalde*** East Ter PH21 1JS ☎(0540) 661266
Closed Nov & Dec
Overlooking the Spey Valley from its elevated position above the High Street, this sturdy Victorian house offers good value holiday accommodation. It has a friendly atmosphere and combines good food with home comforts. Special wildlife and fishing packages are available – details on application.
8hc (3fb)⊁in all bedrooms CTV in 1 bedroom LDO 2pm
𝕄 CTV 8P

GH QQQ Tighvonie West Ter PH21 1HA ☎(0540) 661263
This splendid turreted Victorian house is set in a quiet residential area amid mature pine trees at the southern end of the village. The guesthouse is family run with a friendly and informal atmosphere, and offers good value accommodation in modern style, comfortably furnished bedrooms. Guests should note that this is a no smoking establishment.
5rm(2↱3hc) (1fb) CTV in all bedrooms ® ✱ sB&B£14-£15.15 dB&B£28-£30 dB&B↱£33-£35
𝕄 5P croquet Ⓔ

KINVER Staffordshire Map **07** SO88

INN QQQ Kinfayre Restaurant 41 High St DY7 6HF
☎(0384) 872565 FAX (0384) 877724
A fully modernised inn situated in the heart of the village, with well equipped bedrooms in a separate building. Evenings are busy here with the skittle alley, but peace and quiet can be found in the private gardens which have a heated pool for residents' use only.
11↱ (1fb) CTV in all bedrooms ® ✖ (ex guide dogs) ✱ sB&B↱fr£30 dB&B↱fr£50 WB&Bfr£175 Lunch £4.50-£7.35&alc Dinner fr£4.50&alc LDO 10pm
𝕄 CTV 17P ⛆(heated)
Credit Cards [1]

KIPPFORD Dumfries & Galloway *Kirkcudbright* Map **11** NX85

GH QQQ Boundary Cottage Barnbarroch DG5 4QS
☎(055662) 247
Closed Xmas
This charming roadside cottage is situated on the A710 south of Dalbeattie and close to the picturesque fishing village of Kippford. There are fine views towards the wooded Screel Hill, and the garden is well tended. A comfortable lounge overlooks the garden with its geese, and it is well stocked with potted plants, books, ornaments, games, TV and audio equipment. The ground-floor bedroom has a double-glazed bay window overlooking the front, and the 2 first-floor bedrooms are more compact but still pretty.
3hc (1fb) CTV in 1 bedroom ® ✱ sB&B£20 dB&B£28-£30 LDO am
𝕄 CTV 5P

KIRKBEAN Dumfries & Galloway *Dumfriesshire* Map **11** NX95

SELECTED

GH QQQQ Cavens House DG2 8AA ☎(038788) 234
Peacefully situated in 11 acres of attractive gardens and woodland on the Solway coast, this old country mansion has many historic connections. Bedrooms enjoy garden views, although plainly decorated and simply furnished; they are all spacious and very well maintained and serviced, with en suite facilities, TV and tea making provisions. The comfortably furnished, spacious lounge offers TV, a piano, board games and an honesty bar. Other facilities include an exercise room and putting green. A 4-course dinner features the cooking of the owner Mrs Jeffries, and provides good value.
6rm(4⇌2↱) (1fb) CTV in all bedrooms ® ✱ sB&B⇌↱£30 dB&B⇌↱£40-£50 LDO 7pm
Lic 𝕄 CTV 10P putting green
Credit Cards [1] [3]

KIRKBY LONSDALE Cumbria Map **07** SD67

SELECTED

GH QQQQ *Cobwebs Country House* Leck, Cowan Bridge LA6 2HZ ☎Kirkby Lonsdale(05242) 72141
Mar-Dec rs Sun
This charming 17th-century farmhouse is peacefully located just off the A65 at Cowan Bridge, 2 miles southeast of the town. The house has been carefully furnished, with great success, to create a country house atmosphere, with the friendly young owners Paul Kelly and Yvonne Thompson devoting much attention to their guests' well being. The 5 delightful bedrooms are superbly furnished, with every modern facility and several thoughtful extras. There are 2 charming lounges, one with an open log fire, with plenty of books, magazines and fresh flowers everywhere. Tempting 4-course dinners with a choice of starter are served in the attractive conservatory restaurant, with top quality fresh produce a feature.
5⇌↱ CTV in all bedrooms ® ✖ LDO 7.30pm
Lic 𝕄 20P nc12yrs ♩
Credit Cards [1] [3]

SELECTED

GH QQQQ Hipping Hall Hotel Cowan Bridge LA6 2JJ
☎(05242) 71187 FAX (05242) 72452
Mar-Nov
Hipping Hall is the remnant of a hamlet dating back to the 15th century and is now a handsome country house built of attractive stone and surrounded by well secluded, beautiful gardens. The bedrooms have pretty floral patterned walls and →

most are fitted with antique furniture in keeping with the style of the house. All are en suite and equipped with TV and tea/coffee making facilities. Guests are invited to help themselves to drinks from the sideboard before enjoying a well produced 5-course dinner in the Great Hall, which is complete with a minstrels' gallery and a beautiful high beamed ceiling; several really comfortable armchairs/settees are provided. There is a drawing room available for guests use and a comfortable, friendly atmosphere is created throughout.
7rm(6⇨1↱) CTV in all bedrooms ® sB&B⇨↱£53-£62 dB&B⇨↱£60-£72 LDO 6.30pm
Lic Ⅲ CTV 12P nc12yrs croquet
Credit Cards [1] [3]

KIRKBYMOORSIDE North Yorkshire Map **08** SE68

SELECTED

GH QQQQ Appletree Court Town Farm, 9 High Market Place YO6 6AT ☎(0751) 31536
A delightful little guesthouse, once part of a working farm, at the top end of Kirkbymoorside. It is distinguished by its red painted door and brass knocker, and the 2 large apple signs, cut out of wood, extending from its mellow grey stone walls. Original beams are a feature of both the dining room and lounge; and the bedrooms, each named after an apple, are quite charming with many thoughtful extras. The house is personally run by hospitable hosts Jean and Fred Adamson, and Jean's beautiful embroidery and tapestry can be seen around the house.
4⇨↱ ⊁in all bedrooms CTV in all bedrooms ✖ ✱ dB&B⇨↱fr£40 LDO noon
Ⅲ 2P nc12yrs

KIRKBY STEPHEN Cumbria Map **12** NY70

SELECTED

GH QQQQ The Town Head House High St CA17 4SH ☎(07683) 71044 FAX (07683) 72128
Parts of this lovely house date back to 1724, and the remainder is Victorian, so there is certainly no lack of character and charm here. There are 5 spacious double bedrooms and one single, each with elegant furnishings and excellent facilities, including en suite bathrooms, direct-dial telephones, colour TV and hairdryers. The lounges are comfortable and homely, filled with fresh flowers, books and magazines, and plenty of deep settees and armchairs. A well produced dinner is provided by Mrs Macrae, who cooks with care and pride.
6⇨↱ ⊁in 2 bedrooms CTV in all bedrooms ® T sB&B⇨↱£37-£42 dB&B⇨↱£56.50-£75 WB&B£219-£260 WBDi£330-£400 LDO 4pm
Lic Ⅲ 8P 1⌂ nc12yrs
Credit Cards [1] [3] £

KIRKCAMBECK Cumbria Map **12** NY56

SELECTED

FH QQQQ Mrs M Stobart ***Cracrop*** *(NY521697)* CA8 2BW ☎Roadhead(06978) 245
Jan-Nov
Built in 1847 and surrounded by over 400 acres of pasture grazed by a pedigree Ayrshire milking herd, this delightful farmhouse has been lovingly furnished and combines character and old charm with modern facilities. Bedrooms are pretty, with tea trays, radios and en suite bathrooms. There is a charming lounge, and a dining room with a large communal table. Guests also have the use of a games room and a sauna. The farmhouse is run by Mrs Stobart who is a friendly and caring hostess.
3↱ (2fb)⊁in all bedrooms CTV in all bedrooms ®
✖ (ex guide dogs) LDO 1pm
Ⅲ CTV 3P sauna 425 acres arable beef dairy mixed sheep
Credit Cards [2]

KIRKCUDBRIGHT Dumfries & Galloway Map **11** NX65

SELECTED

GH QQQQ Gladstone House 48 High St DG6 4JX ☎(0557) 31734
Situated in the historic former high street of the small fishing town, this elegant Georgian property has been carefully restored by the present owners, Sue and Jim Westbrook, who warmly welcome guests and provide a high standard of bed and breakfast accommodation in particularly clean and well maintained rooms. While not large, the 3 bright 2nd floor rooms have comfortable beds and colourful fabrics, and the smartly tiled en suite bathrooms are equipped with good towels. There is an attractive first floor lounge, and to the rear of the property a delightful and unexpectedly large garden which guests are welcome to enjoy. This establishment operates a no smoking policy throughout.
3⇨↱ ⊁in all bedrooms CTV in all bedrooms ®
✖ (ex guide dogs) ✱ sB&B⇨↱fr£30 dB&B⇨↱fr£45
Ⅲ nc14yrs

KIRKHILL Highland *Inverness-shire* Map **14** NH54

SELECTED

GH QQQQ *Moniack View* IV5 7PQ
☎Drumchardine(046383) 757
Apr-Oct
Proprietor Mrs Munro offers superior bed and breakfast accommodation at her smart, modern bungalow, which stands in its own neatly maintained garden overlooking the surrounding tree-studded countryside. The individually decorated bedrooms are comfortably furnished in the modern style and are equipped with a choice of books for bedtime reading. There is an elegant lounge, decorated in a soft pink colour scheme, furnished with comfortable settees and easy chairs, which enjoys an outlook over the glorious countryside, and hearty, well cooked breakfasts are served around the communal table in the adjoining, tastefully appointed dining room. Mrs Munro is very affable and extends a warm welcome to all her guests, many of whom return year after year.
3hc ✖
Ⅲ CTV 3P nc12yrs

FH QQQ Mrs C Munro **Wester Moniack** *(NH551438)* IV5 7PQ ☎Drumchardine(046383) 237
A relaxed, friendly atmosphere prevails at this traditional farmhouse which is situated beside the Highland winery at Moniack Castle. The 2 bedrooms are compact but attractive and tastefully furnished, and there is a comfortable lounge. Hearty, home-cooked farmhouse meals are served at a communal table in the smart dining room.
2hc (1fb) ✱ sB&B£13-£15 dB&B£24-£26 WB&B£84-£90 WBDi£126-£136 LDO 8pm
Ⅲ CTV 4P 600 acres arable beef mixed sheep £

KIRK IRETON Derbyshire Map **08** SK25

INN QQ Barley Mow DE6 3JP ☎Ashbourne(0335) 370306
Closed Xmas wk
An inn full of character and charm situated in the small, hilltop village of Kirk Ireton. Built in 1683, this imposing building offers a more modern bedroom annexe that is decorated and furnished to a

country style in keeping with the character of the inn, and all rooms are equipped with TV and tea- making facilities. A small, cosy lounge area is the beamed cottage parlour, with its solid fuel fire and piano. Evening meals are served by arrangement and special diets along with vegetarians can be catered for. Outside, the large walled garden is available for guests to use and there is ample off-street parking.

5rm(4⇐1↱) (1fb) CTV in all bedrooms ® ✻
sB&B⇐↱fr£20.50 dB&B⇐↱fr£35.75 Dinner £8.50
LDO noon
꜠ P

KIRKMUIRHILL Strathclyde *Lanarkshire* Map **11** NS74

FH Q Mrs I H McInally **Dykecroft** *(NS776419)* ML11 0JQ
☎Lesmahagow(0555) 892226

A modern bungalow situated 1.5 miles west of Kirkmuirhill on the A726 Strathaven road, set amidst open farmland. Compact and cosy accommodation is provided, together with modest standards and a friendly environment.

3rm ® ✻ sB&B£14-£16 dB&B£26-£28 WB&B£90-£95
꜠ CTV 4P 60 acres sheep

KIRKOSWALD Cumbria Map **12** NY54

SELECTED

GH QQQQ **Prospect Hill Hotel** CA10 1ER
☎Lazonby(0768) 898500
Closed 24-26 Dec

Situated about a mile north of the village, this family owned and run hotel has been developed from a group of 18th-century sandstone farm buildings. The attractively furnished bar was once the byre, and now houses a collection of interesting farm implements. There are 2 lounges, one with TV and both with open fires and plenty of books and magazines. Many of the bedrooms feature exposed stonework ; all accommodate antique furniture in keeping with the style and age of the house. Seasonal à la carte and vegetarian dishes are served in the spacious half-circle dining room which overlooks the gardens. Isa and John Henderson are caring hosts and will happily loan their guests maps, bicycles and even wellington boots.

10rm(4⇐↱6hc) Annexe 2⇐↱ (1fb) CTV in 2 bedrooms ® ✘ ✻ sB&B£19-£22 sB&B⇐↱£28-£44 dB&Bfr£44 dB&B⇐↱£57-£63 WBDi£189.70-£249.50 LDO 8.45pm
Lic ꜠ CTV 30P 1⛟ (£2) croquet clock golf barbecue patio
Credit Cards [1] [2] [3] £

KIRKWHELPINGTON Northumberland Map **12** NY98

SELECTED

GH QQQQ **Shieldhall** Wallington, Cambo NE16 4AQ
☎Otterburn(0830) 40387
rs Nov-Feb

Stephen and Celia Robinson-Gay have created a charming guesthouse from the original 18th-century house and farm buildings which form 3 sides of a courtyard, and feature low ceilings, beams and natural stone. The delightful reproduction furniture featured in most rooms is made by Stephen whose workshop is on the premises. There are 2 family or group suites, with 2 bedrooms sharing facilities, in addition to the 2 rooms with en suite facilities. There are 2 lounges, one of which has a TV and tea-making facilities, while the quiet lounge is elegantly furnished and has French doors leading out to the patio and lawns. Meals are taken in the beamed dining room on 2 large tables. Quite unique in style and layout, Shieldhall offers a peaceful and relaxing stay amidst beautiful countryside.

6rm(5⇐↱1hc) (1fb) ® ✘ (ex guide dogs) dB&B⇐↱£36-£44 WB&B£126-£154 WBDi£196-£224 LDO noon
Lic ꜠ CTV 10P

KIRTLING Cambridgeshire Map **05** TL65

FH QQ Mrs C A Bailey **Hill** *(TL685585)* CB8 9HQ
☎Newmarket(0638) 730253

Situated midway between Saxon Street and the village of Kirtling, this is a traditional 16th-century farmhouse with a modern exterior, surrounded by arable and pasture farmland. Accommodation is comfortable and clean and the public rooms include a lounge and dining room with open log fires and a games room.

3rm(2↱1hc) CTV in 1 bedroom ® ✻ sB&B£22 sB&B↱£22 dB&B£40 dB&B↱£40 WB&Bfr£270 WBDifr£346
LDO 8.30pm
Lic ꜠ CTV 15P games room 500 acres arable £

See advertisement under NEWMARKET

KIRTON Nottinghamshire Map **08** SK66

GH QQ ***Old Rectory*** Main St NG22 9LP
☎Mansfield(0623) 861540 Telex no 378505
Closed Xmas & New Year

An attractive detached Georgian house standing in its own well maintained grounds, situated on the main street of this small rural village. Sound, clean accommodation is provided, with substantial meals available in the dining room, and snacks in the pleasant lounge bar.

10rm(2↱8hc) (1fb) ✘ (ex guide dogs) LDO 7pm
Lic CTV 18P
Credit Cards [1] [3]

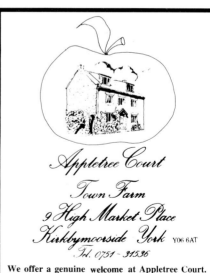

KNARESBOROUGH North Yorkshire Map **08** SE35

GH QQQ ***Newton House Hotel*** 5/7 York Place HG5 0AD
☎Harrogate(0423) 863539 FAX (0423) 869614
Closed 25 & 26 Dec
An attractive Georgian building situated on the A59 York road leaving the town. The owners Len and Jackie Cohen have carefully restored this lovely Grade II listed house, which is decorated throughout in rich prints and stripped pine. Bedrooms are especially spacious: 1 has a half-tester bed and another has a 4-poster. Individually decorated with good quality soft furnishings, each room has TV, direct dial phones, radio alarms, mini bars and tea-making facilities. Good home cooking is provided in the traditional dining room, and there is a car park at the rear.
10rm(9⇌🚿1hc) Annexe 2rm(1⇌1🚿) (3fb) CTV in all bedrooms ® LDO 7pm
Lic 🏨 CTV 7P
Credit Cards [1] [3]
See advertisement under HARROGATE

GH QQQ **The Villa** The Villa Hotel, 47 Kirkgate HG5 8BZ
☎Harrogate(0423) 865370
An interesting and attractive private hotel uniquely situated high above the River Nidd, and conveniently close to the railway station and town centre. Each bedroom is individually decorated and furnished in period style; most have private bathrooms and all have TV, radio alarms, mini-bars and tea and coffee making facilities. The pretty conservatory dining room overlooks the river and there is also a spacious sun terrace.
6rm(4🚿2hc) (1fb) CTV in all bedrooms ® sB&B£16.50 dB&B£36 dB&B🚿£40 WB&B£120-£140
🏨 CTV P̸ Ⓔ

KNOWLE West Midlands Map **07** SP17

GH QQ **Ivy House** Warwick Rd, Heronfield B93 0EB
☎(0564) 770247
A friendly guesthouse just outside Knowle with easy access to the M42, NEC and airport. Rooms are attractively decorated and furnished, with good modern en suite facilities, but a couple of the single rooms are compact.
11🚿 (2fb) CTV in all bedrooms ® sB&B🚿£22-£28 dB&B🚿£36-£44
🏨 CTV 20P ⛳ Ⓔ

KNUTSFORD Cheshire Map **07** SJ77

GH QQ ***Pickmere House*** Park Ln, Pickmere WA16 0JX
☎(0565) 893433
Closed Xmas
A fully modernised 3-storey house in the heart of the village of Pickmere, easily reached off junction 19 of the M6. It is a no-smoking house with 2 comfortable lounges in which to relax.
9rm(5🚿2hc) (3fb)⚡in all bedrooms CTV in all bedrooms ®
🏨 CTV 9P

INN QQQ **The Dog Inn** Well Bank Ln, Over Peover WA16 8UP ☎Chelford(0625) 861421
An attractive village inn that serves good country style food in generous portions. The bedrooms are spacious and well equipped. To find the inn, turn off the A50 at the 'Whipping Stock' inn south of Knutsford, and proceed along this road for about 2 miles.
3⇌ CTV in all bedrooms ® ✈ (ex guide dogs) ✱ sB&B⇌🚿£30-£35 dB&B⇌🚿£55-£60 Bar Lunch £11.50-£14.50 Dinner £12-£14.50 LDO 9.30pm
🏨 30P pool table

KYLESKU Highland *Sutherland* Map **14** NC23

INN Q **Kylesku Hotel** IV27 4HW ☎Scourie(0971) 2231 due to change to (097150) 2231
7hc ® ✱ sB&Bfr£20 dB&Bfr£38 WBDifr£200 Lunch £3.50-£15 Dinner £3.50-£15&alc LDO 9pm
🏨 CTV 12P ⛳ pool table
Credit Cards [1] [3]

LACOCK Wiltshire Map **03** ST96

SELECTED

GH QQQQ **At the Sign of the Angel** 6 Church St SN15 2LA ☎Chippenham(0249) 730230
FAX (0249) 730527
Closed 23 Dec-5 Jan
This ancient property of enormous character is in the centre of the National Trust village of Lacock, which is in itself steeped in history. Access to the M4 is easy via Chippenham, and Bath is only a short drive away. The Sign of the Angel dates back to the 15th century and has been run since 1953 by the Levis family, who are always on hand to offer a friendly welcome to guests. The 2 dining rooms and the first-floor lounge have log fires during the winter months, and the guesthouse has gained a reputation for good traditional English cooking. The set-price menu is good value; a vegetarian or fish dish may be ordered instead of the daily roast, complemented by a wide selection of starters and desserts. Each bedroom has been individually decorated and lavishly furnished with beautiful antique pieces in keeping with the style of the building. There are 4 bedrooms in a cottage annexe, and all the rooms have modern facilities and many thoughtful extras such as fresh flowers and mineral water.
6⇌ Annexe 4⇌ (1fb) CTV in all bedrooms ® T sB&B⇌£55-£70 dB&B⇌£75-£90 LDO 8.15pm
Lic 🏨 P 1🚗 nc10yrs
Credit Cards [1] [2] [3]

LADYBANK Fife Map **11** NO30

GH QQQ **Redlands Country Lodge** KY7 7SH ☎(0337) 31091
Closed 2wks Mar
This attractively maintained development consists of a converted game keeper's house, where meals are served overlooking the colourful gardens, and a Norwegian pine lodge, which has a comfortable lounge and 4 en suite bedrooms, with their own entrances. These rooms have pine walls, polished floors with colourful rugs and pine furniture, and are equipped with extras such as hairdryers and home-made biscuits. Everywhere is kept very clean and guests can be sure of a friendly welcome from the resident proprietors. The lodge is rurally situated, half a mile from the village, beside an unclassified road.
4🚿 (1fb) CTV in all bedrooms ® ✈ (ex guide dogs) ✱ sB&B🚿£21-£23 dB&B🚿£42-£46 WB&B£140-£147 WBDi£224-£238 LDO 2pm
Lic 🏨 CTV 6P

LAMBERHURST Kent Map **05** TQ63

INN QQ **George & Dragon** School Hill TN3 8DQ
☎(0892) 890277
The accommodation is slowly being upgraded at this popular and well managed inn. There are cosy fireside chairs in the beamed bar-lounge and St Georges bar, and the Riverside restaurant offers an à la carte and Sunday carvery menu. Chef/manager Mr J Eaton uses fresh ingredients and local produce, and daily selections can be seen on the blackboard. The hotel is now open all day from 7.30am and serves a good breakfast. There is a pool table and good car parking.
6rm(4⇌🚿2hc) (1fb) CTV in all bedrooms ®
✈ (ex guide dogs) ✱ sB&Bfr£25 sB&B⇌🚿£37.50-£40 dB&B⇌🚿£45-£50 Lunch £1.50-£8.96alc Dinner £5-£30alc LDO 9.30pm
🏨 30P pool table
Credit Cards [1] [3] Ⓔ

LANCASTER Lancashire Map **07** SD46

GH QQQ Lancaster Town House 11/12 Newton Ter, Caton Rd LA1 3PB ☎(0524) 65527

Ideally located for both tourists and business people, this friendly end of terrace establishment offers bright, attractive bedrooms, a comfortable lounge, furnished with a green dralon suite and a nicely appointed dining room where breakfast is taken. Situated one mile from junction 34 of the M6 and only a short distance from the city centre.

6rm(3🛁3🚿) (2fb) CTV in all bedrooms ® 🐕̸ (ex guide dogs) ✱ sB&B🛁🚿£22-£25 dB&B🛁🚿£30-£34.50 ♨ nc4yrs

LANGHOLM Dumfries & Galloway *Dumfriesshire* Map **11** NY38

GH Q Langholm Guest House & Restaurant 81 High St DG13 0DJ ☎(03873) 81343

Situated right beside the main road in the centre of the town, this small, friendly family-owned guesthouse offers modestly appointed accommodation, while a good range of meals are available in the restaurant, which is open from 10am to 9pm.

4hc (2fb) ® ✱ sB&Bfr£16 dB&Bfr£32 LDO 9pm Lic ♨ CTV Ⓔ

LANGLAND BAY West Glamorgan Map **02** SS68

See also Bishopston and Mumbles

GH QQQ Wittemberg Hotel SA3 4QN ☎Swansea(0792) 369696

Closed 24 Dec-4 Jan

The sea is just a short walk away from this family run holiday hotel, set in a quiet area of the town. An ideal base from which to tour the Gower, the hotel provides bright, well-equipped accommodation.

12rm(10🚿2hc) (2fb)🚭in 5 bedrooms CTV in all bedrooms ® 🐕̸ (ex guide dogs) sB&B£25-£30 sB&B🚿£25-£35 dB&B£40 dB&B🚿£45-£50 WB&B£125-£145 WBDi£175-£195 LDO 7pm Lic ♨ CTV 11P nc5yrs Credit Cards 1 3

LANGPORT Somerset Map **03** ST42

SELECTED

GH QQQQ Hillards High St, Curry Rivel TA10 0EY ☎(0458) 251737

This superb Grade II listed building dating back to the late 16th century, was once a large working farm. However, today it is a delightful home to Jeannie Wilkins and Mike Carter who are lovingly restoring the property to an exceptionally high standard; one where guests are invited to enjoy the atmosphere, character and charm of the place. Although the house is in a rural setting in the village of Curry Rivel, its location is convenient for many major routes. Four rooms are expected to be completed early in 1993 as part of the restoration programme which includes extensive landscaping of the grounds. The charm of the oak and elm panelling, beamed ceilings and exposed stonework is enhanced by fresh flowers and fine antiques. Bedrooms are furnished in a luxurious, comfortable style and those en suite have either a spa bath or bath with a separate shower. A hearty breakfast is served, dinner can be booked. This is a no-smoking establishment.

4rm(1🛁🚿3hc) Annexe 2🛁🚿 🚭in all bedrooms 🐕̸ (ex guide dogs) ✱ sB&B£17.50-£25 sB&B🛁🚿£35-£45 dB&B£36 dB&B🛁🚿£46-£55 ♨ CTV 25P nc Ⓔ

See advertisement inside back cover

LARGS Strathclyde *Ayrshire* Map **10** NS25

GH QQQ Whin Park 16 Douglas St KA30 8PS ☎(0475) 673437

Mar-Nov

A detached house, situated 300yds from the main road on the northern side of town. Spotlessly clean and meticulously maintained, the bedrooms are generally very well furnished and thoughtfully laid out; the small single room has different furnishings but still holds appeal, and all the en suite bathrooms are of a high standard. There is a comfortable lounge and neat dining room with individual, well spaced tables.

4🚿 (1fb) CTV in all bedrooms ® 🐕̸ (ex guide dogs) sB&B🚿fr£19 dB&B🚿fr£38 4P

FH QQ Mrs M Watson **South Whittlieburn** *(NS218632)* Brisbane Glen KA30 8SN ☎(0475) 675881

Closed Dec

You are assured of a warm welcome and a home-from-home atmosphere at this roadside farmhouse. There is a comfortable guest lounge and the bedrooms are attractive and thoughtfully equipped, one with a second room adjoining, ideal for a family. The farm lies 2 miles north of Largs on the hill road to Greenock – follow signs to Brisbane Glen.

3rm(1🛁🚿2hc) (1fb) CTV in all bedrooms ® ✱ sB&Bfr£15.50 dB&Bfr£29 dB&B🛁🚿fr£35 ♨ CTV 10P 155 acres sheep Ⓔ

Every effort is made to provide accurate information, but details can change after we go to print. It is advisable to check prices etc. before you make a firm booking.

LATHERON Highland *Caithness* Map **15** ND13

FH QQ Mrs C B Sinclair **Upper Latheron** *(ND195352)* KW5 6DT ☎(05934) 224

May-Oct

A traditional two-storeyed farmhouse in an elevated position enjoying fine views across the North Sea. Situated south of the village off the A9, it offers good value tourist accommodation and is also a popular pony trekking centre.

3rm (1fb) in 2 bedrooms TV in 1 bedroom (ex guide dogs) sB&Bfr£14 dB&Bfr£24 WB&Bfr£84 LDO 6pm

CTV 6P U 200 acres arable beef sheep

LAUNCESTON Cornwall & Isles of Scilly Map **02** SX38

FH QQQ Mrs Margaret Smith **Hurdon** *(SX333828)* PL15 9LS ☎(0566) 772955

May-Oct

An 18th-century stone-built farmhouse on the edge of the town, with easy access to Bodmin Moor and Dartmoor and both the north and south Cornish coasts. The bedrooms are tastefully decorated, and most now have private bathrooms. There is a comfortable lounge, and traditional farmhouse meals are available six nights a week in the dining room.

6rm(4⇌2hc) (1fb) ® (ex guide dogs) sB&B£14-£15 sB&B⇌£16.50-£17.50 dB&B£28-£30 dB&B⇌£33-£35 WB&B£78-£98 WBDi£132-£152 LDO 4.30pm

CTV 10P 400 acres mixed

LAVERTON Gloucestershire Map **04** SP03

SELECTED

GH QQQQ **Leasow House** WR12 7NA (2m SW of Broadway off A46) ☎Stanton(038673) 526

This early 17th-century Cotswold stone farmhouse is situated southwest of Broadway off the A4632 (signposted Worminston and Dumbleton, it is the first farm on the right). Bedrooms are very modern and well equipped, all with en suite facilities, yet the character of the farmhouse has been retained. The comfortable library has a wide range of books and guides. Two new bedrooms have recently been added, and these share a mini kitchen and comfortable lounge.

5⇌ Annexe 4rm(2⇌2) (2fb) CTV in all bedrooms ® * dB&B⇌£45-£65

10P

Credit Cards 1 2 3

See advertisement under BROADWAY

LEAMINGTON SPA (ROYAL) Warwickshire Map **04** SP36

GH QQ **Buckland Lodge Hotel** 35 Avenue Rd CV31 3PG ☎(0926) 423843

Situated on a wide tree lined avenue, this Victorian villa, dating from 1846, was established in 1977 as a hotel by the Chandler family. The bedrooms vary in size offering a mixture of furnishings and most have modern en suite facilities. Breakfast and evening meals are served in the small dining room and a residents' lounge is provided.

10rm(5⇌1 4hc) (2fb) CTV in all bedrooms ® * sB&B£21-£25 sB&B⇌£32-£35 dB&B£36-£42 dB&B⇌£42-£46 WB&B£147-£175 WBDi£179-£207 LDO 2.30pm

Lic 16P

Credit Cards 1 2 3 5 £

GH QQ **Charnwood** 47 Avenue Rd CV31 3PF ☎(0926) 831074

Closed 23 Dec-1 Jan

Charnwood is situated close to the town centre and provides attractive, well equipped accommodation and a comfortable small dining room.

6rm(1⇌1 4hc) (1fb) CTV in all bedrooms ® sB&B£14-£15 sB&B⇌£25-£36 dB&B£27-£32 dB&B⇌£34-£36 WB&B£94.50-£126 WBDi£140-£175 LDO 4pm

CTV 5P

Credit Cards 1 3 5 £

GH QQQ **Coverdale Private Hotel** 8 Portland St CV32 5HE ☎(0926) 330400 FAX (0926) 833388

An attractive and well sited Georgian town house, off Regent Street, offering a high level of comfort and facilities, appealing to commercial and leisure guests alike. Sensitively modernised, accommodation is now almost all en suite.

8rm(2⇌4 2hc) (2fb) CTV in all bedrooms ® T * sB&B⇌fr£31 dB&B⇌fr£42

3P

Credit Cards 1 3 £

GH QQQ **Flowerdale House** 58 Warwick New Rd CV32 6AA ☎(0926) 426002 FAX (0926) 883699

This delightful Victorian property is situated on the Leamington to Warwick road, on the outskirts of town. The accommodation is attractively decorated and the furniture is in keeping with the style of the building, blending nicely with coordinated soft furnishings. A tastefully appointed dining area leads through to the conservatory filled with greenery, and breakfast can sometimes be taken here in the summer. There is a comfortable lounge with an open fire, adjoining a small cosy bar area.

6rm(4⇌2) (1fb) CTV in all bedrooms ® (ex guide dogs) sB&B⇌£22-£26 dB&B⇌£36-£42

Lic 6P

Credit Cards 1 3 £

GH QQ **Glendower** 8 Warwick Place CV32 5BJ ☎(0926) 422784

Situated on the main road into Leamington Spa from Warwick, this guesthouse is just 5 minutes' walk from the town centre. It is a Victorian property offering generally spacious accommodation, and there is an attractive dining room where evening meals are available.

9rm(2⇌7hc) (3fb) CTV in all bedrooms ® * sB&B£14-£18 dB&B£28-£36 dB&B⇌£34-£42 LDO 8pm

Lic CTV 2P £

GH QQQ **Milverton House Hotel** 1 Milverton Ter CV32 5BE ☎(0926) 428335

The friendly proprietors are sure to make guests very welcome at this substantial Victorian property, converted to provide a comfortable, small hotel. The bedrooms are attractively decorated with quality wallcoverings and a mixture of furnishings, plus all have modern, well kept en suite facilities. A particularly good quality lounge provides comfortable sofas and armchairs, and the dining room is in keeping with the style of the building with its impressive fireplace and large brass domed chandelier.

10rm(6⇌4hc) (1fb) CTV in all bedrooms ® T (ex guide dogs) sB&B£20-£24 sB&B⇌£35-£38 dB&B£34-£36 dB&B⇌£42-£48 LDO 5pm

Lic 5P

Credit Cards 1 2 3 £

FH QQQ Mrs R Gibbs **Hill** *(SP343637)* Lewis Rd, Radford Semele CV31 1UX ☎(0926) 337571

Closed Xmas & New Year

Tucked away at the end of Lewis Road, just off the A425 at Radford Semele, this farmhouse is proving popular with business people. The bedrooms have pretty coordinated décor and soft furnishings, most in a honeysuckle print, and modern but compact showers have been added to 3 of them.

6rm(3 3hc) (1fb) in all bedrooms ® * sB&B£15-£20 sB&B£15-£20 dB&B£26-£34 dB&B£26-£34 WB&B£182-£238

CTV 6P 4 350 acres arable beef mixed sheep £

LEDBURY Hereford & Worcester Map **03** SO73

GH QQQ Wall Hills Country Guesthouse Hereford Rd HR8 2PR ☎(0531) 2833 due to change to 632833
Closed 24-31 Dec

Complete with its own 15th-century Cruck barn and near an original Iron Age hill fort, this elegant Georgian mansion overlooking the town centre, provides comfortable, spacious accommodation. There is a small honesty bar for residents, and the chef/proprietor uses fresh home produce in all his cooking, whenever possible. Situated on the A438 Hereford road off the by-pass.

3rm(1⇌1↱1hc) (1fb)⊁in all bedrooms Ⓡ ✗ sB&B£27-£32 sB&B⇌↱£29-£33 dB&B£37-£40 dB&B⇌↱£39-£43
LDO 8.30pm
Lic 🍽 CTV P
Credit Cards 1 3 £

LEEDS West Yorkshire Map **08** SE33

GH QQQ Aragon Hotel 250 Stainbeck Lane, Meanwood LS7 2PS ☎(0532) 759306 FAX (0532) 753300
Closed Xmas

An attractive detached house with a large front garden and a private, locked, car park at the rear. The hotel is well furnished and comfortable, with a good range of facilities including a cocktail bar and small conference room. It is located in the quiet suburb of Meanwood, north of the town centre off the A61.

14rm(8⇌2↱4hc) (1fb) CTV in all bedrooms Ⓡ sB&Bfr£26.08 sB&B⇌↱£32.99-£37.99 dB&Bfr£39.58 dB&B⇌↱£43.74-£48.74 LDO 6pm
Lic 🍽 25P
Credit Cards 1 2 3 5

GH QQQ Ash Mount Hotel 22 Wetherby Road, Oakwood LS8 2QD ☎(0532) 658164

A tall, attractive stone-built house with an extensive front garden and a car park at the rear. Mr and Mrs Spence have gradually been improving their hotel, and the rooms are smart, comfortable and pleasantly furnished. The guesthouse is located off the A58 at Oakwood, northeast of the town centre near Roundhay Park.

12rm(5⇌↱7hc) (2fb) CTV in all bedrooms Ⓡ sB&B£20-£21 sB&B⇌↱£30-£32 dB&B£35-£36 dB&B⇌↱£42-£44
Lic 🍽 CTV 10P
Credit Cards 1 3 £

GH Q Green House 5 Bank View, Stainbeck Ln, Chapel Allerton LS7 2EX ☎(0532) 681380

Just north of the city (off the A61) and tucked away in a residential area along an unadopted lane, is this white painted, early Victorian house with a lovely garden to the rear. Mrs Green (by name and nature) has a strong feeling for the environment and a bold artistic flair which is evident in the unusual but fitting choice of decorative schemes in the simple bedrooms. The book- lined lounge is rather more traditional with William Morris wallpaper and polished parquet flooring. Around the house are meditative shields, based on astrological symbols, made by the proprietor.

2hc ⊁in all bedrooms TV in 1 bedroom Ⓡ ✗ (ex guide dogs) ✱ sB&Bfr£25 dB&Bfr£45 WB&Bfr£133 WBDifr£182
🍽 CTV 4P nc5yrs £

GH Q *Highfield Hotel* 79 Cardigan Road, Headingley LS6 1EB ☎(0532) 752193

A tall semidetached Victorian house set well back from the road, with a car park in front. Located close to the University and county cricket ground, it is just off the A660, north of the town centre. The hotel offers basic, modern accommodation at reasonable prices.

10hc (1fb) Ⓡ LDO 7pm
🍽 CTV 7P

Book as early as possible for busy holiday periods.

GH QQ Holme Leigh Pinfold Ln, Halton LS15 7SX ☎(0532) 607889

A well-run family hotel on the eastern side of Leeds, off the York road, quite easily found by following the signs to Temple Newsam House. Holme Leigh is a 3-storey Edwardian house in a residential road opposite the local school.

8rm(2⇌6hc) CTV in all bedrooms Ⓡ LDO 5pm
Lic 🍽 5P £

GH QQQ *Merevale Hotel* 16 Wetherby Rd, Oakwood LS8 2QD ☎(0532) 658933
Closed Xmas

This large detached house can be found by keeping to the Roundhay road out of Leeds, to the junction with Wetherby Road. Recently taken over by an enthusiastic young couple, Mr and Mrs Jeynes, the house has been refurbished, and improvements are still being made. Bedrooms of various sizes are all coordinated, with crisp navy duvets, starched linens and matching towels. Many of the watercolour landscapes on the walls are the work of Mrs Jeynes.

14rm(6⇌↱8hc) (1fb) CTV in all bedrooms Ⓡ ✗
🍽 CTV 9P
Credit Cards 1 3

GH QQQ Trafford House Hotel 18 Cardigan Road, Headingley LS6 3AG ☎(0532) 752034 FAX (0532) 742422
Closed Xmas

A large, converted Victorian house situated close to the Headingley cricket ground.The accommodation is well furnished and comfortable, and there is ample parking space provided. The hotel is just off the A660, north of the town centre.

18rm(4↱14hc) (4fb) CTV in all bedrooms Ⓡ
✗ (ex guide dogs) ✱ sB&B£21-£23 sB&B↱£37-£42 dB&B£50-£53 LDO noon
Lic 🍽 CTV 30P
Credit Cards 1 3 £

LEEK Staffordshire Map **07** SJ95

GH Q ***Peak Weavers Hotel*** King St ST13 5NW ☎(0538) 383729
A large Georgian house with well kept front gardens situated close to the town centre, backing on to the Catholic church. Built in 1822, it was once a convent. The bedrooms are neat and clean and there is a small bar for residents.
11rm(3🛁1🚿7hc) (2fb) TV in all bedrooms ®
🐕 (ex guide dogs) LDO 8.30pm
Lic 🍽 CTV 8P 4🚗
Credit Cards [1] [2] [3]

INN QQ Abbey Abbey Green Rd ST13 8SA ☎(0538) 382865
Popular locally for its bar food, the inn is just outside Leek (signposted Meerbrook off the A523 Macclesfield road), and provides good parking facilities. The all en suite bedrooms are in converted outbuildings.
Annexe 7🚿 CTV in all bedrooms ® 🐕 (ex guide dogs) ✱
sB&B🚿£25-£27 dB&B🚿£42-£45 LDO 8pm
🍽 60P nc14yrs
Credit Cards [1] [2] [3] (£)

LEICESTER Leicestershire Map **04** SK50

GH QQQ Burlington Hotel Elmfield Av LE2 1RB
☎(0533) 705112 FAX (0533) 704207
Closed Xmas
This small, family-run hotel is situated in a quiet residential road about one mile from the city centre. Public rooms include a small licensed bar and a lounge with a fine wood panelled wall incorporating a fireplace, with stained glass windows. The dining room is in keeping with this late Victorian house, retaining the original cornicing, ceiling roses and beautiful wall panels. A small, good value menu is provided, offering both English and continental home cooking. The majority of bedrooms have en suite facilities and are double glazed; they are all particularly well maintined, with appealing décor and modern fitted furniture. The combination of ample on site car parking and a conference room make this a popular choice for business guests.
16rm(4🛁7🚿5hc) (1fb) CTV in all bedrooms ® 🐕 sB&B£22-£25 sB&B🛁🚿£30-£32 dB&B£32-£35 dB&B🛁🚿£37-£40 LDO 8pm
Lic 🍽 CTV 23P
Credit Cards [1] [3] (£)

GH QQ Croft Hotel 3 Stanley Rd LE2 1RF ☎(0533) 703220 FAX (0533) 706067
A large, detached red-brick Victorian house situated in a quiet residential road just off the A6 London road, 1 mile south of the city centre. Some of the rooms have recently been modernised, with open-plan fitted furniture, pastel décor and coordinated soft furnishings. Other, older rooms are simple, serviceable and well maintained. There is a small lounge with TV and a bar. Dinner is available by prior arrangement, with generous portions of fresh home cooking providing good value-for-money.
26rm(6🛁🚿20hc) (1fb) CTV in all bedrooms ®
🐕 (ex guide dogs) ✱ sB&B£22 sB&B🛁🚿£32 dB&B£34 dB&B🛁🚿£38 LDO 5pm
Lic 🍽 CTV 26P
Credit Cards [1] [3] (£)

GH Q ***Daval Hotel*** 292 London Road, Stoneygate LE2 2AG
☎(0533) 708234
This large Victorian red brick house stands one mile south of the city centre on the busy A6, and is predominantly used by commercial guests. Accommodation is simple, with mixed serviceable furniture, TV and radio alarms. There is a large lounge bar with satellite TV. On site car parking is available, with ample street parking adjacent.
14rm(1🛁13hc) (2fb) CTV in all bedrooms LDO 7pm
Lic 🍽 CTV 20P
Credit Cards [1]

GH QQ Scotia Hotel 10 Westcotes Dr LE3 0QR
☎(0533) 549200
New owners have started upgrading this small family run guesthouse. The refurbished lounge now has a licensed bar and provides a selection of bar snacks to supplement the dinner menu in the dining room. A ground floor bedroom with en suite facilities has been provided for those who find stairs difficult; 6 bedrooms are located in an annexe across the road from the main house. The hotel is conveniently located for access to the M1/M69 junction and city centre.
11rm(2🛁🚿9hc) Annexe 6hc (1fb) CTV in all bedrooms ® ✱
sB&B£17-£22 sB&B🛁🚿£25 dB&B£36-£40 dB&B🛁🚿£40-£45 LDO 9pm
Lic 🍽 5P

GH QQ The Stanfre House Hotel 265 London Rd LE2 3BE
☎(0533) 704294
Closed 24 Dec-2 Jan
This small, friendly, family-run guesthouse is located one mile south of the city centre on the A6. A white painted house slightly set back from the road, it has limited car parking at the front; the majority of bedrooms are located at the rear, thus screened from the traffic noise. Rooms are simply furnished, with bright cheerful décor and spotlessly maintained. The public rooms house a collection of plates and brasses, and guests are welcome to play the electric organ in the breakfast room.
12hc (1fb) CTV in 2 bedrooms TV in 4 bedrooms ✱ sB&B£19 dB&B£30 WB&B£133
Lic 🍽 CTV 6P (£)

GH QQ Stoneycroft Hotel 5/7 Elmfield Av LE2 1RB
☎(0533) 707605 FAX (0533) 706067
This large, cream-washed building is set slightly back from the road in a quiet residential road off the busy A6. Part of a major renovation scheme has recently been completed, providing more en suite facilities. The new rooms are equipped with wooden open plan fitted furniture, colour coordinated soft furnishings, clock radios, TV and tea trays. The older rooms are simply furnished and more compact, with rooms priced accordingly. The public rooms now have good colour schemes and décor throughout. There is a lounge with pool and TV available, and a restaurant and bar offering a choice of menus, together with bar snacks.
44rm(25🛁🚿19hc) (4fb) CTV in all bedrooms ®
🐕 (ex guide dogs) ✱ sB&B£22-£32 sB&B🛁🚿£32 dB&B🛁🚿£38 WB&B£140-£210 WBDi£210-£280 LDO 9pm
Lic 🍽 CTV 20P pool table
Credit Cards [1] [3] (£)

LEIGH Hereford & Worcester Map **03** SO75

FH QQ Mrs F S Stewart ***Leigh Court*** *(SO784535)* WR6 5LB
☎Leigh Sinton(0886) 32275
28 Mar-6 Oct
This large, early 17th-century farmhouse is situated off the A4103 (signposted from Bransford), opposite the parish church, and is set on a sheep and arable working farm. The big bedrooms are furnished with solid period-style furniture. The lounge and dining room are also very spacious, and there are pleasant lawns and a snooker room with a full size table. The farm has a 14th- century timber framed barn built for the monks of Pershore Abbey, which is the largest 'cruck' built structure in Britain.
3rm(1🚿2hc) ® LDO 9am
🍽 CTV 6P 🎣 billiard room library 270 acres arable sheep

LELANT Cornwall & Isles of Scilly Map **02** SW53

INN QQQ ***Badger*** TR26 3JT ☎Hayle(0736) 752181
This village inn is situated in the area of St Ives Bay, close to the Hayle Estuary and the A30. The bars are furnished in a comfortable style, yet retain their character and atmosphere. An extensive selection of dishes is available from the blackboard menus and hot servery. Bedrooms have been tastefully decorated and equipped with many extras such as colour TV, direct dial telephones, tissues and toiletries.

6⇌↱ CTV in all bedrooms ® ✘ (ex guide dogs)
LDO 10.15pm
🅿 100P nc6yrs
Credit Cards 1

LEOMINSTER Hereford & Worcester Map **03** SO45

See also Bodenham

GH QQ ***Knapp House*** Luston HR6 0DB (2.5m N on B4361)
☎(0568) 615705

An impressive 16th-century black and white timbered house in the centre of the village of Luston, a few miles north of Leominster. The sitting room has magnificent original wood panelled walls and a log fire, and the small dining room has a beamed ceiling with a communal dining table. Outside, there are pretty gardens, and the Morris family offer genuine hospitality to their guests.

2hc (1fb) TV in 1 bedroom ® LDO 5pm
🅿 CTV 4P

SELECTED

GH QQQQ ***Withenfield*** South St HR6 8JN
☎(0568) 612011

Part Georgian, part Victorian, the Withenfield is situated on the B4361 (the old A48), just south of the town centre, and is set in half an acre of lawns, with well laid out flower gardens and a recently extended car park. Mr and Mrs Cotton are a charming couple who offer genuine warmth and hospitality, they have had family connections with the house since the 1920s and have lovingly restored it in recent years. The spacious bedrooms are furnished with antiques and good armchairs, 2 have original fireplaces and one a 4-poster bed. Modern facilities include colour TV, direct dial telephones and hairdryers. There is a delightful drawing room with an impressive mirrored marble fireplace and a grand piano that guests may play; and the original conservatory, dating back to 1897, is still in use. French, Spanish and German are spoken here.

4⇌↱ ⊬in all bedrooms CTV in all bedrooms ®
✘ (ex guide dogs) LDO 8.30pm
Lic 🅿 6P
Credit Cards 1 3

FH QQQ Mrs Jane Conolly **The Hills** *(SO564638)* Leysters HR6 9HP ☎Leysters(056887) 205
Mar-Oct

Set in 20 acres of arable farmland with pretty gardens surrounding the house, this 15th-century farmhouse is run by the very friendly Peter and Jane Conolly. The attractively timbered lounge has pretty floral covered settees and a wood burning stove, leading to the slab floored dining room, complete with pine dresser, where good home cooking is prepared by Jane. There are 3 bedrooms, each of them individual in character – one is called the 'Chapel Room' reflecting a previous use and one the 'Tigeen' (Irish for small house) is in a converted barn with an upstairs, pine furnished bedroom. Two rooms are en suite and the third has a private bathroom nearby.

2⇌ CTV in all bedrooms ® ✱ sB&B⇌£23-£24 dB&B⇌£36-£38 WB&B£126-£133 WBDi£210-£217 LDO 5pm
🅿 6P nc12yrs 120 acres arable

FH QQ Mr & Mrs Black ***Wharton Bank*** *(SO508556)* HR6 0NX ☎(0568) 612575

A warm welcome is assured from the friendly Black family at this busy working dairy farm just off the B4361 south of the town. Bedrooms are well decorated and there is a comfortable lounge for residents.

4rm(1⇌3hc) ® ✘ (ex guide dogs)
🅿 CTV 8P 2🚗 nc3yrs ⛱ 🎾(grass)174 acres dairy

LERWICK

See **SHETLAND**

LEVENS Cumbria Map **07** SD48

INN QQQ Gilpin Bridge Hotel & Restaurant Bridge End LA8 8EP ☎(044852) 206

This busy and conveniently situated Cumbrian inn offers a very good range of food, either in the bar or the restaurant. Bedrooms are modern in style, all are en suite and have direct dial telephones and colour TV. The inn is situated just off the A590 in the open countryside of south Lakeland.

10rm(6⇌4↱) CTV in all bedrooms ® ✘ (ex guide dogs) ✱
sB&B⇌↱£29.50 dB&B⇌↱£46 LDO 9pm
🅿 100P pool table darts board
Credit Cards 1 3

LEW Oxfordshire Map **04** SP30

SELECTED

FH QQQQ Mrs M J Rouse **The Farmhouse Hotel & Restaurant** *(SP322059)* University Farm OX18 2AU
☎Bampton Castle(0993) 850297 & 851480 Telex no 83243
FAX (0993) 850965
Closed Xmas & New Year rs Sun

A 17th-century Cotswold stone farmhouse situated 3 miles south of Witney on the A4095 Bampton road in this tiny village; part of the Rouse family's working farm, the attractive gardens and terraces have peaceful country views. Bedrooms are individually furnished and decorated and retain many of the original features, including oak-beamed ceilings, inglenook fireplaces and a Victorian bath; they all have private bathrooms, TV, direct dial telephone and radio alarm; 1 room on the ground floor has been designed for disabled guests. The comfortable sitting room has a splendid inglenook fireplace, and a cosy bar adjoins the beamed restaurant with an attractive conservatory, used mostly as a breakfast room. The restaurant is open to non-residents, and simple farmhouse food is offered, with a daily-changing menu offering a variety of seasonal choices. Smoking is not permitted in the restaurant and bedrooms.

6⇌↱ (2fb)⊬in all bedrooms CTV in all bedrooms ® **T**
✘ (ex guide dogs) sB&B⇌↱fr£39 dB&B⇌↱fr£52
LDO 7.30pm
Lic 🅿 25P nc5yrs 216 acres dairy
Credit Cards 1 3

See advertisement on page 235

LEWDOWN Devon Map **02** SX48

FH Q Mrs M E Horn **Venn Mill** *(SX484885)* EX20 4EB
☎Bridestowe(083786) 288
Etr-Oct

Guest rooms are on ground level at this modern farmhouse, and all have windows opening on to the well kept garden. The bedrooms are bright with coordinating soft furnishings, and there is a pleasant atmosphere in the comfortable lounge. Meals are served in a relaxed and informal dining room, and the house offers easy access to the A30 between Okehampton and Launceston. Trout fishing is available on the farm and there are facilities for coarse fishing and pony trekking nearby.

3rm(2hc) (1fb) CTV in 1 bedroom ® ✘ sB&B£14 dB&B£28
LDO 4pm
CTV 4P 4🚗 ✔ 160 acres beef dairy sheep Ⓕ

LEWIS, ISLE OF Western Isles *Ross & Cromarty* Map **13**

STORNOWAY Map **13** NB43

GH QQ Ardlonan 29 Francis St PA87 2NF ☎(0851) 703482
Closed Xmas & New Year
Situated at the end of a terrace in a residential area close to the town centre, this personally run guesthouse offers comfortable, good value accommodation. The breakfast menu offers a good choice of dishes, while tasty home baking is served to guests in the lounge in the evening.
5hc (1fb) in all bedrooms CTV in 2 bedrooms TV in 2 bedrooms ® sB&B£16 dB&B£32
CTV

UIG Map **13** NB03

GH QQQ Corran View 22a Breasclete PA86 9EF ☎(0851) 72300
Situated 18 miles west of Stornoway in a quiet village overlooking East Loch Roag, a former croft house has been extended and modernised to create this friendly, family-run holiday guesthouse. Bedrooms, though compact, are comfortably furnished in the modern style. There is a small dining room and the comfortable lounge was being extended at the time of our visit.
3 (1fb) CTV in all bedrooms ® dB&B £60 (incl dinner) WBDi£198 LDO 7pm
CTV 6P

LEYBURN North Yorkshire Map **07** SE19

GH Q *Eastfield Lodge Private Hotel* 1 St Matthews Ter DL8 5EL ☎Wensleydale(0969) 23196
An unpretentious guesthouse on the outskirts of this Dales town, providing spacious bedrooms, a comfortable lounge with a bar for guests and an attractive dining room.
8hc (2fb) CTV in all bedrooms ® LDO 8.30pm
Lic 10P
Credit Cards 1 3

INN QQ The Black Swan Hotel Market Place DL8 4NP ☎Wensleydale(0969) 22221
Closed 24-27 Dec
Beams, stone walls and open fires are features of this 17th-century inn situated in the market place of the Yorkshire Dales town, noted for its racehorse training stables. Bedrooms in the older part of the inn are full of character: 2 have 4-poster beds, and all have modern en suite facilities. There is a wide variety of bar meals available, and a cosy dining room for resident guests.
7 (1fb) CTV in all bedrooms ® sB&B £24.50-£25 dB&B £38.50-£39.50 Lunch £7.25-£8.50alc Dinner £7.25-£16.75alc LDO 9pm
Credit Cards 1 3 £

INN QQQ Foresters Arms Carlton-in-Coverdale DL8 2BB ☎(0969) 40272
This attractive, grey stone inn, built in the 17th century, is situated by the roadside in the picturesque village of Carlton. Beams, flagstone floors, farming bric-a-brac and log fires are a feature of the bars, which together with the dining room – furnished with candlelit antique tables – form pleasant public areas. An à la carte menu is available at night and extensive bar meals are served both at lunch and dinner. The bedrooms have recently been restored to a tasteful, modern standard and are attractively decorated, still retaining the character of the period. Outside there is a small beer garden with benches on the grass verge for sunny days.
3rm(2 1hc) CTV in all bedrooms ® ✱ sB&B£21.50-£25 sB&B £21.50-£25 dB&B£40-£50 dB&B £40-£50 WB&B£150 WBDi£250 Bar Lunch £4-£15 High tea £4-£6 Dinner £17-£22.50&alc LDO 10pm
CTV 12P
Credit Cards 1 3

LICHFIELD Staffordshire Map **07** SK10

GH QQ Coppers End Walsall Rd, Muckley Corner WS14 0BG ☎Brownhills(0543) 372910
Three miles southwest of the town, alongside the A461, this small, family-run guesthouse is set in pleasant lawns and gardens with its own car park. Bedrooms are pretty and there is a comfortable lounge for residents.
6rm(1 5hc) in all bedrooms CTV in all bedrooms ® sB&B£20-£22 sB&B £27 dB&Bfr£33 dB&B fr£39 WB&B£104-£170 WBDi£163.50-£229.50 LDO noon
Lic CTV 10P 2 (£1)
Credit Cards 1 3 £

GH QQQ The Oakleigh House Hotel 25 St Chads Rd WS13 7LZ ☎(0543) 262688
rs Sun evening & Mon
Set in attractive lawns and gardens and overlooking Stowe Pool, this family- run hotel provides good modern accommodation. The bar and lounge are comfortable and relaxing, and the restaurant, now independently run, is gaining in popularity.
5rm(3 2hc) Annexe 5rm(1 4) CTV in all bedrooms ® T ✱ sB&B fr£35 dB&Bfr£50 dB&B fr£55 LDO 9.30pm
Lic 20P nc5yrs
Credit Cards 1 3

LIFTON Devon Map **02** SX38

GH QQ Mayfield House PL16 0AN ☎(0566) 784401
A small, detached, family-run guesthouse with its own garden, set back off the main A30 road in the town. Four recently redecorated bedrooms have attractive coordinating soft furnishings, and there is a cosy bar downstairs.
4hc (2fb) in all bedrooms CTV in all bedrooms ® (ex guide dogs) ✱ sB&B£17 dB&B£31.50
Lic 9P 1
Credit Cards 2 £
See advertisement under LAUNCESTON

LIGHTHORNE Warwickshire Map **04** SP35

FH QQ Mrs J Stanton **Redlands** *(SP334570)* Banbury Rd CV35 0AH (on A41, 5m S of Warwick) ☎Warwick(0926) 651241
Closed Xmas
A long drive leads from the A41 to this carefully preserved 16th-century house. The pretty gardens and open-air swimming pool are available to guests, and Mrs Stanton cooks wholesome dishes using home grown produce where possible.
3rm(1 2hc) (1fb) in all bedrooms (ex guide dogs) sB&B£14-£15 dB&B£30-£32 dB&B £30-£35 WB&B£98-£125.50
CTV 6P 100 acres arable £
See advertisement under WARWICK

LINCOLN Lincolnshire Map **08** SK97

GH Q *Brierley House Hotel* 54 South Park LN5 8ER ☎(0522) 526945 & 522945
On a quiet avenue overlooking South Park, south of the city centre, this professionally run hotel offers rooms which are generally well proportioned with some en suite facilities. There is a comfortable lounge and the dining room has a small bar. Brierley House successfully caters for both commercial and weekend visitors to the city.
11rm(2 4 5hc) CTV in 10 bedrooms TV in 1 bedroom ® LDO breakfast
Lic CTV adjacent 18 hole golf course

GH QQQ ***Carline*** 1-3 Carline Rd LN1 1HL ☎(0522) 530422
Closed Xmas & New Year
This double-fronted Edwardian house is located just a short walk from the castle and cathedral, in a quiet residential area. The enthusiastic and friendly proprietors work hard to maintain a high standard throughout, and this is reflected in the good quality accommodation provided. The attractive bedrooms are well equipped and comfortable, the majority having private bathrooms. Annexe rooms in a house opposite are equally well maintained and equipped but slightly old-fashioned, which is reflected in a cheaper tariff. There is a no smoking policy in the main house.
9⇌🚿 Annexe 3rm(1🚿2hc) (2fb)⊬in 9 bedrooms CTV in all bedrooms ®
🛏 7P 2🚗 nc2yrs

SELECTED

GH QQQQ D'Isney Place Hotel Eastgate LN2 4AA
☎(0522) 538881 FAX (0522) 511321
A Georgian town house adjacent to the Minster with a pay and display car park across the road. In the absence of any public areas, the bedrooms, most of which are spacious, have been furnished comfortably in period style. Antiques are set off against lavish fabrics, with which some beds are canopied, and all rooms have modern facilities and excellent en suites. An ample and well presented breakfast is served in the bedrooms.
18rm(15⇌3🚿) (2fb)⊬in 3 bedrooms CTV in all bedrooms ® T ✱ sB&B⇌🚿£39-£53 dB&B⇌🚿£62-£72
🛏 7P
Credit Cards 1 2 3 5

GH QQQ ***Ferncliffe House Hotel*** 2 St Catherines LN5 8LY
☎(0522) 522618
Closed 24 Dec-2 Jan
This guesthouse, once a substantial family home, is situated just on the outskirts of the city centre, with a large private car park and access from Crosscliffe Hill, A15. Its Victorian origins are evident in the high ceilings and spacious bedrooms, which are individually and attractively furnished with comfort in mind. The lounge has a splendid fireplace with an open fire, and there is a separate dining room.
5rm(2🚿3hc) (2fb) CTV in all bedrooms ® LDO 9pm
Lic 8P
Credit Cards 1 2 3

GH QQQ ***Minster Lodge Hotel*** 3 Church Ln LN2 1QJ
☎(0522) 513220 FAX (0522) 513220
Located in the upper part of the city, just a short walk from the cathedral, this is a large semidetached corner house of the late Victorian period. It has had great care and attention lavished on it by owner Ray Brown, which is immediately evident in the neat, colourful garden and the high standard of cleanliness and maintenance inside.
6⇌🚿 (2fb) CTV in all bedrooms ® ✗ (ex guide dogs)
Lic 🛏 CTV 6P
Credit Cards 1 2 3

GH QQQ Tennyson Hotel 7 South Park LN5 8EN
☎(0522) 521624 & 513684
Situated towards the city centre on the inner southern ring road, this extremely well kept and comfortable guesthouse offers bedrooms which are comfortably fitted and furnished and benefit from good, modern en suite facilities. Proprietors Mr and Mrs Saggiorato also provide an à la carte menu in the dining room.
8rm(2⇌6🚿) (1fb) CTV in all bedrooms ® ✗ sB&B⇌🚿£28-£29 dB&B⇌🚿£40-£42 LDO 7.45pm
Lic 🛏 8P
Credit Cards 1 2 3 £

See advertisement on page 237

LINLITHGOW Lothian *West Lothian* Map **11** NS97

FH QQ Mrs A Hay **Belsyde House** *(NS976755)* Lanark Rd EH49 6QE ☎(0506) 842098

Closed Xmas

A period farmhouse with well tended gardens 1.5 miles west of Linlithgow off the A706, its elevated position providing fine views northwards across the Forth valley. Enthusiastically run and neatly maintained it offers 2 spacious rooms and 2 singles, all thoughtfully equipped. There is a comfortable lounge with books and tourist information, and a separate dining room adjoining.

4rm(1⛆3hc) (1fb) CTV in all bedrooms ® ✗ (ex guide dogs) ✱ sB&Bfr£15 dB&Bfr£30 dB&B⛆fr£34 LDO noon

▥ CTV 10P 106 acres beef sheep

LISKEARD Cornwall & Isles of Scilly Map **02** SX26

GH QQ **Elnor** 1 Russell St PL14 4BP ☎(0579) 342472

Closed Xmas

Located conveniently close to the station and not far from the town centre, this neat guesthouse has recently been extended to provide an additional 3 en suite bedrooms. Public areas are cosy and simply styled and a good home-cooked breakfast is served, but now there are more restaurants in the town an evening meal is only available on request. The small rear car park is an added bonus here.

9rm(4⛆5hc) (1fb) ® ✗ sB&B£15.50 sB&B⛆£20.50 dB&Bfr£31 dB&B⛆fr£37 WB&B£101.50-£143.50 WBDi£171.50-£213.50 LDO 5pm

Lic ▥ CTV 6P £

FH QQQ Mrs S Rowe **Tregondale** *(SX294643)* Menheniot PL14 3RG (E of Liskeard 1.5m N of A38) ☎(0579) 342407

Situated 1.5 miles off the A390 at Merrymont, this farmhouse has been well modernised yet retains much character, charm and warmth. Bedrooms are pretty, bright and with tasteful coordinated furnishings. One now has excellent modern en suite facilities and the other has sole use of a nearby bathroom. A cheerful homely atmosphere pervades the public areas which are shared with the friendly Rowe family. Traditional farmhouse food is offered, and guests dine around a large communal table.

3rm(1⇌⛆2hc) (1fb) ® ✗ sB&B£15-£18.50 sB&B⇌⛆£17.50-£18.50 dB&B£30-£35 dB&B⇌⛆£35-£37 WB&B£108-£115 WBDi£150-£170 LDO 6pm

CTV 3P ⚲(hard)shooting pony rides 180 acres arable beef mixed sheep £

LITTLE CHEVERELL Wiltshire Map **03** ST95

GH QQQ **Little Cheverell House** Little Cheverell SN10 4JJ ☎Devizes(0380) 813322

In an elevated position surrounded by 4.5 acres of garden and paddocks, this unspoilt Georgian house has retained its graceful, well proportioned rooms. The 2 spacious bedrooms have antique furnishings and interesting items collected by the owners during their many trips abroad. One room is equipped with a modern en suite bathroom and the other has its own bathroom across the landing. A set menu of 3 courses and coffee is served at dinner using fresh local produce.

2⇌⛆ ⚟in all bedrooms ® ✗ sB&B⇌⛆£33-£38 dB&B⇌⛆£48-£52 LDO 9am

▥ CTV P nc12yrs ⚲(hard) £

LITTLE DEWCHURCH Hereford & Worcester Map **03** SO53

FH QQ Mrs G Lee **Cwm Craig** *(SO535322)* HR2 6PS ☎Carey(0432) 840250

A very attractive Georgian house some 6 miles southeast of Hereford off the A49. The spacious bedrooms are furnished with some interesting antique pieces and there are several very comfortable sitting areas. A games room including snooker is available for guests' use.

3hc (1fb) ® ✗ (ex guide dogs) ✱ sB&B£14-£15 dB&B£26-£28 WB&B£84-£90

▥ CTV 5P 190 acres arable beef £

See advertisement under HEREFORD

LITTLE GRANSDEN Cambridgeshire Map **04** TL25

FH QQQ Peter & Mary Cox **Gransden Lodge** *(TL288537)* Longstowe Rd SG19 3EB ☎Great Gransden(0767) 677365

A warm, friendly atmosphere awaits guests at Gransden Lodge Farm, which is located midway between the villages of Little Gransden and Longstowe on the B1046 road. It is a quiet location in an open rural setting of predominantly arable farming with a herd of Gelbwith cattle. Accommodation is clean and cosy, and guests have the use of a large, comfortable lounge with an open log fire.

3rm(1⇌⛆1hc) ⚟in all bedrooms CTV in all bedrooms ® ✗ ✱ sB&B£15-£17 dB&B£25-£27 dB&B⇌⛆£30-£35 WB&B£79.50-£100

▥ CTV 6P 860 acres arable beef mixed £

LITTLE PETHERICK Cornwall & Isles of Scilly Map **02** SW97

GH QQQ **The Old Mill Country House Hotel** PL27 7QT ☎Rumford(0841) 540388

Mar-Oct rs Nov-Etr

Built in 1563, this fine millhouse was used for grinding corn until the 1940s. The water mill adds a further dimension to the outstanding, walled riverside garden and sun terrace. Many of the original features have been retained in the Grade II listed building, including slate floors, beams and fireplaces. The 7 bedrooms are furnished in oak, satinwood and pine, and 2 rooms have adjacent shower facilities; all the rooms have views of the surrounding countryside. There is a beamed dining room, a sitting area and 2 lounges, 1 with TV. There is a daily 4-course menu, with alternative à la carte dishes available. The hotel is very well run by Michael and Pat Walker, with high standards of personal service and comfort in delightful surroundings.

6rm(1⇌4⛆1hc) ⚟in 1 bedroom ® ✗ (ex guide dogs) sB&B£29.50-£38.25 sB&B⇌⛆£37-£47.70 dB&B£42.50 dB&B⇌⛆£53 WB&B£148.75-£185.50 WBDi£220-£257 LDO 6pm

Lic ▥ CTV 10P nc14yrs £

LIVERPOOL Merseyside Map **07** SJ39

GH QQ **Aachen Hotel** 91 Mount Pleasant L3 5TB ☎051-709 3477 & 1126

Closed 25 Dec-7 Jan

Situated close to the Roman Catholic cathedral and convenient for the city centre, this long established and popular private hotel is run in a friendly and efficient manner. Although accommodation is fairly compact, bedrooms are attractively furnished and offer several extras such as hairdryers, trouser presses and satellite TV. There is a neat breakfast room, and a small lounge bar where a small range of snacks is offered in the evening.

17rm(1⇌6⛆10hc) (6fb) CTV in all bedrooms ® **T** ✗ (ex guide dogs) ✱ sB&B£20-£30 sB&B⇌⛆£28-£30 dB&B£34-£42 dB&B⇌⛆£42-£44 WB&B£140.25-£196 WBDi£180.25-£236.25 LDO 8.30pm

Lic ▥ CTV P (£2.50 day) 🚗 (charged) snooker pool room

Credit Cards 1 2 3 5 £

GH Q **New Manx Hotel** 39 Catherine St L8 7NE ☎051-708 6171 FAX 051-737 2206

The new owners are gradually making improvements to this modestly appointed establishment, situated close to the Anglican Cathedral, which offers reasonably priced accommodation, popular with students and musicians.

11hc (2fb) CTV in all bedrooms ® ✱ sB&B£18.50-£20 dB&B£35-£40 WB&B£105-£120 LDO 9.30pm

▥ 20P

Credit Cards 1 2 3 5 £

LIZARD Cornwall & Isles of Scilly Map **02** SW71

GH QQQ ***The Caerthillian*** TR12 7NQ ☎(0326) 290019
15 Mar-24 Dec rs Feb-14 Mar

This Victorian property is full of character and has recently been upgraded and refurbished. Situated in the centre of the Lizard, it is operated very much as 'a restaurant with rooms' rather than a traditional guesthouse. Worthy home-cooked dishes feature regularly in the elegant restaurant, and service is hospitable. There is a cosy bar lounge on the ground floor, and bedrooms are compact but bright and comfortable.

5rm(2⇌ 3hc) CTV in all bedrooms ® ✗ (ex guide dogs) LDO 9pm
Lic 🍽 3P nc12yrs
Credit Cards 1 3

SELECTED

GH QQQQ Landewednack House Church Cove TR12 7PQ ☎The Lizard(0326) 290909

Peter and Geraldine Tebbitt have created a delightful hideaway hotel at this 17th-century former rectory set in a walled garden overlooking the church. Long-standing links with Brittany are maintained, as the house is the home of Landewednack Boule Club. The bedrooms are comfortable and charmingly furnished and decorated. Geraldine is a talented cook and dinner or supper is served, by arrangement only, from a set menu. A recent meal consisted of individual hot spinach, cheese and crab soufflés followed by fillet of turbot with a light fish mousseline sauce with home-grown vegetables, strawberry mille feuille and a small selection of well kept cheeses completed the meal. Guests sit around one large table, house party-style. Breakfast includes fresh orange juice, home-grown fruit in season, generous portions of freshly cooked bacon and home-made marmalade. There are 2 sitting rooms and a self-catering cottage – an integral part of the house – is available. This is a no-smoking establishment.

3rm(1) CTV in all bedrooms ® ✗ (ex guide dogs) ✱ sB&Bfr£18 dB&B£44-£60 dB&B£50-£60 LDO 9pm
Lic 🍽 CTV 6P 2🚗 nc11yrs boule pentanque
Credit Cards 1 3

GH QQ Mounts Bay House Hotel Penmenner Rd TR12 7NP ☎(0326) 290305 & 290393
Closed Nov

A friendly Victorian guesthouse set on the edge of the village with glorious unrestricted views across the fields to Kynance Cove. Bedrooms are traditionally furnished and spotlessly clean, five have en suite showers. Public rooms are comfortable, and guests are well cared for.

7rm(2 5hc) (1fb) ® sB&B£17-£23 sB&B£18.50-£24.50 dB&B£34-£46 dB&B£37-£49 WB&B£107-£149 WBDi£177-£219 LDO 6.30pm
Lic 🍽 CTV 10P
Credit Cards 1 3

GH QQ Parc Brawse House Penmenner Rd TR12 7NR ☎(0326) 290466
Mar-Nov rs Nov

A comfortable house of character, set back in its own grounds, with commanding views out to sea across farmland. Friendly service is provided by the owners, whose pleasantly refurbished house provides a good base for touring south Cornwall.

6rm(2 4hc) (1fb) ® sB&B£12.50-£16 dB&B£25-£30 dB&B£30-£35 WB&B£80.50-£122.51 WBDi£144.75-£183.75 LDO 5.30pm
Lic CTV 6P
Credit Cards 1 3 £

GH QQQ ***Penmenner House Hotel*** Penmenner Rd TR12 7NR ☎(0326) 290370

This hotel has been transformed into a very comfortable and welcoming retreat. Standing in its own grounds, Penmenner House has panoramic views of the coastline and lighthouse. The excellent accommodation is complemented by fine home cooking using fresh local produce.

8rm(5 3hc) (2fb) CTV in all bedrooms ® ✗ (ex guide dogs) LDO 6pm
Lic 🍽 CTV 10P
Credit Cards 1 3

LLANBEDR Gwynedd Map **06** SH52

INN QQQ Victoria LL45 2LD (Frederic Robinson) ☎(034123) 213

This popular stone-built former coaching inn dates back to the 17th century and is situated in the village centre, on the A496. The modern bedrooms are attractively decorated and well furnished with pine; they are equipped to a high standard and have private bathrooms. Public areas include a choice of bars and a pleasant garden with a children's play area.

5⇌ CTV in all bedrooms ® sB&B⇌£25.50 dB&B⇌£47.50 WB&B£153 Bar Lunch £1.10-£8.75 High tea £3-£5.75 Dinner £6-£10&alc LDO 9.30pm
🍽 CTV 75P 7🚗
Credit Cards 1 3

LLANBERIS Gwynedd Map **06** SH56

GH QQ Alpine Lodge Hotel 1 High St LL55 4EN ☎(0286) 870294
rs 28 Oct-Mar

This small, privately owned and personally run hotel is situated on the High Street, at the northwest end of the town. It provides well equipped accommodation and is equally suitable for both tourists and commercial visitors.

→

6rm(4⇨↖2hc) (2fb) CTV in all bedrooms Ⓡ
✗ (ex guide dogs) ✱ sB&B⇨↖£25-£33 dB&B⇨↖£35-£43
WB&B£122.50-£136.50 WBDi£206.50-£220.50 LDO 6pm
Lic 🍽 10P windsurfers canoes
Credit Cards 1 2 3 5

GH QQ ***Lake View Hotel*** Tan-y-Pant LL55 4EL
☎(0286) 870422
This small stone-built house is privately owned and has been extended to provide modern, well equipped accommodation. All except one of the well equipped bedrooms have en suite facilities, and the cottage-style restaurant is popular with both residents and locals. The hotel is situated on the A4086 to the west of the town, overlooking Lake Padarn.
10rm(9↖1hc) (3fb) CTV in all bedrooms Ⓡ ✗ (ex guide dogs)
LDO 9.30pm
Lic 🍽 CTV 10P
Credit Cards 1 3

LLANDDEINIOLEN Gwynedd Map **06** SH56

FH QQQ Mr & Mrs Pierce ***Ty-Mawr*** *(SH553664)* LL55 3AD
☎Port Dinorwic(0248) 670147
This large house is quietly situated on the B4366, from where there are good views of the Snowdonian range. Though it dates from 1760, the house has been considerably modernised and provides comfortable accommodation.
4rm(1⇨3↖) (1fb)⊬in 1 bedroom CTV in 1 bedroom Ⓡ
✗ (ex guide dogs) LDO 6pm
🍽 CTV 20P 87 acres beef sheep

SELECTED

FH QQQQ Mrs Kettle **Ty'n-Rhos** *(SH548672)* Seion
LL55 3AE ☎Port Dinorwic(0248) 670489
Closed 20 Dec-6 Jan
Little remains of the original late 17th-century farmhouse which occupied this site. Considerable alterations and extensions have been carried out in recent times to provide a large modern house with very good quality, well equipped accommodation. Situated in a quiet rural area, Ty'n-Rhos commands good views of the surrounding countryside. Caernarfon, Llanberis, Snowdon and Anglesey are all within a few minutes drive.
11⇨↖ (3fb) CTV in all bedrooms Ⓡ ✗ (ex guide dogs)
sB&B⇨↖£28.50-£30 dB&B⇨↖£54-£60 WB&B£177-£198 WBDi£270-£288 LDO 6.30pm
Lic 🍽 12P nc5yrs ⌡ 72 acres mixed
Credit Cards 1

LLANDEILO Dyfed Map **02** SN62

GH QQQ Brynawel 19 New Rd SA19 6DD ☎(0558) 822925
rs 25 & 26 Dec
Situated on the main road close to the town centre, this small, mid-terrace, family-run hotel provides a cheerful and friendly service. It has a popular café-style restaurant, which serves a selection of hot and cold food throughout the day. The prettily decorated bedrooms are furnished with modern laminated furniture and all have a TV. There is a quiet, modern lounge available for guests.
5rm(2⇨1↖2hc) (1fb) CTV in all bedrooms Ⓡ
✗ (ex guide dogs) sB&B£19 sB&B⇨↖£23-£24 dB&B£28
dB&B⇨↖£34 LDO 5pm
Lic 🍽 6P
Credit Cards 1 3

LLANDELOY Dyfed Map **02** SM82

GH QQQ Upper Vanley Farmhouse SA62 6LJ
☎Croesgoch(0348) 831418
Mar-Nov
Once part of a working farm, this family-run guesthouse is located a few miles from St Davids and is convenient for tourists with its proximity to the many sandy beaches of North Pembrokeshire. Bedrooms are decorated with a floral theme, and most have good en suite bathrooms; they all have TV and tea making facilities. Enjoyable home cooking is offered, and toys and games are available for children who are made especially welcome. There is a modern, comfortable lounge with a piano.
7rm(6⇨↖1hc) (6fb) CTV in all bedrooms Ⓡ sB&B⇨↖£16-£20 dB&B⇨↖£32-£40 WBDi£135-£190 LDO 4pm
Lic 🍽 CTV 15P beauty treatment room

LLANDOGO Gwent Map **03** SO50

GH Q ***Brown's Hotel & Restaurant*** NP5 4TW
☎Dean(0594) 530262
Feb-Nov
Set alongside the A466 in the beautiful Wye Valley, this modestly furnished guesthouse also has a shop and café providing snacks and teas all day. The bedrooms have good en suite facilities.
7rm(1↖6hc) LDO 7.30pm
Lic CTV 20P nc

INN QQQ The Sloop NP5 4TW ☎Dean(0594) 530291
This roadside inn stands beside a river; once a mill, it has fine views of the Wye Valley. The bedrooms are modern, well furnished and comfortable, and the bars are cosy. A wide range of bar food is offered.
4⇨↖ CTV in all bedrooms Ⓡ ✱ sB&B⇨↖£26.50
dB&B⇨↖£39-£47 Lunch £3.95-£10&alc Dinner £6-£10&alc
LDO 10pm
🍽 40P nc9yrs
Credit Cards 1 2 3

LLANDOVERY Dyfed Map **03** SN73

GH QQ Llwyncelyn SA20 0EP ☎(0550) 20566
Closed Xmas
Run by the friendly Griffiths family, this large detached house has a lovely garden which runs down to the river Towy, with beehives positioned on the lawn. The pretty bedrooms are equipped with solid furniture and duvets can be supplied on request. There is a pleasant lounge furnished with old-fashioned, comfortable suites. Good home cooking is served in the dining room.
6hc (3fb) Ⓡ ✗ (ex guide dogs) ✱ sB&B£17.85-£20.85
dB&B£31.50-£33.60 WB&B£89.20-£120.90 WBDi£168.70-£201.40 LDO 7.30pm
Lic 🍽 CTV 12P ⌡

LLANDRINDOD WELLS Powys Map **03** SO06

See also Penybont

GH QQ Griffin Lodge Hotel Temple St LD1 5HF
☎(0597) 822432
This Victorian house located near the town centre, has pretty, neat lawns and a small car park. There is a comfortable, open-plan lounge and bar, and the dining room has chapel pews for seating. Bedrooms are all freshly decorated and well furnished and maintained by the very friendly Jones family.
8rm(5↖3hc) CTV in 6 bedrooms TV in 2 bedrooms Ⓡ ✱
sB&B£17-£20 sB&B↖£20-£23 dB&B£34-£36 dB&B↖£40-£42
WB&B£102-£126 WBDi£165-£196 LDO 7.30pm
Lic 🍽 CTV 8P
Credit Cards 1 3 £

GH QQQ Guidfa House Crossgates LD1 6RF
☎Penybont(0597) 851241 FAX (0597) 851875
A country guesthouse just 3 miles north of this spa town at the junction of the A483 with the A44. Bedrooms are neat and well appointed, and there is a large residents' lounge with a small dispenser bar. New owners have just taken over and many improvements are planned.
7rm(5⇨↖2hc) CTV in all bedrooms Ⓡ ✗ (ex guide dogs)
sB&Bfr£21 sB&B⇨↖fr£31 dB&B⇨↖fr£44 WB&B£126-£132
WBDi£201-£208 LDO 7pm

Lic 10P
Credit Cards [1] [3]

GH QQ The Kincoed Temple St LD1 5HF ☎(0597) 822656 FAX (0597) 824660
Near the centre of this mid-Wales spa town, the guesthouse offers clean and bright bedrooms all well equipped with modern facilities, some of which are en suite. There is a small bar and the attractive restaurant is also popular locally.
10rm(1⇌4⌐5hc) (3fb) CTV in all bedrooms ® ✱ sB&Bfr£14 dB&Bfr£27 dB&B⇌⌐fr£36 WB&B£80-£108 WBDi£153.58-£181.50 LDO 9.30pm
Lic 10P
Credit Cards [1] [3]

GH QQ *Ty-Cerrig* Tremont Rd LD1 5EB ☎(0597) 822704
9hc (2fb) in all bedrooms CTV in all bedrooms ® LDO 9pm
Lic CTV 10P

FH QQ Mrs R Jones **Holly** *(SJ045593)* Howey LD1 5PP (Howey 2m S A483) ☎(0597) 822402
Apr-Nov
A stone-built farmhouse set in attractive gardens, situated just off the A483 south of the town at Howey. The 3 bedrooms are cosy and well decorated, and the lounge and dining room are both comfortable.
3rm(1⌐2hc) (1fb) ® ✗ dB&B£28-£30 dB&B⌐£32-£34 WB&Bfr£105 WBDifr£140 LDO 5pm
CTV 4P 70 acres beef sheep

FH QQQ Mr & Mrs R Bufton **Three Wells** *(SO062586)* Chapel Rd, Howey LD1 5PB (Howey 2m S A483 then unclass rd, E 1m) ☎(0597) 824427 & 822484
Very much a working farm, the house is situated one mile south of this spa town off the A483 at Howey, and overlooks an attractive lake stocked with tench and carp, with wild fowl including Canada geese. Bedrooms are mainly furnished in pine, and include 4 with private sitting rooms; they are all en suite, with pleasant views. There is a very spacious and comfortably furnished lounge bar. Good home cooking is offered by the very friendly Bufton family, and a stair lift has been installed for less mobile guests. Fishing and ponies for riding are also available.
14⇌⌐ CTV in all bedrooms ® ✗ sB&B⇌⌐£16.50-£19.50 dB&B⇌⌐£33-£39 WBDi£155-£185 LDO 6pm
Lic lift CTV 20P nc10yrs U 50 acres beef mixed sheep

LLANDUDNO Gwynedd Map 06 SH78

See **Town Plan Section**

GH QQ Beach Cove 8 Church Walks LL30 2HD ☎(0492) 879638
Closed Xmas
This small, well maintained, personally run guesthouse is located within a few hundred yards of the pier, and is also conveniently close to most amenities in the town. There is no car park, but street parking can usually be found without difficulty. The guesthouse is equally popular with tourists and commercial visitors.
7rm(5⌐2hc) (2fb) CTV in all bedrooms ® ✗ (ex guide dogs) ✱ sB&B£13 dB&B⌐£32 WB&B£105 WBDi£145 LDO 5.30pm
CTV solarium

GH QQ Bodnant 39 St Marys Rd LL30 2UE ☎(0492) 876936
Jan-Nov rs Feb
This small, pleasant guesthouse is family run and provides well maintained accommodation. It is conveniently situated for access to the town centre and other amenities; smoking is not permitted here. There is a small car park.
5⇌⌐ (2fb) in all bedrooms CTV in all bedrooms ® ✗ ✱ dB&B⇌⌐£32-£44 WB&B£112 WBDi£154 LDO 11.50am
Lic 4P 1 nc12yrs

Ⓔ Remember to use the money-off vouchers.

GH QQ Brannock Private Hotel 36 St Davids Rd LL30 2UH ☎(0492) 877483
Closed Xmas & New Year
A small, friendly, family-run hotel situated within easy reach of the town centre and beaches, with its own small car park.
7rm(4⌐3hc) (1fb) CTV in all bedrooms ® sB&B£12.50-£15.50 dB&B£25-£31 dB&B⌐£31 WB&B£85-£100 WBDi£115-£130 LDO 5pm
5P nc3yrs
Credit Cards [1] [3] Ⓔ

GH QQ Britannia Hotel Promenade, 15 Craig-y-Don Pde LL30 1BG ☎(0492) 877185
Closed Dec
Situated on the promenade, convenient for most of the town's facilities, this small hotel offers attractive, brightly decorated and soundly maintained accommodation. Four bedrooms have sea views, most have en suite facilities and some can accommodate families.
9rm(7⇌⌐2hc) (5fb) CTV in all bedrooms ® ✗ (ex guide dogs) ✱ sB&B£13-£13.50 sB&B⇌⌐£16-£16.50 dB&B£26 dB&B⇌⌐£31.50 WBDi£133 LDO 5pm

GH QQ *Bryn Rosa* 16 Abbey Rd LL30 2EA ☎(0492) 878215
Ths small, privately owned, friendly hotel is conveniently situated for access to the town centre and promenade. Several of the bedrooms have en suite facilities, and it is well maintained, with a cosy atmosphere.
7rm(2⌐5hc) (2fb) CTV in all bedrooms ® LDO 4.30pm
CTV 4P nc2yrs
Credit Cards [1] [3]

Llandudno

GH QQQ Buile Hill Private Hotel 46 St Mary's Rd LL30 2UE
☎(0492) 876972
Mar-Nov
A large, comfortable family-run hotel providing modern accommodation. Bedrooms are well maintained, and several have private bathrooms. It is conveniently located for access to the town centre and other amenities, and has its own small car park.
13rm(3🛁4🚿6hc) ® ✱ sB&B£14.50-£16 dB&B£29 dB&B🛁🚿£38-£42 WBDi£124-£160 LDO 4pm
Lic ♨ CTV 6P nc5yrs

GH Q *Capri Hotel* 70 Church Walks LL30 2HG
☎(0492) 879177
This small, privately owned guesthouse is situated in a quiet side street close to the pier and the Great Orme. It provides simple accommodation and is popular with tourists. There is no car park, but street parking can usually be found nearby.
7hc (5fb) ®
Lic ♨ CTV 3P

GH QQ Carmel Private Hotel 17 Craig-y-Don Pde, Promenade LL30 1BG ☎(0492) 877643
Etr-Oct rs Apr
Situated on the seafront, this large end terraced house is nicely maintained throughout and provides well-equipped accommodation with the advantage of its own small car park.
10rm(5🚿5hc) (2fb) CTV in all bedrooms ® ✱ sB&B£13-£13.50 dB&B£26-£27 dB&B🚿£31-£32 WB&B£91-£94.50 WBDi£126-£129.50 LDO noon
♨ CTV 6P nc4yrs

GH QQ Hotel Carmen Carmen Sylva Rd, Craig-y-Don LL30 1LZ ☎(0492) 876361
Mar-Nov
This small personally run hotel is situated east of the town centre, about 100yds from the promenade. The resident proprietors Mr and Mrs Newberry continue to improve the facilities, and bedrooms, although simple, have modern furnishings and equipment, many with private bathrooms. There is a small bar in addition to the spacious lounge. Most of the customers are holiday-makers, and the location of the hotel provides convenient access to the town centre and other amenities.
18🛁🚿 (4fb)🚭in 3 bedrooms CTV in all bedrooms ® ✱ sB&B🛁🚿£18.50-£20.50 dB&B🛁🚿£35-£38 LDO 6pm
Lic ♨ CTV

GH QQQ Cornerways Hotel 2 St Davids Place LL30 2UG
☎(0492) 877334
Apr-1 Nov
A very pleasant small private hotel situated in a quiet side road just off the town centre and within easy walking distance of the seafront. Bedrooms are attractively furnished with coordinating fabrics and décor and equipped with every modern convenience including trouser presses and hair dryers; each room is en suite.
6rm(5🛁1🚿) CTV in all bedrooms ® ✘ (ex guide dogs) sB&B🛁🚿£25-£32 dB&B🛁🚿£50-£54 (incl dinner) WB&B£126-£140 WBDi£175-£189 LDO 4pm
Lic ♨ 5P nc (£)

SELECTED

GH QQQQ Craiglands Private Hotel 7 Carmen Sylva Rd, Craig-y-Don LL30 1LZ ☎(0492) 875090
Mar-Nov
An extremely warm welcome awaits you at this impeccably maintained, small hotel provided by the proprietor Mrs Mullin, who has recently celebrated 25 years of ownership. Her boundless enthusiasm is still as strong as ever, which is one of the reasons why guests return year after year. The house dates back to Victorian times and is situated at the eastern end of town, close to the promenade. The en suite bedrooms are attractively decorated, with coordinated, soft furnishings. The comfortable lounge is equally attractive and is an ideal place to relax after enjoying one of Mrs Mullins' home-cooked meals, prepared from only the best available fresh produce.
6🚿 (1fb) CTV in all bedrooms ® LDO 4pm
♨ CTV nc4yrs

GH QQQ Cranberry House 12 Abbey Rd LL30 2EA
☎(0492) 879760
Mar-Oct
Named after a very attractive collection of Cranberry glassware, this is a delightful family-run guesthouse, strictly for non-smoking guests. The bedrooms have been attractively decorated with coordinating fabrics and wallpaper, and furnished with pine and some fine antiques. The pleasant sitting room has deep sofas and fresh flowers, and meals are served at round lace-covered tables in the dining room. This Victorian house is conveniently situated in a quiet residential area of the town, within easy walking distance of local amenities, with the advantage of its own car park.
6🛁🚿 (1fb)🚭in all bedrooms CTV in all bedrooms ® ✘ (ex guide dogs) ✱ dB&B🛁🚿£32-£38 WB&B£110-£130 WBDi£162-£185 LDO noon
♨ CTV 4P nc
Credit Cards [1] [3] (£)

GH QQ *Granby* Deganwy Av LL30 2DD ☎(0492) 876095
Apr-Oct
A mid-terrace Victorian house in a quiet residential area within walking distance of the shops and seafront. Well maintained bedrooms all have TV and tea trays, and many have moden en suite facilities. There is a comfortable residents lounge and small cosy bar. The Roberts family have welcomed their guests for many years, and take a pride in providing simple home cooking.
7rm(5🚿2hc) (4fb) CTV in all bedrooms ® ✘ LDO 4.30pm
Lic CTV 6P
Credit Cards [1] [3]

GH QQ Hafod-Y-Mor Hill Ter LL30 2LS ☎(0492) 876925
Mar-Oct rs Mar-Etr & Oct
This large semidetached Victorian house is situated in an elevated position on the slopes of the Great Orme. Bedrooms vary considerably in size, all have modern furnishings and several enjoy spectacular views of the town, the promenade and the mountains beyond. A small bar is situated in the dining room and there is a choice of 2 lounges, one of which is for non smokers. The hotel is privately owned and personally run by Dave and Sue Selby, who have been here since 1987.
11🛁🚿 (2fb)🚭in 1 bedroom CTV in all bedrooms ® ✘ ✱ sB&B🛁🚿fr£24 dB&B🛁🚿fr£44 WB&Bfr£147 WBDifr£224 LDO 5pm
Lic ♨ CTV 4P
Credit Cards [1] [3] (£)

GH QQQ Hollybank 9 St Davids Place LL30 2UG
☎(0492) 878521
Etr-mid Oct
This comfortable, attractive and well maintained private hotel provides good quality, well equipped accommodation. Located in a quiet road convenient for the town centre, it also has a small car park.
7🛁🚿 (2fb)🚭in all bedrooms CTV in all bedrooms ® ✱ sB&B🛁🚿£20-£27 dB&B🛁🚿£36-£44 WB&B£115-£140 WBDi£165-£190 LDO 4pm
Lic ♨ 5P
Credit Cards [1] [3] (£)

GH QQ Kinmel Private Hotel 12 Mostyn Crescent LL30 1AR
☎(0492) 876171
Etr-Sep & Xmas
This mid-terrace Victorian house enjoys an excellent central location on the promenade, within easy reach of the town's amenities. En suite facilities have recently been increased and

rooms enlarged, some having good sea views; many of the rooms are decorated with pretty fabrics and attractive colour schemes. The basement restaurant offers good quality fresh food, and a wide range of bar meals and sandwiches is available in the cottage-style bar/lounge which overlooks Llandudno bay.
16rm(13⇌1♠2hc) (3fb) CTV in all bedrooms ® sB&B£18-£20 sB&B⇌♠£21-£23 dB&B⇌♠£40-£46 WB&B£126-£140 WBDi£170-£190 LDO 5.30pm
Lic 🍽 P̸
Credit Cards [1] [2] [3]

GH QQQ Mayfair Private Hotel 4 Abbey Rd LL30 2EA
☎(0492) 876170
Mar-Oct
This small family-run hotel is well maintained and provides well equipped accommodation, with most bedrooms having en suite facilities. It is conveniently located in a residential area, near the sea and shops.
12rm(9⇌♠3hc) (7fb) CTV in all bedrooms ® * sB&B⇌♠£17-£21 WB&B£108-£130 WBDi£155-£182 LDO 6pm
Lic 🍽 CTV 3P

GH Q *Mayfield* 19 Curzon Rd, Craig-y-Don LL30 1TB
☎(0492) 877427
Etr-Sep
This small, simple family-run guesthouse is located in a quiet side street on the eastern outskirts of the town. The seafront is a few minutes' walk away and there is no private parking available.
8hc (5fb) CTV in all bedrooms ® LDO 6pm
Lic CTV

GH QQ *Minion Private Hotel* 21-23 Carmen Sylva Rd LL30 1EQ ☎(0492) 877740
Etr-mid Oct
A detached Edwardian house situated at the eastern end of the town in a quiet residential area, within a short walk of the promenade. Privately owned and personally run, the accommodation is well maintained and the majority of bedrooms have en suite facilities.
12rm(5⇌7♠) (1fb) ® LDO 4pm
Lic CTV 8P

GH QQ Montclare Hotel North Pde LL30 2LP
☎(0492) 877061
Mar-Oct
A tall, terraced, personally run hotel in a convenient location, close to the main shopping area and overlooking the bay. It is nicely maintained throughout, and offers sound, well equipped accommodation.
15rm(2⇌13♠) (6fb) CTV in all bedrooms ®
🐕 (ex guide dogs) * sB&B⇌♠fr£16 dB&B⇌♠fr£32 WB&Bfr£100 WBDifr£140 LDO 3pm
Lic 🍽 4P

GH QQ Oak Alyn Deganwy Av LL30 2YB ☎(0492) 860320
mid Feb-Nov rs Feb
This privately owned, personally run hotel is situated close to the town centre shopping area; the promenade and other amenities are also within easy reach. Bedrooms vary in size, and whilst not luxurious, they are modern and soundly maintained, each with a private bathroom. The hotel has the advantage of its own private car park.
12rm(4⇌8♠) (1fb) CTV in all bedrooms ® sB&B⇌♠£16-£18 dB&B⇌♠£32-£36 WB&B£100-£120
Lic CTV 16P nc1yr
Credit Cards [1] [3]

GH QQQ Orotava Private Hotel 105 Glan-Y-Mor Rd, Penrhyn Bay LL30 3PH ☎(0492) 549780
An attractive back garden with direct access to the beach is a major attraction of this small, comfortable guesthouse to the east of the town. Four of the 6 bedrooms have sea views, and all have private bath or shower room, one of which is not en suite. Guests can relax in a coffee lounge or a second lounge with panelled walls and sea views. For extra privacy, one bedroom has its own lounge.
6rm(4⇌2♠) ⊬in all bedrooms CTV in all bedrooms ® 🐕 * sB&B⇌♠£18 dB&B⇌♠£36 LDO 6pm
Lic 🍽 CTV 10P nc15yrs
Credit Cards [1] [3]

GH QQ Rosaire Private Hotel 2 St Seiriols Rd LL30 2YY
☎(0492) 877677
Mar-Oct
This small, family-owned hotel is quietly situated in the town centre, with easy access to all amenities. Bedrooms vary in style, and range from traditional to modern; recent improvements include the provision of central heating in all rooms and an increase in en suite facilities.
10rm(2⇌5♠3hc) (1fb) ® sB&Bfr£14 dB&Bfr£28 dB&B⇌♠fr£32 LDO 4pm
Lic 🍽 CTV 6P nc3yrs

GH QQQ St Hilary Hotel 16 Craig-y-Don Pde, Promenade LL30 1BG ☎(0492) 875551
Jan-Nov
This Victorian, family-run terraced hotel is situated on the seafront, at the eastern end of the town, not far from the main shopping area. Refurbished in 1991, the accommodation is well appointed and impeccably maintained; most of the bedrooms now have private bathrooms.
11rm(8♠3hc) (8fb) CTV in all bedrooms ® 🐕 (ex guide dogs) * sB&B£13.25-£24 sB&B♠£16.25-£30 dB&B£26.50 dB&B♠£32.50 WB&B£92.75-£113.75 WBDi£127-£148.25 LDO 5.30pm
Lic 🍽 P̸
Credit Cards [1] [3]

GH QQ Sunnyside Private Hotel Llewelyn Av LL30 2ER
☎(0492) 877150
Etr-Oct & Xmas
Set between Great Orme and the town centre, a few minutes from the seafront, this guesthouse offers well-kept bright rooms, some with en suite facilities. The bar and lounge areas are attractive and relaxing.
26rm(5⇌8♠13hc) (4fb) CTV in all bedrooms ® * sB&B£17-£20 dB&B£34-£40 dB&B⇌♠£35-£42 WB&B£115-£120 WBDi£160-£180 LDO 7.30pm
Lic 🍽 CTV

GH QQ *Thorpe House* 3 St Davids Rd LL30 2UL
☎(0492) 877089
Closed Xmas
This nicely maintained, small, personally run hotel is conveniently situated for access to the town centre and other amenities. Some rooms have en suite facilities, and the guesthouse is well furnished and comfortable.
10rm(1♠9hc) (4fb) 🐕
🍽 CTV P̸

GH QQ Warwick Hotel 56 Church Walks LL30 2HL
☎(0492) 876823
This large Victorian house, now a privately owned and personally run hotel is situated on the lower slopes of the Great Orme, within a few minutes' walk of the pier, promenade and town centre. The bedrooms vary in size, some being very spacious, and whilst not luxurious, they are soundly maintained and have modern furnishings and equipment.
16rm(8⇌5♠3hc) (9fb) CTV in all bedrooms ® * sB&B£18.50-£20 sB&B⇌♠£20.50-£23 dB&B£37-£40 dB&B⇌♠£41-£46 WB&B£111-£138 WBDi£162-£180 LDO 6.45pm
Lic 🍽 CTV P̸

GH QQ Wedgewood Hotel 6 Deganwy Av LL30 2YB
☎(0492) 878016
Etr-Dec
A family run hotel just off the town centre in a quiet residential area of this popular resort. Most bedrooms have private bathrooms and are equipped with TV, radios and tea trays. There is a comfortable modern lounge with attractive plants and flowers, and a small bar for residents.
11rm(2⇨7↱2hc) (1fb) CTV in all bedrooms Ⓡ ✱ sB&B£21 sB&B⇨↱£24 dB&B£42 dB&B⇨↱£48 (incl dinner) WB&B£122 WBDi£168 LDO 3pm
Lic ⛫ CTV 7P

GH QQQ The Wilton Hotel South Pde LL30 2LN
☎(0492) 876086 & 878343
Feb-Nov
This small, privately owned and personally run hotel is situated in a row of Victorian properties, close to the shops, promenade and pier. Bedrooms vary in size and style, but all are modern and attractive with nicely coordinated soft furnishings. Private bathrooms have recently been provided for all rooms, and family rooms are available. Other facilities include a very pleasant comfortable lounge bar decorated with a Victorian theme.
14⇨↱ (7fb) CTV in all bedrooms Ⓡ **T** sB&B⇨↱£20-£22 dB&B⇨↱£40-£44 WB&B£140-£152 WBDi£171-£182 LDO 4.30pm
Lic P̸

GH QQ Winston 5 Church Walks LL30 2HD ☎(0492) 876144
This friendly guesthouse has been run by the Healey family for 20 years, and offers attractive, comfortable accommodation. Bedrooms are prettily decorated, with an attractive use of soft fabrics and canopies. All are well equipped, with extras like TV and hairdryers. The lounge is modern and comfortable, accommodating two 3-piece suites and a piano. The dining room is also attractively decorated, and meals here offer good home cooking. Situated near the pier and the seafront, the guesthouse is also convenient for the town centre and the dry ski slope.
7rm(6↱1hc) (1fb) CTV in all bedrooms Ⓡ ✕ ✱ sB&B£14-£15 dB&B↱£30 WB&B£95 WBDi£130 LDO 4pm
⛫ CTV 2P nc2yrs
Credit Cards 1 3

LLANEGRYN Gwynedd Map **06** SH50

FH QQQ Mrs Griffiths ***Bryn Gwyn Country Farm House*** *(SH610060)* LL36 9UF ☎Tywyn(0654) 711771
Closed Jan-Feb
Set in 4-acres of gardens and paddocks and situated within the Snowdonia National Park, this delightful old house dates back to 1730. The bedrooms may not be luxurious but are well maintained. Public rooms include a lovely dining room with antique furniture, where guests can eat off Minton China, and a choice of lounges. A simple games room has been created from a converted garage.
5rm(1⇨1↱3hc) (1fb) 🚭 in 3 bedrooms CTV in 1 bedroom TV in 1 bedroom Ⓡ ✕ (ex guide dogs) LDO 7.30am
⛫ CTV 7P ⌂ bicycles 4 acres non-working

LLANELLI Dyfed Map **02** SN50

GH Q *Awel Y Mor* 86 Queen Victoria Rd SA15 2TH
☎(0554) 755357
A very friendly, family-run guesthouse a short walk from the town centre. Bedrooms are neat and clean, and there is an open-plan lounge and restaurant and a small bar for residents.
11rm(4⇨3↱4hc) (2fb) CTV in 3 bedrooms ✕ (ex guide dogs) LDO 6pm
Lic ⛫ CTV 13P

This guide is updated annually – make sure you use an up-to-date edition.

LLANFACHRETH Gwynedd Map **06** SH72

SELECTED

GH QQQQ Ty Isaf LL40 2EA
☎Dolgellau(0341) 423261
This typical Welsh longhouse dates from 1624 and stands in a secluded hamlet amidst the magnificent scenery of the Snowdonia National Park. Proprietors Diana and Graham Silverton have extensively and tastefully restored the house, successfully combining modern day comforts with the original charm and character. The 3 bedrooms have pine furniture and attractive coordinating soft furnishings; 1 room is on the ground floor. There is an abundance of exposed beams, and 1 of the 3 lounges has a delightful inglenook fireplace. The standard of service and warm hospitality of the Silvertons make this guesthouse, together with its beautiful large garden, a popular choice.
3⇨↱ 🚭in all bedrooms Ⓡ sB&B⇨↱£22-£32 dB&B⇨↱£44 WB&B£154-£224 WBDi£224-£294 LDO 6pm
⛫ CTV 3P 1🚗 nc13yrs (£)

LLANFAIR CAEREINION Powys Map **06** SJ10

FH QQ Mrs J Cornes ***Cwmllwynog*** *(SJ071065)* SY21 0HF
☎(0938) 810791
Etr-Sep
This 17th-century farmhouse with its exposed beams and inglenook fireplace is just off the B4385. It offers a warm welcome and traditional home cooking using local produce wherever possible.
3rm(1↱1hc) CTV in 2 bedrooms Ⓡ ✕ LDO 4pm
⛫ CTV 3P 105 acres dairy

INN QQ Goat Hotel High St SY21 0QS ☎(0938) 810428
An historic 17th-century village inn almost opposite the church, with a roaring fire in the timbered bar where visitors can enjoy the local atmosphere. There is a small dining room for evening meals and breakfast. The bedrooms have ceiling beams and uneven floors, but are modern otherwise.
6rm(4⇨↱2hc) (1fb) Ⓡ **T** ✕ (ex guide dogs) ✱ sB&B£20 sB&B⇨↱£25 dB&B£30 dB&B⇨↱£35 WB&B£105-£150 Bar Lunch £3.50-£7.50alc Dinner £6-£11alc LDO 9pm
⛫ 10P
Credit Cards 1 3

LLANFYNYDD Dyfed Map **02** SN52

INN QQQ Penybont SA32 7TG ☎Dryslywn(0558) 668292
Built around 1680, the inn has been extended over the years and now provides a large function suite as well as modern bedrooms. It is reached via a minor road 5 miles north of the A40 at Cothi Bridge. The bedrooms all have their own en suite facilities and are well equipped with TV, hair dryers and tea making facilities. There are beamed ceilings and stone walls in the bar and restaurant, where a fixed price set menu is supplemented with à la carte and vegetarian selections. The popular carvery and cabaret evenings are usually held at weekends and there is a large car park close to all the rooms.
8⇨↱ (2fb) CTV in all bedrooms Ⓡ ✱ sB&B⇨↱£20-£27.50 dB&B⇨↱£35-£44 WB&Bfr£122.50 WBDifr£175 Lunch £6.50-£9.50&alc High tea £2.50-£4.50alc Dinner £8.50-£11.50&alc LDO 9pm
⛫ CTV 50P
Credit Cards 1 3

Q is for quality. For a full explanation of this AA quality award, consult the Contents page.

LLANGOLLEN Clwyd Map **07** SJ24

GH QQ Hillcrest Hill St LL20 8EU ☎Wrexham(0978) 860208
This large Victorian house has been tastefully converted and modernised into a small, personally run private hotel. It is quietly located within a few minutes' walk of the A5 and town centre. The well maintained accommodation is suitable for tourists and commercial visitors alike, but smoking is not permitted. There is a private car park to the rear of the property.
7↱ (2fb)⅟in all bedrooms CTV in 1 bedroom ®
✗ (ex guide dogs) ✱ dB&B↱£36 WB&B£126 WBDi£185
LDO noon
CTV 10P

FH Q Mrs A Kenrick ***Rhydonnen Ucha Rhewl*** *(SJ174429)*
Rhewl LL20 7AJ ☎(0978) 860153
Etr-Nov
This large, stone-built 3-storeyed farmhouse was built in 1716 and is part of a 120-acre dairy farm, in a remote location near the village of Rhewl, some 5 miles west of Llangollen. It provides simple but soundly maintained accommodation, with picturesque views across the Dee valley to the Berwyn mountains. Shooting is available on the farm, and trout fishing on the River Dee can be provided with a permit.
4hc (2fb) LDO 3pm
CTV P 125 acres dairy

LLANGURIG Powys Map **06** SN98

GH QQQ Old Vicarage SY18 6RN ☎(05515) 280
Mar-Oct
This detached Victorian vicarage is set in a quiet cul-de-sac near the centre of the village. Bedrooms are all en suite and feature TV, tea trays and comfortable furniture. There are 2 lounges, one of which is designated non- smoking and stacked with books and local information. Afternoon teas consist of home-made jams and scones, and can be taken in one of the 2 comfortable lounges or out on the lawn of the very pleasant garden.
5rm(2⇌2↱1hc) (2fb)⅟in all bedrooms CTV in 4 bedrooms TV in 1 bedroom ® sB&B£15 dB&B⇌↱£36-£40 WB&B£140 WBDi£190 LDO 7pm
Lic CTV 6P nc1yr

LLANIDLOES Powys Map **06** SN98

INN QQ Mount China St SY18 6AB ☎(05512) 2247
Situated in the centre of the town, this family-run inn is believed to date back to the 14th century. It now provides 3 modern bedrooms, all well equipped, and a wide variety of food is always available in the bars.
3↱ CTV in all bedrooms ® ✗ LDO 8.45pm
CTV 15P nc14yrs
Credit Cards 3

LLANON Dyfed Map **02** SN50

INN QQQ Plas Morfa Hotel & Restaurant Plas Morfa SY23 5LX ☎(0974) 202415
This family-run holiday hotel sits on its own well maintained lawns on the edge of Cardigan Bay, just quarter of a mile from the A437. Rooms are bright and comfortable, with en suite facilities, and some with sea views. A full à la carte service is available in the attractive cane-furnished Atlantic restaurant, and there is a smart cocktail bar, a separate Cellar bar, bistro and disco in what was once a brewery and warehouse.
8⇌↱ (2fb) CTV in all bedrooms ® sB&B⇌↱£20.50-£27 dB&B⇌↱£41-£54 WB&B£130-£170 Lunch fr£7.50 Dinner £10.50-£15.50alc LDO 9.30pm
40P £

Book as early as possible for busy holiday periods.

LLANRHYSTUD Dyfed Map **06** SN56

FH QQQ Mrs T T Mizen **Pen-Y-Castell** *(SN539684)*
SY23 5BZ ☎Nebo(0974) 272622
High above Cardigan Bay, just 2.5 miles from the village, and commanding beautiful views, this modernised guesthouse sits in pleasant grounds and boasts its own trout lake. Run by the friendly Mizen family, it offers pretty bedrooms with coordinating colour schemes, and a family unit with a separate bunk-bedded room. The cosy lounge has a cheerful wood-burning stove, and there is also a sun lounge with comfortable cushioned cane seating.
6⇌↱ (1fb)⅟in all bedrooms CTV in 3 bedrooms ®
✗ (ex guide dogs) sB&B⇌↱£24 dB&B⇌↱£48 LDO 6pm
Lic CTV 10P 2 boating lake 35 acres beef sheep

LLANSANTFFRAID-YM-MECHAIN Powys Map **07** SJ22

FH QQ Mrs M E Jones **Glanvyrnwy** *(SJ229202)*
SY22 6SU ☎Llansantffraid(0691) 828258
This stone-built farmhouse, situated on the edge of the village, dates back some 300 years, and three windows are still bricked up from the time of the window tax. The 2 neat bedrooms have a pretty décor, and there is a choice of comfortable lounges. Guests also enjoy the well tended gardens and lawns. Mrs Jones has long extended warm Welsh hospitality, and some guests have been returning regularly for 20 years.
2hc ® ✗ (ex guide dogs) sB&B£15 dB&B£30 WB&B£95
CTV 3P nc3yrs 42 acres beef

'Selected' establishments, which have the highest quality award, are highlighted by a tinted panel. For a full list of these establishments, consult the Contents page.

LLANWDDYN Powys Map **06** SJ01

FH QQ H A Parry **Tynymaes** *(SJ048183)* SY10 0NN
☎(069173) 216
May-Sep
Situated just a few miles from Lake Vyrnwy this cosy farmhouse, run by the Parry family offers a warm welcome. The lounge is spacious and comfortable and the bedrooms are bright and cheerful.
3hc (1fb) ® ✱ dB&B£26-£28 WB&B£90-£95 WBDi£140-£145 LDO 5pm
CTV 4P 420 acres beef sheep

LLANWNDA Gwynedd Map **06** SH45

FH QQQ Mr & Mrs G Rowlands **Pengwern** *(SH459587)* Saron LL54 5UH ☎(0286) 830717
Closed Dec & Jan
Peacefully situated between the mountains and the sea, this beautifully preserved and impeccably maintained, large Victorian house commands wonderful views of Snowdon and the 130 acres of land on which it stands. There are 3 period furnished but modern and well equipped bedrooms in the main house, 2 of which have enormous and luxurious en suite bathrooms and the third has exclusive use of a modern bathroom and toilet. A fourth self-contained unit is located in a single storey cottage to the rear of the house, which comprises of a large double room plus a small twin and has its own spacious lounge, bathroom and kitchen. This is a no smoking establishment. Best Newcomer for Wales 1992–3, see colour section.
3rm(2) Annexe 1 in all bedrooms CTV in all bedrooms ® ✱ sB&B£17 dB&B£32-£34 WB&B£112-£119 WBDi£156-£164
4P 130 acres beef sheep

LLANWRIN Powys Map **06** SH70

FH QQQ Mrs R J Hughes **Mathafarn** *(SN812055)* Cemmaes Rd SY20 8QJ ☎Cemmaes Road(0650) 511226
Standing in pleasant lawns and mature woodland, this impressive, 16th-century ivy-clad house is part of a working farm and Henry VII is reputed to have stayed here en route to the battle of Bosworth. Three nicely equipped bedrooms are available – all prettily decorated and well furnished. The dining room has a beamed ceiling and magnificent inglenook fireplace and the sitting room is furnished with comfortable, floral sofas and armchairs.
3rm(1 2hc) ® (ex guide dogs) ✱ sB&B£15 dB&B£30-£32
CTV 3P 600 acres beef sheep

LOCHINVER Highland *Sutherland* Map **14** NC02

GH QQ Ardglas IV27 4LI ☎(05714) 257
Feb-Nov
Set on a hill overlooking the bay and harbour, this friendly family-run guesthouse offers good value bed and breakfast accommodation in a relaxed atmosphere. The bedrooms are spotless and well looked after, though some are compact. A hearty breakfast is served at shared tables in the bright dining room overlooking the bay. Guests are requested to refrain from smoking in the bedrooms.
8hc (2fb) in all bedrooms CTV in 1 bedroom ® ✱ sB&B£13-£15 dB&B£26-£30
CTV 12P

LOCHRANZA

See **ARRAN, ISLE OF**

LOCHWINNOCH Strathclyde *Renfrewshire* Map **10** NS35

FH QQ Mrs A Mackie **High Belltrees** *(NS377584)* PA12 4JN (situated 1m off the A737 to Largs road) ☎(0505) 842376
The approach to this farm is off the A737 by way of a narrow country road leading high into the hills. The farm offers fine views out across the valley and Castle Semple Loch. Popular with business people as well as tourists, the farm has mostly spacious bedrooms and a cheery informal atmosphere.
4rm(3hc) (2fb) CTV in all bedrooms ® (ex guide dogs) ✱ sB&B£15-£16 dB&B£24-£26
CTV 6P 220 acres dairy mixed sheep

LOCKERBIE Dumfries & Galloway *Dumfriesshire* Map **11** NY18

GH QQQ Rosehill Carlisle Rd DG11 2DR
☎(05762) 2378
On the southern approach to town, this tastefully decorated detached house offers spacious and comfortable accommodation and a friendly atmosphere. Bed and breakfast only is provided.
5hc (3fb) CTV in all bedrooms ® sB&B£15-£16 dB&B£28
CTV 5P

London Plan 1

1 Bryanston Court *(W1)*
2 Camelot Hotel *(W2)*
3 Hotel Concorde *(W1)*
4 Edward Lear Hotel *(W1)*
5 Georgian House Hotel *(W1)*
6 Hart House Hotel *(W1)*
7 Kingsway Hotel *(W2)*
8 Mitre House Hotel *(W2)*
9 Park Lodge Hotel *(W2)*

Details of the establishments shown on this map can be found under the *London Postal District* which follows the establishment name.

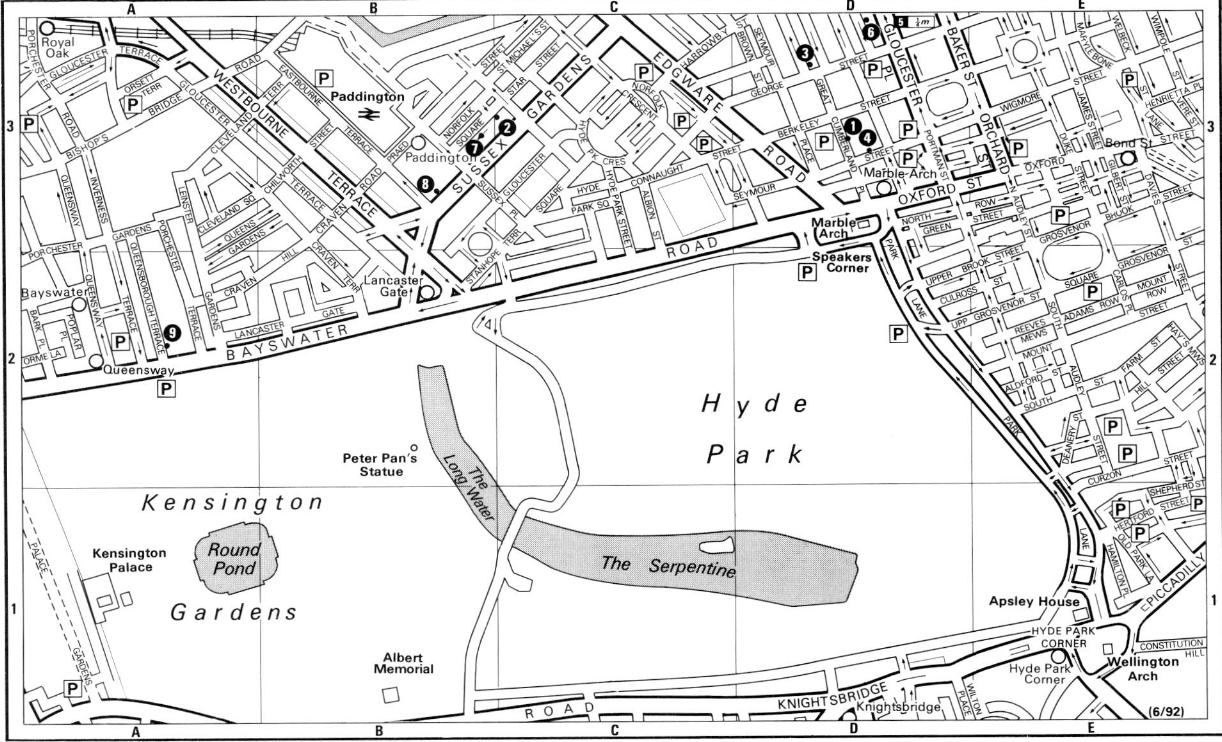

London Plan 2

1 Atlas Hotel *(W8)*
2 Claverley Hotel *(SW3)*
3 Kensington Manor *(SW7)*
4 Knightsbridge Hotel *(SW3)*
5 Swiss House Hotel *(SW5)*

Details of the establishments shown on this map can be found under the *London Postal District* which follows the establishment name.

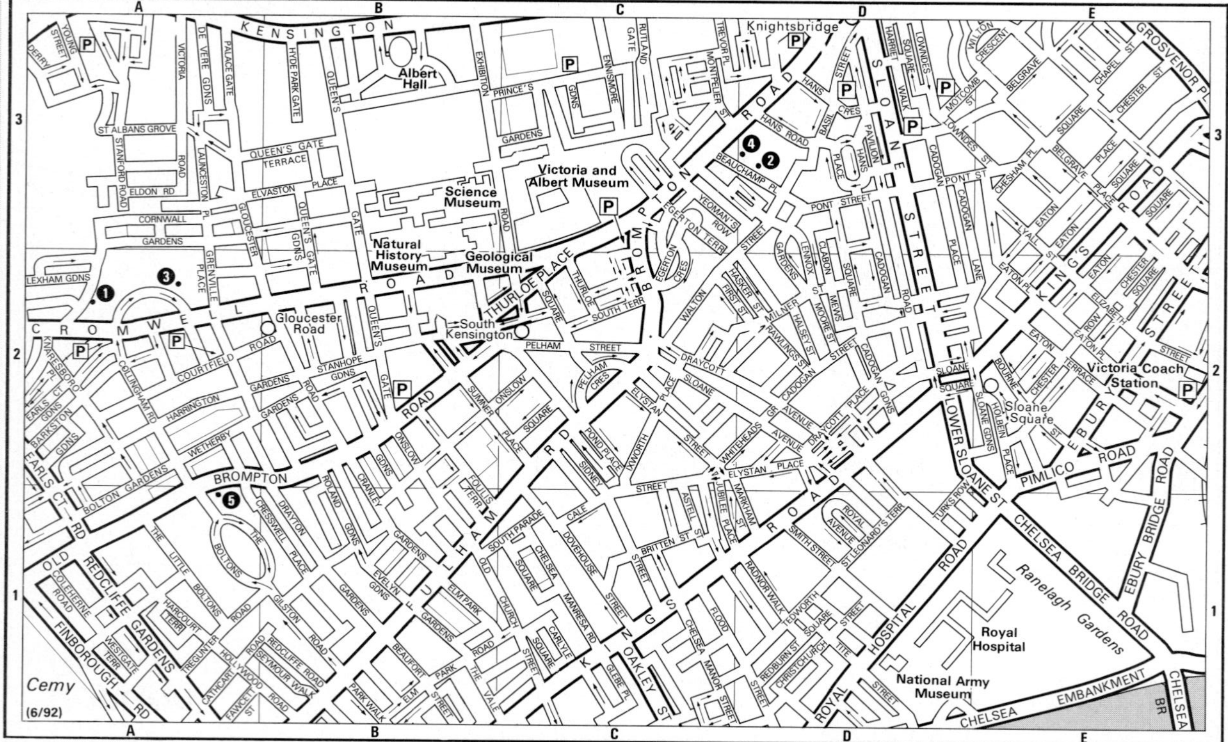

London Plan 3

1 Winchester Hotel *(SW1)*

2 Windermere Hotel *(SW1)*

Details of the establishments shown on this map can be found under the *London Postal District* which follows the establishment name.

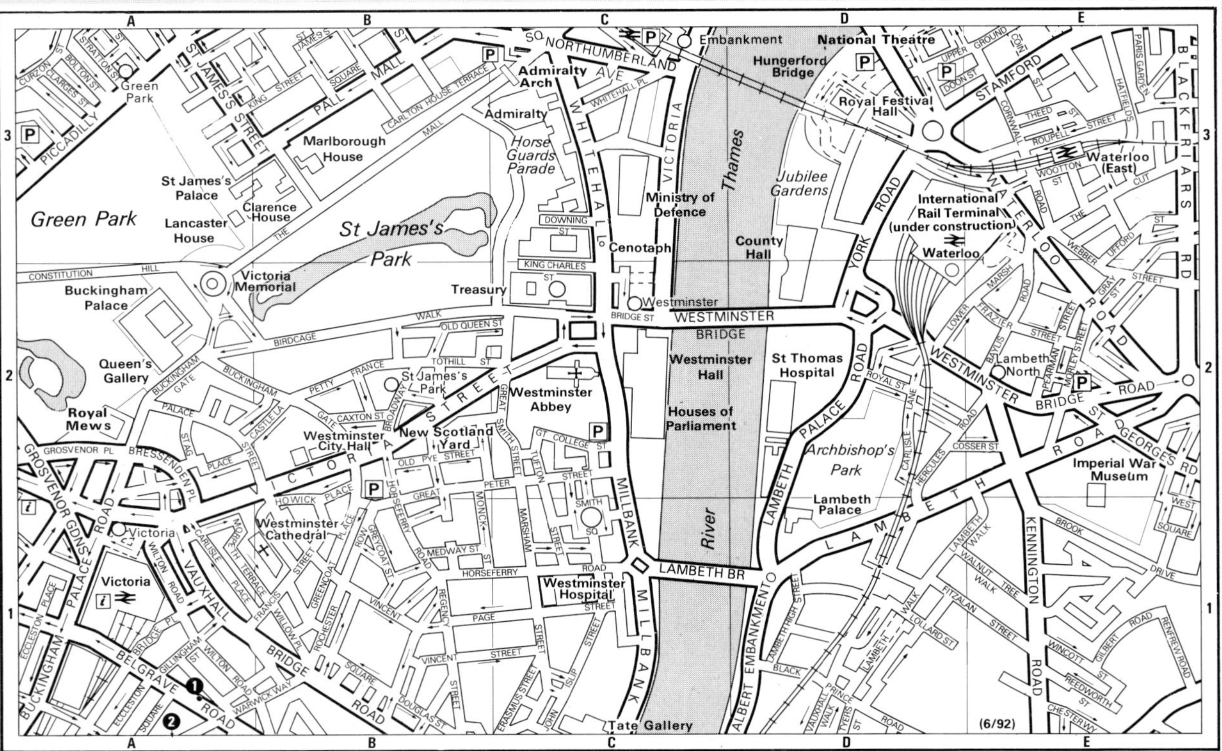

London Plan 4

The placenames highlighted by a **dot** are locations of AA listed establishments outside the Central London Plan area (Plans 1–3). Some of these fall within the London Postal District area and can therefore be found in the gazetteer under **London** in postal district order (see London Postal District map on following page). Others outside the London Postal District area can therefore be found under their respective placenames in the main gazetteer.

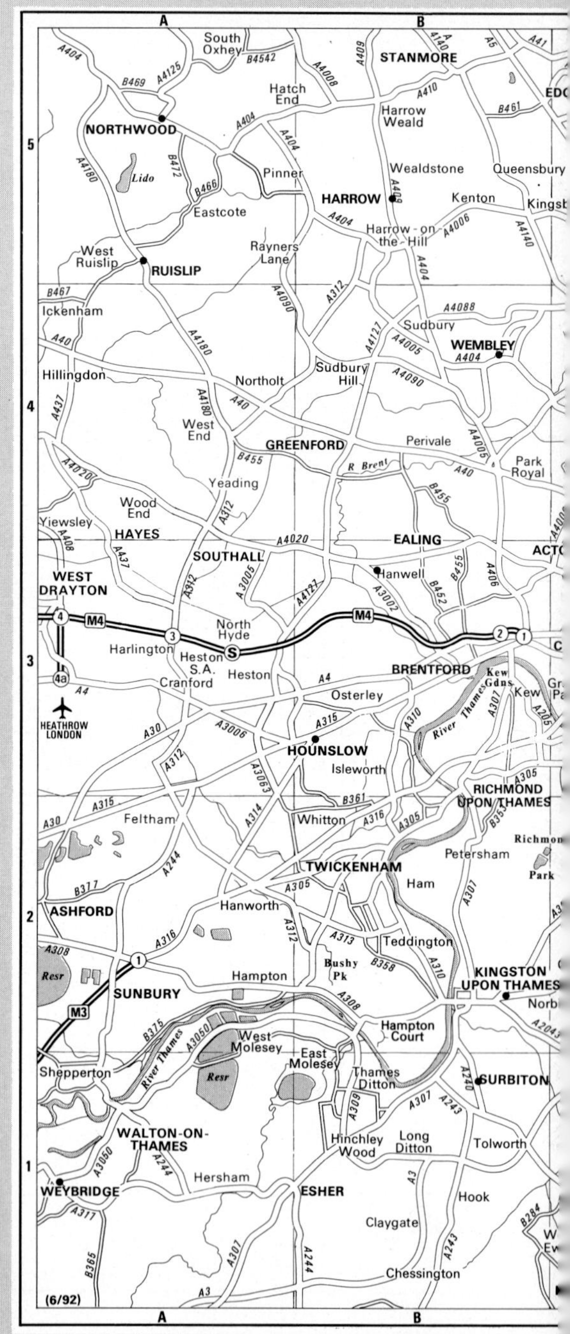

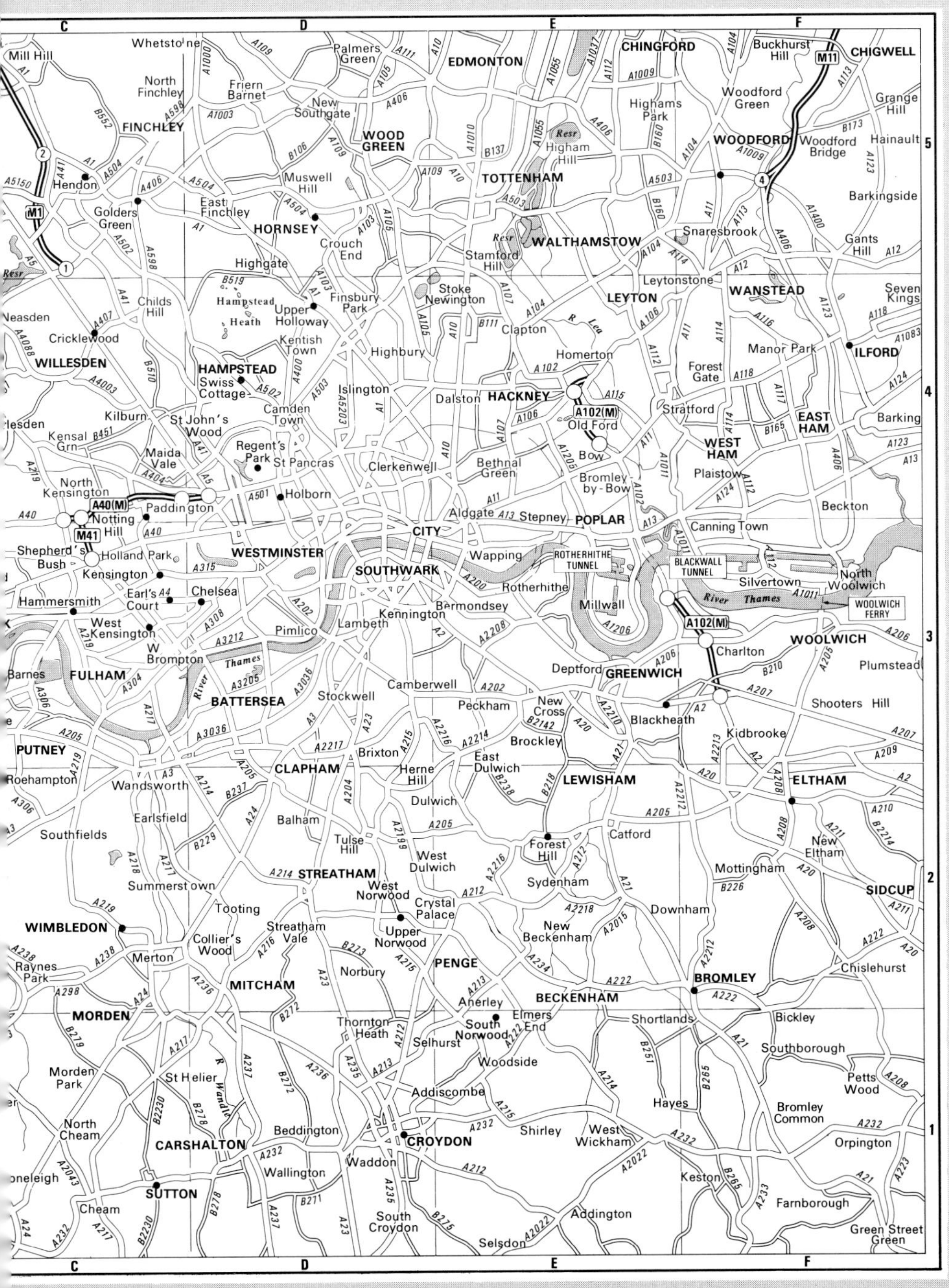
Mill Hill
Whetstone
Palmers Green
EDMONTON
CHINGFORD
Buckhurst Hill
M11
CHIGWELL
North Finchley
Friern Barnet
New Southgate
Woodford Green
Highams Park
Grange Hill
FINCHLEY
WOOD GREEN
Resr
Higham Hill
WOODFORD
Woodford Bridge
Hainault
Hendon
Muswell Hill
TOTTENHAM
Barkingside
M1
Golders Green
East Finchley
HORNSEY
Crouch End
Stamford Hill
WALTHAMSTOW
Snaresbrook
Gants Hill
Highgate
Hampstead Heath
Upper Holloway
Finsbury Park
Stoke Newington
Leytonstone
LEYTON
WANSTEAD
Seven Kings
Neasden
Childs Hill
Cricklewood
Kentish Town
Highbury
Clapton
R Lea
Manor Park
ILFORD
WILLESDEN
HAMPSTEAD
Swiss Cottage
Homerton
Forest Gate
Islington
Dalston
HACKNEY
A102(M)
Stratford
Barking
Kilburn
St John's Wood
Camden Town
Old Ford
EAST HAM
Kensal Grn
Regent's Park
Maida Vale
St Pancras
Clerkenwell
Bethnal Green
Bow
WEST HAM
Plaistow
North Kensington
A40(M)
Paddington
Holborn
Bromley-by-Bow
Beckton
Notting Hill
M41
Aldgate
Stepney
POPLAR
CITY
Canning Town
Shepherd's Bush
Holland Park
WESTMINSTER
Wapping
ROTHERHITHE TUNNEL
BLACKWALL TUNNEL
Kensington
SOUTHWARK
North Woolwich
Silvertown
Hammersmith
Earl's Court
Chelsea
Rotherhithe
River Thames
WOOLWICH FERRY
Millwall
Bermondsey
West Kensington
Kennington
Lambeth
Pimlico
WOOLWICH
W Brompton
Charlton
Plumstead
Barnes
FULHAM
Deptford
GREENWICH
Camberwell
BATTERSEA
Stockwell
Peckham
New Cross
Blackheath
Shooters Hill
Kidbrooke
Brockley
PUTNEY
Brixton
CLAPHAM
East Dulwich
Herne Hill
Roehampton
Wandsworth
LEWISHAM
ELTHAM
Dulwich
Earlsfield
Balham
Catford
Southfields
Tulse Hill
Forest Hill
New Eltham
West Dulwich
Mottingham
STREATHAM
Summerstown
West Norwood
Sydenham
SIDCUP
Tooting
Crystal Palace
Downham
WIMBLEDON
Streatham Vale
Upper Norwood
New Beckenham
Collier's Wood
Raynes Park
Merton
Norbury
PENGE
Chislehurst
MITCHAM
BECKENHAM
BROMLEY
Anerley
MORDEN
Thornton Heath
South Norwood
Elmers End
Shortlands
Bickley
Selhurst
Southborough
Morden Park
St Helier
R Wandle
Woodside
Petts Wood
Addiscombe
Hayes
North Cheam
Bromley Common
Beddington
Shirley
West Wickham
CARSHALTON
CROYDON
Orpington
Wallington
Waddon
Keston
SUTTON
Cheam
South Croydon
Addington
Farnborough
Selsdon
Green Street Green

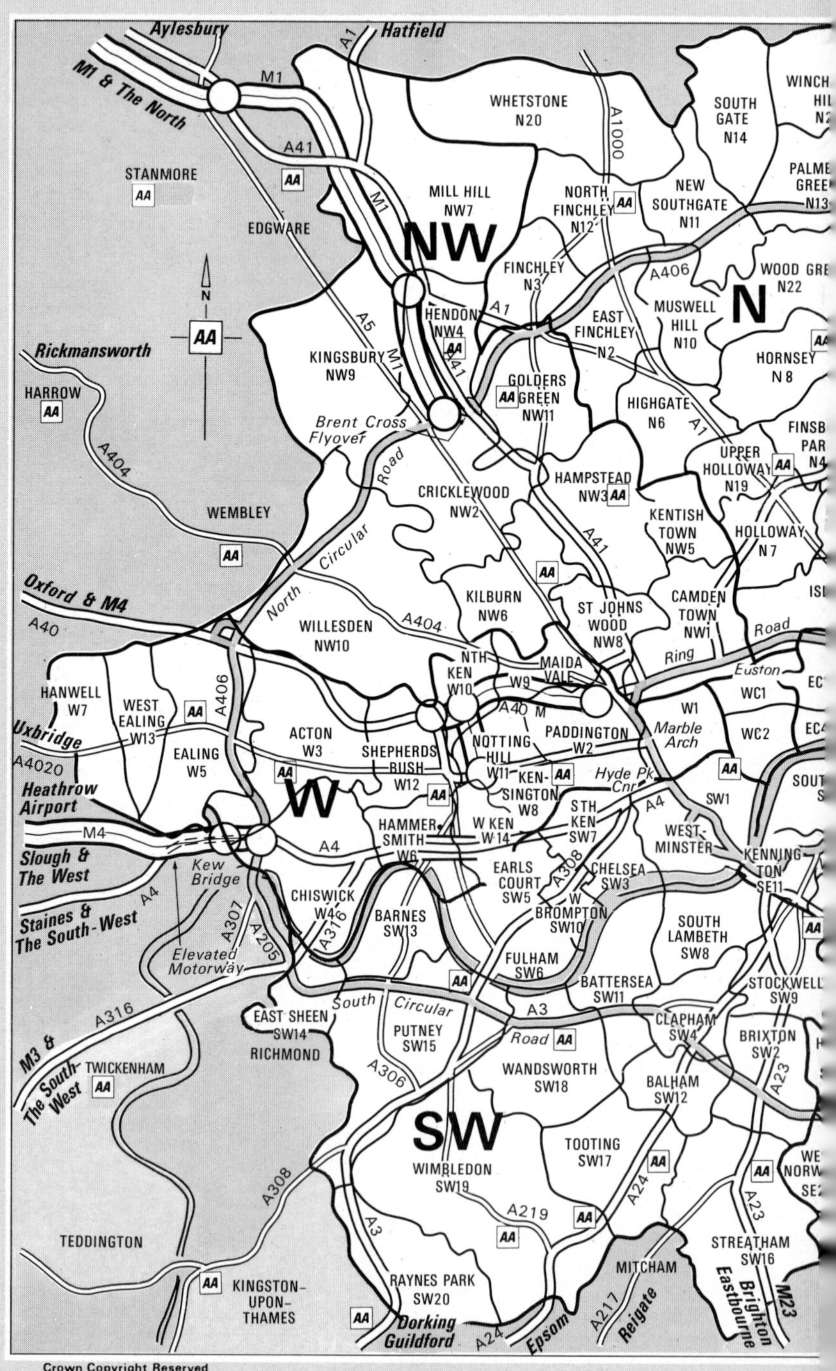
Aylesbury
Hatfield
M1 & The North
M1
A1
A41
STANMORE
EDGWARE
WHETSTONE
N20
A1000
SOUTH
GATE
N14
MILL HILL
NW7
NORTH
FINCHLEY
N12
NEW
SOUTHGATE
N11
NW
FINCHLEY
N3
A406
WOOD GRE
N22
N
HENDON
NW4
EAST
FINCHLEY
N2
MUSWELL
HILL
N10
HORNSEY
N 8
Rickmansworth
HARROW
KINGSBURY
NW9
A5
GOLDERS
GREEN
NW11
HIGHGATE
N6
Brent Cross
Flyover
A404
Road
CRICKLEWOOD
NW2
HAMPSTEAD
NW3
UPPER
HOLLOWAY
N19
KENTISH
TOWN
NW5
HOLLOWAY
N 7
WEMBLEY
Circular
North
Oxford & M4
A40
KILBURN
NW6
ST JOHNS
WOOD
NW8
CAMDEN
TOWN
NW1
WILLESDEN
NW10
Ring
Road
Euston
NTH
KEN
W10
MAIDA
VALE
W9
HANWELL
W7
WEST
EALING
W13
Uxbridge
A4020
A406
ACTON
W3
PADDINGTON
W2
W1
WC1
WC2
Marble
Arch
EALING
W5
SHEPHERDS
BUSH
W12
NOTTING
HILL
W11
KEN-
SINGTON
W8
Hyde Pk
Cnr
Heathrow
Airport
W
SW1
HAMMER-
SMITH
W6
W KEN
W14
STH
KEN
SW7
WEST-
MINSTER
KENNING-
TON
SE11
M4
A4
Slough &
The West
Kew
Bridge
EARLS
COURT
SW5
A308
CHELSEA
SW3
Staines &
The South-West
A307
A205
CHISWICK
W4
A316
BARNES
SW13
W
BROMPTON
SW10
SOUTH
LAMBETH
SW8
Elevated
Motorway
FULHAM
SW6
BATTERSEA
SW11
STOCKWELL
SW9
EAST SHEEN
SW14
South
Circular
A3
A316
PUTNEY
SW15
Road
CLAPHAM
SW4
BRIXTON
SW2
RICHMOND
M3 &
The South
West
TWICKENHAM
A306
WANDSWORTH
SW18
BALHAM
SW12
A23
SW
TOOTING
SW17
WIMBLEDON
SW19
A308
A219
A24
A3
TEDDINGTON
STREATHAM
SW16
MITCHAM
KINGSTON-
UPON-
THAMES
RAYNES PARK
SW20
Dorking
Guildford
A24
Epsom
A217
Reigate
Brighton
Eastbourne
M23
AA

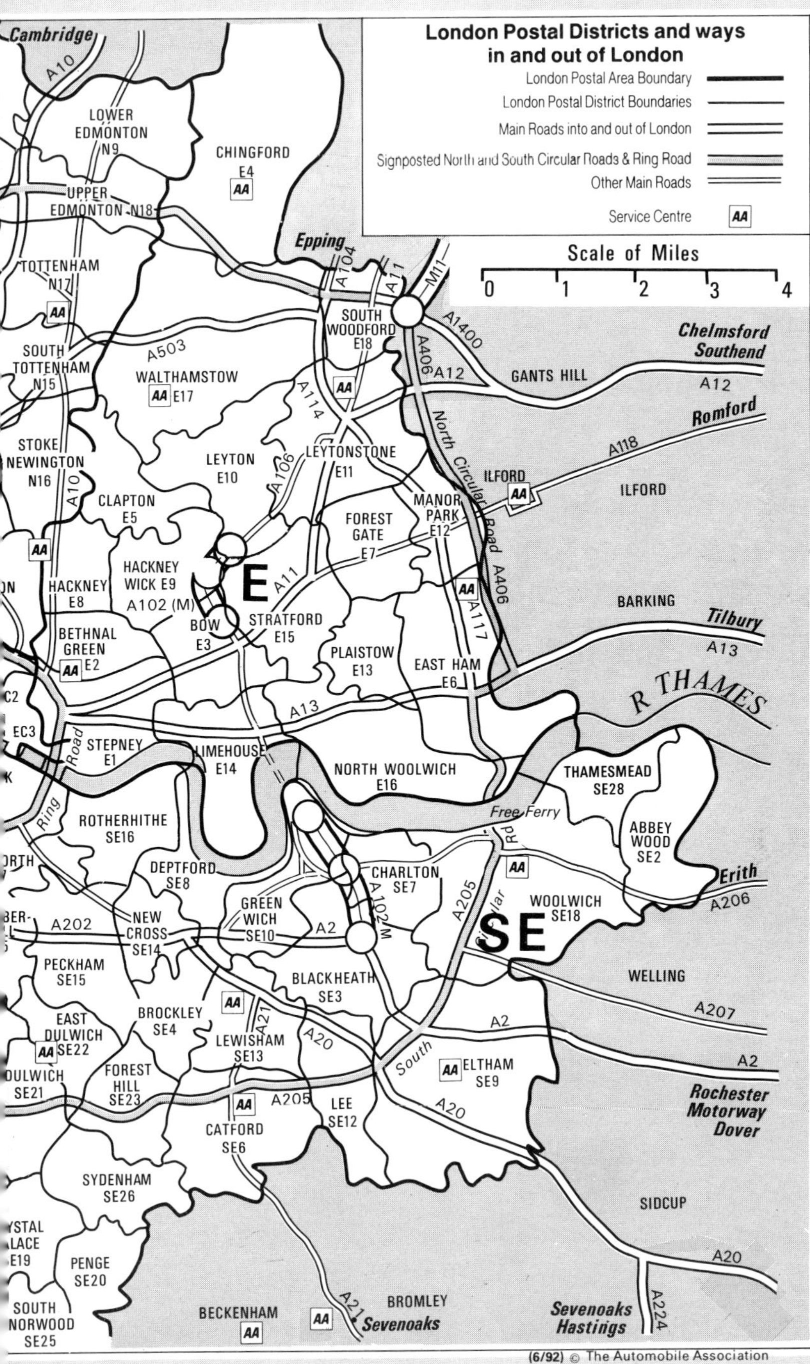
London Postal Districts and ways in and out of London
London Postal Area Boundary
London Postal District Boundaries
Main Roads into and out of London
Signposted North and South Circular Roads & Ring Road
Other Main Roads
Service Centre
Scale of Miles
0 1 2 3 4
Cambridge
LOWER EDMONTON N9
CHINGFORD E4
UPPER EDMONTON N18
Epping
TOTTENHAM N17
SOUTH WOODFORD E18
Chelmsford Southend
SOUTH TOTTENHAM N15
WALTHAMSTOW E17
GANTS HILL
Romford
STOKE NEWINGTON N16
LEYTON E10
LEYTONSTONE E11
ILFORD
CLAPTON E5
FOREST GATE E7
MANOR PARK E12
HACKNEY WICK E9
HACKNEY E8
E
BARKING
Tilbury
BETHNAL GREEN E2
BOW E3
STRATFORD E15
PLAISTOW E13
EAST HAM E6
R THAMES
STEPNEY E1
LIMEHOUSE E14
NORTH WOOLWICH E16
THAMESMEAD SE28
Free Ferry
ROTHERHITHE SE16
ABBEY WOOD SE2
DEPTFORD SE8
CHARLTON SE7
Erith
NEW CROSS SE14
GREEN WICH SE10
WOOLWICH SE18
SE
PECKHAM SE15
BLACKHEATH SE3
WELLING
EAST DULWICH SE22
BROCKLEY SE4
LEWISHAM SE13
ELTHAM SE9
FOREST HILL SE23
LEE SE12
Rochester Motorway Dover
CATFORD SE6
SYDENHAM SE26
SIDCUP
PENGE SE20
BROMLEY
SOUTH NORWOOD SE25
BECKENHAM
Sevenoaks
Sevenoaks Hastings
North Circular Road
South Circular Rd
Ring Road
(6/92) © The Automobile Association

LONDON Greater London Map **04**

See plans 1-4 pages 245-249. A map of the London postal area appears on pages 250-251.
Places within the London postal area are listed below in postal district order commencing East then North, South and West, with a brief indication of the area covered. Detailed plans **1-3** show the locations of AA-listed hotels within Central London and are indicated by a number. Plan **4** highlights the districts. **Other places within the county of London are listed under their respective placenames and are also keyed to this plan or the main map section.**

E18 SOUTH WOODFORD London plan **4** F5

GH QQ Grove Hill Hotel 38 Grove Hill, South Woodford E18 2JG ☎081-989 3344 FAX 081-530 5286
This popular hotel offers compact but well kept bedrooms, each with radio, TV and recently installed telephones. A generous breakfast is included in the room tariff.
21rm(10⇌2♠9hc) (2fb) CTV in all bedrooms ® **T** ✱ sB&B£23.50-£30.55 sB&B⇌♠£35.25 dB&B£41.70 dB&B⇌♠£49.35
Lic 🍽 CTV 8P 4🚘 (£2 per night)
Credit Cards [1] [2] [3] £

N8 HORNSEY London plan **4** D5

GH QQ Aber Hotel 89 Crouch Hill N8 9EG ☎081-340 2847 FAX 081-340 2847
Traditional standards of friendly family service combine with an old-fashioned British atmosphere at the Aber. Value-for-money standard accommodation is provided, and several rooms are suitable for family use. There is a no-smoking breakfast room and colour TV lounge, and service is provided by Mr and Mrs Jenkins who have been host to many overseas visitors over the years. Parking can be difficult at times, but space can usually be found in side streets.
9hc (4fb) 🐕 ✱ sB&B£18-£25 dB&Bfr£34 WB&B£95-£105
🍽 CTV
Credit Cards [1] [3] £

GH QQQ White Lodge Hotel 1 Church Ln, Hornsey N8 7BU ☎081-348 9765
This private family-run guesthouse has been skilfully extended and provides triple-glazed front rooms and an elegant Victorian-style entrance lobby lounge. Bedrooms offer modern levels of comfort, all furnished to the same standard, and a small no smoking breakfast room also has some additional lounge seating. Family bedrooms are available, and the very friendly service is personally supervised by the resident proprietor. A full English breakfast is available at an extra charge.Car parking can be extremely difficult: taxis are advisable.
16rm(8♠8hc) (5fb) CTV in all bedrooms ® 🐕 (ex guide dogs) ✱ sB&B£22-£24 dB&B£32-£34 dB&B♠£38-£40 LDO at breakfast
🍽 CTV 🅿̸
Credit Cards [1] [3] £

N19 UPPER HOLLOWAY London plan **4** D4

GH QQQ Parkland Walk 12 Hornsey Rise Gardens N19 3PR ☎071-263 3228 Telex no 262433 FAX 071-831 9489
The home of Lawrence and Penny Solomons, this house was built about 1880, and has been beautifully restored throughout using period and antique furniture. The bedrooms are sympathetic to the English Town House style, however they have no wash basins but guests (6 max.) share 2 general bathrooms. There is a very comfortable lounge and guests have unrestricted access to the house, although no-smoking is strictly observed throughout. Full English breakfast is included, cooked to order, and local restaurants can be recommended by the proprietors. The service is relaxed and informal provided by very helpful and friendly hosts.
4rm (1fb)🚭in all bedrooms CTV in all bedrooms ® 🐕 ✱ sB&B£17-£22 dB&B£34-£40 WB&B£120-£132
🍽 CTV £

NW1 REGENT'S PARK London plan **4** D4

GH QQ Four Seasons Hotel 173 Gloucester Place, Regents Park NW1 6DX ☎071-724 3461 & 071-723 9471
Just north of the Marylebone Road near Baker Street tube station, this friendly, family-run hotel offers competitively priced bedrooms with very good quality beds. The conservatory-style breakfast room is light and fresh with dazzling white décor, and a Continental-style breakfast is provided consisting of ham, cheeses and eggs. English breakfast can be made available with prior notice.
16rm(14⇌♠2hc) (2fb) CTV in all bedrooms 🐕 ✱ sB&B⇌♠£49.50 dB&B⇌♠£65
🍽
Credit Cards [1] [2] [3] [5]

NW2 CRICKLEWOOD London plan **4** C4

GH Q Clearview House 161 Fordwych Rd NW2 3NG ☎081-452 9773
This peaceful, family-run guesthouse is situated in a quiet residential area. Adequately furnished and well maintained, it offers a choice of bedrooms including more spacious family rooms. There is a combined family lounge and dining room and the friendly and informal atmosphere is augmented by efficient service provided by the very helpful Mr and Mrs Guido Padion. Unrestricted car parking is usually available.
6hc (1fb) CTV in 1 bedroom TV in 5 bedrooms
🐕 (ex guide dogs) ✱ sB&B£18 dB&B£34 WB&B£85
🍽 CTV 🅿̸ nc5yrs £

GH QQ The Garth Hotel 64-76 Hendon Way NW2 2NL ☎081-455 4742

This commercial hotel has recently been extensively redeveloped and completely refurbished, and now offers a variety of bedrooms with all the modern amenities expected of a privately owned and well managed hotel. There is an impressive reception lobby, the Tivoli Restaurant and bar and extensive banqueting and conference facilities with air conditioning, and at the rear of the hotel is a car park, in Garth Road. The hotel is located on the southbound carriageway of the A41 Hendon Way.

53rm(30🛁10🚿13hc) (9fb) CTV in all bedrooms Ⓡ sB&Bfr£42.95 sB&B🛁🚿£59 dB&Bfr£60 dB&B🛁🚿£80 LDO 11pm

Lic 🍴 CTV 58P

Credit Cards [1] [2] [3] [5]

NW3 HAMPSTEAD London plan 4 D4

GH QQ La Gaffe 107-111 Heath St NW3 6SS ☎071-435 4941 & 071-435 8965 FAX 071-794 7592

Annexe 14🛁🚿 CTV in all bedrooms ✖ (ex guide dogs)

Lic

Credit Cards [1] [2] [3] [5]

SELECTED

GH QQQQ The Langorf Hotel 20 Frognal, Hampstead NW3 6AG ☎071-794 4483

This elegant Edwardian building is in a residential side street near Finchley Road and about 15 minutes' from Hampstead village. It has recently been very smartly refurbished. Bedrooms are located from the lower ground floor up to the 3rd floor (there is a lift), half at the front and the rest overlooking the quiet garden behind. Most are a good size and all are attractively decorated and fully equipped, with modern bathrooms and excellent showers. The bedrooms also have the benefit of 24-hour room service. An eye-catching black and white chequered staircase leads up from the road to a blue and white lobby/lounge, with a staffed reception, chesterfield seating and a friendly welcome. There is a bright breakfast room which has small café-styled tables, TV, a licensed bar and a light snack menu. A full English breakfast is available at an extra charge. With good road and rail access to the West End, this hotel offers very good value. Motorists might need to discuss parking options in advance.

31🛁🚿 (2fb) CTV in all bedrooms Ⓡ ✖ ✱ sB&B🛁🚿£61 dB&B🛁🚿£75-£83 WB&B£377 WBDi£464.50

Lic lift 🍴 CTV

Credit Cards [1] [2] [3] [5]

GH QQ Seaford Lodge 2 Fellows Rd, Hampstead NW3 3LP ☎071-722 5032 FAX 071-586 8735

This detached manor house was built 150 years ago and has been completely refurbished. Furnished mainly with antiques, the house retains much of its Edwardian character, and additional facilities include family bedrooms, a baby listening service, ground floor accommodation for the semi-disabled and inclusive English breakfast. Service is personally supervised by the proprietor Miss Caroline Plunkett, and the hotel enjoys a location close to Regents Park.

15🛁🚿 (1fb) CTV in all bedrooms Ⓡ T sB&B🛁🚿£45 dB&B🛁🚿£70 WB&B£255 LDO noon

🍴 3P 2🚗

Credit Cards [1] [3] [5] £

NW4 HENDON London plan 4 C5

GH QQQ Peacehaven Hotel 94 Audley Rd, Hendon Central NW4 3HB ☎081-202 9758 & 081-202 1225

Quietly situated off the A41, west of Hendon Central underground station, this small, friendly guesthouse provides excellent value and has been extensively refurbished. The modern bedrooms are well equipped with many amenities, together with spacious private, but not en suite, bathrooms, some of which are on the ground floor. Service is personally supervised by Mr Summers and an attractive breakfast room overlooks the terraced garden. Unrestricted street car parking is usually available outside the hotel.

13rm(7🛁🚿6hc) CTV in all bedrooms Ⓡ ✖ (ex guide dogs) ✱ sB&B£38-£42 sB&B🛁🚿£48-£50 dB&B£56-£60 dB&B🛁🚿£65-£68

🍴 2P

Credit Cards [1] [2] [3] [5] £

NW11 GOLDERS GREEN London plan 4 C5

GH QQQ *Anchor Hotel* 10 West Heath Dr, Golders Green NW11 ☎081-458 8764 FAX 081-455 3204

12rm(9🚿) (2fb) CTV in all bedrooms

🍴 CTV 6P 3🚗

GH QQ Croft Court Hotel 44 Ravenscroft Av, Golders Green NW11 8AY ☎081-458 3331 FAX 081-455 9175

This small, personally run Kosher hotel has been completely refurbished throughout, and bedrooms are all equipped with every modern facility. The kitchens are run under the supervision of Bethdin and Kashrus Commission; breakfast is inclusive and dinner is available on request. The combined lounge/dining room can be hired for private functions and conferences. The hotel is situated in a convenient location in a residential area just off the Finchley road.

20🛁🚿 (4fb) CTV in all bedrooms Ⓡ T ✖ ✱ sB&B🛁🚿£54 dB&B🛁🚿£60

🍴 CTV 3P

Credit Cards [1] [2] [3] £

SE3 BLACKHEATH London plan 4 E3

GH QQ Stonehall House Hotel 35-37 Westcombe Park Rd SE3 7RE ☎081-858 8706 FAX (0895) 251948

This long-established, quietly situated old-fashioned guesthouse has been extended into the next door property. Bedrooms are functional and modestly furnished, with good standards of housekeeping. Well managed, the accommodation offers good value for money with a very friendly and relaxed informal atmosphere. Car parking is readily available, and there is a railway station nearby.

27rm(1🛁10🚿16hc) (10fb) CTV in all bedrooms ✱ sB&B£20-£22 sB&B🛁🚿£25-£27 dB&B£30-£33 dB&B🛁🚿£35-£37

🍴 CTV P̸

Credit Cards [1] [3] £

SELECTED

GH QQQQ *Vanbrugh Hotel* 21/23 St Johns Park SE3 7TD ☎081-853 4051

Run in conjunction with Bardon Lodge Hotel, this self-contained villa has been extensively upgraded and well furnished to a high standard throughout. There is a choice of comfortable bedrooms, ideal for both tourist and business travellers, and public rooms include a small lounge, separate dining/breakfast room, and a lift to all levels. There are good reception check-in facilities, a rear garden and forecourt car parking.

30🛁🚿 CTV in all bedrooms Ⓡ ✖ (ex guide dogs)

LDO 9.15pm

Lic lift 🍴 CTV 16P

Credit Cards [1] [2] [3]

SE9 ELTHAM London plan 4 F2

GH QQQ *Yardley Court Private Hotel* 18 Court Rd SE9 ☎081-850 1850

In a convenient location off the A20 and close to the shops, post office and main line station, this hotel benefits from its own forecourt car park. Bedrooms are individually furnished and vary

→

in shape and size, but all have colour TV and en suite showers – rooms 4 and 6 being shower only. The conservatory breakfast room overlooks the rear garden and there is a small reception and sitting area. Service is helpful and very well managed, and full English breakfast is included in the room tariff.

9rm(6 3hc) (1fb) CTV in all bedrooms ® (ex guide dogs) 8P

Credit Cards 1 3

SE19 NORWOOD London plan **4** D2

GH QQ Crystal Palace Tower Hotel 114 Church Rd, Crystal Palace SE19 2UB 081-653 0176

This large Victorian family-run guesthouse is close to all amenities and provides easy access to London. Attracting a regular clientèle, good value for money is provided, with free car parking and inclusive full English breakfast. Several family rooms are available, and bedrooms are double glazed. Service is personally supervised by the resident proprietors Mr and Mrs Weir.

11rm(3 4 4hc) (4fb) CTV in 3 bedrooms TV in 8 bedrooms ® * sB&B£21 sB&B £25 dB&B£32-£35 dB&B £36-£39

CTV 10P

Credit Cards 1 3 5 £

SE25 SOUTH NORWOOD London plan **4** E1

GH QQQ Norwood Lodge 17-19 South Norwood Hill, South Norwood SE25 6AA 081-653 3962

This hotel is made up of 3 houses joined together to offer an extensive range of bedrooms, a spacious modern reception, and a lower ground floor dining room overlooking the garden. Bedrooms are located on different levels and are designed to provide every modern amenity, including direct dial telephones and beverage making equipment. All are furnished to the same standard with light wood veneers, bright décor and coordinated fabrics. There are plans to enlarge the dining room into a fully licensed restaurant, which could be completed during 1993. Free car parking and inclusive full English breakfast are provided, and the hotel is ideally located for ready access to London. Staff are friendly, helpful and well managed.

20 (1fb) CTV in all bedrooms ® T sB&B £35-£45 dB&B £45-£55

Lic CTV 16P 1

Credit Cards 1 3 £

SW1 WESTMINSTER London plan **4** D3

GH QQ *Belgrave House* 28-32 Belgrave Rd, Victoria SW1V 1RG 071-828 1563 & 071-834 8620

This 5-storey terraced bed and breakfast establishment has benefited from recent renovation, but bedrooms vary in size and some are very restricted. Continental-style breakfast is provided, but a cooked English breakfast is available by arrangement. Car parking is very difficult and taxi access is recommended.

46rm(2 4 40hc) (8fb) in 25 bedrooms

CTV

GH QQQ The Diplomat 2 Chesham St, Belgravia SW1X 8DT 071-235 1544 Telex no 926679 FAX 071-259 6153

Situated in the exclusive Belgravia area, this listed building offers spacious, attractive bedrooms which have smart, modern bath or shower rooms. All bedrooms are reached via the impressive spiral staircase or alternatively the lift will take you up to all but the 4th floor. A full English breakfast buffet can be enjoyed in the basement dining room.

27 (5fb) CTV in all bedrooms ® T * sB&B £64.57-£83.37 dB&B £99.82-£135.13

lift

Credit Cards 1 2 3 5

GH QQ *The Executive Hotel* 57 Pont St, Knightsbridge SW1X 0BD 071-581 2424

This elegant Victorian town house is situated just a stone's throw from fashionable Knightsbridge and several museums. The bedrooms may be compact but all are en suite and are equipped with every modern facility. A self-service hot and cold breakfast buffet is served in the air-conditioned basement dining room.

29 (1fb) CTV in all bedrooms ® (ex guide dogs)

lift

Credit Cards 1 2 3 5

GH QQ Willett Hotel 32 Sloane Gardens, Sloane Square SW1W 8DJ 071-824 8415 Telex no 926678

Situated just off Sloane Square, this elegant Victorian town house offers smart, modern bedrooms which vary in size, but all are equipped with every modern convenience. English breakfast is taken in the bright basement dining room.

18rm(15 3hc) (6fb) CTV in all bedrooms ® T * sB&B£50-£58.75 sB&B £71.03-£77.49 dB&B£71.03-£77.49 dB&B £90.42

Credit Cards 1 2 3 5

GH QQ Winchester Hotel 17 Belgrave Rd SW1V 1RB 071-828 2972 Telex no 269674 FAX 071-828 5191

This privately owned and long-established guesthouse is conveniently located near Victoria station. The rooms are all furnished to the same standard with every modern amenity, and very high levels of housekeeping are maintained. A generous inclusive English breakfast is served in the pleasant basement dining room. Car parking can be very difficult, but there is a car park in Warwick Way, Pimlico, nearby.

18 (2fb) CTV in all bedrooms sB&B £45-£58 dB&B £50-£58

nc10yrs

GH QQQ Windermere Hotel 142/144 Warwick Way, Victoria SW1V 4JE 071-834 5163 & 071-834 5480 Telex no 94017182 FAX 071-630 8831

A small family-run hotel offering nicely equipped, modern rooms, tastefully furnished, with further improvements planned. A coffee shop is open in the evening, and room service is available during the day. There is a small residents' lounge, and a night porter is usually on hand. Car parking is readily available nearby, and the hotel is well situated for easy access to the West End.

23rm(19 4hc) (7fb) CTV in all bedrooms T (ex guide dogs) sB&B£38-£44 sB&B £42-£49 dB&B£48-£52 dB&B £54-£79 LDO 9.30pm

Lic CTV

Credit Cards 1 2 3

SW3 CHELSEA London plan **4** D3

GH QQQ *Claverley House* 13-14 Beaufort Gardens, Knightsbridge SW3 071-589 8541

Tucked away in a quiet cul-de-sac within minutes' of Harrods, this privately owned town house has been upgraded to a very high standard. Individually decorated bedrooms, though compact, are stylishly furnished with quality fabrics and reproduction furniture, and many have smart marbled bathrooms. There is an elegant ground floor reading room with inviting Chesterfields and facilities for guests to make hot drinks, while a full English breakfast is served by cheerful staff in the recently re-decorated basement breakfast room. Reception is staffed from 7.30am to midnight, and there is a lift to all floors.

36rm(25 11hc) (2fb) CTV in all bedrooms

lift

Credit Cards 3

GH QQQ *Knightsbridge Hotel* 10 Beaufort Gardens SW3 1PT 071-589 9271

This terraced house was built in 1870 and has been extensively upgraded and modernised to provide very comfortable bed and breakfast accommodation. Situated in a quiet tree-lined cul-de-sac

off the Brompton road, it benefits from a convenient location for shopping. Excellent facilities include satellite TV, Teletext and radio, complemented by personal, friendly service. Business services are also available, and there is a well stocked bar. Car parking can be extremely difficult.
20rm(4⇨5♠11hc) (4fb) CTV in all bedrooms ® ✈
LDO 9.30pm
Lic 🛗 ₱
Credit Cards [1] [2] [3]

See advertisement on page 259

SW5 EARLS COURT London plan **4** C3

GH QQ Swiss House Hotel 171 Old Brompton Rd, South Kensington SW5 0AN ☎071-373 2769 & 071-373 9383 FAX 071-373 4983
In the heart of South Kensington, this attractive small hotel with its ivy- clad façade is ideal for both tourists and visitors to nearby exhibitions. Bedrooms are prettily decorated in pastel shades and floral fabrics, most are en suite and all are equipped with modern conveniences. A Continental buffet is provided in the basement dining room and a range of snacks is available all day from room service.
16rm(11⇨♠5hc) (7fb) CTV in 15 bedrooms TV in 1 bedroom
T sB&Bfr£32 sB&B⇨♠fr£45 dB&Bfr£48 dB&B⇨♠fr£58
🛗 CTV
Credit Cards [1] [3] £

SW7 SOUTH KENSINGTON London plan **4** D3

GH QQQ Five Sumner Place Hotel 5 Sumner Place, South Kensington SW7 3EE ☎071-584 7586 FAX 071-823 9962
Forming part of an impressive stucco-fronted Victorian terrace, this small privately owned and run hotel is situated in the heart of South Kensington. Recently restored bedrooms are tastefully furnished with reproduction pieces, elegant drapes and coordinating décor, all complete with smart, modern en suite →

facilities. An enjoyable breakfast is taken in the bright conservatory leading to a small patio which guests can use during summer months.
13⇌ (4fb) in 2 bedrooms CTV in all bedrooms T ✱
sB&B⇌£64-£76 dB&B⇌£82-£98
lift CTV
Credit Cards 1 2 3 5 £

SW19 WIMBLEDON London plan **4** C2

GH QQ *Kings Lodge* 5 Kings Rd SW19 8PJ ☎081-545 0191 FAX 081-545 0381
Closed Xmas
The bedrooms at this guesthouse vary in size, but they have all been furnished to a very high standard and equipped with direct dial telephones, TV and beverage making facilities. A separate front room provides a residents' salon, and a fully inclusive English breakfast is served in the small dining room; there are plans to extend the dining room soon. Car parking can be extremely difficult, although there is a small fore-court: taxis are recommended.
7rm(2⇌5) (2fb) CTV in all bedrooms ® (ex guide dogs) LDO 9pm
CTV 2P 2
Credit Cards 1 2 3 5

GH QQ Trochee Hotel 21 Malcolm Rd SW19 4AS ☎081-946 1579 & 3924 FAX 081-785 4058
Under the same family ownership as Worcester House, this old-fashioned but soundly maintained guesthouse is quietly situated. It offers bed and breakfast accommodation, with modern, simply furnished bedrooms in varying styles, all with full double-glazing. The combined breakfast room/lounge is set off by a garden in the summer, and full English breakfast is inclusive. Additional facilities include some self-catering units. Service is personally supervised by the proprietor Mr Amin Dhala.
17hc (2fb) CTV in all bedrooms ® (ex guide dogs) sB&B£35 dB&B£49
CTV 3P
Credit Cards 1 3 £

GH QQ Wimbledon Hotel 78 Worple Rd SW19 4HZ ☎081-946 9265 081-946 1581
This detached Victorian house, situated on the corner of Elm Grove, offers a choice to suit everyone. The bedrooms are simply furnished to the same standard, with some compact family rooms available. All rooms are equipped with TV, clock alarm radios and tea making facilities and some offer en suite showers. A small lounge and a non smoking breakfast room – offering inclusive, full English breakfast, add to the overall comfort.
14rm(5⇌9hc) (6fb) in 8 bedrooms CTV in all bedrooms ® T ✱ sB&B£45-£48 sB&B⇌£48-£51 dB&B£51-£54 dB&B⇌£58-£59
CTV 10P
Credit Cards 1 3 5

GH QQQ Worcester House 38 Alwyne Rd SW19 7AE ☎081-946 1300 FAX 081-785 4058
This attractive detached house is quietly located in a residential area, and is personally supervised by the proprietor Mrs Rosina Dhala. A choice of brightly decorated bedrooms is offered, all equipped with modern amenities and furnished in a comfortable old-fashioned style. Full English breakfast is served in the small pine furnished dining room. Service is friendly and well managed, but car parking can be difficult at times.
9 (1fb) CTV in all bedrooms ® ✱ sB&B£45-£49.50 dB&B£59.50
CTV P
Credit Cards 1 3 5 £

Book as early as possible for busy holiday periods.

W1 WEST END London plan **4** D3/4

GH QQQ Bryanston Court 60 Great Cumberland Place W1 (Best Western) ☎071-262 3141 Telex no 262076
This long-established, family-run hotel is located in the centre of London, close to all the main shops and department stores. The bedrooms have recently been fitted with new furniture and redecorated, plus all the shower/bathrooms are now upgraded. All rooms are equipped with a telephone, TV/radio, tea making facilities and a hair dryer. A well used bar offers a club-style dimension and the nicely furnished lounge and breakfast room advances the hotel's good facilities. Light refreshments are available throughout the day and there are limited conference facilities offered. Car parking can be difficult at times but there is a NCP near.
54rm(4⇌50) (3fb) CTV in all bedrooms ® ✱
sB&B⇌fr£75 dB&B⇌fr£90 LDO 10pm
Lic lift 2 (£15 per day)
Credit Cards 1 2 3 5

GH QQQ Hotel Concorde 50 Great Cumberland Place W1H 7FD ☎071-402 6169 Telex no 262076
Closed 23 Dec-1 Jan
Adjoining the Bryanston Court hotel which the Theodore family also own, this well managed hotel has been recently renovated and bedrooms are all furnished to the same standard, with good quality, modern showers, direct dial telephone, radio, TV, hair dryer and tea making facilities. There is a lift to all levels, and a small basement breakfast room; a supplementary charge is made for full English breakfast. The Theodore family have managed these hotels for over 2 family generations, and the hotel enjoys an international and loyal returning clientèle. There is a very attractively furnished club-style foyer sitting area, but no car park: parking meters can usually be found nearby and there is a local NCP car park.
28rm(5⇌23) (1fb) CTV in all bedrooms ® ✱
sB&B⇌fr£65 dB&B⇌fr£70
Lic lift CTV 2 (£15 per day)
Credit Cards 1 2 3 5

GH Q Edward Lear Hotel 28-30 Seymour St W1 ☎071-402 5401 FAX 071-706 3766
Named after the artist and writer who lived here from 1812-1888, this conveniently located rambling house offers good basic accommodation on 6 floors. The rooms vary, but most now offer TV and direct dial telephones, and some have private bathrooms. Well managed by John McLaren, the service is friendly and helpful, and with full English breakfast included, the guesthouse provides overall good value for this central location. Car parking can be very difficult at certain times of the day.
30rm(5 25hc) (3fb) CTV in all bedrooms ® T ✱
sB&B£39.75-£45 sB&B£55 dB&B£49.50-£57.50 dB&B£62.50-£67
CTV P
Credit Cards 1 3 £

GH QQ Georgian House Hotel 87 Gloucester Place, Baker St W1H 3PG ☎071-935 2211 Telex no 266079 FAX 071-486 7535
This small, friendly hotel in a central location offers a choice of quiet, modern and well equipped bedrooms with particularly good value family rooms. There is a lift to all floors, and additional facilities include an automatic drinks machine, shoe cleaning service, security video system and very good international guest information. English breakfast can be provided at an additional charge, served in the basement dining room.
19rm(14⇌5) (3fb) CTV in all bedrooms ® ✱
sB&B⇌£45-£50 dB&B⇌£65-£70
Lic lift P nc5yrs
Credit Cards 1 2 3

Visit your local AA Shop.

GH QQ Hart House Hotel 51 Gloucester Place, Portman Sq W1H 3PE ☎071-935 2288 FAX 071-935 8516

A small family-run house on 5 floors, with the building forming part of a Georgian terrace. The bedrooms are slowly being upgraded to a good standard, and all rooms have direct dial telephone, TV, radio and tea making facilities. Personally run by Andrew and Jackie Bowden, the service is friendly, informal and helpful, and full English breakfast is inclusive. Car parking is very difficult, but there is good bus access to all local amenities. Well situated for Central London and Baker Street.

15rm(7⇌↱8hc) (4fb) CTV in all bedrooms ® ✖ sB&B£39-£42 sB&B⇌↱£45-£50 dB&B£50-£60 dB&B⇌↱£65-£75
♨ CTV P̸
Credit Cards 1 2 3 £

W2 BAYSWATER, PADDINGTON London plan **4** C/D3/4

SELECTED

GH QQQQ Byron Hotel 36-38 Queensborough Ter W2 3SH ☎071-243 0987 Telex no 263431 FAX 071-792 1957

This hotel provides bed and breakfast accommodation of an unusual quality for this part of London. Designer furnished to capture the Victorian London town house style, all bedrooms have air conditioning and every modern amenity; they range in size from very compact to luxurious, but all are beautifully furnished and well maintained. Full English breakfast is inclusive, and the elegant sitting room, formal reception, business services and small meeting room all complement the hotel's extensive facilities. There is a lift to all floors, and service is friendly and well managed by Mrs Margaret Moore. There is no car park: taxis are advised.

42⇌↱ (3fb)⊬in 10 bedrooms CTV in all bedrooms ® **T** ✖ (ex guide dogs) ✱ sB&B⇌↱£80-£85 dB&B⇌↱£95-£105 LDO 8pm
Lic lift ♨ CTV P̸
Credit Cards 1 2 3 5 £

GH QQQ Camelot Hotel 45-47 Norfolk Square W2 1RX ☎071-723 9118 & 071-262 1980 Telex no 268312 FAX 071-402 3412

A beautifully restored town house built around 1850 and retaining many original features despite its modern and distinctive refurbishment and upgrading. Bedrooms are furnished to the same general standard and are particularly well equipped. The pine furnished basement breakfast room has a feature fireplace, and a modern automatic lift serves all floors except the 6th. Car parking can be difficult, but the hotel is well situated in a quiet square.

44rm(36⇌↱8hc) (8fb) CTV in all bedrooms ® **T** ✖ (ex guide dogs) sB&B£40.25-£48.50 sB&B⇌↱£55 dB&B⇌↱£77
lift ♨ CTV P̸
Credit Cards 1 3 £

GH QQQ *Kingsway Hotel* 27 Norfolk Square, Hyde Park W2 1RX ☎071-723 7784 & 071-723 5569 FAX 071-723 7317

A small family-run hotel set in an attractive square overlooking the gardens and only a few minutes' walk from Paddington Station. The newly decorated bedrooms are equipped to a good standard with co-ordinating soft furnishings and all modern conveniences. Public areas are somewhat limited but there is a small foyer lounge, and breakfast is served in the basement dining room. Pay and display parking is available.

33rm(30⇌↱3hc) (4fb) CTV in all bedrooms ® ✖ (ex guide dogs)
lift ♨ CTV
Credit Cards 1 2 3 5

GH QQQ Mitre House Hotel 178-184 Sussex Gardens, Hyde Park W2 1TU ☎071-723 8040 Telex no 914113 FAX 071-402 0990

This family-run licensed hotel has recently been refurbished and upgraded, with the addition of 31 new bedrooms. Proprietor Mr A Chris personally supervises a friendly and informal style of service, and the accommodation has steadily improved over recent years. Free forecourt car parking, a lift to all floors and an inclusive English breakfast add to the overall good value being offered. There are plans to develop the restaurant/breakfast room.

70rm(64⇌↱6hc) (3fb) CTV in all bedrooms ✖ sB&B⇌↱£55-£60 dB&B⇌↱£65-£70
Lic lift ♨ CTV 25P jacuzzi
Credit Cards 1 2 3 5

See advertisement on page 263

GH QQQ *Mornington Hotel* 12 Lancaster Gate W2 3LG (Best Western) ☎071-262 7361 Telex no 24281 FAX 071-706 1028
Closed 23 Dec-1 Jan

The Mornington provides a very high standard of accommodation. The bedrooms are furnished in the modern Swedish style and equipped with direct dial telephones, remote control TV, satellite TV, radios, and bathrooms with shower facilities. The Continental breakfast buffet is a feature of the hotel, offering an excellent choice, with full English breakfast available on request. The public rooms have attractive wood panelling, and sandwiches, tea and coffee are available throughout the day from the bar. The friendly, helpful service is particularly well managed by the convivial Mr Robert Bellhouse.

68⇌↱ (6fb) CTV in all bedrooms
Lic lift ♨ P̸ sauna
Credit Cards 1 2 3 5

GH QQQ Norfolk Plaza Hotel 29/33 Norfolk Square, Paddington W2 1RX ☎071-723 0792 Telex no 266977
87⇌↱ (25fb) CTV in all bedrooms ® ✖ (ex guide dogs) ✱ sB&B⇌↱£68-£70 dB&B⇌↱£78-£88 WB&B£272-£317 WBDi£330-£368 LDO 10.30pm
Lic lift ♨
Credit Cards 1 2 3 5

GH QQQ *Norfolk Towers Hotel* 34 Norfolk Place W2 1QW ☎071-262 3123 Telex no 268583

A tastefully restored Victorian house which has benefited from a programme of complete refurbishment and upgrading. Bedrooms are generally furnished to the same standard, and comfortable, well appointed public areas add to the hotel's tourist appeal. The Victorian London-style Cad's Wine Bar offers an alternative to the Arundel Restaurant, but the lift does not serve the lower ground floor restaurant levels. Car parking can be very difficult, but Paddington station is not far away.

85⇌↱ (3fb) CTV in all bedrooms ✖ (ex guide dogs) LDO 10pm
Lic lift ♨ P̸
Credit Cards 1 2 3 5

GH QQ Park Lodge Hotel 73 Queensborough Ter, Bayswater W2 3SU ☎071-229 6424 FAX 071-221 4772

Newly refurbished bed and breakfast accommodation in Bayswater, with bedrooms on 5 floors (no lift) which come in a variety of shapes and sizes. All are neatly decorated, well equipped and have modern tiled en suite shower rooms. There is very limited public space.

29rm(2⇌27↱) (2fb) CTV in all bedrooms ® **T** ✖ (ex guide dogs) ✱ sB&B⇌↱£45-£49 dB&B⇌↱£55-£59 LDO noon
♨
Credit Cards 1 2 3 5 £

GH QQ Parkwood Hotel 4 Stanhope Place W2 2HB ☎071-402 2241 FAX 071-402 1574

This 4-storey terraced house is quietly located yet conveniently close to the West End. It offers bed and breakfast accommodation, with comfortable but variable bedrooms, all with TV, direct dial →

telephone and tea and coffee making facilities. The best bedrooms are on the 2nd floor, furnished with brass beds, and there are 2 ground floor rooms; most rooms have private bathrooms. Both the reception lounge and breakfast room are no-smoking areas. Car parking can be difficult.
18rm(12⇐⌐6hc) (5fb)✗in 3 bedrooms CTV in all bedrooms ® **T** ⊁ ✳ sB&Bfr£39.75 sB&B⇐⌐fr£55 dB&Bfr£54.50 dB&B⇐⌐fr£64.50
⅏ CTV Ⓟ̸
Credit Cards [1] [3] £

SELECTED

GH QQQQ Pembridge Court Hotel 34 Pembridge Gardens W2 4DX ☎071-229 9977 Telex no 298363 FAX 071-727 4982
This privately owned, gracious 19th-century town house has been skilfully extended and is elegantly furnished and beautifully appointed throughout. Proprietor Mr Paul Capra has earned an enviable reputation for his hospitality and services, and complemented by manager Valerie Golliatt, this hotel goes from strength to strength. A new drawing room has been created, and bedrooms range from compact to luxurious, but thoughtful touches improve the degree of comfort, and they are generously furnished and extensively equipped. Caps Restaurant provides freshly prepared traditional fare, and service from this long-standing team continues to be warm and attentive. There is no car park and taxis are strongly recommended.
17⇐⌐ Annexe 4⇐⌐ (4fb) CTV in all bedrooms **T** sB&B⇐⌐£90-£125 dB&B⇐⌐£110-£160 LDO 11.15pm
Lic lift ⅏ 2🚗
Credit Cards [1] [2] [3] [5]

GH QQ Slavia Hotel 2 Pembridge Square W2 4EW ☎071-727 1316 Telex no 917458 FAX 071-229 0803
This long-established, old-fashioned hotel is personally managed by Yugoslavian proprietor Mr Raden, together with a team of young student staff. Bedrooms are slowly being improved, with a lift to all floors, and it now provides good value generous accommodation which includes full English breakfast. The best rooms are on the 3rd floor, and the basement breakfast room has been furnished in Yugoslavian style. There is no car park, but parking meters are available in the square opposite.
31⌐ (8fb) **T** sB&B⌐£30-£45 dB&B⌐£40-£60
Lic lift ⅏ CTV 1P (£6 per day)
Credit Cards [1] [2] [3] [5] £

W4 CHISWICK London plan 4 C3

GH QQQ Chiswick Hotel 73 Chiswick High Rd W4 2LS ☎081-994 1712 FAX 081-742 2585
Recent improvements to this hotel include more en suite facilities and bedroom upgrading. The accommodation has now been well equipped and furnished in the modern style. There is a small dining room combined with a bar, and a cosy, quiet TV lounge. Some car parking is provided on the forecourt, and the Chiswick's location gives ready access to most parts of London.
33⇐⌐ (5fb) CTV in all bedrooms ® **T** sB&B⇐⌐fr£64.50 dB&B⇐⌐fr£82.50 LDO 8.30pm
Lic ⅏ CTV 15P
Credit Cards [1] [2] [3] [5] £

W6 HAMMERSMITH London plan 4 C3 (pages 000-000)

GH QQ Premier West Hotel 28-34 Glenthorne Rd, Hammersmith W6 OLS ☎081-748 6181
Premier West is a popular bed and breakfast hotel which is slowly developing. It comprises a choice of modern and substantially equipped bedrooms ranging from the larger family-style rooms in the lodge annexe to more varied and some quite compact rooms in the main building. Bar snacks and one-dish meals are available throughout the day, there is a night porter service and the proprietors are friendly and helpful. A new conference room is currently under construction and there are plans to provide a car park.
26⇐⌐ Annexe 15⇐⌐ (5fb) CTV in all bedrooms ® ⊁ (ex guide dogs) ✳ sB&B⇐⌐£40-£65 dB&B⇐⌐£45-£75
Lic ⅏ CTV 5P
Credit Cards [1] [2] [3] [5]

W7 HANWELL London plan 4 B3

GH QQQ Wellmeadow Lodge 24 Wellmeadow Rd W7 2AL ☎081-567 7294 FAX 081-566 3468
A charming little guesthouse quietly situated in a residential area, personally supervised by the resident joint proprietors Kennie Hornak and Francis Davey. Fine English breakfasts are served in the kitchen at a communal table, and there is a cosy lounge and individually furnished bedrooms, where smoking is not permitted. There are plans to extend next year, with all bedrooms having private bathrooms. Car parking can be difficult.
5rm(3⇐⌐2hc) ✗in all bedrooms CTV in all bedrooms ® **T** ⊁ sB&B£35-£45 dB&B⇐⌐£61-£70 LDO noon
⅏ CTV
Credit Cards [1] [2] [3] £

W8 KENSINGTON London plan 4 C3

GH QQ Apollo Hotel 18-22 Lexham Gardens W8 5JE ☎071-835 1133 Telex no 264189 FAX 071-370 4853
Closed 24 Dec-1 Jan
The well equipped though old-fashioned bedrooms of this small hotel are gradually being upgraded. A new reception and lobby have recently been completed. Services include a night porter, a small lift and light refreshments, and guests may use the bar in the Atlas Hotel next door.
59rm(40⇐10⌐9hc) (4fb) CTV in all bedrooms **T** ⊁ (ex guide dogs) ✳ sB&B£24-£30 sB&B⇐⌐£34-£46 dB&B⇐⌐£40-£56
Lic lift ⅏ CTV Ⓟ̸
Credit Cards [1] [2] [3] [5] £

GH QQ Atlas Hotel 24-30 Lexham Gardens W8 5JE ☎071-835 1155 Telex no 264189 FAX 071-370 4853
Closed 24 Dec-1 Jan
Benefiting from a bright modern reception and bar, the Atlas like the Apollo next door, has old-fashioned rooms with direct dial telephones and colour TV. A lift, night porter and the availability of light refreshments add to the advantage of a good location.
64rm(15⇐30⌐19hc) (7fb) CTV in all bedrooms ⊁ (ex guide dogs) ✳ sB&B£24-£30 sB&B⇐⌐£34-£46 dB&B⇐⌐£46-£56
Lic lift ⅏ CTV Ⓟ̸
Credit Cards [1] [2] [3] [5] £

GH QQ Observatory House Hotel 37 Hornton St W8 7NR ☎071-937-1577 & 071-937 6353 Telex no 914972 FAX 071-938 3585
An impressive building retaining many of its original features, built in the late 19th century on the site of the old Observatory. Whilst bath and shower rooms generally need to be better maintained, the overall quality of the furnishings is quite good. The basement breakfast room reverts during the day to a coffee lounge, and full English breakfast is inclusive. There is no lift and car parking access can be rather complicated.
24rm(7⇐17⌐) (5fb) CTV in all bedrooms ® **T** ⊁ (ex guide dogs) sB&B⇐⌐£54.95-£61.20 dB&B⇐⌐£69.90-£81.70 WB&B£280-£350
Lic ⅏ Ⓟ̸
Credit Cards [1] [2] [3] [5] £

£ Remember to use the money-off vouchers.

W14 WEST KENSINGTON London plan **4** C3

GH QQQ Aston Court Hotel 25/27 Matheson Rd W14 8SN
☎071-602 9954 Telex no 919208 FAX 071-371 1338
This small, comfortable hotel is situated in a residential area just a few minutes from Olympia. The attractively decorated bedrooms are on several floors and a lift is provided. Although the rooms vary in shape and size, they all have quality furnishings and are fully equipped with modern facilities. The lobby extends into a small bar/lounge area, where light snacks may be obtained, and breakfast is served in a modern conservatory extension. The friendly new owners are continuing to make their mark on this establishment.
29rm(10⇌19♠) (3fb) CTV in all bedrooms ® **T**
✗ (ex guide dogs) ✱ sB&B⇌♠£59.50-£62.50
dB&B⇌♠£69.50-£73
Lic lift ⅏ CTV ℗
Credit Cards [1] [2] [3] [5] £

GH QQQ Avonmore Hotel 66 Avonmore Rd W14 8RS
☎071-603 4296 & 3121 Telex no 945922 FAX 071-603 4035
A delightful little terraced guesthouse only a short walk from the Exhibition Centre at Olympia. Bedrooms are still being upgraded: 2 more rooms now have en suite showers, and rear facing bedrooms are double glazed. A well furnished attractive little breakfast room and a bar add to the facilities, and Miss Margaret McKenzie supervises the friendly service, with light refreshments available most evenings. Car parking is virtually impossible.
9rm(7⇌♠2hc) (3fb) CTV in all bedrooms ® **T** ✗ ✱
sB&B£39-£45 sB&B⇌♠£49-£55 dB&B£50-£52
dB&B⇌♠£59-£65
Lic ⅏ CTV ℗
Credit Cards [1] [3]

GH Q Centaur Hotel 21 Avonmore Rd W14 8RP
☎071-602 3857 & 071-603 5973
This attractive family-run guesthouse is in a quiet residential location close to Olympia and Earls Court. It is run by Yugoslavian proprietor Mrs Murial Stojsavljevic and her husband, and the atmosphere is relaxed and informal. Guests have use of the 'no smoking' lounge, and full English breakfast is inclusive. Bedrooms are modestly furnished but well equipped with TV and direct dial telephones, and most have showers. Car parking is extremely difficult: taxis are strongly recommended.
12rm(3♠9hc) (5fb) CTV in all bedrooms **T** ✗ ✱ sB&B£32-£35
sB&B♠£45-£50 dB&B£45-£50 dB&B♠£55-£60
⅏ CTV £

GH QQQ Russell Court Hotel 9 Russell Rd, Kensington
W14 8JA ☎071-603 1222 FAX 071-371 2286
An extensive programme has been undertaken to upgrade this establishment completely, providing bright, modern and thoughtfully equipped bedrooms. Compact single bedrooms are available, and all rooms are double glazed for extra comfort. Although no dining room is available, continental breakfast is served in the bedrooms or from the bar/lounge buffet. Twenty-four hour service can be provided, and business services are available on request. There is no car park, making parking difficult at times.
18⇌♠ CTV in all bedrooms ® ✗ (ex guide dogs) ✱
sB&B⇌♠£59.50 dB&B⇌♠£69.50
Lic lift ⅏ CTV
Credit Cards [1] [2] [3] [5] £

WC1 BLOOMSBURY, HOLBORN London plan **4** D4

GH QQ Mentone Hotel 54-55 Cartwright Gardens WC1H 9EL
☎071-387 3927 & 071-388 4671
This long-established family-run guesthouse provides a choice of old-fashioned, traditionally furnished bedrooms located on several floors, some having en suite showers. Slowly being refurbished, the accommodation offers good value for money for this part of London, with full English breakfast included. Service is very helpful and friendly, personally supervised by Mrs Tyner and her family. Car parking is usually available by meters.
27rm(15♠12hc) (10fb) CTV in all bedrooms ® ✗ sB&B£25-£32 sB&B♠£35-£48 dB&B£35-£45 dB&B♠£45-£52
WB&B£150.50-£224
⅏ ℗ 🎾(hard)
Credit Cards [1] [3] £

LONGLEAT Wiltshire Map **03** ST84

FH QQQ Mrs J Crossman **Stalls** *(ST806439)* BA12 7NE
☎Maiden Bradley(0985) 844323
This 120-year-old farmhouse is attractively situated in Longleat Park, and was once the home farm for the estate. A warm and friendly welcome is assured, and guests are invited to share the relaxed family atmosphere. Bedrooms are comfortable and public rooms have a home-from-home feeling.
3hc ✗ ✱ sB&Bfr£15 dB&Bfr£30
⅏ CTV 6P table tennis table childrens play area 350 acres dairy

FH QQQ Mrs M A Cottle **Sturford Mead** *(ST834456)*
BA12 7QU ☎Westbury(0373) 832213
Tastefully decorated and furnished bedrooms are a feature of this farmhouse, which overlooks National Trust land and is close to both Longleat House and the safari park. Comfortable, spacious and very well kept accommodation is provided by the friendly owners Mr and Mrs Cottle, and the bedrooms are very well equipped.
4⇌♠ CTV in all bedrooms ® sB&B⇌♠£20-£25
dB&B⇌♠£32-£36
⅏ CTV 10P ⌂ 5 acres pig

LONGSDON Staffordshire Map **07** SJ95

FH QQQ Mr & Mrs M M Robinson ***Bank End*** *(SJ953541)*
Old Leek Rd ST9 9QJ (0.5m SW off A53) ☎Leek(0538) 383638
Closed Xmas wk
This small, family-run hotel is on the A53 about half a mile south of the village, overlooking the Endon Brook valley and Cauldon Canal. The pine-furnished bedrooms are in converted outbuildings, and there is a comfortable lounge bar and a good choice of food. Fishing and riding are available to residents.
9rm(6⇌1♠2hc) (3fb) CTV in all bedrooms ® LDO 8pm
Lic ⅏ CTV 10P ▣(heated) ⌐ 62 acres beef

LONGTOWN Cumbria Map **11** NY36

FH QQQ Mr & Mrs Elwen **New Pallyards** *(NY469713)*
Hethersgill CA6 6HZ (5.5 m E off the A6071 Brampton-Longtown road , take unclass road.)
☎Nicholforest(0228) 577308
This nicely decorated farmhouse offers some spacious bedrooms including a huge family room. Three bedrooms are in a purpose-built annexe next to the main house. The farm lies 6 miles east of Longtown and is best reached by leaving the town by Swan Street and, within a mile, turning right along the Stapleton road.
5rm(2⇌1♠2hc) (2fb) CTV in 2 bedrooms TV in 1 bedroom ®
✱ sB&Bfr£18 sB&B⇌♠£23 dB&Bfr£36 dB&B⇌♠£38
WB&B£105-£120 WBDi£165-£170 LDO 6.30pm
⅏ CTV 8P 1🚗 ⌐ U bowls putting 65 acres beef mixed sheep
£

LOOE Cornwall & Isles of Scilly Map **02** SX25

GH QQQ Coombe Farm Widegates PL13 1QN
☎Widegates(05034) 223
Mar-Oct
An attractive 1920s house with superb views, only a few miles from Looe. Recently renovated, it now provides 10 bedrooms all en suite, with very smart shower rooms; 3 of the rooms are located in a stone annexe building. The lounge is comfortable and stylish, and there is an attractive dining room furnished with antiques and enjoying splendid views, together with a very large games room. The well tended gardens contain an outdoor pool.

7⟨shower⟩ Annexe 3⟨shower⟩ (6fb) CTV in all bedrooms ® **T**
sB&B⟨shower⟩£16.50-£22.50 dB&B⟨shower⟩£33-£45 WB&B£115.50-£157.50
LDO 7pm
Lic ⟨central heating⟩ CTV 12P nc5yrs ⟨pool⟩(heated) games room croquet ⟨£⟩
See advertisement under LOOE

See advertisement on page 267

GH QQ Gulls Hotel Hannafore Rd PL13 2DE
☎(0503) 262531
Etr-Oct & Xmas
This guesthouse is well situated in an elevated position above the town, with wide panoramic views across the bay. Due to its position it is not ideal for those unable to manage steps or stairs, as there are plenty. Bedrooms are fairly compact but well arranged to ensure practicality and comfort; 2 have smart, modern en suite showers. Each room is named after a ship's captain, and many have lovely views. There is a cosy, well stocked bar, and public areas also enjoy fine views. A choice of food is offered from a short table d'hôte menu. This is a no-smoking establishment.
11rm(2⟨shower⟩9hc) CTV in 5 bedrooms TV in 6 bedrooms ® ✱
sB&B£10.50-£15.50 dB&B£21-£31 dB&B⟨shower⟩£26-£36
WB&B£70-£115 WBDi£122-£167 LDO breakfast
Lic ⟨central heating⟩ CTV 3P

SELECTED

GH QQQQ Harescombe Lodge Watergate PL13 2NE
☎(0503) 263158
One and a half miles northwest of Looe off the A387 road towards Polperro, this former shooting lodge dating from 1760 stands in a delightful picturesque setting hidden by woodland and overlooking the River Looe. Bedrooms are cosy and traditionally furnished with some lovely antique furniture, together with country views and modern, well presented private bathrooms. An evening meal is freshly prepared by the charming proprietor Mrs Wynn, using local good quality ingredients and home-grown vegetables. A hearty breakfast is also served, and the atmosphere here is convivial and cosy, resulting in regularly returning guests seeking peace and tranquility.
3rm(2⟨bath⟩1⟨shower⟩) ® ✗ (ex guide dogs) ✱ dB&B⟨bath⟩⟨shower⟩£32-£38
LDO 4pm
⟨central heating⟩ CTV 4P nc12yrs ⟨£⟩

GH Q *'Kantara'* 7 Trelawney Ter PL13 2AG ☎(0503) 262093
This small guesthouse offers an informal, relaxed atmosphere. Bedrooms are simply furnished but bright and fresh. A home-cooked evening meal is offered, and a hearty English breakfast is served. At the time of our inspection, the new owners were planning to build a small bar and to redecorate the entire establishment in the coming months.
6hc (3fb) CTV in all bedrooms ® LDO 5pm
CTV 1P 2⟨garage⟩
Credit Cards [1] [3]

GH QQ Ogunquit Portuan Rd, Hannafore PL13 2DW
☎(0503) 263105
A private hotel in an elevated position in Hannafore, West Looe, close to the seafront. It offers neatly presented bedrooms with fresh décor and simple furnishings. Public areas are comfortably appointed, sunny and bright, with superb views.
5rm(1⟨shower⟩4hc) (2fb) ✱ sB&B£15-£17 dB&B£28-£30
⟨central heating⟩ CTV ⟨no parking⟩

GH QQQ Panorama Hotel Hannafore Rd PL13 2DE
☎(0503) 262123
Feb-Nov
A family run hotel in an enviable position high above the town at Hannafore, with glorious views of the estuary and bay. The bedrooms have been completely upgraded, and provide co-ordinating cottage style décor with spotlessly clean, modern en suite facilities; 3 rooms also have a sun lounge and balcony. Public

→

areas take advantage of the view, with the front sun lounge and bar giving the widest panorama. There is a quiet, cosy lounge and a bright, fresh dining room where a choice of home-cooked dishes is offered by the resident proprietors Mr and Mrs Russell.
10rm(1⇨9↱) (4fb) CTV in all bedrooms ® ✕ sB&B⇨↱£22-£32 dB&B⇨↱£44-£64 WB&B£132-£192 WBDi£186-£250 LDO 6.30pm
Lic CTV 7P
Credit Cards [1] [3] Ⓔ

GH QQQ St Aubyns Marine Dr, Hannafore, West Looe PL13 2DH ☎(0503) 264351
Etr-end Oct
Opposite the seafront, enjoying lovely views out across Hannafore Point and the bay, this Victorian guesthouse has much to offer. Bedrooms and public areas are spotlessly clean and furnished with fine antiques. A substantial freshly cooked breakfast is served, with plenty of choice.
8rm(4⇨↱4hc) (5fb) CTV in 4 bedrooms ® ✕ ✱
sB&B⇨↱fr£20 dB&B⇨↱fr£50
CTV 4P
Credit Cards [1] [3] Ⓔ

GH QQQ Woodlands St Martins Rd PL13 1LP
☎(0503) 264405
Located in an elevated position, above the town of Looe, this Victorian property has a lovely, friendly country house atmosphere. Personally managed by Valerie Corse, the proprietors John and Gill Chapman remain involved and all 3 are genial hosts. The house has been decorated in an elegant and stylish manner, including the no-smoking bedrooms that are very prettily coordinated, and all but the single room are en suite. Every room is nicely presented and equipped. At present no lounge is available but the bedrooms have easy seating and the dining room is comfortably appointed, complete with a cosy open fire for chilly months. Valerie prepares an interesting, varied choice of meals from, wherever possible, fresh local ingredients with vegetables organically grown. Her home-made cakes and puddings are particularly tempting and her delicious breakfast sauce must be tried.
5rm(4↱) (2fb) CTV in 4 bedrooms ® ✕ (ex guide dogs) ✱
sB&B£12-£15 sB&B↱£20-£25 dB&B↱£40-£50 LDO 6.30pm
Lic 🍽 6P

FH QQ Mr & Mrs Hembrow ***Tregoad Farm Hotel*** *(SX272560)* St Martins PL13 1PB ☎(0503) 262718
Etr-Oct
Dating back over 120 years, this farmhouse enjoys both superb views of the surrounding countryside and the convenience of being only 2 miles from the centre of town. Bedrooms have a fresh décor and are neat and well presented. Public areas are comfortable and convivial, and include a neat dining room, a homely lounge and a bar area.
6hc (4fb) CTV in all bedrooms ® LDO 4pm
Lic CTV 15P ⛳ 60 acres dairy sheep beef

LOUGHBOROUGH Leicestershire Map **08** SK51

GH Q De Montfort Hotel 88 Leicester Rd LE11 2AQ
☎(0509) 216061
9hc (1fb) CTV in all bedrooms ® sB&Bfr£19 dB&Bfr£32 WB&Bfr£129.50 WBDifr£178.50 LDO 4pm
Lic 🍽 CTV
Credit Cards [1] [3] Ⓔ

GH QQQ *Garendon Park Hotel* 92 Leicester Rd LE11 2AQ
☎(0509) 236557
The friendly proprietors of the Garendon Park Hotel offer a personal service and make every effort to meet the guests needs. The bedrooms are light and cheerful, as are the public rooms. The lounge is comfortable and provides books, games and satelite T.V.
9hc (2fb) CTV in all bedrooms ® LDO 8pm
Lic 🍽 CTV
Credit Cards [1] [3]

LOUTH Lincolnshire Map **08** TF38

GH QQQ Wickham House Church Ln LN11 7LX
☎North Somercotes(0507) 358465
(For full entry see Conisholme)

INN QQQ Masons Arms Cornmarket LN11 9PY
☎(0507) 609525
Located in the market place, this handsome period inn has been thoroughly restored to offer modern, spacious accommodation with pine furniture, printed fabrics and comfortable seating. Some bedrooms are equipped with en suite facilities and others share a renovated Victorian bathroom, but all are warm and cheerfully decorated. As well as the huge hall, which is the restaurant, there is a choice of the 'Market' or lounge bar and all are popular places for meeting or enjoying a home-cooked meal. The Masons Arms is personally run by Mr and Mrs Harrison, assisted by other members of their family.
10rm(5⇨↱5hc) CTV in all bedrooms ® ✕ (ex guide dogs) ✱
sB&B£19.50-£25 dB&B£29.50-£39.50 dB&B⇨↱£39.50-£49.50 WB&B£125-£200 WBDi£175-£250 Lunch £6.95&alc Dinner £6.75-£14.45alc LDO 10pm
🍽
Credit Cards [1] [3]

LOW CATTON Humberside Map **08** SE75

GH QQQ Derwent Lodge YO4 1EA
☎Stamford Bridge(0759) 71468
Feb-Nov
Just 8 miles south of York towards Pocklington, and in the village centre, Derwent Lodge is owned and run by a charming family and offers a high level of comfort with emphasis on warmth and cleanliness.
6rm(4↱2hc) (1fb)⚟in all bedrooms CTV in all bedrooms ®
dB&Bfr£37 dB&B↱£41-£45 WB&B£129.50-£143.50 WBDi£199.50-£213.50 LDO 4pm
Lic 🍽 8P nc8yrs
See advertisement under YORK

LOWER BRAILES Warwickshire Map **04** SP33

SELECTED

GH QQQQ *Feldon House* OX15 5HW
☎Brailes(060885) 580
Closed 2 wks in Autumn
Hospitable proprietors, Maggie and Allan Witherick, warmly welcome visitors to their comfortable country home, situated next to the village church, which provides accommodation split between the main house and coach house. The main house rooms are prettily decorated and have private bathrooms, although not en suite, while the spacious coach house rooms are equipped with modern, quality en suite facilities. All bedrooms are exceptionally well supplied with a wide range of amenities and many thoughtful extras. There are 2 attractive sitting rooms, burning log fires in winter, and 2 dining areas, that include a conservatory, where breakfast is taken communally around the Victorian table. Great emphasis is placed on providing carefully prepared, enjoyable dinners. Car parking is available on a narrow track in front of the church.
2⇨↱ CTV in all bedrooms ® ✕ (ex guide dogs)
Lic 🍽 9P nc11yrs croquet lawn
Credit Cards [1] [3]

LOWER BEEDING West Sussex Map **04** TQ22

FH QQQ Mr J Christian **Brookfield Farm Hotel** *(TQ214285)* Winterpit Ln, Plummers Plain RH13 6LU ☎(0403) 891568 FAX (0403) 891499
Enjoying attractive, peaceful surroundings, this hotel offers a wealth of activities; an outdoor pool and play area for children and its own lake for boating and fishing. The accommodation is well equipped and there is a bar and a choice of restaurants.
20⇌↱ (2fb) CTV in all bedrooms ® T ✱ sB&B⇌↱£35.25-£41.13 dB&B⇌↱£47-£52.88 LDO 9.30pm
Lic 🍽 CTV 100P ⇝ ▸ ♩ sauna games room putting 300 acres mixed
Credit Cards 1 2 3 5

LOWESTOFT Suffolk Map **05** TM59

GH QQQ ***Albany Hotel*** 400 London Rd South NR33 0BQ ☎(0502) 574394
This guesthouse is situated on the A12, south of the town, just a few minutes' walk from both the shopping centre and beach. Licensed and well run, it suits the commercial visitor and tourist alike, with comfortable, spacious rooms and some en suite facilities.
7rm(3⇌↱4hc) (3fb) CTV in all bedrooms ®
✗ (ex guide dogs) LDO 1pm
Lic 🍽 CTV 2P
Credit Cards 1 3

GH QQ Amity 396 London Rd South NR33 0BQ ☎(0502) 572586
Closed Xmas & New Year
On the A12, the Amity has a distinctive red painted façade. It offers clean and tidy accommodation with some en suite facilities.
12rm(6↱6hc) (3fb) CTV in all bedrooms ® ✱ sB&Bfr£17 sB&B↱fr£24 dB&Bfr£32 dB&B↱fr£36 WB&Bfr£102 WBDifr£136 LDO 2pm
Lic 🍽 CTV ₱ solarium games room
Credit Cards 1 2 3

GH QQ Fairways 398 London Rd South NR33 0BQ ☎(0502) 572659
On the A12 south of the town, this carefully maintained guesthouse has friendly proprietors and offers some en suite facilities.
7rm(3⇌↱4hc) (4fb) CTV in all bedrooms ® sB&Bfr£17 dB&Bfr£32 dB&B⇌↱fr£39 WB&Bfr£110 WBDifr£140 LDO 4pm
Lic 🍽 CTV 3P
Credit Cards 1 2 3 £

GH QQ Kingsleigh 44 Marine Pde NR33 0QN ☎(0502) 572513
Closed Xmas
Central to the town and on the seafront, this is a nicely kept guesthouse with good sea views from the front rooms. The car park is on London Road South near to the building.
6hc (2fb) CTV in all bedrooms ® sB&B£16-£20 dB&B£30-£36 🍽 6P nc3yrs £

GH QQQ Rockville House 6 Pakefield Rd NR33 0HS ☎(0502) 581011 or 574891
rs Oct-Apr
A professional approach and genuine consideration for guests' comfort are demonstrated at this popular guesthouse, with such details as the recently installed grab rails for the elderly and disabled, the crisply laundered linen, en suite facilities and above average cleanliness.
8rm(2⇌1↱5hc) CTV in all bedrooms ® ✗ (ex guide dogs) sB&Bfr£20 sB&B⇌↱fr£31.50 dB&Bfr£34 dB&B⇌↱fr£40 WB&Bfr£102.50 WBDifr£167.50 LDO 10am
Lic 🍽 nc12yrs beach hut
Credit Cards 1 3 £

GH QQQ Somerton House 7 Kirkley Cliff NR33 0BY ☎(0502) 565665
A distinctive white and blue fronted house on the seafront south of the town, with commanding views. The bedrooms are well equipped, comfortable and attractively co-ordinated, and the four-poster room is popular. The Crocker family are enthusiastic and friendly, offering a professional approach and high catering and hygiene standards. The guesthouse benefits from an NCP car park opposite.
8rm(4↱4hc) (4fb)⊁in 2 bedrooms CTV in all bedrooms ® ✱ sB&Bfr£20 sB&B↱fr£25 dB&Bfr£34 dB&B↱fr£39 WB&Bfr£120 WBDifr£168 LDO 5pm
Lic 🍽 CTV 1P
Credit Cards 1 2 3 5 £

LOW ROW North Yorkshire Map **07** SD99

GH QQQ ***Peat Gate Head*** DL11 6PP ☎Richmond(0748) 86388
This enchanting 400-year-old house is situated high on a hillside, overlooking its own sloping garden and the Dales beyond. The unpretentious bedrooms are compact and well tended, while the 2 lounges – one with a TV – offer a wealth of reading material and a peaceful atmosphere. The resident proprietor, Alan Earl, is a delightful host and he personally cooks the delicious, imaginative dinners, for which he has earned a good reputation, encouraging guests to return time and time again.
6rm(3↱3hc) ⊁in all bedrooms ® ✗ LDO 5.30pm
Lic 🍽 CTV ₱ nc5yrs

LUDGVAN Cornwall & Isles of Scilly Map **02** SW53

FH Q Mrs A R Blewett **Menwidden** *(SW502337)* TR20 8BN ☎Penzance(0736) 740415
Closed Dec-Jan
Check for directions to this pebble-dashed family farmhouse, with extensive views. Sound bedroom accommodation lacks only wash basins; downstairs there is a cosy TV lounge.
6rm(1hc) (2fb) ✱ sB&Bfr£13 dB&Bfr£26 WB&Bfr£85 WBDifr£112 LDO 1pm
CTV 6P 40 acres dairy/market gardening
Credit Cards 2 £

LUDLOW Shropshire Map **07** SO57

See also Culmington

GH QQQ Cecil Sheet Rd SY8 1LR ☎(0584) 872442
Closed 20 Dec-6 Jan
A very well maintained modern bungalow on the edge of town, reached via the Ludlow bypass. The resident proprietors Mr and Mrs Phillips offer a friendly welcome and home-cooked meals are served in the attractive dining room which overlooks the colourful mature rear garden. Parking facilities are available.
10rm(3↱7hc) (1fb)⊁in all bedrooms CTV in 3 bedrooms ® sB&B£16.50-£19 dB&B£33-£38 dB&B↱fr£38 WB&B£110-£130 WBDi£164-£184 LDO 9am
Lic 🍽 CTV 10P 1🚘
Credit Cards 1 2 3 £

GH QQQ No. 28 Lower Broad St SY8 1PQ ☎(0584) 876996
This attractive half-timbered town house is within walking distance of the castle and town centre, near the River Teme and Ludford Bridge. The 2 bedrooms are equipped with every modern facility including TV, direct dial telephones and hair dryers. There is a comfortable lounge with book-lined walls, and a small walled garden; ideal for after dinner coffee. The Ross family are most welcoming, and are experienced hoteliers.
2rm(1⇌1↱) CTV in all bedrooms ® T ✱ sB&B⇌↱£40-£45 dB&B⇌↱£60-£70 (incl dinner) WBDi£210-£225 LDO 8.30pm
Lic 🍽 ₱ £

INN QQQ The Church The Buttercross SY8 1AW
☎(0584) 872174
Closed Xmas Day
A smart little hotel in the centre of town, situated behind the Buttercross. Unfortunately there is no private parking, but there is a public car park nearby. The rooms are prettily decorated and have modern facilities. Meals are available in the lounge bar or in the small, attractive restaurant.
8rm(5⇌3♠) (1fb) CTV in all bedrooms ® ✗ (ex guide dogs) ✱ sB&B⇌♠£28 dB&B⇌♠£40 LDO 9pm
ꟻ ⁄P
Credit Cards 1 3

LUTON Bedfordshire Map **04** TL02

GH QQ ***Ambassador Hotel*** 31 Lansdowne Rd LU8 1EE
☎(0582) 31411 or 451656
Closed Xmas
A detached Edwardian house in a quiet residential area, 4 miles from the airport, yet within a few minutes' walk of the town centre. An original feature of the house is an ornate folly tower: the house was converted to a hotel in 1979, with great care taken to preserve the character and charm of the original building. Bedrooms are individually decorated and well equipped with TV, telephone, radio and tea making facilities; most have private bathrooms. Ample private parking is provided, with an attractive rear garden.
14♠ CTV in all bedrooms ® LDO 8.45pm
Lic ꟻ CTV 20P pool table
Credit Cards 1 3

GH QQ Arlington Hotel 137 New Bedford Rd LU3 1LF
☎(0582) 419614 FAX (0582) 459047
Closed 25-26 Dec
This is a detached commercial hotel, set back from the A6 heading towards Bedford, which provides simple, well maintained accommodation. The majority of bedrooms are en suite and equipped with TV, telephones and tea making facilities. In the dining room a table d'hôte menu is available on Monday to Thursday nights, with bar meals available Friday to Sunday.
19rm(2⇌17♠) (3fb) CTV in all bedrooms ®
✗ (ex guide dogs) ✱ sB&B⇌♠£32-£48.90 dB&B⇌♠£46.50-£51.90 LDO 8.30pm
Lic ꟻ 25P
Credit Cards 1 2 3 5 £

GH QQ ***Humberstone Hotel*** 618 Dunstable Rd LU4 8RT
☎(0582) 574399
Conveniently situated on the dual carriageway running from the M1 to Luton town centre, this is a suitably equipped guesthouse, catering generally for commercial visitors. Bedrooms vary in standard and all have TV, telephones and tea-making facilities. The attractive restaurant serves an à la carte menu, plus a comfortable lounge and well stocked bar are available to guests.
9hc Annexe 12rm(2⇌10♠) (4fb) CTV in all bedrooms ®
✗ (ex guide dogs) LDO 5.30pm
Lic ꟻ 35P
Credit Cards 1 2 3 5

LUTTERWORTH Leicestershire

See **Shearsby**

LYDNEY Gloucestershire Map **03** SO60

GH QQQ Lower Viney Country Viney Hill GL15 4LT (2.5m from Lydney on A48 on unclassed road) ☎Dean(0594) 516000
A charming, cottage-style guesthouse just outside the village of Blakeney, off the A48. It has been sympathetically extended and the rooms are quite spacious, many with lovely views of the surrounding countryside. There are 2 lounges and an interesting garden in which to relax. Guests are requested not to smoke.
6♠ CTV in all bedrooms ® ✗ (ex guide dogs) sB&B♠fr£30 dB&B♠fr£40 LDO 1pm
Lic ꟻ CTV 10P
Credit Cards 1 3 £
See advertisement under BLAKENEY

LYME REGIS Dorset Map **03** SY39

GH Q Coverdale Woodmead Rd DT7 3AB ☎(0297) 442882
Mar-Oct
Located high above the town in a quiet residential area, this neat guesthouse has simply furnished, freshly decorated bedrooms with some enjoying superb views across the Golden Cap. En suite shower facilities have recently been added to 4 of the existing bedrooms, and all are no smoking. There is a comfortable lounge area and a rear facing dining room where an evening meal is offered, home cooked by Mrs Harding.
8rm(4♠4hc) (2fb)⚟in all bedrooms ® ✱ sB&B£10-£16 dB&B£20-£29.50 dB&B♠£25-£35.50 WB&B£69-£118.65 WBDi£112-£160.50 LDO 4pm
ꟻ CTV 12P nc18mths £

GH QQQ ***St Michael's Hotel*** Pound St DT7 3HZ
☎(0297) 442503
Situated on a hill, just away from the main street of the town, this small, private hotel is personally run by the Perram family who offer a very warm and friendly welcome. The comfortable bedrooms are neat and very well presented, with en suite facilities or a private bathroom, and are thoughtfully equipped with bubble bath and shampoo. There is a comfortable lounge plus a bright, airy sun lounge, in addition to the cosy cellar bar and the well furnished dining room. Additional facilities include a hairdressing salon and sunbed room. A small car park is provided.
12rm(4⇌6♠2hc) (1fb) CTV in all bedrooms ®
Lic ꟻ 12P 1🚘 nc3yrs ℘(hard)sauna solarium
Credit Cards 1 3

GH QQQ The White House 47 Silver St DT7 3HR
☎(0297) 443420
Apr-Oct
Formerly a Merchant's house, dating back to 1770, this graceful property has been well converted into a very pleasing and nicely maintained, small hotel. The bedrooms are bright, modern and freshly decorated with smart en suite shower rooms that are spotlessly clean. There is a cosy, comfortable lounge filled with fresh flowers, plants, books and ornaments, along with an open fire on chilly days. Breakfast only is served in the bright, well appointed front facing breakfast room, but plenty of information is available on places to eat locally. The attentive proprietors provide a friendly, cheerful atmosphere at this well presented house with plenty of charm and character.
7♠ CTV in all bedrooms ® dB&B♠£36-£40 WB&B£112-£126
ꟻ 7P nc10yrs £

LYMINGTON Hampshire Map **04** SZ39

See also Sway

GH QQ Albany House Highfield SO41 9GB ☎(0590) 671900
Closed 2wks in winter
This centrally situated 3-storey Regency house overlooks municipal gardens at the front and its own lawned garden behind. The comfortable bedrooms are generally of a good size, and this year there are 2 more en suites. Downstairs is a cosy lounge with deep armchairs, books and ornaments.
4rm(2⇌2hc) (2fb) CTV in all bedrooms ® ✱ sB&B£21-£24 dB&B⇌£41-£48 WB&B£143.50-£168 WBDi£196-£234 LDO 7pm
ꟻ CTV 4P £

GH QQQ Our Bench Lodge Rd, Pennington SO41 8HH
☎(0590) 673141
Our Bench is a modern chalet bungalow with an attractive, well kept garden, situated in a quiet residential area. The accommodation has been furnished and decorated to a good standard with modern facilities, and there is a pleasant, comfortably furnished conservatory lounge in addition to the dining room where a 4-course English breakfast is served. Good →

leisure facilities include a small swimming/exercise pool, jacuzzi and sauna. This is a no smoking house.
3hc ⅟in all bedrooms ® ✗ ✱ dB&B£31-£36 WB&B£100-£126 ꟾꟾꟾ CTV 5P nc16yrs ▭(heated) sauna jacuzzi
Credit Cards [3]

LYNDHURST Hampshire Map **04** SU30

SELECTED

GH QQQQ Knightwood Lodge Southampton Rd SO43 7BU ☎(0703) 282502 FAX (0703) 283730
Closed 24-25 Dec
Improvements continue at this friendly small hotel on the edge of the town overlooking open heathland on the Southampton Road. The bedrooms are all prettily furnished and, although they vary in size, several have fine views and they are all well maintained. There is a sunny front-facing dining room where breakfast is served, and a cosy bar for evening meals and a drink. Downstairs there is a well furnished lounge area and a small health suite with sauna, steam room and solarium. Proprietors Mr and Mrs Sanderson are most willing and amiable, and have recently started a new service providing continental breakfast in bedrooms.
15⇌♨ (2fb) CTV in all bedrooms ® T ✗ (ex guide dogs) sB&B⇌♨£28-£36 dB&B⇌♨£42-£52 LDO 8pm
Lic ꟾꟾꟾ 15P sauna solarium turkish steam room
Credit Cards [1] [2] [3] [5] £

GH QQQ Ormonde House Southampton Rd SO43 7BT ☎(0703) 282806 FAX (0703) 283775
Closed 25-26 Dec
This detached late-Victorian house stands back from the A35 and overlooks open heathland, although it is located only a few minutes from the town centre. There is a comfortable lounge and a smart dining room with a bar at one end; a bistro-style menu is offered at dinner. The bedrooms vary in size, outlook and appointment: most are prettily decorated and they are all gradually being upgraded. One of the ground floor bedrooms has been designed for wheelchairs, and all the rooms have TV and tea trays.
15rm(11⇌4♨) (1fb) CTV in all bedrooms ® T ✱ sB&B⇌♨£28-£32 dB&B⇌♨£40-£54 LDO 6.45pm
Lic ꟾꟾꟾ 15P
Credit Cards [1] [3] £

GH QQQ Whitemoor House Hotel Southampton Rd SO43 7BU ☎(0703) 282186
Closed Xmas
This detached house is set on the edge of the town overlooking open heathland. Bedrooms are all of a good size, spotlessly clean and have recently installed en suite facilities. Smoking is only permitted in the lounge, or on the small patio by the pretty water garden.
8rm(1⇌6♨1hc) (2fb)⅟in all bedrooms CTV in all bedrooms ® ✗ (ex guide dogs) ✱ sB&B£25-£30 sB&B⇌♨£25-£30 dB&B£40-£44 dB&B⇌♨£44-£48 WB&B£140-£150
Lic ꟾꟾꟾ CTV 10P ▶18
Credit Cards [1] [3] £

Every effort is made to provide accurate information, but details can change after we go to print. It is advisable to check prices etc. before you make a firm booking.

LYNMOUTH Devon Map **03** SS74

See **Town Plan Section**
See also Lynton

SELECTED

GH QQQQ Countisbury Lodge Hotel Tors Park EX35 6NB ☎Lynton(0598) 52388
Mar-Dec
Formerly a Victorian vicarage, this secluded guesthouse has lovely panoramic views over the picturesque village and harbour of Lynmouth. Owners Margaret and John Hollinshead take great pride in their personal restoration of the house and a high standard of cleanliness is achieved throughout. The bedrooms are individually decorated and attractively coordinated with exposed timbers providing an elegant feature. Most bedrooms are equipped with en suite facilities and all other rooms have hand basins. Several cosy public areas are available, including the small dispense bar which is built around the rock face, adding an unusual aspect. In the pleasant dining room a table d'hôte menu is served and guests must select their dinner in the morning. On offer is a good selection of traditional starters/sweets and the main course may include venison casserole or perhaps foil-wrapped salmon, with a vegetarian choice always available.
6rm(3⇌3♨) (1fb) ® LDO 5pm
Lic ꟾꟾꟾ CTV 8P
Credit Cards [1] [3]

GH QQQ The Heatherville Tors Park EX35 6NB ☎Lynton(0598) 52327
This south-facing, stone-built house is a small family-run holiday guesthouse, tucked away in a secluded spot with commanding views out to sea. It offers spotlessly clean, bright bedrooms which are nicely decorated and furnished. There is a cosy, comfortable lounge and a small bar, with traditional wholesome meals from the set menu. A recent change of ownership has resulted in some upgrading and improvements.
9rm(1⇌4♨4hc) (1fb) CTV in 5 bedrooms ® ✱ dB&Bfr£42 dB&B⇌♨fr£47 WB&Bfr£148 LDO 5.30pm
Lic ꟾꟾꟾ CTV 9P nc7yrs

See advertisement on page 273

INN QQQ *The Village Inn* Lynmouth St EX35 6EH ☎Lynton(0598) 52354
Tucked away behind the main street, the Village Inn has a striking black and gold exterior with hanging baskets and white wrought iron pavement furniture. The 6 spacious bedrooms have recently been upgraded to provide attractive coordinating décor and fabrics with pine furniture; the bathrooms have gold taps and pine fittings. A comprehensive menu of grills and steaks is served in the old world bar or the small enclosed patio garden – the English breakfast is huge.
6⇌♨ (1fb)⅟in 2 bedrooms CTV in all bedrooms ® ✗ (ex guide dogs) LDO 9.30pm
ꟾꟾꟾ P̸ nc
Credit Cards [1] [3]

LYNTON Devon Map **03** SS74

See **Town Plan Section**
See also Lynmouth

GH QQQ Alford House Hotel Alford Ter EX35 6AT ☎(0598) 52359
Set on a hillside overlooking the bay, this handsome Georgian house provides a most relaxing atmosphere created by the location and friendly proprietors. The individually styled bedrooms are most inviting with their attractive décor and furnishings. There is a tastefully decorated lounge with comfortable seating and the softly lit, elegant dining room is a perfect setting for the imaginative, freshly cooked dinners, that can be especially recommended.

→

WHITEMOOR HOUSE HOTEL

LISTED

Southampton Road,
Lyndhurst, New Forest
Hampshire SO43 7BU
Telephone: Lyndhurst (0703) 282186

A beautiful country house hotel, overlooking the New Forest, where a personal service awaits you from this family run hotel.

- Comfortable colour TV lounge with residential licence.
- Tea/coffee facilities in all rooms & colour TV.
- All rooms en-suite and fully central heated.
- Ample private car parking.
- Ideal for business, holidays, golfers and walkers.
- Brochure/tariff on request. All major credit cards accepted.

KNIGHTWOOD LODGE

Southampton Road, Lyndhurst,
Hampshire SO43 7BU
Tel: (0703) 282502
Fax: (0703) 283730

A charming detached residence on the edge of Lyndhurst overlooking the New Forest. Comfortable bedrooms, all en suite, each with colour TV, telephone, hair dryer, mini bar, radio alarm, tea/coffee making facilities. Indoor Leisure Centre includes sauna, Turkish steam room and sun pool. Cosy bar. Evening meals, packed lunches available. Parking. Major credit cards accepted. Member of Guestaccom.

Brochure and tariff on request from proprietors Paul and Jackie Sanderson.

Ormonde House

Southampton Road, Lyndhurst
Hampshire
Tel: (0703) 282806. Fax: (0703) 283775

Ormonde House is an attractive Victorian Bed and Breakfast House situated 5 minutes' walk from Lyndhurst and opposite open Forest land.

The House has been extensively refurbished and all 15 bedrooms are en-suite and are equipped with colour TV, phone and teamaking. One of our ground floor bedrooms has been designed to allow access for wheelchair users. A comfortable lounge is available to our guests.

Residential licence.

Bed & Breakfast Rates 1992
£20-£30 per person per night

THE NURSE'S COTTAGE

★
B & B FROM
£15.00 p.p.
★
LICENSED
★
EVENING MEAL
★

Formerly the District Nurse's residence, this cosy cottage provides the visitor with a high degree of comfort in an ideal touring location.

QQ

Station Road, Sway
Lymington, Hants SO41 6BA
Tel/Fax: (0590) 683402

8rm(1⇌6🚿1hc) CTV in all bedrooms ® 🐕 (ex guide dogs) sB&B⇌🚿£21-£26 dB&B⇌🚿£44-£52 WB&B£135-£165 WBDi£195-£225 LDO 8pm
Lic 🏨 CTV 🅿 nc9yrs
Credit Cards 1 3 £

GH QQQ Hazeldene 27 Lee Rd EX35 6BP ☎(0598) 52364
Closed mid Nov-28 Dec
A very comfortable guesthouse where Mrs Blight, who has been here for 30 years, provides bedrooms with all the modern facilities. The freshly painted lounge and dining room with their abundance of ornaments are most appealing, and the standard of housekeeping throughout is very thorough.
9⇌🚿 (2fb) CTV in all bedrooms ® sB&B⇌🚿£20-£25 dB&B⇌🚿£37-£42 WB&B£126-£140 WBDi£193-£203 LDO 5pm
Lic 🏨 CTV 8P nc5yrs
Credit Cards 1 2 3 £

GH QQQ Ingleside Hotel Lee Rd EX35 6HW ☎(0598) 52223
Mar-Oct
A neat detached Victorian house in its own garden, offering fresh decoration and high standards of housekeeping throughout. The attractive bedrooms are furnished in a modern style, the dining room is light and airy and the lounge has a real fire.
7rm(4⇌3🚿) (2fb) CTV in all bedrooms ® 🐕 sB&B⇌🚿£25-£28 dB&B⇌🚿£44-£50 WB&B£140-£161 WBDi£228-£256 LDO 5.30pm
Lic 🏨 10P nc5yrs
Credit Cards 1 3 £

GH QQQ Lynhurst Hotel Lyn Way EX35 6AX ☎(0598) 52241
Mar-Oct
This elegant Victorian house is set about 500 feet above sea level, giving superb views over the surrounding countryside and the sea. The individually designed bedrooms are quite cosy featuring pretty fabrics and bric-a-brac. There are 2 lounges, both with a comfortable atmosphere, and a neat lower ground floor dining room where home-cooked dinners are served.
7rm(4⇌3hc) (1fb)🚭in all bedrooms CTV in all bedrooms ® ✱ dB&B£36-£40 dB&B⇌£36-£40 WB&B£120-£133 WBDi£155-£189 LDO noon
Lic CTV 🅿

GH QQ Mayfair Hotel Lynway EX35 6AY ☎(0598) 53227
There are wonderful views from this detached Victorian villa set high above the town looking out to sea and over National Trust woodland. Bedrooms offer modern facilities and public rooms include an attractive bar and restaurant and a quiet, comfortable lounge.
9rm(6⇌🚿3hc) (1fb) CTV in all bedrooms ® sB&B£23-£25 dB&B£40-£44 dB&B⇌🚿£46-£50 WB&B£133-£154 WBDi£189-£210 LDO 5pm
Lic 🏨 10P
Credit Cards 1 2 3 £

GH Q Retreat 1 Park Gardens, Lydiate Ln EX35 6DF ☎(0598) 53526
A small terraced property offering very neat and clean accommodation at a reasonable price. The small TV lounge and dining room are both cosy and well decorated. The owners offer a warm welcome, and the guesthouse is popular with walkers.
6hc (2fb) ® sB&B£14-£16 dB&B£28-£32 WB&B£93-£106 WBDi£146-£166 LDO 4pm
🏨 CTV 3P £

GH QQQ St Vincent Castle Hill EX35 6JA ☎(0598) 52244
Apr-Oct
An attractive Georgian house in the centre of the village, next to the Exmoor Museum. There is a small, pretty cottage garden at the front where cream teas are sometimes served. The light, spacious bedrooms are spotlessly clean, and in the basement there is a cosy lounge and separate bar with the original flagstone floors and fireplaces. Home-cooked dinners are served in the elegant dining room.
6rm(1⇌2🚿3hc) (1fb) ® 🐕 sB&B£14-£15 dB&B£28-£30 dB&B⇌🚿£33-£35 WB&B£93-£117 WBDi£153-£180 LDO 4pm
Lic CTV 3P £

GH Q Valley House Hotel Lynbridge Rd EX35 6BD ☎(0598) 52285
Modest but neat accommodation is provided at this stone-built early Victorian house, set in woodland in an elevated position. The atmosphere is peaceful and the service friendly and informal.
6rm(4⇌🚿2hc) (2fb) CTV in all bedrooms ® ✱ sB&B£18.50-£22 sB&B⇌🚿£22.50-£30 dB&B£37 dB&B⇌🚿£43-£45 WB&B£129.50-£157.50 WBDi£213.50-£241.50 LDO 6pm
Lic 🏨 CTV 8P
Credit Cards 1 2 3

SELECTED

GH QQQQ Waterloo House Hotel Lydiate Ln EX35 6AJ ☎(0598) 53391
Reputed to be one of the oldest original lodging houses in Lynton, this 19th- century building has undergone extensive renovations to create a warm and welcoming small hotel. The attractive bedrooms are imaginatively decorated and the larger rooms have separate seating areas. Most have en suite facilities and all are equipped with TV and beverage making equipment. An elegant dining room acts as a tea room during the season from 11am-5pm and the evening meal is a candlelit dinner of 4-courses, chosen from a table d'hôte menu. A sample dinner may include home-made chicken liver pâté with brandy, followed by beef Waterloo cooked in ale with prunes and walnuts, then fruit Pavlova, and finishing with cheese and biscuits. A vegetarian menu is also available. There are two lounges, one for non smokers and one for smokers.
11rm(4⇌4🚿3hc) (2fb)🚭in 2 bedrooms CTV in all bedrooms ® ✱ sB&B£16.50-£19.50 sB&B⇌🚿£21.50-£24.50 dB&B£33-£39 dB&B⇌🚿£43-£52 WB&B£95-£143 WBDi£160-£210 LDO 7pm
Lic 🏨 CTV 3P £

LYTHAM ST ANNES Lancashire Map 07 SD32

GH QQ Cullerne Hotel 55 Lightburne Av, St Annes on Sea FY8 1JE ☎St Annes(0253) 721753
This late Victorian semidetached house with bay windows and a canopied entrance, is situated in a quiet road just off the Inner Promenade, close to the miniature golf course and within walking distance of the town centre. The bright and airy bedrooms have been comfortably furnished, and they all have TV and tea-making facilities. Downstairs there is a lounge, a cosy bar and an attractive dining room with individual tables; special diets are catered for. Reduced rates are available for senior citizens and children, and forecourt parking is also available.
6hc (2fb) CTV in all bedrooms ® 🐕 ✱ sB&Bfr£14 dB&Bfr£28 WB&Bfr£91 WBDifr£112 LDO noon
Lic 🏨 CTV 4P

GH QQQ Endsleigh Private Hotel 315 Clifton Dr South FY8 1HN ☎St Annes(0253) 725622
One of a number of late Victorian houses in the area which have been converted into private hotels or guesthouses. It is very conveniently situated only 2 minutes walk from the seafront and very close to the shops in St Annes Square. Bedrooms are furnished with light fitted units, and all have modern en suite facilities, TV, radio and tea and coffee making provision. Two rooms have been specially designed for families, with separate adjoining bedrooms; there are also some ground floor rooms with private entrances. The attractive dining room with individual tables is situated at the rear, and there is a spacious, comfortable

guests' lounge at the front. Private parking is provided at the front of this family-run hotel.
15⇌↱ (3fb) CTV in all bedrooms ® ⋈ ✻ sB&B⇌↱£19.75 dB&B⇌↱£39 WB&B£119.50 WBDi£144.50-£154.50 LDO 4pm
Lic ⊞ 8P

GH Q *Lyndhurst Private Hotel* 338 Clifton Dr North FY8 2PB
☏St Annes(0253) 724343
This tall, gabled, semidetached Victorian house is situated a few hundred yards north of the town centre, opposite Ashton Gardens. The pleasant bedrooms vary in shape and size with those at the front enjoying views of the park. There is a spacious and comfortable lounge with TV, adjoining the well appointed dining room. Private car parking is provided at the front of the house.
12rm(1⇌3↱8hc) (4fb) CTV in 4 bedrooms ® LDO noon
CTV 11P

GH QQQ Strathmore Hotel 305 Clifton Dr South FY8 1HN
☏St Annes(0253) 725478
A late Victorian property in a very convenient location opposite the general post office and within a short walk of the pier, promenade and shops. Bedrooms are modern in style, comfortable and tastefully furnished; several have private bathrooms and they all have TV, radio alarms and tea and coffee making facilities. There is an elegant lounge downstairs, and good home cooking is served in the dining room, at individual tables: dinner is at 6pm. Private parking is available at the front.
10rm(2⇌3↱5hc) CTV in all bedrooms ® ⋈ ✻ sB&B£18.50 sB&B⇌↱£20 dB&B£37 dB&B⇌↱£40 WB&B£122-£133 WBDi£140-£161 LDO 5pm
Lic ⊞ 10P nc9yrs

Book as early as possible for busy holiday periods.

MACCLESFIELD Cheshire Map **07** SJ97

GH QQ Moorhayes House Hotel 27 Manchester Rd, Tytherington SK10 2JJ ☎(0625) 433228

This large detached house stands in spacious gardens on the A523 Stockport road, just north of the town centre. The accommodation, whilst not luxurious, is modern and soundly maintained: bedrooms vary in size from compact to quite spacious. Proprietors Ann and Owen Thomas aim to provide a 'home from home' atmosphere for their guests, who comprise both commercial visitors and tourists.

9rm(5⫯4hc) CTV in all bedrooms ® sB&B£23-£26 sB&B⫯£32 dB&B£35 dB&B⫯£39.95

15P £

FH QQ Mrs Anne Read **Hardingland** *(SJ958725)* Macclesfield Forest SK11 0ND ☎(0625) 425759

Mar-Nov

A remotely situated farmhouse in the Peak District National Park, overlooking Teggs Nose Country Park. The rooms are tastefully furnished, and the owner is renowned for her cuisine: dinners here have more than a hint of France in the cooking.

3rm(1⇨) ⚟in all bedrooms ® ✱ sB&B£20 sB&B⇨£25 dB&B£35 dB&B⇨£38 WB&B£117-£133 WBDi£185.50-£206.50 LDO 9am

CTV 3P nc16yrs 17 acres smallholding beef sheep

MACHRIHANISH Strathclyde *Argyllshire* Map **10** NR62

SELECTED

GH QQQQ Ardell House PA28 6PT ☎(058681) 235

Closed Xmas & New Year rs Nov-Feb

This fine detached Victorian house is in a wonderful setting, in its own garden overlooking the golf course, with views of the sea and the distant islands of Islay and Jura. Bedrooms vary in size and style from the spacious master bedrooms to the more compact, but equally well equipped chalet rooms in the annexe, which are much in demand. There is a cosy lounge upstairs with a self-service honesty bar, and imaginative Taste of Scotland dishes are served in the attractive dining room. The atmosphere is friendly and relaxed, with many visiting golfers and tourists returning every year to David and Jill Baxter's welcoming home.

7rm(1⇨5⫯1hc) Annexe 3⫯ (1fb) CTV in all bedrooms ® ✱ dB&B⇨⫯£36-£48

Lic 12P

MACHYNLLETH Powys Map **06** SH70

See also Llanwrin

GH QQ Maenllwyd Newtown Rd SY20 8EY ☎(0654) 702928

Closed 25 & 26 Dec

Situated opposite the cottage hospital, this large detached Victorian house was once a manse. Now a family-run guesthouse, it provides good, comfortable accommodation, together with ample car parking and a pleasant lawn area at the rear.

5hc (2fb) CTV in all bedrooms ® ✱ sB&B£16-£18 dB&B£28-£30 LDO 1pm

Lic CTV 10P

Credit Cards 1 2 3

FH QQ Mr & Mrs D Timms **Rhiwlwyfen** *(SH761983)* Forge SY20 8RP ☎(0654) 702683

Apr-Oct rs Oct-Apr

This secluded, remote 17th-century farmhouse lies in the hills above the nearby hamlet of Forge, and is reached across the golf course. There are 3 smart, comfortable bedrooms, and a relaxing lounge with an inglenook log fire.

2rm (2fb) ® ✗ (ex guide dogs) ✱ sB&Bfr£15 dB&Bfr£30 WB&Bfr£105 WBDifr£157.50 LDO 8pm

CTV 6P 100 acres beef sheep £

INN QQQ The White Lion Hotel Heol Pentrerhedyn SY20 8ND ☎(0654) 703455

This former coaching inn stands in the centre of the busy market town near the famous clock, and in recent years has been completely modernised. Bedrooms are attractively furnished in pine, and new en suite rooms have been added. There is a large open plan bar and restaurant, where a wide range of food is available. The hotel also benefits from a large car park.

9rm(6⇨⫯3hc) (2fb) CTV in all bedrooms ® ✱ sB&B£20 sB&B⇨⫯£30 dB&B£37 dB&B⇨⫯£52 WB&B£105-£175 LDO 9pm

CTV 45P

Credit Cards 1 2 3 5

MAIDSTONE Kent Map **05** TQ75

GH QQ Rock House Hotel 102 Tonbridge Rd ME16 8SL ☎(0622) 751616

Closed 24 Dec-1 Jan

A long-established and popular family-run guesthouse benefiting from its own forecourt car parking. Seven of the bedrooms have a shower in the room, and they all have TV and tea making equipment. There is a small, cosy lounge and separate breakfast room. Service is personally managed by the resident proprietors Mr and Mrs Salter.

12hc (2fb) CTV in all bedrooms ® ✗ ✱ sB&B£20-£36 dB&B£34-£44 WB&B£140-£175

CTV 7P nc1yr

Credit Cards 1 3 £

SELECTED

GH QQQQ Tanyard Hotel Wierton Hill, Boughton Monchelsea ME17 4JT ☎(0622) 744705 FAX (0622) 741998

early Feb-mid Dec

This charming timber-framed medieval country house hotel is idyllically situated in the heart of rural Kent with panoramic views across the Weald. The 5 bedrooms, on 2 floors, are individually decorated and furnished with coordinating soft furnishings, antiques and sofas; they all have private bathrooms and the heavily beamed suite has a spa bath. The dining room and lounge are dominated by 2 huge inglenook fireplaces and furnished in period cottage style. Proprietor Jan Davies offers very personal service, with refreshments available all day, and an imaginative set menu is offered in the evening using a variety of local produce; special diets can also be catered for. Directions to find the guesthouse are essential.

6rm(5⇨1⫯) (3fb) CTV in all bedrooms ® T ✗ sB&B⇨⫯£50-£95 dB&B⇨⫯£75-£95 WB&B£262.50-£665 WBDi£402.50-£805 LDO 8pm

Lic 9P nc6yrs

Credit Cards 1 2 3 5

GH QQ Willington Court Willington St ME15 8JW ☎(0622) 38885 due to change to 738885

A Tudor-style listed building built around 1896 and located one and a half miles east of Maidstone town centre on the A20. The no-smoking bedrooms have fresh air units and traditional furnishings, and there is a fine oak staircase with some very narrow steps. The breakfast room has an inglenook fireplace with a log fire, and there is a small token lounge. The number of overnight guests is restricted to 6 at any one time.

4rm(2⇨⫯2hc) (3fb)⚟in all bedrooms ® ✗ (ex guide dogs) sB&B£17-£21 sB&B⇨⫯£25-£27 dB&B£34 dB&B⇨⫯£40-£42 WB&B£105-£175

CTV 6P nc7yrs

Credit Cards 1 2 3 5 £

MALDON Essex Map **05** TL80

INN QQ Swan Hotel Maldon High St CM9 7EP
☎(0621) 853170
A popular inn near the centre of town. Recently completely refurbished, it now offers a smart open-plan bar and dining area, and some bright, simply furnished bedrooms with good facilities.
6hc (2fb)✗in 1 bedroom CTV in all bedrooms ® ✗ sB&B£35-£40 dB&B£48-£55 Lunch fr£3.50 Dinner £5-£7 LDO 9pm
30P 1
Credit Cards 1 2 3 5 £

MALHAM North Yorkshire Map **07** SD96

GH QQQ Sparth House Hotel BD23 4DA
☎Airton(0729) 830315
Parts of this spacious Victorian house, date from 1664, making it one of the oldest in Malham. Some of the bedrooms are situated in a more modern wing at the rear, and have lovely views of the surrounding hills; although rather compact, they are very functional. The bedrooms in the older part of the house are a good, comfortable size and nicely decorated with modern fabrics. All the bedrooms are no smoking. Downstairs, there is a spacious dining room with a cosy bar area and an adjoining games room. Sensible forethought has been given by providing 2 comfortable lounges, one for smokers and one for non smokers and both are equipped with TV.
10rm(4⇌ 6hc) ✗in all bedrooms CTV in 4 bedrooms ®
✗ (ex guide dogs) ✱ sB&B£20.50 dB&B£37 dB&B⇌£50 WBDi£200-£240 LDO 5pm
Lic CTV 7P table-tennis darts £

MALMESBURY Wiltshire Map **03** ST98

FH QQQ Mrs R Eavis **Manor** *(ST922837)* Corston SN16 0HF ☎(0666) 822148
An attractive Cotswold stone-built farmhouse beside the A429 in the village of Corston, 3 miles from both Malmesbury and junction 17 of the M4. The spacious bedrooms have been tastefully decorated and comfortably furnished, each with coordinating colour schemes, and electric blankets. There is a TV lounge, and separate tables are available in the breakfast room.
5rm(1⇌ 4hc) (2fb)✗in 2 bedrooms CTV in 3 bedrooms ® ✗
✱ sB&B£14-£18 dB&B£28-£36 dB&B⇌£36-£40
CTV 8P 436 acres arable dairy
Credit Cards 1 2 3 5 £

FH Q Mrs E G Edwards **Stonehill** *(SU986894)* Charlton SN16 9DY (1m E) ☎(0666) 823310
A 15th-century stone-built farmhouse on the B4040 Cricklade road, 3.5 miles from England's oldest borough of Malmesbury. The bedrooms are clean and comfortable, and breakfast is served around one large table in the dining room. The guesthouse is in a peaceful setting, surrounded by dairy cattle and sheep.
3rm(1) (1fb) CTV in 1 bedroom ® sB&B£15-£20 dB&B£28-£30 dB&B£35-£40
CTV 4P 1 180 acres dairy sheep £

MALPAS Cheshire Map **07** SJ44

SELECTED

FH QQQQ Mrs K M Ritchie **Tilston Lodge** *(SJ463511)* SY14 7DR ☎Tilston(0829) 250223
This delightful house reflects Kathie Ritchie's talent and good taste for interior design, with its carefully chosen period, antique furniture and good quality soft furnishings. Dating back to Victorian times, when it was a shooting lodge, the house was enlarged in 1878, and further extended during Edwardian times. There are 2 good size bedrooms – a twin and a family room with an antique 4 poster bed – plus a small, single room which does not have an en suite. All of the period style bedrooms are equipped with modern facilities in addition to thoughtful extras. Public areas include a choice of lounges, one of which has a solid fuel stove. The breakfast/dining room, where dinner is sometimes available with advance notice, is a lovely old room which will seat up to 8 people at 2 tables, and has antique furniture with heavy drapes and matching soft furnishings. The house is fronted by a mature, attractive garden and is adjacent to 12 acres of land, farmed by Mr and Mrs Ritchie who rear rare breeds of sheep, cattle, fowl and poultry, and guests are more than welcome to explore and get involved in the activities.
3rm(2⇌ 1hc) (1fb) CTV in 2 bedrooms ®
✗ (ex guide dogs) ✱ sB&Bfr£16.50 dB&B⇌£36-£42
CTV 10P 12 acres cattle poultry sheep £

MALVERN Hereford & Worcester Map **03** SO74

GH QQQ Sidney House Hotel 40 Worcester Rd WR14 4AA
☎(0684) 574994
rs Xmas & New Year
A grade II listed house dating from 1823, standing in an elevated position with fine views over the Severn valley towards the Vale of Evesham and the Cotswolds. It stands alongside the A449 just west of the town centre. Tom and Margaret Haggett are hospitable hosts, and the bedrooms are mostly furnished with stripped pine, together with equipment usually attributed to more formal hotels, including samples of the famous Malvern water.
8rm(5 3hc) (2fb) CTV in all bedrooms ® sB&B£20 sB&B£30-£35 dB&B£39 dB&B£44-£49 LDO 3pm
Lic CTV 9P
Credit Cards 1 2 3 £

£ Remember to use the money-off vouchers.

MAN, ISLE OF Map **06**

DOUGLAS Map **06** SC37

GH Q **Ainsdale Guest House** 2 Empire Terrace, Central Prom ☎(0624) 676695
Apr-Sep
Situated just off the central promenade, this friendly, family-run guesthouse has recently been improved, and while standard rooms remain modestly appointed, 6 now offer smart new en suite facilities. There is a pleasant and comfortable lounge, and a freshly decorated and refurbished dining room.
16rm(7⇌↱9hc) (2fb) CTV in 2 bedrooms TV in 4 bedrooms Ⓡ sB&B£12.50 dB&B£25 dB&B⇌↱£33 WB&B£87.50-£115.50 WBDi£122.50-£147.50 LDO 6pm
CTV P Ⓔ

GH Q **All Seasons** 11 Clifton Ter, Broadway ☎(0624) 676323
Situated a short, but steep, walk from the Gaiety theatre, this terraced Victorian property offers a modest standard of accommodation which the friendly young owners are gradually improving. There is a small bar and a dining room furnished with pine tables, plus a no-smoking lounge.
9rm(2↱7hc) CTV in 8 bedrooms TV in 1 bedroom Ⓡ * sB&B£12-£15 dB&B£24-£30 dB&B↱£30-£34 WB&B£84-£105 LDO 9pm
Lic 🅜 CTV P

GH QQ **Edelweiss** Queens Promenade ☎(0624) 675115 FAX (0624) 673194
This friendly, family-run small hotel is set back from the main promenade and offers well equipped bedrooms with all floors being served by a lift. There is a comfortable lounge and 2 restaurants, one of which is open to non-residents.
20rm(3⇌17↱) (3fb) CTV in all bedrooms Ⓡ **T** sB&B⇌↱£28.18 dB&B⇌↱£46.97 WB&B£164.41 WBDi£238.44 LDO 9pm
Lic lift 🅜 CTV P solarium
Credit Cards [1] [3] [5] Ⓔ
See advertisement in colour supplement.

GH QQ ***Hydro Hotel*** Queen's Promanade ☎(0624) 676870
This large Edwardian seafront hotel, which caters for tour groups and large parties, has been gradually and steadily improved over the years. Bedrooms vary in size, but all are well equipped, and are served by a lift. Public areas are spacious and include 2 bars, one of which provides live entertainment.
60rm(11⇌20↱29hc) (17fb) CTV in all bedrooms Ⓡ ✗ (ex guide dogs) LDO 7pm
Lic lift 🅜 solarium pool table darts
Credit Cards [1] [3] [5]

GH QQ **The Laurels** 2 Mona Dr, Central Promenade ☎(0624) 674884
Mar-Nov
Conveniently situated close to the beach, in a one way street just off the central promenade. This attractively maintained property, with its green awnings and colourful flower baskets, offers compact but pleasantly furnished bedrooms, enhanced with cheery coordinated fabrics. There is a comfortable lounge in addition to the cosy bar and neatly set out dining room.
14rm(8⇌↱6hc) (1fb) Ⓡ ✗ (ex guide dogs) * sB&B£16 sB&B⇌↱fr£19.50 dB&Bfr£30 dB&B⇌↱fr£34
Lic CTV

GH Q **Rosslyn Guest House** 3 Empire Ter, Central Promenade ☎(0624) 676056
Closed 29 Nov-2 Jan
This terraced guesthouse is situated close to the seafront, and offers neat though modestly appointed accommodation. Some of the bedrooms have en suite facilities, and there are a cosy bar and a small TV lounge on the first floor.
16rm(4⇌4↱8hc) (3fb) CTV in 5 bedrooms Ⓡ ✗ (ex guide dogs) * sB&B£14.10-£15 dB&B£28.20-£30 dB&B⇌↱£40-£43 WB&B£98.70-£105 WBDi£123.41-£126
Lic 🅜 CTV P Ⓔ

GH QQ ***Rutland Hotel*** Queen's Promenade ☎(0624) 621218
Etr-Oct
Situated on the seafront and overlooking Douglas Bay, this large family-run hotel offers generally spacious accommodation and a good range of services. Bedrooms are neat, well equipped and colour coordinated, and the public areas include a foyer lounge, an attractive restaurant and a choice of bars where live entertainment is provided.
86rm(55⇌25↱6hc) (20fb) CTV in all bedrooms Ⓡ LDO 7.30pm
Lic lift CTV P
Credit Cards [1] [3]

PORT ERIN Map **06** SC16

GH QQ **Regent House** The Promenade ☎(0624) 833454
Mar-Sep
This small, friendly Victorian guesthouse overlooking the bay has been tastefully modernised to provide comfortable accommodation and bedrooms are well appointed, many with en suite facilities. Vegetarian dishes are always offered as an alternative at dinner. Smoking is not permitted.
8rm(6⇌↱2hc) ⊬in all bedrooms CTV in all bedrooms Ⓡ ✗ * sB&B£17-£18 dB&B⇌↱£40-£43 WB&B£143-£153 WBDi£199-£209.50 LDO 6.30pm
🅜 P nc12yrs

MANCHESTER Greater Manchester Map **07** SJ89

GH QQ **Ebor Hotel** 402 Wilbraham Rd, Chorlton Cum Hardy M21 1UH ☎061-881 1911 & 061-881 4855
Closed Xmas
Set back from the A6010 and well placed for both the city centre and airport, this detached house offers comfortable accommodation which includes a small TV lounge, a separate bar and a neat dining room.
16rm(7↱9hc) (4fb) CTV in all bedrooms Ⓡ ✗ * sB&B£19-£21 sB&B↱£26 dB&B£31 dB&B↱£36 WB&B£133-£182 WBDi£171.50-£220.50 LDO 5pm
Lic 🅜 CTV 20P 🚗 nc4yrs darts
Credit Cards [1] [2] [3] Ⓔ

GH Q **Kempton House Hotel** 400 Wilbraham Rd, Chorlton-Cum-Hardy M21 1UH ☎061-881 8766
Closed 25 & 26 Dec
This late Victorian semidetached house stands beside the A6010, 3 miles from the city centre. Family owned and run, it offers modest, compact accommodation at reasonable rates.
14rm(4↱10hc) CTV in 13 bedrooms TV in 1 bedroom Ⓡ ✗ (ex guide dogs) * sB&B£22-£23 sB&B↱fr£28 dB&Bfr£32 dB&B↱fr£37.50 LDO 5pm
Lic 🅜 CTV 9P
Credit Cards [1] [3] Ⓔ

GH QQ **New Central Hotel** 144-146 Heywood St, Cheetham M8 7PD ☎061-205 2169
Situated in a quiet residential area just off the A665 at Cheetham, yet only a mile from the city centre and Victoria Station, this double fronted house offers modest accommodation and a friendly, relaxed atmosphere. Bedrooms, some with shower cubicles, are generally compact, but there is a pleasant lounge and a comfortable small bar for guests' use.
10rm(5↱5hc) CTV in all bedrooms Ⓡ * sB&Bfr£20.50 sB&B↱fr£21.50 dB&Bfr£33 dB&B↱fr£35 LDO 7.30pm
Lic 🅜 CTV 10P Ⓔ

GH QQQ West Lynne Hotel 16 Middleton Rd, Crumpsall M8 6DS ☎061-721 4866 & 061-721 4922
Standing beside the A576 midway between the M62 and the city centre, this renovated, detached house provides practical accommodation. Although the décor and furnishings are rather functional, the bedrooms are comfortable and all have telephones and modern en suite bathrooms. Public areas include a spacious lounge bar and a neat dining room. The hotel has the advantage of its own car park.
12⇌ (2fb) CTV in all bedrooms Ⓡ ✖ (ex guide dogs) ✱
sB&B⇌£25-£37 dB&B⇌£35-£45 WB&B£180 WBDi£230
LDO 8.30pm
Lic 卌 15P
Credit Cards 1 2 3 5 £

MAPPOWDER Dorset Map **03** ST70

FH Q Mrs A K Williamson-Jones **Boywood** *(ST733078)* Sturminster Newton DT10 2EQ (1.5m N unclass rd toward Hazelbury Bryan) ☎Hazelbury Bryan(0258) 817416
This traditional farmhouse is set in peaceful, rural surroundings 1.5 miles north of the village on the unclassified road towards Hazelbury Bryan. Part of a dairy farm, the accommodation offered is simple, and guests can enjoy an informal and relaxing stay 'en famille'.
3rm(2hc) ✱ dB&B£30
卌 CTV P ⊟(heated) ℘(hard)17 acres beef poultry £

MARGARET RODING (NEAR GREAT DUNMOW) Essex Map **05** TL51

FH QQ Mr & Mrs J Matthews **Greys** *(TL604112)* Ongar Rd CM6 1QR ☎Good Easter(024531) 509
Check for directions to this comfortable farmhouse in a rural setting. There are beamed breakfast and sitting rooms downstairs, three simple, bright and clean bedrooms above, and a cheerful welcome from Joyce and Jeffrey Matthews.
3rm(2hc) 🚭in all bedrooms ✖ ✱ dB&Bfr£32
卌 CTV 3P nc10yrs 340 acres arable beef sheep

MARGATE Kent Map **05** TR37

GH QQ Beachcomber Hotel 3-4 Royal Esplanade, Westbrook CT9 5DL ☎Thanet(0843) 221616
This licensed hotel enjoys a good reputation for its cooking, which is complemented by the use of fresh ingredients and the involvement of proprietors Mr and Mrs Philip McGovern. Overlooking the sea, it offers well-maintained, simply furnished rooms and pleasant public areas.
15hc (3fb) Ⓡ ✖ ✱ sB&B£16.50-£17.50 dB&B£33-£35 WB&B£105-£119 WBDi£145-£153 LDO 10am
Lic 卌 CTV 1P

GH Q Charnwood Private Hotel 20-22 Canterbury Rd CT9 5BW ☎Thanet(0843) 224158
This small family-run guesthouse is divided into 2 houses offering adequate bedrooms, many of which are suitable for families with children. Other facilities include reception, a large dining room, TV lounge, a panelled bar and residential licence.
8hc (4fb) Ⓡ ✖ sB&B£14-£17 dB&B£26-£32 WB&B£85-£100 WBDi£110-£125 LDO 4pm
Lic 卌 CTV P̸
Credit Cards 1 3 £

GH QQQ *The Greswolde Hotel* 20 Surrey Road, Cliftonville CT9 2LA ☎Thanet(0843) 223956
This Victorian terrace house is close to the sea at Walpole Bay. The delightful public rooms, filled with Victorian memorabilia, are cosy and welcoming. The lounge has winged armchairs, the original tiled fireplace and a gas fire, and is a pleasant place to enjoy a drink in the evening. The spacious bedrooms offer a good degree of comfort including en suite facilities and are popular with business travellers.
6rm(1⇌5🚿) (2fb) CTV in all bedrooms Ⓡ
Lic 卌 P̸
Credit Cards 1 3

GH Q The Malvern Hotel 29 Eastern Esplanade, Cliftonville CT9 2HL ☎Thanet(0843) 290192
A terraced house, opposite Walpole Bay, on 6 floors with a cosy lounge and basement breakfast room. The bedrooms are adequately furnished and the majority have generous en suite showers. The Malvern overlooks the sea, promenade and bandstand and is close to all the local amenities.
10rm(8🚿2hc) (1fb) CTV in all bedrooms Ⓡ ✖ sB&B£18-£20 sB&B🚿£25-£35 dB&B£32-£36 dB&B🚿£35-£40 WB&B£89-£105 LDO noon
Lic 卌 P̸
Credit Cards 1 2 3 5 £

GH QQ Westbrook Bay House 12 Royal Esplanade, Westbrook CT9 5DW ☎Thanet(0843) 292700
A long-established, friendly and well maintained guesthouse run for many years by Maureen and Ken Richardson. Some bedrooms have private showers and several are suitable for family use, with children made very welcome. There are good sea views from some rooms, and they all have TVs, clock radios and tea trays. The attractive dining room incorporates a small bar with a residential licence, and there is a comfortable, well appointed TV lounge. Unrestricted street car parking is available, and the guesthouse is within easy walking distance of putting and bowling greens, tennis courts and a leisure centre.
11rm(3🚿8hc) (4fb) CTV in 10 bedrooms Ⓡ ✖ (ex guide dogs) sB&Bfr£20 dB&Bfr£40 (incl dinner) WB&Bfr£100 WBDifr£120 LDO 4.30pm
Lic 卌 CTV £

See advertisement on page 279

MARKET DRAYTON Shropshire Map **07** SJ63

FH QQQ Mr J M Thomas **Stoke Manor** *(SH646279)* Stoke-on-Tern TF9 2DU ☎Hodnet(063084) 222
Closed Dec

An 18th-century farmhouse set in 250 acres of arable farmland, situated in the village of Stoke-on-Tern, reached off the A53 at Hodnet. The 3 bedrooms all have en suite bathrooms, and are furnished with stripped pine, TV and tea making facilities. There are lovely views of the Shropshire Plain from the comfortable, modern sitting room. No evening meal is served, but there are ample local restaurants nearby. Artefacts and pottery dating from the 12th century are displayed in the house, and the unusual cellar bar features a collection of old farm implements. The grounds include a lake stocked with crayfish and tench, and there are fishing rights on a stretch of the River Tern.

3⇌ (1fb) in all bedrooms CTV in all bedrooms Ⓡ (ex guide dogs) * sB&B⇌£22-£25 dB&B⇌£40-£48
Lic 20P vintage tractor collection farm trail 250 acres arable Ⓔ

MARKINCH Fife Map **11** NO20

INN QQQ Town House Hotel 1 High St KY7 6QQ ☎Glenrothes(0592) 758459
4rm(3⇌1hc) (1fb) CTV in all bedrooms Ⓡ * sB&Bfr£38 sB&B⇌fr£40 dB&B⇌fr£55 Lunch £8.25-£10alc Dinner £9.50-£16.50alc LDO 9pm
Credit Cards 1 2 3 5

MARKSBURY Avon Map **03** ST66

GH QQ Wansdyke Cottage Crosspost Ln BA2 9HE ☎Bath(0225) 873674

A late 18th-century stone cottage situated on the A39/B3116 crossroads south of Bath. The accommodation is comfortable, and there is a private lounge/dining room available for guests. There are no hand basins in the bedrooms, but sufficient are provided within the general facilities.

4rm(1⇌) Ⓡ * sB&B£15-£20 dB&B£30-£40 dB&B⇌£30-£40 WB&B£95-£120 WBDi£144-£169 LDO 6pm
CTV 4P Ⓔ

MARLBOROUGH Wiltshire Map **04** SU16

See also Burbage

GH QQQ Laurel Cottage Southend, Ogbourne St George SN8 1SG ☎Ogbourne St George(067284) 288
Apr-Oct

This pretty chocolate box, 16th-century thatched flint cottage is just 3 miles north of Marlborough on the A345. The cosy dining room and lounge are beamed and everywhere is spotlessly clean. There's no shortage of character in the bedrooms which are all different in style and the best use has been made of sometimes limited space. Laurel Cottage is a useful location for touring, and walkers from the Ridgeway find it a convenient stop. This is a no smoking establishment.

3rm(1⇌2hc) (1fb) in all bedrooms CTV in all bedrooms Ⓡ sB&Bfr£25 sB&B⇌fr£34 dB&Bfr£32 dB&B⇌£38-£45 LDO 9.30am
5P Ⓔ

GH QQ Merlin Hotel High St SN8 1LW ☎(0672) 512151
Closed Xmas Day

Situated on the south side of Marlborough's High Street, the hotel shares frontage with a wine bar and a small boutique. At the rear is a small restaurant where residents are served breakfast and can choose dinner from a range of home-made dishes. Bedrooms are simply furnished, the majority are en suite and all have TV and tea making facilities.

15rm(13⇌2hc) Annexe 1 (1fb) CTV in all bedrooms Ⓡ sB&B£25-£35 sB&B⇌£30-£40 dB&B£35-£40 dB&B⇌£40-£45 LDO 9.30pm
Lic CTV
Credit Cards 1 3 Ⓔ

MARLOW Buckinghamshire Map **04** SU88

GH QQQ Holly Tree House Burford Close, Marlow Bottom SL7 3NF ☎(0628) 891110 FAX (0628) 481278

A large modern detached property situated close to the M4 and M40. Recently extended, it now provides 5 bedrooms, all with private bathrooms, tastefully decorated and furnished, with every facility from irons and ironing boards to direct dial telephones and hairdryers. Guests have use of an outdoor heated pool and sun patio in the well kept gardens. Breakfast is served in an informal dining room, which is adjacent to a bright, cosy conservatory lounge.

5⇌ CTV in all bedrooms Ⓡ T (ex guide dogs) sB&B⇌£49.50 dB&B⇌£62.50-£67.50
CTV 8P (heated)
Credit Cards 1 2 3 Ⓔ

MARPLE Greater Manchester Map **07** SJ98

FH QQ Mrs M G Sidebottom **Shire Cottage Ernocroft** *(SJ982910)* Marple Bridge SK6 5NT ☎Glossop(0457) 866536

Situated in an elevated position up a small lane off the A626 between Marple and Glossop, this modern bungalow enjoys lovely views over the surrounding countryside. The bedrooms are attractively appointed if not overly spacious.

4rm(2 2hc) (1fb) in 2 bedrooms CTV in all bedrooms Ⓡ * sB&B£16-£18 sB&B£20-£24 dB&B£30-£34 dB&B£34-£38 WB&B£105-£120
CTV 6P 180 acres mixed Ⓔ

MARTON Warwickshire Map **04** SP46

FH QQQ Mrs P Dronfield ***Marton Fields*** *(SP402680)* CV23 9RS ☎(0926) 632410
Closed Xmas

Approaching Marton on the A423 from Southam/Banbury, take the first left into North Street which opens into Church Street. Follow this road to the end fork and bear left. Marton Fields, an attractive red-brick period farmhouse set in delightful gardens, is a mile from the church. Mixed arable/sheep farmland leads to the River Itchen, accessible to visitors. The house is comfortable and well kept by Mrs Dronfield, a charming host and a talented artist. A good breakfast is offered with home-baked bread.

3hc in all bedrooms Ⓡ (ex guide dogs) LDO 6pm
CTV 10P croquet lawn painting holidays 240 acres arable beef mixed sheep

MARY TAVY Devon Map **02** SX57

GH QQQ The Stannary PL11 9QB ☎(0822) 810897 FAX (0822) 810898

This attractive 16th-century property with a Victorian extension is in the village of Mary Tavy on Dartmoor, close to Tavistock. Run as a vegetarian restaurant and guesthouse by resident proprietors Alison Fife, chef, and Michael Cook who is responsible for service, the welcome is warm and the food could be fairly described as creative cuisine that is animal friendly. There is a lot of choice and Michael produces many of his own wines, liqueurs and spirits for sale in the restaurant. The public areas have a Victorian theme, and many of the proprietors' personal pieces have been used to give an individuality to the house and comfort is emphasised throughout. Four bedrooms have been tastefully decorated in a style of simple elegance and there is a garden.

4hc in all bedrooms CTV in all bedrooms Ⓡ (ex guide dogs) * sB&B£25 dB&B£40 LDO 9pm
Lic 20P nc12yrs
Credit Cards 1 3

Book as early as possible for busy holiday periods.

FH QQQ Mrs B Anning **Wringworthy** *(SX500773)* PL19 9LT ☎(0822) 810434
Apr-Oct
An old Dartmoor farmhouse set in a valley a short distance from Tavistock, with views over the countryside. Wringworthy is mentioned in the Domesday Book, and the public areas are full of interesting original features including beautiful flagstone floors, exposed granite walls and linenfold wooden panelling taken from Tavistock Abbey during the reign of Henry VIII. The 3 bedrooms are comfortably furnished, and all have TV and tea making facilities. Outside there is an attractive garden for guests' use.
3rm (1fb)⅟in all bedrooms CTV in all bedrooms ® ✖ (ex guide dogs) ✱ sB&B£14-£15 dB&B£28-£30
CTV 3P 80 acres beef sheep

MASHAM North Yorkshire Map **08** SE28

GH QQQ Bank Villa HG4 4DB ☎Ripon(0765) 689605
Etr-Oct
A well established, popular guesthouse offering personal service from the resident proprietors, quaint bedrooms and comfortable lounges. Dinner can be especially recommended.
7hc sB&B£21 dB&B£33.50 WB&Bfr£112.50 WBDifr£210 LDO noon
Lic CTV 7P nc5yrs

MATLOCK Derbyshire Map **08** SK36

GH QQQ Lane End House Green Ln, Tansley DE4 5FJ ☎(0629) 583981
A small Georgian farmhouse situated in the quiet village of Tansley, on the outskirts of Matlock; set behind the village green, with well tended gardens, it is an ideal base from which to explore the surrounding Peak District. Bedrooms have been carefully decorated and furnished, with many thoughtful extras provided; all the rooms have pleasant views over the countryside. A carefully planned 4-course home-made dinner is served, after which guests can relax in either of 2 comfortable lounges. A no-smoking policy is requested.
3rm(1⇌↱2hc) ⅟in all bedrooms CTV in all bedrooms ® ✱ sB&B£29.50 sB&B⇌↱£32.50 dB&B⇌↱£42-£48 LDO 6pm
Lic CTV 5P nc12yrs croquet
Credit Cards 1 3 £

GH QQQ Robertswood Farley Hill DE4 3LL ☎(0629) 55642
This handsomely proportioned stone-built house dates from the 1880s, and now provides a comfortable retreat. Individually decorated bedrooms offer a good range of modern facilities including en suite bathrooms. A friendly atmosphere is actively encouraged by the resident proprietors, so communal dining is the norm, and the tastefully decorated lounge is an ideal place to relax after a freshly cooked dinner.
7⇌↱ CTV in all bedrooms ® T ✱ sB&B⇌↱£19-£35 dB&B⇌↱£38-£55 LDO noon
Lic 8P nc12yrs
Credit Cards 1 3 £

FH QQ Mrs M Brailsford **Farley** *(SK294622)* Farley DE4 5LR ☎(0629) 582533
Closed Xmas & New Year
This busy working farm, set high in the Derbyshire hills, has bright warm bedrooms, and a cheery welcome awaits guests from Mrs Brailsford and her dogs!
3hc (2fb)⅟in all bedrooms CTV in 1 bedroom ® sB&B£15-£16 dB&B£28 WB&Bfr£98 WBDifr£133 LDO 5pm
CTV 8P U 275 acres arable beef dairy £

FH QQQ M Haynes ***Packhorse*** *(SK323617)* Tansley DE4 5LF (2m NE of Matlock off A632 at Tansley)
☎(0629) 582781
Lovely countryside forms a backdrop to Mrs Haynes's lovingly maintained gardens, and the farmhouse accommodation has splendid views.
5hc (3fb) ® ✖
CTV 20P nc3yrs 40 acres mixed

FH QQ Mrs Janet Hole **Wayside** *(SK324630)* Matlock Moor DE4 5LF ☎(0629) 582967
Closed Xmas & New Year
At Matlock Moor, 2 miles from the town centre, this working farm offers fine views. Cattle byres stand next to the 17th-century farmhouse. A conservatory is soon to provide an attractive dining room to complement the comfortable, simple accommodation.
6hc (2fb) ✖ (ex guide dogs) sB&B£17 dB&B£28-£30
CTV 8P 60 acres dairy £

MAWGAN PORTH Cornwall & Isles of Scilly Map **02** SW86

GH QQQ White Lodge Hotel TR8 4BN
☎St Mawgan(0637) 860512
Mar-Nov & Xmas
A large, detached house situated in an elevated position with glorious views over the beach and cliffs of the bay. The bedrooms are well equipped and in the process of being refurbished. There is a good selection of dishes to choose from at dinner, and the atmosphere is relaxed and friendly.
16rm(11⇌↱5hc) (7fb) CTV in all bedrooms ® sB&B£17.50-£21.50 sB&B⇌↱£20.50-£24.50 dB&B£35-£43 dB&B⇌↱£41-£49 WB&B£102-£132 WBDi£158-£188 LDO 7.30pm
Lic CTV 17P games room
Credit Cards 1 2 3 £

MAXEY Cambridgeshire Map **04** TF10

GH QQ *Abbey House* West End Rd PE6 9EJ
☎Peterborough(0778) 344642
Located in a quiet village in a keen conservation area, this former cell of Thorney Abbey dates in part from 1190 and was extended in the Georgian era. It was in church ownership until it passed from Peterborough Minster to the present owners. Accommodation →

styles differ between the main house which provides sound, modest rooms, and the modern coach house annexe that offers good en suite facilities.
4rm(1↱3hc) Annexe 4↱ CTV in 10 bedrooms ®
✕ (ex guide dogs)
ᛗ CTV 12P

MAYFIELD East Sussex Map **05** TQ52

INN QQQ The Rose & Crown Fletching St TN20 6TE
☎(0435) 872200
Dating back to 1546, this charming village inn is situated in a conservation area, just half a mile from the high street, overlooking the green. Three of the bedrooms are particularly spacious, and all have en suite facilities and are individually furnished, with floral duvets, dried flowers and books adding to their charm. There are a number of cosy bars and eating areas, all full of character with original features and real log fires. Guests can choose to eat in the bars, where bar billiards and shove ha'penny are played by the locals, or enjoy a more formal atmosphere in the separate à la carte restaurant.
3⇌↱ Annexe 2⇌ CTV in all bedrooms ® ✕ (ex guide dogs)
sB&B⇌↱£44.50 dB&B⇌↱£61 WB&Bfr£200 WBDifr£230
Dinner £8-£12.50alc LDO 9.30pm
ᛗ 14P nc7yrs
Credit Cards [1] [3]

MAYFIELD Staffordshire Map **07** SK14

INN Q *Queen's Arms* DE6 2HH ☎Ashbourne(0335) 42271
Standing close to a busy junction, this lively house offers darts and pool, and live entertainment at weekends. Needless to say, it is well-supported by the locals.
4hc (2fb) CTV in all bedrooms ® ✕ (ex guide dogs)
LDO 6.30pm
ᛗ 20P pool table

MELKSHAM Wiltshire Map **03** ST96

GH QQ Longhope 9 Beanacre Rd SN12 8AG ☎(0225) 706737
An attractive Victorian Bath stone house with garden on the A350 towards Chippenham. The spacious and comfortable lounge and dining room, together with well equipped bedrooms, make the Longhope a popular place with business people and tourists alike.
7rm(1⇌5↱) (2fb) CTV in all bedrooms ® ✱ sB&B⇌↱£18-£20 dB&B⇌↱£30-£35 WB&B£110 WBDi£154 LDO 4pm
ᛗ CTV 12P (£)

GH QQ Regency Hotel Restaurant 10-12 Spa Rd SN12 7NS
☎(0225) 702971 FAX (0454) 776445
A Regency period terraced house situated a short walk from the town centre, offering well equipped, comfortable bedrooms, bright public areas and a restaurant open to non-residents.
10rm(2⇌4↱2hc) (1fb) CTV in all bedrooms ® **T** sB&B£20-£25 sB&B⇌↱£30-£35 dB&B£36-£42 dB&B⇌↱£40-£45
WB&B£100-£140 WBDi£160-£200 LDO 10pm
Lic ᛗ P̸
Credit Cards [1] [2] [3] [5] (£)

MELROSE Borders *Roxburghshire* Map **12** NT53

SELECTED

GH QQQQ Dunfermline House Buccleuch St TD6 9LB
☎(089682) 2148
This delightful Victorian house situated close to Melrose Abbey has been sympathetically restored to provide every modern comfort and facility by caring owners Susan and Ian Graham. Bedrooms are spotlessly clean, bright and cheerful, with comfortable modern appointments. There is a small cosy sitting room, and hearty breakfasts are served in the attractive dining room, together with a 3-course table d'hôte dinner using fresh local produce: dinners must be booked in advance. Smoking is not permitted.
5↱ 🚭in all bedrooms CTV in all bedrooms ® ✕ ✱
sB&B↱£19 dB&B↱£38 WB&B£110
ᛗ

MELTON MOWBRAY Leicestershire Map **08** SK71

GH Q Westbourne House Hotel 11A-15 Nottingham Rd
LE13 0NP ☎(0664) 63556 & 69456
Closed Xmas
16hc (1fb) CTV in all bedrooms sB&Bfr£19.50 dB&Bfr£35
LDO 7.30pm
Lic ᛗ CTV 20P

MENDHAM Suffolk Map **05** TM28

FH QQ Mrs J E Holden **Weston House** *(TM292828)* IP20 0PB
☎St Cross(098682) 206
Mar-Nov
This charming 16th-century white-painted farmhouse is situated 2 miles from the village, follow signs to St Cross from Mendham. It has pleasant lawns and is set in 150 acres of a beef and arable farm, where guests are welcome. There are 3 good-sized bedrooms, with pretty floral wallpaper, and public areas include a large, comfortable lounge and an attractive verandah and conservatory.
3rm(1↱2hc) (1fb) ® sB&Bfr£16.50 dB&B£29 dB&B↱£34
WB&B£87.50-£101.50 WBDi£147-£161 LDO 2pm
ᛗ CTV 6P 300 acres arable beef mixed
Credit Cards [2] (£)

MENDLESHAM GREEN Suffolk Map **05** TM06

GH QQQ Cherry Tree Farm IP14 5RQ
☎Stowmarket(0449) 766376
Feb-Nov
This traditional timber framed farmhouse has a wealth of exposed timbers. It offers 3 comfortable bedrooms that are pine furnished and 2 boast en suite facilities, while the third has a private shower room. The lounge features a brick inglenook fireplace, where logs burn during cold weather and guests share a communal table at breakfast and dinner. Food is freshly cooked using good quality ingredients and a selection of English cheeses are available, together with a wine list that includes 11 wines from East Anglian vineyards. Martin and Diana Ridsdale believe in old-fashioned hospitality and happily provide a service of early morning and afternoon teas.
3rm(2⇌↱1hc) 🚭in all bedrooms ✕ (ex guide dogs) ✱
dB&B£33-£37 dB&B⇌↱£37-£44 WB&B£115.50-£129.50
WBDi£199.50-£213.50 LDO 2pm
Lic ᛗ CTV 3P nc

MERE Wiltshire Map **03** ST83

GH QQQ Chetcombe House Hotel Chetcombe Rd BA12 6AZ
☎(0747) 860219
Closed 1-20 Feb
An elegant detached property on the edge of the village, just off the A303 Exeter to London trunk road. The bedrooms are comfortable and spotlessly clean. A small bar is available at reception and access to the beautifully kept gardens is through the attractive lounge. Home-cooked dinners, making use of home-grown vegetables in season, are offered in the informal dining room.
5⇌↱ (1fb)🚭in all bedrooms CTV in all bedrooms ® ✱
sB&B⇌↱£28-£32 dB&B⇌↱fr£48 WB&B£170-£195
WBDi£250-£275 LDO 7pm
Lic ᛗ 10P
Credit Cards [1] [2] [3]

INN QQ ***Talbot Hotel*** The Square BA12 6DR ☎(0747) 860427
This family-owned inn, situated in the heart of the country town of Mere, dates back to the 1580s. Bedrooms are gradually being refurbished and modern facilities upgraded and improved. The public bars have character and charm and some original 16th-century features remain. In addition to extensive bar snacks, there is also a varied table d'hôte lunch and dinner menu. The dining room is nicely appointed and comfortable. The proprietors Mr and Mrs Aylett remain very involved in the day to day running of the hotel.
7rm(4⇔3➦) (3fb) CTV in all bedrooms ® LDO 9pm
⊞ 22P
Credit Cards [1] [2] [3]

MERIDEN West Midlands Map **04** SP28

GH QQ Meriden Hotel Main Rd CV7 7NH ☎(0676) 22005
FAX (0676) 23744
A well established guesthouse just off the A45 with easy access to Coventry and the NEC. Some rooms are compact, but they are all well kept. There is a large dining room and a small bar in addition to the lounge which can double as a meeting room.
13rm(5⇔8➦) (1fb) CTV in all bedrooms ® **T** ✱
sB&B⇔➦£38.80-£50 dB&B⇔➦£64.65 LDO 9pm
Lic ⊞ CTV 15P ♧
Credit Cards [1] [3]

MERTHYR TYDFIL Mid Glamorgan Map **03** SO00

GH QQQ Llwyn On Cwmtaf CF48 2HS ☎(0685) 384384
This establishment is ideally placed for touring the Brecon Beacons, and visiting Swansea and Cardiff. Just 4 miles north of the town on the A470, it perches above the Llwyn On reservoir and enjoys commanding views of the countryside. Bedrooms are spotlessly clean and brightly decorated with attractive pine furnishings and pretty coordinating fabrics. Excellent facilities are provided, and there is a relaxing and congenial atmosphere promoted by the owners Mr and Mrs Evans.
4rm(2⇔➦2hc) CTV in all bedrooms ® ✗ (ex guide dogs)
sB&B£18 dB&B£33 dB&B⇔➦£38
⊞ 4P

INN QQQ Tredegar Arms Hotel 66 High St, Dowlais Top
CF48 2YE ☎(0685) 377467
Conveniently positioned just north of the town close to the junction of the A465/A470, this character inn has recently been upgraded to provide comfortable bedrooms, brightly decorated and well equipped for today's traveller. There is an attractive little restaurant and popular bars, and useful car parking is available on site. The inn is under the same ownership as The Little Diner at Dowlais Top, also AA registered.
5rm(2⇔3➦) CTV in all bedrooms ® ✱ sB&B⇔➦fr£27
dB&B⇔➦fr£37.50 Lunch fr£5.25&alc Dinner fr£5.25&alc
⊞ 6P
Credit Cards [1] [2] [3]

MERTON Devon Map **02** SS51

GH QQ Merton House EX20 3DR ☎Beaford(08053) 364
Apr-Oct
A Georgian residence peacefully situated in its own grounds, halfway between Bideford and Okehampton and affording glorious views of open Devonshire countryside. Bedrooms are comfortable and some have en suite facilities. A choice of menu is available in the restaurant, which is also open to non- residents. Outside, facilities include a swimming pool, tennis court and putting green.
5rm(3⇔2hc) (1fb) ® ✱ sB&B£23-£28 sB&B⇔£29-£34
dB&B£46-£56 dB&B⇔£58-£68 (incl dinner) LDO 10am
Lic ⊞ CTV 8P ≈℘(grass)snooker putting green table tennis
(£)

MEVAGISSEY Cornwall & Isles of Scilly Map **02** SX04

GH QQQ Headlands Hotel Polkirt Hill PL26 6UX
☎(0726) 843453
Mar-Oct & Xmas
This family-run, licensed private hotel enjoys superb views out across the bay – the panoramic views are undoubtedly some of the best in Cornwall. Bedrooms are freshly decorated and are steadily being improved. They are furnished and equipped in a modern style. Public areas are bright and are complemented by a small, cordial bar. A home-cooked evening meal, prepared by proprietor Mrs Grist using fresh, local quality produce, may also be enjoyed by guests.
14rm(8➦6hc) (3fb) CTV in 8 bedrooms sB&B£16-£24
sB&B➦£20-£28 dB&B£32-£40 dB&B➦£40-£48 WB&B£102-£158 WBDi£210.50-£238.50 LDO 7.30pm
Lic ⊞ CTV 11P

GH QQQ Mevagissey House Vicarage Hill PL26 6SZ
☎(0726) 842427
Mar-Oct
A former vicarage dating back to 1832, owned and run by friendly resident proprietors Mr and Mrs Owens. Bedrooms are individually decorated, well furnished and comfortable. Public areas are very elegant and offer views of rolling countryside. There are well tended gardens, a pleasant dining room, sun lounge and cosy bar area, and the spacious sitting room is filled with easy seating, flowers, magazines and ornaments. A home-cooked evening meal is offered.
6rm(1⇔3➦2hc) (2fb) CTV in all bedrooms ®
✗ (ex guide dogs) sB&B£23-£26 sB&B⇔➦£25-£28 dB&B£34-£40 dB&B⇔➦£38-£46 WB&B£112-£154 WBDi£196-£230
LDO 5pm
Lic ⊞ 12P nc7yrs
Credit Cards [1] [3]

GH QQQ Spa Hotel Polkirt PL26 6UY
☎St Austell(0726) 842244
12rm(11⇔➦1hc) (3fb) CTV in all bedrooms ® ✱
sB&B⇔➦£21.50-£25.50 dB&B⇔➦£43-£51 WB&B£127-£157
WBDi£182.50-£209 LDO 7.45pm
Lic ⊞ CTV 14P
Credit Cards [1] [2] [3]

GH QQQ Tremarne Hotel Polkirt PL26 6UY ☎(0726) 842213
Closed Dec rs Jan & Feb
Quietly situated up a private road away from the bustle of the village centre, this small, family-run hotel enjoys a relaxed and friendly atmosphere, and good views across the bay. The young and enthusiastic owners are steadily upgrading the rooms, which now have a fresh, bright décor. All bedrooms are en suite and most now have pretty and coordinated décor and furnishings; those not yet upgraded are still neat and comfortable. Public areas are comfortable and nicely appointed.
14⇔➦ (2fb) CTV in all bedrooms ® sB&B⇔➦£25-£29
dB&B⇔➦£40-£44 WB&B£137-£165 WBDi£181-£217
LDO 5pm
Lic ⊞ 14P nc3yrs ≈(heated)
Credit Cards [1] [2] [3] (£)

FH QQQ Mrs L Hennah **Kerryanna** *(SX008453)* Treleaven Farm PL26 6RZ ☎(0726) 843558
Mar-Oct
This modern, bright and comfortable house is convenient for the centre of the village, yet enjoys peace and tranquility. Bedrooms are neat and fresh, with smart en suite facilities and pretty soft fabrics. The particularly comfortable lounge enjoys superb views, and there is also a cosy bar, and a dining room where home-cooked evening meals and hearty breakfasts are served. One popular feature of this establishment is the outdoor pool, heated to a comfortable temperature.
6⇔➦ (2fb) CTV in all bedrooms ® ✗ dB&B⇔➦fr£36
WB&Bfr£126 WBDifr£180 LDO 5pm

→

Lic 🏨 7P nc5yrs ⛱(heated) games room putting green 200 acres arable beef

FH QQQ Mrs A Hennah ***Treleaven*** *(SX008454)* PL26 6RZ ☎(0726) 842413

Closed 15 Dec-7 Jan

This bright, modern farmhouse offers comfortable accommodation and a relaxed, friendly atmosphere. Bedrooms are fresh and airy, all are en suite and those at the front enjoy lovely views. This is true also of the public areas, which include a comfortable lounge and a dining room which offers a choice of à la carte or table d'hôte menu, and which is open to non-residents. Energetic guests will enjoy the use of the outdoor pool, the putting green and the games room.

6🚿 (1fb) CTV in all bedrooms ® ✗ LDO 8pm

Lic 🏨 CTV 6P ⛱(heated) games room, putting green 200 acres mixed

Credit Cards 1 3

INN QQ ***The Ship*** Fore St PL26 6UQ (St Austell Brewery) ☎(0726) 843324

This historic inn, situated in the heart of the bustling fishing port, offers simple, neat bedrooms, with some modern facilities. The bars are full of character, and popular with locals and visitors alike. Low ceilings, roaring open fires, flagstone floors and scrubbed pine tables add charm, and the management and staff are a friendly team.

6hc (2fb) CTV in all bedrooms ® LDO 8.30pm

🏨 P̸

MIDDLETON-IN-TEESDALE Co Durham Map 12 NY92

GH QQ Brunswick House 55 Market Place DL12 0QH ☎Teesdale(0833) 40393

Incorporating a tearoom, this attractive guesthouse is situated at the western end of the town close to the parish church. The bedrooms have been cheerfully decorated in modern colours, with pine furniture in most pleasing coordinated fabrics. Meals are served at pine tables in the beamed tearoom which, together with the adjoining guests' lounge with its open fire, board games and books, reflect the charm and character of this 18th-century house. There is a small private car park at the rear of the hotel.

4rm(3🚿1hc) (1fb) CTV in all bedrooms ® ✗ (ex guide dogs) ✱ sB&B£25 sB&B🚿£25 dB&B£36 dB&B🚿£36 WB&Bfr£126 WBDifr£175 LDO 7pm

Lic 🏨 4P

MIDDLETON PRIORS Shropshire Map 07 SO69

SELECTED

GH QQQQ Middleton Lodge WV16 6UR (1m NE on unclass rd) ☎Ditton Priors(074634) 228 or 675

Closed Xmas

Set in 20 acres of Shropshire countryside overlooking Brown Clee hill, this 17th century property with its pebble dash frontage, was once a hunting and shooting lodge. Three bedrooms are available, one of which can be made en suite. One of the bedrooms has a four poster bed, the other 2 have brass beds, all of them are well furnished and comfortable with period pieces of furniture and coordinated fabrics. There is a choice of 2 sitting rooms, one of which has an original Knowle settee. The slab floored dining room, featuring a log fire and original bread oven, is furnished with solid oak tables and breakfast only is served. Middleton Lodge is a no smoking establishment.

3rm(2⇌1🚿) CTV in all bedrooms ® ✗ (ex guide dogs) ✱ dB&B⇌🚿£40-£45

🏨 CTV 4P nc5yrs

MIDDLEWICH Cheshire Map 07 SJ76

FH QQ Mrs S Moss **Forge Mill** *(SJ704624)* Warmingham CW10 0HQ ☎Warmingham(027077) 204

Situated in peaceful countryside, to the south of Middlewich, this large Victorian country house is set in spacious, attractive gardens. It is furnished throughout in a style reflecting its period and includes many antique pieces. There are 2 spacious bedrooms – one is a twin and the other will accommodate 3 people.

2hc ✗ (ex guide dogs) ✱ sB&Bfr£16.50 dB&B£28-£30 WB&Bfr£105

🏨 CTV 10P 🎾(grass)150 acres mixed £

MIDHURST West Sussex

See **Bepton** and **Rogate**

MILNATHORT Tayside *Kinross-shire* Map 11 NO10

GH QQ ***Hollyhock Cottage*** 3 Backloan KY13 7YJ ☎Kinross(0577) 64518

Closed Xmas & New Year

An immaculately maintained private house in a narrow side street behind the town hall, offering tastefully appointed bedrooms, decorated and furnished with an expert touch. There is a bathroom on each floor, but no wash basins in the rooms. Breakfast is taken round a communal table in the little dining room which is full of character. This is a no-smoking establishment.

3rm ⊁in all bedrooms CTV in all bedrooms ®
✗ (ex guide dogs)
🏨

MILTON COMMON Oxfordshire Map 04 SP60

INN Q ***Three Pigeons*** OX9 2NS ☎Great Milton(0844) 279247

A small, popular country inn beside the M40 at Junction 7, giving easy access to both Oxford and London. The 3 bedrooms are approached by an exterior stairway, and are due to be renovated. There is a choice of bars, where a varied bar snack menu is available for both lunch and dinner.

3⇌🚿 (1fb) CTV in all bedrooms ® ✗ LDO 10pm

🏨 CTV 20P

Credit Cards 1 2 3 5

MILTON KEYNES Buckinghamshire Map 04 SP83

See also Gayhurst and Whaddon

GH QQQ Thurstons Private Hotel 90 High St, Newport Pagnell MK16 8EH ☎Newport Pagnell(0908) 611377

This establishment is part of a subtantial town house on the High Street of Newport Pagnell. Bedrooms are on 3 floors and are simply appointed with en suite facilities. There is a small lounge area adjoining the breakfast room, and a large car park.

8rm(2⇌6🚿) CTV in all bedrooms ® ✗ (ex guide dogs) ✱ sB&B⇌🚿£27-£42 dB&B⇌🚿£37-£50

Lic 🏨 14P

Credit Cards 1 2 3

MILTON-UNDER-WYCHWOOD Oxfordshire Map 04 SP21

SELECTED

GH QQQQ Hillborough Hotel The Green OX7 6JH (off A424 Burton-Stow village centre) ☎Shipton-under-Wychwood(0993) 830501 FAX (0993) 830646

Closed Jan

A small family-run licensed hotel and restaurant overlooking the village green in this peaceful village, close to Burford. The bedrooms in the main house are simply decorated but pretty, and the 3 family rooms in the annexe cottages are colour coordinated and have direct access to the car park. The bar has a welcoming atmosphere and the bar menu offers a variety

of home-cooked dishes; there is also a choice of menus available in the attractive restaurant, which enjoys a good reputation for fine English cooking using top quality fresh produce; the restaurant is also open to non-residents. There is a spacious conservatory lounge that opens on to the gardens.
6rm(5⇌1↱) Annexe 4⇌ (3fb) CTV in all bedrooms ® T ✻ sB&B⇌↱£39 dB&B⇌↱£54 WB&B£189 WBDi£240-£254 LDO 9.15pm
Lic 🍽 15P ⛳ croquet
Credit Cards 1 3 £
See advertisement under OXFORD

MINEHEAD Somerset Map **03** SS94

See **Town Plan Section**

GH QQQ Avill House Townsend Rd TA24 5RG
☎(0643) 704370
This Victorian semidetached 3-storey house with a brightly painted façade and colourful flower beds, is conveniently located a short walk from the town and seafront. The accommodation is being steadily improved, and bedrooms have smart, functional furniture, pretty coordinating décor and interesting paintings of local attractions; they are all comfortable and kept spick and span. the bar has recently been extended and is cosy and comfortable, and a new sitting room is currently being built. The front-facing dining room is simple in décor, and a small choice for an evening meal is offered, along with a huge breakfast served by Mrs Wood. There is ample forecourt parking.
9rm(3↱6hc) (4fb) CTV in all bedrooms ® ✗ ✻ sB&B£16.50-£17.50 dB&B£26-£29 dB&B↱£32-£35 WB&B£87.50-£112 WBDi£123-£157.50 LDO 5pm
Lic CTV 9P £

GH QQ Bactonleigh Private Hotel 20 Tregonwell Rd TA24 5DU ☎(0643) 702147
This small, well established hotel retains a traditional seaside holiday atmosphere. Guests return year after year for the warm hospitality and such treats as early morning service. Bedrooms are comfortable, there is a TV lounge where guests get to know one another, and a spacious dining room where full English breakfasts are served.
8rm(3↱5hc) (1fb) ® ✻ sB&B£14-£16 dB&B£25-£30 dB&B↱£30-£35 LDO 5pm
Lic 🍽 CTV 8P

GH QQQ Gascony Hotel The Avenue TA24 5BB
☎(0643) 705939
Mar-Oct
Over the years Mr and Mrs Luckett have transformed this Victorian property into a comfortable and appealing small hotel. The lounge bar is warm and inviting with chandeliers and polished brass, and the deep buttoned dralon chairs are quite high to accommodate the older clientèle. The dining room is pretty in pink and green and has some well chosen antiques such as a Welsh dresser with a collection of pewter. Bedrooms are of a good size and have quality beds; now all en suite, the bathrooms are generally modern and well tiled. Standards are high here and there is an easy, good natured atmosphere.
13⇌↱ (2fb) CTV in all bedrooms ® ✻ sB&B⇌↱£24-£26 dB&B⇌↱£44-£46 WBDi£163-£173 LDO 5.30pm
Lic 🍽 15P nc5yrs
Credit Cards 1 3 £
See advertisement on page 285

GH QQ *Marshfield Hotel* Tregonwell Rd TA24 5DU
☎(0643) 702517
Mar-Nov
A well established hotel, personally run by resident proprietors who provide golfing breaks in conjunction with nearby links and parkland courses. The smartly decorated and furnished dining room is complemented by a small sun lounge bar and TV lounge. Bedrooms are freshly decorated and modern, many with private bathrooms.
→

12rm(2⇌6↱4hc) (1fb) ® LDO 6.30pm
Lic 🍽 CTV 7P

SELECTED

GH QQQQ Marston Lodge Hotel St Michaels Rd TA24 5JP ☎(0643) 702510
8 Feb-6 Nov

An Edwardian property dating back to 1905 situated in an acre of gardens, high above the town on North Hill near the famous Church Steps. Under the care of proprietors Mr and Mrs Allen the hotel has been steadily improved to its current excellent standard, and public areas are pretty, elegant and tasteful. Mrs Allen's floristry talents are displayed throughout the house, with dried flower arrangements home grown in the beautifully tended terraced garden, and the bar is decorated with a mural depicting local scenes by Mr Allen. Bedrooms are on 3 floors, each with superb views across town, and are tastefully furnished, with pretty coordinating décor and many thoughtful extra touches. The en suite bath and shower rooms are spotlessly clean, with good quality linen and toiletries. The menu changes daily, with a varied choice using fresh produce and home-grown vegetables, cooked by Mrs Allen and accompanied by a reasonable wine list. This is a no-smoking establishment.

12rm(5⇌7↱) CTV in all bedrooms ® ✗ sB&B⇌↱£35-£37 dB&B⇌↱£70-£74 (incl dinner) WB&B£158-£172 WBDi£228-£242 LDO 7pm
Lic 🍽 7P nc10yrs
Credit Cards 1 3 £

GH QQQ Mayfair Hotel 25 The Avenue TA24 5AY ☎(0643) 702719
Mar-Nov rs Feb

Very neat and nicely presented, this establishment stands on the main avenue and is conveniently close to the seafront and shops. The pretty bedrooms are freshly decorated and well equipped with modern en suite facilities. A further 9 bedrooms are provided in a building just across the road and are similar to those in the main hotel, with front forecourt parking available. The public areas have recently been redecorated to a very good standard and offer 2 lounges with a large dining room. The jovial resident proprietors provide an attentive service for guests and many return time and time again to this well managed hotel.

16rm(5⇌11↱) Annexe 9rm(4⇌5↱) (10fb) CTV in all bedrooms ® ✗ (ex guide dogs) ✱ sB&B⇌↱£23-£25 dB&B⇌↱£45-£48 WB&B£147-£160 LDO 6pm
Lic 🍽 23P
Credit Cards 1 3

INN QQQ Kildare Lodge 18 Townsend Rd TA24 5RQ ☎(0643) 702009 FAX (0643) 706516

This large whitewashed building dates back to 1907 and was built by a student of Edwin Lutyens; it thus offers an abundance of unusual architectural details. The majority of bedrooms are located in the main building and the stable block to the side of the property, along with 2 further rooms with their own private entrances. The rooms are all plainly furnished but with high ceilings, sloping eaves, beams and plenty of nooks and crannies, and are modern in terms of comfort and practicality, being bright, light and comfortable. Some bedrooms have very nice private bathrooms, 3 with bath and separate shower, and family rooms are practically laid out. An extensive bar menu and an á la carte menu is offered, with the choice of eating in the bars or restaurant. Standing just on the edge of the town centre, the inn offers good value for money and a constant source of pleasure architecturally.

5⇌↱ Annexe 5↱ (3fb) ⊬in 2 bedrooms CTV in all bedrooms ® T ✱ sB&B⇌↱£19.50-£27.50 dB&B⇌↱£38.50-£56.50 WB&B£125-£155 WBDi£155-£225 Lunch £3.95-£11.95alc Dinner £11.25&alc LDO 9pm
🍽 30P
Credit Cards 1 3 5 £

MINSTER LOVELL Oxfordshire Map 04 SP31

FH QQQ Mrs Katherine Brown **Hill Grove** *(SP314115)* OX8 5NA ☎Witney(0993) 703120 FAX (0993) 700528
Closed Xmas

This modern, Cotswold stone farmhouse is conveniently situated just off the B4047 towards Crawley, and enjoys views over the Windrush valley. The bedrooms are comfortable and nicely equipped, and guests benefit from the friendly and warm atmosphere.

2⇌↱ ⊬in all bedrooms CTV in all bedrooms ® ✗ (ex guide dogs) dB&B£32-£34 dB&B⇌↱£38-£40
🍽 CTV 3P 300 acres arable beef mixed £

MOFFAT Dumfries & Galloway *Dumfriesshire* Map 11 NT00

GH QQ Barnhill Springs Country DG10 9QS ☎(0683) 20580

This early Victorian house is situated in delightful rural surroundings yet has easy access to the A74 south of Moffat, and offers unpretentious but comfortable and spacious accommodation with a friendly atmosphere.

6rm(1↱5hc) (1fb) ® sB&B£16.50-£17.50 dB&Bfr£33 dB&B↱£35 WB&B£115.50-£122.50 WBDi£185.50-£192.50 LDO 3pm
Lic 🍽 CTV 10P

GH Q *Buchan* Beechgrove DG10 9HG ☎(0683) 20378

Colourful hanging baskets decorate the exterior of this small guesthouse, which is within walking distance of the town centre and offers modest but improving standards of accommodation.

7rm(2⇌↱5hc) (2fb) LDO 5pm
🍽 CTV 10P

SELECTED

GH QQQQ Gilbert House Beechgrove DG10 9RS ☎(0683) 20050

This lovely detached white stone Victorian house is not far from the town centre, yet enjoys a peaceful setting in a quiet residential area with views of the surrounding hills. Modern fabrics have been used to good effect in the individually decorated bedrooms which are comfortably furnished and maintained to a high standard. Smoking is not permitted in the public areas, which include a comfortable lounge and smart dining room, where a delicious home- cooked set dinner is offered. The hotel provides superior accommodation at competitive prices, with personal attention from the enthusiastic owners.

6rm(4↱2hc) (3fb) ® ✱ sB&B£15-£17.50 dB&B£30-£35 dB&B↱£32-£35 WB&B£95-£101 WBDi£154-£160 LDO 5pm
Lic 🍽 CTV 6P
Credit Cards 1 3

GH QQ St Olaf Eastgate, Off Dickson St DG10 9AE ☎(0683) 20001
Apr-Oct

Quietly situated in a side street off the High Street, the house offers pleasant and reliable accommodation which includes bright, cheerful bedrooms and an inviting first-floor lounge.

7rm(1↱6hc) (3fb) ® ✱ sB&B£15 dB&B£25 dB&B↱£27 WB&B£87.50
🍽 CTV 4P 4🚘 £

MOLD Clwyd Map 07 SJ26

FH QQ Mrs A Brown **Hill** *(SJ263265)* Llong CH7 4JP (on A5118 between Chester and Mold) ☎Buckley(0244) 550415

This large Georgian farmhouse stands on the A5118 in an elevated position, about 2 miles southeast of Mold, at Llong. It is well maintained and provides clean, comfortable accommodation.

3hc (1fb)⚟in all bedrooms ® ⊁ (ex guide dogs) sB&B£15-£17 dB&B£26-£30
CTV 5P 300 acres dairy mixed

MOLESWORTH Cambridgeshire Map **04** TL07

INN QQQ Cross Keys PE18 0QF ☎Bythorn(08014) 283
A good range of bar meals and home-made dishes are prepared by Mrs Bettsworth, the friendly proprietress of this archetypal village inn, set just off the A604. It offers a high standard of accommodation, all with good en suite facilities.
4rm(1⇌3♪) Annexe 5rm(2⇌3♪) (1fb) CTV in all bedrooms ® sB&B⇌♪fr£23 dB&B⇌♪fr£38 Lunch £5-£8alc Dinner £5-£8alc LDO 10.30pm
30P
Credit Cards [1] [3]

MONTGOMERY Powys Map **07** SO29

FH QQQ Mrs G M Bright **Little Brompton** *(SO244941)* SY15 6HY ☎(0686) 668371
Little Brompton farm is a delightful early eighteenth century farmhouse with timbered walls, beamed ceilings and stone fireplaces. It has very pretty bedrooms, a comfortable lounge and fresh farm food is served in the attractive dining room. Close to Offa's Dyke it is convenient for walkers.
3rm(2♪1hc) (1fb)⚟in 1 bedroom ® sB&B£15-£18 dB&B£30-£32 dB&B♪£34-£36 WB&B£105-£126 WBDi£160-£180 LDO 4pm
CTV 3P 1 shooting in season 100 acres arable beef mixed sheep

MONTROSE Tayside *Angus* Map **15** NO75

GH QQ ***Linksgate*** 11 Dorward Rd DD10 8SB ☎(0674) 72273
This substantial detached Victorian house is situated close to the golf course and beach. The bedrooms are mainly spacious and comfortable, and the lounge and dining room feature ornate plaster ceilings and fine fireplaces – the one in the lounge now fronted by a small wood-burning stove.
9rm(2⇌7hc) (3fb) CTV in 2 bedrooms LDO 6pm
CTV 9P

MORCHARD BISHOP Devon Map **03** SS70

SELECTED

FH QQQQ Mr & Mrs S Chilcott ***Wigham*** *(SS757087)* EX17 6RJ ☎(03637) 350
This picturesque 16th-century Devon longhouse is set in 30 acres of organic farmland and run by Steve and Lesley Chilcott. Bedrooms are all individually furnished, with en suite bathrooms and modern facilities including TV and video. Public areas are comfortable and feature log fires or wood-burning stoves. All have oak beams and some feature exposed brickwork. There are 2 lounges, a snooker room and a dining room where guests share a communal table. Steve cooks using home-grown produce, including lamb, beef, pork, chicken, butter, cream, yoghurt, free range eggs, vegetables and soft fruit. Dinners consist of a set starter and main course and a choice of puddings, and might include coq au vin or beef with Bernaise sauce followed by bread and butter pudding, fresh fruit pavlova and local cheeses.
5⇌♪ (1fb)⚟in all bedrooms CTV in all bedrooms ® ⊁
Lic 9P nc10yrs (heated) U snooker table 31 acres mixed
Credit Cards [1] [2] [3]

See advertisement on page 287

Ⓔ Remember to use the money-off vouchers.

MORECAMBE Lancashire Map **07** SD46

GH QQQ Ashley Private Hotel 371 Marine Rd Promenade East LA4 5AH ☎(0524) 412034
Apr-Oct
This small, private hotel is situated at the eastern end of the seafront and offers sea views from the majority of bedrooms and public areas. The sleeping accommodation is compact but well furnished and there is a first floor lounge. Downstairs, a nicely appointed dining room and bar are provided.
13rm(3⇌8♪2hc) (3fb) CTV in all bedrooms ® ⊁ sB&B£15-£16 sB&B⇌♪£18-£20 dB&B⇌♪£34-£40 WB&B£116-£130 WBDi£135-£160 LDO 3pm
Lic 5P 1 (£5) Ⓔ

GH QQ Beach Mount 395 Marine Rd East LA4 5AN ☎(0524) 420753
mid Mar-Oct
Situated on the quieter eastern promenade, the wide frontage of this private hotel overlooks the bay, as do many of the bedrooms and the main lounge. The accommodation is mostly compact but comfortably furnished with bright, fresh décor and the majority of rooms have en suite facilities. An attractively appointed dining room also offers lovely views of the sea and the Cumbrian Hills beyond.
26rm(22⇌4hc) (3fb) CTV in 22 bedrooms ® * sB&B£17.50 sB&B⇌£20.50 dB&B£31 dB&B⇌£38 WBDi£155 LDO 7pm
Lic CTV 6P
Credit Cards [1] [2] [3] [5]

GH Q Ellesmere Private Hotel 44 Westminster Rd LA4 4JD ☎(0524) 411881
A small Victorian terraced house situated in a road of similar properties away from the seafront at the western end of the town. Colour television and tea- making facilities are provided in the bedrooms and there is a cosy, attractive lounge on the ground floor. →

6hc (2fb)⊬in 1 bedroom CTV in all bedrooms ® ✗ (ex guide dogs) ✱ sB&B£14-£16 dB&B£22-£24 WB&B£84-£98 WBDi£98-£110 LDO 3pm
CTV
Credit Cards [1] [3] £

GH QQ New Hazelmere Hotel 391 Promenade East LA4 5AN ☎(0524) 417876 FAX (0524) 414488
May-29 Nov
Set in a corner position on the eastern promenade, overlooking the sea, this private hotel features a bar and lounge which contain many antiques with a nautical theme. Most of the bedrooms have views over the bay and are conventional in style but all have modern bathroom suites.
20rm(17⇌3♠) (3fb) CTV in all bedrooms ® sB&B⇌♠fr£17.50 dB&B⇌♠fr£35 WB&B£105-£125 WBDi£150-£160 LDO 5.30pm
Lic CTV 3P
Credit Cards [1] [3] £

GH QQQ Hotel Prospect 363 Marine Rd East LA4 5AQ ☎(0524) 417819
Etr-Oct
Occupying a prime seafront location with fine views over the bay, this friendly, private hotel provides comfortable accommodation in tastefully furnished and decorated bedrooms, equipped with modern facilities. The public rooms include an attractive dining room, a comfortable lounge with TV and a lounge bar which also overlooks the sea.
14⇌ (9fb) CTV in all bedrooms ® sB&B⇌fr£22 dB&B⇌fr£36 WB&Bfr£113 WBDifr£148 LDO 3pm
Lic CTV 6P
Credit Cards [1] [3] £

GH QQQ Wimslow Private Hotel 374 Marine Rd East LA4 5AH ☎(0524) 417804
mid Feb-Nov & Xmas
Situated on the eastern promenade overlooking the bay, with the lakeland hills beyond, this friendly hotel offers modern bedrooms with every modern facility. A feature of the hotel is its attractive, first-floor dining room, with lovely views across the bay. Downstairs, there is an old-world bar and lounge, in addition to a quiet lounge.
13rm(1⇌12♠) (2fb) CTV in all bedrooms ® ✗ ✱ sB&B⇌♠£20-£21 dB&B⇌♠£40-£42 WB&B£120-£125 WBDi£158-£165 LDO 4.30pm
Lic CTV 3P 6
Credit Cards [1] [3] £

MORETONHAMPSTEAD Devon Map 03 SX78

GH QQQ Cookshayes 33 Court St TQ13 8LG ☎(0647) 40374
mid Mar-Oct
A character property on the edge of the town with beautifully kept gardens, the guesthouse is personally run by resident proprietors who extend a warm welcome to guests. The quality bedrooms offer comfort combined with old fashioned charm. An elegant lounge is available and home-cooked dishes are served in the intimate dining room.
8rm(6♠2hc) (1fb) CTV in all bedrooms ® ✱ sB&B£20 sB&B♠£30 dB&B£32 dB&B♠£36-£39 WB&B£105-£119 WBDi£192.50-£217 LDO 5.30pm
Lic CTV 15P nc7yrs putting green
Credit Cards [1] [2] [3] £

GH QQQ Moorcote TQ13 8LS ☎(0647) 40966
Closed Xmas
A Victorian house of character set back off the road, with a small garden. Bedrooms are cosy, comfortable, individually decorated and nicely furnished, combining modern facilities with charm and character. Hearty breakfasts are popular with the numerous Dartmoor National Park walkers and tourists.
6rm(4♠2hc) CTV in all bedrooms ® ✗ ✱ sB&B♠fr£22 dB&Bfr£30 dB&B♠fr£34
CTV 6P nc12yrs

FH QQQ Mrs M Cuming **Wooston** *(SX764890)* TQ13 8QA ☎(0647) 40367
Closed Xmas
A 280-acre mixed farm peacefully situated high above the Teign valley, with glorious open views across the moors. Fine, tastefully decorated bedrooms are comfortably furnished, with many thoughtful extras provided; smoking is not permitted in the bedrooms. There are 2 attractive lounges, 1 for non-smokers, and home cooked farmhouse fare is served around a large table in the dining room.
3rm(2♠1hc) (1fb)⊬in all bedrooms ® sB&B£14.50-£16 dB&B£29-£32 dB&B♠£30-£36 LDO 5pm
CTV 6P 280 acres mixed £

MORETON-IN-MARSH Gloucestershire Map 04 SP13

GH QQ Moreton House High St GL56 0LQ ☎(0608) 50747
A spacious, well established family-owned Cotswold stone house in the town centre, opposite the end of the A44 Evesham road. Bedrooms are simple but soundly appointed, with good en suite facilities. The large, attractive bay- windowed front houses a little tea room on the ground floor, making this a popular location for both tourists and business guests.
12rm(5⇌♠7hc) CTV in all bedrooms ® ✱ sB&B£22.50 dB&Bfr£42 dB&B⇌♠£49-£55 LDO 8pm
Lic 5P
Credit Cards [1] [3] £

MORFA NEFYN Gwynedd Map 06 SH23

GH Q *Erw Goch Hotel* LL53 6BN ☎Nefyn(0758) 720539
Family owned and run, this detached Georgian house stands in its own grounds and provides good home comforts. The facilities provided include a three-quarter size snooker table.
15hc (5fb)
Lic CTV 25P
Credit Cards [1] [3]

MORTEHOE Devon Map 02 SS44

See also Woolacombe

SELECTED

GH QQQQ Sunnycliffe Hotel EX34 7EB ☎Woolacombe(0271) 870597
Feb-Nov
In 1993 the proprietors celebrate 25 years of ownership of this successful small hotel, which is delightfully situated on a hillside overlooking the sea. Bedrooms are very comfortable with lots of thoughtful extras, including quite a range of books, and the lounge bar and restaurant are bright, inviting rooms. Mr Bassett personally prepares all the dishes fresh on the day, even the pudding, and Mrs Bassett ensures that guests are happy and comfortable.
8rm(4⇌4♠) ⊬in 4 bedrooms CTV in all bedrooms ® ✗ sB&B⇌♠£23-£29 dB&B⇌♠£46-£58 WBDi£240-£269 LDO 6pm
Lic 10P nc £

MOUSEHOLE Cornwall & Isles of Scilly Map 02 SW42

GH QQQ *Tavis Vor* TR19 6PR ☎Penzance(0736) 731306
A delightful country house style guesthouse, standing in its own grounds running down to the sea, with commanding and unrestricted views out to St Michaels Mount and across the bay. Bedrooms are bright, cosy and well equipped, and public rooms are comfortable.
8rm(3♠5hc) (1fb) CTV in all bedrooms ® LDO 5pm
Lic 7P nc5yrs

MUDDIFORD Devon Map **02** SS53

FH QQQ Mrs M Lethaby **Home Park** *(SS553360)* Lower Blakewell EX31 4ET ☎Barnstaple(0271) 42955

This small, well modernised farmhouse is set in a quiet position with uninterrupted views of rolling countryside. Mrs Lethaby provides cheerful hospitality and an excellent home-cooked dinner using fresh local ingredients. Two modern bedrooms have en suite facilities and there are plenty of provisions for children

3⇌♠ (2fb) CTV in all bedrooms ® ✗ (ex guide dogs) ✱ sB&B⇌♠fr£15 dB&B⇌♠fr£30 WB&Bfr£100 WBDifr£135 LDO 4pm

CTV 3P 70 acres sheep beef £

MUDFORD Somerset Map **03** ST51

INN QQQ **The Half Moon** Main St BA21 5TF ☎Marston Magna(0935) 850289

This smart, well presented inn dates back to the 17th-century and is conveniently located along the A359, 2 miles northeast of Yeovil. The bedrooms are situated in 2 annexe, stable-style blocks and although rather compact they are nicely furnished and equipped with remote control TV, tea and coffee making facilities, direct dial telephones and shower en suite. Public areas consist of a pretty non smoking dining room, plus a second cosy dining area – where an à la carte menu is served – and also the village bar. Friendly, cheerful staff help to give the inn a relaxed, pleasing atmosphere, which continues to be extremely popular with returning commercial guests.

Annexe 11rm(1⇌10♠) CTV in all bedrooms ® **T** ✱ sB&B⇌♠£30 dB&B⇌♠£40 WB&B£186 WBDi£280 Lunch £10.95&alc Dinner £10.95&alc LDO 9.30pm

40P

Credit Cards 1 2 3 5 £

MUIR OF ORD Highland *Ross & Cromarty* Map **14** NH55

SELECTED

GH QQQQ The Dower House Highfield IV6 7XN ☎(0463) 870090

Closed 1 wk Oct & 2 wks Feb/Mar

Nestling in 3 acres of lawns and wooded grounds, this captivating cottage style house is a haven of peace and quiet. Superior appointments, combined with excellent cuisine and welcoming hospitality add to the appeal of this guesthouse, which is personally run by resident owners Robyn and Mena Aitchison. Individual bedrooms are prettily decorated, fitted with period furnishings and provide a good standard of amenities. One room has a separate sitting area and another has a brass bedstead – all have conventional bathrooms fitted with cast iron baths. The day rooms are limited but quite pleasing, including a cosy sitting room with its welcoming open fire, well filled bookshelves and chintzy seating that invites comfortable relaxation. Robyn is a gifted chef and the elegant, period style dining room is the ideal setting to enjoy his imaginative creations, produced from the best fresh ingredients available. The set price menu changes daily and is supported by an extensive and well chosen wine list.

5rm(4⇌1↱) (1fb) CTV in all bedrooms **T** ✱

sB&B⇌↱£50-£75 dB&B⇌↱£100-£110 WB&B£315-£350 WBDi£507-£525 LDO 8.30pm

Lic 🍴 20P

Credit Cards 1 3

MULL, ISLE OF Strathclyde *Argyllshire* Map **10**

BUNESSAN Map **10** NM32

GH QQQ ***Ardachy*** PA67 6DR ☎Fionnphort(06817) 505 & 506

Peacefully situated between Bunessan and Visken and only minutes from a sandy beach, this converted farmhouse now offers modern style accommodation. Some bedrooms are small but there is a comfortable lounge which offers fine views across to Jura, Colonsay and the mainland.

8rm(7↱1hc) (2fb) ® LDO 6pm

Lic 🍴 CTV 8P ⤴ shooting

Credit Cards 1 3

DERVAIG Map **13** NM45

GH Q ***Ardbeg House*** PA75 6QT ☎(06884) 254

Just through the village, on its western fringe, this white painted house sits in its own elevated grounds, complete with ducks, and garden furniture on the front lawn. Inside, it is immediately apparent that the proprietor is a fan of Charles Dickens, with associated memorabilia everywhere. The lounge, with its small corner bar, is the focal point, though the hall lounge also has some seating. Bedrooms are generally simply furnished though 2 rooms have pine 4- posters. The dining room is boldly decorated, and guests can be expected to share tables.

7rm(3⇌↱4hc) (1fb) ® LDO 6pm

Lic 🍴 P

SALEN Map **10** NM54

GH QQQ Craig Hotel PA72 6JG ☎Aros(0680) 300347 & 300451

Etr-15 Oct

Jim and Lorna McIntyre's small roadside hotel has a picture-postcard setting at the northern edge of the village, at the side of a stream with a narrow bridge and gardens to the rear of the hotel. The comfortable lounge with a wood-burning stove offers a selection of books and board games, and the small dining room is attractively furnished in pine. Bedrooms are bright, cheerful and comfortable.

6hc sB&B£23-£26 dB&B£40-£46 WB&B£140-£160 WBDi£200-£250 LDO 7.15pm

Lic 🍴 CTV 7P

Credit Cards 1 3

TOBERMORY Map **13** NM55

SELECTED

GH QQQQ Fairways Lodge PA75 6PS ☎(0688) 2238 FAX (0688) 2142

Derek and Kathy McAdam built Fairways Lodge in 1991 on a prime site on Tobermory golf course; the 4th green is very close, and the uninterrupted views down to the Sound of Mull are outstanding. Offering bed and breakfast accommodation only, the emphasis is on providing the highest standard of accommodation: bedrooms are well furnished, tastefully decorated and thoughtfully equipped with several extra touches. There is a small conservatory and an upstairs lounge for guests. Breakfasts are cooked to order with a good choice offered, including porridge and kippers. Those seeking dinner are encouraged to dine at Strongarbh House (see separate entry), also owned by the McAdam family, within 15 minutes' walk.

5⇌↱ (1fb) CTV in all bedrooms ® sB&B⇌↱£28 dB&B⇌↱£56 WB&Bfr£176

🍴 CTV 6P 2🚘 Ⓔ

SELECTED

GH QQQQ Strongarbh House PA75 6PR ☎(0688) 2328 FAX (0688) 2142

The McAdam family converted this fine Victorian house (pronounced Strongarve) to a small restaurant with rooms in 1991, and have retained much of the original character. Leading off the flagstone-floored hall is a comfortable sitting room and the restaurant which is split over 2 rooms, all of them have open fires in winter. The lofty bedrooms are typical of the period, 2 being particularly spacious; they are all very comfortable, with private bathrooms. The house is run by son Ian, who is also chef, and his wife Mhairi. The quality of the food is such that it has earned 2 AA rosettes: the emphasis is on fresh seafood and char-grilled local meats, with a tantalising choice of menu offered. Service is friendly and attentive throughout. The house is surrounded by its own gardens at the end of a quiet lane, high above the harbour with superb views out across the bay.

4⇌↱ CTV in all bedrooms ® dB&B⇌↱£64-£72 WBDifr£348.50 LDO 9.45pm

Lic 🍴 6P 1🚘

Credit Cards 1 3 Ⓔ

MUMBLES West Glamorgan Map **02** SS68

See also Bishopston & Langland Bay

GH QQ Harbour Winds Private Hotel Overland Road, Langland SA3 4LP ☎Swansea(0792) 369298

Situated in an elevated position with garden and sea views, this spacious hotel, with good comfortable bedrooms, has very friendly and welcoming owners. Good food is served in an attractive, panelled dining room, and the lounge is very relaxing.

8rm(1⇌5↱2hc) (3fb) CTV in 5 bedrooms ® ✱

sB&B⇌↱£25-£30 dB&B£46-£50 dB&B⇌↱£50-£60 WBDi£190.40-£210 LDO noon

Lic 🍴 CTV 14P

Credit Cards 1 3

GH Q Mumbles Hotel 650 Mumbles Rd SA3 4EA ☎Swansea(0792) 367147
Closed 23-30 Dec
Well sited in a pretty position overlooking the harbour and with views of the bay, this modest little guesthouse has simple bedrooms to suit the budget end of the market. There is a useful little Bistro open all day during the season. Mumbles Hotel is family owned and run, providing a friendly service.
11rm(4⇌7hc) (1fb) CTV in all bedrooms ® ✱ sB&B£18-£28 sB&B⇌£23-£35 dB&B£28-£35 dB&B⇌£35 LDO 9pm
Lic CTV nc5yrs
Credit Cards [1] [3]

GH QQQ *The Shoreline Hotel* 648 Mumbles Road, Southend SA3 4EA ☎Swansea(0792) 366233
Ideally situated opposite the harbour with commanding views out over the bay, this small and friendly, pretty guesthouse is personally run by the resident owners. The clean, compact bedrooms are equipped to a good standard suitable for both tourist and commercial guests. There is an attractive little restaurant with an open plan bar and lounge.
14rm(5⇌9hc) (1fb) CTV in all bedrooms ® LDO 9.30pm
Lic CTV nc3yrs
Credit Cards [1]

MUNDESLEY Norfolk Map 09 TG33

GH QQQ Manor Hotel NR11 8BG ☎(0263) 720309 FAX (0263) 721731
Closed 2-13 Jan
A red-brick Victorian house perched on the cliffside, with its own beach access and a swimming pool in the gardens. A substantial hotel, it offers a full range of services provided by the Bolton family: the restaurant provides a 4-course table d'hôte menu and full à la carte, produce is fresh and the tasty dishes include a vegetarian choice. There is a spacious lounge and bar and bedrooms are simply furnished, the majority having private bathrooms. This unpretentious hotel provides good value for all ages.
24rm(9⇌12⇌3hc) Annexe 4⇌ (2fb) CTV in 4 bedrooms ® ✱ sB&B£26 sB&B⇌£29.50 dB&B£46 dB&B⇌£49.50 WBDi£125-£185 LDO 9pm
Lic CTV 50P (heated)

MUNGRISDALE Cumbria Map 11 NY33

FH QQQ Mr G Weightman **Near Howe** *(NY286373)* CA11 0SH (1.5m from the A66) ☎Threlkeld(059683) 678
Mar-Nov
This very peacefully located establishment is just one mile from the A66 trunk road, and is a traditional Cumbrian farmhouse standing in 380 acres of moorland. Bedrooms are modern in style and have tea-making facilities and central heating. There is a well stocked bar lounge, and a larger TV lounge with an open fire. Good home-cooked evening meals are available except on Sundays, and guests are offered a warm welcome by enthusiastic hosts Mr and Mrs Weightman.
7rm(5⇌2hc) (3fb) ® (ex guide dogs) LDO 5pm
Lic CTV 10P snooker 350 acres beef sheep

NAILSWORTH Gloucestershire Map 03 ST89

GH QQQ Apple Orchard House Orchard Close, Springhill GL6 0LX ☎(0453) 832503 FAX (0453) 836213
Guests can relax in the pleasant front and rear gardens of this large, modern house, set off Springhill in a small residential cul de sac. The bedrooms are modern in style, and there is a resident's lounge and dining room, which have lovely views over the rear garden to the surrounding countryside.
3⇌ in all bedrooms CTV in all bedrooms ® T ✱ sB&B⇌£18-£22 dB&B⇌£28-£32 WB&Bfr£88
LDO 10am
CTV 3P
Credit Cards [1] [2] £

GH QQ Laurels Inchbrook GL5 5HA ☎Stroud(0453) 834021 FAX (0453) 834004
Closed mid Dec-mid Jan
Personally restored by Mr and Mrs Williams-Allen, who are hospitable hosts, this small and friendly rural guesthouse is a good location for touring and with easy access to the M4 and M5. Its bright, warm bedrooms, wood panelled lounge and bright dining room, provide all round comfortable and cosy accommodation.
4⇌ (2fb) in all bedrooms CTV in all bedrooms ® ✱ sB&B⇌£16-£21 dB&B⇌£27-£32 WB&B£94.50-£126 WBDi£164-£192.50 LDO 7pm
Lic CTV 6P £

NAIRN Highland *Nairnshire* Map 14 NH85

GH QQ Ardgour Hotel Seafield St IV12 4HN ☎(0667) 54230
Mar-Oct
Situated in a quiet residential area not far from the seafront, this family- run holiday hotel has a friendly atmosphere and offers traditional services and comforts.
10hc (2fb) ® sB&B£15-£17 dB&B£26-£30 WB&B£86-£110 WBDi£126-£143 LDO 5pm
CTV 8P

GH QQQ Greenlawns 13 Seafield St IV12 4HG ☎(0667) 52738
Excellent value bed and breakfast accommodation is offered at this comfortably appointed family-run guesthouse, which is situated in a residential area close to the beach and various recreational facilities. Bedrooms are comfortably furnished and well equipped, and the lounge is pleasant and quiet. There is also a well stocked gallery featuring the work of local artists, including paintings by Isobel Caldwell, wife of the proprietor.
6rm(2⇌4hc) CTV in all bedrooms ®
→

CTV 8P
Credit Cards [1] [3]

NANTWICH Cheshire Map **07** SJ65

See also Wybunbury

INN QQ *Wilbraham Arms* Welsh Row CW5 5EW
Crewe(0270) 626419

This 3-storey inn is situated on the A51 Chester road, close to the town centre. The rooms have recently been attractively renovated and now offer modern amenities for both business and tourist guests.

7rm(2 5hc) (1fb) CTV in 8 bedrooms ®
12P

NEAR SAWREY Cumbria Map **07** SD39

GH QQQ Buckle Yeat LA22 0LF
Hawkshead(05394) 36446 & 36538

Illustrated in Beatrix Potters 'Tale of Tom Kitten', this 200-year-old-cottage is situated in the centre of the village and is full of charm and character with its log fires and old beams. The bedrooms are prettily furnished and decorated each complete with TV and tea-making facilities. A very pleasant lounge and a spacious dining room is provided along with warm and friendly service.

6 CTV in all bedrooms ® sB&B £17.50-£18 dB&B £35-£36 WB&B£240
CTV 10P
Credit Cards [1] [2] [3]

SELECTED

GH QQQQ Ees Wyke Country House LA22 0JZ
Hawkshead(05394) 36393

Boasting one of the finest views in all of lakeland over Esthwaite Water, this delightful Georgian country house is set in its own grounds, and offers honest, warm hospitality from the resident owners Mr and Mrs Williams. The bedrooms have individual colour schemes and are prettily furnished with modern style furniture. A recently completed extension includes a spacious restaurant and 2 lounges which are decorated and furnished in Geórgian style, with open log fires and lots of reading material provided.

8 CTV in all bedrooms ® * sB&B £34-£48 dB&B £68-£70 WBDi£306-£316 LDO 7.15pm
Lic 12P nc10yrs £

See advertisement under HAWKSHEAD

SELECTED

GH QQQQ *The Garth* LA22 0JZ
Hawkshead(05394) 36373
Closed Dec & Jan

This fine Victorian house stands in its own grounds overlooking Esthwaite Water and the Langdale mountains. Mr and Mrs Sommerville are the friendly caring proprietors. There is a very comfortable lounge with an open fire and lots of family items around. Dinner, freshly cooked and English-style, is taken in the charming dining room. Bedrooms, three with 4-poster beds, are individually decorated and furnished and some have colour TV.

7rm(2 5hc) (1fb) CTV in 4 bedrooms ® LDO 4pm
Lic CTV 10P nc6yrs

See advertisement under HAWKSHEAD

GH QQ High Green Gate LA22 0LF
Hawkshead(05394) 36296
Mar-Oct rs Xmas & New Year

An 18th-century farmhouse, now a cosy well run guesthouse, set in attractive gardens in a peaceful hamlet.

5rm(1 2 2hc) (4fb) sB&Bfr£19 sB&B fr£22 dB&Bfr£32 dB&B fr£38 WB&B£112-£133 WBDi£155-£173 LDO 6pm
CTV 7P £

GH QQQ *Sawrey House Country Hotel* LA22 0LF
Hawkshead(05394) 36387

An attractive house set in well tended gardens in a quiet village, for many years the home of Beatrix Potter. The house is well furnished and there is a lovely lounge overlooking the gardens.

11rm(7 4hc) (3fb) ® LDO 6pm
Lic CTV 15P croquet lawn

NEATH West Glamorgan Map **03** SS79

GH QQ Europa Hotel 32/34 Victoria Gardens SA11 3BH
(0639) 635094
Closed Xmas

Spotlessly clean and very friendly, this little guesthouse is situated in a convenient town location, overlooking an attractive Victorian park. Personally run by the family owners, it offers good value-for-money accommodation, provided by bright comfortable bedrooms, with TV and tea/coffee making facilities. There is a cosy, inviting lounge and a breakfast room, and also a small car park for guests.

12hc (2fb) CTV in all bedrooms ® (ex guide dogs) sB&Bfr£16 dB&Bfr£30
Lic CTV 3P
Credit Cards [1] [3] £

NEATISHEAD Norfolk Map **09** TG32

GH QQ Regency The Street NR12 8AD
Horning(0692) 630233

A 17th century house situated in a popular and picturesque village, ideal for touring the coast or the Broads. Bedrooms are prettily decorated, comfortable and well maintained; some en suite facilities are available.

5rm(1 1 3hc) (1fb) CTV in all bedrooms ® sB&Bfr£19 sB&B fr£21 dB&Bfr£34 dB&B fr£38
CTV 6P £

NEEDHAM MARKET Suffolk Map **05** TM05

SELECTED

GH QQQQ Pipps Ford Norwich Rd Rdbt IP6 8LJ (entrance off rdbt junct A45/A140)
Coddenham(044979) 208 FAX (044979) 561
Closed Xmas & New Year

At the A45/A140 intersection, with access along a lane off the roundabout, this white, timbered Tudor farmhouse is set in open farmland leading to the River Gipping. The house has a lovely atmosphere with fine furnishings to be used rather than admired. The lounge with its plethora of collectables, includes teapots arranged on gleaming antique furniture, and deep sofas set around the inglenook fireplace. The dining room has a communal table, and there is a vine clad conservatory. Bedrooms are colour themed, for example Hollyhock is in pretty pinks, with upholstered ladies' chairs, a hand-made patchwork quilt and period furniture against a 4-poster bed. Morning Glory is blue, with a provincial French upholstered bed and Louis XIV style sofa; a spotlight vanity unit with a double wash hand basin and corner bath. Raewyn Hackett-Jones from New Zealand is a delightful host.

3 Annexe 4 in all bedrooms ® (ex guide dogs) sB&B£17 dB&B £52-£58 WB&B£174.50-£195.50 WBDi£279.50-£300.50 LDO 5pm
Lic CTV 12P nc5yrs (hard)
Credit Cards [3]

NETLEY Hampshire Map **04** SU40

GH QQ La Casa Blanca SO3 5DQ
☎Southampton(0703) 453718
Closed Xmas & New Year
This, cheerful, white, terraced house is only a short walk from Southampton Water and 3 miles from the town centre. Bright, well equipped bedrooms are on several levels, and there is a well stocked bar and a patio downstairs.
10rm(1⇌9hc) (1fb) CTV in all bedrooms ® **T**
⋈ (ex guide dogs) ✱ sB&B£21 sB&B⇌£32 dB&B£34 dB&B⇌£42 WB&B£119-£147 WBDi£154-£182 LDO 9.30pm
Lic ᵭ CTV 2P 1🚗 £

NETTLEBED Oxfordshire Map **04** SU68

GH QQQ *Chessall Shaw* Newnham Hill RG9 5TN (2.5m S)
☎(0491) 641311 FAX (0491) 641819
A comfortable family home set in a peaceful wooded valley, with beautifully kept terraced gardens and an outdoor covered swimming pool. The house is situated on Newnham Hill, just 10 minutes from Henley-on-Thames and convenient for Heathrow Airport. The 2 very comfortable bedrooms are tastefully decorated and furnished, and every facility imaginable has been provided, from ironing boards to sewing kits. The pleasant lounge has a piano and a selction of books, and 1 large table is shared in the dining room, where home-cooked dinners and breakfasts are served.
2⇌⇌ (2fb) CTV in all bedrooms ® LDO am
ᵭ CTV 6P ⌂ ⌂(heated) ℘(hard)

NETTLECOMBE Dorset Map **03** SY59

INN QQ The Marquis of Lorne DT6 3SY
☎Powerstock(030885) 236
Closed 25 Dec
Filled with character, this quiet 16th-century inn is complemented by its peaceful, rural setting. The cosy bars are complete with log fires, where a lengthy menu is available. A spacious, nicely furnished dining room offers a more extensive menu, including tempting dishes prepared with skill by Mr Bone. The bedrooms are simply furnished, freshly decorated and offer good value for money.
6rm(4⇌2hc) (2fb) CTV in 1 bedroom ® ⋈ (ex guide dogs) ✱ sB&B£12.50-£23 sB&B⇌£12.50-£25 dB&B£25-£46 dB&B⇌£25-£50 WB&B£122.50-£140 WBDi£175-£217 Lunch £13.50-£19.95alc Dinner £13.50-£19.95alc LDO 9.30pm
CTV 65P
Credit Cards 1 3 £

NETTLETON Wiltshire Map **03** ST87

SELECTED

GH QQQQ Fosse Farmhouse Country Hotel Nettleton Shrub SN14 7NJ ☎Castle Combe(0249) 782286
FAX (0249) 783066
Deep in the heart of Beaufort hunt country, this attractive 18th-century, Cotswold stone farmhouse is situated close to many areas of interest. The en suite bedrooms are decorated in simple Victorian style and furnished with lovely antique pieces blending nicely with pretty English chintz bed covers. Three rooms are in the main house and the remainder above the tea room across the garden in the converted stables. There is a snug lounge and home cooked meals and teas are served throughout the day in one of the dining rooms, where gingham cloths, open fires and exposed beams give a unique character to the old building.
2⇌⇌ Annexe 3⇌ CTV in all bedrooms ® LDO 8.30pm
Lic ᵭ 10P ⌂ ▶18
Credit Cards 1 2 3

NEWARK-ON-TRENT Nottinghamshire

See **Kirton**

NEWBOLD ON STOUR Warwickshire Map **04** SP24

FH QQ Mrs J M Everett **Newbold Nurseries** *(SP253455)* CV37 8DP ☎(0789) 450285
Mar-29 Oct
A modern farmhouse with a long, pine-tree-lined drive offering spacious, simply appointed bed and breakfast accommodation. Convenient for tourists, it is situated half a mile north of the A429 roundabout on the A34.
2rm(1hc) (1fb) CTV in all bedrooms ® ✱ dB&Bfr£28
ᵭ CTV 2P 25 acres arable tomato nursery £

NEWBROUGH Northumberland Map **12** NY86

GH QQ *The Stanegate* NE47 5AR ☎Hexham(0434) 674241
In the centre of the peaceful village, this attractive stone-built house provides comfortable accommodation, and a popular restaurant offering an interesting daily changing menu.
3⇌ ⊬in all bedrooms CTV in all bedrooms
ᵭ 10P
Credit Cards 1 3

NEWBY BRIDGE Cumbria Map **07** SD38

GH QQ Furness Fells LA12 8ND ☎(05395) 31260
Mar-Oct
A friendly family-run guesthouse with pleasant gardens near the southern outfall of Lake Windermere. It offers well furnished and comfortable accommodation.
3hc ® ⋈ ✱ dB&B£27 WB&B£88
Lic ᵭ CTV 4P nc3yrs £

NEWCASTLE-UNDER-LYME Staffordshire Map 07 SJ84

GH QQQ Clayton Farmhouse The Green, Clayton ST5 4AA ☎(0782) 620401

An attractive 18th-century farmhouse with open fires and exposed timbers, just one and a half miles from the town centre on the A519 half a mile from junction 15 of the M6. Bedrooms are quite spacious and well furnished, and 2 lounges are available for residents.

5rm(1⇌2↱2hc) (2fb) CTV in all bedrooms ® ✗ (ex guide dogs) sB&B£22 sB&B⇌↱£24-£26 dB&B£32 dB&B⇌↱£34-£36 LDO 1pm

CTV 12P

Credit Cards 1 3 £

GH QQ Durlston Kimberley Rd, Cross Heath ST5 9EG ☎Stoke-On-Trent(0782) 611708

This bright and cosy guesthouse is conveniently situated off the A34, just north of the town centre. Run by the friendly Stott family, bedrooms are modern and there is a comfortable lounge for residents where drinks are served.

7hc (2fb)⊬in all bedrooms CTV in all bedrooms ® ✱ sB&B£18 dB&B£33 WB&B£120

Lic CTV

Credit Cards 1 3 £

NEWCASTLE UPON TYNE Tyne & Wear Map 12 NZ26

GH QQQ Chirton House Hotel 46 Clifton Rd NE4 6XH ☎091-273 0407

Standing in its own grounds in a residential area west of the city centre, this large semidetached Victorian house is reached by turning off the A186 opposite the hospital. Individually decorated bedrooms vary in size, but some are spacious and comfortable, with modern shower rooms. Public areas include a cosy bar and comfortable lounges, one of which is for non-smokers.

11rm(2⇌3↱6hc) (3fb) CTV in all bedrooms ® ✱ sB&B£24-£26 sB&B⇌↱fr£34 dB&Bfr£40 dB&B⇌↱fr£50 WB&B£150-£230 WBDi£200-£280 LDO 5.30pm

Lic CTV 12P

Credit Cards 1 3 £

GH QQ *The George Hotel* 88 Osborne Rd, Jesmond NE2 2AP ☎091-281 4442 FAX 091-281 8300

14rm(11⇌↱) (4fb)⊬in 2 bedrooms

GH QQQ *The Rise* The Rise, Woolsington NE13 8BN ☎Tyneside091-286 4963

Adjoining the airport, and with easy access to the A1, this impressive house stands in its own well tended gardens. Individually styled bedrooms are modern, colour coordinated and offer many little extras. Public areas are more traditional, with solid furniture, comfortable seating and tasteful bric-à- brac creating a restful and relaxing atmosphere. This is a totally no smoking house.

5rm(2↱3hc) ⊬in all bedrooms CTV in all bedrooms ✗

7P 2🚗 (£2 per day)

NEWDIGATE Surrey Map 04 TQ14

GH Q Woods Hill Country Village St RH5 5AD ☎(030677) 437

Simple, compact accommodation is offered at this guesthouse, with 2 rooms having en suite facilities. There is a small breakfast room, or early risers can have a continental breakfast served in their room. A full English breakfast is available on request. Snacks are available throughout the day, and car parking can be arranged for those guests flying from Gatwick.

4rm(2⇌↱2hc) (2fb)⊬in all bedrooms CTV in all bedrooms ® ✗ sB&Bfr£40 sB&B⇌↱fr£40 dB&Bfr£54 dB&B⇌↱fr£54

CTV 10P

Credit Cards 1 3

NEWHAVEN East Sussex Map 05 TQ40

GH QQ *Harbour View* 22 Mount Rd BN9 0LS ☎Brighton(0273) 512096

A small bungalow personally run by the resident proprietors, with a relaxed atmosphere. Three well equipped bedrooms share a bathroom with a shower and separate WC. This is a popular overnight stay for people using the ferry. It is situated on the eastern edge of town off the A259 to Seaford: turn north from the A259 signed for Denton, then immediately right; Mount road is the 2nd turning on the left.

3hc (2fb)⊬in 2 bedrooms CTV in 2 bedrooms TV in 1 bedroom ® ✗ (ex guide dogs)

3P

GH QQQ Newhaven Marina Yacht Club Hotel Fort Gate, Fort Rd BN9 9DR ☎(0273) 513976 FAX (0273) 517990

Closed 3 wks Jan

The Newhaven Marina offers bright, fresh bedrooms with modern furniture and attractive co-ordinated fabrics. The Yacht Club bar is open to residents and an extensive range of bar food is available. The Riverside Restaurant has an à la carte menu featuring fresh fish. There are views of the docks and marina from the terrace.

7rm(1↱6hc) CTV in all bedrooms ® ✗ (ex guide dogs) ✱ sB&B£28-£42 sB&B⇌↱£42 dB&B£42 dB&B⇌↱£50 WB&B£190 LDO 9.30pm/10.30pm

Lic 50P marina facilities

Credit Cards 1 3

NEWLYN EAST Cornwall & Isles of Scilly Map 02 SW85

GH QQQ Trewerry Mill Trerice TR8 5HS ☎Mitchell(0872) 510345

Good Friday-Oct

Quietly located in 7 acres of land, displaying beautiful, well tended gardens filled with pretty and unusual plants, this attractive property dates back to 1639 and was originally a water-powered mill. The comfortable bedrooms are nicely coordinated and many enjoy attractive garden views. There are cosy, comfortable public areas with lots of character and charm, where home-cooked meals are served, prepared with fresh, organically grown fruit and vegetables whenever possible. This no-smoking establishment has a friendly atmosphere and upholds very thorough standards of housekeeping.

6rm (1fb)⊬in all bedrooms ✗ ✱ sB&B£13.75-£15.75 dB&B£27.50-£31.50 WBDi£134.75-£148.75 LDO 9am

Lic CTV 12P nc7yrs

FH QQQ Mrs K Woodley **Degembris** *(SW852568)* TR8 5HY ☎Mitchell(0872) 510555

Etr-Oct

A listed, 18th-century Delabole slate-built farmhouse in a peaceful rural location. The bedrooms are bright and attractive and all now have colour TV. There is a comfortable lounge and home-cooked farmhouse fare is served in the character dining room. Degembris offers easy access to the beaches of the north coast of Cornwall.

5hc (2fb) CTV in all bedrooms ® ✗ sB&Bfr£15 dB&Bfr£30 WB&Bfr£105 WBDifr£161 LDO 10am

CTV 8P 165 acres arable

NEWMARKET Suffolk Map 05 TL66

See also Kirtling

GH QQQ Live & Let Live 76 High St, Stetchworth CB8 9TJ ☎(0638) 508153

Closed 20 Dec-3 Jan

The Live & Let Live is less than a mile south of Newmarket in a central village location, and the whitewashed flintstone walls of the original inn are easily spotted. Mr and Mrs Human have furnished each of the bedrooms with great care and attention to detail. The décor and fabrics are colour coordinated down to the towels, and the rooms are strikingly fresh and clean. Guests take breakfast in the small dining room with a dark wood polished table and

cottage-style walls, and smoking is permitted only in the first-floor lounge.
7rm(2⇨↱5hc) (1fb)⊬in all bedrooms ® ✗ sB&B£17-£18 sB&B⇨↱£24-£25 dB&B£32-£34 dB&B⇨↱£36-£38
Ⓜ CTV 5P nc10yrs
Credit Cards [1] [3] £

NEWPORT Gwent Map **03** ST38

GH QQ Caerleon House Hotel Caerau Rd NP9 4HJ
☎(0633) 264869
This well maintained guesthouse has been run for many years by the very friendly Powell family, and it is within walking distance of the town centre. The bedrooms are modern and all have private bathrooms. There is a small bar/lounge for residents.
7⇨↱ (1fb) CTV in all bedrooms ® sB&B⇨↱£25-£30 dB&B⇨↱£40-£45 LDO 9pm
Lic Ⓜ 8P

GH QQQ Kepe Lodge 46a Caerau Rd NP9 4HH
☎(0633) 262351
Closed 22-31 Dec
This neat, well maintained house is set back from the road with a tree-lined private drive, a short walk from the town centre. A comfortable lounge is available for residents, and bedrooms are all well furnished and equipped.
8rm(3↱5hc) CTV in all bedrooms ® ✗ (ex guide dogs) ✱ sB&B£18-£21 sB&B↱£21 dB&B↱£32
Ⓜ 8P £

GH QQ Knoll 145 Stow Hill NP9 4FZ ☎(0633) 263557
Situated near the main shopping centre on Stow Hill, this large Victorian house retains many of its original features. It offers comfortable and well-equipped bedrooms and a spacious, relaxing guest lounge.

→

9rm(7⇌↱2hc) (2fb) CTV in all bedrooms ® T ✳ sB&B£18-£21 sB&B⇌↱£18-£21 dB&Bfr£32
🍽 6🚗

NEWPORT Shropshire Map **07** SJ71

INN QQ ***Fox & Duck*** Pave Ln TF10 9LQ
☎Telford(0952) 825580
A large roadside inn on the old A41, one mile south of the town centre, close to Lilleshall National Sports Centre. The majority of rooms have en suite facilities, but 2 rooms lack wash basins and share a shower room. A smart function room is available for business and social gatherings.
9rm(7⇌↱) (1fb)⚟in all bedrooms CTV in all bedrooms ®
✗ (ex guide dogs) LDO 10pm
🍽 75P
Credit Cards 1 3

NEWQUAY Cornwall & Isles of Scilly Map **02** SW86

See **Town Plan Section**
See also Newlyn East

GH QQ Aloha 124 Henver Rd TR7 3EQ
☎(0637) 878366
Closed annual holidays
This well-maintained guesthouse is conveniently located on the A3058 Henver road, and has been skilfully extended to provide a new conservatory and a very well appointed bar. Bedrooms are all furnished in the modern style, each with TV and tea-making facilities. There is a comfortable TV lounge, a separate games room with pool and darts, a rear garden and ample parking space on the forecourt. Home-cooked food is offered on an à la carte menu, and friendly service is personally provided by the proprietors.
14rm(6↱8hc) (6fb) CTV in all bedrooms ® sB&B£11-£15 sB&B↱£13-£18 dB&B£22-£30 dB&B↱£26-£34 WB&B£66-£115 WBDi£90-£165 LDO 6pm
Lic 🍽 CTV 14P
Credit Cards 1 3 £

GH QQ Arundell Hotel Mount Wise TR7 2BS
☎(0637) 872481
This very informal, family-run hotel has recently been renovated, and offers excellent indoor facilities. The spacious bar has live entertainment and dancing, and an entertainment programme is provided six nights a week throughout the main season. The bedrooms are slowly being upgraded.
36⇌↱ (8fb) CTV in all bedrooms ® T ✳ sB&B⇌↱£19-£27 dB&B⇌↱£38-£54 WB&B£114-£177 WBDi£142-£205 LDO 6pm
Lic lift 🍽 CTV 32P 8🚗 ⛆(heated) snooker sauna solarium gymnasium
Credit Cards 1 2 3

GH QQ Bon-Ami Hotel 3 Trenance Ln TR7 2HX
☎(0637) 874009
Apr-Sep
This well established family-run guesthouse is set in a very peaceful location overlooking the boating lakes and park. Some bedrooms are rather compact but are furnished in the modern style, and public rooms include a small TV lounge, a bar, sun porch and spacious dining room. Varied menus, extensive service and good value are provided by the friendly and helpful proprietors.
9↱ ® ✗ sB&B↱£16-£19.50 dB&B↱£32-£39 WB&B£109-£133.50 WBDi£137-£161.50 LDO 8pm
Lic 🍽 CTV 9P nc11yrs £

GH QQQ Claremont House 35 Trebarwith Crescent TR7 1DX ☎(0637) 875383
Completely upgraded by the new proprietors Mr and Mrs Nunns, the accommodation here offers particularly good value for money, and easy access to the bay and beach. Extensive service is available, including afternoon teas, and the cooking is done by Mr Nunns. There is a small lounge, a delightful little dining room with a residential license, and well furnished bedrooms which vary in shape and size.
7rm(3↱4hc) (3fb) ® ✗ (ex guide dogs) sB&B£15-£19 dB&B£30-£36 dB&B↱£32-£40 WB&B£75-£140 WBDi£95-£165 LDO 4pm
Lic 🍽 CTV £

GH QQQ ***Copper Beech Hotel*** 70 Edgcumbe Av TR7 2NN
☎(0637) 873376
Etr-mid Oct
A well maintained guesthouse occupying a fine location directly opposite Trenance Gardens and tennis courts and run by the Lentern family for over 19 years. Spacious public rooms include a very comfortable bar lounge, and a bright no-smoking, narrow dining room. Bedrooms are modern, bright and airy, with a choice of some family rooms: the accommodation is beautifully maintained to a high standard throughout. There is a large car parking area on the fore-court.
14rm(3⇌11↱) (3fb) ® ✗ LDO 6pm
Lic 🍽 CTV 14P

GH QQ ***Hepworth Hotel*** 27 Edgcumbe Av TR7 2NJ
☎(0637) 873686
Apr-Oct
A well maintained guesthouse comprising modern, bright, double-glazed bedrooms, a cosy, comfortable TV lounge, a cheerful dining room and a separate bar. Outside there is a sun lounge and front garden, and cream teas are available on sunny days. This modern family hotel is in a good location set back from the front but still within walking distance of local amenities. Good car parking facilities are available.
13rm(4↱9hc) (4fb) CTV in all bedrooms ® ✗ LDO 6.30pm
Lic 🍽 CTV 12P

GH QQ ***Kellsboro Hotel*** 12 Henver Rd TR7 3BJ
☎(0637) 874620
Etr-Oct
Friendly and long established, the Kellsboro offers generous public areas and good indoor leisure facilities. Bright, simply furnished bedrooms vary in shape and size and have very good quality en suite facilities. The lounge bar features regular evening entertainment in the summer, and a video film lounge is provided. Good forecourt parking facilities are available.
14rm(10⇌3↱1hc) (8fb)⚟in all bedrooms CTV in all bedrooms ® LDO 7pm
Lic 🍽 20P ⛆(heated)

GH QQ ***Links Hotel*** Headland Rd TR7 1HN ☎(0637) 873211
Apr-Oct
Conveniently located on the Towan Headland, within easy reach of the town, beaches and golf course, this hotel has some rooms with views of the golf course and the sea. Bedrooms are simply furnished and equipped, well maintained and bright, with simple décor. The friendly and informal atmosphere is augmented by a lively bar, pool room and reception facilities.
15rm(10⇌3↱2hc) (3fb) CTV in all bedrooms ® LDO 4pm
Lic 🍽 CTV ⱣP

GH QQQ Pendeen Hotel Alexandra Road, Porth TR7 3ND
☎(0637) 873521
Closed Nov
Enjoying a very good position directly opposite Porth beach, this long- established family-run hotel has built up a reputation for comfort, good food and personal service. The brightly decorated bedrooms are furnished in a modern style, all equipped with TV, tea making facilities and a choice of en suite shower or bathroom. There is a small, well furnished reading lounge and a very popular bar lounge. The attractive, alcoved dining room offers a menu that changes daily, with alternative home-made dishes always available, supplemented by packed lunches, teas and light refreshments throughout the day, all of which can be enjoyed on the sun terrace. A generous full English breakfast is included in the tariff. Good car parking facilities are provided.

15rm(6⇌9↱) (5fb)⊁in 3 bedrooms CTV in all bedrooms ® ✈ (ex guide dogs) ✻ sB&B⇌↱£18.50-£23 dB&B⇌↱£35-£40 WB&B£99-£172 WBDi£120-£192 LDO 6pm
Lic ♨ 15P
Credit Cards [1] [3] £

GH QQQ Porth Enodoc 4 Esplanade Road, Pentire TR7 1PY
☎(0637) 872372
Apr-Oct
Well located overlooking Fistral beach, this elegant property is very well managed by professional proprietors Mr and Mrs Lawson, who have recently taken over. Carefully extended over the years, the accommodation is very neat, clean and well turned out, with spotless en suites in every room. There is a comfortable lounge and a cosy bar, plus the pretty dining room where evening meals are appreciated by guests. A cheerful and relaxed atmosphere prevails throughout this friendly hotel.
15↱ (3fb) TV available ✈ sB&B↱£18.75-£21.35 dB&B↱£37.50-£42.70 WBDi£131.75-£165.70 LDO 6.45pm
Lic ♨ CTV 15P

GH QQQ Priory Lodge Hotel Mount Wise TR7 2BH
☎(0637) 874111
Apr-Oct & Xmas rs Mar & Nov
This converted vicarage beside the church has been skilfully extended and modernised. It comprises comfortable bedrooms, all with metered colour TV, and well proportioned public rooms including a wood panelled lounge and sitting areas, a large dining room with a popular menu, and a bar which features live entertainment and dancing. Four annexe bedrooms overlook the swimming pool and sun terrace, and other facilities include a coin operated laundry and good forecourt parking.
22rm(7⇌13↱2hc) Annexe 4↱ (17fb) CTV in all bedrooms ® **T** ✈ (ex guide dogs) sB&B£31-£33 dB&B£62-£66 dB&B⇌↱£70-£74 (incl dinner) WB&B£150-£170 WBDi£160-£200 LDO 7.30pm
Lic ♨ 30P ⛆(heated) sauna solarium pool table video machines
Credit Cards [1] [3] £

GH QQ Rolling Waves Alexandra Rd, Porth TR7 3NB
☎(0637) 873236
Etr-Nov Closed 2 days Xmas rs Dec-Etr
Situated between Whipsiderry and Porth beaches, this lovely guesthouse has a very pleasant sea view and good access to the sandy beach. Although the bedrooms are on the small side, they are all well furnished and equipped with TV and tea making facilities – convenient ground floor bedrooms are available for the less able. The delightful dining room, complete with a dispense bar, is adorned with wall ornaments and prominent blue tablecloths, where a daily menu offering professional standards of cooking is served. There is a very sunny, double aspect lounge, where cream teas and light refreshments are usually available. Outside there is a nice garden and private car parking is provided.
10rm(6↱4hc) (3fb) CTV in all bedrooms ® sB&B£19.50-£21 sB&B↱£22-£23.50 dB&B£39-£42 dB&B↱£41-£44 WB&B£130-£160 WBDi£146-£185 LDO 6.30pm
Lic CTV 10P
Credit Cards [1] [3] £

GH QQQ Tir Chonaill Lodge 106 Mount Wise TR7 1QP
☎(0637) 876492
Friendly service and value-for-money holiday accommodation are provided by Mr and Mrs Watts at Tir Chonaill. Bedrooms are bright and simple, and most of them have en suite facilities. Public areas are comfortable and the atmosphere is relaxed.
20rm(8⇌12↱) (9fb) CTV in all bedrooms ® sB&B⇌↱£14.50-£20 dB&B⇌↱£28-£40 WB&B£100-£140 WBDi£125-£162 LDO 5pm
Lic ♨ CTV 20P darts pool £

SELECTED

GH QQQQ Towan Beach Hotel 7 Trebarwith Crescent TR7 1DX ☎(0637) 872093

rs Oct-1 Apr

This delightful small terraced guesthouse has been completely renovated and redecorated and is situated in the town centre in a quiet position. Bedrooms vary in size and are light, bright and modern; 3 rooms have private bathrooms and they all have showers, TV, tea-making facilities and clock radios. There is an elegant, well-furnished drawing room with an open fire, and a small conservatory bar. The resident chef/proprietor Andrew Medhurst provides a good choice of menu having worked on the QE2, and meals are served in the candlelit dining room. His partner Tony Baker ensures that guests are well looked after. Barbeques are also provided on the patio on warm summer evenings. Limited car parking can be arranged and the house is very conveniently situated within walking distance of the shops, beach, buses and railway station. The personal attention to details and excellent service provide outstanding value for money.

6rm(3↱3hc) (1fb) CTV in all bedrooms ® ✗ (ex guide dogs) sB&B£19-£26 sB&B↱£21-£28 dB&B£38-£52 dB&B↱£42-£56 (incl dinner) WB&B£85-£139 WBDi£125-£174 LDO 4.30pm

Lic 卌 CTV 2P nc8yrs

Credit Cards 1 3 £

GH QQQ Wheal Treasure Hotel 72 Edgcumbe Av TR7 2NN ☎(0637) 874136

Apr-mid Oct

Standing in its own grounds overlooking Trenance Gardens and boating lake, this elegant, well maintained detached house has been tastefully furnished to a good standard throughout. The bar and lounge have been extended with a new conservatory, and the attractive dining room is kept a 'no smoking' area. There are several family bedrooms available, and good car parking facilities are provided. Mr Franks does the cooking, and service is friendly and very helpful.

12rm(3⇌8↱1hc) (3fb) ® ✗ sB&B£12-£19 sB&B⇌↱£15-£20 dB&B£24-£38 dB&B⇌↱£30-£40 WB&B£115-£140 WBDi£140-£167.50 LDO 5pm

Lic 卌 CTV 10P nc3yrs £

SELECTED

GH QQQQ Windward Hotel Alexandra Road, Porth TR7 3NB ☎(0637) 873185

This very smart, newly designed hotel stands in an elevated position and enjoys lovely views across to Newquay, Porth beach and beyond. The building has been completely renovated and is now exceptionally well presented. The bedrooms are all en suite, with smart modern facilities, mostly showers. Each room is very tastefully furnished with comfort in mind; great care has been taken to coordinate the pretty fabrics, and although compact, they are well serviced and some have some fine views. Public areas are equally well appointed: there is a cosy bar with a quiet TV lounge adjoining, and the bright dining room overlooks the bay. Wholesome and tasty traditional English meals are cooked using fresh local produce. There is a large car park at the rear and the hotel has much to commend it, with very friendly proprietors Carol and Maurice Sparrow providing tremendous care and hospitality.

14⇌↱ (3fb) CTV in all bedrooms ® ✗ (ex guide dogs) dB&B⇌↱£46-£60 WB&B£132-£187 WBDi£160-£215 LDO 6.30pm

Lic 卌 CTV 14P

Credit Cards 1 3 £

FH QQQ J C Wilson **Manuels** *(SW839601)* Ln TR8 4NY ☎(0637) 873577

Closed 23 Dec-1 Jan

Remotely situated in a wooded valley 3 miles from Newquay, this ancient cottage-style farmhouse dates in part from 1617. Family bedrooms offer additional sleeping areas suitable for children, and good bath and shower facilities are available. There is a traditional lounge and a beamed dining room with a large communal table where home produce is usually featured on the menu.

4hc (2fb)⊬in all bedrooms ® ✗ (ex guide dogs) WB&B£98-£119 WBDi£150-£200 LDO 4pm

卌 CTV 6P 44 acres mixed £

NEW QUAY Dyfed Map **02** SN35

SELECTED

GH QQQQ Park Hall Hotel Cwmtydu SA44 6LG ☎(0545) 560306

Once a Victorian gentleman's residence, Park Hall is set amidst 4.5 acres of lawns and woodlands in the picturesque valley of Cwm Tydu. The attractive conservatory restaurant looks out over these lawns with views down to a small cove. There is a fixed price, set menu available, augmented with a small à la carte, featuring such dishes as poached salmon in smoked salmon sauce or kebab of Welsh lamb with cranberry sauce, and Welsh cheeses are much in evidence. As well as the comfortable sitting room, a bar furnished with Chesterfields and antique armchairs, provides ample space to relax. The bedrooms all have en suite bathrooms, with many still retaining the original fireplace and one featuring an antique 4 poster. A warm welcome is extended to all guests by the very friendly McDonnell family.

5⇌↱ ⊬in 1 bedroom CTV in all bedrooms ® ✱ dB&B⇌↱fr£70 (incl dinner) WBDi£245 LDO 7.30pm

Lic 卌 CTV 20P ⤹ U

Credit Cards 1 2 3 5 £

FH QQQ Mr M Kelly **Ty Hen** *(SN365553)* Llwyndafydd SA44 6BZ (S of Cross Inn, A486) ☎(0545) 560346

mid Feb-mid Nov

This old farmhouse is situated 2 miles west of the A487. Modern bedrooms have been created in the old house and in adjoining outbuildings. A separate complex houses the bar and restaurant facilities, and this now includes a fully equipped leisure centre.

5↱ Annexe 2↱ (2fb)⊬in 5 bedrooms CTV in all bedrooms ® ✱ sB&B↱£20-£29 dB&B↱£40-£58 WB&B£120-£190 LDO 6pm

Lic 卌 CTV 20P ▭(heated) sauna solarium gymnasium bowls & skittles 40 acres sheep

Credit Cards 1 3

NEW ROMNEY Kent Map **05** TR02

GH Q ***Blue Dolphins Hotel & Restaurant*** Dymchurch Rd TN28 8BE ☎(0679) 63224

An historic small hotel parts of which date back to circa 1507. The recently renovated bar/lounge augments a popular candlelit à la carte restaurant which features an interesting choice of dishes and wines. Bedrooms vary considerably according to age: the best have the original beams and fireplace, and there are 2 modest ground floor rooms. Service is supervised by the very friendly and helpful Mrs Vivien Dallas, whilst her son Mark is now responsible for most of the cooking. Car parking is available at the rear of the hotel.

8hc (1fb) CTV in 9 bedrooms ® ✗ (ex guide dogs) LDO 9.30pm

Lic 卌 CTV 15P

Credit Cards 1 3

NEWTON Northumberland Map **12** NZ06

FH Q Mrs C M Leech **Crookhill** *(NZ056654)* NE43 7UX ☎Stocksfield(0661) 843117

rs Nov-Mar

A stone-built farmhouse set in an elevated position overlooking open countryside, close to the A69. Well furnished and comfortable, it offers friendly service.

3rm(1hc) (1fb)⊁in all bedrooms ® ⋊ ✱ sB&B£15 dB&B£28-£30 WB&B£84

▥ CTV 4P 23 acres beef mixed sheep (£)

NEWTON ABBOT Devon Map **03** SX87

GH QQ Lamorna Ideford Combe TQ13 0AR (3m N A380) ☎(0626) 65627

A compact, cosy, modern guesthouse offering bed and breakfast accommodation. There are attractive rural views and pleasant gardens available to guests. Smoking is not permitted in the dining room. To find the house, follow signs for Ideford Combe off the A380 Exeter-Torquay dual carriageway, about 3 miles from Newton Abbot.

6hc (1fb) CTV in 2 bedrooms TV in 4 bedrooms ®
⋊ (ex guide dogs) ✱ sB&B£18-£20 dB&B£32-£36 WB&B£112-£126 LDO 6pm

Lic ▥ CTV 15P ⊡(heated)

NEWTOWN Powys Map **06** SO19

FH QQQ David & Sue Jones **Dyffryn** *(SO052954)* Dyffryn, Aberhafesp SY16 3JD ☎(0686) 688817

Dyffryn (valley in English) is a carefully restored half timbered barn dating back to the 17th century. It lies within a working farm along the banks of a small stream called Nant Rhyd Rhoslaw. David and Sue Jones are the welcoming hosts and guests have the freedom of nature walks and, of course, the farm. The exterior and every room boasts a wealth of exposed timbers, and the lounge, with a brick inglenook fireplace, overlooks the stream. Three en suite bedrooms are available, quite spacious with pretty duvet-covered beds and comfortable armchairs. Furniture is mostly pine, and full modern room facilities are on hand. As well as a hearty Welsh breakfast, a 2-choice 3- course dinner is available with an additional vegetarian choice. The house is totally no-smoking, and can be a little difficult to find – situated off the B4568 west of the town (OS reference 052954 essential).

3🛁 ⊁in all bedrooms CTV in all bedrooms ®
⋊ (ex guide dogs) ✱ sB&B🛁£16-£20 dB&B🛁£32-£40 WB&B£112-£140 WBDi£182-£210 LDO 5pm

▥ CTV 3P ⚘ 100 acres beef sheep

NITON

See **WIGHT, ISLE OF**

NORTHALLERTON North Yorkshire Map **08** SE39

GH QQQ Alverton 26 South Pde DL7 8SG ☎(0609) 776207

An attractive Victorian terraced house conveniently situated midway between the railway station and town centre. The rooms are comfortably furnished, and all have TV, radio and tea making facilities; 3 rooms have private bathrooms with a shower and WC. There is a spacious lounge, and the dining room is attractively appointed.

5rm(3🚿2hc) (1fb) CTV in all bedrooms ® ⋊ (ex guide dogs) sB&B£16.50-£18 sB&B🚿£23 dB&B🚿£33.50-£37 WB&B£115.50-£126 WBDi£178.50-£188.65 LDO 1pm

▥ CTV 4P (£)

GH QQ Porch House 68 High St DL7 8EG ☎(0609) 779831

This historic house, situated opposite the church, was built in 1584 and used by Charles I when he was in the area. Modernised in recent years, although still retaining many beams and other original features, it now provides comfortable accomodation in 5 traditional bedrooms, all with private bathrooms. There is also a pleasant lounge with beams and a stone-flagged floor, and an attractive period dining room, with a large communal table.

5🚿 (1fb) CTV in all bedrooms ® **T** ✱ sB&B🚿£24-£28 dB&B🚿£42 WB&B£147-£196 WBDi£209-£252 LDO 4pm

Lic ▥ CTV 8P

Credit Cards [1] [3] (£)

GH QQ Windsor 56 South Pde DL7 8SL ☎(0609) 774100

Closed 24 Dec-2 Jan

This Victorian terraced house is situated just south of the town centre and is convenient for the railway station. Bedrooms are decorated with pretty wallpaper and fabrics, and are thoughtfully furnished and equipped. Public rooms include a comfortable lounge and an attractive dining room provided with pink linen cloths and fresh flowers.

6rm(2🚿4hc) (1fb) CTV in all bedrooms ® sB&B£20 sB&B🚿£25 dB&B£30 dB&B🚿£36 WB&B£140-£175 WBDi£196-£231 LDO 3pm

▥ CTV

Credit Cards [1] [3]

NORTHAMPTON Northamptonshire Map **04** SP76

GH Q Hollington 22 Abington Grove NN1 4QW ☎0604 32584

This predominantly commercial guesthouse is in a residential area, not far from the town centre. The accommodation is modest with no en suite but bathroom facilities are provided. There is a dining room where breakfast only is served. The friendly owners make guests very welcome.

7hc (2fb) CTV in all bedrooms ® sB&B£16-£18 dB&B£25-£30

▥ (£)

GH QQQ Poplars Hotel Cross Street, Moulton NN3 1RZ ☎(0604) 643983

Closed Xmas wk

In a quiet village location, this family-run hotel is only 4 miles from Northampton. Continued improvements result in comfortable bedrooms with a good range of modern facilities. Public areas include a cosy dining room and a television lounge. Personal →

service is provided by friendly proprietors, Peter and Rosemary Gillies.
21rm(2⇌13♠6hc) (4fb) CTV in all bedrooms ® ✱ sB&B£25 sB&B⇌♠£35 dB&B⇌♠£45 WB&B£245 WBDi£315
LDO 6pm
Lic 🏨 CTV 22P
Credit Cards [1] [3] £

NORTH BERWICK Lothian *East Lothian* Map **12** NT58

GH Q Cragside 16 Marine Pde EH39 4LD ☎(0620) 2879
Good value accommodation is provided at this friendly family-run guesthouse. Overlooking the Firth of Forth, the attractive white-painted semidetached villa is on the seafront and is very convenient for the putting green, golf club and tennis courts.
4hc ® ✗ ✱ sB&Bfr£17 dB&Bfr£34 WB&Bfr£97.50
🏨 CTV ₱

NORTH DUFFIELD North Yorkshire Map **08** SE63

FH QQ Mrs A Arrand ***Hall*** *(SE692375)* YO8 7RY
☎Selby(0757) 288301
Etr-Sep
Set in flat, open countryside to the northeast of the village, this is a brick-built Yorkshire farmhouse, offering a sound standard of accommodation. The bedrooms are simply furnished and all have wash-basins. A separate lounge is available and dining is at a large communal table.
3hc (2fb)⊁in all bedrooms ✗
🏨 CTV P 170 acres arable sheep

NORTH ELMHAM Norfolk Map **09** TF92

INN QQQ *Kings Head Hotel* Crossroads NR20 5JE
☎(0362) 668856
This small country inn dates back to the 16th century, but has been much extended over the years, and is now popular locally for its restaurant. There are currently only 2 bedrooms, both quite spacious, with the emphasis on comfort and good facilities including quality en suite bathrooms. Enthusiastic management encourages a relaxed atmosphere and good service. There is a bowling green to the rear of the inn, and good local walks and country pursuits are further attractions.
2⇌♠ (1fb) CTV in all bedrooms ® ✗ (ex guide dogs)
LDO 9.30pm
🏨 30P
Credit Cards [1] [2] [3]

NORTH MOLTON Devon Map **03** SS72

GH QQ Homedale EX36 3HL ☎(05984) 206
Etr-Oct rs Xmas & New Year
This Victorian house is in the centre of the historic village on the edge of the Exmoor National Park. The accommodation consists of 3 comfortable bedrooms, a cosy lounge and a dining room with a communal table for breakfast and dinner. A warm welcome is assured from the resident proprietors.
3rm(1♠2hc) ⊁in all bedrooms TV in 1 bedroom ® ✱ sB&Bfr£14 sB&B♠fr£16 dB&Bfr£28 dB&B♠fr£32
LDO 5.30pm
🏨 CTV 1P 1🚗 nc3-9yrs £

NORTH NIBLEY Gloucestershire Map **03** ST79

GH QQQ Burrows Court Hotel Nibley Green, Dursley GL11 6AZ ☎Dursley(0453) 546230
Set in a quiet rural location, this stone built, converted mill house, whilst retaining many original features, offers well equipped, prettily decorated bedrooms with modern facilities. On reaching North Nibley, follow signs to Berkeley and the house is just past the crossroads, set back from the road in its own grounds.
10rm(6⇌4♠) CTV in all bedrooms ® ✗ ✱ sB&B⇌♠£36-£39 dB&B⇌♠£50-£54 WB&B£147-£161 WBDi£189-£224
LDO 8pm
Lic 🏨 12P nc5yrs ⛱
Credit Cards [1] [2] [3] £

NORTH PERROTT Somerset Map **03** ST40

INN QQQ *The Manor Arms* TA18 7SG
☎Crewkerne(0460) 72901
A Grade II 16th-century village inn located in North Perrott, a sleepy village renowned for its beautifully situated cricket ground. Lovingly restored and refurbished over the last 2 years by the owners, it offers 3 en suite ground-floor rooms in a converted coach house; a self catering flat is also available. The bars and restaurant are full of character and meals are available in both; all the food is home made and good value for money. There is a car park, beer garden and children's adventure play area at the rear. Smoking is not permitted in bedrooms.
3♠ (1fb)⊁in all bedrooms CTV in all bedrooms ®
✗ (ex guide dogs) LDO 9.45pm
🏨 P
Credit Cards [1] [3]

NORTH WALSHAM Norfolk Map **09** TG23

GH QQQ Beechwood Private Hotel 20 Cromer Rd NR28 0HD
☎(0692) 403231
Closed 24 Dec-7 Jan
A charming red-brick detached house set in an acre of beautifully maintained gardens, in a residential area close to the town centre. The Victorian features of the house have been carefully retained, and the décor is light, complementing the spacious accommodation. Many of the bedrooms have private bathrooms, and there are two lounges, one with TV. The emphasis here is firmly on good old fashioned comfort and excellent service.
11rm(3⇌4♠4hc) (5fb) ® sB&B£22 sB&B⇌♠£24 dB&B£44 dB&B⇌♠£48 WB&B£132-£154 WBDi£148-£209 LDO 7pm
Lic 🏨 CTV 12P nc5yrs games room £

NORTH WHEATLEY Nottinghamshire Map **08** SK78

SELECTED

GH QQQQ The Old Plough Top St, North Wheatley DN22 9DB ☎Gainsborough(0427) 880916
The friendly, caring proprietors of this spotlessly clean, listed building have endeavoured to combine comfort and quality throughout. Individually styled bedrooms include a good range of facilities – one room has an en suite shower, the remaining have private bathrooms across the corridor. Smoking is prohibited in the bedrooms and the dining room, where guests dine at a communal table. Mrs Pasley is an excellent cook which is apparent in the imaginative set 4-course menu, that changes constantly. Everything is home made from the apetizers before dinner to the sweets with coffee. A typical meal might start with fish terrine, followed by chicken breast wrapped in ham and perhaps delicious bakewell tart, before a selection of cheeses to finish. The delightful drawing room is furnished with antique pieces that blend with the light, attractive décor. **Best Newcomer for Central England 1992–3, see colour section.**
3⇌♠ (1fb) CTV in all bedrooms ® ✗ (ex guide dogs) sB&B⇌♠£25 dB&B⇌♠£50 WB&B£175 WBDi£262.50
LDO 8.30pm
Lic 🏨 CTV P nc15yrs £

NORTHWOOD Greater London London plan **4** A5 (pages 245-251)

GH Q Frithwood House 31 Frithwood Av HA6 3LY
☎(0923) 827864 24720
A white, Edwardian house situated in a quiet suburban road. The friendly new owners are slowly upgrading the bedrooms. There is a comfortable lounge with TV and a drinks trolley. Breakfast is taken at pine tables in the kitchen.

7hc (4fb) ✗ (ex guide dogs) * sB&B£22 dB&B£38
♨ CTV 10P
Credit Cards 1 3

NORTH WOOTTON Somerset Map **03** ST54

FH QQQ Mrs M White ***Barrow*** *(ST553416)*
☎Pilton(074989) 245
Closed Dec-Jan
On the outskirts of the village to the west, towards Queen's Sedge Moor, this 15th-century stone farmhouse is set on a 120-acre dairy farm. The country- style bedrooms now provide TV and tea-making facilities, and Mrs White keeps very high standards of housekeeping. Both lounges are comfortable and very well furnished, and one has an open fire.
3hc (1fb) CTV in all bedrooms ® ✗ LDO 9am
CTV 4P 150 acres working dairy

NORTON FITZWARREN Somerset Map **03** ST12

GH QQ Old Manor Farmhouse TA2 6RZ
☎Taunton(0823) 289801
This establishment sits at one end of the village on the A361, and offers a warm welcome and a relaxed, friendly atmosphere. Very well equipped bedrooms are neat and en suite, and include such extra facilities as telephones. There is a cosy lounge with a bar in one corner, and a dining room where a choice of menu is offered. Ample car parking is available.
7→↑ CTV in all bedrooms ® T ✗ (ex guide dogs) *
sB&B→↑£32-£36 dB&B→↑£42-£46 WB&B£140-£245
WBDi£231-£336 LDO 4pm
Lic ♨ 12P
Credit Cards 1 2 3 5 (£)

NORWICH Norfolk Map **05** TG20

GH QQ *Caistor Hall Hotel* Caistor St Edmund NR14 8QN
☎(0603) 624406
Caistor Hall is less than three miles from the city centre, yet enjoys a quiet secluded location a short drive off the A140. There has been a house on the site since the Domesday Book and the building was enlarged in 1826. Accommodation varies, but all rooms have en suite facilities and are well equipped. The hotel has a large bar, restaurant and extensive conference facilities.
20→↑ (2fb) CTV in all bedrooms ®
Lic 250P ✿ croquet putting green
Credit Cards 1 3

GH QQ Earlham 147 Earlham Rd NR2 3RG ☎(0603) 54169
Halfway along a pleasant Victorian terrace with attractive gardens front and back, the house is on the B1108 to Earlham which runs from behind the Roman Catholic cathedral on the Inner Ring Road to the Outer Ring Road. A Mary and Martha lintel remains in the hallway together with a rose and bud cornice. Mr and Mrs Wright are a lovely pair and are most hospitable.
7rm(2↑5hc) (1fb) CTV in all bedrooms ® ✗ * sB&B£17-£20
dB&B£30-£34 dB&B↑£36-£38
♨ CTV P̸ (£)

GH QQQ Grange Hotel 230 Thorpe Rd NR1 1TJ
☎(0603) 34734
Closed Xmas wk
A busy commercial hotel on the Great Yarmouth road, close to the city centre and railway station. Bedrooms are well equipped, clean and all with private bathrooms, and public areas have recently been refurbished. Ample car parking is provided.
36rm(4→32↑) (1fb) CTV in all bedrooms ® T
✗ (ex guide dogs) * sB&B→↑£28-£36 dB&B→↑£45-£52
WB&B£175-£196 WBDi£250-£265 LDO 9.30pm
Lic ♨ 40P sauna solarium pool room
Credit Cards 1 2 3 5 (£)

GH QQ Marlborough House Hotel 22 Stracey Road, Thorpe Rd NR1 1EZ ☎(0603) 628005

A cheerful and clean family-owned guesthouse situated just off the Great Yarmouth road, within walking distance of the station and city centre. Some bedrooms are compact, but they are well equipped and modestly furnished, many with private bathrooms. There is a small bar/lounge which leads to the dining room.

12🛁🚿 (2fb) CTV in all bedrooms ® sB&B£16-£20 sB&B🛁🚿£27-£30 dB&B£37-£40 dB&B🛁🚿£37-£40 WB&B£189-£210 WBDi£231-£280 LDO 4.30pm

Lic ♨ CTV 8P 2🚗

NOTTINGHAM Nottinghamshire Map 08 SK54

GH QQ Crantock Hotel 480 Mansfield Rd NG5 2EL ☎(0602) 623294

A large, detached, fully modernised house conveniently set on the A60 just over a mile from the city centre. Bedrooms are all furnished with modern amenities, some with private bathrooms. Ample car parking is available, and the guesthouse is suitable for tourists and commercial guests alike.

10rm(1🛁🚿9hc) Annexe 10rm(7🛁🚿3hc) (5fb)🚭in 10 bedrooms CTV in all bedrooms ® ✱ sB&B£20-£24 sB&B🛁🚿£29-£35 dB&B£30-£38 dB&B🛁🚿£38-£45 WB&B£126-£168 WBDi£161-£203 LDO 9pm

Lic ♨ CTV 70P pool table

Credit Cards [1] [3] (£)

GH QQ Grantham Commercial Hotel 24-26 Radcliffe Rd, West Bridgford NG2 5FW ☎(0602) 811373

A commercial guesthouse very close to the Trent Bridge cricket ground. The rooms are neat and well equipped, and some have en suite facilities.

22rm(14🚿8hc) (2fb) CTV in all bedrooms ® ✱ sB&B£20-£22 sB&B🚿£25-£26 dB&B£32-£34 dB&B🚿£35-£38 WB&B£120-£150

♨ CTV 8P 2🚗 nc3yrs

Credit Cards [1] [3] (£)

GH Q P & J Hotel 277-279 Derby Rd, Lenton NG7 2DP ☎(0602) 783998

rs 24-29 Dec

Located on the main Derby road into the city centre, this small commercial hotel has been converted from a Victorian house. Public areas include a lounge bar where snacks are available in the evening.

19rm(9🚿10hc) (8fb) CTV in all bedrooms ® ✱ sB&B£25-£35 sB&B🚿fr£35 dB&Bfr£40 dB&B🚿fr£50 LDO 9.30pm

Lic ♨ CTV 12P

Credit Cards [1] [2] [3] [5] (£)

GH QQ Park Hotel 7 Waverley St NG7 4HF ☎(0602) 786299 & 420010 FAX (0602) 424358

This period house is set close to the city centre, overlooking a park. Only street parking is available. The bedrooms are well equipped and the annexe rooms all have en suite facilities.

27rm(11🛁🚿16hc) (2fb) CTV in all bedrooms ®
🐕 (ex guide dogs) LDO 9.30pm

Lic ♨ CTV

Credit Cards [1] [2] [3] (£)

GH QQQ *Royston Hotel* 326 Mansfield Rd, Sherwood NG6 2EF ☎(0602) 622947

A detached Victorian house on the A60 out of the city, with a terraced garden and off-street parking. The bedrooms are individually furnished with care and attention, and include a selection of creature comforts.

8rm(6🚿2hc) Annexe 4🚿 (2fb) CTV in all bedrooms ®
🐕 (ex guide dogs)

♨ CTV 16P

Credit Cards [1] [2] [3] [5]

NUNEATON Warwickshire Map 04 SP39

GH QQQ Drachenfels Hotel 25 Attleborough Rd CV11 4HZ ☎(0203) 383030

Situated 10 minutes' walk from the town centre, this imposing Edwardian house has been well modernised to provide comfortable, well-equipped bedrooms and cosy public areas.

8rm(2🚿6hc) (2fb) CTV in all bedrooms ® ✱ sB&B£19.50-£21 sB&B🚿£22.50-£25 dB&B£29-£31 dB&B🚿£32-£35 LDO 8pm

Lic ♨ 8P

Credit Cards [1] [3] (£)

NUNNEY Somerset Map 03 ST74

INN QQQ George at Nunney Church St BA11 4LW ☎(0373) 836458 & 836565

This large and popular inn, located in the centre of a Saxon village near the well known medieval castle provides neatly modernised bedrooms that are nicely equipped and include en suite facilities. There is a small first-floor lounge, which is set away from the busy bars that reflect the 17th-century charm of the George. Family owned and run, this establishment prides itself on offering genuine hospitality to all visitors.

11rm(7🛁4🚿) (3fb) CTV in all bedrooms ® T
🐕 (ex guide dogs) ✱ sB&B🛁🚿£26-£42 dB&B🛁🚿£40-£52 WB&B£127-£140 WBDi£150-£175 Lunch £10-£20alc High tea fr£5alc Dinner £10-£20alc LDO 9.30pm

♨ CTV 30P

Credit Cards [1] [3] (£)

NUTHURST West Sussex Map 04 TQ12

FH QQQ Mrs S E Martin **Saxtons** *(TQ199274)* RH13 6LG ☎Lower Beeding(0403) 891231 FAX (0403) 891116

Closed Xmas

A delightful Georgian farmhouse situated in an unspoilt rural area about 4 miles from Horsham, just off the A281 Brighton road. It offers attractive, comfortable bedrooms, 2 of which are particularly spacious and smartly furnished. There is a combined lounge/dining room where the welcoming owner Mrs Martin offers a hearty farmhouse breakfast, including eggs from their own hens and chunky home-made marmalade.

4hc (1fb)🚭in all bedrooms CTV in all bedrooms ®
🐕 (ex guide dogs) ✱ sB&B£21 dB&B£36 WB&B£126-£147

♨ CTV 6P 2🚗 100 acres deer sheep goats (£)

OAKAMOOR Staffordshire Map 07 SK04

SELECTED

GH QQQQ Bank House Farley Ln ST10 3BD ☎(0538) 702810

Just a few hundred yards out of the village centre, take the Farley road and you will see Bank House behind its sandstone walls and heavy iron gates. The original farmhouse has been considerably extended, creating an imaginative and high quality family home where John and Muriel Orme make guests very welcome. It certainly has the setting, high above the steep wooded slopes of the Churnet Valley, and close to many places of interest. Dinner is in true family style, the menu fixed after discussion with the guests, and everyone sitting together at the beautifully laid table. A typical meal could consist of chilled creme vichyssoise, poached salmon trout, new potatoes, a selection of vegetables, several English cheeses, then a choice of home-made praline ice- cream, lemon sorbet or Bakewell tart. Not all the cooking skills are Muriel's, the breads are made by John, including excellent brioche and croissants served at breakfast. The bedrooms are lovely big old rooms with antique furniture. Extras include bottled water and fresh fruit Apart from the maple floored drawing room, there is a separate library and a terrace for fine weather.

3rm(2⇌↑ 1hc) ⊬in all bedrooms CTV in all bedrooms ® ✗ (ex guide dogs) sB&B£23 dB&B£46 dB&B⇌↑£60 WBDifr£220 LDO 11am
🍽 CTV 6P

INN QQ Admiral Jervis Country Hotel Mill Rd ST10 3AG
☎(0538) 702187
20 Mar-5 Nov
This 18th-century inn overlooks the River Churnet in this picturesque village convenient for Alton Towers. Bedrooms are en suite and some are furnished with pine units and walls. Real ale and basket meals are provided at the friendly bar which features original oak beams, and a wide range of food prepared by the chef/proprietor is served in the restaurant.
6⇌↑ (4fb)⊬in all bedrooms CTV in all bedrooms ® ✗ ✻ sB&B⇌↑fr£25 dB&B⇌↑fr£39 LDO 8.30pm
🍽 20P
Credit Cards [1] [3] £

OAKFORD Devon Map **03** SS92

FH QQQ Anne Boldry **Newhouse** *(SS892228)* EX16 9JE
☎(03985) 347
Closed Xmas
Set back off the old South Molton road in 40 acres within a peaceful valley and bordered by a trout stream, this 17th-century farmhouse retains much of its charm and character whilst providing modern comfort. Two en suites have recently been installed. Home-made soups, patés, bread and preserves, as well as home-produced vegetables can be enjoyed here. The farmhouse is well sited for touring Devon, together with access to Somerset and the coast.

→

3⇔ (1fb) ® ✕ sB&B⇔£18-£19 dB&B⇔£32-£34 WB&Bfr£112 WBDi£165 LDO 4pm
⊞ CTV 3P nc10yrs ♪ 42 acres beef sheep £

OBAN Strathclyde *Argyllshire* Map **10** NM83

GH QQ Ardblair Dalriach Rd PA34 5JB ☎(0631) 62668
Apr-Sep rs Etr
From its elevated position, the Ardblair offers fine views across the town and bay from many of its bedrooms and the sun lounge. The self-service arrangements for snacks and beverages prove popular with children. The municipal swimming pool is within 3 minutes' walk.
15rm(11⇔♪4hc) (3fb) ® ✕ ✱ sB&B£12-£14 sB&B⇔♪£16-£20 dB&B£24-£28 dB&B⇔♪£32-£40 WB&B£84-£126 WBDi£140-£170 LDO 5.30pm
⊞ CTV 10P £

GH QQ Glenburnie Private Hotel The Esplanade PA34 5AQ ☎(0631) 62089
Apr-Oct
A solid stone-built period house on the esplanade overlooking the west bay. Spacious and traditionally furnished, it offers comfortable bedrooms and neatly appointed public rooms.
14rm(10♪4hc) (2fb) CTV in all bedrooms ®
✕ (ex guide dogs) ✱ sB&B£17.50-£20 dB&B£35-£40 dB&B♪£45-£65
⊞ CTV 12P 1🚘 nc4yrs
Credit Cards 1 3

GH QQ Roseneath Dalriach Rd PA34 5EQ ☎(0631) 62929
Closed 24-26 Dec
In an elevated position overlooking the town and bay, this cheery guesthouse is spotlessly maintained. There is a comfortable lounge, and the bedrooms are attractively decorated, some have full en suites and 4 have modern shower cabinets.
10rm(2♪8hc) (1fb) CTV in 3 bedrooms ® ✕ ✱ sB&B£12.50-£15.50 dB&B£25-£31 dB&B♪£30-£35
⊞ CTV 8P

GH QQ Sgeir Mhaol Soroba Rd PA34 4JF ☎(0631) 62650
A well maintained bungalow on the main A816 road leading out of Oban going south. Bedrooms are bright and airy, and there is a cosy lounge and a small attractive dining room.
7rm(5♪2hc) (3fb) CTV in all bedrooms ® ✕ (ex guide dogs) sB&B£13.50-£26.50 dB&B£27-£33 dB&B♪£33-£40 LDO 4pm
⊞ CTV 10P

GH QQQ Wellpark Hotel Esplanade PA34 5AQ ☎(0631) 62948 FAX (0631) 65808
May-Oct rs Etr
Bedrooms offering such conveniences as telephones and radio/clock/alarms are a feature of this mansion which overlooks the Esplanade and West Bay.
17♪ CTV in all bedrooms ® ✱ sB&B♪£29-£32 dB&B♪£40-£58
⊞ 12P nc3yrs
Credit Cards 1 3

ODDINGTON Gloucestershire Map **04** SP22

INN QQQ Horse & Groom Upper Oddington GL56 0XH ☎Cotswold(0451) 30584
8⇔♪ (2fb) CTV in all bedrooms ® ✕ (ex guide dogs) ✱ sB&B⇔♪£27-£29.50 dB&B⇔♪£42-£47 Lunch £1.50-£7.25 Dinner £1.50-£7.25&alc LDO 9.30pm
⊞ 40P
Credit Cards 1 3

OFFTON Suffolk Map **05** TM04

FH QQ Mrs P M Redman **Mount Pleasant** *(SS066495)* IP8 4RP ☎(0473) 658896
Tucked away behind the church, this 16th-century farmhouse has been extended and renovated to provide 3 bedrooms, each with a good range of facilities and prettily decorated using Laura Ashley fabrics. Guests are welcome to view the variety of farm animals roaming the 8 acres, and to sample the local and home-grown produce at dinner (by arrangement).
3rm(2♪1hc) CTV in all bedrooms ® ✕ (ex guide dogs) ✱ sB&Bfr£15 sB&B♪fr£15 dB&Bfr£25 dB&B♪fr£25 WB&B£87.50-£105 WBDi£143.50-£161
Lic ⊞ 6P nc8 acres mixed £

OKEHAMPTON Devon Map **02** SX59

FH QQ Mrs K C Heard **Hughslade** *(SX561932)* EX20 4LR ☎(0837) 52883
Closed Xmas
The location of this farmhouse has been made more peaceful by the completion of the Okehampton bypass. Bedrooms and lounges are spacious and comfortable, home-cooked dinners are served and a Devonshire welcome awaits you.
4hc (3fb) ® sB&B£16-£20 dB&B£32-£40 WB&B£90-£110 WBDi£110-£140 LDO 6pm
CTV 10P U snooker games room horse riding 600 acres beef sheep £

OLD DALBY Leicestershire Map **08** SK62

FH Q Mr & Mrs S Anderson ***Home*** *(SK673236)* Church Ln LE14 3LB ☎Melton Mowbray(0664) 822622
Although mostly Victorian, parts of this ivy and clematis-clad house date back to the 1700s. Set in a small and peaceful village, it provides modest and comfortable accommodation with a wealth of character.
3hc Annexe 2♪ (1fb) CTV in 2 bedrooms ® ✕ (ex guide dogs)
⊞ CTV 5P stables for guests horses 1 acres non-working

OLD SODBURY Avon Map **03** ST78

GH QQ Dornden Church Ln BS17 6NB ☎Chipping Sodbury(0454) 313325
Closed Xmas & New Year & 3 wks in Oct
This former Georgian rectory is situated just off the A432 east of the village. The accommodation retains much of the original charm of the period with bright, spotlessly clean bedrooms, successfully combining character with comfort. The house is set back within pleasant well tended gardens with commanding views across open countryside, making this a convenient location for the M4, Bath and Bristol.
9rm(2⇔3♪4hc) (4fb) CTV in all bedrooms ✱ sB&Bfr£19.50 sB&B⇔♪£30 dB&Bfr£37 dB&B⇔♪£44 LDO 3pm
⊞ 15P ℘(grass) £

GH QQQ The Sodbury House Hotel Badminton Rd BS17 6LU ☎Chipping Sodbury(0454) 312847 FAX (0454) 273105
Closed 27 Dec-10 Jan
Tucked away within its own grounds and gardens, this small country house has, over the recent years, seen commendable upgrading. The accommodation is in 3 sections – the bedrooms in the main house are particularly comfortable, with quality furniture, en suites and little personal touches, while those in the adjacent coach house and stable block are more compact, but all boast an extensive range of facilities that are enhanced with pleasing décor and coordinating fabrics. There is a cosy lounge and dining room that are richly furnished and also nicely personalized. Enthusiastically run by owners David and Margaret Warren, there is a detectable air of hospitality about this cosy retreat, and top marks must be awarded to them for sparkling cleanliness throughout.

6⇌🚿 Annexe 9🚿 (2fb) CTV in all bedrooms ® T
sB&B⇌🚿£36-£45 dB&B⇌🚿£45-£60
Lic 🍴 28P croquet boule
Credit Cards [1] [3]

ONICH Highland *Inverness-shire* Map **14** NN06

GH QQQ ***Cuilcheanna House Hotel*** PH33 6SD ☎(08553) 226
Etr-6 Oct
8⇌ (2fb) ® LDO 7.30pm
Lic 🍴 CTV 10P

GH QQ ***Tigh-A-Righ*** PH33 6SE ☎(08553) 255
Closed 22 Dec-7 Jan
A genuine Highland welcome is shown at this small family run guesthouse which stands beside the A82 just north of the village, 8 miles south of Fort William. Bedrooms, though compact, are comfortable and modern, some with en suite facilities, and are equipped with useful extras. Public rooms include a reading lounge and a spacious dining room where good home cooking is served. The White Corries ski run in Glencoe is within 30 minutes of the guesthouse, and the area also offers hill-walking and climbing, fishing, yachting and canoeing.
6rm(1⇌1🚿4hc) (3fb) ® LDO 9pm
Lic 🍴 CTV 15P

ORFORD Suffolk Map **05** TM44

INN QQ Kings Head Front St IP12 2LW ☎(0394) 450271
A character 13th-century village inn whose proximity to sea and estuary ensures a good supply of fresh fish and oysters in season, which are featured on both the bar and restaurant menu. The accommodation is simple and clean.
6hc (1fb) CTV in all bedrooms ® sB&B£23-£24 dB&B£38-£40
Lunch £5-£20alc Dinner £12-£25alc LDO 9pm

→

🍽 50P 1🚗 nc8yrs
Credit Cards [5] (£)

OSWESTRY Shropshire Map **07** SJ22

GH QQQ ***Ashfield Country House*** Llwyn-y-Maen, Trefonen Rd SY10 9DD ☎(0691) 655200
A friendly, personally run small hotel, just 1 mile out of the town, that has a good reputation for home-made food and personal service. Rooms are well equipped and the large lounge has extensive views over the hotel grounds and the Candy Valley. It is found by following signs to Trefonen for about 2 miles.
12🛁🚿 (2fb) CTV in all bedrooms ® LDO 9pm
Lic 🍽 50P

OTTERY ST MARY Devon Map **03** SY19

GH QQ Fluxton Farm Hotel Fluxton EX11 1RJ ☎(0404) 812818
This 16th-century Devon longhouse is now a small family-run farm hotel in a peaceful setting to the south of the town. The accommodation is neat and cosy, with modestly appointed bedrooms.
12rm(6🛁4🚿2hc) (2fb) CTV in 10 bedrooms ® ✱ sB&B🛁🚿£27.50-£32 dB&B🛁🚿£57-£64 (incl dinner) WB&B£150-£180 WBDi£190-£220 LDO 5.30pm
Lic 🍽 CTV 15P 🎣 putting garden railway (£)

OUNDLE Northamptonshire Map **04** TL08

INN QQ ***The Ship Inn*** 18-20 West St PE8 4EF ☎(0832) 273918
This old world inn is situated at the heart of the picturesque market town. Guest accommodation is provided in 2 stone-built annexes, the coach and boat houses. Rooms have a good range of facilities and most have pine furniture and striking coordinated fabrics; and books, dried flowers and china all help to personalise the décor. Further rooms are available in the cottage, but the accommodation provided was not up to AA standard when inspected; and this annexe also houses a small dining room/ lounge. There is a cosy bar with an inglenook fireplace in the inn, where a range of bar meals and real ales is served.
11rm(1🛁10🚿) (1fb) CTV in all bedrooms ® LDO 10pm
🍽 CTV 70P
Credit Cards [1] [3]

OXFORD Oxfordshire Map **04** SP50

See also Horton-cum-Studley

GH Q Acorn 260 Iffley Rd OX4 1SE ☎(0865) 247998
Closed Xmas-New Year
A Victorian property on the Iffley road, giving easy access to the city centre. Run by the cheerful resident proprietor, bedrooms are simply furnished but well equipped and comfortable. Breakfast is served in a small, modestly appointed dining room.
6hc (3fb) CTV in all bedrooms ® 🚫 ✱ sB&B£18-£24 dB&B£36-£40 WB&B£119-£154
🍽 5P
Credit Cards [1] [3] (£)

GH QQ All Seasons 63 Windmill Rd, Headington OX3 7BP ☎(0865) 742215
A small, welcoming house close to the centre of Headington with its range of shops and restaurants. Three of the bedrooms have been recently decorated and furnished to a very high standard, and provide modern facilities; the remaining 3 are more modestly priced and soundly furnished. The small dining room has also been freshly decorated, and the overall standard of housekeeping is high. This is a no smoking establishment.
6rm(3🚿3hc) 🚭in all bedrooms CTV in all bedrooms ® 🚫 ✱ sB&B£20-£25 sB&B🚿£33-£35 dB&B£35-£38 dB&B🚿£45-£48 WB&B£140-£231
🍽 6P nc12yrs

GH QQ Bravalla 242 Iffley Rd OX4 1SE ☎(0865) 241326 & 250511
A small guesthouse situated along the busy Iffley road, conveniently located for the city centre. Bedrooms are pretty and well equipped, although a few are compact, but they are all comfortable. There is a small parking area at the front of the house, and the resident proprietor is very informative with regard to local tourist attractions.
6rm(4🚿2hc) (2fb) CTV in all bedrooms ® ✱ sB&B🚿£25-£35 dB&B🚿£35-£45
🍽 CTV 6P
Credit Cards [1] [3] (£)

See advertisement on page 307

GH QQ ***Bronte*** 282 Iffley Rd OX4 4AA ☎(0865) 244594
This cosy Victorian semi won first prize in the 1991 'Oxford in Bloom' competition for its attractive flower baskets and tubs. The well polished bedrooms are neatly kept and have sound modern beds.
5rm(1🚿4hc) (1fb) CTV in all bedrooms ® 🚫 (ex guide dogs)
🍽 CTV 5P

See advertisement on page 307

GH QQ ***Brown's*** 281 Iffley Rd OX4 4AQ ☎(0865) 246822
A neat and tidy Victorian property on the Iffley road, a mile away from the city centre, with some off-street parking. Bedrooms are well equipped, bright and clean, with showers but no baths. A cheerful atmosphere prevails in this family-run Bed and Breakfast guesthouse.
6rm(2🚿4hc) (1fb) CTV in all bedrooms ®
🍽 CTV 4P
Credit Cards [1] [3]

Venn Ottery Barton

Venn Ottery, Near Ottery St Mary, Devon EX11 1RZ

Five miles from Sidmouth beach, in its own garden amid unspoilt farmlands. Family run, full central heating and every comfort, with charm of 16th century beams. Bar, lounge with colour TV, large games room, log fires. Ample parking
Open all year for dinner, bed and breakfast. Bargain breaks.

Tel: Ottery St Mary (0404) 812733

King's Head Inn

FRONT ST.
ORFORD, NR. WOODBRIDGE
Telephone: Orford (0394) 450271

Fresh local seafood is a speciality of this small Inn run by Alistair & Joy Shaw. The 13th century smugglers' Inn with its wealth of old beams and candlelit Dining Room, offers comfortable accommodation in 'olde worlde' bedrooms, and full English breakfast.

Lunches 12.00-2.00pm Daily

Bar meals most evenings

Dinner 7-9pm except Sunday & Thursday evening

BOWOOD HOUSE

238 OXFORD ROAD, KIDLINGTON, OXFORD OX5 1EB

Situated on the A4260, 4 miles from Oxford, Bowood House offers accommodation of a high standard and a warm friendly atmosphere.

- ★ Private bathrooms
- ★ Colour TVs
- ★ Direct Dial telephones
- ★ Tea/Coffee making facilities
- ★ Radio alarms
- ★ Residential Licence

OXFORD (0865) 842288

GH QQQ Chestnuts 45 Davenant Rd, off Woodstock Rd OX2 8BU ☎(0865) 53375

Conveniently situated along the Woodstock road, just over a mile from the city centre, this smart, modern guesthouse offers comfortable and well furnished bedrooms, each en suite, with good facilities. Public areas are attractive, and breakfast is taken in the conservatory, which overlooks the well tended garden.

4↱ ⚟in all bedrooms CTV in all bedrooms ®
✗ (ex guide dogs) sB&B↱£28-£32 dB&B↱£44-£50
🍽 5P nc12yrs £

GH QQ Combermere 11 Polstead Rd OX2 6TW ☎(0865) 56971

This fine red brick Edwardian house is situated in a quiet side street, only a 15 minute walk from the city centre. The bedrooms are simply furnished and all have en suite facilities, making space in some rooms rather limited. Breakfast is served in a compact dining room.

9↱ (2fb) CTV in all bedrooms ® sB&B↱£25-£35 dB&B↱£35-£50 WB&B£123-£210
🍽 3P
Credit Cards 1 3

GH QQQ Conifer 116 The Slade, Headington OX3 7DX ☎(0865) 63055

Located outside the city centre in Headington, this family-run guesthouse is spotlessly clean and superbly maintained. Bedrooms are reasonable in size and well presented, with neat and tidy décor. There is a small breakfast room/lounge area, and some car parking is available. In the warmer weather, guests can take advantage of the outdoor swimming pool.

8rm(1⇌2↱5hc) (1fb) CTV in all bedrooms ® ✗ sB&B£21-£25 dB&B£32-£35 dB&B⇌↱£42-£45
🍽 8P ⩯(heated)
Credit Cards 1 3

SELECTED

GH QQQQ Cotswold House 363 Banbury Rd OX2 7PL ☎(0865) 310558

Jim and Anne O'Kane, the resident proprietors, offer friendly, attentive service in a relaxed atmosphere. The bedrooms vary in size but all are comfortable with a high quality of housekeeping and are equipped to a good standard, including a mini fridge. Breakfast is served between 8am and 9am, with a varied choice available, from fresh fruit to several cooked alternatives. After breakfast, the room doubles up as a quiet lounge, and several restaurants can be found only a short walk away. Cotswold House is a no smoking establishment.

7↱ (2fb)⚟in all bedrooms CTV in all bedrooms ® ✗ sB&B↱£32-£35 dB&B↱£47-£50
🍽 6P nc6yrs

GH QQQ Courtfield Private Hotel 367 Iffley Rd OX4 4DP ☎(0865) 242991

An attractive detached 1930s house located on the Iffley Road, within easy access of the city centre. The accommodation is spotless, with all rooms double glazed to combat traffic noise; most of the rooms are en suite. Personal service is provided by the resident proprietors, and breakfast is served in a comfortable dining room which also has a lounge area.

6rm(4⇌↱2hc) (1fb) ✗ sB&B£25-£30 sB&B⇌↱£27-£32 dB&B£38-£42 dB&B⇌↱£40-£44
🍽 CTV 6P 2🚗 nc3yrs
Credit Cards 1 2 3 £

GH QQQ Dial House 25 London Rd, Headington OX3 7RE ☎(0865) 69944

Closed Xmas & New Year

This half-timbered house has been converted into a smart, well maintained and spotlessly clean guesthouse. It is located along the busy London road in Headington, and offers a high standard of accommodation. Bedrooms are freshly decorated and well furnished, with smart en suite facilities. Public areas are comfortable and there is a well tended garden at the rear, with car parking in numbered bays at the front.

8⇌↱ (2fb)⚟in all bedrooms CTV in all bedrooms ® ✱ dB&B⇌↱£45-£50
🍽 8P nc6yrs £

GH QQ Earlmont 322-324 Cowley Rd OX4 2AF ☎(0865) 240236

Closed 24 Dec-1 Jan

A double-fronted house situated along the busy Cowley road to the east of Oxford city centre, with five bedrooms in the main building and the remainder across the road in a small annexe. All bedrooms are regularly redecorated, and have recently been refurbished to ensure that standards remain high. Some of the rooms are fairly compact but comfortable nonetheless. Similarly, public rooms are nicely furnished and decorated if a little limited.

8rm(1⇌3↱4hc) Annexe 7hc (2fb)⚟in 8 bedrooms CTV in all bedrooms ® ✗ sB&B£25-£30 sB&B⇌↱£30-£35 dB&B£36-£40 dB&B⇌↱£40-£45
🍽 CTV 10P 1🚗 nc5yrs
Credit Cards 1 2 3

See advertisement on page 309

GH QQQ Falcon Private Hotel 88-90 Abingdon Rd OX1 4PX ☎(0865) 722995

Situated along the Abingdon road just east of the city, this guesthouse has been created by the conversion of two Victorian houses and carefully refurbished by the new proprietors. Bedrooms are particularly well equipped and comfortable, with excellent en suite facilities. Public areas are comfortable, if a little limited in space. The owners are friendly, helpful and eager to provide for their guests' comfort.

→

11⇌ (4fb)⊁in all bedrooms CTV in all bedrooms ® T ✗ (ex guide dogs) ✱ sB&B⇌£26-£28 dB&B⇌£42-£45 WB&B£129.50-£182 WBDi£178-£231 LDO 5pm
🍽 CTV 10P jacuzzi
Credit Cards 1 3 £

GH QQ Galaxie Private Hotel 180 Banbury Rd OX2 7BT
☎(0865) 515688
This popular, privately-run commercial hotel is situated along the busy Banbury road. The guesthouse has gradually been extended and now offers comfortable, well equipped bedrooms, each with a fresh, bright décor. Breakfast only is served in the rear-facing dining room, which leads into a cosy lounge area.
34rm(21⇌⇌13hc) (3fb) CTV in all bedrooms T ✱ sB&B£25-£45 sB&B⇌⇌£39-£45 dB&B£45-£50 dB&B⇌⇌£55-£60
lift 🍽 CTV 25P
Credit Cards 1 3 £

GH QQ *Green Gables* 326 Abingdon Rd OX1 4TE
☎(0865) 725870
Closed 20 Dec-6 Jan
Situated just south of the city centre, this Edwardian house is set in a mature garden. The accommodation is comfortable, with some good sized bedrooms. The service is friendly and is under the owner's personal supervision.
8rm(3⇌5hc) (2fb) CTV in all bedrooms ® ✗ (ex guide dogs)
🍽 CTV 8P
Credit Cards 1 3

GH QQ Highfield 91 Rose Hill OX4 4HT ☎(0865) 774083 & 718524
Doreen and Bertram Edwards provide a warm welcome at their smart and very well run guesthouse, which is just off the ring road to the east of the city. The bright and freshly decorated dining room is appealing, and there is a pleasant lounge with thick rugs and comfortable sofas. The modern bedrooms are of a high standard, making this a popular choice with the local business community.
7rm(3⇌2hc) (2fb)⊁in 3 bedrooms CTV in all bedrooms ® ✗ ✱ sB&B£18-£20 dB&B£30-£32 dB&B⇌£40-£44
LDO breakfast
🍽 CTV 5P
Credit Cards 1 3

GH QQ Homelea 356 Abingdon Rd OX1 4TQ
☎(0865) 245150
Peggy and John Hogan have created a warm and welcoming home here where generally spacious bedrooms are especially comfortable because of the excellent quality of the beds. Homelea is obviously placed on Abingdon Road and has its own parking and small garden.
6rm(3⇌3hc) (3fb) CTV in all bedrooms ® ✗ (ex guide dogs) ✱ sB&B£18-£20 dB&B£34-£36 dB&B⇌£36-£38
🍽 CTV 6P £

GH QQQ Pickwicks 17 London Rd, Headington OX3 7SP
☎(0865) 750487 FAX (0865) 742208
A family-run guesthouse situated on the London road in Headington, just outside the city centre. Two adjacent Victorian houses have been converted to provide comfortable and bright bedrooms, each of which is well equipped, most with their own bathrooms. Public areas are currently being extended, and these too are bright and nicely decorated.
9rm(3⇌5⇌1hc) Annexe 4rm(2⇌2hc) (2fb)⊁in 2 bedrooms CTV in all bedrooms ® T sB&B£18-£22 sB&B⇌⇌£28-£34 dB&B£36-£40 dB&B⇌⇌£46-£50 WB&B£140-£210 WBDi£196-£280 LDO 1pm
Lic 🍽 CTV 20P
Credit Cards 1 2 3 £

Book as early as possible for busy holiday periods.

GH QQ Pine Castle 290 Iffley Rd OX4 4AE
☎(0865) 241497 & 727230
Closed Xmas
A small Edwardian family home on the Iffley road, just east of the city, in a popular central location. The public rooms are well decorated and comfortably furnished, and the bedrooms are modern, with some coordination of colour schemes. Breakfast is served in the dining area, adjacent to a cosy lounge.
6hc (3fb) CTV in 5 bedrooms TV in 1 bedroom ® ✗ (ex guide dogs) sB&B£20-£23 dB&B£34-£42 WB&B£102-£136.50 LDO 8.30am
🍽 CTV 4P
Credit Cards 1 3 £

See advertisement on page 311

SELECTED

GH QQQQ Tilbury Lodge Private Hotel 5 Tilbury Ln, Eynsham Rd, Botley OX2 9NB ☎(0865) 862138
Just 2 miles west of the city centre, this guesthouse in a quiet residential lane is run by Mr and Mrs Trafford and offers bed and breakfast accommodation only. Bright modern bedrooms are very well equipped and include extras like telephones and hairdryers. One bedroom features a romantic 4-poster bed, and there is a ground floor room for guests unable to use the stairs. A spa bath is available for guests' use between 11am and 6pm. Breakfast is served at 8.30am in the informal breakfast room, and guests can relax in the well appointed lounge which is well stocked with tourist information.
8⇌⇌ (2fb) CTV in all bedrooms ® T ✗ sB&B⇌⇌£33-£36 dB&B⇌⇌£55-£75
🍽 CTV 8P 1🚗 jacuzzi
Credit Cards 1 3 £

See advertisement on page 311

GH QQQ Westwood Country Hotel Hinksey Hill Top OX1 5BG ☎(0865) 735408 FAX (0865) 736536
Closed 22 Dec-6 Jan
Situated midway along Hinksey Hill, this small family-run hotel stands in 4 acres of lovely woodland, now designated a nature reserve. Bedrooms are mostly spacious and well equipped with modern facilities. The restaurant and bar area have recently been refurbished: the bar now has a full licence, allowing less restricted drinking hours. There is a good range of leisure facilities, including a jacuzzi, sauna and mini-gym.
26rm(14⇌12↱) (5fb) CTV in all bedrooms ® **T**
✗ (ex guide dogs) ✱ sB&B⇌↱£50-£60 dB&B⇌↱£72-£90 WBDifr£357 LDO 8pm
Lic ⅲ CTV 50P ⌂ sauna jacuzzi mini gym
Credit Cards 1 2 3 5 £

GH QQ *Willow Reaches Hotel* 1 Wytham St OX1 4SU ☎(0865) 721545 FAX (0865) 251139
In a quiet residential area south of the city, Willow Reaches has been completely refurbished to provide comfortable, well-equipped bedrooms. Public rooms are limited, but the dining room offers a choice of English and Indian cuisine.
9rm(3⇌6↱) (1fb) CTV in all bedrooms ® ✗ LDO 6pm
Lic ⅲ CTV 6P 3⌂
Credit Cards 1 2 3 5

See advertisement on page 313

OXHILL Warwickshire Map **04** SP34

FH QQQ Mrs S Hutsby **Nolands Farm & Country Restaurant** *(SP312470)* CV35 0RJ (1m E of Pillarton Priors on A422) ☎Kineton(0926) 640309
Closed 15-30 Dec
The farm is situated just off the A422, in a tranquil valley. Guest rooms are located in carefully restored stables, totally separate from the owner's accommodation. The comfortable bedrooms are generally spacious: 2 have 4- poster beds and they offer a good range of facilities including private bathrooms. Public areas include a cosy dining room and a small comfortable bar area. There is a well stocked trout lake and clay pigeon shooting and riding can be arranged nearby.
Annexe 9rm(2⇌7↱) (2fb) CTV in all bedrooms ®
✗ (ex guide dogs) sB&B⇌↱fr£20 dB&B⇌↱£30-£44 LDO 6pm
Lic ⅲ 10P 2⌂ nc7yrs ✓ clay pigeon shooting bicycle hire 300 acres arable
Credit Cards 1 3 £

OXWICH West Glamorgan Map **02** SS58

GH QQQ Oxwich Bay Hotel Gower SA3 1LS ☎Swansea(0792) 390329 & 390491 FAX (0792) 391254
Right on the beach of this lovely sandy bay the hotel provides extensive and comfortable bar and function facilities. The bedrooms have all been recently refurbished and offer an abundance of modern comforts.
13⇌↱ (4fb) CTV in all bedrooms ® ✗ (ex guide dogs) sB&B⇌↱£19-£45 dB&B⇌↱£38-£70 WB&B£106.40-£151.20 WBDi£184.80-£229.60 LDO 10pm
Lic ⅲ 300P
Credit Cards 1 2 3 5

PADSTOW Cornwall & Isles of Scilly Map **02** SW97

See also Little Petherick, St Merryn and Trevone

GH QQ *Alexandra* 30 Dennis Rd PL28 8DE ☎(0841) 532503
Etr-Oct
The Alexandra overlooks the beautiful Camel Estuary from an elevated, quiet residential position. Built in 1906, this fine Victorian house is the family home of proprietor Maureen Williams and offers a relaxing, informal atmosphere. The bedrooms are furnished in a traditional style with a TV and tea/coffee making facilities provided. A comfortable sitting room

→

Pine Castle Hotel

290 Iffley Road
Oxford
Telephone:
0865 241497
or 727230

A comfortable, family run Edwardian guest house, 1½ miles from the city centre and on an excellent bus route. Very convenient to Post Office, launderette, etc, and also to the lovely River Thames. Well appointed rooms offer Tea/Coffee making facilities and TV and are accessible to guests throughout the day, as is the attractive TV lounge.

Write or telephone for further details to resident proprietors, Peter and Marilyn Morris.

TILBURY LODGE

PRIVATE HOTEL

TEL: (0865) 862138
(Three lines)

Tilbury Lodge is situated in a quiet country lane just two miles west of the city centre and one mile from the railway station. Good bus service available. Botley shopping centre is a few minutes walk away with restaurants, shops, banks, pubs etc.

All rooms en suite with direct dial telephone colour TV, radio, hair dryer and tea & coffee facilities. Jacuzzi. Four poster. Ground floor bedrooms. Central heating, double glazing. Ample parking.

TILBURY LODGE PRIVATE HOTEL
5 TILBURY LANE, EYNSHAM ROAD,
BOTLEY, OXFORD OX2 9NB

Willow Reaches Hotel

1 Wytham St., Oxford

Tel: Oxford (0865) 721545 Fax: (0865) 251139

English Tourist Board Commended

A private hotel with a high standard of comfort, in a quiet location just a mile south of Oxford city centre.

The hotel is near a fishing lake and a public park with swimming pools and children's boating lake.

Every bedroom has a direct dial telephone, colour television, radio and tea/coffee-making facility; all bathrooms en suite. Bridal suite.

Central Heating throughout. Residents' lounge with teletext TV. Bar, restaurant serving English and Indian meals. A large garden. Children welcome. Parking facilities.

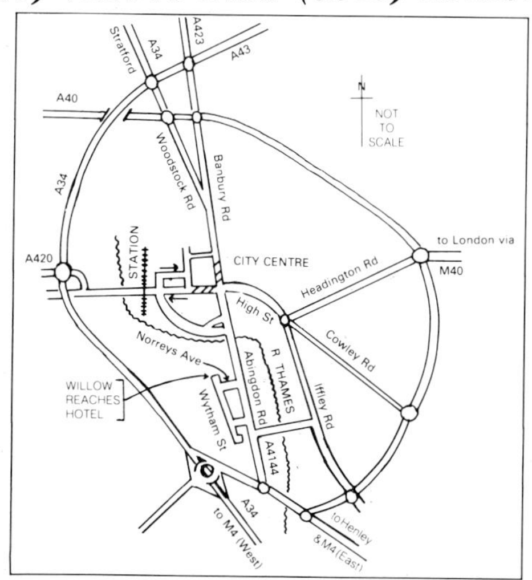

augments a small dining room, and un-restricted parking is available.
6hc (2fb) CTV in all bedrooms ® ✕ LDO noon
5P nc5yrs

GH QQQ Dower House Fentonluna Ln PL28 8BA
☎(0841) 532317
Etr-Oct
Quietly set in its own grounds, this delightful 19th-century house enjoys a fine position overlooking the town and with a south facing terrace, provides an ideal setting for cream teas and light refreshments. The individually furnished bedrooms offer lots of thoughtful extras including fresh fruit and flower arrangements. A TV lounge and separate bar lounge are provided, along with a dining room where a full English breakfast and 4-course dinners are served. Personally run by the proprietor Christine Thomas, this licensed guesthouse provides a friendly service.
8rm(1⇨4↱3hc) (3fb) CTV in 6 bedrooms ® sB&Bfr£23 sB&B⇨↱£30.50 dB&B£34-£40 dB&B⇨↱£48 WB&B£114-£158
Lic ♨ CTV 9P

PAIGNTON Devon Map **03** SX86

See **Town Plan Section**

GH QQQ Beresford 5 Adelphi Rd TQ4 6AW ☎(0803) 551560
Sound accommodation and personal service is provided by this small, friendly guesthouse. It is close to the town, beach and esplanade.
8↱ (1fb)⊁in 2 bedrooms CTV in all bedrooms ® ✕
sB&B↱fr£25 dB&B↱fr£40 WB&Bfr£120 WBDifr£145
LDO 10am
Lic ♨ CTV 3P £

GH QQ Channel View Hotel 8 Marine Pde TQ3 2NU
☎(0803) 522432 FAX (0803) 522323
Located in a quiet cul-de-sac on the esplanade, only a short distance from the hustle and bustle of Paignton, this establishment has been owned for many years by Mrs Teague. The compact bedrooms are bright, airy and freshly decorated, and all are nicely equipped with en suite facilities, some rooms enjoying good sea views. There is a front facing dining room, also with superb sea views, and forecourt parking is available. An amiable, cheery atmosphere prevails here, which draws guests back time after time.
12⇨↱ (3fb) CTV in all bedrooms ® ✕ (ex guide dogs)
dB&B⇨↱£30-£60 WBDi£90-£210 LDO noon
Lic ♨ CTV 10P
Credit Cards 1 3 £

GH Q Cherra Hotel 15 Roundham Rd TQ4 6DN
☎(0803) 550723
Mar-Oct
A small private hotel in a quiet residential area a short distance from the town centre, beaches and harbour. The bedrooms are comfortable though some are compact; all have colour TV. A colourful garden surrounds the property.
14rm(9↱5hc) (7fb) CTV in all bedrooms ® sB&B£16-£23 sB&B↱£20-£27 dB&B£32-£46 dB&B↱£40-£54 (incl dinner) WB&B£90-£140 WBDi£105-£155 LDO 5.30pm
Lic ♨ CTV 15P putting green £

GH QQQ *Clennon Valley Hotel* 1 Clennon Rise TQ4 5HG
☎(0803) 550304 & 557736
A modern-fronted property with its own car park and a terraced garden, in an elevated position on the Dartmouth road. The bedrooms are brightly decorated and several offer family accommodation all with good facilities. The cosy lounge and bar are comfortably appointed and simple dishes are offered on the menu in the informal dining room.
12rm(1⇨9↱2hc) (2fb) CTV in all bedrooms ®
Lic ♨ CTV 12P free access to Torbay leisure centre
Credit Cards 1 3

GH QQQ *Danethorpe Hotel* 23 St Andrews Rd TQ4 6HA
☎(0803) 551251
Away from the hustle and bustle of town but only a short walk to the seafront and harbour, this family-run hotel continues to be steadily upgraded and improved. The bedrooms are a little compact but each is very nicely equipped, most of them have en suite showers and all are neatly presented with pretty coordinated décor. The public areas are comfortable and include a lively, popular bar, a cosy TV lounge and a more spacious lounge. A choice of evening meal is offered from either the table d'hôte or small à la carte menu and proprietors Mr and Mrs Chillcott are amiable, cheery hosts.
10rm(4↱6hc) (2fb) CTV in all bedrooms ® ✕
Lic ♨ 10P
Credit Cards 1 2 3

GH QQQ Redcliffe Lodge Hotel 1 Marine Dr TQ3 2NL
☎(0803) 551394
Apr-mid Nov
A corner plot on Marine Drive, beside the safe, sandy beach and green, and a level walk to the town centre, pier and Festival Theatre. The bedrooms are all en suite with colour TV, and the lounge and dining room are cosy and comfortable. The menu offers simple dishes, and a happy, relaxed atmosphere is created by the friendly resident proprietors.
17rm(10⇨7↱) (2fb) CTV in all bedrooms ® ✕ ✻
sB&B⇨↱£20-£30 dB&B⇨↱£40-£60 WBDi£168-£214
LDO 6.30pm
Lic ♨ CTV 20P
Credit Cards 1 3

GH QQQ Hotel Retreat 43 Marine Dr TQ3 2NS
☎(0803) 550596
Etr-Sep
This comfortable private hotel is family owned and set in pleasant grounds in a secluded position on the seafront. The accommodation is comfortable with cosy, bright and well equipped bedrooms.
13rm(5⇨8hc) (1fb) CTV in all bedrooms ® ✻ sB&B£16-£20 dB&B£32-£36 dB&B⇨£36-£40 WBDi£161-£198 LDO 6pm
Lic CTV 14P
Credit Cards 1 3 £

GH QQQ St Weonard's Private Hotel 12 Kernou Rd TQ4 6BA ☎(0803) 558842
An attractive terraced property in a residential street, close to the town centre and only about 100 yards from the seafront. The bedrooms have been brightly decorated and comfortably furnished and the lounge has a home-like feel. A choice of menu promotes home-cooked dishes, and the resident proprietors extend a warm family welcome to guests.
8rm(4↱4hc) (2fb) ® ✕ sB&B£13-£15.50 dB&B£26-£31 dB&B↱£32-£37 WB&B£86-£102 WBDi£120-£140
LDO 3.30pm
Lic CTV 2P £

GH QQ Sattva Hotel 29 Esplanade TQ4 6BL ☎(0803) 557820
Mar-Oct
An attractive end-of-terrace property on the seafront with a level 2-minute walk to the beach. The bedrooms are simply appointed with good facilities. A lively atmosphere is promoted in the bar/lounge where entertainment is provided during the season.
21rm(2⇨17↱2hc) (2fb) CTV in all bedrooms ® ✕
sB&B⇨↱£22-£28 dB&B£36-£40 dB&B⇨↱£40-£44 WB&B£120-£140 WBDi£148-£180 LDO 5pm
Lic lift ♨ CTV 10P
Credit Cards 1 3

GH QQQ The Sealawn Hotel Sea Front, 20 Esplanade Rd TQ4 6BE ☎(0803) 559031

A semidetached 4-storey establishment on the seafront between Paignton Pier and the Festival Hall, affording views across the greens to the sea. The bedrooms are all well equipped and have en suite facilities. The menu offers a choice of simple dishes which should be ordered in advance.

13rm(6⇌7↱) (3fb) CTV in all bedrooms ® T ✗ sB&B⇌↱£18-£29 dB&B⇌↱£36-£48 WB&B£119-£196 WBDi£161-£238 LDO 5.30pm

Lic 🍴 CTV 13P solarium £

GH QQ *Sea Verge Hotel* Marine Dr, Preston TQ3 2NJ ☎(0803) 557795

Closed Dec

A modern building near the beaches, green and town centre with its own car park and small garden. The bedrooms are brightly decorated and a comfortable atmosphere is created in the public areas by the proprietor's relaxed approach.

12rm(5↱7hc) (1fb) CTV in all bedrooms ® ✗ LDO 5pm

Lic 🍴 CTV 14P nc9yrs

Credit Cards [1] [3]

GH QQQ Torbay Sands Hotel 16 Marine Pde, Preston Sea Front TQ3 2NU ☎(0803) 525568

Vera and Eddie Hennequin have created a hospitable atmosphere at their modern hotel which has panoramic views of the bay. The bright, cosy bedrooms are complemented by comfortable and tasteful public rooms.

14rm(9↱5hc) (4fb) CTV in all bedrooms ® ✱ sB&B£13-£17 sB&B↱£13-£17 dB&B£26-£34 dB&B↱£26-£34 WB&B£90-£112 WBDi£110-£132

Lic 🍴 CTV 5P

Credit Cards [1] [3] £

GH QQ **Waterleat House** 22 Waterleat Rd TQ3 3UQ ☎(0803) 550001

A Spanish-style villa situated in an elevated position overlooking Paignton Zoo, away from the hustle and bustle of the town. Bedrooms are all well equipped, and most have private bathrooms. A small bar lounge is available for guests, and evening bar meals are served until 9.30pm.

6⇌↱ (1fb) CTV in 5 bedrooms ® ✗ (ex guide dogs) sB&B£14-£16 sB&B⇌↱£22.50-£25 dB&B⇌↱£32-£35 WB&B£96-£105 WBDi£151.65-£160.65 LDO 9.30pm

Lic 4P Ⓔ

PANDY Gwent Map **03** SO32

FH Q Mrs Olive Probert ***Oldcastle Court*** *(SO326247)* NP7 7PH ☎Crucorney(0873) 890285

To find this house in its secluded location, leave the A465 at Pandy Inn signed to Oldcastle and proceed along this road for 1.5 miles; bearing left turn into the narrow lane when you see the red letter box and the farm is at the end of the lane. It is a simply furnished, traditional Welsh farmhouse, with the Offa's Dyke walk passing close by.

3rm(2hc) (1fb)

10P 308 acres mixed

PARKHAM Devon Map **02** SS32

SELECTED

GH QQQQ **The Old Rectory** EX39 5PL ☎Horns Cross(0237) 451443

Closed 11 Dec-14 Jan

This Georgian country house, set in its own garden, provides an ideal venue for a few days of pampering in peaceful surroundings. The bedrooms are comfortable and freshly decorated with many thoughtful extras. There is a comfortable lounge with its roaring log fire and a separate study for reading and writing. Dinner is taken around a large table with everybody, including the hosts, enjoying Jean's imaginative cooking. A choice of starters is available, perhaps a home-made soup or cheese puff with gooseberry sauce. Then a set main course is served: a rack of lamb with herb and wine sauce, and loin of pork with a watercress and hazelnut stuffing, are just 2 from this year's selection. A choice of sweets might include grand marnier iced soufflé in brandy-snap baskets.

3rm(2⇌↱1hc) ✗ (ex guide dogs) sB&B⇌↱£45-£52 dB&B⇌↱£65-£72 WB&B£204.75-£226.80 LDO 6pm

Lic CTV 12P nc12yrs

PARKMILL (NEAR SWANSEA) West Glamorgan Map **02** SS58

FH QQ Mrs D Edwards ***Parc-le-Breos House*** *(SS529896)* SA3 2HA ☎Swansea(0792) 371636

This early 19th-century farmhouse is situated in the heart of the Gower and reached by a long, tree-lined farm road. Bedrooms and lounges are comfortably appointed, and the house still retains much of its character. There are pleasant grounds, including a well stocked fish pond, and riding school facilities are available.

8rm(2↱5hc) ✗

CTV U snooker 55 acres mixed

PATELEY BRIDGE North Yorkshire Map **07** SE16

FH QQ Mrs C E Nelson ***Nidderdale Lodge*** *(SE183654)* Felbeck HG3 5DR ☎Harrogate(0423) 711677

Etr-Oct

A large bungalow on a working farm alongside the B6265 at Fellbeck, 2 miles east of Pateley Bridge. All bedrooms have their own wash basin and one has an en suite shower and WC. There is a comfortable lounge and a spacious dining room as well as a small kitchen for guests' use.

3hc (1fb)⊁in all bedrooms ® ✗ (ex guide dogs)

CTV 3P 30 acres mixed

PATRICK BROMPTON North Yorkshire Map **08** SE29

SELECTED

GH QQQQ **Elmfield House** Arrathorne DL8 1NE (2m N unclass towards Catterick Camp) ☎Bedale(0677) 50558 & 50557

Surrounded by fields and in its own secluded gardens, this modern house lies just one mile north of Patrick Brompton. Spacious bedrooms are beautifully furnished and decorated; one has a 4-poster bed and 2 on the ground floor have special facilities for the disabled. All have lovely views of the countryside. Public areas include a very comfortable lounge/bar, with an adjoining, quieter lounge. Home-cooked meals are served in the large, very well appointed dining room, and there is also a games room and a solarium. Edith and Jim Lillie make guests very welcome.

9rm(4⇌5↱) (2fb) CTV in all bedrooms ® T ✗ (ex guide dogs) sB&B⇌↱£25-£27.50 dB&B⇌↱£38-£44 WB&B£126-£147 WBDi£196-£217 LDO before noon

Lic 12P ⌡ solarium games room Ⓔ

PAWLETT Somerset Map **03** ST24

FH QQQ Mrs Worgan **Brickyard** *(ST298421)* River Rd TA6 4SE ☎Puriton(0278) 683381

Set in its own neat gardens that include a children's play area and a fascinating collection of gnomes, this 450-year-old farmhouse is discreetly positioned close to the river. Inside, there is a cosy lounge with a TV and a display of interesting plates on the wall. The no-smoking bedrooms are prettily decorated, as well as spotlessly clean and nicely maintained. The friendly hostess, Ann Worgan, provides a warm, informal atmosphere throughout.

3hc (1fb)⊁in all bedrooms ® sB&B£12.50-£15 dB&B£25-£30 WB&B£87.50-£105 WBDi£115.50-£133 LDO 8pm

Lic CTV 12P ⌡ 2 acres non working Ⓔ

PAYHEMBURY Devon Map **03** ST00

SELECTED

GH QQQQ **Colestocks House** Colestocks EX14 0JR (1m N unclass rd) ☎Honiton(0404) 850633

Closed 22 Dec-4 Jan

Amidst 2 acres of walled gardens, where the emphasis is very much on peace and quiet, this 16th-century thatched cottage offers en suite bedrooms, equipped with good facilities, and most are spacious, enhanced with Laura Ashley soft furnishings. The lounge and bar promote a cosy atmosphere, where a range of reading material is provided, along with comfortable seating and access to the garden during summer. A choice of home-cooked dishes, with a French influence, is served in the relaxed surroundings of the dining room, which boasts a large and attractive inglenook fireplace.

9⇌↱ (1fb) CTV in all bedrooms ® ✗ (ex guide dogs) sB&B⇌↱£29.50-£32.50 dB&B⇌↱£49-£55 WBDi£220-£235 LDO 8pm

Lic 9P nc10yrs putting green

Credit Cards 1 3 Ⓔ

PEEBLES Borders *Peebleshire* Map **11** NT24

GH QQQ **Whitestone House** Innerleithen Rd EH45 8BD (on A72-Peebles to Galashiels Rd) ☎(0721) 20337

A former stone-built manse situated on the A72 Peebles to Galashiels road with its own garden and excellent views over the surrounding hills. Bedrooms vary in size but are comfortably appointed in a mixture of styles and provide good value accommodation and tea-making facilities. Hearty breakfasts are

served in the combined lounge/dining room. Car parking is available. Guests are made very welcome here.
5hc (2fb) ® ✗ (ex guide dogs) ✱ dB&Bfr£26
🏛 CTV 5P

FH QQQ Mrs J M Haydock **Winkston** *(NT244433)* Edinburgh Rd EH45 8PH ☎(0721) 21264
Etr-Oct
Situated in an elevated position beside the A703, 1.5 miles north of the town, this listed Georgian farmhouse offers cosy, well maintained accommodation and a friendly atmosphere. Bedrooms are prettily decorated, and furnished with good beds. There is also a comfortable lounge and a neat dining room.
3hc ⊁in all bedrooms ® ✗ (ex guide dogs) ✱ sB&B£15 dB&B£25-£26
🏛 CTV 4P 40 acres sheep

PEMBROKE Dyfed Map **02** SM90

GH QQ High Noon Lower Lamphey Rd SA71 4AB
☎(0646) 683736 & 681232
Run by the very friendly Mr and Mrs Bryant, this spotlessly clean guesthouse is situated a short walk from the town centre. Extra en suite rooms have recently been added, and bedrooms are neat, bright and modern. There is a comfortable open-plan lounge and dining room, and car parking is available.
9rm(5⇌↱4hc) (2fb) CTV in all bedrooms ® ✱ sB&B£12.60-£16 sB&B⇌↱£15-£16 dB&B£25.20-£32 dB&B⇌↱£27.20-£32 WB&B£84.70-£105 WBDi£120.70-£142.50 LDO 5pm
Lic 🏛 CTV 9P

PENARTH South Glamorgan Map **03** ST17

GH QQ Albany Hotel 14 Victoria Rd CF6 2EF
☎Cardiff(0222) 701598 & 701242 FAX (0222) 701598
This small, friendly and personally run guesthouse is conveniently situated just a short walk from the town centre and railway station. Bedrooms are simply styled and furnished, but well equipped for a small property, with satellite TV, direct-dial telephones and private bathrooms. There is also a comfortable lounge and cosy bar.
13rm(7⇌↱6hc) (4fb)⊁in 2 bedrooms CTV in all bedrooms ® **T** ✱ sB&B£25 sB&B⇌↱£35 dB&B£40 dB&B⇌↱£45 LDO 8.30pm
Lic 🏛 CTV 3P
Credit Cards 1 2 3
See advertisement under CARDIFF

PENLEY Clwyd Map **07** SJ44

GH QQQ *Bridge House* LL13 OLY
☎Overton-On-Dee(097873) 763
Good quality, comfortable modern accommodation is provided at this considerably renovated former farmhouse. It is located 2 miles north of the village, which is midway between Wrexham and Whitchurch, and stands in impeccably kept gardens with a babbling brook at the bottom.
3rm(2hc) ⊁in all bedrooms CTV in all bedrooms ® ✗ LDO noon
🏛 CTV 6P 2🚘 nc10yrs

PENRHYNDEUDRAETH Gwynedd Map **06** SH63

FH QQ Mrs P Bayley **Y Wern** *(SH620421)* LLanfrothen LL48 6LX (2m N off B4410) ☎(0766) 770556
This large stone-built farmhouse dates back to the early 17th century and is situated at the foot of the 'Moelwyns' in a picturesque and peaceful area, 2 miles north of the village, close to the junction of the A4085 and B4410. Retaining much of the original character, the accommodation is comfortable with a mixture of modern and traditional furniture; family rooms are also available. Guests eat in the large farmhouse kitchen.
5rm(2↱3hc) (4fb) ® ✗ sB&B£18 sB&B↱£21 dB&B£27-£30 dB&B↱£33-£36 WB&B£85-£95 WBDi£141-£151
🏛 CTV 6P 110 acres beef sheep

PENRITH Cumbria Map **12** NY53

GH QQ Brandelhow 1 Portland Place CA11 7QN
☎(0768) 64470
Closed 24-26 Dec & 31 Dec
Situated in a terraced row within walking distance of the town centre, this guesthouse has attractively decorated bedrooms with coordinated fabrics. Guests may use the owners' lounge which is tastefully furnished in period style.
6rm(5hc) (3fb)⊁in 2 bedrooms CTV in all bedrooms ® ✱ sB&B£15-£17 dB&B£27-£29 WB&B£91-£98
🏛 CTV 1P Ⓔ

GH QQQ *The Grotto* Yanwath CA10 2LF ☎(0768) 63288 FAX (0768) 63432
A traditional, stone-built small hotel standing in its own secluded grounds next to the west-coast railway line. The bedrooms have good facilities, and public areas are attractive, with several lounges. A home-cooked dinner is provided in the charming restaurant.
6rm(4↱2hc) (2fb) CTV in all bedrooms ® ✗ LDO 6pm
Lic 🏛 12P
Credit Cards 1 3

GH QQ Limes Country Hotel Redhills, Stainton CA11 0DT (2m W A66) ☎(0768) 63343
This attractive Victorian house stands in its own gardens surrounded by open countryside. To find it, follow the A66 off junction 40 of the M6, turning left by the Little Chef, and following signs from there. Bedrooms are equipped with tea-making facilities and have central heating, and the comfortable lounge provides lots of easy chairs.
6rm(1⇌4↱1hc) (2fb) ® ✗ (ex guide dogs) ✱ sB&B£17.50-£22.50 sB&B⇌↱£20-£24 dB&B£30-£35 dB&B⇌↱£34-£40 WB&B£115-£160 WBDi£165-£230 LDO 3pm
Lic 🏛 CTV 7P
Credit Cards 1 3 Ⓔ

GH QQQ Woodland House Hotel Wordsworth St CA11 7QY
☎(0768) 64177 FAX (0768) 890152
This very pleasant family-run small hotel is situated in a side road close to the town centre. Bedrooms are attractively decorated and have good facilities. Public areas include a cosy lounge with a bar and lots of wildlife books to read.
8⇌↱ (2fb)⊁in all bedrooms CTV in all bedrooms ® ✗ sB&B⇌↱fr£22 dB&B⇌↱fr£38 WB&Bfr£146 LDO 4.30pm
Lic 🏛 CTV 10P 1🚘 Ⓔ

PENRUDDOCK Cumbria Map **12** NY42

SELECTED

FH QQQQ Mrs S M Smith **Highgate** *(NY444275)* CA11 0SE ☎Greystoke(07684) 83339
mid Feb-mid Nov
This lovely stone-built Cumbrian farmhouse dating from 1730, is just 4 miles from junction 40 of the M6. Old beams and brasses and brass bedsteads feature in 2 of the tastefully decorated rooms. All rooms have colour TV, hot and cold washbasins and tea and coffee-making facilities. The lounge is delightful, full of kettles, brasses and Victoriana. A filling Cumbrian breakfast is provided, and Mrs Smith is an attentive hostess.
3hc CTV in all bedrooms ® ✗ sB&B£15-£20 dB&B£30
🏛 3P nc5yrs 400 acres mixed Ⓔ

Street plans of certain towns and cities will be found in a separate section at the back of the book.

PENRYN Cornwall & Isles of Scilly Map **02** SW73

SELECTED

GH QQQQ Prospect House 1 Church Rd TR10 8DA
☎Falmouth(0326) 373198

Built around 1830, this handsome house is set back from the A39 in a leafy garden. A listed building, it has been tastefully restored retaining its original mahogany doors, coloured glass and elaborate plaster cornices. Bedrooms are all attractively decorated and furnished, with many thoughtful extras, including teddy bears. The cosy lounge has an open fire, antique furniture, books, dried flowers and ornaments. The flagstoned dining room accommodates a communal table and elegant chairs of Flemish design. A set menu is available in the evening, and guests are welcome to bring their own wine. Cliff Paul and Barry Sheppard are friendly and attentive hosts.

3⇔↑ TV available ® sB&B⇔↑£26-£31 dB&B⇔↑£46-£51 WB&B£145-£195 WBDi£257-£307 LDO noon
ᵯ CTV 4P 1🚗 nc12yrs (£)
See advertisement under FALMOUTH

PENSHURST Kent Map **05** TQ54

SELECTED

GH QQQQ Swale Cottage Old Swaylands Ln, Off Poundbridge Ln TN11 8AH ☎(0892) 870738

Converted from an 18th-century Kentish barn, this delightful cottage guesthouse is peacefully located in 2 acres of well kept garden and paddock, overlooking the Weald of Kent countryside. Bedrooms are beautifully maintained and individually furnished in cottage style each with TV, clock radio and tea tray; one room has a 4-poster bed. There is a large lounge with an inglenook fireplace and beams, and a hearty English breakfast is served at the elegant communal dining table in the beamed breakfast/dining room by proprietor Cynthia Dakin.

3⇔↑ ⊬in all bedrooms CTV in all bedrooms ✗ sB&B⇔↑£26-£32 dB&B⇔↑£40-£50
ᵯ 5P nc10yrs (£)

PENYBONT Powys Map **03** SO16

SELECTED

GH QQQQ Ffaldau Country House & Restaurant LD1 5UD (2m E A44) ☎(0597) 851421

A listed cruck-built long house dating from 1500, set back from the A44 at Llandegley. This picturesque guesthouse is surrounded by very pretty gardens, nestling in the Radnor Hills. The comfortable bedrooms are timbered, each with private bathrooms, and coordinating fabrics are much in evidence. There is a very comfortable small lounge on the first-floor landing, with a sizeable library of books and TV, and a small timbered bar which features a recently exposed log fire. Dinners are prepared by Sylvia Knott, who has earned a well deserved reputation for her cooking; these are served in the dining room which is timbered with the original beams and has a wood-burning stove.

3⇔↑ ® ✗ (ex guide dogs) ✱ sB&B⇔↑£22-£25 dB&B⇔↑£36-£45 LDO 9pm
Lic ᵯ CTV 25P nc10yrs

PENZANCE Cornwall & Isles of Scilly Map **02** SW43

See **Town Plan Section**

GH QQQ Blue Seas Hotel 13 Regent Ter TR18 4DW
☎(0736) 64744 FAX (0736) 330701

A conveniently located family-run guesthouse near the promenade and town centre, facing the sea. Bedrooms are on 3 levels, and many have sea views; they are all tidy and well maintained, each with private bathroom. The Davenports show great attention to detail, with fresh local produce for their home-cooked meals. There is a comfortable lounge and a very pretty front garden.

10rm(2⇔8↑) (3fb) CTV in all bedrooms ® ✗ sB&B⇔↑£15-£17.50 dB&B⇔↑£30-£35 WB&B£200-£245 WBDi£329-£364 LDO 6.30pm
Lic ᵯ CTV 12P nc5yrs
Credit Cards 1 3 (£)

GH QQQ ***Camilla Hotel*** Regent Ter TR18 4DW
☎(0736) 63771

This whitewashed Regency house sits in a quiet terrace overlooking the seafront, close to the parks and town centre. Bedrooms are attractively decorated and well equipped, and there is a comfortable lounge with some period furniture. The accommodation is clean and well kept throughout.

9rm(1⇔4↑4hc) (3fb) CTV in all bedrooms ® LDO noon
Lic ᵯ CTV 6P
Credit Cards 1 3

GH QQ Carlton Private Hotel Promenade TR18 4NW
☎(0736) 62081
Etr-19 Oct rs Mar

This small, modest hotel is positioned right on the seafront and has been personally run by the same family for several years. It offers spotlessly clean, bright and well equipped bedrooms, with commanding views.

10rm(8↑2hc) CTV in all bedrooms ® ✗ (ex guide dogs) sB&Bfr£16.50 dB&B£34-£35 dB&B↑£40-£42
Lic CTV Ᵽ nc12yrs (£)

GH QQQ Chy-an-Mor 15 Regent Ter TR18 4DW
☎(0736) 63441
Closed Dec-Jan

Lew and Anita Hitchens have been here many years and offer a friendly welcome at their terraced guesthouse near the promenade. There is a neat garden at the front, a comfortable lounge and bedrooms on 2 floors.

8↑ CTV in all bedrooms ® ✗ ✱ sB&B↑fr£16.50 dB&B↑fr£33 WB&Bfr£110 WBDifr£169.50 LDO breakfast
Lic ᵯ 10P nc12yrs
Credit Cards 1 3 (£)

GH QQ Dunedin Alexandra Rd TR18 4LZ
☎(0736) 62652
Closed Xmas rs Jan-Etr

A family-run terraced guesthouse midway between the town and seafront. Bedrooms are generally spacious, and they are all comfortable and well equipped. There is a residents' lounge and a licensed bar area adjacent to the dining room.

9rm(1⇔8↑) (4fb) CTV in all bedrooms ® sB&B⇔↑£13-£16 dB&B⇔↑£26-£32 WB&B£90-£110 WBDi£140-£155 LDO 5pm
Lic ᵯ CTV 1🚗 (£3) nc3yrs (£)

GH QQ Georgian House 20 Chapel St TR18 4AW
☎(0736) 65664
Closed Xmas rs Nov-Apr

This friendly guesthouse is centrally situated opposite the famous Admiral Benbow Inn and offers good value for money. Bedrooms are well equipped, and there is a popular family restaurant on the ground floor.

12rm(4⇔2↑6hc) (4fb) CTV in all bedrooms ® ✗ (ex guide dogs) sB&B£18-£24 sB&B⇔↑£24-£26 dB&Bfr£30 dB&B⇔↑fr£37 LDO 8pm

→

Chy-an-Mor *(House by the sea)*

15 Regent Terrace, Penzance TR21 4DW
Tel 0736 63441

* Full central Heating
* Mid week bookings
* Ample private parking
* Licensed
* Special rates for Spring and Autumn
* Evening meals by request

Ideal for touring the West Country we offer modern comfortable en-suite rooms most with lovely sea-views. All rooms have tea making facilities and colour TV's and radio's. Recommended for our friendly atmosphere and good varied cuisine using fresh local produce.

Access/Visa accepted

B & B from £16 per person
No single supplements

Blue Seas Hotel

Regent Terrace, Penzance
Cornwall TR18 4DW
Telephone: (0736) 64744
Fax: (0736) 330701

Access **Visa**

Blue Seas offers a high standard of comfort and friendly service.
All bright attractive bedrooms are en-suite with colour TV central heating.
Tea making facilities. Crisp cotton bed linen.
Set in a quiet terrace overlooking the sea.
Ample private parking.
Bus, rail and boat to Isles of Scilly within easy walking distance.

Resident Proprietors:
Pat and Derek Davenport

Camilla Hotel

Regent Terrace,
Penzance,
Cornwall
TR18 4DW

Tel: Penzance
(0736) 63771

Camilla is a delightful building of the Regency period ideally situated in a quiet terrace overlooking the seafront promenade within easy reach of the rail and coach termini. The shopping centre, parks and harbour departure for the Isles of Scilly are very close at hand. The Hotel is licensed and offers private parking, central heating, en suite facilities. There are colour televisions, tea/coffee making facilities in all bedrooms. Several European languages are spoken by the resident proprietors Brian and Annette Gooding.

OPEN ALL YEAR

Payment in European currency accepted

the·ffaldau

COUNTRY HOUSE

RESIDENTIAL & LICENSED RESTAURANT

Nestling in the lee of the Radnor Hills. This picturesque cruck-built longhouse c1500 with its hanging baskets and window boxes is set in 1½ acres of garden.

3 prettily furnished en suite bedrooms. Our high standards of cooking are reflected in our choice and preparation of fresh local produce and organic vegetables from our own garden when available, complemented by an interesting selection of wines. A la carte menu.

LLANDEGLEY · POWYS · WALES · LD1 5UD
TELEPHONE 0597 851421

Lic CTV 11P
Credit Cards 1 2 3 £

GH QQ **Kimberley House** 10 Morrab Rd TR18 4EZ
(0736) 62727
Closed Dec
This end-of-terrace Cornish granite-built house offers sound accommodation on 2 floors: the second staircase is rather narrow. The bedrooms are tastefully furnished and include personal touches like sewing kits and hot water bottles. Downstairs there is a residents' lounge and a separate bar.
9hc (2fb) CTV in all bedrooms ® (ex guide dogs) sB&B£13-£15 dB&B£26-£30 WB&B£86-£93 WBDi£140-£152 LDO 5pm
Lic CTV 4P nc5yrs
Credit Cards 1 3

GH QQ ***Hotel Minalto*** Alexandra Rd TR18 4LZ
(0736) 62923
Closed 18 Dec-3 Jan
A granite-built house on a corner site in a residential street, only a short walk from the seafront. It offers guests both a lounge and a bar downstairs, and rooms of various sizes and facilities above.
11rm(2 9hc) (1fb) CTV in all bedrooms ® LDO 5.30pm
Lic CTV 10P
Credit Cards 1 3

GH Q **Mount Royal Hotel** Chyandour Cliff TR18 3LQ
(0736) 62233
Mar-Oct
Overlooking Mounts Bay, this solid Victorian house offers simply furnished bedrooms and a spacious dining room, along with a simple lounge.
9rm(5 4hc) (3fb) CTV in 3 bedrooms ® * sB&B£21-£24 sB&B £23-£26 dB&B£34-£38 dB&B £38-£42 WB&B£126-£140
CTV 6P 4 (£3 per night) £

GH QQ **Penalva** Alexandra Rd TR18 4LZ (0736) 69060
This family-run terraced guesthouse lies in a residential road between the shops and the sea. Bedrooms are neat and well kept, and the public areas offer a wide selection of Cornish pictures and information. Smoking is not permitted.
5rm(4 1hc) (3fb) in all bedrooms CTV in all bedrooms ® * sB&B£10-£15 sB&B £10-£15 dB&B£20-£30 dB&B £24-£32 WB&B£80-£98 WBDi£136-£154 LDO 6.30pm
nc3yrs £

GH QQ **Penmorvah Hotel** Alexandra Rd TR18 4LZ
(0736) 63711
Set in a tree-lined road, this family-run terraced private hotel has bedrooms on 3 floors: they are equipped with all modern facilities, and several are arranged for families.
10rm(5 5) (4fb) CTV in all bedrooms ® T
sB&B £12.50-£18 dB&B £25-£36 WB&B£80-£120 WBDi£115-£165 LDO 6pm
Lic
Credit Cards 1 2 3 £

GH QQ **Trenant Private Hotel** Alexandra Rd TR18 4LX
(0736) 62005
A stylish Victorian property, conveniently located close to the seafront and local amenities. Personally run, it has spacious public rooms and well furnished bedrooms of varying sizes.
10rm(5 5hc) (3fb) CTV in all bedrooms ® * sB&B£12.50-£15 dB&B£25-£30 dB&B £32-£38 WB&B£85-£130 WBDi£135-£180 LDO noon
Lic CTV nc5yrs £

GH Q **Trevelyan Hotel** 16 Chapel St TR18 4AW
(0736) 62494
Closed 25 Dec
This 17th-century building is in one of the oldest streets in the town centre. Top-floor rooms enjoy a distant view, and several bedrooms have a shower facility.
8hc (4fb) CTV in all bedrooms ® (ex guide dogs) sB&B£12.50-£13.50 dB&B£25-£27 dB&B£27 WB&B£85-£90 WBDi£140-£145 LDO am
Lic CTV 8P £

GH QQ **Trewella** 18 Mennaye Rd TR18 4NG
(0736) 63818
Mar-Oct
A bright and cheerful little guesthouse in a quiet residential street near the football ground and close to the seafront. There is a lounge and bar decorated with plants and a collection of pictures, and bedrooms are neat and clean.
8rm(4 4hc) (2fb) in 1 bedroom ® sB&B£11.50-£13.50 dB&B£23-£27 dB&B £27-£31 WB&B£78-£85 WBDi£117-£124 LDO noon
Lic CTV nc5yrs £

INN QQQ **The Yacht** The Promenade TR18 4AU
(0736) 62787
Set back from the seafront, this popular pub is an eye-catching thirties design, built in tune with the well known open air lido. The public areas consist of a busy lounge bar, attractively styled with yachting pictures, where snacks are served. The bedrooms on the first floor are very smartly decorated, with good amenities and most have sea views.
7 (1fb) CTV in 6 bedrooms ® (ex guide dogs) *
sB&B £20-£28 dB&B £40-£56 WB&B£130-£170
Lunch £6-£7.50 Dinner £7.50-£9 LDO 9pm
8P
Credit Cards 1 2 3 £

PERRANPORTH Cornwall & Isles of Scilly Map **02** SW75

GH QQ ***Fairview Hotel*** Tywarnhayle Rd TR6 0DX
Truro(0872) 572278
Apr-Oct
Standing in an elevated position with lovely views out to sea, this whitewashed Edwardian property is popular with families. Currently some bedrooms are having smart en suite facilities added, otherwise the rooms are simply furnished and decorated but nicely kept. The attractive, comfortable lounge boasts a bar and pool table at one end, and evening meals are taken in the front-facing dining room, filled with a collection of wall plates and plants. Car parking is available at the rear of the building.
15rm(8 7hc) (6fb) in 2 bedrooms ® (ex guide dogs) LDO 8pm
Lic CTV 8P 3
Credit Cards 1 3

GH QQQ **Villa Margarita Country Hotel** Bolingey TR6 0AS
Truro(0872) 572063
Exceptionally well appointed colonial-style villa in an acre of well tended gardens. Imaginative table d'hôte menus served by caring owners.
5rm(3 2hc) Annexe 1 (1fb) TV in 1 bedroom ®
(ex guide dogs) * sB&B £18.50-£20 dB&B £37-£40 WB&B£11-£120 WBDi£195-£204 LDO 4pm
Lic CTV 8P nc8yrs solarium £

PERTH Tayside *Perthshire* Map **11** NO12

GH QQQ ***Alpine*** 7 Strathview Ter PH2 7HY (0738) 37687
At the northern edge of the city, on the A92, this house offers spotlessly clean accommodation. Bedrooms are nicely decorated and there is a small lounge with tourist information.
6rm(3 3hc) (1fb) in all bedrooms CTV in all bedrooms ® LDO 7pm
Lic 12P nc7yrs

GH QQQ **Ardfern House** 15 Pitcullen Crescent PH2 7HT
(0738) 22259
3rm(1 2hc) in all bedrooms CTV in all bedrooms ®
dB&B £32-£40 LDO noon
CTV 6P nc5yrs putting green

GH QQQ Clark Kimberley 57-59 Dunkeld Rd PH1 5RP
☎(0738) 37406
A warm welcome awaits guests at this friendly guesthouse which has convenient access to the city bypass. Mr and Mrs Cattanach are to be congratulated on the high standard of accommodation they offer, most of the rooms having en suite facilities.
8rm(6↱2hc) (5fb) CTV in all bedrooms ® ✗ (ex guide dogs) * sB&B£15-£16 dB&B↱£30-£32 WB&B£105-£112
♔ CTV 12P

GH QQQ Clunie 12 Pitcullen Crescent PH2 7HT
☎(0738) 23625
Situated on the A94 Braemar road a short way from the town centre, this guesthouse is well furnished in all areas and is mainly modern in style. The resident owners offer warm and friendly service and show great concern for their guests' comfort.
7⇌↱ (3fb) CTV in all bedrooms ® * sB&B⇌↱fr£17 dB&B⇌↱fr£34 LDO noon
♔ CTV 8P

GH QQ The Darroch 9 Pitcullen Crescent PH2 7HT
☎(0738) 36893
This guesthouse offers 3 spacious bedrooms with private bathrooms, and another 3 smaller rooms, more modest in standard.
6rm(3↱3hc) (2fb) CTV in all bedrooms ® sB&B£13.50-£15.50 dB&B£27-£31 dB&B↱£30-£34 LDO 4pm
♔ CTV 9P

GH QQ The Gables 24 Dunkeld Rd PH1 5RW
☎(0738) 24717
This family-run guesthouse is situated on the northern side of the city, at the junction of the Inverness and Crieff roads, and it has convenient access to the ring route and A9. Bedrooms are thoughtfully equipped, and there is a cosy lounge and a small residents' bar in the dining room.
8hc (3fb) CTV in all bedrooms ® sB&B£14-£15 dB&B£26-£28 WB&B£91-£105 WBDi£133-£140 LDO 4pm
Lic ♔ CTV 8P
Credit Cards 3

GH QQ The Heidl 43 York Place PH2 8EH ☎(0738) 35031
This commercial guesthouse on the Glasgow road is just off the town centre. Bedrooms vary in size, some being in the original house and others in a small modern wing. There is no lounge, but meals are served to both residents and non residents.
10rm(1↱9hc) (2fb) CTV in all bedrooms ® * sB&B£18-£20 sB&B↱£26-£30 dB&B£32-£36 dB&B↱£40-£44
Lic ♔ 3P

GH QQ Iona 2 Pitcullen Crescent PH2 7HT
☎(0738) 27261
Featuring an attractive little dining room with lace table cloths and nice, modern bedrooms equipped with good en suite shower rooms, this well looked after Victorian house is situated on the A94, and provides a small parking area at the front.
5rm(2↱3hc) (1fb) CTV in all bedrooms ® sB&B£14 sB&B↱£16 dB&B£28 dB&B↱£32 LDO 4.30pm
♔ CTV 5P

GH QQQ Kinnaird 5 Marshall Place PH2 8AH
☎(0738) 28021
Trisha and John Stiell are the enthusiastic owners of this Georgian town house, which looks out over the local park and is convenient for those coming into the town from the south. Bedrooms are attractively decorated and furnished with modern units. They vary in size but most are compact. There is a small quiet lounge and a dining room with individual and well spaced tables. Parking, including lock-up garaging, is available in the private lane to the rear.
7rm(5⇌↱2hc) CTV in all bedrooms ® ✗ (ex guide dogs) sB&Bfr£18 dB&Bfr£32 dB&B⇌↱fr£36 LDO 4pm
♔ 1P 6🚗 nc12yrs

GH QQQ ***Lochiel House*** 13 Pitcullen Crescent PH2 7HT
☎(0738) 33183
It is difficult to imagine a more welcoming 'home from home' than Lochiel House, a semidetached Victorian property on the A94 on the northern fringe of the town. Rita Buchan's charm, sincerity and affection for her guests makes this a delightful place to stay. Her enthusiasm is also mirrored in lovely personal touches throughout the house, which is a no-smoking establishment. The cosy little lounge has a real fire when weather dictates and a selection of games. Hearty breakfasts are also taken here around 2 lace-covered tables. Bedrooms are immaculately clean and will be remembered not only for their comfort but for all the thoughtful extras such as books, magazines, sweeties, washing-up liquid, shortbread, face cloths, mineral water, pens, tissues and cotton-wool balls, as well as radios. One room has 2 rocking chairs, and while there are no en suites, residents have the use of both a shower room and a bathroom. These are modern and very attractively decorated, and have an array of toiletries as well as radio sets for lingerers.
3hc CTV in all bedrooms ® ✗ (ex guide dogs)
卿 4P

GH QQ Ochil View 7 Kings Place PH2 8AA ☎(0738) 25708
Within a 5-minute walk of the railway station, and looking out across the local park, Ochil View occupies the first and second floors of a semidetached stone house. Bedrooms are brightly decorated and the dining room and lounge share a spacious room with a bay window. There is a small parking area to the front just off the pavement.
5rm(1↱4hc) (2fb) CTV in all bedrooms ® * dB&B£22-£27 dB&B↱£24-£30 WB&B£70-£84
卿 CTV 4P

GH QQQ Park Lane 17 Marshall Place PH2 8AG
☎(0738) 37218 FAX (0738) 43519
20 Jan-12 Dec & Xmas & New Year
Comfortable, nicely appointed bedrooms are a feature of this well maintained terraced house overlooking the links, only minutes' walk from the city centre. The lounge also serves as the breakfast room.
6⇌↱ (2fb)⊬in 2 bedrooms CTV in all bedrooms ® ✗ (ex guide dogs) sB&B⇌↱£16.50-£18.50 dB&B⇌↱£33-£37 WB&B£115-£125
卿 CTV 8P
Credit Cards [1] [3]

GH QQ Pitcullen 17 Pitcullen Crescent PH2 7HT
☎(0738) 26506
A well maintained, family-run guesthouse on the northern edge of the city beside the A94. There is an attractive first-floor lounge, and a high standard of cleanliness and housekeeping makes this a popular base for tourists.
6rm(3↱3hc) (1fb) CTV in all bedrooms ® ✗ * sB&B£20-£25 sB&B↱£25-£30 dB&B£30-£40 dB&B↱£35-£45 LDO 6pm
卿 6P

PETERBOROUGH Cambridgeshire Map **04** TL19

GH QQQ ***Hawthorn House Hotel*** 89 Thorpe Rd PE3 6JQ
☎(0733) 340608
A brick, semidetached Victorian house with some off-street parking, located on the B1179 opposite the hospital and within ten minutes' walk from the city centre and station. Tastefully converted a few years ago, the house incorporates every modern facility whilst retaining the original style and elegance of that period. Bedrooms are well presented and furnished, with a high standard of cleanliness. A well stocked bar opens into the dining room and small lounge area.
8rm(2⇌6↱) (2fb)⊬in 2 bedrooms CTV in all bedrooms ® ✗
Lic 卿 CTV 5P
Credit Cards [1] [3]

PETERSFIELD Hampshire Map **04** SU72

See also **Rogate**

INN QQQ The Master Robert Buriton GU31 5SW
☎(0730) 267275 FAX (0730) 260154
Nestling among the South Downs in the pretty village of Buriton, just south of Petersfield, lies this popular historic inn. The bedrooms are very smart and well equipped and have good modern private bathrooms.
6⇌↱ CTV in all bedrooms ® **T** * dB&B⇌↱£25-£35 Lunch £1.95-£9.95&alc High tea £3.95-£5.95 Dinner £1.95-£9.95&alc LDO 10pm
卿 35P (charged)
Credit Cards [1] [2] [3]

PETHAM Kent Map **05** TR15

SELECTED

GH QQQQ The Old Poor House Kake St CT4 5RY (5m S of Canterbury off B2068) ☎Canterbury(0227) 700413 FAX 071-247 1873
Built in 1769 and at one time housing the parish poor, this delightful house is peacefully set in 3 acres just 1.5 miles from the village of Petham. The 4 bedrooms, all with good en suite facilities, are attractively decorated in coordinating pastel shades and furnished with antique pine. Waltons restaurant is open from Tuesday to Saturday and chef/patron Raymond Kemp combines modern influences with classical cuisine. There is a selection of country-house set menus at varying prices which you can mix and match, or you can choose from the full à la carte.
4rm(2⇌2↱) (1fb)⊬in 2 bedrooms CTV in all bedrooms ® ✗ (ex guide dogs) * sB&B⇌↱£40 dB&B⇌↱£50 WBDi£350 LDO 9.45pm
Lic 卿 CTV 45P
Credit Cards [1] [3] (£)

PEVENSEY East Sussex Map **05** TQ60

GH QQ Napier The Promenade BN24 6HD
☎Eastbourne(0323) 768875
Superbly situated on the beach with its own beach garden, this guesthouse enjoys an away-from-the-crowds location but is only a few miles from Eastbourne. Bedrooms are modern and simply furnished, 2 of them have their own balcony. There is a small bar, dining room and sun lounge, and extensive service is provided by the friendly proprietors.
10rm(5↱5hc) (3fb) CTV in all bedrooms ® ✗ sB&B£16-£19 sB&B↱£16-£19 dB&B£30-£36 dB&B↱£32-£38 WB&B£102-£109 LDO 4pm
Lic 卿 CTV 7P ♪ (£)

PICKERING North Yorkshire Map **08** SE88

GH QQQ Bramwood 19 Hallgarth YO18 7AW
☎(0751) 74066
A listed grey stone Georgian house close to the town centre, Bramwood is ideally situated for touring the moors and coast. Although without full en suite facilities, the bedrooms are particularly spacious and individually decorated. There is a comfortable lounge with a TV and an open fire and English cooking is served in the small dining room.
6hc (1fb)⊬in all bedrooms ® ✗ (ex guide dogs) sB&B£14-£15 dB&B£28-£34 WB&B£84-£96 WBDi£143.50-£155.50 LDO 2.30pm
CTV 6P nc3yrs
Credit Cards [1] [2] [3] [5] (£)

(£) Remember to use the money-off vouchers.

PIDDLETRENTHIDE Dorset Map **03** SY79

INN QQQ The Poachers DT2 7QX ☎(03004) 358

This 16th-century inn has a separate, modern bedroom block, built around the gardens and the outdoor heated swimming pool. The rooms are comfortable and bright with pretty soft furnishings. The bar area is currently being refurbished and a cosy residents' lounge is being built. The Fox family remain very involved in the daily running of the establishment, and create a warm, friendly atmosphere.

2🛁🚿 Annexe 9🛁🚿 (2fb) CTV in all bedrooms Ⓡ ✱
sB&B🛁🚿£30 dB&B🛁🚿£46 WBDi£220 Lunch £5-£10&alc
Dinner £6-£12alc LDO 9pm
🏢 CTV 40P ⛲(heated)
Credit Cards [1] [3] Ⓔ

PITLOCHRY Tayside *Perthshire* Map **14** NN95

GH QQ Comar House Strathview Ter PH16 5AT
☎(0796) 473531 FAX (0796) 473811
Etr-Oct

Dating back to 1910, this imposing, turreted stone house enjoys a fine outlook from its secluded grounds on a hillside above the town. It offers good value bed and breakfast accommodation in bright, cheery bedrooms decorated in pastel colours with mixed, modern furniture, and there is a spacious lounge with a large bay window which invites peaceful relaxation.

6rm(3🛁🚿3hc) CTV in all bedrooms Ⓡ ✱ sB&Bfr£14.50
sB&B🛁🚿£17.50-£19.50
🏢 CTV P
Credit Cards [1] [3]

GH QQQ Craigroyston House 2 Lower Oakfield PH16 5HQ
☎(0796) 472053

A warm welcome awaits you at this comfortable, family-run Victorian house which is set in its own grounds overlooking the town and surrounding hills. The bedrooms are comfortably furnished in Victorian style and most feature Laura Ashley décor and coordinating fabrics. There is a comfortable, quiet lounge and hearty breakfasts are served in the attractive dining room.

8rm(7🛁🚿1hc) (1fb) CTV in all bedrooms Ⓡ
✗ (ex guide dogs) sB&B🛁🚿£16-£23 dB&B🛁🚿£32-£46
WB&B£112-£161
🏢 9P

SELECTED

GH QQQQ Dundarave House Strathview Ter PH16 6AT
☎(0796) 473109

This fine detached Victorian house is set in its own well tended gardens high above the town and commands superb views across the valley. The new owners Mae and Bob Collier have recently taken over the guesthouse and plan to further improve on the already high standards here. The bright, attractive bedrooms are well proportioned and thoughtfully equipped with fresh fruit, shortbread, home-made cake and hairdryers. The comfortable lounge has bay windows and a fine black marble fireplace. Enjoyable breakfasts are served in the small dining room, complete with linen, silver and period chairs.

7rm(5🛁🚿2hc) (1fb) CTV in all bedrooms Ⓡ sB&B£24-£28 dB&B£48-£56 dB&B🛁🚿£48-£56 WB&B£154-£168 WBDi£238-£266 LDO 5pm
🏢 7P 1🚗

See advertisement on page 323

GH QQ Duntrune 22 East Moulin Rd PH16 5HY
☎(0796) 472172
Feb-Oct

This large detached Victorian house sits peacefully in its own gardens in an elevated position which affords fine views across the town and valley. The neat bedrooms are spotlessly clean and the lounge displays mementoes of the owners' time in Hong Kong.

→

7rm(5⛿2hc) (1fb) CTV in all bedrooms ® ✗ sB&B£16-£19 dB&B⛿£32-£39
🛏 8P nc5yrs

GH QQQ ***Fasganeoin Hotel*** Perth Rd PH16 5DJ ☎(0796) 472387
15 Apr-12 Oct
Fasganeoin, which is Gaelic for 'place of the birds', was built as a private house in the 1870s. Bedrooms are spacious and comfortable; several have fine period furniture and original fireplaces, and some have modern private bathrooms. The hotel has a reputation for serving good Scottish afternoon and high teas, the latter taking the place of dinner. Fasganeoin is the first hotel you see if entering the town from the south and it occupies a secluded position in its own grounds, yet is within walking distance of the town centre.
9rm(5⇨⛿4hc) (3fb) ✗ (ex guide dogs) LDO 7.15pm
Lic 🛏 CTV 20P
Credit Cards 1 3

GH QQQ ***Torrdarach Hotel*** Golf Course Rd PH16 5AU ☎(0796) 472136
Etr-mid Oct
A relaxed, friendly atmosphere prevails at Richard and Vivienne Cale's fine Edwardian house, which is set in beautiful wooded gardens close to the golf course. Bright and airy bedrooms with mixed, modern furnishings offer the normal range of amenities. The quiet lounge with comfortable settees and easy chairs, invites peaceful relaxation and a Scottish menu is offered in the neat dining room, overlooking the garden.
7hc CTV in all bedrooms ® ✗ (ex guide dogs) LDO 5.45pm
Lic 🛏 8P nc8yrs

GH QQ Well House Private Hotel 11 Toberargan Rd PH16 5HG ☎(0796) 472239
Mar-Oct
A well run private hotel in a residential area above the town centre, where the bedrooms and spacious public rooms offer a high level of comfort.
6⛿ (1fb) CTV in all bedrooms ® ✱ dB&B⛿£37-£22 WB&B£129.50-£154 LDO 5.30pm
Lic 🛏 8P
Credit Cards 1 3

PLUCKLEY Kent Map **05** TQ94

FH QQQ Mr & Mrs V Harris ***Elvey Farm Country Hotel*** *(TQ916457)* TN27 0SU ☎(0233) 840442 FAX (0233) 840726
rs Nov-Mar
This medieval farmhouse, dating back to 1430, has varied accommodation, with bedrooms in a converted oast house, Kent barn and stables, all spread around the original farmhouse, rather untidy farmyard buildings and old machinery. The spartan-styled bedrooms have every modern amenity and reasonable levels of comfort with night storage heaters. There is a comfortable lounge for residents and the large dining room is popular for local weddings and parties; Mrs Harris provides a relaxed and informal style of service. The farm has 75 acres breeding mostly poultry, Christmas turkeys and sheep.
10rm(7⇨3⛿) (6fb) CTV in all bedrooms ®
Lic 🛏 40P 75 acres mixed

PLYMOUTH Devon Map **02** SX45

See **Town Plan Section**

GH QQQ Bowling Green Hotel 9-10 Osborne Place, Lockyer St, The Hoe PL1 2PU ☎(0752) 667485
Closed 25-30 Dec
This terraced Georgian property overlooks Drake's famous Bowling Green, and is close to the Hoe and the Barbican city centre. The hotel has been extensively refurbished, and bedrooms are attractive and well equipped. Full English breakfast is served in the informal open-plan lounge/dining room, and the accommodation is spotlessly clean.
12rm(8⇨⛿4hc) (3fb) CTV in all bedrooms ® T sB&B£26 sB&B⇨⛿£32 dB&B£34 dB&B⇨⛿£44
🛏 CTV 4🚗 (£2 per night)
Credit Cards 1 2 3 £

GH QQ Cranbourne Hotel 282 Citadel Road, The Hoe PL1 2PZ ☎(0752) 263858 FAX (0752) 263858
Colourful floral pots and troughs attract guests to this end-of-terrace Georgian hotel, just a short walk from the Hoe, Barbican and city centre. Bedrooms are simply furnished and equipped with tea-making facilities.
13rm(5⛿8hc) (3fb) CTV in all bedrooms ® ✱ sB&B£12-£16 dB&B£26-£30 dB&B⛿£30-£40
Lic 🛏 CTV 3🚗
Credit Cards 1 2 3 £

GH QQ Devonshire 22 Lockyer Rd, Mannamead PL3 4RL ☎(0752) 220726
A period, double-fronted, stone-built, terraced property situated in a quiet residential road very close to the Mutley Plain shopping area. The comfortable bedrooms are bright and airy and all have TV and tea-making facilities; there are 3 bedrooms available on the ground floor. A set dinner is served at 6pm in the basement dining room. The lounge bar has a cosy atmosphere, and the guesthouse is personally run by the owners Mary and Phil Collins in a friendly and relaxed style.
10rm(3⛿7hc) (4fb) CTV in all bedrooms ® ✗ ✱ sB&B£13-£15 sB&B⛿£20-£25 dB&B£28 dB&B⛿£32 WB&Bfr£98 WBDifr£154 LDO 2pm
Lic 🛏 CTV 6P £

GH QQ Dudley 42 Sutherland Road, Mutley PL4 6BN ☎(0752) 668322
rs Xmas
This family Victorian home in a residential area, near the station, has 6 simply furnished bedrooms, and there are many personal pieces throughout the public areas.
6hc (3fb) CTV in all bedrooms ® ✱ sB&B£15-£17 dB&B£30-£32 LDO 9am
🛏 CTV P̸
Credit Cards 1 3 £

GH Q Elizabethan 223 Citadel Rd East, The Hoe PL1 2NG ☎(0752) 661672
This small guesthouse is not easy to find due to the road layout, so it is best to ask for directions. The simple, single-fronted Victorian mid-terrace house is a short walk from the Barbican, and bedrooms are compact and simply furnished. Breakfast is taken in the basement dining room.
5hc (1fb) CTV in all bedrooms ® ✗ (ex guide dogs) ✱ sB&B£15 dB&B£24 WB&Bfr£80
🛏

GH QQQ Georgian House Hotel 51 Citadel Rd, The Hoe PL1 3AU ☎(0752) 663237 FAX (0752) 253953
Closed 23 Dec-5 Jan rs Sun
A terraced Georgian house near the famous Hoe and Barbican, with easy access to the city centre. The bedrooms offer modern, simple décor and furnishings, and are well equipped, with en suite facilities. An à la carte menu offers some imaginative dishes in the informal 'Four Poster Restaurant' which is adjacent to the small cocktail bar.
10rm(4⇨6⛿) (1fb) CTV in all bedrooms ® T ✗ (ex guide dogs) ✱ sB&B⇨⛿£31 dB&B⇨⛿£41 LDO 9pm
Lic 🛏 CTV 2P
Credit Cards 1 2 3 5

GH QQ The Lamplighter Hotel 103 Citadel Rd, The Hoe PL1 2RN ☎(0752) 663855
Closed 23 Dec-6 Jan
Peggy and Colin Rowe personally welcome their guests to this small, family-run guesthouse which is within easy walking distance of the city centre and the popular Barbican and Hoe areas of the →

city. The bedrooms are light and airy with the majority having en suite facilities. Limited parking is provided at the rear of the house.
9⇈ (2fb) CTV in all bedrooms ® ✗ (ex guide dogs) ✱
sB&B⇈£18-£20 dB&B⇈£30-£32
CTV 4P sauna
Credit Cards 1 3 £

GH Q Merville Hotel 73 Citadel Rd, The Hoe PL1 3AX
☎(0752) 667595
An end-of-terrace Victorian property providing simple accommodation within easy walking distance of the Barbican, Hoe and city centre. There is a comfortable lounge and fairly compact dining room.
10hc (3fb) CTV in all bedrooms ® ✱ sB&Bfr£11 dB&Bfr£24 LDO 3pm
Lic CTV 2P

GH QQ *Oliver's Hotel & Restaurant* 33 Sutherland Rd PL4 6BN ☎(0752) 663923
This end-of-terrace Victorian property, located near the station, offers 6 bedrooms which are furnished in a traditional style. Some interesting dishes are offered on the menu featured in the attractive restaurant. The resident proprietors extend a warm welcome to guests.
6rm(4⇈2hc) (1fb) CTV in all bedrooms ® ✗ LDO 8pm
Lic 3P nc11yrs
Credit Cards 1 2 3 5

GH QQ Rosaland Hotel 32 Houndiscombe Rd, Mutley PL4 6HQ ☎(0752) 664749
8rm(2⇈6hc) (2fb) CTV in all bedrooms ® ✗ (ex guide dogs) sB&B£16 sB&B⇈£20-£25 dB&B£30 dB&B⇈£32 LDO 5pm
Lic CTV 3P
Credit Cards 1 3 £

GH Q Russell Lodge Hotel 9 Holyrood Place, The Hoe PL1 2QB ☎(0752) 667774
A Georgian mid-terrace property, handy for the ferry terminal, the Hoe, Barbican and city centre. This personally run establishment offers bright accommodation and friendly service. Light snacks are available in the evening.
9rm(5⇈4hc) (2fb) CTV in all bedrooms ® ✗ (ex guide dogs) sB&B⇈£22.50-£23.50 dB&B⇈£35-£36.50 WB&B£135-£142
CTV 3P
Credit Cards 1 2 3 5

GH QQQ St James Hotel 49 Citadel Rd, The Hoe PL1 3AU
☎(0752) 661950
Closed Xmas
A single-fronted Victorian terraced property, conveniently situated for all city amenities. Bedrooms are attractively coordinated, and a good choice is offered at breakfast – including boiled eggs with soldiers. Dinner, prepared from fresh local produce, is available by prior arrangement with Mrs Ford.
10⇈ (2fb) CTV in all bedrooms ® ✗ (ex guide dogs) sB&B⇈£30 dB&B⇈£41 WB&B£136.50-£210 WBDi£241.50-£315 LDO 9pm
Lic P̸
Credit Cards 1 3 £

GH QQ The White House Hotel 12 Athenaeum St PL1 2RH
☎(0752) 662356
Within easy walking distance of the famous Hoe and city centre, this small guesthouse is run by its friendly, caring owners. The comfortable rooms are simply furnished, and a generous breakfast is served in the small rear dining room.
6rm(2⇈4hc) (1fb) CTV in all bedrooms ® sB&B£20-£25 sB&B⇈£25 dB&B£25 dB&B⇈£30 WB&B£70-£100
2P
Credit Cards 1 3 £

POCKLINGTON Humberside Map 08 SE74

FH Q Mr & Mrs Pearson **Meltonby Hall** *(SE800524)* Meltonby YO4 2PW (2m N unclass) ☎(0759) 303214
Etr-Oct
This large Georgian farmhouse is situated on the edge of the village of Meltonby, 2 miles north of Pocklington. It provides 2 traditionally furnished bedrooms, and an evening meal can be served if advance notice is given.
2rm (1fb) ® ✗ sB&B£12.50-£14.50 dB&B£25-£29
CTV 4P 118 acres mixed £

PODIMORE Somerset Map 03 ST52

FH QQ Mrs S Crang **Cary Fitzpaine** *(ST549270)* BA22 8JB (2m N, take A37 at junc. with A303 for 1 mile then turn rt onto unclass rd) ☎Charlton Mackrell(0458) 223250
Closed 23-26 Dec
One mile north of the A303 Podimore roundabout on the A37, this well kept Georgian farmhouse is surrounded by its own mixed farmland. The cosy dining room for breakfast and comfortable lounge complement the well equipped bedrooms.
3rm(1⇌⇈2hc) (1fb) CTV in all bedrooms ®
✗ (ex guide dogs) ✱ sB&B£14.50 sB&B⇌⇈£18 dB&B£29 dB&B⇌⇈£34 WB&B£90-£110
CTV 6P ✔ 600 acres arable beef horses sheep £

POLBATHIC Cornwall & Isles of Scilly Map 02 SX35

GH QQ The Old Mill PL11 3HA
☎St Germans(0503) 30596
This establishment dates back over 300 years and is in a peaceful village setting, providing a convenient resting place close to the main A roads to and from Plymouth. Bedrooms are compact, but neatly presented, and the public areas include a small, well stocked bar and comfortable lounge/dining area.
10rm(7hc) (3fb) ® sB&B£12.50-£14 dB&B£25-£28 WB&B£85-£95 WBDi£130-£165 LDO 8pm
Lic CTV 12P
Credit Cards 1 3 5 £

POLMASSICK Cornwall & Isles of Scilly Map 02 SW94

GH QQQ Kilbol House Country Hotel PL26 6HA
☎Mevagissey(0726) 842481
Dating back 400 years and standing in 2.5 acres of gardens and grounds, with paddocks and fields beyond, this house offers an idyllic setting for a peaceful and relaxing break. Bedrooms are comfortable and offer lovely views, and 2 are located away from the main building in an annexe in the garden. Public areas include a bright sun lounge, a cosy bar with a wood-burning stove and a comfortable lounge with an open fire. Home-cooked meals are taken in the nicely appointed dining room overlooking the garden. There is an outdoor pool, and ample car parking for guests.
8rm(4⇌4hc) (2fb) ® ✱ sB&Bfr£19.77 sB&B⇌⇈£22.85 dB&Bfr£39.54 dB&B⇌⇈£45.70 WB&B£136.93-£159.80 WBDi£193.70-£210.97 LDO noon
Lic CTV 12P 1 (charged) clock golf
Credit Cards 1 2 3

POLPERRO Cornwall & Isles of Scilly Map 02 SX25

GH QQQ Landaviddy Manor Landaviddy Ln PL13 2RT
☎(0503) 72210
Feb-19 Oct
Dating back over 300 years, this lovely manor house sits within 2 acres of well tended gardens on a quiet lane just above the centre of the fishing village, enjoying lovely rural and sea views. Bedrooms are decorated in a feminine style, with coordinated soft fabrics and a mixture of modern and antique furniture. All are nicely equipped, some have en suite facilities and some have 4-poster beds. Public areas are attractive and comfortable, and a relaxed atmosphere pervades throughout, cultivated by the warm and friendly proprietors.

9rm(5🚿4hc) CTV in all bedrooms Ⓡ ✱ sB&B£20-£25 sB&B🚿£25-£30 dB&B£34-£40 dB&B🚿£45-£55 WB&B£117-£170 LDO 10am
Lic 🍽 CTV 12P nc5yrs
Credit Cards 1 3 5 £

SELECTED

FH QQQQ Mrs L Tuckett **Trenderway** *(SX214533)* Pelynt PL13 2LY ☎(0503) 72214
Built in the late 16th century, the Cornish stone buildings of this mixed working farm are set in peaceful, beautiful countryside at the head of Polperro Valley. Bedrooms here are truly superb: the 2 rooms in the main farmhouse are pretty and nicely furnished, each with an individual, stylish theme and décor; there is another room in a recently converted adjacent barn and a fourth room has recently been created with a 4-poster bed, beautiful furniture and attractive colour scheme. A hearty farmhouse breakfast is served in the sunny conservatory, which has lovely views out across the valley. Lynn Tuckett and her family are welcoming, caring hosts, and early reservations are advised as the farmhouse is very popular.
2🛁🚿 Annexe 2🛁🚿 ⊁in all bedrooms CTV in all bedrooms Ⓡ ✗ dB&B🛁🚿£46-£50 WB&B£154-£168
🍽 2P 2🚗 nc10yrs 400 acres arable mixed sheep cattle £

POLRUAN Cornwall & Isles of Scilly Map **02** SX15

GH QQQ ***Polmarine*** West St PL23 1PL ☎(0726) 870459
Etr-Oct
What a delightful place – located down steep steps with half the building backing on to the water's edge and overlooking Fowey harbour. The hotel has recently been converted from a working boat house and the cheerful young proprietors have refurbished it with style. Bedrooms are pretty and bright with good facilities, and public areas are full of character and charm. The breakfast room currently has communal tables, but a conservatory extension will soon allow guests to breakfast separately if they prefer. The hotel's location makes it unsuitable for children and those who find steps difficult. Car parking is at the top of the village but there is easy access by boat and 2 moorings available for guests.
4rm(1🛁3🚿) ⊁in 1 bedroom CTV in 3 bedrooms TV in 1 bedroom Ⓡ ✗
🍽 6🚗 nc10yrs ⚓ 2 moorings

POLZEATH Cornwall & Isles of Scilly Map **02** SW97

GH QQQ ***White Lodge Hotel*** Old Polzeath PL27 6TJ ☎Trebetherick(020886) 2370
9rm(2🛁🚿7hc) (1fb) CTV in 2 bedrooms Ⓡ
Lic 🍽 CTV 12P

PONTRHYDFENDIGAID Dyfed Map **06** SN76

GH QQ ***Llysteg*** SY25 6BB ☎(09745) 697
The Edwards family run this very pleasant guesthouse which is situated on the Aberystwyth side of the village. It provides spotlessly clean and well decorated bedrooms, each with a private bathroom, and a comfortable open-plan lounge and bar. An impressive feature is the carved wooden mantlepiece over the open stone fireplace in the lounge, which was brought in 1948 from Lord Lisburn's house nearby.
6🛁🚿 (4fb)⊁in all bedrooms LDO 10.30pm
Lic 🍽 CTV 6P

PONTRILAS Hereford & Worcester Map **03** SO32

FH QQQ Mr & Mrs Whittal-Williams **Howton Court** *(SO405285)* HR2 0BG ☎(0981) 240249
This charming stone and timber-framed 17th-century farmhouse has been in the Whittal-Williams family for 4 generations, and is steeped in history and character. Situated just off the A465 Hereford to Abergavenny road, the house enjoys glorious rural views and is in an ideal location to explore the Golden Valley, Wye Valley and Brecon Beacons. The 3 bedrooms are individually furnished with antiques and country furniture, and are well equipped and pleasingly decorated in rich coordinating colours and fabrics; one room has an antique Welsh bed and stylish Victorian en suite. The lounge features a flagstone floor, and the oak-panelled dining room has an elegant mahogany table, where imaginative home-cooked food is served. The farmhouse is surrounded by a delightful secluded mature garden with a small covered plunge pool ideal for children.
3rm(1🛁2hc) ⊁in all bedrooms Ⓡ ✱ dB&Bfr£40 dB&B🛁fr£50 LDO 8pm
🍽 CTV 20P 🏠 ⛆ ⚓ U croquet lawn 450 acres arable

POOLE Dorset Map **04** SZ09

See also Bournemouth

GH QQ **Avoncourt Private Hotel** 245 Bournemouth Rd, Parkstone BH14 9HX ☎(0202) 732025
This small private hotel is situated on the A35 main Bournemouth – Poole road but a car park is provided at the rear. Bedrooms are neatly presented and simply furnished, some with private shower rooms. There is a bright, cosy and well decorated combined bar and breakfast room, and the accommodation is spotlessly clean throughout. The resident proprietors, Mr and Mrs Jones, take great pride in their guesthouse and work hard to maintain the high standards.
6hc (3fb) CTV in all bedrooms Ⓡ ✗ ✱ sB&B£16-£20 dB&B£30-£40 WB&B£90-£120 WBDi£105-£140 LDO 10am
Lic 🍽 CTV 5P 1🚗
Credit Cards 1 3 £

GH QQQ ***Seacourt*** 249 Blandford Rd, Hamworthy BH15 4AZ ☎(0202) 674995
This small friendly guesthouse, close to the cross channel ferry terminal, is a popular choice with both business and tourist guests. Standards of housekeeping are very high and the whole house is →

spick and span. Bedrooms are pretty and comfortable, and while the lounge is cosy the breakfast room is airy and bright. The amiable proprietors extend a warm, relaxed welcome to their guests.
6rm(2⇨1♞3hc) (1fb) CTV in all bedrooms ® ✗ (ex guide dogs) 🅿 7P

GH QQ Sheldon Lodge 22 Forest Rd, Branksome Park BH13 6DH ☎(0202) 761186
In a pleasant position in a quiet residential area of Branksome Park, close to both Bournemouth and Poole, this establishment offers simple but well equipped bedrooms with neat décor. Comfortable public areas include a cosy bar and a snooker room with a three-quarter size table.
14rm(8⇨6♞) (1fb)⚟in 4 bedrooms CTV in all bedrooms ® * sB&B⇨♞£21-£23 dB&B⇨♞£42-£46 WBDi£175-£195 LDO 7pm
Lic 🅿 3P solarium
Credit Cards 1 £

PORLOCK Somerset Map **03** SS84

SELECTED

GH QQQQ Gable Thatch Doverhay TA24 8LQ ☎(0643) 862552
6 Mar-Oct, Xmas & New Year rs Nov-4 Jan
Parts of this thatched Grade II listed building date back to 1690. It sits in its own cottage garden down a quiet lane in the popular village. Leaded windows and climbing roses add to a very picturesque image. Anne de Ville and David McWilliam took over the house last year, and have upgraded all the rooms with the emphasis on quality. All rooms are en suite and have thoughtful extras such as baskets of fruit and toiletries. There are 2 lounges with log fires, where a table service of drinks is offered. Interesting 6-course dinner menus are offered, usually set, but with a choice of main course. From the moment guests arrive they are made to feel relaxed and cheerful, immediately offered tea on arrival and cared for by very attentive staff.
5rm(4⇨♞1hc) CTV in all bedrooms ® * sB&B⇨♞fr£38 dB&B⇨♞£76-£86 (incl dinner) WB&B£168-£196 WBDi£238-£273 LDO 8pm
Lic 🅿 ₱ nc10yrs

GH QQ Lorna Doone Hotel High St TA24 8PS ☎(0643) 862404
Dating back to 1886, this property stands in the centre of the village, only 7 miles from Minehead, and has much character and charm. There is a small car- parking area at the rear, with stable blocks and a cottage-style annexe providing 3 more bedrooms. Constant improvements to bedrooms in the main building have now provided the majority with en suite facilities and pretty, fresh and bright décor. The pleasant public areas are charming and cosy, with fresh flowers, pictures and rustic furnishings. The restaurant is open daily to non-residents and has a lively, cheerful ambience, created by the resident proprietors, Mr and Mrs Thornton.
10rm(3⇨4♞3hc) Annexe 3rm(1♞2hc) CTV in 11 bedrooms ® sB&B£18-£19.50 sB&B⇨♞£19 dB&B£36-£39 dB&B⇨♞£39-£47 WB&B£119-£157.50 LDO 9.15pm
Lic 🅿 CTV 9P
Credit Cards 1 3 £

'Selected' establishments, which have the highest quality award, are highlighted by a tinted panel. For a full list of these establishments, consult the Contents page.

PORT ERIN

See **MAN, ISLE OF**

PORTESHAM Dorset Map **03** SY68

GH QQQ Millmead Country Hotel & Restaurant Goose Hill DT3 4HE ☎Abbotsbury(0305) 871432 FAX (0305) 871884
This small hotel is located in a tiny, rural village, and offers good value for money; it is run with pride and care by the amiable proprietors, Peter and Marian Cox. The pretty bedrooms are nicely appointed, with a fresh and bright décor. There is a smart bar area leading into a charming small conservatory, where tempting cream teas are offered, along with a comfortable lounge and dining room where guests enjoy home-cooked meals.
7rm(5♞2hc) ⚟in all bedrooms CTV in all bedrooms ® * sB&B£25.50-£29.50 sB&B⇨♞£28.50-£32.50 dB&B£38.50-£42.50 dB&B⇨♞£44.50-£48.50 WBDi£160-£210
LDO 6.30pm
Lic 🅿 16P nc10yrs
Credit Cards 1 2 3 £

PORTHCAWL Mid Glamorgan Map **03** SS87

GH QQ *Collingwood Hotel* 40 Mary St CF36 3YA ☎(0656) 782899
A family-run guesthouse situated close to the shops and seafront, popular with both tourists and business people alike. There is a comfortable, modern lounge, a small bar and pretty bedrooms.
8hc (4fb)⚟in all bedrooms CTV in 1 bedroom ® ✗ (ex guide dogs) LDO 5pm
Lic 🅿 CTV ₱

GH QQ Heritage 24 Mary St CF36 3YA ☎(0656) 771881
Conveniently situated close to the promenade and pavillion, this small, friendy hotel provides compact but comfortable, nicely equipped bedrooms, that have bright en suites and a TV with satellite channels. There is a cosy bar and an attractively furnished restaurant, with worthy standards of imaginative cuisine from chef patron John Miller, who has established a firm reputation.
8rm(6♞2hc) CTV in all bedrooms ® ✗ * sB&B£16-£21 sB&B♞fr£21 dB&B♞fr£36 WB&Bfr£112 LDO 9pm
Lic 🅿 ₱
Credit Cards 1 3

GH QQ Minerva Hotel 52 Esplanade Av CF36 3YU ☎(0656) 782428
Conveniently positioned just off the promenade and only a short walk from the town centre, this small, family-run guesthouse provides modestly furnished bedrooms which are well equipped. The public rooms consist of a cosy, inviting lounge, a small breakfast room and a bar for residents' use only. The proprietors Mr and Mrs Giblett provide a personal service.
8rm(2⇨2♞4hc) (3fb) CTV in all bedrooms ® sB&B£14 sB&B⇨♞£22 dB&B£28 dB&B⇨♞£38 WB&B£90 WBDi£149.50 LDO 6pm
Lic 🅿 CTV

PORTHCOTHAN BAY Cornwall & Isles of Scilly Map **02** SW87

GH QQ Bay House PL28 8LW ☎Padstow(0841) 520472
Apr-Oct
The accommodation in this guesthouse offers a choice of bright basic bedrooms: the best have front-facing balconies, and rooms on the second floor afford the best sea views. Generous public rooms include sun and TV lounges and a very popular well stocked bar, together with a dining room offering a daily menu. There are also 3 self-catering holiday flats available, and adequate parking.
16hc (1fb) ✗ (ex guide dogs) * sB&B£16-£18 dB&B£32-£36 WB&B£112-£126 WBDi£125-£159 LDO 4.30pm
Lic CTV 17P

PORTHCURNO Cornwall & Isles of Scilly Map **02** SW32

GH Q Corniche Trebehor TR19 6LX ☎Sennen(0736) 871685
Closed 21-31 Dec

Situated within 2 miles of the hamlet of Porthcurno with its popular open air Minack Theatre. John and Wyn Ring are the friendly proprietors of this chalet bungalow set in half an acre of garden with magnificent country and distant sea views. There are 3 ground-floor rooms available, all light and airy, and the lounge/dining room enjoys the superb views. An evening meal is available on request.

6hc (1fb) ✗ (ex guide dogs) ✳ sB&B£11 dB&B£20-£22 WB&B£70 WBDi£105 LDO 3.30pm
Lic ♨ CTV 7P

PORTHMADOG Gwynedd Map **06** SH53

GH Q Oakleys The Harbour LL49 9AS ☎(0766) 512482
Apr-Oct

This large, early-19th-century stone-built house stands close to both the town centre and harbour. The accommodation is very well maintained and represents good value for money. Family bedded rooms are available, and there is a ground-floor bedroom. Private parking is provided, and the house is also close to the Ffestiniog railway terminus.

8rm(1⇔2↱5hc) (3fb) ✗ (ex guide dogs) sB&B£14-£16 dB&B£26-£28 dB&B⇔↱£28-£30 WB&B£90-£100 WBDi£140-£150 LDO 5pm
CTV 18P nc5yrs

GH QQ Owen's Hotel 71 High St LL49 9EU ☎(0766) 512098
Mar-Oct

This small, friendly guesthouse dates back to 1840, when it was known as the Royal Commercial Hotel. It is in the High Street over the proprietor's coffee shop/confectionery business, and a small private car park is located a few yards away. The bedrooms are not modern but soundly maintained, and equipped to satisfy the needs of both tourists and business people requiring bed and breakfast accommodation.

10rm(3⇔4↱3hc) (3fb) CTV in all bedrooms ® sB&Bfr£17 sB&B⇔↱fr£22 dB&Bfr£30 dB&B⇔↱fr£40 WB&Bfr£134
♨ CTV 4P 5🚗
Credit Cards [1] [3]

PORT ISAAC Cornwall & Isles of Scilly Map **02** SW98

GH QQQ Archer Farm Hotel Trewetha PL29 3RU
☎Bodmin(0208) 880522
Etr-Oct

This rambling Cornish farmhouse has been lovingly converted to provide a choice of modern and old bedrooms, some with full en suite facilities, several of the rooms have lovely rural views and a balcony. There is a small TV lounge on the ground floor, and a very comfortable well appointed bar lounge and dining room on the first floor. The atmosphere is very friendly and informal, with the proprietor Vickie Welton personally supervising the service and cooking. A 4-course Cordon Bleu dinner is served using fresh local produce, which is ordered when confirming the booking. Ample car parking and a garden are also available.

7rm(5⇔↱2hc) (2fb)⊘in all bedrooms CTV in 4 bedrooms **T** ✳ sB&B£21-£22.50 sB&B⇔↱£21-£22.50 dB&B£42-£45 dB&B⇔↱£54-£57 LDO 8pm
Lic ♨ CTV 8P Ⓔ

GH Q *Bay Hotel* 1 The Terrace PL29 3SG
☎Bodmin(0208) 880380
Etr-Oct

Enjoying a good position overlooking the sea, this long-established hotel has been run by Mary and Jim Andrews for over 13 years. The bedrooms are furnished to a satisfactory standard in a conventional style and several are suitable for families. There is a comfortable lounge facing the sea, with a separate bar and a plain but practical dining room where an à la carte menu is usually available. Parking can be a little difficult at times but there is a pay and display car park opposite.

10rm(3⇔↱7hc) (5fb) LDO 7pm
Lic CTV 10P

GH QQ Old School Hotel Fore St PL29 3RB
☎Bodmin(0208) 880721

Converted by the present owner 9 years ago, the guesthouse overlooks the picturesque fishing village and harbour. Bedrooms are well equipped, and include 3 self-catering units. Snack and light meals are available throughout the day, local fish being a speciality. Medieval banquets can be arranged, with prior notice, for groups: costumes may be hired from the hotel. Private parking is available.

13⇔↱ (6fb) CTV in all bedrooms ® ✳ sB&B⇔↱£14-£24 dB&B⇔↱£36-£73 WB&B£126-£255.50 WBDi£192-£322 LDO 9.30pm
Lic CTV 20P
Credit Cards [1] [3] Ⓔ

See advertisement on page 329

PORTNANCON Highland *Sutherland* Map **14** NC46

GH QQ Port-Na-Con House IV27 4UN
☎Durness(097181) 367 due to change to (0971) 511367
Apr-Oct

Quietly situated by the picturesque shore of Loch Eriboll, this former custom house and harbour store has been converted and modernised to create this comfortable, family-run guesthouse. The bedrooms have modern furniture and all enjoy loch views, as does the inviting first-floor lounge which also offers access to the adjoining balcony. Ongoing improvements are taking place under the direction of the enthusiastic owners Ken and Lesley Black.

4hc (2fb)⊘in all bedrooms ® sB&B£22 dB&B£32 LDO 5pm
Lic ♨ 6P nc4yrs
Credit Cards [1] [3]

PORT OF MENTEITH Central *Perthshire* Map **11** NN50

FH QQQ Mrs C Tough **Collymoon Pendicle** *(NN591961)* FK8 3JY ☎Buchlyvie(036085) 222
Apr-Oct
A modern bungalow peacefully situated along a turning off the B8034 close to the River Forth. It is surrounded by an attractive garden and offers a good standard of accommodation, including a comfortable lounge and a new conservatory dining room.
3hc (1fb) in all bedrooms ® (ex guide dogs) sB&B£12-£14 dB&B£24-£28 WB&B£84-£98 WBDi£133-£141 LDO 6pm
CTV 3P 500 acres arable mixed

PORTPATRICK Dumfries & Galloway *Wigtownshire* Map **10** NX05

GH QQQ Blinkbonnie School Brae DG9 8LG ☎(077681) 282
Mar-Oct
Standing within its own attractive gardens, high on the shoulder of a thickly wooded glen, this captivating house has commanding views over the town and harbour. The accommodation is modest but comfortable, neat and clean, while the inviting lounge has lovely views from its large windows. A substantial breakfast is served in the pleasant dining room.
6hc (1fb) in all bedrooms ® * sB&B£18-£19 dB&B£32-£34
CTV 10P

PORTREE

See **SKYE, ISLE OF**

PORTSMOUTH & SOUTHSEA Hampshire Map **04** SZ69

See **Town Plan Section**

GH QQ Abbey Lodge 30 Waverley Rd PO5 2PW ☎(0705) 828285 FAX (0705) 872943
This terraced property has a bright, lively appearance, and is ideally situated for the cross channel ferries. Bedrooms have many facilities, including satellite TV and telephones, and are geared towards short-stay guests. Public areas include a dining room, and a small lounge where children are welcome to play computer games.
9rm(1 2 6hc) (2fb) CTV in all bedrooms ®
(ex guide dogs) sB&B£15-£18 dB&B£30-£36 dB&B £35-£45 LDO 9am
CTV
Credit Cards 1 2 3 5 £

GH QQQ Ashwood 10 St Davids Rd PO5 1QN ☎(0705) 816228
This cheerful family-run guesthouse lies in a quiet residential road between the sea and city centre. The bedrooms have very pretty décor with colourful drapes and borders, and everywhere is clean and well looked after.
7hc CTV in all bedrooms ® (ex guide dogs) * sB&B£14-£16 dB&B£28-£32 WB&B£95-£100 LDO 4pm
CTV nc £

GH QQQ Bembell Court Hotel 69 Festing Rd PO4 0NQ ☎Portsmouth(0705) 735915 & 750497
This family-run, detached period house stands near the seafront and offers rooms of various sizes, all of which have a good range of modern facilities. Public areas include a comfortable lounge, small bar and a spacious dining room.
13rm(7 6hc) (4fb) in 1 bedroom CTV in all bedrooms ®
T * sB&B £30-£36 dB&B£38-£42 dB&B £40-£46 WB&B£130-£150 LDO 4pm
Lic CTV 10P
Credit Cards 1 2 3 5 £

GH QQ Birchwood 44 Waverley Rd PO5 2PP ☎(0705) 811337
This Victorian terraced house is situated 5 minutes' walk from the seafront. Bedrooms are well kept and soundly equipped; downstairs there is a comfortable lounge, and an attractive breakfast room.
6rm(3 3hc) (2fb) in 2 bedrooms CTV in all bedrooms ®
(ex guide dogs) * sB&B£13-£15 sB&B £15-£17 dB&B£26-£30 dB&B £30-£34 WB&B£82-£108 WBDi£117-£142 LDO 3pm
Lic CTV
Credit Cards 1 2 3 5 £

GH QQ *Bristol Hotel* 55 Clarence Pde PO5 2HX ☎(0705) 821815
Closed Xmas
Attractive, whitewashed Victorian house, dating back to 1851, overlooking the seafront and Southsea Common. The hotel offers simply appointed but fresh bedrooms, with some modern facilities. There is also a comfortable lounge area, a small bar and a prettily decorated basement dining room. Personally run by resident proprietors for the past 15 years, this hotel has a friendly, relaxed atmosphere.
13rm(9 4hc) (7fb) CTV in 9 bedrooms TV in 4 bedrooms ®
(ex guide dogs)
Lic CTV 7P
Credit Cards 1 3

GH QQ Collingham 89 St Ronans Rd PO4 0PR ☎(0705) 821549
Closed 24-26 Dec
A small terraced guesthouse with a colourful tiny front garden, comfortable modern bedrooms and a combined lounge and breakfast room.
6hc (3fb) in 2 bedrooms CTV in all bedrooms ®
sB&B£13.50-£14.50 dB&B£27-£29 WB&B£80-£82
CTV £

GH Q The Elms 48 Victoria Rd South PO5 2BT ☎(0705) 823924
This owner-run guesthouse offers simple accommodation particularly aimed at families, with several bunk beds, and toys available in the cosy lounge. There is a bar downstairs.
6hc (3fb) CTV in all bedrooms ® (ex guide dogs) sB&B£14-£15 dB&B£26-£28 WB&B£90-£95
Lic CTV 2P £

GH QQ Fortitude Cottage 51 Broad St, Old Portsmouth PO1 2JD ☎(0705) 823748
Closed 25 & 26 Dec
A narrow terraced cottage in Old Portsmouth, opposite the quayside. There are 3 very pretty, bright and airy bedrooms, one of which is small; downstairs the attractive breakfast room has pine furniture, and dried flowers hanging from the beams.
3rm(1 2hc) in all bedrooms CTV in all bedrooms ® *
sB&B£27-£30 dB&B£36-£40 dB&B £38-£42
ncn £

GH QQ Gainsborough House 9 Malvern Rd PO5 2LZ ☎(0705) 822604
Closed Xmas
This Victorian mid-terraced guesthouse in a quiet residential street close to the sea has been run for over 20 years by the friendly Ms Filer. Bedrooms are neat and tidy, and there is a spacious, comfortable lounge.
7hc (2fb) CTV in all bedrooms ® * sB&B£13.50-£14.50 dB&B£27-£29
CTV nc3yrs £

GH QQ Glencoe 64 Whitwell Rd PO4 0QS ☎(0705) 737413
This quietly situated terraced guesthouse offers comfortable bedrooms, and a deceptively spacious open-plan lounge and breakfast room, with family ornaments and a patio view.
7rm(2 5hc) (1fb) in 1 bedroom CTV in all bedrooms ®
* sB&B£15-£16.50 dB&Bfr£30 dB&B fr£32
CTV
Credit Cards 5 £

GH [Q][Q] *Goodwood House* 1 Taswell Rd PO5 2RG
☎(0705) 824734
Closed 24 Dec-2 Jan
This semidetached Victorian house lies in a quiet residential street, close to all amenities. The bedrooms are traditionally furnished, and downstairs there is a small comfortable bar/lounge.
8hc (1fb) TV in all bedrooms ® 🐕 (ex guide dogs) LDO 5pm
Lic 🍽 P̸

GH [Q][Q][Q] **Hamilton House** 95 Victoria Rd North PO5 1PS ☎(0705) 823502
A deceptively spacious Victorian house located in a central residential area. The cheerful bedrooms vary in size, but all are spick and span and well maintained; 3 rooms have private bathrooms. The Tubbs create a friendly atmosphere and continue to make improvements.
8rm(3↑5hc) (3fb) CTV in all bedrooms ® 🐕 sB&B£14-£16 dB&B£28-£32 dB&B↑£35-£39 WB&B£95-£133 WBDi£130-£168 LDO noon
🍽 CTV P̸ Ⓔ

GH [Q][Q] **St Andrews Lodge** 65 St Andrew's Rd PO5 1ER
☎(0705) 827079
Closed 21 Dec-3 Jan
Situated in a residential side street, this guesthouse has well equipped, modern bedrooms, some ideal for families. There is a comfortable ground-floor lounge, and the accommodation is suitable for both tourists and commercial visitors.
8hc (2fb) CTV in all bedrooms ® 🐕 (ex guide dogs) sB&B£13-£18 dB&B£25-£30 WB&B£84-£120 WBDi£120-£150
LDO 5pm
🍽 CTV P̸ Ⓔ

Book as early as possible for busy holiday periods.

GH [Q][Q][Q] *St David's* 19 St Davids Rd PO5 1QH ☎(0705) 826858

This attractive Victorian semidetached house is situated in a quiet street, convenient for the ferry terminals. The new proprietors have set high standards of housekeeping and decoration, and the establishment is popular with both holidaymakers and business people, retaining a friendly atmosphere. A 3-course dinner is available by prior arrangement, and sandwiches can be provided on request.

6hc (2fb)⅄in 4 bedrooms CTV in all bedrooms ®
✘ (ex guide dogs)
CTV 1P

GH [Q][Q] Upper Mount House Hotel The Vale, Clarendon Rd PO5 2EQ ☎(0705) 820456

This listed 3-storey Victorian villa is tucked away in a quiet lane between the shops and the sea. Downstairs there is a comfortable lounge with a small bar area; above are bedrooms of varying size and standards of comfort which are slowly being improved.

12rm(11⇨↱1hc) (3fb) CTV in all bedrooms ®
✘ (ex guide dogs) ✱ sB&B⇨↱£17-£26 dB&B⇨↱£30-£46 WBDi£160-£180 LDO 6pm
Lic ▥ CTV 10P
Credit Cards [1] [3] Ⓔ

GH [Q][Q] *Victoria Court* 29 Victoria Rd North PO5 1PL ☎(0705) 820305

A Victorian semidetached property located in a residential street. The bedrooms, recently refurbished, have simple décor and modern facilities. A basement dining room and small first-floor lounge have also recently been refurbished, and the hotel now offers a home-cooked evening meal, using their own vegetables. The resident proprietors remain very involved in the day-to- day running of the hotel, and are enthusiastically steadily improving the accommodation.

7↱ CTV in all bedrooms ® ✘ (ex guide dogs)
Lic
Credit Cards [1] [3]

PRESTATYN Clwyd Map 06 SJ08

GH [Q] Roughsedge House 26-28 Marine Rd LL19 7HD ☎(0745) 887359

This small, personally run guesthouse is situated on the A548, within easy walking distance of both the beach and town centre. It has a following of regular commercial visitors, but is equally suitable for tourists. There is a small private car park and unrestricted roadside parking is readily available.

9rm(1⇨↱7hc) (2fb)⅄in 2 bedrooms CTV in all bedrooms ®
✘ sB&B£12.50-£13.50 dB&B£25-£27 dB&B⇨↱£32-£35 WB&B£85-£115 LDO 4pm
Lic ▥ CTV 3P
Credit Cards [1] [2] [3] Ⓔ

INN [Q][Q] Bryn Gwalia 17 Gronant Rd LL19 9DT ☎(0745) 852442
Closed 24 Dec-1 Jan

This small, cosy, privately owned and personally run hotel provides well equipped bedrooms, all of which have en suite facilities. The hotel is conveniently close to the town centre, and is equally suitable for tourists and business people alike.

8⇨↱ (2fb) CTV in all bedrooms ® ✘ (ex guide dogs) ✱
sB&B⇨↱£31 dB&B⇨↱£42 WB&Bfr£155 WBDifr£210 Lunch £6.50-£8&alc High tea £2.50 Dinner £7.50-£12&alc LDO 9pm
▥ 24P
Credit Cards [1] [3]

[Q] is for quality. For a full explanation of this AA quality award, consult the Contents page.

PRESTON Lancashire Map 07 SD52

GH [Q][Q][Q] Tulketh Hotel 209 Tulketh Road, Ashton PR2 1ES ☎(0772) 726250 & 728096 FAX (0772) 723743
Closed Xmas-New Year

Personally owned and run by the Hardwick family, this detached Edwardian property is situated in a side road just off the Blackpool road, 2 miles west of the town. The well equipped bedrooms provide good facilities, including TV and direct-dial telephones; some rooms are located in a modern extension. There is a cosy bar/ lounge for guests, and an à la carte menu is served each evening in the pleasant dining room. The spacious entrance hall features a fine stained-glass window.

12rm(11⇨↱1hc) (1fb) CTV in all bedrooms ® T
✘ (ex guide dogs) sB&B£31-£37 sB&B⇨↱£33-£40 dB&B£43-£47 dB&B⇨↱£45-£51 LDO 7.30pm
Lic ▥ CTV 12P
Credit Cards [1] [2] [3] [5] Ⓔ

GH [Q] Withy Trees 175 Garstang Road, Fulwood PR2 4LL (2m N on A6) ☎(0772) 717693

This mainly commercial guesthouse is situated on the A6, 2 miles north of the town centre. Bedrooms are modest but bright and clean, and 2 bedrooms have en suite facilities. There is a comfortable lounge.

11rm(2↱9hc) (2fb)⅄in 5 bedrooms CTV in all bedrooms ® ✱
sB&Bfr£19 sB&B↱£25-£28 dB&B£30-£33 dB&B↱£35-£39 WB&Bfr£110 WBDifr£145 LDO 2pm
▥ CTV 20P
Credit Cards [1] [3] Ⓔ

INN [Q][Q][Q] *Birley Arms Motel* Bryning Ln, Warton PR4 1TN ☎(0722) 679988 FAX (0772) 679435

16↱ CTV in all bedrooms ® ✘ (ex guide dogs) LDO 9.15pm
▥ P
Credit Cards [1] [2] [3] [5]

PRESTWICK Strathclyde *Ayrshire* Map 10 NS32

GH [Q][Q] Fairways Hotel 19 Links Rd KA9 1QG ☎(0292) 70396

This fine semidetached period house, built around the turn of the century, overlooks the golf course and caters well for devotees of the game. There is a relaxing first-floor lounge, and on the ground floor a tasteful dining room with well spaced tables and a beautiful period sideboard. Bedrooms are being upgraded to provide en suite facilities.

5rm(4↱1hc) (1fb) CTV in all bedrooms ® ✱ sB&B↱£22.50 dB&B↱£41 WB&B£125
Lic ▥ CTV 8P

GH [Q][Q][Q] Fernbank 213 Main St KA9 1SU ☎(0292) 75027

This red sandstone house is set beside the main road on the southern side of town. Spotlessly clean throughout it offers variously sized bedrooms all enhanced by colour-coordinated fabrics. Bathrobes are provided for those without en suite facilities, who have the use of an attractive first-floor bathroom complete with bidet. There is a small but comfortable lounge and a lovely pine-furnished breakfast room. Modern wood-strip wall panelling has been used to great effect throughout.

7rm(4↱3hc) (1fb) CTV in all bedrooms ® ✘ ✱ sB&B£14-£15 dB&B↱£34-£36
▥ CTV 7P nc5yrs Ⓔ

SELECTED

GH [Q][Q][Q][Q] Golf View Hotel 17 Links Rd KA9 1QG ☎(0292) 671234 FAX (0292) 671244

Quietly situated, yet convenient for both the airport and railway stations, this semidetached red sandstone house overlooks the Prestwick Golf Club, home of the first Open Championship in 1860. Enthusiastically run by the friendly proprietors, it offers a high standard of bed and breakfast accommodation, and is understandably popular with golfers.

Bedrooms are well appointed and equipped with thoughtful extras. The first-floor lounge overlooks the 14th green, as does the attractive breakfast room.
6rm(5⇌↱) (2fb)⊬in 1 bedroom CTV in all bedrooms ® ✖ (ex guide dogs) ✱ sB&B⇌↱fr£24 dB&B⇌↱fr£46
Lic 🍴 CTV 10P
Credit Cards [1] [3]

GH QQ Kincraig Private Hotel 39 Ayr Rd KA9 1SY
☎(0292) 79480
Situated on the main road, this detached sandstone house has a comfortable lounge and attractive period dining room. Bedrooms in the main are spacious and well furnished.
6rm(3↱3hc) (1fb) CTV in all bedrooms ® ✱ sB&B£14.50-£17.50 dB&Bfr£28 dB&B↱fr£35 LDO 5pm
Lic 🍴 CTV 8P nc3yrs

RAMSGATE Kent Map **05** TR36

GH QQ Eastwood 28 Augusta Rd CT11 8JS
☎Thanet(0843) 591505
rs 25 & 26 Dec
A popular, friendly family-run commercial guesthouse ideally located close to the beach, ferry terminal and town centre. There is a choice of attractively furnished simple bedrooms varying in shape and size; 2 rooms now have private bathrooms and they all come equipped with remote-control satellite TV and video. A set daily dinner is cooked by Caroline Gunnell and served in the attractive dining room, and there is a cosy lounge. The patio garden is available in the summer, and there is unrestricted street parking. →

7rm(2⇌🚿5hc) (4fb) CTV in all bedrooms ® ✱ sB&B£15-£20 dB&B£25-£35 dB&B⇌🚿£35-£40 WB&B£75-£135 WBDi£105-£160 LDO 6pm
🍽 CTV 12P £

GH QQ St Hilary Private Hotel 21 Crescent Rd CT11 9QU ☎Thanet(0843) 591427
rs 25-26 Dec
Cheerful compact bedrooms, basement dining room, situated in residential area.
7hc (4fb) 🐕 sB&B£12.60-£14.40 dB&B£26-£34 WB&B£50-£70 LDO 3.30pm
Lic CTV 🅿 nc4yrs
Credit Cards 1 2 3 £

RASKELF North Yorkshire Map **08** SE47

SELECTED

GH QQQQ Old Farmhouse Country Hotel YO6 3LF ☎Easingwold(0347) 21971
Closed 22 Dec-29 Jan
Ideal for exploring the North Yorkshire Moors and the nearby Hambleton Hills, which are notable for their beauty, this delightful cottage-style hotel was once a farmhouse and still retains much of its original character. The beamed bedrooms, which include 2 family rooms and one with a 4 poster, have been tastefully furnished and decorated with a mixture of styles. There is an extremely comfortable main lounge with winged armchairs and settees, plus a small lounge for those wishing to watch TV. Excellent fixed-price dinners are served in the attractive dining room with lace, green damask cloths, fresh flowers and specially made oak chairs. The menu may include smoked salmon salad with quail eggs or perhaps chicken, farmhouse style and home-made sweets such as Taffety tart. Bill and Jenny Frost are very congenial hosts who assure guests of their fullest attention at this establishment renowned for its hospitality and delicious food.
10rm(6⇌4🚿) (2fb) ® dB&B⇌🚿£67-£80 (incl dinner) WBDi£234.50-£259 LDO 6pm
Lic 🍽 CTV 12P

RAVENSCAR North Yorkshire Map **08** NZ90

GH QQQ The Smugglers Rock Country YO13 0ER ☎Scarborough(0723) 870044
Mar-Nov
Converted and restored farmhouse, close to moors and sea.
10rm(2⇌8🚿) (2fb) CTV in all bedrooms ® sB&B⇌🚿£19-£19.50 dB&B⇌🚿£38-£39 WB&B£125 WBDi£169 LDO 4.30pm
Lic 🍽 CTV 12P nc3yrs snooker £

RAVENSTONEDALE Cumbria Map **12** NY70

FH Q Mrs M Wildman **Ellergill** *(NY737015)* CA17 4LL ☎Newbiggin-on-Lune(05396) 23240
Mar-Nov
A pleasant farmhouse situated in a very rural location among fells. The owners are very friendly and offer a warm welcome.
3hc (1fb)⊁in all bedrooms ® 🐕 (ex guide dogs)
CTV 6P 300 acres dairy sheep £

READING Berkshire Map **04** SU77

GH QQQ Abbey House Hotel 118 Connaught Rd RG3 2UF ☎(0734) 590549 FAX (0734) 569299
This friendly, family-run detached house is located in a residential road close to the town centre. Bedrooms vary in style and price. Standard rooms provide good value accommodation, while the more expensive offer almost 3-star facilities, including trouser presses and telephone computer terminals – ideal for the business guests. Standards of housekeeping are high throughout, and decoration is simple and tasteful. There is a lounge suitable for small meetings, and the bright dining room offers both a set menu and an à la carte in addition to bar snacks.
18rm(7⇌🚿11hc) (1fb) CTV in 24 bedrooms ® T 🐕 (ex guide dogs) ✱ sB&Bfr£28 sB&B⇌🚿fr£42.50 dB&Bfr£44 dB&B⇌🚿fr£52.50 LDO 8.30pm
Lic 🍽 CTV 14P
Credit Cards 1 2 3 £

GH QQQ Aeron Private Hotel 191-193 Kentwood Hill, Tilehurst RG3 6JE (3m W off A329) ☎(0734) 424119 FAX (0734) 451953
Now a sizeable hotel, the Aeron remains a family-run establishment which has been extensively upgraded and redecorated and now offers clean, fresh bedrooms to suit all pockets. The simpler, annexe-style single rooms are popular with people working in the area, while the en suite rooms provide more sophisticated facilities, including writing desks and hairdryers. The attractive dining room has been extended to provide a no-smoking area, and the à la carte menu has a wide choice from plain grill meals and vegetarian choices to more adventurous foreign dishes. There are 2 smartly decorated lounges which provide a relaxing atmosphere.
14rm(7🚿7hc) Annexe 11hc (1fb) CTV in all bedrooms ® T ✱ sB&B£20-£28 sB&B🚿£41-£43 dB&B£43-£45 dB&B🚿£54 LDO 8.15pm
Lic 🍽 CTV 20P
Credit Cards 1 2 3 £

GH QQ *Brackenhurst* 230 Wokingham Rd, Earley RG6 1JS ☎(0734) 667829
Brackenhurst is a large period building on the Wokingham road leaving the town centre, and has an Alpine appearance with its elevated position, gables and balcony. Bedrooms, many with showers, are smartly decorated and of a good size. Newly refurbished last year, everything is in good order.
7hc (1fb)⊁in 4 bedrooms CTV in all bedrooms ® 🐕 (ex guide dogs)
🍽 5P nc3yrs
Credit Cards 1 3

REDCAR Cleveland Map **08** NZ62

GH QQQ *Claxton House Private Hotel* 196 High St TS10 3AW ☎(0642) 486745
Closed 24 Dec-2 Jan
Situated at the end of the High Street, this well established hotel provides well appointed accommodation, with both the business and leisure guest in mind. The spacious, attractive open-plan bar and restaurant are popular, and there is a cosy TV lounge; some rooms enjoy sea views.
17rm(6🚿11hc) (2fb) CTV in 15 bedrooms ®
Lic 🍽 CTV 10P snooker

REDHILL Surrey Map **04** TQ25

GH QQ Ashleigh House Hotel 39 Redstone Hill RH1 4BG ☎(0737) 764763
Closed Xmas
This attractive Edwardian detached house is ideally located for the town centre and station. Modestly furnished bedrooms are well maintained, and TVs and tea-making facilities are soon to be installed. There is a cosy guests' lounge, and a hearty English breakfast is served by the hospitable owners Mr and Mrs Warren. There is also a swimming pool which is open at specific times during the day.
8rm(1⇌3🚿4hc) (2fb) CTV in 7 bedrooms ® 🐕 (ex guide dogs) ✱ sB&B£25-£28 dB&B£38-£44 dB&B⇌🚿£45-£55
🍽 9P ⛱(heated)
Credit Cards 1

The Aeron Private Hotel

191 Kentwood Hill, Tilehurst, Reading.
Tel: (0734) 424119 Fax: (0734) 451953

24 bedrooms some en suite, all with colour TV, telephone and tea & coffee making facilities. Full English breakfast. Dinner served Mon-Thurs inclusive except public holidays. Good class accommodation at highly competitive rates.

BUSINESS & PRIVATE.
SPECIAL WEEK END DISCOUNT.

2 miles M4 exit 12. 45 minutes London Airport via M4. 35 minutes London Paddington via BR.

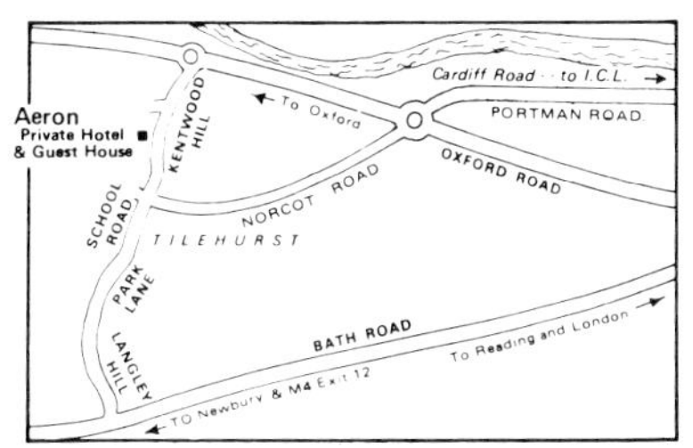

Family Run Hotel **Est 16 Years** **BTA Commended**

Ashleigh House Hotel

39 Redstone Hill, Redhill, Surrey
Tel: Redhill (0737) 764763

This fine Edwardian residence now run as a family hotel offers a genuine friendly atmosphere with the personal attention of the owners at all times. Our English breakfast is our speciality and value for money.

★ Lounge ★
★ Hair dryer, tea/coffee & colour television in all rooms ★ Some en suite
★ Full fire certificate
★ Exit Junction 6 & 8 M25 ★ Junction 8 M23

Gatwick by car 15 minutes by train 10 minutes; London by train 35 minutes.

QQ

EASTWOOD GUEST HOUSE

28 Augusta Road, Ramsgate, Kent CT11 8JS
Telephone: Thanet (0843) 591505

- The house is situated in a lovely position adjacent to the beach, the Ferry port and the town centre.
- Comfortable rooms with satellite TV and hot drink making facilities. En suite rooms available.
- Good food and any special diets happily catered for.

This house is appraised for its unique friendly atmosphere

B & B from £12.00 nightly. Evening meal £5.00
Reduced weekly terms

Send for colour brochure

OPEN ALL YEAR **AMPLE SAFE PARKING**

Proprietor: Mrs Carole Gunnell

GH QQQ Beechwood Hotel 39 Hatchlands Rd RH1 6AP
☎(0737) 761444 & 764277
On the borders of Redhill and Reigate, Beechwood Hotel is only 10 minutes' walk from Redhill railway station for trains to London and Gatwick. Recently renovated and re-opened, it provides hotel standards of accommodation with modern well fitted shower rooms. The attractively decorated dining room has a comfortable small bar and, at present, evening meals are served by prior arrangement only, but greater choice and flexibility are planned.
9rm(7) (2fb) in 7 bedrooms CTV in all bedrooms ® *
sB&B£30-£40 dB&B£45-£55 LDO 10am
Lic 10P
Credit Cards 1 3

GH QQ Lynwood House 50 London Rd RH1 1LN
☎(0737) 766894 & 762804
A small friendly guesthouse just a short walk from the town centre and within easy reach of Gatwick Airport. Owner Mrs Rao has renovated the house, and now most rooms have their own shower, and they are all clean and comfortable. The breakfast room has been newly furnished, and there is a cosy lounge. The car park is a useful bonus.
10rm(2 8hc) (3fb) CTV in all bedrooms ® (ex guide dogs)
* sB&B£20-£28 dB&B£34-£40 dB&B£38-£45
CTV 8P
Credit Cards 1 3 £

REDMILE Leicestershire Map **08** SK73

GH QQ Peacock Farm Guest House & Restaurant NG13 OGQ
☎Bottesford(0949) 42475
4hc Annexe 6 CTV in 4 bedrooms TV in 2 bedrooms ®
(ex guide dogs) sB&B£19.50-£24 sB&B£29 dB&B£32
dB&B£39 LDO 8.30pm
Lic CTV 30P snooker solarium
Credit Cards 1 2 3 £

REDWICK Gwent Map **03** ST48

GH QQ Brickhouse NP6 3DX ☎Magor(0633) 880230
Brickhouse is in a quiet spot on the edge of Redwick village, but only 3 miles from junction 23 of the M4. There has been a house here since 1450 and parts of the original farmhouse remain, but the Georgian façade was built around 1795. Part of a working farm, the guesthouse is run separately and is popular with business travellers. Accommodation is comfortable, with traditional first-floor rooms and more modern second-floor rooms – all no-smoking and spotlessly clean. Public areas include a cosy lounge and a dining room serving breakfast and a set evening meal.
7rm(5 2hc) (1fb) in all bedrooms * sB&B£24
sB&B£29 dB&B£39 LDO 6pm
Lic CTV P
See advertisement under NEWPORT

REETH North Yorkshire Map **07** SE09

SELECTED

GH QQQQ Arkleside Hotel DL11 6SG
☎Richmond(0748) 84200
Mar-Oct rs Nov-Dec
Originally a row of terraced 17th-century cottages, this is now a delightful small, comfortable hotel offering splendid panoramic views of typical Dales countryside. Bedrooms are prettily decorated in different colour schemes and are very comfortably furnished: some have fine antiques and all have TV and radio/alarms. A well produced set 4-course dinner is provided in the richly decorated dining room, which enjoys superb views, and there are 2 comfortable lounges, one with a bar. Malcolm and Sylvia Darby offer a warm welcome to all their guests.
9rm(1 7 1hc) CTV in all bedrooms ® *
sB&B£38-£41 dB&B£52-£60 LDO 7.30pm
Lic 6P 1 nc10yrs (hard)
Credit Cards 1 3 £

REIGATE Surrey Map **04** TQ25

GH QQQ Cranleigh Hotel 41 West St RH2 9BL
☎(0737) 223417 FAX (0737) 223734
Closed 24-26 Dec
Ideally located for the town centre and the M25, this Victorian town house retains many of its original features. Double rooms are generally spacious, while singles are more compact, they are all attractively decorated and most have private facilities. On the ground floor guests have a choice of public rooms, an elegant lounge, cosy bar, and a dining room where a short weekly-changing menu is offered Monday to Thursday. A 1956 Wurlitzer in the adjoining conservatory provides the background music.
10rm(6 1 3hc) (2fb) CTV in all bedrooms ® **T**
(ex guide dogs) * sB&B£35-£40 sB&B£49.50-£55
dB&B£59.50-£65 dB&B£59.50-£65 LDO 9pm
Lic CTV 6P (heated)
Credit Cards 1 2 3 5

RHANDIRMWYN Dyfed Map **03** SN74

INN QQ Royal Oak SA20 0NY ☎(05506) 201
FAX (05506) 332
Reached by a picturesque drive through a wooded valley along the A48 north of Llandovery, this secluded inn has pretty, well equipped bedrooms and a warm, welcoming bar.
5rm(2 1 2hc) (1fb) CTV in 3 bedrooms ® * sB&B£16-£18.50 dB&B£40-£45 LDO 10.30pm
20P pool table clay pigeon wknds
Credit Cards 1 3

RHOSCOLYN

See **ANGLESEY, ISLE OF**

RHOS-ON-SEA Clwyd

See **Colwyn Bay**

RHYD Gwynedd Map **06** SH64

FH QQ Mrs N Griffiths **Bodlondeb** *(SH636420)* LL48 6ST
☎Penrhyndeudraeth(0766) 770640
Surrounded by rugged hills, this small, stone house is part of a 500-acre sheep-rearing farm and has recently been extensively modernised. It now has 2 double bedded rooms, both with en suite shower and toilet, plus a twin room, and all are quite compact but nicely decorated. The attractive lounge has an open fire and TV with lots of ornaments and bric-a-brac that add a cosy feeling. The small, pleasant dining room seats up to 6 people at 2 tables.
3rm(2 1hc) * sB&Bfr£15 dB&Bfr£30 WB&Bfr£95
LDO 6pm
CTV 2P 500 acres sheep hill farm

RHYL Clwyd Map **06** SJ08

GH QQ Pier Hotel 23 East Pde LL18 3AL
☎(0745) 350280
Closed Dec
This small, privately owned hotel provides well equipped accommodation. It is located on the promenade, opposite the 'Ocean World' complex. There is a small car park at the rear.
9rm(3 3 3hc) (3fb) CTV in all bedrooms ® sB&B£13-£14
dB&B£34-£38 WB&B£110-£120 WBDi£135-£140
LDO 3pm
Lic CTV 2P
Credit Cards 1 3

£ Remember to use the money-off vouchers.

RICHMOND North Yorkshire Map **07** NZ10

See also Low Row, Reeth and Thwaite

GH QQQ Pottergate 4 Pottergate DL10 4AB ☎(0748) 823826
A Georgian terraced house on the A6108 as it approaches the town from the east. Bedrooms are comfortable and thoughtfully furnished, all with colour TV and tea-making facilities. Downstairs there is a cosy lounge and a small bar within the neat little dining room.
6hc (2fb)⅟in 3 bedrooms CTV in all bedrooms ® ✗ sB&B£18-£20 dB&B£28-£30 WB&B£90-£110
Lic 🍽 CTV 3P 2🚗 nc2yrs

SELECTED

FH QQQQ Mrs M F Turnbull ***Whashton Springs*** *(NZ149046)* DL11 7JS (3m W on unclass rd)
☎(0748) 822884
Closed Xmas & New Year
Surrounded by tranquil, unspoilt countryside this Georgian farmhouse is situated on a delightful 600-acre mixed farm. A few of the comfortable bedrooms, furnished in a Georgian style (one has a 4-poster bed), are located in the old house, with bay windows overlooking the gardens. The remainder are in a converted stable and are more modern in style but very tastefully furnished and decorated. The lounge is a comfortable, spacious room with views of the garden and again furnished with antique items, plus a cosy log fire which gives it much charm and character. Mouth-watering evening meals and sumptuous breakfasts are served in the attractive dining room, with its polished tables. This is very much a working farm, run by the Turnbull family, with Mrs Turnbull providing hospitality in the farmhouse.
3rm(2⇌1♠) Annexe 5rm(2⇌3♠) (2fb)⅟in 3 bedrooms CTV in all bedrooms ® ✗ (ex guide dogs) LDO am
Lic 🍽 10P nc5yrs 600 acres arable beef mixed sheep

RINGWOOD Hampshire Map **04** SU10

SELECTED

GH QQQQ *Little Forest Lodge Hotel* Poulner Hill BH24 3HS ☎(0425) 478848
An attractive Edwardian-style chalet set back from the A31 eastbound carriageway from Ringwood, surrounded by 3 acres of landscaped gardens. The bedrooms are all prettily furnished and well maintained: 3 are spacious, with private bathrooms, and there are plans to convert the other 2; most are double glazed and equipped with TV and tea-making facilities. There is an oak-panelled dining room, and 4-course dinners or bar snacks are available by arrangement. The Martins offer a friendly welcome, and activities such as fishing, sailing and riding can be arranged.
5rm(2⇌1♠2hc) (2fb)⅟in 2 bedrooms CTV in all bedrooms ® LDO 4pm
Lic 🍽 CTV 10P 2🚗 solarium
Credit Cards 1 3

GH QQQ The Nest 10 Middle Ln BH24 1LE ☎(0425) 476724
This late-Victorian schoolmaster's house is now an appealing and comfortable B&B within walking distance of local pubs and a cosmopolitan range of restaurants. Bedrooms are prettily decorated and there are especially high standards of housekeeping and maintenance. A bright conservatory breakfast room looks out on to a neat garden and breakfast includes fresh filter coffee. The Nest is well placed for local facilities, and just around the corner is the sports hall featured in TV's The Britas Empire. *This is a no-smoking establishment.*

→

3hc ⊁in all bedrooms CTV in all bedrooms ® ✖ ✱ sB&B£18-£22 dB&B£30-£35 WB&Bfr£105
꾸 4P

ROADWATER Somerset Map **03** ST03

FH QQ Mr & Mrs Brewer ***Wood Advent*** *(ST037374)* TA23 0RR ☎Washford(0984) 40920

Set in 340 acres at the foot of the Brendon Hills in Exmoor National Park, this delightful farmhouse has spacious bedrooms, some with en suite facilities, and relaxing public rooms. Mrs Brewer uses home produce whenever possible for the set menu.

5rm(1⇌2⌐1hc) (3fb) ® ✖
Lic 꾸 CTV 10P 2🚗 ⌂ ≏(heated) 𝒫(grass)350 acres arable beef sheep

See advertisement under DUNSTER

ROCHDALE Greater Manchester Map **07** SD81

FH QQ Mrs J Neave **Leaches** *(SD835838)* Ashworth Valley OL11 5UN ☎(0706) 41116 & 228520
Closed 24 Dec-1 Jan

The Neaves have improved the farm track that leads to this 17th-century farmhouse, situated between the A680 and the B6222, enjoying breathtaking views over the Manchester plain. Bedrooms are simple but pleasantly furnished, though the single room is extremely small. There is a comfortable lounge in which to relax and the Neaves are a mine of local information.

3hc (2fb)⊁in all bedrooms CTV in all bedrooms ® ✱ sB&Bfr£18 dB&Bfr£32
꾸 CTV 6P ↲ coarse fishing 140 acres beef sheep £

ROCHE Cornwall & Isles of Scilly Map **02** SW96

GH QQQ ***Asterisk*** Mount Pleasant PL26 8LH ☎St Austell(0726) 890863

This detached stone house stands back from the A30 east of Roche in its own grounds, which contain geese, ducks, goats and Shetland ponies. Proprietors Mr and Mrs Zola are steadily improving the accommodation, with a restaurant and smart lounge/bar new additions this year. The 7 bedrooms are bright and fresh, 2 have private bathrooms, another 2 have showers. Some of the bedrooms have rural views. There is a comfortable TV lounge with TV, books and a log fire, and a cosy bar.

7rm(2⌐5hc) (2fb) ®
Lic 꾸 CTV 10P 2🚗
Credit Cards 1 3

ROCHESTER Northumberland Map **12** NY89

FH QQ Mrs J M Chapman **Woolaw** *(NY821984)* NE19 1TB ☎Otterburn(0830) 20686

This well furnished, comfortable farmhouse is situated off the A68 in a lovely rural setting north of the village. The ground-floor bedrooms are functional and modestly furnished but have private bathrooms, and there is another, large family room.

3rm(2⌐) (1fb) TV available ✖ (ex guide dogs) ✱ sB&B⌐£12-£15 dB&B⌐£24-£30 LDO 5.30pm
꾸 CTV 10P ↲ 740 acres beef sheep

ROCK Cornwall & Isles of Scilly Map **02** SW97

GH Q Roskarnon House Hotel PL27 6LD ☎Trebetherick(0208) 862329
Mar-Nov

Set in an acre of mature grounds, this detached Edwardian house has been owned by the same family for over 35 years. Standing in an elevated position, it has spectacular panoramic views over the Camel Estuary, and offers peaceful relaxation at an affordable price. The bedrooms are being refurbished: two have a private shower, some have TV and 2 are conveniently located on the ground floor. The lounge and dining room overlook the lawns and beach, and most bedrooms have sea views. A table d'hôte menu is served, using home-grown produce, and the friendly service is personally supervised by the proprietor Ian Veall. Table tennis is available in the games room, and local sports including sailing, golf, tennis, riding, water skiing, surfing and fishing can be arranged.

15rm(4⇌3⌐8hc) (5fb) CTV in 6 bedrooms TV in 1 bedroom ✖ ✱ sB&Bfr£17.50 sB&B⇌⌐fr£25 dB&Bfr£35 dB&B⇌⌐fr£40 WB&Bfr£120 WBDifr£180 LDO 8pm
Lic CTV 14P 2🚗 (£1 per night)

ROEWEN Gwynedd Map **06** SH77

GH QQQ Gwern Borter Country Manor Barkers Ln LL32 8YL ☎Tyn-y-Groes(0492) 650360
Closed 23 Dec-2 Jan

Gwern Borter Manor is set in 9 acres of grounds at the foot of Talytan Mountain, north of the village. Short breaks are the main business at the manor house which can be enhanced by supervised horse rides. For complete freedom self-catering units are available.

3rm(1⇌2⌐) (1fb) CTV in all bedrooms ® ✱ dB&B⇌⌐£38-£44 WB&B£100-£140 WBDi£140-£195 LDO 4pm
Lic 꾸 CTV 10P 4🚗 ⌂ U cycle hire £

ROGART Highland *Sutherland* Map **14** NC70

SELECTED

FH QQQQ Mrs J S R Moodie **Rovie** *(NC716023)* IV28 3TZ ☎(0408) 641209
Apr-Oct

Guests return year after year to sample the welcoming hospitality and enjoyable home cooking offered by Christine Moodie, at her delightful lodge- style farmhouse in the picturesque valley of Streathfleet. The comfortable bedrooms are spacious with individual décor and furniture of various styles. The main lounge with its welcoming peat-burning fire is comfortable and pleasantly furnished, inviting peaceful relaxation, and a TV is provided in the cosy timber-lined sun lounge. Hearty breakfasts and enjoyable home-cooked dinners are served at separate tables in the attractive dining room, though at peak times it may be necessary to share a table with other guests. A genuine home-from-home atmosphere prevails and home baking is personally served with morning and evening teas. Fishing and shooting can be arranged.

6hc (1fb) ✱ sB&B£16-£18 dB&B£32-£36 WB&B£112-£126 WBDi£196-£200 LDO 6.30pm
CTV 8P ▸9 ↲ rough shooting 120 acres beef sheep

ROGATE West Sussex Map **04** SU82

SELECTED

FH QQQQ Mrs J C Francis **Mizzards** *(SU803228)* GU31 5HS ☎(0730) 821656
Closed Xmas

A lovely 16th-century house in a tranquil rural setting, with the River Rother forming a boundary on one side of the 13 acres of landscaped gardens which include a swimming pool and lake. The 3 attractively furnished bedrooms vary in size, but are very well equipped: one room has a canopied bed and spacious marble bathroom and they all have antique furniture, TV, tea trays and private bathrooms. There is an elegant drawing room and a spectacular galleried and beamed breakfast room with an inglenook fireplace. Bed and breakfast only is provided, but there are many excellent local pubs and restaurants nearby. Smoking is not permitted.

3⇌⌐ ⊁in all bedrooms CTV in all bedrooms ® ✖ sB&B⇌⌐£28-£33 dB&B⇌⌐£42-£46
꾸 10P 2🚗 nc6yrs ≏(heated) 13 acres sheep non-working £

FH QQQ Mrs J Baigent **Trotton** *(SU835225)* GU31 5EN
☎Midhurst(0730) 813618 FAX (0730) 816093
This pleasant farmhouse was converted 3 years ago from an old cart shed and is situated conveniently on the A272, between Trotton and Rogate. Two bedrooms are beamed, freshly decorated, furnished with antique pine and have smart, modern en suites. Breakfast is taken in the small dining room, with a friendly, family atmosphere. The guests are provided with their own lounge/games room.
3rm(2 1hc) in all bedrooms CTV in 1 bedroom ®
(ex guide dogs) * sB&B£15-£20 sB&B £25-£30 dB&B£35-£40
CTV P table tennis darts 230 acres arable beef mixed

ROMFORD Greater London Map **05** TQ58

GH QQ **The Coach House** 33 Main Rd RM1 3DB
☎(0708) 751901 & 728534 FAX (0708) 730290
A short distance from the town centre, alongside the A118, the Coach House comprises 2 large Victorian buildings with various annexes facing each other across the main road. Most of the bedrooms have been cheerfully renovated with bold floral bedspreads, stripped pine doors and several smartly tiled bathrooms. Breakfast is served on large polished tables in an attractive period room.
32rm(14 4 14hc) in 4 bedrooms CTV in all bedrooms ®
(ex guide dogs) * sB&B£29.50-£35.50 sB&B £49.50 dB&B£39.50 dB&B £49.50
Lic 20P
Credit Cards 1 2 3 5

GH Q **The Orchard Guest House** 81 Eastern Rd RM1 3PB
☎(0708) 744099
Closed Xmas

→

This converted Victorian house lies in a quiet residential street not far from the town centre. Most of the bedrooms are on the first floor, vary in size and are soundly equipped.
5rm(1⛿2hc) (2fb) CTV in all bedrooms ✗ (ex guide dogs) sB&B£25-£30 sB&B⛿£25-£30 dB&B£30-£35 dB&B⛿£35-£40 WB&B£150-£175 WBDi£195-£220 LDO am
CTV 6P

ROMSEY Hampshire Map **04** SU32

GH QQQ Highfield House Newtown Rd, Awbridge SO51 0GG ☎(0794) 40727
From the A31 in Romsey take the A27 signed for Salisbury, after 2 miles take the first right into Danes Road, then the first left signed for Newtown and the house is first on the right. It is a newly built property, attractively hung with Sussex tiles and set in a quiet wooded area with 1.5 acres of garden overlooking Dunwood Manor Golf Club, and just 12 miles from Salisbury and Winchester it is a good touring location. The 3 en suite rooms combine quality modern plumbing with antique furniture and pretty fabrics. There is a well furnished and comfortable lounge with an open fire in a marble surround, while the dining room has one large table for everyone. Pauline Parsons loves to cook and offers a 4-course evening meal of home cooking which can include home-grown items.
3rm(1⇌2⛿) CTV in all bedrooms ® ✗ (ex guide dogs) * sB&B⇌⛿£18-£37 dB&B⇌⛿£40 LDO 4pm
CTV 10P nc14yrs

ROSLIN Lothian *Midlothian* Map **11** NT26

INN QQ *Olde Original Rosslyn* 4 Main St EH25 9LD ☎031-440 2384
An attractive village inn, only 7 miles from Edinburgh, offering pretty, well appointed bedrooms and good value menus in both the bar lounge and restaurant.
6⇌⛿ CTV in all bedrooms ® LDO 10pm
14P
Credit Cards 1 2 3

ROSS-ON-WYE Hereford & Worcester Map **03** SO52

See also St Owen's Cross

GH QQ The Arches Country House Walford Rd HR9 5PT ☎(0989) 63348
This Georgian-style building is set in half an acre of lawns and shrubbery, on the B4228 just south of the town and river. Bedrooms are a bit small but well developed with modern laminated furniture and pretty fabrics. The restaurant is furnished with plush upholstered seating and there is a new conservatory lounge opening on to the lawn.
8rm(2⇌2⛿4hc) (2fb)⊬in 2 bedrooms CTV in all bedrooms ® ✗ (ex guide dogs) sB&B£17-£21 sB&B⇌⛿£21 dB&B£30-£40 dB&B⇌⛿£40 WB&B£108-£138 LDO 5pm
Lic CTV 9P £

GH QQ Brookfield House Ledbury Rd HR9 7AT ☎(0989) 62188
Closed 3 days Xmas rs Nov-Jan
This friendly guesthouse is situated within walking distance of the town centre and has its own car park. Bedrooms are bright and cheerful and there is a pleasant lounge for residents.
8rm(1⇌2⛿5hc) CTV in all bedrooms ® * sB&B£16 dB&B£31 dB&B⇌⛿£35 WB&B£97-£108
Lic 10P nc5yrs
Credit Cards 1 3 £

GH QQQ Edde Cross House Edde Cross St HR9 7BZ ☎(0989) 65088
Feb-Nov
A Georgian Grade II listed building, once the home of the Dame of Sark; it was also used as the summer palace of the Bishops of Hereford. Bedrooms are very pretty and comfortably furnished and well equipped with some thoughtful extras. Some rooms have lovely rural views over the River Wye, and there is an attractive small garden also offering fine views. There is a small lounge for residents, and guests are given a choice of the normal or a vegetarian breakfast. Smoking is not permitted here.
5rm(2⛿3hc) ⊬in all bedrooms CTV in all bedrooms ® ✗ (ex guide dogs) sB&B£18-£19 dB&B£31-£35 dB&B⛿£41-£45 WB&B£119-£143.50
1 (£1 per day) nc10yrs £

GH QQQ *Ryefield House Hotel* Gloucester Rd HR9 5NA ☎(0989) 63030
This large Victorian house is situated on the Gloucester road, in a quiet residential area of the town. It provides modern and very well equipped bedrooms, many with private bathrooms, an attractive restaurant and pleasant lounges.
8rm(5⇌⛿3hc) (4fb) CTV in all bedrooms ® LDO 5pm
Lic CTV 10P 1

GH QQ Sunnymount Hotel Ryefield Rd HR9 5LU ☎(0989) 63880
Closed Xmas
This guesthouse is situated just off the Gloucester road, in a quiet residential area of this pretty town. It is run by the friendly Williams family and bedrooms are cosy and well maintained, with a comfortable residents' lounge.
9rm(6⇌⛿3hc) ® ✗ (ex guide dogs) sB&B£20 sB&B⇌⛿£29 dB&B⇌⛿£44-£48 WB&B£140 WBDi£215-£250 LDO 6.30pm
Lic CTV 7P
Credit Cards 1 2 3 £

ROTHBURY Northumberland Map **12** NU00

SELECTED

GH QQQQ Orchard High St NE65 7TL ☎(0669) 20684
Mar-Nov
This spotlessly clean and meticulously maintained Georgian house lies well back from the main road in this popular market town. Bedrooms are comfortable, airy and well equipped, with electric blankets for the cooler nights, and remote-control TV. Each floor has an 'essentials kit', including useful items such as hairdryer, scissors, plasters and sewing materials. The relaxing lounge accommodates an honesty bar, and there are lots of books, magazines and board games for guests to use. The 4-course dinners provide good home cooking, and can include broccoli flan, roast lamb with fresh vegetables, and rhubarb crumble, cheese or fruit.
6rm(4⛿2hc) (1fb) CTV in all bedrooms ® ✗ sB&B£19.50-£21.50 dB&B£39-£41 dB&B⛿£43-£45 WB&B£136.50-£150.50 WBDi£210-£224 LDO 7pm
Lic P £

ROTHERHAM South Yorkshire Map **08** SK49

GH QQQ *Stonecroft* Main St, Bramley S66 0SF (4m E of Rotherham) ☎(0709) 540922
This delightful stone-built former farmhouse dates back some 300 years and retains much of its original charm and character. The accommodation is cosy, and some bedrooms are in cleverly converted cottages to the rear of the house. A small self-catering cottage is also available. The guesthouse is conveniently located close to the centre of Bramley village, some 4 miles east of Rotherham, within half a mile of junction 1 of the M18.
4rm(1⇌⛿3hc) Annexe 5⇌⛿ (1fb) CTV in all bedrooms ®
Lic CTV 10P

ROTHLEY Leicestershire Map **08** SK51

GH QQQ *The Limes Hotel* 35 Mountsorrel Ln LE7 7PS ☎Leicester(0533) 302531
Closed Xmas
Friendly, efficiently run hotel with comfortable bedrooms and pleasant bars.
→

Sunnymount Hotel

RYEFIELD ROAD
ROSS-ON-WYE HR9 5LU

GUESTACCOM

Ideal for exploring the Wye Valley, Forest of Dean and the Black Mountains. Quietly located on edge of town. Warm, comfortable hotel, with most rooms ensuite. Own & local produce freshly cooked for each meal. English/French cuisine. Licensed. Private parking.

Brochure: ROSS (0989) 63880

Brookfield House

Ledbury Road, Ross on Wye, Herefordshire HR9 7AT
Telephone: (0989) 62188

A Queen Anne & Georgian listed building once part of the Manor of the Bishop's of Hereford.
Bed & Breakfast at its best.
Close to town centre but within easy reach of the A40 M50. **LARGE CAR PARK.**
All rooms H&C, Central Heating, Tea and Coffee facilities, and T.V.. Some rooms with toilet, bath or shower. Licensed. Hostess Josephine Baker extends a warm welcome. Pets with well-behaved owners are welcome!
Travellers Britain Recommended.

Ryefield House Hotel

Gloucester Road, Ross-on-Wye,
Herefordshire HR9 5NA
Telephone: 0989 63030

AA LISTED

Our lovely hotel is efficiently run with warmth and humour – a most relaxing base from which to tour the Wye Valley, Forest of Dean, Malvern Hills and Welsh mountains.

All bedrooms have television, telephone, beverage tray, fresh flowers and fudge! Breakfast when you wish.

We will happily guide you on your choice of pub, restaurant or cafe at which to dine, or tempt you to try one of our mouth watering Aga cooked dinners.

THE ARCHES

Country House Hotel

Small family run hotel, set in 1/2 acre of lawns, ideally situated only 10 minutes walk from town centre and with easy access to many interesting places in the beautiful Wye Valley.

All bedrooms are furnished and decorated to a high standard and have views of the lawned garden. Tea/coffee facilities and CTV are available in bedrooms. Fully licensed. Attractive residents lounge. Full central heating. Renowned for good food, a warm and friendly atmosphere with personal service. Ample parking. Bed and breakfast. Reduced weekly terms available

AA Listed Les Routiers ETB

For brochure or reservations, please write or phone:

Jean & James Jones, The Arches Country House Hotel, Walford Road, Ross-on-Wye, Herefordshire HR9 5PT. Telephone: (0989) 63348

12⇌↑ CTV in all bedrooms ® ✗ (ex guide dogs) LDO 9pm
Lic 🍽 15P nc12yrs
Credit Cards [1] [2] [3]

ROTTINGDEAN East Sussex Map **05** TQ30

GH Q Braemar House Steyning Rd BN2 7GA
☎Brighton(0273) 304263
Peacefully situated close to the village shops and the seafront, this family- run guesthouse offers simple but particularly well kept accommodation. A cosy lounge is provided for residents in addition to the breakfast room.
16hc (2fb) ✱ sB&B£14-£15 dB&B£28-£30
🍽 CTV ⁄P £

GH Q Corner House Steyning Rd BN2 7GA
☎Brighton(0273) 304533
This Victorian end-of-terrace house offers simple, functional bedrooms which have shared use of a public bathroom and separate shower. A full English breakfast is served in the small dining room by friendly proprietor Mrs Lilley.
6hc (1fb) CTV in all bedrooms ✱ sB&B£14.50-£15 dB&B£29-£30
🍽 ⁄P £

ROXTON Bedfordshire Map **04** TL15

FH QQQ Mrs J Must ***Church*** *(TL153545)* 41 High St MK44 3EB ☎Bedford(0234) 870234
This attractive farmhouse has a brick façade, with well tended gardens and a patio. The peaceful village setting means a good night's sleep in the 2 spacious bedrooms, one with grand period furniture. Guests have use of a comfortable lounge with TV and an open fire, and the timbered breakfast room. A warm, friendly atmosphere prevails.
2hc (1fb) ®
🍽 CTV 6P 66 acres arable

RUCKHALL Hereford & Worcester Map **03** SO44

SELECTED

INN QQQQ The Ancient Camp HR2 9QX
☎Golden Valley(0981) 250449
At the edge of an Iron-Age camp from which it takes its name, the inn overlooks the beautiful Wye River and Golden Valley. Two bedrooms offer this view, and one of these has its own sitting room. The bar, separated into several parts, has slab floors and log fires and is furnished with comfortable settees and rustic chairs and tables. It is a popular place to eat and only 10 minutes by car from the centre of Hereford, approached by a private drive. Four hundred yards of the river is available to residents for fishing.
5rm(2⇌3↑) CTV in all bedrooms ® **T** ✗ (ex guide dogs) sB&B⇌↑£36.50-£46.50 dB&B⇌↑£50-£60 Bar Lunch £3-£7alc Dinner £15-£18alc LDO 9.30pm
🍽 30P nc10yrs ⌐
Credit Cards [1] [3] £

RUFFORTH North Yorkshire Map **08** SE55

GH QQ Wellgarth House Wetherby Rd YO2 3QB
☎(090483) 592 & 595
Closed 25-26 Dec
A large well appointed modern house on the edge of the village.
8rm(4↑4hc) (1fb) CTV in all bedrooms ® ✗ (ex guide dogs) sB&B£17-£19 dB&B£28-£32 dB&B↑£30-£36
🍽 CTV 8P nc2yrs
Credit Cards [1] [3] £

RUGBY Warwickshire Map **04** SP57

GH QQ Avondale 16 Elsee Rd CV21 3BA ☎(0788) 578639
Situated in a quiet residential area close to the town centre and Rugby School, the accommodation is neatly maintained and public areas include a combined lounge and breakfast room. There is a rear car park for guests' use.
4rm(1↑3hc) (1fb) CTV in 2 bedrooms ® ✗ sB&Bfr£20 sB&B↑fr£25 dB&Bfr£34 dB&B↑fr£38
🍽 CTV 6P 2🚗 £

GH Q Mound Hotel 17-19 Lawford Rd CV21 2EB
☎(0788) 543486
Closed Xmas
The Mound Hotel is on the A428 close to the town centre. Rooms are individually decorated and named, providing modest guest accommodation.
17rm(6↑11hc) (4fb) CTV in 6 bedrooms TV in 11 bedrooms ✗ (ex guide dogs) sB&Bfr£19.40 sB&B↑fr£25.55 dB&Bfr£32.70 dB&B↑fr£37.30
Lic 🍽 CTV 14P
Credit Cards [1] [3]

RUISLIP Greater London London plan **4** A5 (pages 245-251)

GH QQQ *Barn Hotel* West End Rd HA4 6JB
☎(0895) 636057 Telex no 892514 FAX (0895) 638379
Comprising a small village of buildings set in its own pretty landscaped gardens, this hotel features 6 executive bedrooms housed in 17th-century, black and white converted barns. The majority of the other bedrooms are in 3 modern annexes and all rooms are en suite, equipped to a good standard, especially for the commercial visitor. There is a pleasant reception and a beamed bar for residents' use.
Annexe 66⇌↑ (1fb)⚟in 4 bedrooms CTV in all bedrooms ® ✗ (ex guide dogs) LDO 9.30pm
Lic 🍽 CTV 60P
Credit Cards [1] [2] [3] [5]

RUSHTON SPENCER Staffordshire Map **07** SJ96

FH QQ Mrs J Brown **Barnswood** *(SJ945606)* SK11 0RA
☎(0260) 226261
Closed 24 Dec-5 Jan
A warm welcome is assured from the Brown family at this 300-year-old farmhouse situated alongside the A523 and overlooking Rudyard Lake. Bedrooms are clean and bright and there is a cosy lounge/dining room for residents.
4rm(2hc) (2fb) ® ✗ ✱ sB&Bfr£14 dB&Bfr£24
🍽 CTV 4P 100 acres dairy

RUSTINGTON West Sussex Map **04** TQ00

GH QQQ Kenmore Claigmar Rd BN16 2NL ☎(0903) 784634
Quietly located in a residential area, this detached house has recently undergone an extension, and a new lounge has been created. The majority of rooms are en suite, well equipped with colour TV, tea-making facilities and radio alarms. Rooms are attractively co-ordinated. The new dining room is attractive, and 3-course dinners are available. Mrs Sylvia Dobbs creates a comfortable atmosphere.
7rm(1⇌5↑1hc) (2fb) CTV in all bedrooms ® LDO noon
🍽 CTV 7P
Credit Cards [1] [2] [3]

Street plans of certain towns and cities will be found in a separate section at the back of the book.

RUTHIN Clwyd Map **06** SJ15

SELECTED

GH QQQQ Eyarth Station Llanfair Dyffryn Clwyd LL15 2EE ☎(08242) 3643 due to change to (0824) 703643

As the name would suggest this was once a small railway station and station master's house, which has been cleverly and tastefully converted, and proprietors Jennifer and Albert Spencer continue to improve this delightful guesthouse. All the attractively decorated bedrooms have now been provided with en suite facilities, and 4 are conveniently situated on ground level. There is a conservatory extension containing the dining room which, like the spacious and comfortable lounge, commands lovely views of the valley. Outside is a heated swimming pool, a sun terrace and colourful gardens.

4↱ Annexe 2↱ (2fb) CTV in 1 bedroom ® ✱
sB&B↱£25-£30 dB&B↱£38-£40 LDO 7pm
Lic ⅏ CTV 6P ⛱(heated)
Credit Cards 1 3

RYDAL Cumbria

See **Ambleside**

RYDE

See **WIGHT, ISLE OF**

RYE East Sussex Map **05** TQ92

SELECTED

GH QQQQ Green Hedges Hilly Fields, Rye Hill TN31 7NH ☎(0797) 222185

Closed Xmas

An Edwardian red-brick house set in 1.5 acres of well kept south-facing gardens which include an outdoor pool. Bedrooms are very pretty, coordinated with flair and style and extremely comfortable. Breakfast is the only meal served, but it is a sumptuous affair, with a choice of traditional English breakfast, or a more imaginative menu including organic home-grown fruits with Greek yoghurt, locally baked French pâtisseries, French toast with cinnamon or scrambled egg with cheese sauce. Bookings are advisable as there are only 3 bedrooms, and smoking is not permitted. Green Hedges is quietly situated in a private road along Rye Hill, known as the A268 London road out of the town; the house is located half-way up the hill on the left, in a cul-de-sac marked 'Private': known locally as 'Hilly Fields'; the road is unsigned.

3↱ ⊬in all bedrooms CTV in all bedrooms ® ✗ ✱
dB&B↱£45-£50
⅏ 8P nc12yrs ⛱(heated)

SELECTED

GH QQQQ Holloway House High St TN31 7JF ☎(0797) 224748

This beautiful Tudor house with its ivy-clad Georgian façade is ideally situated in the attractive High Street. It was built over a medieval vaulted cellar, and was once the home of the British historian William Holloway. Proprietor Sheila Brown has tastefully decorated and furnished each room with antiques, together with half-tester, 4-poster and Victorian brass beds, all with private bathrooms. The residents' parlour features the original Elizabethan oak panelling and a stone fireplace. Dinner is served in the summer months, and room-service snacks are available throughout the year.

7rm(5⇌2↱) (2fb) CTV in all bedrooms ®
✗ (ex guide dogs) sB&B⇌↱£39-£65 dB&B⇌↱£50-£90 LDO 8pm
Lic ⅏ P
Credit Cards 1 3

See advertisement on page 343

SELECTED

GH QQQQ Jeakes House Mermaid St TN31 7ET ☎(0797) 222828 FAX (0797) 222623

This delightful listed building dates back in parts to the 17th century and is situated in a picturesque, medieval cobbled street. The oldest part of the house was used as a wool store and later as a Baptist school. Bedrooms are all tastefully furnished with antiques and pretty soft furnishings, and most have smart en suite bathrooms featuring hand painted Rye tiles. Breakfast is served in the 18th-century galleried dining room, formerly a chapel and Quaker meeting house. There is a small bar lounge and a parlour with chintz furnishings and a piano. The house is family owned and run by Francis and Jenny Hadfield and has several literary connections with the past.

12rm(8⇌2↱2hc) (2fb) CTV in all bedrooms ® T
sB&B£21.50 dB&B£39 dB&B⇌↱£53 WB&B£136.50-£185.50
Lic ⅏ P
Credit Cards 1 2 3 £

See advertisement on page 343

GH QQQ ***Little Saltcote*** 22 Military Rd TN31 7NY ☎(0797) 223210

Situated in an elevated position with its own cottage garden, this cosy establishment has well furnished and maintained bedrooms. Parking is available and the town centre is only 5 minutes' walk away.

6rm(2⊓4hc) (2fb) TV in all bedrooms ® ✗
P

GH QQQ Old Borough Arms The Strand TN31 7DB ☎(0797) 222128

Partially built into the medieval town wall at the foot of the famous Mermaid Street, this guesthouse has an appealing dining room combined with a bar on the first floor. It has aged floorboards, beams, and a log fire adds to the 18th-century charm. Bedrooms are all bright and modern with assorted floral fabrics, comfortable cane seating and smart tiled en suite shower rooms. Proprietors Terry and Jane Cox and daughter Vanessa offer an informal friendly atmosphere.

9⊓ (3fb) CTV in all bedrooms ® sB&B⊓£25-£28 dB&B⊓£36-£56 LDO 8pm
Lic CTV 2P
Credit Cards [1] [3] Ⓔ

GH QQQ The Old Vicarage Guesthouse 66 Church Square TN31 7HF ☎(0797) 222119

Closed 22-26 Dec

An attractive, listed, pink house directly opposite St Mary's church in the picturesque Church Square. The pretty bedrooms have been individually decorated in pastel shades, with coordinated soft furnishings and a few thoughtful extras. Two rooms have 4-poster beds, and several have private bathrooms: all bedrooms are no-smoking. Owners Julia and Paul Masters offer a hearty breakfast in the dining room using local free-range eggs, and there is a pleasant lounge.

6rm(4⇌⊓2hc) (1fb)⊬in all bedrooms CTV in all bedrooms ® ✗ (ex guide dogs) sB&B£26-£30 sB&B⇌⊓£35-£45 dB&B£35-£37 dB&B⇌⊓£50-£52 WB&B£110.25-£164
nc10yrs Ⓔ

SELECTED

GH QQQQ The Old Vicarage Hotel & Restaurant 15 East St TN31 7JY ☎(0797) 225131

Closed Jan

Situated just off the High Street, this listed building dates from 1706 and was originally a family home; the American author Henry James lived here briefly. It is now run as a small private hotel by proprietors Mr and Mrs Foster. Each of the 4 bedrooms has its own character and is furnished in period style, with private bathrooms, and equipped with every modern facility and some thoughtful extras; some rooms have tester beds with curtains. An à la carte menu is served in the elegant restaurant which overlooks the River Rother and Romney Marsh, with local lamb and fish featuring when available. There is also an attractive cocktail bar.

4⇌⊓ (2fb) CTV in all bedrooms ® **T** dB&B⇌⊓£56-£80 WB&B£175-£245 WBDi£245-£322 LDO 9pm
Lic P̸
Credit Cards [1] [2] [3] [5]

GH QQQ Playden Cottage Military Rd TN31 7NY ☎(0797) 222234

In a peaceful setting just a short walk from the centre of Rye, this pretty cottage was supposedly written about in Bensons's novels about Mapp and Lucia, where he called it 'Grebe'. The cottage dates back to the 1700s, the bedrooms are comfortable and airy and 2 have views across the country garden, which in summer is flower filled and drenched in sunshine, while the other room looks over woodland. The lounge has a well tuned piano, TV, books and guides to local attractions. A tray of sherry is left out for guests and supper trays are available by prior arrangement. Mrs Fox, the charming hostess, produces a menu of simple home-cooked dishes, but most guests prefer to take pot luck. Breakfast is taken around a communal table and the choice is wide, including fresh fruits and huge black mushrooms cooked in butter, as well as the traditional breakfast dishes.

3⊓ (1fb) ® ✗ (ex guide dogs) ✱ sB&B⊓£30-£56 dB&B⊓£40-£56 LDO by arrangement
CTV 5P
Credit Cards [1] [3]

FH QQ Mrs P Sullivin **Cliff** *(TQ933237)* Iden Lock TN31 7QE ☎Iden(0797) 280331

Mar-Oct

This attractive Sussex peg tile hung farmhouse is in an elevated position with extensive views over Romney Marsh. Find it 2 miles along the Military road from Rye to Appledore. The 3 rooms are furnished in a traditional style with floral décor, woollen bedspreads and period furniture. All have washbasins and there is a shower on the ground floor. Proprietors Pat and Jeff Sullivin offer a hearty breakfast in the cosy dining room and guests have their own lounge with colour TV and log-burning stove.

3hc (1fb) ® ✱ dB&B£27-£29
CTV 6P 6 acres smallholding Ⓔ

SAFFRON WALDEN Essex Map 05 TL53

GH QQ ***Rowley Hill Lodge*** Little Walden CB10 1UZ (2m N on B1052) ☎(0799) 25975 due to change to 525975

A pair of cottages extended and converted to provide 2 pleasant bedrooms, a breakfast room and lounge, situated in a rural setting just south of Little Walden.

2hc ⊬in all bedrooms CTV in 1 bedroom ® ✗ (ex guide dogs)
CTV 4P

ST AGNES Cornwall & Isles of Scilly Map 02 SW75

GH QQ Penkerris Penwinnick Rd TR5 0PA ☎Truro(0872) 552262

Set in an ideal spot for the walking enthusiasts and a good base for touring. The proprietor of this Edwardian residence is able to recommend many pretty walks and places to visit. The accommodation is simple and quite compact, but reasonably equipped. There is a comfortable lounge area and a dining room where an evening meal is offered. Outside, the garden provides children's play apparatus and ample parking facilities.

6rm(2⊓4hc) (2fb) CTV in all bedrooms ® ✱ sB&B£13-£20 dB&B£26-£28 dB&B⊓£30-£35 WB&B£85-£102 WBDi£115-£145 LDO 10am
Lic CTV 8P badminton net
Credit Cards [1] [3]

GH QQQ ***Porthvean Hotel*** Churchtown TR5 0QP ☎(0872) 552581

Closed Dec & Mar

A small personally run hotel in the centre of the village. The public areas, shared with non-residents, offer character dining rooms and a cosy bar area. A choice of dishes is available from various menus.

6rm(5⊓1hc) (3fb) CTV in all bedrooms ® ✗ (ex guide dogs) LDO 9pm
Lic 8P
Credit Cards [1] [3]

GH Q ***St Agnes Hotel*** Churchtown TR5 0QP ☎(0872) 552307

Busy bars are a feature of this little inn at the centre of the village. The bedrooms are more simply furnished, and a lived in residents' lounge is available.

5rm(1⇌2⊓2hc) (5fb) CTV in 3 bedrooms ® LDO 9pm
Lic CTV 50P
Credit Cards [1] [3]

ST ALBANS Hertfordshire Map **04** TL10

GH QQQ Ardmore House 54 Lemsford Rd AL1 3PR
☎(0727) 59313 & 861411
A pleasant hotel with modern accommodation: the majority of bedrooms are en suite and they are all well equipped. The spacious dining room overlooks the garden, and menus are varied. The bar and bar lounge facilities are excellent.
26rm(23⇌🚿3hc) (2fb) CTV in all bedrooms ® **T** ✻ sB&B£32.90 sB&B⇌🚿£47 dB&B£39.95 dB&B⇌🚿£51.70 LDO 8.30pm
Lic 🛏 CTV 30P
Credit Cards [1] [2] [3]

GH QQ Melford 24 Woodstock Rd North AL1 4QQ
☎(0727) 53642 & 830486
An attractive detached house in a pleasant residential area off the A1057 Hatfield road, 5 minutes' drive from the city centre. Bedrooms are clean and brightly decorated, although some rooms are very compact. The comfortable lounge overlooks the rear garden and has TV and a small honesty bar. Breakfast is served in the small dining room.
12rm(4🚿8hc) (3fb) ® ✻ sB&B£24.67-£44.65 dB&B£37.60-£47
Lic 🛏 CTV 12P £

GH Q Newpark House Hotel North Orbital Rd AL1 1EG
☎Bowmansgreen(0727) 824839 FAX (0727) 826700
The only access to Newpark House is from the eastbound carriageway of the A414 North Orbital road. It is a small, family-run hotel with simply furnished but well equipped bedrooms. There is a first-floor lounge with colour TV and an attractive dining room where breakfast is served. Excellent parking facilities are provided.
14hc CTV in 7 bedrooms TV in 7 bedrooms ® ✻ sB&B£20-£23 dB&B£40-£46 LDO 8pm
Lic 🛏 CTV 50P
Credit Cards [1] [3] £

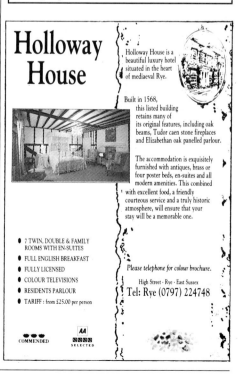

ST ANDREWS Fife Map **12** NO51

GH QQ Albany Private Hotel 56 North St KY16 9AH
(0334) 77737
Situated at the eastern end of the town, this neat and compact terraced house offers well equipped, modestly appointed bedrooms, an inviting and comfortable lounge and a basement dining room.
12rm(6 6hc) (2fb) in 2 bedrooms CTV in all bedrooms ® **T** sB&B£20-£27 dB&B£34-£44 dB&B £44-£58 WBDi£175-£255 LDO 6pm
Lic CTV
Credit Cards 1 3 5

GH QQ Amberside 4 Murray Pk KY16 9AW (0334) 74644
Mar-1st wk Dec also Xmas & New Year
A small, modern, well equipped house, part of a tenement row between the town centre and the sea. It offers compact but well maintained bed and breakfast accommodation, with a small combined lounge/breakfast room.
6rm(5 1hc) (2fb) CTV in all bedrooms ® * sB&B£17-£25 dB&B £34-£50 WB&B£105-£161
CTV

GH QQQ Arran House 5 Murray Park KY16 9AW
(0334) 74724 FAX (0334) 72072
Feb-Nov
Situated in a side street between the seafront and town centre, this well maintained small guesthouse provides neat bed and breakfast accommodation. Bedrooms are furnished in modern style, and there is an attractive first-floor breakfast room.
4rm(3 1hc) (2fb) CTV in all bedrooms ® sB&B£20-£25 sB&B £25-£35 dB&B£34-£38 dB&B £36-£40 WB&B£200-£250
CTV

GH QQ *Beachway House* 6 Murray Park KY16 9AW
(0334) 73319
Neat, compact accommodation with simply furnished bedrooms each with its own shower room characterises this quietly run terraced property which is situated between the town centre and the sea.
6rm(5 1hc) (2fb) CTV in all bedrooms ®

GH QQ Bell Craig 8 Murray Park KY16 9AW (0334) 72962
A small, friendly, centrally situated guesthouse offering a sound standard of well maintained bed and breakfast accommodation. Breakfast is served in the ground-floor lounge/dining room.
5rm(4 1hc) (3fb) CTV in all bedrooms ® sB&B£25 sB&B £25 dB&B£30-£40 dB&B £30-£44 WB&B£90-£140
CTV
Credit Cards 1 3

GH QQ *Burness House* Murray Park KY16 9AW
(0334) 74314
A compact, modernised house situated on a corner site between the town centre and the sea. It offers compact but neat bed and breakfast accommodation, with a small first-floor lounge/breakfast room.
5 (1fb) CTV in all bedrooms ®
CTV

GH QQ Cleveden House 3 Murray Place KY16 9AP
(0334) 74212
Quietly situated in a side street between the town centre and the seafront, this well decorated and maintained small guesthouse offers bed and breakfast with a sound standard of accommodation, in compact but attractive bedrooms.
6rm(4 2hc) (2fb) CTV in all bedrooms (ex guide dogs) sB&B£14-£20 dB&B £28-£44
CTV

GH QQ Craigmore 3 Murray Park KY16 9AW
(0334) 72142 & 77963
This friendly guesthouse is conveniently situated for the town and seafront, and offers spacious, well maintained bed and breakfast accommodation. Bedrooms are smartly decorated, comfortable and well equipped, and there is a combined lounge/breakfast room.
5rm(1 4) (4fb) CTV in all bedrooms ® dB&B £28-£46 WB&B£90-£150
CTV
Credit Cards 1 3 £

GH QQQ Edenside House Edenside KY16 9SQ
Leuchars(0334) 838108
Set back from the A91 enjoying fine views over the Eden Estuary nature reserve and bird sanctuary, this 19th-century Scottish farmhouse has been carefully renovated to provide pleasant, totally non smoking accommodation. The bedrooms are either contained in the main house or in an adjacent, single storey extension, the latter having their own entrance and being generally a little more spacious. All bedrooms are furnished with attractive coordinated fabrics and solid pine furniture, complete with modern, smart shower rooms. The main house contains a cosy lounge and small dining room.
3 Annexe 6 in all bedrooms CTV in all bedrooms ® * sB&B £18-£30 dB&B £32-£44 LDO 7pm
12P nc10yrs
Credit Cards 1 3

GH QQQ Glenderran 9 Murray Park KY16 9AW
(0334) 77951
Conveniently located, this charming, small, no-smoking guesthouse provides bed and breakfast accommodation and is run with style and flair by the resident proprietors, who take great pride in their high standards of housekeeping. The individually decorated bedrooms are thoughtfully equipped, most with private bathrooms. Breakfast is served in an attractive front-facing room which combines as the lounge for residents.
5rm(3) in all bedrooms CTV in all bedrooms ® sB&B £17-£23 dB&B £34-£46 WB&B£112-£140
nc12yrs

GH QQ *Hazlebank Private Hotel* 28 The Scores KY16 9AS
(0334) 72466
Situated on the seafront and enjoying lovely uninterrupted views over the bay, this private hotel offers a sound standard of modern, well equipped accommodation. Meals are served in an attractive ground-floor room which is open during the day for light snacks.
10 (6fb) CTV in all bedrooms ®
Lic CTV
Credit Cards 1 3

GH QQQ Lorimer House 19 Murray Park KY16 9AW
(0334) 76599
Situated in a side street between the town centre and the seafront, this neatly maintained and decorated bed and breakfast establishment offers a sound standard of accommodation. While the bedrooms are not over large, they are pleasantly furnished in a modern style with one being situated on the ground floor. The public areas are limited to a combined breakfast room/lounge with satellite TV available.
5rm(4 1hc) (2fb) CTV in all bedrooms ® * dB&B £30-£40
CTV

GH QQ Romar 45 Main St, Strathkinness KY16 9RZ
Strathkinness(0334) 85308
This modern chalet bungalow is situated in rural surroundings at Strathkinness and offers comfortable, pleasant accommodation. Guests are provided with home baking, and share the lounge with the friendly proprietors. Breakfast is served around a communal table in the small dining room.
4hc (1fb) in all bedrooms CTV in all bedrooms ® (ex guide dogs) sB&B£14-£18 dB&B£24-£30
5P

GH QQ West Park House 5 St Mary's Place KY16 9UY
☎(0334) 75933
Mar-Nov
This attractive small detached 1840s house in the town centre has freshly appointed and neatly tended accommodation. Guests can arrange dinner at the owner's other hotel five minutes' walk away.
5rm(3⬧2hc) (1fb) CTV in all bedrooms ® ✗ (ex guide dogs) dB&B£31-£35 dB&B⬧£33-£40

GH QQ Yorkston Hotel 68 & 70 Argyle St KY16 9BU
☎(0334) 72019
rs Xmas & New Year
This long-established private hotel close to the West Port, offers individually decorated bedrooms ranging from compact singles to large family rooms. There is a choice of dishes on the dinner menu in the neat dining room, and there is a comfortable first-floor lounge.
10rm(1⇌4⬧5hc) (3fb) CTV in all bedrooms ® ✗ (ex guide dogs) sB&B£20-£26 dB&B£38-£44 dB&B⇌⬧£40-£60 WB&B£133-£210 WBDi£220.50-£297 LDO 5pm
Lic

FH QQQ Mrs A E Duncan ***Spinks Town*** *(NO541144)*
KY16 8PN ☎(0334) 73475
Situated in rural surroundings beside the A917 coast road, just 2 miles east of the town, this most attractively appointed modern farmhouse offers comfortable, spacious accommodation of a high standard. Substantial breakfasts are served around a communal table.
3rm(2⇌⬧1hc) ⊬in all bedrooms ✗
CTV 3P 250 acres arable cattle

ST ASAPH Clwyd Map 06 SJ07

SELECTED

FH QQQQ Mrs A Roberts **Bach-Y-Graig** *(SJ075713)*
Tremeirchion LL17 0UH ☎Trefnant(0745) 730627
Closed Xmas & New Year
This delightful old house dates back to 1567 and is reputed to be the first brick-built house in Wales. The 200-acre farm is remotely located, offering accommodation that is tastefully decorated and furnished in a style which is sympathetic to the age of the building. The lounge has a welcoming real fire burning in the magnificent inglenook fireplace. Many lovely antiques are in daily use and include an impressive dining table, although the bedrooms have modern equipment which includes hairdryers and irons in addition to TVs and radios.
3⇌⬧ (1fb)⊬in all bedrooms CTV in all bedrooms ® ✗ ✱ sB&B⇌⬧£20 dB&B⇌⬧£32-£36 WB&B£112-£126
CTV 3P ♩ woodland trail 200 acres dairy

ST AUBIN

See **JERSEY under CHANNEL ISLANDS**

ST AUSTELL Cornwall & Isles of Scilly Map 02 SX05

GH QQ Alexandra Hotel 52-54 Alexandra Rd PL25 4QN
☎(0726) 74242
Closed 23 Dec-6 Jan
A neat, well presented private hotel near the railway station, recently purchased by Mr and Mrs Staples, who are enthusiastic and friendly. The bedrooms, which vary in size, are bright and well maintained, some having en suite showers. There is a comfortable front-facing lounge, a well stocked bar and a nicely appointed dining room, where home-cooked evening meals and an ample breakfast are served. Parking is available at both the front and rear.
14rm(4⬧10hc) (6fb) CTV in all bedrooms ® sB&B£24-£26 sB&B⬧£29-£32 dB&B£46-£48 dB&B⬧£56-£60 WB&Bfr£161 WBDifr£224 LDO 5.30pm
Lic CTV 20P
Credit Cards 1 2 3 £

FH QQQ Mrs J Nancarrow **Poltarrow** *(SW998518)*
PL26 7DR ☎(0726) 67111
Closed 16 Dec-5 Jan
With views over rolling farmland, situated in the scattered hamlet of St Mewen, this wisteria-clad farmhouse is a wonderful base for touring. The high quality bedrooms are individually furnished and decorated with lots of flair. Judith Nancarrow's set 3-course dinners, using local produce, are very popular, with farmhouse cookery being the order of the day. A cosy lounge is provided for guests, with a log fire buring on chilly evenings. There are 3 large, attractive self-catering cottages also available to let.
3⇌⬧ CTV in all bedrooms ® ✗ (ex guide dogs) sB&B⇌⬧£16-£18 dB&B⇌⬧£32 WB&B£112 WBDi£168 LDO noon
Lic CTV 10P pool table 45 acres mixed
Credit Cards 1 3

INN QQQ Rashleigh Arms Quay Rd, Charlestown PL25 3NJ
☎(0726) 73635
Along the A3061 towards Charlestown, this popular inn has a fine selection of real ale on offer. Modern bedrooms are well presented and bright and each has a smart en suite facility. Public areas are numerous, and include a children's room, a choice of 2 public bars and a restaurant area where an extensive menu is offered. There is ample car parking available at the rear.
5⬧ CTV in all bedrooms ® ✗ (ex guide dogs) ✱ sB&B⬧£20-£25 dB&B⬧£40-£50 WB&B£140-£210 Lunch £7.35-£11.15alc Dinner £7.55-£20.75alc LDO 10pm
120P
Credit Cards 1 3

ST BLAZEY Cornwall & Isles of Scilly Map 02 SX05

SELECTED

GH QQQQ Nanscawen House Prideaux Rd PL24 2SR
☎Par(0726) 814488 FAX (0726) 814488
Closed 22-27 Dec
A private drive leads to this delightful Georgian house, peacefully set in 5 acres of grounds and well kept gardens. Keith and Janet Martin and their family extend a warm welcome to guests, inviting them to share in their elegant and comfortable Cornish home, where smoking is not permitted, but the atmosphere is relaxing. Three bedrooms, varying in size, provide the highest standard of cleanliness and good taste in furnishings. The rooms are all en suite, with many thoughtful extra touches provided. There is a spacious drawing room, and Janet's passion for cooking is evident in the set dinner, with fresh local produce and their own fruit and vegetables used to great effect. **Best Newcomer for South West England 1992–3, see colour section.**
3⇌⬧ ⊬in all bedrooms CTV in all bedrooms ® T ✗ ✱ dB&B⇌⬧£60-£70 LDO 9.30am
6P nc12yrs (heated) putting jacuzzi whirlpool
Credit Cards 1 3

ST BRIDES-SUPER-ELY South Glamorgan Map 03 ST07

GH QQQ Sant-y-Nyll CF5 6EZ
☎Peterston-Super-Ely(0446) 760209
This elegant country house is situated in the tranquil Vale of Glamorgan, quite near to the Welsh Folk Museum at St Fagans. There are two comfortable lounges and the bedrooms are spacious and well equipped.
6rm(1⇌⬧5hc) (1fb) CTV in all bedrooms ® sB&Bfr£25 dB&Bfr£35 dB&B⇌⬧fr£45 WB&Bfr£150 LDO 6pm
Lic 20P croquet
Credit Cards 2
See advertisement under CARDIFF

ST CATHERINE'S Strathclyde *Argyllshire* Map **10** NN10

GH QQQ Arnish Cottage, Lochside Guest House. Poll Bay PA25 8BA ☎Inveraray(0499) 2405

Bill and Maisie Mercer run their beautifully restored, converted cottage with commitment and enthusiasm. The cottage lies in a delightful position, on a single-track road, right on the shores of Loch Fyne. A little conservatory has been added to the split-level lounge and dining room, which are adorned with personal items of furniture and ornaments. Of the 4 en suite bedrooms, 2 are on the compact side but all are attractive and well equipped. Maisie's home- cooked dinners receive much praise and you are welcome to bring your own wine. Arnish Cottage is a no smoking establishment.

4⌐ ⅟in all bedrooms ® ✗ (ex guide dogs) sB&B⌐£18-£24 dB&B⌐£32-£44 WB&B£107-£160 WBDi£187-£240

🕮 CTV 3P nc16yrs

GH QQQ Thistle House PA25 8AZ ☎Inveraray(0499) 2209

Etr-Oct

This meticulously maintained detached Victorian mansion sits in its own gardens looking across Loch Fyne; it features a spacious and elegant lounge.

5rm(3⌐2hc) (1fb) ® ✱ sB&B£16.50-£22 sB&B⌐£22-£27 dB&B£33-£38 dB&B⌐£38-£42

🕮 10P ⓕ

ST CLEARS Dyfed Map **02** SN21

INN QQ Black Lion Hotel Pentre Rd SA33 4AA ☎(0994) 230700

In the heart of a quiet town, this pleasant inn offers clean and well cared for bedrooms, fitted with modern furniture. The slab-floored bar features an interesting collection of brass/copper utensils as well as various items connected with horses. A good range of bar and restaurant meals are available and the restaurant has a further collection of jugs. There is also a small residents' lounge.

13rm(4⇌⌐9hc) (1fb) CTV in all bedrooms ® ✱ sB&B£18-£20 sB&B⇌⌐£25-£27 dB&B£35-£37 dB&B⇌⌐£45-£47 WB&B£105-£160 WBDi£150-£170 Lunch £4-£7alc Dinner £8-£15alc LDO 9pm

🕮 25P snooker

Credit Cards 1 3 5

ST DAVID'S Dyfed Map **02** SM72

GH QQ *The Ramsey* Lower Moor SA62 6RP ☎(0437) 720321

This bright, cosy guesthouse is situated at the edge of the city, within easy walking distance of the shops and cathedral. Run by the friendly Thompson family, it has recently been extended, and bedrooms are attractively fitted with full-length mirrored wardrobes, together with new en suite facilities of excellent quality. The open plan lounge/dining room and bar look out on to a neat lawn.

7rm(4⌐3hc) ® LDO 7pm

Lic 🕮 CTV 9P nc12yrs

GH QQ *Redcliffe House* 17 New St SA62 6SW ☎(0437) 720389

Apr-Oct

Run by the friendly Clarke family, this small guesthouse is situated in the centre of the tiny city. Bedrooms and lounge areas are comfortably furnished, bright and cosy.

6hc (2fb) CTV in all bedrooms ® ✗

🕮 CTV 2P nc6yrs

GH QQQ Y Glennydd 51 Nun St SA62 6NU ☎(0437) 720576 FAX (0437) 720184

Closed Jan

Conveniently situated for the cathedral and the shops, this guesthouse offers comfortable accommodation and friendly service by the Foster family. Bedrooms are well maintained and attractively decorated, using some very pretty fabrics, and some have sofabeds for extra guests. The small lounge features an electric organ, and there is a bar at one end of the stone-walled restaurant. Open to non-residents, the restaurant offers a wide selection of dishes, many featuring locally caught lobster, trout and halibut.

9rm(5⇌⌐4hc) (4fb) CTV in 10 bedrooms ®

✗ (ex guide dogs) ✱ sB&B£16.50-£35 sB&B⇌⌐£18.50-£35 dB&B£30 dB&B⇌⌐£35 WB&B£108-£122.50 WBDi£190-£210 LDO 9pm

Lic 🕮 CTV ⅌

Credit Cards 1 3 5

ST ERME Cornwall & Isles of Scilly Map **02** SW84

FH QQQ Mr & Mrs E Dymond ***Trevispian Vean*** *(SW850502)* TR4 9BL ☎Truro(0872) 79514

Mar-Oct

A carefully extended 300-year-old farmhouse, on a working farm, offering a warm family welcome and Cornish hospitality. The bedrooms are comfortable, mostly en suite, and there is a choice of attractive lounges: 2 with colour TV, one no smoking and 2 quiet areas. Home-cooked dinners are served in the spacious dining room.

12rm(2⇌7⌐3hc) (7fb) ✗ (ex guide dogs) LDO 4.30pm

Lic 🕮 CTV 20P ♪ games room 300 acres arable beef pigs sheep

ST HELIER

See **JERSEY under CHANNEL ISLANDS**

ST HILARY Cornwall & Isles of Scilly Map **02** SW53

SELECTED

FH QQQQ S L White ***Ennys*** *(SW559328)* TR20 9BZ ☎Penzance(0736) 740262

Closed 7-30 Nov

A delightful 17th-century stone manor house on a small working farm, set in pretty grounds with a walled garden and grass tennis court. The bedrooms are beautifully furnished with Sanderson and Liberty fabrics and Laura Ashley bed linen; 3 rooms are in the main house and 2 other family letting rooms are in a converted stable, with high ceilings and beams. The comfortable lounge has a log fire, and proprietors Sue and John White offer their guests a down-to- earth, warm and friendly hospitality, whilst continuing to make improvements. Commendable home cooking with good use of home-grown and local produce is served at separate tables, and guests may bring their own wine, as the farm is unlicensed. To find the house, look for a sign off the B road to Relebbus a short distance east of St Hilary, where a long winding lane leads to the farmhouse.

3⇌⌐ Annexe 2⇌⌐ (1fb)⅟in all bedrooms CTV in all bedrooms ® ✗ LDO 7.30pm

🕮 CTV P 🚗 ♧ 🎾(grass)50 acres arable

See advertisement under PENZANCE

ST IVES Cornwall & Isles of Scilly Map **02** SW54

GH QQ Bay View Headland Road, Carbis Bay TR26 2nx ☎Penzance(0736) 796469

A modern family-run establishment in a quiet residential area of Carbis Bay. The bedrooms are comfortable and the public areas have a home-from-home feel to them.

9rm(8⌐1hc) (3fb)⅟in all bedrooms CTV in all bedrooms ® ✗ (ex guide dogs) ✱ sB&B£12.50-£18.50 WB&B£80-£135 WBDi£120-£175 LDO 6pm

Lic 🕮 CTV 9P 2🚗 nc5yrs

GH QQQ Blue Mist The Warren TR26 2EA ☎Penzance(0736) 795209

Etr-Oct

A delightful cottage-style property on the water's edge, affording beautiful views of the harbour. The bedrooms are cosy and well equipped, and a choice of home-cooked meals is offered in the

attractive dining room. The resident proprietors, Kathy and Bob Carr, welcome their guests.
9rm(8⛿1hc) (1fb) CTV in all bedrooms ® T ✗ (ex guide dogs) sB&B£16.50-£19.50 sB&B⛿£18-£22.25 dB&B⛿£36-£48 WB&B£146-£165 LDO 5pm
🅿 4P (£15.50 per wk) nc4yrs
Credit Cards [1] [3]

GH QQ Channings Hotel 3 Talland Rd TR26 2DF
☎Penzance(0736) 795681
Channings Hotel is set in a terrace of hotels an elevated walk from the town centre and harbour. Family run, the emphasis is on a relaxed and informal atmosphere in bright if simply styled surroundings.
12rm(2⇌9⛿1hc) (5fb) ® ✗ LDO 4pm
Lic 🅿 CTV 12P
Credit Cards [1] [3] £

GH QQ Chy-an-Creet Private Hotel Higher Stennack TR26 2HA ☎Penzance(0736) 796559
mid Mar-mid Oct rs mid Nov-mid Mar
A small, family-run hotel on the edge of the town and within a short walk of the beaches, close to Leach pottery. Bedrooms all have private bathrooms, and provide tea-making facilities and alarm clock radios. The public areas are attractive and comfortable, and a choice of menu is available for dinner in the intimate dining room, with orders taken in advance.
10⇌⛿ (4fb) ® sB&B⇌⛿£11.50-£18.50 dB&B⇌⛿£23-£37 WB&B£85-£130 WBDi£130-£195 LDO 4pm
Lic 🅿 CTV 16P
Credit Cards [1] [3] £

GH QQQ Dean Court Hotel Trelyon Av TR26 2AD
☎Penzance(0736) 796023
Mar-Oct
This attractive Cornish stone house stands on the Carbis Bay side of St Ives, in a commanding position with glorious views across St Ives Bay, and close to the Cornish Coastal Path. Bedrooms are bright, well decorated and equipped, and proprietors Joy and Ian Alford keep the spotless accommodation very well maintained; all the rooms have modern en suite bathrooms and some have sea views. The elegant, comfortable lounge and pretty dining room also overlook the bay. There is a delightful terraced garden and a private car park.
12⇌⛿ (2fb) CTV in all bedrooms ® ✗ sB&B⇌⛿£28-£34 dB&B⇌⛿£56-£68 WB&B£170-£200 WBDi£205-£235 LDO 5pm
Lic 🅿 12P nc14yrs

GH QQQ *The Hollies Hotel* 4 Talland Rd TR26 2DF
☎Penzance(0736) 796605
A small semidetached, family-run hotel a short elevated walk from the harbour and town centre. Bedrooms are simply furnished but comfortable and well equipped, and there is a relaxing atmosphere in the bar and lounge. A choice of dishes is offered on the blackboard menu in the informal dining room.
10⇌⛿ (4fb) CTV in all bedrooms ® ✗ LDO 9am
Lic 🅿 CTV 12P

GH QQ *Island View* 2 Park Av TR26 2DN
☎Penzance(0736) 795111
Mar-Oct
Island View is a small, family-run hotel on Park Avenue high above the town, commanding glorious views of the harbour and St Ives Bay. The bedrooms are clean and bright, all have colour TV and 2 now have en suite shower rooms. Dinner is served in the informal dining room.
10rm(2⛿8hc) (4fb) CTV in all bedrooms ® LDO 6.30pm
🅿 P̸

Book as early as possible for busy holiday periods.

GH QQ Kandahar 11 The Warren TR26 2EA
☎Penzance(0736) 796183
Closed Xmas, New Year & owners hols
The accommodation at Kandahar is in a unique position at the sea's edge, directly overlooking the harbour and up the coast to Newquay. There is a comfortable lounge and dining room, and the bedrooms are clean and well maintained.
5rm(2⛿3hc) (1fb) CTV in all bedrooms ® ✗ sB&B£16-£20 dB&B£35-£39 dB&B⛿£39-£43
🅿 CTV 6P (Apr-Oct) £

See advertisement on page 349

GH QQQ Longships Hotel Talland Rd TR26 2DF
☎Penzance(0736) 798180
At the end of a terrace of small hotels, a short hilly walk from the shops and harbour, the Longships offers a lively bar, comfortable public areas and simply furnished bedrooms.
25rm(4⇌21⛿) (7fb) CTV in all bedrooms ® ✱ sB&B⇌⛿£17-£25.25 dB&B⇌⛿£34-£50.50 WB&B£119-£176.75 WBDi£150.50-£208.25 LDO 7pm
Lic 🅿 CTV 17P
Credit Cards [1] [3]

GH QQQ *Lyonesse Hotel* 5 Talland Rd TR26 2DF
☎Penzance(0736) 796315
Apr-Oct
Set high above the town centre and harbour in a terrace of family-run hotels, the Lyonesse provides well appointed bedrooms and attractive public areas where entertainment is provided on some evenings during the season in a cosy bar. Home-cooked dishes are featured on the menu.
15⛿ (4fb) CTV in all bedrooms ® ✗ LDO 6.30pm
Lic 🅿 CTV 10P pool table

🛏 GH QQQ Monowai Private Hotel Headland Road, Carbis Bay TR26 2NR ☎Penzance(0736) 795733
Feb-Oct
A family-run, character establishment in an elevated position commanding glorious views across the bay. The brightly decorated bedrooms have been furnished in a cottage style, and a cosy atmosphere is a feature of the bar and lounge. A choice of home-cooked dishes is offered on the table d'hôte menu with vegetarian specialities. A friendly welcome awaits guests.
9rm(7🚿2hc) (3fb) ® sB&B£14-£20 dB&B£28-£40 dB&B🚿£34-£50 WB&B£125-£180 WBDi£165-£220 LDO 6.30pm
Lic ♨ CTV 7P nc5yrs ≋(heated) pool table darts (£)

GH QQQ The Old Vicarage Hotel Parc-An-Creet TR26 2ET ☎Penzance(0736) 796124
Etr-Sep
This attractive Victorian property is situated away from the town centre in a residential area of St Ives. The bedrooms, some en suite, are comfortable and all have central heating, colour TV and tea facilities. The lounge is attractive with plenty of reading material for guests, and there is also a cosy bar lounge. Snacks are available during the week and more substantial menus are offered at weekends.
8rm(4🛁🚿4hc) (3fb) CTV in 7 bedrooms TV in 1 bedroom ® sB&B£20-£22 sB&B🛁🚿£22-£24 dB&B£36-£40 dB&B🛁🚿£42-£46 WB&B£105-£115 LDO 6.45pm
Lic ♨ CTV 12P putting green
Credit Cards [1] [2] [3] (£)

GH QQQ *Pondarosa Hotel* 10 Porthminster Ter TR26 2DQ ☎Penzance(0736) 795875
Closed 25 Dec
An end-of-terrace family home with a happy and welcoming atmosphere a short walk from the town centre and harbour. Bedrooms are brightly decorated and spotlessly clean. A set dinner is available every evening in the informal dining room.
9rm(1🛁1🚿7hc) (4fb) CTV in all bedrooms ®
✗ (ex guide dogs) LDO 4pm
Lic ♨ CTV 12P nc3yrs

GH QQ *Primrose Valley Hotel* Primrose Valley TR26 2ED ☎Penzance(0736) 794939
Closed Jan-Feb
A small, family-run guesthouse at the end of a steep terrace of houses very close to Porthminster beach, and a level walk from the town. Bedrooms are simply decorated and furnished, and the public areas are comfortable. A large bar and patio is popular in the summer for lunches, coffees and afternoon teas.
11rm(6🛁🚿5hc) (6fb) CTV in all bedrooms ® ✗
Lic CTV 12P

GH QQQ Regent Hotel Fernlea Ter TR26 2BH ☎Penzance(0736) 796195 FAX (0736) 794641
rs Sep-mid May
This friendly, family-run hotel is on the edge of town, close to the bus and railway stations and with easy access to the beaches. Most of the bedrooms have breathtaking views of the harbour and St Ives Bay, all are tastefully decorated and furnished, and several offer en suite shower rooms.
10rm(6🚿4hc) CTV in all bedrooms ® ✗ ✱ sB&Bfr£19 sB&B🚿fr£23 WBDifr£149 LDO 7pm
Lic CTV 12P nc7yrs
Credit Cards [1] [2] [3] [5]

GH QQ Hotel Rotorua Trencrom Ln, Carbis Bay TR26 2TD ☎Penzance(0736) 795419
Etr-Oct
A purpose-built family-run hotel in a quiet wooded lane away from the centre of the town and harbour, but just 20 minutes' walk from Carbis Bay beach. The bedrooms are modern and well equipped and the public areas spacious. Evening meals are available in the informal dining room.
13🛁🚿 (10fb)⊁in 2 bedrooms CTV in all bedrooms ® sB&B🛁🚿£17-£22 dB&B🛁🚿£34-£44 WB&B£119-£152 WBDi£168-£201 LDO 5pm
Lic ♨ CTV 10P ⌂ ≋(heated)

GH QQ *St Merryn Hotel* Trelyon TR26 2PF ☎Penzance(0736) 795767 & 797248
Mar-Nov
A detached property on the main St Ives road offering well equipped bedrooms and comfortable public areas. The hotel is about 15 minutes' walk from the harbour and town centre.
19rm(11🛁8hc) (8fb) CTV in all bedrooms ® ✗ LDO 6pm
Lic ♨ CTV 20P nc4yrs
Credit Cards [1] [3]

GH QQ *Sunrise* 22 The Warren TR26 2AT ☎Penzance(0736) 795407
Jan-Oct
A terraced cottage in the town centre, with glorious views of the harbour from the top-floor bedrooms. The attractive bedrooms are comfortably furnished, with spotless en suite facilities. Traditional English breakfasts are a speciality, and complement the warm welcome offered by Vicki Mason and her daughter.
7rm(4🛁🚿3hc) (2fb) CTV in all bedrooms ®
♨ CTV 4P (£2 day)

GH QQ Thurlestone Private Hotel St Ives Road, Carbis Bay TR26 2RT ☎Penzance(0736) 796369
Mar-Sep
This attractive little stone-built hotel is on the main road into St Ives in the Carbis Bay area. Bedrooms are bright and comfortable and some have en suite facilities. There is a choice of lounges, one with a bar, and home- cooked dishes are served from the predominantly set dinner menu in the relaxed atmosphere of the dining room.
9rm(1🛁4🚿4hc) (3fb) ® ✗ ✱ sB&B£12-£15 dB&B£24-£30 dB&B🛁🚿£28-£34 WB&B£84-£104 WBDi£126-£146 LDO 5pm
Lic ♨ CTV 6P nc3yrs

GH QQ Tregorran Hotel Headland Bay, Carbis Bay TR26 2NU ☎Penzance(0736) 795889
Apr-Oct
An attractive outdoor swimming pool and small gym are features of this small, well appointed hotel which enjoys a scenic location overlooking Carbis Bay.
15rm(13🚿2hc) (5fb) ® sB&B£17-£27 WB&B£119-£189 WBDi£161-£224 LDO 3pm
Lic ♨ CTV 25P ≋(heated) solarium gymnasium pool table (£)

GH QQ *White House Hotel* The Valley, Carbis Bay TR26 2QY ☎Penzance(0736) 797405
Closed Nov-Feb
A detached house standing in its own grounds at the bottom of a wooded valley, affording sea views through the granite arches of a Brunel viaduct. Situated 150 yards from safe, sandy beaches and one mile from the town, it offers bedrooms with private bathrooms and modern décor, and a comfortable lounge and bar. Dinner is available in the dining room.
8🛁🚿 Annexe 2🛁🚿 (2fb) ® ✗ LDO 8pm
Lic ♨ CTV 10P
Credit Cards [1] [3]

INN QQQ Queens Tavern High St TR26 1RR (St Austell Brewery) ☎(0736) 796468
A characterful inn right in the heart of this bustling popular seaside town, amongst shops and close to the harbour. There is a congenial bar and a simply styled restaurant on the first floor. Due to significant refurbishment, bedrooms are cosy, bright and well furnished with pleasing décor and co- ordinating fabrics; each is well equipped with en suite bathrooms. The inn stocks a good range of cask and keg beers, but there is no car park on site.

5🚿 (3fb) CTV in all bedrooms ® ✗ (ex guide dogs) ✻ sB&B🛁🚿£25 WBDifr£117 Lunch £7&alc Dinner £12&alc LDO 8.15pm
🍽 CTV
Credit Cards [1]

ST JUST (NEAR LAND'S END) Cornwall & Isles of Scilly
Map **02** SW33

GH QQQ Boscean Country Hotel TR19 7QP
☎Penzance(0736) 788748
Mar-Nov
This white Edwardian house stands in its own peaceful grounds between St Just and the sea. Extensive public areas include many interesting architectural features, with a wood-panelled entrance hall and lounge, and a licensed bar. Bedrooms are a fair size, and many contain attractive period furniture. The building is surrounded by 3 acres of walled garden, and the Lees have been established here for many years, and offer a warm welcome.
9🛁🚿 Annexe 2🛁 (3fb) ® dB&B🛁🚿£38 WB&B£120 WBDi£190 LDO 7pm
Lic 🍽 CTV 12P 🏠

INN QQQ Wellington Hotel Market Square TR19 7HL
☎Penzance(0736) 787319
Situated right in the heart of the village, this character inn offers a good range of food and has a cosy bar. Six excellent modern bedrooms situated in the small courtyard have been recently added, each offering high standards of comfort, bright en suites and an extensive range of modern facilities including remote-control colour TVs, direct-dial telephones, trouser presses and tea/coffee-making facilities combined with quality décor and co-ordinated furnishings.
Annexe 6🛁🚿 (4fb) CTV in 6 bedrooms ® **T** sB&B🛁🚿£25-£28 dB&B🛁🚿£35-£40 Lunch £1.95-£7.95&alc Dinner £1.95-£7.95&alc LDO 9pm

→

🍽 CTV
Credit Cards [1] [3] (£)

ST JUST-IN-ROSELAND Cornwall & Isles of Scilly Map **02** SW83

SELECTED

GH QQQQ Rose-Da-Mar Hotel TR2 5JB
☎St Mawes(0326) 270450
mid Mar-mid Oct
A pretty and well presented house located along a quiet country lane overlooking the creeks of Carrick Roads Fal Estuary, close to the renowned Roseland peninsula. The bedrooms all have splendid views and are nicely decorated with coordinating fabrics. There is a very pleasant, spacious drawing room, a small cosy bar and a bright sunny dining room where Mrs Brown's interesting 5-course table d'hôte menu is offered. Tea is served on the sun terrace in summer. As this is a very popular hotel, early booking is strongly advised: many guests return year after year.
8rm(4🛁1🚿3hc) (1fb) ® sB&B£40.80 dB&B£75.20-£77.40 dB&B🛁🚿£81.60-£88 (incl dinner) WB&B£165.20-£210 WBDi£256.62-£300.30 LDO 6.30pm
Lic 🍽 CTV 9P nc11yrs (£)

ST KEYNE Cornwall & Isles of Scilly Map **02** SX26

FH QQ Mrs B N Light **Penbugle Farm** *(SX228602)* PL14 4RS
☎Liskeard(0579) 20288
Mar-Oct
This small farmhouse is situated along the Looe-Duloe road and offers spacious rooms, simply presented, with smart modern shower rooms. There is a comfortable lounge with a fire, TV and video. Breakfast is served at a communal table. Part of the Duchy of Cornwall, it is a mixed farm with 287 acres of farmland, in the heart of this pretty area.
2🚿 (2fb) ® 🚫 (ex guide dogs) ✱ dB&B🚿fr£26 WB&Bfr£90
🍽 CTV 4P 287 acres arable beef sheep

ST MARTIN

See **GUERNSEY under CHANNEL ISLANDS**

ST MARY'S

See **SCILLY, ISLES OF**

ST MARY'S LOCH Borders *Selkirkshire* Map **11** NT22

INN QQQ Tibbie Shiels TD7 5NE
☎Capercleuch(0750) 42231
rs Mon Nov-Feb
Situated on the shores of St Mary's Loch, this historic inn has been welcoming guests since 1824, and is named after one of the first inhabitants. Gradually extended, it now offers good accommodation in 5 neat ground-floor rooms, in most attractive surroundings. A good range of bar meals is available, with high teas a speciality. A popular haunt for fishermen, birdwatchers and walkers, it is closed on Mondays in winter.
5hc (1fb) ® 🚫 (ex guide dogs) ✱ sB&Bfr£21 dB&Bfr£34 Lunch £1.50-£6.50alc High tea fr£6.50alc Dinner £8.50-£11.50alc LDO 8.30pm
🍽 CTV 30P 🎣
Credit Cards [1] [3]

ST MAWGAN Cornwall & Isles of Scilly Map **02** SW86

INN QQ The Falcon TR8 4EP ☎Newquay(0637) 860225
A wisteria-covered 16th-century village pub with accommodation for 6 overnight guests. Bedrooms are comfortable, modern and well proportioned. The bar and flagstoned dining area are furnished in pink, offering real ales, good bar meals, an à la carte menu and daily blackboard specials. There is an attractive beer garden with delabole slate tables on granite pillars, a barbecue and play area. Parking can be difficult at busy times but there is a general car park behind the village store.
3rm(2🚿1hc) CTV in all bedrooms ® 🚫 (ex guide dogs) ✱ dB&B£36 dB&B🚿£42-£48 Bar Lunch £6-£10alc Dinner £6-£15alc LDO 10pm
🍽 20P nc14yrs
Credit Cards [1] [3] (£)

ST MERRYN Cornwall & Isles of Scilly Map **02** SW87

INN QQQ ***Farmers Arms*** PL28 8NP (St Austell Brewery)
☎Padstow(0841) 520303
Original low beams, slate floors and cosy firesides with features like the well in the Blacksmiths bar, are part of the atmosphere of this skilfully extended 250-year-old village pub. Bar food served at 12-2pm and 7-9pm, has a good reputation with the locals and summer holidaymakers. Although on the small side, the bedrooms are well equipped with remote-control TV, hairdriers, tea-making facilities and controllable heating. The summer patio, childrens games room and the Stables room which is used for lively functions all add to the good facilities as do real ales and cordial management.
4🚿 CTV in all bedrooms ® LDO 9.30pm
🍽 100P
Credit Cards [1] [2] [3]

ST OWEN'S CROSS Hereford & Worcester Map **03** SO52

FH QQ Mrs F Davies **Aberhall** *(SO529242)* HR2 8LL
☎Harewood End(098987) 256
Mar-Nov
A warm welcome is assured from Freda Davies at this 16th-century, grey stone farmhouse, situated off the B4521, some 5 miles northwest of Ross on Wye on the A49. The bedrooms are comfortable and one features an extra large en suite shower. Very much a working farm, bed and breakfast only are available, but guests have the use of a modern and comfortable lounge, and there are many sports facilities for the energetic, including table tennis, darts and pool in the basement games room, and a hard tennis court in the pleasant garden.
3rm(1🚿2hc) 🚭in all bedrooms ® 🚫 (ex guide dogs) sB&Bfr£20 dB&Bfr£30 dB&B🚿£33-£35
🍽 CTV 3P nc10yrs 🎾(hard)pool & table tennis 132 acres arable beef mixed (£)

ST PETER PORT

See **GUERNSEY under CHANNEL ISLANDS**

ST SAMPSON

See **GUERNSEY under CHANNEL ISLANDS**

SALCOMBE Devon Map **03** SX73

GH QQ Bay View Hotel Bennett Rd TQ8 8JJ ☎(0548) 842238
Mar-Sep
The magnificent views of the estuary are a memorable part of this small privately owned bed and breakfast establishment. The bedrooms are simply appointed but comfortable and the public areas are situated at various levels of the 5-storey building. The resident proprietors have a very relaxed attitude.
5rm(2🛁🚿3hc) (2fb) CTV in 1 bedroom ® 🚫 ✱ dB&B£48-£56 dB&B🛁🚿£50-£60
Lic 🍽 CTV 6P
Credit Cards [1] [3]

GH QQQ Devon Tor Hotel Devon Rd TQ8 8HJ
☎(0548) 843106
Closed 10 Dec-10 Jan rs 28 Sep-1 Nov
A small private hotel with a fine position commanding magnificent views of the estuary from many of the bedrooms. Rooms are cosily decorated, each with its own colour scheme, and there is a sunny dining room and a small but comfortable guests' lounge.

7rm(4🛁🚿3hc) (2fb)🚭in all bedrooms CTV in 4 bedrooms ® 🐕 sB&B£20-£21 dB&B£40-£44 dB&B🛁🚿£40-£50 WB&B£140-£165 WBDi£205-£235 LDO 4.30pm
Lic ♨ CTV 5P nc9yrs (£)

GH QQQ Lyndhurst Hotel Bonaventure Rd TQ8 8BG
☎(0548) 842481
Jan-Oct
Situated in a residential area, this hotel offers wonderful views over the town and estuary. Attractively coordinated bedrooms provide modern facilities with effective showers and all rooms are equipped with TV, radio and tea- making equipment. Geoff and Sheila Sharp have built a good reputation for their 4-course dinners, with a choice always available, and the selection of sweets is notable. Sheila Sharp's cooking has proved so popular that she has published her own cookery book. A comfortable bar lounge is always available for guests.
8🚿 (1fb)🚭in all bedrooms CTV in all bedrooms ® 🐕 sB&B🚿£29-£35 dB&B🚿£58-£70 (incl dinner) WB&B£140-£164 WBDi£203-£231 LDO 4.30pm
Lic ♨ 4P nc7yrs

GH QQQ Torre View Hotel Devon Rd TQ8 8HJ
☎(0548) 842633
6 Feb-4 Nov
Friendly and enthusiastic proprietors, Julie and Arthur Bouttle, run this small hotel, which boasts superb views of the Salcombe estuary. Rooms are mainly en suite and are decorated in a light and airy style. There is a no- smoking lounge, a residents' bar with darts and skittles, and a spacious dining room where the choice for dinner is displayed on a blackboard menu.
8🛁🚿 (2fb) CTV in 2 bedrooms ® 🐕 ✱ sB&B🛁🚿£21-£25 dB&B🛁🚿£42-£50 WB&B£140-£160 WBDi£210-£230 LDO 6pm
Lic ♨ CTV 4P nc4yrs
Credit Cards [1] [3] (£)

GH QQ *Trennels Private Hotel* Herbert Rd TQ8 8HR
☎(0548) 842500
Mar-Nov
A private, licensed hotel conveniently situated for the town centre and harbour in a residential area with superb views over the town, estuary and National Trust land. Bedrooms are all comfortable and simply furnished, the majority having estuary views. Home-cooked meals are served in the dining room, with a set 4-course table d'hôte menu. Smoking is not permitted here.
7rm(1🛁4🚿2hc) (1fb)🚭in all bedrooms CTV in 5 bedrooms ® 🐕 LDO 10am
Lic ♨ CTV 8P nc4yrs

SALEN

See **MULL, ISLE OF**

SALFORD Greater Manchester Map **07** SJ89

GH QQQ *Hazeldean Hotel* 467 Bury New Rd M7 0NX
☎061-792 6667 FAX 061-792 6668
Closed 4 days Xmas
Sound standards of accommodation and friendly service are offered at this well established hotel set back from the A56, 2.5 miles from the centre of Manchester. Bedrooms are both comfortable and attractive and there is a pleasant lounge, bar and small restaurant.
21rm(17🛁🚿4hc) Annexe 3rm(2🛁🚿1hc) (2fb) CTV in all bedrooms ® LDO 9pm
Lic ♨ CTV 21P
Credit Cards [1] [2] [3] [5]

See the regional maps of popular holiday areas at the back of the book.

SALHOUSE Norfolk Map **09** TG31

GH QQQ *Brooksbank Hotel* Lower St NR13 6RW
☎Norwich(0603) 720420
This lovely guesthouse is set in the centre of the village, and is run by the friendly proprietors, Mr and Mrs Coe. The row of white 18th-century cottages retains its appeal, and is surrounded by well tended gardens. The accommodation is of a good quality with the emphasis on comfort.
3rm(2🛁1🚿) (1fb) CTV in all bedrooms ®
♨ CTV 3P

SALISBURY Wiltshire Map **04** SU12

See also Downton (6.5m S off A338)

GH QQQ Byways House 31 Fowlers Rd SP1 2QP
☎(0722) 328364 FAX (0722) 322146
A Victorian house with an adjoining coach house, a short, hilly walk from the city centre. The bedrooms are attractively decorated, comfortably furnished and well equipped. The lounge provides a quiet area, and breakfast and dinner are served, by arrangement, in the informal dining room.
23rm(19🛁🚿4hc) (5fb) CTV in all bedrooms ® sB&Bfr£20 sB&B🛁🚿fr£26.50 dB&Bfr£35 dB&B🛁🚿fr£39 WB&Bfr£122.50 WBDifr£189 LDO 6.30pm
Lic ♨ 15P
Credit Cards [1] [3] (£)

GH QQQ Cricket Field Cottage Skew Bridge, Wilton Rd SP2 7NS ☎(0722) 322595
Well appointed, en suite bedrooms are offered in this modernised game keeper's cottage overlooking the cricket field on the outskirts of the city. Bed and breakfast only is offered, and guests share tables in the dining room.
5rm(1🛁4🚿) (2fb) CTV in all bedrooms ® 🐕 (ex guide dogs) ✱ sB&B🛁🚿£22-£24 dB&B🛁🚿£36-£38
♨ 8P

GH QQ Glen Lyn 6 Bellamy Ln, Milford Hill SP1 2SP
☎(0722) 327880
A substantial Victorian property with its own well kept gardens in a quiet cul-de-sac, a few minutes' walk from the city centre. The bedrooms are comfortable, and the public areas elegantly furnished. The house is no smoking throughout, and offers bed and breakfast only.
9rm(2🛁2🚿5hc) (1fb)🚭in all bedrooms CTV in all bedrooms ® 🐕 (ex guide dogs) ✱ sB&B£18-£20 dB&B£32-£34 dB&B🛁🚿£34-£36 WB&B£120-£140
♨ CTV 6P nc12yrs

GH QQ Hayburn Wyke 72 Castle Rd SP1 3RL
☎(0722) 412627
Situated right by Victoria Park and close to the cathedral, this Victorian brick property offers clean and bright accommodation all equipped with TV and tea-making facilities, some of the bedrooms are en suite. A full English breakfast is served in the dining room, and limited parking is available at the guesthouse. The proprietors Alan and Dawn Curnow warmly welcome guests to their home.
6rm(2🚿4hc) (2fb) CTV in all bedrooms ® 🐕 (ex guide dogs) sB&B£20-£22 sB&B🚿£24-£26 dB&B£30-£33 dB&B🚿£36-£38
♨ CTV 5P 1🚗 ⛳ (£)

GH Q Holmhurst Downton Rd SP2 8AR ☎(0722) 323164
Mar-Oct
A detached red-brick family home situated on the A338, adjacent to the cathedral. Bedrooms are simply appointed and comfortable, and breakfast only is served in the pleasant dining room.
8rm(5🚿3hc) (2fb)🚭in 1 bedroom 🐕 sB&B£18-£30 sB&B🚿£20-£34 dB&B£30 dB&B🚿£34
♨ CTV 9P nc5yrs

See advertisement on page 353

GH QQ Leena's 50 Castle Rd SP1 3RL ☎(0722) 335419
A small guesthouse on the main road leading into Salisbury town centre, with a friendly, relaxed atmosphere. Bedrooms are prettily decorated with good modern facilities. Public areas are comfortable and have many personal touches. A family-run establishment where the family is much in evidence.
6rm(3↱ 3hc) (1fb)⊬in all bedrooms CTV in all bedrooms ® ✗ (ex guide dogs) sB&B£16-£19 dB&B£28-£31 dB&B↱£31-£35
᪥ CTV 6P Ⓔ

GH QQQ The Old House 161 Wilton Rd SP2 7JQ
☎(0722) 333433
Full of character, this attractive brick house is set in its own large gardens, within easy reach of the city and railway station. The en suite bedrooms are brightly decorated, each furnished in its own individual style and all are equipped with remote-control TV and tea-making facilities. A comfortable lounge, featuring exposed beams and brick walls, is available to guests, and home-cooked English breakfasts are served in the tasteful dining room, furnished and decorated in a country-cottage style with china plates on the walls and a Welsh dresser in one corner. Smoking is only permitted in the lounge.
6rm(1⇌4↱) (2fb)⊬in all bedrooms CTV in all bedrooms ® ✗ (ex guide dogs) ✱ sB&Bfr£20 sB&B⇌↱£30 dB&Bfr£32 dB&B⇌↱£35 WB&B£140-£210 WBDi£189-£255.50
LDO noon
᪥ CTV 10P games room table tennis

INN QQ Old Bell 2 Saint Ann St SP1 2DN ☎(0722) 327958
FAX (0722) 411485
This small 14th-century inn is ideally situated close to the cathedral, opposite St Ann's Gate. Each of the bedrooms is comfortable, well decorated and tastefully furnished: many have beams and low ceilings, and 2 house splendid 4-poster beds. The dining room is bright and cheerful and contains an impressive antique mirror and a piano, and the public bar area has a lively atmosphere, with log fires.
7rm(1⇌6↱) ® ✗ dB&B⇌↱£55-£60
᪥ CTV ⁄P nc12yrs solarium
Credit Cards 1 2 3 5

SALTASH Cornwall & Isles of Scilly Map **02** SX45

INN QQQ *The Crooked Inn* Stoketon Cross, Trematon PL12 4RZ ☎Plymouth(0752) 848177
Annexe 8⇌↱ (2fb) CTV in all bedrooms ® LDO 10pm
᪥ P ⛱(heated)
Credit Cards 1 3

SANDBACH Cheshire Map **07** SJ76

GH QQ Poplar Mount 2 Station Rd, Elworth CW11 9JG
☎Crewe(0270) 761268
This large Victorian house, situated just off the A533 and fronted by a private car park, is opposite Sandbach railway station. The proprietors Joan and Ian MacDonald provide clean, comfortable accommodation and the brightly decorated bedrooms have modern furniture, 2 have en suite showers. A selection of handicrafts made by Mrs MacDonald and her daughter is displayed in the lounge and can be purchased by guests. Individual tables are set in the small dining/breakfast room where a good cooked breakfast is served and an evening meal can be provided if prior notice is given.
5rm(2↱ 3hc) (1fb) ® ✱ sB&B£13.50-£15 sB&B↱£22.50-£25 dB&B£26-£30 dB&B↱£28-£32 LDO 7.45pm
᪥ CTV 7P
Credit Cards 1 3 Ⓔ

Street plans of certain towns and cities will be found in a separate section at the back of the book.

SANDOWN

See **WIGHT, ISLE OF**

SANDPLACE Cornwall & Isles of Scilly Map **02** SX25

GH QQQ *Polraen Country House Hotel* PL13 1PJ
☎Looe(05036) 3956
Dating back to 1742, this attractive granite country house is set in 2 acres of pretty, well kept gardens. The spacious bedrooms are well appointed, freshly decorated and comfortable. Public areas are well furnished and cosy, and the proprietress is a warm and welcoming hostess.
5rm(1⇌4↱) (2fb) CTV in all bedrooms ® LDO 8pm
Lic ᪥ 21P
Credit Cards 1 3

SANDWICH Kent Map **05** TR35

INN QQQ *St Crispin* The Street CT14 0DF
☎Dover(0304) 612081
First licenced in 1690, this historic country inn is set in peaceful village surroundings and features heavy oak beams, log fires and antique furniture. Bedrooms are available in the main building or in an annexe which offers more modern accommodation. The restaurant has a very good reputation locally for home-cooked food, and the inn is also popular for its range of ales. There is a large, pretty garden, and golfing facilities and ferry terminals are within easy reach.
4rm(2⇌2↱) Annexe 3⇌ (2fb) CTV in all bedrooms ®
LDO 9.30pm
᪥ 30P
Credit Cards 1 3

SARISBURY GREEN Hampshire Map **04** SU50

GH QQQ Dormy House Hotel 21 Barnes Ln SO3 6DA
☎Locks Heath(0489) 572626
Closed 22 Dec-2 Dec
Mollie and Eddie Rees provide a friendly welcome at this quietly situated small hotel. Bedrooms are well equipped, neat and comfortable; 3 of the rooms are just outside on the ground floor overlooking the garden. Inside is a cosy lounge, and a well organised breakfast room/kitchen. The hotel is conveniently located for Southampton, Portsmouth and Hamble.
10rm(8↱ 2hc) (1fb) CTV in all bedrooms ® ✗ (ex guide dogs) ✱ sB&B£23.50 sB&B↱£37.50 dB&B£40 dB&B↱£42.50
LDO 5pm
Lic ᪥ CTV 18P
Credit Cards 3 Ⓔ

SAUNDERSFOOT Dyfed Map **02** SN10

GH QQ Jalna Hotel Stammers Rd SA69 9HH ☎(0834) 812282
Mar-Oct
Just above the harbour and seafront, this family-run hotel provides modern, quite spacious accommodation. The well equipped bedrooms are all en suite, there is a comfortable lounge and a large bar in the basement.
14rm(8⇌6↱) (8fb) CTV in all bedrooms ® sB&B⇌↱£31-£22 dB&B⇌↱£36-£40 WB&B£120-£130 WBDi£160-£180
LDO 6.30pm
Lic ᪥ CTV 14P solarium
Credit Cards 1 3

GH QQQ The Sandy Hill Sandy Hill Road/Tenby Rd SA69 9DR ☎(0834) 813165
Mar-Oct
This delightful small guesthouse, once a farm, is alongside the A478 before the Tenby roundabout. Bedrooms are pretty and comfortable, and there is a cosy lounge and bar. Good value home cooking is provided, and a swimming pool in the garden for warm days.

5rm(1↱4hc) (3fb) CTV in all bedrooms ® WB&B£98-£105 WBDi£140-£161
Lic ⊞ 7P nc3yrs ≋ Ⓔ

GH QQQ Vine Farm The Ridgeway SA69 9LA
☎(0834) 813543
Apr-Oct
This old farmhouse, dating back in parts to the early 19th century, is now a very pleasant family-run guesthouse, set in well kept lawns and gardens. There is an attractive timbered dining room, a spacious lounge with an open fire, and pretty, well furnished and equipped bedrooms.
5⇌↱ (1fb) CTV in all bedrooms ® ✱ sB&B⇌↱£19-£20.50 dB&B⇌↱£38-£41 WBDi£160-£192 LDO 6pm
Lic ⊞ 10P

SAXELBY Leicestershire Map **08** SK62

FH QQ Mrs M A Morris **Manor House** *(SK701208)*
LE14 3PA ☎Melton Mowbray(0664) 812269
Etr-Oct
The manor house, parts of which date back to the 12th and 15th centuries, is situated on the edge of the village, 5 miles from Melton Mowbray.
3rm(1↱2hc) (2fb) CTV in all bedrooms ® ✖ (ex guide dogs) sB&Bfr£22 dB&Bfr£32 dB&B↱fr£40 WB&Bfr£103 WBDifr£158 LDO noon
⊞ CTV 6P 125 acres dairy sheep Ⓔ

Every effort is made to provide accurate information, but details can change after we go to print. It is advisable to check prices etc. before you make a firm booking.

SCARBOROUGH North Yorkshire Map **08** TA08

See **Town Plan Section**

GH Q Alga Court 5 Alga Ter, off St Martins Square YO11 2DF ☎(0723) 366078

This small terraced house is situated off St Martins Square, only a short walk from the South Cliffs. Bedrooms are unpretentious and have tea and coffee- making facilities. Friendly proprietors welcome senior citizens, families and pets.

6rm(1⇨2↱3hc) (3fb) CTV in all bedrooms ® ✱ sB&B£13-£16 sB&B⇨↱£16-£20 dB&B£26-£32 dB&B⇨↱£32-£40 (incl dinner) WB&B£91-£112 WBDi£112-£140 LDO 3pm

䴍 CTV

GH Q Avoncroft Hotel 5-7 Crown Ter YO11 2BL ☎(0723) 372737

This guesthouse is part of a Georgian terrace and is within a few minutes' walk of the beach and town centre. Bedrooms are centrally heated, many with en suite facilities. There is also a comfortable lounge and a well stocked bar.

34rm(1⇨20↱13hc) (13fb) CTV in all bedrooms ® ✱ sB&B£18.40-£20.40 sB&B⇨↱£22-£24 dB&B£36.80-£40.80 dB&B⇨↱£44-£48 WB&B£128.80-£142.80 WBDi£159-£171 LDO 6.15pm

Lic 䴍 CTV P̸ games room pool table Ⓔ

GH QQQ Bay & Premier Hotels 66/67 Esplanade, South Cliff YO11 2UZ ☎(0723) 501038 & 501062

Mar-Nov

These elegant Victorian hotels, situated next door to each other and under the same ownership, command fine views overlooking the South Bay, the picturesque harbour and the ruins of Scarborough Castle. Bedrooms in both hotels have en suite facilities, colour TV and tea-making equipment. Both are licensed, each hotel having its own bar lounge as well as comfortable residential lounges and well appointed dining rooms.

18rm(2⇨16↱) Annexe 20rm(17⇨3↱) (2fb) CTV in all bedrooms ® sB&B⇨↱£29-£32 dB&B⇨↱£54-£64 WB&B£175-£210 WBDi£231-£266 LDO 6pm

Lic lift 䴍 10P Ⓔ

GH QQQ Burghcliffe Hotel 28 Esplanade, South Cliff YO11 2AQ ☎(0723) 361524

Closed 18 Dec-8 Jan

Prominently situated overlooking the South Bay, this friendly family-owned private hotel provides a good standard of accommodation, with all bedrooms having en suite facilities, TV, radio alarms, hairdryers and tea-making equipment. There is also a comfortable lounge with fine sea views, a cocktail bar and an attractive basement dining room.

12rm(4⇨8↱) (6fb) CTV in all bedrooms ® ✗ ✱ sB&B⇨↱£25-£30 dB&B⇨↱£44-£52 WB&B£147-£175 WBDi£213.50-£241.50 LDO 4pm

Lic 䴍 CTV P̸

Credit Cards 1 3 Ⓔ

GH QQ *Dolphin Hotel* 151 Columbus Ravine YO12 7QZ ☎(0723) 374217

Well equipped bedrooms with private bathrooms are a feature of this small, friendly, mid-terrace private hotel. It is situated close to North Bay and cricket ground, and home-cooked dinners are provided by the resident owners.

6⇨↱ (2fb) CTV in all bedrooms ® ✗ LDO 8.30pm

Lic 䴍 CTV P̸ nc5yrs

Credit Cards 1 3

GH QQ Geldenhuis Hotel 145-147 Queens Pde YO12 7HU ☎(0723) 361677

Etr-early Oct

Distinguished by the gold-coloured canopies over its lower windows, the Geldenhuis overlooks North Bay and has a large car park at the front. Public rooms are spacious, bright and airy, and several of the variably sized bedrooms have views over the sea.

30rm(3⇨6↱21hc) (6fb) ® ✗ (ex guide dogs) sB&B£21.75 dB&B£37.60 dB&B⇨↱£43.45 WBDi£164.50 LDO 6pm

Lic 䴍 CTV 24P nc5yrs Ⓔ

GH QQ Manor Heath Hotel 67 Northstead Manor Dr YO12 6AF ☎(0723) 365720

Closed 19 Nov-5 Dec & 24-25 Dec

An early 1930s detached purpose-built private hotel situated near the North Bay and Peasholm Park. Some of the front bedrooms have sea views, and public rooms include a cosy bar and an attractive dining room. There are gardens at the front and parking to the rear.

16rm(2⇨9↱5hc) (5fb) CTV in all bedrooms ® ✗ sB&B£16-£18 sB&B⇨↱£18-£20 dB&B£32-£36 dB&B⇨↱£38-£40 WB&B£112-£140.50 WBDi£140-£171 LDO 4.30pm

Lic 䴍 CTV 16P Ⓔ

GH Q Meadow Court Queens Ter YO12 7HJ ☎(0723) 360839

A clean, well maintained and soundly decorated guesthouse situated in the North Bay area of the town, but not on the seafront. There is a small bar and cosy lounge, and the hotel is conveniently located, close to the cricket ground and within easy reach of the town centre.

10hc (2fb) ⁄ in 2 bedrooms ® sB&B£13-£15 dB&B£26-£30 LDO 2pm

Lic 䴍 CTV Ⓔ

GH QQQ Mount House Hotel 33 Trinity Rd, South Cliff YO11 2TD ☎(0723) 362967

Mar-Oct

A spacious semidetached Victorian house about 10 minutes' walk from central areas and the beach. The bedroom décor and furnishings have been tastefully coordinated, there is a very comfortable lounge, a quiet conservatory and a cosy bar close to the dining room.

10rm(1⇨3↱6hc) (2fb) ® ✗ (ex guide dogs) ✱ sB&B£16 dB&B£32 dB&B⇨↱£36 WB&B£108-£122 WBDi£154-£168 LDO 4pm

Lic 䴍 CTV 6P

Credit Cards 1 3 Ⓔ

GH QQQ Paragon Hotel 123 Queens Pde YO12 7HU ☎(0723) 372676

2 Jan-Oct

Overlooking the quieter North Bay, this private hotel has been tastefully modernised and provides comfortable well equipped bedrooms, all with baths or showers en suite. There is a relaxing lounge with sea views and a well appointed dining room.

14rm(3⇨11↱) (4fb) CTV in all bedrooms ® sB&B⇨↱£26-£28 dB&B⇨↱£40-£42 LDO 6.30pm

Lic 䴍

Credit Cards 1 3 Ⓔ

GH QQ Parmelia Hotel 17 West St YO11 2QN ☎(0723) 361914

Apr-Oct

This private, family-run hotel is situated on the South Cliff, not far from the Esplanade. It offers pleasant, well maintained accommodation, including 2 lounges, one with a bar, and dinners are excellent value.

15rm(1⇨10↱4hc) (4fb) CTV in all bedrooms ® ✗ (ex guide dogs) sB&Bfr£18 dB&Bfr£36 dB&B⇨↱fr£41 WBDi£157-£175 LDO 4pm

Lic 䴍 CTV Ⓔ

GH QQ The Ramleh 135 Queens Pde YO12 7HY ☎(0723) 365745

rs Dec-Feb

Overlooking the North Bay and close to the cricket ground, this friendly guesthouse is tastefully furnished and decorated throughout. Many of the bedrooms have a sea view as does the dining room, and there is a comfortable guests' lounge with a TV.

10rm(4⨍6hc) (4fb) ® ✗ (ex guide dogs) ✱ sB&B£14-£16 dB&B£28-£32 dB&B⨍£34-£38 WB&B£95-£105 WBDi£120-£133 LDO 2pm
Lic 𝍖 CTV 5P
Credit Cards 1 3 £

GH QQQ *Riviera Hotel* St Nicholas Cliff YO11 2ES
☎(0723) 372277
Closed Xmas & New Year
Recent redecoration has considerably enhanced this private hotel, which is in a prime position close to the south beach, town centre and spa. Bedrooms have full en suite facilities and a good range of equipment.
20rm(15⇌5⨍) (6fb) CTV in all bedrooms ®
✗ (ex guide dogs) LDO 7pm
Lic lift 𝍖 P̸
Credit Cards 1 3

GH Q Sefton Hotel 18 Prince of Wales Ter YO11 2AL
☎(0723) 372310
Mar-Oct
A Victorian terraced house only a short walk from the South Cliff and the Spa Conference Complex. An automatic lift serves all floors, bedrooms are comfortable and there is a spacious dining room with individual tables downstairs, as well as a television lounge on the first floor.
14rm(6⇌8hc) (2fb)⊁in 6 bedrooms ✗ (ex guide dogs) ✱ sB&B£19-£22 dB&B£38-£44 dB&B⇌£40-£46 (incl dinner) WB&B£112-£133 WBDi£133-£154 LDO 6pm
Lic lift 𝍖 CTV nc12yrs £

GH QQ West Lodge Private Hotel 38 West St YO11 2QP
☎(0723) 500754
A semidetached house among other similar properties a short distance from the South Cliff and within walking distance of the town centre and other amenities. Bedrooms are mostly ample in size, all with colour TV and tea- making facilities, and there is a comfortable lounge.
7rm(2⨍5hc) (4fb) CTV in all bedrooms ® ✗ (ex guide dogs) ✱ sB&B£13 sB&B⨍£15 dB&B£26 dB&B⨍£30 WB&B£91-£105 WBDi£112-£126 LDO 10am
Lic 𝍖 CTV £

SCILLY, ISLES OF No map

ST MARY'S

SELECTED

GH QQQQ Brantwood Hotel Rocky Hill TR21 0NW
☎Scillonia(0720) 22531 Telex no 45117
FAX (0720) 22301
May-Sep
Rurally located a short distance outside the town, this is a single-storey country retreat with a small garden. Bedrooms are comfortable and individually styled, providing spotlessly clean accommodation with en suite facilities. There is a small cosy lounge, and a breakfast room with a fine display of William Timyn drawings. Bed and breakfast only are available, but there is a residents' licence. David and Dorothy Oxford offer a cordial welcome and are willing to chauffeur guests into town.
4⨍ CTV in all bedrooms ® ✗ (ex guide dogs) ✱ sB&B⨍£38 dB&B⨍£66 (incl dinner) WB&B£231-£266
Lic 𝍖 P̸ nc10yrs croquet
Credit Cards 1 2 3 £

This guide is updated annually – make sure you use an up-to-date edition.

SELECTED

GH QQQQ Carnwethers Country House Carnwethers, Pelistry Bay TR21 0NX ☎Scillonia(0720) 22415
Apr-15 Oct
Situated near the secluded Pelistry Bay, this former farmhouse offers a comfortable and relaxing retreat. Bedrooms vary in size, but all are tastefully decorated and well equipped, and many have superb sea views. Interesting paintings by local artists adorn the walls, as they do in the dining room where a nautical theme prevails. The spacious lounge has a good range of local information, in books and on videos, and other facilities include a solar-heated pool, a Nordic-style sauna, a croquet lawn and a games room with a pool table and table tennis. Roy and Joyce Graham have offered a warm welcome for 20 years, and greet many returning guests year after year.
9rm(8⇌⨍1hc) Annexe 1⨍ (2fb) CTV in all bedrooms ® ✗ (ex guide dogs) sB&B£32-£40 sB&B⇌⨍£42-£50 dB&B⇌⨍£64-£96 (incl dinner) LDO 6.30pm
Lic 𝍖 CTV 4P nc7yrs ⩦(heated) sauna pool table croquet lawn library

SCOTCH CORNER North Yorkshire Map **08** NZ20

SELECTED

INN QQQQ Vintage Hotel DL10 6NP
☎Richmond(0748) 824424 & 822961
Closed 25 Dec & 1 Jan rs Nov-Feb
A popular hotel situated on the A66, just a few yards from the A1. Bedrooms are compact but neat and cosy and well appointed. The rustic-style lounge and bar feature chunky stone and wood, and are comfortable and inviting. The extensive menus in both bar and restaurant offer freshly cooked food at realistic prices, and light snacks, tea and coffee are also available. Service is friendly and courteous.
8rm(5⇌⨍3hc) CTV in all bedrooms ® T
✗ (ex guide dogs) ✱ sB&B£27-£29.50 sB&B⇌⨍£36-£39.50 dB&B£38-£41 dB&B⇌⨍£45-£47.50 WB&B£130-£200 WBDi£225-£295 Lunch £9.75 Dinner £13.50&alc LDO 9.15pm
𝍖 50P
Credit Cards 1 3 £

SEAFORD East Sussex Map **05** TV49

GH QQ Avondale Hotel 4-5 Avondale Rd BN25 1RJ
☎(0323) 890008
A family-run hotel, close to the town centre, with a range of freshly decorated bedrooms. A small lounge is combined with a dining room, and dinner is available on request. This is a no-smoking hotel.
16rm(4⨍12hc) (8fb)⊁in all bedrooms CTV in all bedrooms ® ✗ (ex guide dogs) sB&B£16-£18 sB&B⨍£30-£35 dB&B£30-£35 dB&B⨍£35-£40 WB&B£112-£120 WBDi£154-£168 LDO 2pm
lift 𝍖 CTV
Credit Cards 1 3

SEASCALE Cumbria Map **06** NY00

GH QQQ Cottage Black How CA20 1LQ ☎(09467) 28416
Well furnished and modern accommodation is provided at this friendly and comfortable house in a quiet part of the village. Bedrooms have good facilities and there is a cosy lounge for guests' use.
8rm(7⇌1⨍) (1fb) CTV in all bedrooms ® ✗ ✱ sB&B⇌⨍£25 dB&B⇌⨍£40
𝍖 CTV 10P £

SEATON (NEAR LOOE; 7M) Cornwall & Isles of Scilly Map **02** SX35

GH QQQ ***Blue Haven Hotel*** PL11 3JQ
☎Downderry(05035) 310

The view is quite magnificent from this hotel on top of Looe Hill. The bedrooms are comfortable, mostly with good en suite facilities, and public areas are bright and sunny. Dinner is available, home-cooked from fresh ingredients.

6rm(5⛿ 1hc) (3fb) CTV in 2 bedrooms TV in 2 bedrooms ® LDO 8pm
Lic CTV 6P
Credit Cards 1 3

SEATON Devon Map **03** SY29

GH QQ Harbourside 2 Trevelyan Rd EX12 2NL
☎(0297) 20085
Mar-Oct

This small, family-run guesthouse is situated in a quiet residential area close to the town centre and overlooking the harbour. Bedrooms are comfortable and clean, and set home-cooked meals are served in the lounge/dining area.

4rm(1⛿ 3hc) (2fb) CTV in all bedrooms ® ✻ sB&B£14-£16 dB&B£26-£28 WB&B£80 WBDi£130-£135 LDO 9pm
Lic 🛏 CTV 8P

GH QQQ Mariners Hotel Esplanade EX12 2NP
☎(0297) 20560

This small, private hotel, personally run by the proprietors, has a superb seafront position overlooking Lyme Bay. Bedrooms are all en suite and a ground-floor room is available. There is a residents' lounge and an additional spacious sun lounge, and a varied choice of menu is offered at dinner.

10⇌⛿ (1fb) CTV in all bedrooms ® sB&B⇌⛿£25-£30 dB&B⇌⛿£41-£44 WB&B£128.50-£140 WBDi£205.50-£217
Lic 🛏 CTV 10P
Credit Cards 1 3 £

SEAVIEW

See **WIGHT, ISLE OF**

SEDBERGH Cumbria Map **07** SD69

GH QQ Cross Keys Hotel LA10 5NE ☎(05396) 20284
Etr, Apr-Dec & New Year

A small 18th-century stone-built house situated on the A683 to the northeast of the town, in beautiful countryside. Owned by the National Trust, this old inn offers good accommodation combined with charm and character, with low ceilings, beams, flagged floors and open fires. Although it is unlicensed, with no TV, bedrooms have modern facilities and a good standard of home cooking is provided. Smoking is not permitted.

5rm(1⇌⛿ 4hc) ⚟in all bedrooms ® ✖ (ex guide dogs) sB&B£23 dB&B£46 dB&B⇌⛿£54 WB&B£161-£189 WBDi£259-£287 LDO 24hr notice
9P £

SEDGEFIELD Co Durham Map **08** NZ32

INN QQQ Dun Cow High St TS21 3AT (RE) ☎(0740) 20894

A charming old inn situated on the fringe of the town, near the racecourse. The unusual bedrooms feature white rough cast walls, heavy beams, red carpets and substantial dark, wood furnishings; all are very well equipped and there are 2 well appointed Victorian-style bathrooms serving the 6 bedrooms. The inn is renowned for its excellent standard of cuisine, with a wide range of bar meals and an appetising à la carte menu in the pretty restaurant.

6hc CTV in all bedrooms ® **T** ✻ sB&Bfr£36.50 dB&Bfr£45 LDO 10pm
🛏 25P
Credit Cards 1 2 3 5

SELBY North Yorkshire Map **08** SE63

GH Q Hazeldene 32-34 Brook St, Doncaster Rd YO8 0AR (A19) ☎(0757) 704809
Closed Xmas wk

A neat late-Victorian semidetached villa on the A19, just south of the centre, with private parking facilities at the rear.

7hc (2fb)⚟in all bedrooms TV in all bedrooms ® ✖ sB&B£15-£17 dB&B£30-£34
CTV 5P

SELKIRK Borders *Selkirkshire* Map **12** NT42

GH QQQ Hillholm 36 Hillside Ter TD7 4ND ☎(0750) 21293
Closed Dec-Feb

A family-run semidetached Victorian house conveniently situated beside the A7 at the south end of the town. Bedrooms are decorated in soft pastel shades with pretty coordinated fabrics, and the guesthouse is clean, comfortable and well maintained. The attractive lounge has comfortable leather chairs, and hearty breakfasts are served at the communal table in the neatly appointed dining room.

3hc ® ✖ ✻ sB&B£18 dB&B£30
🛏 CTV 🅿̸ nc10yrs

SEMLEY Wiltshire Map **03** ST82

INN QQ Benett Arms SP7 9AS ☎East Knoyle(0747) 830221
Closed 25 & 26 Dec

Friendly proprietors, Joseph and Annie Duthie, run this country inn situated in a quiet village between Tisbury and East Knoyle. The well equipped bedrooms are simply furnished and comfortable; 3 rooms are located in a rear annexe on ground-floor level. The friendly informal bar is split level, with an open fire in the bar area. There is an extensive range of bar meals, or the more formal restaurant is available.

2⇌⛿ Annexe 3⛿ CTV in all bedrooms ® **T** sB&B⇌⛿£26-£30 dB&B⇌⛿£40-£44 WB&B£180-£208 WBDi£280-£308 Lunch £7.95-£9.45&alc Dinner £10-£18alc LDO 9.45pm
🛏 30P
Credit Cards 1 2 3 5 £

SENNEN Cornwall & Isles of Scilly Map **02** SW32

GH Q The Old Manor Hotel TR19 7AD ☎(0736) 871280
Closed 23-28 Dec

The Old Manor lies on the road to Lands End, opposite Sennen church. Inevitably bedrooms come in all shapes and sizes, some with en suite facilities, some a floor away from a bathroom, but although modestly decorated, they are well equipped. The public areas are very cosy, with plenty of books, ornaments and mementoes.

8rm(5⛿ 3hc) (3fb)⚟in 1 bedroom CTV in 7 bedrooms ® **T** ✖ sB&B£14-£26 sB&B⛿fr£26 dB&Bfr£32 dB&B⛿£36-£42 WB&B£84-£161 WBDi£136-£213 LDO 6.30pm
Lic 🛏 CTV 50P putting green
Credit Cards 1 2 3 £

GH QQ Sunny Bank Hotel Sea View Hill TR19 7AR
☎(0736) 871278
Closed Dec

An attractive Cornish stone-built detached house in a rural position just outside the village. It offers clean, simple family accommodation complemented by commanding views over the sea and countryside. En route to Lands End, it provides a good base for touring the south-west peninsula.

11hc (2fb) ® ✖ (ex guide dogs) sB&B£14-£16 dB&B£28-£36 WB&B£98-£126 WBDi£125-£150 LDO 7pm
Lic 🛏 CTV 12P

SENNYBRIDGE Powys Map **03** SN92

SELECTED

FH QQQQ Mrs M C Adams **Brynfedwen** *(SN963297)* Trallong Common LD3 8HW ☎(0874) 636505

With superb views across the Usk Valley and the Brecon Beacons, and set in 150 acres, this establishment is very much a working farm, and during the spring guests are welcome to help bottle feed the numerous lambs. There are 2 en suite bedrooms in the main house, furnished in pine with pretty duvet covers. The separate annexe flat can also be used for self catering and includes a small, private sitting room overlooking the lawn and is ideal for disabled guests. There is a modern lounge with an open fire, and proprietor Mary Adams offers genuine, warm hospitality as well as good home cooking. Brynfedwen Farm stands high above the A40 in the village of Trallong, which is signposted off the A40 just 2 miles east of Sennybridge.

2⇌(shwr) Annexe 1(shwr) (2fb) CTV in 1 bedroom ® ✗ (ex guide dogs) sB&B⇌(shwr)fr£15 dB&B⇌(shwr)fr£30 WB&Bfr£105 WBDifr£175 LDO 6.30pm

CTV 6P 150 acres sheep cattle horses £

SETTLE North Yorkshire Map **07** SD86

GH QQ Liverpool House Chapel Square BD24 9HR ☎(0729) 822247

Closed 21 Dec-Jan

A mid-18th-century building originally designed as a gatehouse for the extension to the Leeds-Liverpool canal. Morning coffee, light lunches and afternoon teas are served in the small dining room every day except Wednesday and Thursday, and dinner is also served, for which advance reservation is advisable. There are 7 well maintained bedrooms and 2 cosy bars available for resident guests. Smoking is not permitted.

7hc ⊘in all bedrooms ® ✗ sB&B£17-£19.50 dB&B£34-£39 WB&B£119 WBDi£215 LDO 10am

Lic CTV 8P nc12yrs

Credit Cards 1 3 £

GH QQ The Oast Guest House 5 Pen-y-Ghent View, Church St BD24 9JJ ☎(0729) 822989

Looking down the Ribble Valley with wide views of Pen-y-Ghent, this Edwardian terraced house offers comfortably furnished bedrooms in a modern style with attractively coordinated fabrics. The guests' lounge has comfortable settees and armchairs plus a TV and small dispense bar in one corner. A 3-course evening meal is served in the pleasant dining room with individual tables, and the cooking is English including alternative dishes for those on special diets or vegetarians. There is a small car park at the back of the hotel as well as on-street parking.

5rm(2⇌(shwr) 3hc) ® ✗ (ex guide dogs) * dB&B£34 dB&B⇌(shwr)£39 WB&Bfr£136 WBDifr£196.20 LDO noon

Lic CTV 4P nc5yrs

GH QQ *Whitefriars Country Guesthouse* Church St BD24 9JD ☎(0729) 823753

Closed Xmas Day

Its own spacious gardens provide the attractive setting for this 17th-century family house with monastic origins. There are 2 comfortable lounges, one with an open fire, colour TV and lots of books and tourist information. The sizeable bedrooms – 3 with en suite facilities – are a feature of this friendly house, which is situated in the centre of the town with ample parking within the grounds. This is a no-smoking establishment.

9rm(3(shwr) 6hc) (3fb)⊘in all bedrooms CTV in 3 bedrooms ® ✗ (ex guide dogs) LDO 5pm

Lic CTV 9P

SEVENOAKS Kent

See **Wrotham**

SHALDON Devon

See **Teignmouth**

SHANKLIN

See **WIGHT, ISLE OF**

SHAP Cumbria Map **12** NY51

GH QQQ *Brookfield* CA10 3PZ ☎(09316) 397 due to change to (0931) 716397

Closed 20 Dec-Jan

An attractive detached house situated on the A6 to the south of the village and flanked by a charming garden. It offers a good standard of accommodation and friendly, attentive service from the resident owners. A good range of home-cooked food is served in the pleasant dining room.

6hc (3fb) CTV in all bedrooms ® ✗ LDO 8.15pm

Lic CTV 30P 6 garages

FH Q E & S Hodgson **Green Farm** *(NY565143)* CA10 3PW ☎(09316) 619 due to change to (0931) 716619

Etr-Sep

This Cumbrian farmhouse dates from 1703 and offers friendly hospitality. It is set back from the A6, on the south of the town.

3rm(2hc) (2fb) ® ✗ * dB&B£28

CTV 4P 200 acres mixed

SHAWBURY Shropshire Map **07** SJ52

FH Q Mrs S J Clarkson ***Longley*** *(SJ602228)* Stanton Heath SY4 4HE ☎(0939) 250289
Closed Xmas
An extended family-run farmhouse with a long drive, surrounded by 15 acres. The house is around 250 years old, and is located in the village of Stanton Heath, just off the A53 Shrewsbury-Newcastle road.
2hc Annexe 1⇌ ®
🍴 CTV 4P 15 acres arable sheep

FH QQQ G C Evans ***New*** *(SJ586215)* TF6 6RJ ☎(0939) 250358
A modern farmhouse with an attractive, unusual extension which forms a separate entrance for guests' accommodation. The rooms are individually decorated and well equipped, many with private bathrooms. The farm is reached by following signs to Muckleton, off the A53 Shrewsbury – Market Drayton road.
4rm(3↱1hc) CTV in all bedrooms ® ✗
🍴 CTV 10P nc3yrs 70 acres arable sheep

SHEARSBY Leicestershire Map **04** SP69

FH QQQ Mrs A T Hutchinson **Knaptoft House Farm & The Greenway** *(SP619894)* Bruntingthorpe Rd LE17 6PR ☎Leicester(0533) 478388
Closed Xmas
Surrounded by open countryside and well tended gardens, complete with some well stocked carp ponds (guests can arrange fishing access), this friendly family farm provides a peaceful environment that proves equally popular with business and tourist visitors. The comfortable accommodation and public rooms are in adjoining houses, consisting of light and cheerful bedrooms with matching floral bedspreads and curtains. The majority have a shower facility within the bedroom and all have access to a refrigerator on the landing where fresh milk is provided. A tastefully furnished lounge is equipped with TV, games, reading materials and various prints adorn the walls.
3hc Annexe 3rm(1↱2hc) (1fb) ® ✗ ✱ sB&Bfr£18 sB&B↱fr£25 dB&Bfr£32 dB&B↱fr£36
🍴 CTV 10P nc3yrs ✓ stabling 145 acres mixed Ⓔ

SHEERNESS Kent Map **05** TQ97

GH Q Isle of Sheppey Hotel 214 Queenborough Rd, Halfway ME12 3DF ☎(0795) 665950 FAX (0795) 476709
This late-Victorian detached house is located on the A250 between Minster and Sheerness, and has been converted into a small guesthouse. It offers basically furnished functional bedrooms, family rooms with bunk beds and 2 ground-floor annexe bedrooms. Dinner can be provided by prior arrangement with the proprietor Mrs Sophie Allen; the breakfast room is a no-smoking area. The guesthouse is being renovated by the present owners, and ample car parking is available on the forecourt.
8⇌↱ (3fb) CTV in all bedrooms ® ✱ sB&B⇌↱fr£25 dB&B⇌↱fr£35 LDO 9pm
🍴 CTV 10P ⛆(heated) Ⓔ

SHEFFIELD South Yorkshire Map **08** SK38

GH QQ Lindum Hotel 91 Montgomery Rd S7 1LP ☎(0742) 552356
Closed Xmas
This semidetached, stone-built house is situated in the residential suburb of Nether Edge, a mile southwest of the city centre. It provides simple but modern accommodation and has a small car park.
12rm(1⇌11hc) (1fb) CTV in 11 bedrooms TV in 1 bedroom ®
Lic 🍴 CTV 6P

Ⓔ Remember to use the money-off vouchers.

GH QQ Millingtons 70 Broomgrove Rd S10 2NA (off A625 Ecclesall Rd) ☎(0742) 669549
A small friendly guesthouse, 1.5 miles south west of the city centre via the A625, opposite the polytechnic buildings in a tree-lined side road. It provides simple but sound modern accommodation and is popular with commercial visitors. There is a small car park at the front of the house.
6rm(3⇌↱3hc) CTV in all bedrooms ® ✗ (ex guide dogs) ✱ sB&Bfr£22 sB&B⇌↱fr£22 dB&B⇌↱fr£42
🍴 CTV 4P nc12yrs

SHEPTON MALLET Somerset Map **03** ST64

INN QQ Kings Arms Leg Square BA4 5LN ☎(0749) 343781
Closed Xmas rs Sat lunch
In the quiet, older part of the town, this inn dates back to the 1660's and is well managed and very popular. The bar and other public areas have recently been upgraded to a smart standard. The bedrooms are currently quite comfortable but less modern in décor and style; however they are reasonably equipped and there are plans to update them soon. A comprehensive bar menu is offered with a relaxed and friendly atmosphere throughout.
3↱ CTV in all bedrooms ® ✗ (ex guide dogs) ✱ sB&B↱£25-£33 dB&B↱£33-£40 Lunch £3.25-£16.20 Dinner £16.20 LDO 9.30pm
🍴 6P nc10yrs games room
Credit Cards 1

SHERBORNE Dorset Map **03** ST61

FH QQ Mrs P T Tizzard **Venn** *(ST684183)* Milborne Port DT9 5RA ☎Milborne Port(0963) 250598
Only 3 miles from the famous abbey town of Sherborne, this dairy farm is located on the A30. Bright, neat and pretty bedrooms are provided, with some modern facilities, and a comfortable guests' lounge, complete with a fire and TV, is available. A hearty breakfast is served at one end of the lounge, where the views are lovely. There is a warm, friendly atmosphere and the Tizzard family are pleasant, cheery proprietors.
3hc (1fb) CTV in all bedrooms ® ✗ (ex guide dogs)
🍴 CTV P ⌂ 375 acres dairy/beef Ⓔ

SHERBOURNE Warwickshire

See **Warwick**

SHERIFF HUTTON North Yorkshire Map **08** SE66

GH QQQ Rangers House Sheriff Hutton Park YO6 1RH ☎(03477) 397
Built in 1639 as a brewhouse and stable for the royal hunting lodge, this attractive guesthouse is situated in Sheriff Hutton Park. Adjacent to the hall, its name is derived from the rangers who looked after the park. This friendly, comfortable house contains much period style furniture and although the bedrooms have been modernised, beams and leaded windows help to retain its character. The main hall with its comfortable seating, open fire, TV and lots of literature has a gallery and an 18th-century staircase. The dining room with its yellow painted walls, also contains antique furniture, including spacious, individual tables. The hotel is fully licensed, and children are always welcome.
6rm(2⇌2↱2hc) (1fb) ® ✗ ✱ sB&B⇌↱£32 dB&B£60 dB&B⇌↱£64 LDO 9.30pm
Lic 🍴 CTV 30P Ⓔ

SHERINGHAM Norfolk Map **09** TG14

GH QQQ Beacon Hotel Nelson Rd NR26 8BT ☎(0263) 822019
May-Sep
Beacon Hotel is perched atop Beeston Hill, to the east of the town, a minute from the sea. It is a particularly well cared for establishment with light, fresh décor and furnishings, and a comfortable lounge and dining room.

6rm(3⬏3hc) ⍻in all bedrooms ® ✗ sB&B£29-£30 sB&B⬏£29-£30 dB&B£58-£60 dB&B⬏£58-£60 (incl dinner) WBDi£189
Lic 🏢 CTV 5P nc14yrs
Credit Cards 1 3 £

GH QQQ Fairlawns 26 Hooks Hill Rd NR26 8NL
☎(0263) 824717
Etr-Oct
Fairlawns is situated in a quiet residential cul-de-sac just off the Holt road. The well proportioned rooms are comfortably furnished, colour TVs have recently been installed, and there are excellent en suite facilities providing each room with a bath and shower. Evening meals are freshly prepared and the premises are licensed.
5⇨⬏ CTV in all bedrooms ® ✗ (ex guide dogs)
dB&B⇨⬏£38-£42 WB&Bfr£121 LDO noon
Lic 🏢 6P nc12yrs £

SHETLAND Map **16**

LERWICK Map **16** HU44

GH QQ Glen Orchy House 20 Knab Rd ZE1 0AX
☎Shetland(0595) 2031
Situated in a residential area high above the town, this comfortable guesthouse is a popular base for business people and holidaymakers alike. At the time of our visit, new owners Joan and Trevor Howarth had just begun a programme of refurbishment which includes the creation of a new lounge, and more en suite facilities are planned.
8rm(1⬏7hc) (2fb) CTV in all bedrooms ® sB&B£19.50-£22.50 sB&B⬏£26 dB&B£37 dB&B⬏£43 WB&B£136.50-£157.50 WBDi£190-£211
🏢 CTV ⚑9

SHIFNAL Shropshire Map **07** SJ70

GH QQ Village Farm Lodge Sheriffhales TF11 8RD
☎Telford(0952) 462763 FAX (0952) 677912
This former farm building has been cleverly converted to provide modern, well equipped accommodation with en suite bathrooms. It is located on the B4379 on the northern edge of the village, about 3 miles north of Shifnal. Telford town centre and business areas are within a few minutes' drive, and the guesthouse is understandably popular with commercial visitors.
8⬏ (3fb) CTV in all bedrooms ® sB&B⬏£25-£28.50 dB&B⬏£35-£39.50
Lic 🏢 CTV 12P
Credit Cards 1 2 3 £

SHILLINGFORD Devon Map **03** SS92

SELECTED

GH QQQQ The Old Mill EX16 9BW
☎Bampton(0398) 331064
Originally a water-powered corn mill, the property was purchased in a completely derelict state and has been transformed by Diane and Roger Burnell into a lovely home and very special establishment. The bedrooms are a mixture of suites or family rooms, nicely decorated, furnished and equipped with excellent en suite facilities. All rooms are spacious and some have large, comfortable lounges. There is a comfortable lounge for guests to enjoy, and breakfast/dinner is taken around a communal table (separate tables are available on request), in convivial surroundings and a beautiful setting of lace, sparkling crystal, gleaming silver and fine china. The optional set menu evening meal which Diane Burnell prepares from local, fresh produce, after consulting guests about dislikes or specific dietary requirements, is cooked with care and flair. Breakfast is a hearty affair and the Burnells are on hand to ensure guests have all they require to make their stay thoroughly enjoyable.

→

2⇌ Annexe 2 (2fb) in all bedrooms CTV in all bedrooms ® dB&B⇌£30-£50 WB&B£95-£155 WBDi£189-£250 LDO noon
Lic CTV 20P ♩ ①
See advertisement under BAMPTON

SHIPBOURNE Kent Map **05** TQ55

INN QQQ ***The Chaser*** Stumble Hill TN11 9PE
☎Plaxtol(0732) 810630 FAX (0732) 810941
Built in the 1880s, this colonial-style listed building has been skilfully extended by converting the adjoining stables and hayloft. Bedrooms are particularly well equipped, including one for the disabled, and 6 rooms have full bath and shower facilities. Home cooking, including interesting soups and pies is available in the bar, and the beamed, vaulted restaurant features a fixed-price menu. Harvey's real ale and a well kept cellar complement the personal and attentive service by the resident managers.
15⇌ (1fb) CTV in all bedrooms ® LDO 9.30pm
30P
Credit Cards 1 2 3

SHIPSTON ON STOUR Warwickshire Map **04** SP24

INN QQQ Red Lion Hotel Main St, Long Compton CV36 5JS ☎(060884) 221
5⇌ (1fb) CTV in all bedrooms ® ✱ sB&B⇌fr£30 dB&B⇌fr£50 Bar Lunch £6-£12alc Dinner £11-£15alc LDO 9.30pm
60P
Credit Cards 1 3 ①

SHOTTLE Derbyshire Map **08** SK34

GH QQ Shottle Hall Farm DE5 2EB
☎Cowers Lane(0773) 550276 & 550203
Closed Nov & Xmas
Guests are assured of a warm welcome at this large family home. Surrounded by 3 acres of grounds and a large farm, this is the ideal spot for a relaxing holiday.
11rm(3⇌8hc) (3fb) in all bedrooms ® sB&Bfr£23 sB&B⇌fr£30 dB&Bfr£39 dB&B⇌fr£50 WB&Bfr£154 WBDifr£210 LDO 6pm
Lic CTV 30P

SELECTED

FH QQQQ Mrs J L Slack **Dannah** *(SK314502)* Bowmans Ln DE56 2DR ☎Cowers Lane(0773) 550273 & 550630 FAX (0773) 550590
Closed Xmas
This 18th-century Georgian house sits high above the Ecclesbourne valley amidst beautiful tranquil countryside; a mixed working farm, it is part of the Chatsworth Estate and is situated close to Shottle village. Proprietors Joan and Martin Slack have tastefully furnished the accommodation, and make every effort to provide a genuinely hospitable atmosphere. There are 2 sitting rooms, and a new restaurant serving both residents and locals, aptly named Mixing Place, and popular with both. Good quality fresh produce is carefully cooked and presented, with set menus for the first half of the week and a choice of menus for the other days.
7rm(6⇌1hc) (1fb) in all bedrooms CTV in all bedrooms ® (ex guide dogs) sB&B£29.50-£35 sB&B⇌£29.50-£35 dB&B£50-£70 dB&B⇌£50-£70 WB&B£165-£215 LDO 9.15pm
Lic CTV 20P 128 acres mixed
Credit Cards 1 3 ①
See advertisement under DERBY

SHREWLEY Warwickshire Map **04** SP26

SELECTED

GH QQQQ Shrewley House CV35 7AT
☎Claverdon(092684) 2549 FAX (092684) 2216
A charming listed Grade II Georgian farmhouse dating from the 17th century, set in 1.5 acres of well tended gardens in open countryside. Accommodation in the main house consists of 3 beautifully decorated rooms furnished in pine, 2 with king-sized draped 4-poster beds. Mr and Mrs Green provide an exceptionally wide range of facilities, together with some very thoughtful extras. More compact rooms in annexe cottages are also available for self catering, and each has a kitchen; all the rooms have modern en suite bathrooms. The comfortable drawing room opens on to the gardens, and there is a cosy sitting room with a piano. Breakfast is served in the attractive dining room, and snacks and suppers can be served in rooms by arrangement. Standards here are particularly high and very worthy of our selected award.
3⇌ Annexe 6⇌ (1fb) CTV in 5 bedrooms ® T sB&B⇌£35-£42 dB&B⇌£52-£58 LDO 2pm
CTV 15P 2
Credit Cards 1 3
See advertisement under WARWICK

SHREWSBURY Shropshire Map **07** SJ41

GH Q ***Cannock House Private Hotel*** 182 Abbey Foregate SY2 6AH ☎(0743) 356043
Closed Xmas
A small, modest guesthouse situated on the main road close to the town centre, opposite the Abbey. The accommodation is well maintained, and private parking is available.
7hc (1fb)
CTV 5P

GH QQQ Fieldside 38 London Rd SY2 5NX ☎(0743) 353143
Closed 18 Dec-18 Jan
This large, beautifully maintained and fully modernised Victorian house stands on the A5112, close to the Lord Hill column, east of the town centre. The bedrooms are attractively furnished and well equipped, many with private bathrooms. Smoking is not permitted.
9rm(6 3hc) in all bedrooms CTV in all bedrooms ® sB&B£18-£20 sB&B£28-£30 dB&B£40-£42
Lic 10P 2 nc9yrs
Credit Cards 1 2 3

GH QQ ***Restawhile*** 36 Coton Crescent SY1 2NZ
☎(0743) 240969
A fully modernised terraced house with a friendly family atmosphere. All the bedrooms have private bathrooms and are well equipped. It is found off the A528 Ellesmere road out of the town centre.
4⇌ CTV in all bedrooms ® LDO 6pm
CTV nc11yrs

GH QQ Roseville 12 Berwick Rd SY1 2LN ☎(0743) 236470
Just off the A528 a few minutes' walk from the town centre, this late- Victorian town house is run by Carol and Norman Stening-Rees who extend a warm welcome to their home. Three sparkling pine-furnished bedrooms are available, 2 with modern en suite showers and the third with a private bathroom. The sitting room and breakfast room are combined, modern and comfortable, and guests usually have breakfast together. There are several attractively tiled original fireplaces in the house, which is completely no smoking.
3rm(2 1hc) in all bedrooms sB&B£15.50-£17 dB&B£34-£39
CTV 3P nc12yrs

GH QQQ Sandford House Hotel St Julians Friars SY1 1XL ☎(0743) 343829
A small hotel close to English bridge and river walks, located on a narrow road off the main route into the town centre. There is no parking at the hotel, but there is a public car park nearby. The elegant lounge overlooks a well tended rear garden, and the owners make every effort to ensure a pleasant stay.
10rm(5⇨🚿5hc) (2fb) CTV in all bedrooms ® ✱ sB&Bfr£22.50 sB&B⇨🚿fr£29 dB&Bfr£37 dB&B⇨🚿fr£44
Lic 🍴 CTV 3P
Credit Cards [1] [3] £

GH QQQ Sydney House Hotel Coton Crescent, Coton Hill SY1 2LJ ☎(0743) 354681
Closed 24-30 Dec
A smart, friendly and well run Victorian house with facilities that benefit both the tourist and the business person. It is situated on the northern edge of town, just off the A528 to Ellesmere.
7rm(4🚿3hc) (1fb) CTV in all bedrooms ® T 🐕 (ex guide dogs) ✱ sB&Bfr£32 sB&B🚿£32-£42 dB&B£40 dB&B🚿£54 WB&B£130-£270 WBDi£193-£325 LDO 8.30pm
Lic 🍴 7P
Credit Cards [1] [2] [3] £

GH QQQ Tudor House 2 Fish St SY1 1UR ☎(0743) 351735
Closed Xmas
As the name suggests, this delightful little house dates back to 1460. Although recently extensively renovated by the present owners, it has lost none of its original charm and character, which is enchanced by timber-framed walls and exposed ceiling beams. It provides cosy, well maintained accommodation which is complemented by friendly hospitablity and personal service. The town centre location ensures its popularity with tourists and overseas visitors.

→

3rm(2⌐1hc) CTV in all bedrooms ✗ ✱ sB&B£25-£32 sB&B⌐£30-£32 dB&B£37 dB&B⌐£40-£42 WB&B£150-£210 Lic ♨ CTV Ⓔ

FH QQ Mrs P A Roberts ***The Day House*** *(SJ465104)* Nobold SY5 8NL (2.5m SW between A488 & A49) ☎(0743) 860212

Closed Xmas & New Year

A large farmhouse with spacious public rooms and bedrooms just 2 miles southwest of Shrewsbury town centre in the village of Nobold. To find the farm turn off the A49 into Longden Road (signed to Nuffield Hospital), continue along this road until you see the bed and breakfast sign on a T-junction, then follow the private drive through farmland.

3rm(1⇌1⌐1hc) (3fb) CTV in all bedrooms Ⓡ ✗ (ex guide dogs) ♨ CTV 10P 1🚗 ⌐ rough & game shooting 400 acres arable dairy

FH QQ Mrs J M Jones **Grove** *(SJ537249)* Preston Brockhurst SY4 5QA ☎Clive(093928) 223

Closed Xmas & New Year

A large 17th-century farmhouse with Victorian additions, situated in the village of Preston Brockhurst on the A49, 6 miles north of Shrewsbury. Accommodation is well maintained and traditional, with rural views at the rear of the house, overlooking the attractive garden.

3hc (1fb)⊬in all bedrooms CTV in 1 bedroom Ⓡ ✗ (ex guide dogs) ✱ sB&Bfr£14 dB&Bfr£34 ♨ CTV 4P 320 acres arable mixed

SIDMOUTH Devon Map 03 SY18

GH QQQ ***Canterbury*** Salcombe Rd EX10 8PR ☎(0395) 513373

Mar-Nov

A period house in a residential area close to the river and park, and only a short walk from the town centre and sea front. The bedrooms are well appointed and many have good en suite facilities. The resident proprietors provide a set home-cooked dinner.

8rm(7⇌⌐1hc) (4fb) CTV in all bedrooms Ⓡ LDO 4.30pm Lic CTV 6P

GH QQ ***Mariners*** 69 Sidford High St EX10 9SH ☎(0395) 515876

Closed Nov & Dec

The family home of the resident proprietors, set in well kept grounds in the small village of Sidford, just 1.5 miles from the seafront. The bedrooms are modern and brightly decorated and the lounge cosy. Evening meals are available in the relaxed atmosphere of the dining room.

8⌐ (2fb) CTV in all bedrooms Ⓡ LDO 10am ♨ CTV 8P

GH QQQ The Old Farmhouse Hillside Rd EX10 8JG ☎(0395) 512284

Closed Dec & Jan

An attractive thatched 16th-century farmhouse in a residential area of the town, within easy walking distance of the shops and esplanade. Owners Anne and Peter Williams are totally involved in the day-to-day running of the guesthouse. The dinner menu, cooked by Anne, offers a choice at each course and features home-made soups and pâtés and lovely old-fashioned puddings. The bedrooms have pretty décor: some rooms are in a small cottage approached across the colourful sun-trap patio area; smoking is not permitted in the rooms. This small, family-run hotel also benefits from an abundance of character and charm, with beams and low doorways.

3hc Annexe 4rm(2⇌1⌐1hc) (2fb) Ⓡ ✱ sB&B£18-£23 sB&B⇌⌐£21-£23 dB&B£36-£38 dB&B⇌⌐£42-£46 WB&B£135-£146 WBDi£162-£209 Lic ♨ CTV 4P

GH Q Ryton House 52-54 Winslade Rd EX10 9EX ☎(0395) 513981

This semidetached house is quietly situated in a residential area away from the town centre, one mile from the sea, but still within easy reach of all local amenities. Bedrooms are well maintained, simply appointed, bright and clean, and a set traditional menu is served nightly in the informal dining room, where smoking is not permitted. The resident proprietors Mary and Vic Williams offer a warm, friendly welcome.

9rm(3⌐6hc) (3fb) Ⓡ ✱ sB&B£14.50-£18 dB&B£28-£34 dB&B⌐£30-£36 WB&B£105-£120 WBDi£135-£170 LDO 4.30pm Lic ♨ CTV 9P Ⓔ

SILLOTH Cumbria Map 11 NY15

GH QQ Nith View 1 Pine Ter CA5 4DT ☎(06973) 31542

Set in a wide cobbled street overlooking the Solway Firth, this guesthouse has friendly and attentive service provided by Mr and Mrs Story. Rooms are pleasantly furnished, 5 are en suite. A small bar, pleasant rear dining room and cosy lounge complete the package.

8rm(5⌐3hc) (4fb) CTV in 5 bedrooms Ⓡ ✱ sB&B£16 sB&B⌐£18-£20 dB&B£28 dB&B⌐£32 WB&B£107 WBDi£157 LDO 2pm Lic ♨ CTV 8P 1🚗 Credit Cards 1 2 3 Ⓔ

SIMONSBATH Somerset Map 03 SS73

FH QQQ Mrs A R Brown **Emmett Grange** *(SS753369)* TA24 7LD (2.5m SW unclass towards Brayford) ☎Exford(064383) 282

Mar-Oct

A large Victorian farmhouse approached by an attractive drive situated in unspoilt moorland within Exmoor National Park, with superb views. Bedrooms are comfortable and well equipped, complete with TV and hairdryers. Guests return regularly for the owner's cooking, which comprises 4-course dinners using local produce, and hearty breakfasts. Self-catering cottages are also available.

4rm(2⇌2hc) CTV in all bedrooms Ⓡ ✱ sB&B£20 sB&B⇌£23 dB&B£40 dB&B⇌£46 WB&B£121-£141 WBDi£200-£220 LDO 6.30pm Lic ♨ 6P stabling for guests own hoses 1200 acres hill stock Ⓔ

SITTINGBOURNE Kent Map 05 TR96

SELECTED

GH QQQQ Hempstead House London Rd, Bapchild ME9 9PP ☎(0795) 428020

A Victorian family house situated on the A2 road between Sittingbourne and Canterbury, set well back in 3 acres of attractive gardens and surrounded by beautiful countryside. The 2 bedrooms suites have dressing areas and private bathrooms, and are spacious and comfortable. The spacious public areas include a formal dining room, comfortable drawing room, conservatory and small sitting room with TV, together with a vast kitchen where breakfast is served. Much of the food is home grown or locally produced, and kept simple to show off its freshness; there is a genuinely friendly atmosphere, and guests can dine with the family if desired: the hospitality shown by the Holdstock family is exceptional.

2⇌⌐ (1fb)⊬in all bedrooms CTV in all bedrooms Ⓡ ✱ sB&B⇌⌐£50 dB&B⇌⌐£56 WB&B£177 WBDi£282 ♨ CTV 20P ⛬ ⌂(heated)

Q is for quality. For a full explanation of this AA quality award, consult the Contents page.

SKEGNESS Lincolnshire Map **09** TF56

GH Q Abbey Hotel North Pde PE25 2UB ☎(0754) 763677
Closed Jan-Feb

Located opposite the miniature golf on the North Parade, this interesting guesthouse offers public areas that are themed, with many items of chapel furniture carefully incorporated into the décor and furnishings, such as a pulpit, communion rail and a few pews. The lounge bar, with its open log fire and shaped bar and windows, proves quite a talking point. The dining room is more sober in comparison, with light décor and polished wooden tables, plus a few brasses, plates and ornaments displayed on the walls. A set-price menu features home cooking and is excellent value for money. A small room with a pool table and darts is available for guests' use. The bedrooms come in various sizes and styles consisting of 5 grades of room, from floral-decorated rooms with pine furniture at the front of the house, to the rear-facing, more compact bedrooms and the majority have en suite shower or bathrooms.

24rm(6⇌14⇒4hc) (12fb) CTV in all bedrooms ® ✱ sB&B£15-£18 sB&B⇌⇒£21-£25 dB&B£35 dB&B⇌⇒£35-£40 WB&B£115-£150 WBDi£128-£165

Lic lift ☖ CTV 8P sauna solarium pool table rowing machine
Credit Cards 1 3 £

See advertisement on page 365

GH QQ Crawford Hotel South Pde PE25 3HR
☎(0754) 764215

Situated south of the town centre on the seafront, the Crawford has a particularly high level of cleanliness and hospitality. The varied range of facilities and public areas attracts the holiday maker and the commercial visitor.

20rm(10⇌7⇒3hc) (8fb) CTV in all bedrooms ® ✗ ✱ sB&B⇌⇒fr£27.03 dB&Bfr£44.66 dB&B⇌⇒fr£44.66 WBDifr£184.48 LDO 5pm

Lic lift ☖ CTV ✗P ⊠(heated) sauna jacuzzi games room
Credit Cards 1 3

GH QQ Northdale 12 Firbeck Av PE25 3JY ☎(0754) 610554
South of the town and 2 blocks from the seafront, this nicely maintained guesthouse continually improves its comfort and facilities, and is an ideal place for those seeking a quiet relaxing stay. Good en suite facilities are provided.
12rm(2⇌5↱5hc) (3fb) CTV in 1 bedroom TV in 11 bedrooms
® WBDi£90-£117 LDO 5.30pm
Lic 卌 CTV 8P Ⓔ

SKIPTON North Yorkshire Map **07** SD95

GH QQ Craven House 56 Keighley Rd BD23 2NB
☎(0756) 794657
Closed 24-31 Dec
This double-fronted Victorian end-terrace house is situated on the A629, just on the edge of the town towards Keighley, and provides comfortable accommodation in its traditional and individually styled bedrooms. Rooms at the front are double glazed and have views of the nearby hills. Tables in the bay-windowed dining room are attractively clothed and pictures of farming scenes adorn the walls. There is no lounge, but it is a friendly family-run establishment in a good location for visiting the Yorkshire Dales or shopping in the interesting market town of Skipton.
7rm(2⇌1↱4hc) CTV in all bedrooms ® sB&Bfr£16
sB&B⇌↱£20-£22 dB&B£30-£32 dB&B⇌↱£34-£38
Lic 卌 3P Ⓔ

GH QQ Highfield Hotel 58 Keighley Rd BD23 2NB
☎(0756) 793182
Closed 28 Dec-1 Feb rs 24-30 Dec
This small hotel is situated on the A629 within easy walking distance of the town centre and bus and railway stations. It offers well equipped, nicely appointed bedrooms with private bathrooms, a cosy lounge with bar facilities, and an attractive dining room where dinner and breakfast are served.
10rm(3⇌6↱1hc) (2fb) CTV in all bedrooms ® sB&B£18.50-£19.50 sB&B⇌↱£28-£30 dB&B£37-£39 dB&B⇌↱£37-£39
LDO 8pm
Lic 卌 CTV P̸
Credit Cards 1 3 Ⓔ

INN Q *Red Lion Hotel* High St BD23 1DT (Whitbread)
☎(0756) 790718
Built in 1205, this High Street inn is said to be one of the oldest buildings in Skipton. Recent upgrading of the bars has made it a popular venue for tasty bar food. Upstairs the 3 bedrooms provide comfortable accommodation with private bathrooms. During the winter months, bar meals are only served at lunch time, and residents are offered bed and breakfast accommodation only.
3⇌↱ (1fb) CTV in all bedrooms ® ✗
卌 4P
Credit Cards 1 3

SKYE, ISLE OF Highland *Inverness-shire* Map **13**

DUNVEGAN Map **13** NG24

GH QQ Roskhill Roskhill IV55 8ZD (3m S A863)
☎(047022) 317
Quietly situated 2 miles south of the village, this small friendly family-run licensed guesthouse is an ideal base for the touring holidaymaker. It has a cosy lounge and an attractive stone-walled dining room. Smoking is not permitted in the dining room or bedrooms, which are compact in size.
5rm(3↱2hc) (2fb)⚟in all bedrooms ® dB&B£30-£34
dB&B↱£35-£40 WB&B£115-£122 WBDi£170-£184 LDO 4pm
Lic 卌 CTV 6P
Credit Cards 1 3

PORTREE Map **13** NG44

GH Q Bosville Hotel Bosville Ter IV51 9DG ☎(0478) 2846
FAX (0478) 3434
Closed Jan-Feb
Situated just north of the town centre, this family-run hotel offers practical, good value accommodation. Bedrooms are generally compact and functional, and downstairs there is a combined restaurant and tea room which is open to non-residents.
16rm(10↱6hc) Annexe 3↱ CTV in all bedrooms ® sB&B£22-£27 sB&B↱£27 dB&B£40-£54 dB&B↱£54 WB&B£140-£175
WBDi£195-£245 LDO 8pm
Lic 卌 CTV 10P
Credit Cards 1 3

GH QQQ Craiglockhart Beaumont Crescent IV51 9DF
☎(0478) 2233
Closed Dec
Situated on the waterfront overlooking the picturesque bay and harbour, these 2 adjoining houses enjoy fine views over to the Isle of Raasay. Bedrooms are comfortably furnished and well equipped. Hearty breakfasts are served at shared tables in the neat breakfast room.
10rm(3↱7hc) CTV in 9 bedrooms ® ✗ ✱ sB&B£15-£16
dB&B£32-£36 dB&B↱£36-£40
卌 CTV 4P

GH QQQ Quiraing Viewfield Rd IV51 9ES ☎(0478) 2870
Good value bed and breakfast accommodation is offered at this comfortable and well maintained modern bungalow which is situated beside the main road on the southern outskirts of the town, close to the centre. All the rooms have TV, and each bedroom has its own dining table allocated.
6rm(4↱2hc) (2fb)⚟in all bedrooms CTV in all bedrooms ®
✗ (ex guide dogs) ✱ sB&B£14-£16 dB&B£28-£30 dB&B↱£32-£36
卌 CTV 8P

SLAIDBURN Lancashire Map **07** SD75

SELECTED

GH QQQQ Parrock Head Farm House Hotel
Woodhouse Ln BB7 3AH ☎(02006) 614
Previously a 17th-century 'long' farmhouse, this delightful small hotel is set in open countryside with cattle and sheep in the surrounding fields. There are 3 beautifully furnished bedrooms in the old house, with the remainder in garden cottages, and all have every modern facility. The cottages are furnished mainly in pine with attractive coordinating fabrics, and the rooms in the house are more sumptuous in style. A first-floor lounge, furnished with soft armchairs and settees, features antiques, paintings and a large stone fireplace. The timbered library is full of interesting aspects, along with lots of books and the downstairs, beamed bar/reception lounge provides a relaxed setting for pre-dinner drinks. A daily-changing, English à la carte menu is offered in the elegant dining room, that was once the milking parlour, and Vicky and Richard Umbers are justifiably proud of the high standard of cuisine achieved here.
3⇌↱ Annexe 6⇌↱ (1fb) CTV in all bedrooms ® **T** ✱
sB&B⇌↱£37.50-£39.50 dB&B⇌↱£55-£62 LDO 8.30pm
Lic 卌 20P
Credit Cards 1 2 3 Ⓔ

'Selected' establishments, which have the highest quality award, are highlighted by a tinted panel. For a full list of these establishments, consult the Contents page.

SLEAFORD Lincolnshire Map **08** TF04

See also Aswarby

INN QQ ***Carre Arms Hotel*** Mareham Ln NG34 7JP ☎(0529) 303156

A large Victorian coaching inn situated half a mile from the town centre, close to the railway station. It has been refurbished to a good standard to offer well equipped bedrooms and spacious comfortable public areas which include an á la carte restaurant.

14rm(3⇌11hc) CTV in all bedrooms ® LDO 9pm

CTV 50P

Credit Cards 1 3

SLEDMERE Humberside Map **08** SE96

INN Q **Triton** YO25 0XQ ☎Driffield(0377) 86644

This 18th-century inn, with its cream-washed walls, nestles in the picturesque wolds, and while simple is fastidiously clean and well kept. The bar is oak panelled with a warm open fire and offers hand-pumped real ales and interesting bar meals, hence it is very popular with the locals. There is a separate dining room with deep brown dralon banquettes and light pink flock wallpaper. The bedroom furniture is solid, with floral duvets, plain carpets and light wallpaper – gradually fabrics are being coordinated more fashionably.

7rm(3⇌2🚿2hc) (1fb) CTV in all bedrooms ® LDO 9pm

CTV 30P

Credit Cards 1 3 5

SLOUGH Berkshire Map **04** SU97

GH QQ ***Colnbrook Lodge*** Bath Rd, Colnbrook SL3 0NZ (3m E A4) ☎(0753) 685958

Closed 24-25 Dec

A detached house on the edge of the village of Colnbrook, with easy access to Heathrow and motorways. Bedrooms are comfortable and well equipped, with double glazing to help combat the air-traffic noise. There is a TV lounge, and breakfast is served in the informal dining room.

8rm(3⇌🚿5hc) (2fb) CTV in all bedrooms ®

(ex guide dogs) LDO 7pm

Lic CTV 12P

Credit Cards 1 3

SOLIHULL West Midlands Map **07** SP17

GH QQ **The White House Hotel** 104 Olton Rd, Shirley B90 3NN ☎021-745 3558

A small, family-run hotel conveniently situated close to the A34 in the suburbs of Solihull. Rooms can be compact, but are popular with commercial visitors. Breakfast is served in the cosy dining room, and car parking is available at the front.

8rm(4🚿4hc) CTV in all bedrooms ® (ex guide dogs) *
sB&Bfr£22 sB&B🚿fr£36 dB&Bfr£42 dB&B🚿fr£52

5P

Credit Cards 1 2 3 £

SOLVA Dyfed Map **02** SM82

See also Llandeloy

SELECTED

FH QQQQ Mrs M Jones **Lochmeyler** *(SM855275)* SA62 6LL (4m N on unclass rd) ☎Croesgoch(0348) 837724

A 16th-century farmhouse set in 220 acres of a busy dairy farm. Six miles from St Davids, near the little hamlet of Llandeloy, it provides farm trails, duck ponds and an abundance of wildlife. Bedrooms are large, comfortably furnished and contain every modern facility including videos and free films. Two relaxing lounges are available, and good home cooking is provided by the very hospitable Mrs Jones.

6⇌ (5fb) in all bedrooms CTV in all bedrooms ®
WB&B£140 WBDi£185 LDO 6pm

→

Lic 🍽 CTV P nc10yrs 220 acres dairy
Credit Cards [1] [3]

SOMERTON Somerset Map **03** ST42

GH QQQ Church Farm Compton Dandon TA11 6PE
☎(0458) 72927
Closed 20 Dec-7 Jan
Quietly located in a rural village setting, this delightful cottage offers comfortably furnished, nicely presented bedrooms; most of which are in the old stable block annexe. The breakfast room is bright and sunny and a substantial breakfast is served, complete with home-made marmalade. An evening meal is available on request, by prior arrangement. The conscientious, caring resident proprietors ensure guests have a comfortable stay.
1⇌ Annexe 5⇌ (2fb) CTV in all bedrooms ®
sB&B⇌£20 dB&B⇌£35 LDO 10am
Lic 🍽 6P nc5yrs

SELECTED

GH QQQQ The Lynch Country House 4 Behind Berry TA11 7PD ☎(0458) 72316
This delightful Grade II listed property, is set in its own very pretty garden, complete with ornamental lake and black swans. The house is beautifully presented with excellent housekeeping standards, and a very friendly, warm atmosphere is created by host Mr Copeland and his small team of attentive staff. Both bedrooms and public areas are very prettily decorated, furnished with quality and comfort in mind, with many thoughtful extras provided such as bathrobes, mineral water and magazines, plus all the bedrooms have excellent en suite facilities. A hearty breakfast is the only meal available, which is served at one end of an elegant room, at the other end of which is a small sitting area, comfortably appointed and filled with books. For the more independent, there are 2 equally pleasing, self-catering cottages located in the courtyard.
5⇌ CTV in all bedrooms ® **T** ✱ sB&B⇌£35-£50 dB&B⇌£45-£75
Lic 🍽 15P
Credit Cards [1] [3] £

SOUTHAMPTON Hampshire Map **04** SU41

See **Town Plan Section**

GH QQ Banister House Hotel Banister Rd SO1 2JJ
☎(0703) 221279
Closed 25-27 Dec
Family run and well established, this extended Victorian building is in a residential area just off the Avenue. All the bedrooms are on the ground or first floor, and downstairs there is a combined bar and dining room with polished wood tables.
23rm(11⇌12hc) (3fb) CTV in all bedrooms ® **T**
sB&B£21.50-£24.50 sB&B⇌£25.50-£27.50 dB&Bfr£30.50 dB&B⇌£34.50-£36 LDO 7.45pm
Lic 🍽 14P
Credit Cards [1] [2] [3] £

GH QQ Capri 52 Archers Rd SO1 2LU ☎(0703) 632800
This detached Victorian property is centrally positioned for all amenities, and, despite refurbishment, it still enjoys some period features including stained-glass windows, several fine pieces of furniture and many pictures. The comfortable bedrooms vary in size but are decorated with imagination. The dining room is small but there are plans to extend it. Ample car parking space is available around landscaped gardens.
14rm(10⇌4hc) (2fb) CTV in all bedrooms ® **T** ✗ ✱ sB&B£17-£18 sB&B⇌£17-£18 dB&B£34 dB&B⇌£34 LDO 1pm
Lic 🍽 CTV 14P nc2yrs
Credit Cards [1] [3] £

GH QQ *Edgecombe House* 188 Regents Park Rd, Shirley SO1 3NY ☎(0703) 773760
13rm(5⇌8hc) (1fb) CTV in all bedrooms ® ✗ (ex guide dogs) LDO 7pm
Lic 🍽 CTV 14P
Credit Cards [1] [2] [3]

GH QQQ Hunters Lodge Hotel 25 Landguard Rd, Shirley SO1 5DL ☎(0703) 227919 FAX (0703) 230913
Closed 17 Dec-7 Jan
This canopied and double-fronted hotel offers comfortable rooms and a spacious lounge with a small bar at one end. The dedicated, well established owners, Steve and Veronica Dugdale, are committed to continual improvement.
18rm(8⇌4⇌6hc) (2fb)⊬in 1 bedroom CTV in all bedrooms ® **T** sB&B£20-£23.50 sB&B⇌£25-£33.49 dB&B£40-£44.06 dB&B⇌£40-£52.29 WB&Bfr£164.50 WBDifr£205 LDO 6pm
Lic 🍽 CTV 16P 4🚘 (75p per night)
Credit Cards [1] [2] [3]

GH QQ Landguard Lodge 21 Landguard Rd SO1 5DL
☎(0703) 636904
This quietly located semidetached property lies in a residential area. Recent improvements include new en suite bathrooms, and high standards of housekeeping are very apparent. The cheerful bedrooms are simple and vary in size, but are well equipped.
13rm(4⇌9hc) (1fb) CTV in all bedrooms ® ✗ (ex guide dogs) ✱ sB&B£15 sB&B⇌£17.50 dB&B£28 dB&B⇌£30 WB&B£90 WBDi£120 LDO 9am
🍽 CTV 4P nc5yrs
Credit Cards [1] [2] [3] £

GH QQ Linden 51-53 The Polygon SO1 2BP ☎(0703) 225653
Closed Xmas
Tricia and David Hutchins have run their double-fronted bed and breakfast establishment, in a residential street, for 20 years. They offer bright bedrooms, good housekeeping and a cheerful smile.
12hc (4fb) CTV in all bedrooms ® ✗ ✱ sB&B£13-£14.50 dB&B£26-£29 WB&B£91-£101.50
🍽 CTV 7P £

GH QQ Lodge 1 Winn Rd, The Avenue SO2 1EH
☎(0703) 557537
Closed 23 Dec-1 Jan
This Tudor-style detached house is in a quiet residential street on the outskirts of the city centre. It offers simple accommodation at competitive prices and is popular with students and business people. Bedrooms vary in size but they are all well equipped with modern facilities. There is a small bar, comfortable lounge, and evening meals cooked by the proprietor are served in the dining room.
14rm(2⇌5⇌7hc) (2fb) CTV in all bedrooms ® ✱
sB&Bfr£22.50 sB&B⇌fr£30.50 dB&Bfr£36 dB&B⇌fr£42.50 LDO 9pm
Lic 🍽 CTV 10P
Credit Cards [1] [3] £

GH Q Madison House 137 Hill Ln SO1 5AF ☎(0703) 333374 FAX (0703) 772264
rs 23 Dec-2 Jan
This cosy, simple detached house is set in a busy residential area with easy access to the city centre and docks. Bedrooms are all on the first floor, and there is a piano in the lounge.
9rm(3⇌6hc) (2fb) CTV in all bedrooms ® ✗ ✱ sB&B£13.95-£15.50 sB&B⇌£16-£19 dB&B£25.50-£28 dB&B⇌£29.90-£34.50 WB&B£89.25-£105
🍽 CTV 7P
Credit Cards [1] [3] £

SOUTHEND-ON-SEA Essex Map **05** TQ88

GH QQ Argyle Hotel 12 Clifftown Pde SS1 1DP
☎(0702) 339483
Closed Xmas
A small, comfortable hotel situated in an ideal position overlooking the bandstand and seafront, within walking distance of the town. The accommodation is simple, clean and comfortable.
11hc (3fb) CTV in all bedrooms ® ✗ ✱ sB&B£17-£20 dB&B£34-£40
Lic ♨ CTV P̸ nc5yrs £

GH QQQ *Cobham Lodge Hotel* 2 Cobham Rd, Westcliff On Sea SS0 8EA ☎(0702) 346438
A substantial and attractive guesthouse located in a peaceful residential area a few minutes' walk from the sea. Accommodation is clean, well equipped and comfortable, and public rooms include a choice of lounges, a well stocked bar and a large dining room providing a table d'hôte menu.
30rm(9⇌13↱8hc) (3fb) CTV in all bedrooms ® ✗ LDO 7pm
Lic ♨ CTV P̸ snooker
Credit Cards 1 3 5

GH QQ Marine View 4 Trinity Av, Westcliff on Sea SS0 7PU
☎(0702) 344104
Conveniently situated for both the seafront and town centre, this Edwardian terraced house is run by welcoming proprietors Mr and Mrs Miller. Bedrooms are simply furnished and freshly decorated, and there is a small lounge adjoining the dining room.
6hc (1fb) CTV in all bedrooms ® ✗ (ex guide dogs) ✱ sB&B£15-£17.50 dB&B£28-£32.50 WB&B£85-£98
♨ CTV P̸ nc3yrs

GH QQ Mayflower Hotel 5-6 Royal Ter SS1 1DY
☎(0702) 340489
Closed Xmas
This Grade II Regency house is part of the Royal terrace, and in summer the wrought-iron balconies are festooned with wonderful flowers by the charming proprietors. Bedrooms are on 4 floors, simply furnished, clean and well maintained. The front rooms have sea views, as does the lounge which also offers a pool table.
23rm(4↱19hc) (3fb) CTV in all bedrooms ® ✱ sB&Bfr£21 sB&B↱fr£28 dB&Bfr£32 dB&B↱fr£40
♨ CTV 2P pool table

GH QQ *Terrace Hotel* 8 Royal Ter SS1 1DY ☎(0702) 348143
A most attractive villa-style house built around the end of the 18th century. Situated above the cliff, some bedrooms have excellent sea views, and the accommodation is clean and comfortable.
9rm(3↱6hc) (3fb) CTV in all bedrooms ®
Lic ♨ P̸ nc5yrs

GH QQQ Tower Hotel 146 Alexandra Rd SS1 1HE
☎(0702) 348635 FAX (0702) 433044
Built in 1901, this attractive hotel is situated in the conservation area, not far from the seafront. The bedrooms in the main building and the adjacent annexe are furnished in the modern style with unit furniture – all are en suite and are equipped very adequately, but some are rather compact. There is a smart Victorian style lounge bar on the ground floor and the basement restaurant 'Basils' offers a short table d'hôte menu in elegant surroundings.
16rm(14⇌↱2hc) Annexe 17rm(4⇌13↱) (6fb) CTV in all bedrooms ® **T** sB&B£30-£35 sB&B⇌↱£33-£45 dB&B⇌↱£40-£55 LDO 9pm
Lic ♨ CTV 2P residents membership of nearby sports club
Credit Cards 1 2 3 5 £

Every effort is made to provide accurate information, but details can change after we go to print. It is advisable to check prices etc. before you make a firm booking.

SOUTHPORT Merseyside Map **07** SD31

See **Town Plan Section**

GH QQQ Ambassador Private Hotel 13 Bath St PR9 0DP
☎(0704) 543998 & 530459 FAX (0704) 536269
Closed 20 Dec-7 Jan
Occupying a central position, adjacent to Lord Street and close to the promenade, a warm welcome and high standards await you at this long-established, small private hotel. The en suite bedrooms vary in size but all are tastefully furnished and thoughtfully equipped. There is a cosy bar, where snacks are available and a dining room where guests can choose between English or Continental breakfast. A quiet, first-floor lounge provides peaceful relaxation.
8↱ (4fb)⊬in 4 bedrooms CTV in all bedrooms ® ✱ sB&B↱£29-£30 dB&B↱£46 WB&B£140 WBDi£180
LDO 7pm
Lic ♨ 6P nc5yrs
Credit Cards 1 3 £

GH QQ *Fairway Private Hotel* 106 Leyland Rd PR9 0JQ
☎(0704) 542069
Mar-Nov
Situated in a peaceful residential area close to the Municipal Golf Course, this privately owned, small hotel offers traditionally furnished bedrooms and comfortable public rooms including a small lounge bar.
9rm(4↱5hc) (4fb) CTV in 8 bedrooms ® ✗ (ex guide dogs)
LDO 6pm
Lic CTV 10P

GH QQQ *The Gables Private Hotel* 110 Leyland Rd PR9 0JE
☎(0704) 535554
Apr-Oct

→

Quietly situated off the Northern Promenade, this pleasantly appointed and well maintained guesthouse offers comfortable accommodation for a relaxing holiday with good home cooking being served in the charming dining room.
9rm(2⇌6⮣1hc) CTV in all bedrooms ® ✗ LDO 3pm
Lic ⁂ CTV 9P nc12yrs

GH Q *Lake Hotel* 55-56 The Promenade PR9 0DY
☎(0704) 530996
Situated on the promenade close to the theatre and Floral Hall, this privately owned, pink and white painted guesthouse offers a comfortable lounge, small bar and neat dining room. Bedrooms, although equipped with facilities such as telephones, are simply decorated and furnished.
20⮣ (5fb) CTV in all bedrooms ® LDO 4.30pm
Lic ⁂ CTV 14P
Credit Cards [3]

GH Q Lyndhurst 101 King St PR8 1LQ ☎(0704) 537520
This terraced property is situated in a side street close to the town centre, and offers modestly appointed and compact accommodation.
7hc CTV in all bedrooms ® ✗ (ex guide dogs) * sB&B£14 dB&B£28 WB&B£91 WBDi£124 LDO noon
Lic ⁂ CTV 2P nc5yrs

GH QQQ Oakwood Private Hotel 7 Portland St PR8 1LJ
☎(0704) 531858
Etr-Nov
This friendly, long-established guesthouse is conveniently situated close to the centre of town and offers well maintained and comfortable accommodation which is appreciated by the more mature holidaymaker.
7rm(4⮣3hc) ⊬in all bedrooms CTV in all bedrooms ® ✗ *
sB&Bfr£21 dB&B⮣fr£42 WBDifr£165
Lic ⁂ CTV 8P nc5yrs

GH QQ Rosedale Hotel 11 Talbot St PR8 1HP
☎(0704) 530604
This friendly, family-run guesthouse, close to the town centre, has compact and modestly furnished bedrooms, but a comfortable lounge and a small bar in which to relax.
10rm(7⮣3hc) (2fb) CTV in all bedrooms ® ✗ (ex guide dogs)
* sB&B£19-£21 sB&B⮣£21.50-£25 dB&B£38-£42
dB&B⮣£43-£50 LDO 4pm
Lic ⁂ 8P

GH QQQ Sunningdale Hotel 85 Leyland Rd PR9 0NJ
☎(0704) 538673
Situated in a quiet residential area at the northern end of the town centre, this detached Victorian hotel is personally run and offers generally spacious accommodation attracting both business and leisure guests. Bedrooms are comfortably furnished, mostly in modern style, and are neatly maintained, as is the rest of the house. There is a roomy lounge bar with a pool table and darts, and a separate lounge for those seeking quieter surroundings.
14rm(1⇌11⮣2hc) (4fb) CTV in all bedrooms ® T sB&B£18
sB&B⇌⮣£20 dB&B£38 dB&B⇌⮣£38 WB&B£119-£133
WBDi£161-£175 LDO 4.30pm
Lic ⁂ CTV 10P half size snooker table dart board
Credit Cards [1] [3]

GH QQ The White Lodge Private Hotel 12 Talbot St PR8 1HP
☎(0704) 536320
A long-established, family-run guesthouse situated close to the town centre and offering pleasant, fresh accommodation. Bedrooms are fairly compact but well maintained, as are the attractive and comfortable public areas.
9rm(1⇌4⮣4hc) (3fb) CTV in 4 bedrooms ®
✗ (ex guide dogs) sB&B£16-£22 sB&B⇌⮣£18-£25 dB&B£32-£44 dB&B⇌⮣£36-£50 WB&B£90-£130 WBDi£110-£160
LDO 6pm
Lic CTV 6P £

GH QQ Windsor Lodge Hotel 37 Saunders St PR9 0HJ
☎(0704) 530070
Young owners create a friendly atmosphere at this detached guesthouse situated close to the promenade and marine lake. While bedrooms are modestly furnished, there is a pleasant lounge and dining room in addition to a basement bar and games room.
12rm(3⇌⮣9hc) (1fb) CTV in all bedrooms ®
✗ (ex guide dogs) * sB&B£15.50 sB&B⇌⮣£17.50 dB&B£31
dB&B⇌⮣£35 LDO noon
Lic ⁂ CTV 9P pool table £

INN QQ *The Herald Hotel* 16 Portland St PR8 1LT
☎(0704) 534424
Located close to the town centre, this friendly public house is attractively decorated and offers a sound standard of bedroom accommodation. Rooms without en suite facilities have shower cabinets.
12rm(4⮣8hc) (1fb) CTV in all bedrooms ® LDO 8pm
⁂ 25P

SOUTHSEA Hampshire

See **Portsmouth & Southsea**

SOUTH SHIELDS Tyne & Wear Map **12** NZ36

GH Q Walkerville 125 Ocean Rd NE33 2JL ☎(091456) 5931
This end-of-terrace house is close to the seafront, parks and amusements, and provides friendly service and modest but neat accommodation.
8hc (4fb) CTV in all bedrooms ® * sB&B£16-£18 dB&Bfr£28
⁂

SOUTHWOLD Suffolk Map **05** TM57

INN QQ Kings Head Hotel 23/25 High St IP18 6AD
☎(0502) 723829
This attractive inn of white and red brick dates from the 17th century, and is now furnished in Victorian style with an open-plan lounge bar and cheery fires. Bedrooms, across the road, are spacious and furnished with antiques. Bar meals, offered from a blackboard menu, are freshly prepared and of good quality, ranging from fresh fish to pheasant. Mr and Mrs Atkins are friendly and enthusiastic proprietors.
Annexe 3⇌⮣ CTV in all bedrooms ® LDO 9.30pm
⁂
Credit Cards [3] £

SOUTH ZEAL Devon Map **02** SX69

GH QQQ Poltimore EX20 2PD ☎Okehampton(0837) 840209
A peacefully situated cottage offering character accommodation with easy access to the A30. Bedrooms are compact but clean and comfortable, and there are 2 lounges with exposed timbers and feature fireplaces. A choice of food is served in the informal dining room.
7rm(2⇌2⮣3hc) CTV in all bedrooms ® sB&B£23-£25
sB&B⇌⮣£26-£28 dB&B£48-£50 dB&B⇌⮣£48-£52
WB&B£143-£163 WBDi£220-£240 LDO 9pm
Lic ⁂ CTV 25P nc8yrs
Credit Cards [1] [2] [3] £

SPEAN BRIDGE Highland *Inverness-shire* Map **14** NN28

GH QQ Coire Glas PH34 4EU ☎(039781) 272
Jan-Oct
Situated in its own grounds on the eastern fringe of the village, overlooking the Ben Nevis mountain range, this friendly family-run guesthouse offers good value accommodation. Bedrooms are comfortable with practical furnishings and there is also a well stocked residents' bar as well as an à la carte dinner menu.
14rm(8⮣6hc) (2fb) ® ✗ (ex guide dogs) sB&B£15-£17
dB&B£26-£28 dB&B⮣£32-£34 WBDi£151-£179 LDO 8pm
Lic CTV 20P

GH QQ Inverour PH34 4EU ☎(039781) 218
mid Mar-Oct
Conveniently situated at the junction of the A82/A86, this friendly family-run guesthouse is an ideal touring base. It has a comfortable lounge, and hearty breakfasts are served in the beamed dining room. Bedrooms, with fitted units, are warm and comfortable, though some are compact.
7rm(3↱4hc) TV in all bedrooms ® ✱ sB&B£13-£14 dB&B£26-£28 dB&B↱£30-£32 LDO 6pm
🅜 7P

STAFFORD Staffordshire Map **07** SJ92

GH QQ Leonards Croft Hotel 80 Lichfield Rd ST17 4LP ☎(0785) 223676
Closed Xmas
Friendly hosts ensure that guests feel at home here in a large detached house with extensive and well tended rear gardens which stands on the edge of the town.
12hc (2fb) ® sB&B£17 dB&B£34 LDO 9pm
Lic 🅜 CTV 10P

STAMFORD BRIDGE Humberside

See **Low Catton & High Catton**

STANLEY Co Durham Map **12** NZ15

GH QQQ Tanfield Garden Lodge Tanfield Ln, Tanfield DH9 9QF ☎(0207) 282821
This detached house is situated on the fringe of the village, with its own attractive gardens and a car park. Bedrooms are very neat and well tended, and there is a pleasant dining room. Friendly service is provided by the resident proprietors.
6rm(4⇌↱2hc) (3fb) CTV in all bedrooms ® ✗ ✱ sB&B£22-£28 sB&B⇌↱£28-£30 dB&B£32-£35 dB&B⇌↱£38-£40 WB&B£110-£150
🅜 8P Ⓕ

STANLEY Tayside *Perthshire* Map **11** NO13

FH QQ Mrs D A Dow **Tophead** *(NO080321)* Tullybelton PH1 4PT ☎(0738) 828259
Apr-Oct
Glorious views can be enjoyed from the well tended gardens of this attractive farmhouse, that sits in a peaceful, elevated position, three quarters of a mile west of the A9. The comfortable spacious bedrooms are bright and airy, as are the sitting room and sun lounge. Breakfasts are served around the large communal table.
3rm(1↱1hc) (1fb)⊬in all bedrooms ® ✗ (ex guide dogs) ✱ dB&B↱£32-£36 WB&B£100-£113
🅜 CTV 5P 400 acres arable dairy beef

STANSTED Essex Map **05** TL52

GH QQ The Laurels 84 St Johns Rd CM24 8JS ☎(0279) 813023
Just off the B1383 in the village of Stansted Mount-Fitchet, this small, family house offers nicely equipped bedrooms of different sizes. There is a cheerful lounge and the dining room is now licensed, offering a set dinner of standard English dishes which can be ordered up to 7pm. A free courtesy car to the nearby airport and railway is provided.
7rm(5⇌↱2hc) (2fb)⊬in 6 bedrooms CTV in all bedrooms ® ✱ sB&B£22-£25 sB&B⇌↱£27-£30 dB&Bfr£40 dB&B⇌↱fr£45 LDO 10pm
Lic 🅜 CTV 7P 3🚗 (£15 per wk)
Credit Cards 3 Ⓕ

Street plans of certain towns and cities will be found in a separate section at the back of the book.

STARBOTTON North Yorkshire Map **07** SD97

SELECTED

GH QQQQ Hilltop Country BD23 5HY ☎Kettlewell(0756) 760321
mid Mar-mid Nov
Dating back to the 17th century, this charming farmhouse is situated in the pretty hamlet of Starbotton, on the road between Kettlewell and Buckden. Standing in an elevated position, the house has fine views of the surrounding hills, and the grounds slope down to Cam Gill Beck. Tasteful use of modern fabrics has ensured that the house has retained much of its character. Bedrooms are spacious and comfortable, although one in the converted barn is more compact. The drawing room is comfortable and relaxing, with a log fire for cooler evenings and a small bar for pre-dinner drinks. Excellent meals are taken in the former parlour where guests enjoy superb meals at antique tables. The owners, Mr and Mrs Rathmell, have written a book containing Hilltop recipes, on sale to guests. A typical meal might include smoked fillet of Kilnsey trout, breast of Nidderdale chicken stuffed with mushroom pâté, served with sherry sauce, and followed by lemon meringues and local cheeses.
4rm(1⇌3↱) Annexe 1↱ (1fb)⊬in 4 bedrooms CTV in all bedrooms ® ✗ (ex guide dogs) dB&B⇌↱£50-£56 LDO 6pm
Lic 🅜 6P Ⓕ

STEEPLE ASTON Oxfordshire Map **04** SP42

GH QQQ Westfield Farm Motel The Fenway OX5 3SS ☎(0869) 40591
Situated on the edge of a pretty Cotswold village, this motel was converted from farm buildings and offers 6 bedrooms with direct access from a central car park. The cottage-style rooms have recently been upgraded and now provide modern, tiled shower rooms with larger than average showers and all bedrooms are well equipped with most modern facilities. There is a small breakfast room and a lounge with a counter selling soft drinks.
7↱ (1fb) CTV in all bedrooms ® **T** sB&B↱£32-£36 dB&B↱£42-£46 WB&B£200-£226 WBDi£263-£289 LDO 7pm
Lic 🅜 CTV 12P U
Credit Cards 1 3 Ⓕ

STEPASIDE Dyfed Map **02** SN10

GH QQ Bay View Hotel Pleasant Valley SA67 8LR ☎Saundersfoot(0834) 813417
Apr-Sep
A modern hotel situated in a secluded position in a lovely wooded valley convenient for many fine beaches. Accommodation is simple but clean and bright: there is a large residents' bar, a small TV lounge and an outdoor pool for the summer.
12rm(7↱5hc) (4fb) ® ✗ (ex guide dogs) sB&B£14.45-£17 dB&B£28.90-£34 dB&B↱£31.80-£33.80 WB&B£101.15-£128 WBDi£130-£160 LDO 5pm
Lic 🅜 CTV 14P ⇜(heated)

STEVENTON Oxfordshire Map **04** SU49

GH QQ *Steventon House Hotel* Milton Hill OX13 6AB ☎Abingdon(0235) 831223 FAX (0235) 834689
Set in 2 acres, this small Victorian country house features an outdoor, heated swimming pool situated in the orchard. There are several bedrooms in the main house plus the more modern garden suites, which are spacious and equipped for both business and leisure use. Lunch and dinner are served in the 2 attractive dining rooms which are lofty and well proportioned. While some areas may have a lived-in appearance, there is a genuine warmth and friendliness evident throughout.
8rm(3⇌5↱) Annexe 15⇌↱ (2fb) CTV in all bedrooms ® ✗ (ex guide dogs) LDO 8.30pm

→

Lic 𝌆 50P ⛱(heated)
Credit Cards [1] [2] [3] [5]

STEWARTON Strathclyde *Ayrshire*

See **Dunlop**

STEYNING West Sussex Map **04** TQ11

GH QQ Nash Hotel Horsham Rd BN4 3AA ☎(0903) 814988
Set in 9 acres, including a vineyard, outside the village and off the B2135 to Partridge Green, this attractive house has modestly furnished bedrooms of varying size. One is en suite whilst the others share a functional general bathroom. There is a bright breakfast room and an attractive lounge with co- ordinated décor and comfy sofas. Wine from the vineyard is sampled in the wine-tasting room.
4rm(1⇌3hc) (2fb)⚟in 1 bedroom CTV in all bedrooms ® ✱ sB&B£20-£25 dB&B£43 dB&B⇌£45 LDO 7pm
Lic 𝌆 CTV 18P ⛱℘(hard)wildfowl lake vineyard £

GH QQQ Springwells Hotel 9 High St BN44 3GG
☎(0903) 812446 & 812043
Closed 1 wk Xmas
This attractive Georgian house has a central location in this picturesque market town. The bedrooms are individually furnished and named after trees – many have smart mahogany furniture and all are well equipped. There is a small bar/lounge to the rear and an adjoining conservatory which leads to the patio, walled garden and outdoor swimming pool. At the front of the house there is a bright dining room and an elegant, comfortable lounge in which to relax.
10rm(8⇌↱2hc) (1fb) CTV in all bedrooms ® T ✱ sB&Bfr£20 sB&B⇌↱fr£25 dB&B£36 dB&B⇌↱fr£42 WB&Bfr£140 LDO 8.45pm
Lic 𝌆 CTV 6P ⛱(heated) sauna
Credit Cards [1] [2] [3] [5] £

STIPERSTONES Shropshire Map **07** SJ30

GH QQ Tankerville Lodge SY5 0NB
☎Shrewsbury(0743) 791401
A well hidden house in a rural setting reached by turning off the A488 Shrewsbury to Bishops Castle road, signed to Snailbeach, pass through Stiperstones and in three quarters of a mile you will see the bed and breakfast sign on a bend in the road. The rooms are neat, there is a lounge full of touring information, and a daily weather chart in the country-style dining room. A self-catering cottage is also available.
4hc ® sB&B£14-£16 dB&B£28 WB&B£88.20-£102.20 WBDi£140.70-£154.70 LDO 4pm
Lic 𝌆 CTV 4P nc5yrs £

STIRLING Central *Stirlingshire* Map **11** NS79

See also **Denny**

GH QQQ Castlecroft Ballengeich Rd FK8 1TN
☎(0786) 74933
Closed 23 Dec-4 Jan
In an elevated position under Stirling Castle, this bed and breakfast establishment offers modern accommodation. The spacious lounge provides guests with lovely views of the mountains to the west.
6↱ (1fb) CTV in all bedrooms ® ✱ sB&B↱£25-£32 dB&B↱£36
lift 𝌆 9P

STOCKBRIDGE Hampshire Map **04** SU33

GH QQQ Carbery Salisbury Hill SO20 6EZ
☎Andover(0264) 810771
Closed 2 wks Xmas
This attractive Georgian house lies at the western end of the village High Street with extensive tiered lawned gardens. Bedrooms are restfully rural with pine furniture and pretty floral fabrics, and well arranged with modern amenities. Communal areas include a games room, a sitting room with comfortable burgundy-coloured armchairs and a conservatory entrance hall with bamboo furniture. Ann and Philip Hooper have provided a warm welcome here for many years, and service includes evening meals and a residential licence.
11rm(2⇌6↱3hc) (2fb) CTV in all bedrooms ® ✗ sB&B£20-£27.50 sB&B⇌↱£27.50 dB&B£40-£45 dB&B⇌↱£40-£45 WB&B£130-£182.50 WBDi£200-£250 LDO 6pm
Lic 𝌆 14P ⛱(heated) badminton pool table

GH QQQ Old Three Cups Private Hotel High St SO20 6HB
☎Andover(0264) 810527
24 Dec-early Jan rs Jan
This low, white 15th-century coaching inn stands at the westerly end of the busy High Street. The public rooms have a wealth of beams – some rather low – including the restaurant which offers a wide menu of English and continental dishes. All the bedrooms are on the first floor and vary in size and outlook – many have been upgraded with floral patterns and pine furniture.
8rm(3⇌↱5hc) (2fb) CTV in all bedrooms ✗ (ex guide dogs) ✱ sB&Bfr£25 sB&B⇌↱fr£36 dB&Bfr£36 dB&B⇌↱fr£48 LDO 9.30pm
Lic 𝌆 12P
Credit Cards [1] [3] £

STOCKPORT Greater Manchester

See **Marple**

STOCKTON-ON-TEES Cleveland Map **08** NZ41

GH QQQ *The Edwardian Hotel* 72 Yarm Rd TS18 3PQ
☎(0642) 615655
A late-Victorian terraced house situated on the A135, close to the A66 and A19, west of the town centre. The lounge and dining room have been tastefully decorated featuring Laura Ashley décor. Bedrooms are cosy, bright and very well equipped. Proprietor Mrs Hall will provide dinner on request, using fresh local produce.
6rm(4↱) (3fb) CTV in all bedrooms ® ✗ (ex guide dogs) LDO 7pm
Lic 𝌆 CTV 8P
Credit Cards [1]

STOGUMBER Somerset Map **03** ST03

GH QQQ Chandlers House TA4 3TA ☎(0984) 56580
Apr-Oct
Chandlers House is a white-painted, listed property with a pretty walled garden at the rear, in the centre of the conservation village at the foot of the Quantock Hills, close to Exmoor National Park and just 12 miles from Taunton. Joanna Milward welcomes guests to her home, and most leave as friends. There are 2 comfortable bedrooms, both tastefully decorated and furnished with antique pieces, one has a shower room en suite and the other has the use of a private bathroom across the landing. The elegant lounge is in the Georgian part of the house, while the breakfast room has a more cottagey style with a wood-burning stove during the colder months. Here, English breakfast is served around a large table.
2rm(1↱) ⚟in all bedrooms CTV in all bedrooms ® ✱ sB&Bfr£15 sB&B↱£16 dB&Bfr£30 dB&B↱£32
𝌆 CTV 2P

STOKE-BY-NAYLAND Suffolk Map **05** TL93

INN QQQ The Angel Inn Polstead St CO6 4SA
☎Nayland(0206) 263245
Closed 25-26 Dec & 1 Jan
A popular and at times very busy inn dating from the 16th-century, situated in one of Suffolk's most interesting villages and surrounded by lovely countryside, has been totally restored and refurbished whilst retaining such original features as exposed brickwork, beams, 2 large open fireplaces in the bars and the gallery overlooking the high-ceilinged dining room. Individually decorated and furnished bedrooms of a high standard are provided

with good modern en suite facilities. The restaurant serves the same dishes as are listed on the daily blackboard bar-meals menu – both bars and restaurant being much frequented by local customers.
5⇔↱ Annexe 1⇔↱ CTV in all bedrooms ® T
✗ (ex guide dogs) sB&B⇔↱£44.50 dB&B⇔↱£57.50 Lunch £10-£25&alc Dinner £10-£25&alc LDO 9pm
⅏ 25P nc8yrs
Credit Cards [1] [2] [3] [5]

STOKE HOLY CROSS Norfolk Map **05** TG20

FH **QQ** Mrs Harrold **Salamanca** *(TG235022)* NR14 8QJ
☎Framingham Earl(05086) 2322 due to change to (0508) 492322
Closed 15 Dec-15 Jan & Etr
This large farmhouse is set in the heart of a picturesque village and dates back to the 16th century. Surrounded by well tended gardens, it offers traditional, comfortable accommodation and a pleasant lounge.
3hc Annexe 1⇔ ✗ ✱ sB&Bfr£16 sB&B⇔fr£18 dB&Bfr£28 dB&B⇔fr£32
⅏ CTV 7P nc6yrs 175 acres dairy mixed
See advertisement under NORWICH

STOKE-ON-TRENT Staffordshire Map **07** SJ84

GH **QQQ** **White Gables Hotel** Trentham Rd, Blurton ST3 3DT ☎(0782) 324882 FAX (0782) 598302
A large, fully modernised house in extensive grounds with a rural outlook, set on the A5035 on the outskirts of the city. The rooms are spacious, well equipped and distinctively decorated. Additional facilities include a basement games room.
9rm(3⇔3↱3hc) (2fb) CTV in all bedrooms ® T
✗ (ex guide dogs) sB&B£20-£25 sB&B⇔↱£35-£40 dB&B£38-£45 dB&B⇔↱£45-£52 LDO 7.30pm
→

Lic ♨ CTV 12P 2🚗 ⚲(hard)games room
Credit Cards 1 2 3 £

GH QQ The White House Hotel 94 Stone Rd, Trent Vale ST4 6SP ☎(0782) 642460 & 657189

Conveniently situated north of the ring road at its A34 junction, this family- run guesthouse provides clean, modern bedrooms. There is ample car parking available and, although there is no bar, drinks are available in the lounge.

8rm(3⌐5hc) Annexe 2⌐ (2fb) CTV in all bedrooms ® **T** ✗ (ex guide dogs) sB&B£19-£23 sB&B⌐£30-£34 dB&B£34-£38 dB&B⌐£40-£46 WB&B£200-£300 WBDi£240-£360 LDO 11am
Lic ♨ CTV 12P
Credit Cards 1 2 3 £

STORNOWAY

See **LEWIS, ISLE OF**

STOURBRIDGE West Midlands Map **07** SO98

GH QQ Limes Hotel 260 Hagley Rd, Pedmore DY9 0RW ☎Hagley(0562) 882689

A predominantly commercial guesthouse 1.5 miles from Stourbridge in a pleasant residential area. Owners Mr and Mrs Bibby continue to make improvements.

11rm(2⌐8hc) (1fb) CTV in 10 bedrooms ® **T** ✱ sB&B£22-£27 sB&B⌐£30.50-£33 dB&B£32-£36 dB&B⌐£36.50-£42 LDO 7.30pm
Lic ♨ CTV 12P
Credit Cards 1 2 3

STOW-ON-THE-WOLD Gloucestershire Map **04** SP12

GH QQ Cotswold View Nether Westcote OX7 6SD (4m E, signed from A424) ☎Shipton under Wychwood(0993) 830699

This guesthouse is quietly situated in the small village of Nether Westcote, which is signed from the A424, 4 miles from the town and 5 miles from Burford; its elevated position gives fine rural views across Warwickshire. The simply furnished bedrooms are comfortable, and home-made cream teas are served in the smartly decorated and furnished dining room in the summer. There is a cosy TV lounge with games and a log fire, and a small gift shop.

6rm(3⌐3hc) ⊬in all bedrooms ® ✱ sB&B£20 dB&B⌐£30.50-£38 WBDi£117.50-£165 LDO 4pm
CTV 8P 3🚗 £

GH QQ Limes Evesham Rd GL54 1EJ ☎Cotswold(0451) 30034

Closed 23 Dec-1 Jan

This cosy little house is personally run by the hospitable owners Mr and Mrs Keyte. There are small but comfortable bedrooms and a bright conservatory dining room with good views over an expanse of countryside. A pretty garden surrounds the house, and there is useful car parking. This is a good location for touring the Cotswolds.

2rm(1⌐1hc) Annexe 1⌐ (1fb) CTV in all bedrooms ® dB&B⌐£33-£40
♨ CTV 4P

FH QQ Mr R Smith **Corsham Field** *(SP217249)* Bledington Rd GL54 1JH ☎Cotswold(0451) 831750

This modern house is reached by following signs to Bledington, and is approximately 2 miles out of Stow. One has to drive through the farmyard to reach the house which offers modern bedrooms, most with lovely views of the Cotswold countryside. About 5 minutes' walk away is a pub serving good food.

3rm(1⇌2hc) (1fb) CTV in all bedrooms ® sB&B£14-£20 dB&B£24-£32 dB&B⇌£28-£35
♨ CTV 10P 100 acres arable beef sheep

Book as early as possible for busy holiday periods.

INN QQQ Royalist Hotel Digbeth St GL54 1BN ☎Cotswold(0451) 30670

13rm(8⇌5⌐) (3fb) CTV in all bedrooms ® sB&B⇌⌐£25-£45 dB&B⇌⌐£40-£70 Bar Lunch £5-£10alc
♨ 12P
Credit Cards 1 2 3

STRACHUR Strathclyde Map **10** NN00

INN QQQ Glendale PA27 8BX ☎(036986) 630

Set in its own gardens beside the A815, overlooking Loch Fyne, this sturdy stone-built Victorian house has recently been completely refurbished. The bedrooms are comfortable. Light snacks and meals are available all day in the bright bar which also has a small lounge area. On cooler evenings, a coal fire burns in the cosy dining room. Ian and Evelyn Gordon offer an enthusiastic welcome to their guests.

3⌐ (1fb)⊬in all bedrooms CTV in 2 bedrooms ® ✗ sB&B⌐£25-£30 dB&B⌐fr£50 Bar Lunch fr£6.80 High tea fr£5 Dinner fr£10
♨ 20P games room

STRATFORD-UPON-AVON Warwickshire Map **04** SP25

See **Town Plan Section**

GH QQ *Ambleside* 41 Grove Rd CV37 6PB ☎(0789) 297239 & 295670 FAX (0789) 295670

Closed Xmas

Situated in a pleasant area yet within easy reach of the town centre, this guesthouse is constantly being improved, and the accommodation is attractive, comfortable and well equipped. Public areas are somewhat limited but include a combined lounge and dining room. There is a spacious private car park at the rear.

7rm(3⌐4hc) (3fb)⊬in 3 bedrooms CTV in all bedrooms ®
♨ CTV 15P 1🚗 (50p per night)
Credit Cards 1 3

GH QQ *Avon View Hotel* 121 Shipston Rd CV37 7LW ☎(0789) 297542 (0789) 294550

This small private hotel has the benefit of its own car park and is a short walk from the town centre. Recent improvements have given all the bedrooms en suite facilities. Light meals and snacks can be served in the evening upon request.

9⇌⌐ (1fb)⊬in all bedrooms CTV in all bedrooms ® ✗ LDO 4pm
Lic ♨ CTV 16P nc12yrs
Credit Cards 1 2 3 5

GH QQQ Brook Lodge 192 Alcester Rd CV37 9DR ☎(0789) 295988

Closed Xmas

A well kept guesthouse situated on the Alcester Road close to Anne Hathaway's cottage. Rooms are nicely decorated and furnished with a good range of facilities. There is a split-level dining room and lounge, and public areas are comfortable.

7rm(5⌐2hc) (2fb) CTV in all bedrooms ® dB&B£34-£38 dB&B⌐£36-£40 WB&Bfr£102
♨ CTV 10P
Credit Cards 1 2 3 5 £

GH QQ Courtland Hotel 12 Guild St CV37 6RE ☎(0789) 292401

This Georgian Grade II listed building is situated on a busy road close to the town centre. The bedrooms vary in size and generally offer modest décor and furnishings. Breakfast is served in the small dining room and there is also a comfortable guests' lounge filled with knick-knacks and family mementoes.

7rm(2⇌⌐5hc) (1fb) CTV in all bedrooms ® ✗ (ex guide dogs) sB&B£15-£17 sB&B⇌⌐£30-£35 dB&B£30-£35 dB&B⇌⌐£38-£48 WB&B£105-£245
♨ CTV 2P 1🚗
Credit Cards 2 £

See advertisement on page 375

Stratford-upon-Avon

GH QQQ Craig Cleeve House 67-69 Shipston Rd CV37 7LW ☎(0789) 296573 FAX (0789) 299452

A comfortable guesthouse on the A34 100yds south of Clopton Bridge. Accommodation is bright and fresh with a good range of facilities, and the majority of rooms have en suite facilities. There is an attractive dining room overlooking the rear garden and a lounge bar. Spotlessly clean throughout, the house is a credit to Terry and Margarita Palmer, the hospitable hosts.

15rm(9ſ6hc) CTV in all bedrooms ® sB&B£18.50-£26 sB&Bſ£36 dB&B£37 dB&Bſ£51 WB&B£122.50-£164.50

Lic ℙ 15P

Credit Cards [1] [2] [3] [5] £

GH QQ The Croft 49 Shipston Rd CV37 7LN ☎(0789) 293419

A busy guesthouse situated close to Clopton Bridge with direct access to the tramway, town and theatre from the rear garden. The accommodation offers a good range of modern facilities and there is a lounge for guests' use. Dinner is served by prior arrangement.

9rm(3ſ6hc) (5fb) CTV in all bedrooms ® sB&B£18.50-£28 sB&Bſ£32-£37 dB&B£33-£38 dB&Bſ£40-£47 LDO noon

Lic ℙ 4P

Credit Cards [1] [3] [5] £

GH QQ The Dylan 10 Evesham Place CV37 6HT ☎(0789) 204819

This bright, friendly little guesthouse is centrally located with comfortable, well equipped bedrooms and stylish Victorian fireplaces. There is a congenial breakfast room complete with an old Wurlitzer juke box for those nostalgic for that era. Useful car parking is available at the rear.

5ſ (1fb) CTV in all bedrooms ® ✱ sB&Bſ£16-£24 dB&Bſ£32-£48 WB&B£112-£168

ℙ 3P

GH QQQ Eastnor House Hotel Shipston Rd CV37 7LN ☎(0789) 268115

Closed Xmas

A professionally run guesthouse in a convenient location just 300m from the theatre on the A34. It is a large Victorian house converted to provide comfortable accommodation, and all rooms have good modern en suite facilities. There is a lounge for guests' use and a well furnished breakfast room.

9⇔ſ (3fb) CTV in all bedrooms ® ✱ dB&B⇔ſ£39-£52 WB&Bfr£117

Lic ℙ 9P

Credit Cards [1] [3] £

GH QQ Eversley Bears 37 Grove Rd CV37 6PB ☎(0789) 292334

A privately run guesthouse in a convenient location close to the town centre. The proprietors Mr and Mrs Thomas have a large collection of teddy bears which are very much in evidence throughout the house. The accommodation is modest and rooms vary in size; some are very spacious. Public areas include a separate breakfast room and a lounge full of teddies.

6rm(2ſ4hc) (2fb) ® ✗ (ex guide dogs) ✱ sB&B£18-£20 dB&B£36-£40 dB&Bſ£48-£52

ℙ CTV 3⌂ (50p) nc14yrs £

GH QQQ Gravelside Barn Binton CV37 9TU ☎(0789) 750502 & 297000 FAX (0789) 298056

This clever conversion of an old thatcher's barn is on one of the highest points in the area in the middle of open countryside. Its peaceful location at the end of a private drive belies its accessibility to Stratford, just 4 miles away. Accommodation is spacious and attractive with quality furnishings and an excellent range of modern facilities including fridges with complimentary soft drinks. The barn is self contained with its own lounge and dining areas. This is a no-smoking establishment.

3ſ ⊘in all bedrooms CTV in all bedrooms ®
✗ (ex guide dogs) sB&Bſ£30-£40 dB&Bſ£40-£60 WB&B£125-£175

ℙ 6P nc12yrs

Credit Cards [1] [2] [3] £

GH QQ Hardwick House 1 Avenue Rd CV37 6UY ☎(0789) 204307 FAX (0789) 296760

Closed Xmas

This well established bed and breakfast hotel is just off the Warwick road in a quiet residential area; it is a Victorian property owned by the Coulson family for over 20 years. Bedrooms are generally spacious and comfortable, breakfast is served in the attractive dining room and a lounge is available for guests' use.

14rm(7⇔ſ7hc) (3fb) CTV in all bedrooms ®
✗ (ex guide dogs) ✱ sB&B£16.50-£23 dB&B£33-£48 dB&B⇔ſ£46-£56

ℙ 12P

Credit Cards [1] [2] [3] [5] £

GH QQQ Highcroft Banbury Rd CV37 7NF ☎(0789) 296293

A substantial red-brick country house situated on the A422 Banbury road, 2 miles south of Banbury. The Davies family offer 2 letting bedrooms, one in the main house, the other a ground-floor room with its own entrance. The rooms are spacious and attractive, with coordinating décor and antique or pine furniture, and are well equipped with modern, en suite facilities. Breakfast is served around a communal table in the lounge/dining room, and there is a tennis court for guests' use.

1⇔ſ Annexe 1⇔ſ (1fb) CTV in all bedrooms ® dB&B⇔ſ£30-£35 WB&Bfr£95

ℙ 5P 𝓅(hard) £

GH QQQ *Hollies* 'The Hollies', 16 Evesham Place CV37 6HQ ☎(0789) 266857

A corner property in a convenient location close to the town centre, with its own car park. Much care is taken with the upkeep of the house, and the garden is always colourful. Mrs Morgan is a popular hostess who gives a warm welcome, as comments in her visitors' book will verify.

→

The Croft

BED & BREAKFAST
from £15.50

49 Shipston Road
Stratford-upon-Avon
Warwickshire CV37 7LN
Telephone (0789) 293419

The Croft is a typically Victorian home, which over many years has become established as a friendly, family run guest house, offering its patrons a high standard of food, service and accommodation.

Five minute walk to the theatre through our hotel gardens.

All rooms are tastefully decorated:

- Full central heating
- Wash hand basins
- Colour television
- Tea and coffee making facilities
- Clock radios & hairdryers
- Some rooms are en suite
- Residential licence
- Open all year
- Car parking
- Pre-theatre dinner by arrangement
- Guests' lounge

"Resident proprietors Jeanne and Kevin Hallworth invite you to come and make yourselves at home"

Listed

British Tourist Authority

The Heart of England Tourist Board

Courtland Hotel

12 Guild Street, Stratford-on-Avon CV37 6RE

Bed and Breakfast from/to £14/£24

En suite facilities available.

Personal attention in well appointed Georgian House. Full English & Continental breakfast with home made preserves. All rooms with H&C, central heating, double glazing, colour television, tea & coffee making facilities. Antique furniture. Town centre situation. 3 minutes' level walk to theatre.

Tel: (0789) 292401

Mrs. Bridget Johnson

Recommended by Arthur Frommer

AA LISTED

English Tourist Board HIGHLY COMMENDED

GRAVELSIDE BARN

Stay in the Heart of England

Gravelside Barn, superbly located on a hilltop in open countryside, is an old thatchers barn built from local stone and carefully converted to retain its charm and character; but with all the modern conveniences and creature comforts the discerning traveller of today expects.

Highly recommended by our guests and highly commended by the English Tourist Board. A little haven of tranquility 10-15 mins from the M40, and 5 mins from Stratford- upon -Avon.

For a copy of our brochure contact Denise or Guy Belchambers.

GRAVELSIDE BARN.

Binton, Stratford upon Avon, Warwicks. CV37 9TU
Tel 0789 750502 /297000 Fax 0789 298056

6rm(1⇁5hc) (2fb) CTV in all bedrooms ®
♨ CTV 6P

GH QQ **Hunters Moon** 150 Alcester Rd CV37 9DR
☎(0789) 292888
This guesthouse is situated on the Alcester Road, a short drive from the town centre. Accommodation is functional and well equipped, most rooms having private bathrooms. Public areas are limited and include a combined breakfast room and sitting area.
7rm(5⇁2hc) (5fb) CTV in all bedrooms ® ✱ sB&B£16-£25 dB&B⇁£30-£42
♨ CTV 6P
Credit Cards 1 2 3 5 £

GH QQQ ***Kawartha House*** 39 Grove Rd CV37 6PB
☎(0789) 204469
This cosy, friendly guesthouse is on the Evesham road. The accommodation is attractive with pretty décor and coordinated Laura Ashley soft furnishings. There is a small front-facing dining room where breakfasts are served.
6rm(3⇁3hc) (2fb) CTV in 4 bedrooms ®
♨ CTV 4🚗

GH QQ **Marlyn** 3 Chestnut Walk CV37 6HG ☎(0789) 293752
Closed Xmas
This Victorian terraced property is in a chestnut tree-lined side street, with easy access to the town centre. The accommodation is traditional and well kept, although lacking in modern facilities. Public areas include a TV lounge and a dining room.
8hc (1fb) ® ✗ (ex guide dogs) ✱ sB&Bfr£18 dB&Bfr£34
♨ CTV

GH QQQ **Melita Private Hotel** 37 Shipston Rd CV37 7LN
☎(0789) 292432
Closed Xmas
A friendly family-run guesthouse on the A34 close to the river and major attractions. The bedrooms are exceptionally well equipped, the majority have en suite facilities and 2 newly decorated ground-floor rooms are particularly attractive. Some rooms have been set aside for non-smokers. Public rooms include a cosy dining room and a comfortable lounge bar.
12⇌⇁ (3fb) ⚡in 8 bedrooms CTV in all bedrooms ® T
sB&B⇌⇁£28.50-£40 dB&B⇌⇁£45-£58 WB&B£157.50-£189
Lic ♨ CTV 12P
Credit Cards 1 2 3 £

GH QQQ **Moonraker House** 40 Alcester Rd CV37 9DB
☎(0789) 299346 FAX (0789) 295504
The accommodation arrangement in this professionally run guesthouse is rather unusual, being spread over 4 properties. The attractive bedrooms have coordinating décor and soft furnishings, with modern furniture and a good range of facilities including a hairdryer. Four no-smoking rooms are available in the bungalow, 2 have 4 poster beds, and each has access to a rear patio. There are 2 separate dining rooms where the proprietors provide a helpful and friendly service. Moonraker is conveniently situated just half a mile from the town centre and not far from the railway station.
6⇁ Annexe 9⇌⇁ (1fb) ⚡in 4 bedrooms CTV in all bedrooms ® dB&B⇌⇁£37-£55 WB&B£126-£175
♨ 12P 3🚗 (£1 per night)
Credit Cards 1 2 3 £

GH QQ **Nando's** 18-19 Evesham Place CV37 6HT
☎(0789) 204907
A large guesthouse in a pleasant location close to the town centre. Accommodation is modern and functional, and some rooms have good en suite facilities. Private parking is available nearby.
21rm(1⇌6⇁14hc) (10fb) CTV in all bedrooms sB&B£16-£18 sB&B⇌⇁£25-£30 dB&B£25-£33 dB&B⇌⇁£32-£41
♨ CTV 8P
Credit Cards 1 2 3 £

GH QQ **Parkfield** 3 Broad Walk CV37 6HS ☎(0789) 293313
In a pleasant side street with easy access to the town centre and attractions, just 6 minutes' walk away, this Victorian property is personally run by friendly proprietors Jo and Roger Pettitt. Rooms are neat, with further en suite facilities planned. Traditional or vegetarian breakfasts are served.
7rm(5⇁2hc) (1fb) CTV in all bedrooms ® sB&B£16-£20 dB&B£32-£34 dB&B⇁£38-£40
♨ 8P nc7yrs
Credit Cards 1 3 5

See advertisement on page 379

GH QQQ **The Payton Hotel** 6 John St CV37 6UB
☎(0789) 266442
This Georgian property is in the New Town just minutes from the town centre. Bedrooms are attractively decorated and furnished, and most rooms have en suite facilites, though some are compact. Breakfast is served in the cosy dining room and there is seating in the pleasant entrance hall. Proprietors June and John Rickett are friendly and welcoming.
5rm(4⇁1hc) (1fb) CTV in all bedrooms ® ✗ (ex guide dogs) sB&B⇁£35 dB&B⇁£48
♨ ⅌ nc1-8yrs
Credit Cards 1 2 3 £

GH QQ **Penryn House** 126 Alcester Rd CV37 9DP
☎(0789) 293718
A semidetached house situated one mile from the town centre, on the Alcester road. Continuing improvements include the redecoration of rooms, which are bright, fresh and well equipped. Public areas are small but attractive, and there is a private car park at the rear.
7rm(5⇁2hc) Annexe 1⇁ (3fb) CTV in all bedrooms ® sB&B£15-£20 sB&B⇁£22-£35 dB&B£30-£35 dB&B⇁£30-£45 WB&B£80-£120

→

ꟷ 9P
Credit Cards 1 2 3 5 £

GH QQ Ravenhurst 2 Broad Walk CV37 6HS ☎(0789) 292515
Closed Xmas
Situated in a quiet location yet within easy reach of the town centre, this converted Victorian property offers good accommodation. At the time of our inspection 2 rooms were being upgraded and one is to have a 4-poster bed. Breakfast is served in the spacious dining room.
6rm(4⇨↱2hc) (2fb) CTV in all bedrooms ® ✗ ✱ sB&B£17-£20 sB&B⇨↱£25-£30 dB&B£32-£34 dB&B⇨↱£36-£42
ꟷ 1P 3🚗
Credit Cards 1 2 3 5

GH Q Salamander 40 Grove Rd CV37 6PB
☎(0789) 205728
Conveniently situated a short walk from the town centre, this guesthouse offers modest accommodation in rooms of varying shapes and sizes. There is a lounge for guests' use and a small dining room.
7rm(2↱5hc) (3fb) CTV in 4 bedrooms ® sB&B£12.50-£16 dB&B£25-£30 dB&B↱£30-£40 WB&B£98-£105 WBDi£140-£144 LDO 6.30pm
ꟷ CTV 4P 2🚗

GH QQQ Sequoia House Private Hotel 51-53 Shipston Rd CV37 7LN ☎(0789) 268852
Closed 22-27 Dec
On the A3400 just across the Avon opposite the Royal Shakespeare Theatre, this large hotel has been created from 2 substantial late-Victorian properties. Several room types are available, from the cosy cottage annexe to the exceptionally well furnished, luxury no-smoking rooms. The restaurant is air conditioned and particularly attractive, and the hotel is able to provide facilities for both wedding receptions and conferences. Staff are professional, helpful and friendly.
20rm(16⇨↱4hc) Annexe 5↱ (4fb) CTV in all bedrooms ® **T** ✗ sB&B£27.50-£32.50 sB&B⇨↱£39-£55 dB&B£35-£39 dB&B⇨↱£55-£72 LDO 4pm
Lic ꟷ CTV 26P nc5yrs
Credit Cards 1 2 3 5

See advertisement on page 381

GH QQ Stretton House Hotel 38 Grove Rd CV37 6PB
☎(0789) 268647
This guesthouse, conveniently situated for access to the town centre, is steadily improving with the redecoration of rooms and the addition of en suite facilities. There is a pleasant small dining room complete with fish tank.
6rm(3↱3hc) (2fb) CTV in all bedrooms ® ✗ (ex guide dogs) sB&B£16-£20 dB&B£30-£38 dB&B↱£44 LDO 4pm
ꟷ 3P 1🚗

GH QQQ Twelfth Night Evesham Place CV37 6HT
☎(0789) 414595
A delightfully refurbished Victorian villa built in 1897, in a convenient location. The pretty rooms offer a good range of facilities and some welcome extra touches; the majority of rooms have en suite facilities. Public areas include a very well appointed dining room and a comfortable lounge. Smoking is not permitted.
7↱ (1fb)⊬in all bedrooms CTV in all bedrooms ® ✗ sB&B↱£19-£32 dB&B↱£38-£52
ꟷ 3P 4🚗 nc5yrs
Credit Cards 1 3

GH QQQ Victoria Spa Lodge Bishopton Ln CV37 9QY
☎(0789) 267985 & 204728
Well worth the short drive from the town centre, this private hotel enjoys a peaceful, leafy setting at the side of the Stratford Canal. Victoria Spa Lodge, dating from 1837, has generously proportioned rooms which are decorated and furnished with care and attention to detail, resulting in comfortable and attractive accommodation. The beautiful dining room is the perfect setting in which to start the day with an English, Continental or vegetarian breakfast.
7rm(5⇨↱2hc) (2fb) CTV in all bedrooms ® ✗ ✱ dB&Bfr£41 dB&B⇨↱fr£45
ꟷ 12P
Credit Cards 1 3

GH QQQ Virginia Lodge 12 Evesham Place CV37 6HT
☎(0789) 292157
This well kept guesthouse, close to the centre of Stratford, offers individually styled rooms, an attractive lounge and a cosy dining room. The friendly proprietors make guests very welcome and there is a rear car park for guests' use.
7rm(6↱1hc) (1fb)⊬in 6 bedrooms CTV in all bedrooms ® ✱ sB&B£16-£18 dB&B↱£34-£40
Lic ꟷ CTV 7P 2🚗

See advertisement on page 381

FH QQ Mrs R M Meadows **Monk's Barn** *(SP206516)* Shipston Rd CV37 8NA ☎(0789) 293714
Closed 25-26 Dec
The River Stour runs through the farmland and guests may enjoy the cross- country walk to the nearby village. This farm has foundations dating back to 1560 and is situated 2 miles south of the centre of Stratford. The bedrooms have bright, fresh décor and are generally spacious – 2 rooms have quality en suites. A guests' lounge with its wood panelling has comfortable sofas and armchairs and is split level with a dining area on the higher level.
4rm(2↱2hc) (1fb)⊬in all bedrooms CTV in 3 bedrooms TV in 1 bedroom ® ✗ (ex guide dogs) sB&B£14.50-£15 sB&B↱£16.50-£17 dB&B£26-£27 dB&B↱£30-£31 WB&B£87.50-£100
ꟷ CTV 5P 75 acres mixed

FH QQQ Mr & Mrs R Evans ***Oxstalls*** *(SP217566)*
Warwick Rd CV37 4NR ☎(0789) 205277
Apart from providing an extensive range of accommodation, this farmhouse is also a thoroughbred stud farm. It is situated opposite the Welcombe golf course and just one mile from the town centre. The en suite bedrooms are mostly situated in converted, surrounding outbuildings and offer bright, fresh décor with a mixture of furnishing styles and a good range of facilities. There are 3 dining areas where breakfast is served.
5hc Annexe 13rm(3⇌8♠2hc) (5fb)⅟in all bedrooms CTV in 2 bedrooms TV in 1 bedroom ® ✗ (ex guide dogs)
🅼 CTV P ▶18 ♩70 acres stud farm

STRATHAVEN Strathclyde *Lanarkshire* Map **11** NS74

GH QQ ***Springvale Hotel*** 18 Letham Rd ML10 6AD
☎(0357) 21131
Closed 26-27 Dec & 1-3 Jan
Situated in a residential area some 300yds from the town centre, this converted and extended house offers practical, well equipped bedrooms, a traditional lounge and bright, cheerful dining room overlooking the garden and playing fields. Personal and friendly service is provided by the owners, and home cooking is a feature of the popular high teas. Some long-stay residents are accommodated.
14rm(1⇌10♠3hc) (1fb) CTV in all bedrooms ® LDO 6.45pm
Lic 🅼 CTV 8P

STRATHTAY Tayside *Perthshire* Map **14** NN95

GH QQQ **Bendarroch House** PH9 0PG ☎(0887840) 420
Standing in an elevated position on the northern banks of the River Tay, this imposing Victorian mansion has recently been completely restored to provide superior accommodation in 4 comfortable bedrooms. Each room has been individually decorated and tastefully furnished in period style, with the front-facing rooms enjoying particularly pleasant views of the river. The public areas feature a quiet, comfortable and well appointed drawing room, in addition to a satellite TV lounge complete with piano and a small library of books, whilst home-cooked meals are served in the attractive dining room. Well preserved and spotlessly clean throughout, it is an ideal base for the sportsman who can pursue such activities as hunting, fishing, hill walking, sailing and golf, all within the immediate vicinity.
6♠ ✗ (ex guide dogs) ✱ sB&B♠£16-£24 dB&B♠£32-£48 WB&B£105-£154 LDO 8pm
Lic 🅼 CTV 8P ▶9 table tennis croquet
Credit Cards 1 3

STRATHYRE Central *Perthshire* Map **11** NN51

GH QQQ **Auchtubhmor House** Balquhidder FK19 8NZ
☎(08774) 632
rs Oct-Feb
A genuine welcome awaits guests at the Doyle's attractively situated and comfortably furnished small country house, set in an elevated position just off the A84 by Balquhidder. The well proportioned bedrooms offer fine views of the surrounding countryside, but it is Christine Doyle's enthusiastic cooking that gives rise to most of the favourable comments in the visitors' book.
4⇌♠ (1fb) ® ✱ sB&B⇌♠£18-£22 dB&B⇌♠£32-£34 WB&B£110-£130 WBDi£180-£220 LDO 6pm
Lic 🅼 CTV 6P
Credit Cards 1 2 3 £

STREFFORD Shropshire Map **07** SO48

FH QQQ Mrs C Morgan **Strefford Hall** *(SO444856)*
Strefford SY7 8DE ☎Craven Arms(0588) 672383
Closed Xmas & New Year
In the spring this imposing Victorian farmhouse is surrounded by colourful yellow fields, and the 360-acre farm also has sheep and cattle. There are 3 spacious bedrooms with solid older style furniture, 2 of which have en suite shower rooms and the third has a private bathroom. The comfortable residents' lounge is furnished with modern 3-piece suites and has a log-burning stove. Strefford Hall Farm is set in its own pretty lawns and gardens, and is situated just off the A49.
3rm(2♠1hc) ⅟in all bedrooms ® ✱ sB&Bfr£16 sB&B♠fr£16 dB&Bfr£32 dB&B♠fr£32 WB&Bfr£100
CTV 3P 350 acres arable beef sheep £

STRETTON Leicestershire Map **08** SK91

INN QQ ***The Shires Hotel*** LE15 7QT
☎Castle Bytham(0780) 410332
The Shires Hotel and restaurant is a 200-year-old free house, located on the southbound side of the A1 to the north of Stamford. Whether travelling north or south, leave the A1 at Stretton junction, which is also signposted RAF Cottesmore, then take the slip road for the southbound A1, and it is the second turn on the left before you join the A1. The comfortable lounge bar, with its sofa-style seating, is colour coordinated with pinks and greens throughout, and is currently being extended to provide a bar meal area and games room (to incorporate a snooker table). Bar meals and the restaurant are popular with local people, and the British and French-style menus offer value-for-money set-price meals during the week, with a carvery on Friday when demand is particularly heavy. The restaurant is cottagey in style with bold floral décor, a Welsh dresser and an attractive central stone fireplace. Bedrooms are generally roomy, but tend to be simply furnished, and have colour TV, radio and tea-making facilities.
5rm(4hc) (3fb) CTV in all bedrooms ® LDO 10.30pm
🅼 100P
Credit Cards 1 3

STROUD Gloucestershire Map **03** SO80

GH QQ **Downfield Hotel** 134 Cainscross Rd GL5 4HN
☎(0453) 764496
Closed 2 wks from 25 Dec
This fully extended, period house is situated on the A419, half a mile west of the town centre, and offers good parking facilities. There are spacious public rooms which include a licensed restaurant.
21rm(13⇌♠8hc) (4fb) CTV in 15 bedrooms ® **T** LDO 8pm
Lic 🅼 CTV 25P
Credit Cards 1 3 £

STUDLEY Warwickshire Map **04** SP06

FH QQQ Miss S A Walters **Bug In The Blanket** *(SP089643)*
Castle Farm B80 7AH ☎(0527) 854275 FAX (0527) 854897
Don't be put off by the name, this reflects the quirky but pleasing nature of this farmhouse. Set in the grounds of a 500-acre estate, the majority of accommodation is offered in 'The Wing', converted from old garden buildings. These modern rooms have a good range of facilities including a kitchenette and en suite. Two rooms are situated in the 15th-century black and white cottage, 'The Bug'; these rooms have access to shower facilities only via public areas. 'The Bug' also contains the dining room where appetising meals are served around a commual table, helping to maintain the convivial and fun atmosphere of the place. Continental breakfast can be left in room refrigerators, alternatively, a cooked breakfast is available in the cottage. There is also a cosy lounge and the restaurant is licensed.
2hc (1fb)⅟in 2 bedrooms CTV in 6 bedrooms ®
✗ (ex guide dogs) sB&Bfr£27 sB&Bfr£39.95 dB&Bfr£35 dB&Bfr£51.70 LDO 2pm
Lic 🅼 CTV 15P ⇒(heated) sauna 500 acres arable beef sheep £

'Selected' establishments, which have the highest quality award, are highlighted by a tinted panel. For a full list of these establishments, consult the

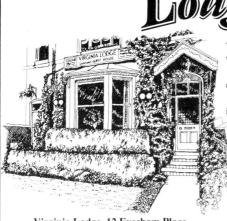

STURMINSTER NEWTON Dorset Map **03** ST71

GH Q Old Bridge Cottage Restaurant The Bridge DT10 2BS ☎(0258) 72689

This 17th-century cottage restaurant offers simple accommodation at a reasonable price. Although simply decorated, the bedrooms have plenty of character, with low ceilings, sloping floors and beams. The chef/patron Mr Botterill creates a relaxed, friendly atmosphere.

3rm(1⇌2hc) CTV in all bedrooms ® ✗ (ex guide dogs) sB&B£23-£27 sB&B⇌fr£27 dB&B£36-£44 dB&B⇌fr£44 WB&B£150-£170 WBDi£200-£230 LDO 8.30pm

Lic 𝍠 8P

Credit Cards 1 3 £

FH QQ Mrs S Wingate-Saul **Holebrook** *(ST743117)* Lydlinch DT10 2JB ☎Hazelbury Bryan(0258) 817348

Closed 25 Dec & 1 Jan rs Nov-Mar

This 18th-century farmhouse is clearly signposted, 3 miles west of the A357 Stalbridge road, and is set in peaceful countryside at the end of a long track. Most of the accommodation is in attractive converted stable bedroom suites, with one room in the main farmhouse and the accommodation is suitable for disabled guests. A hearty breakfast and dinner (during busy summer months) is served by the amiable hosts around the communal kitchen table. In addition to an informal, relaxed and friendly atmosphere, this farmhouse offers leisure facilities including fly fishing, clay-pigeon shooting tuition, a small outdoor swimming pool, games room and the attraction of its quiet position.

2rm(1hc) Annexe 4rm(3♠) CTV in 4 bedrooms ® ✗ (ex guide dogs) ✱ sB&B£19-£22 dB&B£36-£44 dB&B♠£38-£44 WBDi£171.50-£448 LDO 4pm

Lic 𝍠 CTV 12P ⛱clay pigeon shooting games room 126 acres mixed £

STURTON BY STOW Lincolnshire Map **08** SK88

FH QQQ Mrs Brenda Williams **Gallows Dale** *(SK874809)* Stow Park Rd LN1 2AH ☎Gainsborough(0427) 788387

Closed Xmas

A detached 18th-century red-brick farmhouse situated a mile from the village on the A1500 towards Gainsborough. Recently extended and modernised in keeping with its period, the house now provides comfortable, attractive bedrooms. There is a choice of lounges with one permitting smoking, otherwise smoking is not allowed.

3rm(2hc) (1fb)⊁in all bedrooms ® ✗ ✱ sB&B£14-£15 dB&B£28-£30

𝍠 CTV 3P nc6yrs 33 acres cattle £

SUDBURY Suffolk Map **05** TL84

GH QQ Old Bull And Trivets Church St CO10 6BL ☎(0787) 74120 due to change to 374120

Dating from the 16th century, this pink-washed, timbered building is operated as a restaurant, serving a predominantly pizza menu, and a guesthouse. All the rooms are on the first floor and are individually colour themed, those in the main house have more traditional furnishings and the 3 annexe rooms are more spacious. All have a good dressing table/desk facility with modern en suite bathrooms, controllable heating and colour TVs.

7rm(4⇌♠3hc) Annexe 3⇌♠ (5fb) CTV in all bedrooms ® ✱ sB&B£20-£30.55 sB&B⇌♠fr£30.55 dB&B£32-£37.50 dB&B⇌♠fr£42

Lic 𝍠 15P

Credit Cards 1 2 3 5

SURBITON Greater London London plan **4** B1 (pages 245-251)

GH Q Warwick 321 Ewell Rd KT6 7BX ☎081-399 5837 & 2405

This small guesthouse, convenient for the A3, is run by a cheerful proprietress. Bedrooms are clean, simply furnished and best suited for single guests. Public areas are limited.

9rm(1⇌8hc) (1fb) CTV in all bedrooms ® **T** ✱ sB&B£30-£36 sB&B⇌£36 dB&B£40-£46 dB&B⇌£46 WB&B£160-£180 WBDi£190-£210 LDO 2pm

𝍠 CTV 8P

Credit Cards 1 3 £

SUTTON Greater London London plan **4** C1 (pages 245-251)

GH QQQ Ashling Tara Hotel 50 Rosehill SM1 3EU ☎081-641 6142 FAX 081-644 7872

Two detached houses have been converted to make up this hotel on a residential road to the north of Sutton. Various improvements are taking place, which will leave the bar and dining room in one building with some bedrooms, and the remaining bedrooms will be a few doors away. All bedrooms are well maintained and equipped.

10rm(3⇌6♠1hc) Annexe 5rm(4♠1hc) (2fb) CTV in 14 bedrooms ® ✗ ✱ sB&B£30-£65 sB&B⇌♠£52.50-£56 dB&B£60-£70 dB&B⇌♠£56-£65 WB&Bfr£210 WBDifr£270 LDO 9pm

Lic 𝍠 CTV 16P

Credit Cards 1 3

GH Q ***Dene Hotel*** 39 Cheam Rd SM1 2AT ☎081-642 3170

The Dene has been personally run as a bed and breakfast hotel for many years, in a very friendly manner. It is a pair of linked houses, very close to the town centre, opposite the Holiday Inn, offering bedrooms in a variety of sizes, some with garden views.

28rm(8⇌4♠16hc) (3fb) CTV in all bedrooms ® ✗ (ex guide dogs)

𝍠 18P

GH Q Eaton Court Hotel 49 Eaton Rd SM2 5ED ☎081-643 6766

Closed 1 wk Xmas

Located in a quiet residential area, not far from the town centre, this pair of converted Victorian houses offers functional, well equipped bedrooms of varying sizes. Bed and breakfast only is provided, but there is a ground-floor lounge bar for hotel users.

14rm(2♠12hc) Annexe 7rm(1⇌6♠) (3fb) CTV in all bedrooms ® **T** ✱ sB&B£28-£40 sB&B⇌♠£32-£40 dB&B£36-£50 dB&B⇌♠£44-£52

Lic 𝍠 CTV 10P

Credit Cards 1 2 3 £

GH QQQ ***Thatched House Hotel*** 135 Cheam Rd SM1 2BN ☎081-642 3131 FAX 081-770 0684

Lying a short distance outside the town centre, on the A232, this thatched house has been carefully modernised and extended. The Sells are well established here and continue to improve their hotel. Bedrooms, on the ground and first floors, are all comfortably furnished and several overlook the garden and pond, and there is a small beamed bar with a carved oak counter.

27rm(19⇌♠8hc) CTV in all bedrooms ® LDO 8.45pm

Lic 𝍠 CTV 24P

Credit Cards 1 3

SUTTON West Sussex Map **04** SU91

SELECTED

INN QQQQ The White Horse RH20 1PS ☎(07987) 221 FAX (07987) 291

Dating back to 1746, this establishment has all the ingredients of a good village inn: attractive surroundings, interesting fresh food, real ales and bright, friendly staff. There are 5 splendid bedrooms with mahogany furniture, coordinated soft furnishings, smart modern bathrooms and thoughtful extras such as books, magazines, dried flowers and mineral water. Outside, there is a garden with a raised patio, and live music is regularly featured in the evening entertainment diary.

5⇌ CTV in all bedrooms ® **T** ✗ sB&B⇌£44 dB&B⇌£54 WB&B£127-£204 WBDi£199-£276 Lunch £12&alc Dinner £12&alc LDO 9.30pm

🍽 10P
Credit Cards 1 3 £

SUTTON COLDFIELD West Midlands Map **07** SP19

GH Q Standbridge Hotel 138 Birmingham Rd B72 1LY ☎021-354 3007

A friendly, well established guesthouse in a convenient location with easy access to the motorway network. Most of the compact rooms, though not en suite, have private shower facilities. There is a comfortable lounge and an attractive rear garden.

8hc Annexe 1hc CTV in all bedrooms ® sB&B£20-£21 sB&B£26 dB&B£36 WB&B£127.30-£133.70 WBDi£166-£172 LDO 6pm
Lic 🍽 CTV 11P nc5yrs jacuzzi
Credit Cards 1 3
See advertisement under BIRMINGHAM

SWAFFHAM Norfolk Map **05** TF80

GH QQQ Corfield House PE32 2EA ☎(0760) 23636
mid Mar-mid Dec

This red-brick former farmhouse has been carefully converted to provide 5 cottage-style en suite rooms. The rooms are immaculate, and standards of maintenance and housekeeping are exemplary: each is individually styled with pine furniture, Laura Ashley décor and soft furnishings. There is a comfortable guest lounge and a small dining room where set 4-course dinners are served at 7.30pm. Situated in the quiet village of Sporle, just outside Swaffham, the house is well sited for touring northwest Norfolk. Smoking is not permitted.

5rm(2⇌3🚿) ⊬in all bedrooms CTV in all bedrooms ® sB&B⇌🚿£19.50 dB&B⇌🚿£36-£39 WB&B£126-£136.50 WBDi£180-£195 LDO 6pm
Lic 🍽 5P
Credit Cards 1 3

SWANAGE Dorset Map **04** SZ07

GH QQQ *Bella Vista Hotel* 14 Burlington Rd BH19 1LS ☎(0929) 422873
Mar-Oct

Pretty flower-filled gardens and excellent sea views are the setting for this very attractive property, dating back to 1902, which stands on the cliff top beside a path leading to the beach. The bedrooms are freshly decorated, nicely furnished and very well looked after, the majority being en suite with showers. There is a comfortable lounge area with a fire, good easy seating and TV, where guests are served tea on their arrival and bedtime drinks if required. Whilst English breakfast is the only meal available, a varied choice is offered each morning and there is a small bar where, in the evenings, drinks are available. A warm, friendly greeting is assured from the proprietor Mrs Beeston, who works very hard to look after her guests and create a relaxed atmosphere.

6rm(5🚿1hc) (4fb) ® ✗
Lic 🍽 CTV 6P nc4yrs

GH QQQ Burlington House Hotel 7 Highcliffe Rd BH19 1LW ☎(0929) 422422
3 Apr-Oct

This small, personally managed hotel is well placed on the cliff top, with lovely sea views out across the bay. There is also a private cliff-side garden where guests can sit and enjoy the view. Continuing improvements have resulted in bedrooms which are pretty, fresh and nicely appointed, most with smart, modern bathrooms. The recently decorated lounge is bright and fresh, and the cosy bar is well stocked. A 4-course home-cooked evening meal is offered, and car parking is provided at the rear.

9rm(7⇌🚿2hc) (5fb) CTV in 8 bedrooms TV in 1 bedroom ® ✗ sB&B£14.50-£18 dB&B£32-£40 dB&B⇌🚿£35-£43 WB&B£105-£130 WBDi£150-£172 LDO 5pm
Lic 🍽 CTV 9P musical evenings £

GH QQQ Chines Hotel 9 Burlington Rd BH19 1LR ☎(0929) 422457
24 Apr-Sep rs Mar-Oct

This neat 2-storeyed house is situated in a residential area, close to both the sea and town centre. Bedrooms are well equipped and prettily decorated in coordinating fabrics. There is a smart bar area and an evening meal is offered. Outside there are pretty front gardens with a sun terrace.

12rm(8🚿4hc) (3fb)⊬in all bedrooms CTV in all bedrooms ® ✗ ✱ sB&B£17-£20 dB&B£34-£40 dB&B🚿£39-£45 WB&B£119-£133 WBDi£185.50-£199.50 LDO 4pm
Lic 🍽 CTV 9P ✿ £

GH QQQ Crowthorne Hotel 24 Cluny Crescent BH19 2BT ☎(0929) 422108
Closed Dec & Jan

Standing in an elevated position close to the centre of town, yet in a quiet residential area. The proprietors of this Victorian villa have steadily been upgrading and improving the property in keeping with its origins. It offers nicely decorated, comfortably furnished bedrooms and the majority are en suite with smart, modern facilities. There is a choice of 2 lounges, one equipped with TV and the other a quieter room filled with literature. The dining room is where home-cooked and delicious tempting meals are served in a wholesome, imaginative English style, using fresh produce. A welcoming pot of tea is offered to guests on arrival and the attentive proprietors remain involved during their stay. Crowthorne Hotel is a no-smoking establishment.

8rm(2⇌2🚿) (2fb)⊬in all bedrooms ® ✗ ✱ sB&B£25-£32.50 dB&B£50-£65 dB&B⇌🚿£58-£73 (incl dinner) WB&B£96-£150 WBDi£165-£220 LDO 5pm
Lic 🍽 CTV 8P
Credit Cards 1 3

GH QQ *Eversden Private Hotel* Victoria Rd BH19 1LY
☎(0929) 423276
Mar-Nov
Quietly situated in a residential area, this private hotel is a few minutes' walk from the beach and has good sea views. Bedrooms are simply furnished and neatly presented, and public areas include a comfortable TV lounge, cosy bar and a bright dining room. The atmosphere is relaxed and friendly, and many guests return year after year.
12rm(2⇔3↱7hc) (3fb)⊘in 2 bedrooms CTV in 1 bedroom TV in 1 bedroom ® ✗ LDO 6pm
Lic 🍴 CTV 12P

GH QQ Firswood Hotel 29 Kings Rd BH19 1HF
☎(0929) 422306
Closed Xmas
Conveniently situated close to the town centre, seafront and the steam railway, this small family-run establishment continues to be steadily improved and upgraded. The pretty bedrooms are light and airy, equipped to a good standard and only 2 have en suite, although the proprietors are hoping to add more as time progresses. In addition to the freshly decorated, nicely furnished dining room, there is a comfortable first-floor lounge with good sofa seating and TV. Some car parking spaces are provided, and a warm, relaxed and friendly atmosphere is offered throughout.
6rm(1⇔3↱2hc) (3fb) CTV in 5 bedrooms ® ✗ *
sB&B£13.50-£15 dB&B£26-£30 dB&B⇔↱£28-£32
WB&B£94.50-£105 WBDi£143.50-£154 LDO 4.30pm
🍴 CTV 7P nc5yrs

GH QQQ Gillan Hotel 5 Northbrook Rd BH19 1PN
☎(0929) 424548
This substantial corner property has recently been purchased by the Spencer family. Mr and Mrs Spencer are professional hoteliers and have implemented a steady and continued upgrading programme at the hotel. The bedrooms offer fresh, bright décor with most having modern en suite facilities, each well presented and neatly furnished. Public areas include a very welcoming heated outdoor swimming pool and a terrace where snacks and light lunches can be served in warm weather. There is a comfortable lounge with TV, a bright airy dining room and a cosy, snug bar/lounge. Interesting and varied menus are offered in the dining room, which is open to non-residents, and guests greatly appreciate the style and quality of the cuisine.
9rm(3⇔6↱) (4fb)⊘in all bedrooms CTV in all bedrooms ®
✗ sB&B⇔↱£22-£36 dB&B⇔↱£44-£52 WBDi£170-£230
LDO 5.30pm
Lic 10P ⩯(heated)
Credit Cards [1] [3]

GH QQQ Havenhurst Hotel 3 Cranbourne Rd BH19 1EA
☎(0929) 424224
A popular holiday hotel run by resident proprietors Pat Cherrett and Nicola Robson. Since taking over here, they have redecorated and upgraded almost throughout to a well coordinated modern standard. The dining room provides fresh food wherever possible, including home-made bread rolls and fresh fish, meat and vegetables. There is a smart bar lounge sometimes used by outside parties and a warm friendly atmosphere prevails.
17rm(6⇔11↱) (4fb) ® ✗ (ex guide dogs) LDO 7pm
Lic 🍴 CTV 17P

GH QQQ Oxford Hotel 3/5 Park Rd BH19 2AA
☎(0929) 422247
Along a steep hill, just away from the high street, this nicely maintained and presented establishment offers bright, fresh bedrooms, some of which have very smart en suite facilities and all are reasonably equipped. The public areas are comfortably furnished and have a cosy atmosphere. The cheerful, involved proprietors have only recently taken over this small family hotel, and provide a friendly service to their guests.
14rm(7⇔↱7hc) (4fb) CTV in 12 bedrooms TV in 2 bedrooms
® ✗ sB&B£17.50-£19.50 dB&B£35-£39 dB&B⇔↱£41-£45
WB&B£117-£151 WBDi£171-£205 LDO 4.30pm
Lic 🍴 CTV (£)

GH QQQ *St Michael Hotel* 31 Kings Rd BH19 1HF
☎(0929) 422064
Feb-Nov
Situated close to the centre of town and the steam railway, this guesthouse offers clean, bright bedrooms and comfortable public areas. During the busy season a home-cooked evening meal is available, and there is a small car park in addition to the on-street and public car parking close by.
6rm(3↱3hc) (4fb) CTV in all bedrooms ® LDO 2pm
Lic 🍴 5P nc5yrs

GH QQQ Sandringham Hotel 20 Durlston Rd BH19 2HX
☎(0929) 423076
Mar-Nov rs Dec-Mar
A small private hotel quietly located in a residential area, close to the Country Park and seafront. Personally supervised by the resident owners, the housekeeping standards are high, and bedrooms are well furnished and equipped and generally of ample size. Public areas are comfortable, and a home-cooked 4-course evening meal is offered.
11rm(9↱2hc) (5fb) ® ✗ (ex guide dogs) * sB&B£21-£25
dB&B↱£42-£50 WB&B£126-£150 WBDi£180-£210
LDO 6.30pm
Lic 🍴 CTV 8P (£)

GH QQQ White Lodge Hotel Grosvenor Rd BH19 2DD
☎(0929) 422696 & 425510
rs Dec & Feb
Standing in an elevated position above the town centre, this property dates back to 1909 and is now personally run by the Hutchins family, who are steadily improving the guesthouse and offer a warm, cheery and friendly welcome. The majority of bright, freshly decorated bedrooms are en suite and there is one ground-floor room popular with the elderly. There are 2 lounges, both conventional in style with comfortable furniture and it is hoped that a small bar is to be fitted in one of the lounge areas. Very enjoyable home cooking is served in the dining room, chosen from a set menu featuring tasty dishes prepared by Mrs Hutchins. Overall this small, private establishment has much to commend it and is ideal for visitors who require a quiet break, with lots of local attractions near by.
14⇔↱ (4fb) CTV in all bedrooms ® * sB&B⇔↱£24-£31
dB&B⇔↱£48-£58 (incl dinner) WB&Bfr£140 WBDi£160-£190 LDO 6pm
Lic 🍴 CTV 12P
Credit Cards [1] [2] [3]

SWANSEA West Glamorgan Map **03** SS69

See also Bishopston, Langland Bay and Mumbles

GH QQ Alexander Hotel 3 Sketty Road, Uplands, Sketty
SA2 0EU ☎(0792) 470045 & 476012
Closed Xmas
Conveniently situated for the city centre and the Uplands shopping centre, this friendly, family-run hotel offers comfortable accommodation. In addition to the usual facilities, bedrooms include satellite TV.
7rm(6⇔↱1hc) (4fb) CTV in all bedrooms ® T
✗ (ex guide dogs) * sB&B£20 sB&B⇔↱£25-£30
dB&B⇔↱£40-£42 WB&B£100-£150
Lic 🍴 P̸ nc2yrs games room
Credit Cards [1] [2] [3] [5] (£)

GH QQQ Cefn Bryn 6 Uplands Crescent SA2 0PB
☎(0792) 466687
Closed Xmas
Conveniently situated near the Uplands shopping centre, and not far from the city centre, this family-run hotel is spotlessly clean and full of character. Comfortably furnished throughout, rooms

are spacious and bright, retaining many Victorian features including ornate interior plasterwork and large fireplaces. Bedrooms are prettily decorated and furnished with soft fabrics and a good range of facilities. There is also an attractive lawned garden at the front of the building.
6↱ (2fb) CTV in all bedrooms ® ✗ ✱ sB&B↱£20 dB&B↱£40 WB&Bfr£99
CTV ✗P

GH QQ *Channel View* 17 Bryn Rd, Brynmill SA2 0AR ☎(0792) 466834
This friendly guesthouse overlooks the St Helens cricket and rugby ground, with "grandstand" views from many rooms including the breakfast room. Bedrooms are simply furnished in a modern style, and the Parr family are friendly and hospitable hosts.
6hc (1fb)⊁in all bedrooms CTV in all bedrooms ® LDO 10am
CTV

GH QQ Crescent 132 Eaton Crescent, Uplands SA1 4QR ☎(0792) 466814
Closed Xmas & New Year
This friendly, family-run hotel is neatly tucked away in a quiet residential area, convenient for the Uplands shopping centre and not far from the city centre and seafront. Bedrooms are bright and well equipped, and the lounge and dining room are congenial. There is car parking available for guests.
6⇌↱ (1fb) CTV in all bedrooms ® ✱ sB&B⇌↱£20 dB&B⇌↱£32 WB&B£105-£125 WBDi£147-£170 LDO 9am
CTV 4P

GH QQ The Guest House 2/4 Bryn Rd SA2 0AR ☎(0792) 466947
This friendly guesthouse offers value for money and is conveniently situated for the beach, city centre and the cricket and rugby ground which is just across the road. Well managed by the Tough family, accommodation includes good modern bedrooms with all necessary facilities, a cosy bar, and a choice of comfortable lounges.
14rm(6↱8hc) (2fb)⊁in 7 bedrooms ✗ (ex guide dogs) ✱ sB&B£13-£22 sB&B↱£20-£25 dB&B↱£34-£40 LDO 1pm
Lic CTV ✗P nc9yrs
Credit Cards 1 2 3

SELECTED

GH QQQQ Tredilion House Hotel 26 Uplands Crescent, Uplands SA2 0PB ☎(0792) 470766
rs Xmas
Thoughtfully and tastefully converted by the owners Mr and Mrs Mesner into a cosy, comfortable house, this Victorian property has retained much of its distinctive charm and character with pleasing interior plasterwork, cornices, an open staircase and brightly polished wooden floors. The bedrooms are prettily decorated in Liberty-style wall coverings with matching fabrics and duvets, and fitted with complementary antique and reproduction Victorian pine furnishings. All rooms have bright en suites and a high range of facilities including TV, direct-dial telephone and hairdryer, plus nice little personal touches throughout. There is an inviting lounge and an appealing little breakfast room complete with dispense bar. Personal, friendly service is provided by the conscientious owners, who continue to make improvements to their house and always keep it spotlessly clean. Outside there is a pretty little garden at the front, and parking is available.
7⇌↱ (1fb) CTV in all bedrooms ® T sB&B⇌↱£34-£38 dB&B⇌↱£48-£50 WB&B£160-£250 WBDi£240-£335 LDO noon
Lic CTV 8P 1🚗
Credit Cards 1 2 3 5 £

SWAY Hampshire Map **04** SZ29

GH QQ The Nurse's Cottage Station Rd SO41 6BA ☎Lymington(0590) 683402
This small bungalow was formerly the district nurse's home and is situated in the heart of this New Forest village. The neatly decorated bedrooms are clean and offer modern facilities that include TV and tea/coffee-making equipment. There is a small, well furnished breakfast room where dinner is served by prior arrangement, and the garden, incorporating a patio, is available for guests' use. Being a bungalow, this guesthouse has obvious advantages for the less able and is an ideal base for visiting numerous attractions.
3rm(1↱2hc) (1fb) CTV in all bedrooms ® sB&B£17.50-£18.50 dB&B£30-£32 dB&B↱£32.50-£36 WB&B£107-£124.50 WBDi£166.50-£184 LDO 6pm
Lic 5P nc8yrs
Credit Cards 1 3
See advertisement under LYMINGTON

SELECTED

GH QQQQ The Tower Barrows Ln SO41 6DE ☎Lymington(0590) 683034 FAX (0590) 683785
Closed 24 Dec-13 Jan
This magnificent folly, standing over 200ft tall, was built in the 1880s and was one of the first buildings to be created in concrete. Its creator was 'Judge' Peterson, who was reputedly aided in his architectural plans by Sir Christopher Wren, through a medium. Today, after much loving restoration, Paul and Julie Atlas have created something unique: the Tower is appealingly different. The 4 elegant rooms are filled with antiques and facilities include private telephone, answer-phone, mini bar and satellite TV. Gothic moulded arches, unusual pictures and fine antiques and tapestries abound and a trip up the winding staircase to the 13th floor to enjoy the view must not be missed. A delicious supper cooked by the very efficient and charming Sheila is taken in the small, cosy dining room. Smoking is not permitted here. **Best Newcomer for South East England 1992–3, see colour section.**
4⇌↱ ⊁in all bedrooms CTV in all bedrooms ® T ✗ ✱ sB&B⇌↱£49-£65 dB&B⇌↱£98
Lic 5P nc12yrs ⊡(heated) ℘(hard)
Credit Cards 1 2 3 5

SWINDERBY Lincolnshire Map **08** SK86

GH QQQ Halfway Farm Motel & Guest House A46 LN6 9HN (8m N of Newark on A46, 8m SW Lincoln) ☎(0522) 868749 FAX (0522) 868082
Aptly named, as it lies on the A46 midway between Lincoln and Newark. A very well kept 18th-century farmhouse with motel-style accommodation in the nicely converted brick and pantile outbuildings. These offer particularly good comfort and good en suite facilities.
7rm(3↱4hc) Annexe 10↱ (4fb) CTV in all bedrooms ® T ✱ sB&B£18-£20 sB&B↱£27-£28 dB&B£34-£36 dB&B↱£38-£40
CTV 20P nc2yrs
Credit Cards 1 2 3 5 £
See advertisement under LINCOLN

SWINDON Wiltshire Map **04** SU18

GH QQQ Fir Tree Lodge 17 Highworth Rd, Stratton St Margaret SN3 4QL ☎(0793) 822372
Built in the 1930's, this recently extended family home is situated on the edge of the town with easy access to the M4. The en suite bedrooms are modern with simple décor and bright coordinating soft furnishings and all have TV. Breakfast is served at separate tables in the compact dining room, and a warm welcome is assured from the resident proprietors.
→

11🚿 CTV in all bedrooms ® 🚫🐕 (ex guide dogs) ✱ sB&B🚿£20-£25 dB&B🚿£35-£40
🏠 14P £

GH QQ ***Grove Lodge*** 108 Swindon Rd SN3 4PT
☎(0793) 825343
Comfortable accommodation is offered at this family-run roadside hotel on the outskirts of Swindon. Bedrooms are well equipped, and breakfast is served in an informal dining room.
10⇌🚿 (1fb) CTV in all bedrooms ® LDO 6pm
🏠 12P

SYMONDS YAT (EAST) Hereford & Worcester Map **03** SO51

GH QQQ Garth Cottage Hotel HR9 6JL ☎(0600) 890364
Garth Cottage is set on the banks of the River Wye with superb views, and is ideal for anglers, walkers and tourists. The Eden family offer warm and genuine hospitality and the compact rooms are clean and fresh, with welcoming extras, pretty fabrics and cushions. There is a comfortable modern lounge, a pine furnished dining room and a cosy bar. The new conservatory serves as a sun lounge and extension to the dining room.
4🚿 ® 🚫🐕 (ex guide dogs) dB&B🚿£44 WB&B£140 WBDi£234.50 LDO 3pm
Lic 🏠 CTV 9P nc12yrs 🎣

INN QQ ***Saracens Head*** HR9 6JL ☎(0600) 890435
Once a cider mill, this friendly family-run half-timbered inn lies alongside the River Wye at this lovely beauty spot. Many rooms overlook the river and they are all attractively decorated; several have en suite shower rooms. There is an upstairs lounge, again overlooking the river, with books, games and satellite TV. The public bar is long and narrow and features a red GPO box in working order; another lounge bar has a central fireplace. A good choice of menus is available in the restaurant, with bistro meals as well as à la carte and table d'hôte; fresh Wye salmon is a speciality, and there is an extensive seafood menu.
10rm(7🚿3hc) (1fb) ® 🚫🐕 LDO 9.30pm
🏠 CTV 60P 🎣
Credit Cards 1 2 3 5

SYMONDS YAT (WEST) (NEAR ROSS-ON-WYE) Hereford & Worcester Map **03** SO51

GH QQ Woodlea Hotel HR9 6BL
☎Symonds Yat(0600) 890206
Closed 11 Jan-25 Feb
Dating back to the 16th century, with an extension added in 1896, this pleasant house is idyllically situated overlooking the River Wye in wooded slopes above this famous beauty spot. Bedrooms are attractively decorated with pretty wallpaper and fabrics, and most have en suite bathrooms and fine views. There is a comfortable lounge with a copper-hooded log fire, a cosy cottage-style bar and a separate coffee lounge. Owners Val and Tony Blunt offer a genuine welcome to their guests and provide good home cooking. The gardens contain an outdoor swimming pool and terraced lawns.
9rm(6⇌🚿3hc) (2fb) ® **T** sB&B£21.50-£22.50 dB&B£43-£45 dB&B⇌🚿£52-£55 WBDi£195-£240 LDO 6.30pm
Lic 🏠 CTV 9P
Credit Cards 1 2 3 £

TADCASTER North Yorkshire Map **08** SE44

GH QQ Shann House 47 Kirkgate LS24 9AQ ☎(0937) 833931
A Georgian town house in the one-way system with car parking at the rear. The spacious bedrooms all have en suite facilities; there is a small breakfast room with pine furniture and a guests' lounge.
8⇌🚿 (1fb) CTV in all bedrooms ® ✱ sB&B⇌🚿fr£20.50 dB&B⇌🚿fr£36 WB&Bfr£143.50
Lic 🏠 P̸
Credit Cards 1 3 £

TALGARTH Powys Map **03** SO13

FH QQ Mrs B Prosser **Upper Genffordd** *(SO171304)*
LD3 0EN ☎(0874) 711360
Just off the A479 and 3 miles south of Talgarth, these 16th-century farm buildings have been converted to provide farmhouse accommodation. The proprietors provide pretty bedrooms and a lounge with character. A cheerful welcome awaits guests.
2⇌🚿 (1fb) CTV in all bedrooms ® ✱ sB&B⇌🚿£12.50-£13 dB&B⇌🚿£25-£26 WB&B£87.50-£91 LDO 5pm
🏠 CTV 4P 200 acres dairy mixed sheep

TAL-Y-LLYN Gwynedd Map **06** SH60

GH QQQ Dolffanog Fawr LL36 9AJ ☎Corris(0654) 761247
FAX (0654) 761480
Surrounded by attractive gardens, this 17th-century former farmhouse is situated at one end of Tal-y-Llyn Lake, at the foot of Cader Idris Mountain and commands magnificent views of the lake and valley. The new owners Pam and Alan Coulter have made extensive improvements to the 3 bedrooms, inlcuding the provision of en suite facilities and central heating. The brightly decorated rooms have solid pine furniture with pretty coordinated soft furnishings and extra thoughtful touches include a wide variety of toiletry items. A choice of lounges is available for smokers or non-smokers, and a traditionally furnished dining room with a feature stone fireplace seats 6 people at a communal table.
3⇌🚿 🚭in all bedrooms CTV in all bedrooms ®
🚫🐕 (ex guide dogs) ✱ dB&B⇌🚿£31-£35 WB&B£115.50 WBDi£185.50 LDO 5pm
🏠 CTV 6P nc10yrs £

TARRANT MONKTON Dorset Map **03** ST90

INN QQQ Langton Arms DT11 8RX ☎(0258) 89225
In the middle of a tiny village, this inn offers 6 chalet-style bedrooms in a modern annexe complete with courtyard where guests may enjoy the sunshine. The rooms are all very well equipped and each has a useful lobby area and very smart en suite bath/shower rooms. The inn itself has plenty of character and charm. There is a lounge and public bar where an extensive range of bar snacks is served. If more formal dining is preferrred, there is a cosy restaurant with tempting table d'hôte and à la carte menus. Breakfast is served in a sunny conservatory and the atmosphere throughout is relaxed, cheerful and friendly, with locals mingling easily with guests.
Annexe 6⇌🚿 CTV in all bedrooms ® ✱ sB&B⇌🚿£28-£32 dB&B⇌🚿£40-£48 Lunch £8.50-£10 Dinner £11.95-£14.95&alc LDO 9.15pm
80P pool table skittles
Credit Cards 1 2 3

TAUNTON Somerset Map **03** ST22

GH QQ Brookfield 16 Wellington Rd TA1 4EQ
☎(0823) 272786
Situated along the A38 close to the town centre, this small family-run hotel continues to be steadily upgraded. The bedrooms whilst simply furnished, are reasonably equipped, have bright carpeting, a fresh décor and are generally nicely presented. All public rooms are comfortable with a warm, relaxed feel about them. Dinner is occasionally offered, depending on guests' requirements, and smoking is not permitted in the dining room. A small front forecourt parking area is provided.
8hc (2fb) CTV in all bedrooms ® sB&B£15-£18 dB&B£25-£30 WB&B£105-£126 WBDi£140-£161 LDO 2.30pm
Lic 🏠 CTV 8P £

SELECTED

GH QQQQ Meryan House Hotel Bishop's Hull TA1 5EG ☎(0823) 337445

This charming period residence dating back over 300 years is located in the quiet village of Bishop's Hull, a mere mile from the centre of Taunton and major routes. The Clark family have created a very comfortable, attractive and elegant private hotel, so much so, in fact, that early booking is strongly advised. Each of the 12 bedrooms is individually decorated in a pretty feminine style with lots of extra thoughtful touches such as boiled sweets, comfortable cushioned seating, tissues, pot pourri and quality toiletries. Public areas are elegant and very comfortable. A home-cooked 4-course meal is very reasonably priced. Mrs Clark loves cooking and this enjoyment is reflected in the varied and interesting menus.

12⇌↱ (3fb)⊁in 4 bedrooms CTV in all bedrooms Ⓡ T ✱ sB&B⇌↱£36-£38 dB&B⇌↱£45-£49 LDO 6.30pm

Lic ⅢCTV 17P tennis net croquet

Credit Cards [1] [3] Ⓔ

FH QQQ Mrs M Fewings **Higher Dipford** *(ST216205)* Trull TA3 7NU ☎(0823) 275770 & 257916

Closed Feb

Maureen and Chris Fewings extend a warm West Country welcome to guests at their Grade II listed farmhouse, which dates back to the 14th century. It is on a country road at the foot of the Blackdown Hills, just three quarters of a mile from Taunton Deane service area on the M5, and 2.25 miles from the centre of the town. The house is surrounded by the farm buildings, some of which are derelict and one, adjoining the house, has been converted to provide a spacious character lounge with exposed stonework and timbers. The 3 bedrooms upstairs are in a similar style with modern en suite facilities. The accommodation is tastefully furnished and the quality is evident throughout the décor, down to the Aynsley china and the sturgeon prints on the walls. There is a smaller lounge with an honesty bar, and home-cooked, traditional fresh farmhouse fare is served at separate tables in the elegant dining room.

3⇌↱ CTV in all bedrooms Ⓡ ✗ ✱ sB&B⇌↱fr£30 dB&B⇌↱fr£50 WB&Bfr£161 WBDi£259-£273 LDO 8pm

Lic Ⅲ CTV 6P 120 acres beef dairy

Credit Cards [2]

TAVISTOCK Devon Map **02** SX47

See also Mary Tavy

GH QQQ Old Coach House Hotel Ottery PL19 8NS (2mW) ☎(0822) 617515

This former coach house to the adjacent farm has been recently restored and converted into a small hotel of character, situated in the hamlet of Ottery. The three bedrooms on the ground floor are en suite and comfortably furnished. Both the cosy lounge and the intimate restaurant have access to the patio and a set evening dinner is available. Resident proprietors extend a warm welcome to guests.

6rm(4⇌2↱) (1fb) Ⓡ ✗ (ex guide dogs) sB&B⇌↱£19-£27 dB&B⇌↱£38-£54 WB&B£120-£170 WBDi£175-£225 LDO 10pm

Lic Ⅲ CTV 8P nc10yrs ♪

Credit Cards [1] [3] Ⓔ

See advertisement on page 389

TEBAY Cumbria Map **12** NY60

GH QQQ Carmel House Mount Pleasant CA10 3TH ☎Orton(05874) 651

Closed 23 Dec-3 Jan

A very well furnished and comfortable small guesthouse next to the post office, in the village centre. Bedrooms are delightfully furnished, and there is a cosy lounge for guests. Service is friendly and welcoming.

→

5↱ (1fb) CTV in all bedrooms ® ✗ (ex guide dogs) ✱
sB&B↱£15.50-£18 dB&B↱£31-£36 WB&B£105-£115
♨ CTV 6P
Credit Cards [1] [3]

TEIGNMOUTH Devon Map **03** SX97

GH QQQ Fonthill Torquay Rd, Shaldon TQ14 0AX
☎Shaldon(0626) 872344
Closed Xmas/New Year
This Georgian manor house is set in 25 acres of garden and grounds overlooking the River Teign, with fine yew hedges an impressive feature. The 3 comfortable bedrooms are in the west wing along with a breakfast room cum sitting room with colour TV. The Graeme family warmly welcome guests to their no-smoking home.
3rm(1⇌↱2hc) ⊬in all bedrooms ® ✗ ✱ sB&B£25-£28 dB&B£36-£38 dB&B⇌↱£39-£42
♨ CTV 6P ℘(hard)

[⇌▶] GH QQ Hill Rise Hotel Winterbourne Rd TQ14 8JT
☎(0626) 773108
In a quiet residential cul-de-sac, this red-brick Edwardian house offers light, airy accommodation. There is a comfortable guests' lounge with television, and home-made bar snacks are available in the evening. Smoking is not allowed in the hotel except in the bar.
8rm(2↱6hc) (2fb)⊬in all bedrooms CTV in 2 bedrooms ®
✗ (ex guide dogs) sB&B£12.50-£14 sB&B↱£12.75-£14.50 dB&B£25-£30 dB&B↱£30-£35
Lic ♨ CTV 5P Ⓔ

GH QQQ Lyme Bay House Hotel Den Promenade TQ14 8SZ
☎(0626) 772953
Apr-Oct
A large Victorian house overlooking the sea on Den Promenade, next to the church, situated close to the town's amenities. Three of the bedrooms have private bathrooms, and TVs are available in rooms on request. A lift serves all floors.
9rm(3↱6hc) (1fb) ® ✱ sB&Bfr£16 sB&B↱£22 dB&Bfr£32 dB&B↱fr£42 WB&Bfr£100 WBDi£143-£170
Lic lift ♨ CTV ₱

GH QQ Rathlin House Hotel Upper Hermosa Rd TQ14 9JW
☎(0626) 774473
Closed Xmas
This attractive Victorian villa is set in a quiet residential area and has its own gardens and a sun-trap terrace. Bedrooms are simply furnished and well presented, there is a comfortable guests' lounge, and the dining room serves plain English meals.
10rm(5↱5hc) (4fb) CTV in 2 bedrooms ® LDO 6.15pm
Lic CTV 12P Ⓔ

SELECTED

GH QQQQ Thomas Luny House Teign St TQ14 8EG
☎(0626) 772976
Closed mid Dec-mid Jan
Purchased in 1988 by John and Alison Allan, the house took the best part of a year to restore. Now it is much as it would have been when the 18th-century marine artist, whose name it bears, lived there. It is approached through an archway and a courtyard with parking. Guests sit around a large table to enjoy the set menu which might include celery and pepper soup followed by John Dory with an orange and mushroom stuffing and chocolate and cinnamon cream pie. Bedrooms are furnished with great flair and have thoughtful touches like fresh flowers, books and mineral water. Each has direct-dial telephone and remote- control colour TV.
4rm(3⇌1↱) CTV in all bedrooms **T** ✗ (ex guide dogs)
sB&B⇌↱£27.50-£30 dB&B⇌↱£55-£60 LDO 8pm
Lic ♨ 8P nc12yrs Ⓔ

TELFORD Shropshire Map **07** SJ60

GH QQQ Church Farm Wrockwardine, Wellington TF6 5DG
☎(0952) 244917
This attractive Georgian farmhouse is in the heart of the village of Wrockwardine, virtually opposite the church. Each room is individually decorated and all have modern facilities. Recently the remains of a medieval manor house have been found in the grounds, and these are to be made a feature of the garden.
5rm(1⇌↱3hc) Annexe 1↱ (1fb) CTV in all bedrooms ® ✱
sB&Bfr£25 sB&B⇌↱fr£30 dB&Bfr£38 dB&B⇌↱£40-£46 WB&B£110-£133 WBDi£201-£224 LDO 9am
♨ CTV 10P Ⓔ

GH QQQ *West Ridge* TF11 9LB ☎(0952) 581223
A much extended, privately owned and personally run guesthouse set in large gardens, situated on the A4169 close to its junction with the B4379. The accommodation is very well equipped, and all rooms have private bathrooms. Its location close to the A54 and the nearby Halesfield industrial estate in Telford makes it popular with business people; however it is equally suitable for tourists wishing to visit the historic town of Ironbridge.
5⇌↱ CTV in all bedrooms ® ✗ (ex guide dogs) LDO 9pm
Lic ♨ CTV 10P nc10yrs
Credit Cards [1] [2] [3]

INN QQ *Cock Hotel* 148 Holyhead Rd, Wellington TF1 2ED
☎(0952) 244954
This traditional town inn is situated at the busy junction of the B5061 and the A5; close to junction 7 of the M54. Clean, simply furnished bedrooms are available, together with ample parking facilities.
7hc (1fb) CTV in all bedrooms ® ✗ LDO 9pm
♨ 30P 4🚘

INN QQ Swan Hotel Watling St, Wellington TF1 2NH
☎(0952) 223781
Since purchasing the hotel from the brewery, the proprietors have made great improvements to the accommodation; the rooms are now smart and modern, and the meal choices vary from an à la carte menu to lighter bar snacks.
12rm(6↱6hc) (2fb) CTV in all bedrooms ® ✱ sB&B£15-£25 sB&B↱£25-£38 dB&B£30-£36 dB&B↱£30-£40 Bar Lunch £2.50-£9 Dinner £2.50-£9.95&alc LDO 10pm
♨ 150P
Credit Cards [1] [2] [3] Ⓔ

TEMPLE CLOUD Avon Map **03** ST65

FH QQ Mr & Mrs Wyatt **Temple Bridge** *(ST627575)*
BS18 5AA ☎Mendip(0761) 452377
Mar-Oct
This 17th-century white farmhouse with mullion windows and oak beams also has a large garden available to guests. The house is situated south of the village and set back from the A37 road. It is within easy distance of Bath, Wells and Bristol. Simple accommodation is provided in comfortable rooms.
2hc (2fb) ® ✗ sB&B£16-£17 dB&B£28-£32
♨ CTV 2P 1🚘 nc2yrs 250 acres beef arable Ⓔ

TENBY Dyfed Map **02** SN10

GH QQ Castle View Private Hotel The Norton SA70 8AA
☎(0834) 842666
Mar-Oct
A family-run hotel ideally situated overlooking the harbour and North Beach. The first-floor lounge and several bedrooms have lovely views of the beach and harbour, and all the rooms are well equipped and en suite.
10rm(7⇌3↱) (4fb) CTV in all bedrooms ® ✱ sB&B⇌↱£18-£21 dB&B⇌↱£36-£42 WB&B£126-£147 WBDi£168-£189 LDO 6.30pm
Lic CTV 7P
Credit Cards [3]

GH QQ Clarence House Hotel Esplanade SA70 7DU
☏(0834) 844371 FAX (0834) 844372
mid Apr-mid Oct
A large Victorian hotel overlooking the sandy south beach, with good sea views from some rooms and views of the garden from others. Bedrooms are all en suite and well equipped, and there is a bar and a choice of 2 lounges for residents.
68⇌↱ (4fb) CTV in all bedrooms ® sB&B⇌↱£20-£32 dB&B⇌↱£34-£58 WB&B£119-£231 WBDi£175-£287 LDO 7.30pm
Lic lift ♨ CTV nc3yrs
Credit Cards 1 3 £

GH QQ *Gumfreston Private Hotel* Culver Park SA70 7ED
☏(0834) 842871
Closed Nov
Just a short stroll from the south beach you will find this cosy guesthouse, run by the friendly owners, Bill and Dot Tovey. The individually decorated bedrooms have recently been updated with clever use of bed canopies, satin bed covers and matching fabrics. A comfortable residents' lounge and cosy basement bar provide adequate facilities.
11rm(1⇌10↱) (5fb) ® ✗ LDO 4pm
Lic ♨ CTV ℙ
Credit Cards 3

GH QQQ Hildebrand Hotel Victoria St SA70 7DY
☏(0834) 842403
Apr-Oct rs Jan-Mar & Nov
Veronica and Jim Martin have run this small hotel for 2 decades and make every effort to ensure their guests feel at home. It is situated a short walk from the walled town and just 200yds from the golden South Beach. There is an excellent first-floor lounge, a cosy basement bar and a feature of the hotel is the award-winning floral displays, which are on show during the season.

→

10rm(8⇌↱2hc) (5fb)⅟in 3 bedrooms CTV in all bedrooms ® ✕ sB&B£16-£21 sB&B⇌↱£18-£25 dB&B£28-£38 dB&B⇌↱£30-£46 WB&B£85-£136 WBDi£145-£199 LDO 4pm
Lic 🍽 CTV 🅿̸ nc3yrs
Credit Cards [1] [2] [3] [5]

GH QQ Ripley St Marys Hotel Saint Mary's St SA70 7HN
☎(0834) 842837
Apr-Sep rs Feb-Mar & Oct-Nov
Situated within the town walls and less than 100 yards from the sea, this guesthouse offers cosy bedrooms, a comfortable, traditional lounge, and a small bar. It has been run by the same friendly family for over 20 years.
14rm(8⇌↱6hc) (6fb) CTV in all bedrooms ® ✱ sB&B£18 sB&B⇌↱£22 dB&B£36 dB&B⇌↱£40 WB&Bfr£124 WBDifr£180 LDO 5.30pm
Lic CTV 🅿̸
Credit Cards [1] [3]

GH QQ *Sea Breezes Hotel* 18 The Norton SA70 8AA
☎(0834) 842753
Jun-Sep rs Mar-May & Oct-Nov
This small, family-run guesthouse stands a few yards from the sandy North Beach and harbour, 2 minutes from the town centre. Bedrooms are modestly appointed, but all have TV and tea-making facilities. There is a comfortable combined lounge/bar on the 1st floor.
11rm(5⇌1↱5hc) (3fb)⅟in 6 bedrooms CTV in 6 bedrooms TV in 5 bedrooms ® ✕ (ex guide dogs) LDO 4.30pm
Lic 🍽 CTV 🅿̸

GH QQQ Tall Ships Hotel 34 Victoria St SA70 7DY
☎(0834) 842055
Mar-Oct
The sandy South Beach, town centre and bowling green are all within easy walking distance of this guesthouse where a warm welcome is extended by Marianne and Dilwyn Richards. Bedrooms are neat and modern, with attractive flower baskets complementing the pretty duvets. Some have en suite shower rooms. Public areas include a cosy basement 'nautical' bar and a comfortable modern lounge.
8rm(5↱3hc) (6fb) CTV in all bedrooms ® ✕ (ex guide dogs) sB&B£15-£18 sB&B↱£17.50-£20.50 dB&B£26-£32 dB&B↱£31-£37 WB&B£87-£124.50 WBDi£125-£165.50 LDO 5pm
Lic CTV 🅿̸
Credit Cards [1] [3]

TETBURY Gloucestershire Map **03** ST89

SELECTED

GH QQQQ Tavern House Willesley GL8 8QU
☎Westonbirt(0666) 880444
Very well sited for touring the Cotswolds, this attractive stone property stands adjacent to the A433, 3 miles west of Tetbury. The house dates back some 400 years and has recently been restored by the owners, Tim and Janet Tremellen, to provide a very commendable retreat. The cosy beamed bedrooms, which retain much of the original charm, are very comfortably furnished, brightly decorated and boast a high range of facilities. All are spotlessly clean and are equipped with spacious en suites with personalised toiletries. There is a comfortable lounge and an appealing little breakfast room, where a hearty breakfast is served. The Tremellens do not offer dinner but will be happy to advise guests of local eating options. Another bonus is the delightful walled garden where al fresco breakfasts can be taken during warmer weather. Smoking is prohibited in all bedrooms and the breakfast room.
4⇌↱ ⅟in all bedrooms CTV in all bedrooms ® T ✕ ✱ sB&B⇌↱£35-£45 dB&B⇌↱£49-£57 WB&B£161-£189
🍽 8P nc10yrs
Credit Cards [1] [3] ©

TEWKESBURY Gloucestershire Map **03** SO83

GH QQ *The Abbey Hotel* 67 Church St GL20 5RX
☎(0684) 294247
With its attractive restaurant recently opened, this family-run hotel, situated in the main street, offers comfortable bedrooms fitted with many extras. It has a car park at the rear.
16rm(7⇌7↱2hc) (3fb) CTV in all bedrooms ® LDO 9.30pm
Lic 🍽 11P
Credit Cards [1] [2] [3]

FH QQQ Mick & Anne Meadows ***Home*** *(SO933390)* Bredons Norton GL20 7HA ☎Bredon(0684) 72322
Closed Dec
This attractive farmhouse is situated 100yds up a lane which runs beside the village hall. It has pretty bedrooms and a comfortable lounge with French windows that lead to a patio area and gardens.
3rm(2⇌1hc) (1fb) ®
6P 🏠

THAME Oxfordshire Map **04** SP70

GH QQ Essex House Chinnor Rd OX9 3LS ☎(084421) 7567 FAX (084421) 6420
A detached property with a walled garden situated on the bend of the Chinnor road, between Thame and Chinnor. Bedrooms are equipped with TV, direct-dial telephones and tea-making facilities. Most of the rooms have private bathrooms; 6 are in an annexe block across the car park, where smoking is not permitted. There is a cosy bar, and a choice of dishes is offered on the table d'hôte menu in the dining room. Ample car parking is available.
8rm(5↱3hc) Annexe 6rm(3⇌3↱) (1fb)⅟in 5 bedrooms CTV in all bedrooms ® T ✕ (ex guide dogs) ✱ sB&Bfr£35 sB&B⇌↱fr£43 dB&B⇌↱fr£59 LDO 7pm
Lic 🍽 CTV 20P
Credit Cards [1] [2] [3] [5]

SELECTED

FH QQQQ Mrs M Aitken **Upper Green** *(SP736053)* Manor Rd, Towersey OX9 3QR (1.5m E unclass rd)
☎(0844) 212496 FAX (0844) 260399
A most attractive setting, on the edge of the village of Towersey surrounded by open countryside, adds to the appeal of this 15th-century, thatched, whitewashed farmhouse. Some of the bedrooms are situated in a timber-framed barn conversion which also houses the breakfast room and a comfortable lounge, with more lounge area available in the farmhouse. The bedrooms are individual in style and décor, furnished with antiques and bric-a-brac. The farmhouse is full of character, with exposed beams and inglenook fireplaces, tastefully decorated and lavishly furnished with antiques, in keeping with the style of the building, by the resident proprietors Evan and Marjorie Aitken. Children and pets are not accepted, and smoking is not permitted.
3rm(1↱1hc) Annexe 6⇌↱ ⅟in all bedrooms CTV in 7 bedrooms TV in 2 bedrooms ® ✕ ✱ sB&B£20 sB&B⇌↱£28 dB&B£35 dB&B⇌↱£38-£50
🍽 CTV 11P nc13yrs 7 acres poultry sheep

THAXTED Essex Map **05** TL63

GH QQQ Folly House Watling Ln CH6 2QY
☎(0371) 830618
Quietly situated in a lane just off the centre of the village, this modern house, built in 1988, offers 3 comfortably furnished bedrooms, one being en suite and the other 2 sharing a spacious bathroom. Downstairs, guests have their own smart lounge, furnished with some antique pieces and with a real coal fire.

Breakfast is served in the small dining room with its communal oak table (separate tables can be set up if preferred) and French doors lead to the patio and garden which overlook the Chelmer Valley. Hosts Mr and Mrs King will happily transport guests to and from Stanstead Airport which is just 12 minutes away.

3rm(1⇨2hc) (3fb) CTV in all bedrooms ® ✗ ✱ sB&B£18-£20 dB&B£36-£40 dB&B⇨£40-£45 WB&Bfr£70 WBDifr£100 LDO 9.30pm

CTV 6P nc3yrs

SELECTED

FH QQQQ Mr & Mrs Hingston **Piggot's Mill** *(TL608314)* Watling Ln CM6 2QY ☎(0371) 830379

rs Xmas

A range of traditional Essex barns retaining many original features, tastefully developed by the farmer owners Richard and Gillian Hingston. The 2 bedrooms are attractively furnished and well equipped, with views over the neat garden and smart en suite bathrooms. An excellent breakfast is served at a communal table in the dining hall which features a flagstone floor and timbered roof. There is also a spacious, comfortable sitting room with a log- burning stove and piano.

2⇨⇨ ⊁in all bedrooms CTV in all bedrooms ® ✗ sB&B⇨⇨£27-£30 dB&B⇨⇨£39-£42 WB&B£117-£180

6P nc12yrs 850 acres arable Ⓔ

INN QQQ ***Farmhouse*** Monk St CM6 2NR ☎(0371) 830864 FAX (0371) 831196

This attractively extended inn has 16th-century origins and is situated in picturesque Monk street, one mile south of Thaxted off the B184. There is a freehouse bar with local beers, snacks and a pool table. Bedrooms are well equipped and have good en suite facilities.

11⇨⇨ ⊁in 4 bedrooms CTV in all bedrooms

✗ (ex guide dogs) LDO 9.30pm

48P

Credit Cards 1 2 3

THIRLMERE Cumbria Map 11 NY31

FH QQ Mr & Mrs J Hodgson **Stybeck** *(NY319188)* CA12 4TN ☎Keswick(07687) 73232

Closed 25 Dec

This Victorian lakeland stone farmhouse is a friendly 'home from home', and gives a true feeling of being on a working Cumbrian farm. It is set back from the main Ambleside to Keswick road with a dramatic backdrop of fells and crags. A no-smoking house, it offers 3 pretty bedrooms with little extras such as soft toys; and 2 lounges, both with TV and books, and open fires in the winter months.

3rm(1⇨2hc) (1fb)⊁in all bedrooms ® ✗ ✱ sB&B£15-£16 dB&B£30-£34 dB&B⇨£32-£34

CTV 4P nc5yrs 200 acres dairy mixed sheep working

THORNEY Cambridgeshire Map 04 TF20

FH QQ Mrs Y G Baker **Oversley Lodge** *(TF269041)* The Causeway PE6 0QH ☎Peterborough(0733) 270321

Located on the A47 a few miles east of Peterborough on the Wisbech road, this privately owned fenland farmhouse offers a friendly welcome. The good sized bedrooms are comfortable and warm, and the open-plan public room serves as both lounge and dining room. Traditional farmhouse evening meals are available by arrangement.

3hc (1fb)⊁in all bedrooms CTV in all bedrooms ® ✱ sB&B£18-£20 dB&B£30-£35 LDO 7pm

CTV P 260 acres arable Ⓔ

THORNTON Lancashire Map 07 SD34

SELECTED

GH QQQQ The Victorian House Trunnah Rd FY5 4HF ☎Blackpool(0253) 860619 FAX (0253) 865350

Amidst its own secluded gardens, only a short distance from Blackpool, this elegant Victorian house is a delightful place in which to stay and dine. It has 3 luxurious bedrooms – one with a 4 poster – all sumptuously furnished and decorated in Victorian style. There are 2 Victorian parlours adorned with antique furniture, objets d'art, paintings and an abundance of fresh flowers. Pride of place, however, goes to the excellent restaurant in which the 4- course, fixed-price menu has been widely acclaimed. A credit to chef patron Didier Guerin, the menu is French and offers a wide choice of dishes including home-made soups and puddings. Louise Guerin supervises front of the house, assisted by genial waitresses.

3⇨⇨ CTV in all bedrooms ® ✱ sB&B⇨⇨£45-£49 dB&B⇨⇨£69.50-£72 WB&B£315-£343 WBDi£447.65-£475.65 LDO 9.30pm

Lic 20P nc6yrs

Credit Cards 1 3

THORNTON DALE North Yorkshire Map 08 SE88

GH QQQ ***Easthill*** Wilton Rd YO18 7QP ☎Pickering(0751) 74561

Mar-Dec

A large, comfortable family house set in 2.5 acres of gardens alongside the A170 on the eastern edge of the village. Bedrooms are pleasantly decorated and furnished, some with en suite facilities and antique furniture. The spacious lounge overlooks the gardens, meadowland and the wolds beyond. The dining room shares this view and good home cooking is served at individual →

tables. The grounds include a grass tennis court, putting green and childen's play area.
8rm(4⇌4🚿) (2fb) TV in 1 bedroom ✗ LDO noon
Lic 🍽 CTV 12P ♧ 🎾(grass)crazy golf games room

THORPE BAY Essex

See **Southend-on-Sea**

THORPENESS Suffolk Map **05** TM45

INN Q Dolphin Hotel IP16 4NB ☎Aldeburgh(0728) 452681 FAX (0728) 454246
A mile from Aldeburgh on the coast, this 1920s holiday village, with its attractive mock Tudor façade, was built for seasonal use but is now sought after for all year occupation. The Dolphin provides the focal point both as public house and restaurant, and it offers simple, comfortable accommodation. Mr and Mrs Moss are making progress with their plans to update the furnishings and facilities.
18rm(5⇌1🚿12hc) (3fb) CTV in all bedrooms Ⓡ **T** ✱ sB&B£14.95-£28.50 sB&B⇌🚿£21.50-£28.50 dB&B£36.50-£39.50 dB&B⇌🚿£39.50-£46.50 WB&B£104-£199 WBDi£180-£210 Lunch £8.25-£16alc Dinner £8.25-£16alc LDO 9.30pm
🍽 🅿̸ nc3mths
Credit Cards 1 2 3 £

THREE COCKS Powys Map **03** SO13

GH QQQ *Old Gwernyfed Country Manor* Felindre LD3 0SU ☎Glasbury(04974) 376
mid Mar-mid Nov
This Elizabethan manor house lies in several acres of parkland, and has many notable features including a minstrel's gallery, an oak-panelled banqueting hall, a mast from the Spanish Armada, a secret code carved by Shakespeare and a priest's hole. The accommodation is comfortable, with most of the bedrooms en suite, and there is a good range of home-cooked meals.
11rm(7⇌2🚿2hc) (4fb) LDO 7.30pm
Lic 15P croquet
See advertisement under BRECON

THREE LEGGED CROSS Dorset Map **04** SU00

FH QQ Mr & Mrs B Gent **Homeacres** *(SU096054)* Homelands Farm BH21 6QZ ☎Verwood(0202) 822422
This modern-style farmhouse is located along the main road between Three Legged Cross and Ashley Heath. The accommodation is neat and freshly decorated, and the atmosphere is relaxed. There is a choice of first and ground-floor lounges, the ground-floor one, nearest the breakfast room, being the most comfortable. A games room is also available, with table tennis, table football and local tourist information, while in the house there is a wide selection of games and books for guests' use.
6rm(4⇌🚿2hc) (3fb) Ⓡ ✱ sB&B⇌🚿£15-£19.50 dB&B£24-£33 dB&B⇌🚿£30-£39 WB&B£84-£105
🍽 CTV 5P 3🚗 games room 270 acres beef

THRINGSTONE Leicestershire Map **08** SK41

FH Q Miss F E White ***Talbot House*** *(SK423173)* LE6 4NQ ☎Coalville(0530) 222233
Mostly built in Victorian times, around a much earlier building, this large, rambling farmhouse provides simple, old-fashioned and comfortable accommodation. It stands on the B587, 4.5 miles west of M1 junction 23.
4rm (1fb) CTV in 1 bedroom TV in 1 bedroom
✗ (ex guide dogs) LDO noon
🍽 CTV 6P croquet 150 acres dairy

See the regional maps of popular holiday areas at the back of the book.

THURNING Norfolk Map **09** TG02

FH QQ Mrs A M Fisher **Rookery** *(TG078307)* NR24 2JP ☎Melton Constable(0263) 860357
Closed Dec-Jan
A 17th-century detached red-brick farmhouse in a rural, secluded setting, surrounded by well tended gardens. The traditionally furnished accommodation is spacious and comfortable, and there is an attractive lounge/dining room with an open fire. Guests are advised to obtain directions from the proprietor, Mrs Fisher.
2rm(1🚿) (1fb) Ⓡ ✗ dB&B🚿£28
CTV P 400 acres arable

THURSBY Cumbria Map **11** NY35

FH QQ Mrs M G Swainson **How End** *(NY316497)* CA5 6PX ☎Wigton(06973) 42487
This is a typical Cumbrian farmhouse dating back to 1764 and situated on the A595 between Wigton and Carlisle. There are two attractive bedrooms with coordinated fabrics, and facilities include hairdryers. There is also a lounge and a dining room. Mrs Swainson's friendly manner creates a relaxed and informal atmosphere.
2rm (1fb)⊬in all bedrooms ✗ (ex guide dogs) ✱ sB&B£14-£15 dB&B£28-£30 WB&B£95-£100
🍽 CTV 4P 200 acres dairy mixed £

THWAITE North Yorkshire Map **07** SD89

GH QQ Kearton DL11 5DR ☎Richmond (North Yorks)(0748) 86277 FAX (0748) 86590
Mar-Dec
An attractive guesthouse in the pretty village of Thwaite on the B6270 between Kirkby Stephen and Reeth. It features neat bedrooms, a spacious guests' lounge together with a small bar and a large dining room with views of the surrounding hills and where Yorkshire home cooking is given prominence.
13hc (2fb) Ⓡ ✗ (ex guide dogs) sB&B£22-£23.50 dB&B£44-£47 (incl dinner) WB&Bfr£119 WBDifr£154 LDO 6.30pm
Lic 🍽 50P
Credit Cards 1 3 £

TIDEFORD Cornwall & Isles of Scilly Map **02** SX35

FH QQ Mrs B A Turner **Kilna House** *(SX353600)* PL12 5AD ☎Landrake(0752) 851236
Closed Xmas & New Year
This small, stone-built farmhouse is set in a large pleasant garden and overlooks the River Tiddy Valley; it is situated along the busy A38 between Liskeard and Plymouth, just outside the village. Bedrooms are well appointed and comfortable and the public areas simple but neat, with a relaxed atmosphere. The proprietors have run it for the past 20 years and, having made gradual improvments, now enjoy a returning clientèle.
5hc (2fb) CTV in all bedrooms Ⓡ sB&B£15-£17 dB&B£28-£34 WB&B£84-£98
🍽 CTV 6P 12 acres arable pasture £

TIMSBURY Avon Map **03** ST65

GH QQ Old Malt House Hotel & Licensed Restaurant Radford BA3 1QF ☎Mendip(0761) 470106
Closed Xmas
On the outskirts of the village. This former malting house has been renovated to provide spacious public areas and well equipped bedrooms which all have en suite facilities. The Horler family also operate a shire horse stud adjacent to the house.
10⇌🚿 (2fb) CTV in all bedrooms Ⓡ **T** ✗ sB&B⇌🚿£33-£35 dB&B⇌🚿£56-£60 WB&Bfr£178.50 WBDifr£267.75
LDO 8.30pm
Lic 🍽 40P nc3yrs
Credit Cards 1 2 3 5 £

TINTAGEL Cornwall & Isles of Scilly Map **02** SX08

GH QQQ Castle Villa Molesworth St PL34 0BZ
Camelford(0840) 770373 & 770203

Carefully modernised to retain all its original features, this delightful 18th-century stone cottage boasts home-made beer and delicious Cornish ice creams. The skilfully extended dining room offers a good home-cooked menu with a prominent wine list, including several house wines. There is a very cosy TV lounge with a Cornish stone fireplace and the cottage is mostly double glazed, including the individually styled bedrooms, which are all equipped with satellite TV, clock radio and tea-making facilities. Car parking spaces are provided.

5rm(1 4hc) in all bedrooms CTV in all bedrooms ® sB&B£12.50-£14.50 dB&B£25-£29 dB&B £30-£34 WB&B£78.75-£107.10 WBDi£141.75-£176.40 LDO 10am
Lic CTV 6P
Credit Cards 1 3 £

SELECTED

GH QQQQ Trebrea Lodge Trenale PL34 0HR
Camelford(0840) 770410

Originally built in the 14th century on land granted to the Bray family by the Black Prince, this handsome, Grade II listed building was enlarged in the 18th century, and is today a graceful, Georgian-style country residence. The public areas vary from an elegant, sunny first-floor drawing room to a cosy, snug lounge where a fire roars in the grate and an honesty bar stands in one corner. A hearty English breakfast, served from a buffet table, and delicious set meals are greatly appreciated. The menu changes daily and uses fresh, quality produce, home cooked by the cheery, friendly proprietors. Individually decorated and furnished with style and flair, the bedrooms are comfortable and well equipped with lovely views over the rural countryside towards the sea. Trebrea Lodge stands in a beautiful, peaceful setting, enjoying breathtaking views across the rugged North Cornish Coast, and with its relaxed, calming atmosphere provides a perfect place to stay away from the hustle and bustle of everyday life.

6 Annexe 2 (1fb) in all bedrooms CTV in all bedrooms ® T * sB&B £33-£42 dB&B £50-£65 WB&B£157.50-£204.75 WBDi£259-£294 LDO 8pm
Lic 15P
Credit Cards 1 2 3 £

GH QQQ Trewarmett Lodge PL34 0ET
Camelford(0840) 770460
Closed Nov rs Dec-Etr

Overlooking countryside and the sea, this house retains much of its original character with its oak beams, low rafters and slate stone floors. All the spacious bedrooms have lovely views over the valley and one has en suite facilities. The cosy lounge with a feature fireplace, the beamed 'Pig-sty' restaurant and a separate bar all add further dimensions to this very attractive, friendly family-run establishment. A daily menu and à la carte alternatives are offered by Maureen Twitchen, who does all the cooking. The French-style dishes are particularly recommended; our inspector enjoyed her crab bisque followed by ragout of lamb. The service of light refreshments is available throughout the day.

6rm(1 5hc) (2fb) in all bedrooms ® * sB&B£15-£19 sB&B £24 dB&B£30-£36 dB&B £36-£40 WB&B£87.50-£96 WBDi£154-£168 LDO 9pm
Lic CTV 10P
Credit Cards 1 3 £

INN QQQ Tintagel Arms Hotel Fore St PL34 0BD
Camelford(0840) 770780

This very popular and well maintained family-run and fully licensed free house has a good range of individually furnished, well equipped modern bedrooms, with very generous en suite facilities. Zorba's Taverna is open all day during the season, offering bar →

meals and snacks from the blackboard, along with a selection of real ales and local fish, with seafood usually available. There is a Honeymoon Suite, and the hotel's central location gives easy access to all the local attractions.
7🛁🚿 CTV in all bedrooms Ⓡ 🐕✗ (ex guide dogs) ✱
sB&B🛁🚿£25 dB&B🛁🚿£40-£50 Lunch £4.75-£9.75alc Dinner £6.75-£9.75alc LDO 9.30pm
🅿 8P
Credit Cards 1 3 Ⓔ

TINTERN Gwent Map **03** SO50

GH QQ **Valley House** Raglan Rd NP6 6TH ☎(0291) 689652
Situated just 800yds from the A466 and within a mile of Tintern Abbey, this Georgian residence is situated in the tranquil Angiddy Valley. Rooms have been restored to a good standard, all with modern en suite facilities.
3🛁🚿 🚭in all bedrooms CTV in all bedrooms Ⓡ ✱
sB&B🛁🚿£25-£30 dB&B🛁🚿£35-£40 LDO by arrangement
🅿 7P Ⓔ
See advertisement under CHEPSTOW

INN Q **Fountain** Trellech Grange NP6 6QW ☎(0291) 689303
This 17th-century inn is situated two miles west of the village (turn at the Royal George hotel). There is a cosy beamed bar and an attractive restaurant offering a wide range of good value food.
5hc (2fb) CTV in 4 bedrooms TV in 1 bedroom Ⓡ ✱ sB&B£15-£17 dB&B£24-£28 WB&B£93 WBDi£151 Lunch £9 Dinner £13-£20alc LDO 10.30pm
🅿 40P
Credit Cards 1 3

TISSINGTON Derbyshire Map **07** SK15

FH QQQ Mrs B Herridge **Bent** *(SK187523)* DE6 1RD
☎Parwich(033525) 214
Etr-Oct
Part of a country estate within the Peak District National Park, this stone-built house is part of a working farm. Guests will enjoy comfortable accommodation and a charming country garden.
4rm(2🛁2hc) (1fb) Ⓡ 🐕✗ (ex guide dogs) ✱ dB&Bfr£27 dB&B🛁fr£32 WB&Bfr£94 WBDifr£150 LDO 5pm
🅿 CTV 6P nc5yrs 280 acres beef dairy mixed sheep

TIVERTON Devon Map **03** SS91

GH QQQ **Bridge** 23 Angel Hill EX16 6PE ☎(0884) 252804
A family-run guesthouse near the centre of town in an enviable position beside the river with its own small garden. The bedrooms are well decorated and some now have en suite showers. There is a cosy guests' lounge and home-cooked dinners are served in the lower ground floor dining room.
10rm(5🚿5hc) (2fb) CTV in 5 bedrooms TV in 5 bedrooms Ⓡ sB&B£17-£18 sB&B🚿£26-£30 dB&B£32-£34 dB&B🚿£39-£41 WB&B£105-£140 WBDi£150-£190 LDO 6.30pm
Lic 🅿 CTV 6P 1🚗 ⚓ riverside tea garden Ⓔ

FH QQQ Mrs S Hann **Great Bradley** *(SS908135)* Withleigh EX16 8JL ☎(0884) 256946
Mar-Oct
In the heart of mid-Devon yet only 2.5 miles from Tiverton with its easy motorway access, this 16th-century farmhouse offers glorious views of rolling countryside from its elevated position. Bedrooms are comfortable, neatly decorated and simply furnished, and a log fire is lit in the sitting room in cooler months. Mrs Sylvia Hann serves breakfast only, though tea and home- made sponge on arrival was much appreciated. Breakfast is substantial with a wide choice of cereals, fruits and natural yoghurt. Non-smokers only please.
2hc 🚭in all bedrooms TV in 1 bedroom Ⓡ 🐕✗ dB&B£32-£35 WB&B£110 WBDi£155-£175 LDO 9am
🅿 CTV 4P nc7yrs 155 acres dairy Ⓔ

FH QQQ Mrs B Pugsley **Hornhill** *(SS965117)* Exeter Hill EX16 4PL ☎(0884) 253352
Mar-Oct
Parts of this farmhouse date back to the 17th century, and it sits on a hill high above the town in its own gardens, surrounded by farmland now farmed by a neighbour. The bedrooms are comfortable with many facilities that include colour TV, tea-making equipment and electric blankets. One room on the ground floor has its own shower room, while others have private bathrooms across the corridors. The lounge is attractive with floral chintz covered sofas and log fires during cooler evenings. Breakfast is served around one large table and evening dinners are available by prior arrangements. This is a no-smoking house.
3rm(1🚿) 🚭in all bedrooms CTV in all bedrooms Ⓡ 🐕✗ ✱
sB&B🚿£16-£18 dB&B🚿£30-£36 WB&B£105-£115 WBDi£175-£185 LDO 24hr in advance
5P nc8yrs 75 acres beef sheep

🛏☕ **FH** Q Barbara & Len Fullilove **Lodge Hill** *(SS945112)* Ashley EX16 5PA ☎(0884) 252907
This rendered period farmhouse is in an elevated position set well back from the A396 to Crediton, only a mile from the town. Simple bed and breakfast accommodation is offered, and a small kitchen where guests may prepare light meals, sandwiches and baby foods. Lodge Hill has a friendly, relaxed atmosphere.
8rm(6🚿2hc) (2fb) CTV in 4 bedrooms Ⓡ sB&B£13-£14 sB&B🚿£15-£16 dB&B£26-£28 dB&B🚿£30-£32 WB&B£90-£100
Lic 🅿 CTV 12P 2🚗 (£1 per night) 10 acres poultry sheep horses
Credit Cards 1 3

SELECTED

FH QQQQ Mrs R Olive **Lower Collipriest** *(SS953117)* EX16 4PT ☎(0884) 252321
Etr-Oct
The beautiful Exe Valley is the setting of this delightful farmhouse which lies only a mile from Tiverton and has easy access to the North Devon Link and the M5, yet is very much "off the beaten track". Beneath the thatched roof, bedrooms are spacious and very tastefully decorated and have en suite facilities and many thoughtful extras like hairdryers, electric blankets, and biscuits on the tea tray. The comfortable lounge features an inglenook fireplace where logs burn on cooler evenings, and the dining room has a large communal table where guests enjoy good, wholesome farmhouse cooking. Mr and Mrs Olive welcome guests to their peaceful home and offer friendly service.
2🛁🚿 🚭in all bedrooms Ⓡ 🐕✗ (ex guide dogs)
sB&B🛁🚿£26-£27.50 dB&B🛁🚿£51-£55 (incl dinner) WBDi£178.50-£182.50 LDO noon
🅿 CTV 2P 2🚗 nc16yrs ⚓ 220 acres beef dairy

TIVETSHALL ST MARY Norfolk Map **05** TM18

INN QQQ **Old Ram Coaching Inn** Ipswich Rd NR15 2DE ☎Pulham Market(0379) 676794 FAX (0379) 608399
A 17th-century coaching inn on the A140 north of Diss, where good value home- cooked food is available all day in the extended, rustic-style eating area. Be warned – the mixed grill is a truly hearty meal. Bedrooms are excellent, with Laura Ashley furnishings, each room unique and equipped with the latest facilities. There are 2 split-level mini suites and a very attractive 4-poster. The Old Ram offers unrivalled value for money.
5🛁🚿 (1fb)🚭in 1 bedroom CTV in all bedrooms Ⓡ **T**
🐕✗ (ex guide dogs) ✱ sB&B🛁🚿£39.75-£44.75
dB&B🛁🚿£59.50-£64.50 Lunch £5.45-£9alc Dinner £5.45-£14.50alc LDO 10pm
🅿 120P
Credit Cards 1 3

TOBERMORY

See **MULL, ISLE OF**

TONBRIDGE Kent Map **05** TQ54

SELECTED

GH QQQQ Goldhill Mill Golden Green TN11 0BA
☎Hadlow(0732) 851626 FAX (0732) 851881
Closed 11 Jul-Aug & 24-26 Dec
In an idyllic situation beside the river, and set in 20 acres, Goldhill Mill has been lovingly renovated by Shirley and Vernon Cole who invite you to share their home. Bedrooms are furnished to the highest of standards with luxurious bathrooms, 2 of which have double jacuzzis. Guests can enjoy a cup of tea in front of the wood-burning stove in the lounge, or relax in the delightful 'parlour', tastefully furnished with antiques. Breakfast is served in the beamed farmhouse kitchen, where you can watch the mill machinery turn as you tuck into the hearty meal.
3⇌↱ ⊁in all bedrooms CTV in all bedrooms ® **T**
✗ (ex guide dogs) sB&B⇌↱£40-£50 dB&B⇌↱£50-£65 WB&B£140-£280 LDO 48hrs prior
☗ CTV 6P ℘(hard)croquet
Credit Cards 1 3 £

TORBAY Devon

See **Brixham, Paignton and Torquay**

TORQUAY Devon Map **03** SX96

See **Town Plan Section**

GH QQ Avron Hotel 70 Windsor Rd TQ1 1SZ
☎(0803) 294182
May-Sep
Proprietors Len and Audrey Auld are proud of their hotel, and justifiably so. It is quietly located in a residential area overlooking a pleasant green, and is deceptively large, though bedrooms are fairly compact. Dinner is home- cooked and the hotel claims an unbeatable sweet trolley – our inspector certainly liked the look of the lemon meringue pie.
14rm(6↱8hc) (1fb) TV in all bedrooms ® WBDi£115-£150
CTV 8P

GH QQQ Barn Hayes Country Hotel Brim Hill, Maidencombe TQ1 4TR ☎(0803) 327980
rs Nov-Feb
This detached 1920s country hotel is located along a quiet lane leading to Maidencombe beach and village, and stands in pretty sloping gardens with spectacular sea views. Bedrooms are pretty and bright, a few are compact, but they are all neat, with smartly tiled shower rooms and 2 have bathrooms. Three of the rooms are in nearby chalets, which are ideal as family garden suites with self-catering facilities. Public areas are spacious, with a comfortable bar/lounge, a tiny TV lounge and a larger lounge area with an open fire. The Gownes family provide a warm and friendly atmosphere, with a simple menu offered in the dining room including a Healthy Option dish. Most of the rooms have extensive sea and country views and there is a small outdoor pool, with the local beach a short stroll from the hotel.
10rm(8↱2hc) Annexe 3rm(2⇌1↱) (5fb) CTV in 3 bedrooms ® ✱ sB&B£20-£22 sB&B⇌↱£22-£24 dB&B£40-£44 dB&B⇌↱£44-£48 WB&B£147-£161 WBDi£216-£231 LDO 7pm
Lic ☗ CTV 16P ⛆
Credit Cards 1 3 £

GH QQ Beauly 503 Babbacombe Rd TQ1 1HL
☎(0803) 296993
A Victorian single-fronted, end-of-terrace house situated 600yds from the harbour, and within easy reach of the major shops. Bedrooms vary in size but are all very well equipped and comfortable. A hearty breakfast is served in the lounge/dining room.
5⇌↱ (3fb) CTV in all bedrooms ® sB&B⇌↱£18-£22 dB&B⇌↱£36-£44 WB&B£116-£144 LDO noon
☗ CTV £

GH QQQ ***The Berburry Hotel*** 64 Bampfylde Rd TQ2 5AY
☎(0803) 297494
Closed 3 wks during Dec-Jan
This attractive detached property stands in its own grounds in an excellent position overlooking the Torre Valley Sports Grounds, with the seafront and English Riviera Centre nearby. Bedrooms are well equipped and pretty, with en suite facilities. Public rooms include a comfortable lounge, where smoking is not permitted, a cosy dining room and small bar. Proprietors Bernard and Rosemary Sellick provide friendly and attentive service, and well presented enjoyable food is served, cooked by Rosemary.
10⇌↱ (3fb) CTV in all bedrooms ® ✗ LDO 5pm
Lic ☗ CTV 10P nc7yrs
Credit Cards 1 3

GH QQQ ***Braddon Hall Hotel*** Braddons Hill Rd East TQ1 1HF ☎(0803) 293908
Within easy reach of the harbour and beaches, this quietly set hotel has en suite facilities and public areas of a high standard. The resident proprietors provide a choice of menu and a warm welcome.
11⇌↱ (3fb) CTV in all bedrooms ® LDO 5pm
Lic ☗ 8P

GH QQQ Burley Court Hotel Wheatridge Lane, Livermead TQ2 6RA ☎(0803) 607879
mid Mar-mid Nov
Set in three quarters of an acre of grounds with views over Torbay, the hotel offers comfortable and well presented public areas and all en suite bedrooms. In the dining room great emphasis is placed on the use of fresh local produce prepared and presented by the chef/patron.
11↱ (5fb) CTV in all bedrooms ® **T** ✗ (ex guide dogs) ✱ sB&B↱£27-£32 dB&B↱£54-£64 (incl dinner) WB&B£130-£150 WBDi£170-£190 LDO 6.30pm
Lic ☗ 25P ⛆(heated) ⛆(heated) solarium gymnasium
Credit Cards 1 £

GH QQQ Chesterfield Hotel 62 Belgrave Rd TQ2 5HY
☎(0803) 292318
A Victorian mid-terrace with colourful floral displays in front, just 4 minutes' level walk from the seafront and gardens. Two ground-floor rooms are available, and home-cooked meals are served in the lower ground-floor dining room.
12rm(10↱2hc) (5fb) CTV in all bedrooms ® sB&B£12-£20 sB&B↱£15-£25 dB&B£24-£34 dB&B↱£28-£42 WB&B£74-£130 WBDi£104-£170 LDO 4pm
Lic ☗ CTV 3P
Credit Cards 1 3 £

GH Q Clovelly 91 Avenue Rd TQ2 5LH ☎(0803) 292286
A small, family-run guesthouse with a friendly atmosphere. Bedrooms are simply appointed, but all have TV and tea-making facilities. An evening meal is served at 6pm, with choices for each course. A comfortable lounge is available for guests, featuring a wide variety of pot plants.
6hc (2fb) CTV in all bedrooms ® sB&B£11-£13 dB&B£22-£26 dB&B£24-£28 WB&B£77-£91 WBDi£119-£133 LDO 5pm
☗ CTV 4P
Credit Cards 1 3 £

GH QQQ ***Hotel Concorde*** 26 Newton Rd TQ2 5BZ
☎(0803) 292330
Standing on the outskirts of town, this guesthouse has been well modernised and offers spacious public areas, well equipped bedrooms and a sheltered sun- trap garden area with an outdoor heated pool.
22rm(14⇨↱8hc) (7fb) CTV in all bedrooms ® LDO 6pm
Lic ⊘ CTV 18P ≏(heated)
Credit Cards [1] [3]

GH QQQ Craig Court Hotel 10 Ash Hill Rd, Castle Circus TQ1 3HZ ☎(0803) 294400
Etr-Oct
An early Victorian detached house in an elevated position, with distant views of Torquay and Torbay beyond, situated in a residential area, close to the shopping centre. Four of the comfortable bedrooms are on the ground floor, and there is a choice of 2 lounges. There is a narrow gauge railway track in the garden, and Craig Court is a centre for model railway enthusiasts.
10rm(5↱5hc) (2fb) ® ✕ (ex guide dogs) sB&B£16-£19 sB&B↱£24-£26 dB&B£32-£38 dB&B↱£38-£44 WB&B£112-£133 WBDi£150.50-£189 LDO noon
Lic CTV 8P model railway in garden (£)

GH QQQ Cranborne Hotel 58 Belgrave Rd TQ2 5HY
☎(0803) 298046
Closed Dec
A regular award winner in Torquay in Bloom, this Victorian mid-terrace house has been sympathetically modernised by Betty and Keith Dawkins. Great care is taken with the preparation and presentation of food served in the lower ground floor dining room, and puddings are a particular talking point.
12rm(11⇨↱1hc) (6fb) CTV in all bedrooms ® ✕ sB&B£16-£19 sB&B⇨↱£19-£22 dB&B⇨↱£38-£42 WB&B£102-£129 WBDi£123-£153 LDO 3pm
Lic ⊘ CTV 3P
Credit Cards [1] [3] (£)

GH QQQ Cranmore 89 Avenue Rd TQ2 5LH
☎(0803) 298488
An attractive semi-detached house set on a main road, a short walk to the town centre. Bedrooms are well equipped with orthopaedic beds, and the open plan public areas have a Tudor theme. A home-cooked 4-course dinner is served nightly which is optional, but proving popular.
9rm(5⇨↱4hc) (2fb) CTV in all bedrooms ®
✕ (ex guide dogs) sB&B£12-£14 dB&B£24-£28 dB&B⇨↱£28-£32 WB&B£84-£112 WBDi£126-£154 LDO 5pm
⊘ CTV 4P
Credit Cards [1] [2] [3]

GH QQQ ***Daphne Court Hotel*** Lower Warberry Rd TQ1 1QS
☎(0803) 212011
mid-Mar-mid-Oct
An elegant detached Victorian villa situated in a peaceful area of town, known as 'the Warberries', yet conveniently close to the shops, beaches, harbour and amenities. Bedrooms are comfortable and nicely appointed and equipped, with 4 new 'Jardinière' bedrooms offering attractive coordinated décor and luxury facilities at a small extra charge. There is a comfortable, quiet lounge, a separate lounge/bar and a pleasant traditional dining room where simple, home- cooked food is served. Personally run by proprietors Geoff and Jenny Langley, the atmosphere here is cheerful and friendly. The large south-facing garden has a heated swimming pool and sun patio.
16rm(2⇨14↱) (8fb) CTV in all bedrooms ®
✕ (ex guide dogs) LDO 7.30pm
Lic ⊘ CTV 15P ≏(heated) games room
Credit Cards [1] [3]

Book as early as possible for busy holiday periods.

GH QQ Devon Court Hotel Croft Rd TQ2 5UE
☎(0803) 293603
Etr-Oct
In a quiet but central location the hotel is within easy walking distance of Torre Abbey Gardens, Abbey Sands and all the town's facilities. Some ground- floor bedrooms are available, and there is an outdoor heated swimming pool set in sheltered gardens. Varied home cooking is prepared by the family partnership.
13rm(8↱5hc) (3fb) CTV in all bedrooms ® ✕ ✱
sB&Bfr£12.50 dB&Bfr£25 dB&B↱fr£29.40 WB&B£86-£141 WBDi£112-£169 LDO 4.30pm
Lic ⊘ CTV 14P ≏(heated)
Credit Cards [1] [3] (£)

GH QQQ Elmdene Hotel Rathmore Rd TQ2 6NZ
☎(0803) 294940
Mar-Oct
Elmdene is conveniently situated near the railway station and the cricket ground, and within easy walking distance of Abbey Sands. Spacious public areas include a bar lounge and separate sun lounge. Five-course table d'hôte meals are offered with additional dishes carrying a supplementary charge. Many of the comfortable bedrooms have en suite facilities.
12rm(2⇨5↱5hc) (3fb) CTV in all bedrooms ® sB&B£18.50-£21 sB&B⇨↱£24.50-£27 dB&B£37-£42 dB&B⇨↱£43-£48 WB&B£126-£143.50 WBDi£196-£213.50 LDO 5pm
Lic ⊘ CTV 12P nc5yrs
Credit Cards [1] [3] (£)

GH QQ Exmouth View Hotel St Albans Rd, Babbacombe Down TQ1 3LG ☎(0803) 327307
FAX (0803) 329967
This large detached family hotel, converted from 2 buildings, is situated 100yds from Babbacombe Downs and the picturesque cliff railway and beach. Bedrooms are comfortable, well equipped and vary in size; continuing renovation is providing the majority of rooms with private bathrooms. There is a bright and airy lounge bar, and various public rooms include an open-plan lounge area complete with dance floor. A simple home-cooked menu is served in the spacious dining room, with a choice of dishes.
32rm(22⇨↱10hc) (7fb) CTV in all bedrooms ®
✕ (ex guide dogs) sB&B£14-£28 sB&B⇨↱£16-£30 dB&B£28-£56 dB&B⇨↱£32-£60 (incl dinner) WB&B£90-£175 WBDi£105-£210 LDO 6.30pm
Lic ⊘ CTV 25P
Credit Cards [1] [3] (£)

GH QQ Fairways Hotel 72 Avenue Rd TQ2 5LF
☎(0803) 298471
Conveniently positioned for the town centre and English Riviera, this central guesthouse offers compact bedrooms that are light and airy, equipped with colour TV and tea-making facilities, and hot water bottles are provided on a do-it-yourself basis. During summer months only, a set dinner is served in the no-smoking dining room. A spacious, comfortable lounge is available, and there are good parking facilities on site.
6rm(4↱2hc) (2fb) CTV in all bedrooms ® sB&B£13-£14 dB&B£26-£28 dB&B↱£30-£32 WB&B£86-£106 WBDi£130-£154 LDO 4pm
⊘ 7P
Credit Cards [1] [3] (£)

SELECTED

GH QQQQ Glenorleigh Hotel 26 Cleveland Rd TQ2 5BE ☎(0803) 292135
6 Jan-14 Oct
Away from the hustle and bustle of the seafront and town centre, this friendly family holiday hotel is run by Michael and Maureen Rhodes and offers lots of holiday facilities. There is an outdoor pool, a solarium, a games room with pool, darts and video games, and live entertainment 2 evenings each week. Bedrooms are neatly decorated and furnished, and most

have en suite facilities. There is a 'dry' lounge with TV, a bright, neat dining room, and a bar complete with small dance floor. Outside, the Spanish-style patio looks out over the beautiful, expertly tended garden, 8 times winner of the Torbay in Bloom award.

16rm(9⬏7hc) (5fb) ® ✗ (ex guide dogs) sB&B£16-£25 sB&B⬏£20-£27 dB&B£32-£50 dB&B⬏£40-£54 (incl dinner) WB&B£112-£175 WBDi£120-£220 LDO 6pm

Lic ♛ CTV 10P ⛱(heated) solarium pool table

See advertisement on inside front cover

GH QQQ Grosvenor House Hotel Falkland Rd TQ2 5JP ☎(0803) 294110

This small, friendly and comfortable hotel is situated a short walking distance from the town and beaches, and is run by Jock and Evelyn Ballantyne. There are ground-floor bedrooms available, and the comfortable, attractive lounge has a separate bar. A short table d'hôte is offered, with a choice of main course, in the basement dining room.

11⬏ (4fb) CTV in all bedrooms ® ✗ (ex guide dogs) sB&B⬏£17-£21 dB&B⬏£34-£42 WB&B£108-£132 WBDi£157-£181 LDO 4.30pm

Lic ♛ CTV 7P

Credit Cards 1 3 £

GH QQQ Hotel Trelawney 48 Belgrave Rd TQ2 5HS ☎(0803) 296049

A family-run hotel conveniently located just 200yds from Torre Abbey Sands and the English Riviera centre. The bright and airy bedrooms are all en suite, the majority with showers, and are equipped with a range of facilities including satellite TV, video, direct-dial telephones and tea-making provision. The set traditional roast dinner is served at 6pm in the basement dining room, and a choice of breakfast is offered.

14rm(13⇌⬏1hc) (2fb) CTV in all bedrooms ® **T** ✗ (ex guide dogs) sB&B£14-£16 dB&B⇌⬏£32-£44 WB&B£90-£140 WBDi£140-£190 LDO 2pm

Lic ♛ CTV 3P

Credit Cards 1 3 5 £

GH QQ *Ingoldsby Hotel* 1 Chelston Rd TQ2 6PT ☎(0803) 607497

This quietly situated guesthouse has lovely views over the bay, yet is only 200yds from the beach. The majority of bedrooms have private bathrooms, and 4 of the rooms are on the ground floor. The spacious public areas are simple but comfortable, and a choice of menus is offered at dinner. The hotel is run by a friendly team of proprietors in a relaxed atmosphere.

15rm(3⇌9⬏3hc) (5fb) ® ✗ (ex guide dogs) LDO 7pm

Lic ♛ CTV 15P

Credit Cards 1 3

GH Q Jesmond Dene Private Hotel 85 Abbey Rd TQ2 5NN ☎(0803) 293062

rs Oct-Apr

This guesthouse is situated within easy walking distance of the town centre and harbour, and offers clean, comfortable and simply furnished bedrooms. There is a TV lounge, and a pleasant dining area: dinner is available for guests during summer months.

11hc (3fb) ® sB&B£13-£16 dB&B£26-£32 WB&B£78-£82 WBDi£100-£105 LDO noon

♛ CTV 3P £

SELECTED

GH QQQQ Kingston House 75 Avenue Rd TQ2 5LL ☎(0803) 212760

Apr-Oct

Efficiently run by the cheerful, jolly hosts Anita and Brian Sexon, this small, semidetached Victorian-style villa has been completely renovated to justify the high standard of accommodation they offer. The pretty, well coordinated bedrooms vary in size but all are comfortably furnished with a practical layout and nicely equipped. A beautiful piano stands in one corner of the quiet lounge, which is pleasantly decorated. Anita produces very tasty, enjoyable home-cooked evening meals from the highest quality of produce available and a choice is offered at each course. The proprietors provide a cordial, pleasant atmosphere, making this guesthouse a delightful place to stay.

6rm(5⇌⬏1hc) (3fb) CTV in all bedrooms ® ✗ sB&B£15-£19.50 sB&B⇌⬏£15-£21.50 dB&B£23-£31 dB&B⇌⬏£27-£35 WB&B£77-£119 WBDi£119-£159 LDO noon

♛ 6P nc8yrs

Credit Cards 1 3

GH QQQ Lindum Hotel Abbey Rd TQ2 5NP ☎(0803) 292795

Mar-Nov

This is a long-established, centrally situated hotel with soundly furnished bedrooms. A comfortable TV lounge is available, with a sun lounge off. There is a residents' bar, and a choice of menu is offered at each meal.

20rm(14⇌⬏6hc) (2fb) CTV in all bedrooms ® sB&B£12-£21 sB&B⇌⬏fr£15.40 dB&Bfr£24 dB&B⇌⬏£30.80-£42 WB&Bfr£84 WBDi£140-£176.50 LDO 7.15pm

Lic ♛ CTV 14P

GH QQQ Mapleton Hotel St Lukes Rd North TQ2 5PD ☎(0803) 292389

Mar-15 Nov, Xmas & New Year

This Victorian property is in a central location in a quiet residential area above the town, with wide views across to Dartmoor. Recently purchased by the enthusiastic proprietors Jamie and Cheryl Holden, the hotel has a lively, convivial atmosphere and is well managed. Bedrooms are light and bright with high ceilings and pretty floral décor; they are reasonably equipped, including TV and video and the majority have smartly tiled en suite facilities; there are also a few ground-floor rooms available. A choice of home-cooked dishes is served each evening, using good quality fresh produce. This pleasant, small hotel provides a large private car park and lawned gardens with a sunny patio.

11rm(1⇌7⬏3hc) (2fb) CTV in all bedrooms ® ✗ ✱ sB&Bfr£17.50 dB&Bfr£30 dB&B⇌⬏fr£35 WB&Bfr£122.50 WBDi£180 LDO 6.30pm

Lic ♛ 10P nc14yrs

Credit Cards 1 3 £

GH QQQ Olivia Court Upper Braddons Hill Rd TQ1 1HD ☎(0803) 292595

A Grade II listed Victorian villa set in a quiet residential area close to the town centre, with a secluded garden. The owners Malcolm and Althea Carr took over in 1991 and have made improvements to the hotel, creating a new reception area, lounge and small dispense bar. The bedrooms are furnished to a high standard and are attractively coordinated; most are en suite. A 4-course table d'hôte menu is served in the attractive dining room.

13rm(12⇌⬏1hc) (2fb)⊁in 4 bedrooms CTV in all bedrooms ® sB&B⇌⬏£17.50-£20.50 dB&B⇌⬏£35-£41 WB&B£107-£128 WBDi£151-£171 LDO 4pm

Lic ♛ CTV 4P

Credit Cards 1 2 3 £

GH QQ The Porthcressa Hotel 28 Perinville Road, Babbacombe TQ1 3NZ ☎(0803) 327268

This family-run hotel is located in a quiet, residential part of the town and provides bright bedrooms with attractive soft furnishings and colour TVs. The public areas are comfortable, and a lively bar proves popular with guests.

→

13rm(2↑11hc) (3fb) TV in all bedrooms Ⓡ ✕ (ex guide dogs) ✱ sB&B£15-£18 dB&B£30-£33 dB&B↑£34-£37 WB&B£75-£90 WBDi£90-£135 LDO 8pm
Lic ⅏ CTV 6P

GH [Q][Q][Q] Rawlyn House Hotel Rawlyn Road, Chelston TQ2 6PL ☎(0803) 605208
Apr-Oct & Xmas
A Victorian country house set in secluded grounds, with an attractive heated swimming pool. Bedrooms are individually furnished and comfortable : the majority have private bathrooms, and all are well equipped. There is a bar lounge, and a small TV lounge. A choice of breakfasts is offered, and a short table d'hôte menu is available for dinner ; a vegetarian menu can also be prepared by chef/proprietor Tony Cox.
17rm(4⇨10↑3hc) (3fb) CTV in all bedrooms Ⓡ ✕ ✱ sB&B⇨↑fr£26 dB&B⇨↑fr£52 (incl dinner) WBDifr£180 LDO 7.15pm
Lic ⅏ CTV 15P ⛆(heated) games room badminton Ⓔ

GH [Q][Q][Q] Richwood Hotel 20 Newton Rd TQ2 5BZ ☎(0803) 293729
This popular family holiday hotel is open throughout the year. The brightly decorated bedrooms are cosy and compact ; the old Tavern Bar is full of character, and there is a games room for guests' enjoyment. The heated outdoor pool, built on the south side of the hotel, is quite a sun trap. Dinner is available in the relaxed atmosphere of the dining room.
21rm(3⇨15↑3hc) (9fb) CTV in all bedrooms Ⓡ ✱ sB&B£12-£20 sB&B⇨↑£14-£22 dB&B£24-£40 dB&B⇨↑£28-£44 WB&B£70-£130 WBDi£99-£179 LDO 6.30pm
Lic ⅏ CTV 14P ⛆(heated) pool table games room
Credit Cards [1] [3] Ⓔ

GH [Q][Q][Q] *Seaway Hotel* Chelston Rd TQ2 6PU ☎(0803) 605320
A spacious Victorian house with an attractive garden and terrace in a quiet position only 200 yards from the sea. Bedrooms vary in size, many are en suite, and tea facilities are planned. The dining room is light and airy and choices are provided for each course. There is a comfortable lounge and a bar adjoining the dining room.
14rm(1⇨6↑7hc) (3fb) LDO 7pm
Lic ⅏ CTV 15P
Credit Cards [1] [3]

[🛏♥] GH [Q][Q][Q] Sevens Hotel 27 Morgan Av TQ2 5RR ☎(0803) 293523
This small hotel is situated in a quiet avenue within easy walking distance of the town centre. It is supervised by the friendly proprietors, Mr and Mrs Stephens, who create a relaxed, informal atmosphere. There are simple, comfortably furnished bedrooms and a lower ground floor bar lounge where guests can play pool and darts.
12rm(3↑9hc) (3fb) ✕ sB&B£15-£18 sB&B↑£17.50-£21 dB&B£28-£34 dB&B↑£33-£40 WB&B£105-£126 WBDi£126-£150 LDO 4.30pm
Lic ⅏ CTV 10P Ⓔ

GH [Q][Q] Silverlands Hotel 27 Newton Rd TQ2 5DB ☎(0803) 292013
This well maintained guesthouse is situated within walking distance of the town and beaches. Bedrooms are compact but well furnished, and equipped with TV and tea-making facilities. Breakfast is served in the light and airy dining room by proprietors Wendy and Ray Porthouse.
11rm(6↑5hc) (2fb) CTV in all bedrooms Ⓡ ✱ sB&B£12-£15 sB&B↑£17-£21 dB&B£24-£30 dB&B↑£30-£36 WB&B£84-£126
⅏ 13P

GH [Q][Q] Skerries Private Hotel 25 Morgan Av TQ2 5RR ☎(0803) 293618
Family run, this cosy private hotel has comfortable public rooms and well- maintained, compact bedrooms. It is conveniently close to the town centre and has parking facilities.
12rm(3↑9hc) (3fb) CTV in all bedrooms Ⓡ ✱ sB&B£13-£17 dB&B£25-£31 dB&B↑£32-£38 WB&B£87-£113 WBDi£111-£130 LDO 2pm
Lic ⅏ CTV 7P Ⓔ

GH [Q] Torbay Rise Old Mill Rd TQ2 6HL ☎(0803) 605541
Apr-Oct
A Victorian house situated in an elevated position overlooking Torquay harbour and the sea. The atmosphere is informal, under the supervision of resident proprietors Vivienne and Alan Plewes. Bedrooms are simply furnished, though a 4-poster bedroom is available, and there is an outdoor pool set in a patio in the garden.
15rm(9⇨6↑) (2fb) CTV in all bedrooms Ⓡ ✱ sB&B⇨↑£17-£23 dB&B⇨↑£32-£44 WBDi£133-£182 LDO 11am
Lic 8P nc3yrs ⛆(heated)
Credit Cards [1] [3]

GH [Q][Q] Trouville 70 Belgrave Rd TQ2 5HY ☎(0803) 294979
Closed Dec
A single-fronted, Victorian, mid-terrace house located within easy distance of the town's amenities. One room features a 4-poster bed, and they all have showers and metered satellite TV. The dining room is comfortable and houses a collection of decorative plates, and there is a cosy lounge with TV. Run by Doug Cumpstey and Col Paxton, the guesthouse has a friendly relaxed atmosphere.
7rm(2↑5hc) (2fb) CTV in all bedrooms Ⓡ ✱ sB&B£11-£16 dB&B£22-£32 dB&B↑£26-£36
⅏ CTV 5P
Credit Cards [1] [3]

GH [Q][Q][Q] *Villa Marina Hotel* Cockington Ln, Livermead TQ2 6QU ☎(0803) 605440
Apr-Oct
A modern holiday hotel located in Cockington Lane, close to Livermead Beach, privately owned and personally supervised by the Harrison family. The spacious open-plan public areas offer superb views over Torbay, and bedrooms are all en suite and very well equipped. A choice of menu is offered at dinner, and live entertainment provided. Outside, there is a heated swimming pool with a sunbathing area.
26rm(20⇨6↑) (6fb) CTV in all bedrooms Ⓡ LDO 6.45pm
Lic ⅏ CTV 20P
Credit Cards [1] [3]

GH [Q][Q][Q] Westgate Hotel Falkland Rd TQ2 5JP ☎(0803) 295350
This relaxed and friendly holiday hotel, run by amiable proprietors, is in a tree-lined road close to Torre Abbey and Garden and the English Riviera Centre. A choice of menu is offered at dinner, specialising in traditional English home cooking. Bedrooms are comfortable, and the new bar and lower ground floor games room are useful additional facilities.
13↑ (2fb) CTV in all bedrooms Ⓡ ✕ ✱ sB&B↑£19-£23 dB&B↑£38-£46 WB&B£130-£147 WBDi£190-£210 LDO 8pm
Lic CTV 14P nc5yrs games room pool table
Credit Cards [1] [3]

TORRINGTON, GREAT Devon Map 02 SS42

GH [Q][Q] Smytham Manor EX38 8PU (2m S A386) ☎Torrington(0805) 22110
Mar-Oct
An attractive manor house set in 15 acres of well kept grounds which incorporate a campsite and self-catering cabins. The range of facilities include an outdoor heated pool and bar area. The bedrooms are clean and comfortable, and there is a cosy lounge and full-size snooker table. A range of menus offer a comprehensive choice of dishes served in the dining room.
7rm(3⇨2↑2hc) Ⓡ ✱ sB&B£13-£14 sB&B⇨↑£17-£19 dB&B£26-£28 dB&B⇨↑£34-£38 WB&B£79-£125 WBDi£130-£175 LDO 9pm

Lic CTV 14P (heated) snooker croquet mini golf table tennis games room
Credit Cards [1] [3] £

FH Q Mrs E J Watkins **Lower Hollam** *(SS501161)* Little Torrington EX38 8QS (on unclass rd 3m S of Torrington off A386) ☎(0805) 23253
Mar-Oct
An extended 18th-century farmhouse, located down a long unclassified road about 3 miles from the town. The bedrooms are simply appointed, and the lounge and dining room are comfortable.
3hc (1fb)⊁in all bedrooms ® ⊁ (ex guide dogs) ✱ sB&B£11-£12 dB&B£22-£24 WB&B£70 WBDi£91-£98 LDO 5pm
CTV 3P rough shooting 220 acres beef cereal sheep £

TOTLAND BAY

See **WIGHT, ISLE OF**

TOTNES Devon Map **03** SX86

SELECTED

GH QQQQ **Lyssers Hotel** 4 Chapel Ln, Bridgetown TQ9 5AF ☎(0803) 866513 FAX (0803) 865156
A charming small hotel and restaurant tucked away in Chapel Lane, close to the River Dart. Originally a rope works, when hemp boats used to discharge their cargoes in the port of Totnes, it has recently been converted by Mr and Mrs Lysser, and has already established a reputation for its cuisine, using fresh produce and seafood supplied locally. The spacious bedrooms are all en suite and comfortable, with a good all-round standard of housekeeping. The Bothy is a separate unit in the garden providing an ideal family room with cooking facilities. On the lower ground floor, accessible from the side street, there is a spacious lounge, bar and restaurant: an open-plan area with well spaced separate tables. There is also a no-smoking lounge, and excellent parking facilities are available. To find the hotel, travel towards Torquay over the old bridge from the centre of Totnes and take the first left down Rowsells Lane.
6 Annexe 1 (1fb)⊁in all bedrooms CTV in all bedrooms ® ✱ sB&B £35-£37.50 dB&B £50-£55 LDO 9pm
Lic 20P
Credit Cards [1] [3] £

SELECTED

GH QQQQ **The Old Forge** Seymour Place TQ9 5AY ☎(0803) 862174
rs Xmas wk
Quietly located in this Edwardian town, the Old Forge dates back some 600 years and is the only selected guesthouse in a working forge – complete with its own prison cell. The bedrooms are individually decorated and furnished in a cottage style, having numerous thoughtful extras. Breakfast here is a special occasion, with a wide choice including a vegatarin option, and is served in the Tudor-style dining room where cream teas, home-made jams and a wide variety of teas are also available and can be enjoyed in the garden if preferred. Dinner is not provided, but the area is renowned for its eating places and a list is featured in the bedroom folder. It is requested guests refrain from smoking anywhere inside the house.
10rm(8 2hc) (4fb)⊁in all bedrooms CTV in all bedrooms ® ⊁ (ex guide dogs) ✱ sB&B £30-£42 dB&Bfr£40 dB&B £50-£60 WB&B£133-£210
Lic CTV 8P putting
Credit Cards [1] [3] £

SELECTED

INN QQQQ The Watermans Arms Bow Bridge, Ashprington TQ9 7EG ☎Harbertonford(0803) 732214

This famous old country inn has an interesting past; it has been a blacksmiths, a brewhouse and even a prison during the Napoleonic war. Situated on the banks of the River Dart at the head of Bow Creek, and next to the Bow Bridge which dates back to Domesday, the inn is full of character. Bars have exposed beams and open fires, and offer an extensive snack menu and daily blackboard specials. A more sophisticated table d'hôte menu can be found in the informal restaurant which is separate from the bustling bars. Bedrooms have been tastefully decorated with floral paper and drapes, and are comfortably furnished with reproduction antique furniture. All have shower rooms en suite, TV and telephones. Phoebe and Trevor Illingworth extend a warm welcome to guests, and their team of staff provide a friendly and caring service.

10 CTV in all bedrooms ® sB&B£25-£32 dB&B£50-£64 WB&B£165-£205 WBDi£235-£275 Bar Lunch fr£9alc Dinner fr£14.95 LDO 9.30pm

60P

Credit Cards 1 3 £

TOTTENHILL Norfolk Map **09** TF61

GH QQ Oakwood House Private Hotel PE33 0RH
☎Kings Lynn(0553) 810256

This elegant Georgian house of mellow brick with a slate roof is set in its own well tended gardens, and Mr and Mrs Britton have made steady improvements over the 3 years of their ownership. The bedrooms have been professionally fitted with good rattan-faced laminated furniture, with white woven bed covers, fresh décor and matching pastel headboards and curtains. Good framed prints relieve the plainness of the annexe room walls and enhance the pleasant blue and cream colour scheme. Bathrooms are all tiled and have modern suites. A 6-course à la carte menu is offered in the dining room, which has an attractive Victorian fireplace with a mirrored mantel, shuttered windows and white linen covered tables.

7rm(5 2hc) Annexe 3 CTV in all bedrooms ® ✱ sB&B£22 sB&B£36-£38 dB&B£28 dB&B£46-£48 WBDi£220 LDO 8.30pm

Lic 20P

Credit Cards 1 3 £

TREARDDUR BAY

See **ANGLESEY, ISLE OF**

TREGARON Dyfed Map **03** SN65

FH QQ Mrs M J Cutter **Neuadd Las Farm Country Guest House** *(SN663620)* SY25 6JL ☎(0974) 298905 & 298965

This well maintained guesthouse is set in its own grounds a short distance from the Teifi River, with panoramic views of the Cumbrian mountains. Situated just one mile from the town, off the Aberystwyth road, it offers bright and comfortable accommodation. Private fishing is available, and the Cors Caron Nature Reserve is near by.

4rm(3 1hc) (2fb) CTV in 1 bedroom ® ✱ sB&B£15-£18 sB&B£17-£20 dB&B£30-£36 dB&B£34-£40 WB&B£105-£140 WBDi£154-£189 LDO 9pm

CTV 10P 25 acres mixed

Street plans of certain towns and cities will be found in a separate section at the back of the book.

TRENEAR (NEAR HELSTON) Cornwall & Isles of Scilly Map **02** SW63

FH Q Mrs G Lawrance **Longstone** *(SW662319)* TR13 0HG
☎Helston(0326) 572483

Mar-Nov

A simple but comfortable farmhouse, part of a working farm in a peaceful, remote setting amidst beautiful countryside. There is ample space both inside and out for families, and facilities include a playroom and sun lounge.

5hc (2fb) ✱ sB&B£13-£15 dB&B£26-£30 WB&Bfr£85 WBDifr£120 LDO 4pm

CTV 6P 62 acres dairy £

TREVONE Cornwall & Isles of Scilly Map **02** SW87

GH QQ Coimbatore Hotel West View PL28 8RD
☎Padstow(0841) 520390

Situated 150 yards from the beach, this large white detached villa, named after a railway town in India, has generous public areas including a bar lounge which overlooks the garden and catches the sun. Bedrooms are individually furnished and brightly decorated. Six have good sized en suite showers. Two ground-floor bedrooms are available. Chrissie Knutsen does all the cooking on an Aga. The car park is located behind the hotel with access (first left) up Sandy Lane and not down the cul-de-sac.

10rm(7 3hc) (3fb) ® sB&B£20 dB&B£40 WB&B£140 WBDi£189 LDO 4.30pm

Lic CTV 4P 6

Credit Cards 1 3 £

GH QQQ Green Waves Private Hotel PL28 8RD
☎Padstow(0841) 520114

Etr-Oct

In a quiet residential area, only a few minutes from 2 beaches, one of which has a natural bathing pool, this hotel has well-equipped, comfortable rooms, some with lovely coastal views. There is a small bar for residents, a very comfortable lounge and a billiard room. Mrs Chellew supervises the kitchen, and has a good reputation for her meals and home-made bread. A selective wine list complements her cooking skills.

20rm(17 3hc) (3fb) CTV in all bedrooms ® sB&B£17.50-£23 sB&B£17.50-£23 dB&B£35-£46 dB&B£35-£46 WBDi£140-£170 LDO 7pm

Lic 17P nc4yrs half size snooker table

Credit Cards 1 3

See advertisement under PADSTOW

TRINITY

See **JERSEY under CHANNEL ISLANDS**

TROON Cornwall & Isles of Scilly Map **02** SW63

GH Q Sea View TR14 9JH ☎Praze(0209) 831260

Closed Dec

Lying south of Troon village this small, simply furnished guesthouse is in a peaceful location, with an adjacent farm and fine views.

7hc (3fb) in all bedrooms ® sB&B£11-£15 dB&B£22-£30 WB&B£70-£85 WBDi£126-£141 LDO 6pm

Lic CTV 8P (heated) £

TROTTON West Sussex Map **04** SU82

FH QQ Mrs J R Field ***Mill*** *(SU832224)* GU31 5EL
☎Midhurst(0730) 813080

This 1930s farmhouse, situated on a working farm in a slightly elevated position, overlooks attractive open countryside. The house has a comfortable family atmosphere, with open fires and an elegant lounge. The bedrooms are cosy and well equipped.

2hc (1fb) in all bedrooms CTV in all bedrooms ®
(ex guide dogs)

CTV 8P (grass)15 acres sheep beef

TRURO Cornwall & Isles of Scilly Map **02** SW84

GH QQ ***Abbey View*** 32 Tregolls Rd TR1 1LA ☎(0872) 223763
Situated on the main A390 into Truro, this simple, clean and well maintained guesthouse has an easy-going, relaxed atmosphere. The freshly decorated bedrooms offer en suite or private bathrooms and they are furnished in a practical, modern style. Breakfast is the only meal served but there are several local eating places near by. Some useful private parking is available at the front of the house.
6rm(1⇌3⌐2hc) (1fb) CTV in all bedrooms ®
✗ (ex guide dogs)
6P

GH QQQ Conifers 36 Tregolls Rd TR1 1LA ☎(0872) 79925
Situated along the main road into Truro, from the A39 St Austell route, this elegant Victorian guesthouse has been tastefully refurbished in keeping with its era. Mrs Gibbons and her family offer a warm welcome, and the atmosphere in the house is a happy one. Bedrooms are very pretty, bright and fresh, and the public areas are pleasantly decorated and well presented. There is some car parking at the rear (take the private lane alongside the adjacent house). Many of the guests are regulars, and most are business people, but Mrs Gibbons also caters well for leisure guests.
4hc CTV in all bedrooms ® ✗ (ex guide dogs) ✱ sB&B£16-£17 dB&B£32-£34 WB&B£112-£119
꘎ CTV 3P Ⓔ

GH QQQ Lands Vue Lands Vue, Three Burrows TR4 8JA ☎(0872) 560242
Closed Xmas & New Year
An attractive country house set in 2 acres of well tended gardens, with lovely peaceful, rural views. Ideally situated, it is just of the A30, only 3 miles from the sea and 4 miles from Truro. The 3 bedrooms are compact but prettily decorated, and there is an annexe cottage room. The spacious dining room has panoramic rural views and there is a cosy TV lounge with an open fire. The large gardens include an outdoor swimming pool, croquet and other games, and a large parking area. To find the house from the A30 take the A390 then the first left turning to Tregevathen; stay on that road and Lands Vue is on the left: ignore further signs to Tregevathen.
3rm(1⌐2hc) Annexe 1⌐ CTV in 1 bedroom ®
✗ (ex guide dogs) ✱ sB&B£14-£16 dB&B£28-£32 dB&B⌐£32-£36 WB&B£98-£105 LDO 4pm
꘎ CTV 6P nc8 yrs ⩳croquet Ⓔ

TUNBRIDGE WELLS (ROYAL) Kent Map **05** TQ53

See also Frant

SELECTED

GH QQQQ Danehurst House 41 Lower Green Rd, Rusthall TN4 8TW ☎(0892) 527739 FAX (0892) 514804
Quietly situated this small Victorian Tudor-style house, with its own garden and fish-pond, provides the perfect atmosphere to unwind and get away from it all. Old-fashioned furnishings are coordinated throughout, using a choice of styles in the bedrooms, which are all equipped with TV, radio and tea-making facilities. Dinner can be taken at the communal dining room table, with breakfast served in the sunny conservatory. All the food is prepared and cooked fresh by the proprietor Angela Godbold, using home-made recipes; also light refreshment is usually available throughout the day. Danehurst House is a licensed establishment and the house wine is particularly good value at £5.95 per bottle. A no-smoking policy is strictly observed.
6rm(4⇌⌐2hc) (1fb)⊁in all bedrooms CTV in all bedrooms ® ✗ sB&B£27.50 sB&B⇌⌐£43.50 dB&B£39.50 dB&B⇌⌐£52.50 WBDi£333.20-£445.20 LDO 6pm
Lic ꘎ CTV 6P
Credit Cards [1] [3]

TWO BRIDGES Devon Map **02** SX67

GH QQQ ***Cherrybrook Hotel*** PL20 6SP
☎Tavistock(0822) 88260
Closed 20 Dec-4 Jan
A small family-run hotel set high on Dartmoor, with panoramic views across the moors, yet within easy reach of the north and south coasts of Devon. Seven bedrooms have been redecorated by the proprietors, and all have private showers and WCs. There is a characterful bar/lounge, and a choice of home- cooked fare is offered in the relaxed atmosphere of the dining room.
7⌐ (2fb) CTV in all bedrooms ® LDO 7.15pm
Lic ꘎ 12P

TWYNHOLM Dumfries & Galloway *Kirkcudbrightshire*
Map **11** NX65

SELECTED

GH QQQQ Fresh Fields DG6 4PB ☎(05576) 221
Mar-Oct
Conveniently situated, just minutes from the A75, in this relatively undiscovered region of Scotland, is Len and Ivy Stanley's attractive home, where they successfully create a relaxed, informal atmosphere. It is a distinctive, 3-gabled detached house with a pleasant garden, which is tastefully decorated and furnished throughout. Nowhere is over spacious but it is all most comfortable. The thoughtfully equipped bedrooms are delightful and all have private facilities. There is a comfortable sitting room and dining room, where a 5-course dinner is served. The menu features sound home cooking and is changed every day.
5⌐ ⊁in 2 bedrooms ® ✱ sB&B⌐£39 dB&B⌐£78 (incl dinner) WBDi£273 LDO 5.30pm
Lic ꘎ CTV 10P nc5yrs

TYNEMOUTH Tyne & Wear Map **12** NZ36

GH QQQ Hope House 47 Percy Gardens NE30 4HH
☎091-257 1989

A spacious end-of-terrace Victorian house overlooking the sea and sandy beach, yet within 20 minutes' drive of Newcastle. Antiques feature in all the rooms, which are tastefully enhanced by stylish décor and fine fabrics. The 2 front-facing rooms are particularly comfortable, with private bathrooms and sea views; a stair chair lift operates to all floors. Meals are served on Japanese porcelain at a handsome Georgian dining table.

3rm(1⇌2↑) (1fb) CTV in all bedrooms ® ✖ (ex guide dogs) sB&B⇌↑£35-£42.50 dB&B⇌↑£37.50-£47.50 WBDi£243.25 LDO 9pm
Lic ♨ 3P 3🚗 (£1.50 per night)
Credit Cards [1] [2] [3] £

TYWARDREATH Cornwall & Isles of Scilly Map **02** SX05

GH QQQ Elmswood Tehidy Rd PL24 2QD
☎Par(0726) 814221

Sitting in the quiet village, opposite the church, this very attractive hotel offers excellent standards, a friendly atmosphere and good value. Bedrooms are individually decorated, and furnished with pretty coordinated fabrics and modern en suite facilities. One or two also offer a flower-filled balcony to add to guests' enjoyment of the lovely rural views. Public areas are comfortable and have a fresh, pretty décor, and there is a colourful garden with tables and chairs set out for guests in good weather.

7rm(1⇌4↑2hc) (1fb) CTV in all bedrooms ®
✖ (ex guide dogs) ✱ sB&B£17 sB&B⇌↑£24 dB&B£34 dB&B⇌↑£36 WB&B£119 WBDi£171.50 LDO noon
Lic ♨ CTV 8P

UCKFIELD East Sussex Map **05** TQ42

SELECTED

GH QQQQ Hooke Hall 250 High St TN22 1EN
☎(0825) 761578 FAX (0825) 768025
Closed Xmas

This delightful Queen Anne house stands at the top of the High Street, and is run by owners Mr and Mrs Percy. Named after famous mistresses and lovers, bedrooms are furnished and decorated with considerable style – not surprising as Mrs Percy runs an interior design business as well. Antique furniture, modern comforts and many thoughtful extras combine to render this accommodation outstanding. Pre-dinner drinks can be sipped in the cosy panelled study, while interesting home cooking can be sampled Tuesday to Saturday in the elegant dining room, which is full of pictures and curiosities collected by the couple over the years. A real luxury is the option for guests to enjoy breakfast in bed.

9rm(7⇌1↑1hc) CTV in all bedrooms ® **T** ✖ sB&B£35-£60 sB&B⇌↑£35-£60 dB&B£50-£95 dB&B⇌↑£50-£95 LDO 8.30pm
Lic ♨ 8P nc10yrs
Credit Cards [1] [3]

SELECTED

GH QQQQ South Paddock Maresfield Park TN22 2HA
☎(0825) 762335

This delightful country house is set in 3.5 acres of landscaped gardens, found down a peaceful private road opposite the church in the centre of Maresfield village. There are 2 bedrooms, both facing south, attractively furnished and decorated, and sharing the large bathroom across the hall. They are twin-bedded rooms, but other beds are available to accommodate families. There is a comfortable lounge with a real log fire, and breakfasts, featuring home-made preserves, are taken around the large antique dining table. Major and Mrs Allt are friendly hosts and always available to provide local information and anything else guests might need.

2hc CTV in all bedrooms ® ✖ (ex guide dogs) sB&B£27-£34 dB&B£42-£50 WB&B£145-£215
♨ CTV 6P nc5yrs croquet
Credit Cards [1] [3] £

UFFCULME Devon Map **03** ST01

FH QQ Mrs M D Farley **Houndaller** *(ST058138)* EX15 3ET ☎Craddock(0884) 40246

A 16th-century Devonshire longhouse, just a quarter of a mile from junction 27 of the M5. Bedrooms are spacious and comfortable; there is a cosy guests' lounge where you are treated as part of the family, and the dining room has a large communal table.

3hc (2fb) ® sB&B£12.50-£16 dB&B£25-£30 LDO 6pm
♨ CTV 3P 1🚗 176 acres arable beef dairy sheep
Credit Cards [1] [2] [3] £

UIG

See **LEWIS, ISLE OF**

ULLAPOOL Highland *Ross & Cromarty* Map **14** NH19

GH QQQ The Sheiling Garve Rd IV26 2SX ☎(085461) 2947
Closed Xmas & New Year

Situated on the western fringe of the village, this modern purpose-built house is set in an acre of grounds beside the picturesque shore of Loch Broom. It has a relaxed friendly atmosphere, is comfortably appointed, modern, and offers excellent value bed and breakfast accommodation. Smoking is not permitted here.

7rm(2⇌5↑) ⊁in all bedrooms ® ✖ (ex guide dogs) ✱ sB&B⇌↑£16-£30 dB&B⇌↑£32-£40
♨ CTV 7P ✓

ULLINGSWICK Hereford & Worcester Map **03** SO54

SELECTED

GH QQQQ The Steppes HR1 3JG
☎Hereford(0432) 820424
Closed 2 wks before Xmas & 2 wks after New Year

This 17th-century country house, with some 14th-century parts, is situated a short distance from the A417, signposted Ullingswick, 1.5 miles northwest of its junction with the A465. The dining room has a low beamed ceiling, an inglenook fireplace and an original tiled floor, the cooking is imaginative and a daily changing gourmet menu is offered as well as an à la carte. The cellar bar was originally a dairy and cider-making cellar and retains the original cobble and flagstone floor, stone walls, oak timbers and inglenook fireplace, and has comfortable lounge seating. A further ground-floor lounge is available with modern sofas and a wood-burning stove. The 3 bedrooms in the main house with en suite showers are shortly to be taken over by the family. These will be replaced by 4 new rooms in a converted Tudor barn and another barn imported from Normandy. All the rooms will then surround a courtyard, including the 2 existing annexe rooms, which again are beamed, with some antiques and stripped pine furniture, settees, armchairs and pretty fabrics. There are plants and flowers everywhere, and all the rooms have teddy bears, bookshelves and a good range of modern facilities.

Annexe 6⇌↑ (1fb)⊁in 4 bedrooms CTV in all bedrooms ® **T** sB&B⇌↑£35 dB&B⇌↑£60-£70 (incl dinner) WB&B£190 WBDi£300-£315 LDO 6.30pm
Lic ♨ 8P nc10yrs
Credit Cards [1] [3] £

UNDERBARROW Cumbria Map **07** SD49

FH QQQ Mrs D M Swindlehurst **Tranthwaite Hall** *(SD469930)* LA8 8HG ☎Crosthwaite(04488) 285 due to change to (05395) 68285

A lovely Cumbrian farmhouse, dating back to the 14th century, full of character and charm. There are 2 delightful bedrooms and a very attractive lounge.

2hc (1fb) ® ✗ (ex guide dogs) * sB&B£15-£16 dB&B£27-£30

CTV 2P 200 acres dairy sheep

UPPINGHAM Leicestershire Map **04** SP89

GH QQQ Rutland House 61 High St East LE15 9PY ☎(0572) 822497

Located at a quiet end of the High Street in the busy market town, Rutland House provides comfortable and spacious accommodation with en suite bathrooms and many thoughtful extras. A ground-floor room would be suitable for some elderly and disabled guests, though not specifically designed to be. Breakfast is the only meal served (strictly no smoking in the dining room), but Mrs Hitchen is only too pleased to direct guests to local pubs and restaurants just a short walk away.

4⇌ (1fb) ⁄in 1 bedroom CTV in all bedrooms ® sB&B⇌£27 dB&B⇌£37

3P (£)

UPTON PYNE Devon Map **03** SX99

FH QQ Mrs Y M Taverner **Pierce's** *(SK910977)* EX5 5JA ☎Exeter(0392) 841252

Etr-Sep

A 16th-century oak-beamed farmhouse set in the centre of the village, only 3 miles from Exeter. The bedrooms are comfortable, and guests have the use of an attractive lounge. Breakfast is served at separate tables and a warm welcome awaits guests from the Taverner family.

2rm(1↱ 1hc) (1fb) ® ✗ dB&B£28-£32 dB&B↱£34-£38 WB&B£95-£115

CTV 2P 300 acres mixed (£)

UPTON UPON SEVERN Hereford & Worcester Map **03** SO84

GH QQQ Pool House WR8 0PA ☎(0684) 592151

Closed Xmas

This lovely Queen Anne house is set in attractive grounds on the banks of the River Severn. The pleasant bedrooms are spacious and comfortable, and there are 2 lounges available for residents. The house is located just off the town centre on the B4211, signposted to Lower Malvern.

9rm(3⇌3↱ 3hc) (2fb) ⁄in all bedrooms CTV in 1 bedroom ® ✗ * sB&B£22-£24 sB&B⇌↱£31.50-£34.50 dB&B£35-£38.50 dB&B⇌↱£46-£50 WB&B£105-£180

Lic CTV 20P

Credit Cards [1] [3] (£)

UTTOXETER Staffordshire Map **07** SK03

GH QQ *Hillcrest* 3 Leighton Rd ST14 8BL ☎(0889) 564627

Closed Xmas Day

This family-run guesthouse is situated in an elevated position a few minutes' walk from the town centre. Bedrooms are now all en suite and equipped with modern facilities such as TVs and hairdryers. There is a spacious lounge and a small bar for residents.

7⇌↱ (6fb) CTV in all bedrooms ® ✗ (ex guide dogs) LDO 4pm

Lic CTV 10P 2

Credit Cards [1] [2] [3]

VENN OTTERY Devon Map **03** SY09

GH QQQ Venn Ottery Barton Country Hotel EX11 1RZ ☎Ottery St Mary(0404) 812733

Quietly situated in the centre of the charming village, this is a listed building, parts of which date back to 1530, set in about 2 acres of gardens. Freshly prepared, home-cooked food, including locally caught fish, is served in the dining room and choices are offered at each course. Ground-floor rooms are available.

16rm(5⇌6↱ 5hc) (3fb) ® * sB&B£21.50-£23.50 sB&B⇌↱£25.50-£27.50 dB&B£39-£43 dB&B⇌↱£47-£51 WBDi£203-£259 LDO 7.30pm

Lic CTV 20P large games room

Credit Cards [1] [3] (£)

See advertisement under OTTERY ST MARY

VENTNOR

See **WIGHT, ISLE OF**

VOWCHURCH Hereford & Worcester Map **03** SO33

SELECTED

GH QQQQ The Croft Country House HR2 0QE ☎Golden Valley(0981) 550226

Croft Country House is situated at the junction of the B4348 and the B4347 in the centre of beautiful Golden Valley, 10 miles southwest of Hereford. It is a small country house, parts of which date back to the 18th century, set in 7 acres of grounds with lawns, 2 lakes, a pond and tennis court. The large vegetable garden supplies the cottage-style restaurant, now popular with the locals, which offers a fixed-price menu with additional items. Public rooms have log fires or wood burners, and include a small pine bar and a comfortably furnished lounge with several settees and a good choice of books. The main house bedrooms have pretty floral décor with a mixture of stripped pine and antique furniture, and there are 3 new pine-furnished bedrooms in a converted coach house, one with its own private lounge.

4⇌↱ Annexe 4⇌↱ (1fb) ⁄in all bedrooms CTV in all bedrooms ® ✗ (ex guide dogs) * dB&B⇌↱£44-£54 WB&B£150-£185 WBDi£230-£269 LDO 9pm

Lic CTV 15P 2 nc10yrs (grass)croquet lawn

Credit Cards [1] [3] (£)

WADEBRIDGE Cornwall & Isles of Scilly Map **02** SW97

INN QQQ Swan Hotel PL27 7DD (St Austell Brewery) ☎(0208) 812526

Recently restored to a good standard, the pine furnished bedrooms are all equipped with a hairdryer, remote-control TV and tea-making facilities. There is a comfortable, beamed bar that is furnished in a modern style and is very much the focal point with its popular real ales, home-cooked bar meals and daily blackboard specials. The very attractive, Victorian-style 'Cob and Pen' restaurant offers a good value à la carte menu. Service is supervised by the friendly resident managers Allan and Diana Biggs.

6⇌ (1fb) CTV in all bedrooms ® ✗ (ex guide dogs) LDO 9pm

6P

Credit Cards [1] [2] [3] (£)

WANSFORD Cambridgeshire Map **04** TL09

INN Q Cross Keys PE8 6JD ☎Stamford(0780) 782266

2hc Annexe 5hc (2fb) CTV in all bedrooms ® ✗ sB&B£18-£22 dB&B£36-£40 Bar Lunch fr£5.25 LDO 9.30pm

pool table

WARE Hertfordshire Map **05** TL31

INN QQQ ***Feathers Hotel*** Wadesmill SG1 2TN
☎(0920) 462606

This coaching inn is situated beside the A10 on the Cambridge side of Ware. An adjacent modern accommodation annexe provides attractive cottage-style rooms and an excellent array of modern facilities. There is a breakfast room also located in the annexe, in addition to the dining room which provides a popular carvery in the main building, where the bars remain open all day.

Annexe 22rm(11⇔4↱7hc) CTV in all bedrooms ®
✕ (ex guide dogs) LDO 10.30pm
⌂ 100P
Credit Cards [1] [2] [3] [5]

WAREHAM Dorset Map **03** SY98

FH QQ L S Barnes **Luckford Wood** *(SY873865)* East Stoke BH20 6AW ☎Bindon Abbey(0929) 463098

This modern farmhouse is a friendly, informal place, ideal for children or those who enjoy being in touch with nature. It is very much a family house, filled with the sound of children and their laughter, and the Barnes are open, convivial people who enjoy welcoming guests to their home. Bedrooms are pretty, public areas comfortable, and reservations are advisable. The farm, predominantly dairy, is found by taking the A352 from Wareham (2 miles), turn left at the church on the left, go over the manually operated level crossing, and the house is on the right-hand side half a mile along the lane.

5rm(1↱2hc) (3fb)⊘in 1 bedroom CTV in all bedrooms ® ✻
sB&B£17-£20 dB&B£30-£34
⌂ CTV 5P 167 acres dairy (£)

SELECTED

FH QQQQ Mrs J Barnes ***Redcliffe*** *(SY932866)*
BH20 5BE ☎(0929) 552225
Closed Xmas

Standing at the edge of Wareham Yacht Club lake with good views over the River Frome, this modern farmhouse offers a peaceful, quiet and relaxed atmosphere, coupled with a warm, cheery welcome which guests return time and time again to enjoy. There are 3 very pretty bedrooms, plus one simpler single room, and all share a modern well kept bath/shower room. Two of the bedrooms have balconies. Whilst they lack many modern facilities, they are all very comfortable. Breakfast is served at a communal table, although sometimes tables are set out on the sun patio, and a family lounge filled with photographs and ornaments is greatly appreciated by guests, where they can watch TV in comfort. This established farmhouse remains a popular holiday choice, not least due to the friendly proprietors and the comfortable home they happily share with their visitors.

4rm(1⇔1↱2hc) ⊘in 3 bedrooms ✕ (ex guide dogs)
⌂ CTV 4P 250 acres dairy mixed

WARKWORTH Northumberland Map **12** NU20

GH QQQ North Cottage Birling NE65 0XS
☎Alnwick(0665) 711263
Closed Xmas & 2wks Nov

A charming, rambling cottage situated on the fringe of the village in an elevated position overlooking its own tiered patios and garden. Bedrooms are cosy and attractive and the spacious comfortable lounge overlooks the gardens.

4rm(2↱2hc) (4fb)⊘in all bedrooms CTV in all bedrooms ® ✕
✻ sB&B£13.50 dB&B£27 dB&B↱£30 WB&B£88-£98
⌂ CTV 4P nc14yrs

Book as early as possible for busy holiday periods.

WARREN STREET (NEAR LENHAM) Kent Map **05** TQ95

INN QQQ Harrow Hubbards Hill ME17 2ED
☎Maidstone(0622) 858727 FAX (0622) 850026
Closed 25 & 26 Dec

Enjoying a very good local reputation for good food, the accommodation here has recently been extended to provide 10 new en suite bedrooms, a conservatory restaurant and new reception. The beamed and very popular bar with its log- burning stove offers an extensive range of bar meals, together with pumped ales and local cider. The Harrow is situated high on the North Downs off the A20 amidst farmland, and was once the forge and rest-house for travellers en route to Canterbury. The bedrooms are particularly well equipped to a high standard.

15⇔↱ (6fb) CTV in all bedrooms ® **T** ✕ (ex guide dogs) ✻
sB&B⇔↱£35-£45 dB&B⇔↱£45-£59 Lunch £6.50-£12.50alc
Dinner £9.50-£20alc LDO 10pm
⌂ CTV 80P
Credit Cards [1] [2] [3] (£)

WARSASH Hampshire Map **04** SU40

GH QQQ Solent View Private Hotel 33-35 Newtown Rd
SO3 6FY ☎Locks Heath(0489) 572300

This friendly and well kept small hotel is situated in the village centre, a short walk from the River Hamble. Bedrooms are comfortable, prettily decorated and well equipped. There is a bar and lounge available for guests.

6rm(1⇔5↱) CTV in all bedrooms ® LDO noon
Lic ⌂ CTV 12P
Credit Cards [1] [3] (£)

WARWICK Warwickshire Map **04** SP26

See also Lighthorne

GH QQ Austin House 96 Emscote Rd CV34 5QJ
☎(0926) 493583

Conveniently situated for the town centre, this guesthouse offers modest accommodation. Most rooms have en suite shower facilities and all have metered colour TVs, and there is a TV lounge for guests' use.

6rm(4↱2hc) (3fb) CTV in all bedrooms ® ✻ dB&B£27-£33
dB&B↱£27-£33
⌂ CTV 8P 2⊗
Credit Cards [1] [2] [3] [5] (£)

GH QQ Avon 7 Emscote Rd CV34 4PH ☎(0926) 491367

A large Victorian terraced house half a mile from the town centre on the Leamington road, offering clean and simply appointed bed and breakfast accommodation close to amenities and with the advantage of a good car park.

7hc Annexe 3hc (4fb) ® ✕ sB&B£15 dB&B£30 WB&B£98
WBDi£147 LDO 8pm
Lic ⌂ CTV 6P 1⊗ (£)

GH QQ ***Cambridge Villa Private Hotel*** 20A Emscote Rd
CV34 4PL ☎(0926) 491169

A double-fronted Victorian terraced house, half a mile east of the town centre on the Leamington Spa road, offering simply appointed bedrooms and a bright basement dining room where the enthusiastic Italian owner offers specialities from her homeland.

16rm(4↱12hc) (2fb) CTV in all bedrooms ® LDO 10pm
Lic ⌂ CTV 28P ⌂
Credit Cards [1] [3]

GH QQQ The Old Rectory Vicarage Ln, Sherbourne
CV35 8AB (off A46 2m SW)
☎Barford (Warwicks)(0926) 624562
Closed 24-27 Dec

Tastefully restored house offering very comfortable accommodation and home- cooked food.

7⇔↱ Annexe 7⇔↱ (2fb) CTV in all bedrooms ®
sB&B⇔↱£30-£38 dB&B⇔↱£39-£50 LDO 8pm

Lic 🍽 CTV 14P
Credit Cards 1 2 3 £

See advertisement on page 407

INN QQ Tudor House West St CV34 6AW ☎(0926) 495447
FAX (0926) 492948
This Tudor house, still retaining much wattle and daub and timbers, was built in 1472. The bedrooms are of a cosy nature, being equipped with good en suite facilities. Its attractive public rooms are complemented by traditional wholesome food.
11rm(8⇌🚿3hc) (1fb) CTV in all bedrooms ® **T**
🐕 (ex guide dogs) sB&Bfr£24 sB&B⇌🚿fr£38
dB&B⇌🚿fr£54 Lunch fr£5&alc Dinner fr£10&alc
LDO 10.30pm
🍽 5P
Credit Cards 1 2 3 5

WASHFORD Somerset Map **03** ST04

INN QQQ Washford TA23 0PP ☎(0984) 40256
The Inn is in a village location on the A39 next to the restored steam railway and station, and some bedrooms have good views of the line. A modern open-plan bar serves a range of popular pub dishes. The pretty, converted bedrooms have modern tiled shower rooms and comfortable beds.
8🚿 CTV in all bedrooms ® **T** 🐕 (ex guide dogs) sB&B🚿£21-£26 dB&B🚿£38-£42 LDO 9pm
🍽 30P nc12yrs
Credit Cards 1 2 3 5

WATERHOUSES Staffordshire Map **07** SK05

GH QQ Croft House Farm Waterfall ST10 3HZ (1m NW unclass) ☎(0538) 308553
This stone-built farmhouse is about a mile north of the A523 at the hamlet of Waterfall. Partly dating from 1520, it now provides neat bedrooms, a small residents' lounge and a cosy bar.

→

6hc (2fb) CTV in all bedrooms ® ✗ sB&B£16.50-£21.50 dB&Bfr£33 LDO 8pm
Lic 🍽 CTV 15P

INN Q **Ye Olde Crown** ST10 3HL ☎(0538) 308204

Dating back in parts to the 17th century, this popular village inn is easily accessable alongside the A523. Bedrooms are modern and there are two characterful bars which are popular with locals.

7rm(5⇌🚿2hc) (1fb) CTV in all bedrooms ®
✗ (ex guide dogs) ✱ sB&B£15 sB&B⇌🚿£21.50 dB&B£33 dB&B⇌🚿£33 Lunch £5.50-£15alc Dinner £5.50-£15alc LDO 10pm
🍽 50P

See advertisement under ASHBOURNE

WATERMILLOCK Cumbria Map **12** NY42

SELECTED

GH QQQQ **The Old Church Hotel** CA11 0JN ☎Pooley Bridge(07684) 86204 FAX (07684) 86368

Apr-Oct

This haven of tranquillity is situated in its own grounds on the very edge of Lake Ullswater, enjoying spectacular views from all sides. It is an elegant white-painted Georgian house, converted into a small hotel, 3 years ago by the present owners Kevin and Maureen Whitemore. Maureen is responsible for the interior design and she made all the soft furnishings. Public areas feature bold designs and colour schemes, while the bedrooms are in a softer vein, all individually decorated and thoughtfully furnished.

10⇌ CTV in all bedrooms ✗ (ex guide dogs) ✱ sB&B⇌£45-£75 dB&B⇌£90-£150 LDO 7.30pm
Lic 🍽 30P boating, moorings & jetties
Credit Cards 1 3

GH QQ **Waterside House** CA11 0TH ☎Pooley Bridge(07684) 86038

Closed Xmas

This charming house dates back to 1771 and retains much of its original character. Old beams abound, and there are 2 lounge areas, one with a piano for musical guests. Bedrooms are bright and fresh and being refurbished. A good Cumbrian breakfast is provided, and the owner Mrs Jenner is always on hand to chat. The grounds extend to 10 acres and go down to the shores of Lake Ullswater.

7rm(2⇌1🚿4hc) (1fb)⊁in all bedrooms ® ✱ sB&B£15-£20 sB&B⇌🚿£20-£25 dB&B£30-£40 dB&B⇌🚿£40-£50
7P
Credit Cards 1 3

WATERROW Somerset Map **03** ST02

INN QQ **The Rock** TA4 2AX ☎Wiveliscombe(0984) 23293

A character inn with low beams and open fireplaces offering good value, clean and tidy accommodation. The proprietor has gradually improved the establishment over the last 5 years, and while bedrooms vary in size and comfort, most now have en suite facilities and modern equipment. There is a small dining area, set away from the public bar, and the food is home-prepared, simple and wholesome.

7rm(6⇌🚿1hc) (1fb) CTV in all bedrooms **T** sB&B⇌🚿£20-£21.50 Lunch £5.50-£6alc Dinner £5-£12.50alc LDO 10pm
🍽 CTV 20P
Credit Cards 1 3 £

See advertisement under TAUNTON

WEETON Lancashire Map **07** SD33

FH Q Mr & Mrs J Colligan **High Moor** *(SD388365)* PR4 3JJ ☎Blackpool(0253) 836273

Closed Xmas & New Year

Although no longer on a working farm, this 150-year-old brick farm house is situated in a rural location and there are plenty of chickens, turkeys, geese and ducks to be seen. The 2 bedrooms are cosy with comfortable furniture and equipped with modern facilities. Downstairs the breakfast room only has 2 tables and a freshly cooked breakfast is served every morning. Behind the house, on the B5260, there is a touring caravan site.

2rm (1fb) CTV in all bedrooms ® ✗ ✱ dB&Bfr£25
🍽 CTV 10P 7 acres non-working

WELCOMBE Devon Map **02** SS21

FH QQQ Mrs P Tunnicliffe ***Henaford Manor*** *(SS249187)* EX39 6HE ☎Morwenstow(028883) 252

Built in the 13th century, this farmhouse has an elegant dining room and comfortable lounge. One of the nicely appointed bedrooms has en suite facilities and all are equipped to modern standards. There is also a self- catering cottage next to the house.

3rm(1⇌2hc) (1fb) CTV in all bedrooms ® ✗ LDO 6pm
🍽 CTV 6P 226 acres dairy mixed

WELLINGBOROUGH Northamptonshire Map **04** SP86

GH QQQ **Oak House Private Hotel** 8-11 Broad Green NN8 4LE ☎(0933) 271133

Closed Xmas

This well established, professionally run guesthouse is situated in the older part of Wellingborough on the former village green, yet is convenient for the town centre. Rooms can be compact, but accommodation is functional and all rooms have private showers. Home-cooked meals are served in the split-level dining room and a comfortable guests' lounge is available.

16rm(15🚿1hc) (1fb) CTV in all bedrooms ® ✱ sB&B🚿£28-£32 dB&B£38 dB&B🚿£38-£42 WB&B£196-£224 WBDi£255.50-£283.50 LDO noon
Lic 🍽 CTV 12P
Credit Cards 1 2 3 £

WELLINGTON Shropshire

See **Telford**

WELLINGTON Somerset Map **03** ST12

FH QQQ Mrs Howe **Gamlins** *(ST082194)* Greenham TA21 0LZ ☎Greenham(0823) 672596

Closed Xmas

A well presented farmhouse set on the Somerset/Devon border offering good value for money. Facilities include a heated covered swimming pool, rough shooting and coarse fishing available on site, and there are 3 self-catering cottages. There is a selection of local pub and restaurant menus on view in the lounge for dinner.

3rm(1⇌🚿2hc) (1fb) CTV in 2 bedrooms TV in 1 bedroom ® ✗ ✱ sB&B£18 dB&B⇌🚿£30-£36
🍽 CTV 6P nc2yrs ⛆(heated) ⚲ 116 acres poultry

FH QQQ Mrs N Ash **Pinksmoor Mill House** *(ST109198)* Pinksmoor TA21 0HO (2m W off A38 at Beam Bridge Hotel) ☎Greenham(0823) 672361

Closed 23-29 Dec

Convenient for junctions 26 and 27 of the M5, this white-painted millhouse is believed to be of Saxon origin and dates back to the 13th century. Although the old mill is no longer in use, the wooden gearing and large millstones remain as they were when last used to grind corn in the 1940s. Now a working farm, all areas are open for guests to explore; kingfishers and heron are to be seen by the water, and commercial animals include a herd of dairy cattle and a flock of ewes. The accommodation inside the farmhouse is very comfortable. Bedrooms have tea trays and TV and 2 are en suite, while the other has a private bathroom. Of the 2 lounges, one is designated as non smoking and the other features a beautiful fireplace with exposed red brickwork. Home-cooked meals are served around one large table in the dining room. The owner, Mrs Ash, ensures that guests relax and enjoy themselves in this friendly, family farmhouse.

3rm(2🛁🚿1hc) (1fb)🚭in all bedrooms CTV in all bedrooms ®
sB&Bfr£18.50 sB&B🛁🚿£19.50 dB&Bfr£32 dB&B🛁🚿£34
WB&B£105-£126 WBDi£178-£206.50 LDO 4pm
♨ CTV 6P 98 acres dairy sheep (£)

See advertisement on page 409

WELLS Somerset Map **03** ST54

GH QQQ Bekynton House 7 St Thomas St BA5 2UU
☎(0749) 672222
rs 24-26 Dec

Standing on the fringe of the lovely cathedral city, this well appointed guesthouse is steadily being improved to an even higher standard. This year more en suite facilities have been provided and these are very smart, spacious and practical. The bedrooms are all no smoking and well coordinated as are the public rooms. Mr and Mrs Gripper remain very personally involved and many of their guests return time after time to enjoy the relaxed and friendly atmosphere here.

8rm(6🛁🚿2hc) (2fb)🚭in all bedrooms CTV in all bedrooms ®
🐕 sB&B£21-£25 dB&B£36-£39 dB&B🛁🚿£38-£46
♨ 6P nc5yrs
Credit Cards [1] [3] (£)

See advertisement on page 409

Q is for quality. For a full explanation of this AA quality award, consult the Contents page.

SELECTED

GH QQQQ Coach House Stoberry Park BA5 3AA ☎(0749) 676535
Closed 24-31Dec
A converted coach house standing in 6 acres of attractive grounds in the Mendip Hills, 15 minutes walk from the city centre; with superb views over the city across to Glastonbury Tor. The spacious bedrooms are nicely presented and equipped, each with private bathrooms; standards of housekeeping are excellent throughout. Public areas are spacious, with various seating areas and an open- plan staircase. The hearty breakfast is the only meal served and includes local bacon and sausages from free range pigs. The charming owners Mr and Mrs Poynter enjoy welcoming guests into their home, many of whom return regularly; they are both well travelled, and speak French, Spanish and German. Mr Poynter is creating a beautiful garden at the rear of the house, making this a delightful place to stay in a glorious location. To find the house, take the turning to College Road, then follow the turning into a private drive marked Stoberry Park at one end. Drive across open parkland for a quarter of a mile along the drive until it forks; take the right-hand road marked to the Coach House.
3⇌ ⚟in all bedrooms CTV in all bedrooms ® dB&B⇌£36-£40 WB&B£112
♨ CTV 6P nc3yrs £

GH QQ Tor 20 Tor St BA5 2US ☎(0749) 672322
A neatly presented charming 17th-century house standing close to the cathedral along the A371 Shepton Mallet road. Tasteful restoration has provided comfortable accommodation retaining the original character of the period, with double glazing being a modern benefit.
9rm(6↱3hc) (2fb) CTV in all bedrooms ® ✗ sB&B£25 dB&B£34-£38 dB&B↱£40-£48 WB&B£140-£175 WBDi£210-£245 LDO 10am
♨ CTV 11P 1🚗 nc5yrs £

FH QQ Mrs P Higgs **Home** *(ST538442)* Stoppers Ln, Upper Coxley BA5 1QS (2m SW off A39) ☎(0749) 672434
Closed 1wk Xmas
Only 2 miles from Wells town centre, this very nicely presented farmhouse has much to commend. Mrs Higgs is a friendly, cheery lady who extends a warm welcome to her guests and takes great pride in the farmhouse. Accommodation offered is prettily decorated and some bedrooms have a newly fitted en suite; each room being comfortable and spotlessly clean. A home-cooked breakfast is served and there is a cosy TV lounge, complete with open fire.
7rm(2⇌5hc) (1fb) ® ✱ sB&B£15-£16 dB&B£30-£32 dB&B⇌£35-£38
Lic ♨ CTV 12P nc5yrs 15 acres pigs

SELECTED

FH QQQQ Mr & Mrs Gnoyke **Littlewell** *(ST536445)* Coxley BA5 1QP (2 miles SW on A39) ☎(0749) 677914
Closed Jan
The well tended orchard garden gives an early indication of the quality accommodation within this 200-year-old, whitewashed farmhouse, that lies back from the A39. There is a comfortable lounge and a dining room displaying pretty ornaments and flower arrangements, where guests share an antique polished table. The good size, individual bedrooms are attractively decorated, fitted with well chosen pieces of furniture and all have their own bathrooms, although 2 are not en suite. Gerry and Di Gnoyke offer friendly and relaxing hospitality along with good standards of maintenance and housekeeping.
4rm(1⇌3↱) CTV in all bedrooms ® ✗ (ex guide dogs) ✱ sB&B⇌↱£19.50-£22 dB&B⇌↱£33-£41
Lic ♨ 4P 4🚗 nc10yrs 2 acres non-working

FH QQQ Mrs J Gould **Manor** *(ST546474)* Old Bristol Rd, Upper Milton BA5 3AH (1m W A39 towards Bristol, 200 yds beyond rdbt) ☎(0749) 673394
Closed Xmas
This historically interesting 16th-century Grade II listed building is on a large beef farm with footpaths across the fields to Wookey Hole and Wells. The 3 spacious bedrooms are spotlessly clean, freshly decorated and have excellent quality beds. There is a colour TV in the small lounge cum breakfast room.
3hc (1fb) ® ✗ (ex guide dogs) sB&B£15.50-£17.50 dB&B£26-£28 WB&B£87-£96
♨ CTV 6P 130 acres beef

FH QQQ Mr & Mrs Frost ***Southway*** *(ST516423)* Polsham BA5 1RW (3m SW off A39) ☎(0749) 673396
This is a Georgian farmhouse about 3 miles outside the cathedral city along the A39. It is very well kept and presented by Mrs Frost with prettily furnished bedrooms coordinated in quality fabrics. The lounge area is extremely comfortable with fire, TV and record player, the dining room, where breakfast is served is also an elegant room. Overall, the atmosphere is cheerful and friendly.
3hc ✗ (ex guide dogs)
♨ CTV 5P 170 acres dairy

WELLS-NEXT-THE-SEA Norfolk Map 09 TF94

GH QQ Mill House Northfield Ln NR23 1JZ ☎Fakenham(0328) 710739
Closed 8 Nov-14 Dec, 24-27 Dec rs 15 Dec-29 Feb
Sadly, the mill itself no longer stands, but this splendid red-brick Georgian house remains, with three quarters of an acre of garden, just a couple of minutes' walk from the quay off Standard Road. Mrs Fisher is the cheerful and enthusiastic proprietor who goes out of her way to look after her guests. The most recently decorated bedrooms are the most attractive, but they are all warm and comfortable. Evening meals may be available on request.
7rm(2⇌2↱3hc) Annexe 1⇌ (3fb) CTV in all bedrooms ® sB&B£15.50-£18.50 dB&B£30-£33 dB&B⇌↱£37-£45 WB&B£105-£149
Lic ♨ CTV 10P nc6yrs

GH QQQ The Normans Invaders Court, Standard Rd NR23 1JW ☎Fakenham(0328) 710657
Situated 50yds from the quay, this is a lovely red-brick Georgian residence with a cobbled courtyard at the front. Mr and Mrs Burns, the proprietors, have kept the spacious reception area and accentuated the period features, such as the Adams fireplace and dining room mouldings, with sensitive décor. The lounge is comfortable with large armchairs and sofas, and the bedrooms have been thoughtfully furnished. Rooms at the rear have splendid views over the quay.
7rm(2⇌↱5hc) (2fb) CTV in all bedrooms ® dB&B£33-£36 dB&B⇌↱£41-£44 WB&B£112-£151 WBDi£189.50-£235 LDO 5pm
♨ CTV 7P 1🚗 nc10yrs

GH QQQ Scarborough House Clubbs Ln NR23 1DP ☎Fakenham(0328) 710309 & 711661
This is a popular guesthouse, quietly situated a few minutes from the quay. A Victorian detached house, it is furnished comfortably and attractively with antiques and collectables of the era. There are some en suite facilities, and a delightful lounge and carvery restaurant. There are immediate plans to extend the accommodation.
11rm(5⇌6↱) (2fb) CTV in all bedrooms ® sB&B⇌↱£29-£35 dB&B£36 dB&B⇌↱£48-£54 WB&B£161-£196 WBDi£241-£276 LDO 8.30pm

→

HOME FARM

Wells, Somerset Farmhouse accommodation
Details and terms, Mrs Pat Higgs,
Home Farm, Stoppers Lane, Coxley, Wells,
Somerset BA5 1QS.
Tel: Wells 0749 72434

Pat Higgs offers a relaxed holiday, long or short stay, in a peaceful spot just 1½ miles from the City of Wells, slightly off the A39, with extensive views of the Mendip Hills.

Somerset offers a varied type of holiday, with the popular city of Bath only ½ hour ride, there are National Trust properties, Cheddar Gorge, The Fleet Air Arm Museum, Wookey Hole Caves, also many other attractions.

We have all facilities including a shower.
Bed & Breakfast only.

Many good restaurants and pubs within easy reach.

BEKYNTON HOUSE

7 ST THOMAS STREET
WELLS, SOMERSET
BA5 2UU

English Tourist Board COMMENDED

A delightful setting close to the Cathedral and Bishop's Palace makes our period home an ideal choice for a special holiday. Comfortable pretty bedrooms with en-suite facilities, colour TV and complementary hot drinks trays. An attractive sitting room and pleasant dining room for your chosen breakfast add to your pleasure.

An ideal touring centre and walkers' paradise.

Desmond & Rosaleen Gripper
Wells (0749) 672222

Tor Guest House

20 Tor Street, Wells, Somerset BA5 2US
Telephone: Wells (0749) 672322

Delightful 17th century family run guest house set in attractive grounds overlooking Wells Cathedral/Bishop's Palace and borders National Trust woodland. Comfortable, centrally heated and tastefully furnished rooms (many en suite) enjoying fine views and equipped with beverage making facilities. Excellent home cooking including vegetarian cuisine. 3 minute walk alongside Palace moat to town centre. Large car park. Open all year. Ideal centre for touring Somerset with Bath and Bristol 30 minutes by car.

Resident Proprietors: Albie and Letitia Horne

Take a stroll along the old millstream . . .

13c. Pinksmoor Mill

The haunt of kingfisher, heron, snipe and mallard.
Go badger watching –
or just wander where you please, around this 'family run' dairy farm.

Then return to the homely atmosphere of the farmhouse, for good food and a peaceful nights rest.

Just ten minutes from junction 26 - M5

Mrs. Nancy Ash
Pinksmoor Farm
Wellington Somerset
(0823) 672361

AA LISTED QQQ

COMMENDED

Lic ▥ 10P nc7yrs
Credit Cards 1 2 3 £

WELSHPOOL Powys Map **07** SJ20

FH QQQ Mrs E Jones **Gungrog House** *(SJ235089)* Rhallt SY21 9HS (1m NE off A458) ☎(0938) 553381
Apr-Oct
Providing good quality bedrooms and public rooms this guesthouse has superb views from its elevated position over the Severn Valley. It is reached via a country lane opposite to the junction of the A483 and A458.
3rm(2↱1hc) ✖ ✱ dB&B↱£32 WB&Bfr£100 WBDifr£170 LDO 5pm
▥ CTV 6P 21 acres mixed

FH QQ Mr & Mrs M C Payne **Heath Cottage** *(SJ239023)* Kingswood, Forden SY21 8LX (3m S off A490) ☎Forden(093876) 453
Etr-Oct
This former country pub, just yards away from Offa's Dyke, is run by the friendly Payne family. There is a comfortable lounge available for guests, and the bedrooms have recently been improved with all rooms now having en suite facilities.
3⇌↱ (1fb) ® ✖ sB&B⇌↱£16 dB&B⇌↱£32 WB&B£100 WBDi£156
▥ CTV 4P 6 acres poultry sheep

FH QQQ Mr & Mrs G Jones **Lower Trelydan** *(SJ225105)* Lower Trelydan, Guilsfield SY21 9PH (3.5m N off A490) ☎(0938) 553105
This 16th-century black and white timbered farmhouse is set in pleasant lawns and gardens. The accommodation is spacious and comfortable with a panelled lounge and a dining room still with its original butler's pantry. An unusual feature of the house is the licensed bar which has been built into the 400- year-old inglenook fireplace. The house is located at Guilsfield, 2 miles off the A490, signposted off the B4392 at the 30mph sign before entering the village.
3rm(2⇌1↱) (1fb) CTV in 2 bedrooms ® ✱ sB&Bfr£15 sB&B⇌↱fr£17 dB&Bfr£28 dB&B⇌↱fr£32 WB&Bfr£112 WBDifr£175 LDO 5pm
Lic CTV P 108 acres beef dairy sheep

FH QQQ Mr & Mrs W Jones **Moat** *(SJ214042)* SY21 8SE ☎(0938) 553179
Apr-Oct rs Feb, Mar & Nov
One mile south of Welshpool, this working farm dates back to the 16th century and provides comfortable accommodation. The Jones family are welcoming and a tennis court and pool table are available. The River Severn runs through the grounds.
3⇌↱ (1fb)⊬in all bedrooms CTV in all bedrooms ® ✖ ✱ dB&B⇌↱£32-£36 WB&B£112-£120 WBDi£168-£175 LDO 2pm
▥ 3P ♩(grass)pool table croquet 260 acres dairy

FH QQQ Mrs F Emberton **Tynllwyn** *(SJ215085)* SY21 9BW ☎(0938) 553175
Providing good comfortable bedrooms and spacious lounge this large 18th- century farmhouse is situated off the A490 North of Welshpool with good rural views.
6hc (3fb) CTV in all bedrooms ® ✖ ✱ sB&Bfr£14 dB&Bfr£28 WB&Bfr£90 WBDifr£130 LDO 6.30pm
Lic ▥ CTV 20P 150 acres mixed

WEM Shropshire Map **07** SJ53

FH QQQ Mrs A P Ashton **Soulton Hall** *(SJ543303)* Soulton SY4 5RS ☎(0939) 232786
A manor house steeped in history on the B5065 Wem to Market Drayton road. During the summer guests can relax in the walled garden and in the winter a welcoming log fire blazes in the hall/lounge.
3rm(2⇌1hc) Annexe 2⇌↱ (2fb)⊬in 1 bedroom CTV in all bedrooms ® ✱ sB&B£21.50-£27.50 sB&B⇌↱£25.50-£31.50 dB&Bfr£43 dB&B⇌↱fr£51 WB&B£135.45-£160.65 WBDi£220.50-£245.70 LDO 9pm
Lic ▥ 10P 2🚗 ⌂ ♩ U 560 acres mixed
Credit Cards 1 3 £
See advertisement under SHREWSBURY

WEMBLEY Greater London London plan **4** B4 (pages 245-251)

GH QQ Arena Hotel 6 Forty Ln HA9 9EB ☎081-908 0670 & 081-908 2007
This detached house is usefully situated for the stadium and conference centre, a short drive off the North Circular. It has recently been modernised throughout and most rooms are en suite. There is a comfortable small lounge and meals are provided by arrangement.
10rm(3⇌4↱3hc) (1fb) CTV in all bedrooms ®
✖ (ex guide dogs) ✱ sB&B£25-£28 sB&B⇌↱£32-£35 dB&B£38-£39 dB&B⇌↱£45-£49 LDO 10.30pm
▥ CTV 10P
Credit Cards 1 3
See advertisement under NW4 HENDON

WEOBLEY Hereford & Worcester Map **03** SO45

SELECTED

INN QQQQ Ye Olde Salutation Market Pitch HR4 8SJ ☎(0544) 318443
Created from the combination of a former ale and cider house, this model of an English inn with magpie colours, misshapen walls and timber, has been a centre of attraction here for about 500 years. The present hosts Christopher and Frances Anthony have added to its already substantial reputation, and are making alterations to release 2 more bedrooms for guests' use as well as providing a lovely new lounge. Oak beams, chintzy soft furnishings, armchairs and comforts like tea-making equipment, TV and hairdryer are standard in all bedrooms, and some have excellent en suite bathrooms. Humorous names are given to the bedrooms, such as the 4-poster favoured by honeymooners, called after Richard Tonkins, a local character who fathered 30 children. While ales and beer are the usual attraction, the imaginative bar food is well worth a visit with such treats as roast lamb with honey and rosemary or a French stick stuffed with hot roast beef, vegetarian meals are also available. The restaurant has a lengthy menu with portions that are real trencherman sizes and local produce is used whenever possible.
3rm(2↱1hc) ⊬in all bedrooms CTV in 2 bedrooms ® ✱ dB&B£31.50 dB&B↱£52.50 Lunch £14.50-£20alc Dinner £14.50-£20alc LDO 9.30pm
▥ CTV 14P nc14yrs
Credit Cards 1 3 £

WEST BAGBOROUGH Somerset Map **03** ST13

GH QQQ Higher House TA4 3EF ☎Bishops Lydeard(0823) 432996
Closed Xmas rs Dec-Mar
Originally dating back to 1661, Higher House stands at one end of the village, nestling at the foot of the Quantock Hills and enjoying superb views. The comfortable bedrooms are pretty and nicely coordinated – offering good facilities. There is a choice of spacious and charming lounge areas, consisting of a drawing room, complete with snooker table and a cosy morning room, with a log fire and pretty garden views. Evening meals are served on a long polished communal table and a dinner-party atmosphere is promoted by the proprietors, who remain charming and helpful throughout their guests' stay. A heated, outdoor swimming pool adds an extra bonus.

6rm(3⇌1↱2hc) (1fb) CTV in all bedrooms ® T ✱ sB&Bfr£27 sB&B⇌↱fr£32 dB&B£38-£43 dB&B⇌↱£48-£53
LDO 4.30pm
Lic ꟾꟾꟾ CTV 13P ⩡(heated) three quarter snooker table
Credit Cards [1] [3]

WEST BUCKLAND Devon Map **03** SS63

FH QQ Mrs J Payne **Huxtable** *(SS666308)* EX32 0SR
☎Filleigh(0598) 760254
Closed 25 Dec
This medieval longhouse is found down a farm lane opposite the village school, going towards East Buckland from West Buckland. Bedrooms vary from cosy farmhouse rooms to those in an adjacent, recently converted barn, which have private bathroom and TV. The well appointed dining room has a flagstone floor and a large table where dinner by candlelight is served. A choice of starters is offered, with a set main course and a choice of puddings and cheese; owner Dr Payne's home-made wine is included with dinner. Children are especially catered for, with children's breakfast and high tea available by arrangement. There is a sauna and games room which includes snooker, bar billiards and table tennis.
3hc Annexe 3⇌↱ (2fb) CTV in 3 bedrooms ®
✗ (ex guide dogs) sB&B⇌↱£19-£24 dB&B⇌↱£36-£42
WB&B£133-£168 WBDi£196.70-£245 LDO 6pm
ꟾꟾꟾ CTV 8P ⌂ sauna games room 80 acres mixed sheep
Credit Cards [2]

WEST CHILTINGTON West Sussex Map **04** TQ01

FH QQQ Mrs A M Steele ***New House*** *(TQ091185)*
Broadford Bridge Rd RH20 2LA ☎(0798) 812215
Closed Dec
A charming 15th-century farmhouse situated in a picturesque village. Bedrooms are all comfortably furnished, each with a private bathroom, one of which contains a corner spa bath. The cottage annexe provides a more modern, compact room. Log fires burn in the cosy combined sitting/dining room, where breakfast is served at a communal table, provided by welcoming hosts Mr and Mrs Steele.
3⇌↱ (2fb) CTV in all bedrooms ® ✗
CTV 4P 2⛍ nc9yrs 50 acres mixed

WESTCLIFF-ON-SEA Essex

See **Southend-on-Sea**

WEST DOWN Devon Map **02** SS54

SELECTED

GH QQQQ The Long House EX34 8NF
☎Ilfracombe(0271) 863242
early Mar-early Nov
In a peaceful village on the fringes of Exmoor, and within easy reach of the sandy beaches, this converted village smithy has comfortable, individually designed bedrooms with many thoughtful little extras as well as all the facilities one would expect of an award-winning establishment. The quaint teashop is changed into an attractive dining room at night offering inspired home-cooked dinners, and there is also a cosy lounge where guests can relax over coffee. Friendly and attentive service is provided by the resident proprietors Pauline and Rob Hart.
4⇌↱ ⚟in 1 bedroom CTV in all bedrooms ®
✗ (ex guide dogs) dB&B⇌↱£74 (incl dinner)
WBDi£241.50 LDO 8pm
Lic ꟾꟾꟾ CTV 4P
Credit Cards [1] [3] £

GH QQ Sunnymeade Country House Hotel Dean Cross EX34 8NT (1m W on A361) ☎Ilfracombe(0271) 863668
Apr-Nov
Set back from the road, with gardens to the front, this family-run guesthouse is conveniently situated for access to Ilfracombe and Braunton. The friendly and courteous proprietors offer neat and well maintained accommodation.
10rm(8↱2hc) (2fb) CTV in all bedrooms ® ✗ ✱ sB&B£15-£15.50 dB&B↱£34-£36 WBDi£140-£162 LDO 6pm
Lic ꟾꟾꟾ CTV 14P
Credit Cards [1] [2] [3] [5]

WESTGATE ON SEA Kent Map **05** TR37

GH QQ White Lodge 12 Domneva Rd CT8 8PE
☎Thanet(0843) 831828
This guesthouse provides a choice of well equipped bedrooms furnished in the modern style, with pretty fabrics and good, controllable heating levels. A spacious beamed lounge augments the combined bar/dining room, and there is a peaceful and relaxing atmsophere. Unrestricted street car parking is available.
7rm(5⇌↱2hc) (2fb) CTV in all bedrooms ® sB&B£18 sB&B⇌↱£25 dB&B£37 dB&B⇌↱£42 WB&B£113-£132 WBDi£162-£181 LDO 7pm
Lic ꟾꟾꟾ CTV 3P £

WEST GRAFTON Wiltshire Map **04** SU26

SELECTED

FH QQQQ Mrs A Orssich **Mayfield** *(SU246598)*
SN8 3BY ☎Marlborough(0672) 810339
Closed Xmas
A delightful thatched farmhouse surrounded by well kept grounds and gardens in a rural area. The property has been carefully extended by the present proprietors to provide 3 comfortably sized bedrooms and 2 bathrooms. There is a choice of lounges and guests share a single table in the breakfast room. Mayfield is decorated with taste and style, and furnished with antiques. Chris and Angie Orssich welcome guests with open arms, and the family kitchen, where there is a relaxed party atmosphere, is the heart of the place.
3rm ⚟in all bedrooms CTV in all bedrooms ® T
sB&B£23-£28 dB&B£36-£42
ꟾꟾꟾ CTV 6P ⌂ ⩡(heated) ℘(hard)table tennis play area 8 acres non-working £

WEST LINTON Borders *Peeblesshire* Map **11** NT15

SELECTED

GH QQQQ Medwyn House Medwyn Rd EH46 7HB
☎(0968) 60542 & 60816 FAX (0968) 60005
Closed mid Jan-mid Mar
A large country house set in 30 acres of gardens and woodlands adjoining the golf course, 18 miles south of Edinburgh on the A702. Situated on an old Roman road, the house was originally known as the Bridgehouse Inn, dating back to the 15th century. The 3 spacious bedrooms are comfortably appointed and thoughtfully equipped, each with large private bathrooms. There is a fine panelled hall with a welcoming log fire and comfortable chintz-covered chairs. The spacious, sunny drawing room has a Victorian atmosphere, furnished with fine antiques, and the elegant dining room has attractive blue and yellow soft furnishings and lace-covered tables, where hostess Anne Waterston offers her set 4-course dinner which is carefully prepared from fresh local produce. Smoking is not permitted in the bedrooms.
3⇌ ⚟in all bedrooms TV available ® T dB&B⇌fr£68
LDO noon
→

CTV 12P 2 nc12yrs sauna

WEST MALLING Kent Map **05** TQ65

SELECTED

GH QQQQ Scott House High St ME19 6QH
☎(0732) 841380 & 870025
Closed 24 Dec-1 Jan
Home to friendly proprietors Mr and Mrs Smith, this delightful Grade II listed Georgian town house is now a combined antique shop and bed and breakfast business. The bedrooms are all on the first floor and each is individually furnished with antique pieces, coordinated fabrics and smart modern en suites, and guests can help themselves to fresh milk and iced mineral water from a fridge tucked away in the hall. There is a large, elegant lounge with period furnishings and a real log fire, and a hearty breakfast is served downstairs in the sunny dining room which doubles as the Smiths' lounge in the evening. Readers should note that this is a no-smoking establishment.
3 in all bedrooms CTV in all bedrooms ®
(ex guide dogs) sB&B£30-£39 dB&B£50
nc
Credit Cards 1 3 £

WEST MERSEA Essex Map **05** TM01

GH QQQ Blackwater Hotel 20-22 Church Rd CO5 8QH
☎Colchester(0206) 383338 & 383038
Closed 8 Jan-5 Feb
Situated in the heart of the village and close to West Mersea beach, this late-Victorian building with its attractive ivy-clad façade was previously a coaching inn. Comfortable bedrooms are simply furnished but freshly decorated, and most have private bathrooms adjacent. The Champenois restaurant offers genuine French cooking in an authentic and friendly atmosphere, and there is a cosy bar and a comfortable lounge. Ample car parking is available at the rear.
6rm(1 3hc) CTV in 4 bedrooms TV in 2 bedrooms ®
(ex guide dogs) sB&B£30-£50 sB&B£30-£50 dB&B£40-£68 dB&B£57-£68 WB&Bfr£192 WBDifr£244 LDO 10pm
Lic 20P
Credit Cards 1 2 3 £

WESTON-SUPER-MARE Avon Map **03** ST36

See **Town Plan Section**

GH QQQ Ashcombe Court 17 Milton Rd BS23 2SH
☎(0934) 625104
This popular and spotlessly clean family-run hotel has benefited from further improvements and upgrading. Bedrooms are bright and individually styled and decorated, combining the character of the Victorian building with modern creature comforts. An ideal small holiday hotel with a very hospitable congenial atmosphere created by Sian and Tom Bisdee.
6rm(1 5) (1fb) in all bedrooms CTV in all bedrooms ®
(ex guide dogs) ✱ sB&B fr£17.50 dB&B fr£35 WBDi£134-£144 LDO 6pm
CTV 9P
Credit Cards 2 £

GH QQ Baymead Hotel Longton Grove Rd BS23 1LS
☎(0934) 622951
Closed Jan & Feb
A popular, family-run holiday hotel in a central location close to the town centre and all amenities. It offers bright, well equipped bedrooms with private bathrooms and modern facilities. The lively bars provide entertainment 3 nights a week.
33rm(30 3hc) (3fb) CTV in all bedrooms ® sB&B£15-£22.50 sB&B£22.50-£25 dB&B£35-£40 WB&B£110-£170 WBDi£135-£195 LDO 6.30pm
Lic lift CTV 4P half size snooker table

GH QQQ Braeside 2 Victoria Park BS23 2HZ
☎(0934) 626642
This delightful family-run hotel is set in a quiet elevated position with views over Weston Bay to Brean Down. Full of character, it offers bright well furnished bedrooms, all en suite and equipped for the modern traveller. Public rooms are cosy, and good home cooking and services are provided by conscientious owners Mr and Mrs Wallington. There is no car park, but there is unrestricted parking on the street opposite.
9 (3fb) CTV in all bedrooms ® sB&B fr£22.50 dB&B fr£45 WB&B£135 WBDi£180 LDO 6pm
Lic £

GH Q Clifton Lodge 48 Clifton Rd BS23 1BN
☎(0934) 629357
Closed 25-31 Dec
This friendly little bed and breakfast establishment is in a quiet residential area, but close to the seafront and Tropicana leisure centre. The compact but brightly styled bedrooms are ideally suited to shorter stay guests. Unrestricted parking is permitted in the street opposite.
5rm(1 4hc) (3fb) CTV in 4 bedrooms TV in 1 bedroom ®
(ex guide dogs) sB&B£13.50-£15 dB&B£27-£30 dB&B£34-£36
£

GH QQ Kara Hewish BS24 6RQ (1m E of junc 21 M5 on A370) ☎Yatton(0934) 834442
Alongside the A370 some 3 miles from the resort, on the Bristol side of its junction with the M5 (junction 21), this is a family-run guesthouse set in pleasant secluded lawns and gardens. Bedrooms are bright and cosy and there is a comfortable lounge/diner with a log fire in cooler weather.
6rm(2 4hc) (3fb) CTV in all bedrooms ® ✱ sB&B£15-£16 dB&B£30-£32 dB&B£33-£35 WB&B£100-£109
Lic CTV 5P small putting green swing

GH QQQ *Lewinsdale Lodge Hotel* 5-7 Clevedon Rd BS23 1DA
☎(0934) 632501
Mar-Nov
Just a few paces from the seafront, beach, lawns and Tropicana leisure centre, this very personally run hotel offers good value and spotlessly clean accommodation. The building is full of character and the cosy public rooms are tastefully decorated and furnished.
5 CTV in all bedrooms ® (ex guide dogs) LDO noon
4P

GH QQQ Milton Lodge 15 Milton Rd BS23 2SH
☎(0934) 623161
Apr-Sep rs Oct-Mar
A charming Victorian house which has been sympathetically restored to combine its original character with modern facilities. The accommodation is bright, comfortable and spotlessly clean throughout, and the well equipped bedrooms all have private bathrooms. Personally run by enthusiastic proprietors, the hotel is conveniently situated for the town centre, parks and all amenities.
6rm(3 3) CTV in all bedrooms ® sB&B£16-£17 dB&B£32-£34 WB&B£102 WBDi£136-£147 LDO 10am
CTV 6P nc9yrs £

GH QQ Newton House 79 Locking Rd BS23 3DW
☎(0934) 629331
A small family-run holiday hotel in a convenient location close to the town centre and all amenities. Bedrooms are compact but bright and well equipped and spotlessly clean. The public rooms are cosy and there is useful car parking on site.
8rm(5 3hc) (4fb) CTV in all bedrooms ® sB&B£16-£25 sB&B£16-£25 dB&Bfr£32 dB&B£38 WB&B£100-£120 WBDi£150-£170 LDO 2pm

Lic CTV 9P
Credit Cards 1 2 3 5 £

GH QQ Saxonia 95 Locking Rd BS23 3EW ☎(0934) 633856 FAX (0934) 623142
A small guesthouse with well equipped, soundly furnished bedrooms, suitable for commercial visitors. Situated reasonably close to the town centre, there is limited car parking on site.
8rm(5 3hc) (4fb) CTV in all bedrooms ® sB&B£17-£22 sB&B £17-£22 dB&B£34-£44 dB&B £34-£44 WB&B£100-£150 WBDi£150-£170 LDO 2pm
Lic CTV 4P
Credit Cards 1 2 3 5 £

GH QQQ Wychwood Hotel 148 Milton Rd BS23 2UZ ☎(0934) 627793
Closed 23 Dec-2 Jan
A spacious Victorian house situated on the outskirts of town, personally run by Mr and Mrs Whitehouse. It offers comfortable well equipped bedrooms, pleasant public rooms and an outside heated swimming pool. There is useful car parking on site.
10rm(1 7 2hc) (2fb) CTV in all bedrooms ® (ex guide dogs) * sB&B£20-£24 sB&B £24 dB&B £40 WB&B£132-£160 WBDi£189.50-£228 LDO 6.30pm
Lic 14P (heated)
Credit Cards 1 3 £

FH QQ Mrs T G Moore **Purn House** *(ST331571)* Bleadon BS24 0QE ☎Bleadon(0934) 812324
Feb-Nov
An attractive creeper-clad 17th-century farmhouse situated 3 miles from Weston in the peaceful village of Bleadon, close to the A370. Bedrooms are bright and mostly spacious, with TV, clock radios and modern fittings, whilst retaining some of the original character and charm of the period. There is a cosy comfortable lounge, panelled breakfast room and a pretty lawned garden full of colour surrounding this family-run house.
6rm(3 3hc) (3fb) in all bedrooms CTV in 3 bedrooms ® (ex guide dogs) dB&B£32-£34 dB&B £40-£44 WB&B£90-£110 LDO 10am
CTV 10P 450 acres arable dairy

WEST STOUR Dorset Map 03 ST72

INN QQ The Ship SP8 5RP ☎East Stour(074785) 640 due to change to (0747) 838640
This inn was built in 1750 and has fine views of Blackmore Vale. A series of cosy bars have log fires and there is an extensive range of bar food available. The attractive dining room features a working hand pump for the well. Bedrooms are light and fresh with pretty soft furnishings; some have old fireplaces and they all have modern facilities such as double glazing.
6 (2fb) CTV in all bedrooms ® (ex guide dogs) * sB&B £28 dB&B £38-£42 Lunch £1.75-£8.50 Dinner £1.75-£13&alc LDO 9.30pm
CTV 50P
Credit Cards 1 3 £

WESTWARD HO! Devon Map 02 SS42

GH QQQ The Buckleigh Lodge 135 Bayview Rd EX39 1BJ ☎Bideford(0237) 475988
A late 19th-century detached house in a large garden on the edge of the village with some fine sea views. Here spacious bedrooms are freshly decorated and furnished with antiques. The dining room is more modern but serves traditional English food with mouthwatering home-made puddings. There is a comfortable TV lounge and a smartly furnished bar in keeping with the age of the building.

6rm(3 3hc) (1fb) CTV in all bedrooms ® (ex guide dogs) sB&B£16-£18 sB&B fr£18 dB&B£32-£36 dB&B fr£36 WB&B£105-£120 WBDi£160-£175 LDO 4pm
Lic CTV 8P

WETHERBY West Yorkshire Map 08 SE44

GH Q Prospect House 8 Caxton St LS22 4RU ☎(0937) 582428
This large house close to the town centre offers simple, clean bedrooms. There is a fragrant rose garden at the front, and a private car park. To find Prospect House, turn into St James Street and it is on the corner opposite the county primary school.
6hc (1fb) CTV in 1 bedroom * sB&B£15-£15.50 dB&B£30-£31 WB&B£105-£108.50
CTV 6P £

WEYBRIDGE Surrey London plan 4 A1 (pages 245-251)

GH QQ Warbeck House Hotel 46 Queens Rd KT13 0AR ☎(0932) 848764 FAX (0932) 847290
This attractive Edwardian house is situated in a residential area but close to the town centre, and benefits from ample car parking at the front. Bedrooms are simply furnished but provide adequate comfort. Breakfast is served in the Barclay Room which has a conservatory extension overlooking the landscaped gardens.
10rm(1 9hc) (1fb) CTV in all bedrooms ® * sB&Bfr£32.90 sB&B fr£39.95 dB&Bfr£45.83 dB&B fr£49.35
Lic CTV 20P

WEYMOUTH Dorset Map 03 SY67

GH QQ Andena 18 Abbotsbury Rd DT4 0AE ☎(0305) 772030
During the summer months, the garden of this brightly painted, terraced guesthouse, which has won awards for its appearance, is very colourful and attractive. The bedrooms, whilst compact, are well equipped and the public areas are rather limited but adequate. The entrance hall has a wealth of tourist information about the area. A home-cooked evening meal is offered and there is a car park.
8hc (3fb) in all bedrooms CTV in all bedrooms ® *
sB&B£16 WBDi£154 LDO 4pm
6P

SELECTED

GH QQQQ Bay Lodge 27 Greenhill DT4 7SW ☎(0305) 782419 FAX (0305) 782828
rs Nov
This lovely Victorian residence overlooks the tennis courts and the sea. It has its own car park and garden. More bedrooms and a larger restaurant are being built by Barbara and Graham Dubben, the proprietors, whose personable and cheerful presence is an asset. Evening meals can be arranged; summer menus change every day, in the winter an à la carte menu is provided. Bedrooms are all equipped to a very high standard and there is no supplementary charge for a sea view. Many original Victorian features have been retained including cosy fires and a central glass dome over the staircase. Decoration is attractive with Laura Ashley fabrics. The Bay Lodge is equally attractive to families with children or business people. Barham's Cottages are also available for self-catering guests. The hotel is licensed and has a selection of good value wines.
6 in 5 bedrooms CTV in all bedrooms ® T sB&B £21-£26 dB&B£35-£40 dB&B £42-£52 WBDi£189-£219 LDO 5pm
Lic CTV 15P
Credit Cards 1 2 3 5

GH QQ Birchfields 22 Abbotsbury Rd DT4 0AE ☏(0305) 773255
rs Oct-Apr
Not far from the centre of town, in a residential area, this corner property provides limited car parking for guests. Bedrooms, while a little compact, have pretty, fresh décor. There is a cosy bar/lounge area and an evening meal is offered.
9rm(3🚿6hc) (4fb) TV available Ⓡ sB&B£14-£20 sB&B🚿£18-£24 dB&B£32-£40 dB&B🚿£36-£48 WB&B£78-£120 WBDi£118-£150 LDO 3pm
Lic 🍽 CTV 3P Ⓔ

GH QQQ Channel View 10 Brunswick Ter, The Esplanade DT4 7RW ☏(0305) 782527
This neat and comfortably appointed hotel is found in a 'no through road', only yards from the seafront, which is opposite the front of the guesthouse. Bedrooms are well equipped and nicely decorated, complete with teddy bears on the beds. Cosy public areas include a pretty dining area, small lounge and a tiny but very well stocked bar. A 4-course home-cooked evening meal is offered, using good quality fresh produce.
7hc (2fb)⊬in all bedrooms CTV in all bedrooms Ⓡ ✗ (ex guide dogs) LDO 4pm
Lic 🍽 CTV nc12yrs
Credit Cards 1 3 Ⓔ

GH QQ Ferndown 47 Walpole St DT4 7HQ ☏(0305) 775228
Closed 25 Dec-7 Jan
A neat little guesthouse situated in a quiet residential area, close to the seafront and town centre. It offers pretty, individually decorated bedrooms with some welcoming extra touches. Public areas are compact, but offer a comfortable and friendly atmosphere. A home-cooked evening meal is provided by Mrs Waddell using good quality fresh produce. The whole Waddell family are involved in running this guesthouse, and the atmosphere is friendly and relaxed.
8hc (1fb) CTV in 4 bedrooms Ⓡ ✱ sB&B£11-£15 dB&B£22-£30 WB&B£72-£85 WBDi£100-£115
CTV Ⓔ

GH QQ Hazeldene 16 Abbotsbury Rd, Westham DT4 0AE ☏(0305) 782579
This cosy seaside guesthouse is located a short distance from the centre of town and the seafront. The bedrooms are compact but spotlessly clean and neat, with bright, cheerful décor. Public areas include a comfortable lounge area with TV and a small dining room.
7hc (4fb) Ⓡ ✗ sB&B£13-£15 dB&B£26-£30 WB&B£75-£90 WBDi£125-£135 LDO noon
Lic 🍽 CTV 7P 1🚗 nc5yrs Ⓔ

GH QQQ Kenora 5 Stavordale Rd DT4 0AB ☏(0305) 771215
Etr & 9 May-4 Oct
A Victorian house in a quiet cul-de-sac with views of the harbour from rear rooms. Bedrooms vary in size but are neat and clean. Public rooms include a bar lounge and a spacious dining room where a traditional English menu is served. Guests can relax in the award-winning garden, which also has a children's play area.
15rm(4⇌9🚿2hc) (5fb) Ⓡ ✗ (ex guide dogs) sB&B£18.50-£22 sB&B⇌🚿£25.50-£29 dB&B⇌🚿£41-£48 WB&B£132-£156 WBDi£154-£177 LDO 4.30pm
Lic 🍽 CTV 20P
Credit Cards 1 3

GH QQ Kings Acre Hotel 140 The Esplanade DT4 7NH ☏(0305) 782534
Closed 15 Dec-5 Jan rs Oct, Nov & Dec
Located along the Esplanade at one end of the town centre, this small family- run hotel offers bright, neat bedrooms and cosy public areas. Every year upgrading and improvements are being made, and although the quality is simple, presentation and maintenance of this 1850s building is good. The 9-space car park at the rear is invaluable in the summer months.
13rm(5🚿8hc) (4fb) CTV in all bedrooms Ⓡ ✗ ✱ sB&Bfr£19 sB&B🚿fr£28 dB&Bfr£34 dB&B🚿fr£40 WB&Bfr£119 WBDifr£150 LDO 4.30pm
Lic 🍽 CTV 9P
Credit Cards 1 3

GH QQQ Sou'west Lodge Hotel Rodwell Rd DT4 8QT ☏(0305) 783749
Closed 21 Dec-1 Jan
A small family-run hotel situated above the Old Quay, along the main route from the town towards Portland. Continuing improvements have recently provided private bathrooms for all rooms, which are reasonably equipped with useful facilities, and have fresh, pretty décor. The public areas are very comfortable, with ample sofa seating in the lounge and bar, and a neat well decorated dining room. The cheerful proprietor maintains the hotel very well, and there is convenient front-forecourt parking.
8⇌🚿 (2fb) CTV in all bedrooms Ⓡ ✱ sB&B⇌🚿£19-£21 dB&B⇌🚿£38-£42 WB&B£105-£139 WBDi£148.75-£180 LDO 3pm
Lic 🍽 CTV 12P Ⓔ

GH QQQ Sunningdale Private Hotel 52 Preston Rd, Overcombe DT3 6QD ☏(0305) 832179
Mar-Oct
A family holiday hotel set back from the main Preston road, in an elevated position. Public areas are smartly furnished and include a comfortable lounge and well appointed dining room. The freshly decorated bedrooms vary in size, and many have private bathrooms. The garden contains an outdoor pool with seating, and a putting green.
20rm(5⇌2🚿13hc) (8fb) CTV in 16 bedrooms TV in 2 bedrooms Ⓡ sB&B£20-£25 sB&B⇌🚿£30-£35 dB&B£40-£50 dB&B⇌🚿£45-£55 WB&B£123-£155 WBDi£153-£193 LDO 6.30pm
Lic CTV 20P ⇋(heated) putting green table tennis pool table games room
Credit Cards 1 3

GH QQQ Tamarisk Hotel 12 Stavordale Rd, Westham DT4 0AB ☏(0305) 786514
Mar-Oct
A Victorian house in a quiet cul-de-sac close to the harbour, a short walk from the town centre. Bedrooms are freshly decorated and well maintained, many with private bathrooms, and there is an attractive and spacious dining room and a comfortable bar lounge.
16rm(4⇌8🚿4hc) (7fb) CTV in 6 bedrooms Ⓡ ✗ ✱ sB&B£17-£20 sB&B⇌🚿£19-£22 dB&B£34-£40 dB&B⇌🚿£38-£44 WB&B£100-£120 WBDi£125-£155 LDO 2pm
Lic 🍽 CTV 19P

GH QQ Trelawney Hotel 1 Old Castle Rd DT4 8QB ☏(0305) 783188
10⇌🚿 CTV in all bedrooms Ⓡ ✱ sB&B⇌🚿£22-£26 dB&B⇌🚿£40-£46 WB&B£146-£156 WBDi£175-£195 LDO 7pm
Lic 🍽 CTV 13P putting green
Credit Cards 3

GH QQ *The Westwey* 62 Abbotsbury Rd DT4 0BJ ☏(0305) 784564
A small, friendly, family-run hotel offering comfortable accommodation: most bedrooms have private bathrooms and TV, although they vary in size.
11rm(1⇌8🚿2hc) (2fb) CTV in all bedrooms Ⓡ ✗ LDO 6.30pm
Lic 🍽 CTV 10P nc6yrs

WHADDON Buckinghamshire Map **04** SP83

INN QQQ ***Lowndes Arms & Motel*** 4 High St MK17 0NA
☎Milton Keynes(0908) 501706 FAX (0908) 504185
This is a traditional, rural village inn complete with inglenook fireplace. The bedrooms are in a separate converted stable block; they are attractively decorated and equipped with all modern comforts. Bar meals are available and consist primarily of steak grills. The accommodation is not suitable for children or pets.
Annexe 11🚿 CTV in all bedrooms ® 🐕 (ex guide dogs) LDO 9.30pm
🅿 30P nc14yrs
Credit Cards 1 3 5

WHEDDON CROSS Somerset Map **03** SS93

GH QQQ The Higherley TA24 7EB
☎Timberscombe(0643) 841582
This modern farmhouse and small fruit farm is beautifully positioned with extensive views across Exmoor. Small, fresh bedrooms are neatly furnished and share modern bathroom facilities. The lounge is very comfortable and has a real fire and colour TV. The dining room also serves morning coffee and cream teas.
6hc (1fb) CTV in 2 bedrooms ✱ sB&B£16.75-£18.75 dB&B£33.50-£38 LDO 9pm
Lic 🅿 CTV 25P 6🚗 nc3mths
Credit Cards 3 £

WHIMPLE Devon Map **03** SY09

GH QQQ Down House EX5 2QR ☎(0404) 822860
Apr-Sep rs Oct-Mar
This delightful Edwardian farmhouse is set in 5 acres of gardens and paddocks surrounded by open Devonshire countryside. There is a choice of elegant lounges, where guests can enjoy the house party style hospitality of Alan and Vicky Jiggins. Bedrooms are spacious and brightly decorated, and most are either en suite or have the use of private shower rooms. Evening meals include home-made bread and all fresh fare cooked in the farmhouse kitchen, and are served 'en famille' in the relaxed atmosphere of the dining room.
4rm(2🚿2hc) (1fb) CTV in 3 bedrooms TV in 1 bedroom ® 🐕 (ex guide dogs) ✱ sB&B£13-£17 sB&B🚿£16-£20 dB&B£26-£34 dB&B🚿£32-£40 LDO 4.30pm
🅿 CTV 8P games lounge £

WHITBY North Yorkshire Map **08** NZ81

GH QQQ Corra Lynn Hotel 28 Crescent Av YO21 3EW
☎(0947) 602214
Closed Dec-Jan rs Nov & Feb
A small, friendly hotel, with attractively decorated and tastefully appointed bedrooms, most with private bathrooms and all with TV and beverage-making facilities. There is a spacious, comfortable lounge and a pleasant dining room. The guesthouse is conveniently located for the west cliffs and shops in the town, and provides private parking.
6🛁🚿 (1fb) CTV in all bedrooms ® sB&B🛁🚿£18-£20 dB&B🛁🚿£36-£46 WB&B£119-£140 WBDi£199-£220 LDO 3.30pm
Lic 🅿 CTV 4P nc5yrs £

SELECTED

GH QQQQ Dunsley Hall Dunsley YO21 3TL
☎(0947) 83437
Built at the turn of the century, the hotel is in a delightful rural setting, with fine views over landscaped grounds to the sea. It is signposted off the A171 west of the city, just over a mile from the main road, with easy access to the town and seafront. Tastefully converted, the hotel features a wealth of mellow oak panelling in the public areas, and the spacious, →

impressive snooker room has a full-size table and a delightful inglenook fireplace. The individually designed bedrooms are nicely decorated and well equipped, with many extra touches. The 4-course dinner menu changes daily and offers a choice of freshly cooked dishes. Leisure facilities include an indoor swimming pool, fitness room, tennis court, croquet and putting green.
7⇌🚿 (2fb) CTV in all bedrooms ® sB&B⇌🚿£40-£45 dB&B⇌🚿£70-£80 WB&B£230-£250 WBDi£315-£350 LDO 6pm
Lic 🍽 10P (heated) (hard)snooker gymnasium croquet putting green
Credit Cards [1] [3] £

GH QQQ Europa Private Hotel 20 Hudson St YO21 3EP ☎(0947) 602251
mid Jan-end Oct
A friendly, comfortable and attractively decorated small private hotel situated in a quiet road close to West Cliff. Bedrooms all have beverage- making facilities and TV. There is a very comfortable lounge on the first floor, and the dining room on the ground floor has been nicely decorated.
9rm(2🚿7hc) (1fb) CTV in all bedrooms ® ✗ ✻ sB&Bfr£16 dB&Bfr£30 dB&B🚿fr£35 LDO 11am
🍽 CTV nc3yrs

GH QQ Glendale 16 Crescent Av YO21 3ED ☎(0947) 604242
Apr-Oct
Glendale is a very comfortable and friendly guesthouse with neat bedrooms. It offers very good value for money.
6rm(3🚿3hc) (3fb) CTV in all bedrooms ® sB&B£15-£17 dB&B🚿£36 WB&B£145 WBDi£165 LDO 4.15pm
Lic CTV 6P £

GH QQ Haven 4 East Crescent YO21 3HD ☎(0947) 603842
rs Nov-Jan
Situated in an elevated crescent high on the West Cliff, this cosy guesthouse has fine views over the harbour and sea. Bedrooms are unpretentious but well equipped. Substantial home-cooked dinners and breakfasts are provided, and service from the resident proprietors is friendly and helpful.
8rm(5⇌🚿3hc) (1fb) CTV in all bedrooms ® ✗ sB&B£17-£18.50 dB&B£31-£34 dB&B⇌🚿£33-£38 WB&B£119-£133 WBDi£175-£189 LDO 4pm
Lic 🍽 CTV nc5yrs £

GH QQQ Sandbeck Hotel 2 Crescent Ter, Westcliff YO21 3EL ☎(0947) 604012
15⇌🚿 (5fb) CTV in all bedrooms ® ✗ (ex guide dogs)
Lic 🍽 CTV nc6yrs
Credit Cards [1] [2] [3]

GH QQQ Seacliffe Hotel North Promenade, West Cliff YO21 3JX ☎(0947) 603139
Situated high on the West Cliff, this very well appointed private hotel commands fine views over the sea. Although some of the bedrooms are compact, they all have private baths or showers, TV, telephones and tea-making facilities. The à la carte restaurant offers a wide range of dishes to suit all tastes, including vegetarian. There is also a small cocktail bar, a comfortable residents' lounge and a private car park.
19⇌🚿 (4fb) CTV in all bedrooms ® T ✻ sB&B⇌🚿£29.50-£32.50 dB&B⇌🚿£53-£55 WB&B£185-£193 LDO 8.45pm
Lic 🍽 CTV 8P
Credit Cards [1] [2] [3] [5] £

GH QQQ Waverley Private Hotel 17 Crescent Av YO21 3ED ☎(0947) 604389
Mar-Oct
This large mid-terrace house is in a quiet residential area with easy access to the seafront and town centre. It has bright, inviting bedrooms, a delightful first-floor lounge, attractive dining room and small cocktail bar. The friendly service and home-cooked meals ensure an enjoyable stay.
6rm(5🚿1hc) (4fb) CTV in all bedrooms ® ✗ dB&B£28-£30 dB&B🚿£32-£34 WB&B£90-£105 WBDi£128-£143 LDO 5.45pm
Lic 🍽 CTV nc3yrs

WHITCHURCH Hereford & Worcester Map **03** SO51

GH QQ Portland HR9 6DB ☎Symonds Yat(0600) 890757
Closed Jan rs Nov-Mar
This family-run guesthouse is situated just off the A40 between Ross-on-Wye and Monmouth. There is a pleasant lounge and bedrooms are well equipped.
8hc (2fb) CTV in all bedrooms ® ✻ sB&B£16-£19 dB&B£30-£34 WB&B£98-£112 WBDi£149-£185 LDO 6pm
Lic 🍽 CTV 7P

INN Q Crown Hotel HR9 6DB ☎Symonds Yat(0600) 890234
Closed 25-26 Dec
A large inn situated in the centre of the village alongside the A40 between Ross-on-Wye and Monmouth. Bedrooms are modest but well equipped with modern facilities. The hotel is a popular stopping place for bar meals and refreshments.
5rm(1⇌4🚿) (3fb) CTV in all bedrooms ® sB&B⇌🚿£25-£28 dB&B⇌🚿£40-£45 WB&B£140-£150 WBDi£170-£180 Lunch £5.50-£7.50&alc Dinner £7.50-£10.50&alc LDO 9pm
🍽 CTV 40P skittle alley pool room
Credit Cards [1] [2] [3] [5] £

WHITCHURCH Shropshire Map **07** SJ54

FH QQ Mrs M H Mulliner **Bradeley Green** *(SJ537449)* Waterfowl Sanctuary, Tarporley Rd SY13 4HD ☎(0948) 3442
Closed Xmas
The farm is on the A49 Tarporley road, 2 miles from Whitchurch, and as well as warm rooms and a cosy atmosphere, guests will find a waterfowl sanctuary, nature trail and ponds teeming with ornamental fish. Conducted tours and slide lectures can be arranged.
3rm(2⇌🚿1hc) ⅟in all bedrooms ® ✻ sB&B⇌🚿fr£18 dB&Bfr£36 dB&B⇌🚿fr£36 WB&Bfr£115 WBDifr£174 LDO 9am
🍽 CTV 6P ✓ water gardens 180 acres dairy waterfowl fish farming £

WHITESTONE Devon Map **03** SX89

FH QQ Mrs S K Lee **Rowhorne House** *(SX880948)* EX4 2LQ ☎Exeter(0392) 74675
This red-brick Victorian farmhouse has splendid rural views, and on a clear day the Exe estuary is visible. A warm Devonshire welcome awaits guests at Rowhorne House; to find it take the old Okehampton road out of Exeter, at Whitestone Cross fork right and follow the narrow road to the farm. Bedrooms are spacious, and tea and coffee are available at all times on the landing on a self-service basis. Breakfast is taken around a large table in the dining room, and a comfortable lounge with a television is provided for guests' use.
3hc (2fb) CTV in 1 bedroom TV in 1 bedroom ✗ ✻ sB&B£13.50 dB&B£27 WB&B£94.50 WBDi£129.50
CTV 6P 103 acres dairy
Credit Cards [1] [2] [3] [5] £

WHITEWELL Lancashire Map **07** SD64

INN QQ *The Inn at Whitewell* BB7 3AT ☎Dunsop Bridge(02008) 222
This enchanting country inn, full of character and charm is set in the beautiful Forest of Bowland. Most of the bedrooms have been upgraded in a splendid Victorian style with antique furniture. Telescopes, binoculars and old telephones are all supplied together with sophisticated hi-fi equipment and TV. Oak beams, wood-

panelled walls, old paintings and blazing log fires are a feature of the bars, where a wide choice of highly commended bar meals is available. The restaurant which looks out over the river provides a more formal setting for evening meals. Dogs are welcome but certain breeds are not allowed in public areas.
9⇔♠ (4fb) CTV in all bedrooms LDO 9.30pm
🍴 CTV 60P ✔ clay pigeon shooting by arrangement
Credit Cards [1] [2] [3] [5]

WHITHORN Dumfries & Galloway *Wigtownshire* Map **10** NX44

FH QQ Mrs E C Forsyth ***Baltier*** *(NX466429)* DG8 8HA
☎Garlieston(09886) 241
Mar-Nov
This extended traditional farmhouse, situated off the B7004, offers comfortable accommodation and fine views of the surrounding countryside.
2hc (1fb) ® ✗
🍴 CTV 4P 220 acres dairy sheep

WHITLAND Dyfed Map **02** SN21

GH QQQ Llangwm House SA34 0RB ☎(0994) 240621
As you turn right after passing over the level crossing you will find this large, fully modernised farmhouse, set in 15 acres of land mostly used for breeding and training sheep dogs. The accommodation comprises of quite spacious bedrooms with comfortable duvet covered beds and good wicker chairs, along with 2 lounges, one with a feature stone fireplace and chimney piece. Breakfast is always available but evening meals are only served if prior notice is given.
5rm(2⇔♠3hc) (1fb) CTV in 2 bedrooms ® **T** sB&B£15 dB&B£30 dB&B⇔♠£34-£36 WB&B£105-£126
🍴 CTV 6P nc5yrs

FH QQ C M & I A Lewis **Cilpost** *(SN191184)* SA34 0RP
☎(0994) 240280
Apr-Sep
Run by the friendly Lewis family, this working farm provides clean and well maintained bedrooms with imaginative and enjoyable home cooking offered in the spacious dining room. Comfortable public areas include an excellent snooker room and an indoor swimming pool. The farmhouse is situated north of the village, signposted off the Henllan Amgoed road.
7rm(3⇔3♠1hc) (3fb) ✗ ✱ sB&B£16-£22 sB&B⇔♠£20-£22 dB&B£40-£44 dB&B⇔♠£40-£44 WB&B£84-£154 WBDi£120-£215
Lic 🍴 12P ⊡(heated) ✔ snooker 160 acres dairy mixed

WHITLEY BAY Tyne & Wear Map **12** NZ37

GH QQ Cherrytree House 35 Brook St NE26 1AF
☎091-251 4306
Situated just off the seafront in a quiet residential area, this corner property offers neat, unpretentious accommodation and friendly service.
4rm(2♠2hc) CTV in all bedrooms ® sB&B£14-£16 sB&B♠£18-£20 dB&B£26-£28 dB&B♠£32-£36 LDO 9.30am
🍴 CTV (£)

GH QQ Lindisfarne Hotel 11 Holly Av NE26 1EB
☎091-251 3954 & 091-297 0579
A small, friendly terraced guesthouse situated in a quiet part of the town, yet within easy reach of the sea and shops. Bedrooms are bright and fresh, with attractive fabrics, and there is an attractive dining room, complemented by friendly service.
9rm(4⇔♠5hc) (1fb) CTV in all bedrooms ® ✱ sB&B£14-£20 sB&B⇔♠£20-£30 dB&B£28-£38 dB&B⇔♠£36-£56 LDO 8.30pm
Lic 🍴 CTV Ᵽ
Credit Cards [1] [3] (£)

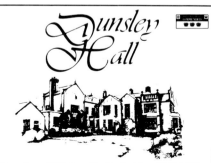

GH QQQ **Marlborough Hotel** 20-21 East Pde, Central Promenade NE26 1AP ☎091-251 3628
A family-owned double-fronted private hotel situated on the seafront. The spacious accommodation includes 2 comfortable lounges with sea views. Bedrooms vary in size and standard of furnishings, but are gradually being improved. Home-cooked evening meals are available on request, and private parking is provided in front of the hotel.
15rm(10⇌🚿5hc) (4fb)⚡in all bedrooms CTV in all bedrooms ® ✗ (ex guide dogs) sB&B£20 sB&B⇌🚿£30 dB&B⇌🚿£40-£45 LDO noon
Lic CTV 7P
Credit Cards [1] [3]

GH QQ **White Surf** 8 South Pde NE26 2RG ☎091-253 0103
This neatly maintained terraced house is situated between the seafront and the town centre. It offers bright and fresh, plainly decorated and furnished accommodation, with generally compact bedrooms, all with TV. The attractive dining room has a continental atmosphere, with white walls and a tiled floor, and the lounge has comfortable leather seating and a small pool table.
7hc (2fb)⚡in 8 bedrooms CTV in all bedrooms ®
✗ (ex guide dogs) ✱ sB&B£15.50-£16.50 dB&B£31-£33 WB&B£105-£110 WBDi£147-£155 LDO 6pm
🍽 CTV 7P 2🚗 ⓔ

GH QQQ **York House Hotel** 30 Park Pde NE26 1DX ☎091-252 8313 & 091-251 3953
Situated in a quiet residential area close to the town centre, this small, terraced, family-run guesthouse offers sound accommodation. Pleasantly decorated bedrooms are compact but thoughtfully equipped, some with private bathrooms. A reasonably priced dinner menu offers a choice of home-cooked dishes, and a ground-floor room has special facilities for disabled guests.
8rm(7🚿1hc) (2fb) CTV in all bedrooms ® **T** ✱ sB&B£21.50-£22 sB&B🚿£26-£28 dB&B🚿£36-£40 WB&B£150.50-£154 WBDifr£180 LDO 7pm
Lic 🍽 CTV 2P
Credit Cards [1] [2] [3]

WHITNEY-ON-WYE Hereford & Worcester Map 03 SO24

SELECTED

INN QQQQ **The Rhydspence** HR3 6EU (2m W A438) ☎Hay(0497) 831262
Dating from the 14th century, this black and white timbered inn is situated alongside the ***A438*** *a mile west of the village. The lawns run down to a stream that is the English/Welsh boundary, making the inn the first and last in England. Peter and Pamela Glover have worked hard to create an inn of character, there are plenty of beams, a recently acquired 4-poster bed, and a roaring log fire in the lounge to welcome guests. There is a locals' bar as well and several restaurants where a wide choice of food is served.*
5rm(4⇌1🚿) CTV in all bedrooms ® ✗
sB&B⇌🚿£27.50-£35 dB&B⇌🚿£55-£75 Lunch £15-£25alc Dinner £15-£25alc LDO 9.30pm
🍽 60P
Credit Cards [1] [2] [3]

WIDDINGTON Essex Map 05 TL53

FH QQQ Mrs L Vernon **Thistley Hall** *(TL556311)* CB11 3ST ☎Saffron Walden(0799) 40388
Mar-Oct
A drive lined with chestnut trees leads guests to this friendly 17th-century farmhouse, surrounded by lovely gardens, working pastureland and quiet countryside. The 3 bedrooms are spacious, traditionally furnished and very clean. Downstairs in the breakfast room there is a communal table for eating, some armchairs and a television. The atmosphere here is warm and the proprietors are charming.
3rm(2hc) ⚡in 2 bedrooms ® ✗ (ex guide dogs) dB&B£30-£32 WB&Bfr£102
🍽 CTV 4P nc8yrs 30 acres mixed working ⓔ

WIGAN Greater Manchester Map 07 SD50

GH QQ ***Aalton Court*** 23 Upper Dicconson St WN1 2AG ☎(0942) 322220
Popular with commercial guests, this Victorian terraced house is convenient for both the town centre and rugby ground. Bedrooms tend to be small but are equipped with modern amenities and there is a small comfortable lounge.
6rm(2⇌4🚿) (1fb) CTV in all bedrooms ® ✗ LDO 2pm
Lic 🍽 CTV 11P

WIGHT, ISLE OF Map 04

BRADING Map 04 SZ68

GH QQQ **A La Carte** 10 High St ☎(0983) 407307
This popular, well managed restaurant has 3 letting bedrooms located in the rear 'Sun Deck' annexe. The well equipped, beamed bedrooms are mostly furnished in the modern style, and offer good value for money. An extensive choice of freshly prepared food and a Sunday lunch carvery are features, and good car-parking facilities are provided at the rear.
3⇌🚿 CTV in all bedrooms ® sB&B⇌🚿fr£25 dB&Bfr£45 dB&B⇌🚿fr£45 WB&Bfr£150
Lic 🍽 14P
Credit Cards [1] [3] ⓔ

FRESHWATER Map 04 SZ38

GH QQQ **Blenheim House** Gate Ln PO40 9QD ☎(0983) 752858
May-Sep
Long established and run by the Shakeshaft family for many years, this pleasant, detached residence promotes a welcoming, home-from-home atmosphere. The nicely maintained bedrooms are equipped with a TV and tea/coffee-making facilities, and some have en suite showers. There are lovely, comfortable public areas, comprising a traditional-style lounge, and a popular bar and attractive dining room that overlooks the garden. A weekly changing menu is provided, freshly prepared by Mrs Shakeshaft. Additional facilities include a heated swimming pool, extra ground-floor shower and toilets, plus a games room.
8🚿 (4fb) CTV in all bedrooms ® ✗ sB&B🚿£23 dB&B🚿£46 WB&B£161 WBDi£217 LDO noon
Lic 🍽 6P nc14yrs ⛱(heated) table tennis billards darts

NITON Map 04 SZ57

GH QQQ **Pine Ridge Country House** Niton Undercliff PO38 2LY ☎(0983) 730802
Quietly situated in 3.5 acres of mature, well kept grounds, this large detached establishment stands in an elevated position, looking majestically out to sea. Bedrooms are tastefully furnished and decorated, and offer good facilities including TV, telephone and hairdryer. All enjoy sea views, and one also has a large balcony. A comfortable lounge overlooks the garden, and there is a small bar lounge adjoining the well appointed dining room. The menu changes daily, and there is an à la carte alternative. Service is supervised by the proprietors, John and Rita Lake.
9rm(6⇌🚿3hc) (2fb) CTV in all bedrooms ® ✱
sB&B⇌🚿£28-£30 dB&B⇌🚿£56-£60 WB&B£180-£198 WBDi£235-£249 LDO 9pm
Lic 🍽 CTV 10P 🏠
Credit Cards [1] [3] ⓔ

See the regional maps of popular holiday areas at the back of the book.

RYDE Map **04** SZ59

GH Q ***Dorset Hotel*** 31 Dover St PO33 2BW ☎(0983) 64327

A friendly, small, privately run hotel, modestly furnished but with a good standard of facilities. It has been partly refurbished to provide more private bathrooms. A choice of food is offered for evening meals, and entertainment is provided 6 nights a week.

25rm(1⇌6↱18hc) (4fb) CTV in all bedrooms ®
Lic CTV 25P ⛱ ⚑

GH QQQ Teneriffe Hotel 36 The Strand PO33 1JF
☎(0983) 63841
Closed Jan-Feb

A substantial, long-established family-run holiday hotel, with modern en suite rooms serviced by a lift. Recent refurbishment and extensions have increased the number of bedrooms, and enlarged the restaurant and ballroom. Service is friendly and helpful, making this a popular choice for both commercial and leisure guests.

50⇌↱ (7fb) CTV in all bedrooms ® ✗ (ex guide dogs) ✱
sB&B⇌↱£17.25-£21.15 dB&B⇌↱£34.50-£42.30
WB&B£120.75-£148.05 WBDi£164.50-£182 LDO 7pm
Lic lift ⅏ CTV 9P
Credit Cards 1 3 £

SANDOWN Map **04** SZ58

GH QQQ ***Braemar Hotel*** 5 Broadway PO36 9DG
☎(0983) 403358
rs Dec-Jan

Well situated on the main road this detached, and very well kept, Victorian house has been skilfully extended and comprises variably sized, nicely furnished, modern bedrooms all equipped with telephone, TV and radio, (several good value family rooms are available). The very comfortable lounge adds a further dimension to the cocktail bar and bright dining room. Dinner is available by prior arrangement and the service is personally provided by the proprietors.

15rm(5⇌9↱1hc) (4fb) CTV in all bedrooms ® ✗ LDO 7pm
Lic ⅏ CTV 10P nc5yrs

GH Q Chester Lodge Hotel Beachfield Rd PO36 8NA
☎(0983) 402773
mid Mar-mid Oct

Situated in a residential street, within easy reach of the shops and Cliff Walk, this large guesthouse has been owned by the Hayward family for many years. Bedrooms are simply furnished and decorated, with some modern facilities. Public areas are spacious and an evening meal is served in the dining room. Whilst some refurbishment has taken place, certain areas of the hotel are in need of renovation, and it is hoped the upgrading programme will continue.

19rm(2⇌11↱6hc) (5fb)⚟in all bedrooms CTV in all bedrooms ® ✱ sB&B⇌↱£23.50-£25.50 dB&B⇌↱£47-£51
WB&B£119 WBDi£177.66
Lic ⅏ CTV 19P
Credit Cards 1 3 £

GH QQQ Culver Lodge Hotel Albert Rd PO36 8AW
☎(0983) 403819 & 402902
Apr-Oct Closed Nov-Mar

Situated conveniently close to the centre of town, the hotel offers comfortable and nicely presented public areas and bright, well equipped bedrooms. There is a first-floor guest laundry which is popular, and a games room on the ground floor with a pool table and games machines. The staff are friendly and helpful.

21rm(20⇌↱1hc) (2fb) CTV in all bedrooms ® ✗ sB&B£19-£22.50 sB&B⇌↱£19-£22.50 dB&B£38-£45 dB&B⇌↱£38-£45
WB&B£125-£150 WBDi£170-£196 LDO 7pm
Lic ⅏ CTV 20P pool room darts video games
Credit Cards 1 2 3 £

GH QQ Rose Bank Hotel 6 High St PO36 3DA
☎(0983) 403854

A small cottage-style hotel – the oldest property in the town. Peace and tranquillity are offered here, along with comfortable, neat bedrooms and public rooms with views out to sea and across the well kept gardens. The resident proprietors enjoy welcoming guests into their home and ensure a good standard of service.

6rm(1⇌5hc) Annexe 2⇌ (2fb) ® ✱ sB&Bfr£15 sB&B⇌fr£18
dB&Bfr£30 dB&B⇌fr£36 WB&Bfr£84 WBDifr£102
LDO 7pm
Lic ⅏ CTV ℗̸ nc6yrs

SELECTED

GH QQQQ St Catherine's Hotel 1 Winchester Park Rd
PO36 8HJ ☎(0983) 402392
Closed 24 Dec-2 Jan rs Nov

This well presented guesthouse is situated on the main road to Shanklin, and is run by the genial Mr and Mrs Barker. Bedrooms, some of which have been recently redecorated, are all very fresh, pretty and bright, and equipped with many facilities, including telephones. Public areas are very comfortable and attractively decorated, with pretty floral displays made by Mrs Barker. She also produces the enjoyable meals, while Mr Barker serves guests. Good car parking is available.

19⇌↱ (3fb) CTV in all bedrooms ® T ✗
sB&B⇌↱£17.50-£21 dB&B⇌↱£35-£42 WB&B£113.75-£136.50 WBDi£159.25-£198.25 LDO 7pm
Lic ⅏ CTV 8P
Credit Cards 1 3 £

Book as early as possible for busy holiday periods.

GH Q *Seacourt* Cliff Path PO36 8PN ☎(0983) 403759
FAX (0983) 7815
A small family-run hotel in a secluded setting along the cliff path, which is being refurbished. The bedrooms are reasonable in size and are very well equipped with modern facilities. Public areas include a games room and a small bar.
12rm(11⇌1hc) Annexe 9rm(8⇌1↱) CTV in all bedrooms Ⓡ LDO 7pm
Lic 25P (heated) snooker sauna solarium pool table tennis petanque hydro spa multi-gym
Credit Cards 1 2 3

SEAVIEW Map **04** SZ69

GH Q ***Northbank Hotel*** Circular Rd PO34 5ET
☎(0983) 612227
Etr-Sep
Northbank is an old Victorian house with a garden sloping down to the seashore. Splendid views are enjoyed from the traditional lounge, the cosy bar crammed with memorabilia, and many of the bedrooms. The latter vary in size, some have fine old furniture, but most are fairly simple.
18hc (6fb) CTV in 3 bedrooms Ⓡ LDO 8pm
Lic CTV 8P 4 snooker

SHANKLIN Map **04** SZ58

See **Town Plan Section**

GH QQQ ***Apse Manor Country House*** Apse Manor Rd PO37 7PN ☎(0983) 866651
A 16th-century manor house peacefully set in 2 acres of grounds, 1.5 miles from the town (A3020 Godshill). The accommodation is comfortably furnished, with good en suite facilities. The restaurant is now open to non-residents.
7⇌ (2fb) CTV in all bedrooms Ⓡ LDO 7.30pm
Lic 10P nc6yrs
Credit Cards 1 3

GH QQQ **Aqua Hotel** The Esplanade PO37 6BN
☎(0983) 863024
Etr-5 Nov
A friendly, modern hotel situated on the Esplanade, in a prime position directly on the seafront. Bedrooms are modern and comfortable, simply furnished and well presented; the sizes vary, but each is well equipped with facilities and 6 of the front-facing rooms have balconies. Public areas enjoy sea views and Boaters restaurant offers a choice of table d'hôte or à la carte menus. There is a bar/lounge area and a smaller, quiet lounge with TV. Long-term improvements are planned to further upgrade the hotel.
22⇌↱ (4fb) CTV in all bedrooms Ⓡ ✗ sB&B⇌↱£18-£24 dB&B⇌↱£36-£48 WB&B£126-£168 WBDi£150-£195 LDO 4.30pm
Lic CTV 2P
Credit Cards 1 2 3 5

GH QQQ ***Bay House Hotel*** 8 Chine Av, Off Keats Green, PO36 6AN ☎(0983) 863180 FAX (0983) 866604
On the edge of Keats Green with superb views far out to sea, this family-run hotel offers a relaxed and friendly atmosphere. Bedrooms are simply decorated and appointed, and each is equipped with modern facilities. Public areas include a spacious open-plan dining room and bar area, a quiet lounge and a smart indoor heated swimming pool, sauna and solarium.
22rm(21⇌↱1hc) (1fb) CTV in all bedrooms LDO 7pm
Lic 16P (heated) sauna solarium
Credit Cards 1 2 3

GH QQQ **Carlton Hotel** 9 Park Rd PO37 6AY
☎(0983) 862517
This hotel enjoys a peaceful location behind the town centre, with excellent sea views. The whole hotel has been recently refurbished, and all areas are very smart and well presented. Bedrooms are well equipped with modern en suite facilities, and are attractively decorated. Public areas are very comfortable and include 2 lounges overlooking the garden and sun terrace, and there is a very well stocked bar offering an international selection of bottled beers. Mrs Brotherton cooks evening meals using local produce, while her husband serves the guests. In all, a friendly and relaxed atmosphere prevails here.
12rm(7⇌5↱) (1fb) CTV in all bedrooms Ⓡ ✗ (ex guide dogs) sB&B⇌↱£26-£30 dB&B⇌↱£52-£60 (incl dinner) WB&B£154-£182 WBDi£180-£210 LDO 6.30pm
Lic CTV 10P
Credit Cards 1 3 £

SELECTED

GH QQQQ **Chine Lodge** East Cliff Rd PO37 6AA
☎(0983) 862358
Closed Dec
Quietly tucked away in the old village of Shanklin, this lovely establishment is well cared for and personally run by Mr and Mrs May. Bedrooms are prettily furnished and well equipped with modern facilities. Two rooms have 4-poster beds and one has a spa bath. Public areas are elegant and comfortable. Both the drawing room and the dining room enjoy beautiful views across the well tended gardens and Shanklin Chine. A peaceful atmosphere and genuine care and attention draw guests back year after year.
7⇌ CTV in all bedrooms Ⓡ ✗ sB&B⇌£22-£25 dB&B⇌£44-£56 WB&B£154-£175 WBDi£202.50-£248
Lic 7P nc £

GH QQQ **Culham Lodge** 31 Landguard Manor Rd PO37 7HZ ☎(0983) 862880
Apr-Oct
Quietly situated, this small Victorian house has been tastefully restored and extended to provide comfortable accommodation. Three of the bedrooms are on the ground floor, and all provide good facilities. There is a cosy lounge and, overlooking the terrace and heated pool, an attractive dining room offers a daily table d'hôte menu with a good choice of dishes. Other features include good car parking and a day shower on the ground floor.
10rm(1⇌7↱2hc) Ⓡ ✗ (ex guide dogs) sB&B£14-£15.50 sB&B⇌↱£16.50-£18 dB&B£28-£31 dB&B⇌↱£33-£36 WB&B£95-£105 WBDi£130-£145 LDO 4pm
CTV 8P nc12yrs (heated) solarium £

GH QQ **Curraghmore Hotel** 22 Hope Rd PO37 6EA
☎(0983) 862605
Mar-Oct
This licensed hotel occupies an elevated position overlooking the beach, only 150 yards away. Most of the bedrooms have en suite facilities and owners Margaret and Colin Andrews have plans to install more in the future. There are some ground-floor rooms, although disabled guests should know that there are steps up to the main entrance. Spacious public areas include a popular bar and ballroom that offers entertainment every other night during the season. There is also a small roof-top sun lounge. The atmosphere here is very relaxed and informal, making it an ideal base for family holidays.
26rm(10⇌8↱8hc) (9fb) CTV in all bedrooms Ⓡ sB&B£18-£20 sB&B⇌↱£20-£22 dB&B£36-£40 dB&B⇌↱£40-£44 WB&B£142-£154 WBDi£177-£189 LDO 6pm
Lic 20P putting £

GH QQQ **Edgecliffe Hotel** Clarence Garden PO37 6HA
☎(0983) 866199 FAX (0983) 404812
Closed Nov-Dec
A 'haven for non-smokers', this establishment offers a choice of modern bedrooms, some of which are quite compact but are well furnished with extra facilities, including a radio and intercom system. An open-plan dining room augments the quiet lounge, and also accommodates a bar. A choice of dishes is provided on the daily changing table d'hôte menu, and light refreshments can be

ordered throughout the day. Service is personally supervised by the friendly proprietors, Peter and Beryl Couchman.
10rm(2⇌4↱4hc) (2fb)⊁in all bedrooms CTV in all bedrooms ® ✗ ✱ sB&B£18-£20 sB&B⇌↱£23-£28 dB&B£36-£40 dB&B⇌↱£40-£46 WB&B£115-£140 WBDi£126-£194 LDO 6.30pm
Lic ⅏ 3P nc3yrs cycles for hire
Credit Cards [1] [2] [3] £

GH QQQ Hambledon Hotel Queens Rd PO37 6AW
☎(0983) 862403 & 863651 FAX (0983) 867894
Personally run by the proprietors Norman and Beryl Birch, this distinctive looking hotel offers a good level of service with a home-from-home atmosphere. The majority of bedrooms are suitable for families, including 2 conveniently situated ground-floor rooms and all are equipped with TV, direct-dial telephones and several little extras. A very comfortable, new no-smoking lounge augments a separate bar and the recently improved dining room, where the menu is changed every 2 weeks and offers a very good choice of vegetarian meals. Light refreshments are available throughout the day. Car ferry bookings can be made by the hotel if required.
11↱ (4fb) CTV in all bedrooms ® T ✗ (ex guide dogs) sB&B↱£17-£22 dB&B↱£34-£44 WB&B£110-£140 WBDi£135-£179 LDO 6pm
Lic ⅏ CTV 8P ♤
Credit Cards [1] [3] £

GH QQ Kenbury Private Hotel Clarence Rd PO37 7BN
☎(0983) 862085
Etr-Oct
Quietly positioned in its own mature gardens, this small private hotel has been run by Mr and Mrs Perez for some time. The bedrooms are modern, bright and functional, complemented by public rooms which include a comfortable, traditional lounge, separate bar with dance floor and pool table, and a candlelit basement dining room. The guesthouse has a residential licence, and ample car parking.
18rm(15⇌↱3hc) (3fb)⊁in 3 bedrooms CTV in all bedrooms ® ✗ (ex guide dogs) ✱ sB&B£22-£27.50 sB&B⇌↱£23-£28.50 dB&B⇌↱£46-£57 (incl dinner) WB&B£136-£154 WBDi£160-£190 LDO 6.30pm
Lic ⅏ CTV 8P nc3yrs
Credit Cards [1] [3] £

GH QQ Mount House Hotel 20 Arthurs Hill PO37 6EE
☎(0983) 862556
This guesthouse is in an ideal location, fairly close to all the amenities. Family run, it provides good value modern, compact accomodation, with spacious TV and bar lounges. Mrs Sandie McLoughlin does the cooking, and breakfast orders are requested the day before. The bar is particularly well stocked; there are some car parking spaces to the side of the building.
10↱ (2fb) CTV in all bedrooms ® ✗ (ex guide dogs) sB&B↱£23-£27.50 dB&B↱£46-£55 WB&B£110-£140 WBDi£143-£179 LDO 4pm
Lic ⅏ CTV 8P
Credit Cards [1] [3] £

SELECTED

GH QQQQ Osborne House Esplanade PO37 6BN
☎(0983) 862501
Jan-24 Oct
Standing in a flower-filled garden on the esplanade at Shanklin, this gabled Victorian house boasts a verandah and sun terrace, from which wide views of the sea and the pier can be enjoyed. Bedrooms are bright, fresh and pretty with modern facilities. Public areas are comfortable and filled with flowers and plants, and the atmosphere is warm, cheerful and relaxed. The restaurant is popular with guests and locals; summer meals consist of an extensive hot and cold buffet, while a 6-course candlelit dinner is served at other times. The cheerful and enthusiastic proprietors, Mike and Liz Hogarth, obviously enjoy caring for their guests, many of whom return year after year.
12⇌↱ CTV in all bedrooms ® ✗ ✱ sB&B⇌↱fr£30 dB&B⇌↱fr£60 LDO 8pm
Lic ⅏ ⱣP nc13yrs
Credit Cards [1] [3] £

GH QQ Rowborough Hotel 32 Arthurs Hill PO37 6EX
☎(0983) 866072 FAX (0983) 864000
Mar-Oct
A convivial, well stocked bar and candlelit dinners are features of this friendly family-run hotel. Bedrooms are furnished in the modern style, and there is a residents' lounge in addition to the banquette seating in the reception lobby. A well kept garden overlooks the main road, and the hotel has its own side car park. Good home cooking is provided by members of the proprietor's family.
8rm(3⇌4↱1hc) (3fb) CTV in all bedrooms ® ✗ sB&B£14-£18 dB&B⇌↱£34-£46 WB&B£103-£135 WBDi£145-£177
Lic ⅏ CTV 5P nc5yrs
Credit Cards [1] [3] £

GH QQQ Soraba Private Hotel 2 Paddock Rd PO37 6NZ ☎(0983) 862367
Mar-Nov
An attractive detached Victorian house in a mainly residential area on the Old Village side of the town and within easy reach of the beach, shops and amenities. The bedrooms are tastefully coordinated, the décor light and fresh. The proprietors maintain a high standard of care and cleanliness, and provide wholesome evening meals and friendly service.
7rm(4⇌↱3hc) CTV in 4 bedrooms TV in 1 bedroom sB&B£14-£16.50 dB&B£28-£33 dB&B⇌↱£34-£39 WB&B£90-£110 WBDi£115-£132 LDO 3pm
Lic ⅏ CTV 4P nc7yrs
Credit Cards [1] [3] £

TOTLAND BAY Map 04 SZ38

GH QQQ Frenchman's Cove Country Hotel Alum Bay Old Rd PO39 0HZ ☎(0983) 752227
Situated in a quiet country lane with super views across the rolling meadows, this small, friendly hotel offers comfortable bedrooms, with fresh décor and modern facilities. The public rooms are pretty and cosy and include a small bar, a simple dining room and a smart lounge.
13rm(2⇌7↱4hc) (11fb) CTV in all bedrooms ® ✗ (ex guide dogs) sB&B£22.50 sB&B⇌↱£26 dB&B£45 dB&B⇌↱£52 WB&B£130 WBDi£225 LDO 8pm
Lic ⅏ CTV 30P badminton net & play equipment
Credit Cards [1] [3] £

GH QQ Lismore Private Hotel 23 The Avenue PO39 0DH
☎(0983) 752025
Closed Nov-Dec
This villa dates back to 1896 and has been lovingly modernised by the resident proprietors. Bedrooms are functional and simple in décor and design; each is well equipped with modern facilities and spotlessly clean. A daily changing menu offers 4 courses of traditional fare, using fresh produce. Personally run for the past 16 years by Mr and Mrs Nolson, this simple hotel enjoys a regular following of returning clientèle.
7rm(5↱2hc) (3fb) CTV in all bedrooms ® ✗ (ex guide dogs) sB&B£25-£26 dB&B↱£54-£58 (incl dinner) WBDi£154-£175 LDO 3pm
Lic ⅏ 8P nc5yrs £

GH QQQ Littledene Lodge Granville Rd PO39 0AX
☎(0983) 752411
Mar-Oct
Whilst located in a quiet residential area on the peaceful side of the island, where the countryside is truly picturesque, this efficiently
→

run establishment is conveniently close to the Yarmouth ferry terminal. The bedrooms are neatly presented with pretty, fresh décor and nicely maintained en suite facilities. Mrs Wright is a local lady who can offer lots of advice on places of interest, and she loves to cook the fresh, 5-course evening meal her guests greatly enjoy. The public areas are comfortable and cosy including a TV lounge and a spacious dining room with a small bar, where guests return time and time again to enjoy the relaxed, friendly atmosphere.

6rm(2⇌3🚿1hc) (3fb) ® ✱ sB&B⇌🚿£22.50 dB&B⇌🚿£37 WB&Bfr£123 WBDi£160-£168 LDO 4.30pm

Lic 🍽 CTV 5P nc3yrs

GH QQ The Nodes Country Hotel Alum Bay Old Rd PO39 0HZ ☎(0983) 752859 FAX (0705) 201621

A Victorian country house set in a peaceful rural location, backing on to Tennyson Down, with over 2 acres of grounds. The wood-panelled, cosy courtyard bar is the hub of the hotel, with a warm and lively atmosphere. Bedrooms are simply decorated and furnished in a comfortable manner, and public areas are traditional in design. Young families are especially welcome, with facilities such as cots, highchairs, high teas and a baby listening service readily provided. The traditional English country cooking uses fresh local produce to great effect.

11rm(3⇌6🚿2hc) (5fb) CTV in all bedrooms ® sB&B£28-£29.50 sB&B⇌🚿£29.50-£34.50 dB&B£56-£59 dB&B⇌🚿£59-£69 (incl dinner) WB&B£115.50-£175.50 WBDi£175-£235 LDO 3pm

Lic 🍽 CTV 15P badminton table tennis

Credit Cards 1 3

GH QQQ Sandford Lodge Hotel 61 The Avenue PO39 0DN ☎(0983) 753478

rs Nov-Dec

This Edwardian house is situated in a quiet residential street and is well kept and nicely presented. Bedrooms are pretty and comfortable, with modern facilities. There are 2 comfortable lounges at this exclusively no-smoking hotel.

6rm(3⇌2🚿1hc) (2fb)⊬in all bedrooms ® ✗ (ex guide dogs) sB&B£21-£25 sB&B⇌🚿£21-£25 dB&B£29-£34 dB&B⇌🚿£34-£39 WB&B£130-£155 WBDi£189-£225 LDO 4pm

Lic 🍽 CTV 6P £

VENTNOR Map 04 SZ57

GH QQ *Channel View Hotel* Hambrough Rd PO38 1SQ ☎(0983) 852230

Apr-19 Oct rs Mar

This family-run hotel enjoys a prominent position overlooking the sea, and offers simply appointed accommodation, with freshly decorated and well presented bedrooms. The public areas are sunny and bright, with pleasant sea views; there is a cosy bar and a nicely appointed restaurant where evening meals are served.

14rm(2🚿12hc) (6fb) ® ✗ (ex guide dogs) LDO 8pm

Lic CTV P̸

Credit Cards 1 3

GH QQQ *Glen Islay Hotel* St Boniface Rd PO38 1NP ☎(0983) 854095

Mar-Oct

Built on several levels, this friendly and informal family-run guesthouse offers family accommdation, equipped with TV and tea/coffee-making facilities, while shoe-cleaning materials and an iron are also available for use. There is an exceptionally comfortable TV lounge and a large bar that contains a pool table and dart board. The popular dining room features home-made and freshly prepared food, selected from a weekly changing menu. Car parking is available on the forecourt.

10rm(1⇌8🚿1hc) (8fb) CTV in all bedrooms ® ✗ (ex guide dogs)

Lic 🍽 CTV 6P

GH QQQ Hillside Private Hotel Mitchell Av PO38 1DR ☎(0983) 852271

This unique 18th-century, 3-storey thatched house is set in 3 acres of mature grounds and garden, overlooking the sea. A comfortable no-smoking lounge augments the separate bar with a sunny conservatory. The menu features vegetarian dishes, and is served in the attractive dining room and light refreshments are available throughout the day. In addition to one convenient ground-floor bedroom, the comfortable bedrooms have sole use of private bath/shower facilities and are equipped with TV and tea/coffee-making amenities – some enjoy sea views over the garden.

11rm(4⇌7🚿) (2fb) CTV in all bedrooms ® sB&B⇌🚿£18.50-£20.50 dB&B⇌🚿£37-£41 WB&B£129.50-£143.50 WBDi£189-£203 LDO 6.30pm

Lic 🍽 16P nc5yrs

Credit Cards 1 2 3 £

GH QQQ Lake Hotel Shore Rd, Bonchurch PO38 1RF ☎(0983) 852613

Mar-Oct

This family-run hotel is quietly situated in over an acre of lovely terraced gardens, in the village of Bonchurch. Bedrooms are prettily and tastefully decorated in coordinated Laura Ashley prints, and many have en suite facilities. The public areas include 2 sunny conservatory-style lounges, a TV lounge and a comfortably appointed larger seating area; there is also a cosy bar area with a range of bar games.

11rm(10⇌🚿1hc) Annexe 10⇌🚿 (7fb) ® sB&B£17-£20 sB&B⇌🚿£17-£20 dB&B£34-£40 dB&B⇌🚿£34-£40 WB&B£120-£150 WBDi£157.50-£175 LDO 6.30pm

Lic 🍽 CTV 20P nc3yrs

GH QQQ Llynfi Hotel 23 Spring Hill PO38 1PF ☎(0983) 852202

Etr-Oct

A well maintained and nicely presented private hotel in a residential street behind the centre of town. The bedrooms are bright, nicely decorated and offer good facilities, and there are lounges for non-smokers, a dining room and a separate bar. The cooking is of a good standard, enjoyed by many guests who return year after year.

10rm(7🚿3hc) (2fb) CTV in all bedrooms ® ✗ (ex guide dogs) ✱ sB&B£15-£18 sB&B🚿£18-£20 dB&B£30-£36 dB&B🚿£36-£40 WB&B£105-£120 WBDi£140-£175 LDO 7pm

Lic CTV 7P

Credit Cards 1 3 £

GH QQ Penshurst 24 Spring Hill PO38 1PF ☎Isle of Wight(0983) 852910

Mar-Oct

Located at the bottom of Spring Hill, only a short walk from the town centre and close to the promenade, this guesthouse is a small family-run establishment with the young, enthusiastic proprietors steadily improving the property and providing an attentive service, along with a relaxed and friendly atmosphere. Some of the bright, fresh bedrooms have smart en suite facilities and each one is comfortable and equipped to a reasonable standard. All public areas are neatly presented and with exception to the lounge, are no smoking (including the bedrooms). Guests greatly enjoy the home-cooked meals prepared for them, using fresh, local produce. Car parking can be provided but it is advised to enquire when booking.

6rm(1⇌2🚿3hc) (2fb)⊬in all bedrooms CTV in all bedrooms ® ✗ (ex guide dogs) ✱ sB&Bfr£13.50 dB&B£27-£29 dB&B⇌🚿£30-£32 WB&B£84.50-£102 WBDi£126-£144

Lic CTV

GH QQQ Hotel Picardie Esplanade PO38 1JX ☎(0983) 852647

Mar-Oct

This hotel enjoys a prime location directly facing the seafront on the Esplanade. Bedrooms are simply and comfortably furnished: some are small but they are all well equipped and neatly presented. In addition to a comfortable, sunny lounge overlooking the seafront, there is also a small, bright bar area – the only room

where smoking is allowed – and a simply appointed dining room where evening meals are offered as well as a traditional English breakfast.
10⇌↱ (3fb)✗in all bedrooms CTV in all bedrooms ®
sB&B⇌↱fr£17.25 dB&B⇌↱fr£34.50 WB&Bfr£115
WBDifr£166 LDO 4.30pm
Lic CTV
Credit Cards [1] [3]

GH QQ Richmond Hotel The Esplanade PO38 1JX
☎(0983) 852496
Enjoying a prime position along the Esplanade and only yards from the beach, the public areas and front bedrooms at this pleasant hotel take advantage of the wide sea views. The freshly decorated bedrooms are simple in style but nicely equipped and the majority benefit from en suite facilities, plus 2 have a balcony where guests can sit. In addition to a comfortable lounge, there is a well stocked bar and a cosy dining room where a good choice of evening meals is offered, and a cheerful, relaxed atmosphere prevails throughout the public areas.
12rm(9⇌↱3hc) (3fb) CTV in all bedrooms ® ✱
sB&Bfr£16.95 sB&B⇌↱fr£19.45 dB&Bfr£33.90
dB&B⇌↱fr£36.40 WB&Bfr£115 WBDifr£165 LDO 5pm
Lic CTV 6P
Credit Cards [1] [3] [5]

GH QQ St Martins Hotel The Esplanade PO38 1JX
☎(0983) 852345
May-Oct
This small, privately owned hotel occupies a prime position on the seafront, and the sea-facing terrace allows guests to sit and watch the world go by. Bedrooms are bright and fresh, furnished in a simple modern style. Public areas are limited in size but are sunny and comfortable. A home-cooked evening meal is offered.
6rm(4⇌2hc) (1fb) CTV in all bedrooms ® ⊘ sB&B£18-£26
dB&B£36-£52 dB&B⇌£40-£72 WB&B£126-£182 WBDi£224-£280 LDO 8.30pm
Lic ♨ nc9yrs
Credit Cards [1] [2] [3] [5] (£)

GH QQQ St Maur Hotel Castle Rd PO38 1LG
☎(0983) 852570
Feb-Nov
Peacefully situated on a hillside, overlooking the park, this private hotel offers bright and freshly decorated bedrooms with simple, modern furniture. The public rooms are comfortable and traditional in style, with a cosy bar area complementing the spacious lounge and dining room. The well managed service is personally supervised by the proprietor.
14rm(13⇌↱1hc) (4fb) ® ⊘ sB&B⇌↱£27-£28 dB&B£54-£56
dB&B⇌↱£54-£56 (incl dinner) WB&B£154-£161 WBDi£189-£196 LDO 7pm
Lic ♨ CTV 12P nc3yrs
Credit Cards [1] [2] [3] (£)

WIGMORE Hereford & Worcester Map **07** SO46

INN Q Compasses Hotel HR6 9UN ☎(056886) 203
Believed to date back to around 1700, this ivy-clad village inn was once a bakery and farmhouse. There are 2 bars where locals congregate, a pleasant restaurant and simple accommodation, together with an abundance of ceiling beams and wall timbers. Set in a pleasant village close to the Herefordshire/Shropshire border, the hotel is popular with walkers exploring the beautiful countryside of this area.
3hc (1fb) CTV in all bedrooms ® ✱ sB&Bfr£20 dB&Bfr£40
Lunch fr£7.25&alc Dinner fr£7.25&alc LDO 9.30pm
♨ 70P
Credit Cards [1] [2] [3] [5] (£)

WILBERFOSS Humberside Map **08** SE75

FH Q Mrs J M Liversidge ***Cuckoo Nest*** *(SE717510)* YO4 5NL
☎(07595) 365
Closed Xmas
This small traditional farmhouse, with a pantiled roof, dates back some 200 years. It is a mixed farm on the A1079, close to the village of Wilberfoss. The accommodation is simple but well maintained.
2hc (1fb)✗in all bedrooms ⊘
♨ CTV P nc2yrs 150 acres arable beef dairy mixed sheep

WILLAND Devon Map **03** ST01

FH QQ Mrs J M Granger **Doctors** *(ST015117)*
EX15 2QQ ☎Tiverton(0884) 820525
Mar-Oct
An attractive Devonshire farmhouse dating in parts back to the 15th century, peacefully set at the end of an unmade raod, surrounded by well kept gardens and 95 acres of pastureland, close to Junction 27 of the M5. The bedrooms are comfortably decorated and furnished and share the family bathroom. An inglenook fireplace gives character to the guests' lounge, and traditional breakfasts are served around one table in the dining room.
3rm (1fb)✗in all bedrooms ® ⊘ sB&B£14 dB&B£28
WB&B£90
CTV 6P ✓ 95 acres dairy (£)

WILLERSEY Gloucestershire Map **04** SP13

SELECTED

GH QQQQ Old Rectory Church St WR12 7PN
☎Broadway(0386) 853729
Closed Xmas
In the shadows of the Norman church in the centre of the village, the Old Rectory is an impressive 17th-century house from which John and Helen Jones have created a small private hotel with its own gardens and car park. Guest rooms are generally spacious with good quality, attractive décor and coordinating soft furnishings, and they have an impressive array of modern facilities and thoughtful extras. There is a comfortable lounge with an open fire, overlooking the gardens. Breakfast is served in the oak-beamed dining room, and the welcoming hosts not only provide information on local restaurants, but also offer a personal chauffeur service.
6⇌↱ Annexe 2⇌↱ ✗in 6 bedrooms CTV in all bedrooms ® T ⊘ ✱ sB&B⇌↱fr£59 dB&B⇌↱£59-£95
♨ CTV 10P nc9yrs
Credit Cards [1] [3]
See advertisement under BROADWAY

WILLEY Warwickshire Map **04** SP48

FH QQQ Mrs Helen Sharpe **Manor** *(SP496849)* Willey
CV23 0SH ☎Lutterworth(0455) 553143
A traditional 18th-century red-brick farmhouse set in a peaceful location overlooking pastureland in an unspoilt village, yet within 5 miles of the M1, M6 and M69 and very close to the A5. The bedrooms are all thoughtfully furnished with coordinated décor and soft furnishings. Guests have the use of a large lounge with an open fire, and breakfast is taken around a communal table in the adjacent dining room. Smoking is not permitted.
3rm(1↱2hc) ✗in all bedrooms CTV in 1 bedroom ®
⊘ (ex guide dogs) sB&B£20-£21 sB&B↱£25-£40 dB&B£30-£32 dB&B↱£40 WB&Bfr£105
♨ CTV 3P nc93 acres sheep

WILLITON Somerset Map **03** ST04

SELECTED

GH QQQQ Curdon Mill Vellow TA4 4LS (2m SE off A358) ☎Stogumber(0984) 56522 FAX (0984) 56197

This centuries' old mill, complete with 100-year-old water wheel, is owned and run by Richard and Daphne Criddle. It is in the tiny village of Vellow, about 2 miles from Williton, surrounded by its own 200 acres of mixed farmland and adjacent to the Donniford trout stream in the foothills of the Quantocks. There are 6 simply coordinated, en suite bedrooms, and guests have use of the comfortable sitting room at any time of day. From mid-April to mid-September the heated outdoor pool is available. The spacious restaurant features the original mill workings and an attractive collection of plates. As a general rule, Daphne Criddle likes to discuss dinner menus with guests at breakfast. A choice is offered and could include pears in tarragon cream; chicken livers with puff pastry; pheasant with Calvados and apples, or Gressingham duck with Cointreau and orange, plus fresh vegetables. Puddings such as Baileys Irish Cream cake, sticky toffee pudding or home-made ice cream are offered, and cheeses from an excellent local supplier. Mrs Criddle runs a successful outside catering business from Curdon Mill, using the mill and its grounds for many wedding receptions. Smoking is not permitted in the dining room or bedrooms.

6rm(1⇌5↱) ⊬in all bedrooms CTV in all bedrooms ® ✗ (ex guide dogs) ✱ sB&B⇌↱fr£30 dB&B⇌↱£42-£60 WBDi£216-£273 LDO 8.30pm

Lic 🍽 100P nc8yrs ⇌(heated) 𝒫(hard&grass) ⌡ U

WILMCOTE Warwickshire Map **04** SP15

GH QQ Swan Cottage The Green CV37 9XJ ☎Stratford-Upon-Avon(0789) 266480

Just 3 miles from Stratford, this cottage, with original beams and flagstone floors, overlooks Mary Arden's house and the Elizabethan museum. The accommodation offers a self-contained room at the rear of the property, plus 2 rooms situated in the main house which share a bathroom. There is a cosy lounge/dining room, with comfortable seating and lots of personal touches, where hearty breakfasts are served at a communal table. All the guests' rooms are plainly decorated and modestly appointed with a mixture of furnishings. The proprietors Veronica and Bill Stevenson warmly welcome guests to their home.

2rm Annexe 1↱ CTV in 1 bedroom ® ✗ dB&B£28 dB&B↱£37

🍽 CTV 4P

WILMSLOW Cheshire Map **07** SJ88

GH QQQ Fernbank 188 Wilmslow Rd, Handforth SK9 3JX ☎(0625) 523729 & 539515

Closed Xmas-New Year

A large detached house on the A34 Wilmslow to Manchester road, an ideal location for the airport. Rooms are spacious and well equipped and residential ceramic courses are held periodically.

3⇌↱ CTV in all bedrooms ® ✱ sB&B⇌↱£28-£30 dB&B⇌↱£38-£44

🍽 CTV 3P china restoration and weekend leisure courses

WILTON Wiltshire Map **04** SU03

INN QQ The Swan Stoford SP2 0PR (3m N off A36) ☎Salisbury(0722) 790236

A popular roadside inn on the A36 6 miles west of Salisbury. An extensive choice of dishes is offered from various menus and the restaurant has access to the gardens via a patio. The bedrooms are comfortable and those at the front are double glazed to combat road noise.

8rm(5↱3hc) (3fb) CTV in all bedrooms ® ✗ (ex guide dogs) ✱ sB&B£20 dB&B£40 dB&B↱£40 WB&B£140 Lunch £5-£15alc Dinner £5-£15alc LDO 10pm

🍽 CTV 100P ⌡ skittle alley pool table

WIMBORNE MINSTER Dorset Map **04** SZ09

GH Q Riversdale 33 Poole Rd BH21 1QB ☎(0202) 884528

Closed Xmas rs Nov-Feb

This pleasant, popular guesthouse has been owned and managed by Mr and Mrs Topham for many years. Parts of the house date back 350 years, so some of the bedrooms have interesting features such as winding staircases and sloping ceilings. Other bedrooms are more practical in shape and size, but all are brightly decorated and simply furnished. Public areas include a pleasant breakfast room and a cosy lounge area. Plenty of tourist information is provided for guests, many of whom have stayed before, though the establishment is particularly favoured by business people.

8rm(1↱7hc) (3fb) CTV in all bedrooms ® ✱ sB&B£14.50-£22 dB&B£29-£44 LDO 10am

🍽 CTV 3P nc3yrs

Credit Cards 1 3

GH QQ Stour Lodge 21 Julian's Rd BH21 1EF ☎(0202) 888003

Closed 20 Dec-5 Jan

Positioned alongside the A31 Dorchester road, close to the centre of town but enjoying rural views, this handsome house offers neat bedrooms and a relaxed, informal atmosphere. There is a comfortable drawing room and conservatory, and dinner, taken around a communal dining table, is available by prior arrangement.

3rm(1⇌2hc) (2fb) CTV in all bedrooms ® sB&Bfr£25 sB&B⇌£30 dB&Bfr£50 dB&B⇌£60 WB&B£150-£180 WBDi£200-£220 LDO 9pm

Lic 🍽 CTV 4P croquet £

WIMPSTONE Warwickshire Map **04** SP24

FH QQ Mrs J E James **Whitchurch** *(SP222485)* CV37 8NS ☎Alderminster(0789) 450275

A lovely Georgian farmhouse built in 1750, very much part of a working farm, situated a few miles south of Stratford-on-Avon. Bedrooms have recently been improved, with good en suite facilities added. There is a small but comfortable lounge with a collection of toys for children.

3rm(2↱1hc) (2fb) ® ✗ sB&B£14-£17 sB&B↱fr£17 dB&B£28-£34 dB&B↱fr£34 LDO 6.30pm

🍽 CTV 6P 220 acres arable beef sheep £

WINCANTON Somerset Map **03** ST72

FH QQQ Mrs A Teague **Lower Church** *(ST721302)* Rectory Ln, Charlton Musgrove BA9 8ES ☎(0963) 32307

Closed Xmas & New Year

This small and very welcoming farmhouse dates from 1738 and retains many old features including beams, bare brickwork and fireplaces. Bedrooms are neat and clean with comfortable, good quality beds and extras such as fresh flowers and magazines. The dining room has one large table and carved wooden chairs, and the lounge has a vast open fireplace and a colour TV. Guests also have the use of a pretty cottage garden.

3rm(2↱1hc) ⊬in all bedrooms ® dB&B£25-£27 dB&B↱£28-£30 WB&B£90-£95

🍽 CTV 3P nc6yrs 60 acres dairy sheep

WINCHCOMBE Gloucestershire Map **04** SP02

GH QQQ Pilgrims Bistro 6 North St GL54 5LH ☎Cheltenham(0242) 603544 & 604194

Closed Xmas rs Sun (Etr-Oct)

This cosy, friendly little bistro in the centre of the village has 3 bright and comfortable bedrooms on the first floor. Each room is individually styled and decorated in pleasing colours and rich

fabrics, and combines the character of the building with modern comfort ; they are all well equipped and provide good quality en suite showers. The popular bistro offers imaginative menus and good standards of cooking. Typical daily dishes include curried pumpkin and tomato soup, spaghetti with a fresh pesto sauce, beef and Beamish casserole with button mushrooms, and cheese and tomato loaf served with a sweet pepper sauce. These are complemented by a well balanced, reasonably priced wine list. There is no private parking, but local parking is available.
3↱ (1fb) CTV in all bedrooms ® sB&B↱fr£27.50
dB&B↱£40-£44 LDO 9.30pm
Lic ⅏
Credit Cards [1] [3]

WINCHELSEA East Sussex Map **05** TQ91

SELECTED

GH QQQQ ***The Country House at Winchelsea*** Hastings Rd TN36 4AD ☎Rye(0797) 226669
Closed Xmas
Dating from the 17th century, this delightful farmhouse is set back from the A259 in 2 acres of grounds. Bedrooms are attractively decorated and have every modern facility including private bath or shower rooms. There is a choice of 2 lounges, each with a country house appeal and one of which features a small bar. Good home cooking is served in the elegant candlelit dining room by the welcoming proprietor, Mrs Carmichael.
4rm(2↱2hc) CTV in all bedrooms ® ✗ LDO 7.30pm
Lic ⅏ 3P 3⌂ nc9yrs

GH QQ The Strand House TN36 4JT ☎Rye(0797) 226276
Dating back to the 15th century, this guesthouse has been sympathetically modernised, retaining all the original architectural features. The low- ceilinged bedrooms are furnished in traditional style, and all but one have compact but private shower rooms. There is a comfortable and elegant lounge with an inglenook fireplace, a hospitality bar and a smart dining room where proprietor Mrs Pownall offers her home cooking. Service is helpful, and there is a pleasant garden and ample parking.
10⇒↱ (1fb) CTV in all bedrooms ® sB&B⇒↱£25-£30
dB&B⇒↱£35-£50 WB&B£135-£175
Lic ⅏ 15P nc7yrs Ⓔ

WINCHESTER Hampshire Map **04** SU52

GH QQQ Aerie 142 Teg Down Meads, (off Dean Lane) SO22 5NS ☎(0962) 862519
Situated in a quiet residential area (check for directions), this modern detached property, has some far-reaching views. It offers immaculate rooms which are light, airy and well equipped, and a shared shower room. There is a no-smoking policy throughout the house.
4hc ⊁in all bedrooms CTV in all bedrooms ® ✗ ✱ sB&B£16-£18 dB&B£31-£36
⅏ 6P nc10yrs

GH QQ ***Harestock Lodge Hotel*** Harestock Rd SO22 6NX (situated 2m N of the city on the B3420) ☎(0962) 881870
Closed 24 Dec-3 Jan
This large house lies on the rural edge of the city. The Bishop family are gradually making improvements to both the spacious public areas and the bedrooms. The conference room is popular with business people, while families enjoy the summer pool.
20rm(9↱11hc) (5fb) CTV in all bedrooms ®
✗ (ex guide dogs) LDO 9.15pm
Lic ⅏ CTV 20P ≈spa pool
Credit Cards [1] [2] [3]

GH QQQ Markland 44 St Cross St SO23 9PS
☎(0962) 854901
This detached Victorian house, with a beautiful stained glass window in the front door, is situated in a residential area on the road running to the city centre from the south. Bedrooms are spacious and simply furnished with good beds; the ground-floor room offering some facilities for the disabled. There is a friendly welcome, parking access to the rear, and a garden to enjoy in the warmer months.
4⛆ (1fb) CTV in all bedrooms ® sB&B⛆£32 dB&B⛆£42
CTV 4P
Credit Cards 1 3

GH QQ Number Fifty Hotel 50 Christchurch Rd, St Cross SO23 9SU ☎(0962) 852628
This attractive house dates from the end of the last century and is in a quiet residential road not far from the city centre. There is a garden and patio, a comfortable lounge adorned with pictures and ornaments, and mostly first-floor bedrooms.
10rm(8⛆2hc) (1fb) CTV in all bedrooms ® ✱ sB&Bfr£25 sB&B⛆£27 dB&B£34-£38 dB&B⛆£38-£40 LDO 7.30pm
CTV 8P
Credit Cards 1 3 £

GH QQQ Shawlands 46 Kilham Ln SO22 5QD
☎(0962) 861166
Shawlands is situated off the Romsey Road in a quiet residential area overlooking open farmland on the edge of Farley Mount, just a short walk from a regular bus service to the city centre. It is a detached family house offering very comfortable bedrooms with quality beds and modern well tiled bathrooms. Special diets can be catered for at breakfast, where home-made bread and preserves are served together with stewed fruit from the garden.
4rm(1⇌⛆3hc) (2fb)⅟in all bedrooms CTV in all bedrooms ® ✗ (ex guide dogs) sB&Bfr£18 sB&B⇌⛆fr£18 dB&B⇌⛆£32-£26 WB&B£107-£126
CTV 3P

SELECTED

INN QQQQ The Wykeham Arms 73 Kingsgate St SO23 9PE ☎(0962) 853834 FAX (0962) 854411
Centrally located in the oldest part of the city between the cathedral and the college, this 250-year-old pub offers real ale, an extensive wine list, and a standard of cuisine that has won it our rosette award. The ground floor of the building is divided into a series of small eating and drinking areas, many of them no smoking. The walls are decorated with a vast collection of pictures, hats and tankards, and there are 4 log fires which burn merrily in winter months. Bedrooms all have en suite facilities, and lots of extras such as minibar, telephone and fresh flowers. There is a separate breakfast room for guests, featuring splendid pine panelling and dresser, and crisp linen cloths. Graeme and Anne Jameson and their team of young staff take great care of their customers in a busy hospitable atmosphere.
7⇌⛆ CTV in all bedrooms ® T ✱ sB&B⇌⛆£62.50 dB&B⇌⛆£72.50 Lunch £11-£15&alc Dinner £15-£18alc LDO 8.45pm
14P nc14yrs sauna
Credit Cards 1 2 3

WINCLE Cheshire Map **07** SJ96

GH QQ Four Ways Diner Motel Cleulow Cross SK11 0QL (1m N of A45) ☎(0260) 227228
This small motel-type operation was developed from former garage and showroom premises. It stands on the A54 Congleton/Buxton road, south of Macclesfield, and from its isolated position there are impressive views of the Dane Valley. The accommodation comprises simple modern bedrooms, each with its own entrance. Four of them have small kitchen areas, and 3 rooms are located in a separate building about 150yds from the main block. The combined bar/restaurant is busy with non-resident travellers, and Sunday lunch is particularly popular. The proprietor is a compulsive collector of all manner of bric-a-brac, much of it displayed in the hotel.
6rm(1⇌5⛆) Annexe 5⛆ (2fb) CTV in all bedrooms ® sB&B⇌⛆£25-£30 dB&B⇌⛆£35-£40 LDO 7.30pm
Lic 50P
Credit Cards 1 2 3 5 £

WINDERMERE Cumbria Map **07** SD49

See **Town Plan Section**

GH QQ Aaron Slack 48 Ellerthwaite Rd LA23 2BS
☎(05394) 44649
Part of a Victorian terrace, this small friendly guesthouse provides clean, freshly decorated accommodation combined with personal service. The 3 bedrooms are prettily furnished, each with TV and tea-making facilities, and 2 are now en suite. There is a small lounge and a separate breakfast room. Smoking is not permitted and pets are not accepted.
3rm(2⇌⛆1hc) ⅟in all bedrooms CTV in all bedrooms ® ✗ sB&B⇌⛆£12-£20 dB&B⇌⛆£24-£34 WB&B£84-£135 LDO noon
nc12yrs
Credit Cards 1 3 £

GH QQQ Applegarth Hotel College Rd LA23 3AE
☎(05394) 43206
A Victorian lakeland stone hotel situated in an elevated position yet close to the town centre and railway station. The modern bedrooms are very spacious, all with private bathrooms and TV: 4 have 4-poster beds and several have fine views towards the lake and fells. The lounge/bar and restaurant are all elegantly furnished and comfortable, and there is a notable stained glass window over the original oak staircase. Bed and breakfast accommodation only is provided, but there are ample restaurants near by open for dinner.
15⛆ (4fb) CTV in all bedrooms ® T sB&B⛆£20-£35 dB&B⛆£40-£70 WB&B£140-£245
Lic CTV 20P
Credit Cards 1 2 3 £

GH QQQ Archway Country College Rd LA23 1BY
☎(05394) 45613
A charming and quite unique guesthouse, furnished in Victorian style, on a side road in Windermere town. It offers interesting and comfortable accommodation with lots of Victoriana around, including books, plants, pictures and patchwork quilts on the beds; good facilities are also provided. The cooking is excellent, using organically grown produce in the preparation of the fine dinners. Breakfast is a marathon event, the meal includes home- made yoghurt and preserves, as well as poached kippers.
6rm(5⛆1hc) ⅟in all bedrooms CTV in all bedrooms ® T ✗ sB&B⛆£22-£25 dB&B⛆£44-£50 LDO 3pm
Lic 3P nc12yrs
Credit Cards 1 £

GH QQQ The Beaumont Hotel Holly Rd LA23 2AF
☎(05394) 47075
This elegant detached Victorian house, with a distinctive entrance porch, small gardens and a car park to the side, is situated close to Windermere village (go through the village one-way system, take the 2nd turning on the left and first left again). Recently opened, the bedrooms have been tastefully furnished and decorated, with modern furniture and attractive coordinated fabrics – one has a 4-poster bed. The guests' lounge has been sumptuously furnished with soft sofas and armchairs, and gracefully decorated in character with the period. There is an attractive breakfast room on the lower ground floor.
11rm(3⇌8⛆) (4fb)⅟in all bedrooms CTV in all bedrooms ® ✗ (ex guide dogs) ✱ sB&B⇌⛆£25-£45 dB&B⇌⛆£36-£70 WB&B£125-£240
Lic CTV 10P nc2yrs
Credit Cards 1 3

GH QQQ Belsfield House 4 Belsfield Ter LA23 3EQ ☎(05394) 45823

This attractive black and white Victorian house is situated in the centre of the village. There are 2 lovely Victorian fireplaces, one in the cosy lounge and one in the dining room. The mainly spacious bedrooms have en suite facilities, attractive coordinated fabrics and modern furniture. Service is warm and friendly.

9 (4fb) CTV in all bedrooms (ex guide dogs) * sB&B£21.50-£23 dB&B£36-£44 WB&B£126-£140 9P £

GH QQQ Blenheim Lodge Brantfell Rd, Bowness on Windermere LA23 3AE ☎(05394) 43440

A comfortable house in a quiet location just above the town centre. It offers friendly service from the resident proprietors, well furnished bedrooms and a comfortable lounge and dining room. The set dinner, all home cooked, is good value for money.

11 (1fb) in all bedrooms CTV in all bedrooms ® * sB&B£23-£25 dB&B£40-£54 WB&B£137-£185 WBDi£215-£265 LDO 7pm

Lic 12P 2 nc6yrs

Credit Cards 1 2 3 £

GH QQQ Brendan Chase 1&3 College Rd LA23 1BU ☎(05394) 45638

A charming family-owned and run guesthouse in a quiet side road close to the town centre, furnished and decorated throughout to a high standard. The bedrooms are decorated with pretty coordinating fabrics, and each room has a TV and tea-making facilities; the beds are of notable quality. The bathroom is home to a delightful collection of ceramic frogs. The dining room is Edwardian in style, and there is a cosy and comfortable lounge. The games room in the basement is a new addition, with a full-sized snooker table.

8rm(4 4hc) (4fb) in 1 bedroom CTV in all bedrooms ®

CTV 8P £

GH QQ Broadlands 19 Broad St LA23 2AB ☎(05394) 46532

A well furnished and comfortable small guesthouse, owned and personally run by the resident proprietors. It is situated in a side road just a short walk from Windermere village.

5rm(3 2hc) (1fb) CTV in all bedrooms ® dB&B£24-£32 dB&B£28-£40

CTV

Credit Cards 1 3 £

GH QQQ Brooklands Ferry View, Bowness LA23 3JB ☎(05394) 42344

A delightful small family-owned and run guesthouse in a lovely rural setting, situated south of Bowness on the Kendal road at the top of Longtail Hill. Bedrooms have individual colour schemes, with pretty prints and TV; most are now en suite. A good lakeland breakfast is provided in the cosy dining room, and there is a comfortable lounge. Parking is available alongside the house.

6rm(5 1hc) (3fb) CTV in all bedrooms ® sB&B£18-£20 dB&B£36-£38

CTV 6P £

GH QQ *Clifton House* 28 Ellerthwaite Rd LA23 2AH ☎(05394) 44968

This Lakeland stone, semidetached house is set in a quiet side road close to the centre of Windermere. There is a cosy lounge for guests' use and a breakfast room to the rear. The bedrooms are bright and fresh with modern furniture, colour TV and tea/coffee-making facilities, and guests can be sure of helpful and friendly service from the resident owners.

5rm(1 4hc) (1fb) CTV in all bedrooms ®

CTV 5P nc5yrs

GH QQQ Cranleigh Hotel Kendal Road, Bowness LA23 3EW ☎(05394) 43293

Situated 2 minutes' walk from Lake Windermere and the village centre of Bowness, this Lakeland stone house offers clean, comfortable bedrooms with colour TV. There are 2 good lounges with plenty of easy chairs, and dinner is available in the pleasant dining room. Service is friendly and attentive.

9 Annexe 6 (1fb) CTV in all bedrooms ® (ex guide dogs) sB&B£19-£30 dB&B£38-£60 WB&B£120-£200 WBDi£190-£270 LDO 7.30pm

Lic CTV 15P

Credit Cards 1 3 £

GH QQQ Fayrer Holme Upper Storrs Rd, Bowness on Windermere LA23 3JP ☎(05394) 88195

Closed 2 Jan-4 Feb

An elegant Lakeland stone country house standing in over 5 acres of grounds overlooking Lake Windermere. Bedrooms are beautifully furnished and have very good facilities provided. There is an elegant lounge and breakfast is served in the conservatory looking out over fields towards the lake.

Best Newcomer for North of England 1992–3, see colour section.

9 (2fb) in 3 bedrooms CTV in all bedrooms ® T sB&B£29.50-£39.50 dB&B£39-£59 LDO 7pm

Lic 20P

Credit Cards 1 3 £

GH QQQ Fir Trees Lake Rd LA23 2EQ ☎(05394) 42272

A very well furnished, comfortable small hotel situated on the main road between Windermere and Bowness. The bedrooms are spacious and all have private bathrooms and provide TV and tea-making facilities. A notable hearty English breakfast is offered in the elegant dining room, accompanied by warm hospitality from the resident owners Mr and Mrs Fishman.

7 (2fb) in 3 bedrooms CTV in all bedrooms sB&B£22.50-£28.50 dB&B£35-£47 WB&B£115-£160 8P

Credit Cards 1 2 3 £

See advertisement on page 429

GH QQQ Glencree Private Hotel Lake Rd LA23 2EQ ☎(05394) 45822
Mar-Dec rs Feb
Glencree is in a very convenient location, midway between Bowness and Windermere, and overlooks a wooded valley with a stream to the rear. It is a Victorian house of Lakeland stone, well furnished in all areas, with a comfortable lounge and cosy breakfast room. The bedrooms are generally spacious, all en suite, and equipped with colour TV and tea-making facilities.
5rm(3⇌2↱) CTV in all bedrooms ® ✗ (ex guide dogs) sB&B⇌↱£29-£35 dB&B⇌↱£39-£60 WB&Bfr£129.50
Lic 8P nc9yrs
Credit Cards 1 3 £

GH QQQ Glenville Hotel Lake Rd LA23 2EQ ☎(05394) 43371
Feb-Nov
Well positioned between Bowness and Windermere, this stone house is well furnished and stands in its own grounds. The atmosphere is friendly and there are 2 lounges – one for non-smokers. All attractive bedrooms have colour TV and tea-making facilities. Hearty breakfasts are a speciality.
9rm(1⇌8↱) (1fb)⅄in 2 bedrooms CTV in all bedrooms ® ✗ sB&B⇌↱£17.50-£22.50 dB&B⇌↱£35-£45 WB&B£122-£155 LDO 2pm
Lic 12P £

GH QQQ *Green Gables* 37 Broad St LA23 2AB ☎(05394) 43886
Closed Xmas & New Year
Situated in a quiet side road close to Windermere village centre and facing Elleray Garden and the local park, Green Gables offers good value accommodation. Bedrooms are prettily furnished and equipped with colour TV, tea-making facilities and hairdryers. A cosy lounge is provided and the resident owners are friendly and helpful.
6rm(2↱4hc) (2fb)⅄in 3 bedrooms CTV in all bedrooms ® ✗ (ex guide dogs)
CTV 2P

GH QQQ *Greenriggs* 8 Upper Oak St LA23 2LB ☎(05394) 42265
This attractive family-owned and run guesthouse has recently been completely refurbished to a very high standard. Set in a quiet and peaceful side road close to the town centre, it offers very friendly and attentive service.
7rm(4↱2hc) (1fb) CTV in all bedrooms ® LDO noon
CTV 4P nc5yrs

SELECTED

GH QQQQ The Hawksmoor Lake Rd LA23 2EQ ☎(05394) 42110
Feb-Nov
The owners, Barbara and Bob Tyson are very friendly hosts who have created a delightfully comfortable small hotel between Bowness and Windermere. Bedrooms are en suite, and are attractively appointed with matching fabric and wallpaper, and each has colour TV and tea-making facilities. Home cooking is of a good standard and served in a well furnished and comfortable dining room matched by an elegant lounge.
10⇌↱ (3fb)⅄in 3 bedrooms CTV in all bedrooms ® ✗ (ex guide dogs) ✱ sB&B⇌↱£23-£35 dB&B⇌↱£42-£55 WB&B£126-£173 LDO 5pm
Lic 12P nc6yrs £
See advertisement in colour supplement

GH QQQ Hazel Bank Hazel St LA23 1EL ☎(05394) 45486
The resident owners of this detached Victorian house are life-long walkers and can give guests excellent advice on this subject. Mr Mathews also leads guided walking tours. The house has generously sized bedrooms and all are en suite with good quality, individual décor and furniture. A very pleasant lounge is provided and contains a lovely log fire plus a good range of hiking books. Although mainly bed and breakfast, evening meals are served at certain times and supper each evening includes home-made cakes and biscuits, all provided with a friendly, attentive service.
3⇌↱ ⅄in all bedrooms ® ✗ dB&B⇌↱£30-£38 WB&B£102-£130 LDO 10am
CTV 4P nc7yrs £

GH QQ Holly Lodge 6 College Rd LA23 1BX ☎(05394) 43873
This is one of the oldest Victorian houses in Windermere, which stands in a quiet road close to the town centre and is owner run by 2 very pleasant, attentive couples. The bedrooms have been recently decorated, offering mixed styles of furniture, plus all are equipped with TV and tea-making facilities. There is a cosy, comfortable lounge, with breakfast and dinner served in an intimate dining room.
10rm(4↱6hc) (3fb) CTV in all bedrooms ® ✗ (ex guide dogs) sB&B£15-£18 dB&B£30-£36 dB&B↱£36-£40 WB&B£105-£140 WBDi£171.50-£206.50 LDO 10am
Lic 7P £

GH QQQ Holly Park House 1 Park Rd LA23 2AW ☎(05394) 42107
Mar-Oct
This attractive Lakeland stone house is in a quiet side road close to Windermere village. Bedrooms are very well furnished and there is a comfortable lounge. Friendly service is provided by the resident owners.
6⇌↱ (4fb) CTV in all bedrooms ® ✗ (ex guide dogs) ✱ sB&B⇌↱£25-£30 dB&B⇌↱£30-£40 WB&B£97.50-£130
Lic 4P £

GH QQ Kenilworth Holly Rd LA23 2AF ☎(05394) 44004
This is a very pleasant little guesthouse, which is well looked after by the owners, Mr and Mrs Gosling. It is situated in a quiet side road, yet close to Windermere town centre. The bedrooms are mainly modern in style and are prettily decorated. A cosy lounge, with colour TV, is provided and service is very friendly.
6rm(3↱3hc) (1fb)⅄in all bedrooms ® ✗ (ex guide dogs) sB&B£13.50-£16 dB&B£27-£32 dB&B↱£32-£38 WB&B£90-£120
CTV 3P £

GH QQQ Kirkwood Prince's Rd LA23 2DD ☎(05394) 43907
This pleasant Lakeland stone house is situated in a quiet part of Windermere, and the resident owners, Mr and Mrs Cox, are friendly hosts. The Victorian- style public areas are comfortably furnished and offer a cosy lounge and an attractive dining room. Bedrooms are more modern in style and have pretty bed covers, colour TV and tea-making facilities.
7↱ (6fb)⅄in 3 bedrooms CTV in all bedrooms ® ✱ dB&B↱£34-£48 WB&B£115-£160
1P
Credit Cards 1 3 £

GH Q Latimer House Lake Rd LA23 2JJ ☎(05394) 46888
A Lakeland stone building on the main approach to Bowness from Windermere village. There is no breakfast room, so cooked breakfasts are served to bedrooms each morning and a good choice is offered. The house is exclusively no smoking.
6rm(2↱4hc) (1fb)⅄in all bedrooms CTV in all bedrooms ® ✗ dB&B£30-£42 dB&B↱£39-£57 WB&B£101.50-£160
CTV 4P 2🚗 nc8yrs £

GH QQQ Laurel Cottage Saint Martins Square LA23 3EF ☎(05394) 45594
A quaint cottage-style guesthouse in Bowness close to the shops and lake. Bedrooms are attractively furnished, the lounge features oak beams and there is a cosy dining room. Freindly service is provided by Mrs Mary Bunker, the charming owner.
→

HAWKSMOOR

Lake Road, Windermere, Cumbria LA23 2EQ
Telephone: (05394) 42110

Large ivy-clad house with every modern facility and superb private car park. Ideally situated between Windermere and Bowness. All rooms en-suite, some ground floor rooms. All rooms have colour TV and tea/coffee facilities.

See colour advertisement in colour section.

GLENVILLE

Lake Road, Windermere LA23 2EQ
Tel (05394) 43371

A delightful country house retaining a host of original features combining the highest standards of comfort and cleanliness. En-suite bedrooms with colour T.V. complementary tea & coffee. Licensed with comfortable lounge. Large private car park. Close to all amenities within walking distance of the lake. Ideally situated for walking and touring. Mid week & short stay bookings welcome. AA QQQ

Please telephone for room availability.
Proprietors: Joseph & Vera Crawford.

Green Gables Guest House

37 Broad Street, Windermere, Cumbria LA23 2AB
Telephone: Windermere (05394) 43886

Family run guest house situated in a pleasant position. Shops, restaurants, bus and railway stations are all nearby. TV lounge, separate dining room, central heating, first class bathrooms, toilets and showers. All our cosy bedrooms have colour TV, hair dryers and tea/coffee making facilities. Some rooms en-suite. Family rooms available.

Cleanliness, friendliness and a good hearty breakfast is the key to our success

A warm welcome awaits you from Sheila and Joe Lawless.

LAKE ROAD
WINDERMERE
CUMBRIA
LA23 2EQ
Telephone:
WINDERMERE
(05394) 42272

Charming Victorian guest house of considerable character and furnished with antiques throughout. Within easy walking distance to Windermere, Bowness, or the lake. Luxurious accommodation with spacious and lovely bedrooms, all with private bath/shower rooms en suite and colour televisions. Simply scrumptious breakfasts. Most of all, old-fashioned hospitality. Recommended by major prestige guides.

15rm(10⬚ 5hc) (2fb) CTV in 6 bedrooms ® ✕ (ex guide dogs) ✱ sB&B£20-£22 dB&B£35-£38 dB&B⬚ £42-£50 WB&B£110-£155
CTV 8P £

GH QQQ Lynwood Broad St LA23 2AB ☎(05394) 42550
A well furnished and comfortable guesthouse in a quiet side road a short walk from the town centre. The Lynwood offers modern, well equipped bedrooms, friendly family service and good value for money.
9rm(4⬚ 5hc) (4fb) in all bedrooms CTV in all bedrooms ® ✕ (ex guide dogs) ✱ sB&B⬚ £13-£20 dB&B£22-£30 dB&B⬚ £30-£40
2P 2 nc5yrs £

GH QQQ Meadfoot New Rd LA23 2LA ☎(05394) 42610
Feb-Nov & Xmas
A friendly house offering excellent comforts, situated in pleasant grounds close to Windermere village. Bedrooms have good facilities and a delightful lounge overlooks well tended gardens.
8rm(4⬚ 4hc) (1fb) CTV in all bedrooms ® ✕ (ex guide dogs) ✱ sB&B£16-£18 dB&B£28-£30 dB&B⬚ £30-£40 WB&B£84-£112
9P nc3yrs £

GH QQ Mylne Bridge House Brookside, Lake Rd LA23 2BX ☎(05394) 43314
Mar-Oct
A very pleasant and comfortably furnished family-run guesthouse in a quiet location close to Windermere centre.
10rm(7⬚ 3hc) (1fb) CTV in all bedrooms ® sB&B£15-£17 sB&B⬚ £17-£19 dB&B£30-£34 dB&B⬚ £34-£38 WB&B£99-£125
Lic 10P £

GH Q Oakthorpe Hotel High St LA23 1HF ☎(05394) 43547
Closed 25 Dec-24 Jan
A family-run guesthouse in the town centre with its own car park. There is an interesting old chest in the foyer which features in Beatrix Potter's Ginger and Pickles.
16rm(4⇌3⬚ 9hc) (3fb) CTV in all bedrooms ® sB&Bfr£19 sB&B⇌⬚ £26 dB&Bfr£38 dB&B⇌⬚ £52 WBDi£168-£220 LDO 8.30pm
Lic 18P
Credit Cards 1 3

GH QQQ Oldfield House Oldfield Rd LA23 2BY ☎(05394) 88445
This charming Victorian house is situated in a quiet side road a short way from Windermere village. The pleasant hallway leads to a cosy lounge with books and newspapers, and an attractive dining room with a stone fireplace. The bedrooms have modern furniture, with good beds, pretty covers and curtains. Telephones have recently been installed, and one room has a 4 poster. This warm, comfortable house offers very good value for money, with friendly hospitality from resident owners Mr and Mrs Theobald.
7rm(1⇌4⬚ 2hc) (2fb) in 2 bedrooms CTV in all bedrooms ® T ✕ (ex guide dogs) sB&B£16-£21 sB&B⇌⬚ £18-£24 dB&B£32-£40 dB&B⇌⬚ £36-£44 WB&B£100.80-£151.20
CTV 7P nc2yrs free membership to leisure club
Credit Cards 1 3 £

GH QQQ Parson Wyke Country House Glebe Rd LA23 3HB ☎(05394) 42837
Formerly the rectory to St Martins church, this Grade II listed building, which stands in 1.5 acres of lovely grounds close to the lake, is now the house of Jean and David Cockburn. Parts of the house date back to the 15th century and it has the style of a medieval cottage. There are 3 spacious bedrooms furnished with antique pieces and old bedsteads, with coordinated décor and soft furnishings, all equipped with TV and en suite facilities. A comfortable lounge, decorated in red, overlooks the garden, and breakfast is served in the delightful dining room, complete with beams and a lovely old fireplace. Considerate and attentive service is provided at all times.
3rm(2⇌1⬚) (1fb) CTV in all bedrooms ® ✕ (ex guide dogs) sB&B⇌⬚ £25-£35 dB&B⇌⬚ £40-£55
CTV 9P £

GH QQQ Rosemount Lake Rd LA23 2EQ ☎(05394) 43739
A comfortable small hotel midway between Bowness and Windermere, it offers well furnished and equipped bedrooms, a cosy lounge and a pretty breakfast room. This is a no-smoking house.
8rm(5⬚ 3hc) in all bedrooms CTV in all bedrooms ® ✕ sB&B⬚ £17.50-£23 dB&B⬚ £35-£46 WB&B£116-£153
Lic 6P 2
Credit Cards 1 3 £

GH QQQ St Johns Lodge Lake Rd LA23 2EQ ☎(05394) 43078
Feb-Nov
Resident owners Mr and Mrs Gregory take pride in their guesthouse, a semidetached property of Lakeland stone situated between Bowness and Windermere, and good quality furnishings and decorations have been used in all parts of the hotel. Bedrooms are brightly decorated and have coordinated fabrics; the good beds have headboard drapes in some rooms, and 2 rooms have 4 posters. There are big armchairs in the cosy lounge, and the pleasant basement dining room has a bar, beams and mirrors.
14rm(1⇌13⬚) (3fb) in 3 bedrooms CTV in all bedrooms ® ✕ sB&B⇌⬚ £20-£25 dB&B⇌⬚ £37-£46 WB&B£128-£140 WBDi£189-£210 LDO 6pm
Lic 11P nc3yrs

GH Q Thornleigh Thornbarrow Rd LA23 2EW ☎(05394) 44203
Feb-Nov
A small, friendly and well run guesthouse in a quiet side road between Bowness and Windermere. Bedrooms are provided with good facilities.
6hc (4fb) CTV in 5 bedrooms ® ✕ (ex guide dogs) sB&B£15-£18 dB&B£30-£36
CTV 5P
Credit Cards 1 3 £

GH QQQ Westlake Lake Rd LA23 2EQ ☎(05394) 43020
A well furnished and comfortable small hotel, midway between Bowness and Windermere, providing good friendly service.
8⇌⬚ (2fb) CTV in all bedrooms ® ✕ sB&B⇌⬚ £18-£24 dB&B⇌⬚ £36-£48 WB&B£126-£154 LDO 3.30am
Lic CTV 8P nc5yrs £

See advertisement on page 433

GH QQQ White Lodge Hotel Lake Rd LA23 2JJ ☎(05394) 43624
Mar-Nov
A comfortable small hotel with its own car park just north of Bowness centre. It offers good bedrooms with well designed facilities. There is a cosy lounge and an attractive dining room.
12⇌⬚ (3fb) CTV in all bedrooms ® ✕ (ex guide dogs) sB&B⇌⬚ £23-£29 dB&B⇌⬚ £42-£54 WB&B£144-£182 WBDi£214-£250 LDO 6.30pm
Lic CTV 14P
Credit Cards 1 3

See advertisement on page 433

GH QQQ Woodlands New Rd LA23 2EE ☎(05394) 43915
A very comfortable small hotel, family owned and run, offering friendly, attentive service. Bedrooms are well equipped, there is a delightful lounge and good home cooking is provided.
15⬚ (2fb) in 2 bedrooms CTV in all bedrooms ® ✕ (ex guide dogs) ✱ sB&B⬚ £18-£27 dB&B⬚ £36-£54 LDO 3pm

→

THORNLEIGH GUEST HOUSE

Thornbarrow Road,
Bowness-on-Windermere

Cumbria LA23 2EW Tel: (05394) 44203

A small, friendly guest house, offering bed and breakfast at very reasonable rates. Comfortable, well appointed bedrooms, with colour TV and tea/coffee making facilities. Some rooms with private showers. Fully centrally heated, private parking, colour TV lounge. Pleasantly situated in good residential area, just off the main road, and close to both Bowness and Windermere.

Rosemount

PRIVATE HOTEL

NON SMOKING

Lake Road, Windermere,
Cumbria LA23 2EQ

VISA

Telephone Windermere (05394) 43739

Delightful guest house built in traditional Lakeland style, ideally situated between Windermere village and the Lake, offering warm and comfortable accommodation. Bedrooms are immaculate and attractively furnished, all with private facilities, colour television and tea trays. Scrumptious sizzling breakfasts (or refreshing fruit alternative) – above all else, friendly and personal attention from the resident owners, Alan and Dorothy Fielding. Licensed Bar. Car Parking. Recommended by all major guides.

St John's Lodge

Lake Road, Windermere LA23 2EQ
Telephone: (05394) 43078

English Tourist Board
COMMENDED

Ideally situated mid way between Windermere and Bowness. Comfortable private hotel managed by resident chef proprietor. All rooms are en suite and include a colour TV and tea/coffee making facilities. Residents' lounge plus dining room and bar. Four poster beds. Excellent cuisine and wine list. Reduced off season rates. Facilities of private sports/leisure club available to guests.

Send for brochure to: Doreen and Ray Gregory.

B E D & B R E A K F A S T

We would like to welcome you to Oldfield House, which has a friendly, informal atmosphere within a traditionally-built Lakeland residence.

7 Bedrooms, most en-suite, four poster room, all with Colour TV & Telephone • Quiet central location • Leisure Club facilities • Car Park

VISA

Bob and Maureen Theobald,
Oldfield House, Oldfield Road,
Windermere, Cumbria LA23 2BY

(05394) 88445

Lic ♨ 15P nc5yrs
Credit Cards [1] [3]

WINDSOR Berkshire Map **04** SU97

GH QQ Clarence Hotel 9 Clarence Rd SL4 5AE
☎(0753) 864436 FAX (0753) 857060

The Clarence Hotel is centrally placed close to the attractions and popular with both tourists and business people. Because of the age of the building, bedrooms come in a variety of shapes and sizes, some compact, but all are en suite and a programme of upgrading and modernisation is producing attractive, well coordinated rooms with 24-channel cable TV. A newly decorated breakfast room and friendly bar complete the picture.

21⇔↱ (6fb) CTV in all bedrooms ® ✱ sB&B⇔↱£30 dB&B⇔↱£49
Lic ♨ CTV 2P
Credit Cards [1] [2] [3] [5]

GH QQQ Melrose House 53 Frances Rd SL4 3AQ
☎(0753) 865328

This elegant, detached Victorian house lies in a residential street some 10 minutes' walk from the town centre. Bedrooms, decorated in pinks and greens, are bright, clean and very well equipped. Downstairs is a spacious breakfast room, a mirrored reception hall and a cosy TV lounge. Mrs Daniel, the manageress, offers a warm and cheery welcome.

9⇔↱ (2fb)⅄in 2 bedrooms CTV in all bedrooms ® **T**
♨ CTV 10P
Credit Cards [1] [3] £

WINSTER Derbyshire Map **08** SK26

GH QQQ The Dower House Main St DE4 2DH
☎0629 650213 FAX (0629) 650894
Mar-Oct

This Elizabethan country house with its walled garden stands in the heart of the Peak District village. It has spacious bedrooms and a lounge with a log fire. Breakfast is served 'en famille'.

3rm(1↱2hc) ⅄in all bedrooms CTV in all bedrooms ® sB&Bfr£30 sB&B↱£35 dB&B£45-£50 dB&B↱£50-£55
Lic ♨ 4P nc10yrs

WINTERBOURNE ABBAS Dorset Map **03** SY69

GH QQ Churchview DT2 9LS ☎Martinstown(0305) 889296
rs Nov-Feb

Ideally situated for those who enjoy lovely, rural walks, yet conveniently located on a major route, this delightful, cottage-style hotel is run by pleasant, friendly proprietors Mr and Mrs Deller. The double-glazed bedrooms have a wealth of character and charm, including beams, sloping ceilings and uneven floors, hence the cosy, cheery feeling that prevails, and 3 rooms have very smart, modern en suite facilities. There is a choice of 2 lounges, one with a TV, the other being a no-smoking room, and a nicely appointed dining room where a home-cooked evening meal is offered.

10rm(2⇔2↱6hc) (1fb) ® sB&B£15.50-£17.50 sB&B⇔↱£19.50-£21.50 dB&B£31-£35 dB&B⇔↱£39-£43 WB&B£102-£114 WBDi£154-£170 LDO 7pm
Lic ♨ CTV 9P 1⌂ nc3yrs
Credit Cards [1] [3] £
See advertisement under DORCHESTER

WISBECH Cambridgeshire Map **05** TF40

FH QQQ Mrs S M King ***Stratton*** *(TF495140)* West Drove North, Walton Highway PE14 7DP ☎(0945) 880162

A modern bungalow-style farmhouse set within 22 acres of grazing; it is situated 4 miles northeast of Wisbech and 8 miles from Kings Lynn; take the first left after the village of Wallon Highway from the A47. A superior style of accommodation is offered: bedrooms are spacious, well equipped and decorated with pretty coordinating soft furnishings, and all are en suite. There is also a covered, heated swimming pool and a small lake for fishing.

3⇔↱ ⅄in all bedrooms CTV in all bedrooms ®
✖ (ex guide dogs)
♨ CTV 6P nc5yrs ≈(heated) ⌐ 22 acres beef dairy pigs

WITHERIDGE Devon Map **03** SS81

INN QQQ ***Thelbridge Cross*** Thelbridge EX17 4SQ On the B3042 ☎Tiverton(0884) 860316
rs 25 & 26 Dec

This recently renovated inn is full of character and has a reputation for good food. It is beside the B3042, about a mile from Witheridge, surrounded by countryside. The bedrooms are brightly decorated in a modern style, and the bars are cosy and attractive with exposed beams and stone walls.

8⇔↱ (1fb) CTV in all bedrooms ® ✖ (ex guide dogs)
LDO 9pm
♨ CTV 50P
Credit Cards [1] [3]

WITNEY Oxfordshire Map **04** SP30

GH QQQ ***Greystones Lodge Hotel*** 34 Tower Hill OX8 5ES
☎(0993) 771898
Closed 2wks Xmas

The outdoor swimming pool in a sun trap sheltered by trees is an inviting feature of this 1930s, creeper-clad detached house. The cosy dining room has fresh linen and the 2-course menu at £8.50 may contain Italian specialities from Ernesto Ceccarelli's home town. Freshly decorated bedrooms have modern furniture and shower units in the room. The hotel has ample parking available.

11hc (1fb) CTV in all bedrooms ® LDO 7.30pm
Lic ♨ CTV 15P ≈
Credit Cards [1] [2] [3] [5]

WIVELISCOMBE Somerset Map **03** ST02

GH QQ Deepleigh Langley Marsh TA4 2UU ☎(0984) 23379
3↱ (2fb) CTV in all bedrooms ® ✖ (ex guide dogs) ✱ sB&B↱£24-£28 dB&B↱£40-£44 LDO noon
Lic ♨ 5P ℛ(hard)U £

WIX Essex Map **05** TM12

FH QQQ Mrs H P Mitchell **New Farm House** *(TM165289)* CO11 2UJ (0.5m N off Wix-Bradfield road) ☎(0255) 870365 FAX (0255) 870837

Easily found just off the Wix to Bradfield road, this modern farmhouse is run by friendly proprietor Mrs Mitchell and caters well for families, the semi- disabled and those with special dietary requirements. The bedrooms are freshly decorated and the 6 annexe rooms all have smart en suite facilities. Traditional home-cooked evening meals are available throughout the year, and guests have a choice of 2 lounges, one designated for smokers.

6rm(1↱5hc) Annexe 6↱ (5fb)⅄in 10 bedrooms CTV in all bedrooms ® ✱ sB&Bfr£18.50 sB&B↱fr£21 dB&Bfr£35 dB&B↱fr£40 WB&B£116.50-£132.30 WBDi£179.50-£195.30 LDO 5.30pm
♨ CTV 20P ⌂ 52 acres arable non-working
Credit Cards [1] [3] £

WOKING Surrey Map **04** TQ05

GH QQQ ***Glen Court*** St Johsn Hill Rd GU21 1RQ
☎(0483) 764154

This attractive Edwardian house is set in 1.5 acres of gardens and woodland, and benefits from ample car parking to the front. The spacious, comfortable bedrooms are traditionally furnished and are all en suite. Three annexe bedrooms are compact but furnished in a more modern style. Breakfast is served in the main house, while next door the Fountain restaurant offers an extensive continental-style à la carte menu, in elegant surroundings. There is also a cosy bar and a small room available for private dining or meetings.

9rm(6⇔3↱) Annexe 3⇔ (1fb) CTV in all bedrooms ®
LDO 10pm

→

Lic 🍽 29P table tennis
Credit Cards [1] [3]

WOODBRIDGE Suffolk Map 05 TM24

GH QQ ***Grove House*** 39 Grove Rd IP12 4LG ☎(0394) 382202
A well sited guesthouse on the A12, a modern bungalow extended to provide thoughtfully furnished accommodation with some en suite facilities. Furnishings are light and coordinated with a fresh, clean feel. Mr and Mrs Kelly are friendly, concerned hosts who work hard to maintain a good standard of repair.
9rm(5🚿4hc) (1fb) CTV in all bedrooms ® LDO 6.30pm
Lic 🍽 CTV 12P
Credit Cards [1] [3]

WOODSTOCK Oxfordshire Map 04 SP41

GH QQQ The Laurels Hensington Rd OX20 1JL
☎(0993) 812583
Closed Xmas
This Victorian family home is just a short walk from the centre of this historic Cotswold village and Blenheim Palace. Comfortable, well furnished bedrooms retain original features and are freshly decorated, clean and appealing. The dining room, too, is furnished in keeping with the house. Evening meals are not provided but Woodstock offers a range of pubs and restaurants. The Laurels is popular with British and overseas tourists, and a comprehensive and inexpensive bus service is available to Oxford then London and Stratford.
3rm(2🚿1hc) (1fb) ⊬ in all bedrooms ® 🐕 sB&B🚿£25-£35 dB&B🚿£32-£40 LDO 10am
🍽 3P nc7yrs
Credit Cards [1] [3]

WOODY BAY Devon Map 03 SS64

GH QQ ***The Red House*** EX31 4QX ☎Parracombe(05983) 255
Apr-Oct
In a superb location above a quiet wooded valley (National Trust land) and with fine sea views, the house is 100 years old and provides spacious, airy bedrooms with comfortable beds and conventional bedding. A good choice for a peaceful stay.
6rm(3🛁1🚿2hc) (1fb) CTV in all bedrooms ® LDO 6.30pm
Lic 🍽 CTV 8P nc4yrs

WOOLACOMBE Devon Map 02 SS44

See also Mortehoe

GH QQ Camberley Hotel Beach Rd EX34 7AA
☎(0271) 870231
In an elevated position with some lovely views, this family-run hotel offers a warm welcome and well equipped accommodation. A choice of menu is available and orders for dinner are taken after breakfast.
6🛁 (3fb) CTV in all bedrooms ® dB&B🛁£32-£40 WB&B£130 WBDi£175 LDO 6.30pm
Lic 🍽 CTV 6P nc7yrs Ⓔ

GH QQQ ***The Castle*** The Esplanade EX34 7DJ
☎(0271) 870788
Apr-Oct
Occupying an elevated position overlooking the sea, this impressive castle- style building provides an overall comfortable atmosphere, complemented by friendly service. The attractive bedrooms are pleasingly furnished and there is an unusual lounge with ornate wood ceilings and copper inset panels to the windows.
8🚿 (2fb) ® 🐕 (ex guide dogs) LDO 6pm
Lic 🍽 CTV 8P nc5yrs

GH QQ Combe Ridge Hotel The Esplanade EX34 7DJ
☎(0271) 870321
Apr-Sep
Providing comfortable well tended accommodation throughout, this professionally managed house is situated on the outskirts of town. The bedrooms are extremely neat and clean, as are the guests' lounge and dining room.
7rm(1🛁4🚿2hc) (3fb) CTV in all bedrooms ® sB&B£18-£21 dB&Bfr£36 dB&B🛁🚿£42 LDO 5pm
Lic 🍽 CTV 7P
Credit Cards [1]

GH QQQ Holmesdale Hotel Bay View Rd EX34 7DQ
☎(0271) 870335 FAX (0271) 870088
Closed Feb
Undoubtably a feature of this well managed guesthouse is the interesting, good value restaurant menu, provided by the cheerful, friendly proprietors who are also responsible for the unpretentious and very nicely maintained accommodation.
15🚿 (10fb) CTV in all bedrooms ® ✱ WBDi£155-£169 LDO 8.30pm
Lic 🍽 CTV 14P
Credit Cards [1] [3]

GH QQQ ***Pebbles Hotel & Restaurant*** Combesgate Beach, Mortehoe EX34 7EA ☎(0271) 870426
Closed Jan
Overlooking the sea on the outskirts of the town, this small, privately owned hotel provides well furnished bedrooms, a spacious lounge bar and an attractive dining room, offering a good value menu with a wide selection of dishes.
12rm(11🛁1hc) (5fb) CTV in all bedrooms ® LDO 9.30pm
Lic 25P 1🚗
Credit Cards [1] [3]

GH QQ ***Seawards*** Beach Rd EX34 7AD ☎(0271) 870249
Tom and Win Cooper provide a warm welcome at their delightful seaside family holiday guesthouse. The spotlessly clean bedrooms and bathrooms are freshly painted, the pleasant lounge has TV, and there is a residents' bar in the dining room. The house is situated only 10 minutes from the beach and backs on to National Trust farmland.
5hc (3fb) 🐕 (ex guide dogs) LDO 5pm
Lic 🍽 CTV 7P nc5yrs

WOOLHOPE Hereford & Worcester Map 03 SO63

INN QQ Butchers Arms HR1 4RF ☎Fownhope(0432) 860281
Situated in a very rural area but close to Hereford, this 14th-century inn was once a row of cottages and a slaughter house for local farmers. There is a wealth of beams and timbers, and bedrooms are bright and cosy. The inn offers extensive bar and restaurant menus, with some unusual choices. Bar meals are served at all times, and the à la carte restaurant is open Wednesday to Saturday inclusive.
3hc CTV in all bedrooms ® **T** 🐕 (ex guide dogs) ✱ sB&Bfr£25 dB&Bfr£39 LDO 9.30pm
🍽 80P nc14yrs

WOOLSTONE Oxfordshire Map 04 SU28

SELECTED

INN QQQQ The White Horse SN7 7QL
☎Farringdon(0367) 820566 & 820726
A quaint 16th-century partly thatched inn near the White Horse Hill, from where the inn derives its name, tucked away amidst pretty rolling countryside. The bedrooms are located in an adjoining annexe, and are comfortable and well equipped, with TV, direct-dial telephone, radio and tea-making facilities. An imaginative choice of bar meals is served in the popular oak-beamed bar, together with a range of malt whiskies and real ales. A changing selection of roasts and home-made pies is offered, with a choice of vegetarian and children's meals also available. The well appointed restaurant

provides a more formal choice, offering à la carte and table d'hôte menus.
Annexe 6⇌↱ CTV in all bedrooms ® T
✗ (ex guide dogs) ✱ sB&B⇌↱fr£40 dB&B⇌↱fr£50
Lunch fr£8.50&alc Dinner fr£14.95&alc LDO 10pm
60P
Credit Cards 1 2 3 5 £

WORCESTER Hereford & Worcester Map **03** SO85

See also Leigh

GH QQQ *40 Britannia Square* WR1 3DN ☎(0905) 611920 FAX (0905) 27152
This 18th-century gentleman's residence is situated in one of the town's famous squares. The attractively decorated lounge and other areas of the main house reflect the owner's interior design background, with clever use of wall stencilling, marbled doors and rag rolling. Some of the bedrooms are in converted outbuildings and these are neat and cosy.
1⇌↱ Annexe 2⇌↱ (2fb)⁄in 1 bedroom CTV in all bedrooms ® ✗
CTV P

GH QQ Wyatt 40 Barbourne Rd WR1 1HU ☎(0905) 26311
This well maintained guesthouse is situated next to the A449 Kidderminster road, opposite the eye hospital. Bedrooms are clean and well decorated, and provide tea-making facilities and TV. There is a spacious lounge with comfortable modern sofas and armchairs, and the tables in the pretty dining room are covered with attractive lace cloths.
8rm(4↱4hc) (4fb) CTV in all bedrooms ® sB&B£16-£18 dB&B£28-£30 dB&B↱£30-£32 LDO 5pm
CTV
Credit Cards 1 3 £

WORKINGTON Cumbria Map **11** NX92

GH QQ Morven Hotel Siddick Rd CA14 1LE
☎(0900) 602118 & 602002
This detached, late-Victorian house with a rear extension stands beside the Silloth road to the north of the town. There are 4 ground-floor bedrooms and 2 upstairs; all have good facilities including TV and hairdryers. The dining room is spacious and modern and 2 comfortable lounges are provided, one of which is no smoking. The resident owners are a caring couple, and adequate parking is provided.
6rm(4⇌2hc) (1fb) CTV in all bedrooms ® ✱ sB&B£18-£20 sB&B⇌£20-£30 dB&B£30-£35 dB&B⇌£36-£40 LDO 4pm
Lic 🍽 CTV 20P

WORTHING West Sussex Map **04** TQ10

GH QQQ Blair House 11 St Georges Rd BN11 2DS
☎(0903) 234071
This small guesthouse is situated in a peaceful, predominantly residential area, close to the seafront. Bedrooms are all freshly decorated and well maintained, all except one have a private bathroom. There is a small comfortable lounge bar, and home-cooked meals are available. Street car parking is unrestricted.
7rm(2⇌4↱1hc) (1fb) CTV in all bedrooms ®
✗ (ex guide dogs) sB&Bfr£20 sB&B⇌↱£25 dB&Bfr£35 dB&B⇌↱£40 WB&B£140-£150 WBDi£196-£206 LDO 6.30pm
Lic 🍽 3P 1🚗 (£5 per day)
Credit Cards 1 2 3 £

GH QQQ Delmar Hotel 1-2 New Pde BN11 2BQ
☎(0903) 211834 FAX (0903) 850249
Peacefully situated overlooking the sea, this small family-run licensed hotel offers a friendly and welcoming atmosphere. Bedrooms are continually being upgraded; they are all particularly well equipped, and most are now en suite. Public areas include a cosy lounge, small bar, and a pleasant roof terrace, and home-cooked evening meals are available in the spacious dining room.
13rm(11⇌↱2hc) (3fb)⚟in all bedrooms CTV in all bedrooms ® ✗ (ex guide dogs) ✱ sB&B⇌↱£24.50 dB&B⇌↱£45 WB&B£154.35 LDO noon
Lic 🍽 CTV 5P 1🚗
Credit Cards 1 2 3 £

GH Q *Osborne* 175 Brighton Rd BN11 2EX ☎(0903) 235771
Situated in a prime position overlooking the sea, this guesthouse offers a pleasant patio to the front where guests can sit out during the summer months. The bedrooms are fairly basic but offer adequate comfort. Snacks are available throughout the day.
8rm(2↱6hc) (4fb) CTV in all bedrooms ®
Lic 🍽 CTV ⅊ nc9yrs
Credit Cards 1 2 3

GH QQ Wolsey Hotel 179-181 Brighton Rd BN11 2EX
☎(0903) 236149
Closed mid-end Dec
Commanding a good seafront position, this family-run guesthouse offers simple but comfortable accommodation. There is a residents' lounge with adjoining bar, and dinner is served by arrangement.
13rm(3↱10hc) (2fb) CTV in all bedrooms ® sB&B£19.50 sB&B↱£27.50 dB&B£39 dB&B↱£55 WB&B£130-£182.50 WBDi£182.50-£235 LDO 6.30pm
Lic 🍽 CTV ⅊
Credit Cards 1 2 3 £

GH QQ Woodlands 20-22 Warwick Gardens BN11 1PF
☎(0903) 233557
Located only a few minutes' walk from the seafront and town centre, this is an ideal base for a restful holiday or business visitors. The bedrooms are well maintained and offer a good level of comfort, as do the separate lounge and no-smoking dining room. The daily set evening meal is cooked by Jill Stoner and a short wine list is available. A friendly service is provided by Alan Stoner, who looks after the guests, creating a relaxed and informal atmosphere.
12rm(1⇌5↱6hc) (3fb) CTV in all bedrooms ® sB&B£16-£21 dB&B£30-£40 dB&B⇌↱£38-£48 WB&Bfr£105 WBDifr£135 LDO 6pm
Lic 🍽 CTV 8P £

WREXHAM Clwyd

See **Hanmer & Penley**

WROTHAM Kent Map **05** TQ65

INN QQ The Bull Hotel Bull Ln TN15 7RF
☎Borough Green(0732) 885522
This 14th-century inn has been lovingly restored by the proprietors Mike and Elaine Dunnell, and whilst the accommodation retains much of its original character, bedrooms all have direct-dial telephone, TV and tea-making facilities. Its reputation for real ales and good food served in the beamed à la carte restaurant is well deserved. Adjoining the hotel is 'The Buttery' with its own bar, which is available for private meetings and functions. The hotel is easily located on the right going into the village, and there is ample car parking space.
10rm(6⇌4hc) (1fb) CTV in all bedrooms ® **T** sB&Bfr£35 sB&B⇌£40 dB&Bfr£45 dB&B⇌£50 Lunch £7.95-£12.50&alc Dinner £12.50&alc LDO 10pm
🍽 50P
Credit Cards 1 2 3 5 £

WYBUNBURY Cheshire Map **07** SJ64

FH QQ Mrs Jean E Callwood **Lea** *(SJ717489)* Wrinehill Rd CW5 7NS ☎Crewe(0270) 841429
A fully operational 130-acre dairy farm, with landscaped gardens around the house where a family of peacocks roam. The rooms are clean and well furnished, and the family really make guests feel welcome.
3rm(1↱2hc) (1fb) CTV in all bedrooms ® ✱ sB&B£13-£15 sB&B↱£15-£16 dB&B£25-£27 dB&B↱£27-£29 WB&B£90-£100 WBDi£130-£150 LDO 5pm
CTV 22P 2🚗 ⚲ snooker pool tables 150 acres dairy £

WYE Kent Map **05** TR04

INN QQ New Flying Horse Upper Bridge St TN25 5AN (Shepherd) ☎(0233) 812297 FAX (233) 813487
Ownership has now reverted to the brewery, and this long-established, popular little village inn is scheduled for a complete refurbishment with more bedrooms being added. Bar meals chosen from the blackboard are still a feature, and the daily specials are recommended. There is also an attractive beer garden, and ample car parking is available. Service, supervised by Mr and Mrs Evans, is friendly and helpful.
4hc Annexe 4⇌ (1fb) CTV in all bedrooms ® ✱ sB&B£31 sB&B⇌£36 dB&B£41 dB&B⇌£46 Lunch £8-£15 Dinner £8-£15 LDO 9.30pm
🍽 20P
Credit Cards 1 2 3 £

YARMOUTH, GREAT Norfolk Map **05** TG50

GH QQ Balmoral Private Hotel 65 Avondale Rd NR31 6DJ
☎(0493) 662538
A cheerful, modest guesthouse in a good position close to the seafront. It maintains a consistent standard, with light, fresh décor in compact rooms.
7rm(4↱3hc) (3fb) CTV in all bedrooms ® ✱ sB&B£15-£22 sB&B↱£18-£25 dB&B£30-£44 dB&B↱£36-£50 WB&B£95-£120 WBDi£125-£150 LDO 4pm
Lic 🍽 CTV ⅊ £

GH Q ***Frandor*** 120 Lowertoft Rd NR31 6ND (2m S off A12)
☎(0493) 662112
Situated close to the town centre, this is a simply furnished guesthouse with a relaxed atmosphere.
6rm(2↑4hc) (3fb)⊬in 4 bedrooms CTV in all bedrooms ® LDO 6.30pm
Lic ♨ CTV 12P
Credit Cards [1] [3]

GH QQ Georgian House NR30 4EW ☎(0493) 842623
Closed Xmas-Feb rs Nov-Etr
A family-run seafront guesthouse on the quieter north side of the resort. It offers some spacious and well furnished rooms with en suite facilities. The proprietors work hard to improve the quality of the accommodation and the standard of cleanliness is commendable. This is a popular, good value establishment.
19rm(11⇔6↑2hc) (1fb) CTV in all bedrooms ® ✖ dB&B£32-£36 dB&B⇔↑£35-£45 WB&B£100-£130
Lic ♨ 18P nc5yrs

GH QQ ***Helm House*** 2 Trafalgar Rd NR30 2LD
☎(0493) 843385
Cheerful, energetic Mrs McWilliam runs this guesthouse with care and attention to detail. The accommodation is attractively furnished in pastels and pretty prints.
11hc (5fb) CTV in all bedrooms ® ✖ (ex guide dogs) LDO 5pm
♨ CTV ₱

GH Q Jennis Lodge 63 Avondale Rd NR31 6DJ (2m S off A12)
☎(0493) 662840
A well located guesthouse a few steps from the seafront in a quiet area. Mr and Mrs Alexander have worked hard to improve the house and have recently installed colour TV in all the rooms.
11hc (4fb) CTV in all bedrooms ® ✱ sB&B£14-£18 dB&B£28-£36 WB&B£85-£115 WBDi£100-£140 LDO 4pm
Lic ♨ CTV ₱ Ⓔ

GH QQ Spindrift 36 Wellesley Rd NR30 1EU
☎Great Yarmouth(0493) 858674
Sparklingly clean and with en suite facilities, this establishment has been run by Mrs Wells for 10 years. It is a semidetched Victorian building on a tree-lined avenue parallel with the seafront.
8rm(5⇔↑3hc) (3fb) CTV in all bedrooms ®
✖ (ex guide dogs) ✱ sB&B£17-£25 sB&B⇔↑£20-£30 dB&B£28-£32 dB&B⇔↑£32-£40 WB&B£89-£120
♨ nc3yrs
Credit Cards [1] [3]

GH QQ Squirrels Nest 71 Avondale Rd NR31 6DJ
☎(0493) 662746 FAX (0493) 662746
Friendly proprietor Mrs Squirrel offers a level of services and facilities which appeals to holidaymakers, particularly families, at her guesthouse a few steps from the beach in a quiet area of Gorlestone.
9rm(1⇔8↑) (1fb) CTV in all bedrooms ® ✱ sB&B⇔↑£16-£27 dB&B⇔↑£32-£64 WB&B£100-£180 WBDi£179-£220 LDO 9.30pm
Lic ♨ 5P
Credit Cards [1] [2] [3] Ⓔ

YARNTON Oxfordshire Map **04** SP41

GH QQ ***Eltham Villa*** 148 Woodstock Rd OX5 1PW
☎Kidlington(08675) 6037
This newly converted cottage with a garden and terrace offers light bedrooms with smartly tiled shower rooms. The attractive dining room is furnished in pine and there is a small lounge for guests' use.
3↑ CTV in all bedrooms ® ✖
♨ CTV 6P
See advertisement under WOODSTOCK

YEALAND CONYERS Lancashire Map **07** SD57

GH QQ The Bower LA5 9SF ☎Carnforth(0524) 734585
This delightful Georgian residence is situated in spacious grounds in an attractive village setting within easy reach of southern Lakeland. It is a family home with just 2 guest bedrooms, one with full en suite facilities, the other with its own private bathroom just down the corridor. The larger of the rooms has a double and a single bed for family occupancy, and both rooms are comfortable, with pine and antique furniture prominently featured. Breakfast is taken in the kitchen with the family, and dinner is served in the attractive period-style dining room overlooking the garden, and should be arranged with the proprietor in advance. Guests are also welcome to share the elegant drawing room. To find the Bower, leave the M6 at junction 35 then follow the A601 (M) to the A6, proceed in the Milnthorpe direction and in 2 to 3 miles the village is signposted.
2⇔↑ (1fb)⊬in all bedrooms CTV in all bedrooms ®
✖ (ex guide dogs) sB&B⇔↑£29.50-£34 dB&B⇔↑£44-£53 WB&B£140-£210 LDO noon
♨ 6P nc12yrs croquet lawn Ⓔ

YELVERTON Devon Map **02** SX56

GH QQQ Harrabeer Country House Hotel Harrowbeer Ln PL20 6EA ☎(0822) 853302
Closed Xmas & New Year
A small, family-run hotel full of character, situated on the edge of Dartmoor, and an easy drive from the centre of Plymouth. The bedrooms all have private bathrooms and provide TV and direct-dial telephones. The public areas are comfortably furnished with a lively atmosphere in the bar. Home-cooked dishes are served in the attractive beamed restaurant.
7rm(4⇔↑3hc) (1fb) CTV in all bedrooms ® **T** ✱ sB&Bfr£23.50 sB&B⇔↑£25.50 dB&B£51 dB&B⇔↑£51-£54 WB&B£164-£178 WBDi£224-£255 LDO 6pm
Lic ♨ CTV 6P

→

Credit Cards [1] [2] [3] (£)
See advertisement under PLYMOUTH

FH QQQ Mrs B Cole **Greenwell** *(SX536659)* Nr Meavy PL20 6PY ☎(0822) 853563
Closed Xmas
Greenwell Farm is situated 2 miles from Yelverton on the Cadover Bridge road on the edge of Dartmoor and has parts dating from the 15th century. The bedrooms are attractively coordinated and there are books and games for children on the landing. Traditional farmhouse cooking is provided and a set menu is served by arrangement only.
3⇌↱ (1fb)⊬in all bedrooms CTV in 2 bedrooms Ⓡ ✖ ✱
sB&B⇌↱£24-£35 dB&B⇌↱£37-£40 WB&Bfr£133
WBDi£196-£210 LDO 4pm
Lic ℳ CTV 10P stabling for guests horses 220 acres beef sheep

YEOVIL Somerset Map **03** ST51

See also Halstock
FH QQQ Mrs M Tucker **Carents** *(ST546188)* Yeovil Marsh BA21 3QE (2m N of Yeovil off A37) ☎(0935) 76622
Feb-Nov
In a quiet, rural setting this sturdy, mellow stone farmhouse, which dates back to the 15th century, offers nicely decorated, bright bedrooms. Mrs Tucker provides a hearty breakfast in the attractive dining room, and a comfortable sitting room, complete with open fire, creates an easy relaxed atmosphere.
3hc ⊬in all bedrooms Ⓡ ✖ sB&B£15-£16 dB&B£30-£31
CTV 6P 350 acres arable beef

YORK North Yorkshire Map **08** SE65

See also Acaster Malbis, Copmanthorpe & Rufforth
GH Q ***Aberford Hotel*** 35 East Mount Rd YO2 2BD ☎(0904) 622694
A terraced house situated in a cul-de-sac west of the city centre, but only a short walk from the main attractions. Some bedrooms have recently been redecorated and although simple, are bright and cheerful: others are in need of improvement. Downstairs public areas are in the process of being upgraded. There is a cosy cellar bar for resident guests, and private parking facilities are available at the rear.
12rm(2⇌↱10hc) (1fb)⊬in 6 bedrooms CTV in all bedrooms Ⓡ ✖ (ex guide dogs)
Lic ℳ CTV 7P 1🚗
Credit Cards [1] [2] [3]

GH QQQ **Acer Hotel** 52 Scarcroft Hill, The Mount YO2 1DE ☎(0904) 653839 & 628046 FAX (0904) 640421
A comfortable house offering compact but well appointed bedrooms, a very good value dinner menu with a good choice of dishes and friendly service from the proprietors.
6rm(2⇌4↱) (1fb) CTV in all bedrooms Ⓡ **T** ✱
sB&B⇌↱£27.50 dB&B⇌↱£41-£51 WB&Bfr£140
WBDi£215-£240 LDO 6.30pm
Lic ℳ CTV 4P 1🚗
Credit Cards [1] [3] (£)

GH Q ***Acomb Road*** 128 Acomb Rd YO2 4HA ☎(0904) 792321
The simple accommodation at this guesthouse is good value for money. It is about one mile from the city centre.
12rm(6↱6hc) (3fb) CTV in all bedrooms Ⓡ LDO 7.30pm
Lic CTV 20P

GH QQ **Acorn** 1 Southlands Rd, Bishopthorpe Rd YO2 1NP ☎(0904) 620081
A small terraced house situated in a quiet area about 10 minutes' walk from the city centre and the racecourse. Bedrooms are well maintained and nicely decorated.
6rm(3↱3hc) (3fb) CTV in all bedrooms Ⓡ ✖ (ex guide dogs)
sB&B£12.50-£16 dB&B£23-£30 dB&B↱£27-£34
WB&B£80.50-£105 WBDi£129.50-£154 LDO 10am
ℳ CTV (£)

GH QQ ***Adams House Hotel*** 5 Main Street, Fulford YO1 4HJ ☎(0904) 655413
Closed Xmas
Conveniently situated in a pleasant area, one mile south of the town centre, this comfortable hotel offers well appointed bedrooms, a spacious lounge and friendly proprietors. There is also a car park for guests.
7rm(2⇌4↱1hc) (2fb) CTV in all bedrooms Ⓡ
Lic ℳ 8P

GH QQ **Alcuin Lodge** 15 Sycamore Place, Bootham YO3 7DW ☎(0904) 632222
Closed 24-26 Dec
This early Edwardian house is situated in a quiet area of the city, within easy walking distance of the central attractions. The accommodation is comfortable and some bedrooms have en suite facilities. Parking is easier than in some parts of the city and there is private space for 2 cars.
6rm(2↱4hc) (1fb) CTV in all bedrooms Ⓡ ✖ (ex guide dogs)
✱ sB&B£15-£17 dB&B£26-£29 dB&B↱£30-£36
Lic ℳ 2P nc10yrs (£)

GH QQQ **Alfreda** 61 Heslington Ln, Fulford YO1 4HN ☎(0904) 631698
A pair of Edwardian houses in Regency style, surrounded by spacious, attractive gardens in a quiet location, with easy access to the town centre. Bedrooms are pleasant and comfortable with modern equipment and several extras, and there is an impressive dining room.
10rm(8⇌↱2hc) (4fb) CTV in all bedrooms Ⓡ **T**
dB&B⇌↱£28-£48 WB&B£125-£168
ℳ CTV 20P 2🚗 (£2 per night)
Credit Cards [1] [3] (£)

GH QQ **Ambleside** 62 Bootham Crescent YO3 7AH ☎(0904) 637165
This compact house is well maintained by the friendly owners who offer neat, bright bedrooms and a comfortable lounge which has retained its fine Victorian fireplace.
8rm(4↱4hc) (1fb) CTV in all bedrooms Ⓡ ✖ ✱ dB&B£28-£34
dB&B↱£34-£40 WB&B£190-£270
ℳ CTV ₱ nc9yrs

SELECTED

GH QQQQ **Arndale Hotel** 290 Tadcaster Rd YO2 2ET ☎(0904) 702424
Closed Xmas & New Year
A distinctive mock-Tudor gable and an arch at one side, leading to the garden, adds to the delightful character of this Victorian residence. The spacious bedrooms are all beautifully furnished, mainly in the style of the period but with tastefully matching modern fabrics. Several have antique 4-poster and half-tester beds – some are also canopied. The bathroom fitments are in a Victorian style and a number are equipped with whirlpool systems. There is a spacious, elegant lounge complete with winged armchairs, paintings and a small dispense bar, which overlooks the gardens and York's famous race course. A substantial English breakfast and a set 4-course evening meal are served in a very attractive dining room, which features lace cloths and plates on the wall. Willing hosts, David and Gillian Reynard, provide hospitable and attentive service.
10⇌↱ (1fb) CTV in all bedrooms Ⓡ ✖ (ex guide dogs) ✱
dB&B⇌↱£44-£60 WB&B£136.50-£171.50
Lic ℳ 15P nc5yrs (£)

GH QQ **Arnot House** 17 Grosvenor Ter, Bootham YO3 7AG ☎(0904) 641966
Feb-Nov
This is a comfortable, privately run guesthouse, situated in a Victorian terrace, with views over Bootham Park and the Minster.

The bedrooms are individually furnished and decorated, complete with at least one easy chair, and a selection of books is provided. Breakfast offers a choice of dishes and is served in the bay-windowed dining room, with its tables covered in crisp linen cloths. Evening meals can be provided on request. There are some private parking spaces, which should be reserved in advance.
6hc (2fb) CTV in all bedrooms ® ✗ sB&B£12.50-£15 dB&B£25-£30 WB&B£87.50-£105 WBDi£155.75-£173.25 LDO 1pm
Lic 🅼 2P nc5yrs Ⓔ

See advertisement on page 441

GH QQ Ascot House 80 East Pde, Heworth YO3 7YH
☎(0904) 426826
This large semidetached Victorian house is about 10 minutes' walk east of the city centre, it features lofty bedrooms, mostly en suite, and many with 4- poster and canopied beds. There is a private car park at the back of the hotel.
15rm(5⇌7♰3hc) (3fb) CTV in all bedrooms ® ✱ sB&B£16-£18 sB&B⇌♰£18.50-£23 dB&B⇌♰£32-£36 WB&B£105-£126
🅼 CTV 14P sauna
Credit Cards 1 3 Ⓔ

See advertisement on page 441

GH QQQ *Ashbourne House* 139 Fulford Rd YO1 4HG
☎(0904) 639912
Located in a quiet area on the fringe of the city, with easy access to both the centre and the ring road, the Ashbourne offers neat modern bedrooms, a spacious lounge and dining room, and friendly service.
6rm(1⇌5♰) (1fb) CTV in all bedrooms ® LDO 7pm
Lic 🅼 CTV 5P 1🚗
Credit Cards 1 3

See advertisement on page 441

GH Q Avenue 6 The Avenue, Clifton YO3 6AS
☎(0904) 620575
This pantiled, late-Victorian mid-terrace house is situated in a quiet tree- lined avenue just off the A19 at Clifton, about 10 minutes' walk from the city centre. There is a combined lounge and dining room, and simple bedrooms recently redecorated by the new owners – all with colour TV and one with an en suite shower. Unrestricted kerbside parking is allowed in the avenue.
7rm(1↱6hc) (3fb) CTV in 1 bedroom TV in 6 bedrooms ® ✖ (ex guide dogs) * sB&B£15-£18 dB&B£26-£30 dB&B↱£30-£36
ꟿ CTV (£)

GH QQ Barclay Lodge 19/21 Gillygate YO3 7EA
☎(0904) 633274
Barclay Lodge consists of 2 converted Georgian town houses situated close to the Minster and the city centre. All the bedrooms have colour TV, tea-making facilities and central heating, there is a comfortable lounge and an attractive dining room. There is also a small bar for residents.
10rm(1⇌9hc) (3fb) CTV in all bedrooms ® ✖ * sB&B£17.50 dB&Bfr£35 dB&B⇌fr£42
Lic ꟿ CTV

GH QQ The Beckett 58 Bootham Crescent YO3 7AH
☎(0904) 644728
Closed 15 Dec-13 Jan
A privately owned terraced Victorian property situated in a quiet residential road off the A19 and convenient for the city centre. Although some bedrooms are fairly compact, they are pleasantly furnished and well maintained. There is also a comfortable lounge and a small breakfast room.
7rm(5↱2hc) (2fb) CTV in all bedrooms ® ✖ (ex guide dogs) sB&B£15-£17 dB&Bfr£30 dB&B↱£32-£36
ꟿ CTV 3P (£)

GH QQQ Bedford 108/110 Bootham YO3 7DG
☎(0904) 624412
Skilfully converted from 2 Victorian houses, this private hotel is nicely decorated and neatly maintained throughout. The bedrooms have good en suites supplied with large bath towels. Public areas consist of an attractive dining room, a lounge and a lounge bar (for residents only). The hotel has a large car park to the rear and is only a short walk from the city centre.
14rm(3⇌11↱) (3fb) CTV in all bedrooms ® ✖ (ex guide dogs) sB&B⇌↱£28-£34 dB&B⇌↱£40-£50 WB&B£140-£175 WBDi£199.50-£234.50 LDO 1pm
Lic ꟿ CTV 14P
Credit Cards 1 3 (£)

GH QQQ Beech House 6-7 Longfield Terrace, Bootham YO3 7DJ ☎(0904) 634581 & 630951
Closed Xmas & New Year
This family-run, Victorian terraced house is situated in a quiet street, 10 minutes' walk from the town centre. The en suite bedrooms are modern in style and are equipped with TV, telephones, radio alarms and tea/coffee-making facilities. Downstairs there is an attractive dining room and a cosy lounge.
9↱ CTV in all bedrooms ® T ✖ * sB&B↱£18-£24 dB&B↱£34-£46 LDO breakfast
ꟿ 5P nc10yrs (£)

GH QQQ Bootham Bar Hotel 4 High Petergate YO1 2EH
☎(0904) 658516
Closed 7-13 Jan
This delightful 18th-century house is just inside one of the fortified gateways to the city. It is well furnished with good facilities and a Victorian Parlour tea room which is open all day.
9rm(1⇌8↱) (2fb) CTV in all bedrooms ® ✖ (ex guide dogs) dB&B⇌↱£48-£64 LDO 7.30pm
Lic ꟿ 4P
Credit Cards 1 3 (£)

See advertisement on page 443

GH QQ *Brönte House* 22 Grosvenor Terrace, Bootham YO3 7AG ☎(0904) 621066
Closed 25 Dec
This Victorian terraced town house is situated just off the A19 on its approach to the town from the north, just 5 minutes' walk from the town. The family-run accommodation provides cheerful bedrooms, most with private bathrooms, and all having TV and tea-making facilities. There is an attractively decorated breakfast room and combined lounge.
8rm(5↱3hc) (1fb) CTV in all bedrooms ® ✖ (ex guide dogs)
ꟿ CTV 3P
Credit Cards 1 2 3

GH QQQ Byron House Hotel 7 Driffield Ter, The Mount YO2 2DD ☎(0904) 632525
Closed 24-26 Dec
This elegant late Regency-style end-of-terrace house has particularly lofty and spacious bedrooms of a modern design which will please both business and leisure guests. There is also a comfortable lounge and bar combined, with a number of dralon upholstered Chesterfields, where one can enjoy pre and after-dinner drinks. The dining room, with wheelback chairs and individual tables is situated on the lower ground floor. Private parking is provided at the front, and the hotel is conveniently situated west of the city centre, standing back from the A1036.
10rm(7⇌↱3hc) (4fb)⊁in 2 bedrooms CTV in all bedrooms ® T sB&B£25-£30 dB&B⇌↱£60-£70 WB&B£140-£200 WBDi£245-£305 LDO noon
Lic ꟿ 6P
Credit Cards 1 2 3 5 (£)

GH QQ Carousel 83 Eldon St, off Stanley St, Haxby Rd YO3 7NH ☎(0904) 646709
Closed Xmas & New Year
This friendly licensed guesthouse is situated within 10 minutes' walk of the city centre in an area of neat terraced houses. All →

Beech House

6-7 Longfield Terrace, Bootham, York
Tel: (0904) 634581

Beech House is family run and situated in a quiet tree lined street, less than ten minutes' walk from York Minster and the city centre.

- All rooms have ensuite shower and toilet
- Colour TV and clock radio in all rooms
- Direct dial telephone
- Tea & coffee making facilities
- Central heating & double glazing in all bedrooms
- Full English breakfast

Bed & breakfast, ensuite £17-24
Special Winter Breaks

Proprietors: Bill and Sheila Stratton

Ascot House

80 East Parade, Heworth, York YO3 7YH
Tel. 0904 426826

Within 15 minutes walk of the City Centre this family-run Victorian Villa offers many four poster or canopy beds, all usual en suite facilities and a large private car park.

Write or phone Mrs June Wood for a brochure.

FIRE CERTIFICATE

Ashbourne House Hotel

139 Fulford Road
York
YO1 4HG
Tel: 0904 639912

Lovely family run hotel.
Close York city. On-site parking. Convenient for the University and close to Fulford International Golf Course. Evening meals available. Licensed lounge bar. Full central heating. All rooms have wash hand basins, shaver point, colour TV, tea/coffee trays. All en-suite. Open all year. Reductions for children. Bargain Winter/Spring Breaks. Major credit cards accepted.

Arnot House

17 Grosvenor Terrace
York YO3 7AG
Telephone:
(0904) 641966

Spacious and tasteful, Arnot House aims to provide hotel comforts at guest house prices. Overlooking Bootham Park and the Minster, only 400 yards from the ancient city walls, it offers an ideal base from which to explore both York itself and the surrounding countryside. Brochure available.

• Full central heating • Evening meals on request • Vegetarian and special diets catered for • Tea/Coffee facilities and colour television in all rooms • Residential licence • Morning newspapers

bedrooms have en suite facilities and colour TV, there is a comfortable guests' lounge and an attractive dining room. A private car park is provided for residents.
9↱ (2fb) CTV in all bedrooms ® ✗ sB&B↱£15-£17.50 dB&B↱£30-£35 WB&B£100-£117.50 WBDi£156-£173.50 LDO 9.30am
Lic 𝍖 CTV 9P £

GH QQQ Cavalier Private Hotel 39 Monkgate YO3 7PB
☎(0904) 636615 & 640769
Closed 22 Dec-2 Jan
An early Georgian listed building situated close to the Minster and York's medieval streets and shopping centre. The comfortable accommodation has recently been completely renovated; most rooms have private bathrooms and all have TV and tea and coffee-making facilities. There is a comfortable lounge and an attractively appointed dining room, and car parking is provided.
10rm(2⇌5↱3hc) (4fb) CTV in all bedrooms ®
✗ (ex guide dogs) sB&B£18-£20 dB&B£36-£40 dB&B⇌↱£40-£44
Lic 𝍖 CTV 2P 3🚘 sauna

GH QQ City 68 Monkgate YO3 7PF ☎(0904) 622483
The City Guesthouse is an early Victorian terraced house situated close to the city walls and only 5 minutes' walk from the Minster. Most of the bedrooms have en suite facilities, and a private car park is available at the rear.
8rm(1⇌4↱3hc) (4fb)⚟in all bedrooms CTV in all bedrooms ® ✗ sB&B£11.50-£20 sB&B⇌↱£15-£20 dB&B£28-£36 dB&B⇌↱£28-£40 WB&B£105-£140
𝍖 6P 1🚘 nc5yrs
Credit Cards 1 3 £

GH QQ Clifton 127 Clifton YO3 6BL ☎(0904) 634031
Just a brisk 20 minutes' walk from the Bootham Bar (one of the city's gates), this end-terrace brick-faced house is on the A19 northern approach to the town, opposite the parish church. Bedrooms vary in size, some furnished in traditional style, and most have comfortable seating. Proprietor Jaqueline Jessup keeps a cosy house with personal touches such as potted plants and fresh flowers throughout. It is hoped that by 1993 all but one bedroom will have en suite facilities. Car parking is provided behind the house.
7rm(1⇌2↱4hc) CTV in all bedrooms ® ✗ ✱ sB&Bfr£15 sB&B⇌↱fr£15 dB&Bfr£30 dB&B⇌↱fr£30
𝍖 CTV 6P 1🚘

GH QQ Clifton Green Hotel 8 Clifton Green, Clifton YO3 6LH ☎(0904) 623597
Overlooking Clifton Green, just off the A19, and forming part of an attractive Victorian house, this friendly guesthouse is conveniently situated for the city centre and the northern ring road.
8rm(2↱6hc) CTV in all bedrooms ® ✗ (ex guide dogs)
Lic 𝍖 CTV 5🚘 £

See advertisement on page 445

GH QQQ *Coach House Hotel* Marygate YO3 7BH
☎(0904) 652780
The attractive interior, with beams, exposed brickwork and horse brasses, adds character to this hotel and restaurant situated only a few minutes' walk from the city centre. Many of the bedrooms have beams and most have en suite facilities. There is a cosy guests' lounge and the restaurant provides a wider than usual range of dishes.
13rm(5⇌6↱2hc) ® ✗ (ex guide dogs) LDO 9.30pm
Lic 𝍖 CTV 13P
Credit Cards 1 3

GH QQQ Collingwood Hotel 163 Holgate Rd YO2 4DF
☎(0904) 783333
This listed Georgian house is set in its own grounds on the A59 as it leaves the city in the direction of Harrogate, and has its own private car park at the side. All the bedrooms have en suite facilities, colour TV, clock radios and beverage trays, and one now →

has a 4-poster bed. There is an attractive dining room with individual tables, and a comfortable bar lounge opening onto a lawn and patio at the rear.
10rm(4⇌6♪) (2fb)⁄in 1 bedroom CTV in all bedrooms ® ✗ (ex guide dogs) sB&B⇌♪£36-£40 dB&B⇌♪£46-£54 WB&B£161-£189 LDO 8.30pm
Lic 卌 CTV 10P
Credit Cards [1] [2] [3] [5] £

GH Q Coppers Lodge 15 Alma Terrace, Fulford Rd YO1 4DQ ☎(0904) 639871
This former police station is situated in a quiet side road off the A19 close to the River Ouse, a short walk from the city walls. Bedrooms are simple, but there is an attractive breakfast room and cosy lounge.
8rm(1⇌♪7hc) (5fb) CTV in all bedrooms ® ✱ sB&B£15-£16 dB&Bfr£25 dB&B⇌♪fr£30 WB&B£91-£105 WBDi£133-£140 LDO 2pm
卌 CTV 2P £

GH QQ Crescent 77 Bootham YO3 7DQ ☎(0904) 623216
Very close to the city walls and within walking distance of the centre, this guesthouse provides modern well furnished bedrooms and friendly service.
10rm(9⇌♪1hc) (5fb) CTV in all bedrooms ® T ✗ ✱ sB&B⇌♪£15-£24 dB&B£28-£36 dB&B⇌♪£33-£48 WB&Bfr£105 WBDifr£168 LDO noon
Lic 卌 3P 1🚗
Credit Cards [1] [2] [3] [5] £

GH QQ Crossways 23 Wiggington Rd YO3 7HJ ☎(0904) 637250
A Victorian end-of-terrace house on the A1363 signed Helmsley, just a 10 minute walk from the minster. All rooms have en suite facilities as well as colour TV and tea-making facilities. There is also an attractive breakfast room.
6♪ CTV in all bedrooms ® ✗ (ex guide dogs) ✱ dB&B♪£28-£32 WB&Bfr£100
卌 3🚗

GH QQQ Curzon Lodge and Stable Cottages 23 Tadcaster Rd, Dringhouses YO2 2QG ☎(0904) 703157
Closed Xmas-New Year
A most attractive whitewashed listed building surrounded by its own well tended gardens, standing close to the race course on the main route into the city. The bedrooms feature stripped pine furniture and antique beds, and some in a converted stable block have the original beams.
5rm(3⇌2♪) Annexe 5rm(3⇌2♪) (1fb) CTV in all bedrooms ® T ✗ sB&B⇌♪£29.50-£38 dB&B⇌♪£42-£56
卌 16P nc7yrs
Credit Cards [1] [3] £

GH QQQ Dray Lodge Hotel Murton YO1 3UH (3m E off A166) ☎(0904) 489591 FAX (0904) 488587
This small hotel is in the village of Murton, just off the A166 close to its junction with the A64 and near to the Yorkshire Museum of Farming, about 3 miles east of the city. It was built in 1830 as a carriage or rulley works, and many original features including oak and pitch pine beams have been retained. Bedrooms are attractively decorated and have en suite facilities as well as colour TVs, telephones and radios. There is a nicely furnished restaurant, a cosy bar and a comfortable guests' lounge, with ample parking at the rear.
8rm(7⇌♪1hc) (1fb) CTV in all bedrooms ® T sB&B⇌♪£25-£30 dB&B⇌♪£36-£44 LDO 8pm
Lic 卌 CTV 15P gymnasium fitness training room beauty salon
Credit Cards [1] [2] [3] £

GH QQQ *Field House Hotel* 2 St George's Place YO2 2DR ☎(0904) 639572
Closed Xmas
Conveniently situated for both the racecourse and the town centre, this impressive house provides spacious bedrooms, a comfortable lounge and an attractive dining room.
17rm(1⇌10♪6hc) CTV in all bedrooms ® ✗ (ex guide dogs) LDO 7pm
Lic 卌 20P
Credit Cards [1] [2] [3]

GH QQQ *Four Poster Lodge* 68-70 Heslington Rd, off Barbican Rd YO1 5AU ☎(0904) 651170
This Victorian villa has been tastefully restored by hosts Peter and Judith Jones; it is situated in a residential area of the city, yet within a short walk of the city's tourist attractions and shops. Many of the bedrooms have 4- poster beds, and are very attractively decorated. Some rooms have private bathrooms, TV, radio alarms, hairdryers and tea and coffee-making facilities; some feature antique fireplaces. Downstairs there is a very comfortable bar/lounge, and hearty English breakfasts are served in the dining room. There is a private car park at the rear of the guesthouse.
10rm(8♪2hc) (2fb) CTV in all bedrooms ® LDO 6pm
Lic 卌 5P 3🚗
Credit Cards [1] [3]

GH QQ Four Seasons Hotel 7 St Peters Grove, Clifton YO3 6AQ ☎(0904) 622621 FAX (0904) 430565
Closed 24 Dec-1 Jan
A handsome house situated in a tree-lined Victorian cul-de-sac just off the A19 on the outskirts of the city centre offers spacious, well maintained bedrooms, a comfortable lounge, and friendly service from its proprietors.
5♪ (2fb) CTV in all bedrooms ® ✗ (ex guide dogs) ✱ sB&B♪fr£27 dB&B♪£44-£50 WB&B£154-£175
Lic 卌 CTV 6P
Credit Cards [1] [3] £

Four Poster Lodge Hotel

A Victorian villa lovingly restored and furnished, situated between the university and York's historic centre. Enjoy our relaxing atmosphere, good food, (English breakfast a speciality) and quality service.

Our amenities include a residents licence and private car park. The four poster bedrooms have private facilities and are fully equipped for your comfort.

Yours hosts Mr & Mrs Peter Jones

70 Heslington Road, off Barbican Road, York, YO1 5AU.
Telephone: 0904 651170

Derwent Lodge

Low Catton, Stamford Bridge, York YO4 1EA
Tel: (0759) 71468

Comfortable, spacious country house in small village, 8 miles east of York. Full central heating, open fires, fresh home cooked food. Tea/coffee and colour TV in all rooms. 4 rooms have private facilities and 1 ground floor bedroom. After sampling the delights of historic York, return to country house hospitality at its best. Dinner, afternoon tea, snacks and packed lunches available. Open Feb-Nov inc.

Field House Hotel

2 St. George's Place, Tadcaster Road, York YO2 2DR
Tel: 0904-639572

Owner-Managers: Ernie and Susan Wright

Discover for yourself the delights of the Field House Hotel, tucked away from the hustle and bustle of city life, yet within easy walking distance of all York's historic attractions. this charming Victorian residence offers you tasteful accommodation whilst retaining the warmth and friendly atmosphere of a family-owned and managed hotel. All bedrooms en suite with colour television, radio, direct dial telephone and tea/coffee trays. There is easy access from the A64 on the A1036.

Clifton Green Hotel

8 CLIFTON GREEN, YORK YO3 6LH
Tel: 0904 623597

Small elegant hotel, attractive location overlooking Clifton Village Green, just ten minutes' walk City Centre and York Minster.

Spacious comfortable bedrooms some with en-suite bathroom, and all with colour television.

The restaurant offers a varied menu.

The hotel is licensed and bar meals are also available.

The owner gives careful attention to the comfort and needs of her guests.

Private parking.

GH QQ Freshney's Hotel 54 Low Petergate YO1 2HZ ☎(0904) 622478 FAX (0904) 426931
12rm(5↱7hc) (1fb) CTV in all bedrooms ® T ✱ sB&B£25 dB&B£30-£40 dB&B↱£50-£55 LDO 9.30pm
Lic 𝍔 9P (£2 per day)
Credit Cards 1 3 £

SELECTED

GH QQQQ Grasmead House Hotel 1 Scarcroft Hill, The Mount YO2 1DF ☎(0904) 629996
Just outside the city walls but within easy walking distance of all the central attractions, this delightful small, family-run hotel is owned by the warm and friendly Eileen and Len Spray. Bedrooms feature antique furniture and 4-poster beds, one of which dates from 1730, and offer every modern convenience including en suite bathrooms and tea-making facilities. Some rooms also have views of the distant Minster. Downstairs, there is a comfortable lounge with a small bar in one corner, and an attractive dining room where a full English breakfast is served.
6⇌↱ (2fb)⊬in 3 bedrooms CTV in all bedrooms ® ✗ dB&B⇌↱£54 WB&B£170
Lic 𝍔 CTV 1P
Credit Cards 1 3 £

GH QQ Greenside 124 Clifton YO3 6BQ ☎(0904) 623631
This attractive detached conservation house is situated on the A19, north of the city centre overlooking Clifton Green. The good sized bedrooms, all with central heating and colour TV, are mostly on the first floor, but there is one on the ground floor at the rear with an en suite shower and WC. The pretty dining room features separate tables with lace cloths and wheelback chairs, and there is a comfortable guests' lounge with TV. Private parking facilities are available at the rear.
6rm(3↱3hc) (2fb) CTV in all bedrooms sB&Bfr£15 sB&B↱fr£28 dB&Bfr£25 dB&B↱fr£28
Lic 𝍔 CTV 5P 1🚗 £

GH QQQ The Heathers 54 Shipton Rd, Clifton – Without YO3 6RQ ☎(0904) 640989
Situated on the A19 York to Thirsk road, this 1930s detached house is a comfortable family home, with many thoughtful touches provided and tastefully decorated throughout. The bedrooms have been furnished to a high standard and are decorated with designer fabrics and antique furniture. Those at the rear overlook a large garden and the front rooms have views of meadowland and in the distance a cricket field. There is a breakfast room on the ground floor which also contains lounge furniture and a TV.
5rm(2↱3hc) (1fb)⊬in all bedrooms ® ✗ ✱ dB&B£26-£30 dB&B↱£34-£40
𝍔 CTV 6P nc4yrs

GH Q *Heworth* 126 East Pde YO3 7YG ☎(0904) 426384
A small friendly, family-run guesthouse in a quiet residential area about 15 minutes' walk from the city centre. Bedrooms are attractively decorated, and in addition to the traditional breakfast various vegetarian dishes are available.
6hc CTV in all bedrooms ®
Lic 𝍔 1P 1🚗

GH Q Hillcrest 110 Bishopthorpe Rd YO2 1JX ☎(0904) 653160
This Victorian terraced house has high ceilings and large windows, making the bedrooms appear more spacious and freshly decorated. They are well equipped with TV and beverage trays, and 2 have en suite showers. There is a large, comfortable lounge, an attractive dining room and a private car park at the rear.
12rm(2↱10hc) (4fb) CTV in all bedrooms ® sB&B£13-£17 dB&B£24-£30 dB&B↱£28-£34 WB&B£91-£119 WBDi£136.50-£164.50 LDO 3pm
𝍔 CTV 8P 1🚗
Credit Cards 1 3 £

GH QQ The Hollies 141 Fulford Rd YO1 4HG ☎(0904) 634279
Closed Xmas
This comfortable family-run guesthouse is situated on the A19 about a mile from the city centre and a similar distance from the southern bypass, convenient for the university. All rooms have colour TV and tea-making facilities and 2 have en suite showers. There is also a spacious guests' lounge.
5rm(2↱3hc) (3fb) CTV in all bedrooms ® ✱ sB&B£15-£23 sB&B↱£17-£26 dB&B£28-£38 dB&B↱£32-£44
𝍔 CTV 5P
Credit Cards 1 3 £

GH QQQ Holmwood House Hotel 112-114 Holgate Rd YO2 4BB ☎(0904) 626183 FAX (0904) 670899
rs 25-31 Dec
This delightful private hotel was converted from 2 early Victorian terraced houses and is conveniently situated on the A59 Harrogate road, within easy walking distance of the city centre. Bedrooms are spotlessly clean and well equipped, there is a small garden, and ample parking at the rear. Friendly hosts Christina and Roberto Gramellini are always willing to give advice on York's many attractions.
11⇌↱ (1fb)⊬in 6 bedrooms CTV in all bedrooms ® T sB&B⇌↱£35-£42 dB&B⇌↱£48-£65 WB&B£160-£180 WBDi£226-£245 LDO 7pm
Lic 𝍔 9P nc8yrs
Credit Cards 1 3

GH QQ Inglewood 7 Clifton Green YO3 6LH ☎(0904) 653523
This friendly and comfortable guesthouse is just off the A19 overlooking Clifton Green. It is a convenient location within easy reach of the city centre and outlying areas.
7rm(3↱4hc) (2fb) CTV in all bedrooms ✗
𝍔 CTV 1🚗 £

GH QQ Jubilee 120 Haxby Rd YO3 7JP ☎(0904) 620566
Closed Xmas & New Year
A late-Victorian terraced house with private parking at the rear, situated 10 minutes' walk away from the Minster and city centre. Three rooms have full en suite facilities, and all have TV and provisions for making tea and coffee.
5rm(3↱2hc) (1fb) CTV in all bedrooms ® ✗ (ex guide dogs) sB&B£14-£18 dB&B£24-£30 dB&B↱£26-£34
𝍔 4P nc4yrs £

GH QQ Limes Hotel 135 Fulford Rd YO1 4HE ☎(0904) 624548
Situated on a corner plot, to the south side of the city, this large detached house is conveniently positioned for both the bypass and University. The majority of bedrooms are a good size and offer satellite TV. There is a comfortable lounge bar (for residents only) and an attractive dining room where it may be necessary to share a table at certain times.
10↱ (2fb)⊬in all bedrooms CTV in all bedrooms ® ✗ sB&B↱£16-£46 dB&B↱£30-£48 WB&B£100-£300 WBDi£150-£350 LDO 6.30pm
Lic 𝍔 14P
Credit Cards 1 3 £

See advertisement on page 449

GH QQ Linden Lodge Hotel Nunthorpe Avenue, Scarcroft Rd YO2 1PF ☎(0904) 620107
Closed 23 Dec-9 Jan
In a quiet residential area close to the city centre, this cosy establishment offers neat bedroom accommodation and a spacious lounge and dining room.
12rm(5↱7hc) (3fb) CTV in 4 bedrooms ® ✗ sB&B£16-£18 sB&B↱£20-£25 dB&B£30-£34 dB&B↱£36-£42

→

Inglewood

GUEST HOUSE

7 Clifton Green, York
York 0904 653523

In this charming Victorian House guests will instantly feel completely at home.

The friendliness and warmth of your host will ensure an enjoyable and relaxing stay.

Spacious accommodation, some bedrooms en-suite, all with colour TV and modern amenities.

An ideal base from which to visit the many attractions of York.

Greenside

124 Clifton, York. Telephone York 623631

Greenside is a charming detached conservation house fronting on to Clifton Green.

Situated in a most convenient location just outside the city walls close to the many attractions that York has to offer.

Spacious fully equipped large bedrooms are all situated on ground or first floor. All rooms centrally heated. Early morning tea available on request. Ample bath, shower and WC facilities. Spacious lounge with colour TV. Enclosed car park. First class English Breakfast and Evening Meals. Registered with English Tourist Board. Fire Certificate. Licensed.

HEWORTH GUEST HOUSE

126 East Parade Heworth
York YO3 7YG
Telephone: 0904 426384

A small friendly guest house within walking distance of the city centre. Ample car parking, all rooms have colour TV, tea and coffee making facilities. A full English breakfast or Continental is included. We can also cater for vegetarians or vegans etc.

The resident proprietors Chris and Sue will ensure a warm friendly welcome.

A small family owned and run hotel situated within easy walking distance of the City Centre. Restful nights are assured in our luxurious centrally heated bedrooms, all with antique four-poster beds. All bedrooms have private bathroom, tea and coffee making facilities, colour TV.

The resident Proprietors, Eileen and Len Spray ensure that a real welcome and personal service awaits each and every guest.

GRASMEAD HOUSE HOTEL
1 Scarcroft Hill
York YO2 1DF
Telephone York (0904) 629996

Lic 🍽 CTV ⚘
Credit Cards [1] [3] £

GH QQQ Midway House Hotel 145 Fulford Rd YO1 4HG
☎(0904) 659272
This detached Victorian house has been tastefully modernised to offer well appointed and comfortable accommodation and an attractive dining room where a choice of menus is available offering reasonably priced dinners.
12rm(11 1hc) (2fb) in all bedrooms CTV in all bedrooms ® (ex guide dogs) dB&B£34-£42 dB&B £38-£50 LDO 7pm
Lic 🍽 14P
Credit Cards [1] [2] [3] [5] £

GH Q Minster View 2 Grosvenor Ter YO3 7AG
☎(0904) 655034
This tall, Victorian terraced house is situated close to the town centre and offers neat, clean bedrooms and a most attractive dining room.
9rm(5 4hc) (4fb) CTV in all bedrooms ® ✻ sB&B£14-£17 dB&B£28-£32 dB&B £30-£38 WB&B£98-£119 WBDi£161-£182 LDO 5.30pm
Lic 🍽 CTV 6P £

GH Q *Moat Hotel* Nunnery Ln YO2 1AA ☎(0904) 652926
Very conveniently situated, the Moat Hotel is close to the railway station and city centre, and has its own private car park. Once a hospital for underprivileged ladies, rebuilt in the 1860s, it provides comfortable accommodation with mostly en suite bedrooms.
9rm(6 3hc) (1fb) CTV in all bedrooms ® (ex guide dogs)
Lic 🍽 CTV 10P
Credit Cards [1] [2] [3] [5]

GH QQ Monkgate Lodge 51 Monkgate YO3 7PB
☎(0904) 631501
This small family-run guesthouse is conveniently situated close to the city centre. There are 2 well furnished bedrooms and a good breakfast is served in the attractive dining room.
2 (1fb) in all bedrooms CTV in all bedrooms ®
🍽 CTV nc5yrs £

GH QQQ Orchard Court Hotel 4 St Peters Grove YO3 6AQ
☎(0904) 653964
A large, impressive Victorian house set within its own garden in a tree-lined avenue, close to the town centre. The accommodation is generally spacious; bedrooms are well appointed and the lofty public rooms are tastefully decorated.
11rm(8 3hc) (4fb) CTV in all bedrooms ®
(ex guide dogs) sB&Bfr£20 sB&B £25-£30 dB&B £44-£58 LDO 7.30pm
Lic 🍽 CTV 12P
Credit Cards [1] [3] £

GH QQQ *Le Petit Hotel & Reataurant Francais* 103 Mount Rd YO2 2AX ☎(0904) 647339
Conveniently situated between the town centre and racecourse, this small guesthouse has neat accommodation and the resident proprietor gives guests a warm welcome.
6 (1fb) CTV in all bedrooms ® LDO 7pm
Lic 🍽 CTV 1
Credit Cards [1] [2] [3]

GH QQ Priory Hotel 126 Fulford Rd YO1 4BE
☎(0904) 625280
Closed Xmas
A pair of large double-fronted Victorian town houses have been converted into a very comfortable hotel with rear gardens, and situated near the city centre. Bedrooms are neat and well appointed, and menus are interesting, extensive and good value.
20 (5fb) CTV in all bedrooms ® (ex guide dogs) ✻ sB&B £25-£30 dB&B £45-£50 LDO 9.15pm
Lic 🍽 CTV 25P
Credit Cards [1] [2] [3] [5] £

See advertisement on page 451

GH QQQ St Denys Hotel St Denys Rd YO1 1DQ
☎(0904) 622207
Closed 2wks Xmas
Former vicarage offers comfortable spacious accommodation and cosy lounge.
10 (4fb) in 2 bedrooms CTV in all bedrooms ® **T** sB&B £25-£35 dB&B £40-£50 LDO noon
Lic 🍽 CTV 9P
Credit Cards [1] [3] £

GH QQ St Georges House Hotel 6 St Georges Place, Tadcaster Rd YO2 2DR ☎(0904) 625056
A large, semidetached Victorian house situated in a quiet residential area just off the A64 on its approach to the city from Leeds, and close to the racecourse. Most bedrooms have en suite facilities, and they all have TV, radio alarms and provisions for making tea.
10rm(1 7 2hc) (5fb) CTV in all bedrooms ® ✻ sB&Bfr£22 sB&B £27 dB&B£30-£40 dB&B £35-£45 WB&Bfr£140 WBDifr£180 LDO 7pm
Lic 🍽 6P (charged) 1
Credit Cards [1] [3] £

GH QQ St Raphael 44 Queen Anne's Rd, Bootham YO3 7AF
☎(0904) 645028
This is a gabled semidetached house with a mock-Tudor façade, situated in a quiet cul-de-sac. The modern bedrooms are brightly decorated with comfortable furnishings and all are centrally heated. There is no lounge, although the dining room is a good size, with individual tables. Kerbside parking is allowed in the road outside the house.
8rm(3 5hc) (2fb) CTV in all bedrooms ® ✻ sB&B£14-£17 dB&B£24-£29 dB&B £29-£34 LDO 4pm
🍽 CTV ⚘
Credit Cards [1] [3]

GH QQQ *Scarcroft Hotel* 61 Wentworth Rd, The Mount YO2 1DG ☎(0904) 633386
Situated in a quiet residential area, this red-brick terraced house has been carefully and tastefully restored by the present owners, who are always on hand to attend to the guests' needs, in a friendly and helpful manner. The bedrooms are all attractive and individually decorated, although they do vary in size from compact singles to the more elegantly furnished doubles – one of which has a 4-poster bed and sunken bath. There is a comfortable lounge and pretty breakfast room, with a small bar and French windows overlooking the patio – where guests may sit on warm days. The house is well cared for with high standards of housekeeping throughout.
7rm(1 6) in all bedrooms CTV in all bedrooms ® (ex guide dogs)
Lic 🍽 CTV

See advertisement on page 450

GH QQ Sycamore 19 Sycamore Place YO3 7DW
☎(0904) 624712
Closed Dec
Boasting a most attractive front garden displaying lots of flowers and an old street gas lamp, this delightful little guesthouse, with its mock tudor gable, is situated in a quiet cul-de-sac only a short walk from the city centre. The bedrooms are attractively decorated with comfortable furnishings and family rooms are available. Providing an attractive setting for the first meal of the day, the breakfast room has individual tables. There is no lounge but guests have access to their bedrooms at all times.
6rm(2 4hc) (1fb) CTV in all bedrooms ® sB&B£15-£20 dB&B£28-£32
🍽 3P nc5yrs

See advertisement on page 450

Book as early as possible for busy holiday periods.

ORCHARD COURT HOTEL

Delightful small Victorian hotel with PRIVATE car park. Pleasantly situated in QUIET location within easy walking distance of City Centre. Comfortable centrally heated en suite bedrooms all with colour TV & complimentary Tea/Coffee trays. A friendly family run hotel with a relaxed atmosphere offering full English breakfast and traditional home cooked evening meals.

ST. PETERS GROVE, BOOTHAM, YORK YO3 6AQ
Tel: 0904 653964

LINDEN LODGE HOTEL

Proprietors: Joan and Bill Wharton

6 Nunthorpe Avenue, Scarcroft Road, York Tel: (0904) 620107

Family run hotel. Licensed.
2 crown status ETB. AA 2 QQ.
En suite, standard single, twin, double & family rooms.
Situated in a quiet cul de sac 10-15 minutes walk from rail station, city centre, racecourse and places of historic interest.

MOAT HOTEL

Nunnery Lane, York, YO2 1AA
Telephone: (0904) 652926

City centre hotel, adjacent to medieval city walls, five minutes walk from Station and Castle Museum.
PRIVATE PARKING
All rooms with private facilities, colour TV and tea/coffee making.
Licensed lounge bar.
Bed and English Breakfast from £18.00.

The Limes

135 Fulford Road, York YO1 4HE
Telephone: (0904) 624548

A small family run hotel with private car parking. Close to Fulford Golf Course and York University and within easy walking distance of the City centre. Most of our 10 rooms are with private facilities all with full central heating and colour, satellite television. The bar lounge is situated on the ground floor where tea, coffee or alcoholic beverages are served. Evening meals available. Children welcome. **No pets. No smoking in bedrooms or dining room.**

GH QQ Tower 2 Feversham Crescent, Wigginton Rd
YO3 7HQ ☎(0904) 655571 & 635924
Closed 25 Dec-Jan

Distinguished by its blue window canopies, this Edwardian house is within easy walking distance of the city centre. The bedrooms provide all contemporary comforts and have been tastefully modernised with white furniture, bright wall coverings and attractive curtains. A spacious dining room is provided, enhanced by small flower arrangements and paintings hanging on the wall. Private parking is available at the front of the hotel.

6⇌↱ (4fb) CTV in all bedrooms ® ✗ (ex guide dogs)
sB&B⇌↱£16-£20 dB&B⇌↱£30-£38 LDO 10.30am
6P
Credit Cards [1] [3]

'Selected' establishments, which have the highest quality award, are highlighted by a tinted panel. For a full list of these establishments, consult the Contents page.

IRELAND

USEFUL INFORMATION - IRELAND

In most instances, the details for establishments in the Irish directory are as outlined in 'Your stay - what you need to know' on page 14, the explanation of Symbols and Abbreviations and the 'How to use the Guide' section on page 33.

1 Town and Country
In the Republic of Ireland establishments classified as Town & Country Houses are indicated by the abbreviation T&C. Because of statutary regulations regarding operation, these properties cannot be officially classified as Guesthouses although their facilities are similar.

2 Map references
In the Irish Directory the six figure map references shown against establishments have been taken from the Irish National Grid.

3 Prices
In the Republic of Ireland prices are quoted in Punts, indicated by the symbol IR£. The rates of exchange between Pounds Sterling and Punts is liable to fluctuate.

In the Republic of Ireland, as part of the registration scheme operated by 'Bord Failte', establishments must display tariffs; these are usually shown in bedrooms or reception. The application of VAT and service charges varies, but all prices quoted must be inclusive of VAT.

4 Telephone Numbers
The area codes shown against the numbers in the Republic of Ireland are applicable within the Republic only. Similarly, the area codes shown for entries in Great Britain and Northern Ireland. Check your Telephone Directory for details.

5 Fire Precautions
In Northern Ireland the Fire Precautions Act 1971 does not apply. The Fire Services (NI) Order 1984 covers hotel and boarding houses providing sleeping accommodation for more than six persons, which must have a fire certificate issued by the Northern Ireland Fire Authority. Properties that sleep less must satisfy the Authority that they have adequate exits. In the Republic of Ireland AA officials inspect emergency notices, fire-fighting machinery and fire exits, although fire safety regulations are a matter for local authority fire services. You are strongly urged to read and understand emergency notices for your own and other people's safety.

6 Licensing Regulations
In Northern Ireland public houses open 11.30-23.00 Monday-Saturday, 12.30-14.30 and 19.00-22.00 Sunday. Also Christmas Day 12.30-22.00. Hotels can serve residents seven days a week without restriction. On Sundays non-residents may be served 12.00-14.30 and 19.00-22.00, and on Christmas Day 12.30-22.00. Children under 18 not allowed in the bar area of licensed premises, neither can they buy or consume liquor in hotels.

In the Republic of Ireland general licensing hours under present legislation are
10.30-23.00 Monday-Saturday winter and 10.30-23.30 summer. On Sundays and St Patrick's Day 12.30-14.00 and 16.00-23.00. No service on Christmas Day and Good Friday.

ACHILL ISLAND Co Mayo Map **01** A4

SELECTED

GH QQQQ ***Gray's*** Dugort ☎(098) 43244 & 43315
Mar-7 Oct
Comfortable accommodation in a quiet location with ample lounge space. Family holidays especially catered for.
8hc Annexe 7rm(5↑2hc) ✗ LDO 6pm
ΨΨ CTV 18P table tennis pool table

🛏☎ **T&C QQ West Coast House** School Rd, Dooagh
☎(098) 43317
This smart new house is in an elevated position giving superb views over Dooagh to the sea. It is furnished to a high standard, and no effort is spared to make guests comfortable.
4rm(2↑2hc) (1fb)⊘in all bedrooms ✗ (ex guide dogs) sB&BIR£14-IR£15 sB&B↑IR£16-IR£18 dB&BIR£24-IR£25 dB&B↑IR£26-IR£28 WB&BIR£75-IR£80 WBDiIR£140-IR£150
ΨΨ 4P

ADARE Co Limerick Map **01** B3

T&C QQQ Coatesland House Killarney Rd, Graigue
☎Limerick(061) 396372
Closed 25 Dec
Coatesland House, situated on the main Killarney road (N21) 5 minutes from Adare village, is a very well appointed house with attractive bedrooms, all en suite. Proprietors Florence and Donal Hogan are welcoming and friendly and give superb attention to detail. Dinner is available. Nearby activities include hunting, fishing, golf and there is also an equestrian centre.
6↑ (3fb) CTV in 3 bedrooms ® **T** sB&B↑IR£18 dB&B↑IR£30 WBDiIR£175 LDO noon
ΨΨ CTV 25P 🐎
Credit Cards [1] [2] [3]

ANNAMOE Co Wicklow Map **01** D3

T&C Q Carmel's ☎(0404) 45297
Etr-Oct
Modern bungalow with nice gardens situated in scenic touring area of Co Wicklow on R755 route. Easy access to all areas of local interest.
4rm(3↑1hc) (2fb) ✗ ✻ dB&BfrIR£24 dB&B↑frIR£30 WB&BfrIR£100 LDO noon
ΨΨ CTV P

ANTRIM Co Antrim Map **01** D5

GH QQ The Beeches Dunadry Rd, Muckamore BT41 2RR
☎Temple Patrick(08494) 33161
Quietly situated in very well tended gardens with open country aspects, this 2-storey, red-brick Edwardian family home is just off the A6, close to the airport. Proprietor Marigold Allen has recently extended the property to provide 3 new bedrooms with en suite showers and all rooms have comfortable seating. Hearty breakfasts are served in the Ulster tradition and evening meals can be provided with advance notification. The furniture and décor throughout is cosy and the guests' lounge is no exception with its comfortable armchairs.
6rm(5↑1hc) ⊘in all bedrooms CTV in all bedrooms ® ✗ (ex guide dogs) sB&B£30 sB&B↑£30 dB&B↑£50 LDO 3pm
ΨΨ 8P
Credit Cards [1] [3]

Book as early as possible for busy holiday periods.

ARDARA Co Donegal Map **01** B5

T&C QQQ Bay View Country House Portnoo Rd
☎(075) 41145
Mar-5 Nov
Large, modern bungalow, on the outskirts of a small town, overlooking the sea.
6↑ (2fb)⊘in all bedrooms ✗ sB&B↑IR£17 dB&B↑IR£27 LDO noon
ΨΨ CTV 20P

ARDEE Co Louth Map **01** C4

SELECTED

GH QQQQ ***The Gables House*** Dundalk Rd
☎Drogheda(041) 53789
Closed first 2wks in Jun & Nov
Smart, comfortable house with a historic past. Very fully equipped bedrooms and a popular restaurant offering excellent food.
5rm(2⇨1↑2hc) (2fb) CTV in all bedrooms ® ✗ (ex guide dogs) LDO 9.30pm
Lic ΨΨ 20P
Credit Cards [1] [2] [3] [5]

ARKLOW Co Wicklow Map **01** D3

FH QQ M T Bourke ***Killinskyduff*** *(T254731)*
☎(0402) 32185
Jun-Sep
Large, modern farmhouse with well-tended lawns and garden, in peaceful surroundings, convenient to the sea.
3hc (3fb)⊘in 2 bedrooms ✗ LDO 4pm
ΨΨ CTV 20P 2⌂ nc12yrs 165 acres hens tillage
Credit Cards [1] [2] [3] [5]

ATHLONE Co Westmeath Map **01** C4

T&C QQ ***Rocwal*** The Beeches, Coosan ☎(0902) 75640
Apr-Oct
Modern bungalow in quiet location on outskirts of town.
4rm(2↑2hc) (1fb) ® ✗ (ex guide dogs)
ΨΨ CTV 6P

AVOCA Co Wicklow Map **01** D3

🛏☎ **T&C QQQ Ashdene** Knockanree Lower
☎Arklow(0402) 35327
Apr-Oct
Modern dormer bungalow in scenic countryside; ideal centre for touring the beauty spots of Co Wicklow.
5rm(4↑1hc) (2fb)⊘in all bedrooms ✗ sB&BIR£14-IR£18 sB&B↑frIR£18 dB&BfrIR£24 dB&B↑frIR£29 WB&BfrIR£87 WBDifrIR£160 LDO noon
ΨΨ CTV 5P 🎾(grass)

T&C QQ ***Riverview House*** ☎Arklow(0402) 35181
Apr-Oct
A split-level house on the side of a hill overlooking the river and the village of Avoca.
5hc (1fb)
CTV 8P 1⌂

BALLINA Co Mayo Map **01** B4

T&C QQ Whitestream House (N57) Foxford Rd
☎(096) 21582
Imposing large modern house situated on main Dublin road into Ballina. Specially geared for fishing fraternity.
6rm(5↑1hc) (2fb) ® ✗ ✻ sB&BfrIR£16 sB&B↑frIR£18 dB&BfrIR£24 dB&B↑frIR£28 LDO 4pm

→

CTV 10P
Credit Cards 3

BALLINADEE Co Cork Map **01** B2

SELECTED

T&C QQQQ Glebe House ☎(021) 778294
FAX (021) 778456
Closed 2wks Xmas
Lovely old house in well kept gardens. Beautifully furnished rooms with many antiques and proprietors looking for ways to spoil guests.
4rm(2⇌2) (2fb) CTV in 1 bedroom ® T
(ex guide dogs) sB&B⇌frIR£25 dB&B⇌frIR£40
LDO noon
Lic 30P croquet lawn badminton
Credit Cards 1 3

BALLINHASSIG Co Cork Map **01** B2

T&C Q Blanchfield House Rigsdale ☎Cork(021) 885167
Mar-Oct rs Nov-Feb
In quiet and peaceful setting. Trout and salmon fishing.
6rm(2⇌4hc) (2fb) (ex guide dogs) * sB&BfrIR£21
sB&B⇌frIR£26 dB&BfrIR£32 dB&B⇌frIR£37
WB&BfrIR£100 WBDifrIR£175 LDO 9pm
Lic 20P
Credit Cards 1 2 3 5

BALLINSKELLIGS Co Kerry Map **01** A2

GH Q Sigerson Arms ☎(0667) 9104 FAX (0667) 9171
May-Sep
Simple, family-run guesthouse with good sea views from bedrooms. Good home cooking.
8hc (ex guide dogs) * dB&BfrIR£37.40 WB&BfrIR£138.60
LDO 9pm
Lic CTV 50P (charged) sauna
Credit Cards 1 3

BALLYBUNION Co Kerry Map **01** A3

T&C QQQ *The Country House* Rahavanig, Car Ferry Rd
☎(068) 27103
Modern house built in neo-Georgian style convenient for Tarbert Car Ferry.
4rm(3 1hc) (1fb) CTV in 1 bedroom (ex guide dogs)
CTV 5P
Credit Cards 1

GH QQ Eagle Lodge ☎(068) 27224 & 27403
Mar-Nov
Off main street in seaside resort. Comfortable accommodation.
8 * sB&BIR£20-IR£30 dB&BIR£30-IR£50
WBDifrIR£180 LDO 9pm
Lic CTV 11P

BALLYCASTLE Co Antrim Map **01** D6

GH Q *Hilsea* 28 Quay Hill BT54 6BH ☎(02657) 62385
Run by the same family for many years, this large, white-painted Victorian villa overlooking Ballycastle Bay offers ample public areas and modest bedrooms.
19hc (4fb) LDO 7.30pm
CTV 70P
Credit Cards 1 2 3

BALLYMACARBRY Co Waterford Map **01** C2

GH QQQ Clonanav Farm Nire Valley
☎Clonmel(052) 36141
Feb-Nov
Modern bungalow in peaceful location with panoramic views.
10 (1fb) (ex guide dogs) sB&BIR£25 dB&BIR£40
WB&BIR£130 WBDiIR£214
Lic CTV 10P (grass)

BALLYMURN Co Wexford Map **01** D3

SELECTED

FH QQQQ Mr & Mrs J Maher **Ballinkeele House** *(T030334)* ☎(053) 38105 FAX (053) 38468
Mar-12 Nov rs Feb & Oct-11 Nov
Built in 1840, designed by Daniel Robertson and standing in 360 acres. This classical house has been lovingly restored by owners John and Margaret Maher, completely retaining its ambience while providing today's comforts. Lovely drawing and dining room. Very comfortable bedrooms with decanter of sherry to welcome you.
4 (ex guide dogs) sB&BIR£30-IR£32
dB&BIR£52-IR£56 WB&BIR£165-IR£180 LDO noon
Lic 20P (hard)snooker croquet 350 acres arable
Credit Cards 1 3
See advertisement under WEXFORD

BALLYVAUGHAN Co Clare Map **01** B3

SELECTED

T&C QQQQ Rusheen Lodge ☎(065) 77092
FAX (065) 77152
Closed 17 Dec-Jan
A charming house nestling in the valley of the Burren Limestone mountains, an area famous for its Arctic and Alpine plants in spring and summer. The McGann family were founders of the famous Aillwee Caves and are a fund of local folklore. The bedrooms are excellent, large and well equipped with attractive décor and all the little extras that ensure a comfortable visit. The cosy dining room has patio gardens leading off. Car parking is available.
6⇌ (3fb) ® T (ex guide dogs) * sB&B⇌IR£20-IR£30 dB&B⇌IR£32-IR£36
CTV 12P
Credit Cards 1 3

BANGOR Co Down Map **01** D5

GH QQQ *Shelleven House* 59/61 Princetown Rd BT20 3TA
☎(0247) 271777
Situated in a residential area, this Victorian end-of-terrace property consists of 2 houses joined together to provide spacious and tasteful accommodation. The majority of bedrooms have en suite facilities and are decorated in coordinating styles, the most spacious rooms, which overlook the sea, are suitable for families. Frances Davis prides herself on the quality of food served to her guests, which includes a hearty Ulster breakfast. The lounge, which adjoins the neatly laid out dining room, has comfortable winged Queen Anne chairs with a bay window overlooking the gardens and is equipped with TV and a selection of books. Plenty of parking is available within the grounds.
14⇌ (3fb) CTV in all bedrooms ®
CTV 12P

BANSHA Co Tipperary Map **01** B3

SELECTED

FH QQQQ J & M Marnane **Bansha House** *(R962320)* ☎(062) 54194 FAX (062) 52499
Closed Xmas

Situated in a very scenic area on the N24, this award-winning Georgian house is approached by an avenue of beech trees, and has 100 acres of land where visitors can roam. It is comfortable, very well furnished and noted for its home baking.

7rm(4⮣ 3hc) (1fb) ✗ (ex guide dogs) sB&BIR£15-IR£16 dB&BIR£28-IR£32 dB&B⮣frIR£32 LDO 7pm
CTV 10P 100 acres mixed

BANTRY Co Cork Map **01** A2

T&C QQQ Shangri-La Glengarriff Rd ☎(027) 50244
Closed Xmas

Bungalow overlooking Bantry Bay. Spacious gardens. Ideal centre for touring Cork and Kerry.

7rm(4⮣ 3hc) (1fb) ® ✗ * sB&BIR£19 dB&BIR£28 dB&B⮣IR£32 WB&BIR£90
Lic CTV 12P
Credit Cards [1] [3]

BELFAST Map **01** D5

GH Q Camera 44 Wellington Park BT9 6DP
☎(0232) 660026 & 667856

In a quiet residential area between the Lisburn and Malone roads and close to the university, this end-of-terrace Victorian house offers simple bed and breakfast accommodation together with a relaxed and friendly atmosphere.

11rm(2⮣ 9hc) (2fb) CTV in all bedrooms ✗ (ex guide dogs) sB&B£21.50-£29 sB&B⮣£27.50-£37.50 dB&Bfr£34 dB&B⮣fr£37.50 LDO 9am
CTV
Credit Cards [1] [3]

GH QQQ Malone 79 Malone Rd BT9 6SH ☎(0232) 669565
Closed 2wks Jul & 2wks Xmas

Situated to the south of the city centre, close to the university halls of residence, this detached Victorian villa offers spacious and comfortable bed and breakfast accommodation, which is kept in particularly good order by the resident proprietress.

8⮣ CTV in all bedrooms ® ✗ sB&B⮣£23-£28 dB&B⮣£37-£43
9P nc12yrs

BENNETTSBRIDGE Co Kilkenny Map **01** C3

T&C QQ Norely Theyr Barronsland
☎Kilkenny(056) 27496

This attractive, modern house is located in a quiet road surrounded by farmland and provides comfortable bedrooms and an excellent lounge.

4hc (2fb) ⊬ in all bedrooms ® ✗ (ex guide dogs) sB&BIR£13 dB&BIR£26 WB&BIR£82 WBDiIR£155 LDO 8.45pm
Lic CTV 10P
Credit Cards [1] [3]

BLARNEY Co Cork Map **01** B2

T&C Q Casa Della Rosa Carrigrohane ☎(021) 385279
May-Oct

Victorian house with well kept gardens, convenient to Cork City and Blarney Castle.

4rm(1⮣ 3hc) (2fb) ⊬ in 1 bedroom ✗ (ex guide dogs) sB&BIR£17 dB&BIR£25 dB&B⮣IR£28 WB&BIR£77 WBDiIR£150 LDO 4pm
CTV 6P

BOYLE Co Roscommon Map **01** B4

FH Q Rushfield *(M850971)* Croghan ☎(079) 62276
Mar-Oct

Large old-style farmhouse situated near Lough Key Forest Park.

4hc (2fb) * sB&BfrIR£14 dB&BfrIR£24 WB&BfrIR£90 WBDifrIR£150
CTV 10P 80 acres dairy sheep

BUNCRANA Co Donegal Map **01** C6

T&C Q ***St Bridget's*** Cockhill Rd ☎(077) 61319

Large, modern bungalow set back from main road. Ideal touring centre.

4hc (3fb) ✗ (ex guide dogs)
CTV 6P

BUSHMILLS Co Antrim Map **01** C6

SELECTED

GH QQQQ White Gables 83 Dunluce Rd BT57 8SJ
☎(02657) 31611
Apr-Sep

A modern villa situated in its own well maintained grounds beside the A2 and enjoying dramatic views over the lovely Antrim coastline. The house is attractively decorated and furnished, with a particularly comfortable lounge where a powerful telescope enables guests to pinpoint details along the coast or across the sea to the isles of Islay. Pleasant bedrooms also have fine views and are thoughtfully equipped. The Johnstons are most hospitable hosts, and Mrs Johnston produces excellent home-cooked meals, including an award-winning Irish breakfast to set guests up for exploring the many local places of interest. It is little wonder that visitors from all over the world return to this delightful spot – but it does mean that reservations should be made well in advance.

4rm(3⮣ 1hc) (1fb) ⊬ in all bedrooms ® ✗ * sB&B£25 sB&B⮣£25 dB&B⮣£37 WB&B£129.50-£175 WBDi£200-£280 LDO 2pm
CTV 10P 2 nc5yrs

CAHERDANIEL Co Kerry Map **01** A2

T&C QQ O'Sullivan's Country House ☎(066) 75124

This house is situated on the Ring of Kerry and provides a country house welcome, with home cooking a feature of Mrs O'Sullivan's hospitality. Sandy beaches, fishing, golf and boat trips can be found near by, and it is possible to arrange hill walking holidays.

6rm(1⮣ 5hc) (3fb) * sB&BfrIR£16 sB&B⮣frIR£19 dB&BfrIR£26 dB&B⮣frIR£30 WB&BfrIR£90 WBDifrIR£145
CTV 8P

CAHIRCIVEEN Co Kerry Map **01** A2

FH QQQ T Sugrue **Valentia View** *(V457773)* ☎(066) 72227
Mar-Oct

Fine old country farmhouse on Ring of Kerry. Rooms overlook Valentia island and Bay. Warm and hospitable atmosphere.

6rm(5⮣ 1hc) (2fb) * sB&BfrIR£17 sB&B⮣frIR£18 dB&BfrIR£28 dB&B⮣frIR£28 WB&BfrIR£98 WBDifrIR£165 LDO 7pm
Lic CTV 20P nc2mths 38 acres beef

Every effort is made to provide accurate information, but details can change after we go to print. It is advisable to check prices etc. before you make a firm booking.

CAPPOQUIN Co Waterford Map **01** C2

SELECTED

GH QQQQ Richmond House ☎(058) 54278
FAX (058) 54988
Feb-Nov
A three-storey house, standing in its own extensive parkland, approx 0.25 mile from the village. The house is comfortably furnished and decorated in warm colours.
10⇌↱ (2fb) ® T ✘ ✱ sB&B⇌↱IR£20-IR£30 dB&B⇌↱IR£50-IR£60 WB&BIR£140-IR£160 WBDiIR£240-IR£260 LDO 8pm
Lic 𝍖 CTV 15P 2⌂
Credit Cards [1] [2] [3] [5]

CARLOW Co Carlow Map **01** C3

T&C QQQ Barrowville Town House Kilkenny Rd ☎(0503) 43324 & 41953
This lovely Georgian house, situated on the edge of town, offers a high standard of comfort and convenience in well furnished accommodation.
6⇌↱ (3fb) CTV in all bedrooms ® T ✘ (ex guide dogs) ✱ sB&B⇌↱IR£17.50-IR£25 dB&B⇌↱IR£32-IR£35
𝍖 9P

T&C Q *Dolmen House* Brownshill ☎(0503) 42444
Jul-Sep
Very large and luxurious modern house on high ground on edge of town. Fine gardens and broad view over local countryside.
6hc ® ✘
𝍖 CTV 8P

CARRIGALINE Co Cork Map **01** B2

T&C QQ *Beaver Lodge* ☎(021) 372595
Closed Xmas
An old ivy-clad house in own grounds off main street.
6rm(2⇌2↱2hc) (5fb)⊘in 1 bedroom CTV in all bedrooms ® ✘ (ex guide dogs) LDO 4pm
𝍖 CTV 14P
Credit Cards [1] [2] [3]

CARRIGANS Co Donegal Map **01** C6

T&C QQQ Mount Royd Country Home ☎Letterkenny(074) 40163
Situated off N13, N14 and A40 a large attractive creeper-clad house surrounded by a well tended garden. Very well appointed bedrooms and excellent home cooking. Caters for tourist and business guests.
4rm(2↱2hc) (3fb) CTV in 1 bedroom ✘ (ex guide dogs) sB&BfrIR£13 dB&BfrIR£26 dB&B↱frIR£26 LDO noon
𝍖 CTV 6P 1⌂

CASHEL Co Tipperary Map **01** C3

FH QQ E O'Brien ***Knock-Saint-Lour House*** *(S074390)* ☎(062) 61172
Apr-Oct
8rm(4⇌↱4hc) (2fb) CTV in 1 bedroom ✘ (ex guide dogs)
𝍖 CTV 20P 30 acres mixed

CASTLEDERMOT Co Kildare Map **01** C3

T&C QQQ *Woodcourte* Castledermot ☎Athy(0507) 24167
7rm(3⇌↱4hc) (2fb) ® ✘ (ex guide dogs) LDO 8.45pm
Lic 𝍖 CTV 25P snooker
Credit Cards [3]

CASTLEFINN Co Donegal Map **01** C5

FH QQ D Taylor ***Gortfad*** *(J265960)* ☎(074) 46135
Closed Nov-Feb
A 200-year-old two-storey farmhouse in a very quiet and secluded location.
5rm(2↱3hc) (3fb) CTV in 2 bedrooms ✘ (ex guide dogs) LDO 4pm
𝍖 CTV P 140 acres mixed

CASTLEGREGORY Co Kerry Map **01** A2

FH Q Mrs C Griffin ***Griffin's*** *(Q525085)* Goulane ☎(066) 39147
Apr-Oct
Two-storey farmhouse situated on the Dingle Peninsula.
8rm(4⇌4↱) (3fb)⊘in all bedrooms LDO 5pm
𝍖 CTV 10P 150 acres dairy sheep

CHEEKPOINT Co Waterford Map **01** C2

GH QQQ Three Rivers ☎(051) 82520 FAX (051) 82542
Superbly located overlooking the 3 rivers, Barrow, Nore and Suir, this enchanting house has nicely furnished bedrooms, together with a lounge and dining room positioned to take full advantage of the magnificent views beyond the attractive gardens and sun balcony. The twinkling lights of Passage East can be seen in the distance, where the ferry to Ballyhack is available, providing quick access to Rosslare Port.
14↱ (3fb) T ✘ sB&B↱frIR£19 dB&B↱frIR£34 WB&BfrIR£105
𝍖 CTV 15P
Credit Cards [1] [3]

CLIFDEN Co Galway Map **01** A4

T&C QQQ Connemara Country Lodge Westport Rd ☎(095) 21122
This is a very comfortable house, purpose built to a high standard, on the main Clifden/Westport road. Charming and hospitable owners provide a warm welcome and home cooking. French and German are spoken here.
6↱ (4fb)⊘in all bedrooms CTV in 3 bedrooms ✱ sB&B↱IR£25 dB&B↱IR£34 WB&BIR£119 LDO noon
𝍖 CTV 12P
Credit Cards [2] [3]

T&C QQQ Failte Ardbear, Ballyconneely Rd ☎(095) 21159
Mar-Oct
Modern bungalow in scenic location on edge of Clifden. Excellent standards of comfort and welcoming hosts. Ideal touring centre.
5rm(2↱3hc) (2fb) ✘ (ex guide dogs) sB&BIR£13 dB&BIR£26 dB&B↱IR£30 WB&BIR£77
𝍖 CTV 15P
Credit Cards [1] [2] [3]

T&C QQ Kingstown House Bridge St ☎(095) 21470
Closed Xmas
Situated just off Clifden's main street and centrally located close to all amenities, this pleasant guesthouse offers a warm welcome from the friendly proprietors Mary and Joe King, who provide comfortable accommodation.
8rm(6↱2hc) (3fb) ✘ (ex guide dogs) sB&BfrIR£16 dB&BfrIR£26 dB&B↱frIR£28
𝍖 CTV
Credit Cards [1] [3]

Street plans of certain towns and cities will be found in a separate section at the back of the book.

CLIFFONY Co Sligo Map **01** B5

T&C QQ Villa Rosa Bunduff, Bundoran Rd ☎Sligo(071) 66173
May-Nov rs Oct, Nov & Mar-Apr
This comfortable house is situated on the main Sligo/Donegal route and has good parking facilities to the rear. The surrounding area is famous for is historic folklore, walks and beautiful scenery.
6rm(2⇌↱4hc) (2fb) ✗ (ex guide dogs) sB&BIR£16 sB&B⇌↱IR£17.50 dB&BIR£26 dB&B⇌↱IR£30 WB&BIR£85 WBDiIR£160 LDO noon
CTV 20P 1🚗
Credit Cards 1 2 3

CLONAKILTY Co Cork Map **01** B2

FH QQ D Jennings **Desert House** *(W390411)* Ring Rd ☎Bandon(023) 33331 FAX (023) 33048
Georgian farmhouse, overlooking Clonakilty Bay. Ideal centre for touring West Cork and Kerry.
5rm(4⇌↱1hc) Annexe 3hc (3fb) CTV in 3 bedrooms ® LDO 5pm
CTV P 100 acres dairy mixed
Credit Cards 1 3

FH QQ Mrs P Beechinor **Liscubba** *(W346463)* Liscubba, Rossmore ☎Bandon(023) 38679
Two-storey farmhouse on beef-rearing farm. Ideal touring centre for West Cork.
6hc (3fb) ✱ sB&BIR£11.50 dB&BIR£23 WB&BIR£80 WBDiIR£148
CTV P 🚗 180 acres beef
Credit Cards 1

CLONBUR Co Galway Map **01** B4

GH Q Fairhill ☎Galway(092) 46176
Etr-19 Oct
Owned and run by Mrs Lynch, who offers a most hospitable service, this village guesthouse is presently being refurbished and boasts a cosy bar which serves food throughout the day.
11rm(2↱9hc) (1fb) CTV in 1 bedroom ® ✗ (ex guide dogs) ✱ sB&B↱IR£13-IR£15 dB&BIR£26-IR£30 LDO 9pm
Lic CTV 10P outdoor pursuit centre pitch & putt

CORK Co Cork Map **01** B2

T&C QQQ Antoine House Western Rd ☎(021) 273494 FAX (021) 273092
Converted four-storey house close to the University, catering for both tourist and commercial clientele.
7↱ CTV in all bedrooms ® **T** ✱ sB&B↱frIR£25 dB&B↱frIR£30
CTV 8P
Credit Cards 1 2 3 5

GH QQQ Garnish House 1 Aldergrove, Western Rd ☎(021) 275111 FAX (021) 273872
Three-storey house opposite University on main Cork/Killarney road.
15rm(10↱5hc) (1fb) CTV in all bedrooms ® **T**
✗ (ex guide dogs) ✱ sB&BIR£23-IR£25 sB&B↱IR£25-IR£28 dB&BfrIR£32 dB&B↱frIR£40
CTV 10P
Credit Cards 1 2 3 5

T&C QQ ***Killarney House*** Western Rd ☎(021) 270179 & 270290
Closed 25-26 Dec
Three-storey terrace house facing University College.
19rm(8↱11hc) (3fb) CTV in all bedrooms ®
✗ (ex guide dogs)
CTV 20P
Credit Cards 1 2 3 5

GH QQQ ***Lotamore House*** Tivoli ☎(021) 822344 FAX (021) 822219
Two-storey Georgian manor set in own grounds overlooking River Lee and Blackrock Castle.
21⇌↱ (7fb) CTV in all bedrooms
CTV 40P
Credit Cards 1 2 3

T&C QQ Roserie Villa Mardyke Walk, off Western Rd ☎(021) 272958 FAX (021) 274087
This bright new guesthouse is conveniently situated for the city centre and offers good car parking facilities.
16rm(12↱4hc) (3fb) CTV in all bedrooms ® **T**
✗ (ex guide dogs) ✱ sB&BIR£16.50-IR£17.50 sB&B↱IR£21-IR£22.50 dB&B↱IR£33-IR£35
CTV 8P
Credit Cards 1 2 3 5

See advertisement on page 461

GH QQQ St Kilda's Western Rd ☎(021) 273095 & 275374 FAX (021) 275015
Approached via the city centre on the N22 route, this comfortable guesthouse is situated opposite University College. Under the personal supervision of the hospitable owners, Pat and Pauline Hickey. St Kilda's offers pleasant, nicely appointed accommodation.
13rm(12⇌↱1hc) (1fb) CTV in all bedrooms **T**
✗ (ex guide dogs) ✱ sB&BIR£18-IR£20 sB&B⇌↱IR£20-IR£25 dB&BIR£30-IR£33 dB&B⇌↱IR£34-IR£38
CTV 14P
Credit Cards 1 3

COROFIN Co Clare Map **01** B3

FH ★★ Mary Kelleher **Fergus View** *(R265919)* Kilnaboy ☎Limerick(065) 27606
Etr-Sep
Recently renovated old farmhouse. Two miles north of Corofin on L53.
6rm(5↱1hc) (4fb)🚭in all bedrooms ✗ ✱ sB&BfrIR£16.50 sB&B↱frIR£18.50 dB&BfrIR£25 dB&B↱frIR£29 WB&BfrIR£101.50 WBDifrIR£165 LDO noon
Lic ⊞ CTV 8P 17 acres non-working

FH ★★★ Mrs B Kelleher ***Inchiquin View*** *(R270916)* Kilnaboy ☎(065) 27731
Apr-Sep
Modern farmhouse overlooking the Fergus river on L53 in the Burren Country.
5rm(3↱2hc) (2fb) ✗ (ex guide dogs) LDO 5pm
⊞ CTV 8P 15 acres beef mixed

CROSSHAVEN Co Cork Map **01** B2

GH ★★ ***Whispering Pines*** ☎Cork(021) 831448 & 831843
Apr-Oct rs Nov & Feb
Modern house in its own well-maintained grounds with a backdrop of mature trees overlooking river and harbour.
15rm(11⇨4↱) (6fb) ✗ LDO 9.30pm
Lic ⊞ CTV 40P
Credit Cards [1] [2] [5]

CRUSHEEN Co Clare Map **01** B3

FH ★★ Dilly Griffey **Lahardan** *(R397889)* Lahardan ☎Ennis(065) 27128 FAX (065) 27319
rs 23-26 Dec
Comfortable two-storey farmhouse 1.5 miles off main Ennis/ Galway road (N18). A quiet and peaceful setting.
8rm(6⇨2↱) (4fb) ✱ sB&B⇨↱frIR£18 dB&B⇨↱frIR£36 LDO 3pm
Lic ⊞ CTV P 230 acres beef
Credit Cards [1] [3]

DINGLE Co Kerry Map **01** A2

GH ★★★ **Alpine** Mail Rd ☎(066) 51250
Mar-Nov
A large, three-storey building on the outskirts of Dingle, situated in its own grounds.
15↱ (4fb) ✗ ✱ dB&B↱IR£30
⊞ CTV 20P
Credit Cards [1] [3]

T&C ★★★ **Ard-na-Greine House** Spa Rd ☎(066) 51113 & 51898
This modern bungalow is situated on the edge of town towards Connor Pass. All the rooms are en suite and offer an unrivalled range of facilities.
4↱ (2fb) CTV in all bedrooms ® **T** ✗ (ex guide dogs) sB&B↱IR£20 dB&B↱IR£30-IR£32
⊞ CTV 4P nc7yrs
Credit Cards [1] [2] [3]

T&C ★★★ **Cleevaun** Lady's Cross, Milltown ☎(066) 51108
mid Mar-mid Nov
Luxury bungalow on a one-acre site with superb views of Dingle Bay and surrounding mountains.
9rm(4⇨4↱1hc) (2fb) CTV in 4 bedrooms ® ✗ (ex guide dogs) ✱ dB&B⇨↱IR£32-IR£40
⊞ CTV 9P nc3yrs
Credit Cards [1] [3]

GH ★★★ **Doyles Town House** 4 John St ☎Tralee(066) 51174 FAX (066) 51816
mid Mar-mid Nov
8⇨↱ CTV in all bedrooms ✗ (ex guide dogs) sB&B⇨↱IR£37 dB&B⇨↱IR£59 LDO 9pm
Lic ⊞
Credit Cards [1] [3] [5]

GH ★★★ **Milltown House** Milltown ☎Tralee(066) 51372
Etr-Oct
Situated on a sea channel to the west of town in an ideal situation for sightseeing and exploring.
7rm(2⇨5↱) (3fb) ✗ (ex guide dogs) ✱ sB&B⇨↱IR£21-IR£23 dB&B⇨↱IR£28-IR£32
⊞ CTV 10P nc5yrs mini golf
Credit Cards [1] [3]

GH ★★★ **Scanlon's** Mail Rd ☎(066) 51883 FAX (066) 51297
This comfortable modern house overlooks the bay, and has fine sea and country views.
6↱ (3fb) ✗ (ex guide dogs) sB&B↱IR£20-IR£30 dB&B↱IR£30-IR£40
⊞ CTV 10P nc9yrs
Credit Cards [1] [3]

DONEGAL Co Donegal Map **01** B5

T&C ★★ **Ardeevin** Lough Eske, Barnesmore ☎(073) 21790
Apr-Oct
Comfortable homely house in a lovely location on a height above Lough Eske and with superb views of lake and mountain. Well appointed bedrooms with en suite facilities.
5⇨↱ (2fb) ® ✗ sB&B⇨↱IR£18 dB&B⇨↱IR£29 LDO noon
⊞ CTV 8P 2🚗 nc9yrs

DOOLIN Co Clare Map **01** B3

T&C ★★★ **Doonmacfelim House** ☎Ennistymon(065) 74503 FAX (065) 74421
This large new 2-storey house is on the edge of the tiny west coast village. It offers comfortable, well planned accommodation, car parking and a friendly welcome from the owners Frank and Majella Moloney.
6↱ **T** ✗ (ex guide dogs) ✱ sB&B↱IR£20 dB&B↱IR£28-IR£32 LDO 2pm
⊞ CTV 20P
Credit Cards [1] [3]

FH ★★★ J Moloney ***Horse Shoe*** *(R073971)* ☎(065) 74006 FAX (065) 74421
Closed Dec
Modern bungalow situated 0.5 mile from main road between Cliffs of Moder and Lisdoonvarna village.
5↱ ✗ (ex guide dogs)
⊞ CTV P boat trips 20 acres dairy
Credit Cards [3]

DOWNPATRICK Co Down Map **01** D5

FH ★★★ Mrs Macauley ***Havine*** 51 Bally Donnel Rd ☎Ballykinlar(0396) 85242
Closed Xmas wk
A modernised farmhouse dating back 200 years in parts, situated 3.5 miles southwest of Downpatrick, off the A25. Take the Ballykibeg road signed Tyrella past the Ramblers Inn, and the farm is about a mile further, on the left. Bedrooms are well furnished, with many thoughtful extras, including dressing gowns, sewing materials and radios.
4hc (1fb) ® LDO 4.40pm
⊞ CTV 10P 2🚗 125 acres arable

DUBLIN Co Dublin Map **01** D4

T&C QQ ***Aaronmor House*** 1c Sandymount Av ☏(01) 687972 FAX (01) 682377

Family run house comfortably furnished and decorated. Situated close to the Royal Dublin Society Showgrounds and Lansdowne Rugby grounds.

6rm(5 1hc) (2fb) CTV in 1 bedroom TV in 1 bedroom ® LDO 10am

CTV 8P nc5yrs

Credit Cards [1] [3]

SELECTED

GH QQQQ ***Aberdeen Lodge*** 53/55 Park Av ☏(01) 2838155 FAX (01) 2837877

An Edwardian house which has been tastefully refurbished to the highest standards, situated on a tree-lined avenue close to the Royal Dublin Society showgrounds and Lansdowne Road rugby grounds. It combines old-world charm with modern comforts. The excellent bedrooms have every facility. Good off-street car parking is available.

16 (8fb) in 2 bedrooms CTV in all bedrooms

Lic CTV 16P

Credit Cards [1] [2] [3] [5]

See advertisement on page 463

'Selected' establishments, which have the highest quality award, are highlighted by a tinted panel. For a full list of these establishments, consult the Contents page.

SELECTED

GH QQQQ Ariel House 52 Lansdowne Rd
☎(01) 685512 FAX (01) 685845
A luxurious Victorian mansion built in 1850, situated beside Lansdowne Rugby grounds. Charming proprietors ensure guests every comfort. Attractive bedrooms with authentic antiques of the period.
28⇌🚿 CTV in all bedrooms **T** ✗ ✱ sB&B⇌🚿IR£33-IR£60 dB&B⇌🚿IR£60-IR£100
Lic 🍴 CTV 40P nc5yrs
Credit Cards 1 3

GH QQQ Beddington 181 Rathgar Rd ☎(01) 978047 FAX (01) 978275
Closed 23 Dec-13 Jan
14🚿 (1fb) CTV in all bedrooms ® **T** ✗ sB&B🚿IR£27.50 dB&B🚿IR£45-IR£50
Lic 🍴 CTV 10P nc7yrs
Credit Cards 1 3

GH QQQ Charleville Guest Inn 268/272 North Circular Rd ☎(01) 386633 FAX (01) 385854
Situated close to the city centre, this elegant terrace of Victorian houses has been completely renovated and offers a high standard of accommodation, business and conference facilities with a large car park for guests.
18🚿 (4fb) CTV in all bedrooms **T** ✗ ✱ sB&B🚿IR£27 dB&B🚿IR£44
CTV 30P
Credit Cards 1 2 3 5

GH QQQ Egan's 7/9 Iona Park, Glasnevin ☎(01) 303611 & 303818 FAX (01) 303312
Situated in a quiet suburb on the north side of the city, this Victorian, red- brick, streetside house has large, comfortable rooms and relaxing lounges and good gardens at rear. A family-run house renowned for its friendly and cheerful atmosphere. Conveniently located for National Botanic Gardens and Airport.
25🚿 (4fb) CTV in all bedrooms ® ✱ sB&B🚿IR£25-IR£32 dB&B🚿IR£44-IR£55 LDO 8pm
Lic 🍴 8P
Credit Cards 1 3

GH QQQ *The Fitzwilliam* 41 Upper Fitzwilliam St ☎(01) 600199 FAX (01) 767488
5 Jan-15 Dec
Situated in the heart of Georgian Dublin, this house has been newly renovated to a very high standard. Ideal for business people and tourists. Close to National Concert Hall.
12rm(2⇌10🚿) (1fb) CTV in all bedrooms LDO 10.30pm
Lic 🍴 CTV 4P
Credit Cards 1 2 3 5

GH QQQ Georgian House 20 Baggot St Lower ☎(01) 618832 FAX (01) 618834
Large Georgian house on streetside, situated close to city centre. Catering for tourists and commercials.
17🚿 Annexe 17⇌🚿 (27fb) CTV in all bedrooms **T** ✗ (ex guide dogs) ✱ sB&B⇌🚿IR£34.98-IR£49 dB&B⇌🚿IR£53.68-IR£79.20 LDO 10.30pm
Lic 🍴 18P
Credit Cards 1 2 3 5

SELECTED

GH QQQQ The Grey Door 22/23 Upper Pembroke St ☎(01) 763286 FAX (01) 763287
rs Bank Hols
This elegant, tastefully restored town house is a jewel in the heart of Georgian Dublin. The extremely attractive bedrooms are decorated in green and coral giving a warm, pleasing appearance, with comfort a priority, and each room is equipped with a luxurious bathroom. There is a delightful upstairs sitting room in addition to a residents' lounge on the first floor and both are fitted to a high standard using antique furnishings. A choice of 2 restaurants is offered, the formal 'Grey Door' and the informal rendezvous 'Blushers'.
Best Newcomer for the Republic of Ireland 1992–3, see colour section.
7⇌🚿 (2fb) CTV in all bedrooms ® **T** ✗ (ex guide dogs) sB&B⇌🚿IR£81.95-IR£91.95 dB&B⇌🚿IR£101.95-IR£111.95 WB&BIR£480 WBDiIR£580 LDO 11.30pm
Lic 🍴
Credit Cards 1 2 3 5

GH QQQ Iona House 5 Iona Park ☎(01) 306217 & 306855 FAX (01) 306732
Closed Dec-15 Jan
Situated in a quiet residential suburb on the north side of the city, this family-run Victorian red-brick house has large modern bedrooms, comfortable lounge and small garden for exclusive use of guests. Conveniently located for National Botanic Gardens and Airport.
14rm(12🚿2hc) (1fb) CTV in 11 bedrooms **T** sB&BIR£23-IR£26.50 sB&B🚿IR£31-IR£34.50 dB&BIR£46-IR£53 dB&B🚿frIR£48
🍴 nc3yrs
Credit Cards 1 3

GH QQQ Kingswood Country House Old Kingswood, Naas Rd, Clundalkin D22 ☎(01) 592428 & 592207
Closed 25-28 Dec
7⇌🚿 (2fb) CTV in all bedrooms **T** ✗ ✱ sB&B⇌🚿IR£35-IR£45 dB&B⇌🚿IR£55-IR£70 LDO 10.30pm
Lic 🍴 60P
Credit Cards 1 2 3

T&C QQQ Marelle 92 Rathfarnham Rd, Terenure ☎(01) 904690
Attractive house recently refurbished. Set back from road in own gardens. Good parking facilities.
6rm(5🚿1hc) (1fb) CTV in 5 bedrooms TV in 1 bedroom ✗ ✱ sB&B🚿frIR£25 dB&B🚿frIR£40 LDO 10am
🍴 CTV 8P nc5yrs
Credit Cards 1 3

T&C QQQ Morehampton Lodge 113 Morehampton Rd, Donnybrook ☎(01) 2837499 FAX (01) 2837595
Totally restored to a high standard, this Victorian house is very conveniently situated near the city centre and good bus routes. Excellent bedrooms are provided, and off-street parking is available.
5⇌🚿 (3fb) CTV in all bedrooms ® **T** ✗ ✱ sB&B⇌🚿IR£34-IR£39 dB&B⇌🚿IR£50-IR£57
🍴 CTV 7P
Credit Cards 1 3

GH QQQ Mount Herbert 7 Herbert Rd ☎(01) 684321 Telex no 92173 FAX (01) 607077
144rm(122⇌3🚿19hc) (9fb) CTV in all bedrooms **T** ✗ (ex guide dogs) ✱ sB&BIR£19-IR£37 sB&B⇌🚿IR£32-IR£53 dB&BIR£37-IR£59 dB&B⇌🚿IR£45-IR£64 LDO 9.30pm

Lic lift ᛘ CTV 80P sauna solarium
Credit Cards [1] [2] [3] [5]

GH QQQ St Aiden's 32 Brighton Rd, Rathgar
☎(01) 902011 & 906178 FAX (01) 92034
10rm(2⇨5↱3hc) (3fb)⊬in 1 bedroom CTV in all bedrooms **T**
✗ ✱ sB&BIR£20-IR£25 sB&B⇨↱IR£25-IR£30
dB&B⇨↱IR£45-IR£50
Lic ᛘ CTV 8P
Credit Cards [1] [2] [3]

DUNCORMICK Co Wexford Map **01** C2

FH Q E Burrell **Ingleside** *(S914090)* The Hill ☎(051) 63154
Mar-Oct
Situated on L128A en route to Passage East Car Ferry, this modern farm bungalow is set in peaceful surroundings. It provides comfortable accommodation, and trips are arranged to Saltee Islands Bird Sanctuary.
6hc (3fb) ® ✗ (ex guide dogs) ✱ sB&BfrIR£13 dB&BfrIR£24
WB&BfrIR£80 WBDifrIR£148 LDO 8.30pm
ᛘ CTV 8P U 90 acres mixed

DUNGANNON Co Tyrone Map **01** C5

SELECTED

GH QQQQ Grange Lodge 7 Grange Rd BT71 7EJ
☎Moy(08687) 84212 FAX (08687) 23891
Closed 20 Dec-1 Jan
Natural warmth and friendliness is extended by Ralph and Norah Brown at their delightful Georgian house, set in well cared for, extensive grounds offering exquisite peace and tranquillity. There are 2 lounges – one with a TV and the other more spacious – both full of the owners' personal items giving a true home-from-home feeling. Norah is a fine cook and enjoys producing interesting set evening meals, plus breakfast is a delight (particularly Bushmills porridge). Two bedrooms are en suite and all are prettily furnished with matching fabrics. Lots of extras are provided including TV, hairdryer, good seating and fresh flowers. This guesthouse is a pleasurable, relaxing and friendly place to stay and fully deserves selected status.
Best Newcomer for Northern Ireland 1992–3, see colour section.
3rm(2⇨↱1hc) CTV in all bedrooms ® ✗ (ex guide dogs)
sB&Bfr£25 sB&B⇨↱fr£30 dB&Bfr£45 dB&B⇨↱fr£49
LDO 1pm
ᛘ CTV 12P nc12yrs ℘(hard)
Credit Cards [1] [3]

DUNGARVAN Co Waterford Map **01** C2

FH Q Miss B Lynch **Killineen House** *(X302963)* N 25, Waterford Rd ☎Waterford(051) 91294
Attractive house with well-tended gardens and views of Comeragh mountains. Situated 4m east of town on Waterford road.
5rm(3↱2hc) (3fb)⊬in 2 bedrooms ® ✱ sB&BIR£12-IR£15
dB&BIR£24 dB&B↱IR£26 WB&BIR£90 WBDiIR£148
LDO 5pm
ᛘ CTV 10P 50 acres grass

DUN LAOGHAIRE Co Dublin Map **01** D4

T&C QQ Ferry 15 Clarinda Park North ☎(01) 2808301
Mar-Nov
Large Victorian house overlooking People's Park.
6rm(2↱4hc) (2fb) CTV in all bedrooms ✗ (ex guide dogs) ✱
dB&BIR£29-IR£30 dB&B↱IR£35-IR£37
ᛘ CTV
Credit Cards [1] [3]

T&C Q ***Tara Hall*** 24 Sandycove Rd, Sandycove
☎(01) 2805120
Large Victorian house on main road catering for tourist and commercial business.
6rm(1⇌5hc) (3fb) ®
CTV 4P
Credit Cards [1] [3]

DUNMORE EAST Co Waterford Map **01** C2

T&C QQQ ***Hillfield House*** Ballymabin ☎(051) 83565
Closed Dec & Jan
This luxury new dormer bungalow is set back from the Waterford road in its own grounds. It offers lovely bedrooms and public rooms with a strong emphasis on comfort.
4⇌ (1fb) CTV in 1 bedroom
CTV 20P nc10yrs

FERNS Co Wexford Map **01** D3

SELECTED

FH QQQQ Mrs B Breen ***Clone House*** *(T022484)*
☎Enniscorthy(054) 66113
Mar-Oct
An award-winning farmhouse in which the hospitable Mrs Breen takes great pride and where fine furniture from past generations enhances the modern day comforts. The prize-winning gardens are a delight.
5rm(4⇌1hc) (4fb) in all bedrooms CTV in 1 bedroom TV in 2 bedrooms (ex guide dogs) LDO 4pm
CTV P (hard) 280 acres mixed

FOULKESMILL Co Wexford Map **01** C2

FH Q Mrs J Crosbie ***Crosbie's*** *(S857185)*
☎Waterford(051) 63616
Mar-Oct
Old-style farmhouse situated in quiet surroundings.
10hc (3fb) LDO 3pm
CTV 150 acres mixed

FH QQ Mrs Vera Young ***Horetown House*** *(S870189)*
☎Waterford(051) 63633 & 63706
Mar-mid Jan (ex Xmas day)
An 18th-century manor house on 214 acres of farmland with its own equestrian centre and cellar restaurant. The Young family are hospitable hosts and the farmhouse makes an ideal touring centre.
12hc (10fb) LDO 9pm
Lic CTV 15P U all weather indoor riding arena outdoor riding 214 acres beef dairy mixed

GALWAY Co Galway Map **01** B4

T&C QQ ***Bay View*** Gentian Hill, Upper Salthill
☎(091) 22116
Feb-Nov
Modern house situated on edge of Salthill. Ideal touring centre.
6rm(5⇌1hc) (2fb) in 5 bedrooms
CTV 6P nc5yrs

T&C QQ **Inishmore House** 109 Fr. Griffin Rd, Lower Salthill
☎(091) 62639
16 Mar-16 Dec
Mature, two-storey house with nice garden situated on outskirts of Salthill; ideal touring centre.
8rm(5⇌3hc) (3fb) CTV in all bedrooms ® * dB&BIR£26-IR£28 dB&B⇌IR£29-IR£32
8P

GH Q **Knockrea House** 55 Lower Salthill ☎(091) 21794
Situated in a quiet residential part of Salthill, convenient to beach and city.
9hc (2fb) (ex guide dogs) * sB&BIR£12.50-IR£14
CTV 10P nc4yrs

T&C QQQ **Roncalli House** 24 Whitesand Av, Lower Salthill
☎(091) 64159
Modern, two-storey, neo-Georgian house in quiet locality overlooking Galway Bay.
6⇌ (1fb) * dB&B⇌IR£28
CTV 5P

GLENEALY Co Wicklow Map **01** D3

FH QQ Mrs Mary Byrne ***Ballyknocken House*** *(T246925)*
☎Wicklow(0404) 44627 & 44614
Closed 21 Dec-1 Feb
8⇌ (1fb) LDO 5pm
Lic CTV 10P (hard)200 acres dairy sheep
Credit Cards [1]

GOREY Co Wexford Map **01** D3

SELECTED

FH QQQQ P O'Sullivan **Woodlands** *(T163648)*
Killinieril ☎Arklow(0402) 37125 & 37133
Georgian-style residence 1.5km off the N11. Excellent accommodation, 3 rooms have balcony. Charming dining room run by chef Gara, daughter of the proprietor, Mrs O'Sullivan. All fresh produce assured. Award-winning gardens enhance the house where relaxation is the priority of the family.
6⇌ (3fb) CTV in all bedrooms (ex guide dogs) * sB&B⇌IR£21-IR£22 dB&B⇌IR£32-IR£33 WBDiIR£190-IR£195 LDO 8pm
Lic CTV 6P (hard)pool table play room pony rides 8 acres beef (non-working)

INISTIOGE Co Kilkenny Map **01** C3

T&C Q ***Ashville*** Kilmacshane ☎(056) 58460
Mar-Oct
A bungalow overlooking the River Nore, with well-maintained gardens and situated 0.5m south of village.
5rm(3⇌2hc) (1fb) TV in 1 bedroom (ex guide dogs) LDO 8pm
CTV 5P
Credit Cards [1] [3]

KANTURK Co Cork Map **01** B2

SELECTED

GH QQQQ **Assolas Country House** ☎(029) 50015
FAX (029) 50795
13 Mar-1 Nov
17th-century manor house in a sylvan setting on a tributary of the River Blackwater, surrounded by prize-winning gardens, parkland and rolling country. Magnificent public rooms with log fires. Fresh garden and local produce are creatively presented in the restaurant.
6⇌ Annexe 3⇌ (3fb) T (ex guide dogs) * sB&B⇌IR£50-IR£60 dB&B⇌IR£80-IR£140 LDO 8.30pm
Lic 20P (grass) croquet clock golf boating
Credit Cards [1] [3] [5]

KENMARE Co Kerry Map **01** A2

T&C QQQ ***Ceann Mara*** ☎Killarney(064) 41220
Etr-Oct rs Mar & Nov
Luxury, split-level bungalow with pleasant gardens in a quiet location off Kenmare-Cork road.
6rm(1⇌3↱2hc) (2fb) ®
ꟾꟾꟾ CTV P ℘(grass)

GH QQQ **Foleys Shamrock** Henry St ☎(064) 41361
FAX (064) 41799
Town-centre guesthouse over pub/restaurant. All bedrooms have been recently refurbished and are very comfortable. A good food service is available via the bar and restaurant.
10⇌↱ CTV in all bedrooms ✗ (ex guide dogs)
sB&B⇌↱IR£15-IR£20 dB&B⇌↱IR£30-IR£38
WB&BIR£99-IR£110 LDO 10pm
Lic ꟾꟾꟾ CTV
Credit Cards 1 3

FH QQ M P O'Sullivan **Sea Shore** *(V899705)* Tubrid
☎(064) 41270
May-Sep
Modern bungalow in own grounds on edge of town overlooking Kenmare Bay.
4↱ (3fb) ✗ (ex guide dogs) LDO 3pm
ꟾꟾꟾ CTV 12P 32 acres dairy

FH QQQ Mrs R Doran **Templenoe House** *(V840693)*
Greenane ☎(064) 41538
Etr-Oct
Two-storey farmhouse reputed to be about 200 years old. Situated on the Ring of Kerry about 4m west of Kenmare.
5rm(2↱3hc) (2fb) ® ✗ (ex guide dogs) dB&BfrIR£26
dB&B↱frIR£30 LDO 3pm
CTV 8P 50 acres dairy

KILCULLEN Co Kildare Map **01** C3

FH QQQ B O'Sullivan ***Chapel View*** *(N856055)*
Gormanstown ☎Curragh(045) 81325
May-Dec
6↱ (2fb) LDO 4pm
ꟾꟾꟾ CTV 20P 22 acres beef
Credit Cards 1 3

KILGARVAN Co Kerry Map **01** A2

FH QQQ E Dineen ***Glanlea*** *(W070745)* ☎(064) 85314
Feb-Oct
Two-storey farmhouse, situated in a peaceful valley.
8rm(3↱5hc) (3fb) ® ✗ (ex guide dogs) LDO 3pm
Lic ꟾꟾꟾ CTV 6P 4🚗 nc10yrs 500 acres

FH QQQ K Dineen **Hawthorn** *(W064754)* ☎(064) 85326
Apr-Sep
Modernised, two-storey farmhouse, in a quiet and peaceful valley.
6rm(3↱3hc) (2fb) ✗ (ex guide dogs) LDO 4pm
ꟾꟾꟾ CTV 12P 87 acres sheep

KILKENNY Co Kilkenny Map **01** C3

GH QQQ **Lacken House** Dublin Rd ☎(056) 61085 & 65611
FAX (056) 62435
A family-run guesthouse/restaurant on outskirts of city.
8⇌↱ CTV in all bedrooms ® T ✗ (ex guide dogs) ✱
sB&B⇌↱IR£31-IR£33 dB&B⇌↱IR£48.40-IR£55
WB&BIR£165-IR£220 LDO 10pm
Lic ꟾꟾꟾ CTV 30P
Credit Cards 1 2 3 5

T&C QQQ Shillogher House Callan Rd ☎(056) 63249
Closed 20-31 Dec
A lovely new house in its own gardens on the road to Clonmel. Tastefully furnished and decorated and Mrs Kennedy has a keen eye to her guests' comfort.
5⇌↱ (1fb)⊁in 4 bedrooms CTV in 1 bedroom TV in 1 bedroom ® ✗ ✱ sB&B⇌↱IR£15-IR£20 dB&B⇌↱IR£26-IR£30 LDO 2pm
♨ CTV 10P
Credit Cards [1] [3]

KILLARNEY Co Kerry Map **01** A2

GH QQ Glena House Muckross Rd ☎(064) 32705
FAX (064) 34033
Closed Xmas
Large, comfortable house close to town. All rooms en suite and good parking facilities.
18rm(3⇌15↱) (3fb) **T** ✱ sB&B⇌↱IR£16-IR£22 dB&B⇌↱IR£30-IR£34 WB&BfrIR£112 WBDiIR£175-IR£196 LDO 8.30pm
Lic ♨ CTV 25P
Credit Cards [1] [2] [3] [5]

T&C QQ Glendale House Dromadessart, Tralee Rd
☎(064) 32152
Mar-15 Dec
Large luxury house situated on Killarney/Tralee road. Set in farming land. Ideal touring centre.
5⇌↱ (2fb) CTV in 3 bedrooms ® ✗ (ex guide dogs) ✱ sB&B⇌↱IR£15-IR£18 dB&B⇌↱IR£27-IR£30 WB&BIR£91-IR£95 WBDiIR£165-IR£170 LDO 4pm
♨ CTV 8P
Credit Cards [3]

T&C QQ Green Acres Fossa ☎(064) 31454
Closed Xmas
Modern house situated on Ring of Kerry and 1.5m outside town.
8rm(6↱2hc) (2fb) ✗ sB&BfrIR£20 sB&B↱frIR£20 dB&BIR£26 dB&B↱IR£29
♨ CTV 12P

SELECTED

GH QQQQ Kathleen's Country House Tralee Rd
☎(064) 32810 FAX (064) 32340
17 Mar-5 Nov
An exclusive, modern, purpose-built guesthouse set in its own lovely gardens 1m from town centre on Tralee road. Family-run, luxury accommodation in scenic countryside. Ideal touring centre.
16⇌↱ (2fb)⊁in 3 bedrooms CTV in all bedrooms ® **T** ✗ ✱ sB&B⇌↱IR£30-IR£45 dB&B⇌↱IR£45-IR£55 WB&BIR£130-IR£168 WBDiIR£255-IR£280.50 LDO 6pm
Lic ♨ 20P nc8yrs lawn croquet
Credit Cards [1]

T&C QQQ Killarney Villa Cork-Waterford Rd (N72)
☎(064) 31878
Mar-Oct
Luxury, two-storey house in beautiful landscaped gardens. Ideal touring centre.
13rm(11⇌↱2hc) (1fb) ® ✱ sB&BIR£14-IR£16 sB&B⇌↱IR£18-IR£20 dB&BIR£25-IR£28 dB&B⇌↱IR£29 WB&BIR£95 WBDiIR£165 LDO 6.30pm
♨ CTV 20P nc6yrs
Credit Cards [1] [2] [3]

GH QQQ Loch Lein Golf Course Rd, Fossa ☎(064) 31260
17 Mar-Sep
A single-storey bungalow on the shores of the Lower Lake. Well maintained lawns and flower beds. Situated in a very quiet and peaceful location.
15rm(2⇌10↱2hc) (5fb)⊁in 2 bedrooms ✗ ✱ sB&BIR£15 sB&B⇌↱IR£17.50-IR£20 dB&B⇌↱IR£26-IR£30
♨ CTV 15P

T&C QQQ Lohan's Lodge Tralee Rd ☎(064) 33871
Situated on Tralee Road, this very attractive bungalow is set in its own well kept gardens and offers nicely decorated accommodation throughout. Proprietors Cathy and Mike Lohan are very dedicated to the needs of their guests.
5↱ (1fb) CTV in all bedrooms ® ✗ ✱ dB&B↱IR£25-IR£27 WB&BIR£87.50-IR£94.50 WBDiIR£157.50-IR£164.50 LDO noon
♨ CTV 7P nc7yrs

T&C QQQ *Mulberry House* Ballycasheen Rd
☎(064) 34112 & 32534
Closed Xmas & New Year
Luxurious, modern house in quiet residential district on the edge of town. En suite spacious rooms with good mountain views.
4rm(2⇌2↱) (1fb) ✗
♨ CTV 7P ℛ(grass)

T&C QQ The Purple Heather Gap of Dunloe ☎(064) 44266
Etr-Sep
Modern bungalow by roadside among spectacular mountain scenery. Ideal touring centre.
5rm(4↱1hc) (1fb)⊁in 2 bedrooms ® ✗ ✱ sB&BfrIR£13 sB&B↱IR£17 dB&BfrIR£23 dB&B↱IR£26 WB&BIR£81.50-IR£91 WBDiIR£150-IR£155 LDO 7pm
♨ CTV 6P ℛ(hard)

T&C QQ *St Rita's Villa* Mill Rd ☎(064) 31517
Feb-8 Dec
A modern bungalow in a very quiet and secluded location on the outskirts of the town.
6rm(4↱2hc) (2fb)
♨ CTV 6P

T&C QQQ Shraheen House Ballycasheen ☎(064) 31286
Closed Xmas & New Year
Modern, two-storey house in a quiet and peaceful location.
6rm(2⇌4↱) (2fb) ✗ sB&B⇌↱IR£20 dB&B⇌↱IR£30
♨ CTV 8P

KILLEAGH Co Cork Map **01** B2

T&C QQQ Tattans Main St ☎(024) 95173
Mar-Oct
Very comfortable bedrooms are a feature of Tattans Town House on the main Cork-Rosslare road, N25. There is a TV room, large attractive gardens, a hard tennis court and an adjoining bar where snacks are available all day. Evening meals are served to residents. Mrs Tattan takes pride in running the hotel, is very welcoming and serves good food.
5rm(4↱1hc) (3fb) ✗ ✱ sB&BfrIR£17 sB&B↱frIR£17 dB&BfrIR£30 dB&B↱frIR£30 WB&BIR£105 WBDiIR£195 LDO 10pm
Lic ♨ CTV 8P ℛ(hard)

FH QQQ Mrs Browne **Ballymakeigh House** *(X005765)*
☎Youghal(024) 95184
Hospitable Margaret Browne, winner of many awards, will make you feel very much at home in her delightful, 250-year-old farmhouse. The cheerful bedrooms are attractively decorated and an elegant dining room provides the setting for a 5-course dinner served every evening.
5⇌↱ (5fb) ✗ (ex guide dogs) sB&B⇌↱frIR£22 dB&B⇌↱frIR£37 WBDifrIR£231 LDO 6pm
Lic ♨ CTV 10P ℛ(hard)snooker 180 acres dairy

KILLESHANDRA Co Cavan Map **01** C4

FH Q K H Locher **Derreskit** *(H290068)* ☎(049) 34156 & 34154
Two-storey modern farmhouse situated 2m from Killeshandra.
7rm(1↱6hc) ✗ ✱ sB&BIR£13.50 dB&BIR£24 dB&B↱IR£25 WB&BIR£77 WBDiIR£133 LDO 8pm
Lic ♨ 5P 1🚗 ⌡ 161 acres beef mixed sheep

KILLORGLIN Co Kerry Map **01** A2

T&C QQQ ***Torine House*** Sunhill Rd, Ring of Kerry ☎(066) 61352
Large, luxurious bungalow in own grounds, situated in a quiet location on edge of town. Homely atmosphere.
6↱ (6fb) ® ✗
⌂ CTV 10P

KILMALLOCK Co Limerick Map **01** B3

FH QQQ Mrs Imelda Sheedy King **Flemingstown House** *(R629255)* Blackpool ☎(063) 98093 FAX (063) 98546
Mar-Oct
Lovely, modernised, 250-year-old farmhouse set amid scenic countryside near edge of town. Homely atmosphere.
5rm(4↱1hc) (2fb) ® ✗ (ex guide dogs) ✱ sB&BIR£15 dB&BIR£26 dB&B↱IR£26 WB&BfrIR£90 WBDifrIR£180 LDO 8pm
Lic ⌂ CTV P ▶18 ℘(hard&grass)♩ squash ∪ gymnasium 102 acres dairy
Credit Cards [1]

KILMEADEN Co Waterford Map **01** C2

T&C Q ***Hillview Lodge*** Adamstown ☎(051) 84230
Mar-Oct
Roadside dormer bungalow with large rear garden of lawns and shrubs.
5rm(1↱4hc) (2fb) CTV in 1 bedroom ✗ (ex guide dogs) LDO 10am
⌂ CTV 10P

KILMEENA Co Mayo Map **01** A4

FH QQQ M O'Malley **Seapoint House** *(L972897)* ☎Westport(098) 41254
Apr-Oct
Large and luxurious modern, two-storey farmhouse set in 40 acres on Clew Bay.
7rm(3⇌2↱2hc) (4fb) CTV in 2 bedrooms ® ✗ ✱ sB&BIR£13 sB&B⇌↱IR£15-IR£18 dB&BIR£25-IR£26 dB&B⇌↱IR£29-IR£30 WB&BIR£85-IR£100 WBDiIR£170-IR£180 LDO 1pm
⌂ CTV 8P sea angling 40 acres mixed

KILRANE Co Wexford Map **01** D2

FH QQ K O'Leary **O'Leary's** *(T132101)* Killilane, St Helen's Bay ☎(053) 33134
Located in a quiet and peaceful setting overlooking St George's Channel.
10rm(7↱3hc) (3fb) ✱ sB&BIR£14-IR£16 sB&B↱IR£16-IR£18 dB&BIR£23-IR£27 dB&B↱IR£27-IR£31 LDO noon
⌂ CTV P 97 acres arable

KINSALE Co Cork Map **01** B2

SELECTED

GH QQQQ Old Bank House 11 Pearse St ☎(021) 774075 & 772502
Under the personal supervision of Marie and Michael Riese, this delightful Georgian house – once a bank house – has been restored to its former elegance. The en suite bedrooms, with period furniture and attractive décor, combine charm with modern comforts. Dinner is offered in the owners' restaurant.
9⇌↱ (2fb) CTV in all bedrooms **T** ✗ (ex guide dogs) sB&B⇌↱IR£40-IR£50 dB&B⇌↱IR£60-IR£80 WB&BIR£185-IR£256 LDO 10pm
Lic ⌂ P nc12yrs
Credit Cards [1] [2] [3]

KINSALEBEG Co Waterford Map **01** C2

T&C Q Blackwater House ☎(024) 92543
Modern bungalow situated at Youghal Bay.
5hc (3fb) ✗ (ex guide dogs) ✱ dB&BfrIR£26 LDO 6pm
⌂ CTV 6P ▶18 ℘(hard)squash ∪

T&C QQ Gables Rath ☎Cork(024) 92739
May-Oct
Large, luxurious, modern house situated on N25.
5rm(1↱4hc) (1fb) ✗ (ex guide dogs) ✱ sB&BfrIR£16.50 sB&B↱frIR£17.50 dB&BfrIR£26 dB&B↱frIR£28 WB&BfrIR£80 WBDifrIR£150 LDO 6pm
⌂ CTV 8P 🚗 ℘(hard)
Credit Cards [1]

KNOCKFERRY Co Galway Map **01** B4

FH QQ D & M Moran **Knockferry Lodge** *(M238412)* ☎Galway(091) 80122 FAX (091) 80328
May-Sep
Situated on the shores of Lough Corrib, this farmhouse offers good food, cosy turf fires and a welcome that is warm and sincere. Fishing is available outside the door.
10⇌↱ (1fb) ✗ (ex guide dogs) ✱ sB&B⇌↱IR£24 dB&B⇌↱IR£40 WB&BIR£140 WBDiIR£182 LDO 8pm
Lic ⌂ CTV 12P boats for hire games room pool table 35 acres mixed
Credit Cards [1] [2] [3] [5]

LARAGH Co Wicklow Map **01** D3

T&C QQQ Laragh Trekking Centre Glendalough ☎(0404) 45282 FAX (0404) 45365
Run by husband and wife team Noreen and David McCallion. Their joint skills, Noreen's experience in the hotel industry and David's love and knowledge of horses, combine to make a holiday spent with them a memorable occasion. David personally leads the rides around 600 acres of mountains and forests of Co Wicklow.
4rm(1↱3hc) (1fb)⊘in 2 bedrooms CTV in all bedrooms ® ✱ sB&BIR£16-IR£20 sB&B↱IR£20-IR£25 dB&BfrIR£28 dB&B↱IR£32-IR£34 WB&BfrIR£196 WBDifrIR£280 LDO noon
⌂ CTV 10P 2🚗 ♘ ♩ ∪
Credit Cards [1] [2] [3]

LARNE Co Antrim Map **01** D5

GH QQ Derrin 2 Prince's Gardens BT40 1RQ ☎(0574) 273269 & 273762
Situated in a residential area just off the coast road and convenient for the town centre, this detached Victorian villa offers well proportioned and comfortable accommodation. Bedrooms vary in size and while they are simply furnished they are spotlessly clean.
7rm(4↱3hc) (2fb) CTV in all bedrooms ✱ sB&Bfr£15 sB&B↱fr£17 dB&Bfr£25 dB&B↱fr£30
⌂ CTV 3P 2🚗

LETTERKENNY Co Donegal Map **01** C5

T&C QQQ Hill Crest House Lurgybrack, Sligo Rd ☎(074) 22300 & 25137
rs Xmas wk
6rm(5↱1hc) (3fb) ✗ (ex guide dogs) ✱ sB&BIR£13-IR£17 sB&B↱IR£14-IR£18 dB&BIR£24-IR£26 dB&B↱IR£26-IR£28 WB&BfrIR£85
⌂ CTV 10P 1🚗
Credit Cards [1] [2] [3]

This guide is updated annually – make sure you use an up-to-date edition.

LISBURN Co Antrim Map **01** D5

SELECTED

FH QQQQ Mrs D Moore **Brook Lodge** *(J315608)* 79 Old Ballynahinch Rd, Cargacroy BT27 6TH
☎Bailliesmills(0846) 638454
This modern farmhouse is peacefully situated in a rural position just off the A49, 3 miles south of junction 6 of the M1. It offers comfortable accommodation including a pleasant lounge with particularly good views of the surrounding countryside. Bedrooms are compact but prettily decorated and well furnished. The farmhouse offers excellent value for money, and Mrs Moore is a most friendly and hospitable host and provides guests with good home-cooked meals.
5rm(1♠4hc) ✗ (ex guide dogs) ✱ sB&B£15 dB&B£30 dB&B♠£32 WB&B£105 WBDi£147
CTV 10P 65 acres mixed

LISDOONVARNA Co Clare Map **01** B3

GH QQ ***Ballinalacken Castle*** ☎(065) 74025
May-Oct
Fine old house standing in its own grounds in the shadow of the 16th-century O'Brien stronghold of the same name. Open fires in lounges and good sea views from bedrooms.
6rm(1⇌3♠2hc) (3fb) ✗ (ex guide dogs) LDO 8.15pm
Lic CTV
Credit Cards 1 3

T&C Q **Sunville** off Doolin Rd ☎(065) 74065
Modern house in pleasant gardens reaching to roadway. Ideal touring centre.
5⇌♠ (3fb) ✗ (ex guide dogs) sB&B⇌♠frIR£17 dB&B⇌♠frIR£26 WB&BfrIR£90 WBDifrIR£155 LDO noon
CTV 10P
Credit Cards 1

LISTOWEL Co Kerry Map **01** A3

T&C QQ **North County** 67 Church St ☎(068) 21238
Comfortable streetside house in centre of market town. Convenient to Shannon car ferry and all amenities.
8rm(2♠6hc) (2fb) ✗ (ex guide dogs) ✱ sB&BIR£12.50-IR£17 dB&BIR£25-IR£34 dB&B♠IR£28-IR£36 WB&BfrIR£85 WBDifrIR£150 LDO noon
CTV

MILFORD Co Carlow Map **01** C3

SELECTED

T&C QQQQ ***Goleen Country House*** ☎(0503) 46132
Closed Dec-1 Jan
This is a lovely house, tree-screened from the Carlow/Waterford road (N9) and with substantial well tended gardens to the front. The Mulveys have done everything possible to make guests comfortable and the bedrooms especially reflect this concern – being very fully and comfortably equipped. Mrs Mulvey is a charming hostess.
6rm(4♠2hc) ⊬in 2 bedrooms CTV in all bedrooms ® ✗
CTV 12P
Credit Cards 1 3

MONAGHAN Co Monaghan Map **01** C5

T&C QQ **Willow Bridge Lodge** Silver Stream, Armagh Rd ☎(047) 81054
Bill and Ann Holden are the friendly, welcoming proprietors of this comfortable house, situated on the main Armagh Road outside Monaghan town.
4rm(2♠2hc) (1fb) CTV in 2 bedrooms ® ✗ (ex guide dogs) ✱ sB&BIR£15 dB&BIR£27.50 dB&B♠IR£35 WB&BIR£45
CTV 8P nc5yrs

MOUNTRATH Co Laois Map **01** C3

T&C QQQ ***Roundwood House*** ☎(0502) 32120 FAX (0502) 32711
Closed 25 Dec
This Palladian villa, in a secluded woodland setting, transports one back in time to an era of grace and leisure. Excellent hospitality and good food are offered by hosts Frank and Rosemarie Keenan.
6⇌ (2fb) ✗ (ex guide dogs) LDO 5pm
Lic P
Credit Cards 1 2 3 5

MOYARD Co Galway Map **01** A4

FH QQQ Mrs M O'Toole **Rose Cottage** *(L673565)* Rockfield ☎(095) 41082
May-Sep
Comfortable farm bungalow on Clifden/Leenane road, N59, near new National Park.
6♠ (2fb) ® ✗ (ex guide dogs) ✱ dB&B♠frIR£30 WBDifrIR£179 LDO 3pm
CTV 10P 36 acres mixed

NAAS Co Kildare Map **01** C3

FH QQQ Mrs J McLoughlin **Setanta** *(N857230)* Castlekeely, Caragh ☎(045) 76481
Mar-Oct
A modern farm bungalow in a quiet, peaceful area.
5rm(3♠2hc) (4fb) ® ✗ (ex guide dogs) ✱ sB&BIR£13 dB&B♠IR£28 LDO noon
CTV 4P 2🚗 43 acres dry stock

FH QQ M & E Nolan ***Westown*** *(N921214)* Johnstown ☎(045) 97006
Closed 16 Dec-Jan
Modern two-storey house 0.5m off N7.
5hc (3fb) ✗ LDO noon
CTV 9P 92 acres arable mixed

NEW ROSS Co Wexford Map **01** C2

T&C Q ***Inishross House*** 96 Mary St ☎Waterford(051) 21335
Smart and comfortable house in the centre of town.
6hc (2fb) ® ✗ (ex guide dogs) LDO 6pm
CTV 6P 2🚗

FH QQQ Miss B Merrigan **Milltown House** *(S690275)* Milltown ☎(051) 80294
Breda Merrigan, daughter of the owners, successfully looks after the guests, along with other members of the family, at this attractive new establishment located on a busy dairy farm. Large bedrooms that are pleasantly furnished provide comfortable accommodation.
3♠ (4fb) CTV in 2 bedrooms ® ✗ (ex guide dogs) ✱ dB&B♠IR£25 WB&BIR£87.50 WBDiIR£119
CTV 10P 2🚗 80 acres dairy

NINE MILE HOUSE Co Tipperary Map **01** C3

T&C QQ **Grand Inn** ☎(051) 47035
17th-century historic Bianconi Inn situated in scenic Valley of Slievenamon, on the N76.
5rm(3♠2hc) (3fb) ✱ sB&BfrIR£15 sB&B♠frIR£17 dB&BfrIR£26 dB&B♠frIR£30 WB&BfrIR£91 WBDifrIR£154 LDO 7pm
CTV 5P

OGONNELLOE Co Clare Map **01** B3

T&C QQQ Lantern House ☎Scarriff(0619) 23034 & 23123 FAX (061) 923139
mid Feb-Oct & Dec
Situated overlooking Lough Derg, in a very scenic setting on the R436 route, this very comfortable house offers nicely furnished and decorated bedrooms, together with a popular restaurant. The well tended gardens provide a marvellous view of the lake.
6🚿 (2fb) **T** ✗ (ex guide dogs) ✱ sB&B🚿IR£20 dB&B🚿IR£32 WB&BIR£98 WBDiIR£189 LDO 9.30pm
Lic ♨ CTV 25P
Credit Cards [1] [2] [3] [5]

OUGHTERARD Co Galway Map **01** B4

GH QQQ The Boat Inn ☎(091) 82196 FAX (091) 82694
The Boat Inn has recently been refurbished to a very high standard, with attractive and comfortable bedrooms. Hosts Anne and Tom Little provide a friendly welcome and are sure to make your visit a memorable one.
11rm(6🛁5🚿) (4fb) CTV in all bedrooms **T** ✱ sB&B🛁🚿IR£25-IR£28 dB&B🛁🚿IR£39-IR£45 WB&BIR£115-IR£135 WBDiIR£185-IR£195 LDO 10pm
Lic ♨ CTV
Credit Cards [1] [2] [3] [5]

OVENS Co Cork Map **01** B2

T&C QQ Milestone Ballincollig ☎(021) 872562
Large, modern, detached roadside residence in a quiet and peaceful setting; well-maintained lawns and gardens.
5hc (2fb)🚭in 2 bedrooms ✗ ✱ sB&BIR£15-IR£16.50 dB&BIR£25 WB&BfrIR£85 WBDifrIR£150 LDO noon
♨ CTV 8P 🏡

PORTLAOISE Co Laoise Map **01** C3

T&C QQQ ***Aspen House*** Rock of Dunamase ☎Portlaois(0502) 25405
Mar-Oct
Large luxury bungalow on outskirts of town with lovely gardens.
4rm(1🛁2🚿1hc) (2fb)🚭in all bedrooms ✗ (ex guide dogs)
♨ CTV 10P
Credit Cards [1] [3]

T&C QQ Knockmay Town House Marian Av ☎(0502) 22509
Closed 20 Dec-1 Jan
Modern house situated close to town.
6hc (1fb)🚭in all bedrooms CTV in 1 bedroom ✗ ✱ sB&BfrIR£13.50 dB&BfrIR£25
♨ CTV 10P

T&C Q O'Sullivan 8 Kelly Ville Park ☎(0502) 22774
Family-run, two-storey, semidetached house on outskirts of town; homely atmosphere.
6🛁 (1fb) ✗ (ex guide dogs) ✱ sB&B🛁frIR£17.50 dB&B🛁frIR£30
♨ CTV 6P

T&C QQ ***Vicarstown Inn*** Vicarstown ☎(0502) 25189
17 Mar-Oct
200-year-old roadside village inn, situated on banks of Grand Canal. Well appointed bedrooms and public rooms. Ideal centre for coarse fishing.
8rm(2🛁🚿6hc) Annexe 3hc (3fb) ® ✗ (ex guide dogs) LDO noon
Lic ♨ CTV P
Credit Cards [3]

Book as early as possible for busy holiday periods.

PROSPEROUS Co Kildare Map **01** C4

FH QQQ Mrs K Phelan ***Silverspring House*** *(N860266)* Firmount ☎Naas(045) 68481
Mar-Nov
Modern, two-storey house set in peaceful location. Own garden with well-kept lawns.
4hc (2fb)🚭in all bedrooms ® ✗ LDO 10am
♨ CTV 12P 12 acres cattle sheep

RATHDRUM Co Wicklow Map **01** D3

T&C QQQ Abhainn Mor House Corballis ☎(0404) 46330
Feb-13 Nov
Two-storey, modern house with well-tended gardens. Peaceful and scenic location on Avoca/Rathdrum road.
6🛁 (2fb) ® ✗ ✱ sB&B🛁IR£21-IR£22 dB&B🛁IR£28-IR£30 WB&BIR£95-IR£100 WBDiIR£175 LDO noon
♨ CTV 10P 🎾(grass)

GH QQQ Avonbrae House ☎Wicklow(0404) 46198
15 Mar-15 Nov
A small, exclusively run guesthouse nestling in the Wicklow Hills amid mountains, rivers and forests. Situated on the Glendalough road from Rathdrum, this is an ideal touring base, and walking holidays are a speciality. The Avonbrae has a heated indoor swimming pool.
6🚿 (2fb) ® ✱ sB&B🚿IR£23.80 dB&B🚿IR£39.60 WB&BIR£124 WBDiIR£214 LDO noon
Lic ♨ CTV 6P 🏊(heated) 🎾(grass)solarium games room
Credit Cards [1] [2] [3]

T&C QQ St Bridget's Corballis ☎Wicklow(0404) 46477
Closed 23-31 Dec
Large, luxurious bungalow situated in open countryside outside town.
3hc (2fb) ✗ (ex guide dogs) ✱ sB&BfrIR£18 dB&BfrIR£27 WB&BfrIR£91 WBDifrIR£162 LDO noon
♨ CTV 10P ⛳ 18 squash U snooker

ROSSDUFF Co Waterford Map **01** C2

FH QQ Mrs J Richardson **Elton Lodge** *(S665059)* ☎(051) 82117
Jun-Sep
Old-style period farmhouse in quiet and peaceful location.
5🛁🚿 (1fb) ✗ ✱ dB&B🛁🚿IR£28 WBDiIR£150 LDO 3pm
♨ CTV P 200 acres dairy

ROSSNOWLAGH Co Donegal Map **01** B5

T&C QQ ***Ardeelan Manor*** ☎Bundoran(072) 51578
Jun-Aug
Restored early 19th century house situated on outskirts of village. Attractive house with all modern comforts.
5rm(4hc) (3fb)🚭in all bedrooms
♨ P stabling available
Credit Cards [1]

See advertisement on page 471

SHANAGARRY Co Cork Map **01** B2

GH QQQ ***Ballymaloe House*** ☎Cork(021) 652531 Telex no 75208 FAX (021) 652021
Closed 24-26 Dec
The house is part of the old Geraldine Castle rebuilt and modernised. the 14th-century keep remains in its original form. The large, high-ceilinged rooms look out over the 4 acre farm. The food in the award-winning restaurant is based on the produce of the farm, gardens and surrounding district.
18🛁🚿 Annexe 12🛁🚿 (1fb) ✗ (ex guide dogs) LDO 9pm
Lic ♨ CTV P 🏡 🏊(heated) ⛳ 7 🎾(hard)
Credit Cards [1] [2] [3] [5]

SKERRIES Co Dublin Map **01** D4

T&C Q ***Teresa's*** 9 Thomas Hand St ☎(01) 491411
Mar-Sep
Comfortable streetside house convenient to all amenities.
4rm(1🚿3hc) 🐕
♨ CTV

SKIBBEREEN Co Cork Map **01** B2

FH Q Mrs M McCarthy **Abbeystrewery** *(W101339)* Abbey ☎(028) 21713
Jun-Sep
Two-storey farmhouse off Skibbereen/Ballydehob road N71, overlooking the River Llen.
4hc (2fb) 🐕 (ex guide dogs) ✱ sB&BIR£12 LDO am
TV P 20 acres dairy
Credit Cards [1]

SLIGO Co Sligo Map **01** B5

T&C QQQ **Aisling** Cairns Hill ☎(071) 60704
Bungalow overlooking Sligo Bay and near Lough Gill.
6rm(3🚿3hc) (2fb) 🐕 ✱ sB&BIR£16 sB&B🚿IR£18 dB&BIR£26 dB&B🚿IR£29
♨ CTV 6P nc6yrs

T&C QQQ **Tree Tops** Cleveragh Rd ☎(071) 60160
Modern home in sylvan setting on road to Lough Gill and Isle of Innisfree.
6rm(4🚿2hc) (2fb) T 🐕 ✱ sB&BIR£16-IR£17.50 sB&B🚿frIR£17.50 dB&BfrIR£24 dB&B🚿frIR£27
♨ CTV 6P
Credit Cards [1]

FH QQ Mrs E Stuart **Hillside** *(G720394)* Enniskillen Rd ☎(071) 42808
Apr-Oct
Situated in the heart of Yeats Country on the Sligo/Enniskillen road (N16) offering comfortable accommodation. Pony and donkey for children.
4rm(2🚿2hc) (4fb)🚭in all bedrooms 🐕 (ex guide dogs) ✱ sB&BfrIR£15 sB&B🚿frIR£20 dB&BfrIR£26 dB&B🚿frIR£29 WB&BfrIR£145 WBDifrIR£150 LDO 3pm
♨ CTV 8P 3🚗 70 acres beef dairy
Credit Cards [3]

SPIDDAL Co Galway Map **01** B3

T&C QQ **Ard Aoibhinn** Cnocan-Glas ☎Galway(091) 83179
Modern bungalow set back from road in lovely garden. Fine views over Galway Bay and Aran Islands.
6🚿 (3fb) 🐕 (ex guide dogs) ✱ dB&B🚿IR£26-IR£28 WB&BIR£175-IR£185 LDO noon
♨ CTV 6P

T&C QQQ **Ardmor** Greenhill ☎Galway(091) 83145
Mar-Nov
Luxury, split-level bungalow on edge of village. Bright, comfortable rooms and lounge. Sun balcony and fine views over Galway Bay and Aran Islands.
8rm(2🛁6🚿) (4fb)🚭in 7 bedrooms 🐕 (ex guide dogs) ✱ sB&B🛁🚿IR£18-IR£20 dB&B🛁🚿IR£30
♨ CTV 20P
Credit Cards [3]

STREAMSTOWN Co Westmeath Map **01** C4

FH QQ Mrs M Maxwell **Woodlands** *(N286426)* ☎Mullinngar(044) 26414
Mar-Oct
Large, attractive house in a sylvan setting off Mullingar/Athlone road.
6rm(2🚿4hc) (2fb) ✱ sB&BIR£14 dB&BIR£24 dB&B🚿IR£28 WB&BIR£65 WBDiIR£148 LDO 3pm
♨ CTV P 120 acres mixed
Credit Cards [3]

SUMMERHILL Co Meath Map **01** C4

FH QQQ Mrs J Hughes ***Cherryfield*** *(N831504)* Dangan ☎(0405) 57034
Apr-Oct
Impressive, large, two-storey house, nice frontage, with farm buildings in background.
4rm(2🚿2hc) (2fb) 🐕 (ex guide dogs) LDO noon
♨ CTV P ⌂ 75 acres dairy

TAGOAT Co Wexford Map **01** D2

FH QQ Mrs E Doyle **Orchard Park** *(T101120)* Rosslare ☎Wexford(053) 32182
Enlarged farm bungalow in a quiet location, convenient to beach and Rosslare car ferry.
8rm(3🚿5hc) (2fb) ✱ sB&BIR£13-IR£18 sB&B🚿IR£16-IR£20 dB&BIR£25-IR£30 dB&B🚿IR£30-IR£35 LDO noon
CTV 20P 🎾(hard)🎣 trampoline 80 acres arable

TAHILLA Co Kerry Map **01** A2

GH Q ***Tahilla Cove*** ☎Killarney(064) 45204
Etr-Oct
Family-run, split-level bungalow in idyllic setting on a sandy cove on Kenmare Bay.
3🛁 Annexe 6rm(4🛁2🚿) (4fb) LDO 10am
Lic ♨ CTV 10P
Credit Cards [1] [2] [3] [5]

THE ROWER Co Kilkenny Map **01** C3

T&C Q **Hillcrest** ☎(051) 23722
Modern, two-storey house with well-tended gardens situated in a rural setting on T20.
4🛁🚿 (2fb)🚭in 1 bedroom CTV in 1 bedroom TV in 1 bedroom ® 🐕 (ex guide dogs) ✱ sB&B🛁🚿IR£12.50 dB&B🛁🚿IR£25 LDO 10.30pm
♨ CTV 6P 2🚗
Credit Cards [1] [3]

FH QQ Mrs J Prendergast ***Garranavabby House*** *(S708346)* ☎Waterford(051) 23613
Apr-Oct
Two-storey, old-style farmhouse situated in scenic setting between Rivers Nore and Barrow.
3hc (2fb) LDO noon
♨ CTV P 84 acres sheep

TIPPERARY Co Tipperary Map **01** B3

GH QQ **Ach-na-Sheen** Clonmel Rd ☎(062) 51298
Closed 23-31 Dec
Large, modern bungalow, five minutes' walk from main street.
10rm(2🛁2🚿6hc) (2fb)🚭in all bedrooms ✱ sB&BIR£14.50-IR£15 sB&B🛁🚿IR£18-IR£19 dB&BIR£25.50-IR£26 dB&B🛁🚿IR£30-IR£32 LDO 3pm
♨ CTV 10P
Credit Cards [1] [3]

TOBERCURRY Co Sligo Map **01** B4

T&C QQ **Cruckawn House** Ballymote/Boyle Rd ☎(071) 85188
The Walsh family offer a warm welcome at this guesthouse on the outskirts of town, in a scenic area which offers good fishing, horse riding and pony trekking.

5rm(4🚿1hc) (1fb)⁄in 2 bedrooms CTV in all bedrooms ✗ (ex guide dogs) * sB&BfrIR£17 sB&B🚿IR£18 dB&BfrIR£26 dB&B🚿frIR£29 WBDifrIR£165 LDO 6pm
▥ CTV 8P ▸9 ℘(hard)squash snooker sauna gymnasium
Credit Cards [1] [3]

TRALEE Co Kerry Map **01** A2

T&C Q Cnoc Mhuire Oakpark Rd ☎(066) 26027
Closed Xmas
Modern home on the Listowel road backed by a pleasant park. Convenient for Shannon car ferry.
5rm(3🚿2hc) (5fb) Ⓡ sB&BfrIR£16 sB&B🚿frIR£17.50 dB&BfrIR£26 dB&B🚿frIR£28
▥ CTV 6P
Credit Cards [1] [2] [3]

TRAMORE Co Waterford Map **01** C2

T&C QQ Rushmere House Branch Rd ☎Waterford(051) 81041
Closed Xmas & New Year
Three-storey, 100-year-old semidetached house situated on main road overlooking sea. Well-tended gardens.
6rm(3🚿3hc) (2fb) Ⓡ ✗ (ex guide dogs) * sB&BIR£16 sB&B🚿IR£20 dB&BIR£25 dB&B🚿IR£29
▥ CTV

TULLAMORE Co Offaly Map **01** C3

SELECTED

GH QQQQ Moorhill Country House Moorhill, Clara Rd (N80) ☎(0506) 21395 FAX (0506) 52424
Period country residence, set in own secluded gardens, on edge of town.
4🛁🚿 Annexe 8🛁🚿 (1fb) CTV in all bedrooms Ⓡ T ✗ * sB&B🛁🚿IR£25-IR£30 dB&B🛁🚿IR£54-IR£60
LDO 9.30pm
Lic ▥ CTV 50P ℘(grass)
Credit Cards [1] [2] [3] [5]

WATERFORD Co Waterford Map **01** C2

GH QQQ Diamond Hill Diamond Hill, Slieverue ☎(051) 32855 & 32254
A 2-storey house in its own well maintained grounds with well tended flower beds and lawns. Situated on Waterford/Wexford Road.
10🛁🚿 (2fb) Ⓡ ✗ (ex guide dogs) * sB&B🛁🚿IR£18-IR£20 dB&B🛁🚿IR£28-IR£32 WBDiIR£150-IR£185
20P
Credit Cards [1] [3]

T&C QQ *Dunroven* Ballinaneesagh, 25 Cork Rd ☎(051) 74743
Closed 24-26 Dec
Modern house on outskirts of town close to Waterford glass factory. Catering for tourist and commercial trade.
7rm(4🚿3hc) (2fb) ✗ (ex guide dogs) LDO noon
▥ CTV 7P

T&C QQ Knockboy House Dunmore Rd ☎(051) 73484
Closed Dec-Jan
Two-storey house with well-tended gardens, overlooking 'Little Island' and the estuary.
6rm(2🚿4hc) (1fb) ✗ * sB&BfrIR£17 sB&B🚿frIR£19 dB&BfrIR£24 dB&B🚿frIR£28 WB&BfrIR£84.98 WBDifrIR£150
▥ CTV 12P nc3yrs

T&C QQ Villa Eildon Belmont Rd, Ferrybank ☎(051) 32174
Jun-Oct
Excellent house situated on New Ross/Waterford road. Beautifully furnished and decorated with a nice outlook from bedrooms.
4rm(1⌐3hc) ✗ ✱ dB&BIR£29 dB&B⌐IR£34
CTV 6P nc7yrs

FH QQ Mrs A Forrest **Ashbourne House** *(S631140)* Slieverue ☎(051) 32037
Apr-Oct
A comfortable ivy-clad house on the main N25 Waterford/Wexford road. Turn off at the Slieverue sign 2 miles from Waterford. Hospitality is guaranteed from the charming owner Mrs Forrest.
7rm(6⌐1hc) (5fb) sB&BIR£11.50-IR£15.50 sB&B⌐IR£13-IR£17 dB&BIR£23 dB&B⌐IR£26 WB&BIR£75-IR£84 WBDiIR£140-IR£148 LDO 3pm
CTV 8P U 20 acres beef

WATERVILLE Co Kerry Map **01** A2

GH QQQ *Smugglers Inn* Cliff Rd ☎(0667) 4330 & 4422
Mar-14 Dec
Beachside guesthouse/restaurant;, family run and very popular. Owner/chef.
10rm(3⇌7⌐) (4fb) ✗ (ex guide dogs) LDO 9.30pm
Lic CTV 40P ▶18
Credit Cards 1 2 3 5

WESTPORT Co Mayo Map **01** A4

FH QQQ Mrs M O'Brien **Rath-a-Rosa** *(L953822)* Rossbeg ☎(098) 25348
Mar-Oct
A modern bungalow on T39, overlooking Clew Bay.
6rm(4⇌⌐2hc) (2fb) ✗ (ex guide dogs) ✱ sB&BfrIR£17 sB&B⇌⌐frIR£20 dB&BfrIR£26 dB&B⇌⌐frIR£32
LDO 11am
CTV 6P 20 acres mixed
Credit Cards 1 3

WEXFORD Co Wexford Map **01** D2

SELECTED

T&C QQQQ Ardruagh Spawell Rd ☎(053) 23194
Closed 17 Dec-7 Jan
A former Vicarage, this magnificent house on the edge of Wexford looks out over the roofs of houses to the estuary in Wexford. The bedrooms and public rooms are spacious and luxurious and the Corish family take a particular pride in looking after their guests.
5⌐ (2fb) CTV in 3 bedrooms ® ✗ (ex guide dogs) ✱ dB&B⌐frIR£30
CTV 10P
Credit Cards 1 3

GH QQ Faythe Swan View ☎(053) 22249
Closed 23 Dec-4 Jan
Fine old house in quiet part of town. Modest comfort and pleasant atmosphere.
11rm(1⌐10hc) (4fb) CTV in 1 bedroom ✗ (ex guide dogs)
LDO 7.30pm
Lic CTV 30P snooker
Credit Cards 1 2 3 5

T&C QQQ Rathaspeck Manor Rathaspeck ☎(053) 42661 & 45148
Jun-Oct
Standing in its own grounds, which feature an 18-hole, par-3 golf course, this 300-year-old restored Georgian country house is situated half a mile from Johnstown Castle. The comfortable, spacious bedrooms are en suite and the public rooms are appointed with period furnishings. Hospitable Mrs Cuddihy will provide dinner by arrangement and the guesthouse holds a wine licence. Good parking is available.
7⇌⌐ (3fb) CTV in all bedrooms ✗ ✱ sB&B⇌⌐frIR£22 dB&B⇌⌐frIR£40 WBDifrIR£200 LDO noon
8P nc10yrs ▶18 (hard)

T&C QQ Tara Villa Larkins Cross, Barntown ☎(053) 45119
Situated on main Wexford/New Ross route (N25) go past the sign for Barntown, continue on main road until a large pink house is reached where a warm welcome awaits the traveller from proprietors Mr and Mrs Whitty.
5⌐ (3fb) ✗ (ex guide dogs) ✱ dB&B⌐IR£27-IR£32
LDO 8pm
Lic CTV 10P 3
Credit Cards 1 3

T&C Q Villa Maria Coolcots ☎(053) 45143
This pleasant, well furnished house is situated off the old road to New Ross. It is good, clean and comfortable.
4rm(3⌐1hc) (2fb) ✗ (ex guide dogs) ✱ sB&BfrIR£14 sB&B⌐frIR£15 dB&BfrIR£24 dB&B⌐frIR£26

SELECTED

GH QQQQ *Whitford House* New Lime Rd ☎(053) 43444 & 43845
Closed 20 Dec-8 Jan
Smart, modern house, with recent extensions, on outskirts of town. Indoor swimming pool and tennis available.
27⇌⌐ (10fb) CTV in all bedrooms ✗ (ex guide dogs)
LDO 8pm
Lic CTV 100P
Credit Cards 1 3

WICKLOW Co Wicklow Map **01** D3

SELECTED

GH QQQQ The Old Rectory Country House & Restaurant ☎(0404) 67048 FAX (0404) 69181
Etr-mid Oct
A fine restored Georgian country house in its own grounds on the edge of Wicklow town. Large airy bedrooms and comfortable public rooms with log fires. Good food from fresh local produce.
5⇌⌐ (1fb) CTV in all bedrooms ® T ✗ sB&B⇌⌐IR£59 dB&B⇌⌐IR£84 WB&BIR£224-IR£238 WBDiIR£350-IR£371 LDO 6pm
Lic 12P
Credit Cards 1 2 3 5

T&C QQ Thomond House St Patrick's Rd Upper ☎(0404) 67940
Mar-Oct
A modern two-storey house with commanding view over the seashore, the surrounding countryside, lakes and mountains.
5rm(2⌐3hc) (1fb) ✗ (ex guide dogs) sB&BIR£16.50-IR£17 dB&BIR£25-IR£26 dB&B⌐IR£29-IR£30 LDO noon
CTV 5P
Credit Cards 1

FH QQQ Mrs P Klaue **Lissadell House** *(T302925)*
Ashtown Ln ☎(0404) 67458
Mar-Dec
Two-storey modern house in own grounds situated in scenic location on the outskirts of town.
4rm(1⇌1♠2hc) (1fb) ✗ (ex guide dogs) dB&BIR£28 dB&B⇌♠IR£32 LDO noon
CTV P 285 acres mixed

YOUGHAL Co Cork Map **01** C2

SELECTED

GH QQQQ Ahernes 163 North Main St ☎(024) 92424 FAX (024) 93633
Closed Xmas & Good Friday
Offering accommodation in spacious bedrooms, furnished to the highest standard with antiques and modern facilities, this pleasant guesthouse boasts an award- winning restaurant, well known for its seafood specialities. There is a cosy drawing room provided for guests and parking is available.
10⇌♠ CTV in all bedrooms T ✗ (ex guide dogs) sB&B⇌♠IR£43 dB&B⇌♠IR£75 LDO 9.30pm
Lic 10P
Credit Cards 1 2 3 5

T&C QQ Carriglea Ballyvergan East, Summerfield ☎(024) 92520
Jun-Sep
Well appointed modern bungalow situated on the outskirts of Youghal on the N25 overlooking the sea. Mr and Mrs Walsh are a hospitable friendly couple who will ensure your every comfort.
4hc (1fb) sB&BIR£13 dB&BIR£22 WB&BIR£70
CTV 8P

T&C Q Devon View Pearse Square ☎(024) 92298
6⇌♠ (2fb) CTV in all bedrooms ® ✱ sB&BIR£15 dB&B⇌♠IR£26 WB&BIR£91 WBDiIR£154 LDO 5pm
CTV 8P
Credit Cards 1 3

FH QQ Mrs E Long **Cherrymount** *(X071823)*
☎(024) 97110
The house is reputed to be about 500 years old but much modernised in recent times.
5hc (2fb) sB&BfrIR£10 dB&BfrIR£20 WB&BfrIR£70 LDO 5pm
CTV 10P ▶18 ℘(hard)70 acres dairy
Credit Cards 1 2 3

This is one of many guidebooks published by the AA. The full range is available at any AA Shop or good bookshop.

BEST VALUE ACCOMMODATION

The county index that follows is a list of guesthouses, farmhouses and inns that offer bed and breakfast accommodation for under £15 per person per night. For more details about the establishments listed, turn to their entries in the Directory.

ENGLAND

AVON

Cromhall	FH	Kimber's Lea
Weston-Super-Mare	GH	Baymead Hotel
Weston-Super-Mare	GH	Clifton Lodge

BUCKINGHAMSHIRE

Gayhurst	FH	Mill

CORNWALL & ISLES OF SCILLY

Bodmin	GH	Mount Pleasant Morland Hotel
Boscastle	GH	Melbourne House
Boscastle	GH	Old Coach House
Bude	GH	Pencarrol
Grampound	GH	Perran House
Launceston	FH	Hurdon
Liskeard	FH	Tregondale
Lizard	GH	Parc Brawse House
Newlyn East	FH	Degembris
Newquay	GH	Aloha
Newquay	GH	Claremount
Newquay	GH	Tir Chonaill Lodge
Newquay	GH	Wheal Treasure Hotel
Penzance	GH	Blue Seas Hotel
Penzance	GH	Dunedin
Penzance	GH	Kimberley House
Penzance	GH	Penmorvah Hotel
Penzance	GH	Trevelyan Hotel
Penzance	GH	Trewella
Polbathic	GH	The Old Mill
St Ives	GH	Chy-an-Creet Private Hotel
St Ives	GH	Monowai Private Hotel
Sennen	GH	The Old Manor House
Sennen	GH	Sunny Bank Hotel
Tideford	FH	Kilna House
Tintagel	GH	Castle Villa
Troon	GH	Sea View Farm

CUMBRIA

Carlisle	FH	Blackwell
Carlisle	GH	East View
Carlisle	GH	Kenilworth
Kendal	FH	Gateside
Keswick	GH	Clarence House
Keswick	GH	Edwardene
Keswick	GH	Fell House
Keswick	GH	Latrigg House
Keswick	GH	Richmond House
Keswick	GH	Twa Dogs
Penruddock	FH	Highgate
Windermere	GH	Aaron Slack
Windermere	GH	Holly Lodge
Windermere	GH	Kenilworth
Windermere	GH	Mylne Bridge House
Windermere	GH	Thornleigh

DERBYSHIRE

Matlock	FH	Farley

DEVON

Abbots Bickington	FH	Court Barton
Barnstaple	GH	Cresta
Barnstaple	FH	Rowden Barton
Barnstaple	GH	West View
Bridestowe	FH	Little Bidlake
Brixham	GH	Harbour Side
Ilfracombe	GH	Collingdale Hotel
Ilfracombe	GH	Strathmore Private Hotel
Lewdown	FH	Venn Mill
Lynton	GH	Retreat
Lynton	GH	St Vincent
Moreton-hampstead	FH	Wooston
Paignton	GH	St Weonard's Private Hotel
Paignton	GH	Waterleat House
Teignmouth	GH	Hill Rise Hotel
Tiverton	FH	Lodge Hill
Torquay	GH	Chesterfield Hotel
Torquay	GH	Clovelly
Torquay	GH	Cranmore
Torquay	GH	Exmouth View Hotel
Torquay	GH	Fairways Hotel
Torquay	GH	Hotel Trelawney
Torquay	GH	Jesmond Dene Private Hotel
Torquay	GH	Kingston House
Torquay	GH	Lindrum Hotel
Torquay	GH	Sevens Hotel
Uffculme	FH	Houndaller

Willand	FH	Doctors

DORSET

Bournemouth	GH	Cransley Private Hotel
Bournemouth	GH	Derwent House
Bournemouth	GH	Dorset House
Bournemouth	GH	Mayfield Private Hotel
Bournemouth	GH	Norland Private Hotel
Bournemouth	GH	Hotel Sorrento
Bournemouth	GH	Telstar
Swanage	GH	Burlington House
Weymouth	GH	Birchfields
Weymouth	GH	Hazeldene

GLOUCESTERSHIRE

Cheltenham	GH	Knowle House
Stow-on-the-Wold	FH	Corsham Field

HAMPSHIRE

Portsmouth & Southsea	GH	Abbey Lodge
Portsmouth & Southsea	GH	Collingham
Portsmouth & Southsea	GH	The Elms
Portsmouth & Southsea	GH	Hamilton House
Portsmouth & Southsea	GH	St Andrews Lodge

HUMBERSIDE

Pocklington	FH	Meltonby Hall

KENT

Dover	GH	Charlton Green
Dover	GH	Dell
Dymchurch	GH	Waterside
Margate	GH	Charnwood Private Hotel
Ramsgate	GH	St Hilary Private Hotel

LANCASHIRE

Blackpool	GH	Brooklands Hotel
Blackpool	GH	The Colby
Blackpool	GH	The Garville Hotel
Blackpool	GH	Woodleigh Private Hotel
Morecambe	GH	Ashley Private Hotel

LINCOLNSHIRE

Hainton	GH	The Old Vicarage

MAN, ISLE OF

Douglas	GH	Ainsdale

NORFOLK

Hunstanton	GH	Pinewood Hotel
King's Lynn	GH	Fairlight Lodge
King's Lynn	GH	Havana
King's Lynn	GH	Maranatha

SHROPSHIRE

Dorrington	GH	Ashton Lees
Stiperstones	GH	Tankerville Lodge

SOMERSET

Pawlett	FH	Brickyard
Taunton	GH	Brookfield
Yeovil	FH	Carents

SUFFOLK

Hitcham	FH	Wetherden Hall

SUSSEX (EAST)

Bexhill	GH	The Arosa
Hastings & St Leonards	GH	Argyle

TYNE & WEAR

Whitley Bay	GH	Cherrytree House

WARWICKSHIRE

Claverdon	GH	Woodside Country
Ettington	FH	Whitfield
Leamington Spa	GH	Charnwood
Lighthorne	FH	Redlands
Stratford-upon-Avon	GH	Courtland Hotel
Stratford-upon-Avon	FH	Monk's Barn
Stratford-upon-Avon	GH	Penryn House
Stratford-upon-Avon	GH	Salamander
Warwick	GH	Avon
Wimpstone	FH	Whitchurch

WIGHT, ISLE OF

Shanklin	GH	Culham Lodge
Shanklin	GH	Rowborough Hotel
Shanklin	GH	Soraba Private Hotel

WILTSHIRE

Malmesbury	FH	Stonehill

YORKSHIRE (NORTH)

Bell Busk	GH	Tudor House
Pickering	GH	Bramwood
Scarborough	GH	Meadow Court Hotel
Selby	GH	Hazeldene
Whitby	GH	Glendale
York	GH	Acorn
York	GH	Arnot House
York	GH	The Beckett
York	GH	Carousel

York	GH	City
York	GH	Greenside
York	GH	Hillcrest
York	GH	Jubilee
York	GH	Sycamore

YORKSHIRE (SOUTH)

Doncaster	Inn	Nelsons Hotel

WALES

CLWYD

Corwen	GH	Corwen Court Private Hotel
Denbigh	GH	Cayo
Holywell	FH	Green Hill
Mold	FH	Hill
Prestatyn	GH	Roughsedge House
Rhyl	GH	Pier Hotel

DYFED

Cardigan	GH	Brynhyfryd
Stepaside	GH	Bay View Hotel
Tenby	GH	Tall Ships
Whitland	GH	Llangwm House

GWYNEDD

Abersoch	GH	Ty Draw
Betws-y-Coed	GH	Bryn Llewelyn
Betws-y-Coed	GH	The Ferns
Dolgellau	FH	Glyn Farm
Llandudno	GH	Brannock Private House
Llandudno	GH	Rosaire Private Hotel
Porthmadog	GH	Oakleys

MID GLAMORGAN

Porthcawl	GH	Minerva Hotel

POWYS

Brecon	GH	Flag & Castle
Church Stoke	FH	The Drewin
Llangurig	GH	Old Vicarage
Llansantffraid-ym-Mechain	FH	Glanvyrnwy
Montgomery	FH	Little Brompton
Sennybridge	FH	Brynfedwen

SCOTLAND

CENTRAL

Callander	GH	Greenbank
Port of Menteith	FH	Collymoon Pendicle

DUMFRIES & GALLOWAY

Dalbeattie	Inn	Pheasant Hotel
Lockerbie	GH	Rosehill

FIFE

St Andrews	GH	Clevedon House
St Andrews	GH	Romar

HIGHLAND

Beauly	GH	Heathmount
Carrbridge	GH	Carrmoor
Glencoe	GH	Scorrybreac
Inverness	GH	Hebrides
Latheron	FH	Upper Latheron
Nairn	GH	Ardgour Hotel
Spean Bridge	GH	Coire Glas

LOTHIAN

Edinburgh	GH	Daisy Park House
Edinburgh	GH	Ellesmere House

STRATHCLYDE

Abington	FH	Craighead
Ayr	GH	Craggallan
Connel	GH	Ronebhal
Glenmavis	FH	Braidenhill
Oban	GH	Sgeir Mhaol

TAYSIDE

Cortachy	FH	Cullew
Perth	GH	The Darroch
Perth	GH	The Gables
Perth	GH	Iona

REPUBLIC OF IRELAND

CORK

Youghal	T&C	Carriglea
Youghal	FH	Cherrymount

DONEGAL

Carrigans	T&C	Mount Royd Country Home

GALWAY

Clifden	T&C	Failte

KERRY

Kenmare	GH	Foleys Shamrock

KILKENNY

Bennettsbridge	T&C	Norely Theyr

MAYO

Achill Island	T&C	West Coast House

TIPPERARY

Bansha	FH	Bansha House

WATERFORD

Waterford	FH	Ashbourne House

WICKLOW

Avoca	T&C	Ashdene

*O*NE STAR HOTELS

The following is a list in county order of one-star hotels offering good value accommodation. The hotels are taken from the 1993 edition of the AA Hotels and Restaurants in Britain and Ireland. They are not listed in the A-Z directory. For more details about the establishments listed, contact them direct.

ENGLAND

AVON

Bath	Royal	(0225) 463134

CAMBRIDGESHIRE

Chatteris	Cross Keys	(0354) 693036
Ely	The Nyton	(0353) 662459
March	Olde Griffin	(0354) 52517

CHESHIRE

Chester	Leahurst Court	(0244) 327542
Chester	Weston House	(0244)326735
Warrington	Kenilworth	(0925) 262323
Warrington	Ribblesdale	(0925) 601197

CLEVELAND

Middlesbrough	The Grey House	(0642) 817485

CO DURHAM

Durham	Redhills	091-386 4331

CORNWALL & ISLES OF SCILLY

Bodinnick	Old Ferry Inn	(0726) 870237
Bude	Edgcumbe	(0288) 353846
Bude	Maer Lodge	(0288) 353306
Bude	Meva Gwin	(0288) 352347
Gwithian	Sandsifter	(0736) 753314
Harlyn Bay	Polmark	(0841) 520206
Lizard	Kynance Bay House	(0326) 290498
Mevagissey	Sharksfin	(0726) 843241
Mount Hawke	Tregarthen Country Cottage	(0209) 890399
Newquay	Lowenva	(0637) 873569
Newquay	Trevone	(0637) 873039
Padstow	St Petroc's House	(0841) 532700
Penzance	Estoril	(0736) 62468
Penzance	Tarbert	(0736) 63758
Perranporth	Beach Dunes	(0872) 572263
Perranuthnoe	Ednovean House	(0736) 711071
Polperro	Claremont	(0503) 72241
St Agnes	Sunholme	(0872) 552318
St Austell	Selwood House	(0726) 65707
St Ives	Dunmar	(0736) 796117
St Wenn	Wenn Manor	(0726) 890240
Talland Bay	Allhays Country House	(0503) 72434
Torpoint	Whitsand Bay , Golf & Country Club	(0503) 30276

CUMBRIA

Appleby-in-Westmorland	Courtfield	(07683) 51394
Beetham	Wheatsheaf	(05395) 62123
Brampton	Howard Arms	(06977) 2357
Broughton in Furness	Old King's Head	(0229) 716293
Carlisle	Vallum House Garden	(0228) 21860
Coniston	The Old Rectory	(05394) 41353
Grange-over-Sands	Clare House	(05395) 33026
Grasmere	White Moss House	(05394) 35295
Keswick	Highfield	(07687) 72508
Keswick	Linnett Hill	(07687) 73109
Keswick	Priorholm	(07687) 72745
Keswick	Swinside Lodge	(07687) 72948
Kirkby Lonsdale	Cobwebs Country House	(05242) 72141
Loweswater	Grange Country House	(0946) 861211
Maryport	Waverley	(0900) 812115
Mungrisdale	The Mill	(07687) 79659
Penrith	Glen Cottage	(0768) 62221
Ravenglass	Pennington Arms	(0229)717222
Windermere	Willowsmere	(05394) 43575
Witherslack	Old Vicarage Country House	(044852) 381 *due to change to* (05395) 52381

DERBYSHIRE

Buxton	Hartington	(0298) 22638
Chesterfield	Abbeydale	(0246) 277849
Hartington	Charles Cotton	(029884) 229

DEVON

Barnstaple	Halmpstone Manor	(0271) 830321
Bigbury-on-Sea	Henley	(0548) 810240
Brixham	Smuggler's Haunt	(0803) 853050
Clovelly	Red Lion	(0237) 431237
Exmouth	Aliston House	(0395) 274119
Fenny Bridges	Fenny Bridges	(0404)850218
Fenny Bridges	Greyhound Inn	(0404) 850380
Ilfracombe	Torrs	(0271) 862334
Lifton	Thatched Cottage Country	(0566) 784224
Lynmouth	Rock House	(0598) 53508
Lynton	Chough's Nest	(0598) 53315
Lynton	Combe Park	(0598) 52356
Lynton	Fairholme	(0598) 52263
Lynton	North Cliff	(0598) 52357
Lynton	Rockvale	(0598) 52279
Lynton	Seawood	(0598) 52272
Newton Abbot	Hazelwood	(0626) 66130
Paignton	Oldway Links	(0803) 559332
Paignton	South Sands	(0803) 557231
Plymouth	Drake	(0752) 229730
Plymouth	Imperial	(0752) 227311
Plymouth	Victoria Court	(0752) 668133
Salcombe	Sunny Cliff	(0548) 842207

Salcombe	Woodgrange	(0548) 842439
Staverton	Sea Trout Inn	(080426) 274
	due to change to	(0803) 762274
Teignmouth	Bay	(0626) 774123
Teignmouth	Belvedere	(0626) 774561
Teignmouth	Glenside	(0626) 872448
Torcross	Grey Homes	(0548) 580220
Torquay	Ashley Rise	(0803) 327282
Torquay	Fairmount House	(0803) 605446
Torquay	Fluela	(0803) 297512
Torquay	Shelley Court	(0803) 295642
Torquay	Sunleigh	(0803) 607137
Torquay	Sunray	(0803) 328285
Torquay	Westwood	(0803) 293818
Woolacombe	Crossways	(0271) 870395

DORSET

Bournemouth	Lynden Court	(0202) 553894
Bournemouth	Taurus Park	(0202) 557374
Bridport	Bridge House	(0308) 23371
Bridport	Bridport Arms	(0308) 22994
Charmouth	Hensleigh	(0297) 60830
Lyme Regis	Tudor House	(0297) 442472
Poole	Fairlight	(0202) 694316
West Lulworth	Shirley	(092941) 358
Weymouth	Alexandra	(0305) 785767

ESSEX

Frinton-on-Sea	Rock	(0255) 677194
Southend-on-Sea	Balmoral	(0702) 342947

GLOUCESTERSHIRE

Gloucester	Rotherfield House	(0452) 410500

GREATER MANCHESTER

Altrincham	The Unicorn	061-980 4347
Bolton	Broomfield	(0204) 61570
Bury	Woolfield House	061-797 9775
Marple	Springfield	061-449 0721
Salford	Beaucliffe	061-789 5092

HAMPSHIRE

Brockenhurst	Cloud	(0590) 22165
Farnborough	Alexandra	(0252) 541050
Ringwood	Moortown Lodge	(0425) 471404

HEREFORD & WORCESTER

Knightwick	Talbot	(0886) 21235
Leominster	The Marsh Country	(0568) 613952
Malvern	Deacons	(0684) 566990
Worcester	Park House	(0905) 21816

HUMBERSIDE

Flamborough	Flaneburg	(0262) 850284

LANCASHIRE

Blackpool	Kimberley	(0253) 41184
Chipping	The Brickhouse Country	(0995) 61316
Lytham St Annes	Carlton	(0253) 721036
Lytham St Annes	Ennes Court	(0253) 723731
Lytham St Annes	Lindum	(0253) 721534
Morecambe	Channings	(0524) 417925
Silverdale	Silverdale	(0524) 701206

LEICESTERSHIRE

Groby	Brant Inn	(0533) 872703
Uppingham	Crown	(0572) 822302

LINCOLNSHIRE

Alford	White Horse	(0507) 462218
Osbournby	Whichcote Arms	(05295) 239

LONDON (GREATER)

Croydon	Central	081-688 5644
(Postal Districts)		
SW1	Ebury Court	071-730 8147

MERSEYSIDE

Rainhill	Rockland	051-426 4603

NORFOLK

Cawston	Grey Gables	(0603) 871259
Downham Market	Crown	(0366) 382322
East Dereham	George	(0362) 696801
Horning	Swan	(0692) 630316
Hunstanton	Wash & Tope	(0485) 532250
Thetford	Wereham House	(0842) 761956
Wells-next-the-Sea	Crown	(0328) 710209
Wroxham	Kings Head	(0603) 782429

NORTHUMBERLAND

Bamburgh	Sunningdale	(06684) 334
Bamburgh	The Mizen Head	(06684) 254
Bardon Mill	Vallum Lodge	(0434) 344248
Berwick-upon-Tweed	Queens Head	(0289) 307852
Corbridge	Riverside	(0434) 632942

OXFORDSHIRE

Oxford	River	(0865) 243475
Oxford	The Palace	(0865) 727627

SHROPSHIRE

Bridgnorth	Whitburn Grange	(0746) 766786
Telford	Arleston Inn	(0952) 501881
Whittington	Ye Olde Boot Inn	(0691) 662250

SOMERSET

Bilbrook	Bilbrook Lawns	(0984) 40331
Cheddar	Gordons	(0934) 742497
Waterrow	Hurstone Country	(0984) 23441
Wells	Ancient Gate House	(0749) 672029
Yeovil	Little Barwick House	(0935) 23902
Yeovil	Preston	(0935) 74400

SUFFOLK

Clare	The Clare	(0787) 277449
Lavenham	Angel	(0787) 247388
Leiston	White Horse	(0728) 830694
Lowestoft	Denes Toby	(0502) 564616
Mendham	Sir Alfred Munnings Country	(0379) 852358
Saxmundham	Bell	(0728) 602331

SURREY

Horley	Langshott Manor	(0293) 786680

SUSSEX (EAST)

Eastbourne	Downland	(0323) 32689
Eastbourne	Lathom	(0323) 641986
Eastbourne	Oban	(0323) 31581
Rye	Playden Oasts	(0797) 223502

SUSSEX (WEST)

Arundel	Burpham Country	(0903) 882160
Bognor Regis	Black Mill House	(0243) 821945
Chichester	Bedford	(0243) 785766

TYNE & WEAR

Newcastle upon Tyne	Osborne	091-281 3385
Sunderland	Gelt House	091-567 2990
Whitley Bay	Cavendish	091-253 3010

WARWICKSHIRE

Atherstone	Chapel House	(0827) 718949
Royal Leamington Spa	Lansdowne	(0926) 450505
Warwick	Penderrick	(0926) 499399

WIGHT, ISLE OF

Chale	Clarendon & Wight Mouse Inn	(0983) 730431
St Lawrence	The Lawyers Rest Country House	(0983) 852610

WILTSHIRE

Trowbridge	Hilbury Court	(0225) 752949

YORKSHIRE, NORTH

Austwick	The Traddock	(05242) 51224
Filey	Sea Brink	(0723) 513257
Goathland	Whitfield House	(0947) 86215
Grassington	Black Horse	(0756) 752770
Harrogate	Alvera Court	(0423) 505735
Harrogate	Aston	(0432) 564262
Harrogate	Britannia Lodge	(0423) 508482
Harrogate	Cavendish	(0423) 509637
Harrogate	Gables	(0423) 505625
Harrogate	Grafton	(0423) 508491
Harrogate	The Croft	(0423) 563326
Leyburn	Golden Lion	(0969) 22161
Malton	Wentworth Arms	(0653) 692618
Robin Hood's Bay	Grosvenor	(0947) 880320
Smallways	A66 Motel	(0833) 27334
Thirsk	Old Red House	(0845) 524383
Thornton	Watlass Buck Inn	(0677) 422461
York	Fairmount	(0904) 638298

YORKSHIRE, WEST

Bradford	Park Grove	(0274) 543444
Ilkley	Grove	(0943) 600298
Ilkley	Moorview House	(0943) 600156

WALES

CLWYD

Colwyn Bay	Glyndwr Private	(0492) 533254
Colwyn Bay	Marine	(0492) 530295
Colwyn Bay	West Point	(0492) 530331
Colwyn Bay	Whitehall	(0492) 547296
Nannerch	The Old Mill	(0352) 741542

DYFED

Aberporth	Glandwr Manor	(0239) 810197
Fishguard	Abergwaun	(0348) 872077
Llanelli	Miramar	(0554) 754726
Tresaith	Bryn Berwyn	(0239) 811126

GWYNEDD

Aberdovey	Maybank	(0654)767500
Barmouth	Bryn Melyn	(0341) 280556
Barmouth	Llwyndu Farmhouse	(0341) 280144
Barmouth	Marwyn	(0341) 280185
Beddgelert	Sygun Fawr Country House	(076686) 258
Beddgelert	Tanronen	(076686) 347
Betws-y-Coed	Fairy Glen	(0690) 710269
Caernarfon	Chocolate House	(0286) 672542
Criccieth	Abereistedd	(0766) 522710
Criccieth	Caerwylan	(0766) 522547
Dolgellau	Clifton House	(0341) 422554
Harlech	Noddfa	(0766) 780043
Llanberis	Gallt-y-Glyn	(0286) 870370
Llandudno	Banham House	(0492) 875680
Llandudno	Branksome	(0492) 875989
Llandudno	Brigstock	(0492) 876416
Llandudno	Bryn-y-Mor	(0492) 876790
Llandudno	Clontarf	(0492) 877621
Llandudno	Concord	(0492) 875504
Llandudno	Crickleigh	(0492) 875926
Llandudno	Epperstone	(0492) 878746
Llandudno	Gwesty Leamore	(0492) 875552
Llandudno	Heath House	(0492) 876538
Llandudno	Hilbre Court	(0492) 876632
Llandudno	Min-y-Don	(0492) 876511
Llandudno	Quinton	(0492) 876879
Llandudno	Ravenhurst	(0492) 875525
Llandudno	Stratford	(0492) 877962
Llandudno	Tan-y-Marian Private	(0492) 877727
Llandudno	White Lodge	(0492) 877713
Mallwyd	Brigand's Inn	(06504) 208
Nefyn	Caeau Capel	(0758) 720240
Pwllheli	The Seahaven	(0758) 612572
Red Wharf Bay	Min-y-Don	(0248) 852596
Tal-y-Llyn	Minffordd	(0654) 761665
Tywyn	Greenfield	(0654) 710354

MID GLAMORGAN

Porthcawl	Brentwood	(0656) 782725
Porthcawl	Rose & Crown	(0656) 784850

POWYS

Brecon	Lansdowne	(0874) 623321
Llanwrtyd Wells	Carlton House	(05913) 248

SOUTH GLAMORGAN

Penarth	Walton House	(0222) 707782

WEST GLAMORGAN

Mumbles	St Anne's	(0792) 369147
Swansea	Parkway	(0792) 201632
Swansea	Windsor Lodge	(0792) 642158

SCOTLAND

BORDERS

Hawick	Hopehill House	(0450) 75042

CENTRAL

Callander	Highland House	(0877) 30269
Lochearnhead	Lochearnhead	(05673) 229
Lochearnhead	Mansewood Country House	(05673) 213
Rowardennan	Rowardennan Loch Lomond	(036087) 273
Strathyre	The Inn	(08774) 224

DUMFRIES & GALLOWAY

Crocketford	Lochview Motel	(055669) 281
Dumfries	Skyline	(0387) 62416
Lockerbie	Ravenshill House	(05762) 2882
	due to change to	(0576) 202882
Moffat	Well View	(0683) 20184
Portpatrick	Mount Stewart	(077681) 291
Thornhill	George	(0848) 30326

FIFE

Crail	Croma	(0333) 50239

GRAMPIAN

Bridge of Marnoch	The Old Manse of Marnoch	(0466) 780873
Old Meldrum	Meldrum Arms	(06512) 2238

HIGHLAND

Ardelve	Loch Duich	(059985) 213
Culnacnoc	Glenview Inn	(047062) 248
Fort William	Factor's House	(0397) 705767
Grantown-on-Spey	Tyree House	(0479) 2615
Harlosh	Harlosh House	(047022) 367
Inverness	Redcliffe	(0463) 232767
Isle Ornsay	Eilean Iarmain	(04713) 332
Kingussie	Osprey	(0540) 661510
Portree	Isles	(0478) 2129
Uig	Ferry Inn	(047042) 242

LOTHIAN

Dunbar	The Courtyard	(0368) 64169
Edinburgh	Iona	031-447 6264

STRATHCLYDE

Ayr	Aftongrange	(0292) 265679
Ayr	Almont	(0292) 263814
Dervaig	Druimard Country House	(06884)345
Inveraray	Fernpoint	(0499) 2170
Oban	Foxholes	(0631) 64982
Rothesay	St Ebba	(0700) 502683
Scalasaig	Colonsay	(09512) 316
Tarbert Loch Fyne	West Loch	(0880) 820283
Tobermory	Mishnish	(0688) 2009
Tobermory	Ulva House	(0688) 2044

TAYSIDE

Aberfeldy	Guinach House	(0887) 820251
Bridge of Cally	Bridge of Cally	(0250) 886231
Carnoustie	Station	(0241) 52447
Crieff	Gwydyr House	(0764) 3277
Crieff	Locke's Acre	(0764) 2526
Fearnan	Tigh-an-Loan	(0887) 830249
Kirkmichael	Strathlene	(0250) 881347
Pitlochry	Craig Urrard	(0796) 472346

NORTHERN IRELAND

ANTRIM

Carrickfergus	Dobbins Inn	(09603) 51905

FERMANAGH

Enniskillen	Railway	(0365) 22084

REPUBLIC OF IRELAND

CLARE

Kilkee	Halpin's	(065) 56032

CORK

Inchigeela	Creedon's	(026) 49012

DONEGAL

Malin	Malin	(077) 70606
Rathmullan	Pier	(074) 58178

GALWAY

Galway	Atlanta	(091) 62241

LIMERICK

Abbeyfeale	Leen's	(068) 31121

TIPPERARY

Tipperary	Royal	(062) 51204

WATERFORD

Ardmore	Cliff House	(024) 94106
Dunmore East	Candlelight Inn	(051) 83215

WICKLOW

Ashford	Cullenmore	(0404) 40422

INDEX OF TOWN PLANS

KEY TO TOWN PLANS

Recommended Route
Other Routes
Restricted Roads
Churches

Tourist Information Centre
AA Centre
Car parking

Guesthouse, inn, etc
Distance to guesthouses, etc, from edge of plan
ASHFORD 16m Mileage to town from edge of plan

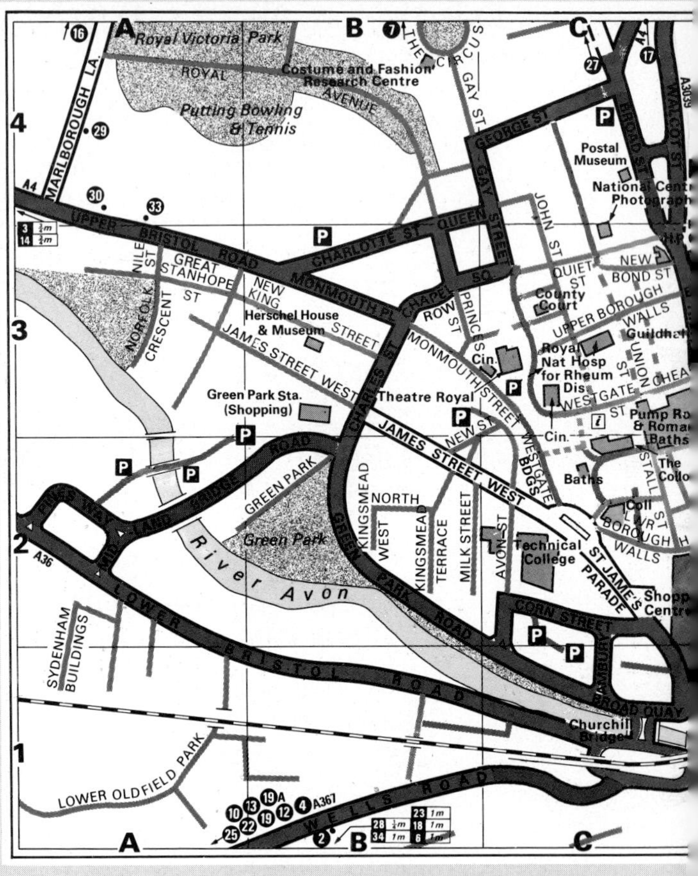

		Bath
D4	**1**	Arden Hotel
B1	**2**	Arney
A3	**3**	Ashley Villa Hotel
B1	**4**	Astor House
F4	**5**	The Bath Tasburgh
B1	**6**	Bloomfield House
B4	**7**	Brocks
D4	**8**	Brompton House Hotel
D4	**9**	Carfax Hotel
A1	**10**	Cheriton House
E3	**11**	County Hotel *(Inn)*
B1	**12**	Devonshire House
B1	**13**	Dorian House
A3	**14**	Dorset Villa
E4	**15**	Edgar Hotel
A4	**16**	Gainsborough Hotel
C4	**17**	Grove Lodge
B1	**18**	Haydon House

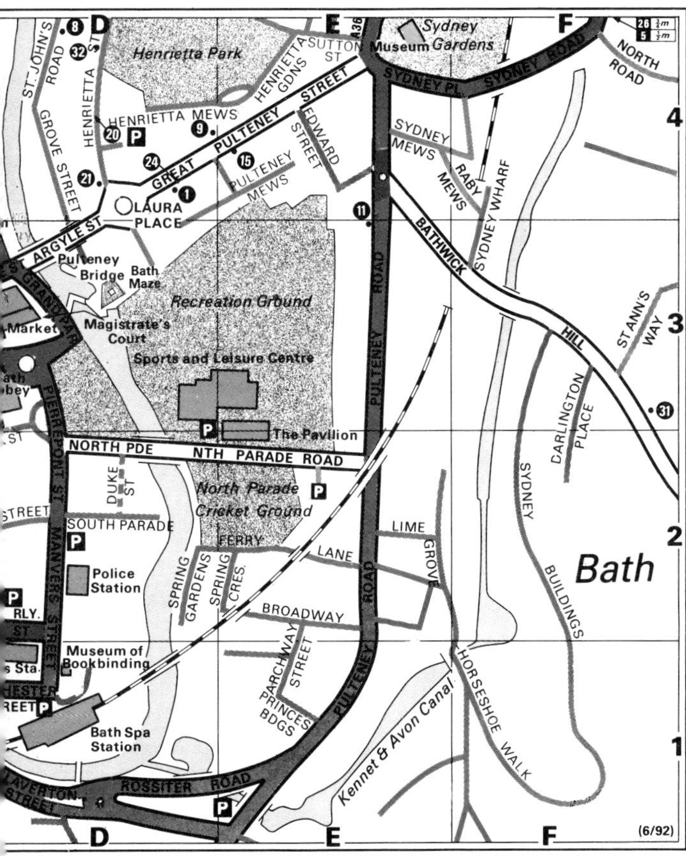

B1	**19**	Highways House	*C4*	**27**	Oxford Private Hotel
B1	**19A**	Holly Lodge	*B1*	**28**	Paradise House Hotel
D4	**20**	Kennard Hotel	*A4*	**29**	Parkside
D4	**21**	Laura Place Hotel	*A4*	**30**	Hotel St Clair
B1	**22**	Leighton House	*F3*	**31**	Somerset House, Hotel & Restaurant
B1	**23**	Meadowland	*D4*	**32**	Villa Magdala Private Hotel
D4	**24**	Millers Hotel	*A4*	**33**	Waltons
A1	**25**	Oldfields	*B1*	**34**	Wentworth House
F4	**26**	Orchard House Hotel			

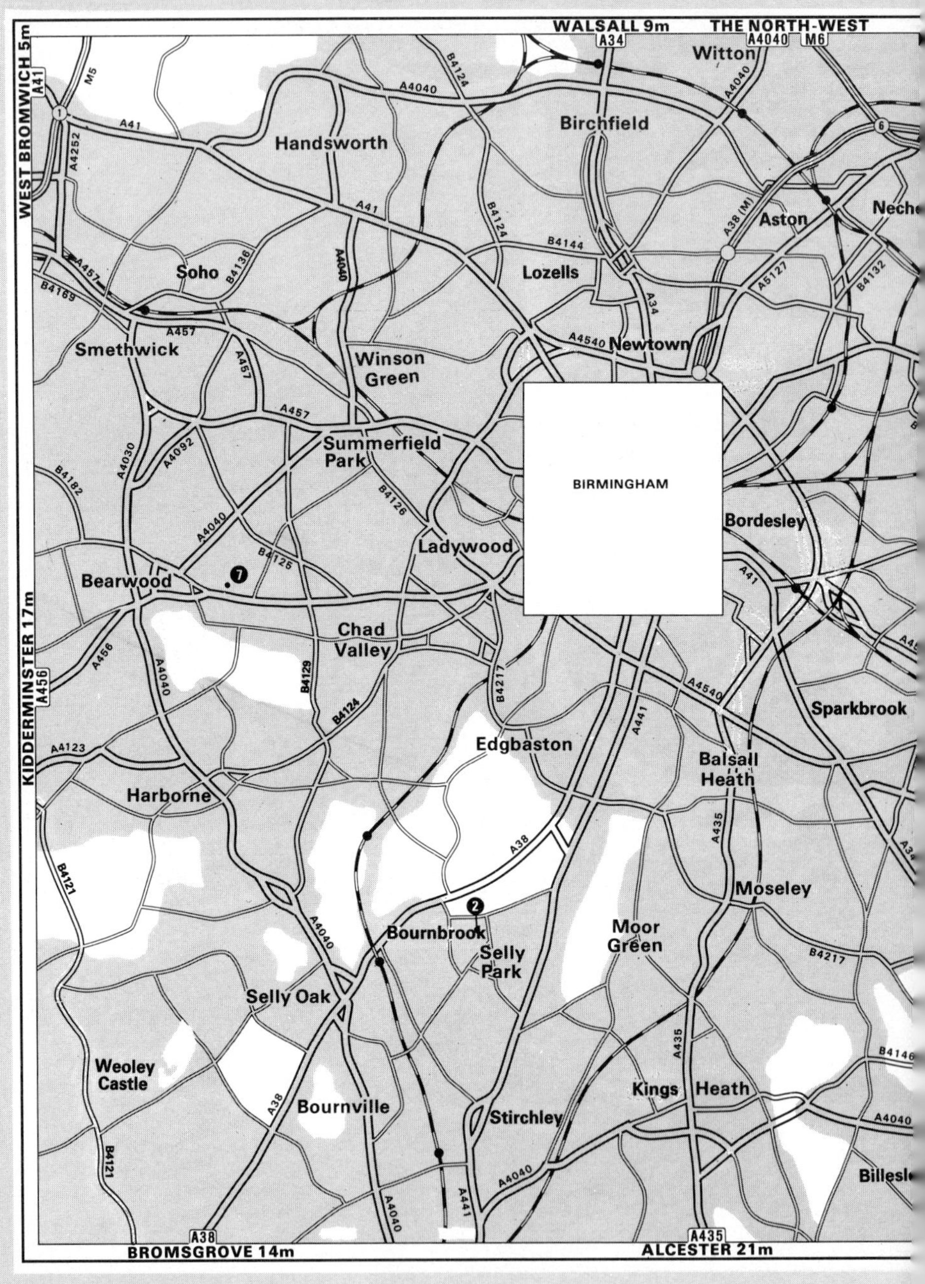

Birmingham & District

1 Ashdale House Hotel	2 Awentsbury Hotel	5 Cape Race Hotel
	3 Beech House Hotel	6 Elston
	4 Bridge House Hotel	7 Fountain Court Hotel

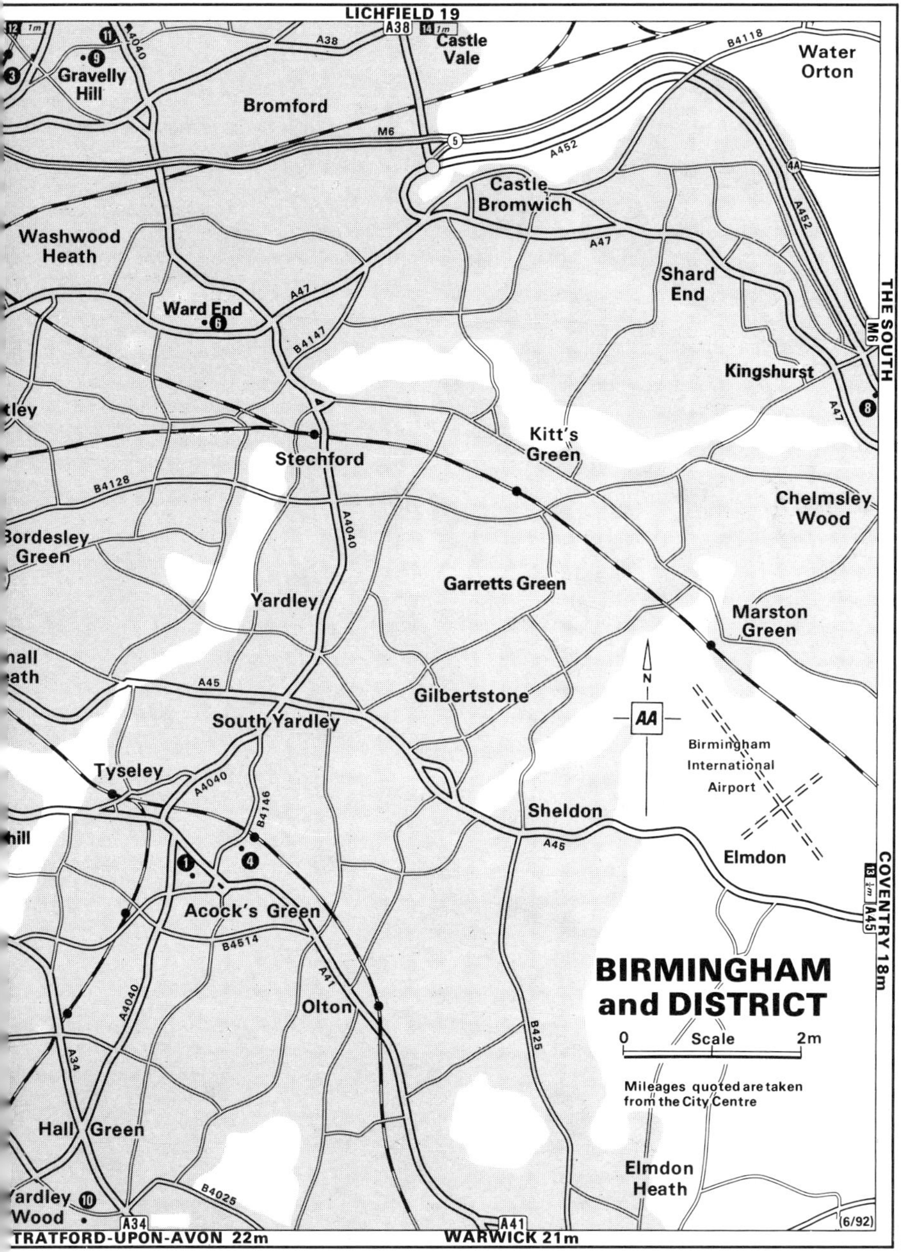

LICHFIELD 19

A38 | 14 1m | Castle Vale | 12 1m | 11 | A4040 | 9 Gravelly Hill | 3 | A38 | Bromford | B4118 | Water Orton | M6 | 5 | A452 | 4A | Castle Bromwich | Washwood Heath | A47 | A452 | Shard End | Ward End 6 | A47 | B4147 | THE SOUTH M6 | Kingshurst | A47 | 8 | tley | Kitt's Green | Stechford | B4128 | Chelmsley Wood | A4040 | Bordesley Green | Garretts Green | Yardley | Marston Green | nall eath | A45 | Gilbertstone | N | AA | South Yardley | Birmingham International Airport | Tyseley | A4040 | B4146 | Sheldon | hill | A45 | 1 | 4 | Elmdon | COVENTRY 18m | 13 ½m | A45 | Acock's Green | B4514 | A41 | A4040 | Olton | A34 | B425 | Hall Green | Elmdon Heath | ardley Wood | 10 | B4025 | A34 | A41 | (6/92)

BIRMINGHAM and DISTRICT

0 Scale 2m

Mileages quoted are taken from the City Centre

TRATFORD-UPON-AVON 22m | WARWICK 21m

8	Heath Lodge Hotel	11	Rollason Wood Hotel	13	Tri-Star Hotel
9	Lyndhurst Hotel	12	Standbridge Hotel *(listed under Sutton Coldfield)*	14	Willow Tree Hotel
10	Robin Hood Lodge Hotel				

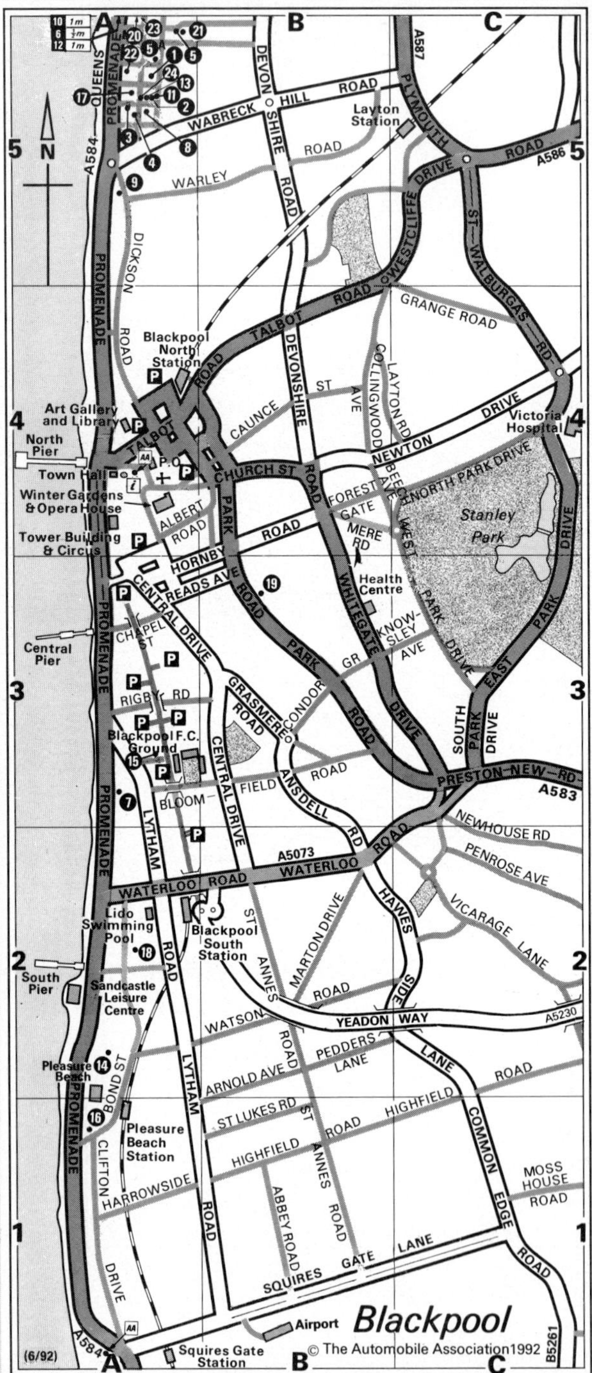

Blackpool

A5	**1**	Arosa Hotel
A5	**2**	Ashcroft Private Hotel
A5	**3**	Berwick Private Hotel
A5	**4**	Brooklands Hotel
A5	**5**	Burlees Hotel
A5	**5A**	Claytons
A5	**6**	Cliff Head Hotel
A3	**7**	The Colby Hotel
A5	**8**	Denely Private Hotel
A5	**9**	Derwent Private Hotel
A5	**10**	The Garville Hotel
A5	**11**	Hartshead Hotel
A5	**12**	Inglewood Hotel
A5	**13**	Lynstead Private Hotel
A2	**14**	Lynwood
A3	**15**	Motel Mimosa
A1	**16**	The New Esplanade Hotel
A5	**17**	North Mount Private Hotel
A2	**18**	The Old Coach House
B3	**19**	Park Lodge
A5	**20**	Sunny Cliff
A5	**21**	Sunray Private Hotel
A5	**22**	Surrey House Hotel
A5	**23**	The Windsor & Westmorland Hotel
A5	**24**	Woodleigh Private Hotel

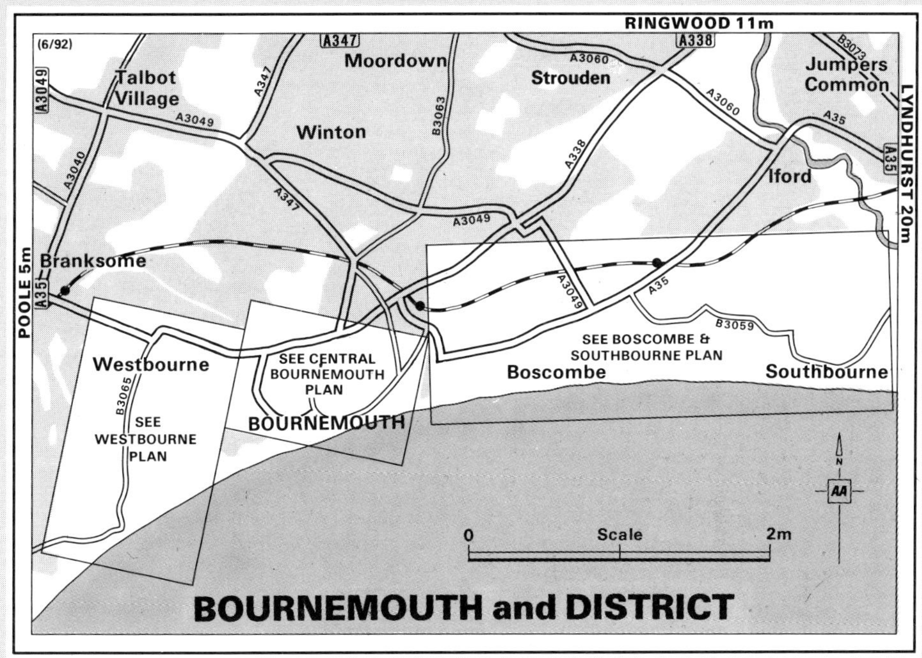
RINGWOOD 11m
(6/92)
A347
A338
Moordown
A3060
Strouden
B3073
Jumpers Common
Talbot Village
A3049
A347
A3049
A3060
A35
LYNDHURST 20m
Winton
B3063
A338
A35
A3040
Iford
A347
A3049
POOLE 5m
Branksome
A35
A3049
A35
B3059
SEE BOSCOMBE & SOUTHBOURNE PLAN
Westbourne
SEE CENTRAL BOURNEMOUTH PLAN
Boscombe
Southbourne
B3065
SEE WESTBOURNE PLAN
BOURNEMOUTH
N
AA
0
Scale
2m
BOURNEMOUTH and DISTRICT

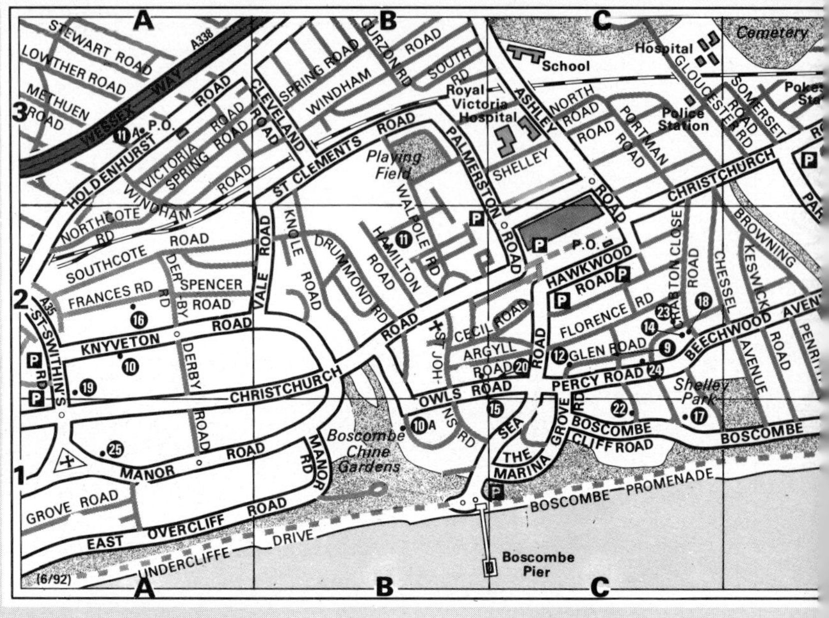

Boscombe & Southbourne

E3 **8** Amitie
C2 **9** Braemar Private Hotel
A2 **10** Cransley Private Hotel
B1 **10A** Dene Court Hotel
B2 **11** Derwent House
A3 **11A** Dorset House
C2 **12** Hawaiian Hotel
F2 **13** Kelmor Lodge
C2 **14** Linwood House Hotel
B2 **15** Lynthwaite Hotel

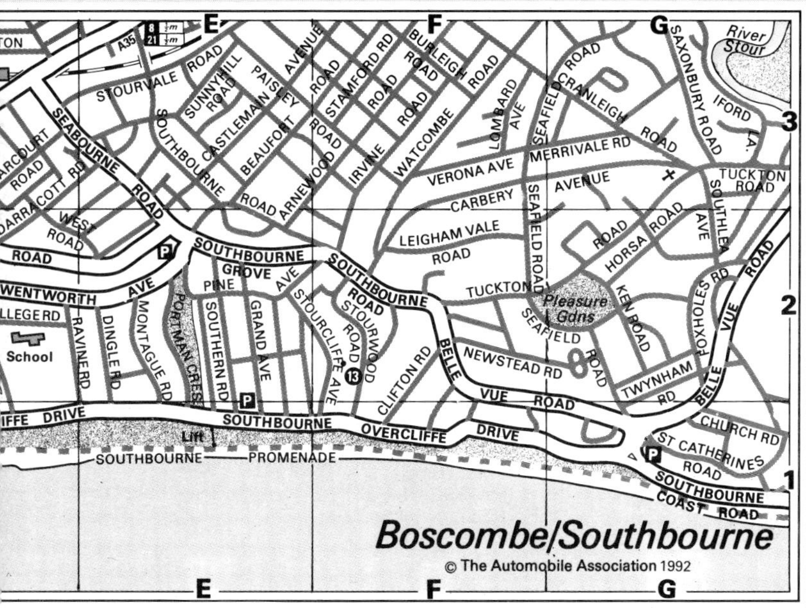

A2	**16**	Mayfield Private Hotel
C1	**17**	Norland Private Hotel
C2	**18**	Oak Hall Private Hotel
A2	**19**	St John's Lodge Hotel
C2	**20**	Hotel Sorrento
E3	**21**	Telstar
C1	**22**	Valberg Hotel
C2	**23**	Weavers Hotel
C2	**24**	Woodlands Hotel
A1	**25**	Wood Lodge Hotel

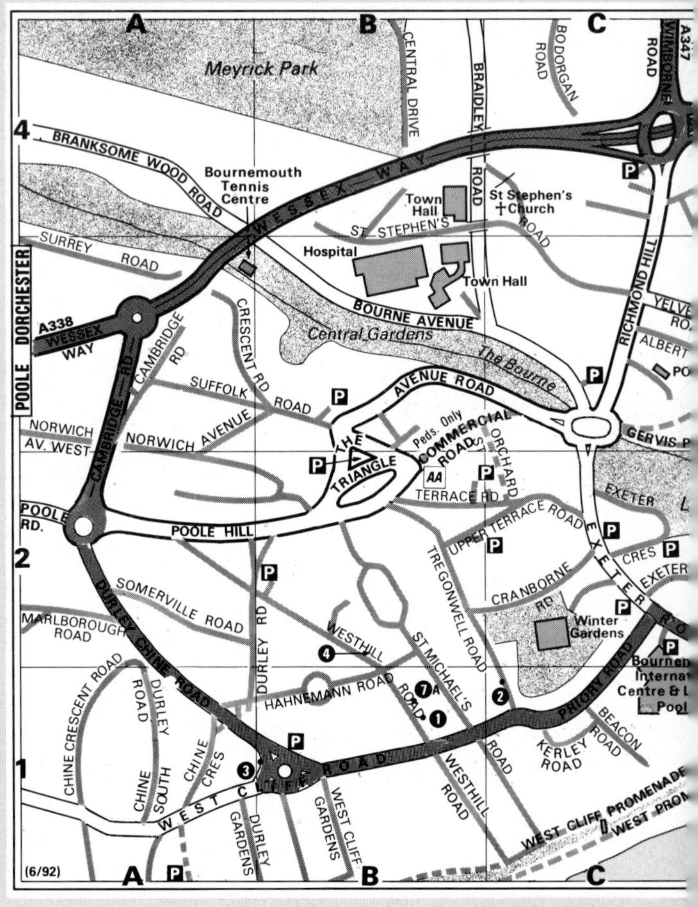

Central Bournemouth

B1 **1** Albemarle Private Hotel
C1 **2** Carisbrooke Hotel
B1 **3** Croham Hurst Hotel
B2 **4** Mae-Mar Hotel

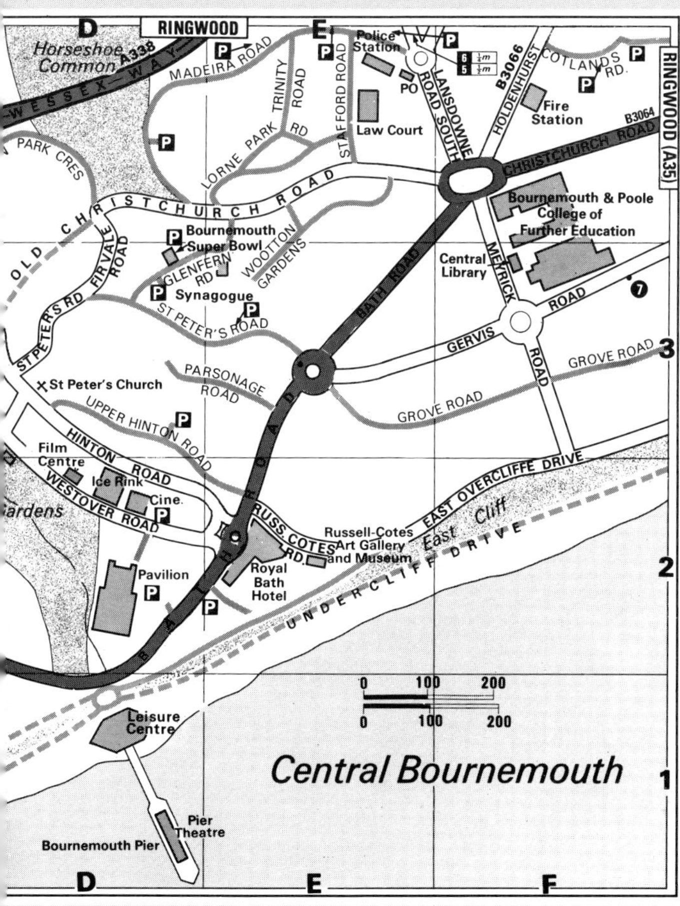

F4	**5**	New Dorchester Hotel	*F3*	**7**	Tudor Grange Hotel
F4	**6**	Silver Trees Hotel	*B1*	**7A**	West Hill Court Hotel

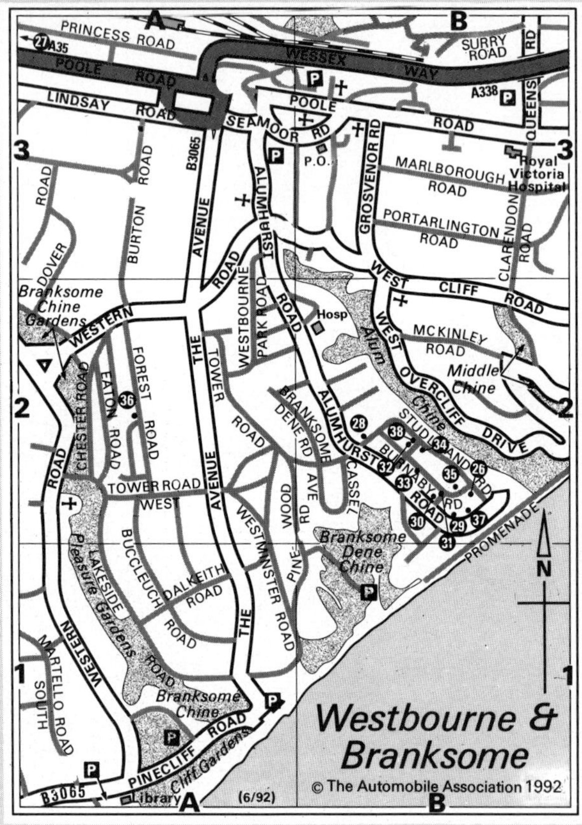

Westbourne & Branksome			*B2* **29**	Cliff House Hotel		*B2* **35**	Sea-Dene Hotel
			B2 **30**	Golden Sands Hotel		*A2* **36**	Sheldon Lodge *(listed under Poole)*
B2 **26**	Alum Grange Hotel		*B2* **31**	Highclere Hotel			
A3 **27**	Avoncourt Private Hotel *(listed under Poole)*		*B2* **32**	Holmcroft Hotel		*B2* **37**	West Dene Private Hotel
			B2 **33**	Newfield Private Hotel			
B2 **28**	Cairnsmore Hotel		*B2* **34**	Northover Private Hotel		*B2* **38**	Woodford Court Hotel

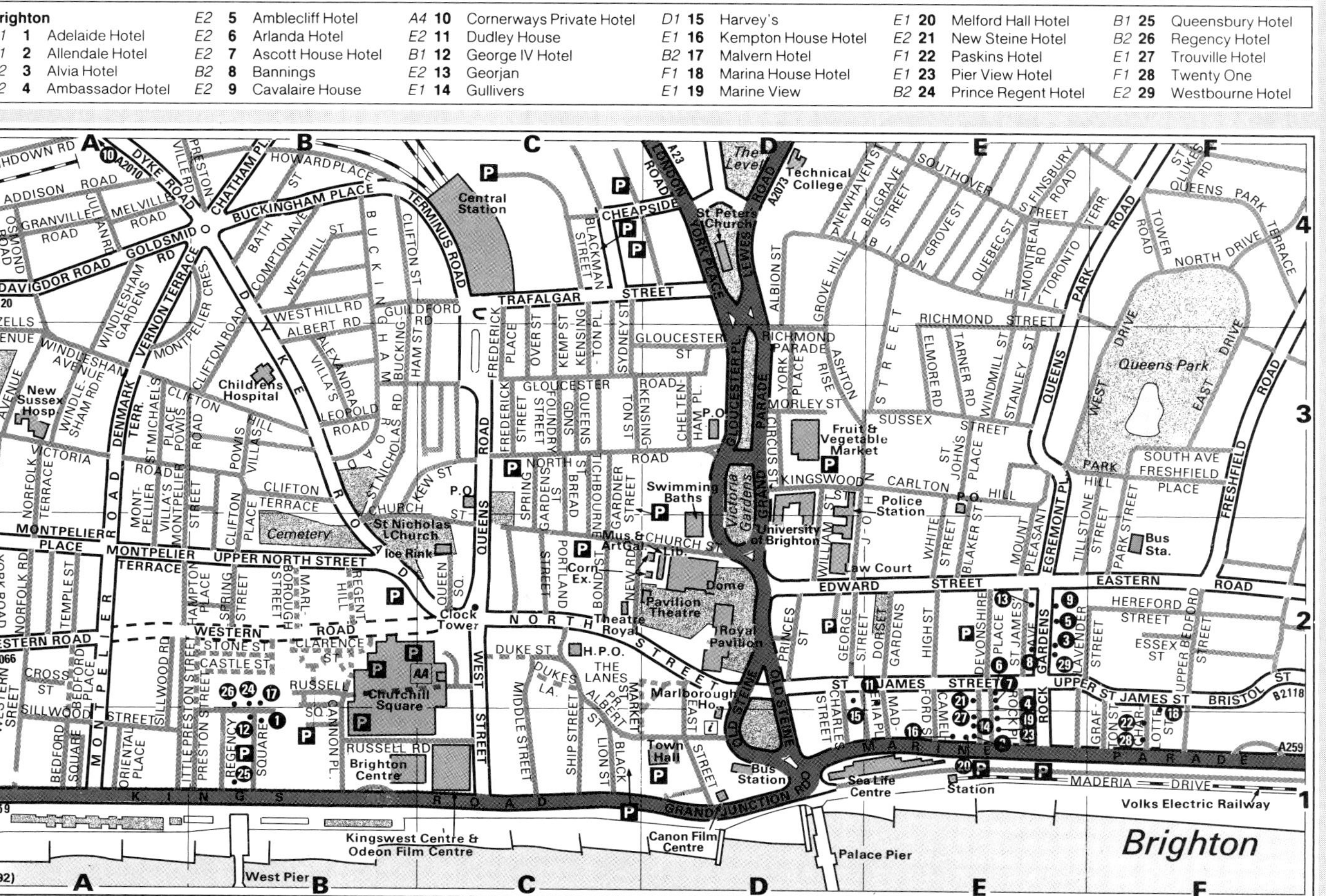

Brighton

Grid	No.	Hotel	Grid	No.	Hotel	Grid	No.	Hotel
B1	**1**	Adelaide Hotel	*E2*	**11**	Dudley House	*E2*	**21**	New Steine Hotel
E1	**2**	Allendale Hotel	*B1*	**12**	George IV Hotel	*F1*	**22**	Paskins Hotel
E2	**3**	Alvia Hotel	*E2*	**13**	Georjan	*E1*	**23**	Pier View Hotel
E2	**4**	Ambassador Hotel	*E1*	**14**	Gullivers	*B2*	**24**	Prince Regent Hotel
E2	**5**	Amblecliff Hotel	*D1*	**15**	Harvey's	*B1*	**25**	Queensbury Hotel
E2	**6**	Arlanda Hotel	*E1*	**16**	Kempton House Hotel	*B2*	**26**	Regency Hotel
E2	**7**	Ascott House Hotel	*B2*	**17**	Malvern Hotel	*E1*	**27**	Trouville Hotel
B2	**8**	Bannings	*F1*	**18**	Marina House Hotel	*F1*	**28**	Twenty One
E2	**9**	Cavalaire House	*E1*	**19**	Marine View	*E2*	**29**	Westbourne Hotel
A4	**10**	Cornerways Private Hotel	*E1*	**20**	Melford Hall Hotel			

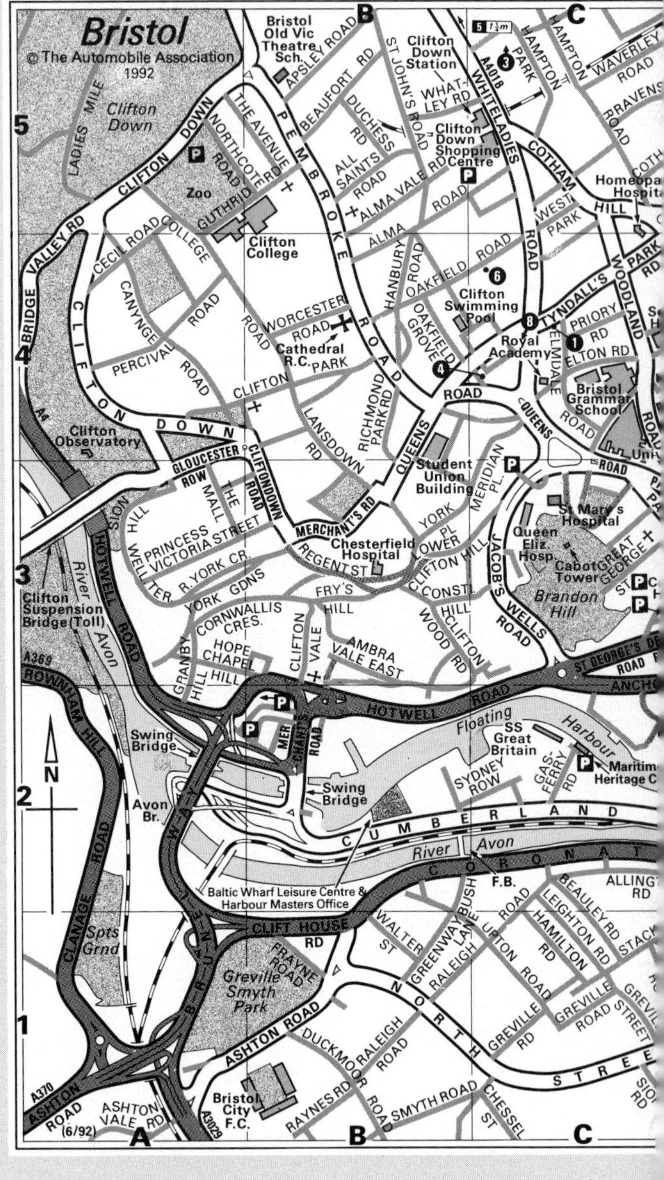

Bristol

C4 **1** Alandale Hotel

F4 **2** Alcove

C5 **3** Birkdale Hotel

C4 **4** Chesterfield Hotel

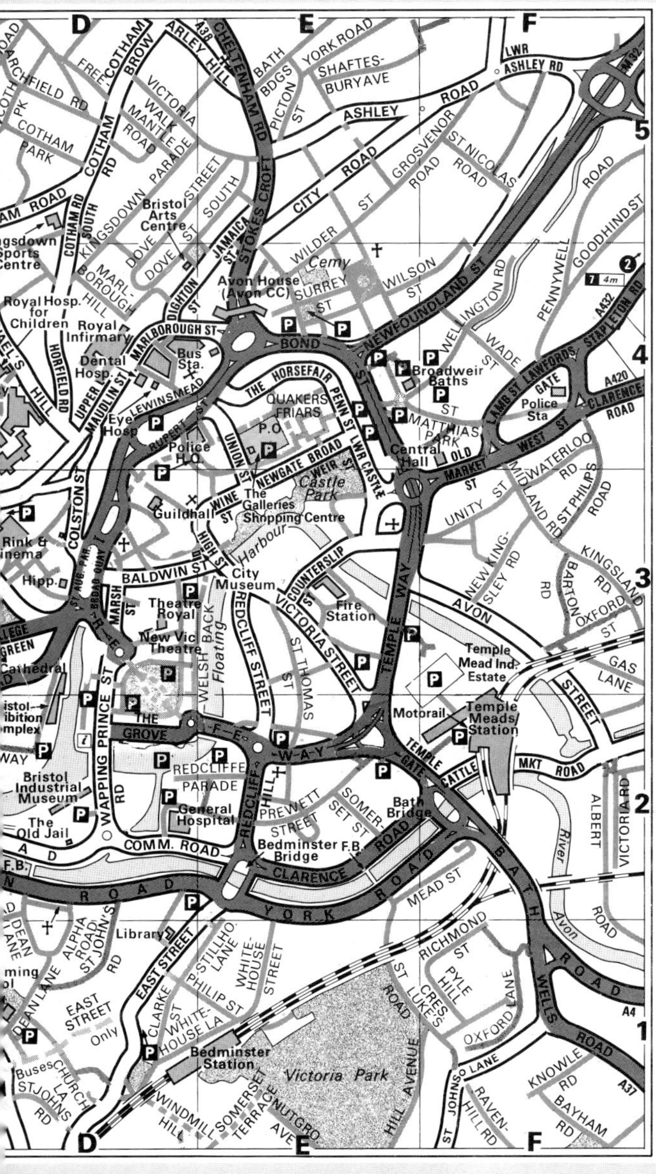

C5	**5**	Downlands	*F4*	**7**	Rowan Lodge
C4	**6**	Oakfield Hotel	*C4*	**8**	Washington Hotel

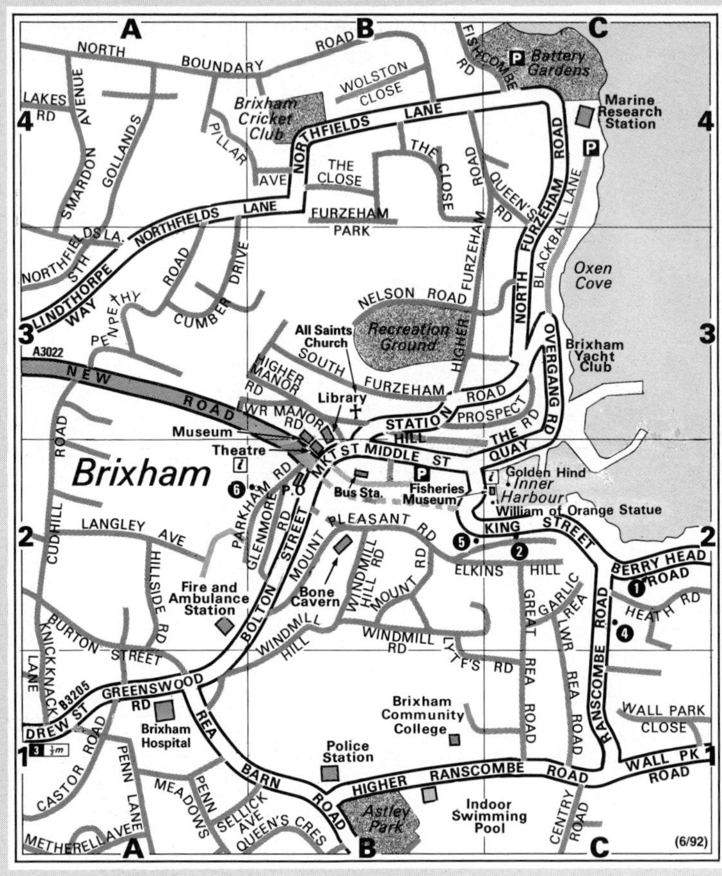

Brixham

C2	**1**	Harbour Side	*A1*	**3**	Raddicombe Lodge
C2	**2**	Harbour View Hotel	*C2*	**4**	Ranscombe House Hotel
			B2	**5**	Sampford House
			B2	**6**	Woodlands

Eastbourne

E3	**1**	Bay Lodge Hotel
A1	**2**	Beachy Rise
D3	**3**	Bourne House Private Hotel
B4	**4**	Chalk Farm Hotel & Restaurant
E4	**5**	Far End Hotel
C3	**6**	Flamingo Private Hotel
D2	**7**	Hotel Mandalay
D2	**8**	Mowbray Hotel
C1	**9**	Saffrons Hotel
D3	**10**	Stirling House Hotel

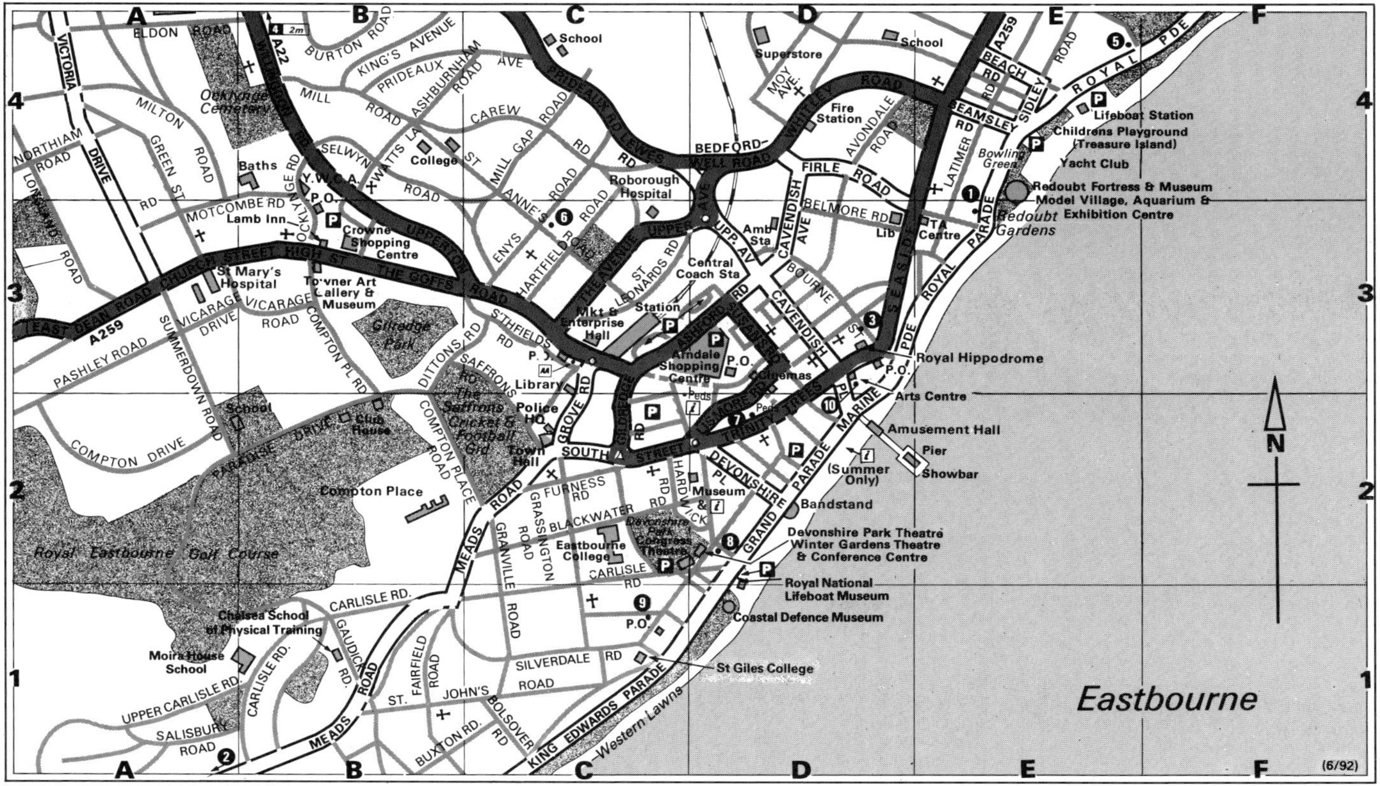

Eastbourne

(6/92)

Edinburgh

F6	**1**	The Adria Hotel
A1	**2**	Anvilla
D6	**3**	Bonnington
A3	**4**	Clifton Private Hotel
F1	**5**	Dalwin Lodge & Restaurant
E6	**6**	Elder York
A6	**7**	Galloway
F1	**8**	Glenorchy Hotel
F6	**9**	Greenside Hotel
F6	**10**	Halcyon Hotel
A1	**11**	Kariba
F1	**12**	Kilmaurs
F1	**13**	Kingsley
A3	**14**	The Lairgs
C1	**15**	Meadows
E6	**16**	Mrs Rooneys
A3	**17**	Rosebery Private Hotel
F1	**18**	Rowan
F1	**19**	Salisbury View Hotel
F1	**20**	Strathmohr
E6	**21**	Stuart House

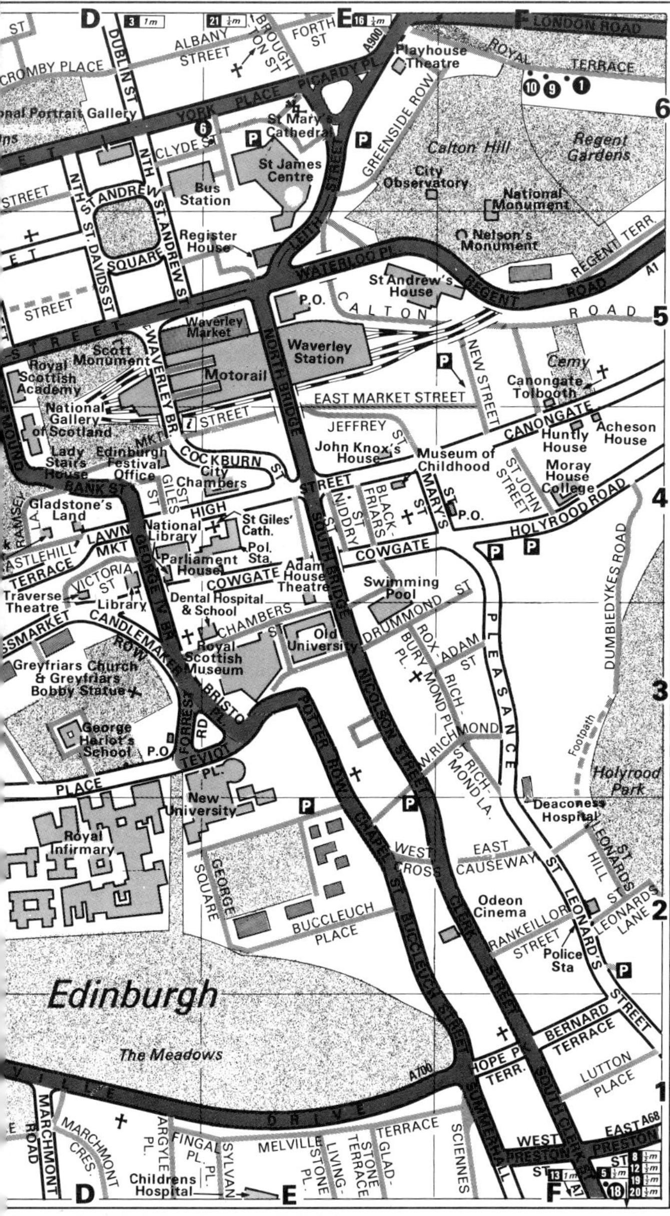

Edinburgh
The Meadows
Calton Hill
Regent Gardens
Holyrood Park
Playhouse Theatre
St Mary's Cathedral
St James Centre
Bus Station
Register House
City Observatory
National Monument
Nelson's Monument
St Andrew's House
Waverley Market
Waverley Station
Motorail
Scott Monument
Royal Scottish Academy
National Gallery of Scotland
Lady Stairs House
Edinburgh Festival Office
City Chambers
Gladstone's Land
National Library
St Giles' Cath.
Parliament House
Pol. Sta.
Adam House Theatre
Swimming Pool
Traverse Theatre
Library
Dental Hospital & School
Royal Scottish Museum
Old University
Greyfriars Church & Greyfriars Bobby Statue
George Heriot's School
New University
Royal Infirmary
John Knox's House
Museum of Childhood
Canongate Tolbooth
Huntly House
Acheson House
Moray House College
Deaconess Hospital
Odeon Cinema
Police Sta
Childrens Hospital
Cemy
P.O.
LONDON ROAD
ROYAL TERRACE
REGENT TERR.
REGENT ROAD
WATERLOO PL.
CALTON ROAD
NORTH BRIDGE
SOUTH BRIDGE
NICOLSON STREET
CLERK STREET
SOUTH CLERK ST
LEITH STREET
GREENSIDE ROW
PICARDY PL.
YORK PLACE
ALBANY STREET
DUBLIN ST
BROUGHTON ST
FORTH ST
CLYDE ST
ST ANDREW SQUARE
NTH ST ANDREW ST
STH ST ANDREW ST
STH ST. DAVIDS ST
WAVERLEY BR.
EAST MARKET STREET
NEW STREET
JEFFREY ST
CANONGATE
HOLYROOD ROAD
ST JOHN STREET
ST MARY'S ST
BLACKFRIARS ST
NIDDRY ST
COWGATE
COCKBURN ST
BANK ST
HIGH STREET
LAWNMKT
GEORGE IV BR
VICTORIA ST
CANDLEMAKER ROW
CHAMBERS ST
DRUMMOND ST
ADAM ST
ROXBURY PL.
RICHMOND PL.
W. RICHMOND
ST RICHMOND LA.
PLEASANCE
DUMBIEDYKES ROAD
Footpath
POTTER ROW
CHAPEL ST
BRISTO PL.
FORREST RD
TEVIOT PL.
GEORGE SQUARE
BUCCLEUCH PLACE
BUCCLEUCH STREET
WEST CROSS CAUSEWAY
EAST CAUSEWAY
RANKEILLOR STREET
ST LEONARD'S STREET
ST LEONARDS HILL
ST LEONARDS LANE
BERNARD TERRACE
LUTTON PLACE
HOPE PK TERR.
MELVILLE DRIVE
MARCHMONT ROAD
MARCHMONT CRES.
ARGYLE PL.
FINGAL PL.
SYLVAN PL.
MELVILLE TERRACE
LIVINGSTONE PL.
GLADSTONE TERRACE
SCIENNES
SUMMERHALL
WEST PRESTON ST
EAST PRESTON ST
A1
A68
A700
A900
D
E
F
1
2
3
4
5
6

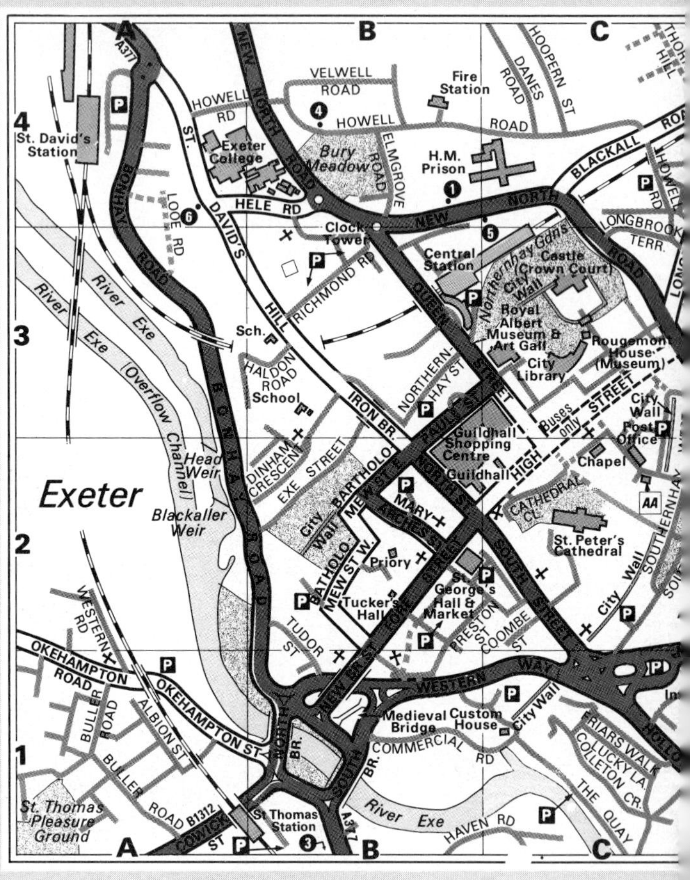

Exeter

B4	**1**	Braeside
D3	**2**	The Edwardian
B1	**3**	Hotel Gledhills
B4	**4**	Park View Hotel

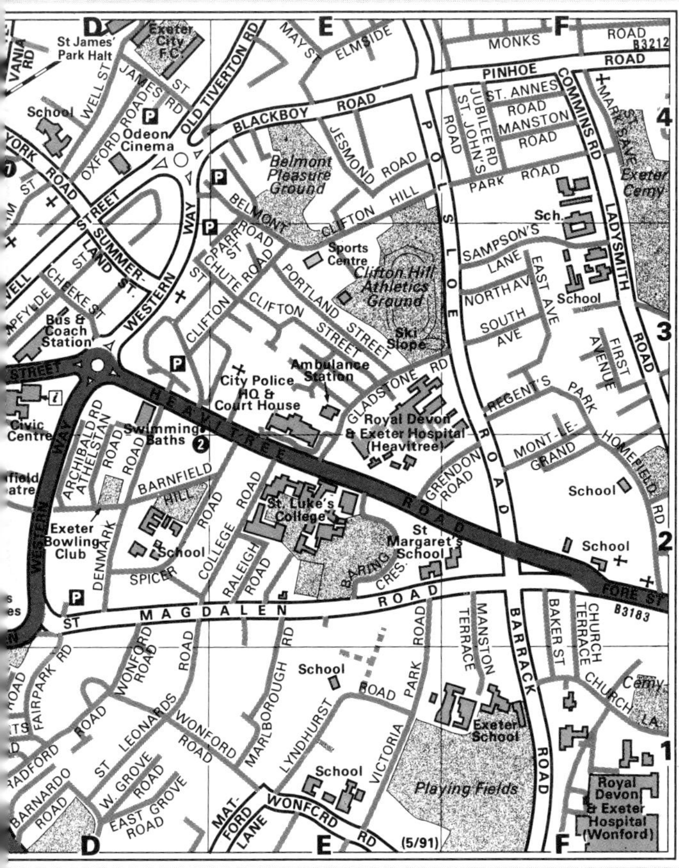

C4 **5** Sunnymede
A4 **6** Telstar Hotel
D4 **7** Trees Mini Hotel
D4 **8** Trenance House Hotel

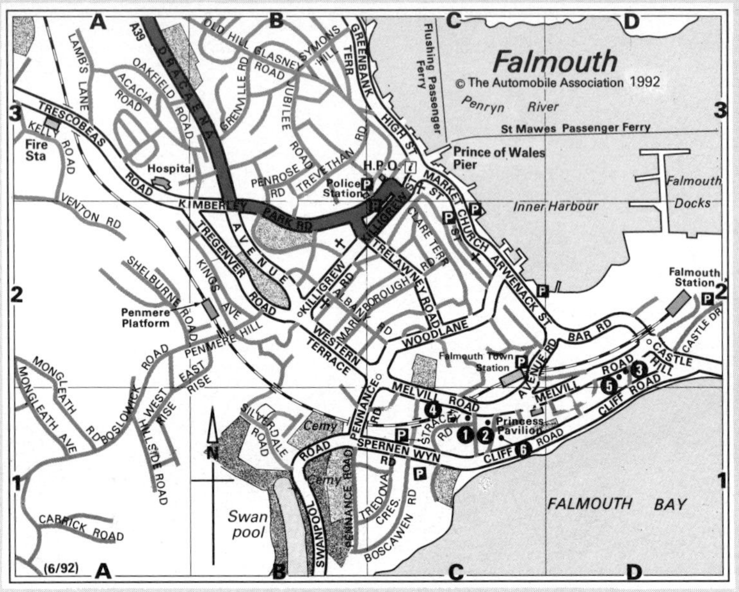

Falmouth					
		C1	**2**	Gyllyngvase House Hotel	
		D3	**3**	Ivanhoe	
C1	**1**	Cotswold House Hotel	*C1*	**4**	Melvill House Hotel
D2	**5**	Penty Bryn Hotel			
C1	**6**	Westcott Hotel			

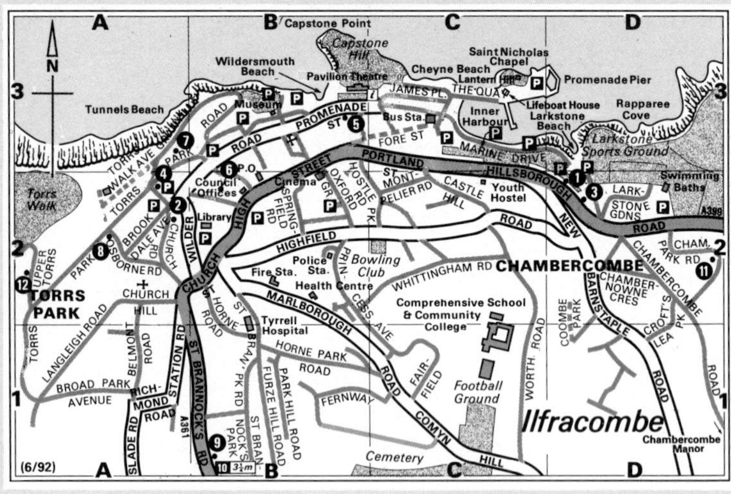

Ilfracombe								
			A2	**4**	Cresta Private Hotel	*B1*	**9**	Strathmore Private Hotel
			B3	**5**	Dedes Hotel	*B1*	**10**	Sunnymeade County House Hotel *(listed under West Down)*
D2	**1**	Cavendish Hotel	*B2*	**6**	Lympstone Private Hotel			
A2	**2**	Chalfont Private Hotel	*A3*	**7**	Merlin Court Hotel	*D2*	**11**	Varley House
D2	**3**	Collingdale Hotel	*A2*	**8**	Southcliffe Hotel	*A2*	**12**	Westwell Hall Hotel

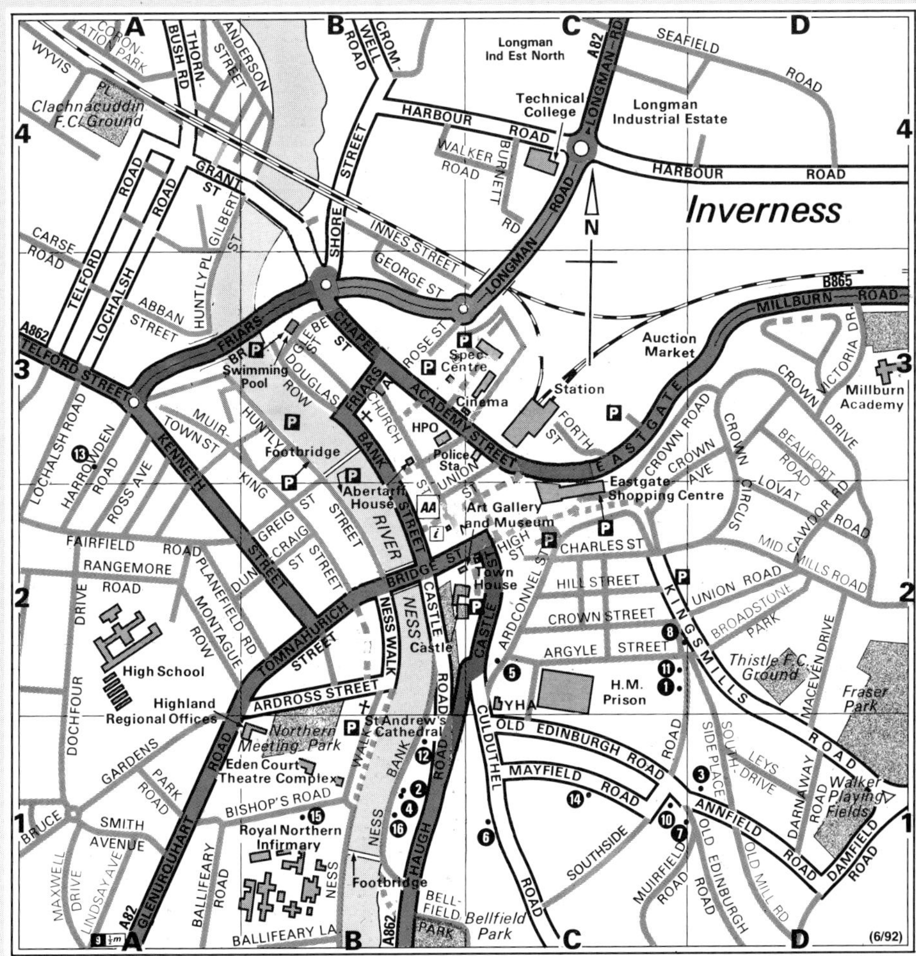

Inverness

C2	**1**	Aberfeldy Lodge
B1	**2**	Ardmuir House
D1	**3**	Ardnacoille House
B1	**4**	Brae Ness Hotel
C2	**5**	Craigside
C1	**6**	Culduthel Lodge
C1	**7**	Four Winds
C2	**8**	Heathmount
A1	**9**	Hebrides
C1	**10**	Leinster Lodge
C2	**11**	The Old Rectory
B1	**12**	Riverside House Hotel
A3	**13**	St Ann's Hotel
C1	**14**	Sunnyholm
B1	**15**	Villa Fontana
B1	**16**	Windsor House Hotel

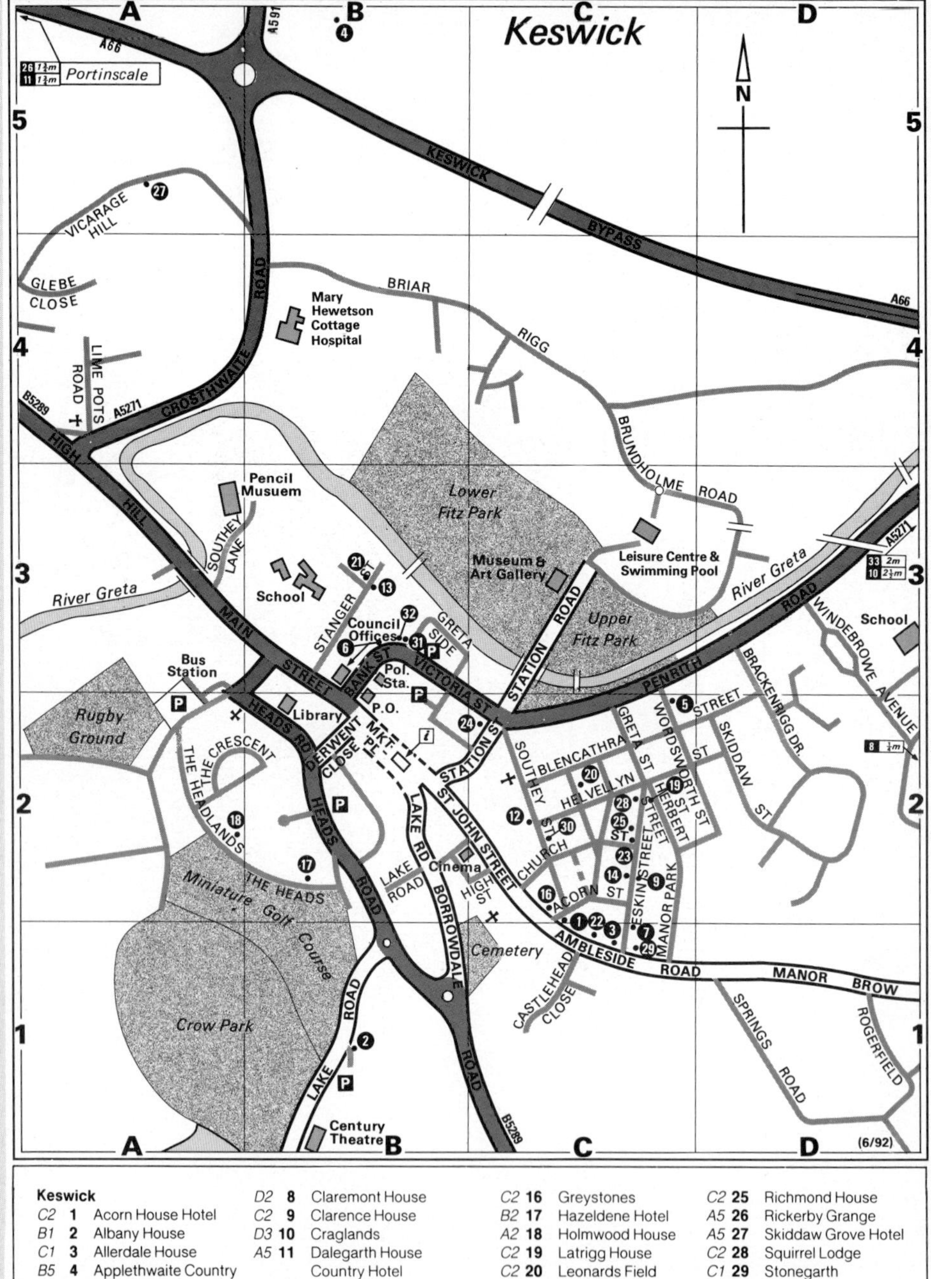

Keswick

C2	**1**	Acorn House Hotel	*D2*	**8**	Claremont House	*C2*	**16**	Greystones	*C2*	**25**	Richmond House
B1	**2**	Albany House	*C2*	**9**	Clarence House	*B2*	**17**	Hazeldene Hotel	*A5*	**26**	Rickerby Grange
C1	**3**	Allerdale House	*D3*	**10**	Craglands	*A2*	**18**	Holmwood House	*A5*	**27**	Skiddaw Grove Hotel
B5	**4**	Applethwaite Country House Hotel	*A5*	**11**	Dalegarth House Country Hotel	*C2*	**19**	Latrigg House	*C2*	**28**	Squirrel Lodge
			C2	**12**	Edwardene	*C2*	**20**	Leonards Field	*C1*	**29**	Stonegarth
C2	**5**	Beckside	*B3*	**13**	Fell House	*B3*	**21**	Lincoln House	*C2*	**30**	Sunnyside
B3	**6**	Brierholme	*C2*	**14**	Foye House	*C1*	**22**	Lynwood	*B3*	**31**	Swiss Court
C1	**7**	Charnwood	*B2*	**15**	The Great Little Tea Shop	*C2*	**23**	Melbreck House	*B3*	**32**	Thornleigh
						C2	**24**	Ravensworth Hotel	*D3*	**33**	Twa Dogs

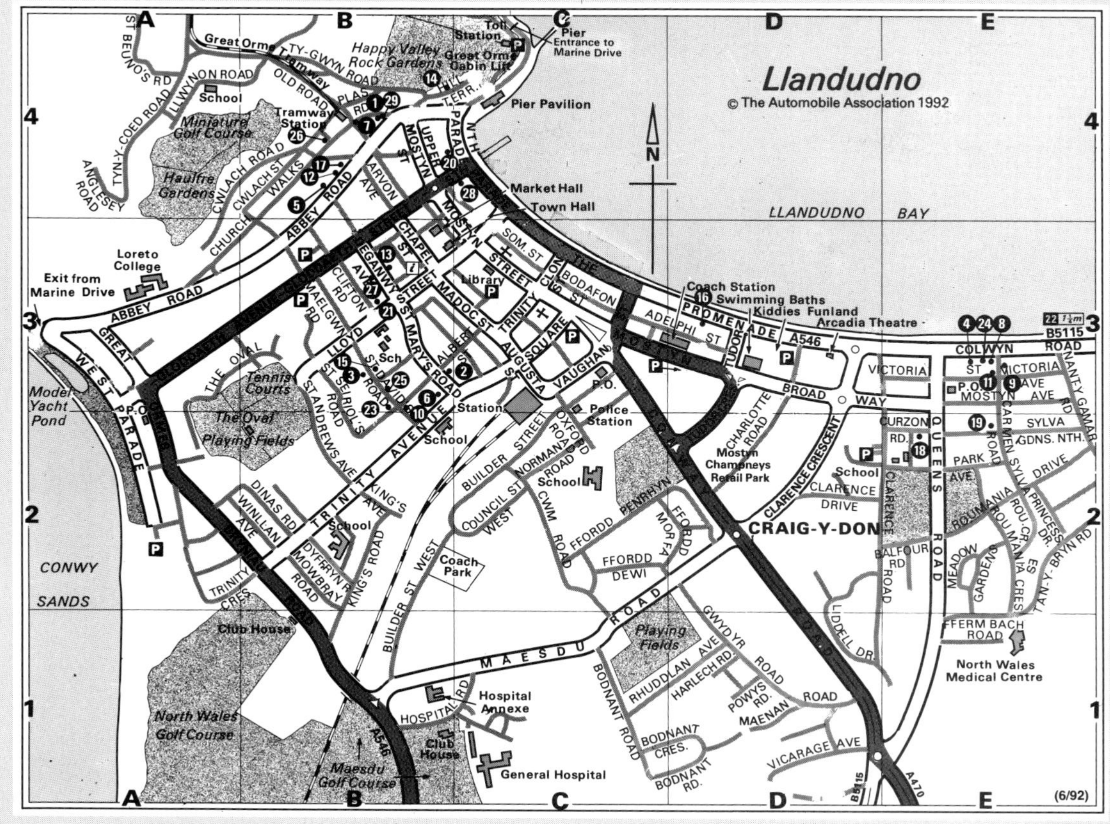

Llandudno

B4	**1**	Beach Cove
B3	**2**	Bodnant
B3	**3**	Brannock Private Hotel
E3	**4**	Britannia Hotel
B4	**5**	Bryn Rosa
B3	**6**	Buile Hill Private Hotel
B4	**7**	Capri Hotel
E3	**8**	Carmel Private Hotel
E3	**9**	Hotel Carmen
B3	**10**	Cornerways Hotel
E3	**11**	Craiglands Private Hotel
B4	**12**	Cranberry House
B3	**13**	Granby
B4	**14**	Hafod-y-Mor
B3	**15**	Hollybank
D3	**16**	Kinmel Private Hotel
B4	**17**	Mayfair Private Hotel
E2	**18**	Mayfield
E2	**19**	Minion Private Hotel
B4	**20**	Montclare Hotel
B3	**21**	Oak Alyn
E3	**22**	Orotava Private Hotel
B3	**23**	Rosaire Private Hotel
E3	**24**	St Hilary Hotel
B3	**25**	Thorpe House
B4	**26**	Warwick Hotel
B3	**27**	Wedgewood Hotel
C4	**28**	The Wilton Hotel
B4	**29**	Winston

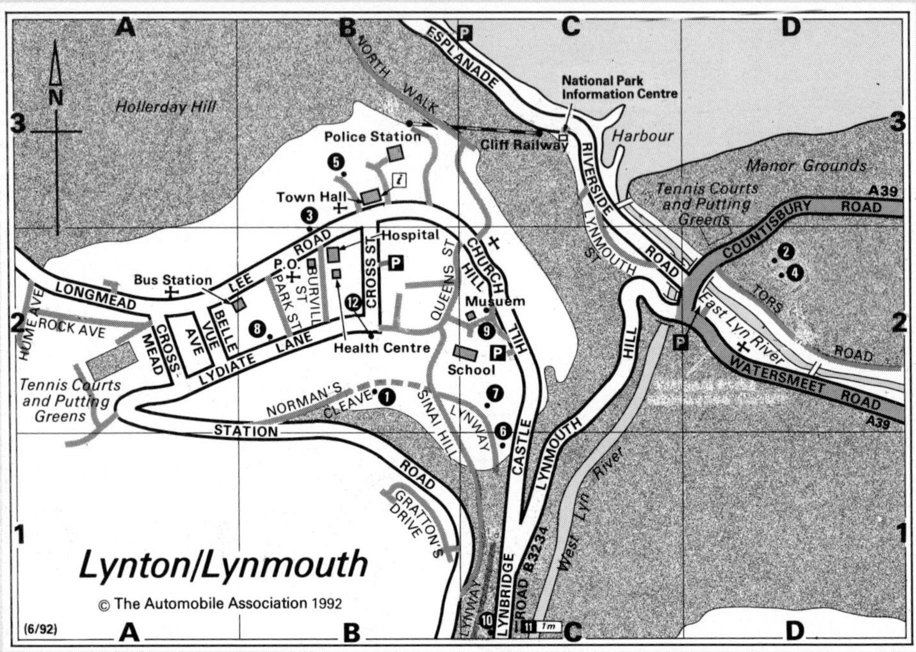

Lynton & Lynmouth

B2	**1**	Alford House Hotel *(see under Lynton)*
D2	**2**	Countisbury Lodge Hotel *(see under Lynmouth)*
B2	**3**	Hazeldene *(see under Lynton)*
D2	**4**	The Heatherville *(see under Lynmouth)*
B3	**5**	Ingleside Hotel *(see under Lynton)*
C1	**6**	Lynhurst Hotel (see under Lynton)
C2	**7**	Mayfair Hotel *(see under Lynton)*
B2	**8**	Retreat *(see under Lynton)*
C2	**9**	St Vincent *(see under Lynton)*
C1	**10**	Valley House Hotel *(see under Lynton)*
C1	**11**	The Village Inn (*see under Lynmouth*)
B2	**12**	Waterloo House Hotel *(see under Lynton)*

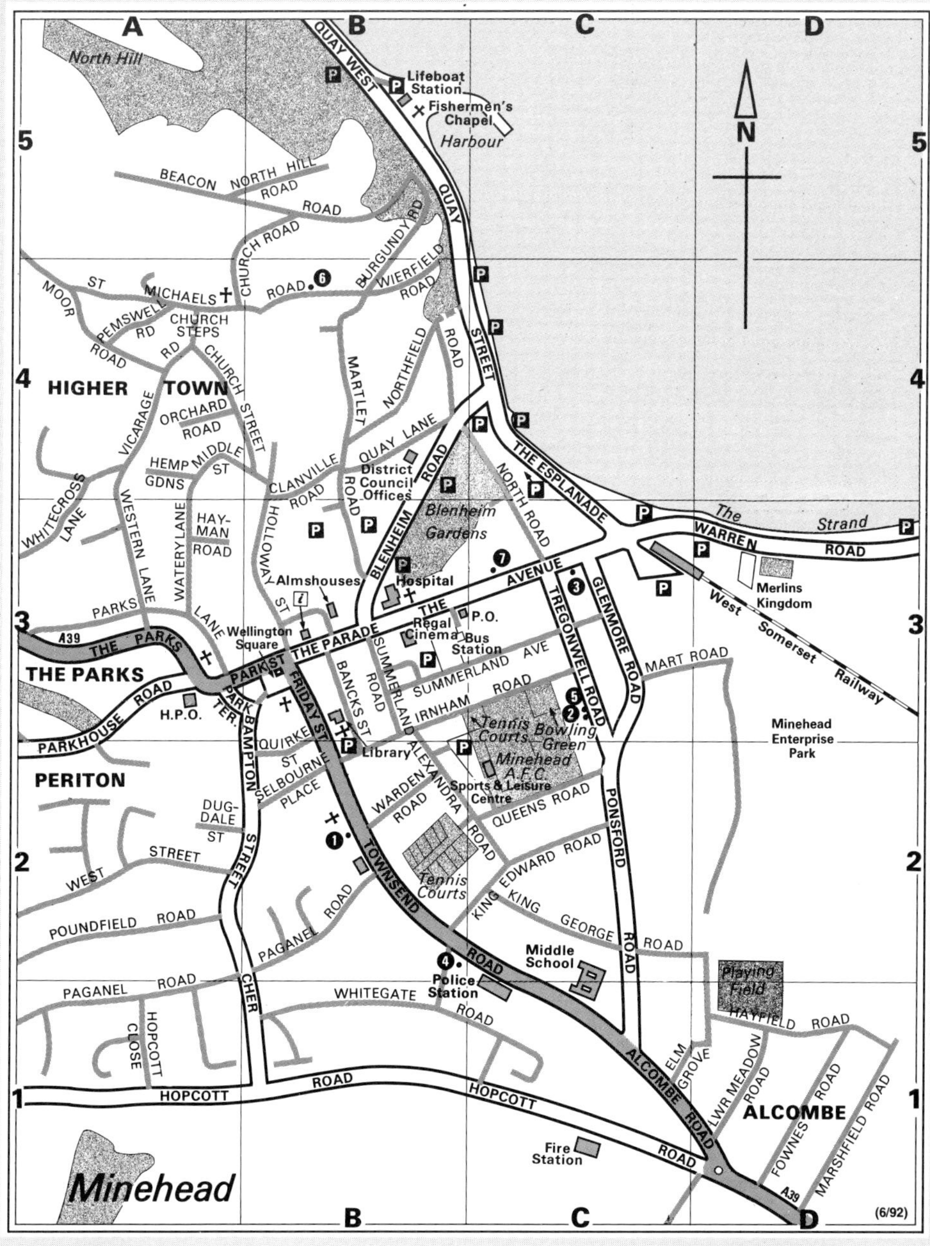

Minehead

B2	**1**	Avill House
C3	**2**	Bactonleigh Private Hotel
C3	**3**	Gascony Hotel
B2	**4**	Kildare Lodge
C3	**5**	Marshfield Hotel
B4	**6**	Marston Lodge Hotel
C3	**7**	Mayfair Hotel

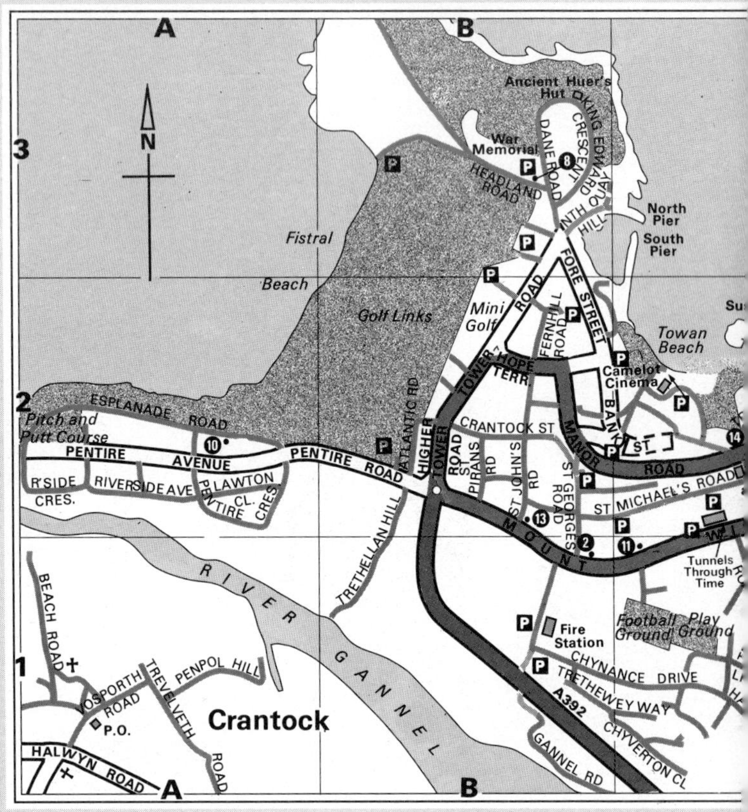

Newquay

E2	**1**	Aloha
B1	**2**	Arundell Hotel
D1	**3**	Bon-Ami Hotel
C2	**4**	Claremont House
D2	**5**	Copper Beach Hotel
D2	**6**	Hepworth Hotel
E3	**7**	Kellsboro Hotel
B3	**8**	Links Hotel

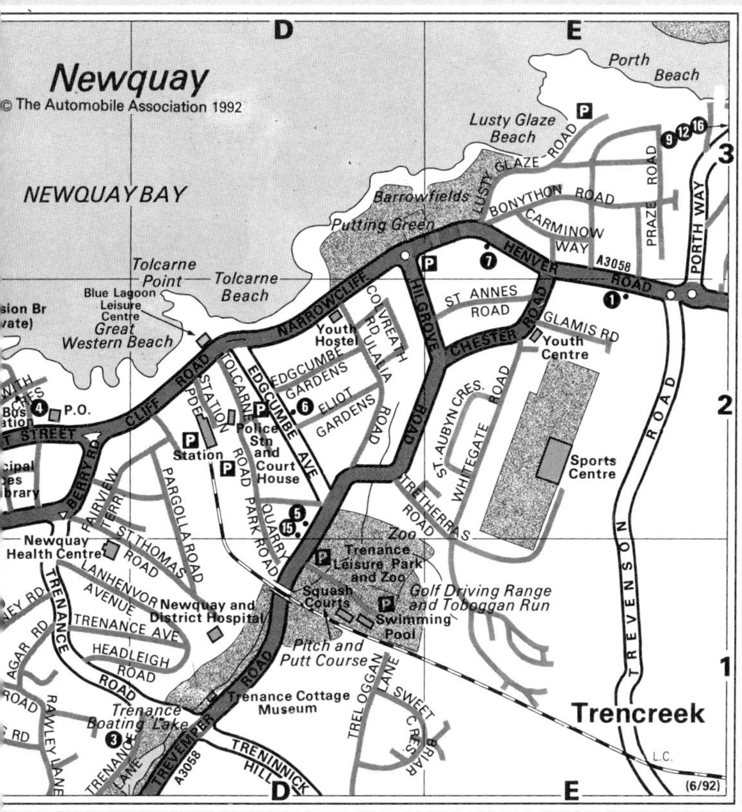

E3	**9**	Pendeen Hotel	*B2*	**13**	Tir Chonaill Lodge
A2	**10**	Porth Enodoc	*C2*	**14**	Towan Beach Hotel
C1	**11**	Priory Lodge Hotel	*D2*	**15**	Wheal Treasure Hotel
E3	**12**	Rolling Waves	*E3*	**16**	Windward Hotel

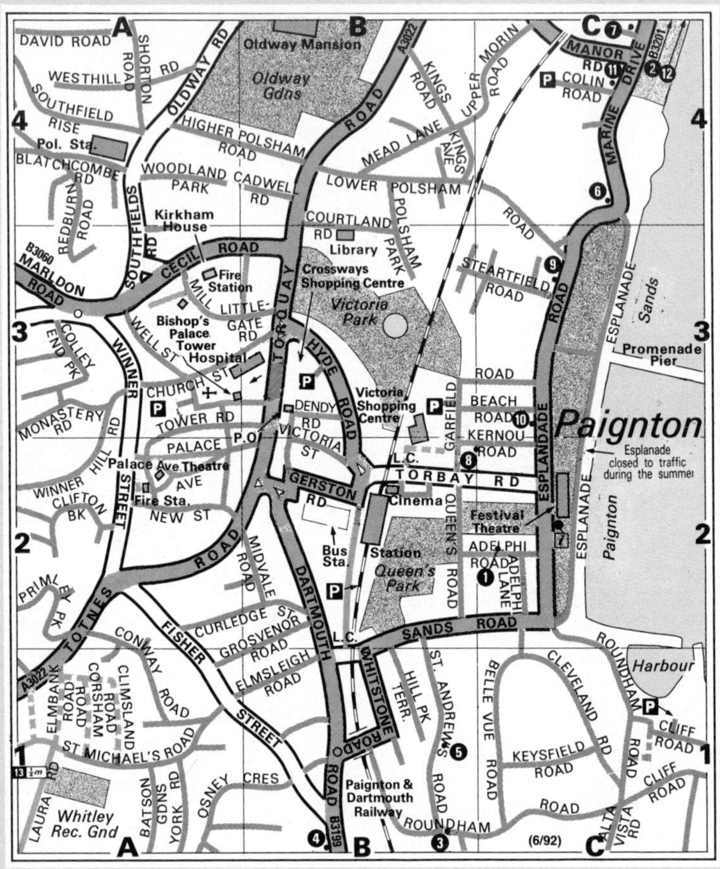

Paignton

C2	**1**	Beresford
C4	**2**	Channel View Hotel
B1	**3**	Cherra Hotel
B1	**4**	Clennon Valley Hotel
B1	**5**	Danethorpe Hotel
C4	**6**	Redcliffe Lodge Hotel
C4	**7**	Hotel Retreat
B2	**8**	St Weonard's Private Hotel
C3	**9**	Sattva Hotel
C3	**10**	The Sealawn Hotel
C4	**11**	Sea Verge Hotel
C4	**12**	Torbay Sands Hotel
A1	**13**	Waterleat House

Penzance

D2	**1**	Blue Seas Hotel
C2	**2**	Camilla Hotel
B1	**3**	Carlton Private Hotel
C2	**4**	Chy-an-Mor
A2	**5**	Dunedin
C3	**6**	Georgian House
C2	**7**	Kimberley House
B2	**8**	Hotel Minalto
D4	**9**	Mount Royal Hotel
A2	**10**	Penalva
A2	**11**	Penmorvah Hotel
B2	**12**	Trenant Private Hotel
C3	**13**	Trevelyan Hotel
B2	**14**	Trewella
D2	**15**	The Yacht *(Inn)*

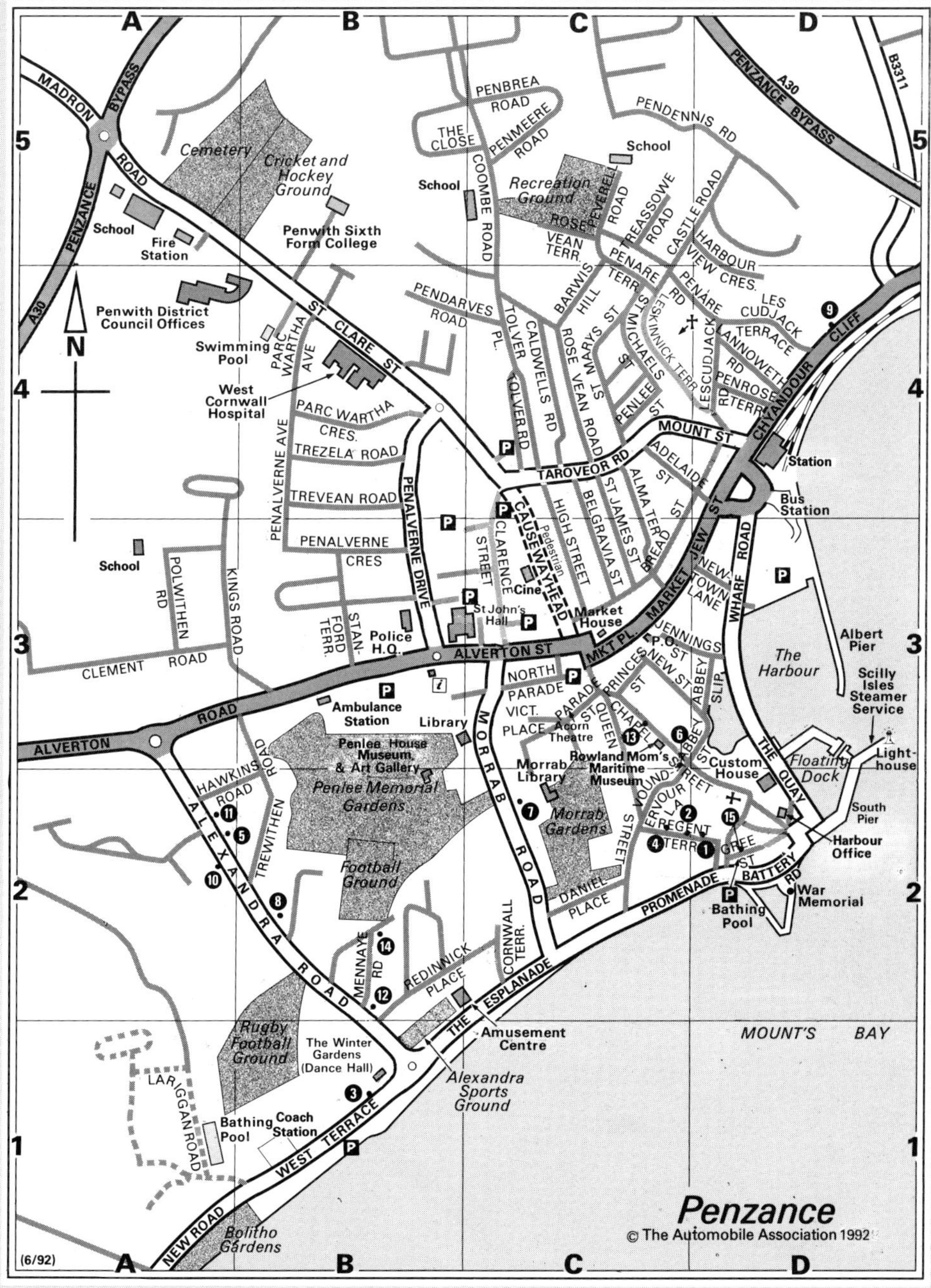
Penzance
© The Automobile Association 1992
(6/92)
A
B
C
D
1
2
3
4
5
N
MADRON
PENZANCE BYPASS
A30
B3311
Cemetery
Cricket and Hockey Ground
School
Fire Station
Penwith Sixth Form College
Penwith District Council Offices
Swimming Pool
West Cornwall Hospital
PENBREA ROAD
THE CLOSE
PENMEERE ROAD
COOMBE ROAD
Recreation Ground
PEVERELL ROAD
PENDENNIS RD
TREASSOWE ROAD
CASTLE ROAD
HARBOUR VIEW CRES.
ROSE VEAN TERR.
PENARE TERR.
PENARE RD
PENDARVES ROAD
BARWIS HILL
ST MARYS ST
ST MICHAELS ST
LESKINNICK TERR
LESCUDJACK RD
LES CUDJACK TERRACE
LANNOWETH RD
PENROSE TERR
CHYANDOUR CLIFF
TOLVER PL.
TOLVER RD
CALDWELLS RD
ROSE VEAN ROAD
PENLEE ST
MOUNT ST
ST CLARE ST
PARC WARTHA AVE
PARC WARTHA CRES.
TREZELA ROAD
TREVEAN ROAD
PENALVERNE AVE
PENALVERNE CRES
PENALVERNE DRIVE
TAROVEOR RD
ADELAIDE ST
ALMA TERR
ST JAMES ST
BELGRAVIA ST
HIGH STREET
CAUSEWAYHEAD
Pedestrian
CLARENCE STREET
Cine
St John's Hall
Market House
BREAD ST
JEW ST
MARKET
NEW TOWN LANE
WHARF ROAD
Station
Bus Station
School
POLWITHEN RD
KINGS ROAD
CLEMENT ROAD
FORD TERR.
STAN-
Police H.Q.
ALVERTON ST
MKT PL.
JENNINGS ST
P.O.
NEW ST
PRINCES ST
ABBEY
SLIP
Albert Pier
The Harbour
Scilly Isles Steamer Service
ALVERTON ROAD
Ambulance Station
NORTH PARADE
VICT. PLACE
PARADE ST
QUEEN ST
CHAPEL ST
Library
Penlee House Museum & Art Gallery
Penlee Memorial Gardens
Acorn Theatre
Rowland Mom's Maritime Museum
Custom House
Floating Dock
THE QUAY
Light-house
HAWKINS ROAD
TREWITHEN ROAD
Morrab Library
Morrab Gardens
MORRAB ROAD
VOUNDERVOUR LA
REGENT TERR
GREEN ST
ABBEY STREET
South Pier
Harbour Office
ALEXANDRA ROAD
Football Ground
DANIEL PLACE
STREET
PROMENADE
BATTERY RD
Bathing Pool
War Memorial
MENNAYE RD
REDINNICK PLACE
CORNWALL TERR.
THE ESPLANADE
Amusement Centre
MOUNT'S BAY
Rugby Football Ground
The Winter Gardens (Dance Hall)
Alexandra Sports Ground
LARIGGAN ROAD
Bathing Pool
Coach Station
WEST TERRACE
NEW ROAD
Bolitho Gardens

Plymouth

C3	**1**	Bowling Green Hotel
C3	**2**	Cranbourne Hotel
D8	**3**	Dudley
E3	**4**	Elizabethan
B3	**5**	Georgian House Hotel
C3	**6**	The Lamplighter Hotel
B3	**7**	Merville Hotel
D8	**8**	Oliver's Hotel & Restaurant
D8	**9**	Rosaland Hotel
C2	**10**	Russell Lodge Hotel
B3	**11**	St James Hotel
C3	**12**	The White House Hotel

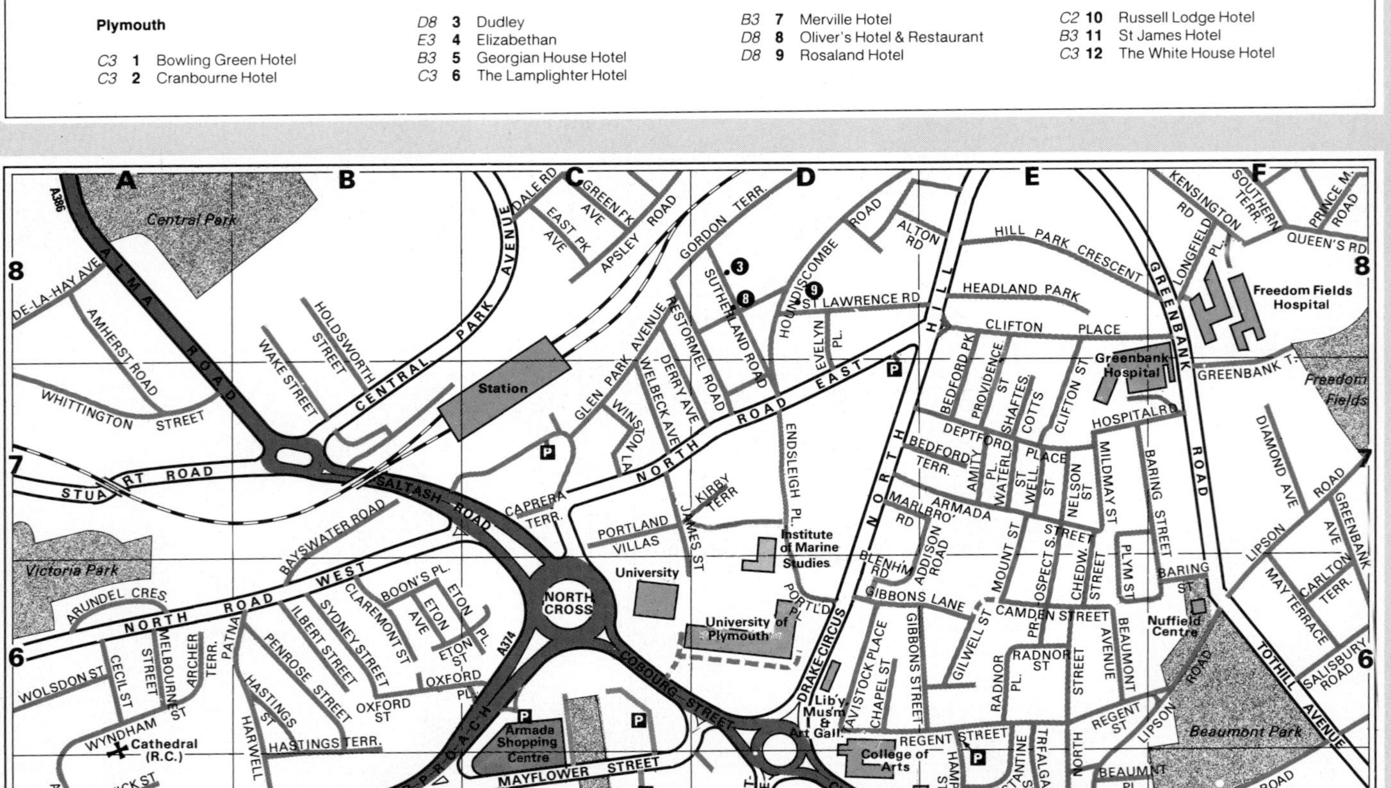

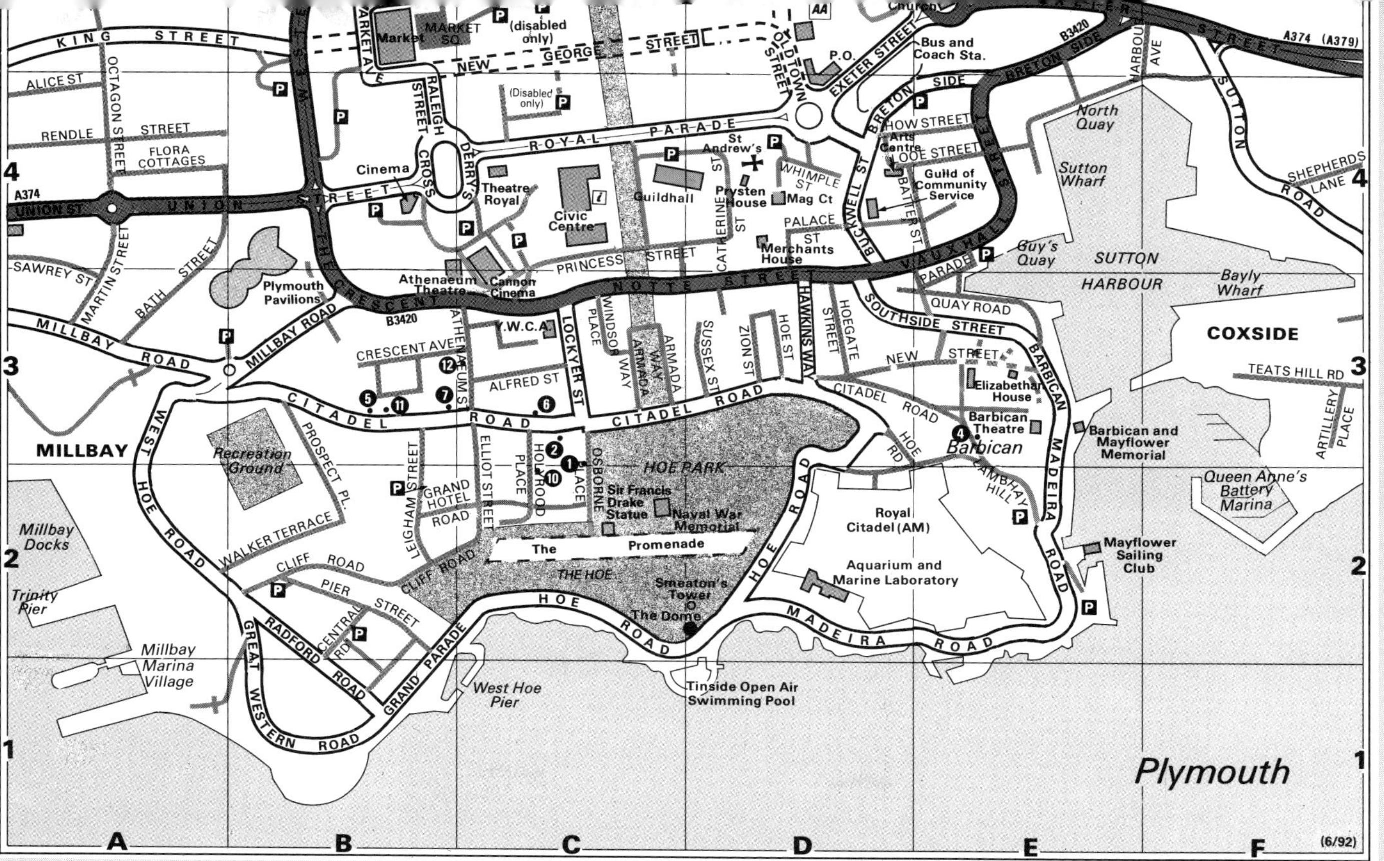
Plymouth
(6/92)
A374 (A379)
SUTTON ROAD
SHEPHERDS LANE
ARTILLERY PLACE
TEATS HILL RD
COXSIDE
Bayly Wharf
Queen Anne's Battery Marina
HARBOUR AVE
SUTTON HARBOUR
North Quay
Sutton Wharf
Barbican and Mayflower Memorial
Mayflower Sailing Club
Guy's Quay
BRETON SIDE
B3240
Bus and Coach Sta.
HOW STREET
LOOE STREET
Guild of Community Service
Arts Centre
BATTER ST
VAUXHALL STREET
QUAY ROAD
PARADE
SOUTHSIDE STREET
NEW STREET
Elizabethan House
Barbican Theatre
Barbican
BARBICAN
MADEIRA ROAD
LAMBHAY HILL
CITADEL ROAD
HOE RD
Royal Citadel (AM)
Aquarium and Marine Laboratory
EXETER STREET
BUCKWELL ST
P.O.
AA
OLD TOWN STREET
WHIMPLE ST
Mag Ct
PALACE ST
Merchants House
HOEGATE STREET
HAWKINS WAY
HOE ST
ZION ST
SUSSEX ST
HOE PARK
HOE ROAD
Tinside Open Air Swimming Pool
St Andrew's
Prysten House
CATHERINE ST
ST
Guildhall
NOTTE STREET
ARMADA WAY
WINDSOR PLACE
Naval War Memorial
Sir Francis Drake Statue
Promenade
Smeaton's Tower
The Dome
NEW GEORGE STREET
ROYAL PARADE
Civic Centre
PRINCESS STREET
LOCKYER ST
OSBORNE PLACE
HOLYROOD PLACE
THE HOE
The
(disabled only)
(Disabled only)
Theatre Royal
Cannon Cinema
Y.W.C.A.
ALFRED ST
ELLIOT STREET
West Hoe Pier
MARKET SQ.
Market
DERRY'S CROSS
Athenaeum Theatre
ATHENAEUM ST
CRESCENT AVE
GRAND HOTEL ROAD
CLIFF ROAD
GRAND PARADE
RALEIGH STREET
Cinema
B3420
LEIGHAM STREET
PIER STREET
CENTRAL RD
MARKET AVE
WESTERN APPROACH
THE CRESCENT
CITADEL
PROSPECT PL.
WALKER TERRACE
CLIFF ROAD
RADFORD ROAD
GREAT WESTERN ROAD
Plymouth Pavilions
MILLBAY ROAD
Recreation Ground
KING STREET
STREET
FLORA COTTAGES
UNION STREET
BATH STREET
WEST HOE ROAD
Millbay Marina Village
OCTAGON STREET
MARTIN STREET
MILLBAY
ALICE ST
RENDLE
SAWREY ST
A374
UNION ST
Millbay Docks
Trinity Pier
A
B
C
D
E
F
1
2
3
4

Central Portsmouth

F2	**1**	Abbey Lodge
E5	**2**	Ashwood
F3	**3**	Bembell Court Hotel
F2	**4**	Birchwood
E2	**5**	Bristol Hotel
F3	**6**	Collingham
E3	**7**	The Elms Hotel
A5	**8**	Fortitude Cottage
E2	**9**	Gainsborough House
F2	**10**	Glencoe
E3	**11**	Goodwood House
E5	**12**	Hamilton House
E5	**13**	St Andrews Lodge
E5	**14**	St David's
D3	**15**	Upper Mount House Hotel
E5	**16**	Victoria Court

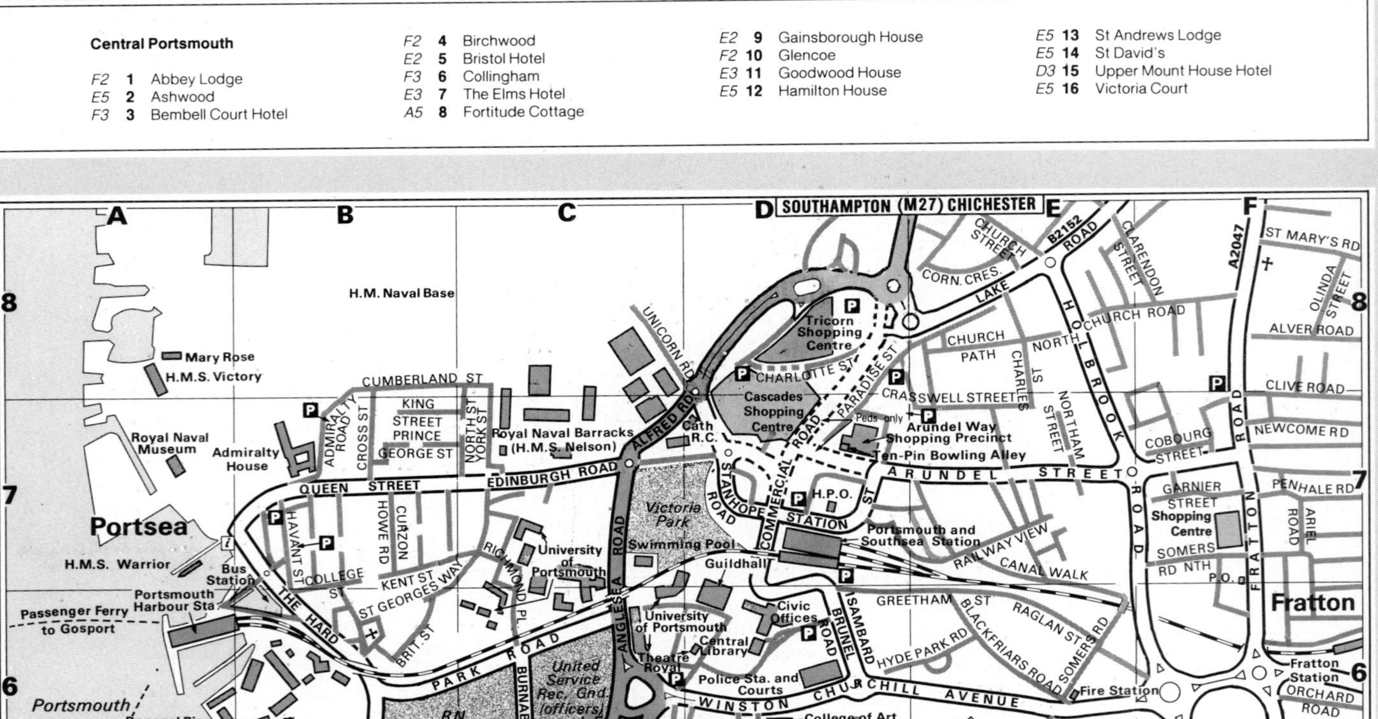

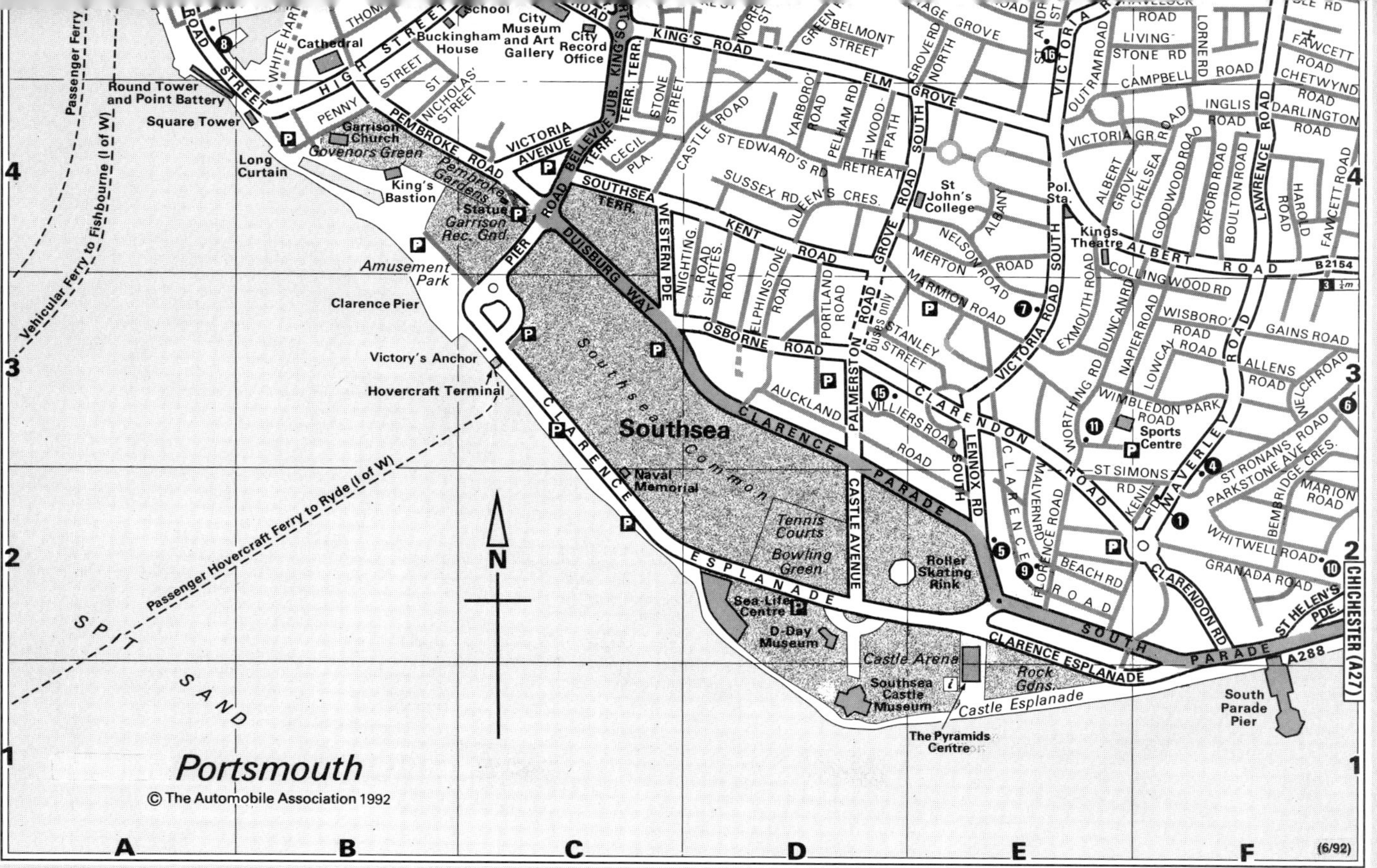
Portsmouth
© The Automobile Association 1992
(6/92)
CHICHESTER (A27)
A288
B2154
Southsea
Southsea Common
South Parade Pier
Southsea Castle Museum
Castle Arena
D-Day Museum
Sea-Life Centre
The Pyramids Centre
Castle Esplanade
Rock Gdns.
Roller Skating Rink
Tennis Courts
Bowling Green
Naval Memorial
Victory's Anchor
Hovercraft Terminal
Clarence Pier
Amusement Park
Garrison Rec. Gnd
Statue
Pembroke Gardens
King's Bastion
Govenors Green
Garrison Church
Cathedral
Long Curtain
Square Tower
Round Tower and Point Battery
Buckingham House
School
City Museum and Art Gallery
City Record Office
St John's College
Kings Theatre
Pol. Sta.
Sports Centre
Passenger Hovercraft Ferry to Ryde (I of W)
Vehicular Ferry to Fishbourne (I of W)
Passenger Ferry
SPIT SAND
CLARENCE PARADE
SOUTH PARADE
CLARENCE ESPLANADE
CLARENCE ESPLANADE
DUISBURG WAY
PIER ROAD
WESTERN PDE
SOUTHSEA TERR.
CASTLE AVENUE
PALMERSTON ROAD
OSBORNE ROAD
KENT ROAD
CLARENDON ROAD
VICTORIA ROAD SOUTH
ALBERT ROAD
LAWRENCE ROAD
WAVERLEY ROAD
CLARENDON RD
HIGH STREET
PEMBROKE ROAD
KING'S ROAD
ELM GROVE
GROVE ROAD SOUTH
ST HELEN'S PDE.

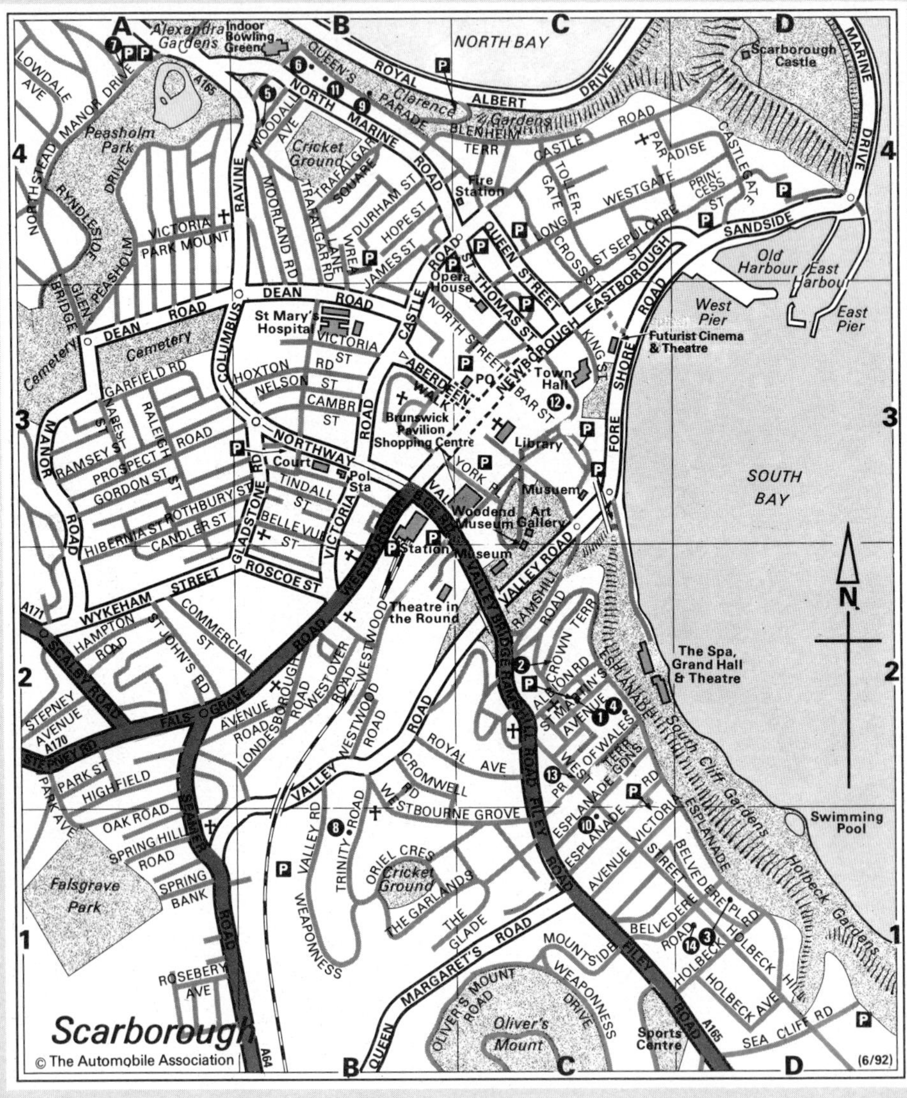

Scarborough

C2	**1**	Alga Court
C2	**2**	Avoncroft Hotel
D1	**3**	Bay & Premier Hotels
C2	**4**	Burghcliffe Hotel
B4	**5**	Dolphin Hotel
B4	**6**	Geldenhuis Hotel
A4	**7**	Manor Heath Hotel
B1	**8**	Mount House Hotel
B4	**9**	Paragon Hotel
C1	**10**	Parmelia Hotel
B4	**11**	The Ramleh
C3	**12**	Riveria Hotel
C2	**13**	Sefton Hotel
D1	**14**	West Lodge Private Hotel

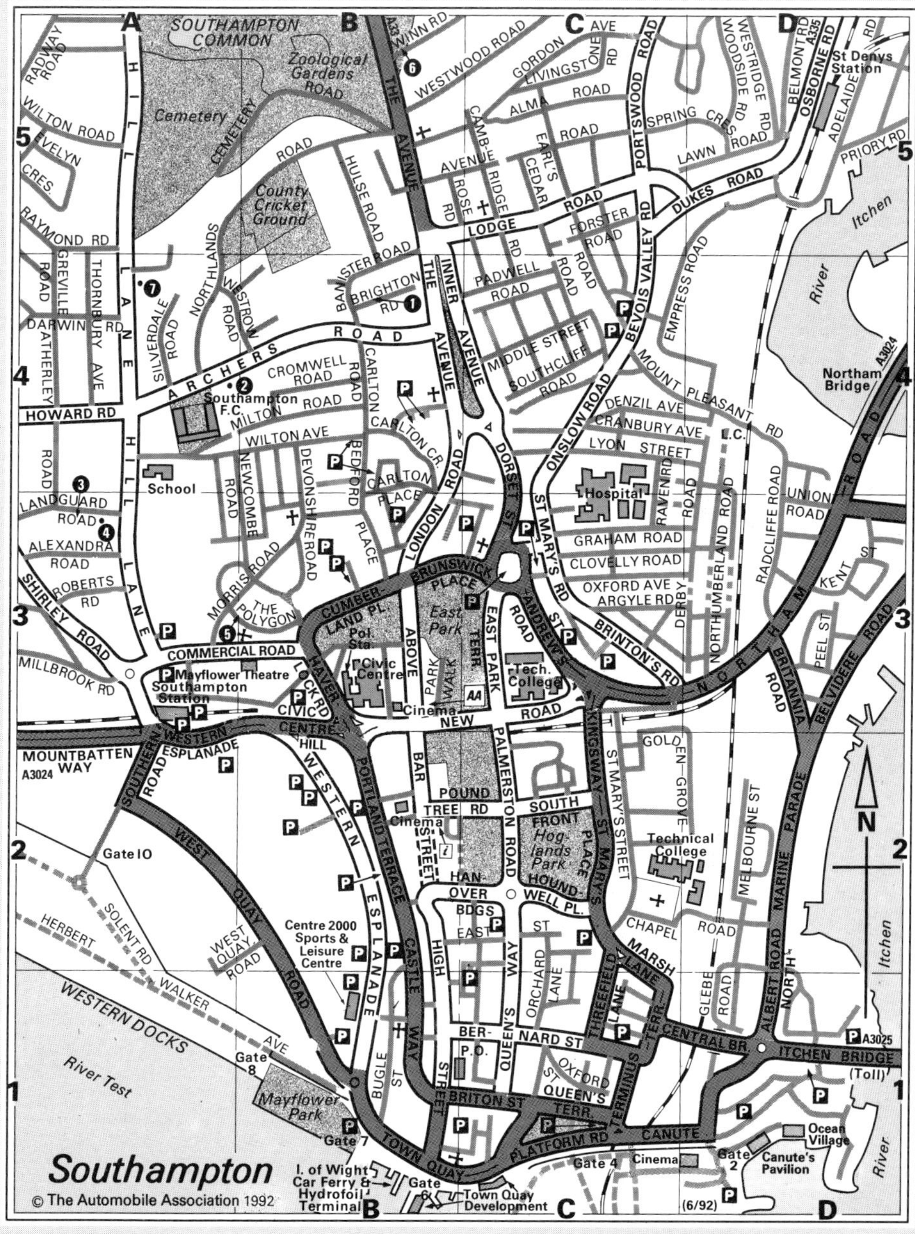

Southampton

B4	**1**	Banister House Hotel
A4	**2**	Capri
A3	**3**	Hunters Lodge Hotel
A3	**4**	Landguard Lodge
A3	**5**	Linden
B5	**6**	Lodge
A4	**7**	Madison House

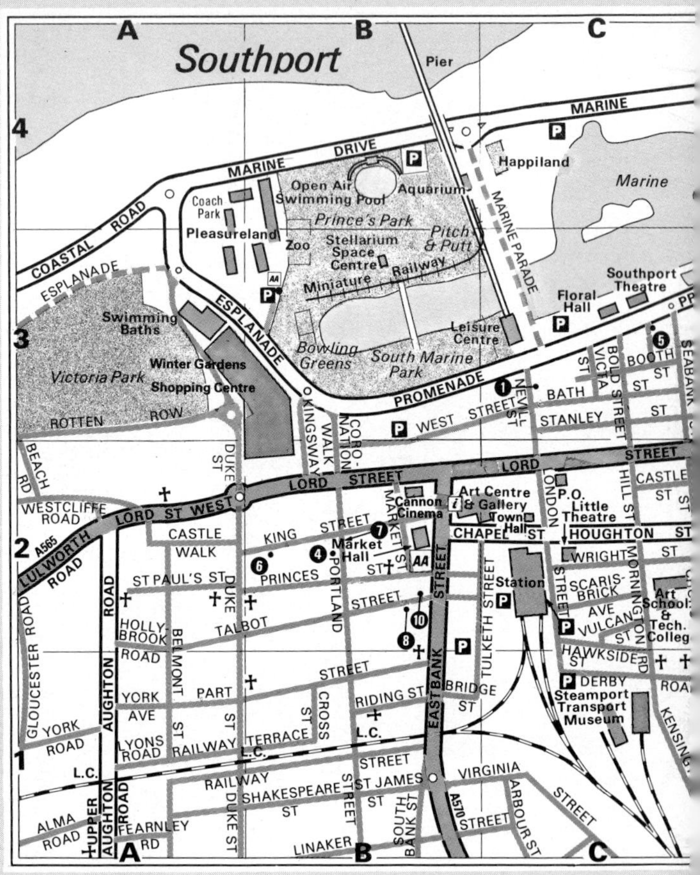

Southport

C3	**1**	Ambassador Private Hotel
D3	**2**	Fairway Private Hotel
D3	**3**	The Gables Private Hotel
B2	**4**	The Herald Hotel
C3	**5**	Lake Hotel
B2	**6**	Lyndhurst

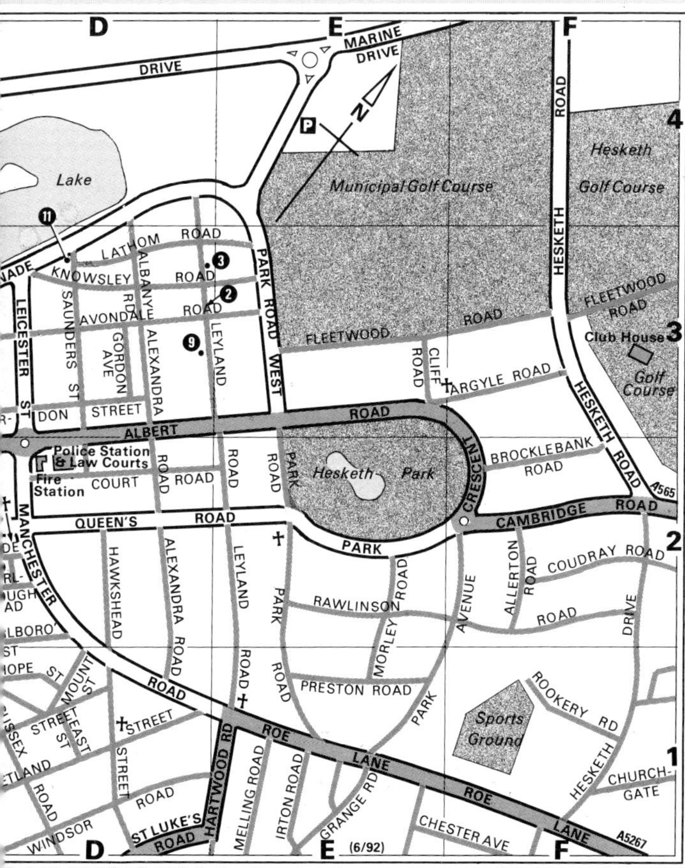

B2	**7**	Oakwood Private Hotel	*B2*	**10**	The White Lodge Private Hotel
B2	**8**	Rosedale Hotel	*D3*	**11**	Windsor Lodge Hotel
D3	**9**	Sunningdale Hotel			

Stratford-upon-Avon

A2	**1**	Ambleside
C1	**2**	Avon View Hotel
A3	**3**	Brook Lodge
B3	**4**	Courtland Hotel
C1	**5**	Craig Cleeve House
C1	**6**	The Croft
A2	**7**	The Dylan
C1	**8**	Eastnor House Hotel
A2	**9**	Eversley Bears
C4	**10**	Hardwick House
C1	**11**	Highcroft
A2	**12**	Hollies
A3	**13**	Hunters Moon
A2	**14**	Kawartha House
A2	**15**	Marlyn
C1	**16**	Melita Private Hotel
A3	**17**	Moonraker House
A2	**18**	Nando's
A1	**19**	Parkfield
B3	**20**	The Payton Hotel
A3	**21**	Penryn House
A1	**22**	Ravenhurst
A2	**23**	Salamander
C1	**24**	Sequoia House Private
A2	**25**	Stretton House Hotel Hotel
A2	**26**	Twelfth Night
A3	**27**	Victoria Spa Lodge
A2	**28**	Virginia Lodge

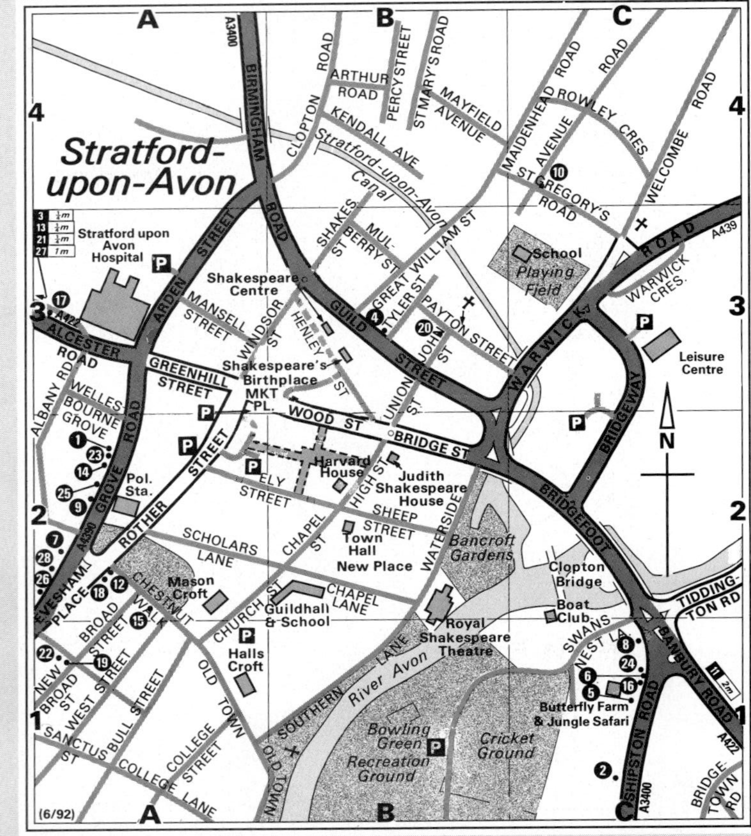

Torquay

F3	**1**	Beauly
B2	**2**	The Berburry Hotel
F3	**3**	Braddon Hall Hotel
B3	**4**	Chesterfield Hotel
A3	**5**	Clovelly
A4	**6**	Hotel Concorde
D4	**7**	Craig Court Hotel
B3	**8**	Cranborne Hotel
A4	**9**	Cranmore
F4	**10**	Daphne Court Hotel
C3	**11**	Devon Court Hotel
B1	**12**	Elmdene Hotel
B3	**13**	Fairways Hotel
B3	**14**	Glenorleigh Hotel
B3	**15**	Grosvenor House Hotel
B1	**16**	Ingoldsby Hotel
D3	**17**	Jesmond Dene Private Hotel
A4	**18**	Kingston House
C3	**19**	Lindum Hotel
D3	**20**	Mapleton Hotel
E2	**21**	Olivia Court
A1	**22**	Rawlyn House Hotel
A4	**23**	Richwood Hotel
B1	**24**	Seaway Hotel
C4	**25**	Sevens Hotel
A4	**26**	Silverlands Hotel
C3	**27**	Skerries Private Hotel
A2	**28**	Torbay Rise
B3	**29**	Hotel Trelawney
B3	**30**	Trouville
B3	**31**	Westgate Hotel

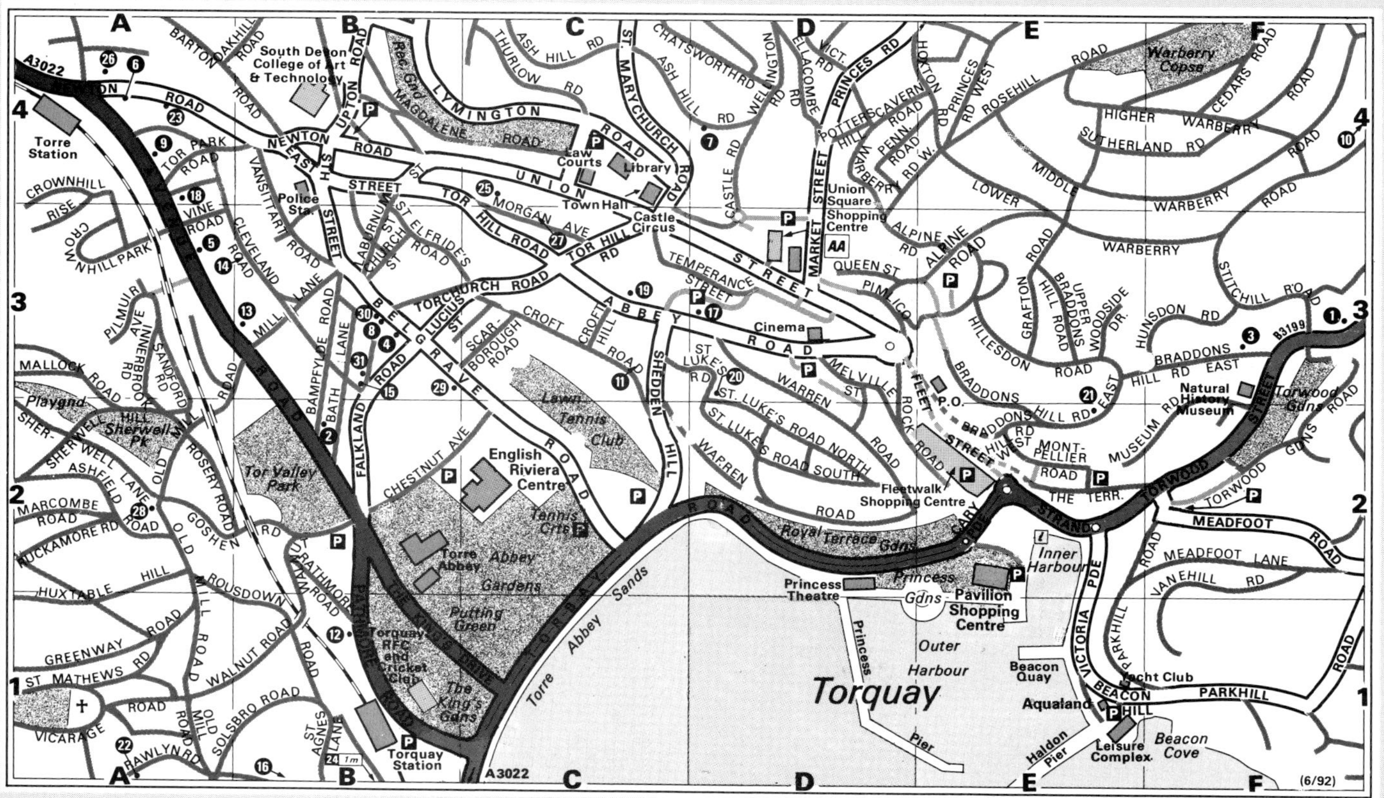
Torquay
Outer Harbour
Inner Harbour
Princess Pier
Haldon Pier
Beacon Quay
Beacon Cove
Torre Abbey Sands
Torre Abbey Gardens
Torre Abbey
Putting Green
The King's Gdns
Torquay RFC and Cricket Club
Torquay Station
Torre Station
English Riviera Centre
Tennis Crts
Lawn Tennis Club
Princess Gdns
Royal Terrace Gdns
Princess Theatre
Pavilion Shopping Centre
Fleetwalk Shopping Centre
Union Square Shopping Centre
Leisure Complex
Aqualand
Yacht Club
Natural History Museum
Torwood Gdns
Warberry Copse
Rec. Gnd
Tor Valley Park
Sherwell Hill Pk
Playgnd
South Devon College of Art & Technology
Police Sta.
Law Courts
Library
Town Hall
Castle Circus
Cinema
P.O.
A3022
B3199
TORBAY ROAD
THE KING'S DRIVE
NEWTON ROAD
AVENUE ROAD
UNION STREET
FLEET STREET
TORWOOD STREET
VICTORIA PDE
STRAND
CARY PDE
ABBEY ROAD
BELGRAVE ROAD
SHEDDEN HILL
ST. MARYCHURCH ROAD
LYMINGTON ROAD
MAGDALENE ROAD
MARKET STREET
PRINCES RD
MEADFOOT ROAD
MEADFOOT LANE
PARKHILL ROAD
BRADDONS HILL RD EAST
WARBERRY ROAD
STITCHILL ROAD
PIMLICO
MELVILLE ST
WARREN ROAD
ST. LUKE'S ROAD NORTH
ST. LUKE'S ROAD SOUTH
FALKLAND ROAD
PATHMORE ROAD
WALNUT ROAD
OLD MILL ROAD
ST MATHEWS RD
(6/92)

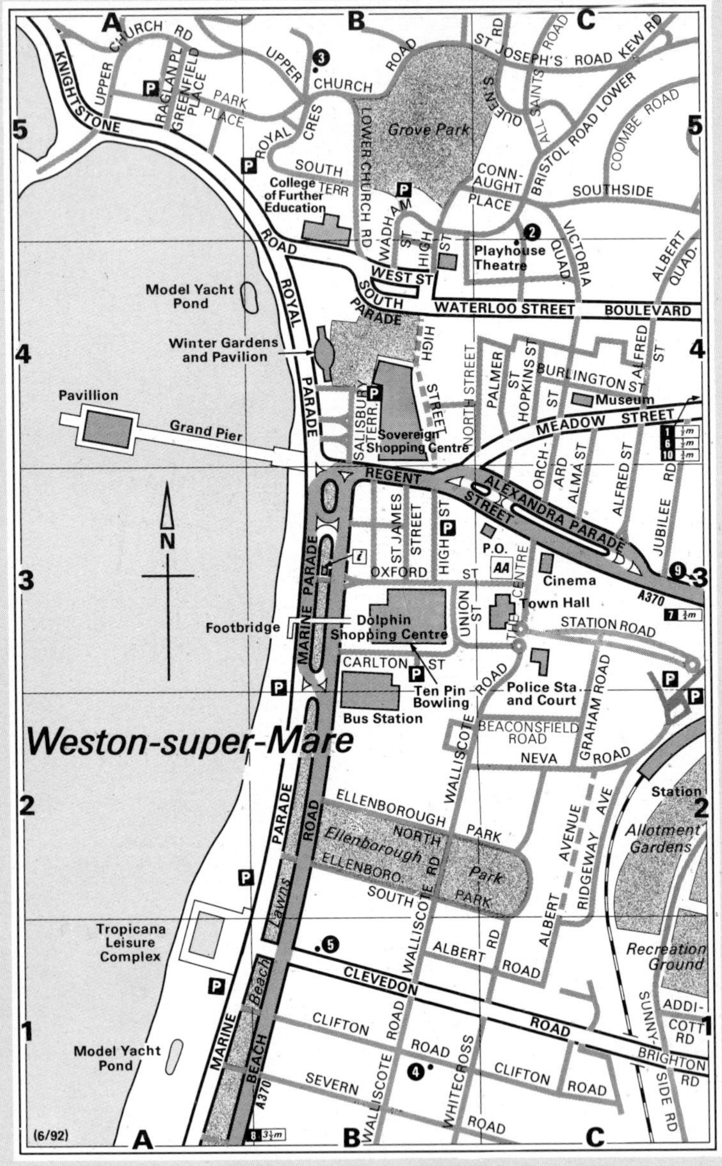

Weston-super-Mare

C4	**1**	Ashcombe Court
C4	**2**	Baymead Hotel
B5	**3**	Braeside
B1	**4**	Clifton Lodge
B1	**5**	Lewinsdale Lodge Hotel
C4	**6**	Milton Lodge
C3	**7**	Newton House
B1	**8**	Purn House
C3	**9**	Saxonia
C4	**10**	Wychwood Hotel

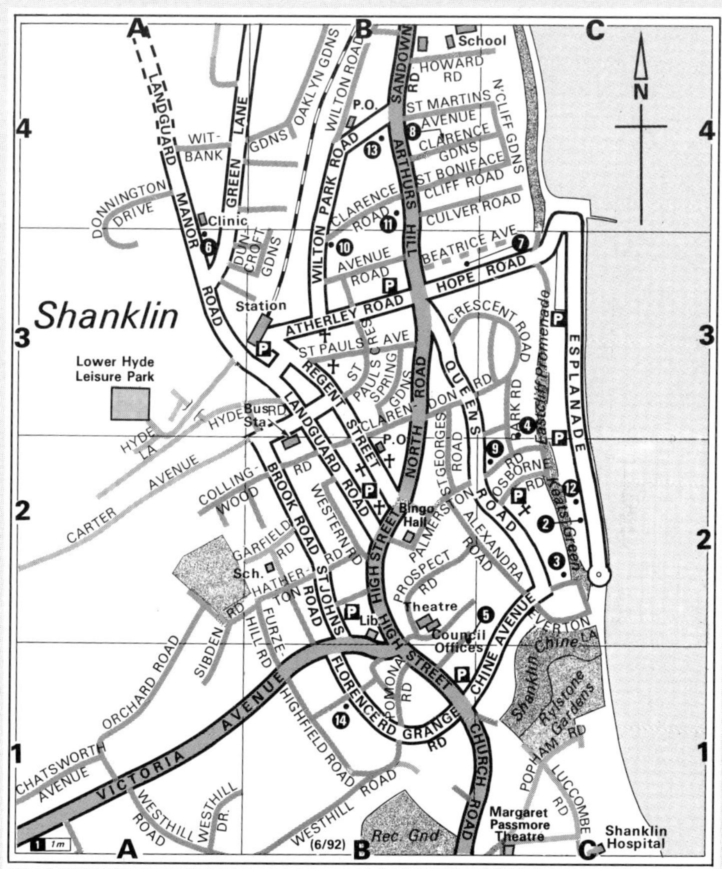

Shanklin

A1	**1**	Apse Manor Country House
C2	**2**	Aqua Hotel
C2	**3**	Bay House Hotel
C3	**4**	Carlton Hotel
B2	**5**	Chine Lodge
A3	**6**	Culham Lodge
B3	**7**	Curraghmore Hotel
B4	**8**	Edgecliffe Hotel
C2	**9**	Hambledon Hotel
B3	**10**	Kenbury Private Hotel
B4	**11**	Mount House
C2	**12**	Osborne House
B4	**13**	Rowborough Hotel
B1	**14**	Soraba Private Hotel

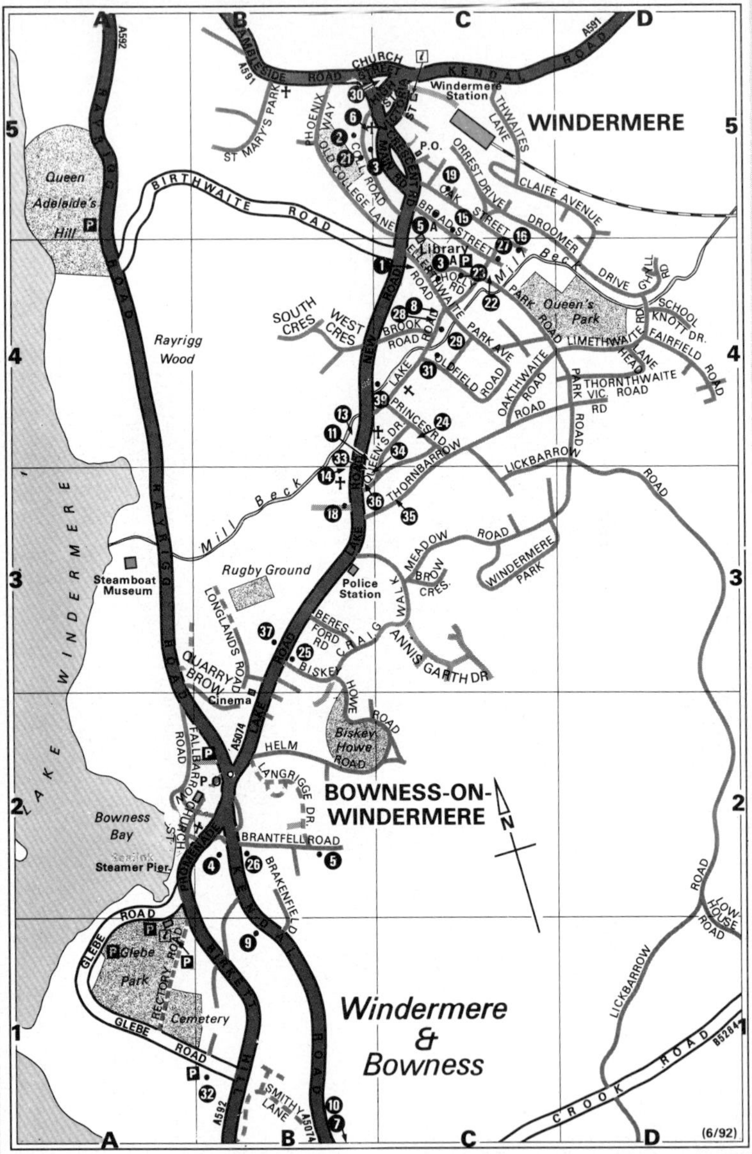

Windermere & Bowness

BOWNESS-ON-WINDERMERE

WINDERMERE

(6/92)

Windermere

Grid	No.	Name
C4	**1**	Aaron Slack
B5	**2**	Applegarth Hotel
B5	**3**	Archway Country
C4	**3A**	The Beaumont Hotel
B2	**4**	Belsfield House
B2	**5**	Blenheim Lodge
C5	**5A**	Broadlands
B5	**6**	Brendan Chase
B1	**7**	Brooklands
C4	**8**	Clifton House
B1	**9**	Cranleigh Hotel
B1	**10**	Fayrer Holme
B4	**11**	Fir Trees
B4	**13**	Glencree Private Hotel
B3	**14**	Glenville Hotel
C5	**15**	Green Gables
C4	**16**	Greenriggs
B3	**18**	The Hawksmoor
C5	**19**	Hazel Bank
B5	**21**	Holly Lodge
C4	**22**	Holly Park House
C4	**23**	Kenilworth
C4	**24**	Kirkwood
B3	**25**	Latimer House
B2	**26**	Laurel Cottage
C4	**27**	Lynwood
C4	**28**	Meadfoot
C4	**29**	Mylne Bridge House
C5	**30**	Oakthorpe Hotel
C4	**31**	Oldfield House
B1	**32**	Parson Wyke Country House
B3	**33**	Rosemount
B3	**34**	St Johns Lodge
C3	**35**	Thornleigh
B3	**36**	Westlake
B3	**37**	White Lodge Hotel
C4	**39**	Woodlands

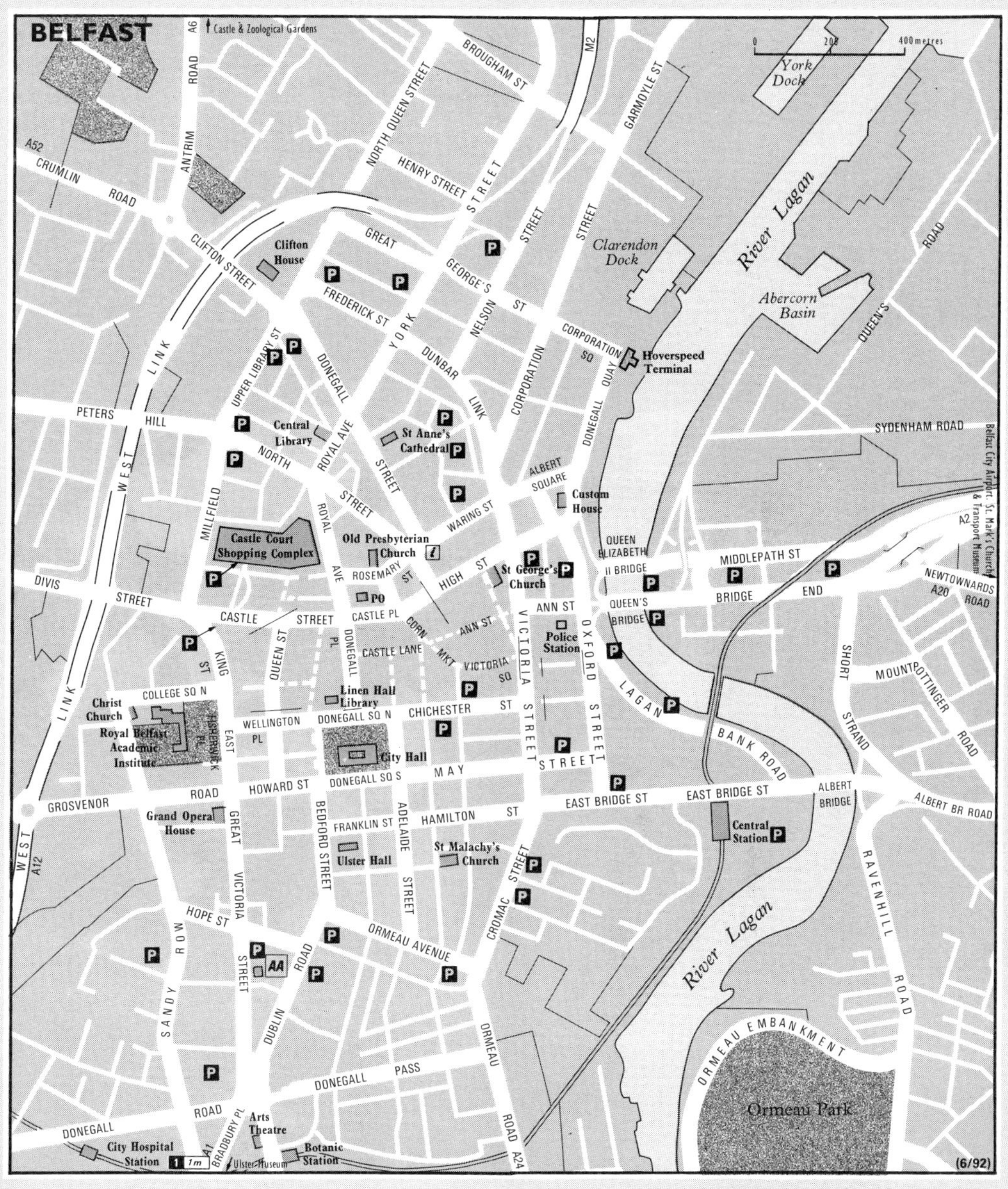

Belfast

1 Camera

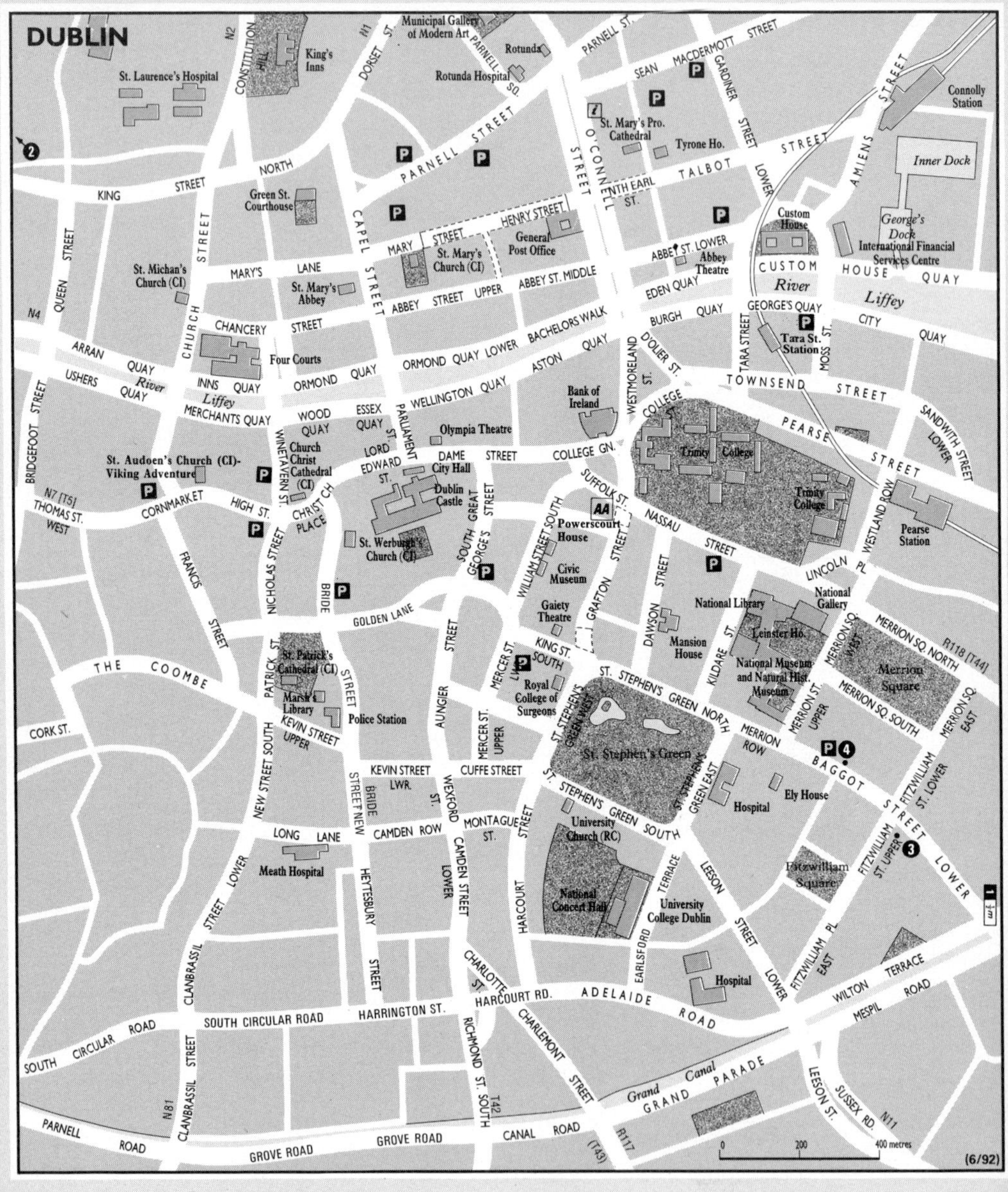

Dublin

1 Ariel House
2 Charleville
3 The Fitzwilliam
4 Georgian House

KEY TO ATLAS

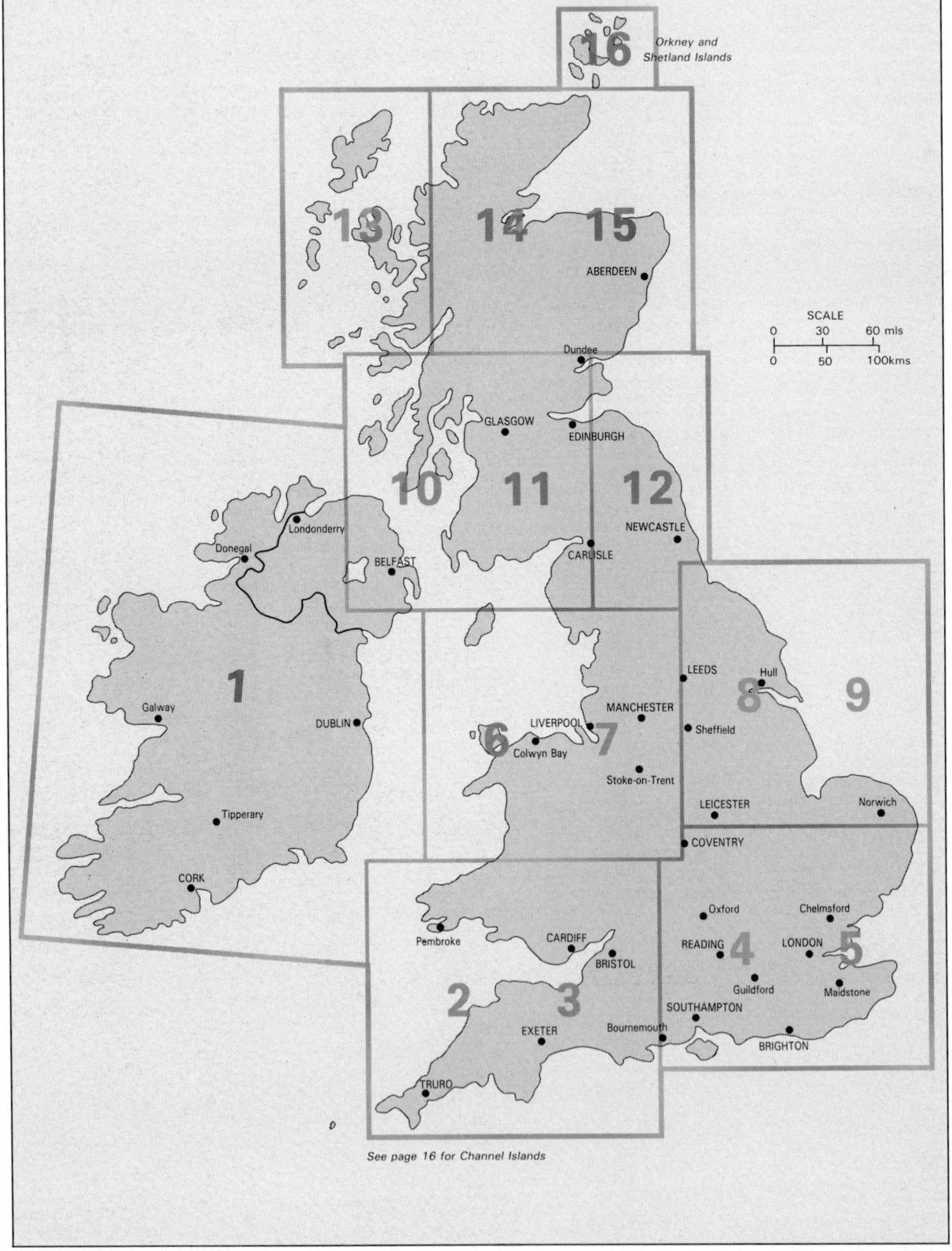

16 Orkney and Shetland Islands
13
14
15
ABERDEEN
SCALE
0 30 60 mls
0 50 100kms
Dundee
GLASGOW
EDINBURGH
10
11
12
Londonderry
Donegal
BELFAST
NEWCASTLE
CARLISLE
1
Galway
DUBLIN
Tipperary
CORK
LEEDS
Hull
8
9
MANCHESTER
LIVERPOOL
6
7
Colwyn Bay
Sheffield
Stoke-on-Trent
LEICESTER
Norwich
COVENTRY
Oxford
Chelmsford
READING
4
LONDON
5
Pembroke
CARDIFF
BRISTOL
Guildford
Maidstone
2
3
SOUTHAMPTON
EXETER
Bournemouth
BRIGHTON
TRURO

See page 16 for Channel Islands

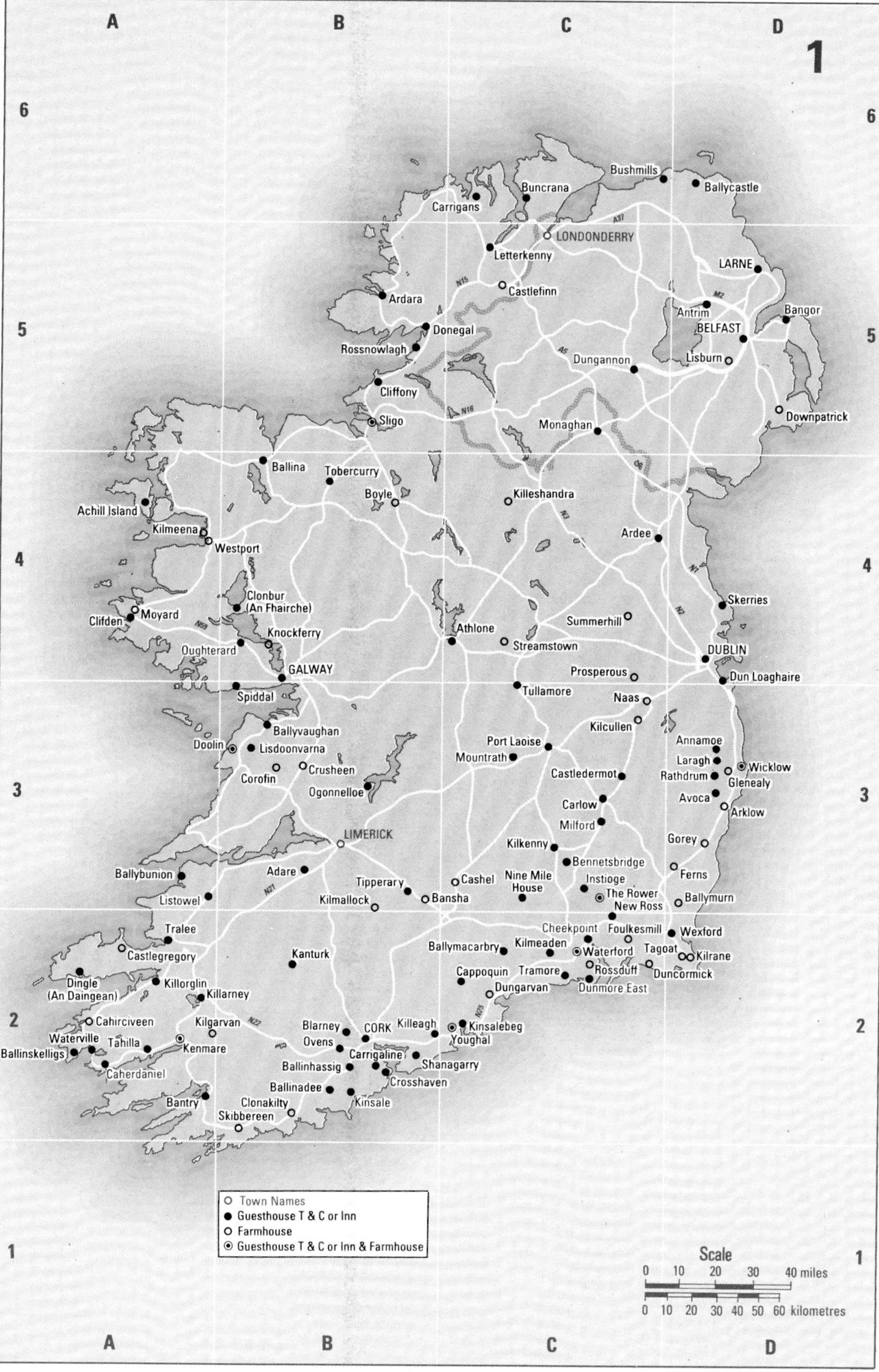
1
A
B
C
D
6
5
4
3
2
1
Bushmills
Ballycastle
Buncrana
Carrigans
LONDONDERRY
Letterkenny
LARNE
Castlefinn
Ardara
Antrim
Bangor
Donegal
BELFAST
Rossnowlagh
Dungannon
Lisburn
Cliffony
Downpatrick
Sligo
Monaghan
Ballina
Tobercurry
Boyle
Killeshandra
Achill Island
Kilmeena
Westport
Ardee
Clonbur
(An Fhairche)
Skerries
Clifden
Moyard
Summerhill
Knockferry
Athlone
Oughterard
Streamstown
DUBLIN
GALWAY
Prosperous
Dun Loaghaire
Spiddal
Tullamore
Naas
Kilcullen
Ballyvaughan
Annamoe
Doolin
Lisdoonvarna
Port Laoise
Laragh
Mountrath
Wicklow
Crusheen
Rathdrum
Corofin
Castledermot
Gleneally
Ogonnelloe
Avoca
Carlow
Arklow
Milford
LIMERICK
Gorey
Kilkenny
Bennetsbridge
Ballybunion
Adare
Ferns
Cashel
Nine Mile
House
Instioge
Tipperary
The Rower
Listowel
Bansha
Ballymurn
Kilmallock
New Ross
Tralee
Cheekpoint
Foulkesmill
Wexford
Ballymacarbry
Kilmeaden
Tagoat
Castlegregory
Waterford
Kilrane
Kanturk
Tramore
Rossduff
Duncormick
Dingle
(An Daingean)
Cappoquin
Dunmore East
Killorglin
Dungarvan
Killarney
Cahirciveen
Kilgarvan
Blarney
CORK
Killeagh
Kinsalebeg
Waterville
Tahilla
Youghal
Ballinskelligs
Kenmare
Ovens
Carrigaline
Shanagarry
Caherdaniel
Ballinhassig
Crosshaven
Ballinadee
Kinsale
Bantry
Clonakilty
Skibbereen
N15
N16
N17
N59
N21
N22
N25
A37
A5
M2
N3
N1
N2
Town Names
Guesthouse T & C or Inn
Farmhouse
Guesthouse T & C or Inn & Farmhouse
Scale
0 10 20 30 40 miles
0 10 20 30 40 50 60 kilometres

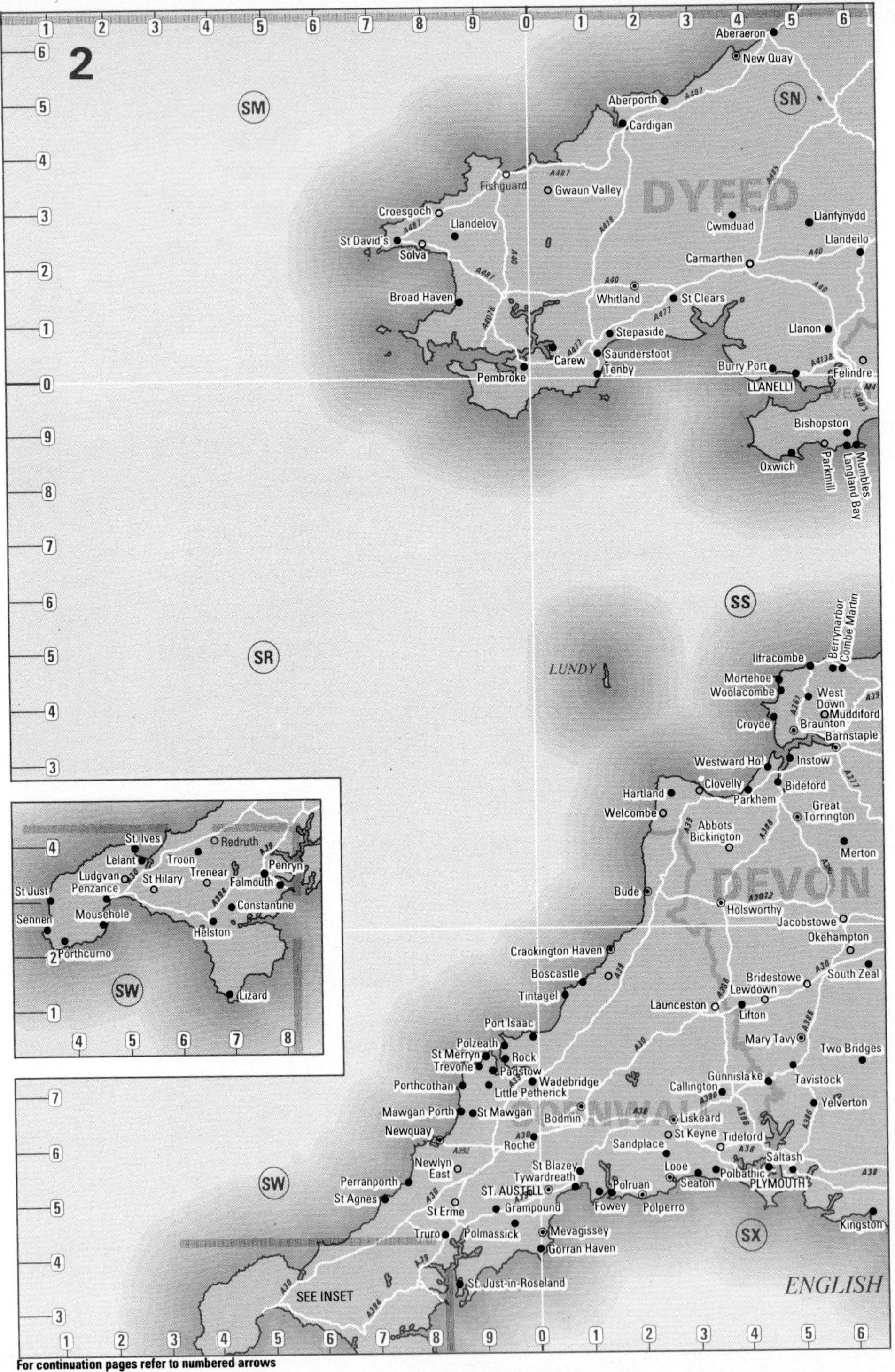
2
SM
SN
SR
SS
SW
SX
DYFED
DEVON
CORNWALL
LUNDY
ENGLISH
Aberaeron
New Quay
Aberporth
Cardigan
Fishguard
Gwaun Valley
Croesgoch
Llandeloy
St David's
Solva
Cwmduad
Llanfynydd
Llandeilo
Carmarthen
Broad Haven
Whitland
St Clears
Stepaside
Carew
Saundersfoot
Tenby
Pembroke
Llanon
Burry Port
LLANELLI
Felindre
Bishopston
Oxwich
Parkmill
Mumbles
Langland Bay
Ilfracombe
Berrynarbor
Combe Martin
Mortehoe
Woolacombe
West Down
Muddiford
Croyde
Braunton
Barnstaple
Westward Ho!
Instow
Clovelly
Hartland
Parkhem
Bideford
Welcombe
Abbots Bickington
Great Torrington
Merton
Bude
Holsworthy
Jacobstowe
Okehampton
Crackington Haven
Boscastle
Tintagel
Bridestowe
South Zeal
Lewdown
Launceston
Lifton
Port Isaac
Polzeath
St Merryn
Rock
Trevone
Padstow
Mary Tavy
Two Bridges
Porthcothan
Wadebridge
Little Petherick
Gunnislake
Callington
Tavistock
Yelverton
Mawgan Porth
St Mawgan
Bodmin
Liskeard
Newquay
Roche
St Keyne
Tideford
Sandplace
Saltash
Newlyn East
St Blazey
Tywardreath
Looe
Seaton
Polbathic
PLYMOUTH
Perranporth
St Agnes
ST. AUSTELL
Polruan
Fowey
Polperro
St Erme
Grampound
Kingston
Truro
Polmassick
Mevagissey
Gorran Haven
St. Just-in-Roseland
SEE INSET
St. Ives
Redruth
Lelant
Troon
Ludgvan
Trenear
Penryn
Penzance
St Hilary
Falmouth
St Just
Constantine
Sennen
Mousehole
Helston
Porthcurno
Lizard
For continuation pages refer to numbered arrows

6
7
3
Tregaron
Llandrindod Wells
Penybont
Eardisland
Leominster
Clifton upon Teme
Droitwich
Himbleton
Warwick
Stratford-upon-Avon
Docklow
Bromyard
Weobley
Bodenham
Ullingswick
Leigh
WORCESTER
Bishampton
Builth Wells
POWYS
Whitney-on-Wye
Bredwardine
Great Malvern
Hanley Castle
Upton upon Severn
Evesham
Rhandirmwyn
Hay-on-Wye
Glasbury
Three Cocks
Bronllys
Talgarth
Ruckhall
HEREFORD
Ledbury
Vowchurch
Fownhope
Woolhope
Llandovery
Sennybridge
Brecon
Little Dewchurch
Kings Caple
Hoarwithy
Tewkesbury
4
Pontrilas
Bishops Cleeve
Pandy
Ross-on-Wye
St Owen's Cross
CHELTENHAM
SN
SO
Crickhowell
Abergavenny
Whitchurch
West Symond Yat
East Symond Yat
GLOUCESTER
Gilwern
Colesbourne
Coleford
GLOUCESTERSHIRE
MERTHYR TYDFIL
GWENT
Clearwell
Llandogo
Tintern
Lydney
Stroud
Cirencester
Neath
Cwmbran
Dursley
Nailsworth
MID GLAMORGAN
Blackwood
Berkeley
North Nibley
SWANSEA
Chepstow
Charfield
Tetbury
Falfield
Cromhall
Malmesbury
NEWPORT
Redwick
Almondsbury
SWINDON
St Brides-Super-Ely
Old Sodbury
Alderton
Bridgend
Porthcawl
SOUTH GLAMORGAN
CARDIFF
Nettleton
BRISTOL
Flax Bourton
Chippenham
SS
Penarth
Clevedon
AVON
Keynsham
BATH
Lacock
Melksham
Weston-super-mare
Marksbury
Farmborough
Bradford-on-Avon
WILTSHIRE
BRISTOL CHANNEL
Blagdon
Timsbury
Hinton Charterhouse
Woody Bay
Lynton
Lynmouth
Countisbury
Temple Cloud
Little Cheverell
Erlestoke
Axbridge
Chewton Mendip
Wells
ST
Frome
Nunney
Brendon
Porlock
Minehead
Pawlett
Williton
Washford
Kilve
Cannington
Shepton Mallet
Simonsbath
Roadwater
Stogumber
North Wootton
Glastonbury
Longleat
Wheddon Cross
Bridgwater
Heasley Mill
West Buckland
Butleigh
Castle Cary
Dulverton
Brompton Regis
West Bagborough
Burrowbridge
Somerton
Mere
Semley
Ansty
SALISBURY
North Molton
SOMERSET
Wiveliscombe
TAUNTON
Wincanton
Shillingford
Waterrow
Norton Fitzwarren
Langport
Podimore
Oakford
Bampton
West Stour
Wellington
Beercrocombe
Mudford
Henstridge
Chiselborough
YEOVIL
Millborne Port
Witheridge
Tiverton
Sherborne
Uffculme
Sturminster Newton
Morchard Bishop
Willand
Crewkerne
Tarrant Monkton
Cheriton Fitzpaine
Cullompton
Chard
North Perrott
Halstock
Evershot
Mappowder
4
DEVON
Blandford Forum
Payhembury
Honiton
Bettiscombe
Beaminster
DORSET
Crediton
Upton Pyne
Whimple
Axminster
Charmouth
Nettlecombe
Piddletrenthide
Bere Regis
Whitestone
EXETER
Ottery St Mary
Colyford
Lyme Regis
Chideock
Bridport
Winterbourne Abbas
Dorchester
Chagford
Venn Ottery
Seaton
Beer
Burton Bradstock
BOURNEMOUTH
Moretonhampstead
Sidmouth
Wareham
Exmouth
Budleigh Salterton
Portesham
Bovey Tracey
WEYMOUTH
Dawlish
Bickington
Teignmouth
Ashburton
Newton Abbot
SY
Holne
Buckfast
Buckfastleigh
Dartington
TORQUAY
Totnes
Paignton
Harberton
Brixham
Halwell
Dartmouth
Bantham
Kingsbridge
Frogmore
Salcombe
SX
CHANNEL
Town Names
Guesthouse or Inn
Farmhouse
Guesthouse or Inn & Farmhouse
Scale
0 10 20 miles
0 10 20 30 kilometres

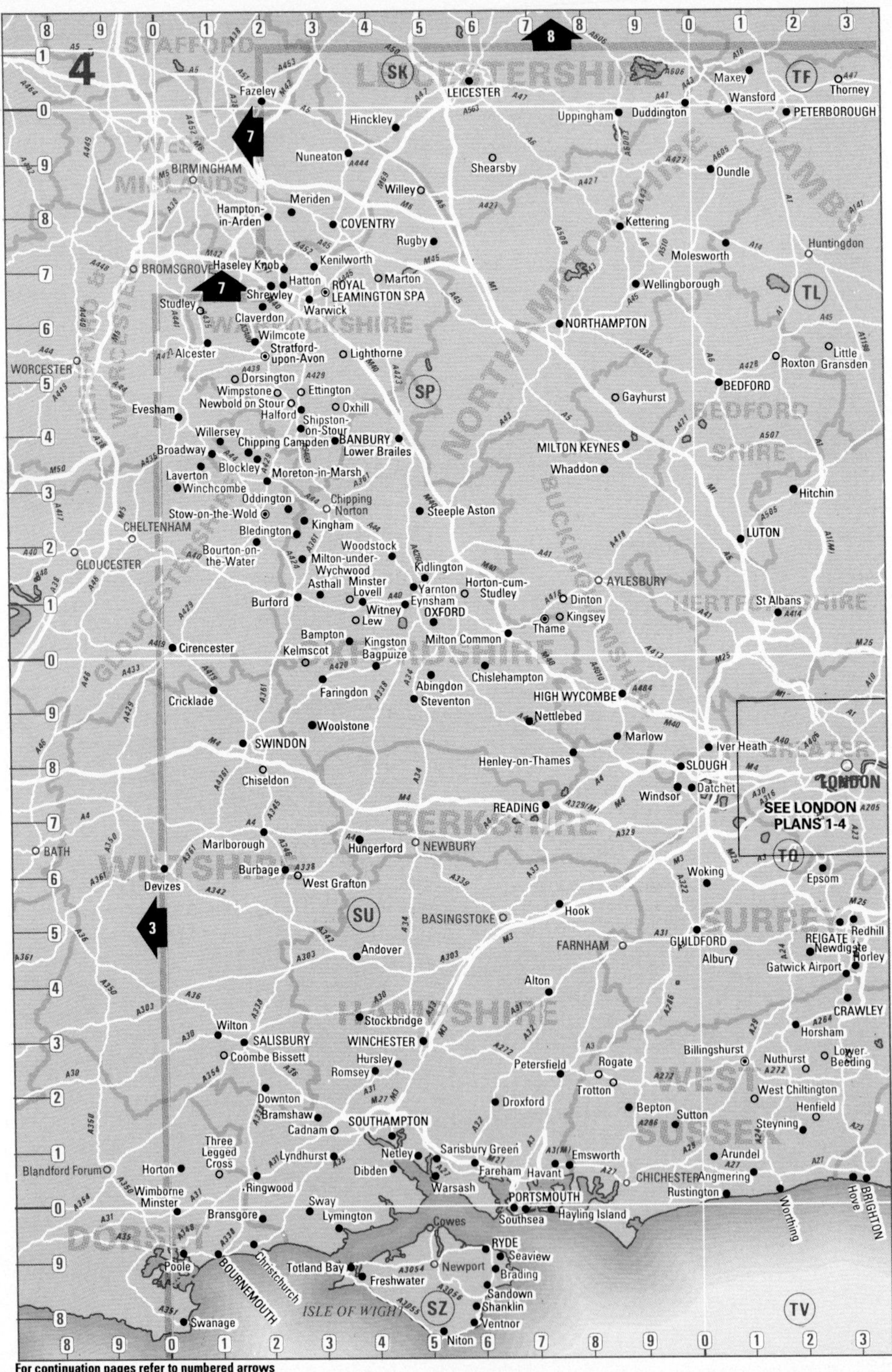

For continuation pages refer to numbered arrows

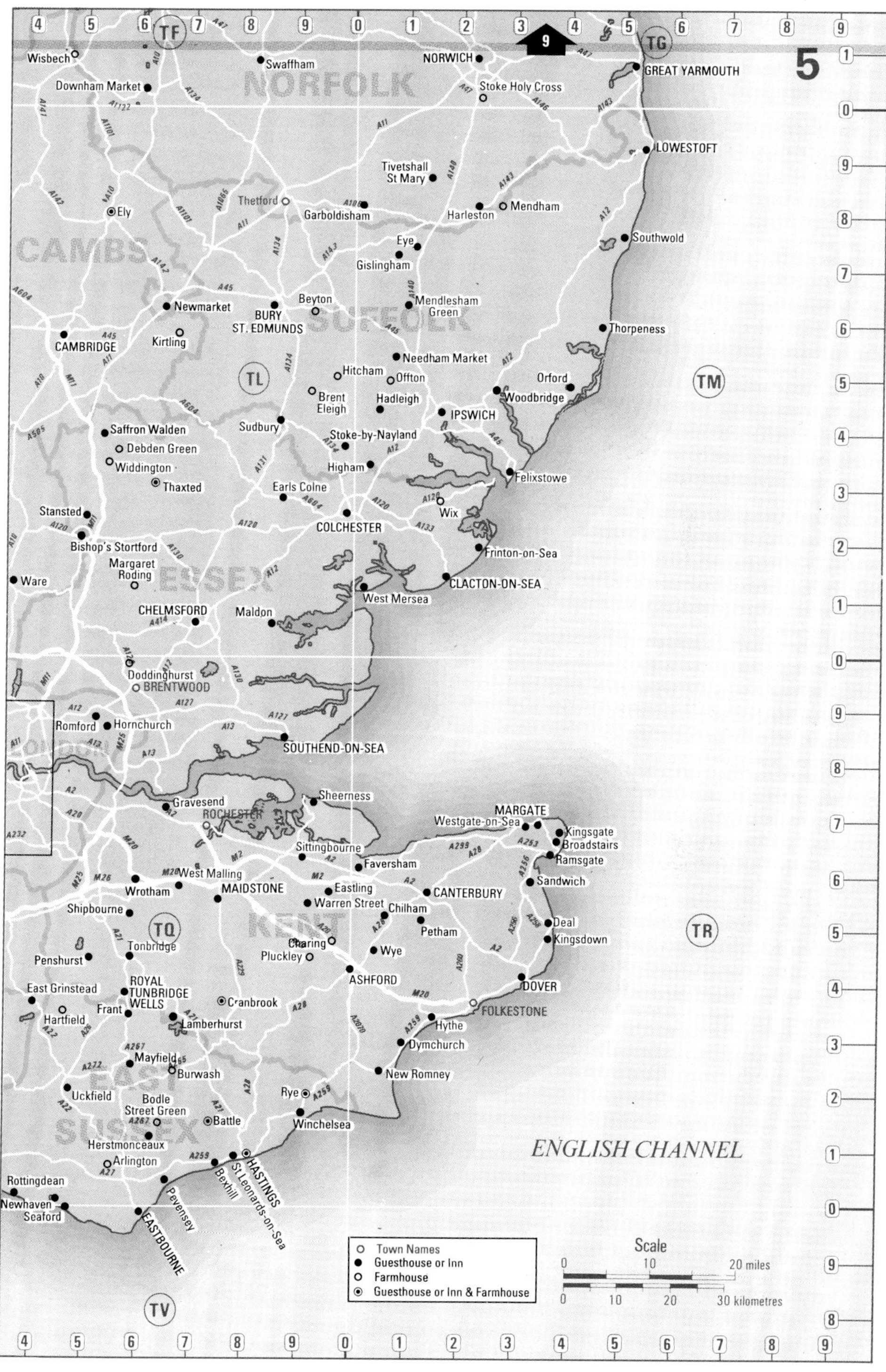

5
9
TF
TG
TL
TM
TQ
TR
TV
NORFOLK
CAMBS
SUFFOLK
ESSEX
KENT
EAST SUSSEX
Wisbech
Swaffham
NORWICH
GREAT YARMOUTH
Downham Market
Stoke Holy Cross
LOWESTOFT
Tivetshall St Mary
Thetford
Garboldisham
Harleston
Mendham
Ely
Southwold
Eye
Gislingham
Newmarket
BURY ST. EDMUNDS
Beyton
Mendlesham Green
CAMBRIDGE
Kirtling
Thorpeness
Needham Market
Hitcham
Offton
Orford
Brent Eleigh
Hadleigh
Woodbridge
IPSWICH
Saffron Walden
Sudbury
Stoke-by-Nayland
Debden Green
Widdington
Higham
Felixstowe
Thaxted
Earls Colne
Wix
Stansted
COLCHESTER
Bishop's Stortford
Frinton-on-Sea
Margaret Roding
Ware
CLACTON-ON-SEA
West Mersea
CHELMSFORD
Maldon
Doddinghurst
BRENTWOOD
Romford
Hornchurch
SOUTHEND-ON-SEA
Sheerness
Gravesend
ROCHESTER
MARGATE
Westgate-on-Sea
Kingsgate
Broadstairs
Sittingbourne
Ramsgate
Faversham
West Malling
Sandwich
Wrotham
MAIDSTONE
Eastling
CANTERBURY
Shipbourne
Warren Street
Chilham
Deal
Petham
Tonbridge
Charing
Kingsdown
Penshurst
Pluckley
Wye
ASHFORD
DOVER
ROYAL TUNBRIDGE WELLS
East Grinstead
Cranbrook
Frant
FOLKESTONE
Hartfield
Lamberhurst
Hythe
Dymchurch
Mayfield
Burwash
New Romney
Rye
Uckfield
Bodle Street Green
Battle
Winchelsea
Herstmonceaux
HASTINGS
Arlington
St Leonards-on-Sea
Bexhill
Rottingdean
Pevensey
Newhaven
Seaford
EASTBOURNE
ENGLISH CHANNEL
Town Names
Guesthouse or Inn
Farmhouse
Guesthouse or Inn & Farmhouse
Scale
0 10 20 miles
0 10 20 30 kilometres

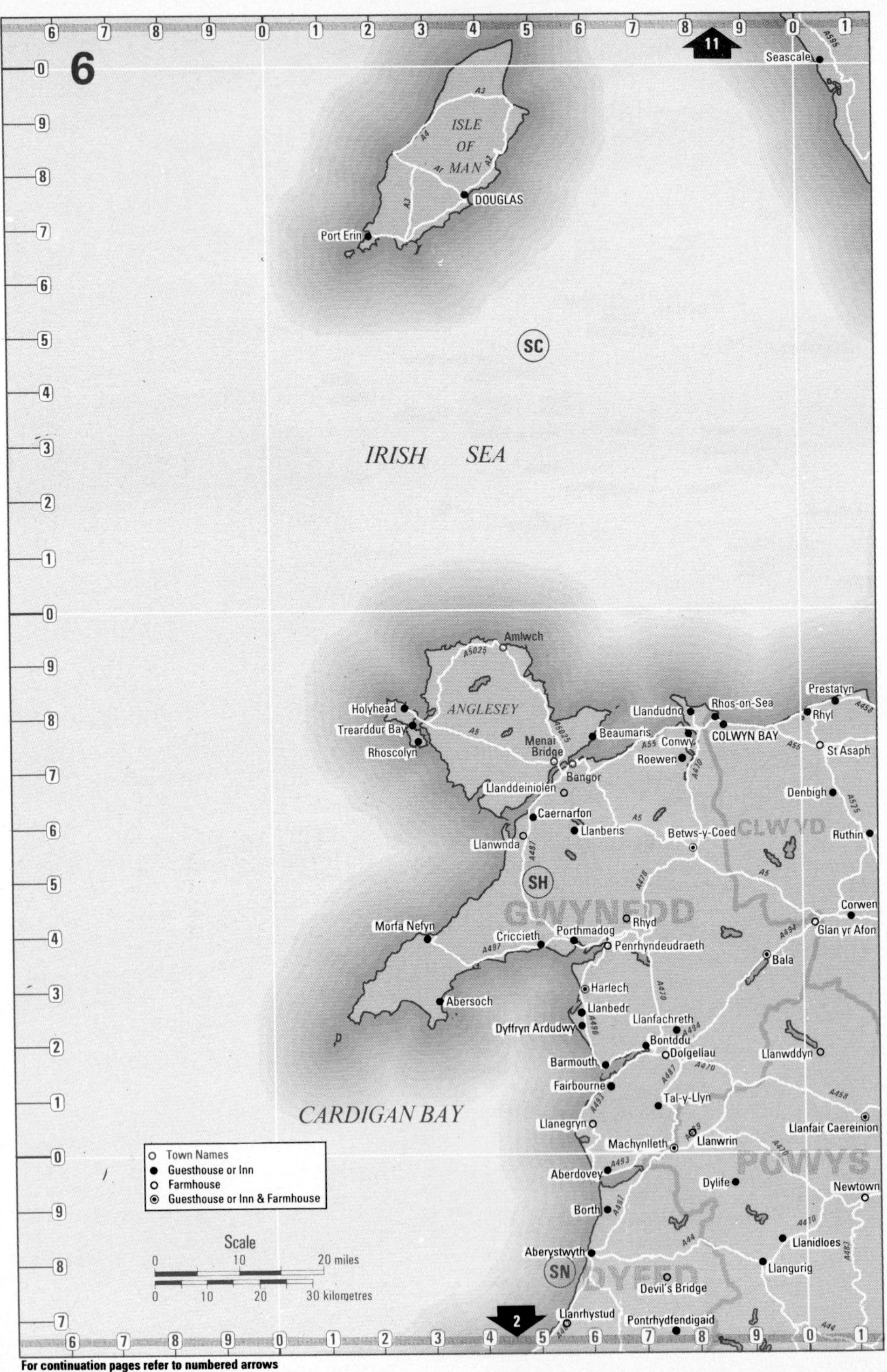

For continuation pages refer to numbered arrows

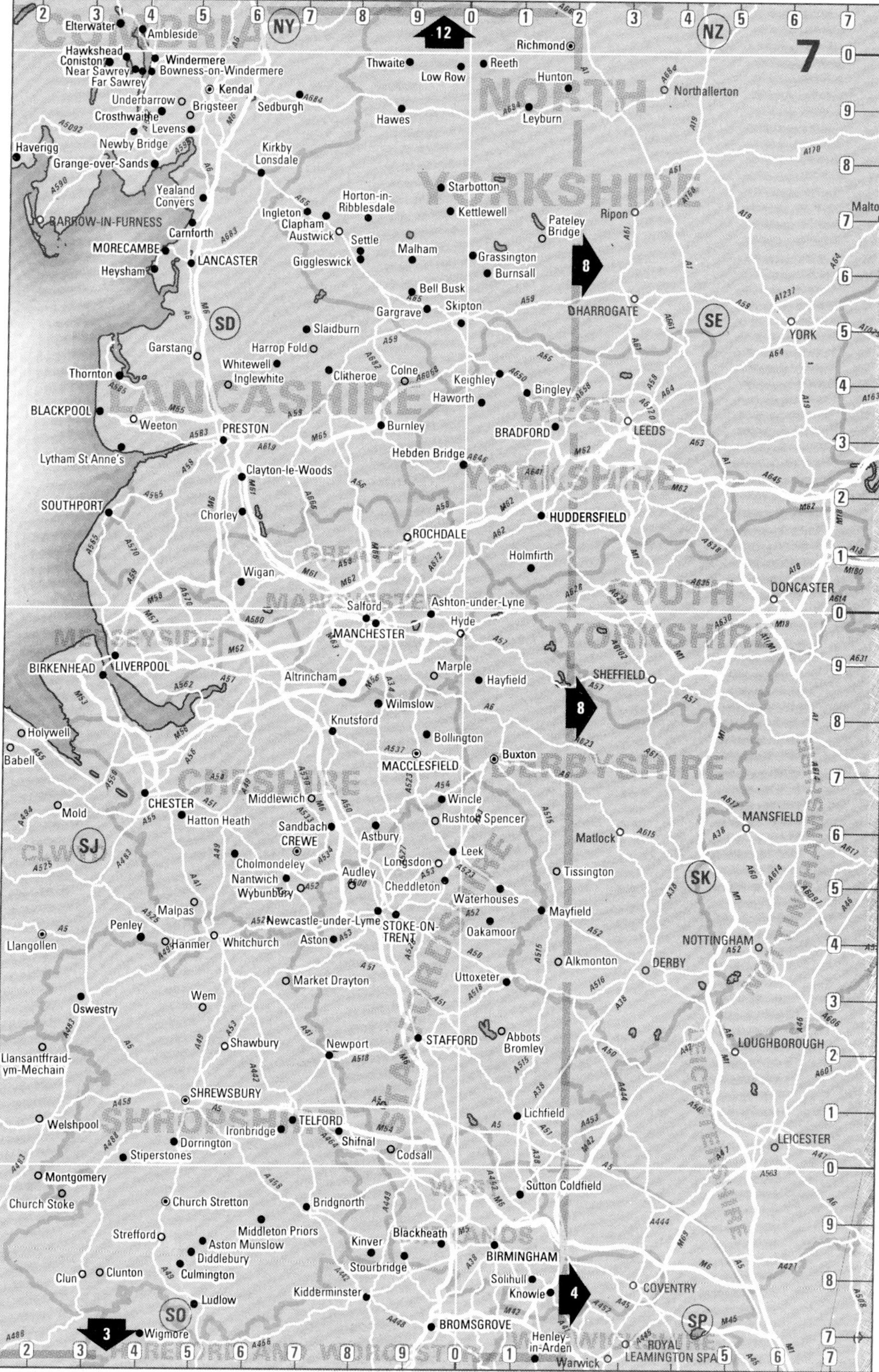

7
12
NY
NZ
SD
SE
SJ
SK
SO
SP
8
8
4
3
CUMBRIA
NORTH YORKSHIRE
LANCASHIRE
WEST YORKSHIRE
GREATER MANCHESTER
SOUTH YORKSHIRE
MERSEYSIDE
CHESHIRE
DERBYSHIRE
CLWYD
STAFFORDSHIRE
SHROPSHIRE
WEST MIDLANDS
NOTTINGHAMSHIRE
LEICESTERSHIRE
HEREFORD AND WORCESTER
WARWICKSHIRE
Elterwater
Ambleside
Hawkshead
Coniston
Windermere
Near Sawrey
Bowness-on-Windermere
Far Sawrey
Kendal
Underbarrow
Brigsteer
Sedburgh
Crosthwaite
Levens
Newby Bridge
Haverigg
Grange-over-Sands
Kirkby Lonsdale
Yealand Conyers
BARROW-IN-FURNESS
Carnforth
MORECAMBE
LANCASTER
Heysham
Richmond
Thwaite
Low Row
Reeth
Hunton
Northallerton
Hawes
Leyburn
Starbotton
Horton-in-Ribblesdale
Ingleton
Clapham
Austwick
Kettlewell
Ripon
Pateley Bridge
Malton
Settle
Giggleswick
Malham
Grassington
Burnsall
Bell Busk
Gargrave
Skipton
HARROGATE
YORK
Slaidburn
Garstang
Harrop Fold
Whitewell
Thornton
Inglewhite
Clitheroe
Colne
Keighley
Bingley
Haworth
BLACKPOOL
Weeton
PRESTON
Burnley
BRADFORD
LEEDS
Lytham St Anne's
Hebden Bridge
Clayton-le-Woods
SOUTHPORT
Chorley
HUDDERSFIELD
ROCHDALE
Holmfirth
Wigan
DONCASTER
Salford
Ashton-under-Lyne
MANCHESTER
Hyde
BIRKENHEAD
LIVERPOOL
Altrincham
Marple
Hayfield
SHEFFIELD
Wilmslow
Knutsford
Holywell
Babell
Bollington
MACCLESFIELD
Buxton
CHESTER
Middlewich
Wincle
Mold
Hatton Heath
Sandbach
Rushton Spencer
MANSFIELD
CREWE
Astbury
Matlock
Cholmondeley
Leek
Longsdon
Tissington
Nantwich
Audley
Cheddleton
Wybunbury
Waterhouses
Malpas
Mayfield
Newcastle-under-Lyme
STOKE-ON-TRENT
Oakamoor
Penley
Llangollen
Hanmer
Whitchurch
Aston
NOTTINGHAM
Alkmonton
DERBY
Market Drayton
Uttoxeter
Oswestry
Wem
STAFFORD
Abbots Bromley
Shawbury
Newport
LOUGHBOROUGH
Llansantffraid-ym-Mechain
SHREWSBURY
Lichfield
Welshpool
TELFORD
Ironbridge
Shifnal
Dorrington
Codsall
LEICESTER
Stiperstones
Montgomery
Church Stoke
Sutton Coldfield
Church Stretton
Bridgnorth
Middleton Priors
Strefford
Aston Munslow
Kinver
Blackheath
BIRMINGHAM
Diddlebury
Stourbridge
Clun
Clunton
Culmington
Solihull
COVENTRY
Knowle
Ludlow
Kidderminster
BROMSGROVE
Wigmore
Henley-in-Arden
ROYAL LEAMINGTON SPA
Warwick

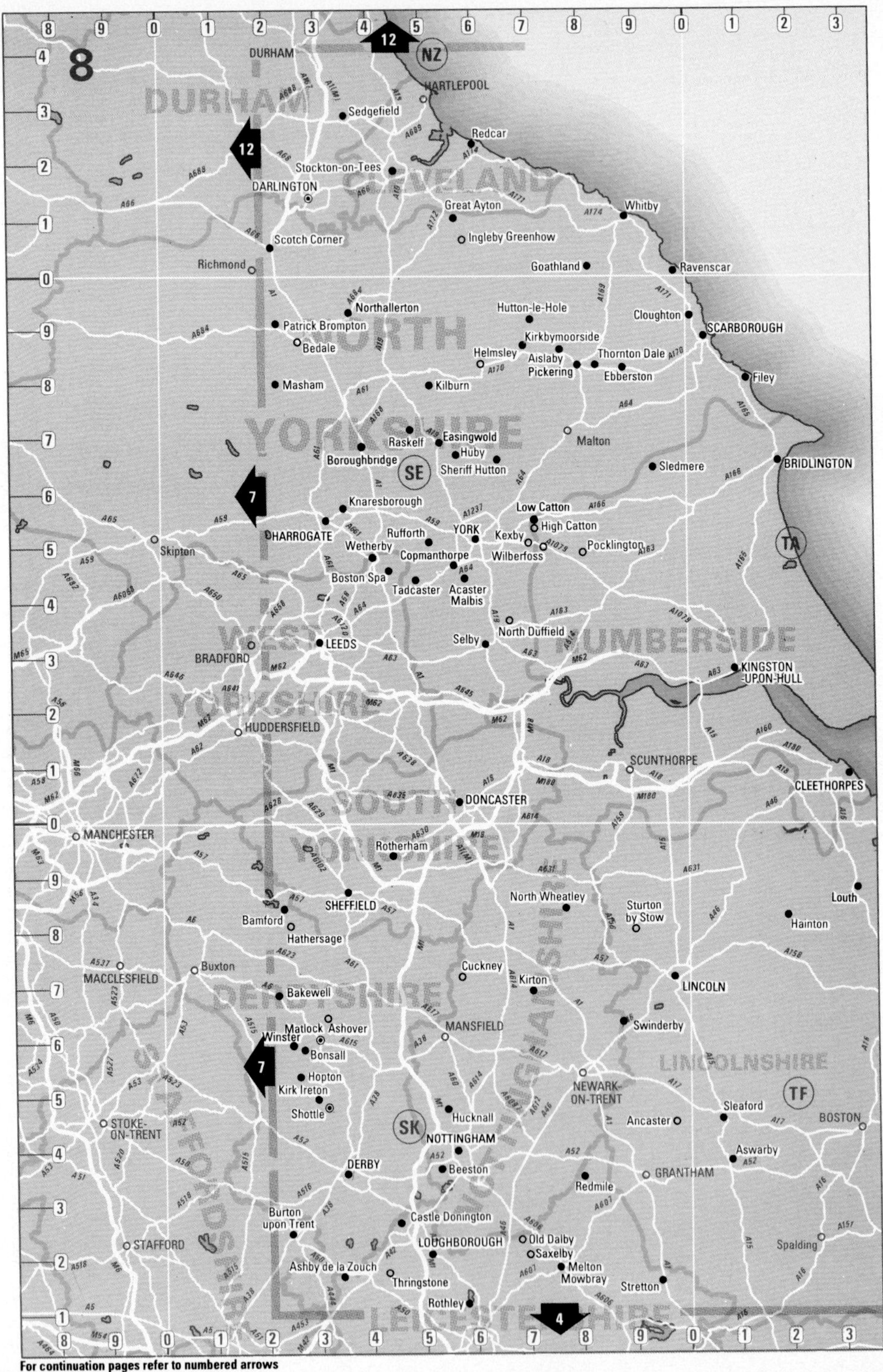

For continuation pages refer to numbered arrows

9
Scale
0
10
20 miles
0
10
20
30 kilometres
Town Names
Guesthouse or Inn
Farmhouse
Guesthouse or Inn & Farmhouse
NORTH SEA
TA
TF
TG
THE WASH
LINCS
NORFOLK
Conisholme
Skegness
Hunstanton
Holbeach
KING'S LYNN
Tottenhill
Wells-next-the-Sea
Blakeney
Sheringham
Cromer
Holt
Mundesley
Barney
Thurning
Blickling
North Walsham
North Elmham
Neatishead
Salhouse
East Dereham
Horsford
Horsham St Faith
NORWICH
5

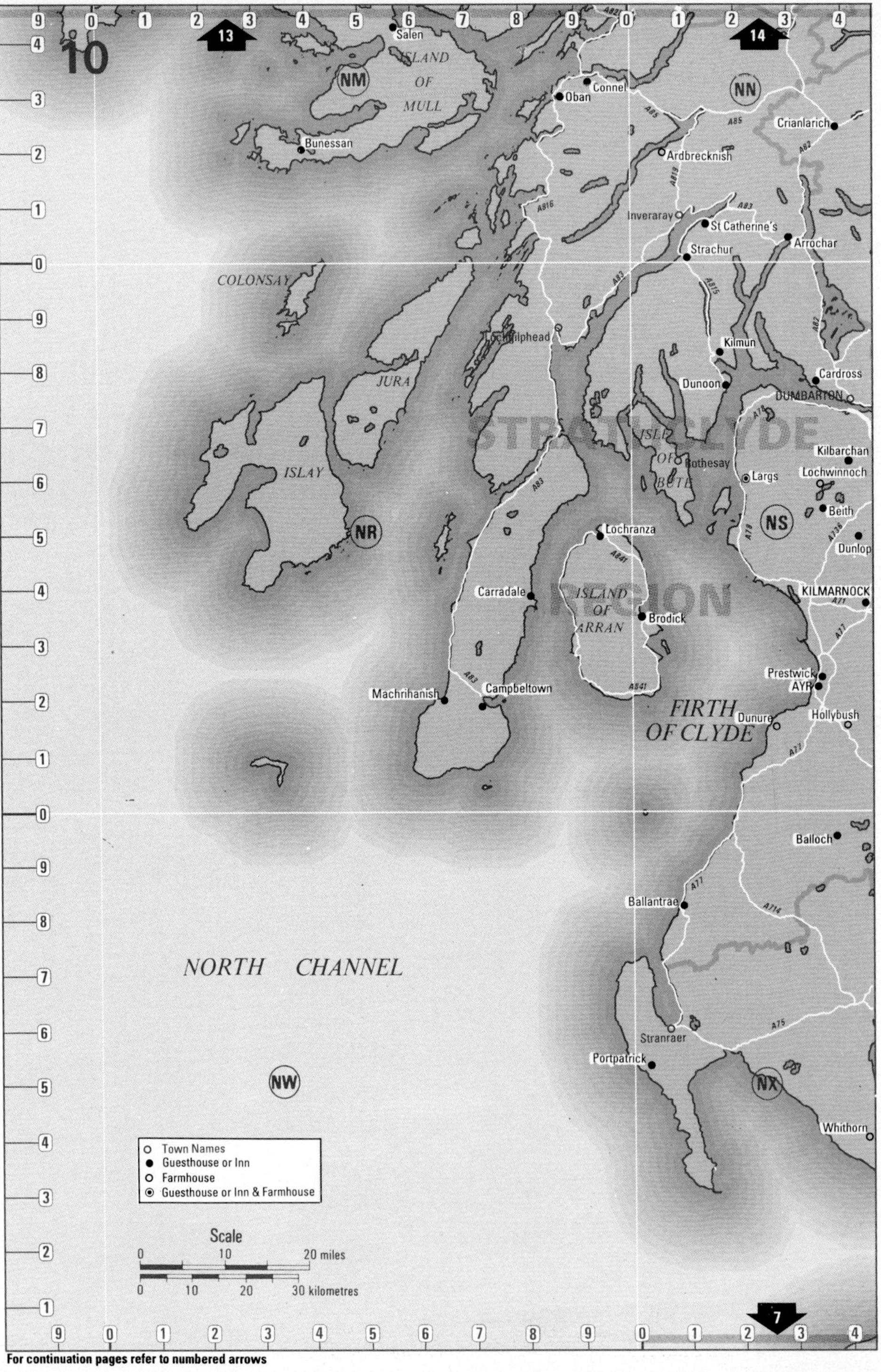

For continuation pages refer to numbered arrows

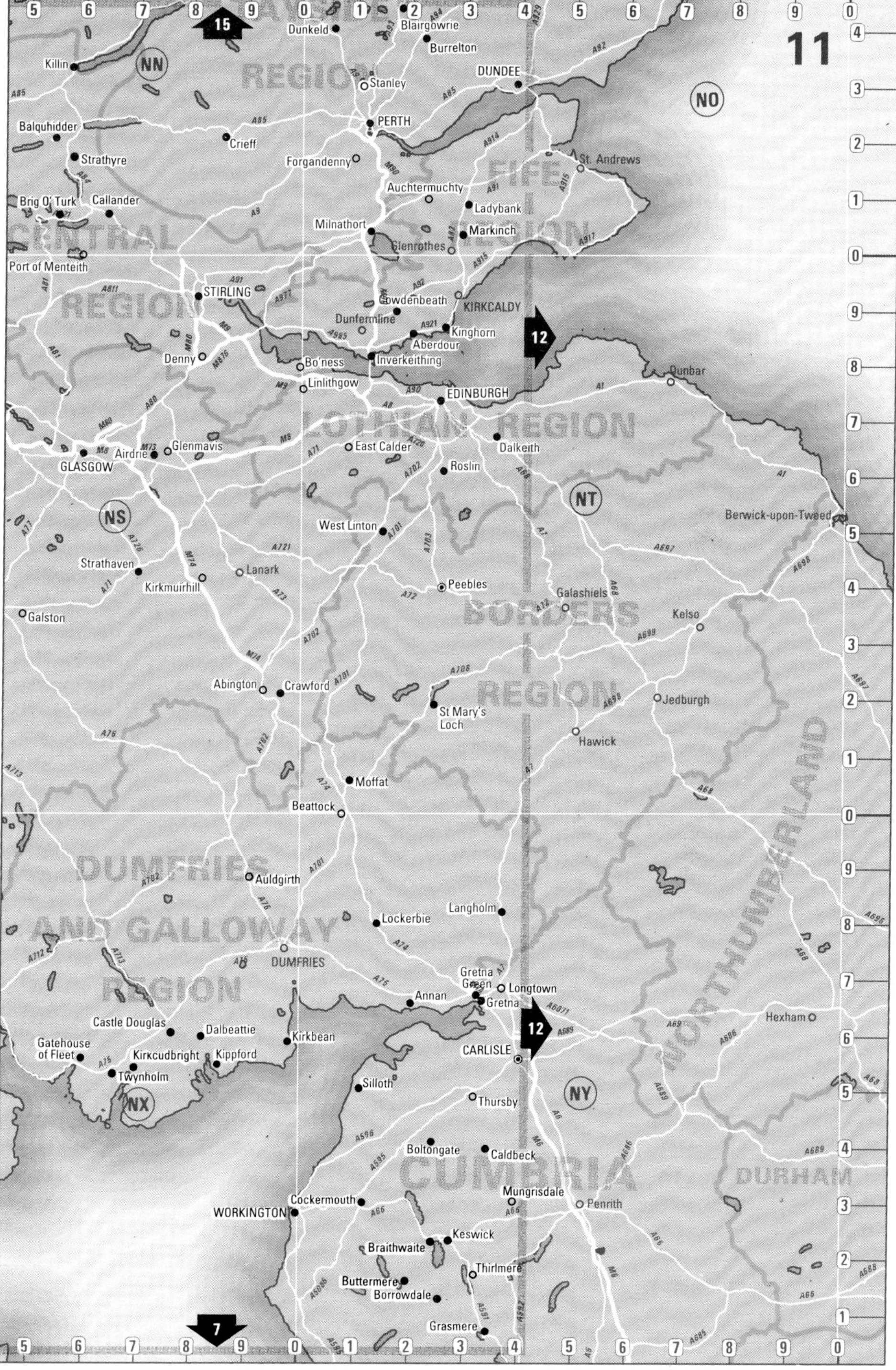

11
15
12
12
7
TAYSIDE
REGION
CENTRAL
REGION
FIFE
REGION
LOTHIAN REGION
BORDERS
REGION
DUMFRIES
AND GALLOWAY
REGION
CUMBRIA
NORTHUMBERLAND
DURHAM
NN
NO
NS
NT
NX
NY
Killin
Dunkeld
Blairgowrie
Burrelton
Stanley
DUNDEE
Balquhidder
Crieff
PERTH
Strathyre
Forgandenny
St. Andrews
Brig O' Turk
Callander
Auchtermuchty
Ladybank
Milnathort
Markinch
Glenrothes
Port of Menteith
STIRLING
Cowdenbeath
Dunfermline
KIRKCALDY
Kinghorn
Aberdour
Denny
Bo'ness
Inverkeithing
Dunbar
Linlithgow
EDINBURGH
GLASGOW
Airdrie
Glenmavis
East Calder
Dalkeith
Roslin
West Linton
Berwick-upon-Tweed
Strathaven
Kirkmuirhill
Lanark
Peebles
Galashiels
Galston
Kelso
Abington
Crawford
St Mary's
Loch
Jedburgh
Hawick
Moffat
Beattock
Auldgirth
Langholm
Lockerbie
DUMFRIES
Gretna
Green
Longtown
Annan
Gretna
Castle Douglas
Dalbeattie
Kirkbean
Hexham
Gatehouse
of Fleet
Kirkcudbright
Kippford
CARLISLE
Twynholm
Silloth
Thursby
Boltongate
Caldbeck
Mungrisdale
Cockermouth
WORKINGTON
Penrith
Keswick
Braithwaite
Thirlmere
Buttermere
Borrowdale
Grasmere

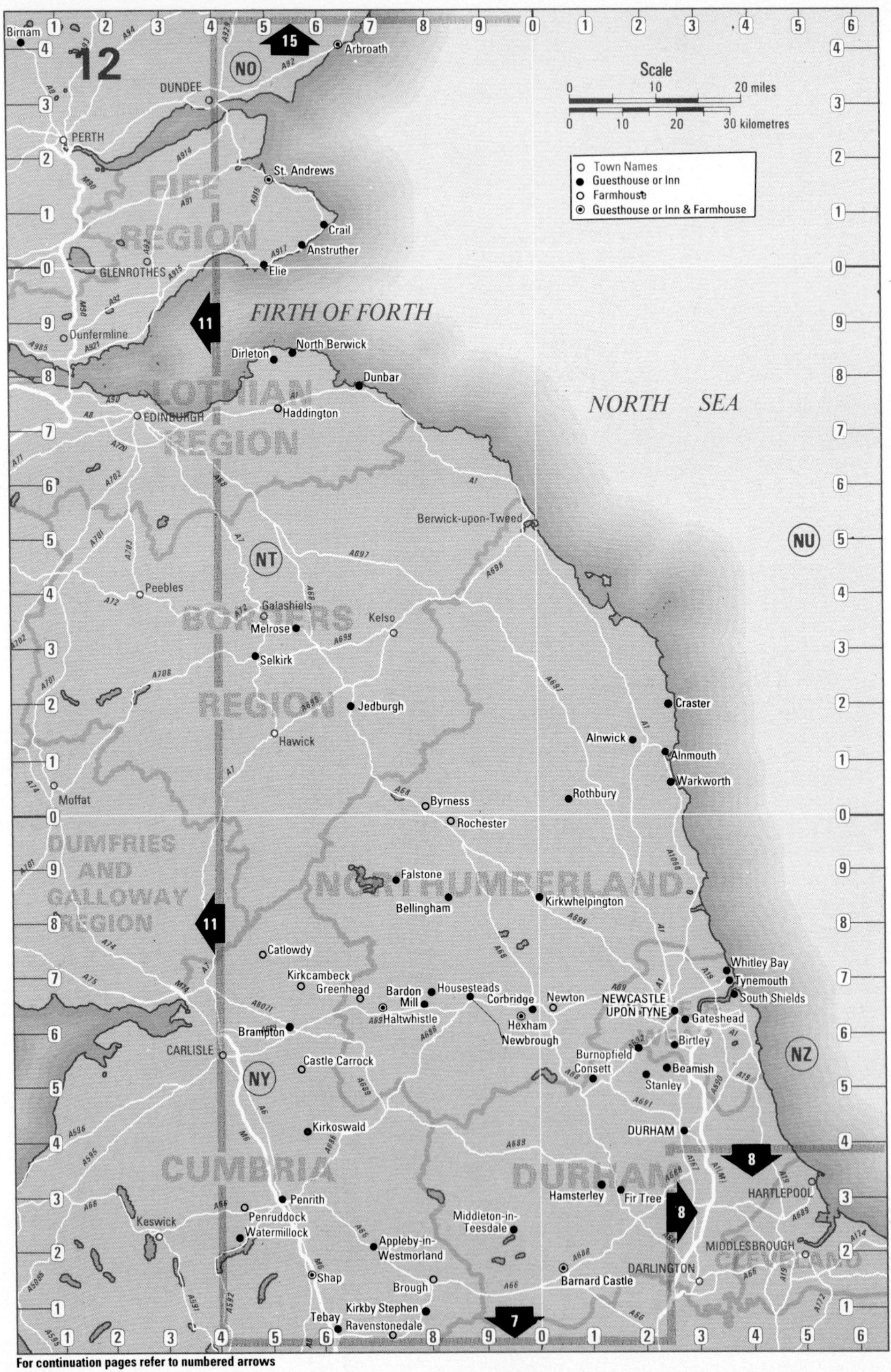

For continuation pages refer to numbered arrows

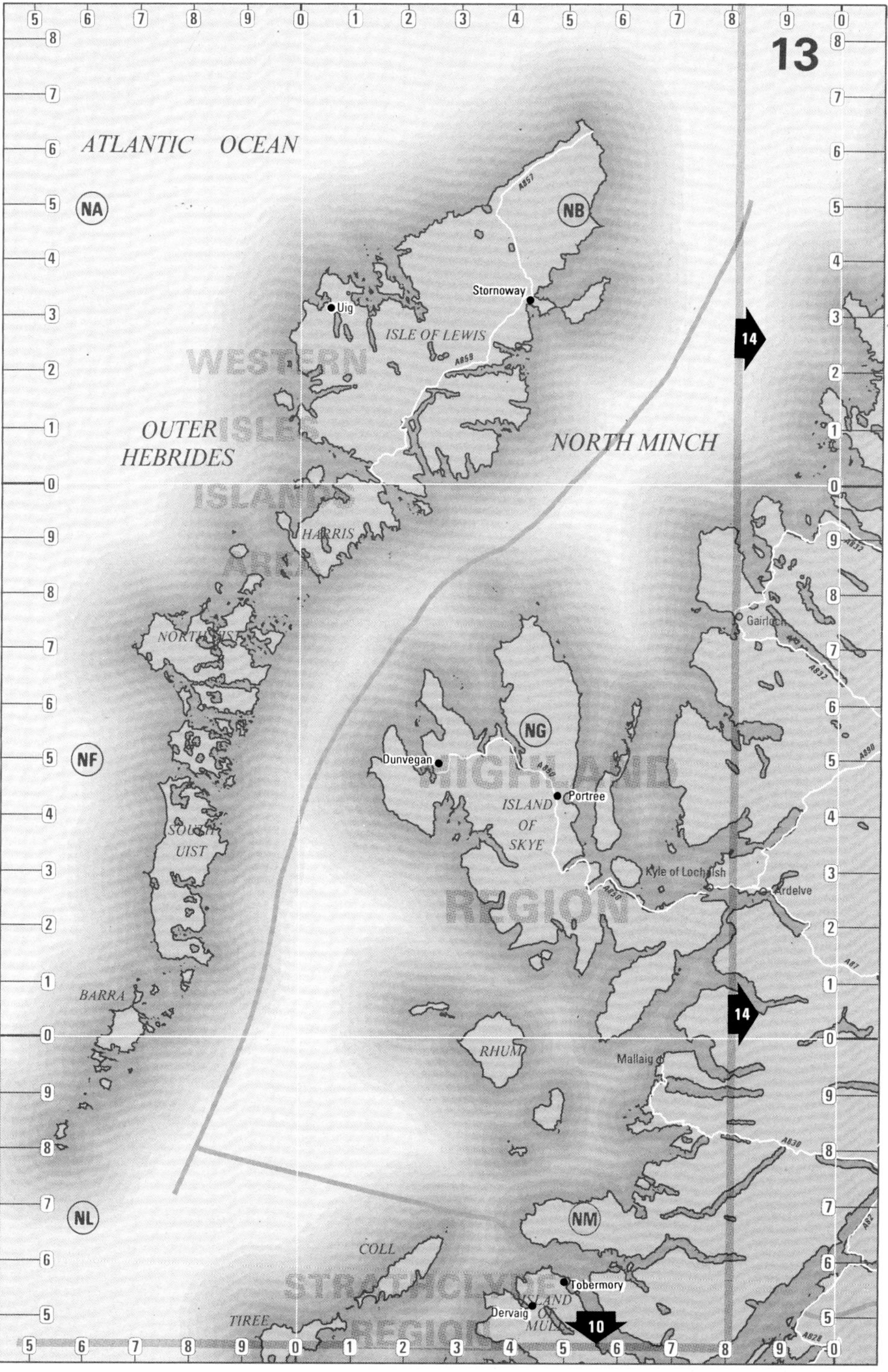
ATLANTIC OCEAN
NA
NB
A857
Stornoway
Uig
ISLE OF LEWIS
A859
WESTERN
OUTER
HEBRIDES
ISLES
ISLANDS
AREA
HARRIS
NORTH MINCH
14
NORTH UIST
NF
SOUTH UIST
BARRA
NG
Dunvegan
HIGHLAND
A850
Portree
ISLAND
OF
SKYE
Kyle of Lochalsh
Ardelve
REGION
Gairloch
A832
A896
A87
RHUM
Mallaig
A830
NL
NM
COLL
TIREE
STRATHCLYDE
REGION
Tobermory
ISLAND
OF
MULL
Dervaig
10
A82
A828

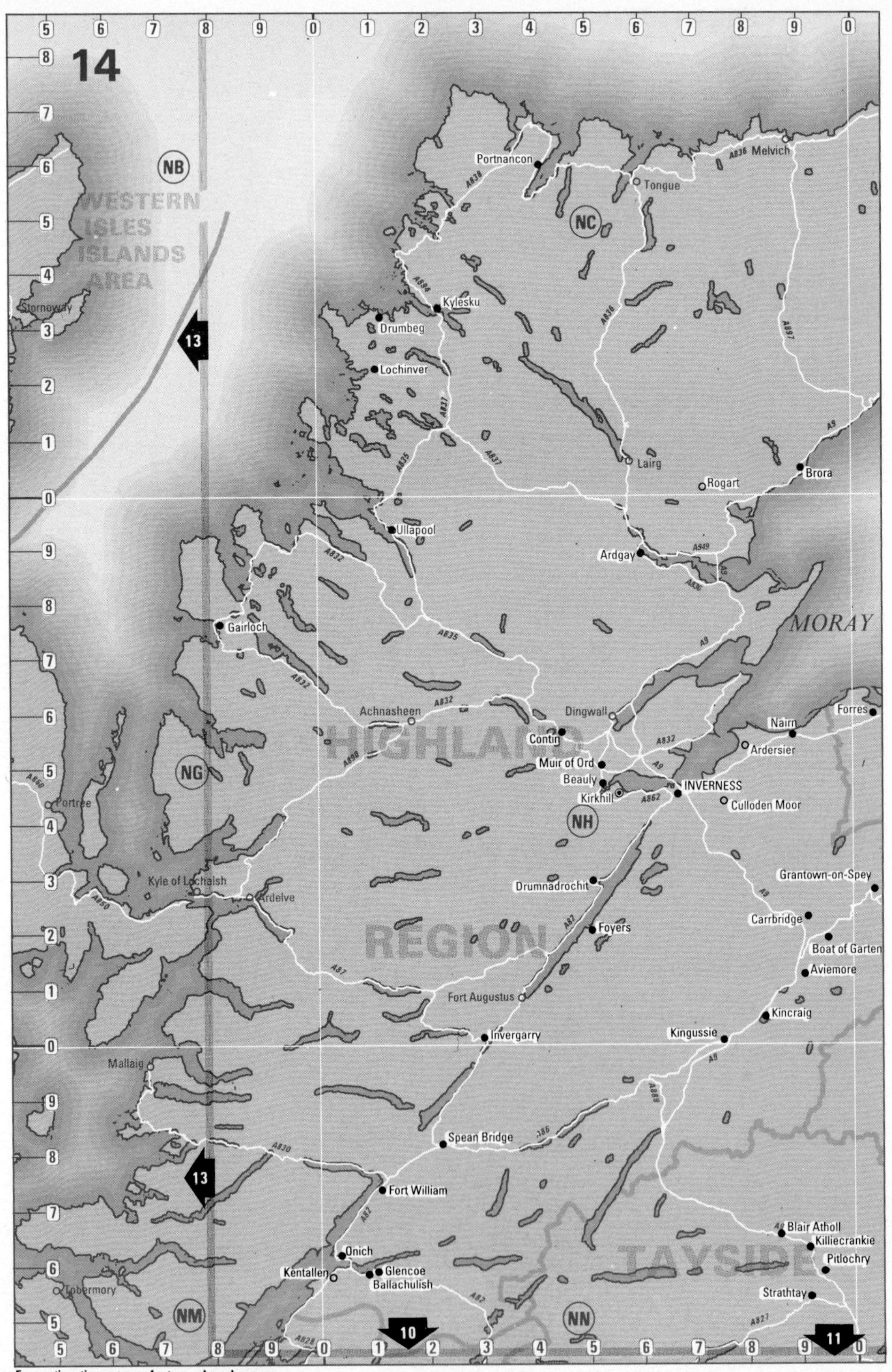

14
WESTERN ISLES ISLANDS AREA
NB
NC
NG
NH
NM
NN
HIGHLAND REGION
TAYSIDE
MORAY
Stornoway
Portnancon
Tongue
Melvich
Kylesku
Drumbeg
Lochinver
Lairg
Rogart
Brora
Ullapool
Ardgay
Gairloch
Achnasheen
Dingwall
Contin
Muir of Ord
Beauly
Kirkhill
INVERNESS
Nairn
Forres
Ardersier
Culloden Moor
Portree
Kyle of Lochalsh
Ardelve
Drumnadrochit
Foyers
Grantown-on-Spey
Carrbridge
Boat of Garten
Aviemore
Fort Augustus
Kincraig
Invergarry
Kingussie
Mallaig
Spean Bridge
Fort William
Onich
Glencoe
Kentallen
Ballachulish
Tobermory
Blair Atholl
Killiecrankie
Pitlochry
Strathtay
13
10
11

For continuation pages refer to numbered arrows

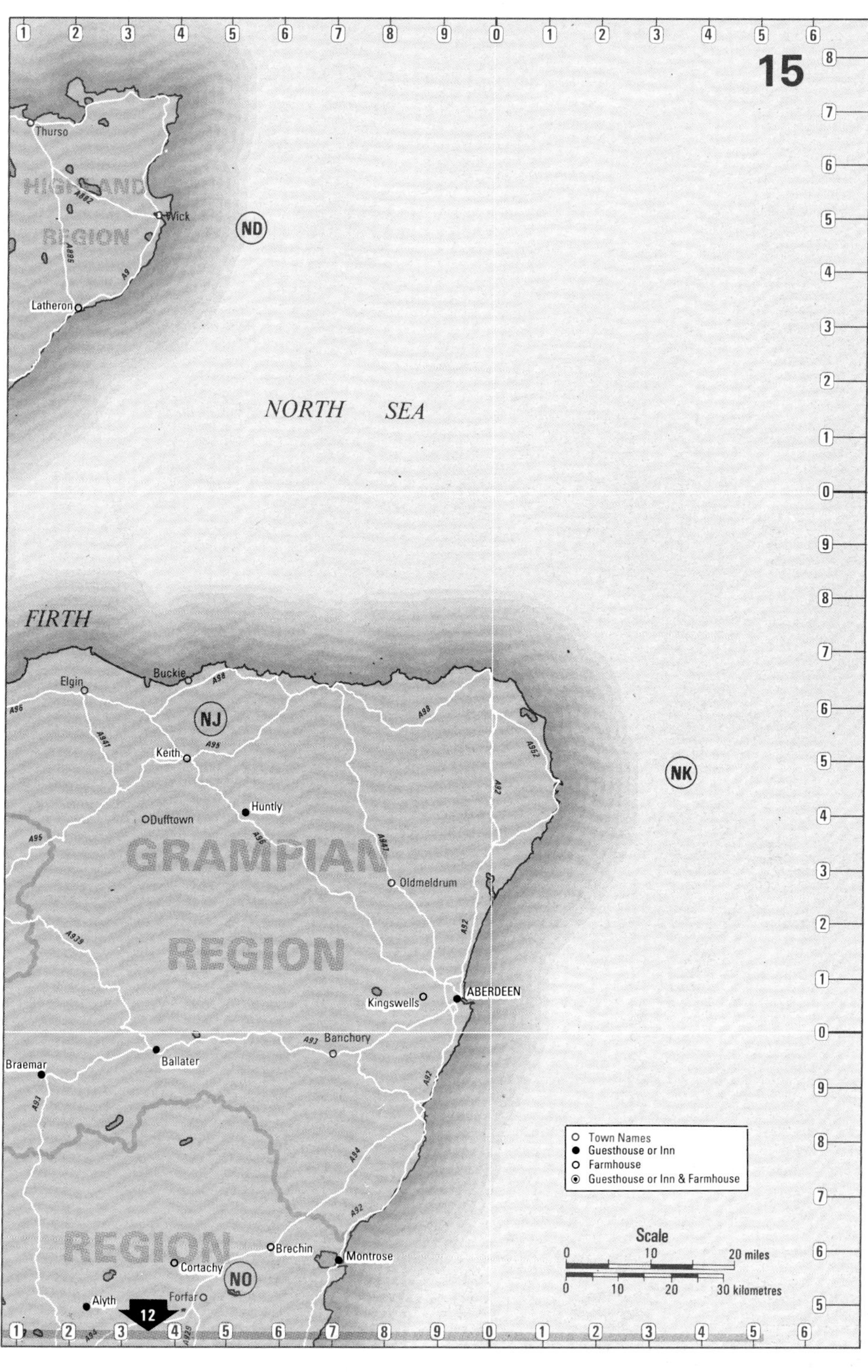
15
Thurso
HIGHLAND
REGION
Wick
ND
Latheron
NORTH SEA
FIRTH
Buckie
Elgin
NJ
Keith
Huntly
Dufftown
NK
GRAMPIAN
REGION
Oldmeldrum
ABERDEEN
Kingswells
Banchory
Ballater
Braemar
Brechin
Montrose
Cortachy
NO
Forfar
Alyth
12
REGION
Town Names
Guesthouse or Inn
Farmhouse
Guesthouse or Inn & Farmhouse
Scale
0 10 20 miles
0 10 20 30 kilometres

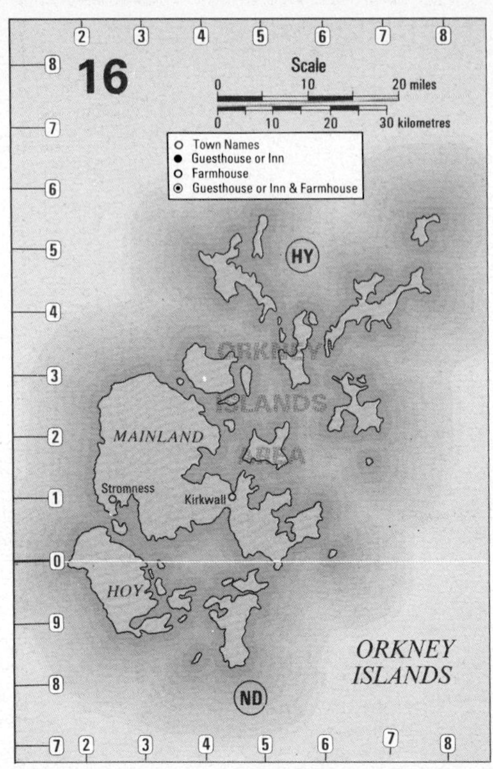

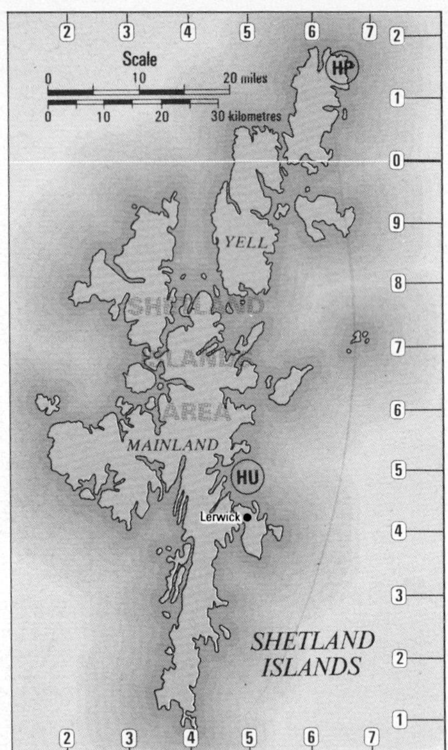

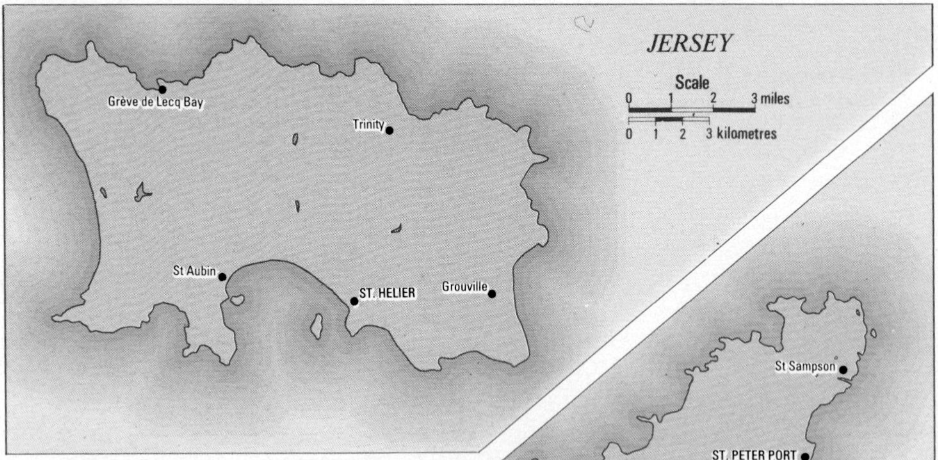

JERSEY

Scale
0 1 2 3 miles
0 1 2 3 kilometres

Grève de Lecq Bay
Trinity
St Aubin
ST. HELIER
Grouville

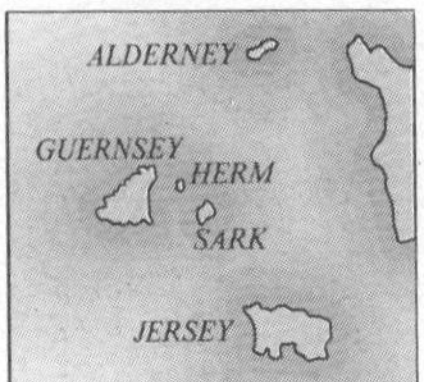

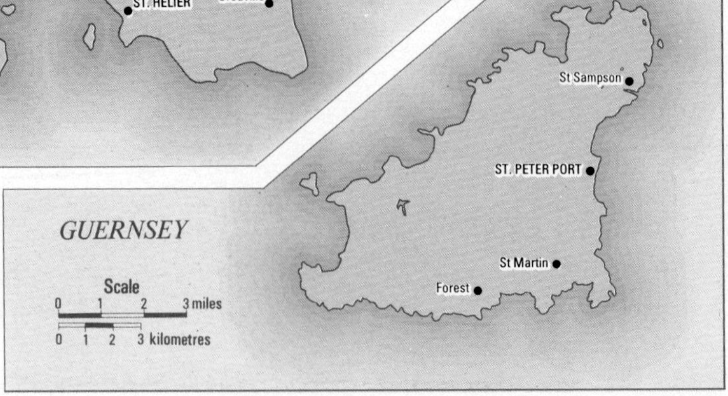

GUERNSEY

Scale
0 1 2 3 miles
0 1 2 3 kilometres

St Sampson
ST. PETER PORT
St Martin
Forest

ALDERNEY
GUERNSEY
HERM
SARK
JERSEY